Sermons very fruitfull, godly and learned
by Roger Edgeworth

Preaching in the Reformation
c.1535–c.1553

This edition, published in 1557, is a rare collection of Catholic Reformation sermons consisting of two series: six sermons on the seven gifts of the Holy Ghost preached at Redcliffe Cross, Bristol, from c.1535, and twenty sermons on St Peter's First Epistle preached in Bristol Cathedral where Edgeworth was canon from 1542 to c.1559. There is also a sermon on the creed and another on ceremonies. Edgeworth opposed Latimer and his confederacy in the 1530s and suffered persecution and imprisonment at Wells under Bishop Barlow in Edward's reign. But his career concluded triumphantly for he was Chancellor of Wells Cathedral under Mary I until his resignation from conscience just before his death in 1560. As one of the architects of the *King's Book*, the third Henrician formulary of the faith, he preaches as a moderate apologist: purgatory, defended in c.1537, thereafter disappears, while little attempt is made to uphold images, pilgrimage and other ceremonies which were abolished by 1548. Although he continues Thomas More's apologetics by objecting on hermeneutic grounds to the reformers' interpretations of controversial words like *imago* and *episcopus* he comes to accept many other translations of the Great Bible. By c.1553 he is outspoken in his complaints at, although powerless to prevent, Protestant attacks on the conservative clergy in Bristol and the confusion created by the Edwardian liturgical reforms. Traditional clerical authority did in fact decline in the West Country, but the rich blend of preaching styles displayed in these twenty-eight sermons suggests that Reformation polemics also moulded the vernacular along new contours. In his hieratic elevated mode which he uses for traditional devotional themes, Edgeworth recalls Bishops Fisher and Longland and anticipates the Elizabethan Euphuists, while his popular voice is notable for its native speech rhythms, proverbs and colloquialisms. He can lament the passing of bygone glories with poignant eloquence, yet with all the colloquial vigour that made him a match for Latimer, can denounce heresy equally fluently.

DR JANET WILSON teaches in the Department of English, University of Otago. She graduated D.Phil. from St Catherine's College, Oxford, and subsequently taught in Oxford and at Trinity College, Dublin, before returning to her native New Zealand.

This book is dedicated
to my father

Sermons very fruitfull, godly and learned

by Roger Edgeworth

Preaching in the Reformation
c.1535–c.1553

Edited by
JANET WILSON

D. S. BREWER

Editorial matter © Janet Wilson 1993

First published 1993 by D. S. Brewer, Cambridge

D. S. Brewer is an imprint of Boydell & Brewer Ltd
PO Box 9, Woodbridge, Suffolk IP12 3DF, UK
and of Boydell & Brewer Inc.
PO Box 41026, Rochester, NY 14604, USA

ISBN 0 85991 336 8

British Library Cataloguing-in-Publication Data
Edgeworth, Roger
Sermons very fruitfull, godly and learned:
Preaching in the Reformation, c.1535–c.1553
I. Title II. Wilson, Janet
252.009
ISBN 0–85991–336–8

Library of Congress Cataloging-in-Publication Data
Edgeworth, Roger, d. 1560.
Sermons very fruitfull, godly, and learned : preaching in the
Reformation, c. 1535–c. 1553 / by Roger Edgeworth ; edited by Janet
Wilson.
   p.   cm.
Includes bibliographical references and index.
ISBN 0–85991–336–8 (alk. paper)
1. Fruit of the Spirit – Sermons – Early works to 1800. 2. Bible.
N.T. Peter, 1st – Sermons – Early works to 1800. 3. Catholic Church –
Sermons – Early works to 1800. 4. Sermons, English – Early works to
1800. I. Wilson, Janet, 1948– . II. Title.
BT122.E33 1993
252'.02 – dc20   92–6238

The paper used in this publication meets the minimum requirements
of American National Standard for Information Sciences –
Permanence of Paper for Printed Library Materials, ANSI Z39.48–1984

Printed in Great Britain by
St Edmundsbury Press Ltd, Bury St Edmunds, Suffolk

CONTENTS

ACKNOWLEDGEMENTS

I remain grateful for the assistance of colleagues in the Department of English at the University of Otago who work on the Tudor Glossary Project: in particular Dr Seymour House for his unfailing patience throughout many discussions, Dr Gregory Waite who answered queries of a lexical nature, and Professor Alistair Fox. I have also appreciated valuable comments made by Professor J.M. Fletcher of the University of Aston, Birmingham, who read the Oxford University section, and by Keith Maslen, formerly of the Department of English at the University of Otago, who read the chapter on the text. Special thanks are due to Jane Jones and Mary Sullivan for their invaluable assistance with the preparation of the text and glossary concordance. I should like to thank the archivists at the Bodleian Library for permission to use the Registers of Oxford University, at Oriel College, Oxford for granting me access to the college Treasurers' Accounts, and at the Public Record Office and Bristol Record Office for answering queries and providing information. Finally to the reference librarians at the Bodleian Library, the British Library and at the University of Otago, especially Frieda Fueron, I should also like to express my appreciation.

ABBREVIATIONS

APC *Acts of the Privy Council of England* (1452–1628), ed. J. Dasent et al, 32 vols, NS (London, 1890–1907)

Aquinas, *ST Summa Theologiae*, gen. ed. and tr., T. Gilby, 61 vols (London, 1964–81)

AV Authorised Version of the Bible

BCP Book of Common Prayer

BHA Historical Association, Bristol Branch

Blench J.W. Blench, *Preaching in England in the later 15th and 16th centuries* (Oxford, 1964)

BL British Library, London

BLR Bodleian Library Record

Bodl. Bodleian Library, Oxford

BRO Bristol Record Office, Bristol

BRUO I–III A.B. Emden. *Biographical Register of the University of Oxford to A.D. 1500*. 3 vols (Oxford, 1957–9)

BRUO IV ———. *Biographical Register of the University of Oxford from A.D. 1501–1540* (Oxford, 1974)

Concilia Concilia, Magnae Britanniae et Hiberniae a Synodo Verolamiensi, A.D. CCCXLVI ad Londinensem A.D. MDCCXVII, ed. D. Wilkins, 4 vols (1733–7, London, facs. repr. 1964)

CPR *Calendar of the Patent Rolls preserved in the Public Record Office. Edward VI, 1547–1553*, ed. R.H. Brodie, 5 vols (London, 1924–9); *Philip and Mary, 1553–8*, ed. M.S. Giuseppi, 4 vols (London, 1937–9); *Elizabeth I, 1558–78*, ed. J.H. Collingridge *et al*, 7 vols (London, 1939–)

Cranmer, *Works* I & II *The Works of Thomas Cranmer*, ed. J.E. Cox, 2 vols PS (Cambridge 1844–5). I, *Miscellaneous Writings and Letters*; II, *Writings on the Sacrament of the Lord's Supper*

CS Camden Society

CU *The Collegiate University*, ed. J. McConica (Oxford, 1986). Vol. III of *The History of the University of Oxford*, gen. ed. T. Aston, (Oxford 1984–)

DB *A Dictionary of the Bible*, ed. J. Hastings, 4 vols (Edinburgh, 1900–1904)

DCB *Dictionary of Christian Biography*, ed. W. Smith and H. Wace, 4 vols (London, 1877–87)

Dict. Bibl. Dictionnaire de la Bible, ed. F. Vigoroux, 5 vols (Paris, 1895–1912)

DNB *Dictionary of National Biography*, ed. L. Stephen and S. Lee, 63 vols (London, 1885–1900)

DRO *The Dean's Register of Oriel, 1446–1661*, ed. G.C. Richards and H.E. Salter, OHS, 84 (Oxford, 1926)

DTC *Dictionnaire de Théologie Catholique*, ed. A. Vacant et al, 15 vols (Paris, 1903–50)

EETS *Early English Text Society*

EHR *English Historical Review*

Enc. Bib. Encyclopaedia Biblica, ed. T.K. Cheyne and J.S. Black, 4 vols (London, 1899–1903)

Enc. Brit. *The New Encyclopaedia Britannica*, 30 vols, 15th ed. (Chicago, 1975)

EOS *The Early Oxford Schools*, ed. J. Catto (Oxford, 1984). Vol. I of *The History of the University of Oxford*, gen. ed. T. Aston (Oxford, 1984–)

Erasmus, *CWE* *The Collected Works of Erasmus* (Toronto 1974–)

ES Extra Series

Formularies *Formularies of Faith put forth by authority in the reign of Henry VIII*, ed. C. Lloyd (London, 1856)

Frere and Kennedy *Visitation Articles and Injunctions of the Period of the Reformation*, ed. W.H. Frere and W.M. Kennedy, 3 vols, Alcuin Club, 14–16 (London, 1910). II, 1536–1558

Hughes and Larkin *Tudor Royal Proclamations*, ed. P.L. Hughes and J.F. Larkin, 3 vols (New Haven, 1964). I, *The Early Tudors* (1485–1553). II, *The Later Tudors* (1553–1587)

ICC International Critical Commentary

JEH *Journal of Ecclesiastical History*

Latimer, *Works* I & II *The Works of Hugh Latimer*, ed. G.E. Corrie, 2 vols., PS (Cambridge 1844–5). I, *Sermons*. II, *Sermons and Remains*

Le Neve, III J. Le Neve, *Fasti Ecclesiae Anglicanae 1300–1541*, III, *Salisbury Diocese*, comp. J.M. Horn (London, 1962)

———, V J. Le Neve, *Fasti Ecclesiae Anglicanae, 1541–1857*, V, *Bath and Wells Diocese*, comp. J. Horne and D.S. Bailey (London, 1979)

———, VIII J. Le Neve, *Fasti Ecclesiae Anglicanae, 1300–1541*, VIII, *Bath and Wells Diocese*, comp. B. Jones (London, 1964)

LP *Letters and Papers Foreign and Domestic of the Reign of Henry VIII*, ed. J. Gairdner and J.S. Brewer, 21 vols (London, 1863–1932)

ME Middle English

MLR *Modern Language Review*

More, *CW* *The Yale Edition of the Complete Works of St.Thomas More* (New Haven, 1963–)

———, *CW5* *Responsio ad Lutherum*, ed. J.M. Headley (New Haven, 1969). Vol. 5

———, *CW6* *The Dialogue concerning Heresies*, ed. T.M. Lawlor, G. Marc'hadour, R. C. Marius (New Haven, 1981). Vol. 6

———, *CW8* *The Confutation of Tyndale s Answer*, ed. L.A. Schuster, R.C. Marius, J.P. Lusardi, R.J. Schoeck (New Haven, 1973). Vol. 8

———, *CW9* *The Apology*, ed. J.B. Trapp (New Haven, 1979). Vol. 9

n. note

NCE *The New Catholic Encyclopaedia*, 10 vols (Washington, 1967)

NS New Series

NT New Testament

OC Arch. Archives of Oriel College, Oxford

OCCL *The Oxford Companion to Classical Literature*, ed. Sir P. Harvey, 2nd ed. rev. M. Howatson (Oxford, 1989)

OCD *The Oxford Classical Dictionary*, ed. N.G.L. Hammond and H.H. Scullard, 2nd ed. (Oxford, 1979)

ODEP *The Oxford Dictionary of English Proverbs*, ed. F.P. Wilson, 3rd ed. rev. (Oxford, 1970)

ODS D.H. Farmer, *The Oxford Dictionary of Saints* (1978, repr., Oxford, 1979)

OED *The Oxford English Dictionary*, ed. J.A.H. Murray, H. Bradley, W.A. Craigie, C.T. Onions (Oxford, 1933)

OHS   Oxford Historical Society

OL   H. Plechl, *Orbis Latinus*, 3 vols (Braunschweig, 1972)

OS   Original Series

OT   Old Testament

OU Arch.   Archives of Oxford University

Owst, *LPME*   G.R. Owst, *Literature and Pulpit in Medieval England*, 2nd ed. (Oxford 1961)

PCC   Wills proven in the Prerogative Court of Canterbury held in the Public Record Office, London

PG   Patrologiae Cursus Completus: Series Graeca, ed. J. Migne, 161 vols (Paris, 1857–66)

PL   Patrologiae Cursus Completus: Series Latina, ed. J. Migne, 221 vols (Paris, 1844–64)

PMLA   Publications of the Modern Language Society

Pocock-Burnet   G. Burnet, *The History of the Reformation in England*, ed. N. Pocock, 7 vols (London, 1865)

PRO   Public Record Office, Chancery Lane, London

PS   Parker Society

REB   Records of the English Bible: the documents relating to the translation and publication of the Bible in English, 1525–1611, ed. A.F. Pollard (1911, repr. London, 1966)

RES   Review of English Studies

RH   Recusant History

SRO   Somerset Record Office, Taunton

SRS   Somerset Record Society

STC   The Short-Title Catalogue of Books Printed in England, Scotland, and Ireland and of English Books Printed Abroad, 1475–1640, ed. A.W. Pollard and G.R. Redgrave, 2nd ed., rev. by W.A. Jackson, F.S. Ferguson, K. Pantzer, 2 vols (London, 1976–86)

TB   Textus Biblie

TBGAS   Transactions of the Bristol and Gloucester Archaeological Society

Townsend-Foxe   J. Foxe, *Acts and Monuments*, ed. G. Townsend, 8 vols (London, 1841, repr., New York, 1965)

VCH   Victoria County History

Vg.   The Vulgate version of the Bible

Wells II   Calendar of the Manuscripts of the Dean and Chapter of Wells, 2 vols, Historical Manuscripts Commission (London, 1907–14). Vol. II

INTRODUCTION

THE TEXT

Printed and manuscript versions of the *Sermons*

The edition of 1557

Sermons very fruitfull, godly and learned, published by Robert Caly, is not entered in the *Stationers' Register*, but the imprint gives the date of publication as September 1557. For the present semi-diplomatic edition the Bodleian copy has been used as the copy-text. The quarto volume is made up as follows:

TITLE-PAGE: [Within an architectural woodcut border, 140 x 85 mm.][1]
Sermons | very fruitfull, godly, | and learned, preached and | sette foorth by Maister Roger | Edgeworth, doctoure of diuini= | tie, Canon of the Cathedrall | churches of Sarisburie, Welles | and Bristow, residentiary in the | Cathedrall churche of Welles, | and Chauncellour of the same | churche: With a repertorie | or table, directinge to ma= | ny notable matters ex= | pressed in the same | sermons. *Excuſum Londini in aedibus Roberti* [swash R] | *Caly, Tipographi. Menſe Septemb.* | *Anno. 1557.*

COLOPHON: Imprinted at | London by Robert Calye, within | the precinct of Christes | Hospitall. | *Cum priuilegio ad imprimendum* | *solum.*

COLLATION: 4⁰. π⁴ <π>A⁴ <π>B⁶ A–4I⁴ 4K⁶; 332 leaves (the last leaf is blank); folios [14] i to cccxvii[i] (misnumbering l as lii, lii as xlx, cviii as cvii, cxxiii as cxii, cxxiv as cxxvi, cxxvi as cxxviii, cxliv as cxliii, cli as cxlxi, clvii as cxlvii, clix as cxlix, clxxxxiii as clxxxxii, clxxxxiv as clxxxxiiii, clxxxxv as clxxxxiiii, clxxxxvii as clxxxxvi, ccxxxvii as ccxxxviii, ccxxxix as ccxl, ccliii as ccxxxviii, ccxxxiv as ccliiii, ccxv as ccxl, cclx as cclix, cclxxii as cclxvii, cclxxxxviii as cclxxxxix, cccxiii as cccxiiii, cccxiv as cccxv, cccxv as cccxvi, cccxvi as cccxvii).[2]

CONTENTS: π1ʳ, title-page; π1ᵛ, Latin quotation (Ecclus 5:13); π2ʳ–π3ᵛ, 'The preface of the aucthor'; π4ʳ, 'The contentes of this boke'; verso, blank; <π>A1ʳ–<π>B6ᵛ, 'The repertorie'; A1ʳ–S2ᵛ, Six sermons on the seven gifts of the holy ghost; S3ʳ–Y3ᵛ, 'An homilie . . . on the articles of our Christian faythe'; Y4ʳ–2B2ʳ, 'An homilie . . . of Ceremonies and mannes lawes'; 2B2ᵛ–4K5ʳ, 'An exposition of the first epistle of Saynt Peter the apostle'; 4K5ᵛ, Colophon; 4K6, blank.

NOTES: 1. *Types:* The title-page and colophon are printed in four varieties of type, the largest of which is *lettre bâtarde* (230 Fraktur), a type from the Low Countries but of French origin. The others are 116, 74, and 72 textura and 95 italic.[3] The preface, repertory and running titles are in 95 roman type with

[1] R.B. McKerrow and F.S. Ferguson, *Title-Page Borders used in England and Scotland 1485–1640*, Bibliographical Society, Illustrated Monographs, XXI (London, 1932), no. 63, pp. 66–7.
[2] For inconsistencies in signatures, variations in catchwords, and a list of the running titles see J.M. Wilson, 'An Edition of Roger Edgeworth's *Sermons very fruitfull, godly and learned*', 2 vols (D.Phil. thesis, Oxford University, 1985), I, 6–7.
[3] See F.S. Isaac, *English and Scottish Printing Types 1501–35, 1508–41*, Bibliographical Society,

occasional use of italic type; the text is in Gothic black letter type, 94 textura, and 95 roman is used for scriptural quotation and often for proper names.[4]

2. I have been unable to trace any copies of the 8º edition cited by W. Herbert in J. Ames's *Typographical Antiquities* in 1810 and by E.G. Duff in 1895. As Herbert had not seen the edition and as Ames's articles are known to have been imperfect, it is probable that such an edition never existed.[5]

Census and description of existing copies

Of Caly's edition sixteen copies are known to survive.[6] They are located in the following libraries:[7] shelf marks and abbreviations are supplied.

Bodleian Library, Oxford.   Douce E. 236; Bodl.
British Library.   227 b. 29; BL.
Balliol College, Oxford.   585 a. 2; Balliol.[8]
Corpus Christi College, Oxford.   G 3–7; Corpus.
Emmanuel College, Cambridge.   S.10 3 432; Emman. Lacks π1–4, title leaf, preface, and 'The contentes of this boke' which are supplied in a nineteenth-century hand. Bound in with the *Sermons* is *Fyue Homiles* by Leonard Pollard, printed by William Gryffyth in 1556.[9]

Pepysian Library, Magdalene College, Cambridge.   No. 1285; Pepys. The volume has been rebound with two additional leaves in the front and three at the back. On the verso of the second leaf in front is a picture of Pepys with a motto; and on the verso of the first of the four blank leaves which follow the colophon is a Latin inscription.[10]

Bristol City Library Copy 1.   SR 90; Bristol 1.[11]
Bristol City Library Copy 2.   SR 4 A; Bristol 2. Lacks 2B2–2C4, 3B–3C4, 3D2–3E2, 4A1–4K6.

St Cuthbert's College.   XVIII. F. 6.3; Ushaw. Lacks π1–3, title-leaf and preface. Beneath the colophon is inscribed the date 1547.

St Edmund's College, Ware.   T4 21; Ware. Lacks 2Y4 and the contents are

Facsimiles & Illustrations, II (Oxford, 1930), fig. 57b; *English and Scottish Printing Types 1535–58, 1552–58*, Vol. III (Oxford, 1930), figs 46, 39.
4 *Ibid.* figs 40, 37.
5 J. Ames and W. Herbert, *Typographical Antiquities*, ed. T.F. Dibdin, 4 vols, 3rd ed. (1810, repr., London, 1969), IV, 463 (cited hereafter as Ames, *Typ. Ant.*); E.G. Duff, *Hand-lists of English Printers, 1501–1556*, 4 vols, Bibliographical Society (London, 1895–1913), IV.
6 STC 7482. The exact size of the edition is unknown and cannot be estimated.
7 I have examined every copy in the United Kingdom and have received written information about those held in the American libraries.
8 The volume is listed in the 1709 manuscript catalogue of the library, fo. 81, and in the 1871 *Catalogue of Balliol College Library*, p. 135.
9 See J.B. Pearson, *Index to English Books and Pamphlets in the Library of Emmanuel College, Cambridge printed before 1700* (London, 1869), p. 25; P. Worsley Wood, *Hand-List of English Books in the Library of Emmanuel College* (Cambridge, 1915), p. 52.
10 See *Catalogue of the Pepysian Library at Magdalene College, Cambridge*, 7 vols (Cambridge, 1978–), I, *Printed Books*, comp. N.A. Smith (Cambridge, 1978), p. 57; E.G. Duff, A *Descriptive Catalogue of the Library of Samuel Pepys*, 2 vols (London, 1914), II, 20–21.
11 See *Books in the Bristol Reference Library printed in England and Ireland up to the year 1640 and of English Books printed abroad during the same period* (Bristol, 1954), p. 19.

supplied in a recent hand. The preface and repertory have been bound in after the colophon.[12]

Trinity College, Dublin. OLS L–2–594; TCD. Lacks E3–F3, H4, K1, K4, 2A1–2, 2C2, 2P1–4, 3G1 and E1, G2, H3, Q2, Q3, 2A3 are either missing or partly torn. This volume has two sheets 2Q and lacks sheet 2P owing to a binding error. It came into the Edgeworth family library in the nineteenth century and is listed in an unpublished catalogue compiled by Maria Edgeworth and others in 1831. All references to the Mass and other forms of Catholic ceremony have been struck through or excised.

Worcester Cathedral. Y.E. 14; Worcs. Lacks 2D1–2K4; 2V1–3T4; 4K1–4K4.

York Minster Library. XII. P. 19; Yk. The repertory precedes the title-page, which exists only in fragments, and the preface.[13]

Folger Shakespeare Library; Folg. Lacks 2A2 which is supplied in facsimile.

University of Texas at Austin; Tex.

Yale University Library. Mhc 5 Ed37. Se7; Yale.

Brasenose College Library, Oxford. Two leaves, 3C1 and 3C3, which have been used as pastedowns, are available from the librarian on request.

Printing and proof-reading of the 1557 edition

The Bodleian copy was chosen to represent the 1557 edition as the copy-text as it is a perfect copy, conveniently located. The copies examined have only minor variants and no important textual divergence. Bodl., BL, Balliol, Corpus, Pepys, Bristol 1, Tex., and Yale are all apparently perfect copies; Emman., Bristol 2, Ushaw, Ware, TCD, Worc., Folg., and Yk. are imperfect owing to wear and tear. A collation of the copy-text against three other copies (BL, Corpus and Balliol) revealed the following minor variants:

1. Sig. L2^r, l. 32: 'artificer' has a misplaced final 'r' in Bodl., Balliol, Bristol 1, Emman., Ushaw, Ware, Worc., Pepys.
2. Sig. 3K2^r: this signature appears as K2 in BL, Folg., Bristol 1, Pepys, Ware, Yk.
3. Sig. 2T1^r: a damaged 'h' in the title 'The seuenth treatise' in Bodl. and BL.
4. Sig. 3N2: the signature appears as Nan in Yk.

The first gathering (π), of which the title-page is the first leaf, also exists in three variant stages:

1. In Yk. the date is printed as 1567. This must be a printing error as there was no second edition and Caly ceased printing after 1558.
2. In BL and Folg. the quotation from Ecclus. 5:13 on the verso of the title-page is omitted.
3. The copy-text and all other copies.

These variants may be the result of errors occurring during the process of printing.[14] The final 'r' of 'artificer' was probably dislodged from the forme during

---

[12] See *Catalogue of English Books before 1640 in the Library at St. Edmund's College, Old Hall, to the year 1640*, comp. E. Burton (Ware, 1902), no. 12.

[13] J. Raine, *A Catalogue of the Printed Books in the Library of the Dean and Chapter of York* (London, 1896), pp. vi–x, 152.

[14] R.B. McKerrow, *An Introduction to Bibliography* (London, 1927), pp. 177–9; F. Bowers, *Principles of Bibliographical Description* (New Jersey, 1949), pp. 46–7.

printing while the other variants suggests that some if not all of the gatherings were proof-read and corrected during the process of printing. Approximately 180 literals appear in 658 pages (excluding the running titles and page numbering) indicating that the volume was probably hastily checked and given only a cursory proof-reading.[15]

Manuscript versions

(i) *Bodl. MS Rawl. D. 831*: on paper, bound in leather and wooden boards. In folio, 305 x 21 mm. ff. 327.

This collection of theological treatises contains 'De Ceremonijs traditionibus' (fos 1–6) and 'De Articulo Fidei' (fos 7–13), versions of 'The articles of our Christian faythe' and 'Of Ceremonies and mannes lawes' (*Sermons*, pp. 168–190).[16] Both are signed by Edgeworth and 'De Articulo Fidei' is holograph. The engrossing Elizabethan secretary hand in which they are written suggests a date sometime in the late 1550s with a *terminus ad quem* of 1560.[17]

The relationship of MS Rawl. D. 831 to the 1557 edition

The sermons in MS Rawl. D. 831 display minor variations from the 1557 edition in spelling and punctuation, but 'De Articulo Fidei' lacks five passages which appear in the printed text and contains one additional passage. The changes in the 1557 edition are as follows:

1 & 2. The addition of two passages on sigs S3ᵛ, S4ᵛ–T1ʳ (*Sermons*, pp. 168–9) on the necessity of belief and of upholding the faith. Both employ extended images: the man almost dead for hunger who refuses sustenance until he knows its source illustrates the importance of belief prior to understanding; the fortress or hold which must be guarded demonstrates the need for the 'watch of the soul' against the incursion of heresies. The date of the sermon, 1546, appears in a reference to the effect of heresies on the church over the previous forty or fifty years.

3. An explanation on sigs V1ʳ⁻ᵛ (*Sermons*, pp. 172–3) of the title 'Lorde' applied to God with an acknowledgement of the Royal Supremacy.

4. The omission of a long exegesis on the cross on fo. 11ᵛ of MS. Rawl. D. 831.

5. The addition on sigs V4ᵛ–XIᵛ (*Sermons*, pp. 175–6), after a quotation from Zechariah, of a passage from I Pet. 3:19–20 on the harrowing of hell. A quotation from St. Basil follows (this precedes the quotation from Zachariah in the manuscript).

6. The addition on sigs X4ᵛ–Y1ʳ (*Sermons*, pp. 178–9) of a reference to Col. 1:4

---

15 P. Simpson, *Proof Reading in the Sixteenth, Seventeenth and Eighteenth Centuries* (Oxford, 1935), pp. 3–31; P. Gaskell, *A New Introduction to Bibliography* (Oxford, 1972), pp. 114–16.
16 The paper is the same as that used in Caly's edition and the water mark (hand and star) is similar to, but not identical with, one of those in the printed text (see C.M. Briquet, *Les Filigranes*, ed. A.H. Stevenson, 2 vols (Amsterdam, 1968), II, no. 11365).
17 The homilies are the only sixteenth century items in a mixed volume of manuscript materials. See A.G. Petti, *English Literary Hands from Chaucer to Dryden* (London, 1977), pp. 16–17 and R.B. McKerrow, 'Note on Elizabethan Handwriting' in his *Introduction to Bibliography*, pp. 341–350; the hands are described by Wilson in 'Edgeworth's *Sermons*', I, 10–11.

on the necessity of faith adorned with charity in conforming to the unity of the church.

The additions in the 1557 text of the sermon on the creed such as the reference to the Supreme Head to whom allegiance is due while 'professing our due subiection to almightye God', identify the sermon as Henrician; the injunction to remain steadfast in the faith gives it an apologetic slant. The omission of the devotional passage on the meaning of the cross in the manuscript version suggests that this form of allegorical exegesis was unfashionable by 1557. These changes may be regarded as editorial emendations. The manuscript may be either an earlier or a later version of the 1557 text although the additions in Caly's 1557 text may have come from another source. In the case of 'De Ceremoniis' the lack of substantive variants and the presence of some editorial or printing marks suggest that the manuscript may have been the source of the printed text.

(ii) *MS Bodl. James 29*: In Latin and Old English on paper: written in 1620–38 by Richard James. Loosely bound in cardboard. 335 x 215 mm. vi & 84 pp.[18]

This manuscript compiled by Richard James, nephew of Bodley's first librarian and fellow of Corpus Christi College in 1618, consists of his own writings and extracts from manuscript sources of medieval chronicles for the most part unfavourable to the Roman Catholic church. On fos 32–3 are three passages from the *Sermons*:

1. 'And this is ye verie propertie of heresyes . . . *obiuit*'. In margin: 'The varietie of our refor/mation in taking away/ ye papistical su/ perstition of/ ye sacrament'. Concludes with a reference to the 'XX sermon' and the date and title of the volume (sigs 4I4^v–4K1^v; *Sermons*, pp. 365–6).
2. 'I have knowne many in this towne, Bristowe . . . trumpery. serm. 4.' In margin: 'Divinitie vndoeth trade' (sig. L3^v; *Sermons*, p. 146).
3. 'In ye actes of Parliaments . . . end. 20 ser in Pet. ib.' In margin: 'destruction of mon^{asteries}' (sig. 4I1^v; *Sermons*, p. 363).

The context in which these extracts occur and the marginal comments reveal an interest in the Reformation. If the materials collected in MS James 29 were intended for an ecclesiastical history of England or a history of the monastic orders then such a work would have reflected the Protestant interests of James and his circle. This included the distinguished antiquarians Sir Robert Cotton and Sir Henry Spelman.[19]

The history and reputation of the *Sermons*

Preaching and printing in the reign of Mary I

Robert Caly printed from July 1553–1558 in Christ's Hospital in the precinct of the recently dissolved Grey Friars where he succeeded the Protestant printer R. Grafton.[20] As the chief Catholic printer of Mary's reign he enjoyed royal patronage

---

[18] See *ibid*. 14–15; F. Madan *et al.*, *Catalogue of Western MSS in the Bodleian Library at Oxford*, 7 vols (Oxford, 1922–53), II, no. 3866, for descriptions of the manuscript.
[19] See *DNB* s.v. 'James, Richard'.
[20] See CPR *(1553–4)*, p. 53. Although Cawood was appointed official printer after Grafton was

and maintained a continuous output of Catholic works, some of which had previously been banned.[21] He held a privilege or patent to print works of theology and so did not require the protection of the Stationers' Company.[22]

The prominence of homily collections in the outputs of Caly and John Cawood, the other main Catholic printer, indicates the importance the Marian church attached to authorised sermons which after 1554 were used to provide systematic and elementary instruction in the Catholic faith. As early as 1542 Bishop Bonner in his injunctions to the clergy had prohibited the use of old homilies.[23] By the time of Queen Mary's accession the dearth of catechetical works meant that the need for new Catholic homilies and expositions of the faith was urgent.[24] The injunctions of March 1554 enjoining that a uniform doctrine be set forth by the bishops of each diocese was reinforced by the fourth decree of the legatine court of 1555.[25] Notable among the works specially prepared for publication is Bonner's A profitable and necessary doctrine (1555), often printed with his Homilies, a work of composite authorship on topics such as the supremacy, the authority of the church, the sacrament of the Altar, transubstantiation, and the Real Presence.[26] Leonard Pollard's Fyue Homilies of 1556 comprises simple sermons on single topics: the sacraments of the Altar and Mass, the primacy, confession, 'fayth and knowledge of God'.[27] Other collections such as Thomas Watson's Two notable sermons (1554) on the Mass and the Real Presence were originally preached before the queen at court. That Watson's sermons on the sacraments, Holsome and Catholic Doctrine, published in 1558, ran to four editions in this year is an indication of the demand for prescriptive homilies.[28]

---

deprived for supporting Lady Jane Grey, Caly used Grafton's device with the monogram and his woodcut borders. See E.G. Duff, A Century of the English Book Trade, Bibliographical Society (London, 1905), pp. 21–2; McKerrow and Ferguson, Title-Page Borders, no. 63, pp. 66–7; Ames, Typ. Ant. III, 453.

[21] See ibid. IV, 457–64 and Duff, Hand-lists, IV for Caly's output. He printed thirty-eight works in six years.

[22] See F.B. Williams, Index of Dedications before 1641, Bibliographical Society (London, 1962), p. 126. Caly's name is not given in the Charter of Incorporation of 1557, but is recorded in Transcript of the register of the Company of Stationers of London 1554–1640, ed. E. Arber, 5 vols (London, 1875–94), I, 70, 94, 316. He took the freedom of the Company in 1559 after having given up printing.

[23] Frere and Kennedy, p. 88.

[24] Ibid. p. 328; on the clergy's need for homilies see J. Loach, 'The Marian Establishment and the Printing Press', EHR 101 (1986), 139–40; J.W. Martin, 'The Marian Regime's Failure to Understand the Importance of Printing' in Religious Radicals in Tudor England (London, 1989), p. 111. The lack of catechetical works under Mary I is pointed out by P. Tudor in 'Religious Instruction for Children and Adolescents in the Early English Reformation', JEH 35 (1984), 391–43.

[25] Hughes and Larkin, II, 407, p. 38. The Synod's twelve decrees, dated 4 February 1556, were published under the title Reformatio Angliae ex decretis Reginaldi Poli Cardinalis, sedes Apostolical Legati Anno MDLVI (Rome, 1562; facs. repr. London, 1962); they are reprinted in Concilia IV, 121–6 and in Documentary Annals of the Reformed Church of England, 1546–1716, ed. E. Cardwell, 2 vols (Oxford, 1844), I, no. XXXVII (cited hereafter as Cardwell, Doc. Ann.); see P. Hughes, The Reformation in England, 3 vols (London, 1954), II, 234.

[26] Bonner's A profitable and necessary doctrine was printed as Pt. 1 with separate colophon with certayne homelies in five editions by Cawood in 1555 (STC 3281.5–3283.7); the homilies were also published separately in eight editions in the same year (STC 3285.1–3285.10).

[27] Leonard Pollard, Fyue homilies (W. Gryffyth,) 1556. STC 20091.

[28] Thomas Watson, Twoo notable sermons concernynge the reall presence (J. Cawood, 1554). STC 25115, 25115.3, 25115.5. See Ames, Typ. Ant. IV, 463–4. The four editions of Holsome and catholyke doctryne concerninge the seven sacramentes (STC 25112–14) also included a pirated edition printed by J. Kingston (STC 25113).

Although the early Marian preachers, John Feckenham, John Harpesfield and James Brooks, aimed at restoring the people into the unity of the Catholic church, unauthorised preaching, teaching the scriptures or points of doctrine were prohibited in 1553.[29] Fox records only one 'popish' sermon by Bishop Weston and another by Leonard Pollard approving purgatory.[30] These restrictions and the corresponding emphasis on catechetical homilies were probably due to the influence of Cardinal Pole who had come to distrust unsupervised preaching after his experience in Italy, and regarded the pulpit less as a tool for pastoral regeneration than for defending the ceremonies, laws and constitutions of the church.[31] After the reconciliation with Rome his priorities were the restoration of ecclesiastical discipline and the training of an orthodox clergy. Although he envisaged doctrinal sermons playing some part in his programme of ecclesiastical and legislative reform, his untimely death prevented the fulfilment of this intention: the Catholic translation of the New Testament, the treatise on the seven sacraments, the Catholic catechism and collection of homilies authorised by the legatine synod never reached print.[32]

The homily collections of 1554–8 emphasise doctrines which had been attacked in the Edwardian reforms such as the sacraments of the Mass and the Altar, but the limited treatment of observances which the Henrician church had dispensed with – image veneration, purgatory and pilgrimages – shows the lines along which ceremony and worship had fragmented during the Reformation. Bishop Fisher's 1521 sermon against Luther, reprinted by Caly in 1554 and 1556, is exceptional in its focus on justification.[33] For the Marian clergy instruction in topics such as the Catholic doctrine of the Mass, the primacy, or the unity of the church seems to have constituted the recovery of Catholic doctrine, just as in the country at large restoration of traditional sacramental ritual was regarded as equivalent to a return to the Catholic faith.[34] The extant sermons convey the impression of a church still in a state of transition.[35]

[29] See James Brooks, A Sermon very notable . . . made at Paules Crosse, the xii daie of November, in the first yere of . . . Quene Marie (Caly, 1553). STC 3838–3839.3. On the preaching of Brooks and Watson see J. Strype, Ecclesiastical Memorials relating chiefly to religion and the reformation of the church of England, 3 vols (Oxford, 1822), III, i, 113–22, 164 (cited hereafter as Strype, Ecc. Mem); on their themes Blench, pp. 272–87.

[30] Townsend-Foxe, VI, 391–3; Hughes and Larkin, II, 390; D. Loades, 'The Press under the early Tudors: A Study in Censorship and Sedition', Transactions of the Cambridge Bibliographical Society IV (1964), 29–50.

[31] John Guy, Tudor England (Oxford, 1988), p. 236; Dermot Fenlon, Heresy and Obedience in Tridentine Italy: Cardinal Pole and the Counter Reformation (Cambridge, 1972), p. 255. Pole's policies are discussed by Rex H. Pogson, 'The Legacy of the Schism: Confusion, Continuity and Change in the Marian Clergy' in The Mid-Tudor Polity, c.1540–1560, ed. J. Loach and R. Tittler (London, 1980), pp. 116–36 and 'Reginald Pole and the Priorities of Government in Mary Tudor's Church', Historical Journal 18 (1975), 3–21. On Pole's vernacular sermons in Bodl. MS Lat. Vat. 5968 see Blench, pp. 50–1, 54, 164–6, 278–9.

[32] Prescriptions on preaching were given in the Synod's fourth decree and by the convocation of 1 January 1557 (Concilia IV, 123, 156; Cardwell, Doc. Ann. I, no. XXXVII, pp. 151–2). Pole planned four books of homilies: 1. Dealing with controverted points. 2. The creed, ten commandments, lord's prayer, sacraments and salutation of the blessed virgin. 3. Saint's days, Sundays, holy-days for explaining the epistles and gospels. 4. The vices and virtues, ceremonies of the church.

[33] The sermon of Johan the bysshop of Rochester made agayn ye pernicyous doctryn of M. luuther was printed by Wynkyn de Worde in 1521?, 1522?, 1527? and by Caly in 1554 and 1556 (STC 10894–7).

[34] Guy, Tudor England, p. 237; on Pole's policies see Pogson, 'Priorities', 9–15, D. Loades, 'The Enforcement of Reaction, 1553–1558', JEH XVI (1965), 54–66.

[35] For assessments of the Marian writings see Martin, Religious Radicals, pp. 118–20; cf. Loach, 'Marian Establishment', 140–2; see Loades, 'Enforcement', 64 and The Reign of Mary Tudor (Lon-

The *Sermons*, preached throughout twenty years of religious conflict, differ from the prescribed homilies, however, in showing conservative 'survival' and in emphasising controverted points.[36] Edgeworth's mild Erastianism also distinguishes him from other conservatives like Bishops Bonner, Tunstal and Gardiner whose strong anti-papal statements would have made publication of their Henrician sermons embarassing. He continues Thomas More's apologetics by asserting the unwritten verities of the church, by defending the role of the priesthood and the Real Presence, and speaking out against Lutheran and Anabaptist heresies. His single allusion to the Pope is probably a later interpolation made out of respect to the Marian Restoration.[37]

The history of the *Sermons* in the reign of Elizabeth

Caly's edition of the *Sermons* enjoyed only a brief period of use before suffering the fate which befell all other Catholic treatises, devotional works, sermons and catechisms which came to be treated as pro-papist propaganda following the Elizabethan Settlement. On 1 March 1569, after a raid on the study of John Stow, the eminent antiquary and bibliophile, a proclamation was passed proscribing such works and ordering all existing copies to be burnt.[38]

The legislation was an inevitable consequence of the official programme of censorship mounted from the outset of Elizabeth's reign, aimed at suppressing seditious literature, especially Catholic writings which were smuggled in from abroad. The 1559 injunctions which set out a licensing system for the press decreed that all works, including religious treatises, be printed subject to official approval.[39] Following the injunctions of 20 June 1566, that all printed books were to be inspected by the wardens of the Stationers' Company, the campaign against imported Recusant works intensified.[40] Customs officers were appointed, 'promoters' and 'waiters' were assigned to inspect books at the ports, booksellers were alerted and informers encouraged.[41] A campaign by Bishop Grindal to enforce conformity in religion commenced the following year.[42]

Although censorship of the press was reinforced until 1577, 1569 was a year of mounting tension due to fears of Catholic insurgency at home and a dissolution of

don, 1979), pp. 463–72; Guy, *Tudor England*, pp. 227–49, for recent analyses of the failure of the Marian Restoration.
[36] As the two sermons on ceremonies and the creed fall into the categories of homilies authorised by convocation in 1557, the versions in manuscript Rawl. D. 831 may have been circulated for the purposes of instruction.
[37] *Sermons*, p. 193. On the mediocre quality of the writings of the Marian Catholic apologists see J. Loach, 'Pamphlets and Politics 1553–8', *Bulletin of the Institute of Historical Research* 48 (1975), 32.
[38] Hughes and Larkin, II, 561; Arber, *Register* I, 430; A.F. Allison and D.M. Rogers, *A Catalogue of Catholic Boooks in English printed abroad or secretly in England, 1558–1640*, 2 parts (Bognor Regis, 1956). Cited hereafter as A&R.
[39] Hughes and Larkin, II, 460, pp. 128–9; F.S. Siebert, *The Freedom of the Press in England: 1476–1776* (Urbana, University of Illinois Press, 1965), pp. 56–7, H.S. Bennett, *English Books and Readers: 1558–1603* (Cambridge, 1965), p. 57; Guy, *Tudor England*, pp. 292, 297.
[40] Arber, *Register* I, 322; Siebert, *Freedom of the Press*, pp. 58–9. The order of 1566 is printed by G.R. Elton in *The Tudor Constitution: Documents and Summary* (Cambridge, 1963), no. 49.
[41] Leona Rostenberg, *The Minority Press and the English Crown: A Study in Repression, 1558–1625* (Nieuwkoop, 1971), pp. 43–4; A.C. Southern, *English Recusant Prose, 1559–1582* (1950, repr. London, 1978), pp. 33–8.
[42] J. Strype, *The History of the Life and Acts of Edmund Grindal* (Oxford, 1821), pp. 180–3; Rostenberg, *Minority Press*, pp. 44–5.

the Anglo-Spanish détente abroad. A dispute over the ownership of Spanish treasure in the straits of Dover had strained relations between the English government and the Duke of Alva: when a manifesto was written by the Spanish ambassador De Spes in favour of the Duke, the Privy Council was greatly offended.[43] It was Stow's alleged complicity in the circulation of the document which led to an official enquiry into his activities. But although depositions were taken from his guild of Merchant Taylors, and Stow was called before the Lord Mayor, little evidence of any involvement could be discovered.[44] Nevertheless, his great collection of books and manuscripts provided an excuse for his study to be ransacked on 21 February.[45] Grindal's commissioners, Bedel, Williams and his chaplain, Archdeacon Watts, compiled an inventory of forty books and manuscripts to prove him 'a great fauourr of papistry'.[46] Among the controversial writings on the Mass by Stephen Gardiner and Dr Richard Smith, Recusant works of 1564–8 written in response to Bishop Jewell's challenge sermon, manuscripts of chronicles collected by Stow, were Marian treatises of Catholic doctrine; Edgeworth's Sermons, and others by Edmund Bonner, Walter Pollard, Thomas Watson, John Feckenham, Hugh Glasier, and James Brooks.[47]

After the Northern rebellion of 1570 increasingly severe measures were devised to stamp out all signs of 'papistry'.[48] Walsingham, Bishop of Winchester, employed a network of spies to search out proscribed books; the official programme was carried out by pursuivants and government undercover agents. The right to search printing houses was renewed in 1576, and after lists of Catholics in the various dioceses were compiled in 1577–8, searches of their households became commonplace.[49] Although Elizabeth's and Burghley's policies were not always successfully enforced, they effectively reduced the English Catholics to a persecuted minority and inhibited access to Catholic records, documents and treatises of the sort that Stow was collecting.[50] It was the English exiles at Douai and Louvain, in particular

43 Reprisals were ordered against Spanish shipping on 6th January; De Spes' manifesto was issued on the 10th; see Hughes and Larkin, II, 556; Conyers Read, Mr. Secretary Cecil and Queen Elizabeth (Oxford, 1956), pp. 431–4; Paul Johnson, Elizabeth (London, 1974), pp. 149–50.
44 Stow, originally a tailor by profession, was admitted to the freedom of the Merchant Taylors Company in 1547; see C.M. Clode, Memorials of the Guild of Merchant Taylors (London, 1875), pp. 183–6; J. Strype, 'Life of Stow' in his edition of Stow's Survey of the Cities of London and Westminster, 2 vols (London, 1720), I, iv–v, xxi–ii; C.L. Kingsford's introduction to his edition of Stow's A Survey of London, 2 vols (London, 1908), I, xvi–iii. The depositions are printed by C.M. Clode, The Early History of the Guild of Merchant Taylors, 2 vols (London, 1888), II, 300–302.
45 See DNB s.v. 'Stow'; Rostenberg, Minority Press, p. 48; Kingsford, Survey I, xix, lxxxvii, on the extent of Stow's library.
46 Watts to Grindal, BL MS Lansdowne 11, art. 3, fo. 5; see Strype, 'Life of Stowe', I, iv; Grindal, pp. 184–5; Kingsford, Survey I, xvi–ii.
47 The inventory, Grindal's letter to Cecil and the Privy Council of 24 February, and Watt's report to Grindal are printed by Arber with his notes from BL MS Lansdowne No. 11 arts. 2–3, fos 4–8 in Transcript I, 393–4; and by Strype in Grindal, pp. 516–19. The inventory is partly analysed by Rostenberg, Minority Press, p. 218. See the transcript newly made from MS Lansdowne No. 11 fos 7–8 by J.M. Wilson in 'A Catalogue of the prohibited books found in the study of John Stow in 1568(9)', RH XX, i (1990), 1–30 (cited hereafter as Wilson, 'Catalogue').
48 Hughes and Larkin, II, 577; C. Cross, Church and People, 1450–1660 (London, 1976), p. 143; Guy, Tudor England, p. 248. G. Anstruther, Vaux of Harrowden, A Recusant Family (Newport, Mons., 1953), p. 83, estimates that as many as six hundred papists were hanged and their possessions looted following the Northern Rebellion.
49 Ibid. pp. 151–2, 168–71, 180–2; Rostenberg, Minority Press, pp. 43–50; Bennett, English Books, pp. 73–8; Southern, Recusant Prose, pp. 35–41.
50 Ibid. p. 68; he estimates that at least 20,000 Recusant works were imported into England before

Nicholas Sander who wrote *De Visibili Monarchia Ecclesiae* (1571) and *De Schismate* (1585), who finally provided a contemporary Catholic history of the Reformation.

The reputation of the *Sermons*

The comparative rarity of the 1557 edition of the *Sermons* due to its proscription in 1569 has meant that Edgeworth's homilies like those of Edmund Bonner, Leonard Pollard and Thomas Watson, have been largely neglected. Moreover the continued fame of Hugh Latimer as the great popular preacher of the Reformation has eclipsed the works of his lesser contemporaries. The extracts printed in MS James 29 are the only known indication of an historical interest in the *Sermons* and they have received only passing mention subsequently. Although the Edgeworth family was aware of their existence in the nineteenth century, their contents were ignored until T. Dibdin drew attention to them in 1824 and T.E. Bridgett assessed Edgeworth's reputation as a minor Catholic apologist in 1879.[51] It was not until 1954, however, that J.W. Blench established the literary and historical importance of the *Sermons*.[52]

A note on dates

Although only the sermon on the creed is dated (1546), approximate dates can be suggested for some of the others. A *terminus ad quem* for the sermon on ceremonies is 6 February 1548, when many of the ceremonies referred to were abolished by Royal Proclamation. The first sermon on the seven gifts of the Holy Ghost was preached in c.1535–6. References to the dispute over purgatory in the second suggest a date of preaching in late 1536 or early 1537 following the Ten Articles. The monastic dissolutions in Bristol in 1539 and 1540 and legislation limiting reading of the vernacular Bible passed in April 1539 provide a date for the fourth, whereas the lack of topical allusions in the fifth and sixth sermons suggest dates in the early 1540s after the earlier controversies had been silenced. The series on St Peter's First Epistle was preached intermittently in Bristol Cathedral from c.1554/5 to c.1553. Sermons eighteen to twenty, preached in c.1553 after a break of five or six years, are Edwardian; so in all likelihood are the twelfth, which alludes to the Merchant Venturers, incorporated into a Society in Bristol in December 1552; the thirteenth, which refers to the Anabaptist heresy denying the incarnation of Christ (a controversial issue in 1552); and the seventeenth, which alludes to events which followed the 1547 Chantries Act.

1580; see Rostenberg, *Minority Press*, pp. 31–9; cf. Guy, *Tudor England*, p. 299 on the minority status of Catholics.
[51] R.L. Edgeworth, *Memoirs*, 2 vols (London, 1820), I, 1; T.F. Dibdin, *The Library Companion*, 2 vols (Oxford, 1824), I, 73–85; T.E. Bridgett, 'The Bristol Pulpit in the Days of Henry VIII', *Dublin Review* 3rd ser. i (1879), 73–95.
[52] J.W. Blench, 'Roger Edgeworth and John Longland, two forgotten preachers of the early sixteenth Century', *RES NS*, v (1954), 123–43.

THE BIOGRAPHY OF ROGER EDGEWORTH

Early years: Oriel College, Oxford, c. 1503–1525

Roger Edgeworth was born in about 1488[1] at Holt Castle within the Marches of Wales in the county of Denbigh and the diocese of Chester.[2] His family, however, may originally have come from the village of Edgeworth in Gloucestershire.[3] He was perhaps the oldest of three or four brothers. His brother John's family evidently became Protestants:[4] one son, Edward, was the first Bishop of Down and Connor in Ireland in 1593 and another son, Francis, who also settled in Ireland, became clerk of the Hanaper in 1616.[5] From the issue of Francis was descended Richard Lovell Edgeworth, noted for his advanced views on education, and Maria Edgeworth, who gained fame as a novelist.[6] Another brother, Robert, recorded as being feoffed the use of land in Warwickshire in 1530 and of holding two pastures in Claredon in Warwick in 1553, evidently predeceased Roger because he makes provision for his family in his will.[7] He also names as a beneficiary, 'my Cosen Sir Richarde Edgeworthe', a relative who like Edgeworth was a fellow of Oriel College, Oxford from 1557 to 1565 and who in later life became a coroner.[8]

In the *Sermons* Edgeworth expresses gratitude to his parents who 'set me to schole in youth' and to Bishop Smyth, 'my bringer vp & exhibitoure . . .tyl I was maister of Arte'.[9] He was doubly fortunate in receiving from an early age the

[1] Edgeworth's age has been calculated from the date of his matriculation in c.1503 and ordination in 1512 (for which the average ages were fifteen and twenty four years); see J.A. Weisheipl, 'Curriculum of the Faculty of Arts at Oxford in the early Fourteenth Century', *Medieval Studies* 26 (1964), 146–7 (cited hereafter as Weisheipl, 'Curriculum'); P. Heath, *The English Parish Clergy on the Eve of the Reformation* (London, 1969), p. 15.

[2] *DNB* s.v. 'Edgeworth': On Holt Castle and the parish of Holt, lying northeast of Wrexham and E. southeast of Denbigh, see S. Lewis, *A Topographical Dictionary of Wales*, 2 vols (London, 1849), I, s.v. 'Holt'. In his will Edgeworth makes provision for his copies of the works of St Chrysostom and St Ambrose to go to a fellow, an MA student in divinity, 'borne nexte to the Castell of holte in the marches of wales beside Westechester', if Oriel College already has them (Appendix, p. 448).

[3] See *The Black Book of Edgeworthstown and other Edgeworth Memories, 1585–1817*, ed. H.J. and H.E. Butler (London, 1927), p. 7 on the family tradition that Edgeworths lived in the village of Edgeware in Middlesex during Henry VIII's reign; J. Maclean, 'The Aid levied in Gloucestershire in the 20th Edward III (1349)', *TBGAS* X (1885–6), 288.

[4] It is not clear whether the John Edgeworth who matriculated at Oriel College determining MA on 6 March 1519, and who succeeded Roger as vicar of Chalfont St Peters from 1528–1532, was his brother and the father of Francis and Edward; his vocation makes it unlikely that he married. See the Transcript of OU Arch. Reg. H, pp. 31, 52 (cited hereafter as *Reg. Congreg. 1518–35*); *The Register of the University of Oxford*, Vol. I, *1449–1463; 1505–71*, ed. C.W. Boase, OHS, 1 (Oxford, 1885), p. 107 (cited hereafter as Boase, *Register*); G. Lipscombe, *The History and Antiquities of the County of Buckingham*, 4 vols (London, 1847), III, 245; Butler, *Edgeworthstown*, pp. 7–8.

[5] *Ibid.*; Bodl. MS. Dep. C. 136.

[6] Butler, *Edgeworthstown*, pp. 8–10, 223–6.

[7] *LP* IV, iii, 6751; g. 8; *CPR (1553–4)*, p. 366; Appendix, p. 449.

[8] Richard Edgeworth supplicated for his BA in 1556 and for his MA in 1563; see Boase, *Register*, p. 234; *DRO*, pp. 143, 146; G.C. Richards and C.L. Shadwell, *The Provosts and Fellows of Oriel College* (Oxford, 1922), p. 69; *CPR (1562)*, p. 379; Appendix, p. 450.

[9] *Sermons*, p. 155.

patronage of William Smyth, Bishop of Coventry from c.1492–5, who was famed for his educational philanthrophy. Edgeworth's educational progress coincided with and benefited from the bishop's advance through the episcopal hierarchy. When Smyth refounded St John's hospital in Lichfield as a free grammar school in 1495 he may have attended as a pupil and, had he already been marked out for the priesthood, would have accompanied the bishop on his translation to the diocese of Lincoln in the same year or followed soon after.[10] Edgeworth's allusion to John Stanbridge confirms that he was one of the first students at the grammar school attached to St John's Hospital, Banbury, which the bishop founded in 1501. Banbury Grammar became famous both for its advanced methods of teaching and for the influence of John Stanbridge's grammars.[11]

From 1500 to 1503 Smyth was Chancellor of Oxford University and acted as Visitor of Oriel and Lincoln Colleges.[12] Edgeworth matriculated as his exhibitioner in c.1503 and for the next four years studied for the degree of BA.[13] The grace for his determination as BA, granted on 16 January 1507/8, lists the duties he has completed:[14] namely, attendance at lectures (in studiis et ordinariis); performing one responsion to a determining bachelor in Lent; one creacio generalis; two variations; one opposition and one responsion in Alberto in the disputations of the scholars amongst themselves (known as the 'Parvisus' exercises); that is he disputed in linguistic grammar-logic probably based on the tractate of Thomas von Erfurt, De Modis Significandi.[15] He determined with credit in Lent.[16] On 8 November 1508 he was unanimously elected to one of the two new Oriel fellowships founded by Bishop Smyth in 1507 with the dispensation that he was not from the Lincoln diocese, as decreed by the ordinances, and with the further dispensation

[10] J. McConica, 'The Rise of the Undergraduate College', CU, pp. 9–10; R. Churton, The Lives of William Smyth, Bishop of Lincoln and Sir Richard Sutton, Knight, Founders of Brasen Nose College (Oxford, 1800), pp. 80–1, 89; DNB s.v. 'Smith'; on early education see N.I. Orme, Education in the West of England, 1066–1548 (University of Exeter, 1976), pp. 20–2; English Schools in the Middle Ages (London, 1973), pp. 59–86 (cited hereafter as Orme, Education and English Schools); Heath, Parish Clergy, p. 13. Edgeworth's early departure from the Welsh Marches makes it unlikely that his sympathies remained with Wales; cf. Glanmor Williams, The Welsh Church from Conquest to Reformation (Cardiff, 1976), pp. 504, 532 (cited hereafter as Williams, Welsh Church).
[11] A. Beesley, The History of Banbury (London, 1841), pp. 194–6; BRUO III, 1754–5; DNB s.v. 'Stanbridge'; on allusions to Stanbridge's grammars in other sixteenth century school statutes see B. White, ed. The Vulgaria of John Stanbridge and the Vulgaria of Robert Whittinton, EETS, OS, 187 (London, 1932), pp. 17–18 (cited hereafter as White, Vulgaria); R.S. Stanier, Magdalen School, OHS, NS, 3 (Oxford, 1940), pp. 33–6, 57–70; Orme, English Schools, pp. 107–9.
[12] McConica, 'Undergraduate College', CU, p. 9; Churton, Lives, p. 227; J.R.L. Highfield, 'The Early Colleges', EOS, p. 243.
[13] Matriculations at Oxford are first recorded in 1565, but this date has been estimated from Edgeworth's supplication to determine as BA in 1507; see Statuta Antiqua Vniversitatis Oxoniensis, ed. S. Gibson (Oxford, 1931), pp. lxxxii–iii (cited hereafter as Gibson, Statuta Antiqua); on patronage J.I. Catto, 'Citizens, Scholars and Masters', EOS, pp. 168–9.
[14] On the requirements of the undergraduate and the cursory and ordinary lectures see Weisheipl, 'Curriculum', 147, 150–1, 153–6; J.M. Fletcher, 'The Faculty of Arts', EOS, pp. 375–7, 386. The ordinary lectures were given by regent masters in the mornings on dies legibiles (fixed days) at fixed hours on the texts; then questions were raised by them on points from the texts on which they had lectured. The cursory lectures, consisting of a running commentary on a text, were delivered at other times by the bachelors.
[15] Transcript of OU Arch. Reg. G, pp. 205–6 (cited hereafter as Reg. Congreg. 1505–17). He was to determine next Lent and perform his exercises in the bachelors' disputations within a year. On admission to determine see Gibson, Statuta Antiqua, pp. lxxxviii–xci; Fletcher, 'Arts', EOS, pp. 379–82; Weisheipl, 'Curriculum', 156–7.
[16] Reg. Congreg. 1505–17, pp. 224, 228–9; on determination see Fletcher, 'Arts', EOS, pp. 381–3.

that there were already two fellows from the Lichfield diocese. He was made full fellow on 11 June 1510.[17] The entries in the university Registers of Congregation and Convocation and in the *Dean's Register of Oriel* give a picture of his studies for the degrees of MA and D.Th. and his life in college until his resignation in 1519 and departure from Oxford to Bristol in 1525.

The degree of MA required a further three years' residence and attendance at the masters' lectures, as well as delivering cursory lectures and opposing and responding publically for two years;[18] for the exercises candidates had also to observe and participate in the annual Lenten and 'Austin' disputations of the bachelors, and the solemn disputations held weekly by the masters.[19] In a ceremony on 18 December 1511 Edgeworth and four other bachelors were awarded by the provost Oriel College's licence to incept as MA.[20] The *Dean's Register of Oriel* prints in full the *forma inceptorum* stating the conditions of inception and imposing the duty of lecturing and disputing in college every term during the two year period of 'necessary regency'.[21] The texts and methods of delivering the twenty four 'ordinary' lectures on the seven arts and three philosophies are prescribed: '*exponendo textum, et movendo dubia textualia, & soluciones dubiorum recitatorum consequenter adiungendo*'. For the public lectures on a work of Aristotle, the four other Oriel scholars are assigned either the works of Aristotle or Duns Scotus, but Edgeworth '*quod sit iunior*' is given the lesser task of elucidating a commentator; he is given leave for two years to lecture on the commentary on Aristotle's *Physics* by Johannes Canonicus, known also as John Marbres.[22] The five Oriel men were also obliged to respond to a formal disputation in the schools held by some master and as necessary regents and members of congregation to participate in the election of the proctors and other university officers. Following this they were granted the licence to incept in the Faculty of Arts on 9 February 1512.[23] They proceeded to the final stage, the ceremony of inception itself, on 6 February and were admitted to the Faculty of Theology.[24]

---

[17] BRUO IV, 184; Churton, *Lives*, pp. 232–5; D.W. Rannie, *Oriel College* (London, 1900), pp. 70–71; DRO, pp. 17, 28. The new fellow was to be from the diocese of Lincoln and a BA who had determined with credit while the original college statutes decreed that there be not more than two fellows from the diocese of Lichfield (also known as Chester) at the same time; see Richards and Shadwell, *Provosts and Fellows*, Appendix III, p. 104.
[18] On the statutory requirements for MA and the set texts see Fletcher, 'Arts', EOS, pp. 384–6; Weisheipl, 'Curriculum', 159–61.
[19] *Ibid.* 162–3; Fletcher, 'Arts', EOS, pp. 386–7; Gibson, *Statuta Antiqua*, pp. xciii–xcvi.
[20] DRO, pp. 28–30; on the four other fellows see Richards and Shadwell, *Provosts and Fellows*, pp. 47–9. Students usually incepted after their seventh year; this was a separate licence from the one imposed by the faculty of arts and it was designed to secure adequate collegiate teaching in the arts; see S.L. Greenslade, 'The Faculty of Theology', CU, p. 298; on the licence see Fletcher, 'Arts', EOS, pp. 388–9; Gibson, *Statuta Antiqua*, pp. xcvi–cxviii.
[21] The terms *pro forma* or *forma inceptorum* refer to the standard by which one proceeded to the status of master and to the set texts; see Weisheipl, 'Curriculum', 149, n. 14, 161; Fletcher, 'Arts', EOS, p. 376.
[22] DRO, p. 29; on the lecturing duties, Gibson, *Statuta Antiqua*, pp. c–cii, 235–6, 263; on John Marbres see BRUO, III, 346–7, s.v. 'Canon, John'. His commentary was a well used text in the Oxford Faculty of Arts. I am grateful to Professor J.M. Fletcher for bringing his name to my attention.
[23] *Reg. Congreg. 1505–17*, p. 296. See *The Register of the University of Oxford*, 5 vols (Oxford, 1885–9), II, i, *1571–1622*, ed. A. Clark, OHS, 10 (Oxford, 1887), pp. 80–1 (cited hereafter as Clark, *Register*); on the prescribed Aristotelian books for the study of the three philosophies see Weisheipl, 'Curriculum', 173–6; Gibson, *Statuta Antiqua*, pp. xcv (n. 3), cviii (n. 3), 32, 34.
[24] *Reg. Congreg. 1505–17*, pp. 298, 301; on the ceremony of inception see Fletcher, 'Arts', EOS, pp. 389–91; Clark, *Register*, pp. 82–5.

In the early sixteenth century the full two year period of necessary regency was often not observed and graces and dispensations were frequently granted to candidates who sought to modify their time and the academic exercises and adminstrative duties incumbent upon them.[25] On 4 February 1511 Edgeworth and other regents were dispensed from disputing in *quodlibets* – disputations or exercises raised 'from the floor'[26] – and in July they were excused from purchasing *capa regentie*, the costly special dress of the regents, permitted to absent themselves from funerals and processions, always an unpopular duty, and at the same time to cast votes, to seek and grant graces in congregation as non-regents and to read one ordinary *dispensativum* as their final lecture because of the long vacation.[27] Edgeworth also performed certain judicial or legal duties: on 16 February 1512 he was appointed to a court of regents to hear an appeal for a case which had been tried in the Vice-Chancellor's court, and the following year as one of the *iudices ad inquirendum de pace* – the officers who helped the proctors maintain order. He frequently acted as guardian of the university chests, and in 1517 was one of three masters appointed as *scrutatores* to check the guardians' accounts of the chests.[28]

As a resident MA Edgeworth was obliged by statute to enter into a higher faculty and on 10 May 1513 after completing his regency he and John Morys entered into the Faculty of Theology having been excused necessary regency and with dispensation from the *lecture minute*; that is, lectures on the *Parva Naturalia*, the small Aristotelian treatises on psychology.[29] For the baccalaureat in theology he had to spend a further seven years in residence, attending lectures on the Bible for three years;[30] he was also required to participate in the terminal disputations in theology and in two *pro forma* disputations in the theology school, opposing not before his fifth year and responding not before his seventh.[31] On 13 October 1519

[25] A master had to fulfil the two year 'necessary regency' before he could proceed to a higher faculty such as theology; on the duties of the necessary regents, see Clark, *Register*, p. 90 ff; on the break-down of the system from c.1500, *ibid.* p. 391; J.M. Fletcher, 'The Faculty of Arts', *CU*, pp. 185–6; Greenslade, 'Theology', *CU*, p. 305; on graces and dispensations see Gibson, *Statuta Antiqua*, pp. cxviii–cxxii; E. Mallet, *A History of the University of Oxford*, 3 vols (London, 1924–7), I, 199–200.

[26] Fletcher, 'Arts', *EOS*, pp. 392–3; Weisheipl, 'Curriculum', 182–5.

[27] *Reg. Congreg. 1505–17*, pp. 303–4, 330, 334, 336; see Gibson, *Statuta Antiqua*, pp. xxvii (n. 2) on the ceremonial dress of the regent masters of arts; c (n. 4) on funerals and processions. The *ordinarium dispensativum* was one lecture required by Congregation which concluded the master's lecturing obligations as a necessary regent.

[28] *Reg. Congreg. 1505–17*, pp. 368–9, 319–20, 398, 430, 634, 671, 728, 744; he was keeper of the *Antiqua Universitatis* in May 1512 (although exempted from duty that year), of the Rothbury Chest in 1513 and 1516, of the Winton Chest in 1515 and 1516, and of the Chicheley Chest in 1516; see Clark, *Register*, pp. 101–4; Gibson, *Statuta Antiqua*, pp. lxxviii–lxxx on law and order; lxxvi on the *scrutatores*.

[29] *Reg. Congreg. 1505–17*, pp. 403–4, 405. On the *Parva Naturalia* (known as the *libri minuti*) see Weisheipl, 'Curriculum', 174–5. On 17 May 1513 the men were given permission to attend congregation when graces were granted by the proctors; see Gibson, *Statuta Antiqua*, pp. cii, lxxv–xxvi on the proctors' duties.

[30] Greenslade, 'Theology', *CU*, pp. 295–8, mentions an intermediate stage at Oriel when the graduate was dispensed from lecturing and allowed to attend the biblical lectures, although still required to particpate in the college's arts disputations.

[31] *Ibid.* p. 296; *Reg. Congreg. 1505–17*, pp. 411, 423, records that on 5 June 1513 Edgeworth and other bachelors were granted permission to read only one ordinary lecture because they were responding in the formal disputations of the masters; on 30 June they were dispensed from pronouncing graces verbatim while seeking to offer determination if any of them was elected proctor; see Clark, *Register*, pp. 109–10, 132–5; Gibson, *Statuta Antiqua*, pp. cix–x (on the conditions for B.Th.)

he and two other Oriel fellows, John Stevyns and Thomas Ware, were admitted as bachelors to lecture on a book of the *Sentences* of Peter Lombard.[32] Edgeworth was granted permission to preach the sermon in Latin required within a year of admission on Corpus Christi Day at the monastery of St Frideswide instead of St Mary's; he disputed for the degree on 29 April 1520 and for the final exercise, the determination, preached the *concio ad clerum* in Latin at St Mary's on 13 May.[33]

Four years' study was required for the doctorate of theology; this included lecturing on the *Sentences* of Peter Lombard *vel fere* and on some book of the Bible and performing eight responsions.[34] Upon his supplication to incept for the D.Th. on 31 March 1521, Edgeworth preached the required probationary sermon in Latin at Paul's Cross.[35] On 7 November 1525 he was licensed for the degree; he disputed sometime early in 1526 and incepted on 2 July.[36] These formal preaching requirements mark the beginning of Edgeworth's reputation as a preacher. He probably preached university sermons at St Mary's, Christ Church and St Peter's in the East during term and the long vacations and he possibly held a licence to preach independently of the degree in theology, issued under the university seal.[37] The extent of his commitments is suggested by the dispensation postponing his inception as D.Th. because he had undertaken to preach outside the university and could not easily be present.[38]

A theological training in the early sixteenth century was still preeminently scholastic and the traditional influence of Duns Scotus and his followers meant that the moderate realism of the teaching programme was undiminished: university lectures were delivered on the Bible or alternatively on Scotus. Continuous exposition of a book of the New Testament may have been offered unofficially as an alternative to the *Sentences*, but otherwise the curriculum remained unchanged from medieval times.[39] Moreover Oriel College, renowned as a centre for study in divinity, retained its innately conservative character despite the encroachment of humanism and took steps to resist the new learning which was enshrined in the statutes of Corpus Christi and Cardinal's Colleges.[40] The new lectureships founded by Wolsey and Bishop Fox had effectively silenced the opposition to the study of Greek mounted by the 'Trojans', whose attitudes and those of the university

[32] *Reg. Congreg. 1518–35*, p. 69; *DRO*, p. 38; see Greenslade, 'Theology', *CU*, pp. 298–300 on the prerequisites for reading the *Sentences* at Oriel.
[33] *Reg. Congreg. 1518–35*, pp. 148, 154a; theologians were permitted to count a sermon delivered elsewhere as equivalent to one given in St Mary's. The *sermo excusatorius* (i.e. the small task undertaken at the insistence of the university to compensate for any omission of the statutory requirements) at St Mary's was considered to complete his full course. On the *conciones ad clerum* see Greenslade, 'Theology', *CU*, p. 311; Clark, *Register*, pp. 136–8; Gibson, *Statuta Antiqua*, pp. cx–cxi (n. 7), 267–8. G.R. Owst, *Preaching in Medieval England, an Introduction to the Sermon Manuscripts of the Period c. 1350–1450* (Cambridge, 1926), pp. 153–4, discusses Latin and vernacular sermons at Oxford.
[34] *Ibid.* pp. 296, 308–9; on the requirements for the D.Th. see Clark, *Register*, pp. 139–42; Gibson, *Statuta Antiqua*, pp. cx (n. 6)–cxi.
[35] *Reg. Congreg. 1518–35*, p. 592. The Paul's Cross sermon could count *pro forma* for the degree in place of the one at Oxford; see Greenslade, 'Theology', *CU*, p. 312.
[36] *Reg. Congreg. 1518–35*, p. 716; Greenslade, 'Theology', *CU*, pp. 311–12; Boase, *Register*, p. 56.
[37] See Anthony a Wood, *Atheniae Oxonienses . . . to which are added* The Fasti *or Annals*, ed. P. Bliss, 4 vols, 3rd ed. (London, 1813, facs. New York, 1967), I, 315; Clark, *Register*, pp. 130–2; Gibson, *Statuta Antiqua*, pp. cxi–ii.
[38] *Reg. Congreg. 1518–35*, p. 676; Clark, *Register*, p. 144.
[39] Fletcher, 'Arts', *CU*, p. 159; Greenslade, 'Theology', *CU*, p. 314; Lupton, A *Life of Dean Colet* (London, 1887; repr. New York, 1974) p. 59; Clark, *Register*, pp. 76–8, 140.
[40] Highfield, 'Early Colleges', *EOS*, pp. 237, 245.

authorities in tolerating them Thomas More had deplored in 1518.[41] But Bishop Longland's visitation injunctions of 1531 recommended that the new learning (*recentiores litteras*) or classical studies, be abandoned in favour of the regular medieval curriculum.[42] A catalogue of the college library holdings in 1375 listing nearly one hundred manuscripts of works required by the medieval curriculum includes treatises by Priscian and Aristotle, texts for the study of civil and canon law, and about forty works of theology; notable is the lack of any classical texts.[43] The college's reputation for orthodoxy was reinforced by the standing of many fellows and visitors such as Edmund Wylsford, Provost from 1507–16 and confessor of Lady Katherine of Aragon, who gave the first university lectures in Divinity in 1497; Edmund Powell, who defended university Catholicism against Lutheran heresy in 1521; and Dr Roper, a resident from 1507–1512 who occupied the Lady Margaret Chair in Divinity in 1500.[44] The staunch resistance of its members to the religious changes of the Reformation is striking: Edward Powell and George Crofts, a former fellow, were both executed for denying the Royal Supremacy, while Richard Crispin, fellow from 1516 to 1527, later Canon of Exeter, was imprisoned for his part in the Western insurgence of 1549 and died in the Tower.[45]

From 1508 to 1519 Edgeworth was one of the college fellows or *socii*, a close knit circle owing to Oriel's relative financial independence from the rest of the university.[46] The offices he held establish the pattern of administrative responsibilities that recurs throughout his career. After being ordained in 1512 he was appointed as college chaplain.[47] By 1513 he was one of the two college treasurers after the previous treasurers, held liable for the college's debts, were dismissed from office.[48] In this year he acted as collector of accounts, probably holding one of the three pedes which were customarily presented at each audit, and he may have repre-

41 On the revival of Greek see C. Cross, 'Oxford and the Tudor State, 1509–1558', CU, pp. 120–1; on the opposition of the 'Trojans' see McConica, 'Undergraduate College', CU, p. 67; More's famous letter is printed in The Correspondence of Sir Thomas More, ed. E.F. Rogers (New Jersey, 1947), no. 60, pp. 111–20; and in Latin with a translation in T. More, In Defense of Humanism, ed. D. Kinney, CW15 (New Haven, 1986), pp. 130–49.
42 Rannie, Oriel, pp. 79–80;
43 C.L. Shadwell, Collectanea I, ed. C.R.L. Fletcher, OHS, 5 (Oxford, 1885), Pt. II, pp. 57–70; a seventeenth century catalogue, Bodl. MS Tanner 269, shows a similar dearth of classical texts; cf. the catalogue in DRO, Appendix II, pp. 386–97. On the addition of theological works to the library in 1544 see DRO, p. 124; N. Ker, 'Oxford college libraries in the sixteenth century', BLR 6 (1959), 468.
44 BRUO III, 1510–1; Oriel College Records, ed. C.L. Shadwell and H.E. Salter, OHS, 85 (Oxford, 1926), p. 41; Richards and Shadwell, Provosts and Fellows, Appendix III, p. 204; on the Lady Margaret professorship see G. Duncan, 'Public Lectures and Professorial Chairs', CU, pp. 347–50. See Williams, Welsh Church, p. 532, for the view that Edgeworth and Powell belonged to a circle of Welsh Catholic humanists.
45 Richards and Shadwell, Provosts and Fellows, pp. 51, 53; BRUO IV, 150, 155–6; DNB, s.v. 'Crofte'. Edgeworth may have met Crofts when he was Master of St Bartholomew's Hospital in Bristol from 1525 to c.1532; he also held two benefices in Somerset.
46 Rannie, Oriel, pp. 72–3; G.K. Richards, 'Oriel in Tudor and Stuart Times', The Oriel College Record (1920), 167; A. Clark, The Colleges of Oxford (Oxford, 1891), pp. 105–6.
47 BRUO IV, 184; Highfield, 'Early Colleges', EOS, p. 251.
48 Richards and Shadwell, Provosts and Fellows, p. 48. In 1513 Ware and Stevyns were treasurers (OC Arch. Transcript of The Treasurers' Accounts VIII (1512–15), 734 (cited hereafter as Treasurers' Accounts); Edgeworth witnessed the replacement of the senior treasurer (DRO, pp. 35–6). OU Arch. Reg. F Rev. (cited hereafter as Chanc. Court Reg. 1506–1515), p. 211, records two payments made on 11 January 1513 by commoners, 'Joan Malerer, widow, and William Ryxston to magister Egeworth, bursar of Oriel.'

sented the college in legal proceedings in the Vice-Chancellor's court.[49] He was inevitably caught up with college affairs, such as appointing probationary scholars, electing a new provost in 1517, administering the college farms at Wadley and Deane, and representing the college interests to the Bishop of Lincoln.[50] The *Treasurers' Accounts of Oriel College* record the payments made to the fellows for expenses incurred in discharging these duties in addition to their quarterly stipends of 13s 4d.[51]

Some of Edgeworth's time was spent in imposing disciplinary measures against troublesome colleagues, Thomas Heritage and John Lewis, for bad debts and other misdemeanours such as disorderly behaviour. Heritage, who was Principal of St Mary's, college chaplain from 1507 to 1512, and senior proctor in 1512, was to be expelled in 1512, but Edgeworth, James More and Stevyns, acting on behalf of Provost Wylsford, pleaded with the Visitor for a delay; however, his continued non- payment of debts led to a second application for his expulsion in 1513.[52] John Lewis was expelled from the college on 11 June 1510 principally for disorderly behaviour. A request made the following April for his readmission seems to have been unsuccessful and so were the fellows' attempts to assist him; Thomas Ware's offer of legal advice was reprimanded by the provost, while the *Dean's Register* records that Edgeworth and his colleagues were reimbursed twenty shillings each in 1511 for expenses incurred in his cause.[53]

From the time he incepted as MA Edgeworth resided in the college and from 1513 he probably lived with three other scholars in a tenement in High St.[54] In 1517, after six years of adminstering the college estates of Wadley, Shenington and Deane, he and another Oriel fellow, Cannyngs, were admitted to the livings of Wadley and Deane.[55] Wadley estate in the parish of Faringdon yielded a rent from tenants of £8 and the *valet clare* was £50; the property was in a state of decay and requests for reparation continued until 1533. Edgeworth may have resided there intermittently until October 1525.[56] But in years when the sweating sickness and plague visited Oxford, as in 1513 and 1518–19, he may have retired to the college farm at Deane in the parish of Spelsbury and Chipping Norton or to Bartlemas, the hospital of St Bartholomew on Headington Hill, with the small allowance and dispensation from formal lectures which the college granted the fellows.[57] Edge-

---

[49] For the treasurers' duties see T.H. Aston and R. Faith, 'University and College Endowments', *EOS*, p. 304; Rannie, *Oriel*, p. 79; *Chanc. Court Reg. 1506–1515*, p. 225, records that 'Rogerus Barbar' was suspended for contumacy at the request of 'magister Egeworth' on 20 July 1513.

[50] Shadwell and Salter, *Oriel College Records*, pp. 69–72; DRO, pp. 33–5, 380–2; *Treasurers' Accounts* VII (1504–12), 694. In 1512 Edgeworth and Ware, deputising for the provost, made presentments to tenants at Wadley.

[51] *Ibid.* 696; VIII, 709–10, 738–9; 774–5; IX (1515–22), 507–8, 538–9, 569–70, 601–2.

[52] DRO, pp. 8–10, 33–5; Richards and Shadwell, *Provosts and Fellows*, p. 44.

[53] Lewis's licence for MA was revoked in 1508. See the accounts in *Calendar of the Chancellor's Court Register, 1506–1515*, pp. 37–8, 165, 178, 210; DRO, pp. 16–28; *Treasurers' Accounts* VII, 611, 660, 665, 696.

[54] *Ibid.* 629; Richards and Shadwell, *Provosts and Fellows*, p. 48; Shadwell and Salter, *Oriel College Records*, pp. 213–14. This and two other grants were made to the fellows in perpetuity in August–September 1513 by William Lynche, a former fellow and the king's physician; cf. DRO, p. 47.

[55] DRO, pp. 35, 41; on the college's purchase of Wadley manor in 1440 see Clark, *Colleges*, p. 104. *Treasurers' Accounts* VII, 694; VIII, 716–18; IX, 515, 551.

[56] Shadwell and Salter, *Oriel College Records*, p. 429; DRO, pp. 35, 51, 63, 66, 91, 93, 97; *Treasurers' Accounts* IX, 583.

[57] DRO, p. 32 and n; H. Maxwell Lyte, *A History of the University of Oxford* (London, 1886), pp. 431–4; on Bartlemas see Rannie, *Oriel*, pp. 20–5, 82; Aston and Faith, 'Endowments', *EOS*, p. 303.

worth resigned his fellowship on 15 March 1519 (with a year's grace in order to take the B.Th.), but continued his association with Oriel College until 1530.[58] During this period he may have resided temporarily at Eton College to which he was appointed as fellow in 1518 and where he was precentor from 1520–1, but he returned to Oriel in 1524 to read for the D.Th., this time as a distinguished lodger bringing prestige and some income to the college as well as contact with the outside world.[59] He rented a small room and was granted a larger one in St Martin's Hall on 20 December; however he was apparently away on other duties for periods after 1524 and his residence until 1530, when it is recorded that he was granted permission to hear and participate in college disputations, was probably intermittent.[60]

Despite the narrowness of his formal theological training and the conservative climate which prevailed at Oriel College, Edgeworth's intellectual development was undoubtedly influenced by the Christian humanism which is strongly attested at Oxford among the generation which succeeded Erasmus, Colet and More.[61] In 1523 he may have attended the public lectures of the reader in theology at Corpus Christi College or those on rhetoric and classical literature by the Spanish humanist, Juan Luis Vives, who succeeded Thomas Lupset as Wolsey's reader in humanity.[62] If the medieval curriculum was already partially reinterpreted so that the Bible was made the focus of study for the D.Th. and lectures were read on individual books rather than on the Sentences (as suggested by the statutes of Corpus Christi College for the reader in theology), then Edgeworth's method of preaching the twenty sermons on St Peter's First Epistle secundum ordinem textus may have evolved at this time; while the series on the seven gifts of the Holy Ghost, drawing on Thomistic theology, might also reflect his study of Summa Theologiae.[63] Certainly his use of Erasmus' biblical scholarship and the historico-critical method of biblical exegesis, as well as his preference for lecturing cursorie as Colet did in his famous lectures on Romans and Corinthians in 1497–1504, suggest the influence of this school.[64] Further signs of the new learning can be

---

[58] DRO, p. 47.

[59] Registrum Regale, ed. J. Pote Williams (Eton, 1847), p. 11; W. Sterry, 'Notes on the early Eton fellows', Etoniana 60 (1935), 158. Edgeworth was not one of the old type of 'battelar', who waited on the fellows, but did not eat with them (BRUO IV, 184).

[60] Treasurers' Accounts X (1522–26), 721, 737–8, 748; DRO, p. 83; Richards and Shadwell, Provosts and Fellows, p. 48.

[61] On the influence of the humanists see A. Hyma, 'Erasmus and the Oxford Reformers, 1493–1503, 1503–19', Nederlands Archief voor Kerkgeschiedenis 25 (1932), 97–134; 38 (1952), 65–85. See Williams, Welsh Church, pp. 504, 532 on the Welsh Catholic humanists.

[62] Duncan, 'Public Lectures', CU, pp. 336–7; The Life and Works of Thomas Lupset, ed. J.A. Gee (New Haven, 1928), pp. 101–2; Foster Watson, ed. Vives: On Education. A Translation of the De Tradendis Disciplinis of Juan Luis Vives (Cambridge, 1913), pp. lxvii–ix and Juan Luis Vives, 1492–1540 (Oxford, 1922), pp. 74–80. The period between 1523–8 has been called the age of pietas litterata; according to White (Vulgaria, p. xv), this was a Tudor educational ideal.

[63] McConica, 'Undergraduate College', CU, p. 22. The Royal Injunctions of 1535 to Oxford and Cambridge stopped the study of Canon Law; divinity lectures were to be on the Old and New Testaments; see J.B. Mullinger, The University of Cambridge, 3 vols (Cambridge, 1873), I, 630; Mallet, History II, 62–3. In the revised statutes of 1549, the grace for taking B.Th. was changed to ad lectionem alicuius Epistolarum Divi Pauli; this may have ratified an alteration already accepted informally; it was endorsed at Oriel in 1550 (Greenslade, 'Theology', CU, pp. 297, 314). In the nova statuta of 1565 bachelors gave six public lectures on some part of scripture or expounded cursorie one of the epistles; ibid. p. 308; Clark, Register, pp. 76, 136, 140. On the changing attitude to Aquinas see below, p. 52.

[64] Strype, Ecc. Mem. I, i, 74; on Colet's methods see The Exposition of St. Paul's Epistle to the

traced in the range of his classical allusions, his reference to the patristic fathers who were valued by Erasmus and Colet, and the impression of only a passing interest in scholasticism.[65]

These leanings would have been encouraged during his time as fellow of Eton College in 1518 and precentor from 1520–1.[66] The master then was Robert Aldridge, friend of Erasmus and contemporary of Croke, and an ardent promoter of the new learning. Both he and Edgeworth were appointed to Cranmer's commission to investigate the sacraments and the role of the clergy in 1540 and the similarity of their answers associates them with the humanist circle whose liberal educational views were underpinned by theological conservatism.[67] Another distinguished humanist and fellow of the college was William Horman, also a former pupil of John Stanbridge, known chiefly for his grammar *Vulgaria Puerorum*.[68] During these years Horman and Aldridge became involved in the celebrated 'Grammarians War' in support of William Lily whose method of teaching grammar by imitation rather than by precept was attacked by Robert Whittinton, the arch-conservative grammarian and friend of the poet, John Skelton. In 1521 Horman wrote a treatise, *Antibossicon*, to which Aldrich contributed a verse epistle.[69]

Bristol and Wells, c.1525–1547

The years following Edgeworth's inception as B.Th. saw the beginnings of his ecclesiastical career. On 13 June 1521 he was presented by Eton College to the living of Christchurch in Monmouthshire in Wales and from 1523 to 1528 he was vicar of Chalfont St Peter's in Buckinghamshire.[70] The incomes from these livings were modest: the vicar of Chalfont St Peter's received £3 1s 0d in returns from farms and tithes in 1535 and the rectory received annually from its farm a rent of

---

Corinthians, ed. and tr. J.H. Lupton (London, 1873, repr., New Jersey, 1965), pp. xx–xxi; Lupton, *Life*, pp. 63–87; P.A. Duhamel, 'The Oxford Lectures of John Colet. An Essay in Defining the English Renaissance', *Journal of the History of Ideas* 14 (1953), 493–510; F. Seebohm, *The Oxford Reformers, John Colet, Erasmus and Thomas More*, 2nd ed. (London, 1869), pp. 33–42; Blench, pp. 29–30.

[65] *Sermons*, pp. 95, 151, 156–7, 301, 345 etc.; there is only one reference to Duns Scotus (*ibid.* p. 116). Most of the classical and patristic authors whom Edgeworth refers to are listed in the statutes of Corpus Christi College; see McConica, 'Undergraduate College', *CU*, pp. 21–2; *The Foundation Statutes of Bishop Fox for Corpus Cristi College in the University of Oxford, A.D. 1517*, ed. and tr. G.M. Ward (London, 1843), pp. 99–200, 204.

[66] There were seven fellows at Eton College in 1535; see J. Ecton, *Liber Regis vel Thesaurus Rerum Ecclesiasticarum*, rev. J. Bacon (London, 1786), p. 491.

[67] *DNB*, s.v. 'Aldrich'; *Annals of Eton College*, ed. W. Sterry (London, 1898), p. 69; Aldrich's answers are printed in Pocock-Burnet, IV, 442–96.

[68] On Horman's association with Eton until his death in 1535 see *DNB* s.v. 'Horman'; BRUO II, pp. 963–4; Sterry, *Annals*, pp. 66–7; Rev. Radford, 'The Early History of Eton', *Etoniana* 93 (1942), 687–8; 95 (1943), 719–20; 96 (1943), 743–6. His *Vulgaria* (1495) has been edited by M.R. James, The Roxburghe Club, 149 (London, 1926); on the various *vulgaria* see *A Fifteenth Century Schoolbook*, ed. W. Nelson (Oxford, 1956), pp. 9–12; N. Orme, *Education and Society in Medieval and Renaissance England* (London, 1989), pp. 67–70, 78–112 (cited hereafter as Orme, *Education and Society*); White, *Vulgaria*, pp. 17–25.

[69] *Ibid.* pp. 28–32; Nelson, *A Fifteenth Century Schoolbook*, pp. 12–13.

[70] The presentation to the living of Christchurch was made by Eton College; see Sterry, 'Fellows', 158; Lipscombe, *History . . . of Buckingham* III, 245; Lincoln Archives Office, Reg. Longland, Lincoln, XXVII, fo. 210ᵛ.

£11.[71] The net income from the parish church of Christchurch in the diocese of Llandaff was £19 7s 1d.[72] But it was his appointment in 1525 as prior of the guild of Kalendars in Bristol which first took him to the West Country.[73] The guild was traditionally a brotherhood of the clergy and laity and a centre of orthodox study and preaching. To the office of prior, who was required to say divine service and to celebrate mases and obits, were attached special duties: to remain in daily attendance on the library, to preach a weekly lecture there, and to explain disputed points of scripture. He was also to be of the status of MA: Edgeworth was the prior of greatest academic distinction in the last forty years of the guild's existence.[74] After his resignation in 1528 little is known of his moves although it is likely that he entered the service of John Longland, Bishop of Lincoln. Like many churchmen at this time he became caught up in the burning issue of the day, the King's 'Great Matter'. He was employed, possibly by Wolsey, as a minor official of the legatine court which met at Blackfriars in May 1529 to discuss the king's divorce from Katherine of Aragon.[75]

This event plunged Edgeworth into the milieu of the group of churchmen now known as the 'conservative Henricians' whose service to the king's cause was amply rewarded with appointments to livings, episcopal sees and diplomatic missions abroad. Theologically and politically conservative they publically acclaimed the Royal Supremacy by preaching, contributing to the Henrician settlement of religion, and writing treatises which elevated obedience to the crown to a political principle.[76] Edgeworth's association in the court proceedings with Thomas Arundell, at that time gentleman of the chamber to Wolsey and a friend of Stephen Gardiner, may have led to the friendship that Winchester claimed with him in the 1540s.[77] He was to meet Bishops Bonner and Bell again in 1540 on the

---

[71] *Valor Ecclesiasticus temp. Henry VIII, auctoritate regia institutus*, ed. J. Caley and J. Hunter, 6 vols (1810–34), IV, 246–7 (cited hereafter as *Valor*). The living was in the property of St John's College, Oxford.
[72] *Ibid*. 374. The gross income was £23 9s 4d; and deductions were £3 10s 6d in tithes and 3s 9d in procurations. Edgeworth probably never resided, but his bequest of £3 4s to the parish church suggests that he maintained an association with the parish after he resigned; see Appendix, p. 448.
[73] Hereford and Worcester Record Office, Reg. Jeronimo Ghinucci, Worc., fo. 36. Edgeworth is named as prior on an indenture of a lease from the Guild of a messuage in High St, dated 10 June 1525; see BRO 12966 (37). *DRO*, p. 66, records that on October 26 1525 *uno socio* was appointed to adminster the cure at Wadley.
[74] For accounts of the guild see N.I. Orme, 'The Guild of Kalendars, Bristol', *TBGAS* 96 (1978), 35–52; 'A Bristol Library for the Clergy' in *Education and Society*, pp. 209–19. Eight books and manuscripts of theology which may have once belonged to the guild's library are listed by T.W. Williams in 'Gloucestershire Medieval Libraries', *TBGAS* 31 (1908), 87–90; cf. N. Ker, *The Medieval Libraries of Great Britain*, 2nd ed. (London, 1964), p. 13; Orme, *Education and Society*, p. 215. On the dissolution of the guild see J. Maclean, 'Chantry Certificates of Gloucestershire', *TBGAS* 8 (1883–4), 246–7.
[75] Edgeworth attended the presentation of the Pope's commission to Campeggio and Wolsey at the Dominican Priory of Blackfriars on 31 May 1529; see BL MS Royal 7c. xvi. fo. 254; *LP* IV, iii, 5613; G. de C. Parmiter, *The King's Great Matter: A Study in Anglo-Papal Relations, 1527–34* (London, 1967), pp. 96–7. The reference in his will to John Williams, formerly one of Wolsey's chaplains and crossbearers, suggests an association with the Cardinal; see Appendix, p. 449.
[76] On the 'conservative Henricians' see L. Baldwin Smith, *Tudor Prelates and Politics, 1536–1558* (New Jersey, 1953), pp. 42–68.
[77] *LP* IV, iii, 5184; *DNB* s.v. 'Arundel'; *Letters of Stephen Gardiner*, ed. J.A. Muller (Cambridge, 1933), p. 531 (To Somerset from the Clynke between 19 January and 20 February 1549): 'Withowt the Universities I know Doctor Cockes, Doctor Robinson, Doctor Crome, the Deanes of Exiter, Westminster and Powles, Layton, the Archdeacon of London, with Edgeworth and Marshall, and these be all thacquaintance I have in England . . .'.

commission of enquiry into the sacraments and John Clerk, Bishop of Bath and Wells through his appointment as canon residentiary of Wells Cathedral by 1536. The court proceedings would also have brought him to the attention of Thomas Cromwell whose acquaintance he fostered between 1536 and 1539 on behalf of the Wells chapter. Although Edgeworth apparently made no such formal commitment to Henry's policies as Bishops Bonner, Tunstal, Richard Sampson, Stephen Gardiner and Edward Fox, all of whom wrote treatises in defence of the Royal Supremacy, allusions to the king and exhortations of obedience to the crown in the *Sermons*, as well as his role in preparations for the third Henrician formulary, the *King's Book*, indicate that he was of their persuasion.[78]

The fruits of service to the crown came in the form of further favours over the next five years: the prebend of Slape in Salisbury, the prebend of Warminster alias Luxville in Bath and Wells, and the rectory of Brandesburton in Holderness, Yorkshire.[79] Edgeworth's association with Wells Cathedral as a canon residentiary commenced sometime between 1535–6; it was to culminate in his appointment as Chancellor under Mary I.[80] If he was in the West Country before this time then he was apparently not involved in the 1533 crisis in Bristol caused by the seditious preaching of the reformer Hugh Latimer, then rector of West Kington.[81]

Bristol was particularly susceptible to religious conflict: it was a traditional centre of Lollard heresy and was able to maintain independence in religious matters due to its division between the dioceses of Worcester and Bath and Wells and its distance from episcopal supervision.[82] In Lent 1533 Latimer preached against the Blessed Virgin, purgatory and images. This was met with disfavour by the conservative clergy who had originally invited him and when he was allowed to preach again, they sent in their own preachers to counter-attack.[83] But conservative preaching became associated with treason. The upshot of the ensuing hearing was that the corporation of Bristol, after a promise of support from Cromwell, came to side with Latimer because he supported the royal divorce. The reformer returned to London, while one of his conservative opponents, William Hubberdyne, was sent to the Tower for pro-papal assertions and conservative statements on the authority of the church.[84]

[78] *Sermons*, p. 208; on Gardiner and other Henrician political pamphleteers see Dickens, *English Reformation*, pp. 173–4; Franklin le van Baumer, *The Early Tudor Theory of Kingship*, Yale Historical Publications, XXXV (New Haven, 1940), ch. 3; Gardiner's treatise is edited by P. Janelle in *Obedience in Church State: Three Political Tracts by Stephen Gardiner* (Cambridge, 1930).
[79] Le Neve, VIII, 70; III, 87; *Valor* I, 134, 231; V, 119; see Rev. N.A.H. Lawrance, *The Clergy of the Archdeaconry of the East Riding in the Diocese of York* (York, 1966), I, s.v. 'Brandesburton'. The date of Edgeworth's institution is not given.
[80] Le Neve, V, 104; *Wells* II, 246.
[81] A. Chester, *Hugh Latimer, Apostle to the English* (Philadelphia, 1954), p. 88; *The History of the County of Gloucester*, ed. W. Page *et al.* 11 vols, VCH (London, 1907–76), II, 24; W. Hunt, *Bristol* (London, 1887), p. 116, all erroneously assume Edgeworth's presence in the affair.
[82] On Lollardy in Bristol see J.A.F. Thomson, *The Later Lollards, 1414–1530* (Oxford, 1965), pp. 20–51; K.G. Powell, 'The Social Background to Protestantism in Gloucestershire', *TBGAS* 92 (1973), 98–100. M. Skeeters, 'The Clergy of Bristol, c.1530–c.1570' (unpublished Ph.D. thesis, University of Austin at Texas, 1984), pp. 38, 227 ff. outlines Bristol's situation and the complications in the 1533 crisis because of the two diocesan authorities.
[83] Skeeters reinterprets the Bristol crises of the 1530s in 'Clergy of Bristol', pp. 50–91 (pp. 51–71 on the 1533 crisis); see G. Elton, *Policy and Police: The Enforcement of the Reformation in the Age of Thomas Cromwell* (Cambridge, 1972), pp. 112–17.
[84] The affair is fully documented in Townsend-Foxe, VII, Appendix of documents (which is unpaginated). See Latimer, *Works* I, 225–39, 357–66 for the charges and Latimer's defence; *Concilia* III, 747–8.

Despite his absence from this crisis, Edgeworth claims that he opposed Latimer and his followers in the 1530s:

> I preached at Redcliffe crosse, in the good and worshipfull citie of Bristow . . . although I was interrupted many yeares by the confederacie of Hughe Lathamer then aspiringe to a bisshopriche and after being bishop of worcester, and ordinary of the greatest part of the sayd Bristow, and infecting the whole.[85]

As Bishop of Worcester from 1535–9 Latimer licenced 'light' preachers to spread the new doctrines around the diocese: they included the martyrs-to-be Thomas Garrett and Robert Barnes, dispossessed friars such as Dr John Joseph, last warden of the Worcester Franciscans, and John Erley, and Latimer's disciples like his chaplain Thomas Bennet, Sir Antony Saunders, curate of Winchcombe, and James Asche, parson of Stanton.[86] This 'confederacy' incurred the hostility of the secular and ecclesiastical authorities such as John Bell, Bishop of Worcester from 1539 to 1543, and the conservative sheriff of Gloucester, Thomas Bell, who complained to Bishop Stokesley of London that Latimer favoured his own men at the expense of the conservative clergy. Bell petitioned the Duke of Norfolk and in order to silence 'horeson heretics and chaplains' appointed two men whom Edgeworth would encounter in the 1540s, Gilbert Bourne, later Bishop of Bath and Wells, and Henry Joliffe, later Dean of Bristol Cathedral.[87]

But after 1533 the conservative reaction in Bristol was no longer a matter of large-scale resistance. The clerical body, which had marshalled all its resources to oppose the corporation, lost autonomy and its traditional authority in administering and regulating the religious life of the town was diminished. The corporation, after Cromwell proved an unreliable ally, failed to sustain a consistent religious policy and became vulnerable to local pressure groups: the local clergy, diocesan authorities and different groups of townspeople. In another controversy in 1537 a groundswell of opinion against Latimer once more associated his name with seditious preaching. Following Cromwell's investigations into diocesan affairs four men were imprisoned for challenging royal religious policy, either for supporting the Northern rebels or for speaking out against the bishop. Edgeworth's 'apology' for purgatory in the second sermon may belong to this dispute.[88] In 1539 George Wishart, the Scottish Protestant radical, was imprisoned for his preaching by the corporation, then strongly conservative in composition, but was later released when local pressure created a fear of widespread disorder.[89]

Between c.1535 and 1542 when he was preaching at Redcliffe Cross in Bristol,

---

[85] *Sermons*, p. 96; below pp. 37–8; on local responses to Latimer's preaching in Exeter in 1534 see R. Whiting, *The Blind Devotion of the People: Popular Religion and the Reformation* (Cambridge, 1989), pp. 245–6, 255 (cited hereafter as Whiting, *Blind Devotion*).

[86] G. Baskerville, 'The Dispossessed Religious of Gloucestershire', *TBGAS* 49 (1927), 79; K.G. Powell, 'The Beginnings of Protestantism in Gloucestershire', *TBGAS* 90 (1971), 146, 149–51; 'Social Background', 107, 110, 114–17; Elton, *Policy and Police*, pp. 30–1, 35–7, 117, 121–3; *LP* VI, 1192, VIII, 171; IX, 747, XI, 1424, XIV, ii, 804; on Barnes's moves see Lusardi's introduction to More, *Confutation*, CW8, 1403–4.

[87] *LP* X, 1099; in 1533 the vicar-general of Worcester licensed five friars to preach against the Protestants; see VCH, *Gloucester* II, 25.

[88] Skeeters, 'Clergy of Bristol', pp. 75–81; Elton, *Policy and Police*, pp. 117–19; *LP* XII, i, 508, 1147; *Sermons*, pp. 128–9; see below, pp. 38–9.

[89] Skeeters, 'Clergy of Bristol', pp. 81–8; Elton, *Policy and Police*, pp. 119–20; *LP* XIV, i, 184.

Edgeworth witnessed the beginning of a period of episcopal decline at Wells as the bishop, John Clerk, gradually transferred authority into the hands of the vicegerent.[90] Although his over-zealous support of the queen in the royal divorce had made Clerk vulnerable to Cromwell's demands, his policy of propitiation in order to buy protection and security suggests that the bishopric's wealth and power had already been threatened by the crown. Edgeworth's was the last appointment made according to the dean and chapter's wishes since from 1536 Cromwell systematically acquired the right to present his own candidates to vacant benefices.[91] The dean and chapter also favoured appeasement and Edgeworth's prominence in the subsequent negotiations suggests that he was either capitalising on a personal acquaintance with Cromwell or was influential in determining the chapter's policy. On 22 April 1536 he and another canon residentary, Richard Eryngton, handed over to Cromwell 'omnia et singula scripta, cartas sive monumenta originalia dicte ecclesie, donationes, appropriationes, portiones et pensiones, omnium et singularum ecclesiarum parochialium', an act which effectively deprived the chapter of all its muniments from 1514.[92] The following year when a new dean was to be elected, Clerk appointed Cromwell since it was the king's pleasure, and the canons residentiary expressed their pleasure to which the king replied with a letter of thanks.[93] The flourishing relations between the vicegerent and the Wells chapter can be discerned from the chapter's request of October to present their 'litigious controversies' to him in person to save them the expense of retaining legal counsel; it was their representative Dr Edgeworth for whom they desired credence and the chapter accounts for that year include a 'Fee to the noble man Thomas Crumwell – £4.'[94] The vicegerent's responsibility for the admission of the residentaries, traditionally a duty of the dean, is also acknowledged by the sub-dean and chapter in a letter of 15 April 1539 which begs him to continue his favour 'to the avoydynge of such danger in tyme to com as we did nowe by the aduertisement our cownsell mistrust'; once more Dr Edgeworth and Mr Eryngton are their representatives who will exhibit their submission under the chapter seal.[95] In March Cromwell had made encroachments on the cathedral wealth sending Drs Tregonwell and Petre to carry out an investigation. With the inventory of the treasure taken for the king's use was included a letter from the chapter to Cromwell complaining of this deprivation and hoping for his intervention with the king on their behalf to see if any remained to 'the honour of God and the necessary use of the church'.[96] Despite these confiscations Clerk continued to make concessions in the forms of grants to Cromwell and the rights of presentation to vacant prebends to his subordinates.[97]

Edgeworth's exercise of authority on behalf of the Wells chapter in dealing with Cromwell illustrates the complex network of relationships which existed between the government and diocesan powers. But his connections locally as well as

[90] On Clark's episcopacy see P.M. Hembry, The Bishops of Bath and Wells, 1540–1640 (London, 1967), pp. 51–4, 59–67.
[91] On grants and leases to the crown between 1536–40 see Wells II, 246–9; Hembry, Bishops, pp. 62–4.
[92] Wells II, vii, 246.
[93] Ibid. 247; LP XII, ii, 753, 768, 797.
[94] PRO SP 1/125, fos 266–7; LP XII, ii, 960; Wells II, 249.
[95] PRO SP 1/242, Pt. 2, fo. 232; LP, Addenda I, ii, 1409.
[96] LP XIV, i, 448.
[97] Wells II, 250–2; Hembry, Bishops, pp. 65–6.

nationally probably made him influential within the diocese. Among those he counted as his friends was the layman, Thomas Clerk, brother of Bishop Clerk and one of the most powerful men in Wells; his influence in local affairs and control over the episcopal estates had originally been acquired during the bishop's absences. This 'pluralist in episcopal administration' continued to increase his estates and to maintain a high standing in local affairs after John Clerk's death; his many offices included that of MP for Wells for six years from 1547. Clerk also enjoyed a personal relationship with Thomas Cromwell (described as one of 'servancy') not unlike that which Edgeworth fostered with the vicegerent through the Wells chapter.[98] Of all the beneficiaries of Thomas Clerk's will, drawn up on 24 November 1554, Edgeworth alone is mentioned as 'my frende' and he received a 'pott of silver marked with I and C'.[99]

In these years Edgeworth also acted as arbitrator in local disputes in the capacity of magistrate or judge. As prebend of Slape at Salisbury Cathedral he was involved in a dispute concerning the tenants of his farm of Slape in Netherbury (near Dorset) either over non-payment of rents or claims for special privileges.[100] A special hearing was held at a local court at Cerne, Dorset on 27 September 1539, but the matter was unresolved and there is no surviving record in the courts of equity of the 'sayd hoole matter in wryting' which was sent to Cromwell. Nevertheless the commissioners' fragmentary report 'of the mater . . . betwene doctor Eggeworthe prebendary of the prebende of Slape and his tenantes of the same' states that Edgeworth was 'confirmable in all thinges' whereas the tenants were considered excessive in their demands and unable to be 'reformed from theyr opynyon'.[101] This verdict of Edgeworth's fairness in legal and financial matters is not so clear from the second case over which he arbitrated, probably at a manorial court held at his farm at Slape.[102] The dispute with Henry Daubeney, Earl of Bridgewater, concerned the custody of a minor, a child of eight years, whom Edgeworth had evicted from his farm with an injunction, then calling Daubeney and others to Westminster with a subpoena.[103] Daubeney had asked that the child be restored and the matter settled at Edgeworth's court 'according to the custome of the same countre'.[104] It is possible that the case was never heard in a central court, for no record of it appears to exist among those of the Courts of Wards, King's Bench or Chancery. Throughout the 1530s Daubeney was involved in protracted disputes to protect his inheritance; but of more interest for the case are the reports of his delicate health and unsound character at this time.[105] John Husee's comment in June 1538 that 'no man will deal with him except he be out

98 Ibid. pp. 54–9; Elton, Policy and Police, p. 332.
99 Somerset Medieval Wills, 1531–1558, ed. F. Weaver, SRS, 21 (1905), pp. 159–60.
100 See S. Lewis, A Topographical Dictionary of England, 4 vols (London, 1849), III, s.v. 'Netherbury'. The rent received was £20 in 1535; see Valor I, 231; J. Hutchins, The History of Dorset, 4 vols, 3rd ed. rev. by W. Shipp and J.W. Hodson (London, 1973), II, 108 (Edgeworth is not among the prebendaries listed).
101 PRO SP 1/54, fos 53–4; LP XIV, ii, 350.
102 PRO SP 1/142, fos 198–9; LP XIV, i, 183 (3).
103 See G.E. Cokayne, The Complete Peerage, ed. V. Gibbs, 13 vols, rev. ed. (London, 1912), II, s.v. 'Bridgwater'; the earldom was awarded on 19 July 1538; LP XV, 541 (3); XIII, i, 1519 (g. 61).
104 PRO SP 1/142, fos 198–9; LP XIV, i, 183 (3).
105 Although twice married Henry Daubeney was childless, and in the event of his death without male issue his lands were to revert to John Bassett (who had settled the Beaumont lands on Henry's father, Giles Daubeney, and his heirs in c.1500); throughout the 1530s and 1540s the Lisle family endeavoured to protect their rights of reversion. See The Lisle Letters, ed. M. St Clair Byrne, 6 vols (Chicago, 1981), IV, 7–9; LP XIV, i, 118; XIII, i, 1183, 1189, 1201.

of his wit' at least offsets the letter's plea that Edgeworth 'cease his such extremity'.[106]

By the 1540s Edgeworth's links with London and the court had developed beyond the ordinary run of capitular business. It is perhaps during this decade that he preached the sermons which he planned to publish in a second volume: 'made in verie solempne audiences on the dominicall epistles and gospelles, some in the vniuersitie of Oxforde, some at Paules Crosse . . . some in the courte afore . . . Henry the eighte'.[107] He was in London as proctor at the convocation of the clergy in 1539 and again in 1545 and he was present at Westminster on 9 July 1540 when the king's marriage to Anne of Cleves was nullified.[108] In the same year he was appointed by Cromwell to a commission of twenty five bishops and clergymen to deliberate things 'quae ad institutionem viri attinent'; that is, to define ceremonies and true doctrine.[109] Without doubt this part in the formation of ecclesiastical policy was Edgeworth's most distinguished contribution to the Reformation. Some of his answers with those of the more conservative commissioners are included in the third and last Henrician formulary, the King's Book of 1543. In terms of temporal benefits his return to the milieu of national affairs brought in its wake another spate of preferments.

When Henry VIII executed his plan to augment the country's bishoprics and formed the diocese of Bristol from those of Gloucester and Worcester Edgeworth was instituted to Bristol Cathedral as a prebendary of the second stall by the charter of erection on 4 June 1542; his sequence of twenty sermons on St Peter's First Epistle, preached in the cathedral according to the statutes' prescriptions four times annually, can be dated from this time.[110] The following year he was appointed a royal chaplain and on 10th October was instituted to the living of St Cuthbert's in the town of St Andrew's in Wells; the presentation was made by the king at Hampton Court.[111] The living was valued at £33 13s 6d in 1535 and Edgeworth's net income was £28 6s 2d;[112] the prebend of Warminster alias Luxville yielded £11 6s 8d gross (£9 6s 0d net) and the canon residentiary of Wells, £100 p.a.[113] He continued to receive gross £23 5s 7d p.a. for the living of Christchurch, Monmouthshire until he vacated it in 1544 and £24 14s 4d p.a. from the rectory of

106 PRO SP 1/142, fos 198–9; Byrne, Lisle Letters V, nos 1174, 1174b, 1331.
107 Sermons, p. 97.
108 Wells II, 250, 261; LP XV, 861; Pocock-Burnet, IV, 431.
109 Edgeworth was one of the original group of eight bishops and twelve theologians named in parliament on 12 April 1540; see House of Lords' Journal, p. 129; LP XV, 826 for summarised answers; below pp. 43–7.
110 J. Le Neve, Fasti Ecclesia Anglicanae, corrected by T. Hardy, 3 vols (Oxford, 1854), I, 228 (cited hereafter as Le Neve–Hardy); LP XVII, 443 (g. 9, 19, 34); 1154 (g. 60). The charter of erection is printed in Foedera conventiones, literae et cuiuscunque generis acta publica inter reges Angliae et alios imperatores . . . ed. T. Rymer, 20 vols, 3rd ed. (London, 1745), XIV, 748–53; the statutes, translated by Canon Norris, were printed in Bristol in 1870 (BRO DC/A/7/1/5); see Sermons, p. 192.
111 The Registers of Thomas Wolsey, Bishop of Bath and Wells 1518–23, John Clerke, Bishop of Bath and Wells 1523–1541, William Knyght, Bishop of Bath and Wells 1541–1547 and Gilbert Bourne, Bishop of Bath and Wells 1554–1559 ed. Sir H. Maxwell Lyte, SRS, 55 (1940), p. 104 (cited hereafter as Bishops' Registers); PRO Pat. Roll, 35 Hen. VIII, pt. 16, m. 12; Wells II, 254; LP XVIII, i, 981 (g. 61).
112 Valor I, 139: the income was £67 13s 6d; outgoings were £34; yearly tenths were £5 7s 4d; see Somerset Chantries: Survey and Rental, ed. E. Green, SRS, 2 (1888), pp. 153–5.
113 Valor I, 134; yearly tenths were £1 10s 8d; the 40s paid to the vicar choral is confirmed in the breakdown in Valor II, 102; the vicar of Corsley, William Bennett, Wolsey's chaplain and archdeacon of Dorset, also paid to Edgeworth a tithe in private composition or rent from farms (ibid.).

Brandesburton in Holderness in Yorkshire.[114] He drew an annual stipend of £20 as a canon of Bristol Cathedral and the same amount as prebendary of Slape in the gift of the bishop of Salisbury; had his application of 1544 to become canon residentiary at Salisbury Cathedral been successful, this sum would undoubtedly have been increased.[115] By the end of Henry's reign Edgeworth was grossing an annual income of approximately £234 4s 7d, a salary which ranked him among the better-to-do clergy. Although all his cures, including St Cuthbert's, were administered by deputy priests or curates, whether he deserved the reputation of being a great pluralist and absenteeist given him by Dean Turner in 1554 is questionable:[116]

> ... the greatest wolfe in Welles (ye wolfe is of Winchester's commissioners) hath one benefice in Holdernesse and two in Somersetshire, he is residentiari both in Bristow and Wells and hath iii Prebendes, one in Welles, one in Bristow and one in Salesburye (& paradventure he hath more).[117]

His income and preferments are modest by comparison to some of the more prominent Henrician and Edwardian churchmen, figures such as George Carewe, prebendary of Wells from 1549–1554, canon of Salisbury from 1554–1555, dean of Bristol in 1552, dean of Windsor in 1560 and of Exeter in 1571, who enjoyed multiple benefices and livings throughout three reigns.[118]

The Edwardian years, 1547–1553

The considerable financial and legal concessions made to the crown during the Henrician reformation, both by John Clerk and his successor William Knight, undoubtedly contributed to the relative calm enjoyed at Wells Cathedral during the Henrician reformation.[119] But all this came to an abrupt end in Edward VI's reign when the whole complex of religious attitudes and beliefs which had survived came under attack. The changes in Wells were effected by Bishop Knight's successor, the arch-Protestant William Barlow, whose effect on the bishopric and on the dean and chapter has been described as 'equally disastrous'.[120] Barlow's episcopacy was marked by his extreme subservience to Somerset as the Protector attempted to enlarge his power in the West Country. During his five and a half

---

[114] On Christchurch see above n. 72; on Brandesburton, Valor V, 119; income from rents was £30 12s; deductions were £15 3s 8d; yearly tenths £4 1s 4d. G. Poulson, Beverlac; or the antiquities and history of the town of Beverley . . . and of the Provostry and Collegiate Establishment of St. John's, 2 vols (London, 1829), I, 641, states that in 1532 the temporalities were 40s and the spiritualities 13s.
[115] Valor I, 231; II, 75; Le Neve, III, 87; Salisbury Cathedral Chapter Act Book, 14, fos 74–5; Edgeworth was refused because there was no vacancy amongst the domus canonicalis.
[116] Green, Somerset Chantries, p. 155; Inventories of Church Goods . . . for the Counties of York, Durham, and Northumberland, ed. W. Page, Surtees Society, 97 (1897), p. 43.
[117] W. Turner, The huntyng of the romyshe vuolfe (Emden, 1555?), STC 24356, sig. D8. The second living in Somerset may be the emolument from the rectory of Corsley (in Salisbury) due to the vicar of Warminster (Valor I, 102; see above n. 113).
[118] BRUO IV, 101–3; C. Field, The Province of Canterbury and the Elizabethan Settlement of Religion (Robertsbridge, 1973), pp. 13–14; Le Neve–Hardy, I, 223; III, 374.
[119] Wells II, 255–62; Hembry, Bishops, pp. 74–7.
[120] Ibid. p. 78; Le Neve, V, 1; Wells II, 264, 266; the petition of the dean and chapter for licence to elect the bishop was rejected.

years in office, in the tradition of his predecessors and in order to repay the debt for his promotion, he freely handed over to him and the crown the greater part of the episcopal endowment. This wholesale transfer began just four months after he took up office in February 1548 and by the time he vacated the see in July 1553 the twenty four episcopal manors were reduced to five; most of this property fell into the hands of the Seymour family.[121]

In great dismay the dean and chapter agreed to this wholesale transference of episcopal lands and reluctantly confirmed three grants made to the Protector in 1548–9.[122] But Barlow made himself even more unpopular by openly preferring his Protestant protégés, many of whom were married, in making capitular appointments. Factions developed in the chapter and resentment towards the bishop surfaced over the appointment of a new dean when the office became vacant on 13 March 1547. Somerset, who was granted the dignity and its dependencies, appointed John Goodman, a protégé of his steward, by an act of parliament on 7 January 1548 without prior consultation with the chapter.[123] Goodman's faction then re-erected the deanery into a royal donative, increasing the quotidians of the deanship out of the portions of the canons.[124] But when in 1550 Barlow tried to oust Goodman, a conservative in religion, in favour of his protégé, the Protestant William Turner, the dean started an action for damages and a writ of praemunire was issued against Barlow.[125] Goodman encouraged the receiver of the county of Somerset, John Barwick of Easton in Wiltshire to tell the Protector the truth about Barlow:

> They hate him and not only for religion, for those who used to favour the reformed religion as much as he or more and used to come to his sermons have now nearly forsaken him: for whereas the whole church was too little to receive the congregation that used to resort to him, now they might be received in a little chapel.[126]

Barlow's unpopularity in the diocese at large was due to his unfairly rejecting many of his tenants from their holdings in order to improve his own standing. He may also have used the pulpit to control local opinion by preaching the official Edwardian homilies and forcibly obstructing any attempts by the conservatives to persuade his disaffected audience to return to their Catholic beliefs. Edgeworth complains that he suffered the same interruptions at Wells that he had in Bristol:

> I preached . . . at the cathedrall Churche there (Bristol) . . . in this also I was manie times and longe discontinued by the odious scisme that was nowe lately, and by the doers of the same. And . . . in the Cathedrall

---

[121] Cross, *Church and People*, p. 91; a full list of the episcopal estates surrendered and their fates is given by Hembry, *Bishops*, pp. 106–17.
[122] *Ibid.* p. 114; *Wells* II, 266–8, 272; *The History of the County of Somerset*, 5 vols, ed. W. Page, VCH (London, 1906–85), II, 36–7.
[123] *Wells* II, 266; Le Neve, V, 5.
[124] *Wells* II, 269; Hembry, *Bishops*, pp. 117–18.
[125] *Ibid.* pp. 118–20; on Goodman's fate see Field, *Elizabethan Settlement*, pp. 5, 7, 8, 12, 110.
[126] PRO SP 10/10/19 and 20, fos 50–4; *Calendar of State Papers. Domestic Series of the Reigns of Edward VI, Mary and Elizabeth, 1547–1580*, ed. R. Lemon (London, 1856), p. 28; cited hereafter as *Cal. SP Dom.*

Churche of Wells . . . I lacked no trouble by bishop Barlow and his officers.[127]

Turner was installed as dean by the king's command on 24 March 1551 despite the opposition of the Wells chapter, while Goodman was deposed by the Privy Council for holding the prebend of Wiveliscombe in plurality and sent to the Fleet.[128] But Turner, one of the new type of clergy in that he was married and had studied medicine prior to turning to theology, was ostracised by the other canons, Goodman's friends, so that he could not take up residence in the deanery.[129] His complaints to Cecil on 22 May suggest that the conservatives' unwillingness to preach reflected their continued allegiance to Goodman and opposition to Barlow:

. . . they are all against Mr Cardmaker and me whom they handle as wards. I have preached eight times since Easter; but I could not make one of them preach saving Master Cardmaker.[130]

His bitterness at this treatment may have prompted his vituperative attack on Edgeworth as a great pluralist in 1554.

From 1545 until his institution as chancellor in 1554, there is no reference to Edgeworth in the Wells capitular records.[131] It is probably during this period that he was prohibited from preaching and imprisoned:

. . . I haue inuehied ernestlie and oft in my sermons in disputacions and reasoninge with the protestauntes, vntill I haue be put to silence either by general prohibitions to preache, or by name, or by captiuitie and imprison- ment, of all whiche . . . I haue had my parte.[132]

As Edgeworth's name does not appear on the list of those licenced to preach under the ecclesiastical seal in July 1547 and as seditious preaching was liable to im- prisonment following two proclamations of 1548 he may have been effectively silenced or imprisoned from this time.[133] In the exordium to the eighteenth ser- mon on St Peter, preached early in 1553, Edgeworth states that his licence had been restored by the same authorities who had revoked it five or six years earlier.[134] This may have been the result of a change in the political climate – the downfall of Northumberland was eminent – rather than to any intercession on his behalf. Edgeworth's 'disputacions . . . with the protestauntes' may also belong to this

127 Sermons, p. 96. The injunction to read Cranmer's Homilies every Sunday was issued in Novem- ber 1547 (Hughes and Larkin, I, 287, p. 402) and again on 23 September 1548 (ibid. 313).
128 Hembry, Bishops, pp. 121–2; J. Ridley, Thomas Cranmer (Oxford, 1962), pp. 310–11; Wells II, 273; Le Neve, V, 5.
129 See DNB s.v. 'Turner'; Troubles Connected with the Prayer Book of 1549, ed. N. Pocock, CS, NS, 38 (London, 1884), pp. 3–4, 131–4; P.F. Tytler, England under the Reigns of Edward VI and Mary, 2 vols (London, 1839), I, 333–7.
130 Wells II, 273; APC (1550–2), p. 218; Tytler, Edward VI and Mary, I, 372–4; for a list of canons see Le Neve, V, 105; they rejected Turner's application to reside in the dean's house, and Goodman sold back to them the three quotidians and three dividends so they would not fall to him.
131 See Bishops' Registers, p. xiii; Field, Elizabethan Settlement, p. 1, on the disappearance of the Edwardian register.
132 Sermons, p. 95.
133 Wells, II, 265; PRO SP 10/2/34, fos 1–4; 10/9/48, fos 91–95ᵛ; Cal. SP Dom. p. 5; Hughes and Larkin, I, 303, 313. On the imprisonment of conservative preachers Richard Crispin, canon of Exeter, and John Moreman following this prohibition, see Whiting, Blind Devotion, pp. 242–3.
134 Sermons, p. 338.

period as well as to the 1530s. Jean Veron, French reformed prebendary of Worcester, and William Turner debated with the well known Anabaptist, Robert Cooche, on the doctrines of original sin and infant baptism in 1550. The same topics were disputed at Worcester in 1552 between the cathedral prebendarys Henry Joliffe and Robert Jonson, and Bishop Hooper.[135] In the Edwardian sermons, particularly in the twelfth and thirteenth on I Peter, allusions to the anabaptist heresy of denying Christ, an issue during the drafting of the Forty Two Articles in 1552, and defences of transubstantiation, auricular confession and works of supererogation reveal a familiarity with these contemporary controversies.[136]

Some record of Edgeworth's association with Bristol Cathedral for the period 1550–1556, however, can be found in the *computa* accounts for this period, that is, the annual payments made to the dean and chapter. These were prepared each fiscal year (from Michaelmas) by or on behalf of the treasurer and certified by the other members of the chapter.[137] Typically they record the annual stipend of £20 due to the canons residentary and payments for minor offices.[138] As sub-dean in 1550 and 1554 Edgeworth's stipend was increased to £2 2s 8d; he was treasurer in 1544 and again in 1552.[139] Entries in 1544 recording payment by various canons to Edgeworth of arrears amounting to £40 and his discharging of a debt owed by George Carewe to another prebendary, Thomas Baylie, suggest that he also acted unofficially as auditor.[140]

The *computa* illustrate the intricacy of the relationships between the canons. During this period Edgeworth became closely associated with two prebendaries, John Cottrell, who was to be vicar general in Wells during the reign of Queen Mary, and Thomas Silke.[141] An incident in 1552 concerning a deal on the sale of stone from a projected cathedral extension discredits this group and the dean John Whitheare, all of whom received £20 each at the expense of the rest of the chapter, and it points to the weakness of diocesan leadership under the moderate Catholic bishop Paul Bush.[142] The deal only became public in the reign of Elizabeth when a suit for the delivery of the stone was brought in the chancery court. The canons were typical of those moderate Catholics who became entrenched in local capitular affairs and survived the Reformation by a mixture of prudence and political strategies. The exploitation of cathedral wealth and treasure became commonplace during the Edwardian confiscations and the incident is

---

[135] See G.H. Williams, *The Radical Reformation* (Philadelphia, 1962), p. 781; I.B. Horst, *The Radical Brethren: Anabaptism and the English Reformation to 1558* (Nieuwkoop, 1972), pp. 115–17 on Turner and Cooche; *DNB* s.v. 'Joliffe'; Field, *Elizabethan Settlement*, p. 26; F. Price, 'The Gloucester Diocese under Bishop Hooper', *TBGAS* 60 (1938), 127.
[136] *Sermons*, pp. 280–1, 282, 289, 290, 291, 333, 351, 363, 365; see above p. 12.
[137] BRO DC/A/9/1/1, fos 3, 7.
[138] BRO DC/A/9/1/1, fos 3, 7, 17, 41; DC/A/9/1/2, fos 11ᵛ, 26, 40ᵛ, 57; Bacon, *Liber Regis*, p. 107; *Foedera* XIV, 748.
[139] BRO *Capituli Actorum Liber, 1542–1573*; DC/E/1/1, fo. 75; DC/A/9/1/1, fos 4, 22ᵛ, 42, 43, 70. See E.T. Morgan, *Bristol Cathedral: An Annotated Catalogue of Deeds and Documents* (Bristol, 1912), pp. 3, 116.
[140] BRO DC/A/9/1/1, fos 22ᵛ, 43.
[141] See *DNB* s.v. 'Cotterell'; *BRUO* IV, 140–1; J. Strype, *Memorials of Cranmer*, 2 vols (Oxford, 1890), I, 459; *Ecc. Mem.* III, i, 39, 352; *Bishops' Registers*, p. 120; Le Neve, V, 9–10, 81; Le Neve–Hardy, I, 225, 230; Field, *Elizabethan Settlement*, pp. 1, 21.
[142] Skeeters, 'Clergy of Bristol', p. 234, citing PRO Court of Requests, 340 (1559 cont. 1561). I am grateful to Dr Skeeters for bringing this to my attention. For other examples of clerical embezzlement see Whiting, *Blind Devotion*, p. 264; J.J. Scarisbrick, *The Reformation and the English People* (Oxford, 1984), pp. 93–6, 99–108.

symptomatic of the general lowering of moral standards. In 1552 parish churches became a source for spoil and church plate was seized; in 1553 everything except linen, chalices and bells was to be confiscated.[143] At a ceremony in May 1553 the commissioners for the county of Gloucester returned to Bristol Cathedral from among the goods they had plundered two chalices for divine service and one great bell for the clock and four other bells – this was all that remained of the original ring of eight bells. Edgeworth, the dean, George Carewe, Thomas Cotterell and Thomas Silke signed the chapter's receipt.[144]

The reign of Mary I: Chancellor of Wells Cathedral, 1554–c.1560

While Edgeworth retained close links with the Bristol chapter under Edward, on Queen Mary's accession he renewed his association with the chapter at Wells where, after the dramatic disapearance of Bishop Barlow and the Protestant John Cardmaker in July 1553, the see was vacant from July 1553 to March 1554. On 8 April 1554 he and John Bowerman witnessed John Cotterell's acceptance of the office of Master of Spiritualities.[145] The new bishop, the queen's candidate, Gilbert Bourne, had been elected by papal provision on 28 March and was consecrated in London.[146] On 20 April 1554 Edgeworth received the highest ecclesiastical office of his career, collation to the dignity of Chancellor of Wells, vacant by the deprivation of the Protestant, John Taylor alias Cardmaker.[147] As this position carried with it the rectory of Kingsbury in Wells he probably resigned the prebend of Warminster and in 1556 the living of Brandesburton in Holderness.[148] The emoluments from these new offices were not insubstantial; the rectory of Kingsbury in the archdeaconry of Taunton was valued at £40 5s p.a. of which £4 0s 6d went in yearly tenths.[149]

There is little evidence that the chancellorship at Wells was redefined in Mary's reign in order to further the restoration of Catholicism. An exhaustive investigation into cases of heresy and clerical marriage took priority over retraining the clergy and re-educating the laity in the principles of the Catholic faith. An early proclamation prohibiting the married clergy from administering and saying mass was followed on 20 December 1553 by the Statute of Repeals, enacted against the Edwardian Act of 1547 permitting the clergy to marry.[150] The first commission to deal with the cases of the married clergy in the consistorial courts in the diocese of Bath and Wells was directed to John Cotterell and his assistants in August 1553.[151]

[143] Guy, *Tudor England*, pp. 223–4.
[144] J. Maclean, 'Inventories of, and Receipts for, Church Goods in the County of Gloucester and Cities of Gloucester and Bristol', *TBGAS* 12 (1888), 73–5, 81–4; Page, *Inventories*, pp. 1–5. On appropriations of plate and jewellery see Green, *Somerset Chantries*, pp. xv–xvii; the returns for Bristol are listed by Maclean, 'Chantry Certificates', 232–61.
[145] *Bishops' Registers*, p. 120; Strype, *Ecc. Mem.* III, i, 352.
[146] *DNB* s.v. 'Bourne'; *Wells* II, 277; Hembry, *Bishops*, pp. 89–90; Le Neve, V, 1.
[147] *Bishops' Registers*, pp. 120–1; Le Neve, V, 12.
[148] *Ibid.*; *Bishops' Registers*, p. 85; cf. Le Neve, VIII, 70 who says he probably held the living until he became Chancellor; *CPR (1555–7)*, p. 527; Poulson, *Beverlac*, I, 282; his successor, Thomas Lante, was presented by the crown to the rectory on 7 December 1556. Edgeworth still owned at the time of his death the 'grey amblinge mare that I boughte in holdernes' (Appendix, p. 448).
[149] *Valor* I, 133.
[150] See J. Loach, *Parliament and Crown in the Reign of Mary Tudor* (Oxford, 1986), pp. 77–8, for the passage of this bill through parliament; Guy, *Tudor England*, p. 234.
[151] W.H. Frere, 'The Marian Reaction in its relation to the English Clergy: a study of the episcopal

They were to inquire into those who had obtained *de facto* parish churches, 'to deprive and remove (them) from the said churches and dignities . . . And those so convicted to separate and divorce from their women, or their wives or rather their concubines'.[152] Dean Turner's claim that Edgeworth was one of Gardiner's commissioners implies that he played a substantial part in this investigation although, as a friend of the Chancellor, Edgeworth may also have accepted separate commissions from him. Turner hints darkly at subterfuge saying that Gardiner acted without 'the knowledge of the reste of counsell'; but there is apparently no record surviving of any commission which Edgeworth may have delivered in Wells.[153]

The Marian period at Wells is notable both for the large-scale clerical deprivations and the large number of subsequent institutions: Bishop Bourne, for example, appointed thirteen new canons between May and November 1556. As Barlow had freely instituted married clergy to benefices and permitted those already incumbent to marry, the large number of eighty six deprivations between 1554–5 is not surprising.[154] Some submitted to sentences of divorce; others took oaths of perpetual chastity. Many of the latter were rapidly reinstituted to benefices as was Reynald Slatter, vicar of Rowborough, whose case in the consistory court was adjucated by Edgeworth in 1554. Having agreed to preach two sermons and seeking absolution and suspension from his benefice until this penance was commuted he was instituted by Bishop Bourne to the vicarage of Otherye on 12 March 1555 'in his collation by lapse of six months'.[155] It was one of the anomalies of the investigation that fulfilment of a penance was sufficient for offenders to be re-instituted rather than any other sign of commitment to Roman Catholic doctrines. Nor was any provision made for the dispossessed wives of the Edwardian clergy.

Cases of heresy and of suspected witchcraft were also investigated in the visitation and on 19 March 1555 Edgeworth and Cotterell heard the testimony of one Hanna Turrye who healed a woman of an ailment allegedly brought upon her by a neighbour who had bewitched her (and her husband's cattle).[156] But there is no evidence that the final penalty of burning for heresy took place in Bath and Wells as it did in Bristol.[157] Foxe notes only that two men were delivered to the sheriff in

registers', *Church Historical Society*, XVIII (1896), Appendix VII, pp. 173–4; the Statute of Repeals is printed in abridged form by G.R. Elton in *The Tudor Constitution: Documents and Commentary* (Cambridge, 1965), pp. 359–63. See Hughes and Larkin, II, 407 (esp. p. 37) for the injunctions of 4 March 1554; *Bishops' Registers*, p. xiv.
[152] Strype, *Ecc. Mem*. III, i, 352.
[153] See above p. 30; W. Turner, *A New Book of spirituall physik for diuerse diseases of the nobilitye and gentlemen of England* (Basle, 1555), fos 88–9: '. . . the hyghe chancellor of England and president of the counsell . . . so lordlye behaveth hymself, that wythout the knowledge of the reste of the counsell, he sendeth forth commissioners (as he dyd of late to Welles by Dr. Edgeworthe) . . .'. J.A. Muller, *Stephen Gardiner and the Tudor Reaction* (London, 1926), p. 325, points out that Gardiner signed many letters from the Privy Council and sent others out in the queen's name of which only drafts and minutes remain in the PRO.
[154] Lists of deprivations are printed in VCH, *Somerset* II, Appendix I, pp. 65–6. See A.G. Dickens, *The Marian Reaction in the Diocese of York*, 2 vols, St Anthony's Hall Publications, 11–12 (1957), I, *The Clergy*, pp. 9–21. For Edgeworth's single presentation see *Bishops' Registers*, pp. xv, 134.
[155] SRO DD/VC/66, fo. 29; *Bishops' Registers*, pp. xiv–v, 137. A.G. Dickens, *The English Reformation* (1964, London, 1968), pp. 278–9.
[156] SRO DD/Ca/22, fo. 70.
[157] Chancellor William Dalby sentenced four men to death in 1556; see K.G. Powell, *Marian Martyrs*, BHA, 31 (1972), p. 9 ff; Field, *Elizabethan Settlement*, p. 26. Hembry, *Bishops*, p. 98, claims that nine clergy were burnt in Wells; but VCH, *Somerset* II, 38, and *DNB* s.v. 'Bourne' deny that any burnings for heresy took place during Bourne's espicopacy.

1554 and although another, Richard Lush, was condemned by him in 1556, the sentence appears not to have been carried out.[158] Bishop Bourne had the reputation for clemency and his name has never been associated with burnings; such cases would have been sent to Bishop Bonner for trial in London.

Edgeworth resided in the chancellor's residence adjacent to the deanery on the West as the inscription *Ricardus Edgeworth Cancellarius 1557* on a stone mantel in one of the chimneys attests.[159] He also sublet from the dean and chapter a toft or cottage with a garden at Torr Bridge for the sum of 3s 4d although this was no longer in his tenure by 1559.[160] After the decree in 1554 that all Protestants be removed from teaching positions, he appointed in 1556 as new master of the grammar school Master William Good, an MA from Corpus Christi College, Oxford and reader in the humanities there in the 1550s, and William Absolon, a fellow of Corpus and BA as his usher.[161] These positions traditionally attracted highly qualified men. Good, furthermore, was of sound Roman Catholic belief; both men became canons in the cathedral.[162] As chancellor Edgeworth may also have been obliged to deliver lectures in theology to the clergy and to instruct the laity, confused by twenty years of religious change, in the rudiments of the Catholic faith.[163] This duty undoubtedly made him aware of the serious decline in learning and encouraged him to gather together his sermons for publication in 1557. But there was no major development in higher education in Wells under his aegis and the seminary recommended by the synod of the clergy in 1556 was never established.[164]

At the Elizabethan Settlement most of the Marian clergy in Wells conformed under pain of deprivation, or like George Carewe who changed his allegiance in order to advance himself, seized the opportunity to take up new preferments. Edgeworth is perhaps unique in resigning both the vicarage of St Cuthbert's in March 1559 and the office of chancellor.[165] As this latter is now accepted indubitably as a resignation of conscience it can be assumed that in all probability he would have resigned his prebend of Salisbury and canonry of Bristol Cathedral as well had the settlement in these dioceses taken place before his death in 1560.[166] The last record of his association with Bristol Cathedral is the *computum* of 1559 listing payment of his stipend.[167] Like others of his generation and persuasion he may have felt that his life's work was at an end and that without risk to his personal safety he could publically endorse his true commitment. There is no indication that he ever took the oath of supremacy.

[158] Townsend-Foxe, VII, 377–8; *Bishops' Registers*, p. 120.
[159] *73rd and 74th Annual Report of the Wells Natural History and Archeological Society, 1961–2* (Affiliated to the Somerset Archaeological and Natural History Society), pp. 5–6.
[160] Wells Cathedral Library, *Communars Rolls, 1559–1560*, p. 54.
[161] Hughes and Larkin, II, p. 38; Orme, *Education and Society*, pp. 20–21; *Education*, pp. 83–9. Tytler, *Edward VI and Mary I*, 372 discusses the intrigues surrounding the office of schoolmaster in Edward's reign.
[162] On Good's career see Field, *Elizabethan Settlement*, pp. 6, 9, 10.
[163] Orme, *Education*, pp. 23, 82–3; on other duties of the chancellor at Wells see VCH, *Somerset* II, 15; Smith, *Tudor Prelates*, pp. 287–9.
[164] Hughes, *Reformation* II, 235–6; R. Pogson. 'Legacy of the Schism', pp. 130–2.
[165] Field, *Elizabethan Settlement*, pp. 13, 16, 18–19; *Bishops' Registers*, p. 154.
[166] Edgeworth is not listed among the deprivations for Bristol and Salisbury (Field, *Elizabethan Settlement*, pp. 26, 254–7). A new prebendary of Slape was instituted on 23 June 1559 (Hutchins, *Dorset* II, 108).
[167] BRO DC/A/9/1/2, fo. 57 (although there are no signatories to payments made between 1556–9); Field, *Elizabethan Settlement*, p. 26.

Edgeworth died sometime between 24 December 1559 and 17 January 1560 probably from the same influenza epidemic that carried off Cardinal Pole and Queen Mary and which swept through the ranks of the parish clergy.[168] His will, drawn up on 24 December and proven on 11 June 1560, reveals that he died in a state of material affluence and social eminence. Bequests of 40s each are made to the cathedral churches of Wells and Salisbury and to his former parish church of Christchurch in Wales. To Oriel College is left his copies of the works of St Chrysostom and St Ambrose and to one of his executors, Thomas Jury, a friend and canon of Wells, the works of St Gregory. His immediate family are well catered for; to his nephew Roger is left 40s and to his sister-in-law Margaret and his nieces a piece of plate each and 40s towards their marriages as 'when I am gone they be like to have small succour'. Those most likely to further his theological interests, however, are the greatest beneficiaries; to his cousin Richard are be-queathed the insignia of his office: his furred, murray and scarlet gownes and £10; to his nephew Edward, who became an Anglican bishop under Elizabeth and emigrated to Ireland, £10 to be given him by his brother Francis when he came of age.[169] Although the desire expressed in the will for burial in Wells Catheral might at first sight suggest a change of belief, communion and burial services were still conducted at Wells by 'validly ordained priests and clerics professing the Catholic faith' for the see was then vacant.[170] Furthermore, Edgeworth's provision for his soul in the form of small bequests to the choir and priests for morning and evening prayers and for saying the psalter at his burial is also found in other extant wills of this period.[171]

The Sermons offer final proof that, although driven by the necessity to conform, and to adjust his beliefs, Edgeworth never fundamentally changed them. The outbursts against Protestant doctrines and theology, the extolling of the Royal Supremacy, testify to the form of Catholicism with which he came to identify: the dogma in which he was educated and the political subservience to the king which was the legacy of the submission of the clergy in 1532. While at times he has profile of a moderate apologist or time-server, he also offers the compensating evidence that he was persecuted for his beliefs; by the ruthless and self-serving standards of the Edwardian Reformation his personal and ideological lapses into pragmaticism seem modest. It was undoubtedly due to his prudence and tenacity that he managed to survive three decades of religious and social upheaval, and to conclude his career with greater dignity of office. His life achievements rest on the accomplishments of Henry VIII s reign – the contribution to redefining the faith in 1540–3, undertaken for that distinguished monument to Henrician Catholi-cism, the King's Book – rather than on the suffering for his convictions in Edward's reign or the attempt to restore Catholicism in Mary's reign. He belonged to the last of the great age of churchmen who under Henry VIII were uniquely privileged in their temporal powers and who survived the Reformation through their caution and restraint. Endowed with the perspicacity of Cuthbert Tunstal, Edmund

---

[168] Ibid. pp. 336–7; see M. Zell, 'The Personnel of the Clergy in Kent in the Reformation Period', EHR 89 (1974), 513 ff.
[169] Appendix, p. 448; the five volumes of Chrysostom's works are still in the Oriel College Library, rebound in three volumes; see BRUO IV, 184.
[170] Bridgett, 'Bristol Pulpit', 93, points out that Elizabeth's policy in cases like Edgeworth's was to 'make death void his preferments'.
[171] Ibid. 92–4.

Bonner and Stephen Gardiner rather than the heroic saintliness of Fisher or More, he remained committed to his faith insofar as it was permitted to survive. The *Sermons*, his finest legacy, record his losing battle to ensure the preservation of that faith.

CHANGES IN DOCTRINE AND WORSHIP, 1536–1553

The Ten Articles and the *Sermons*

From c.1535 to c.1542, in the wake of the Bristol preaching crisis of 1533, Edgeworth preached his sermon sequence on the seven gifts of the Holy Ghost at Redcliffe Cross. Latimer had attacked saints, pilgrimages and purgatory, and after the break from Rome these topics came under increasing criticism because their official status became subject to doubt. Measures were taken to control the widespread turbulence caused by 'inflammable' preaching, and conflicts between Catholic and Protestant clergy.[1] In June 1534 preaching for or against purgatory, saints, clerical marriage and justification by faith was prohibited for one year and the act was renewed by Cromwell in 1536. A redefinition of these practices was urgently required in order to establish the relationship of the English church to the Crown and to restore a measure of order.[2] But the first Henrician formulary of the faith, the Ten Articles of 1536, failed to establish a consistent policy; it betrayed signs of a German Protestant influence, and the articles on salvation, in particular those on purgatory and the veneration of saints, were so ambiguously worded as to be capable of interpretation along either Protestant or Catholic lines.[3]

In Bristol after 1533 conservative preaching in favour of traditional ceremonies and practices became increasingly hazardous. Disputes between Catholic and Protestant were now an issue of law and order, and hence subject to regulation by the secular authority, the town Corporation. The conservative clergy, already suffering from economic inflation and a decline in educational standards, began to lose their traditional authority in regulating the religious life of the community.[4] Furthermore as Cromwell's campaigns of propaganda and enforcement which followed the Ten Articles slowly took effect in the south, they were gradually obliged

---

[1] See Elton, *Policy and Police*, ch. 1; *LP* X, 45, 172, 528 for disturbances in early 1536. Edgeworth's preaching demonstrates the persistence of conservatism in Bristol after 1536 despite the national policies. The view that the Reformation was unpopular among the majority of Englishmen and slow to take root despite the coercive powers of Tudor Government has been developed over the last twenty years. For a summary of this revisionist approach see the essays in *The English Reformation Revised*, ed. C. Haigh (Cambridge, 1987); see also G. Redworth, 'Whatever happened to the English Reformation?', *History Today* (Oct. 1987), 29–35.

[2] See *LP* IX, 704, 742, 1059, for seditious preaching prior to this prohibition; M. Bowker, *The Henrician Reformation: The Diocese of Lincoln under John Longland, 1521–1547* (Cambridge, 1981), pp. 142–6; A. Kreider, *English Chantries: the road to dissolution* (New Haven, 1979), pp. 104–16. Henry lifted Cromwell's ban in May 1536 (*LP* X, 752, 831, 1043).

[3] For assessments of the Ten Articles see Smith, *Tudor Prelates*, pp. 189–91; Hughes, *Reformation* I, 349–53; N.S. Tjernagel, *Henry VIII and the Lutherans, A Study in Anglo-Lutheran Relations from 1521–1547* (St. Louis, 1965), pp. 163–6; Dickens, *English Reformation*, pp. 175–6; M. Dowling, *Humanism in the Age of Henry VIII* (Kent, 1986), pp. 58–9.

[4] On the conservative clergy in Bristol see Skeeters, 'Clergy of Bristol', chs. 2 & 4; J.M. Wilson: 'The *Sermons* of Roger Edgeworth: Reformation Preaching in Bristol' in *Early Tudor England*, ed. D. Williams (Woodbridge, 1989), pp. 223–40; above, pp. 23–4.

to accept the Crown's religious policies.[5] The vicegerent's intrusion into local affairs during the crises of the 1530s, and the Corporation of Bristol's cultivation of his support, meant that preaching in favour of the older ceremonies and forms of worship in opposition to royal policy, would be treated as either heretical or treasonable.

Edgeworth's position exemplifies the dilemma of the conservative clergy. As he espoused the Royal Supremacy in all its political and constitutional implications, he was obliged to preach pragmatically by couching his Catholic views in terms which would not contradict official lines. Fear of official reprisal undoubtedly led him to abandon many of the beliefs which Thomas More defended in his controversial writings, although in his later opposition to the Edwardian liturgical and doctrinal reforms, he would come to renew More's apologetics. Not surprisingly, given his growing concern for the status of the conservative clergy and for the effects of Protestantism on his audience, he was at first reluctant to endorse the royal policies. But in the face of popular religion, institutional change and national policies, he reflects rather than refutes the upheavals of the Reformation:

> Here among you in this citie som wil heare masse, some will heare none . . . som wil be shriuen, som wil not, but for feare or els for shame, some wyll pay tithes & offeringes, som wil not. . . . Som wil prai for the dead, som wil not, I heare of muche suche discension among you.[6]

In the first sermon on the seven gifts Edgeworth avoids any overt reference to the contemporary controversies. But in the second sermon, preached between July 1536 and early 1537, he presents a defence of purgatory which concedes to the redefinition of the doctrine in the first Henrician formulary, the Ten Articles. His apology opens with an attack on 'a famous preacher' who had impugned the traditional idea of purgatory by saying it was 'a place of ease, quietnesse, and rest'.[7] His target is probably Latimer who had renewed his assault on the doctrine in 1536 and who was once more associated with seditious preaching in the Bristol crisis of 1537.[8] But the rest of Edgeworth's defence is controlled by the formulation of the tenth article which recommends prayers for the dead but claims 'the place where they be, the name thereof and kinds of pain there also be uncertain to us by scripture'.[9] His analogy with the word 'Trinity', a doctrine which was also accepted without scriptural authority, and the renaming of purgatory as 'A', add little to his

---

[5] See Guy, *Tudor England*, pp. 178–9; D. Palliser, 'Popular Reactions to the Reformation', *Reformation Revised*, pp. 94–6; C. Haigh, *Reformation and Resistance in Tudor Lancashire* (Cambridge, 1975), pp. 111–13; Elton, *Policy and Police*, pp. 14–27, 113–16, 118–19, 388, 401; Bowker, *Henrician Reformation*, pp. 138–42, 168–9, 178, for measures taken against pro-papal preaching and denial of the Ten Articles and the Six Articles.

[6] *Sermons*, pp. 280–1.

[7] *Ibid.* p. 129. A three month ban on preaching imposed after the passing of the Ten Articles in July 1536 gives a *terminus a quo* of November 1536 (Kreider, *Chantries*, p. 125). In April 1536 the king admitted 'at least a third place neither paradise nor hell' (*LP* X, 752).

[8] See above p. 24 on Latimer's position in 1537; Commentary, pp. 380–1 on his Convocation sermon of 1536. For Henry's vacillations in 1536 over the doctrine of purgatory see *LP* X, 282, 308, 528, 831, 1043; and Latimer's attempts to persuade him, *Works* II, 245–9; Kreider, *Chantries*, pp. 101–3, 119–20.

[9] *Formularies*, p. 17. Another slightly different version of the Ten Articles, published by Berthelet in 1536, entitled *Articles devised by the Kynges highness majestie to stablyshe christen quietnes*, is printed on pp. xv–xxxii. *STC* 10033.4. They are reprinted in Pocock-Burnet, IV, 272–85 (Berthelet's version, p. 272 n.).

argument. Unable to confirm the traditional view of purgatory as a place of fires, torments and pains since this was abandoned in the tenth article, he refers disapprovingly instead to the 'new' Protestant purgatory, 'a place of tranquillitie, a place of lyght, and a place of rest and peace'.[10] This, he claims, denies the Catholic scheme of salvation:

> To denye the sayde A. . . . geueth man occasion boldly to continue in sinne to hys liues ende . . . I trow they meane to go by and by to heauen, as well as he or she that hath liued in vertue & prayers, paine, and penaunce all the dayes of their liues.[11]

In sermons preached after 1540, when the word 'purgatory' had been dropped from the official teaching of the church, he refers to the place euphemistically as 'the skyrte of hell'.[12] In 1537 a conservative defence was possible because the tenth article admitted some latitude of interpretation. But Edgeworth's subsequent silence testifies to his acceptance of the new definition and his inability to defend the doctrine any longer.

Although the Ten Articles laid the foundation for the official teaching on purgatory, it was the destruction of the physical fabric of the medieval church between 1536 and 1540 which decided the future of the doctrine and the practices associated with it.[13] The dissolutions were able to be used by the reformers to justify their onslaught on image veneration as a form of superstition.[14] The First Royal Injunctions of 1536, issued to enforce the Ten Articles, forbade relics, miracles, pilgrimages and images to be used 'for any superstition or lucre . . . seeing all goodness, health and grace ought to be . . . looked for only of God'.[15] Like all

[10] *Sermons*, p. 129. On the Protestant view of purgatory see Simon Fish, *A Supplicacyon for the Beggers; A disputacion of purgatorye* [London? 1537?], and *The Preparacyon to the crosse and to Deathe* [in aed. T. Bertheleti, 1540], a translation printed under the name of Richard Tracey. STC 11387, 11393.

[11] *Sermons*, p. 128. Thomas More in *The Supplication of the Souls* (1529) and Bishop Fisher in *Here after ensueth two fruytfull sermons* (W. Rastell, 1532), sigs C1ᵛ–C2ᵛ, give conventional depictions of purgatory (STC 10909); cf. W. Marshall's translation of Erasmus' *Catechismus, A playne and godly exposytion or declaration of the comune crede and of the .x. comaundementes.* (R. Redman) [f. W. Marshall, 1534], sig. M1ᵛ, which says of souls that: 'if they be defiled wᵗ any smalle spottes/ they are borne into the clensynge fyere of purgatory what so euer or what maner one so euer that fyere of purgatory be' (STC 10504). On the tenth article see Kreider, *Chantries*, pp. 122–3; E.C. Messenger, *The Reformation, the Mass and the Priesthood*, 2 vols (London, 1936), I, *The Revolt from the Medieval Church*, p. 251.

[12] *Sermons*, pp. 175, 293; in the *King's Book* of 1543 the relevant article is entitled 'Of Prayers for the Souls Departed'; see *Formularies*, pp. 375–7; Kreider, *English Chantries*, p. 151.

[13] G.W.O. Woodward, *The Suppression of the Monasteries* (London, 1966), pp. 171–2; see further, D. Knowles, *The Monastic Orders in England*, 3 vols (Cambridge, 1959), III. Edgeworth's view (*Sermons*, p. 126) that men were 'reasoning agaynst Purgatory because they would by that destroye prayers for the dead, and so . . . put downe abbeys, & chauntries whiche were founded for such praiers' was evidently a commonplace. See Latimer, *Works* II, 249; *LP* XII, i, 1312; XIV, ii, 804; Kreider, *Chantries*, p. 127.

[14] Latimer called images 'deceitful and juggling' in his Convocation sermon of 1536 (*Works* I, 53–5). W. Marshall's translation of the treatise probably by M. Bucer, *A treatise . . . that pyctures and other ymages are in no wise to be suffred in churches* [T. Godfray] (f. W. Marshall,) [1535] was reprinted in 1537. STC 24238–9.

[15] That images be used as commemorative aids only was enjoined in the Ten Articles and in the 1536 Injunctions; see Frere and Kennedy, pp. 5–6; *Formularies*, pp. 13–14; M. Aston, *England's Iconoclasts: Laws Against Images*, 2 vols (Oxford, 1988), I, *Images and Literacy*, pp. 223–5 (cited hereafter as *England's Iconoclasts*).

the Henrician church's pronouncements on ceremony and worship this teaching was influenced by the 'adiaphorist' theory of the Swiss reformer Melanchthon. Distinguishing between the divine law of nature which transcended all human institutions, and customs which are arbitrated by human legislation, Melanchthon evolved the principle of 'things good, things ill and things indifferent to salvation'. Images, relics, and fasts, considered indifferent to the law of nature, were allowable only if they supplemented, but did not supplant the essential.[16] The full implications of his adiaphorist theory were realised in the Second Royal Injunctions of 1538 which condemn as idolatry the use of images for any other purposes than as 'remembrances'; and the theory became the intellectual justification for Henrician iconoclasm.[17]

Edgeworth, therefore, lacking recourse to the arguments which More had provided only five years earlier in *Confutation of Tyndale's Answer and Dialogue against Heresies* – in particular that image worship is lawful when directed to that which the image represents – resorts to hermeneutics and criticises the teaching of the reformers that images and idols are one and the same thing.[18] In the fourth sermon, preached during the dissolutions in Bristol in 1539–40, he complains at the townspeople's abuse of images, attributing this confusion to the translators of the Protestant Bibles who 'would haue this latine worde *Imago* signifieth an Idole', and accusing them of perpetrating the error 'that to set vp Images, or to haue Images is idolatrye'. But his 'defence' merely comprises an elementary distinction between the two.[19]

This ideological compromise with Protestantism deepens in the sermons on St Peter's First Epistle. He not only admonishes superstitious veneration of images but, following the Second Royal Injunctions, teaches that they exist only as commemorative aids:

> You make an Image an Idole, geuyinge diuine honoure vnto it, or lokynge for helpe of it, or thinkinge that one Image of our Ladie can helpe thee better then an other, for there is in the Image no suche diuine power . . .

[16] Melanchthon's principle was first applied to English problems in Thomas Starkey's treatise, *An Exhortation to the people instructyinge them to unitie and obedience*, published by Berthelet in 1536 (STC 23236); see Smith, *Tudor Prelates*, pp. 197–9; J.K. McConica, *English Humanists and Reformation Politics Under Henry VIII and Edward VI* (Oxford, 1965), p. 171; W.G. Zeeveld, *Foundations of Tudor Policy* (New Haven, 1948), pp. 149–55; on the use of Melanchthon's distinction in the Ten Articles see *Formularies*, p. 4; on the *Bishops' Book*'s condemnation of images, *ibid.* pp. 135–8; on continental influences, Aston, *England's Iconoclasts*, pp. 35–43.

[17] *Ibid.* pp. 226–9. The injunctions are printed in Frere and Kennedy, p. 38. An anonymous translation of Erasmus's colloquy *The Pilgrimage of Pure Devotion* may have been used by the reformers as propaganda in c.1536–7; see H. White, *Tudor Books of Saints and Martyrs* (Madison, 1963), pp. 80–2; McConica, *English Humanists*, pp. 189–90. On the humanists' attack on ceremonies see J. Phillips, *The Reformation of Images: Destruction of Art in England, 1535–1660* (Los Angeles, 1973), pp. 35–40, 48–50; *English Humanism: Wyatt to Cowley*, ed. J. Martindale (Kent, 1985), p. 40.

[18] See More, *Dialogue*, CW6, 748–59; Tyndale, *An Answer to Sir Thomas More's Dialogue called the Supper of the Lord*, ed. H. Walter, PS (Cambridge, 1850), pp. 56–7, 60–2, 64, 80, 89 (cited hereafter as Tyndale, *Answer*); Phillips, *Reformation of Images*, pp. 42–8. Aston, *England's Iconoclasts*, pp. 393–5. The reformers believed that the Greek *eikon* and *eidolon* could be used interchangeably but the Protestant Bibles are inconsistent. On Cranmer's assertion in 1541 that *imago* and *idolum* meant the same thing, see Ridley, *Cranmer*, p. 230.

[19] *Sermons*, pp. 45–6; Aston, *England's Iconoclasts*, pp. 173–88 (on More's defence of images); 395–9 on Edgeworth's position (*Sermons*, pp. 143–4). More objected to Tyndale's translation of *idolum* as 'image' in *Confutation* (CW8, 173–5).

Make no more of an Image but onelye take it as a representer to signifye
. . . and to put you in remembraunce of the thinge that it is made after.[20]

The *Bishops' Book*, the second Henrician formulary of 1537, permits intercession
of the saints to be asked for but not the invocation of any particular saint for any
particular thing.[21] Edgeworth criticises this habit and in denying the intercessory
power traditionally ascribed to the Blessed Virgin suggests that her cult was no
longer a special subject of veneration:

> This obsecration or beseching signifyeth a certayne vehemencie in desiring
> as it wer for Gods sake, or for the loue of our Lady, or of al the sayntes of
> heauen . . . bi which thei trusted to be saued.[22]

Edgeworth's reference in the fifth sermon on the seven gifts to 'Pylgrymes (who)
vsed to go in flockes togither' testifies to the demise of this observance. Pilgrimages
and worshipping at shrines were deprecated in the Edwardian injunctions of July
1547 which instructed the clergy 'to recant and reprove the extolling . . . of
pilgrimages, relics or images'.[23] In a later sermon he corrects the popular miscon-
ception:

> An old vse hath peruerted the name of a Pilgryme, because folke were
> wont to go from place to place to honour saintes in places dedicate for their
> honour and to kisse theyr images and they only in times past were called
> Pilgrimes. . . . this worde Pilgrime . . . (now) signifieth a wayfaringe man or
> woman . . .[24]

Although the formularies entrusted the clergy to make rules concerning holy
days, rogation days and fasting, the observance of these ceremonies was left to the
individual conscience on the grounds that as 'mean and indifferent things' they
lacked the power to remit sin.[25] As early as 1537 Edgeworth attacks Protestant
denial of the Lenten observance as:

> . . . a clooke for malyce or euil liuinge as these that call theim selues
> euangellicall brothers doth nowe adayes, which counteth them selues by
> their fayth at libertie to eat when they wyll, and what they wyll, . . .
> wythout anye exception, choyse, or diuersity puttyng, betwyxt any kindes
> of meats, fisshe, or flesshe, indifferentlye at all times.[26]

In his sermon on ceremonies, preached around Lent 1548 after the fast was
reinforced, he condemns those who deny it.[27] But it is the persecution of pious

---

[20] *Sermons*, p. 302; Frere and Kennedy, p. 38.
[21] *Formularies*, pp. 141–2, 304–5; Aston, *England's Iconoclasts*, pp. 239–42. Edgeworth does not
follow the *King's Book* retreat from the *Bishops' Book*'s prohibitions against images.
[22] *Sermons*, p. 251. The cult of the Virgin was attacked by Latimer in Bristol in 1533.
[23] *Ibid.* p. 148; *Formularies*, pp. 137, 301; Hughes and Larkin, I, 287; on official disapproval of
pilgrimage images see Aston, *England's Iconoclasts*, p. 243; cf. Tyndale, *Answer*, pp. 63–4.
[24] *Sermons*, p. 252.
[25] *Formularies*, pp. 15–16, 115–16.
[26] *Sermons*, p. 128. For an incident in 1539 see Elton, *Policy and Police*, pp. 98–9.
[27] *Sermons*, p. 189; the Lenten fast was redefined in the 1547 Edwardian Royal Articles (Hughes
and Larkin, I, 287, pp. 400–1; Frere and Kennedy, pp. 107–8) and reasserted in 1548. On the
abolition of ceremonies in 1548 see *Formularies*, pp. 110–11, 114–15 (on the clergy); 147–8,
310–11 (on ceremonies).

Catholics, following radical Protestant preaching against the fast, which invokes his sternest imprecations:

> . . . if you absteyne from fleshe, and from whitmeate in the holy time of Lent; or yf you faste Fridayes and Wednesdaies, or more dayes in the weke in that holy time, or in this holy weke nowe present called the Rogation weke, the procession weke, . . . you shalbe called hipocrites, and folish phariseis, w^t suche other odious names[28]

Commensurate with his reluctance to abandon ceremonies and observances defined by the formularies as 'indifferent to salvation' is Edgeworth's adherence to orthodox doctrines asserted in the Act of Six Articles of 1539: transubstantiation, communion in one kind, clerical celibacy, private masses, the Real Presence and auricular confession.[29] But although he provides basic instruction on the Mass and the Real Presence, upholds penance and confession, and is, on one occasion, outspokenly critical of clerical marriage which was permitted in Edward's reign, he seldom develops his expositions and he avoids theologically complex topics such as justification and free will. Instead it is his defence of sacramental theology and the consecrating powers of the Catholic clergy which best identify his theological conservatism.

The *Sermons* illustrate the ambiguities inherent in Edgeworth's position: he complains at the Edwardian liturgical changes, and condemns the Protestant denial of ceremonies and observances while simultaneously conceding to the very secular authorities whose arbitrations diminished the traditional pietistic value of both. Indeed in the sermon on ceremonies his words echo the phrasing of the injunctions and formularies:

> . . . for our conscience sake we must obey the iust ordinaunces of our rulers . . . for obseruing and keping of the ceremonies of the churche, . . . as for other lawes temporall, godly deuised for the quietnes of the kinges sub-iectes spirituall and temporall, is necessarie for our soule health.[30]

Against the broader outline of national religious change he paints a picture of mounting local conflict between Catholic and Protestant clergy as the different injunctions and proclamations enforced Henrician and the Edwardian religious policies. In Bristol the continuing Protestant challenge to the status of the traditional clergy through the 1540s and 1550s was a legacy of the 1533 crisis: Edgeworth speaks out against Protestant extremists, amateur expositors of scripture who challenge the authority of the parish priest, or who refuse to wear clerical vestments. In c.1552–3 he complains at the confusion caused by the *Order of Communion* and by the 1549 *Book of Common Prayer*, but it is the degradation of the clerical vocation in Bristol which really concerns him. His target is the newly ascendant Protestant clergy, recently recruited from the lay professions, who flaunting 'theyr shameful and incestious bawdry, which they would couer wyth the name of matrimony', displaying 'gredie appetite . . . to get winning at dise and

---

[28] *Sermons*, p. 333; see also pp. 288–9.
[29] Dickens, *English Reformation*, p. 177; Dowling, *Humanism*, p. 61. The Six Articles are printed in *Tudor Constitutional Documents, 1485–1603*, ed. J.R. Tanner, 2nd ed. (London, 1930), pp. 95–8.
[30] *Sermons*, p. 188.

cardes', and 'hongrie for monie and lucre', compete with the Catholic clergy to preach endowed sermons, and interrupt Catholic services.[31]

The years during which the *Sermons* were preached saw in fact a marked decline in the status and functions of the secular clergy in Bristol, as in other dioceses in England.[32] In 1557 when the collection was published many Bristol parish livings fell vacant for lengthy periods and the parishes were served instead by untenured stipendiary curates who were paid by the parishioners and who, unlike the clergy whom they replaced, were poorly educated.[33] Edgeworth's anxiety was well founded, for the conservative clergy was powerless to halt this decline, and to prevent the accession of the Protestant clergy as the regulation of religious life in Bristol fell gradually into the hands of the laity.

Cranmer's questionnaire and the *King's Book*

Edgeworth's participation in 1540 in preparations for the third and final Henrician formulary was undoubtedly his most significant contribution to the Reformation at the national level. The *King's Book* originated as a revision of the *Bishops' Book* of 1537 (properly entitled *The Institution of a Christen Man*). This, the second formulary, had restored the four sacraments omitted from the Ten Articles: confirmation, orders, extreme unction and matrimony. But in reprinting the articles on justification (from the Augsburg Confession) and on purgatory, it had remained a 'cloudy compromise' between the demands for further reform and the principles of continental Protestantism.[34] Now, however, the third formulary would depart from this more radical position by expounding the creed, the seven sacraments, the ten commandments and the Lord's Prayer according to the Six Articles. Of all three formularies it is the most independent of German influence in stating the English church's position and defining its doctrine. Acclaimed as 'the handsomest monument of Henry's experiment in Anglo-Catholicism'[35] the *King's Book* remains a crowning achievement of the programme of conservative reform in the period 1541–7.[36]

The twenty five commissioners including Edgeworth met at Lambeth Palace between 17 September and 29 December 1540 for discussions on the sacraments and on the roles of bishops and priests. Their summarised answers were to be used

---

31 *Ibid.* pp. 351, 346, 365, 140, 187, 289, 333.
32 See Whiting, *Blind Devotion*, pp. 230–1, 264; on the question of clerical decline see C. Haigh, 'Anticlericalism and the English Reformation', *Reformation Revised*, pp. 70–2; on the figures for Lincoln, M. Bowker, 'The Henrician Reformation and the Parish Clergy', *ibid.* pp. 75–93; on clerical poverty, R.H. Pogson, 'Revival and reform in Mary's Tudor Church: a question of money', *JEH* XXV, 3 (1974), 251–2 (repr. in *Reformation Revised*, pp. 139–56); F. Heal, 'The Economic Problems of the Clergy' in *Church and Society in England; Henry VIII to James I*, ed. F. Heal and R. O'Day (London, 1977), pp. 108–13.
33 See Skeeters, 'Clergy of Bristol', pp, 147–51.
34 Dowling, *Humanism*, pp. 59–60. Without the king's approval, or any instruction as to its use, the *Bishops' Book*'s teaching was never enforced. For assessments see Dickens, *English Reformation*, p. 176; H. Maynard Smith, *Henry VIII and the Reformation* (London, 1948), p. 370; Hughes, *Reformation* II, 42–5; Guy, *Tudor England*, pp. 179–80. The *Bishops' Book* (STC 5163–7) is reprinted in *Formularies*, pp. 21–211.
35 Dickens, *English Reformation*, p. 185. For assessments see Kreider, *Chantries*, pp. 150–1; Hughes, *Reformation* II, 46–57; H. Maynard Smith, *Henry VIII*, pp. 375–81; Messenger, *Reformation*, . . . *and the Priesthood* I, 292–300.
36 Guy, *Tudor England*, pp. 193, 480, citing Redworth, 'English Reformation?', 29–35.

as guidelines in revising the section on the seven sacraments in the *Bishops' Book*. Cranmer's reason for having these topics aired was to attempt to establish a scriptural basis for doctrine and to investigate the extent of the king's jurisdiction over the clergy.[37] In devising a questionnaire with which to canvas scholarly opinion he had no doubt been encouraged by the king's swing towards a more radical interpretation of the sacraments, especially holy orders, in his annotated emendations to the *Bishops' Book* of 1537.[38] Despite Henry's apparent dissatisfaction with the earlier formulary he did not dispute the Protestant emphasis in the section on orders, which ranked preaching above the ministration of the sacraments, eliminated distinctions between bishops and priests and used Lutheran terminology in defining bishops as 'superintendants' and 'overseers'. Furthermore, in his revisions he deleted the traditional Augustinian theology that the sacrament was instituted by Christ and a visible sign of an invisible grace; also the word 'holy' from the phrase 'Holy Orders'.[39]

The phrasing of questions nine to fourteen, therefore, represent Cranmer's attempt to push the king's enquiry into the royal jurisdiction even further: they ask whether the sovereign can appoint bishops on his own authority, whether he has the right under any circumstances to create priests, to preach and to administer the sacraments. The other questions are less politically weighted: the first seven ask what the word 'sacrament' means according to scripture and to the Church Fathers, whether it is confined to the seven sacraments only, and if so whether it is taught as a doctrine; questions eight, fifteen and seventeen ask what authority exists for confirmation *cum chrismate*, auricular confession and extreme unction.

The lines along which Anglo-Catholic and reformist opinion divided are revealed in the commissioners' answers. These are preserved in Lambeth MS Stillingfleet with summaries in English and Latin.[40] Edgeworth's conspicuous orthodoxy aligns him with the prominent conservatives: Dr Tresham and Dr Redmayn, Bishop Bonner and Archbishop Lee of York. While the majority of this party upheld the seven sacraments including confirmation with chrism and relied on the belief in the oral traditions of the church, they also reflected the scriptural emphasis of the Henrician religious reforms. They asserted episcopal powers of ordaining on the grounds that these were bestowed upon the apostles; claimed that kings and princes had the power to excommunicate but could not ordain

---

[37] In a House of Lords debate on sacraments and the validity of unwritten ceremonies held in 1537, the king would only admit articles defined by scripture (Guy, *Tudor England*, pp. 179–80); cf. his defence in *Assertio* of the church's authority in defining the saraments; see J. Pelikan, *The Christian Tradition: A History of the Development of Doctrine*, 5 vols (London, 1971–), IV, *Reformation of Church and Dogma (1300–1700)*, pp. 256–7 (cited hereafter as Pelikan, *Church and Dogma*).
[38] Henry also considered criticisms of the articles on the sacraments made by Cranmer and Bishops Heath and Sampson (summarised in BL MS Royal 7c. xvi. fos 199–212). Henry's annotated copy of the *Bishops' Book* is in the Bodleian Library, 4°. Rawl. 245. For discussions of his 'revisions' see J.J. Scarisbrick, *Henry VIII* (1968, repr. London, 1976), pp. 524–7, 531–7; Kreider, *Chantries*, pp. 132 ff. They are printed with Cranmer's annotations in Cranmer, *Works* II, 83–114.
[39] *Ibid.* 97–8; Formularies, pp. 109, 112, 118; Scarisbrick, *Henry VIII*, pp. 534–7.
[40] MS Lambeth Stillingfleet 16 is printed in Pocock-Burnet, IV, Collection III, no. 21, pp. 443–96. BL MS Cleop. E. 5 (*ibid.* VI, Collection III, nos 69–71, pp. 241–7) contains Cranmer's answers, Henry's annotations to another set of answers, the questions and summaries of answers with further comment, and a copy of the points of agreement in the Lambeth MS. The questions and summarised answers are also printed in Cranmer, *Works* II, 115–17. Thirlby's title, the 'Elect of Westminster', which he held only during these months, has established the date of the commission (*LP* XV, 766, 860; Pocock-Burnet, IV, 460).

except in special cases; and maintained that confession is obligatory. Their strong-est opponents were the most Erastian of the reformers: Archbishop Cranmer, Bishop Barlow of St David's (whose answers are preserved in the summaries only), Bishop Skipp of Hereford and Dr Cox.

The questions concerning the revision of the *Bishops' Book*'s article on the sacrament of holy orders and whether the king should possess a *potestas ordinis* were those which most strenuously exercised the commissioners. The latter divided both parties, for only the most extreme of the reformers ascribe the king this power. Cranmer's answer to question nine: 'Whether the apostles . . . not having a Christian king . . . made bishops by that necessity or by God's authority?' is so strongly biased towards an assertion of the royal jurisdiction that it has been condemned as a 'peremptory denial of the sacrament'. He asserted that a priest is equal to a civil minister as both are appointed by the crown, and that ordination is neither necessary nor a rite conferring grace.[41] In his reply Edgeworth insists, like Archbishop Lee and Bishop Thirlby, that divine authority is necessary in ordain-ing, as in this way the apostles made bishops and priests. Dr Redman, by contrast, compromises with the reformers by distinguishing between the acts of ordaining or consecrating (pertaining to the apostles and their successors only) and appointing or naming to the office (pertaining to princes as supreme heads of the church).[42] Edgeworth, moreover, in answering question sixteen along the lines of Archbishop Lee and Bishop Tunstal – that laymen cannot excommunicate as this power was given only to the apostles and their successors – disagrees both with two other members of his party, Thirlby and Tresham, who concede that the power was given to the church and such as the church shall appoint, and with the reformers who add 'only if they be appointed by the high ruler'.[43] It is an indication of his commitment to the principle of clerical autonomy that he resolutely opposes royal jurisdiction in ordination. Like most of his party he insists that this is not the prerogative of the Christian prince, although he could baptise, instruct, choose bishops and regulate their functions.[44]

Edgeworth's answers to the first seven questions on the sacraments are consist-ent with the Anglo-Catholic position. He concedes that the sacraments are ad-mitted in both scriptural and patristic sources, and with Dr Tresham and Dr Oglethorpe opposes Cranmer in confirming, in answer to question two, that Augustine's definition of them as a visible form of invisible grace applies exclu-sively to the seven sacraments. And while he leans towards the reformers' view in denying that the 'determinate number' of seven sacraments is taught by scriptural and patristic authorities, his assertion that the 'doctrine' of the sacraments should nevertheless be taught because they are 'spoken of here and there' is in line with the opinion of his party.[45]

In summary, then, Edgeworth's refusal to concede any secular control in ordina-

---

[41] G. Constant, *La Réforme en Angleterre*, 2 vols (Paris, 1929), I, *Le Schism Anglais (1509–1547)*, tr. R.E. Scantlebury, I, *The English Schism (1509–1547)* (London, 1934), p. 426; cited by Messenger, *Reformation*, . . . *and the Priesthood* I, 287. See Pocock-Burnet, IV, 467–8. Maynard Smith, *Henry VIII*, p. 373, points out that the section on orders in the *King's Book* was most probably written by Cranmer.
[42] Pocock-Burnet, IV, 469–71; Scarisbrick, *Henry VIII*, p. 539; F. le van Baumer, *Early Tudor Theory*, p. 80.
[43] Pocock-Burnet, IV, 490–4.
[44] See Messenger, *Reformation*, . . . *and the Priesthood* I, 278–91; F. van le Baumer, *Early Tudor Theory*, pp. 79–81 for analyses of the answers.
[45] See Pocock-Burnet, IV, 443–64 (esp. 448–9, 459, 460).

tion, arguing from the extra-scriptural traditions, distinguishes his conservatism. He confirms the practices of the early church, saying, in reply to question ten on whether priests made bishops if priests were the first, 'that priests . . . made bishops, I think no inconvenience'; and he agrees with Dr Robertson and Bishop Bonner that Christ made his bishops and priests all at once.[46] He argues that the layman requires a special commission from God to ordain, and like the rest of his party claims that appointment to a bishopric is not sufficient without consecration (whereas Cranmer, Cox and Barlow state that appointment or naming to the office, pertaining to princes as supreme heads of the church, is sufficient). He adds that the Christian prince cannot consecrate without a commission grounded in scripture or authority by tradition, and that he cannot administer the sacraments, other than baptism, unless he has received a special commission from God, as Moses did.[47]

Edgeworth's views are widely represented in the summarised answers of the Anglo-Catholic party: consecration, not appointment alone, is necessary in ordination; absolution is necessary; the layman cannot ordain or excommunicate.[48] That his orthodoxy conferred authoritative status is suggested by the use of his answer on confession in the final version of the formulary – that contrition is only one way to obtain remission of sins, but the absolution of the priest is necessary and the only sure way.[49]

Although the Anglo-Catholic party appears to represent the majority view in the summarised answers, the king's annotations to the questionnnaire insist on scriptural proof and question the functions of the clergy, moving towards the *potestas ordinis* which Cranmer appears to have ascribed to him. Henry challenges the summarised response to question nine, that only by God's authority could the apostles ordain with: 'Where is this distinction found? Now, since you confess that the Apostles did occupate the one part which now you confess belongeth to princes, how can you prove that ordaining is only committed to you bishops?'; and, on the statement that grace was conferred upon the Apostles in ordering, he writes '*Ubi hic?*'[50] The bias displayed in his emendations of the *Bishops' Book* reappears in the formulary's article on holy orders: the sacramental theology that they are a visible sign of an invisible grace which he had earlier deleted, is omitted and 'holy' is not used of holy orders.[51] That the article on the ministry is as much, if not more, Protestant in emphasis than it is in the *Bishops' Book* may therefore be attributable to the king's influence. Although greater authority is attributed to the

[46] *Ibid.* 472–4.
[47] *Ibid.* 475–87 (on answers to questions eleven to fourteen).
[48] F. le van Baumer claims, *Early Tudor Theory of Kingship*, pp. 78, 84, that the Henrician pamphleteers and legislators reserved to the clergy the *potestas ordinis* as the only sphere which was unmolested by secular encroachments; cf. below, n. 52.
[49] Pocock-Burnet, IV, 487–9 (p. 489); this definition of penance as 'sacramental absolution' comes from Duns Scotus (Pelikan, *Church and Dogma*, pp. 95–6, 129–30). The *King's Book (Formularies*, p. 257) states that contrition, confession and satisfaction are 'ways and means expedient and necessary to obtain the said absolution'; Henry comments on the answer to question fifteen that scripture speaks of absolution manifestly: 'Then penance is changed to a new term, viz. absolution' (BL MS Cotton Cleop. E. v. fo. 36).
[50] BL MS Cotton Cleop. E. v. fo. 42; cited by Scarisbrick, *Henry VIII*, p. 539.
[51] See Cranmer, *Works* II, 97–8; Scarisbrick, *Henry VIII*, p. 540, who notes the consistency of his anticlericalism. On the similarities between Henry's revisions of the *Bishops' Book* and the 1543 version of the *King's Book* see Kreider, *English Chantries*, pp. 132–4, and G. Redworth, *In Defence of the Church Catholic: the life of Stephen Gardiner* (Oxford, 1990), p. 168.

office of the priest, the royal prerogative is emphasised: bishops and priests may be appointed by the positive laws of men and bishops may be deposed by the same authorities for these, not God, confer their powers upon them. In short, the activities of the clergy are subject to the temporal jurisdiction of the realm.[52]

For the final stages of preparing the *King's Book* a committee was appointed by Convocation in 1543. The articles on the sacraments were overseen by Cranmer, Thirlby, Skipp, Heath and Salcot and the formulary was drawn up by three bishops – Nicholas Heath, Thomas Thirlby and George Day – and three doctors: John Redman, Richard Cox and Thomas Robinson.[53] But whether Gardiner, who also attended the meeting in 1543, had any part in the final version is questionable, despite Protestant charges and his defence of its doctrines in 1547.[54] Each section of the formulary was approved of by the bishops before being sent to Convocation. It was published in May with a preface by the king under the title *A Necessary Doctrine and Erudition for any Christian Man* and remained in use until his death in 1547.[55]

The King's Book and the Sermons

The *King's Book* and to a lesser extent the *Bishops' Book* were Edgeworth's primary authorities on matters of doctrine and usage in all the sermons he preached after 1543. The *Bishops' Book*'s redefinition of the Catholic church, as a loose grouping of national churches, spread throughout the world and, together with an explicit denial of the church of Rome which is seen as 'a particular member thereof', was repeated in the *King's Book*. In the sermon on the creed of 1546, Edgeworth bypasses the issue of the Catholic church's universal preeminence to declare: 'it is called catholike, that is to saye, vniuersall or whole over all the world'.[56] He also upholds the formularies' teaching on the tenth article, that the Catholic faith is a unity of Christians partaking in the sacraments and that the church is maintained by the doctrine and profession of the Christian faith as taught by the scriptures and the doctrine apostolic. The point of this ecclesiology is to affirm a spiritual unity of Christians through the Holy Ghost.

> And by the vnitie and communion in the fayth and Sacramentes of this holye Churche we receaue as well the merite of Christes passion and of his holy lyfe, as of the good liuinge, and good dedes of all holy people, beynge all one, knitte together by the livelye fayth of the sayde catholike Churche.[57]

---

[52] *Formularies*, pp. 277–89, esp. pp. 278–9, 282, 287. The article, avoiding the word 'consecration', implies that clerical appointment and deposing is subject to the jurisdiction of the state; see Messenger, *Reformation . . . and the Priesthood* I, 296–8.
[53] *LP* XVIII, ii, 68. Henry described the committee as 'men of indifferency for judgement in learning'; Kreider, *Chantries*, p. 150.
[54] Muller, *Gardiner*, pp. 106–7; *Letters*, pp. 299–302, 325. See Maynard Smith, *Henry VIII*, pp. 375, 380–1; J. Ridley, *Thomas Cranmer* (Oxford, 1962), p. 239; cf. Redworth's argument in *Church Catholic*, pp. 167–73, that Gardiner's part in the formulary's production has been exaggerated and that he merely presented it with Cranmer to Convocation.
[55] *Concilia* III, 868; *LP* XVIII, i, 365. The *King's Book* (STC 5168–5177) is reprinted in *Formularies*, pp. 213–377. A Latin translation, *Pia et Catholica Christiani Hominis*, appeared in 1544 (STC 5178).
[56] See J. Pelikan, *Church and Dogma*, p. 99, on the development of this ecclesiology; *Formularies*, pp. 54–5; *Sermons*, p. 179.
[57] *Ibid.* This teaching appears in the official treatises which supported the *Bishops' Book*; see *The Pater noster. ye crede. and the comaundementes in englysh* (J. Byddell, 1537), sigs F1^{r–v} (STC 16820).

Although Edgeworth's treatment of the sacraments usually corresponds to his answers to Cranmer's questionnaire, in his sermon on ceremonies he apparently concedes to Protestant theology by ranking only baptism and confession as essential to salvation and excluding the sacrament of the altar.[58] And while pointing out that penance, especially confession, is the hardest sacrament, he omits the section of his answer to question fifteen (included in the King's Book) to the effect that absolution is the 'only sure way of confession'.[59] But his treatment of orders in the eighteenth sermon on I Peter, emphasising the sacramental duties of the priesthood above those of preaching, implicitly denies the formularies' ranking of preaching and teaching the word of God as the first duty, and ministration of the sacraments as the second.[60] He also reimposes the distinctions between bishops and priests which the formularies had removed, and ascribes to bishops the functions conferred upon bishops by the English church: to ordain and confirm.[61]

But his contrasting definitions of consecration in two different sermons reflect the confusion found in the commissioners' answers to question twelve. If *impositione manu et de oratione* (as found in scripture) was a sign of appointment only, then consecration would mean also anointing with oil. But in the formularies consecration was considered to be made by imposition of the bishop's hand with prayer, and anointing with oil was omitted.[62] In the seventh sermon Edgeworth distinguishes 'the priesthoode of them that by materiall oyle and imposicion of the bishoppes hands be consecrate and made priestes' from the spiritual priesthood of the laity.[63] But in the eighteenth sermon, using the Lutheran terms 'elected' and 'congregation', he states that a priest is 'by prophecye, or election and imposition of a prelates hande is piked out & chosen . . . to be a minister of God in the Churche or congregation'. Furthermore he mentions the 'imposition and laiyng on of the prelates handes' and 'other ceremonies longyng to the same' by which the gift of grace is conferred, without any reference to anointing with oil.[64] This sermon, preached in c.1552–3, attempts to defend the apostolic origin of orders, perhaps in response to the Anglican ordinal of 1550 which has been described as making 'priests presbyters in the sense of Reformation theology instead of consecrating and sacrificing priests in the sense of the Catholic Church'.[65]

The systematisation of faith and worship under Henry VIII, and the Edwardian

---

On this ecclesiology see Scarisbrick, Henry VIII, pp. 506–7. F. le van Baumer, Theory of Kingship, pp. 45–8, claims that the Marsilian redefinition of the church proved the king's right to plenitudo potestas.
[58] Formularies, p. 293; on Henry's orthodoxy concerning Eucharistic doctrine see C.W. Dugmore, The Mass and the English Reformers (London, 1958), pp. 107–10.
[59] Sermons, pp. 186–7; Formularies, p. 257 (cf. pp. 96–8); Bishop Watson defines penance in Holsome and Catholyke doctryne as 'sacramental confession . . . made to a priest for the attaining of absolution'; see his Sermons on the Sacraments, ed. T.E. Bridgett (London, 1876), p. 203.
[60] Sermons, pp. 340–1, 349–50; also 249–50; Watson, Sermons, pp. 292–4; Bonner, A profitable . . . doctryne, ed. cit. sig. 2A5; Formularies, pp. 109, 278.
[61] Sermons, pp. 342, 344; Formularies, pp. 118–19, 121, 282, 286–7; Watson, Sermons, p. 294, upholds the distinction between bishops and priests.
[62] Pocock-Burnet, IV, 480–1; Formularies, pp. 104–5, 277–8; Maynard Smith, Henry VIII, pp. 373–4. According to More in Confutation (CW8, 194–8) anointing with oil is not the sensible sign of the sacrament of order; see Tyndale, Answer, pp. 19–20. It is also omitted by Watson (Sermons, pp. 288, 294) and Bonner in A profitable . . . doctryne, sig. 2A2ᵛ.
[63] Sermons, p. 247.
[64] Ibid. p. 340.
[65] Ibid. pp. 341–9; Edgeworth draws on his answer to question ten that priests in the primitive

liturgical changes, meant that the basis of More's polemics – the appeal to the authority of the church to justify many practices – was effectively eroded. Edgeworth's refutation, in the seventh sermon, of Tyndale's heresy of a 'priesthood of all believers', and his discussion, in the eighteenth sermon, of the translation of *seniores* as 'elders', reveal only a limited application of More's arguments.[66] Crucial to his case is his recognition of the *potestas jurisdictionis* of the king in parliament in church administration. His belief in clerical obedience due to the Crown explains both his silence on secular control over election to the ministry and over the jurisdiction of bishops and priests, and his use of key texts in redefining the relationship between church and Crown.[67] The sequence on St Peter's First Epistle, preached in honour of the king, the founder of Bristol Cathedral, celebrates the principles of Henrician Catholicism enshrined in the *King's Book*, and implicitly affirms the limited doctrine of sovereignty propounded by the Henrician political writers; namely that the king, or the king in parliament, had supreme jurisdiction over ecclesiastical affairs within the confines of the state.[68]

> If God had not preserued our mooste gratious Soueraigne Kinge Henry the eyght, whiche by his princelie zele, loue, and deuotion to God, hath erecte this Cathedrall Churche of Bristowe, and manye other suche within this Realme, God knoweth what case diuine seruice should haue bene in.[69]

church made bishops (Pocock-Burnet, IV, 471–4); see F.J. Clark, *Eucharistic Sacrifice and the Reformation*, 2nd ed. (London, 1963), p. 197; ODCC s.v. 'Orders and Ordination'.
[66] *Sermons*, pp. 245 ff; 340.
[67] *Ibid.* pp. 188, 260, 359. The texts are Rom.13:1–2 and 5.
[68] le van Baumer, *Early Tudor Theory*, pp. 83–4; on the ideological ambiguity within the Royal Supremacy see Scarisbrick, *Henry VIII*, pp. 508–11.
[69] *Sermons*, p. 208. On the practical nature of Henry's ecclesiastical reforms see Redworth, 'English Reformation?', 34.

SOURCES OF THE *SERMONS*

Scriptural and patristic sources

Edgeworth's familiarity with the scholarly practices of early sixteenth-century humanism is nowhere more apparent than in his methods of sermon construction. The series on the seven gifts of the Holy Ghost and the sermon on the creed are preached under headings; the twenty sermons on the First Epistle of St Peter use the historico-critical approach popularised by Colet in his Pauline sermons of 1503–4.[1] Edgeworth explains in the preface his preference for preaching *secundum ordinem textus*:

> And when I shoulde preache oftentimes in one place, I vsed not to take euery day a distinct epistle or gospell, or other text, but to take some proces of scripture, and to prosecute the same, part one day and parte another daye[2]

His preaching techniques were probably developed at Oxford, but he may also have known *Ecclesiastes* (1535), Erasmus' tract on preaching which recommends the 'ancient' method of sermon construction.[3] Certainly his use of Erasmus' biblical scholarship for the sermons preached at Bristol Cathedral suggests that editions of contemporary printed Bibles, with their medieval and sixteenth century commentaries, were available to him in the mid-1540s.[4] In addition to using alongside the Vulgate the *Novum Instrumentum*, Erasmus' edition of the Greek New Testament (1516), he consults the *Annotationes* for difficult words such as *aduena* and *dyscholis*.[5] But like Gardiner he disapproved of Erasmus' *Paraphrases* which he uses critically as when refuting the espousal of *solafideism* in the paraphrase on I Pet. 1:5: *in vobis qui in virtute Dei custodimini per fidem*, 'you are preserved, not through your owne merites, but by faith and vnfained trust', with an orthodox assertion of merit theology.[6] He interprets the text of I Peter using these sixteenth century preaching aids in conjunction with the medieval Bible glosses: the *Glossa Ordinaria* of Walfridus Strabo, the *Glossa Interlinearis* of Anselm of Laon, the *postilla* of Nicholas of Lyra and Hugh of St Cher.[7]

[1] *Sermons*, p. 193. On Colet's disciples see Blench, pp. 28–31.
[2] *Sermons*, p. 96.
[3] For definitions see Siegfried Wenzel, *Preachers, Poets, and the Early English Lyric* (New Jersey, 1986), p. 62; Blench, pp. 71–8 (including practictioners).
[4] D. Erasmus, *Ecclesiastae sive de Ratione Concionandi Libri Quatuor*, ed. F.A. Klein (Leipzig, 1820); see H. Caplan, 'A Late Medieval Tractate on Preaching, the Pseudo Aquinas Tract' in *Of Eloquence, Studies in Ancient Medieval Rhetoric* (Ithaca, 1970), p. 50.
[5] *Sermons*, pp. 195, 260–1; see Jerry H. Bentley, *Humanists and Holy Writ: New Testament Scholarship in the Renaissance* (Princeton, 1983), pp. 123 ff. on Erasmus' *Annotationes*.
[6] *Sermons*, p. 209. Edgeworth apparently did not use the Protestant translations of the *Paraphrases* of 1548–9 which Gardiner and his party condemned; see Strype, *Cranmer* I, 214–5, 218; II, 785–92; Townsend-Foxe, II, 42; McConica, *English Humanists*, pp. 246–9.
[7] Lyra's *postilla*, the *Glossa Ordinaria* and *Interlinearis* are included in *Textus Biblie cum glossa ordinaria etc.* which Edgeworth probably used for this series. On the *postilla* of Lyra, Hugh of St Cher

The *Sermons* betray other signs of his training in scholastic theology. This would have provided him with instruction in the medieval *artes praedicandi*, the fourfold method of biblical exegesis, and the 'modern' method of *divisio thematis*: dividing and subdividing the theme.[8] Several of the recommended methods of amplification or dilation provide variation. The different meanings of 'heaven' in the sermon on the creed and 'pilgrim' in the eighth sermon on I Peter are distributed under headings. Other definitions are provided by contraries (the virtue *modestia* is introduced with its corresponding vice *nimietas*). Some terms are given with their etymologies or simple moralisations, as that Peter's original name, Simon-bar-Jonah, means 'obedience is the child of the doue'; and the properties of natural objects and concepts are given with analogies of natural truths.[9] For such material he would have referred to a preachers' manual or commonplace book such as Bromyard's *Summa Praedicantium* or an alphabetical reference book (a collection of *auctoritates*, preaching *exempla*, or biblical *distinctiones*) of the sort which were provided in the *florilegia* of the twelfth and thirteenth centuries.[10] But like the humanists in general he avoids the *distinctio* and the complex moralisations found in these collections and in compilations of nature *moralisée* such as the *Contes Moralisés* of Nicole de Bozon or the *Liber Sapientiae* of Robert Holkot.[11]

Sometimes Edgeworth integrates these preaching techniques with humanist ones recommended by Erasmus, Valla and Colet which are appropriate to his preferred methods of *dispositio* and exegesis. The geographical and historical background to the First Epistle of St Peter identifies the countries in Asia Minor for which the Epistle is intended and attempts to establish the sequence of Peter's movements following the resurrection; but it also includes spiritual interpretations of the names of Christ and St Peter taken from the *postilla* of St Cher and Lyra.[12] In the earlier series on the seven gifts and in the later 'Edwardian' sermons, by contrast, instead of these exegetical techniques there is a dependence on the Church Fathers, and apologetic interpretations of controversial texts or complaints at contemporary religious changes. Such variation between a philological

and the *Glossa Ordinaria* see B. Smalley, *The Study of the Bible in the Middle Ages*, 3rd ed. rev. (Oxford, 1983), pp. 274, 366–7; on Lyra's *postilla litteralis* see Bentley, *Humanists and Holy Writ*, pp. 20–31.
[8]   The classic treatment of the *artes praedicandi* is by Th. M. Charland, *Artes Praedicandi: Contribution à l'Histoire de la Rhétorique au Moyen Age* (Paris, 1936), pp. 21–6. See also W.O. Ross (ed.), *Middle English Sermons*, EETS, OS, 209 (1940, repr., London, 1960), pp. xliii–lv; J.J. Murphy, *Rhetoric in the Middle Ages: A History of Rhetorical Theory from St. Augustine to the Renaissance* (Los Angeles, 1974), pp. 269–343 (including a translation of Robert of Basevorn's *Forma Praedicandi* (1322), pp. 344–55); E. Gilson, 'Michel Menot et la technique du sermon médiéval' in *Les Idées et les Lettres* (Paris, 1932), pp. 193–154; Wenzel, *Preachers*, pp, 61–3, 67–79; Marianne G. Briscoe, 'Preaching and Medieval Drama' in *Contexts for Early English Drama*, ed. M. Briscoe and John C. Caldeway (Indiana University Press, 1989), pp. 150–72, on the 'modern' method of sermon construction; Blench, pp. 72–3, 79–86, 95–9 for sixteenth century examples.
[9]   *Sermons*, pp. 171, 252–3, 284–5, 194, 122, 210, 262, 290–1, 308, 311. The eight modes of amplification are outlined in several treatises such as Richard of Thetford's *Ars Dilatandi Sermones*. See Murphy, *Rhetoric in the Middle Ages*, pp. 326–8; Caplan, 'Medieval Tractate', pp. 40–78; 'Henry of Hesse on the Art of Preaching', *PMLA* 48, ii (1933), 340–61; Wenzel, *Preachers*, pp. 76–7.
[10]   On Bromyard's *Summa Praedicantium* (1518) see Owst, *Preaching in England*; on handbooks for preachers, H.G. Pfander, 'The Medieval Friars and some Alphabetical Reference-Books for Sermons', *Medium Aevum* 3 (1943), pp. 19 ff.
[11]   Edgeworth may have used the older compilations for their bestiary material as the moralisations were added separately; see J.A. Mosher, *The Exemplum in the Early Religious and Didactic Literature of England* (New York, 1911), p. 3; see below pp. 65–6 on Edgeworth's use of allegory.
[12]   *Sermons*, pp. 194–200.

and historical approach which uses the scriptural glosses, and a thematic, exhortatory approach which draws on the Church Fathers, sometimes even within one sermon, no doubt reflects the vicissitudes of his circumstances and the comparative availability of his preaching aids. The collection's unique span over three reigns and almost twenty years makes a clear perspective difficult, but this diversity of approach is certainly rare in Catholic homilies of the period and it seems not to exist at all in the Protestant ones.

Edgeworth's answers to Cranmer's questionnaire of 1540 on the role of the clergy demonstrate his familiarity with the writings of the Church Fathers, and the provision made at his death for his copies of the works of St Ambrose, St Gregory and St Chrsyostom suggests he had acquired the nucleus of a patristic library. In the series on the seven gifts of the Holy Ghost he is clearly indebted to the *Summa Theologiae* of Thomas Aquinas for his Catholic theology. The 'Angelic Doctor' continued to be highly ranked in the universities; tributes such as More's and Fisher's as 'the very floure of theology' were more widespread than Colet's distaste for him as one of the scholastic writers.[13] But St Augustine, whose preeminence as 'father of the Christian West' was undiminished in the sixteenth century, is the most frequently quoted patristic writer. He draws on his *Sermo de Symbolo* for the sermon on the creed and on his tracts on St John's Gospel and first Epistle for expounding the Real Presence and the gift of fear in the sixth sermon; this sermon also opens with the story of Aristippus taken from *De Civitate Dei*, a favourite treatise of the humanists. In the fifth sermon it is Augustine's account of his difficulty in translating the Greek *latria* in Books IV and IX which underpins his discussion on translating *pietas* into English.[14] Augustine provides a simple philosophy of acceptance of and resignation to God's will; that is, God's indifference creates prosperity and adversity for all men whether good or evil. From *De Civitate Dei* comes this striking illustration of the contrasting effects of adversity:

> As if a man chafe in his hand, or els against the fyre talow or greace, it giueth an horrible stinckynge smell, where as if you likewise chafe by the same fyre a pleasant oyntment, it giueth a fragraunt and swete sauour.[15]

Edgeworth's eschatalogy is also Augustinian; from *De Doctrina Christiana* comes the view that men receive good and bad deaths indiscriminately, and that therefore, to achieve a good death, the Christian must lead a virtuous life following the example of Christ; for '*non potest male mori qui bene vixerit*, he can not die ill that hath liued well'.[16]

Many of the collection's defences of clerical duty and authority derive from St Chrysostom's writings on the priesthood. In the first sermon on the seven gifts Chrysostom's treatise *De Spiritu Sancto* lies behinds Edgeworth's reflections on the role of the preacher, distinguishing between sapience or wisdom, 'the armour of the mouth', and intelligence, 'the harneys of the hert', and concluding with a summary of pastoral duties translated from the pseudo-Chrysostom homily *Primo*

---

[13] On the humanists' attitude to Aquinas see E. Surtz, *The Life and days of John Fisher* (Camb., Mass., 1967), p. 162; ' "The Oxford Reformers" and Scholasticism', *Studies in Philology* 47 (1950), 547–56; Marc'hadour's introduction to More's *Confutation*, *CW*6, 533–5.

[14] On More's and Vives' use of Augustine see Marc'hadour's introduction to *Dialogue*, *CW*6, 526–9; see *Sermons*, pp. 172, 174, 176–8, 164–6, 156, 147–8.

[15] *Ibid.* p. 306.

[16] *Ibid.* p. 307.

Concio de Lazaro. Chrysostom's treatise *De Sacerdotio*, which appears in the *King's Book*'s teaching on orders, is the basis for Edgeworth's treatment of this sacrament in the eighteenth sermon on St Peter.[17] But in asserting the ecclesiastical hierarchy, his quotation from Jerome's epistle *Ad Evangelium* that, in the early church, bishops were chosen as 'overseers' over the other members to avoid heresies, departs from the formulary. He had included this quotation in his answer to question ten of Cranmer's questionnaire.[18]

Although Edgeworth owned a copy of Gregory's works at the time of his death he makes little use of them, using his theology on salvation by merit to counter Erasmus' paraphrase on I Pet. 1:5 and to confirm the orthodoxy of the writings of Dionysius the Areopagite.[19] But he seems to have had a particular fondness for Ambrose from whose commentary on Psalm 118:86 comes the important image in the sermon on the creed, of faith as the 'watch' of men's souls which, like a fortress, must protect them against heresies; and he attacks Tyndale's Lutheran interpretation of I Pet. 2:9, as describing 'a priesthood of all believers', by referring to Ambrose's rule of expounding scripture outlined in *De Vocatione Gentium*.[20] Another Ambrosian treatise, *De Officiis Ministris*, is the source of a discussion on obedience in the fifth sermon on piety, and from his commentary on St Luke's Gospel comes his comments on hospitality. Ambrose is also an authority for his patriarchal views on women, and Edgeworth adapts from the *Hexameron* a striking *exemplum* of the mating habits of the lamprey and her mate, the adder, to exhort better connubial relations between husbands and wives. Finally, sensitive to the humanists' disapproval of using *exempla* of the fantastic and marvellous, he defends his use of fables by citing St Ambrose's commentary on Ephesians.[21]

The Fathers are cited as authorities for orthodox Catholic practices in the face of the Protestant challenge to traditional clerical authority. Jerome is invoked on the dangers of uninformed reading in the vernacular Bible; and Edgeworth, perturbed at the sight of the laity instructed by 'green diuines' and 'pseudapostles', who apparently include women preachers, quotes Jerome's words that in the early church women were merely 'well exercised in holye scriptures' but 'not . . . readers, preachers, or disputers of scriptures'.[22] Tertullian's condemnation as heretics in his *Liber de Prescriptionibus contra Hereticos*, of those who have wavered in the faith inspires Edgeworth's complaints at the liturgical reforms of Edward's reign in the twentieth sermon; while St Basil's epistles on Bishop Eustathius, a disciple of Arius, provide him with a parallel between the Protestants' replacement of altars by communion tables in 1549 and heretics from Dardania who overturned altars and set up tables in c.362.[23] Elsewhere the Fathers confirm the moral virtues of the Christian life. Cyprian's *Liber de Habitu Virginum*, for example, is used for the lengthy denunciation of extravagance in women's apparel, hairstyle and cosmetics in the eleventh sermon, while Jerome's recommendations on the reclusive life, and

---

[17] *Ibid.* pp. 121–2; 347–9; *Formularies*, pp. 277–81; on sixteenth century translations of Chrysostom see Greenslade, 'Theology', *CU*, p. 321.

[18] *Sermons*, p. 344; Pocock-Burnet, IV, 474.

[19] Appendix, p. 449; *Sermons*, pp. 209, 296. See Bentley, *Humanists and Holy Writ*, pp. 186–7, on the problems of identifying the Pseudo-Dionysius.

[20] *Sermons*, pp. 169, 245–6.

[21] *Ibid.* pp. 150, 320, 277–8, 160–1.

[22] *Ibid.* pp. 139–40; Edgeworth may be correcting Erasmus' view in *An exhortacyon to the study of the Gospell*, ed. cit. sigs E1^{r-v}, that 'saint Hierome . . . exhorteth bothe vyrgynes and wydowes/ & wedded wyues to the redynge of holy scripture'.

[23] *Sermons*, pp. 364, 366.

on women in the primitive church, are quoted to illustrate the virtue of piety as a
reverent honour to God.[24] These and other brief allusions to the Fathers suggest
that Edgeworth consulted a preacher's handbook or *florilegium* of *auctoritates*.

Classical sources

Instruction in the classics was frowned upon at Oriel College in the early sixteenth
century, and Edgeworth's sketchy allusions to the ancient writers suggest a second-
hand acquaintance through a popular sixteenth-century compilation such as
Erasmus' *Apophthegmata*. Cicero, for example, appears to be a favourite author, yet
it is unlikely that he had read his works. The Stoic theory of the four passions is
found in *Tusculan Disputations* and *De Finibus Bonorum et Malorum*, but this
version is blended, in the sixth sermon on fear, with that from St Augustine's *De
Civitate Dei* which he appears to know better. It is equally doubtful that he turned
directly to the *Atticae Noctae* of Aulus Gellius for the anecdote of Socrates and his
wife Xantippe; he may have drawn on Jerome's account in *Adversus Jovinianum*,
although his source is probably Erasmus' *Apophthegmata*.[25] Edgeworth charac-
teristically adapts *exempla* from classical *dicta* and stories to his own times. His
narration of Cicero's story of the two Roman praetors in *De Officiis* to illustrate the
virtue of *modestia*, includes an application of the corruption and decadence of
Rome to what he perceives as the delining morality of Bristol. In the fifth sermon
he anecdotes of Codrus, King of Athens, and the Phileni – the two Carthaginian
brothers who died for their country – both from Valerius Maximus' *Dicta et Facta
Memorabilia*, illustrate the virtue of patriotism; this treatise is also the source of
admonitions against lechery and gluttony and of the explanation of the origin of
the word *caeremonia* in the sermon on ceremonies.[26]

Like the Church Fathers, classical writers are moral authorities for reproving
what he regarded as excessive or undesirable behaviour. Book VI of Aristotle's
Nichomachean Ethics, a text which he would have studied for the MA at Oxford, is
the source of discussions on the virtue of prudence which, in the sermon on the
gift of counsel, are aimed at the rash rebels of the Pilgrimage of Grace who have
threatened the realm with instability in 1536–7.[27] His disapproval, in 1539–40, of
lay teaching of the scriptures is bolstered by the opinion of Book I that 'younglinges' are unfit to study moral philosophy or the science of divinity. In the
eighteenth sermon (c.1553), Book IV is the source of a denunciation of *turpe
lucrum*, 'filthy or vnhonest gaines', enjoyed by prelates who play at cards and dice,
and of *illiberales*, those churls who have plundered church treasure.[28]

Edgeworth appears most at home with material of an encyclopaedic nature such
as Pliny's *Naturalis Historia* or Bartholomaeus Anglicus' *De Proprietatibus Rerum*.

[24] *Ibid.* pp. 273–4, 153–4.
[25] *Ibid.* pp. 155, 277.
[26] *Ibid.* pp. 283–5, 150–1, 301, 182.
[27] *Ibid.* p. 124; see also p. 308. On the prescribed Aristotelian texts see Weisheipl, 'Curriculum',
159, 161, 173–6; J. McConica, 'Humanism and Aristotle in Tudor Oxford', *EHR* 94 (1979),
291–317; C.B. Schmitt, 'Towards a Reassessment of Renaissance Aristotelianism', *History of
Science* 11 (1974), 159–93.
[28] *Sermons*, pp. 137–8, 346, 355; the *King's Book*'s article on order states that priests or bishops
should not be 'greedy of filthy lucre' (*Formularies*, p. 279).

His account of the harshness of Rehoboam (III Kings 12:11), for example, dwells on the properties of the scorpion:

> These scorpions be scourges hauyng knottes of wire or leadde on the coardes, . . . so called after a certayne venemous Worme, whiche when he stingeth, turneth vp his tayle ouer his heade, and so styngeth, and so perelouslye, that withoute there bee hadde by and by a certaine Oyle of scorpions . . . there is no healpe nor remedye, but present death.[29]

Pliny's *Naturalis Historia*, and the treatises *De Situ Orbis* and *Polyhistor* by the fourth century cosmographers Pomponius Mela and Julius Solinus, provide geographical, historical, and legendary material for the first sermon on I Peter, although the information that the local name for the isle of Cadiz is *Calis Malis* because of the rocks surrounding it must have come from Bristol merchants. In the fourth sermon on the seven gifts Mela's *De Situ Orbis* is also used in teaching on idols and images to differentiate Chimera, the beast of Greek fable, from 'Chimera', the mountain in Lycia.[30]

However apt their application, most of Edgeworth's classical allusions are used in a simple illustrative manner and, like the medieval preachers, he shows little appreciation of the spirit of the ancient writers; thus in the sixteenth sermon he dismisses Cicero's commendation of hospitality as being too worldly in motive. The impression of his lack of familiarity with their work is reinforced by many inaccuracies: in references to the Stoics, and in misquotations from Horace's epistles, and Martial's epigrams.[31]

Vernacular sources

Edgeworth's failure to acknowledge works of Reformation controversy and Catholic apology reflects the limitations of his apologetics following More's martyrdom: outright championship of his cause was impossible. Yet his dependence on More's arguments in the *Dialogue against Heresies* and *The Confutation of Tyndale's Answer* suggests their pervasiveness, despite the unavailability of More's writings.[32] Another shaping influence on Edgeworth's polemics was Barlow's *A dialogue against these Lutheran faccions* of 1531, written before his conversion to Protestantism. This text echoes so many of Thomas More's opinions that at one time it was thought to be written by the Chancellor himself. Edgeworth repeats More's and Barlow's condemnation of the multitude of sects in Germany, and like them disparages 'carnall liberty' and 'euangelicall brothers'.[33] But these and other attitudes, such as that Luther was 'disdayning at other mens exaltation, auauntage, and profites', and that it is 'rather good and profitable that holie Scripture shoulde

---

[29] *Ibid*. p. 355.
[30] *Ibid*. pp. 199–200; 144.
[31] *Ibid*. pp. 95, 156, 217, 302.
[32] *Ibid*. pp. 137, 340. Tyndale's polemical works were banned and Thomas More's were not reprinted after his death until Rastell's edition of *English Works* in 1557; but overt reference to their works would have been unsafe. Edgeworth mentions by name Protestant opponents, Hugh Latimer and William Barlow only in the Marian preface (*ibid*. p. 96).
[33] *Ibid*. pp. 127–8, 137, 140, 142, 187, 280. Stokesley, Bishop of London, ordered all curates to read Barlow's *A dialoge*; see I.B. Horst, *The Radical Brethren. Anabaptism and the English Reformation to 1558* (Nieuwkoop, 1972), pp. 45–9.

be hadde in the mother tong . . .' were commonplace among the conservative Henricians in the 1530s, and he may not have used written sources.[34]

Edgeworth apparently also knew Erasmus' treatises on the vernacular scriptures, the *Paraclesis* (the preface to the *Novum Instrumentum*) and the preface to his Paraphrase on St Matthew; their English translations, *An exhortacyon to the study of the Gospell* and *An exhortacyon to the dylygent study of scripture*, enjoyed a certain vogue in the 1530s, but he treats Erasmus' views on ceremony and worship with caution.[35] His insistence on forebearance when reading 'hard' passages of scripture, and the recommendation that a teaching ministry trained in theology should explicate their meaning, reflects More's critique of Erasmus in the *Dialogue*. Erasmus' promotion of an interiorised expression of faith through claims such as in *An exhortacyon to . . . study of scripture* that the inspiration of the Holy Spirit makes every man 'a very and true deuyne/ thoughe he be a weuer: yea thoughe he dygge and delue' was ambiguous in the light of Protestant beliefs such as a 'priest-hood of all believers', and this aspect of his piety became unacceptable to the apologists.[36] Citing Jerome's epistles, as Erasmus does in *An exhortacyon to the study of the Gospell*, Edgeworth cautions the laity, especially women, against presumption in teaching and preaching the scriptures.[37] But he was not always critical of Erasmian humanism which he acknowledges in the third sermon on the seven gifts; its influence is apparent in his limited use of scholastic philosophy, his emphasis on Christian revelation, and his theory and practice of rhetoric.[38]

Edgeworth's dependence on the newly available vernacular preaching aids is apparent in the saturation of his prose with proverbs, epithets and pithy sayings. Handbooks of classical material such as the *Adagia* of Erasmus, the *Adagia Sacrorum et Humanorum* of Polydore Vergil, and vernacular proverb collections such as John Heywood's *A Dialogue . . . of prouerbes* (c.1546), were important new sources for the sixteenth century preacher. Another rich quarry were the translations of the *Adagia* and *Apophthegmata* made by Richard Taverner and Nicholas Udall in the 1540s.[39] Edgeworth may have consulted a compilation of the sayings of the

---

[34] *Sermons*, pp. 127, 137; cf. Longland's views in Bowker, *Henrician Reformation*, pp. 161–2.

[35] *Paraclesis, id est, adhortatio ad Christianae philosophiae studium*, was published with the *Novum Instrumentum* in 1516; the translations, *An exhortation to the dylygent study of scripture* and *An exhortacyon to the study of the Gospell*, were probably made by William Roy; see McConica, *English Humanists*, pp. 24, 26, 114.

[36] On Erasmus' contribution to attitudes that led to Protestant iconoclasm see Carlos M.N. Eire, *War against the Idols: The Reformation of Worship from Erasmus to Calvin* (Cambridge, 1986), pp. 52–3. More's doubts about the Erasmian programme are discussed by A. Fox in 'Interpreting English Humanism' in Alistair Fox and John Guy, *Reassessing the Henrician Age: Humanism, Politics and Reform 1500–1550* (Oxford, 1986), pp. 19–21.

[37] For comments on the Protestant Bibles see *Sermons*, pp. 137, 140, 141, 143, 146, 149, 218, 333, 358; for More's views see M. Deansley, *The Lollard Bible* (Cambridge, 1901), pp. 1–17, 364–73; for his views on women priests see *Confutation*, CW8, 190–1; on the limitations of Erasmian humanism in the practical sphere see A. Fox, 'English Humanism and the Body Politic' in *Reassessing the Henrician Age*, pp. 35–41.

[38] *Sermons*, pp. 116, 133, 141–2, 191–2, 284.

[39] The translations by R. Taverner are *Prouerbes or adagies with newe addicions gathered out of the Chiliades of Erasmus*, R. B[anks,] 1539. STC 10436–10441; *The garden of wysdom* [R. Bankes,] 1539 (based on the *Apophthegmata*); printed in two parts separately and together in five editions by 1556. STC 23711a–23716; [tr.] *Flores aliquot sententiarum ex variis collecti scriptoribus* ex aed. R. Taverner, [R. Bankes,] 1540. Selections from the *Apophthegmata*. STC 10445; and by N. Udall, *Apophthegmes . . . First gathered by Erasmus, now translated by N. Udall*, Grafton, 1542. STC 10443. See W.G. Crane, *Wit and Rhetoric in the Renaissance: the Formal Basis of Elizabethan Prose Style* (New York, 1937), pp. 26–31; McConica, *English Humanists*, pp. 184–5, 189, 200.

philosophers and Fathers for proverbs attributable to Jerome, such as *Ne quid nimis*; *Par pari referre*, and to Aristotle:

> *Quod fere fit non fit, sed quod vix fit, fit.* That is almost done or wel nere done, is not done; but that is scarsely done, yet it is done thoughe it be w[t] muche a do.[40]

'All virtues consisteth in the meane and middle betwixt two vices', and the now familiar definition of prudence, 'A prouision for thinges to come bi remembrance of thyngs past', both come from the *Nichomachean Ethics*, while from Boethius' *A Consolation of Philosophy* is adapted the proverb 'Nature is content with a very litle'.[41] As a conscientious neologiser he introduces his vernacular renditions prefaced by their Latin originals: for example, from the *Adagia*, '*Et qui multorum est dominus, idem multorum seruus esse cogitur*: He that is maister of much is compelled to be seruant to many'; and Cato's precept taken from Erasmus' *Praise of Folly*, '*Stultitiam simulare loco prudentia summa est*, To fayne foolishnesse in some cases, is verye highe wisdome'.[42]

The variety of proverbs in the sermons on I Peter exemplify Edgeworth's linguistic innovativeness. He uses scriptural sayings, fashionably, to amplify sententious utterance: 'A little fire burneth a whole grove, or a greate wodde' (Jas. 3:5); 'A fool at forty is a fool indeed' (III Kings 11:42); '*Num & Saul inter Prophetas?* . . . What is Saule amonge the Prophetes' (I Kings 10:11); 'Life is a pilgrimage' (I Pet. 2:11); 'Vice is often clothed in virtue's (liberty's) habit' (I Pet. 2:16).[43] Others are commonplace: 'Iniquity is so aboundant that charity is all colde' (Matt. 24:12), is attested in the works of Skelton, Latimer and Crowley; and 'in a twinkelinge of an eye' (I Cor. 15:32), is time-honoured in the medieval pulpit tradition. Tyndale first used the phrase 'as clear as the sun', while 'as bright as the day' is recorded in the popular drama. Edgeworth's 'as bright as the sun' is closer to the *Ancrene Wisse*'s 'brihtere þen þe sunne is'.[44]

His most colourful aphorisms, however, are those drawn from the vernacular proverb collections. Thomas Heywood's influential *A Dialogue conteinying . . . all the . . . prouerbes in the English tonge* (1546), reprinted four times in Edgeworth's lifetime, barely antedates many of Edgeworth's: for example, 'thinkynge our feete there, as our head wil neuer come', phrases such as 'vse him as an abiect', 'wyll breake a loueday', 'when their prouender pricked them' and 'benchewhystler' or 'a good for nothing fellow'. Others such as 'to rub on the gall' and 'poste to pyller', first recorded by Heywood, are attested in the popular drama of the period.[45] The

---

[40] *Sermons*, pp. 284, 286, 336; although by 'the logition' (*ibid.* pp. 150, 191, 246) Edgeworth probably means Aristotle, he would have known Boethius' *De Differentiis Topicis* Bk IV, a standard authority for the study of dialectic and rhetoric; see R. McKeon, 'Rhetoric in the Middle Ages', *Speculum* 17 (1942), 1–32; M.C. Leff, 'Boethius' *De differentiis topicis* Bk IV' in *Medieval Eloquence: Studies in the Theory and Practice of Medieval Rhetoric*, ed. J.J. Murphy (Los Angeles, 1978), pp. 3–24; on its importance for the liberal arts courses see E. Stump, 'Dialectic' in *The Seven Liberal Arts in the Middle Ages*, ed. D.L. Wagner (Bloomington, 1983), pp. 125–46; Fletcher, 'Arts', *EOS*, pp. 376, 385.

[41] *Sermons*, pp. 133, 308, 218; see pp. 257–8 for other Aristotelian proverbs.

[42] *Ibid.* pp. 324, 230.

[43] *Ibid.* pp. 287, 356, 303, 251, 260. Taverner, *Commonplaces of Scrypture*, 1538 (STC 19494); Edgeworth also used Polydore Vergil's *Adagiorum aeque humanorum ac sacrorum* (Basle, 1550).

[44] *Sermons*, pp. 155, 183, 233, 180, 285, 209; see *Proverbs in the Earlier English Drama*, ed. B.J. Whiting, Harvard Studies in Comparative Literature, XIV (Cambridge, Mass., 1938), p. 309; 'Proverbs in *AR* and *The Recluse*', *MLR* 30 (1935), 504; *OED* s.v. 'Iniquity'.

contemptuous term 'dogboltes' also appears in Udall's *Apophthegmes*. Several versions of the adage, 'You can't teach an old dog new tricks' were then current, Edgeworth's being: 'And though it will be hard to make an olde dog to stoupe, yet stoupe he must that will be saued'. Also familiar is:

> There muste be a consente of the will, or els vertue will not bee there, no more than thou canste make of a horse to drinke of the water if his appetite be not to drinke[46]

Commonplace phrases like 'as blind as the molle', 'while his cups be in' and 'be in his dumps' probably had a literary transmission as the latter acquired some popularity among the Euphuists.[47] But the mid-sixteenth century was the high tide of the fashion for recording proverbs and pithy sayings and, as many had existed for centuries, first recorded usage is often a matter of chance; Edgeworth may not always have borrowed from Heywood. The number of proverbs which in their written form originate from the *Sermons* constitute a substantial contribution to the language.

The *Sermons* confirm that humanist biblical scholarship, vernacular preaching aids such as proverb collections and pre-digested classical material contributed to a revolution in mid-Tudor homiletics. No longer is there the medieval celebration of the marvellous and supernatural. Although Edgeworth dips into the *Legenda Aurea* of Jacobus de Voragine, the traditional repository of the miraculous and legendary happenings of the saints, he tells only one saints' tale, when he exemplifies hospitality with the story of St Cuthbert (of whose parish church in Wells he was vicar) entertaining guests in the guise of angels.[48] *Exempla* or narrations are cautiously introduced, on one occasion with an argument taken from St Ambrose that would have been familiar to Tudor schoolmasters who taught Aesop; on another, with an appeal to his audience to identify with the protagonists. Tales are told without their medieval moralisations.[49] This shift in taste suggests a more discriminating laity, no longer able to be awed by the magus-like, hieratic image of the preacher. Edgeworth's many asides and appeals to his audience effectively narrow the rhetorical distance between them, just as allusions to their Bristol vocations – sailors, merchants, sheriffs, grocers, tailors, husbandmen, physicians, carpenters, and smiths – signify the impact of their presence on his discourse.[50]

Sermon themes with a practical and socially concerned bias, as well as 'authentic' narrations, replace the entertainment offered by fables and legends: examples are the advice offered to apprentices, complaints at the decline of hospitality, pleas for charity to students, and the single autobiographical interpolation expressing gratitude for his education. Criticism of local events – the incorporation of the

---

45 *Sermons*, pp. 358, 289, 217, 160, 298, 368, 298; see *John Heywood's* A Dialogue of Proverbs, ed. R.E. Habenicht, (Los Angeles, 1963), pp. 72, 78–9, 177, 125, 153, 140; Whiting, *Proverbs in . . . Drama*, p. 358.
46 *Sermons*, pp. 365, 356, 162; Udall, *Apophthegmes*, fos. 44, 56.
47 *Sermons*, pp. 117, 217, 284; *OED* s.v. 'Dumps' *sb.*; on the sixteenth century commonplace books see Crane, *Wit and Rhetoric*, pp. 33–48; on the need for a further survey see W.J. Ong, 'Oral Residue in Tudor Prose Style', *PMLA* 80 (1965), 152, 154.
48 *Sermons*, p. 323; cf. pp. 126, 197, 200, 266, 355. On the waning of the saints' legend see White, *Tudor Books*, pp. 67–73; Mosher, *Exemplum*, pp. 113–14; J. Th. Welter, *L'Exemplum dans la littérature religieuse et didactique du moyen âge* (Paris, 1927), pp. 449–52.
49 *Sermons*, pp. 161–2, 209, 270.
50 *Ibid.* pp. 122–3, 140, 146, 161, 255, 345, 354.

Merchant Venturers' Association in 1552, of Protestant plays, and of attacks on the conservative clergy – also move beyond traditional themes.[51] This focus on contemporary issues, due partly to the pressures of Reformation debate as Protestant and Catholic vied for supremacy in the pulpit, partly to humanist rejection of the more extreme forms and sentiments of the medieval homily, is also found in the Edwardian Protestant sermons of Latimer, Thomas Lever and William Peryn. The mid-sixteenth century homilies are distinguished by a greater informality of style, a correspondingly looser structure, debate on controversial issues, personal anecdotes, and reminiscences instead of tales, fables and moralising *exempla*; and all are notable for their denunciation of social ills.[52]

[51] *Ibid.* pp. 144–5, 261–2, 269, 276, 155, 283, 282, 246–7, 140, 333. The Protestant view that the money spent on pilgrimages and at shrines might be better spent on God's living poor, argued by Simon Fish in 1529 in A *Supplicacyon for the Beggers*, ed. J. Furnivall, EETS, ES, 13 (London, 1871), given official status in the formularies and Royal Injunctions of 1536 (Frere and Kennedy, pp. 10–11), encouraged the new sermon themes. See Dickens, *English Reformation*, p. 101; Blench, pp. 245–6.

EDGEWORTH'S USE OF THE BIBLE

The oral traditions of the church

Like other conservative theologians Edgeworth subscribed to the belief in the extra-scriptural traditions which Thomas More and Bishop Fisher had used to validate the practices of Catholicism in opposing the Protestant doctrine of *scriptura sola*.[1] They held that the unwritten verities through which the church preserved certain dogmas inherited from the apostles possessed an authority equal to that of the scriptures themselves. After More's death this doctrine was less openly acclaimed as the *priority of scripture* became fundamental to Henrician religious reform.[2] It was, however, reaffirmed in the Council of Trent's decree on Holy Scripture promulgated in 1546; following this two treatises upholding the oral traditions, written by Dr Richard Smith, the first Regius Professor of Divinity at Oxford in 1536, were immediately published.[3] Early in Edward's reign they were seized on Cranmer's orders and burnt at Paul's Cross on 15 May 1547 in a ceremony at which Smith was forced to recant his views.[4]

Edgeworth's use of the extra-scriptural traditions lacks the polemical urgency of More's, Fisher's and Smith's. He neither refers to the theory, nor attempts to justify it, as More did, by asserting the infallible authority of the church and the church's common unity – the *consensus fidelium* – through the agency of the Holy Ghost.[5] Nevertheless the outlines of the belief are visible in his references to the legend of

---

[1] For More's doctrinal views see A. Fox, *Thomas More: History and Providence* (Oxford, 1982), pp. 151–60; B. Gogan, *The Common Corps of Christendom: Ecclesiological Themes in the Writings of Thomas More* (Leiden, 1982), pp. 270–5. On his controversy with Tyndale see R. Pineas, *Thomas More and Tudor Polemics* (Bloomington, 1968), pp. 44–5, 107–112; E. Flesseman-Van Leer, 'The Controversy about Scripture and Tradition between Thomas More and William Tyndale', *Nederlands Archief voor Kerkgeschiedenis* NS, 43 (1959), 143–65; and 'The Controversy about Ecclesiology between Thomas More and William Tyndale', *Nederlands Archief voor Kerkgeschiedenis* NS, 44 (1960), 65–86; H. Oberman, *Forerunners of the Reformation, The Shape of Late Medieval Thought* (London, 1967), pp. 51–66. For a summary of the historiography of More's ecclesiology see Gogan, *op cit.* pp. 9–16. On Fisher's belief in the oral traditions see his 1521 sermon against Luther in *The English Works of John Fisher*, Pt. 1, ed. J.E.B. Mayor, EETS, ES, 27 (London, 1876), pp. 331–6 (cited by Gogan, p. 315).
[2] On the importance of scripture to the Henrician ecclesiastical settlement, see Redworth, 'English Reformation?', 32–4.
[3] See *The Canons and Decrees of the Sacred and Oecumenical Council of Trent*, tr. J. Waterworth (London, 1848), pp. lxxxvi–viii, 18. On Richard Smith (Smyth) see BRUO IV, 524–5.
[4] *A breif treatyse settynge forth divers truthes . . . left to ye church by the apostles tradition* (T. petit,)1547, STC 22818; *A defence of the sacrifice of the masse* (J. Herforde,) 1546, STC 22820a. See Wilson, 'Catalogue', 9–10.
[5] On the *consensus fidelium* see Marc'hadour's introduction to *Dialogue*, CW6, 498–501; as applied to the Church as the criterion of God's word see Gogan, *Common Corps*, pp. 90–103, 145–8, 191–212; on his use of the Church Fathers as witnesses of them see Trapp's introduction to *The Apology*, CW9, lxviii–lxxi;14–32; R.C. Marius, 'Thomas More and the Early Church Fathers' in *Essential Articles in the Study of Thomas More*, ed. R.S. Sylvester and G.P. Marc'hadour (Connecticut, 1972), pp. 411–420; Flesseman-Van Leer, 'Scripture and Tradition', 160.

the apostles' joint authorship of the creed in the sermon on the Articles of the Faith (preached in 1546); the Paraclete's mission to the apostles at Pentecost; the authority of the pseudo-Dionysian writings; and in his defence of traditional ceremonies such as the Lenten fast and the wearing of liturgical vestments.[6] More's ecclesiology, which emphasised the priority of the church's role in transmitting the revelation of God through Jesus Christ, was discredited by the legislation of the Reformation Parliament. But his persistent identification of the unwritten gospel with the Holy Spirit (or the spirit of God) as the source of divine revelation in the individual's 'Gospel of the heart' or 'inward Gospel', was important in the apologetic tradition which continued after his death, as Edgeworth's sermons on the seven gifts of the Holy Ghost testify.[7] His Thomist theology of the gifts treating the question of the Holy Ghost in men's souls stems from the same premise as More, that the divine truths were unavailable to men through their own natural powers. Only by the gifts of grace, the infused theological virtues, faith, hope and charity, can men receive the supernatural gifts and become capable of actions which surpass their ordinary virtuous capacities.[8]

The first sermon of the series opens with an exposition of Christ's words to the apostles on the Paraclete's mission; for only after Christ's departure can the true *imitatio Christi* begin.[9] Edgeworth's text, John 16:13, which he translates: 'I haue yet many thynges to teache you but as yet ye can not bear them away, but when the spirit of truth the holy ghost commeth, he shall teache you all truthes necessarye for you to knowe' was crucial to More's teaching on revelation.[10] More had provoked controversy by interpreting it, with Matt. 28:20, in Book III of *The Confutation of Tyndale's Answer*, as proof of Christ's promise that he would validate the church's teaching for ever.[11] If Edgeworth had read George Joye's lengthy attack in *The Subuersion of Moris false foundacion*, a treatise published secretly abroad in 1534, then he may have intended this first sermon, preached in c.1535, to be a Catholic response to Joye.[12] His allusion in the second sermon to Henry's

---

[6] *Sermons*, pp. 169, 113–14, 295–6, 187, 189; see Flesseman-Van Leer, 'Scripture and Tradition', 145–148, for More's views on the origins of the unwritten traditions.

[7] See Gogan, *Common Corps*, pp. 90–2, 128–6, 141–3, 145, 192–4, 198, 274–5, on More's belief in the Holy Spirit as the source of individual revelation.

[8] *Ibid.* p. 232; Gogan points out that More and Tyndale essentially agreed in this respect; see *Sermons*, pp. 113, 116.

[9] *Ibid.* pp. 113–14.

[10] *Ibid.* p. 113. More uses this text frequently; in *Responsio ad Lutherum*, CW5, 90, 191; *Dialogue*, CW6, 119, 145, 177–8; *Confutation*, CW8, 45, 107–8, 226, 259, 286, 313, 332, 1481, etc.; it features prominently in Fisher's 1521 sermon against Luther, and Colet cites it in his treatise on the *Hierarchies* of the pseudo-Dionysius, saying:

> we must believe that it was by the teaching of the Holy Spirit that they (i.e. the apostles) ordained all things in the Church . . . It is because their most holy traditions have been superseded and neglected and men have fallen away from the Spirit of God to their own invention that, beyond doubt, all things have been wretchedly disturbed and confounded.

See 'The Ecclesiastical Hierarchy' in *Ioannis Coletus super Opera Dionysii*, ed. and tr. J.H. Lupton (London, 1869, repr., New Jersey, 1966), p. 136; G.P. Marc'hadour, *The Bible in the Works of Thomas More: A Repertory*, 5 vols (Nieuwkoop, 1969–72), II, 190–2 (cited hereafter as Marc'hadour, *Bible*)

[11] More, *Confutation*, CW8, 107–8; Cranmer in *Confutation of Unwritten Verities* (*Works* II, 54) denounces it as a text commonly alleged by the papists. On the importance of these texts to More's belief in the authority of the church see Marius, 'Thomas More', pp. 411–12; his introduction to *Confutation*, CW8, 1279; Flesseman-Van Leer, 'Scripture and Tradition', 147.

[12] *The subuersion of Moris false foundacion* (Emdon, J. Aurik, 1534), sigs A8ᵛ–D4. STC 14829; A. Hume, CW8, Appendix B, no. 31. Joye accused More of dishonesty in translating *omnem veritatem*

treatise against Luther, *Assertio Septem Sacramentorum*, a work which strongly valued the extra-biblical tradition and which uses John 16:13 as a staple text, contributes to the impression that this belief was prominent in the circles in which More and probably Edgeworth moved in the 1520s.[13]

It is not surprising that a conservative like Edgeworth, preaching at a time of violent social and religious upheaval, should return to the beliefs which had shaped his theological views when attempting to defend controversial topics like purgatory and image worship. In addressing the question of whether the scriptures should be available in English in the fourth sermon, he turns once more to More's views on revelation. His belief that it was the conservative clergy's prerogative to transmit the divine message underpins the condemnation of the newly learned Bible clerks of Bristol, 'greene Diuines' who teach their disciples to oppose the best priest of the parish and . . . tel him he lieth'. In his opinion such misguided 'pseudapostles' who trust in the authority of *scriptura sola* will misinterpret obscure and difficult passages to the laity.[14] Again, outlining a programme for lay reading of the vernacular scriptures Edgeworth is guided by the rhetorical principle behind More's teaching on the Bible in the *Dialogue concerning Heresies*, that the revelation of God's Word is accommodated to human nature through divine rhetoric.[15] He exhorts his audience when encountering dark texts, 'not to determine yourself to an vnderstanding after your owne fancie, but abyde a tyme with longanimitie and easy sufferaunce' and he adapts the analogy that More used in *Confutation* of Christ's withholding from the apostles the mystery of the Eucharist because they would not be able to bear it, adding that Peter's faith in Christ's obscure words assisted his understanding them. The need that he perceives for an official teaching ministry is asserted with an expanded interpretation of Ps. 54:21–22:

> *Molliti sunt sermones eius super oleum, et ipsi sunt iacula.* The wordes of God in scripture which afore were hard, by the exercise and labour of catholike clerkes be made very soft, yea more softe, easye, and soople then oile, and be made harnes and dartes, or weapons for the preachers . . . *Et iacta super dominum curam tuam & ipse te enutriet* . . . caste thy care vpon GOD, and he will nourish thee . . . prouiding for the some man that is wel learned & substancially exercitate in the scriptures to teache thee.[16]

The misinterpretation of 'hard' texts is also the focus for an attack in the seventh sermon on I Peter on the reformers' use of I Pet. 2:9: *Vos autem genus electum, regales sacerdotium* [AV 'But ye are a chosen generation, a holy priesthood'] to justify the belief in 'a priesthood of all believers'. He applies Ambrose's

---

as 'every truth' (implying more truths were still to be revealed) and preferred 'all truth' (i.e. the whole truth contained in the Gospel). Edgeworth translates it 'all truths'; he prefers Vg *docebit* to *ducet* (More uses both) and avoids More's term 'Paraclete'. See *ibid.* sigs. B2ᵛ–B3, B5ᵛ, B8ᵛ; G.C. Butterworth and A.G. Chester, *George Joye 1495?–1553. A Chapter in the History of the English Bible and the English Reformation* (Philadelphia, 1962), pp. 109–111; Marc'hadour, *Bible* II, 189, 190–2.
[13] *Sermons*, p. 127; the reference to the *Assertio* was probably a Marian addition. See Gogan, *Common Corps*, pp. 272, 314.
[14] *Sermons*, p. 140; Edgeworth's 'false preachers' resemble More's Messenger who fallaciously dismissed all other forms of learning and in reading the scriptures 'laboured . . . to encerche the sentence and understandynge therof as ferre as he might perceyue by hym selfe'; see *Dialogue*, CW6, 33–4, 122–4.
[15] *Ibid.* 339–40; see Marc'hadour's introduction, 516–23, on More's 'sure way' to read scripture in Book I.
[16] *Sermons*, pp. 141–2; More, *Dialogue*, CW6, 145.

interpretation of Tichonius' rule, 'In scripture many times that thing is said and spoken vniuersally of the whole, which is verified and true onely of the part', to prove the principle of election which lies at the heart of the Catholic sacrament of orders.[17] Preaching on another disputed text, I Pet. 1:2, he translates *electi* as 'elect and chosen' to emphasise, as Thomas More had done, that the election was the call on earth to the Christian life and not to salvation as the reformers taught.[18]

The Protestant Bibles

Edgeworth's reservations about the laity's unsupervised reading of the vernacular scriptures stemmed partly from his concern at the lack of a reliable Catholic translation. More had recommended an independent translation be made in 1531 and discussions were held by the bishops in 1534. Preaching in 1539–40 Edgeworth laments that:

> holie Scripture should be hadde in the mother tong, and with holden from no manne . . . specially if we coulde get it well and truely translated, whyche wyll be very harde to be hadde. But who be meete and able to take it in hand, there is the doubte.[19]

His party's failure to produce an English Bible was a signficant one because after the English Church came to rely on the Protestant Bibles in 1538 the ground was never recovered.[20] The conservative criticism of errors of translation in the Great Bible made in the Convocation of 1542 is now recognised as merely an attempt to improve its English rather than to reduce its newly official status. Although Gardiner proposed a list of words to be retained in their original form or 'Englished with the least alteration', his recommendations were apparently ignored.[21] Edgeworth's inconsistent treatment of disputed translations shows that the English Church came to accept certain words espoused by the reformers, and hence the practices which they signified. General complaints about erroneous Protestant translations were renewed in Mary's reign, notably by John Standish in *A discourse wherin it is debated whether . . . the scriptures should be had in the mother tonge* (1553) and a Catholic translation was authorised at the National Synod of the Clergy in

---

17 *Sermons*, pp. 245–6.
18 *Ibid*. pp. 201–2; on More's concepts of election see Marius's introduction to *Confutation*, CW8, 1329–32.
19 *Sermons*, p. 137; on More's views see *Dialogue*, CW6, 336–44; on Barlow's, *A dialoge, ed. cit.* sigs K8–L1ᵛ. Cardinal Pole had similar reservations about lay reading of the scriptures although he approved in theory; see Bodl. MS Lat. Vat. 5968, fo. 416ʳ (cited by Blench, p. 50). John Standish, *A discourse*, sigs A3–3ᵛ, states:

> if all men were good and catholike, then were it lawfull, . . . that the scripture shoulde be in Englishe, so that the translation were trew and faythfull: But neyther all the people be good and catholyke, nor the translations trewe and faythfull.

20 On More's advocacy for an English translation see *Dialogue*, CW6, 341–4, 519–22. The Great Bible was officially approved and ordered to be put into every church in the Injunctions of 1538; in 1543 it was decreed that passages from both Testaments be read every Sunday; see Hughes and Larkin, I, 192, 200; J.F. Mozley, *Coverdale and his Bibles* (London, 1953), pp. 272–8; REB, no. 43.
21 Gardiner headed the New Testament committee which Convocation set up to correct errors of translation in the Great Bible; see *Concilia* III, 861 (repr. in REB, no. 45). For a critique of the myth about Gardiner's position in the campaign against the Bible, fostered by Wilkins and others, see Redworth, *Church Catholic*, pp. 159–64; see also 'English Reformation?', 35.

1555–6.[22] But the premature deaths of Cardinal Pole and Queen Mary in 1558 prevented its completion.[23]

The lack of a Catholic vernacular Bible, therefore, means that Edgeworth's defence of More's position in his controversy with Tyndale over scriptural translation is fundamentally vitiated. His objections to the Protestant 'mistranslations' remain purely semantic and hardly discredit the new authority which the English Bible gave to disputed words. Preaching in the eighteenth sermon on the disputed text I Pet. 5:2: *Seniores ergo, qui in vobis sunt, obsecro consenior* [AV: 'The elders who are among you, I exhort who am also an elder'] he draws on the same argument with which More refuted Tyndale's translation of the Greek *presbyteros* by 'senior' or 'elder', that 'elder' merely implies age and lacks the connotation of authority conveyed by *presbyteros*: 'Albeit euery olde man, or auncient man is not a Prieste, but onely suche as by prophecye, or election and imposition of a prelates hande is piked out & chosen . . . '. But he undermines his argument by using Tyndale's translation, 'these seignours or elders that we call priests', as this had appeared in all the Protestant Bibles except Taverner's Bible of 1539.[24]

It is likely that Edgeworth attended sessions of the 1542 Convocation and agreed with the objections of Gardiner and the conservative clergy since *presbyteros*, *senior* and other words discussed in the *Sermons* such as *idolum*, *pietas* and *religio*, were among those listed as requiring more 'conservative' translations. The reformers' use of 'godliness' for *pietas* leads him in the fifth sermon on the gifts first to consider the problems that St Augustine found in translating the Greek *latria*, and then the various meanings of 'piety' – mercy, pity and compassion – which may convey the nuances of dutifulness and worship. Turning to *religio*, however, he derives a translation which resembles the modern meaning of piety: '. . . a manne or woman hauing it, is inclined to goodnesse, and made well disposed . . . to serve GOD and to do hym worshippe'; but there is no indication that this was ever accepted.[25] Another controversial translation, that of *imago* by 'idol', provokes the complaint which became standard after the 1538 injunctions forbade veneration of images – that the reformers' refusal to distinguish between the two had encouraged the people to iconoclasm:

> They would haue that this latine worde *Imago* signifieth an Idole, and so these new translations of the english bibles hath it in all places, where the translatours would bring men to beleue that to set vp Images, or to haue Images is idolatrye.[26]

Edgeworth implicitly condemns Tyndale's translations by preferring 'grace' to 'favour', 'confession' to 'knowledging', 'penance' to 'repentance'.[27] Words with Protestant connotations usually appear coupled with the traditional alternative. Out of forty occurrences of the word 'favour', for example, only three appear (in the collocation 'grace and favour'), with the Protestant meaning. But although he

22 A *discourse*, sig. A3ᵛ.
23 *Concilia* IV, 121–6; Cardwell, *Doc. Ann.* I, XXXVII.
24 *Sermons*, p. 340; see Tyndale, *Answer*, pp. 16–18; More, *Dialogue*, CW6, 286, 289–90; *Confutation*, CW8, 182–9; J. Mueller, *The Native Tongue and the Word: Developments in English Prose Style, 1380–1580* (Chicago, 1984), p. 207.
25 *Sermons*, pp. 147–8.
26 *Ibid.* p. 143.
27 On 'grace and favour' see *Sermons*, pp. 184, 207, 220, 274 etc.; on 'repentance', *ibid.* pp. 232, 293, 325, 343; More, *Confutation*, CW8, 203–5; Tyndale, *Answer*, pp. 22–4.

nowhere refers to the famous controversy over Tyndale's translation of *caritas* by 'love' instead of 'charity', his preference is confirmed by the consistent use of 'charity' for *dilectio* or *caritas*, with the exception of Gal. 5:6, 'Faith worketh by love' (a text which More in *Confutation* also renders by 'love'). On the other hand the collocation 'love and charity' occurs twelve times in the *Sermons*.[28] In *Confutation* More criticised the Lutheran translation of 'bishop' as 'overseer' (which Tyndale used in *Obedience*), but Edgeworth s use of the word (on six occasions as an alternative to 'bishop' or 'ruler') reflects the influence of the formularies' definition of bishops as 'overseers' and 'superattendants'.[29] Similarly 'congregation', Tyndale's translation of *ecclesia* to which More had objected, appears thirteen times out of seventeen coupled with 'church', confirming that acceptance of this word had been virtually guaranteed by its use in the *Great Bible*.[30] This gradual assimilation of some 'objectionable' words, and a receptive attitude towards others, therefore, show the growing respectability of the translations in the Protestant Bibles and the Henrician formularies.

Scriptural interpretation and themes in the *Sermons*

Although Edgeworth was trained in the 'Old Learning' and knew of the fourfold method of scriptural interpretation, he stresses the priority of the literal sense of scripture, following the humanists and the Edwardian reformers as he does in preaching *secundum ordinem textus*.[31] His position is made clear in the sixth sermon on I Peter: '. . . the misticall senses and vnderstandinge of the Scriptures, whether it be morall sence, allegory or anagogicall sence, presupposeth a true literall sense on whiche they be grounded'.[32] Like Aquinas, he understands the content of the 'letter' as the whole meaning intended by the author (whether it be expressed in plain language or through allegory or symbol), and the spiritual meaning as referring to the historical events whose significance is known only to God, which the human author records.[33] He is at pains, nevertheless, to draw attention to figurative language when it appears in the text, as in I Pet. 2:6: 'Christe is here called

[28] *Sermons*, pp. 136, 138, 165 etc.; More, *Dialogue*, CW6, 286–8, 512–6; *Confutation*, CW8, 199–203; Tydnale, *Answer*, pp. 20–21; Marc'hadour, *Bible* III, 100.
[29] W. Tyndale, *Obedience of a Christian Man in Doctrinal Treatises*, ed. H. Walter, PS (Cambridge, 1848), pp. 279–80; More, *Confutation*, CW8, 187; *Formularies*, pp. 109, 121, 287; *Sermons*, pp. 197, 267, 344 etc.
[30] *Ibid.* pp. 244, 257, 312, 321, 336 etc. (cf. p. 141); see the homily on the creed (1546): 'the belefe of the vniuersal church . . . the merite of the whole congregation of Christen people' (p. 170). More, *Dialogue*, CW6, 286, 289; *Confutation*, CW8, 145–8, 164–72, 189; Tyndale, *Answer*, pp. 13–15.
[31] The appearance of traditional allegorical exegesis of the cross in the version of the sermon on the creed in MS Rawl. D. 831, which is omitted in the 1557 text, suggests that although such interpretations were not favoured in 1546 they returned to fashion in the Marian period. On the Henrician practitioners of the literal approach see Blench, pp. 28–37; on More's avoidance of allegory Marius' introduction to *Confutation*, CW8, 1358–90; on Erasmus' use of the literal sense in the *Annotationes* Bentley, *Humanists and Holy Writ*, pp. 184–9; on the dispute over scriptural interpretation between Erasmus and Colet, Seebohm, *Oxford Reformers*, pp. 121–25; on Colet's exegetical views, E.W. Hunt, *Dean Colet and his Theology* (London, 1956), pp. 88–102.
[32] *Sermons*, p. 23; he therefore refuses to accept the tradition that there was a particular stone which the builders rejected (Ps. 118:2) when preparing the temple in King's David time because 'this narration hath no euidence of scripture' (*ibid.* p. 237).
[33] *Sermons*, p. 236; see Aquinas, ST Ia. 1.10 (*ed. cit.* I, 36–41); Smalley, *Bible*, pp. 41, 300; on the two schools of scriptural interpretation see Blench, p. 2.

a lyuinge stone . . . but this is a maner of speaking by a metaphor or a similitude'.[34] In interpreting the difficult text, I Pet. 3:19, on Christ's preaching to the spirits in prison he dismisses the 'good & catholike', allegorical exposition in favour of the literal sense because it:

> semeth more moral then litteral, because it taketh the name of the prison, . . . morally for the custom & vse of sinne, . . . & it taketh the prisoner for him that is intangled, poluted, & defaced with the deformity of customable sinne . . . . I thinke .s. Peter speaketh of the spirits or soules of them that woulde not regard the exhortation of Noe made vnto them for amendment of their liues, tyll the very floude came vpon them.[35]

Aquinas also states that doctrine can only be founded on the literal sense, and the spurious interpretation of Peter's name *Cephas* (rock) as *caput* (head) in order to prove the papacy provokes Edgeworth's condemnation of 'summalistes' in the first sermon on I Peter. When he does use allegorical interpretations they are often familiar explanations of basic Catholic doctrines; the waters of the flood signify the sacrament of baptism and Noah's ark the Catholic church in the thirteenth sermon on I Peter.[36] Joshua's taking the town of Hay (Josh. 8:1–29), signifying the conquest of the forces of confusion, is associated with Christ's victory and told in remembrance of the Passion. The story of the widow of Sarepta (III Kings 17:10–14) demonstrates the virtues of hospitality and leads into an exposition of the Real Presence.[37]

As with his other preaching techniques, humanist practices also dominate his forms of scriptural interpretation. Preaching on I Pet. 2:2: *Sine dolo lac* and I Pet. 2:18: *Prauis, dyscholis*, he collates the Erasmian version with the Vulgate, and sometimes adds a scriptural gloss to enable the reader to determine the moral sense.[38] In using the form of the *distinctio* to describe the four small creatures of Prov. 30:24–30 who exemplify the four types of prudence, he provides a justifica-tion of allegories based on the natural properties of 'these dumme creatures':

> we consider theyr naturall disposicions, examinyng and discussing and searching out theyr naturall operacions and vertues. And then they answer vs and teach vs, when by consideracion of them we ascende and rise vp to the knowledge of god.

But Edgeworth's exposition is in fact predominantly philological; focusing on the different translations in the Vulgate of the Hebrew *saphan* (*lepusculus* and *herina-cius* or *hericiis & Mus.*) he then introduces the moralisation that the hare 'signi-fieth the weake good Christen people . . . [who] putte theyr trust principally in our redemer & sauioure Iesus Christe, sygnified by the stone or rocke in whiche (as it is sayde here) the Hare maketh hys bed or forme'.[39]

---

[34] *Sermons*, pp. 236, 308, etc.
[35] *Sermons*, p. 293. Aquinas, *ST, loc cit.*; Blench, p. 17.
[36] *Sermons*, pp. 294–5. On the Henrician exponents of 'Old Learning' and the use of typology and allegory by the Marian preachers see Blench, pp. 3–28, 53–7; H. Caplan, 'The four senses of scriptural interpretation and the medieval theory of preaching', *Speculum* IV (1929), 282–90.
[37] *Sermons*, pp. 298–9, 320–1.
[38] *Ibid.* pp. 232, 260–1. On More's disapproval of this practice see *Dialogue*, CW6, 34, 122–3, 167–71; *ibid.* 522 on Erasmus' recommendation of this method in his colloquy 'The Godly Feast' (1522).
[39] *Sermons*, pp. 311–12. As Edgeworth's allegories are usually based on the medieval Bible glosses he may not have used an alaphabetical spiritual dictionary.

Edgeworth uses Erasmus' New Testament, 'the newe translation', alongside the 'vulgate and comon text' for the sequence on I Peter to draw attention to variations between them. His practice is to offer both alternatives, as with Rom. 1:29: '*deo odibiles* they be odious to God or as the other translation [i.e. Erasmus'] hath *dei osores* suche as hateth God'; but he prefers 'haters of God'.[40] On one occasion when translating Hosea 13:14 he substitutes St Augustine's gloss on this text from his *Sermo de Symbolo*, a practice of Thomas More's but not usually a habit of Edgeworth's.[41] But the translation of John 19:38, *propter motum Judaeorum* [AV 'for fear of the Jews'] as 'shrewes' rather than 'Jews' seems to be a deliberate substitution. 'Shrews', elsewhere a synonym for 'noughty liuers', may refer derisively to Edwardian iconoclasts who have looted shrines, despoiled tombs, removed church plate, and upturned crosses on the wayside.[42]

Although he expounds I Peter *secundum ordinem textus* as a baptismal treatise and a *vade mecum* of instruction for the Christian life, Edgeworth loses no opportunity of explaining and defending Catholic doctrines and practices. *Qui secundum suam magnam regenerauit nos in spem viuam* . . . (I Pet. 1:3) [AV 'Who according to his abundant mercy hath begotten us again into a lively hope'], yields an exposition of the Roman Catholic theology of original righteousness and the doctrine of baptismal regeneration. The necessity of receiving correct doctrine from 'the good Catholike clerkes', a dominant theme of the fifth sermon inspired by I Pet. 2:2, *sine dolo lac concupiscite* [AV 'desire the sincere milk of the word'], evokes the memorable comparison of those who cannot weigh and judge the matters of scripture to 'yonge infantes [who] many tymes wyll sitte moyling in the axen, & put earth or coles into their mouthes'.[43] Some texts recur with a different emphasis: in the second sermon on the gift of counsel, *Quasi liberi & non quasi velamen habentes malicie libertatem sed quasi serui dei* (I Pet. 2:16) [AV 'As free, and not using your liberty for a cloke of maliciousness, but as the servants of God'] prompts an attack on 'euangelical liberty' and those who ignore the Lenten fast; but in the ninth sermon on I Peter it supports a positive interpretation of 'evangelical liberty', in terms of obedience due to the king, by contrast to the 'pretensed libertie' of the Lutherans.[44]

Despite reminders that this Epistle was written in a time of persecution, Edgeworth rarely argues against Protestant theology. The attack inspired by I Pet. 1:23, *Renati non ex femine corruptibili, sed incorruptibili* . . . [AV 'Being born again, not of corruptible seed, but of incorruptible'], on the Anabaptist heresy which denied infant baptism, is exceptional.[45] More characteristic is his treatment of I Pet. 1:6 on the trial of the faith, *In quo exaltabitis modicum nunc si oportet contristari in variis tentationibus* [AV 'Wherein ye greatly rejoice, though now for a season, if need be, ye are in heaviness through manifold temptations'] in which an outburst against heresy culminates in an orthodox treatment of man's salvation and the Last

---

[40] *Sermons*, pp. 202, 231. See Bentley, *Humanists and Holy Writ*, pp. 161–3 on Erasmus' attitude to the Vulgate. For the series on St Peter's First Epistle he probably used the parallel text edition of the Erasmian NT and the Vulgate, *Biblie utriusque Testamenti*, printed in Basle in 1538.
[41] *Sermons*, p. 176; On More's use of the Church Fathers see Marius's introduction to *Confutation*, CW8, 1354–5; 'Church Fathers', 403–7, 412–15.
[42] *Sermons*, pp. 176, 291, 297, 331, 362.
[43] *Ibid*. pp. 205–7, 233.
[44] *Ibid*. pp. 127–8, 259.
[45] *Ibid*. pp. 224–5.

Judgement.[46] Contemporary changes usually evoke moral complaint. *In fide autem omnes vnanimes . . .* (I Pet. 3:8) [AV 'Finally be ye all of one mind'] leads to denigration of Bristol layfolk who have abandoned their traditional forms of worship. But his real target here is the powerful Protestant dominated guilds whose brotherhood was incorporated as the Merchant Venturers Association in 1552. The twentieth sermon on 1 Pet. 5:8, *Aduersarius vester diabolus tanquem leo rugiens circuit quaerens quem deuoret* [AV 'your adversary the devil, as a roaring lion, walketh about, seeking whom he may devour'], directed at the Duke of Northumberland, inspires complaints at recent acts of parliament and the various ways of administering the communion service.[47]

Dominant in Edgeworth's exposition are themes of conventional piety such as the Passion – the subject of the tenth, fourteenth and eighteenth sermons on I Peter. His affective descriptions, equal in emotive power to those of John Longland or Bishop Fisher, demonstrate that this topic was still a focus for devotion in 1552–3. Another traditionally important theme was the Four Last Things, and the *Sermons* confirm that the questions of heaven, hell, death and judgement which loomed large in men's minds in the late Middle Ages retained their emotive force throughout the Reformation. Edgeworth lavishes his full rhetorical powers on them as, in the seventeenth sermon where the approach of the Day of Judgement is examined with reference to *vix saluabitur iustus* of I Pet. 4:18 [AV 'if the righteous scarcely be saved'].[48] The theme of the heavenly inheritance inspires his most imaginatively eloquent writing such as, in the second sermon on the transitory earthly kingdom (I Pet. 1:4) a lyrical threnody which concludes with an *ubi sunt* in traditional elegaic style; and the affective description of the heavenly joys in the tenth sermon.[49] Death and the manner of dying, in contemplation of which men should prepare and order their lives, often receive graphic treatment. *Omnium autem finis appropinquabit* (I Pet. 4:7) [AV 'But the end of all things is at hand'], evokes Age, a harbinger of death, 'whiche daielye creapeth vppon vs, aduertisynge vs of oure ende to whiche he daielye driueth vs' and the infirmities of age, 'sickenes, soores & malenders . . . hed ache, colick, ye stone, gowts, & running legges, dropsye, and palsye' in the fifteenth sermon. Edgeworth avoids the horrors which lie beyond the grave which appear in earlier treatments such as Bishop Fisher's but, modifying the conventions of the *ars moriendi*, he dilates upon the Augustinian maxim that it is necessary to live well in order to die well.[50]

The epistle's ethical injunctions, stemming from its social or domestic Code of Subordination, inspire Edgeworth to adapt to contemporary interests the apostle's sympathy for potentially oppressed social groups.[51] Christian wives who exert a

---

[46] *Ibid.* pp. 211–13.

[47] *Ibid.* pp. 280–2, 361, 363, 365; other comments (*ibid.* pp. 334, 359, 364–5) on the perseuction of heretics and the Protestant martyrs, made with reference to the Petrine text, remain in the realm of complaint.

[48] *Ibid.* pp. 336–7.

[49] *Ibid.* pp. 208–9, 268; on the survival of the *ubi sunt* theme see Blench, pp. 228–34.

[50] *Sermons*, pp. 304, 305, 306–8. *Ars moriendi* treatises were commonplace in the sixteenth century; see Thomas Lupset's *A . . . treatyse, teachyng the waye of dyenge well* (Berthelet, 1534), STC 16934; R. Whitford, *A dayly exercyse and experyence of dethe* (Waylande, 1537), STC 25414; Erasmus' treatise, *De Praeparatione ad Mortem* was translated by T. Paynell as *Preparation to deathe*, and printed by Berthelet in 1538 and 1543 (STC 10505–6). See John X. Evans, 'The Art of Rhetoric and the Art of Dying in Tudor Recusant Prose', *RH* X, 5 (1970), 247–272.

[51] Cf. Col. 3:19; Ephes, 5:25. On the domestic Code of Subordination, characteristic of the Apostolic church, see E.G. Selwyn, *The First Epistle of St. Peter*, 2nd ed. (London, 1947), pp. 425,

beneficial influence upon unbelieving gentile husbands (I Pet.3:1–2) are compared to Bristol wives who will restrain their husbands from heretical opinions; but consistent with his disapproval of women preaching and teaching the vernacular scriptures (I Tim. 2:11–12), expressed in the fourth sermon on the seven gifts, he believes such persuasion should be restricted to conversation only.[52] The apostle's empathy with slaves or domestic servants (I Pet. 2:18–19) whom he exhorts to suffer patiently even when treated unjustly by their masters, is reinterpreted in terms of advice for Bristol apprentices, and includes injunctions on the duties of servants and masters following the recommendations in the Henrician formularies that this theme be preached upon.[53] The formularies' teaching also underlies his preaching on the theme of civil obligation (I Pet. 2: 13–14) in terms of clerical obedience due to the crown, drawing upon Rom. 13:5, *Non solum propter iram, sed propter conscientiam* [AV 'Whereas ye must needs be subject, not only for wrath, but also for conscience sake'].[54] And Edgeworth follows the article on orders in the *King's Book* when listing the attributes required of a bishop in the primitive church in the eighteenth sermon on I Pet. 5:1.[55] The exhortation of I Pet. 4:9, *Hospitales* [AV 'Use hospitality'], that members of a community treat each other with Christian charity and hospitality, leads to a distinction between evangelical hospitality, as taught in the gospel, and spiritual hospitality; but in the eleventh sermon he voices the complaint, common among the Edwardian preachers, that hospitality in his own time was being abused.[56]

The themes of the twenty sermons on St Peter, therefore, reflect the ethical and social emphases of this Christian diaspora letter, which is addressed to a predominantly Christian gentile audience. But Edgeworth also interprets the text in its broadest sense to include topics of contemporary complaint, expositions of Catholic doctrine, and admonitions to his audience on lapses from observances such as the Lenten fast.

Although Edgeworth exemplifies the initial conservative response to the Protestant Bibles in rejecting on doctrinal grounds translations such as 'idol' for *imago*, his silent acceptance of some disputed words on grounds of common usage points to the irrevocable disadvantage his party suffered after the Great Bible became assimilated into English life. Of some compensation for the lack of a standard Catholic translation are the benefits of free paraphrase. Edgeworth's excellence as a prose writer, perhaps the most important legacy of the collection, is amply exhibited in his scriptural translations, most impressively in his treatments of Pauline texts. The numerous scriptural proverbs which he coins is but one feature of the richly decorated and amplified style which reached its apogee in the Elizabethan era.[57] He testifies to the development of a conservative tradition of

429–30; J. Ramsey Micahels, *I Peter*, Word Biblical Commentary, 49 (Texas, 1988), pp. 155–6, 171–2.
52 *Sermons*, pp. 272, 139–40.
53 *Ibid.* pp. 260–2, 145–6; cf. Eph. 6:5 and 9. Cited by J. Vanes, *Education and Apprentices in Sixteenth-Century Bristol*, BHA, 52 (1982), 21.
54 *Sermons*, pp. 259–60; see *Formularies*, pp. 121, 287.
55 *Sermons*, pp. 343–6.
56 *Ibid.* pp. 323–4, 276.
57 Cf. the contrasting renditions of Phil. 2:8 which introduce and conclude the series on the seven gifts of the Holy Ghost (*ibid.* pp. 113, 167) and of I Cor. 13:12 in the *exordia* of the sermons on the creed and the first sermon on I Peter, and in the exposition of the Real Presence in the sixteenth sermon (*ibid.* pp. 168, 191, 322).

Bible translation and the formation of a diction which by the time of Queen Mary had come to be associated with the beliefs of his party.[58] This includes the principles of translation which were fully expressed in the first Catholic Bible, the Douai-Rheims Bible of 1581 and 1609.[59]

---

[58] On Protestant attacks on the alleged élitism of the Catholics with respect to scriptural translation see R.F. Jones, *The triumph of the English language: a survey of opinions concerning the vernacular from the introduction of printing to the Restoration* (Oxford, 1953), pp. 109–114.
[59] The principles of translation agree essentially with those of Gardiner and his party; the 'old vulgar Latin text' rather than the Greek text is used and many words are retained in their untranslated form. See Gregory Martin's preface to *The Holie Bible: The New Testament*, sig. c3ᵛ; printed in *REB*, no. 54, pp. 305–6; and D.M. Roger's discussions of Martin's translations in his prefaces to *The Holie Bible: The Old Testament*, 2 vols, English Recusant Literature, 265, 266 (Kellam, Douai, 1609–10, facs., London, 1975), STC 2207; A&R 107; *The New Testament*, English Recusant Literature, 267 (Rheims, 1581; facs. London, 1975), STC 2884; A&R 265–7; Southern, *English Recusant Prose*, pp. 231–54; Mueller, *Native Tongue*, pp. 208–9.

THE STYLE OF THE *SERMONS*

A colloquial voice: humanism and the Reformation

Edgeworth often writes with an appealing immediacy, illuminating his expositions with flashes of verbal sprezzatura or colloquial expressions. In the only significant assessment of his preaching style to date, J.W. Blench has praised him as a notable exponent of the popular style, implying that he may have been a Catholic counterpart to Hugh Latimer, the most famous of the colloquial preachers.[1] In this focus Blench is essentially in agreement with other critical appreciations of early Tudor prose in which the benchmark of excellence is also the use of native speech forms. The verisimilitude of Tyndale's renditions of direct address and dialogue and the colloquial vigour and speech-based prose of his scriptural translations means that he is now venerated as the major Tudor prose writer. The conflicting claims made for Thomas More as a stylist have agreed in one essential respect: his mastery of a colloquial idiom is the most felicitious aspect of his prose.[2]

The collection as a whole, however, reveals that Edgeworth's colloquial voice was but one option among the range of stylistic resources available to him of which the most notable was the formal, oratorical, pre-Reformation style celebrated in the homilies of Bishop Fisher. Edgeworth introduces his popular idioms with artful calculation to further his rhetorical purposes. These were moulded by the demands of competitive preaching against Latimer, Barlow and other West Country Protestants, in which his role as a Catholic apologist led him to promote conservative clerical authority. His real literary achievement, therefore, lies in his facility in manipulating the stylistic variables available to him, adjusting rhetorical theory to the demands of his preaching milieu and moving between the poles of formal exposition and informal address. For just as religious controversy on issues of ceremony and worship, ecclesiastical authority, the royal supremacy and its practice restricts his apologetics, so it arbitrates his stylistic choices.

His preaching career coincided with a period of remarkable linguistic and literary fertility characterised by an outpouring of vernacular works aimed at a popular audience. The Reformation played a major role, along with printing and humanism, in generating a more inclusive readership for vernacular writings. Bishop Tunstal's choice in 1528 of English as the vehicle for all written

---

[1] Blench, pp. 121–6; 'Longland and Edgeworth', 123–43; Dibdin, *Library Companion*, p. 87, writes: 'Edgeworth is less nervous and familiar than Latimer; less eloquent than Fox; and less learned and logical than Drant. He is, however, a writer of a fine fancy and an easy and flowing diction'. Bridgett commends his 'lively style' and 'striking applications' in 'Bristol Pulpit', 83.

[2] Mueller, *Native Tongue*, pp. 186–7, 201–25. Cf. J. Delcourt, *Essai sur la langue de Sir Thomas More* (Paris, 1914), pp. 303, 311, who sees More as the first master of modern English prose. R.W. Chambers locates More within the native homiletic and devotional tradition in *The Continuity of English Prose from Alfred to More and his School* in Harpsfield's *Life of More*, ed. E.V. Hitchcock, EETS, OS, 186 (London, 1931); and reissued separately in EETS, OS, 192A (London, 1932), p. liv. See C.S. Lewis, *English literature in the sixteenth century excluding drama* (Oxford, 1954), p. 180. On More's use of the resources of the vernacular see Delcourt, *Essai*, pp. 230–52; 'Some Aspects of Sir Thomas More's English', *Essays and Studies* 21 (1935), 21–30.

controversy, and the assimilation of the Great Bible into the mainstream of English life and language after 1539, were decisive factors in broadening the basis of the vernacular as a medium for literature and polemic.[3] The wider use of English also created a closer alignment between oral and written forms of the language. Linguistic studies by N. Davis and I.A. Gordon have established that the sixteenth century was one of the periods when this adjustment was made.[4] Sermons which preserve oral forms of speech illustrate this development more effectively than other forms of discourse. The 1557 text of Edgeworth's collection, for example, undoubtedly retains some fidelity to the spoken forms of his discourse, for he says of his method of delivery in the Preface:

> I euer fearinge the labilitie of my remembraunce, vsed to pen my sermons muche like as I entended to vtter them to the audience: others I scribled vp not so perfitlie, yet sufficientlie for me to perceiue my matter and my processe.[5]

Preached over a twenty year period between c.1535 and c.1553 during which the pulpit became an important platform for religious controversy, his sermons reflect this major adjustment as well as the impact of changing preaching styles.

Although contemporary linguistic changes inevitably broadened the range of Edgeworth's stylistic choices, the moral basis of his colloquial voice can be traced to the homiletic tradition of Gospel translation which favoured a simple, commonplace diction to exemplify the practical goals of the Christian life.[6] But his practice was undoubtedly shaped by humanist teaching and the Renaissance theories of language which reinterpreted the precepts of classical rhetoric.

The humanists advocated verisimilitude, variety, vividness and concrete force in making appeals, and so created the vogue for a more natural form of utterance in preaching which Reformation debate reinforced in practice.[7] Erasmus lampoons the pulpit oratory of his day in Praise of Folly, and recommends a naturalness and sincerity of utterance while Vives in De Tradendis Disciplinis advises that the circumstances of delivery and the personalities of the speaker and listener should be considered.[8] But it was Erasmus' precepts on imitating the classics, and his fusion of the Ciceronian ideal of oratory with the values of Christian piety which most strongly influenced the Renaissance theorists. In his famous textbook, De duplici copia verborum ac rerum, he reorients the inquiry into the problems of

---

[3] See the famous comments on the English language made by Tyndale, Obedience, pp. 148–9; More, Dialogue, CW6, 337. On C. Tunstal's commission to More to use English see Pineas, Thomas More, pp. 39–40; Jones, Triumph of . . . English, pp. 56–7; C. Barber, Early Modern English (London, 1976), pp. 55–6, 58; Mueller, Native Tongue, p. 206.

[4] N. Davis, 'Styles in English Prose of the Late Middle and Early Modern Period', Langue et Littérature: Actes du VIIIe Congres de la Fédération Internationale des Langues et Littératures Modernes, Les Congres et Colloques de l'Université de Liège, 21 (Université de Liège, 1961), 180; I.A. Gordon, The Movement of English Prose (London, 1966), p. 86; Delcourt, 'Aspects', 22; cf. Mueller, Native Tongue, p. 104.

[5] Sermons, p. 96.

[6] Features of Edgeworth's plain style – expletives, direct address, colloquialisms – conform to Mueller's description of Scripturalism: the style modelled on models from the Old and New Testaments. Associated with Protestant writers and humanists in the sixteenth century, this prose is 'overtly rhetorical; it seeks to persuade, whatever its subject' (Native Tongue, pp. 246–7).

[7] H.H. Gray, 'Renaissance Humanism: The Pursuit of Eloquence', in Renaissance Essays from the Journal of the History of Ideas, ed. P.O. Kristeller and P.P. Wiener (New York, 1968), 208, 213.

[8] Erasmus, Moriae Encomium, ed. and tr. Betty Radice, CWE27 (Toronto, 1986), pp. 126–7, 132–41; Vives: On Education, ed. Foster Watson, p. 182.

writing in Latin through the sixteenth century literary and cultural context. In developing a creative method for the art of imitation which uses the resources of *copia* or the abundant style, he recommends committing classical precepts to memory and making as many variations on them as possible. In aiming for *varietas*, the stylistic vice of extension or fruitless repetition might be bypassed when improving on the style of good authors, and the faculty of elegant writing developed.[9]

That these humanist reinterpretations of classical precepts influenced Edgeworth's rhetorical practice is apparent from his comments made in the twelfth sermon preached c.1552. Citing Cicero's *De Officiis* and using Cicero's source, Quintilian's *Institutio Oratio*, he pays tribute to the principle of decorum; the appropriate matching of language and form to subject and ideas. This he sees as inseparable from fitting behaviour:

> *Modestia sit scientia earum rerum quae agentur aut dicentur loco suo collocandarum*, it is a knowledge to set in theyr owne place al things that shalbe done or saide, to place al our doings & sayings according to the oportunitie of the time as occasion shal serue. It is a foul thing & great faut to bring in light language, & to speake gestingly as it wer in an alehouse when men be in communication of an earnest & sad matter.[10]

Decorum, a central term both in rhetoric and moral philosophy, is a concept that pervades all Erasmus' writings on rhetoric and *imitatio*. It is sufficiently attested in works of other humanists like Thomas Elyot and Vives to be regarded as a stylistic principle common to them all.[11] In *De copia* it is intrinsic to the abundant style which Erasmus sees as efficacious only if discriminately applied.[12] In his recommendations on imitating the spirit of the classics in *Ciceronianus* (1527), he defines Cicero's use of decorum, his ability to adapt speech to circumstance, as his greatest virtue. 'Ciceronianism' is therefore exemplified in the speech of those people who take account of changed circumstances and speak as Christians:

> There is nothing to stop a person speaking in a manner that is both Christian and Ciceronian, if you allow a person to be Ciceronian when he speaks clearly, richly, forcefully and appropriately, in keeping with the subject and with the circumstances of the times and of the persons involved.[13]

---

[9] See *De copia rerum ac verborum*, ed. and tr. C.R. Thompson, CWE24 (Toronto, 1978), pp. 301–2, 307, 572–4 for Erasmus' principles. Edgeworth would have found Erasmus' writings available at Oxford; the 1520 catalogue of a bookseller, John Dorne, included seventeen copies of *De Copia* (*ibid.* 283). Its importance in providing a generative method for imitation is established by T. Cave, *The Cornucopian Text* (Oxford, 1979), ch. 1.

[10] *Sermons*, p. 284. See also Cicero's statement on decorum in *Orator*, tr. H.M. Hubbell (London, 1942), 21, 70–72. Cited by V. Kahn, *Rhetoric, Prudence and Skepticism in the Renaissance* (Ithaca, 1985), p. 34. A. Vos, 'Humanistic Standards of Diction in the Inkhorn Controversy', *Studies in Philology* 73 (1976), 380, identifies *propria verba* as a classical principle of diction.

[11] Gray, 'Renaissance Humanism', 208, identifies the fusing of rhetorical and ethical models as a feature of humanism.

[12] See Cave, *Cornucopian Text*, pp. 3–5, 11, 21; Erasmus, *De Copia*, CWE24, 304, 574, 658.

[13] Erasmus, *Dialogus Ciceronianus*, ed. and tr. B.I. Knott, CWE28 (Toronto, 1986), p. 400; see p. 399: 'It may well be that the most Ciceronian person is the one least like Cicero, the person . . . who expresses himself in the best and most appropriate way'. For a discussion of Cicero's view that

Erasmus believed that out of a true appreciation of decorum, the rhetorical ideal of eloquence, defined by humanists as 'wisdom speaking copiously', can be achieved:[14]

> ... let us first take care of what to say and only then of how to say it, and let us fit words to matter, not the other way round, and while we are speaking let us never lose sight of what is appropriate to the subject. A speech comes alive only if it rises from the heart, not if it floats on the lips.[15]

Erasmus' rhetorical theories were assimilated and debated by successive generations of Tudor schoolmasters, by Roger Ascham in *The Schoolmaster*, and by Thomas Elyot in *On the true orator*. *Elocutio* itself was revalued in the 1540s. Edgeworth's twelfth sermon on I Peter was preached at about the time they received more systematic treatment in two vernacular manuals of rhetoric: Richard Sherry's *A Treatise of Schemes and Tropes* (1550) and Thomas Wilson's *The Arte of Rhetorique* (1553).[16] Both schoolbooks are largely devoted to medieval *amplificatio* (the 'ornaments of sentence') and they stress *elocutio* in its relationship to *dispositio* (form) and *inventio* (theme). Sherry's treatise was strongly influenced by *De copia* while Wilson, drawing on Sherry and Erasmus' *Ecclesiastes*, elevates to a new importance the teaching of Cicero and Quintilian. He reinterprets the notion of decorum when treating 'Elocucion' under the heading of 'Aptenese' – the selection and fitting together of words and phrases. 'Apt wordes' are those that 'properly agre unto that thyng, whiche thei signifie, and plainly expresse the nature of the same.'[17]

Decorum is a guiding principle in Edgeworth's rhetorical practice, apparent in his discriminating use of the colloquial style which he reserves for direct address to his audience when driven to complain, or to denounce Protestant heresy, or for biblical paraphrase. But his belief that rhetorical decorum necessarily reflects and endorses propriety of behaviour creates a subjective bias in his handling of language. The view of the Christian orator as the man who combines wisdom and eloquence and seeks to persuade his hearers toward a better life, developed from the Ciceronian ideal of the orator, was central to the Erasmian synthesis of Christian piety and classical paganism. This ideal also assumed that true decorum

---

oratory should be adapted to the understanding of the crowd, see J.E. Seigel, *Rhetoric and philosophy in Renaissance humanism: the union of eloquence and wisdom, Petrarch to Valla* (New Jersey, 1968), pp. 7–8; on decorum see Gray, 'Renaissance Humanism', 215–16.

[14] *Ibid.* 200; on Wilson's humanism see T.J. Derrick's introduction to *Thomas Wilson's Arte of Rhetorique*, The Renaissance Imagination, 1 (Garland, New York, 1982), pp. lxix–lxxii. See Erasmus, *De Copia*, CWE24, 559: 'the fundamental requirement for eloquence is to speak as the occasion demands, and no utterance is well spoken which is lacking in this quality of appropriateness'.

[15] Erasmus, *Ciceronianus*, CWE28, 402.

[16] STC 22428; 25799. See B. Vickers, 'On the Practicalities of Renaissance Rhetoric' in *Rhetoric Revalued*, ed. B. Vickers, Medieval and Renaissance Texts and Studies, 19 (New York, 1982), pp. 136–7 on the revaluing of *elocutio* and the rhetorical goal of *movere* after 1540; on Sherry's and Wilson's treatises, Crane, *Wit and Rhetoric*, pp. 98–104; Derrick's introduction to *Arte of Rhetorique*, pp. lxvi–iii.

[17] Wilson, *Arte of Rhetorique*, p. 332; on Wilson's adaptation of Cicero's norms to the vernacular and his recommendation of 'heaping' of 'matter' see Mueller, *Native Tongue*, pp. 350–3.

or propriety arose from pre-existing moral rectitude.[18] Edgeworth, like the classical orator who also enacted his rhetoric within the realm of probable virtuous action, was undoubtedly conscious that his rhetorical standard of decorum would be effective only insofar as it endorsed a norm of behaviour.[19] In the opening sermon of the sequence on the seven gifts he locates the preacher's moral norms within a Christological framework, defining them as divinely santioned. His aim is to persuade his audience to pursue virtue actively by following the example of Christ and to exercise it in their lives by means of the gifts of the Holy Spirit.[20] In expounding the gifts of wisdom and understanding he attributes true eloquence and hence true wisdom to God alone who 'sendeth . . . to the learner the gifte of intelligence that he may perceiue suche thynges as be Godlye'. The gifts may be attained through living accordynge to God's eloquence and to his holy worde and the preacher, God's deputy, who receives from God the 'spirite of sapience' is chosen to persuade men to the exercise of greater virtue:

> . . . although by my preaching I make not all men better, yet some men be the better therefore, and they that be good, be more modest and vertuous by my sayings. . . . although I haue not perswaded men to daye, yet to morowe I maye peraduenture . . .[21]

But in the sermons he preached after c.1535, unable to draw either on More's ecclesiology or on the extra-scriptural traditions of the church for his apologetics, he uses this concept of moral rectitude as a polemical fulcrum and reinterprets the rhetorical ideal of eloquence. He makes clear in the Preface the ideological position which led him to compromise and redefine his norm of moral goodness in terms of the system he was bound to defend:

> And because these sermons were made in Englishe, and toucheth some-time amonge, suche heresies as hath troubled English folke, I thought it best to set them forth in suche language as might presentlie best edifie the multitude.[22]

The underlying Ciceronian ideal that the orator was necessarily a good man was imperfectly enacted in the world of Reformation politics in which conflicts be-tween Protestant and Catholic led to competition for the attention of West Country audiences after 1533. Pragmatic considerations, therefore, guide his stylis-tic choices in favouring a homely diction and familiar idioms. In pointing out the disastrous effects of the new learning on Bristol trade in the fourth sermon, preached in c.1538–9, he solicits the critical attention of his audience by using native speech rhythms, pungent phrases and West Country dialect forms:

> I haue knowen manye in this towne, that studienge diuinitie, hath kylled a marchaunt, and some of other occupations by theyr busy labours in the

---

[18] Erasmus, *Enchiridion Militis Christiani*, LB V, 32B, tr. C. Fantazzi, CWE66 (Toronto, 1988), p. 73; cited by Kahn, *Rhetoric*, p. 92.
[19] See *ibid.* pp. 34–5. In *De Officiis*, 1. 27. 94, Cicero makes the point that moral goodness and decorum (*honestas* and *utilitas*) cannot conflict.
[20] On the Ciceronian model of the orator see Gray, 'Renaissance Humanism', 206–7; Kahn, *Rhetoric*, pp. 33–6; Seigel, *Rhetoric and philosophy*, ch. 1; *English Humanism: Wyatt to Crowley*, ed. J. Martindale (London, 1985), pp. 32–3.
[21] *Sermons*, p. 122.
[22] *Ibid.* p. 95.

scriptures, hath shut vp the shoppe windowes, fayne to take Sainctuary, or els for mercerye and groserye, hath be fayne to sell godderds, steanes, and pitchers, and suche other trumpery.[23]

Associating colloquial speech with evangelical teaching in Bristol, he imitates the accents of conversation between children and their parents in order to reflect to his hearers their folly in believing the reformers' erroneous definition of images as 'idols':

> when [the chyldren] haue theym in theyr handes, dauncynge theim after their childyshe maner, commeth the father or the mother and sayth: What nasse, what haste thou there? the child aunsweareth (as she is taught) I haue here myne ydoll, the father laugheth and maketh a gaye game at it. So saithe the mother to an other, Iugge, or Thommye, where haddest thou that pretye Idoll? Iohn our parishe clarke gaue it me, saythe the childe, and for that the clarke muste haue thankes and shall lacke no good chere.[24]

The urgency with which Edgeworth addresses his audience and represents local speech can be attributed to the pressures of defensive preaching. The Protestant challenge inspires inventive expressions such as his now proverbial description of 'leude and folyshe priestes, that . . . geue them selues to walkinge the stretes, and beatinge the bulkes with theyr heeles, clatteringe lighte and leude matters' (c.1548).[25] This linguistic vitality also surfaces in his scriptural translations as in the following chastisement of Bristol apprentices (I Pet. 2:20). Native speech forms and idioms are used to dramatise moral deficiencies:

> *Quae est enim gratia si peccantes & collaphisati sufferis?* What thanke shall you haue, yf you do noughtelye and play the sluggardes, or the false bribers in your maisters busynes, and then for your noughtye doyng be well boxed, beaten, and canueste, and so suffer as you deserue? What thanke shall you haue for your suffering? none at all.[26]

Noun phrase lists, familiar in scriptural translation, show affinities with the language of popular drama as in the vilification of Christ, where he compares Christ's tormentors to Protestants who harass Catholics observing their Lenten fast:

> When he was railed agaynste, and called a heretike, and traytourer, a benchewhystler, a blowboll, a felowe with ribaldes, knaues, whores, and drabbes . . .[27]

Here as in other passages, the rhetorical structure of the language of abuse is preserved, enlivened by colloquial epithets like 'blowboll' and 'benchwhystler', which were no doubt familiar to his audience.

Edgeworth's popular preaching therefore developed out of tendencies in the medieval homiletic tradition which were intensified and sharpened by religious conflict. His activity in censoring and judging popular Protestantism effectively redefines the moral basis of his colloquial style; but the channelling of his

---

[23] *Ibid.* p. 146.
[24] *Ibid.* p. 143.
[25] *Ibid.* p. 331.
[26] *Ibid.* p. 263.
[27] *Ibid.* p. 298; nouns phrase lists are used for moral rebuke; see, for example, pp. 128, 238, 316.

emotional response to Protestant attacks into a rhetorical form gives vividness and vitality to much of his prose.

The style of ecclesiastical authority

Although the demands of preaching against heresy inevitably shaped Edgeworth's rhetorical practices, they never completely overwhelmed his principal homiletic goals: Christian revelation and the assertion of clerical authority. Whereas Latimer's popular preaching reflects his dynamic personality and became identified with his evangelical mission, that of Edgeworth constitutes a departure from his staple homiletic style of sententious assertion which was traditionally used to confirm a hierarchical value system.[28] Mingled with his Catholic apologetics and propagandist teaching inherited from Thomas More are affective expositions notable for features which Januel Mueller has identified with the ecclesiastical authoritative style: 'pattern loading' (distensions or interrruptions within a clause which obscure its perception as a unit), pleonasm and parenthetical locutions.[29] He expounds the essential values behind secular ideals of conduct such as piety and patriotism. But he aims at maximal articulation of Christian *de contemptu mundi* through expressing themes such as the *ubi sunt*, the Passion, worldly transience, and the promise of the heavenly kingdom by means of grandiloquent and magisterial assertion. In the following passage on the transience of the earthly kingdom the syntactic parallelism expanded with correlative clauses demonstrate the binary symmetric cast of the correlative style which is associated with William Tyndale.[30] Phonological patterning by means of cross alliteration ('peck', 'bestowen', and 'purchase') and alliteration with syllabic variation ('reapeth', 'redde', 'rye'), embellishes the underlying theme of death and decay:

> Third, if it be suche a grounde where all thinge withereth, and dryeth awaye for lacke of moysture, where hearbes proueth not, and trees groweth not to theyr naturall quantitite, where the leues waxeth yelowe and falleth at Lammas tyde, where men soweth a busshel and reapeth a peck, and for redde wheate reapeth like rye or otes, that is bestowed on suche a purchase, is but caste awaye.[31]

The foundation of this style is the *schemata verborum*, figures of sound, in particular the scheme known as *paramoion* consisting mainly of *similiter cadentes* or *similiter desinentes* (alliteration and *homoioteleuton*); as well as the more elaborate schemes of *isocolon* (clauses of equal length) and *parison* or *compar* (corresponding members with the same form).[32] Precedents are found in the vernacular writings of

---

[28] The title of this section, the style of ecclesiastical authority, is inspired by Mueller's work which identifies aureation with ecclesiastical authority; see *Native Tongue*, pp. 162–77.

[29] *Ibid.* pp. 164, 165, 168 on the classical and English origins of this style.

[30] *Ibid.* pp. 17–201, 205–9, 225–39 on Tyndale's prose style.

[31] *Sermons*, p. 208.

[32] I have used the definitions provided by M.W. Croll, 'The Sources of the Euphuistic Rhetoric' in *Style, Rhetoric and Rhythm*, ed. J.M. Patrick and R.O. Evans (New Jersey, 1966), pp. 241–3; for other terms used in this chapter see Cicero, *Ad C. Herennium Libri IV* (Cambridge, Mass., 1954), pp. 275–405; repr. by J.J. Murphy in the Appendix to *Rhetoric in the Middle Ages* (Berkeley and Los Angeles, 1974). See also Lee A. Sonnino, *A Handbook to Sixteenth Century Rhetoric* (London, 1968).

Caxton and Malory and the officially inspired homilies of bishops John Longland, John Alcock and John Fisher. Their styles reflect the hierarchic value system that temporal ecclesiastical authority endorsed.[33] Like them, when applying the *schemata* in combination for oratorical display, he repeats a single figure over and over and provides variation by using another form of the same scheme or another scheme.[34] The following exhortation to live well in order to have a good death concludes with *rogatio*:

> All things that a man loueth he would fayne haue them fayre and good, as in example: If thou loue thy coate or thy gown, thou wouldest fayne haue it fayre and good. Thou louest thy friende, thou wouldest fayne have him good. Thou louest thy sonne or thy childe, thou wouldest be glad he were good. Thou louest thy house or thy chamber, thou wouldest fayne haue it fayre and good. Then how is it that thou woldest fayn haue a fayre and a good death at thine ending?[35]

Although Edgeworth's failure to integrate the *schemata* with native prose rhythms means that they control the syntax of his public, oratorical style, in passages of Biblical exposition or paraphrase whose structure is provided by the original he adapts them skilfully to the purposes of instruction. Various devices of repetition, doubling, and circumlocution in his lengthy paraphrase of John 16:15 in the first sermon on the seven gifts, preached before the vernacular scriptures were made available to the laity, identify the loaded patterns associated with aureation:

> *Omnia que habet pater mea sunt, propterea dixi de meo accipiet & annunciabit vobis.* All thinges that my father hath, be myne: all power, all knowledge, all connyng be equally, and aswel in the sonne as in the father, and in the sonne from the father, like as he hath his generacion, production, & beyng of the father, therfore sayth Christ, the holy gost shall take of myne and shall shewe it you & teach it you, for when he shal sensibly come among you he shall shewe you my fathers pleasure, which is all one with my pleasure. All that he shal teache you he shall take and learne of my father and of me. Like as he hath his beyng of my father and of me, and as he is the infinite and ineffable loue of my father and of me.[36]

This explanation of the trinity and divine omniscience combines *parison*, the most familiar of the *schemata*, with *conversio* (repetition of final words in a clause),

---

[33] The *schemata* may have developed from the prose of Church Fathers such as Augustine and Cyprian, but they also appear in the 'Euphuistic' tendencies of the medieval homiletic and devotional writers. Edgeworth would have studied them in the grammars of Donatus and Priscian and in the *Doctrinale* of Alexander de Villa Dei; see Mallet, *History* I, 180; Gibson, *Statuta Antiqua*, pp. xciv, 33–4; Croll, 'Euphuistic Rhetoric' pp. 257–8. Mueller, *Native Tongue*, pp. 247–8 summarises critical views on the origins of Euphuism. See A. Feuillerat, *John Lyly contribution à l'Histoire de la Renaissance en Angleterre* (Cambridge, 1910), pp. 458–91, for examples from the prose of Fisher, More and Thomas Elyot; Delcourt, *Essai*, pp. 288–93, on More's prose; Blench, 'Longland and Edgeworth', on Longland's preaching style.
[34] On Latimer's use of the schemes 'to heighten the effectiveness of a rattling invective or to wing the shafts of ridicule' see Croll, 'Euphuistic Rhetoric', p. 279; P. Janton, *Eloquence et Rhétorique dans les Sermons de Hugh Latimer*, Faculté des lettres et Sciences Humaines de L'Université de Clermont-Ferraud, 2nd ser., Fas. 27 (Paris, 1968), pp. 130–2, 147–62.
[35] *Sermons*, p. 307. In the Reformation period only the Protestant preacher, Thomas Lever, assimilates the *schemata* to the native prose rhythms; on his style see Blench, p. 156.
[36] *Sermons*, p. 113.

and *homoioteleuton* ('in the father . . . from the father . . . of the father'; 'you'; 'pleasure' and 'of me'). These three structurally identical measures which parallel the first three sense units demonstrate the interdependence of the three figures of the Trinity. As in the prose of Bishop Fisher the features of pleonasm and semantic redundancy serve devotional ends.[37]

Edgeworth's rhetorical aims of authoritative articulation and grandiose expression lead him to exploit the possibilities of grammatical variation. Thus he places adjectives in the postnominal position in phrases adapted from the French: 'times conuenient', 'causes reasonable', 'causes emergent', 'death temporal'.[38] Conventional religious usage in phrases such as 'reward euerlastynge' dignifies this preference. But when 'euerlastynge' is coupled with the substantives 'life' and 'death', semantic contrast as well as the demands of stress is a controlling factor:

> It were better to dye for truth, & to saue the life of the soule, by which thou mayst come to euerlastinge life, then to loose that life and to be brought to death euerlasting.[39]

Another favourite device is to place the object in a position of emphasis; 'Such a zeale and loue to learnyng hathe manye now adayes'; 'onelye one thinge I warne the that my face thou shalt neuer se', or, following the Old English word order, to invert object and subject after an initial adverbial: 'In like maner be al nacions bounde by the lawe of Nature'. He also freely observes the position of prepositional and adverbial phrases in order to heighten antithesis and to achieve weighty, sententious utterance. He places the prepositional phrase in an emphatic position between clauses: 'Menne can tell well inough by science and good learnynge what to make of it (purgatory), but by experience no man can tell what it is'. This is a device for creating cadence as in 'the lawe of Nature shoulde moue them to staye all suche daungers, and to the vttermost of their powers to resist them'.[40]

These contrived grammatical and syntactical irregularities contribute to the deliberate authorial instrusiveness which is characteristic of this style. But Edgeworth succeeds in achieving balance through the use of rhetorical tropes and other familiar forms of phonological patterning. Inversion of adverb and the infinitive combined with *anaphora* emphasise the inviolability of God's word: 'God . . . commaundeth you, thus to doe, and thus to saye, and thus to lyue'. Grammatical inversion may also be elaborated by a play on sound likenesses and differences as in this case of transverse cross alliteration combined with *homoioteleuton*:

> And the more perfectly that this gifte is inspired into man, by the holy gost: the more distinctly and plainely he shal perceiue such hie secrets, though perceue them as he shall do hereafter in glory, we can not yet.[41]

or by emphasis and *parison*: 'Repugne it may . . . but preuaile it can not'. Antithesis is also heightened by chiastic constructions: 'they haue (diuellishe wisdome) that

---

[37] On Fisher's prose see Mueller, *Native Tongue*, pp. 170–4; Croll, 'Euphuistic Rhetoric', p. 274, on its significance for the development of Euphuism.
[38] Davis, 'Tyndale's English', 11; Delcourt, *Essai*, pp. 183–5; *Sermons*, pp. 263, 137, 132, 133.
[39] *Ibid*. p. 329. Of the ninety five occurrences of 'everlasting' twice as many appear in the post-nominal as in the pre-nominal position.
[40] *Ibid*. pp. 166, 128, 152.
[41] *Ibid*. pp. 242, 120.

be wise and wittye inough to do mischief, but good they can do none'; and in 'And although I haue not set vp them that be sycke, yet thcm that be whole I haue made stronger . . .'.[42] *Hyberbaton*, in which a crucial grammatical element is trans-ferred to the end of the sentence, creates the most dramatic interruption of the clausal unit: 'for without charitie this gifte of science comminge of the holy gooste will not be, no more then other vertues infused'; and 'If thou beleue on God, thou must beleue he is of infinite power, . . . for it is not possible twoo powers infinite to be'.[43]

Without the controlling influence of rhetorical colours and phonological pat-terning, this grammatical variation and syntactic and lexical elaboration can extend the length of sentences, either contribute to distortions in their shape, or cause them to be incomplete. A predisposition to prolixity is the most prominent of Edgeworth's stylistic vices. But another, *anacoluthon*, the syntactic irregularity which causes a sentence to end other than it begins or be incomplete, may be attributed either to poor punctuation or the circumstances of oral delivery.[44] Nevertheless Edgeworth does show mastery of the syntax of compound declarative sentences. When preaching on the resurrection in the sermon on the creed he disrupts the regular subject-verb-object order using *parison* in his final three clauses to achieve cadence and affirm a communal celebration of the faith:

> And this mortification we must buselye and continuallye beare vpon vs, and then we shal be sure to liue with him, by renewinge of our liuinge contrarie to vice, vsing iustice and vertue, that so we may giue light of good example to all others, that they may glorifie and laude God in vs, that finally we, and they with vs, may ryse to immortall glorye.[45]

In the sermons on I Peter, by contrast, linguistic experimentation is shaped to meet the aesthetic demands of a less hortatory, more mellifluous religious style. This exploits the possibilities of decoration. His binary, symmetrical form of com-position using conjunctions and correlatives reappears in the following translation of Is. 40:6–8. It is elaborated with *parison* combined with *adnominatio* or *polyptoton* (repetition of the stem); the verbal auxiliary 'doth', alternating with the more commonly used -eth ending of the third person singular, varies the stress pattern:

> All fleshe is lyke grasse of the medowe, and hys glori (that is to sai) carnal lust or pleasure, is like the floure of the medow that maketh a pleasant shewe for the time and so doth carnall delectation content and please for a while, but euen as the floure within a while withereth and falleth away, so doth carnall ioye fade and fall.[46]

---

[42] *Ibid.* pp. 126, 118, 122.

[43] *Ibid.* pp. 145, 170.

[44] See the exordium of the fourth sermon on the seven gifts; three other cases occur in this sermon (*Sermons*, pp. 136, 137, 138, 140), most frequently in clauses of condition and concession. Without a knowledge of Edgeworth's part in the production of the 1557 text, these errors cannot be confidently attributed to him; problematic punctuation may be the result of the demands of line justification. On the compositors of the 1557 edition see Wilson, 'Edgeworth's Sermons', I, 26–38.

[45] *Sermons*, p. 177. See Croll, 'Euphuistic Rhetoric', 253, on the syntax characteristic of Euphuism. Blench, pp. 130, 188–9, claims that the full Ciceronian period is not produced until the sermons of Hooker; cf. Dom. Hilary Steuert, 'The Prose Style of Bishop Watson of Lincoln 1557', *MLR* XLI, 3 (1946), 225–36.

[46] *Sermons*, p. 225; Mueller, *Native Tongue*, pp. 193–4; Davis, *Tyndale's English*, 10; this passage is

Edgeworth's experimentation with the grammatical and syntactic variables of which the language was then capable had the ethical justification of advancing his doctrinal and devotional beliefs, and thereby promoting the authority of the conservative clergy in Bristol. But the heavier embellishment of his prose in the late 1540s and early 1550s suggests that aureation was becoming a rhetorical end in itself. His delight in linguistic variety emerges, for example, in the conspicuous reduplication of participles and gerunds. Gerunds form new substantival forms, such as 'noughtye doyng' from 'do noughtelye' and 'euil occasions giuing'. Participles are used for transition and to add colour, as in the description of the heavenly kingdom as 'a place of cooling and refreshing'. In combination they form word lists as in this description of excess:

> . . . drinking men vnder the borde, of ryottinge and surfettinge, and of wastfull bankettinge, and of theyr pryde & malicious taunting of pore men, & of sclaunderinge and backebiting.[47]

As tautological word pairs they intensify hortatory and affective appeal as in this exposition of the Passion:

> remembre the heauy burden of the crosse that was layd on his shoulders when he was not able to beare it, but fell downe vnder it, he was so faint and wearye with long abstinence and with watching al the night afore, and with much rude handling . . . & with much haling & pullinge of him from one iudge to another, and then with the ache & smarting of mani sore stripes that he suffered, and wyth shedyng of his blood at his scourging when he was whypped.[48]

The habit of grouping words in pairs and threes, a widespread phenomenon in fifteenth century and Tudor prose, has been identified as a staple of the Catholic, authoritative style.[49] Its use by Catholic translators of the scriptures, was criticised by Protestants as a sign of élitism when an austere, unadorned style came to be the hallmark of Protestant liturgical and scriptural translation during the reigns of Edward VI and Mary I.[50] In Edgeworth's prose this feature is so pervasive that it cuts across the boundaries of his colloquial and expository styles and cannot be associated conclusively with the exercise and affirmation of ecclesiastical authority. He uses doublings locally, invariably linking them with assonance and rhyme to intensify his syntactic patterns of parallelism or antithesis by concentrating stress on key lexical items:

---

notable for syllabic antithesis ('flesche', 'grasse'); assonance and alliteration ('within', 'while', 'withereth'); *polyptoton* or *adnominatio* ('pleasure', 'pleasant', 'please'); and *homoioteleuton* ('carnal', 'falleth', 'fall').

[47] *Sermons*, pp. 263, 117, 129, 316. Analogous gerundive forms are 'extreme and gredie asking' (188); 'resorting and commyng' (149); 'example geuinge' (255).

[48] *Sermons*, p. 265; for other treatments of this theme, see D. Gray, *Themes and Images in the Middle English Religious Lyric* (London, 1972), pp. 122–45.

[49] Mueller, *Native Tongue*, pp. 147–61, 172, 219–20; Ong, 'Oral Residue', 152.

[50] See Jones, *Triumph of . . . English*, pp. 58–60, 67; on the plain style see J.N. King, *English Reformation Literature: The Tudor Origins of the Protestant Tradition* (New Jersey, 1982), pp. 138–42. Mueller avoids this term but see *Native Tongue*, pp. 245–6, on Scripturalism and its impact on English prose style.

With hys blewe wales and scarres in hys fleshe after the scourges, stripes
and strokes that made his skinne to ryse, and to bee blacke and blewe, wee
were healed from the syckenes of our soules; that that made his body sycke
and sore, made vs whole & sound.[51]

While the incidence of doublings is greatest in devotional passages, in his
expositions he aims for semantic incrementation: Christ has 'his generacion, production & beyng from the father'; 'homely and familiar examples' are for all to
'take, sucke and vnderstande'. Tautological combinations show rhythm as well as
sound-effect to be a guiding influence: 'defaced and defowled'; 'firme, fast and
certaine'; 'compasse, cast & contriue'; 'displeasures, dispites and paynes'; the
heavenly joys will 'neuer fade, welowe, or widder awaye'; grounds be 'morish,
maresh or otherwise vnholsome'.[52]

The various figures of adornment also contribute to a densely rhetorically pat-
terned surface, although he displays little of the verbal ingenuity of More, Tyndale
and Skelton.[53] Favourite devices are alliteration with assonance as in 'neyther
fauour nor feare mede nor dreade'; adnominatio or polyptoton (using the same stem
with different endings) as in 'pleasure', 'pleasant', and 'please'. This might include
pleonasm as in this translation of Matt. 18:10: 'The angels see and desire to see,
desiereth to see, and seeth', or word play with anaphora as in the following:

for by oft doyng wel for feare, we may gendre a loue to wel doing, & so at
last we shal do wel for loue, and shal haue a swetenes in wel doinge.[54]

Finally Edgeworth also follows the practice of neologisers like Lord Berners and
Elyot by coupling synonyms with new or unfamiliar words, or by introducing
familiar words with new meanings. The word 'nuzzle' in the sense of 'nurture',
which had a vogue between 1530–1650, occurs in the phrase 'noseiled, brought vp
and be vsed to'. Words of classical origin are grouped with one or more of their
native counterparts; thus 'batilnes', from the Latin vbertas appears with 'frutfulnes';
'solidate' with 'staye it & settle vs sure'; 'assuefaction' with 'exercise, vse or
custom'.[55]

Edgeworth's authorial intrusiveness, visible in linguistic and stylistic features
such as phonological patterning, grammatical variation and syntactic irregularity,
is most notable in the Henrician sermons when he was preaching as spokesman for
officially sanctioned doctrines and ceremonies. It may be identified as a residue of
the hieratic style developed by the earlier prose writers such as Bishop Fisher and
Pecock, and its disappearance in the later sermons, probably corresponds to the
decline in power of the conservative Henricians after 1547. Nevertheless his use of
the schemata for grandiloquent statement and as a source of embellishment provides essential continuity in the development of the florid, decorative mode which
culminated in the writings of the Marian preachers and Elizabethan Euphuistic
writers.[56]

---

[51] Sermons, p. 267.
[52] Ibid. pp. 113, 232, 231, 120, 124, 341, 359, 351.
[53] More's pun on 'heresy' and 'heresay' which runs throughout Dialogue Concerning Heresies like a
leitmotiv, may be alluded to in Sermons, p. 168; see More, Dialogue, CW6, 449.
[54] Sermons, pp. 266, 225, 215, 317; cf. p. 166.
[55] Ibid. pp. 354, 156, 366, 124; the Sermons antedate the OED first use citations of 'solidate' and
'assuefaction'; a list of these and other ante-datings is forthcoming in Notes and Queries.
[56] See Blench, pp. 157, 192–202 on the Marian and Elizabethan Euphuistic preachers.

The imagery of the *Sermons*

While doublings, word play, and neologisms contribute to the articulate energy of
Edgeworth's prose, his use of images and *exempla* serve the purpose of encouraging
faith and good works. As with the Ciceronian orator, the preacher's use of the
faculty of judgement in creating analogies to determine the likenesses between
things is intrinsic to rhetorical decorum. But Edgeworth justifies the use of figurative language as a way of increasing devotion:

> naturall reasons and familier examples may do much to declare and to set
> furth the thinges that we beleue, and to declare the possibilitie of theim
> that such thinges maye bee, and then ioyne yᵉ veritie of this scripture to
> this possibilitie, and this shall make a man more swetelye and louingly to
> beleue the thing that he beleued afore.[57]

Many of his more commonplace analogies and *exempla* of the natural world would
have come from a preacher's handbook. One group draws on the lore of animals,
traditionally a popular source of pulpit moralisation. The pig or hog, compared
with 'the murmurer & grudger' who is ill disposed to do good deeds, remains an
emblem of sloth. The blindness of the burrowing mole symbolises those worldly
wise spiritually blind men who do not attend sermons. He illustrates those who
lack the virtue of circumspection with an example which also appears in *Ancrene
Wisse*:

> [they] be like a skittish starting horse, whiche coming ouer a bridge, wil
> start for a shadowe, or for a stone lying by him, and leapeth ouer on the
> other side into the water, & drowneth both horse and man.[58]

Also familiar is the industry of the bee, invoked in the exhortation to the pilgrim
to increase daily in virtue:

> . . . lyke as a Bee tarieth not styll on one Flower, but flyeth frome Flower to
> flower to gather her Waxe and Honye. Vertue dooeth strengthen our
> Soules in the exyle and banishemente of thys worlde.[59]

Another group is drawn from the domestic sphere. Those who are strengthened by
adversity differ from those who are enfeebled by impatience 'like as the pitchers
that be whole & sound be made faster, harder and stronger by the fyre, so they that
be cracked or broken, flyeth in peces'.[60]

The imagery of his exposition of I Peter provides a picture of Catholic eschato-
logy. Man's true home is not this world, for we are 'pilgrims and strangers euer
laboring through the troublous stormes of thys world, to come to our inheritance
and dwelling place that God hath made for vs'. This present life is like a summer,
hot with the heat of temptations: 'Therefore . . . we must take a tre to shadowe vs,
& to kepe our beautie, that the deuelish heate of temptation do not marre our

---

[57] See Kahn, *Rhetoric*, p. 49; *Sermons*, pp. 290–1; Erasmus recommends introducing fables by
commending the genre in *De Copia*, see CWE24, 632.
[58] *Sermons*, pp. 325, 117, 313.
[59] *Ibid.* p. 252; cf. Erasmus, *Ciceronianus*, CWE28, 402.
[60] *Sermons*, p. 211; see others on pp. 233, 277, 306 etc.; Blench, pp. 123–6; Owst, *LPME*, p. 34.

colour'. Man should make provision for winter or the day of doom by storing up good works in this life; he should follow the example of Christ, 'our chiefe captayne in our dayly battel against our gostly enemyes'.[61] The emotive and visual power of these images may be heightened by idiomatic touches as in the following refutation of those who mistakenly believe that heaven is a wilderness who had:

> leauer keepe the brode waye of pleasure, easelye hopping and dauncing to hell, and therefore to them heauen is a wildernes, and in the wooddes of the wyldernes there be many birdes that singeth swetely, with many and diuers swete tunes: so in heauen where the *inhabitaunts shall prayse the Lorde God worlde without ende.*[62]

Edgeworth's figurative language conveys a deeply felt piety. The focussing tenor of his imagery, stemming from his major preoccupation with the role of the preacher, is the husbandman or farmer, vocational types who formed a large part of his audience. Their tools, useless without their owners, symbolise the indispensability of the Christian faith. The axe without the carpenter is a figure for the seven gifts without the theological virtues. The ploughman's share or coulter of his plough which requires constant use to remain 'fair and bright' symbolises the necessity of good works: 'So with labour a man shall be shininge and bright afore God and man, and shal do muche good where the slothfull man shall be euer vnprofitable . . .'.[63] The husbandman's or ploughman's tending of his land, crops, animals and plants provides an analogy for the pastoral duties of the preacher; for just as his reward is seen in the flourishing fields so the preacher's is found in the succouring and saving of souls. Edgeworth enjoins preachers to direct their flocks to safe pastures, that is, to nourish them with good Catholic doctrine, and urges his audience to heed their words:

> That they maie be glad of their labours taking among you, like as an husbandman which is glad to do his work, when he seeth the trees of his setting & graffing proue well, & beare fruites, When he seeth the fieldes of his tillynge beare plentifullye suche Corne or grayne as hee hath sene, then he perceiueth that he hath not laboured in vayne . . .[64]

It is not surprising that Edgeworth's most 'striking applications' are drawn from the world of nature and refer to the ways of animals and methods of farming and gardening. Bristol was still largely a rural, agricultural society in the sixteenth century.[65] But in placing the figure of the ploughman at the centre of his imaginative world-view he draws on a rich vein of imagery: the traditional typology of the ploughman which originated in conventional scriptural exposition of Luke 9:62 ('No man having put his hand to the plough, and looking back, is fit for the kingdom of God') and Luke 17:7 as a figure for the preacher.[66] The fourteenth century allegorical poem, *Piers Plowman,* reinforced this exegesis through the

---

[61] *Sermons,* pp. 251–2, 319, 264, 208, 331–2.

[62] *Ibid.* p. 268.

[63] *Ibid.* pp. 116, 253.

[64] *Ibid.* pp. 353–4.

[65] This point is made by Blench, p. 125.

[66] Jerome (PL 30, 591) states that ploughing is synonymous with preaching; Bede on Luke 17:7 (PL 92, 540), identifies the ploughman with the *ecclesiae doctor* of the church; see D.W. Robertson and B.F. Huppé, *Piers Plowman and Scriptural Tradition* (New Jersey, 1951), pp. 17–20.

figure of Piers, a type of the ideal Christian who embodies the doctrine of honest toil and comes to symbolise the ultimate recognition of God living in man.[67] In the sixteenth century revival of the poem, it was once more associated with the movement of popular dissent.[68] Even though the ploughman figure was debased into a 'harsh anticlerical spokesman', as Crowley's polemical preface to his edition of 1550 attests, the symbolic overtones of pastoral care were not diminished.[69] Latimer's 'Sermon on the Plowers' of 1548, not only cultivates the archaic dialect of the English peasant as the Lollards did but, drawing on Luke 8:5 and 9:62, it preaches the same doctrine of virtuous toil for the preacher as Edgeworth does:

> And well may the preacher and the ploughman be likened together: first, for their labour of all seasons of the year; . . . then . . . for the diversity of works and variety of offices that they have to do. For as the ploughman first setteth forth his plough, and then tilleth his land, and breaketh it in furrows, and sometime ridgeth it up again; and at another time harroweth it and clotteth it, and sometime dungeth it and hedgeth it, diggeth it and weedeth it, purgeth and maketh it clean: so the prelate, the precher, hath many diverse offices to do.[70]

Edgeworth's prose is enlivened with colourful epithets, racy idioms, and rhymed catchphrases absorbed from popular discourse and vernacular writings. But his stock epithets, *sententia* and aphoristic phrases, used for magisterial utterance conform to a simple pattern of parallelism and antithesis.[71] 'Sobernes may be called the mother of all vertues, and dronkennesse mother of all vices'; 'Amende thy yll lyfe, and neuer feare an yll death'; 'Il wordes declareth an ill hart, & good words declareth a good hart'.[72] The heaping up of *exempla*, analogies of natural truths, images, and proverbial phrases anticipates, by contrast, the figured oratorical style of Rainolds and Lyly, as in this reference to the Stoic theory of the four passions: 'as it is natural for a heart to be fearful, & to an addre to be venemous, to a spaniel to be gentle & familiar, so it is natural for a man to desire', or in the following cluster:

> A goodlie Rose springeth vp amonge the thornes, and a goodlye Oke amonge the rughe bryer bushes. A candle geueth best lyghte in the darke, and the Starres shewest fayrest in the night.[73]

[67] E. Salter, *Piers Plowman – An Introduction* (Oxford, 1969), pp. 84–5; Owst, *LPME*, pp. 548–9; on the poem's relation to preaching see *Piers Plowman by William Langland: an edition of the C-Text*, ed. D. Pearsall (London, 1978), pp. 18–19; A.C. Spearing, 'The Art of Preaching and Piers Plowman' in *Criticism and Medieval Poetry*, 2nd ed. (London, 1972), pp. 107–34.
[68] For example, *Pierce the Ploughmans crede* (R. Wolfe, 1553), STC 19904; see the edition by W.W. Skeat, EETS, OS, 30 (London, 1867), p. i; other imitations are mentioned by King, *Reformation Literature*, pp. 51–2; H. White, *Social Criticism in Popular Religious Literature of the Sixteenth Century* (London, 1944), pp. 26–40.
[69] King, *Reformation Literature*, p. 323; see *The vision of Pierce Plowman. The B Text* [R. Grafton f.] (R. Crowley, 1550), STC 19906–7a; Crowley's preface is printed by W.W. Skeat (ed.), *The Vision of William Langland Concerning Piers the Plowman*, 2 vols (Oxford, 1886, repr. 1979), II, lxxiii–iv.
[70] Latimer, *Works* I, 61; King, *Reformation Literature*, pp. 142–3.
[71] Edgeworth probably used a commonplace collection of *Epitheta*; see Ong, 'Oral Residue', 152. See Erasmus' recommendations on maxims and commonplaces in *De Copia*, CWE24 627–30, 637–8; Habenicht's introduction to Heywood's *Dialogue*, p. 64.
[72] *Sermons*, pp. 218, 307, 287.
[73] *Ibid.* pp. 156, 256; on Euphuism see Blench, pp. 124, 192–3, 197–202; M.W. Croll, 'Euphuistic Rhetoric', pp. 241–3; 210.

The piling up of proverbs for variety and copiousness is another feature of Edgeworth's style which came to be associated with Euphuism.[74] In translating from the *Apophthegmata* the anecdotes of Socrates and Xanthippe he links 'after thunder clappes woulde come a showre' with 'trouble worketh patience' and 'turninge necessitie into vertue', amplifying them with: 'I haue a iewell of her'; 'Adultery may departe bedde and boorde'. In the twelfth sermon the sayings 'in his dumps' and '*Ne quid nimis* do in nothing to muche' are followed by 'liueth from hand to mouth' and 'at every twinckling of an eye'. A further refinement is to group proverbs from classical sources with those from everyday speech: '*Sicut simpliciter ad simpliciter, sic magis ad magis & maxime ad maxime*'; 'thinkynge our feete there, as our head wil neuer come' and 'to kepe a low saile'.[75] Despite some dependence on the new proverb collections, Heywood's *Dialogue*, and Erasmus' *Apophthegmata*, the *Sermons* introduce a large number of proverbs into the written language; the collection records sayings like 'all this wind shook no corne' which soon after disappeared from the language, as well as little known ones such as 'Don't make the foot the head'. Edgeworth's scriptural translations are the first recorded source of many. Others are inspired by his translations from the classics and the Church Fathers while proverbs like 'to kepe a low saile' and 'beatinge the bulkes with theyr heeles' may have sprung from contemporary religious disputes.[76]

It is clear that Edgeworth's characteristic forms of embellishment inherited from the pre-Reformation homiletic tradition, with an additional linguistic fullness attributable to humanist practices and the newly available vernacular compilations of classical material, anticipate the Euphuistic style of the Protestant preachers and secular writers of Elizabeth's reign as well as the adorned sermons of the Recusants.[77] But his decorated style never becomes intrusive as in the prose of the Marian preachers because in observing his twin models of *varietas* and decorum, he adjusts the precepts of religious oratory to his practice. He accommodates the circumstances of delivery to the perceived needs of his audience by moving between the stylistic variables that were available to him: popular speech, declamatory rhetoric using the *schemata*, aureate diction, or an amplified style which employs proverbs, *sententia*, and word pairs. Just as the need to preach strategically to defend his authority contributes to the piquancy of his colloquial voice, and its growing urgency, so the elaborately adorned mode of the later sermons that emerges from the sententious and magisterial style of the earlier ones coincides with the decline of Catholic authority during the Edwardian Reformation.

Latimer, Edgeworth's celebrated opponent, developed a distinctive style of pulpit oratory aimed at stirring the social conscience. Preaching 'a nipping sermon, a rough sermon and a sharp biting sermon', Latimer also mastered the art of storytelling, and like Tyndale invented such catch-phrases as 'strawberry preachers' and 'purgatory pick-purse'.[78] From his polemic the character of a man who will digress,

---

[74] *Ibid.* p. 239.
[75] *Sermons*, pp. 277, 284–5, 357–8; other proverb clusters are on pp. 133, 154, 217–18, 230, 289, 303, 319–20, 333.
[76] *Ibid.* pp. 298, 132–3, 358, 333.
[77] Blench, p. 113, distinguishes three different styles, but some mixture appears in most homelies of the period; on the Recusant writers see Southern, *Recusant Prose*, pp. 181–230, 260–2; Evans, 'Tudor Recusant Prose', 251–66.
[78] Latimer, *Works* I, 240; for assessments see F.E. Hutchinson, 'The English Pulpit from Fisher to Donne', in *The Cambridge History of English Literature*, ed. A.W. Ward and A.R. Waller, 15 vols

reminisce,or introduce autobiography vividly emerges. But Edgeworth, a cautious apologist relying on the scriptures, the Church Fathers, and tried and true Catholic defences, lacks the sharp wit of the debater and the expansive rhetoric of the evangelist. Despite some forceful denunciations, his persona remains shadowy; conventional self-declaimers such as 'the labilitie of my remembraunce' and 'the capacitie of my poore witte', underline his intermediary role between the greater authorities – of scripture and the ecclesiastical and temporal hierarchies – and the laity whose faith he wished to sustain.[79] His rhetorical skills are lavished on the older preaching themes such as the heavenly joys, the transience of earthly goods, fear and piety, often producing prose of lyrical beauty.[80] But although his depiction of the unchanging truths of the natural and celestial worlds, manifested in the variety of proverbs, maxims, *sententia*, and images is an important legacy of this collection, it is the points of disruption within the pre-Reformation *Weltanschauung* of which the Catholic faith was an integral part, which lead to stylistic areas of development. When his rhetorical goal of asserting ecclesiastical authority is overcome by the need to preach pragmatically then he introduces into his prose the stylistic features – word pairs, image and proverb clusters, a homely diction and native speech rhythms – which give his *Sermons* their unique place at the midpoint of the development of Tudor style.

(1908, repr., London, 1980), IV, 229–31; *The Selected Sermons of Hugh Latimer*, ed. A.G. Chester (Charlottesville, 1968), pp. xxviii–xxxi; Janton, *Hugh Latimer*, pp. 130–62; W.K. Jordan, *Edward VI: The Threshold of Power* (London, 1970), pp. 279 ff.
[79] *Sermons*, pp. 96, 147, 192; see Jones, *Triumph of . . . English*, pp. 27–31, on the relation of the modesty topos to the concept of the language as uneloquent.
[80] Blench, p. 231; 'Longland and Edgeworth', 133.

SERMONS VERY FRUITFULL, GODLY AND LEARNED

NOTE ON THE TEXT

The present edition is based on the Bodleian copy of the 1557 edition (*STC* 7482). The following editorial principles have been employed. Superscript letters in the abbreviations y^e, y^t, w^t have been retained; ∫ has been transcribed as modern s except on the title page. The ligatures ct, œ and æ have not been preserved, but the i/j and u/v distinctions of the 1557 text have been retained. The spelling of running titles has been standardised. Marginal notes have been indented within the text at the point where they occur in the 1557 edition. The bold type corresponds to those portions of the 1557 edition in 95 roman type. In the preface, 'contentes', and repertory it corresponds to those in 95 italic type. The * symbol refers the reader to the commentary; the † symbol to the critical apparatus. Material in square brackets refers to conjectural letters and emendations. A space between square brackets indicates a word break. Material in angle brackets is redundant in the original. Breaks between words now treated as single words or as compounds have been preserved as they occur in the 1557 text. The index has been keyed to the signatures rather than to the foliation of the 1557 edition since the original is often in error. These errors have not been recorded. The index or repertory follows the preface as in the 1557 edition.

Sermons
very fruitfull, godly,
and learned, preached and
sette foorth by Maister Roger Edgeworth,
doctoure of diuinitie, Canon of the Cathedrall
churches of Sarisburie, Welles and Bristow,
residentiary in the Cathedrall churche of
Welles, and Chauncellour of the same
churche: With a repertorie or table,
directinge to many notable
matters expressed
in the same
sermons.

¶ Excuſum Londini in aedibus Roberti
Caly, Tipographi. Menſe Septemb.
Anno. 1557.

Eccles. v.
Esto mansuetus ad audiendum verbum dei,
vt intelligas, & cum sapienta proferas†
responsum verum.*

---

† proferas] proferes

The preface of the
aucthor to them that shall rede these
sermons folowinge.

IT is honourable and worthye praise, to confesse and declare the woorkes of
almightie GOD, as the blessed Angell sayd vnto holye Thoby.* And therfore they
that sawe the miracle done by our sauioure Christ vpon the man that was both
deafe and domme, and was restored vnto his sight, and also to his speach, although
they were bidde to make no wordes thereof, yet they consideringe the excellencie
of the miracle, and perceiuinge the humilitie of the doer of the same, as intendinge
more the occultation of his facte, for the auoidinge of worldlie praise, to geue vs
example of like humilitie, then to hide his gratious cure, as thinkinge they shoulde
not haue done well to let suche a marueilous worke vanish to obliuion, were the
busier to diuulge and publishe, not onelie that miracle, but others withall, sayinge:
Bene omnia fecit, & surdus fecit audire, & mutos loqui. This man hath done all
thinges [π2ᵛ] wel, he hath made the deafe to heare, and the domme to speake.* So
I consideringe that it hath pleased almightie God of his plentuous mercie and
goodnes, to open my mouth, and to make me occupied in preachinge his holie
worde nowe by the space of fortie yeares and more, I thoughte it not good to
permitte such matters as I haue (throughe Goddes helpe) set forth in my sermons,
vtterly to rotte and perishe, and left (as the morall Poete saieth) **Deferar in
uicum, uendentem tus & odores,***† I haue therfore perusing, yea rather superfi-
ciallie runninge ouer suche sermons as I haue preached in times past, founde much
good matter in them, right worthie to be had in memorie, and so compact and set
together, that nowe in my olde age I reioyce in God that gaue me his gratious gift,
so to trauayle in suche studie while I was yonge and lustie. These my longe labours
hath be* in the mooste troubleous time, and moste cumbarde with errours and
heresies, chaunge of mindes and scismes that euer was in this realme for so longe
time together, that any man can rede of. While I was a yonge student in diuinitie,
Luthers heresies rose and were scattered here in this realme, whiche in lesse space
then a man woulde thinke, had so sore infected the christen flocke, first the youth,
and consequentlie the elders, where the children coulde sette the fathers to scole,*
that the kinges maiestie, and all the catholike clerkes in the realme had muche a
do to extinguishe them, which yet they could not so perfitlie quenche, but that
euer still when they might haue any maintenaunce by men or women of greate
power, they [π3] burste out a freshe, euen like fire hidde vnder chaffe, whiche
sometimes amonge will flame oute and do hurt if it be not loked to. Against such
errours with their appendeceis I haue inuehied ernestlie and oft in my sermons in
disputations and reasoninge with the protestauntes, vntill I haue be put to silence,
either by general prohibitions to preache, or by name, or by captiuitie and imprisonment, of all whiche (I thanke God) I haue had my parte* And yet euer
when I might haue any clere time, I haue retourned to the same exercise more
vehementlie then afore, and so will do while I may haue strength to speake. And
because these sermons were made in Englishe, and toucheth sometimes amonge,
suche heresies as hath troubled English folke, I thought it best to set them forth in
suche language as might presentlie best edifie the multitude. Moreouer pleaseth

† tus & odores] thus, & arhoma

95

you to be aduertised, that when I shoulde preache in any solempne and learned audience, I euer fearinge the labilitie of my remembraunce, vsed to pen my sermons muche like as I entended to vtter them to the audience: others I scribled vp not so perfitlie, yet sufficientlie for me to perceiue my matter and my processe. And of these two sortes I haue kept (as grace was) a greate multitude, whiche nowe helpeth me in this my enterprise of imprintinge a boke of my saide exhortations. Moreouer I haue made innumerable exhortations at my cures, and in other places where I haue dwelled, and in the countreis there aboute, and in my iourneis, where it hath chaunced me to be on sondaies, or other holie daies, of whiche I haue no [π3ᵛ] signes remaininge in writinge, althoughe I thinke verelie some of them were as fruitfull, as others in whiche I toke more labours, I praye God they maye be written and registred in the boke of life euerlastinge. And when I shoulde preache oftentimes in one place, I vsed not to take euery day a distinct epistle or gospell, or other text, but to take some proces of scripture, and to prosecute the same, part one day and parte another daye, and so you shall perceiue by my declaration of the .vii. giftes of the holy Gooste, whiche I preached at Redcliffe crosse, in the good and worshipfull citie of Bristow, in sundry sermons, although I was interrupted many yeares by the confederacie of Hughe Lathamer,* then aspiringe to a bisshopriche, and after beinge bishop of worce[s]ter, and ordinary of the greatest part of the sayd Bristow, and infecting the whole. And so by the exposition of the first epistle of S. Peter, whiche I preached also in manye sermons at the cathedrall Churche there, where I am one of the Canons, in this also I was manie times and longe discontinued by the odious scisme that was nowe lately, and by the doers of the same. And in like maner in the Cathedrall Churche of welles, on the first and second sondaies of Aduent, on Axewednisdaye, and others, and there I lacked no trouble by bishop Barlowe and his officers,* of which suche as be not perfourmed, I intend (if it shall please God) to perfourme and finishe hereafter.

Of all my saied sermons you shall now receiue
in this boke, as hereafter foloweth.

The contentes of this
boke.

A Declaration of the seuen giftes of the holy gost in syxe sermons.

An homilie of the articles of our Christen faith.

An homilie of Ceremonies, and of mans lawes.

A parfite exposition of S. Peters fyrst epistle, in twentie treatises or sermons.

I haue besyde these many sermons, made in verie solempne audiences on the dominicall epistles and gospelles, some in the vniuersitie of Oxforde, some at Paules crosse in London: some in the courte afore my mooste honourable Lorde and Maister kinge Henry the eighte: some in the cathedrall churche of welles, where hath ben euer sith I knew it a solempne and a well learned audience, whiche I purpose (God willinge) to set forth hereafter, as I maye haue oportunitie.

A repertorie or table,
directinge to manye notable
matters expressed in this booke
folowinge.

A.

† counterfeiter] counterfetter

Aucthoritie of the maister, geueth the scoler a courage to
    learne in all faculties.   [4A3ᵛ]   338
Aulters pulled downe, and bordes† put vp for the
    communion with much mutabilite about the same.   [4K1]   365
Aulters pulled downe by heretikes of Arrius secte, in saint
    Basilles time.   [4K1ʳ⁻ᵛ]   365–6

B.

BAbilon was build .cxxxi. yere after Noes flud by Nembroth.   [4K2]   366
Baptisme of infantes, contrary to the Anabaptistes.   [2N1ᵛ]   225
Baptisme clenseth all sinnes,   [2G3]   207
Bezeleel had the spirits of science.   [L2ᵛ]   145
to Beleue there is one god, or to beleue god, is not sufficient,
    but we must beleue on one god.   [T1ᵛ]   170
Beleue on the holy churche, may be saied.   [Y1]   178–9
Beleue the resurrection .&c. is necessarye to take awaye the
    feare of death.   [Y2ᵛ]   179
Bithinia lieth ouer yᵉ streictes against Constantinople.   [2E2ᵛ]   200
Better it is to shine with laboure, then to rouste for idlenes.   [2X2ᵛ]   253
Bearing one with another easeth the burden, & so doth
    compassion in infirmities of the soule.   [3G2]   281
Beutie of face must not be vsed as an instrumente of mischeif.   [3X3ᵛ]   328
Bilders bad and good.   [2Q4ᵛ]   237
Bishoppes must not be to easy or rasshe in orderinge
    prei[π A2]stes, and their perill in so doinge.   [2V2ᵛ]   249
Bishops and preistes were al one in old time.   [4C2ᵛ]   344
Bishoppes may commaund, and compell, when?   [2V4]   251
Bloud of Abell cried for vengeaunce, the bloud of Christe
    cried for mercye.   [2F2]   202–3
Blessinge is diuersely vnderstande and taken.   [2F4]   205
Blessinge and well sayinge by our neighbours, shalbe requited
    with blessinge euerlastinge.   [3H4]   286
Blessed be they that suffreth for iustices sake.   [3I3]   289
Blessed be they that god correcteth, and why?   [3Z3ᵛ]   335
Bodily members applied to the soule.   [2K2]   216
Bondage came other by iniquite or by aduersitie.   [2Z4]   261
Body of sinne.   [X2ᵛ]   176–7
Bristow was ful of diuersitie of errours.   [3G1ᵛ]   280–1
Brotherhed is to be loued, and not only the brothers   [3G2ᵛ]   281
Brotherhead of heretikes and scismatikes is but a cantell† or
    patche of the very true brotherheade, and like a rotten
    bowe broken of from the tree.   Eodem   281

C

CAre and solicitude we muste caste vpon god.   [4H3]   361
Calling, or election, of two maners,   [2E4ᵛ]   201–2
Cain for lacke of Goddes feare, was punished with feare.   [P3]   158–9

† bordes] birdes; cantell] cancell

D.

G.

† Guyde] Goyde

I.

K.

L.

M.

† Obseruaunces] obseruauncee

P.

R.

S.

Sapience or wisedome is of foure maners. [B2] 116–17
Sacramentes of the olde law. [Z2ᵛ] 183–4
Sacrifices. [Z2ᵛ] 184
Sacred or halowed thinges. [2A2ᵛ] 187
Sacrifices of Christes churche be many. [2A1ᵛ] 186
Sacramentes of Christes churche be seuen. [2A2] 186
Sanctus, holy, signifieth firme, fast & sure in goodnes, [2K4ᵛ] 218
Saba, where it lieth. [2S1] 241
Samaritanes were as it were halfe Iewes, why<¿> [3B2ᵛ] 266
Sara called her husband lorde, yet husbandes must not be
  lordly towarde their wyues. [3E4] 276
Sacrament of baptisme was signified by the water that in
  Noes time saued eyght persons in the shippe. [3L2ʳ⁻ᵛ] 294–5
Sacrament of the aulter is signified by the steene of meale
  and the gear of oyle, & is likewise preserued and continued. [3T3] 321
Science of scripture is in worse case then any other facultie. [I4] 140
Science the gift of yᵉ holy gost extendeth to handy craftes, [L2ʳ⁻ᵛ] 145
Scripture, he that foloweth not holy scriptures knoweth
  not Christ, [L2ᵛ] 145
Scripture sometimes speaketh that of the whole, that is
  verified onely in the part. [2T2] 245
Searche the Scriptures, why? [2B4] 192
Seuen times a day falleth a iust man, is expounded. [4C1ᵛ] 343
Sermons, the quene of Saba shal condempne them that wil
  not take labours to come to heare sermons. [2S1] 241
Seruauntes must obey although their maisters be
  vnreasonable harde, [3A1ʳ⁻ᵛ] 261–2
[π B5ᵛ] Seruauntes must haue a louinge feare towarde their
  maisters, example of Ioseph. [3A2ᵛ⁻3] 263
Seruauntes many times become better then their maisters
  & bieth their maisters childrens inheritaunce. [3C3] 269
Sicknes bringeth ill tidinges to the sensuall appetite, but
  to reason they shoulde be welcome. [3O3ʳ⁻ᵛ] 305
Shipwracke or perill on the sea, wyll make a marchaunt
  to know God more then sermons. [Q4] 162
Semiramis quene of Babilon reigned there victoriousely
  by the space of .xlii. yeares. [4K2ᵛ] 366
Signe of the crosse, saueth vs from the deuel. [V3] 174
Sit, or stand in heauen, is vnderstande. [X3ʳ⁻ᵛ] 177
Simon the sonne of Ionas, is expounded morally. [2C2ʳ⁻ᵛ] 193–4
Simon Magus was driuen from Antioche, and afterward
  from Rome by S. Peter. [2D1ᵛ] 196
Socrates learned sufferaunce by his frowarde wyues. [3E4ᵛ] 277
Sobrietie is temperaunce the cardinal vertue. [4H3ᵛ] 361
Solicitude that is to be exchued. [4H3ᵛ] 361
Spirite is diuersly taken in scripture. [2F1] 202
Sprinklinge of the bloud of Christe and of Abel, haue
  contrary effectes. [2F2] 202–3
Spiritual in liuinge, and spiritual in knowledge. [2P3ᵛ] 233
Spiritual who be called. [3M1] 297

X.

Y.

Finis.

[A1]   ¶The first sermon,* containing an introduction
                 to the whole matter of the vii. giftes of the
                 holy goste,* And treatyng of the two first
                 giftes called the spirite of sapience,
                 and the spirite of intelligence.*

THe blessed euangelist sanct Iohn in the first chapiter of hys gospel, after he had
somewhat touched the ineffable coeternitie of the second person in trinitie, the
sonne of God, with God the father,* consequently he descendeth to his temporall
generacion in fewe woordes, comprising the same, **verbum caro factum est et
habitauit in nobis,** That worde of God the second person in trinitie was content to
come alowe and to take our mortal nature vpon him, and to dwel among vs* not
with any diminution or decay of the godhead, for the infinite glorye of God
suffereth neither augmentacion or increase, neither decreasyng or decay. It is euer
one & after one maner, though it pleased him to hyde the glory of his godhead for
a season, as condescending to the infirmitie of them that he should be conuersaunt
withall, and to teache vs the waye of humilitie: and that is it [A1ᵛ] that saint Paule
sayth, **semet[ ]ipsum exinaniuit formam serui accipiens,** He withdrewe his mightie power from his operacion, for if he had shewed it in his owne lykenes, all the
worlde had not been able to haue receiued him. He kept a lower port, euer vsing
humilitie and lowlynes, & sufferyng the paynes of our mortalitie, with all the
despites that the Iewes did to him, tyll in conclusion he came to his paynes on the
crosse in his painefull passion.* And that he withdrewe his power from his operacion in the tyme of his bodily presence heare on yerth appeareth euidently by
this, that if it had pleased him, he might aswel haue indued his disciples with the
comforte of the holy ghost whyle he bodily taried among them, as to haue differed
it tyll the commyng of the holy ghost by sensible signes at this holy tyme of
whytsontide.* In a long sermon that he made to his disciples afore his passion
among other holesome lessons he sayd thus vnto them: **Expedit vobis vt ego
vadam &c.** It is for your profite that I go from you, for if I go not from you the holy
ghost wyll not come to comfort you.* I haue yet many thynges to teache you, but
as yet ye can not bear them away, but when the spirit of truth the holy ghost
commeth, he shall teache you all truthes necessarye for you to knowe.* But good
lorde what sayst thou? Nowe we can not vnderstande suche thinges as we be to be
taught,* & then we shal vnderstand: How may this be? Is he greater of power then
thou art? Can he do more in teching vs then thou canst do thy selfe good maister?
Christ [A2] to auoyde this scruple & doubt answereth saying: No syrs, I do not say
this for any impotencie in me, or for any inequalitie betwixt the holy ghost and
me, for the thinges that he shall teache you & shewe you, he shall not speake them
of him selfe but of me.* The cause why I say so, is this. **Omnia que habet pater
mea sunt, propterea dixi de meo accipiet & annunciabit vobis.** All thinges that
my father hath, be myne: all power, all knowledge, all connyng be equally, and
aswel in the sonne as in the father, and in the sonne from the father, like as he
hath his generacion, production, & beyng of the father, therfore sayth Christ, the
holy gost shall take of myne and shall shewe it you & teach it you,* for when he
shal sensibly come among you he shall shewe you my fathers pleasure, which is all
one with my pleasure. All that he shal teache you he shall take and learne of my
father and of me. Like as he hath his beyng of my father and of me, and as he is the
infinite and ineffable loue of my father and of me.* Thus sayd Christ vnto his

disciples, for in very deede all the workes of the whole trinitie be al one vndiuidid outfurth among creatures. Loke what one person doth, the same thyng doth all thre persones likewise. Therfore there was nothing that the holy gost taught ye Apostles, but Christ could haue taught it them if it had pleased him. But he reserued & left this power of instructing and comfortyng the Apostles and others by them, vnto the holy gost the third person in trinitie, lest if Christ had done all himselfe, they woulde peraduenture haue [A2^v] thought there had be no holy ghost at all, or els that the holy spirit had not been of equal power with Christ, and with the father of heauen. In very dede afterward there risse a pernicious sect of heretikes, as Arrius and his faction whiche merueilously troubled al the world in their time, saiyng: that the seconde person in trinitie was but a creature and lesse of nature & power then the father,* And that the holy ghost was also a creature, and a minister and messager of the father and of the sonne, and lesse of power then either of them both.* Because Christ would not haue his disciples to erre in this point, he reserued the best porcion of learnyng & of godly comfort from them, that the holy spirit might teache it them for their comforte, that so they might knowe the dignitie of the holy ghost, and might haue cause to glorifie and honoure him, likewise as they honoured the sonne, and the father by the doctrine of Christ, whiche euer attributed and imputed all his lore & instruction, preaching & miracles doyng, vnto the father, as it is plaine in many places in the gospels. Therfore in as muche as they had heard muche of the power of the father, and had heard many holesome exhortacions of their maister Christ, & had seen many merueilous woorkes & miracles done by Christ the very sonne of God the father, and knewe very litle manifestly & plainely of the holy spirit third person in trinitie: therfore as at this tyme by the high wisedome and counsell of the godhead, the holye ghost shewed himselfe lighting vpon the [A3] Apostles in firie tongues,* geuing them suche instruction and knowledge, suche comfort & boldnes, as they neuer had before. And againe, because they should not thinke the holy ghost greater of power then the father or the sonne, he warned them afore, saiyng: **Quecunque audiet loquetur.** All that he shall heare, he shall speake to you. As who should say, tho the giftes that he shal inspire you withall shall be wonderous, yet like as he hath his beyng of my father and of me, so al cunning, knowledge and other giftes he hath of vs and equally with vs, like as he is equal and one in substaunce with vs. And in signe and token of his godhead and godly power, it foloweth there **Et quae ventura sunt annunciabit vobis.*** In this he shall specially shewe his godhead, because it accordeth most & cheifly to God to knowe secretes to come after, and of his godhead it commeth that men haue suche knowledge reueled vnto them, therfore Esaie sayth .xli. **Annunciate quae ventura sunt in futurum, & sciemus quia dij estis vos.** Tell vs what thinges shall come after, and so wee shall surely knowe that you bee goddes.* This quickned their spirites that our sauiour Christ tolde them, that the holy ghost should instruct them of thynges to come after, for there is nothing that mans mynde desireth more then to knowe what world shalbe hereafter, and what shall fall after our daies. And the Apostles were verye inquisitiue in suche thinges, therfore many tymes they asked of Christ whether he went, and which was the way, and when he would come to the iudge[A3^v]ment, and when Ierusalem should be destroyed and not one stone left on another. And when he would come to take his kyngdome vpon him, and what signe therof they shuld haue,* with many suche other questions concernyng thinges to come. Of this thought & carke of mynde our sauiour Christ dispatched them, when he tolde them that the holy ghost should teache them & instruct them of all thynges to

come that were mete and conuenient for them to knowe.* Nowe this presupposed
of the godly power of our sauior Christ by whiche he might haue made his disciples
as parfite in all giftes of grace as yᵉ holy ghost did, and the cause why he did not so,
descending to my principal purpose I will speake according to this holy tyme and
solemne feast of the aboundance & plentie of grace, with whiche his manhode was
indued aboue al other men and wemen that euer had grace,* And which he
deriueth & distributeth to all his faythfull people that receiueth grace. Of him the
Prophet sayth, **Psalmo .xliiii. Vnxit te deus, deus tuus oleo letitiae prae consortibus tuis.*** Kynges and preistes whiche bore the figure of Christe were annoynted
with material and corruptible oyle,* but Christ was annoynted of god the father wᵗ
the oyle of gladnes, that is to say, with the holy ghost, which was figured and
signified by the sayd material oyle. With this oyle of gladnes he was enbrued aboue
al his felowes* more excellently then any man whiche he is content to take and
vse as his felowes coinheritors and copartners of the ioyes of heauen. They haue
[A4] graces distributed to them seuerally by partes, and the graces that one man
hath, another man lacketh, and men hath them after a remisse and slacke maner,
not fully nor perfitely: And they that haue graces of one kynde, yet some hath
them more fully and perfitely then some other hath.* But Christes manhode had
all graces after the highest maner that could bee geuen to any creature. He was full
of grace, not by measure, but aboue measure.* Saint Stephan was full of grace,
Stephanus plenus gratia. Act. vi.* But howe? He had as much grace as was
sufficient for him to preache Christ, and to suffre persecution and martyrdome
paciently for Christes sake. And so is euery good man and woman full of grace after
a certaine sufficiencie, according to their nede, and as it is profitable for them. The
blessed virgin Marye was called in Gabriels salutation **plena gratia**, full of grace,*
by a special prerogatiue or afore others, in asmuche as it pleased him of whom
commeth all grace and goodnes, to take her in so gracious fauoure as to take his
fleshe and bloud of her most pure virginal body. But the manhode of Christ had all
the giftes of grace after a certaine excellencie and superaboundance, by which he
might deriue and distribute grace to all faithfull people, euen like as the head in vs
geueth influence to al partes of the body in the vse and exercise of all sensible
mouinges as appeareth, for when the head is a slepe or mortified with Palseies or
suche diseases, all other partes of the body be astonied and can do litle or nothing.
And [A4ᵛ] contrary, when the head is of good temperature and well at ease, al the
body is the better & more apt in euery membre to do his office, by reason of suche
influence as is deriued from the head vnto them.* Suche influence of grace doth
our sauior Christ geue to all christen people, for he is oure head and we his lymmes
or membres, and that godly liuelynes of grace that we haue, we haue it of his store
and plentie of grace. Of this store and plentie of Christes grace the blessed prophet
Esay maketh mencion, speaking of the misterie of Christes incarnation, saiyng:
capi. xi. **There shal a slyppe or rodde spryng out of the rote of Iesse and a floure
shall ascende out of his rote, and on him shall rest the spirit of God, the spirite
of sapience and of vnderstanding, the spirite of counsell and of fortitude, the
spirite of science and of pietie, and the spirite of the drede of God shall
replenishe him.*** By this slyppe or rodde is vnderstand the humble virgin Mary
very flexible and plyant by humilitie. The floure ascending out of that rote signifieth the swete floure of our redemption, our sauiour Iesus Christ whiche rose and
sprong out of the Stocke and roote of Iesse otherwise called Isai, kyng Dauids
father by the sayd slyppe or rodde Mary discending lyneally of Iesse by Dauid and
by other holy patriarkes,* And on this floure shal the holy ghost rest, with the

seuen giftes of grace whiche be there called seuen spirites, because thei be the
giftes of the holy spirite by appropriation* thoughe they come of the whole trinitie
as is afore sayd.* Of these vii. giftes of grace that were [B1] so excellently in oure
sauiour Christ, and by him were distributed and diuided to all them that be apt to
receiue them, I purpose (God helping) to intreate, partly this day, differring vntil
another tyme or tymes (when it shall please God) them that I shall not haue
leysure or oportunitie to speake of nowe. And here is to be noted for them that be
learned, that the scholastical doctours be of diuers opinions in conferryng and
comparing these seuen gyftes of the holye gost, to the seuen principal vertues, thre
theological, Fayth, Hope and Charitie, & foure cardinall, Prudence, Iustice, Fortitude, and Temperaunce.* And also to the viii. beatitudes that Christe speaketh of,
Matth. v.* And to the fruites of the spirite spoken of, **Gala. v.*** So that by many
diuisions and subdiuisions they reduce al these seuen giftes of the holy gost vnto
the seuen principal vertues aforesayd, & also to the sayd beatitudes and fruites.*
And contrarywise they reduce all the sayd seuen principal vertues, beatitudes, and
fruites, vnto these seuen gifts of the holy gost, considering the scriptures expressing
all one thing in substance, expresseth it in diuers places by diuers wordes.* And
now with more words, now w^t fewer: And in some place omitting that they
expresse in other places. Other sayth ful reasonably, that Fayth, Hope, and
Charitie be presupposed to all these seuen giftes,* as the rote in a   **Sco. iii.**
tree or in a plant is presupposed if the tree shall bryng furth   **di. xxxiiii.**
leaues, blossoms† or fruites.* And as we see that the Carpenters   **& xxxv.***
axe or tole can do no worke except it be [B1^v] handled of the workeman, and
ioyned to him by such handeling or touchyng, euen so our soules be not moued to
the exercise of any of these seuen gifts:* except they be after some maner ioyned to
the holy gost, which must be by faith, hope, & charitye. These be the very meanes
to ioyne man to god & to al godly exercise, therfore wher these be not, there the
holy goste doth not inspire anye of his seuen giftes. Example we haue of S. Paule
which though he were a vessel chosen to be replenished with grace, yet he had not
hys gyftes of grace furthwith after his stroke that he had as he was commyng vnto
Damascus: but he was three dayes starke blinde and sore astonyed and afrayd, & by
this feare with praier & fasting, he was prepared to faith, hope, and charitie, &
consequently to aboundance and plenty of grace superadded to the graces of faith,
hope & charitye.* Then seing that these three most necessary vertues be presupposed to the other gifts of the holy gost, if I should do **quemadmodum sapiens
architectus,** like a wise maister of the works,* I should first intreate of them, as to
lay the foundation afore I begin to garnish the ouer and hier part of our spirituall
building. But because I dout not but ye haue oft and many tymes heard of them at
large, omitting them as presupposing the foundacion to be alredy sufficiently layd,
I will descend to my principal purpose, aduertising you, that who so euer lacketh
the said graces of faith hope, and charitie, and will not dispose hym selfe by prayer
to obtaine them: he shall vnprofitably [B2] heare any preaching of the foresaid
seuen giftes of the holy goste.* Then supposing the best that euery one of vs hath
them, let vs prosecute & procede to intreate of these seuen giftes, and first of the
first gift, that is, the **spirite of sapience,** or the gift of sapience.* And because that
(after the minde of the Logicions) where is anye equiuocation, first we must make
a distinction* afore we giue definitions, therfore it is to be noted that **sapience or
wisdome** is taken foure maner of waies, as appeareth **Iacob .iii.*** where the apostle

† blossoms] blossons

asketh this question: Is there anye one amonge you wise or wellearned? If ye will say yea, then sayth the apostle, let him shew that by his workes, **In mansuetudine sapientie,** curteisly, tractably, or gentlely ordering his wysedome. Where contrarye if ye haue bitter zeale and enuye in your hartes with striuing and brawling, you nede not to be proud, deceiue not your selues, for thoughe you thincke your selfe neuer so wise and iolye fellowes,* and thou scolding woman neuer so iolye a dame, yet this is not the wisedome that commeth from aboue, from God almighty, the giuer of all goodnes: But this is earthly wisedome, beastly wisedome, and diuelish wisedome, where ye haue expressed foure maner of wisdomes, **wisedome that commeth from heauen*** of Gods gift, and three other wisdomes that commeth of our gostly enemies. Let vs exclude these three, and we shal the soner perceyue, vnderstande, and beare awaye what the godly wisedome is. One of these three noughtie wisdomes S. Iames calleth earthlye [B2ᵛ] wisedome, and that is it that couetous men be combred with all, whych be euer like wantes or Moles moiling in the grounde, and when they shuld ascend aboue such worldlines to godly meditacions, as to here sermons or diuine seruice, they be as blinde as the Molle.* Either they cannot perceiue any thing of godly or heauenly counsail, or if they perceiue it, yet they haue no swetenes in it, but down they would headlong to their lucre and aduauntages againe, like as a Molle if a man would feede her with wine and wastel, she will none thereof, but downe againe to the ground she will, and there she is more strong then a Lion, and after her maner wiser then anye other beast.* Example of this earthlye wisedome we haue in the gospel **Luc. xvi.** when Christ said **No man can serue two masters, and ye cannot serue God and your riches,** it foloweth, **the Phariseis that were riche, heard al these thinges, & laughed Christ to scorne.*** So if a man do preach or exhort the couetous men not to put to muche affiaunce and confidence in the vncerteinty of their riches a man shall haue a mocke or a shrewd word, But let them beware of the comminacion that is writ. **Luk. vi Ve vobis diuitibus qui habetis hic consolationem vestram.** Wo be to you riche men, whiche haue your consolation and comfort here in this world.* **Ve,** is a comminacion of payne euerlasting, whyche shall fall vpon theym, beside the temporall woe and pain that they haue in keping their goodes: for they be rather possessed and holden of theyr goodes, then possedeth and holdeth them. And [B3] they haue their goodes, as we say a man hath a paire of fetters or shackels vpon his legges, more to his paine then to his pleasure. This considered S. Paule, writing to Timothe **.i. Timo. vi. diuitibus huius seculi precipe non sublime, sapere, neque sperare in incerto diuitiarum, sed . . . diuites fieri operibus bonis facile tribuere. &c.** Commaund the rich men of this world not to be proude in their own conceiptes, neither to trust in the vncertaintie of their riches, but to be riche in good woorkes and good deedes, to geue gentlely without frowardnes. &c.* The other wisedome called beastly wisedome they haue, that be ouer muche geuen to the pleasure of their bellies, and consequently to the pleasure of the flesh and lechery. For of glotony foloweth lecherye, and this is the wisedome of them that studieth nothinge so muche, as howe they may please their bellies, as where to get a delicate cup of wine and good chere.* These S. Iude in his epistle calleth spottes, for they spotteth and defouleth them selues by ebrietie and surfets, and spotteth other men by their yll examples and euill occasions geuing. **Hi sunt (inquit) in epulis maculis conuiuantes sine timore se[met]ipsos pascentes.*** Against al these speaketh our sauiour Christ. **Luc. vi. Ve qui saturati estis, quia esurietis.** Wo be to you that be farced, stuffed, and full fed, for you shall be a hungred at your iudgement, when ye shall beg refreshing, and none shalbe giuen you,* and this paine with which Christ doth threaten voluptuous persones is inflict and laid on mens neckes, somtimes here in this world as we haue [B3ᵛ] seen by many men which hath mispende all that their fathers left them, goodes, and landes, and all, and haue be ready to begge or steale for very nede, and for very lack of their accustomed fare. Much like vnto Esau, whyche for a messe of potage* sold his first frutes. **Gene. xxv. et contempsit quod . . . vendidisset:** And he litle estemed, yea rather despised that he had so sold them.* So these yong ruflers be not sory, but rather doth maligne and freate and chafe, and be readye to fighte when a man would vmbrayde them for so mispendynge all their substance, worse then the prodigall and wastefull sonne that is spoke of in the gospel, which after that he had scattered and wasted by his lose liuing, all the goodes that his father left hym, yet at the last he tooke remorse and repentaunce, and returned home to his father againe.* The third euill wisdome is called **diuellishe wisdome,** which they haue that be wise and wittye inough to do mischief, but good they can do none: They be wylye to circumuent men, and to deceiue them in all busynes, exchaunges, bargayning, bying and selling, and such other exercyse. And such be they also that by oppression leapeth vpon mens shoulders like Apes* as muche as in them is, keeping them downe that they shall neuer come vppe a lofte to anye thrifte or ryches, and that wyll be gladde to wayte men a shreud turne,* so that no man shall espye them, or knowe that they do it, and many times when they haue done a man a shreude turne will make a man beleue that they be their best frendes. All these be [B4] carnall wysedomes and worldlye wysedomes, that bringeth a man to death euerlasting. **Rom. viii. prudentia carnis mors est,** And it is counted very folyshenes afore God. Of suche wisedome speaketh Christe. **Luc. xvi. The chyldren of thys wicked worlde** all sette in malignitie and myschiefe **be wyser then the chyldren of light,** the children of grace, the children of God. And he geueth laude and prayse to the father, because he hath hid the misteries and secretes of the trewe faith of Christ from them that be worldly wyse and farre casting, and hath reueled, vttred, and declared them to suche as be chyldren, that is to saye small and little in malice, humble and lowlye in harte and spirite. For on suche the holye goste wyll spredde hys gyftes<.> and on none of theym that thyncke theym selues so worldlye wyse, whyche be verye fooles afore God. The apostle Saynte Iames **capit. iii.** declareth what is this godlye sapience or wisedome commynge from almightye GOD aboue, by the effectes and properties of it. Firste (saithe he) **it is chaste** in deedes and in exteriour behauiour, for where the filthynesse of lecherye is, there is no vertue that can please God, and thys is contrarye to beastlye wysedome. **Then it maketh peace,** as wel wythin a mannes selfe, or in a mannes owne conscience, as outwarde to others, dyrectlye agaynst dyuellysh wysdome, that is euer quarelyng and waytyng shrewd tournes. **It keepeth a measure and good manner in worde and deedes.** [B4ᵛ] And so doth nother beastly wisedome nor diuellish wisedome. **Easye to be counselled or intreated,** where earthly wisedome (according to the properties of the earth) is hard to be perswaded agaynste his lucre or aduauntage. **Agreing with good men,** as none of the other three wisedomes doth, **And full of mercy** in hart and dede, **And full of good fruites,** that is to say, good workes, wher as of the other wisedomes commeth no goodnesse but it be colourable & vainglorious, or for some sinistre purpose, **Iudging without simulacion,** or faining. Not shewing iustice and indifferencye outward, bearing indignacion and parciality in hart inward. Such an humble hart had Salomon when he made his supplicacion and peticion to God in Gabaon .iii. **Regum .iii.** where he offered to God a thousand hostes or beastes to be all burned

in Gods honour (as the maner was then) sayinge: I am but yonge, and knowe not
how to beginne, nor how to procede or make an ende of my matters: Therfore giue
vnto me thy seruaunt (O good Lorde) a disciplinable hart, ready and apt to learne
what and howe I ought to doe, that I maye iudge thy people, and dyscerne or put
difference betwyxte good and yll, wythoute whyche no man can be able to iudge
these people, they be so many in nomber. Thys desyre and prayer of thys yonge
kynge Salomon pleased GOD wonderouselye well. And because he asked not long
life, nother riches nother the death of his enemies, but onely wisdome to geue
discrete iudgement, Almighty god [C1] said to him: I haue done as thou hast said.
**Dedi tibi cor sapiens & intelligens in tantum vt nullus ante te similis tui fuerit
nec post te futurus sit.** I haue geuen thee a heart indued with Sapience and
intelligence, in so muche that among all the kinges of Israell that haue bene afore
thee, or that shall come after thee, there was neuer none like thee.* Here ye haue
expresse mencion of the two firste giftes of the holy gost, **Sapience** and **Intelligence,** wittines or fine and cleare vnderstandyng. Of the which, Sapience
properly serueth for iudgement in speculatiue causes, chiefely concernyng almighty God, and celestiall creatures and verities or truthes about the same, iud-
gyng and determining that to them a man shold surely adhere & leyne, & to refuse
the contraries, as false & repugnant to the truth.* And I must nowe speake vnitely
or ioyntly of the gift of sapience & of ye gift of intelligence or vnderstandyng, as
the prophet Esay rehearseth them coupled and linked together, because one of
them adourneth and helpeth another. For Sapience is much the lesse if it lack
Intelligence or wittines. And wittinesse without discrete iudgement of Sapience is
very vnprofitable. And euen like, the gift of counsayle without fortitude or manlinesse is of no price: Nother manlines without counsell or good aduisement. No
more is science without pietie or pietie without the discretion of science. And fear
muste haue some of the saide giftes concurrent with it, or els no good will come of
it.* Then to our purpose. Because that our knowlege natu[C1^v]rally beginneth at
some of our fiue exteriour or outward senses, which we call the .v. wits, if our
knowledge shall be eleuate aboue that his common course to heauenly matters, as
be thinges parteyning to our fayth, it hath nede of some supernaturall light, by
whiche it may ascende and pearce into the knowledge of such thinges as by his
natural power he can not attayne to.* As that there be three persons in one
substaunce of the Godhead. And that the father by his fecund and fruteful memory produceth and getteth his onely begotten sonne the second person in trinitie:
And that the father and the sonne by their fecunde and frutefull will bringeth
forth the holye gost coeternall, and of equall might and power with them both.
And y^t that one God thus distinct in thre persons by his endles and mighty power
at his pleasure, and when he thought good, made all the world of nought. And
that by his onelye goodnes he mainteneth and preserueth the same so that if he
would once withdrawe his hande of maintenaunce but one little moment from hys
creatures, they should sodainely fall to nought as they came fro. And that all the
glorious company of aungels he made to honour him, like as all other creatures,
after their kindes and maners doth.* And where as some of the aungelles swarued
from the grace that they were creat in, and were damned to be the horriblest
creatures and in most payne of all creatures of the world, the others persistyng &
standinge in their goodnesse, were confirmed in grace, so that now they [C2] can
not fall, but continuallye remayneth in the glorious fruition, sighte, and loue of
God, euer ready to do his commaundement in heauen, and at his pleasure here in
earth toward vs mortall men. **Hebr. i.*** These and such high misteries of heauenly

matters to perceiue, and as it were by the sharpenes of mans witte to pearce into
them, (as man may here in this grose and corruptible bodye) perteyneth properly
to the gifte of vnderstandynge, **Ad donum intellectus**. And the more perfectly
that this gifte is inspired into man, by the holy gost: the more distinctly and
plainely he shal perceiue such hie secrets, though perceue them as he shall do
hereafter in glory, we can not yet. And by mature and wise iudgement to discerne
these verities from their contraries, perteyneth properly to the gifte of Sapience, or
godly wisdome. **Ad donum sapientie.*** As to discerne one God from the false
Gods: To know that the .iii. persons in Trinitie be equall in power, and not one of
them minister or seruaunt to the other, as **Arrius** saide.* To know that there is but
one maker of all thinges, & no more, and not to put two creatours, one of good
thinges, an other of euyl thinges, as **Manicheus** saide.* And to iudge when the
angels of God doth trulye Gods message. And to discerne them from the aungels of
darknes, which many times disguise them selues into the fashion of the angels of
light. These and such other hye iudgementes in heauenly causes, perteineth
properly to the gift of sapience or godly wisdome. For this supernaturall gift of
Sa[C2ᵛ]pience the wise man prayed. **Sapi. ix. Da mihi sedium tuarum assistricem
sapientiam.** Geue me the wisdome from aboue that is euer assistent bi thy seat of
glory, and from thence is deriued and infused or send downe to menne. Because
that, **Si quis erit consummatus inter filios hominum, si ab illo fugerit sapientia
tua in nihilum computabitur.** If a man be neuer so profound and excellent in
mans wisdome, if he lacke this godlye wisdome (good Lord) he shall not be
estemed wise, but rather a fole,* in as much as worldly wisdome is counted but
folishnes afore God. **i. Corin. iii.*** And the prophet Dauid prayed that he might
obtayne thys supernaturall gift called **Donum intellectus,** the gift of intelligence,
wittinesse, or fine and cleare vnderstanding, saying: **Psal. cxviii. Da mihi intellectum vt discam mandata tua.** Geue me intelligence that I may learne thy comman-
dementes.* Where it is highly to be noted that this noble king and prophet
whiche so well knew Gods lawes, and that saide he had kept Gods eloquent
sayinges, yet nowe he prayed for finer and clearer vnderstandyng, by whiche he
might yet better ascende and pearce into the same. And we haue nede so to pray as
the prophet did, that this gift of Intelligence may be geuen vs to helpe our fayeth,
like as in many cases our faith helpeth our intelligence or vnderstanding, accordyng to the saying of **Esay .vii. Nisi credideritis, non intelligetis.** As saint
Augustine and others redeth that letter. Excepte ye beleue, ye shall not vnderstande.* For many thinges there be whiche except ye be[C3]leue, ye can not
vnderstande, as the articles of our fayeth, with other like. And many truthes there
be, that we can not beleue except we haue vnderstandyng, either by hearyng the
preacher, by instruction, or by study, as Paule sayth: **Ro. x. Fides ex auditu auditus
autem per verbum Christi.*** And this is acquisite fayth gotten by laboure, studie,
or hearyng: and so is vnderstandyng proporcionablye to the same, whiche bothe be
made more firme, fast, and certaine, by fayth infused, and by Intelligence or
vnderstandynge infused and geuen from aboue of the holy gost.* And this gift of
Intelligence is neuer withdrawen from good men, specially about such thinges as
be necessary for mannes saluation to be knowen, although some men haue it in a
higher degree then some other haue: but about other thinges not necessary to be
knowen, it is withdrawen, to pul men downe, that the matter & occasion of pride
and curiositie may be taken away, and lest men should be to proud of gods gifts:*
and accordyng to this speaketh saint Iohn **.i. Ioh .ii. Vnctio eius docebit vos de
omnibus.** The oyntment, infusion, or inspiration of the holy goste will teach you

in all thinges necessary to be learned,* although very good men hauyng the grace that maketh them acceptable and in the fauour of God, may be dul and little or nought perceiue of other truthes, without whose knowledge a man maye come to heauen wel inough. Chrisostome in a sermon **De spiritu sancto**, vseth a more familier & playner distinction of these two giftes, Sapience, and In[C3ᵛ]telligence, saiyng: When it besemeth a doctour or a teacher to speake plainely, his gifte is called the spirite of Sapience. And where nede is that the hearer do wittily perceiue that is spoken, the gifte that he muste have, is named the spirite of vnderstanding, which also is called the spirite of reuelation, when nede is to learne profound matters.* **Reuela oculos meos & considerabo mirabilia de lege tua.** sayth the Prophet. Reuele or vncouer mine eyes, drawe the curtayne from afore the eyes of my soule by this gift of intelligence, and I shal consider marueylous thinges of thy law.* The spirite of Sapience (sayth Chrisostome) is geuen to the teachers, and the spirite of Intelligence and vnderstandyng is geuen to the hearers. I preache, thou vnderstandest, and takest the minde of my saiynges hauynge the gifte of Intelligence, although thou canst not teach. As the Preacher by the spirite of Sapience iudged what was best to be vttred and expressed for thy erudicion: so thou by the grace of Intelligence takest his words as they be meant, and learnest that is for thy soule health. Almighty God willynge to shewe, that as he sendeth the spirite of Sapience to the teacher, so he sendeth to the learner the gifte of Intelligence, that he maye perceiue suche thynges as be Godlye. Geueth to the mouth of the Preacher the grace of Sapience and to the hearte of the Learner the grace of Intelligence. Sapience is the armour of the mouth, and Intelligence is the har[C4]neys of the hert.* Therfore sayeth the Prophete. **Os meum loquetur sapientiam & meditatio cordis mei prudentiam. Psal. xlviii.** My mouth shall speake Sapience or wisdome, and the recordyng of my hert shall shew prudence, intelligence, or vnderstandyng,* perceiuyng the thyng yᵗ I am taught. Yet here you must diligentlye note, that perfite Sapience is not so much to knowe Goddes eloquence, as for to liue accordynge to Gods eloquence and to his holy worde: And Intelligence is little worth, where a man worketh not accordyng to that he hath learned.* But what shall I say of them, that hearyng Gods eloquence dayly declared vnto them, yet hauyng their mindes occupied aboute other businesse, regardeth not to beare away that they heare, and will not learne and vnderstande to do well accordynge to that they learne. And what shall I saye of them that may get vnderstandyng, and wil not come wher as they maye haue it? but when they heare of a sermon toward, will get them selues out of the church, fainyng some busines to excuse their absence, or els will get them to the Alehouses, or tauernes, or els wil sit talkynge on the crosse in the churchyard, or on the churchyard walls, makynge other as lewde as they be them selues by their yll examples, so that for all the preachinge that is in their townes where they dwel, they be neuer the better, but much the worse, whose iust damnation by gods iuste iudgment must nedes folow as I could declare abundantly if yᵉ time wold [C4ᵛ] permit.* Yet one thing I wold faine discusse by yᵉ way without any great digression from my principal matter: & it is this: in this case now touched, that is to say, when the person, vicare, curate, or preacher, perceiueth that few men or none be the better for his preachynge, whether then and in that case the preacher ought or may ceasse from preachyng, as thinkyng his sapience, his iudgement, and his learnynge in Gods scriptures yll bestowed amonge them, because they regarde it not, and be neuer the better for it, hauyng none intelligence or godly wittinesse gendred or conceiued in their mindes, neither any reformation or amendement in their liuings, nor in their

manners, by al the labours of the curate, or the preacher? For this ye shall vnderstande, that though the negligence of the audience discomforteth and discoura-
geth the preacher greatly, yet he can not so geue ouer and ceasse, bicause of Gods
commination and threatening by his prophet **Ezech. iii.** saiyng: **that if the watch
of Israel, the curate, or preacher se his flocke do noughtielye, and will not tell
them of their fault, nor rebuke them that they may amend, he will require and
aske their bloud of him.*** He shall aunswere for them at the day of dome, Naturall
examples we haue to encourage and comfort the preachers in this behalfe, that he
be not dismayed but take pacience. For we se by experience that the veynes of
waters floweth and runneth, although no manne come to water his cattell at them:
and welles although no manne draw vp water at them, yet they sprinkleth,
boi[D1]leth and welleth vp. And brookes, although neither man nor beast drinke
of them, yet neuer the lesse they kepe their course and floweth. So he that
preacheth must lette hys veyne of sapience flow and runne among his audience,
althoughe no man drinck of it, take hede vnto it, or receiue it.* In this case was
Hieremy the prophet, when he saw no profitte or encrease of vertue come by hys
prophecienge and preachynge, but rather persecution and trouble, mockinge,
laughinge, and scornynge, by whyche he was once mynded to surceasse and leaue
of, preaching, Yet he saith: that **sermo domini . . . factus est in corde meo, quasi
ignis exestuans claususque in ossibus meis, et defeci fere non sustinens. cap. xx.**
The woorde of God was like flaming fyre in my hart (saith this prophet) and it was
closed wythin my bones, so that I left my former purpose, and coulde not forbeare
to speake in Gods name.* Then if he were thus vexed in kepyng silence, what
shall become of vs if we ceasse, specially where none such persecution is as he
suffered, but rather where manye taketh good heede and would fayn learne? Many
profites commeth by declaryng the woorde of God, which shoulde comfort and
encourage the preacher to be doing, not wythstanding that the audience be
negligent: One is, that noughty persones remembring a sermon wil be abashed and
ashamed of them selfe, and will not be so shamelesse to do as they were wont to
doe. As when the preacher speaketh against riatours, and tauerne hunters, the
vnthrifte remembringe the [D1ᵛ] holy word, will be more ashamed when he goeth
into the tauern then he was wont to be. This is a certeine kinde of feare called
verecundia, bashfulnes or shamefastnes, it is **timor ex expectatione connicij,** a
feare of reproche or rebuke, least anye man would chide or checke him, or say yl by
him. This is a very good affection, therfore, if by our preaching yet at the least wise
such an affection may be striken into the hart of any one of our audience, we may
be glad of it. An other vtilitie & profit is, although by my preaching I make not all
men better, yet some men be the better therefore, and they that be good, be more
modest and vertuous by my sayings. And although I haue not set vp them that be
sycke, yet them that be whole I haue made stronger to stande in theyr goodnes,
and more stedfast. The third profit, although I haue not perswaded men to daye,
yet to morowe I maye peraduenture, and if not to morow, I may the next day after,
or the fourth day, or in tyme to come. Example we maye take of a Fisher and the
fish that longe nibleth at his bayte, yet at the last he is taken and cast on lond.
Likewise a husbandman, if he wold giue of going to ploughe, because he seeth
distemperaunce and troublous weather manye tymes, and looseth hys labour and
cost, we shoulde all dye for hunger. Lykewyse the shypman or the marchaunt, if for
one storme or twayne, or one losse or twayne, he should abhorre and giue of goyng
to the sea, there would at the last no man auenture to the seas, and then farewell
this citye of [D2] Bristowe and all good trade of marchaundyse and occupying by

sea. The husbandman often laboreth and breaketh one peece of grounde, and litle or nothing gayneth, yet at last recouereth in one yeare the losse of many yeres afore. And the Marchaunt man although he hath had losse by shipwracke diuers times, yet he absteineth not to passe and seke out straunge portes, and many times auentreth on hys olde busynes with a Cabao gathered of borowed money, and dothe full well, and commeth to great substaunce and riches.* Then considering that these men bestoweth so great studie and labours about transitorie things that will perish: shall we by and by surcesse and leaue preaching, if we be not hearde as we woulde be. Their condicion and ours is not like: they lose both labours and cost, but we shall be sure to receiue rewarde of God for oure labours, for we haue done that we be bounde to do, we haue layde our Lordes money to vsurye and for increase, as he biddeth vs do.* Moreouer consideryng that the diuel neuer des-payreth our destruction, but euer looketh for it wythout rest, shall we despayre the health & saluation of our brothers? Christ that knew well al thinges that should come after, ceassed not to admonishe and teach Iudas, whom he knew wold neuer be good, then what shal we do toward our brothers which we knowe not whither they will be good or no? of Iudas he spoke: **One of you shall betray me, I speake not of you al, for I know whom I haue chosen: One of you is the dyuell.*** He cast them al in an [D2ᵛ] anguish, lest he should publish and vtter the traitour, and should make him past shame by manyfest and open reprofe. The apostle according to this sayth: **ii. Tim. ii. Goddes seruaunt must be no wrangler, but gentle toward al men, teaching them that resyste the truthe, if peraduenture God wyll giue them penaunce towarde the knowledge of truthe.*** And thus I truste thys doubt is solued, which I nowe moued, and that we must do our dutie, still preaching and teaching, and let God alone with the profit and increase to grow therof. And here for thys tyme I must surceasse, because I haue long protract the time, perceiuing your attentiue eares and diligent audience, not doubting but that you will kepe in remembrance that I haue sayd of the introduction and entring into the whole matter of the seuen giftes of the holy gost, and of two of the same: One called the sprite of sapience, the other the sprite of vnderstanding. Of the other ye shall heare more hereafter by the grace and helpe of the holye gost, who wyth the father and with the sonne lyueth and reygneth one God for euer and euer. Amen.

WOrshipfull audience, when I preached last in this place, I promised to declare
vnto you the seuen gifts of the holy gost, which (as the prophet Esaye saith) rested
on the humanitie of our sauiour Christ most abundantly. And entring that matter,
I spoke of the coeternitie, and of the equall power of the holye goste, with the
father and the sonne. And how the manhood of our sauiour Christ had all graces
after a higher maner than euer had any other creature. And then howe all these
seuen giftes presupposeth faith, hope, and charitie, in him that shall receiue them.
And then I declared what sapience is, and howe manye wayes it is taken. And
then ioyntly of the gifte of intelligence or vnderstanding, and why I shoulde so
vnitely or ioyntlye speake of theym.* Nowe consequentlye I muste speake of the
third gifte of the holye gost called the spirite of counsaile, or the gyft of counsaile,*
which like as all the other giftes were giuen to the manhood of Christ, and by him
to vs, like as the holy gost by him is spred on vs, and from him as from the head, be
all giftes of grace deriued vnto vs as to his limmes or members, as I haue afore
said.* For declaration of this **gift of counsel** ye shal vnderstand that this gift of the
holy gost like as all the seuen gyftes be gyuen to man to help all other vertues that
man hath, whether they be naturall, or gotten by assuefaction, exercise, vse, or
custome, and also to make man more [D3ᵛ] pliant, apt & easy to be styrred &
moued to goodnes by the inspiration or mouing of the holy gost as the children of
God. **Quicumque enim spiritu dei aguntur, hij sunt filij dei. Rom. viii.** * God is
euer redy to moue vs to goodnes, thoughe we of our selfe be full dull to go forward,
**hauing al the studie of our hartes set to yll at all times, rather then to goodnes.
Gene. vi.** * Yet where the lyght of reason ouercommeth sensualitie, some intellectual & morall vertues springeth furth, as it was in the paygnim Philosophers, of
which some were taken for excellent in the vertue of temperaunce, some in
liberalitie or other vertues, whiche yet for all their good qualities and vertues
gotten by their great paynes and labours, lacked the grace that shoulde make them
good men and acceptable in the sight of God, because they lacked faithe, the
foundation and grounde of all sure spirituall and gostly building. To helpe the said
gifts gotten naturally or by assuefaction greatly auaileth this gift of the holy gost
the gift of counsail, which is a supernaturall gift of deliberacion or aduisement
superadded to that natural gift of reason,* of which the philosopher speaketh .vi.
Eth. oportet prudentem esse bene consiliariu<u>m. A prudent man, a well
practised man (saith he) must be far casting & a good counseller.* But this
property of reason called counceling, or forecasting, or worldly policie that the
philosopher speaketh of<.> maye be without this supernaturall gyft of counsail
that we now speake of, for a man may compasse, cast, & contriue alwaies (be they
neuer [D4] so many) to bring his purpose or his frends purpose to passe, and yet
may faile of his intent if he lacke this godly counsail that we now speake of.* And
the waies that he thinketh to make for his purpose, shal make cleane contrary
against him, as it is written: **Psal. ii. Populi meditati sunt inania: Astiterunt reges
terrae & principes conuenerunt in vnum aduersus dominum, et aduersus
Christum eius,** Which to the letter was writ by prophecie of the conspiracie of the
chiefe rulers amonge the Iewes with Herod and Pilate againste our sauiour
Christe.* For they had contryued by theyr counsail how to destroy Christ (as
appeareth by the Euangelistes) as it wer by destroying of him to saue them selues
that they should not lose their place and the people. Ioh. xi. * Lest if the

Romaines should heare of such a man to be in their countrey that had so great a
retinew of disciples as Christ had, they might peraduenture surmise a conspiracie,
& consequently some commocion & rebellion against the Emperours power,
which might be occasion that he should send an army into the countrey & destroy
the countrey, and take them & all the people into captiuitie. This was a far cast &
a far fet counseil,* but it was not the gift of counseil comming of the holy gost, &
therefore it proued not with them but went all against theym, for the feare that
they feared, fortuned to them cleane contrary to their miscontriued counsell. For
in deede the Romains came at length and destroyed the countrey & toke the
p[e]ople into miserable captiuitie, & because none that had to do in thys matter
[D4ᵛ] should scape vnpunished, the vengeaunce began at the great men that were
taken for chief Iudges in the condempnation of Christ. For Herode was depriued of
his kyngdome, by **Caius** the emperour, and was banished perpetually to Lions in
Fraunce, and with him Herodias his incestious concubine, by whose meanes
blessed S. Iohn baptist was beheaded. As **Iosephus antiquitatum. lib. xviii. ca
xiiii.** writeth. And Pilate after he had ruled in Iewrye ten yeares, was dryuen
home to Rome by **Vittellius** general gouernour of Siria, to answer to such iniuries
and tirannye as he had done in the countrey: As **Iosephus** writeth **Antiquitatum.
lib. eodem. cap. vii.** And at Rome (because he was an vniust Iudge against
Christ) he was vexed and put to so much trouble, sorowe, and mischiefe: that
desperatlye he beat hym selfe to death with his owne handes, as **Eusebius** wryteth
in the ecclesiasticall storye, the second boke and .vii. chapter.* And the citie of
Ierusalem, and the people of the Iewes for their iniquitie against Christ, were by
the Emperour **Vespasian** and **Titus** hys sonne subdued and destroyed, euen in the
time of theyr Paschal feast, at which time they had done their malice against
Christe, because the tyme of vengeaunce might answer & agree to the time of the
cause of the same.* At the paschal time they shed the most innocent blood of
Christ, & euen then the vengeance for his bloud fel vpon them & vpon their
children and issue, according to their own desire, saying: **Sanguis eius super
nos<.> & super filios nostros.** [E1] Let the vengea[u]nce for his bloud (sayd they)
lye vpon vs and vpon our children.* And so it did, for euen at the same time of the
yere .xlii. yeres after the Emperoure **Vespasian,** and his sonne **Titus,** after they had
destroyed the chiefe Townes and strongest fortalicies and holdes of the Realme,*
came to besiege that citie, and in the whole tyme of that battaile toke prisoners
.lxxxxvii. thousand. And at the same siege were slaine, and that dyed by famine
and moreyne, commyng chiefely of the stinche of the dead corpses liyng vnburied
to the number of a .xi.C. thousand, as Iosephus writeth in the seuenth boke of the
Iewes battayle, and .xvii. Chapter.* Therfore it foloweth in the psalme rehersed.
Qui habitat in coelis, irridebit eos. Almightye God that dwelleth in heauen wyll
laugh them to scorne,* as he did in dede when he rose from death to life againe,
notwithstandyng yᵗ they thought him sure inough being once dead, & notwithstandyng al the kepers that were set to kepe his body from stealyng.* **Et dominus
subsannabit eos.** Our Lorde will wring the nose at them,* which wordes importeth
a greater indignation & anger then derision dothe, and was put in execution at
thys moste horrible<,> strage, and destruction of that citie, and at the takyng away
of the saide prisoners, whiche they feared, when they said, that if they let Christ
scape their handes, the Romayns would come and take their citie, and carye away
the people.* Here you may see what it is to take counsaile against god. The wise
man saith. **Pro. xxi. Non est sapientia, non est prudentia, non est consilium
[E1ᵛ] contra dominum.** There is no sapience, there is no wittines, there is no

counsayle against our lord God.* Sapience is the cognition and iudgement of diui[n]e and high causes, which is not amonge heretiks that soweth cocle & yl sedes among the corne, settyng forth sectes and diuisions Suche wisdome how well learned soeuer it semeth to be, is not the true sapience, because it is againste our lord God, which is the god of peace and not of dissention. Also be thy capacite neuer so quicke to perceiue and vnderstande the lessons of holye scripture. Yet if thou haue **amarum zelum,** a bitter affection,* trustyng by thy learning to checke & rebuke other men, or to allure other to thy sect, faction, or opinion, as some men haue done, reasoning agaynst Purgatory because they would by that destroye prayers for the dead, and so consequently put downe abbeys, & chauntries whiche were founded for such praiers,* or if thou glory to much in thy learnyng, al this maketh **contra dominum,** against God,* and is not the true vnderstandyng or wittines, that is the gifte of the holye goste. And likewise of the thirde gyfte (of whiche wee nowe entreate) **Donum consilii,** As longe as thy caste leaneth ouer muche to mannes imagination, and setteth not God afore, but rather worketh agaynste God, as ye hearde of these that compassed and counsayled for the deathe of Christe, so to saue theim selues, it is not the counsaile that is the gyfte of the holye Gooste, for it is agaynste our Lorde GOD. It leaneth to muche to worldlinesse, and to mannes [E2] caste, grounded on malyce and euyll will, therefore it coulde not holde. Accordynge the saiynge of Gamaliell that honourable learned manne among the Iewes:* when the chiefe rulers among them laied their heads together, & toke theyr counsayle how to put yᵉ apostles to death for preching the fayth of Christ, Vp stode this **Gamaliell,** and gaue them better counsayle, aduertising them to beware how they ordred these men (meanyng) the apostles of Christe, & not sodainly to precipitate their iudgment against them (for this precipitacion of sentence sodaynelye wythout mature deliberation or aduisement, is the contrary to the gyft of counsayle that we now speake of, that is, the thirde gyfte of the holye gost.) Thys he persuaded by two examples, firste of one **Theudas,*** whyche (after Iosephus) vsynge superstitious craftes, toke vpon hym to be a great Prophet and so deluded the people, that he made manye of theim to sell their goodes, and care for nothynge but to folowe hym. And so brought a greate multitude after hym to the water side of Iordane, to the noumber of foure hundred disciples, where he promised them wythin thre dayes nexte folowynge, to deuide the water, and to go ouer with them drye shodde as Iosue did wyth hys companye. But whyle they were tariynge for thys myracle, came on them the Capitayne of the countrey wyth hys Armye, and strooke of **Theudas** heade, and destroyed and scattered all his secte and retinue. After him came an other, **Iudas Galileus*** which brought [E2ᵛ] vp among the people a pernitious errour, that it was not lawfull for them to pay any tribute to the Emperour, or to any other alien, because thei were the elect people of God, and payed to God first fruites, tithes, and offerynges, with other dueties. This pleased the people wonderouslye well, because it set them at an vnlawfull liberty whiche carnall people moste desireth. And so a great multitude folowed him, whiche sone after were all destroyed wyth hym. To my purpose (saith Gamaliel) it is best ye let these men alone, for if the counsayle and way that they take and folow, come of mannes inuention by any carnall and worldlye cast, it will be broken, it will not hold nor continue, no more then the enterprise of **Theudas,** or of **Iudas Galileus** did. But if it come of God ye can not breake it, it will stande, it will prospere and go forwarde, ye can not let it, except ye will repugne against God, which no mans power is able to do & to preuaile: repugne it may as al sinners doth, but preuaile it can not* Of these thre stories compact in one ye se plainly that where so euer in any counsaile men work on Gods halfe, hauyng Gods pleasure afore their eyes, the counsayle goeth forward.* And contrary, where men haue no respect to god, but rather to worldlines, it is not the counsaile comming of the holy gost, and it will not hold, but shal proue contrarye to the entent of the counsailers<.> as we haue sene by many other examples in our tyme.* And suche miscontriued counsayles be and euer hath bene the confederacies and counsails of he[E3]ritiks, therfore they haue not continued nor holden, but euer haue bene dissolued and broken. Examples of **Arrius** and his confederacy, Pelagius, **Manes** otherwise called **Cubricus** or **Manicheus, Sabellius,** and suche like: And here in our realme of Wicliffe,* whose heresies sore troubled this realme in the time of Kinge Edwarde the thirde,* and worse afterwarde in the tyme of king Henry the fift, when a great multitude of that faction conspired against the king. But because this counsayle came of man and not of god, it would not hold, their counsaile was detecte, the captaynes taken, hanged, and burned.* Likewise nowe in our time, Luther in Saxony hath taken to his counsaile and confederacy, many of our Englishe men beside them that he hath infected within this our realme,* their counsaile and confederacy hath no part of this gift of the holy gost, that I call the spirite of counsayle, because it is grounded on carnalitie, and therfore finally it will be broken, thoughe almighty God for our synnes suffre vs to be flagelled & troubled w^t it, how long no man knoweth but god alone, though we trust in God their time be short, for their errours commeth to lighte euerye daye more and more. And by the diligent and studious labours of our soueraigne & most gracious Prince king Henry the eyght, and his encouragyng of **King Henry** greate clerkes to inuestigate, trye, and searche oute the **the eight set** mere and sure truthes of the scriptures,* they be so manif- **forthe a boke** estlye impugned, that no man can be inuegled or deceiued **against Luther,** with them, but such a one as [E3^v] in the cleare light will **in defence of the** not open his eyes to se the daylight. That the counsaile **popes aucthority.*** and confederacye of all suche heretyks is grounded on carnalitie, it can not be hyd. **Arius** heresy rose by occasion that he could not be promoted to the bishopprick of Alexandria, where he was priest and reader.* **Inimicitia,** Enmitye that he had then against Alexander, whiche was then promoted and made Bisshoppe, and also his owne pride, ambicion, and auarice, these be called **Opera carnis. Gala. v,** They cometh of carnal man.* Likewise Wicliff, because he was disappoynted of the promotion that he would haue had to be heade of a house in Oxforde.* And Luther disdayning at other mens exaltation, auauntage, and profites, and others hath maligned here tofore for like occasions and suscitate and sette furthe their heresies for lyke occasions,* whiche be all carnall, and for carnall libertie la- boureth with al their might, vnder the pretensed colour of euangelicall libertie.* In verye dede the fayth of Christe, and the gospell of Christe geueth vs a libertie, but not that liberty that they claime by it. It setteth vs at libertie, out of the deuils daunger that we were in afore Christes comming. It setteth vs at libertie and not bounde to the ceremonies of Moyses lawe, but to saye that it setteth vs so at libertie y^t wee may do what we will, they sclaunder the gospel of Christe, and falsely be lye it. **Gala. v. Vos in libertatem vocati estis fratres, tantum ne liberta-** **tem in occasionem detis carnis sed per charitatem spiritus seruite inuicem.** Ye be called to a libertye by the [E4] fayth of Christ, but beware that by your libertie ye take no occasion of carnalitie or sensuall luste or pleasure, but one helpe an other by the spirite of charitie.* And saint Peter saythe. **i, Pet. ii. Quasi liberi & non** **quasi velamen habentes malicie libertatem sed quasi serui dei.** I woulde (sayth saynte Peter) ye shoulde order your selues as free men and as menne at libertye, but not to take your libertye as a clooke for malyce or euyll liuynge,* as these that call theim selues euangelicall brothers* doth nowe adayes, whiche counteth them selues by their fayth at libertie to eat when they wyll, and what they wyll, wythout anye delect choise or exception of dayes or tymes, wythout anye exception, choyse, or diuersity puttyng, betwyxt any kindes of meats, fisshe, or flesshe, indifferentlye at all tymes.* Yea, and that is more horrible and shamefull to rehearse it (if they were anye thinge a shame to saye it) that all flesshe is free for all fleshe to eate it, that the pleasure of the bellye desireth or to vse in carnall luste, whether it be syster with the brother, and yet more horrible then so, the parentes with their owne chyldren, and the chyldren wyth the parentes, if bothe partyes be agreed.* A sore stroke of God, that he hath suffered menne to runne so at large, and to fall to such shamefull and beastly blindnes against nature, & all for lacke of this gracious spirite of counsaile that we now speake of. Likewise of purgatory which some men make so ragged & iagged* that a man can not tel what to make of it. [E4ᵛ] Menne can tell well inough by science and good learnynge what to make of it, but by experience no man can tell what it is, but he that hath bene there. But now to declare and to proue Purgatory by scriptures with the expositions of autenticall doctours, thoughe it be very easy, because the matter hath bene so laboured among clerks,* yet I should make to great a digresson digress[i]on from my principall purpose, which is to declare vnto you this thirde gyft of the holy gost, the gift of counsayle, whiche as I saide, is not grounded on carnalitie, nor bringeth any man to carnall liberty. As in very dede this opinion of no Purgatorye dothe. Here I will not contende aboute this vocable Purgatory, I meane the middle or meane place betwixt heauen and hell, in whiche some soules be stayd afore they can come to that most pure and cleane citye, into which nothing can enter excepte it be of the cleanest sorte.* For whiche place if I coulde imagine a more accommodate and conuenient vocable or terme, I woulde be glad to vse it, bicause the scriptures hath not the sayd word Purgatory.* Albeit, I knowe ryght well that in all Scripture wee reade not this worde **Trinitas,*** or thys woorde **Consubstancialis,** yet God forbid that we should denye the blessed Trinitie in the Godhed, the sonne to be consubstanciall and of one substance with the father, or the holye gost to be of one substance with the father and the sonne, **Arrius** that pernicious heretike when he was conuinced and compelled by aucthorities and reasonynge to graunte that all [F1] three persons in trinitie were of one and equall substance, had none other refuge, but to sticke in the vocable or terme **homousion,** that we call in latine **consubstantialis, or vnius substantiae,** and in Englyshe, **of one substance,** because that word is not vsed in scripture, he would none therof, althoughe he could not denye the thinge:* a poore cloke of defence (God knoweth) to graunte the thinge, and to varye in the name. Therfore so that I might agree with this audience, and they with me, that there is suche a staye and a meane place of punishment after this life, I would not care thoughe I neuer called it Purgatorye, but let A. be his name.* To denye the sayde A. and to say yᵗ there is no such thing, bringeth a man to a carnall libertye, and geueth man occasion boldly to continue in sinne to hys liues ende, trusting then to crye God mercye for his misliuynge, and then to go through (as they speake) I trow they meane to go by and by to heauen, as well as he or she that hath liued in vertue & prayers, paine, and penance all the dayes of their liues.* And so shoulde they be in beste case, that be lechers, aduouterers, brybers, and oppressioners and extorcioners, vserers, periurers, dicers, and carders, hunters, and haukers, and all suche of the worst sort: where contrarye the true beleue that he that hath not done condigne and conuenient penaunce here, shall be punished greuously, accordynge to the grauitie of his misliuynge, afore he enter into that most clere and pure city, (though god may of his absolute power forgeue [F1ᵛ] such a longe misliuer for one woorde of repentaunce at his laste ende.) Yet this will make a manne beware of him self, and to amende his liuynge, surely thinkyng (as the truth is) that for his vicious pleasures in whiche he hath delited in his lyfe tyme, and hath not sufficiently satisfied for hys faulte he shall haue afore he come to heauen, suche punishement and payne as the lest parte therof shall greue hym more then all his vnlawefull pleasures haue done hym solace or comforte. Thys counsayle and conformitie of good and faythfull people wythdraweth menne from sinne, where contrarye, **Consilia impiorum frau-dulenta,** the disceiptful counsayles and conuenticles of wycked menne,* rather prouoketh, and geueth menne comforte to continue in sinne. I was once in a soleme audience, where I hearde a famous preacher laboure sore to impugne the sayde meane place, saiynge, that if† there were anye such place at all, it is a place of ease, quietnesse, and rest, alledgyng for his purpose the woordes of the Canon of the Masse, after the seconde memento.* **Qui nos precesserunt cum signo fidei & dormiunt in somno pacis** Where we praye for them that begone afore vs wyth the caracter, printe, and signe of christes fayth, and sleapeth in the sleape of peace.* These menne lyke as they take the wordes of the Masse, and of the seruyce of the churche when they semeth to make for theyr purpose, woulde GOD they coulde be so contente to alowe and admit the same in other tymes and [F2] places. It foloweth there right. **Ipsis domine & omnibus in Christo quiescentibus locum refrigerij lucis & pacis, vt indulgeas deprecamur.** Where we pray our Lord God, fauourably and with cheryshing to giue them a place of cooling and refreshing contrarie to heate, a place of light contrarye to darkenes, a place of peace contrary to trouble and vnquietnes, either by perplexitie and confusion of minde, or by terrible visions or otherwise.* Now if their new purgatory be a place of tranquil-litie, a place of lyght, and a place of rest and peace, it should be but al labour lost for vs so besyly to pray that they may come to suche a place, seyng that they haue it alredy.* Then to theyr allegacion, **Dormiunt in somno pacis,** you must vnder-stand these wordes by a like saying of our sauiour Christ **Ioh. xi.*** After that he had a messager sent to him from Martha and Mary, that Lazar their brother was sore sicke, he taried in the place where he was then beyonde Iordaine, for the space of two dayes, and then sayd to his dysciples **Lazarus amicus noster dormit,** Lazar oure frende sleepeth. I will go into Ieurye where he dwelleth and wake him of his slepe. Then sayde his disciples: **Sir if he sleepe, he will be safe anone,** when he hath slept inough. They were as wyse then, as oure newe purgatorye menne be nowe. They thoughte Christe had spoken of that rest that man and beast must nedes haue after theyr labours, or els shall fayle and dye, whyche wee call com-monlye sleepe.

[F2ᵛ] But Christe meaned of the sleape of deathe. **Dixerat autem Iesus de morte euis,** As he expressed by and by playnely, saiynge: **Lazarus mortuus est,** Lazarus is deade.* And thys is it that holye churche in that place of the masse calleth sleapynge in the sleape of peace, as Christe spoke in like case. And as the Prophete speaketh in hys persone. **Psal. xv. Caro mea requiescet in spe.** My bodye shal rest in hope to ryse againe.* Then consideryng that holy church after the maner of holye scripture, vseth to call death by the name of sleape, wee muste be

† if] it

wise and well ware to what thinges, what wordes may agree, and by reason wherof they do agre, or els by our words we maye deceiue our audience, as well as oure selues. If we thinke that this slepe or death commeth to man by reason of the soule, we erre very sore, for the soule neuer dyeth, but is immortall*, as well by the consent of the paynym Philosophers, as by the auctoritie of holy scripture. **Deus Abraham, deus Isaac, & deus Iacob. Exod. iii. Non est autem deus mortuorum sed viuentium. Mat. xxii*** Abraham slepeth, and Abraham is wakyng, Abraham is dead, and Abraham is aliue. The one parte you wyll graunte for it is true, the other is the saiynge of Christe whiche can not be false. The firste is true by reason of the bodie. The seconde is true, by reason of the soule.

The soule is departed from the body, the body lacketh his life, therfore we saye the manne is deade. The soule is immortall, and cannot dye, therefore by that reason Christe sayde Abraham is a[F3]liue. So now because the bodies be out of pain, we say the men rest or slepe in the slepe of peace. And because the soules be departed in the state of grace, and in the way of saluation which they haue not yet perfitly obtained: we pray that thei may come to the place of refreshing, to the place of light, and to the place of peace euerlasting in heauen.* And thus we must take the woordes of the masse aboue rehersed as they were meaned, and we shall gyue no handfast to the contrarye errour. And I would they should not so rashely precipitate their sentence in such weighty matters, except they had some better ground. Thys **precipitatio** headlong shofyng out mens sentence without iudgement, is contrarie to thys gift of the holy gost, that we now entreate of the gyft of counsaile, as I touched afore. This was the faut of Iepthe **Iud. xi.*** which when he should procede to battell against the Ammonites, he made his vow to God **precipitanter** headlong and rashly, without counsel or aduisement, yᵗ what so euer came first against him to meete him at his dore, after his comming home, he would kill it & offer it vp to be burned in sacrifice to almyghtye God. So it chaunced that when he came home after his victory, his own doughter (which he had and no mo children) met him with timbers and such instrumentes of melodie as she had to welcome him home. When he saw her, he tore his clothes and cryed: alas my doughter, thou hast deceiued me, and art deceiued thy selfe. This precipitation hurt king Dauid, notwithstanding his great [F3ᵛ] wisedome and manyfolde vertues, when he fled from the persecution and commotion that hys own sonne Absolon raysed against him, one **Seba** that was seruant to Miphiboseth (Ionatha[n]s sonne, neuew to Saul the kyng) came to kynge Dauid, and brought him presents of such dainties as myght do hym pleasure, and to hys seruantes in that distres and trouble. As Asses for them to ride on, breade and wine and fruites to refresh them in their iourny, fleyng from the host of Absolon. King Dauid asked him, where is thy master Miphiboseth? He made a lye on hys maister, saying: he tarieth behinde in Ierusalem, trusting now to be restored to yᵉ kingdome of Saul his graundfather. King Dauid by and by rashly without iudgement or further aduisement (the partie neither called nor heard) precipitate thys sentence, **Tua sint omnia que fuerunt Miphiboseth. ii. Reg. xvi.** Take thee al that Miphiboseth had.* And so he gaue awaye to a lying knaue all that good gentlemans goodes, whiche he was sorye for afterward when he knew the truth. He shuld not a neded to haue be sory* if he had auoided this precipitacion by the gift of counsell, whiche the holy gost for then, withdrew from him, he had it not. For such causes saith **Ecclesiasticus: Sine consilio nihil facias, et post factum non penitebis xxxii.** Without counsell and aduisement do nothing, & after thy deede thou shalt not repent or be sorye.* These giftes of the holy ghost be not so coherent or linked together, that who so

euer hath one of them must neades haue all the other. The Pro[F4]phete Esay
sayth, that our sauiour Christe had them all, and so he had superabundantly. **Et de
plenitudine eius [n]os omnes accepimus. Iohn. i.** and of his plentye all we take
our giftes.* Of others we reade not that had them all continually, but we finde that
some that were excellent in sapience, or iudgement in Godly causes and heauenly
matters, and coulde instruct and teach noblely well, lacked the gyft of counsayle to
direct and order hym selfe and others accordyngly, and had nede of other mennes
counsayle. And contrarye he that is excellent in geuyng counsayle maye be weake
in the speculation or iudgement of heauenly or Godly matters. **Exo. xviii.*** It is
writ of Moyses* which had receiued of God the spirite of sapience, by whiche he
was able to geue vnto the people the lawes of God, and to teache them the same,
yet he vsed to sit from mornynge to night hearynge causes, and geuyng sentences
and iudgementes betwixte parties amonge the people, and so fatigated and weried
him self and the people also. **Iethro** his father in law consideryng how that labour
was to great for any one manne to sustaine, and also how the people were
combred, tariynge so longe for decision of their causes, while they might haue
bene soner sped, that so they myght haue departed euery man to his owne, and
haue bene better occupied at home sayde playnelye to hym. **Stulto labore con-
sumeris. &c.** Both thou and thys people spende and waste your selues in a
foolyshe laboure,* for thys busynesse is aboue thy power and myghte, [F4ᵛ] thou
art not able alone to sustaine all this busie labour, but heare my wordes and my
counsayl, and our Lord shalbe with thee. Let this people haue the in suche thynges
as pertayne to God, that thou mayst shew vnto him what they saye, and mayst
shewe vnto the people againe the ceremonies and the rites and maner of worshipping God, and the waye that they shall go, and the workes that they shall doe.
And prouide among al this people men of power and that feareth God, and that
haue truth in them, and that hate auarice or couetousnes, and make of them
officers, some ouer a thousande of thys people, some ouer a hundred, some ouer
fiftie, some ouer ten, which may iudge the people at al times, and what so euer
great matter ryseth among them, let them referre it to thee, and let them iudge the
smaller matters and none other, & so thou shalt be more lightned and eased when
thy burden is deuyded amonge other. If thou doe thys, thou shalt be able to fulfill
Gods empery and authoritie, and shalt be able to sustaine that God byddeth thee
doe, and all thys people shall returne with peace to their houses or lodgynge at
tyme conuenient. When Moyses had heard Iethroes counsail, he did all thinges as
he counseld hym. Nowe to my purpose, because no man shall be proude of the
giftes that God hath gyuen hym, we maye see here that Moyses hauyng so excellently the gift of sapience to iudge and discerne and also to teache and instruct in
Godly causes, yet as then he lacked the gift of counsail, which [G1] this straunger
Iethro an alien, and not of the people of Israell (tho as then he was conuerted to
the faythe of one God) had, as appeareth by the holesome counsaile that he gaue
vnto Moyses, by which as well Moyses selfe, as all his whole host were noblye
releued of almyghtye God, the mouthe of **Iethro** his father in lawe, geuyng hym
that good counsail. Therefore I shall most intierly desire you to pray to God for
this gratious gift of counsail, and according to the same to procede in all your
assembles, consultacions, deuisinges, in al thinges that you shal go about, euer
auoyding precipitacion and rashe settinge on in anye of your doinges, and so you
shall not afterwarde repent your doinges or your sayings through the help of God,
to whom be al honour and glory for euer. Amen.

¶The thirde sermon, treating of the fourth gift
of the holy gost called the spirite of
fortitude.

GOod and worshipfull audience, because it is long sith I preached among you of
the giftes of the holye gost which heretofore I promised to declare vnto you, as
oportunitie would serue. Nowe I trust you remember that in my last sermon that I
preached of that mat[G1ᵛ]ter I spoke chiefely of the gift of **godly counsail**, which
(as I said) is a supernaturall gift of deliberation or aduisement, superadded to the
gyft of prudence or policye, that some men haue naturally or by exercise, or
worldly compasyng or casting, for al these may faile and deceiue men, if this gift of
godly counsail be away, as appeareth plainly by the counsail of the Iewes against
Christ to put him to death, for feare that els the Romaines would come vpon them
and destroy their citie, and driue al the people into captiuity, and so vpon thys
they rested not tyll they had slaine Christ vpon the crosse, and then thoughte
them selues safe inough, til the Romaines came within a season after, and destroyed the chief citie Ierusalem, and toke the people that wer left to most
miserable bondage, as I said in my last sermon of that matter.*

By thys it is moste euydentlye true that the wyseman saythe: **Non est sapientia,
non est prudentia, non est consilium, contra dominum. Prouerb. xxi.** There is
no sapience, there is no wyttines, there is no counsaile agaynste oure Lorde God.*
As longe as thy cast leaneth ouer much to mans imagination, and setteth not god
afore, but rather worketh against God: thys is not the counsail that is the gift of
the holy gost. No more is the counsail or confederacie of heretikes, for they be euer
groun ded on carnall lustes enmitie, malice, or some other carnalitie, and nothing
godly, but inducing men to carnall lybertie, as I declared of diuers heresies, and
specy[G2]allye of the heresye that denieth purgatorye, settyng men at loose libertie, spending theyr lyues in voluptuousnesse, trustyng by one woorde of repentaunce to come to heauen, as soone as they that haue lyued in vertue and
penaunce all dayes of their lyues. Then I declared that to shoofe furthe or shoote
furthe mennes sentence vnaduisedly, which is called precipitacion, is contrarie to
this godlie gift of counsail, and howe that hurted king Dauid the Prophet and
made hym to gyue awaye to a false lying wretche all the goodes of Miphiboseth,
whiche afterwarde he repented and was sor. Then fynallye I tolde you that Moyses
lacked thys gifte of counsaile when he satte all daye longe hearing the causes of the
people, and geuing sentences on the same, wearying him selfe, and the people also,
when **Iethro** by the holye spirite of counsaile (whiche he then had) aduised hym
to constitute and sette vnderofficers to beare part of hys paines and labours. And
then Moyses without anye disdayning, without any obstinacye or sturdynesse,
lowlye and obedientlye dyd thereafter, and constantlye by the spirite of **Fortitude**
broughte that to effecte that **Iethro** hadde counsailed hym. And lyke as thys
counsailler **Iethro** had the spirite of GOD, the spirite of counsaile, so had Moyses
the spirite of **fortitude**, strength or manlynesse, to sette thys order amonge the
people, as hys father in lawe hadde counsailed him.*

It was no small enterprise among so vnruly, [G2ᵛ] wilfull and sturdye a multitude
as that people were, to bring such a newe rule, and to set so ordinate a Ierarchie
among rulers, of which some should be lower, some higher, ordinatelye vntyll they
came to Moyses in arduous matters, and causes of difficultie, and at the last to
almightye God, where the causes emergent were aboue Moyses capacitie: For that

people was so hye harted that they would not easely go to the fote, but they would for euery trifle go to the head,* or els they woulde not be ruled nor pleased. Fortitude is a morall vertue, and fortitude is a gyfte of the holye goste.* That morall vertue maye be where this gift of the holy gost is away. **Fortitudo** (after **Aristotle iii. Eth.) Est virtus secundum quam fortis sustinet timet & audet que oportet, cuius gratia oportet, vt oportet, & quando oportet.** Fortitude is the vertue by whiche a manlye man or a verye man susteineth or suffreth, feareth & auentureth on, or dare do such things as he ought to suffer, feare, or aduenture on, & for that cause, for which he ought so to do, & as he ought, & when he ought to suffer, feare, or auenture.* But the philosopher doth so exactlye trym and pare this vertue, that he pareth almost all away. And yet we Christen Philosophers* muste pare away somewhat more of that he leaueth, and so afore we haue al do[n]e, we shall see that this morall vertue like as all other morall vertues withoute the assistence and grace of the holye goste be as Esaye sayth .lxiiii. **Quasi pannus menstruate omnes iustitiae nostre,*** be filthy and very vile in the sight of God. All ver[G3]tues consisteth in the meane and middle betwixt two vices,* and because the extremities somtime haue no name, we expresse them by circumlocution, sometime by two or three thinges for one, and sometime by negatiues: As here **inpauidus** wythout feare, is one extremitie of this vertue fortitude, such a one is he that nothing feareth, neither earthquakes, fire, nor water, but suche a one semeth rather insensate and mad, then bold. Likewise in boldnes or venturousnes, he that will auenture where is no likelyhoode to scape, is in thys extremitie of fortitude, and is called folishehardye, and semeth to be proude and presumptuous rather then bold, a fainer or counterfaiter of boldnes, rather then truly bold or manly. For comonly such men hath a certein feare of hart inwardly annexed to their boldnes, begynning boldly, and at the last will run awaye with shame. He that excedeth in the other extremitye and contrary part, that is feare is called comonly **timidus**, a cowarde, afrayde of his shadowe, or where is no cause why he should feare. Such be they that in all perils despayreth, their hart fayleth them, cleane contrary to fortitude or manlynes, whyche hathe euer good hope to ouercome, where by the iudgement of reason is any likelyhood to ouerco[m]e. So that generallye fortitude is exercised about feares and boldnes or hardynes, as it were to suppresse and correct feare, and to moderate and measure hardines or boldnes. Certein conclusions the Philosopher putteth in which we Christen men varie from him. One is [G3ᵛ] this: He that desireth rather to dye then to sustaine aduersitie, as pouertie, shame, reproche, or rebuke, is not manly, for such (after him) haue a certain feare in them, and worketh rather of a tendernesse or nashnes of hart, then of fortitude or manlinesse.* Contrary to this we rede of Iudas Machabeus* the valiant captaine, that when Lisias protectour of that huge part of Asia, betwixt the riuer of Euphrates, and the ryuer of Nilus, in the absence of Anthiocus the king* had send by the commaundement of the sayde kyng into the land of Iuda .xl. M. footemen, and .vii. M. horsemen to inuade that land, and to destroy it handsmothe, so that there should remayne no memorie of the Iewes in all that lande. Then this noble captain Iudas Machabeus gathered his people together, and after fasting that daye, with feruent and deuout prayer to God, made a solempne exhortacion to hys people, where he saide to my purpose: **Melius est nos mori in bello quam videre mala gentis nostre et sanctorum .i. Mach. iii.** It is better for vs to dye in battail, then to se the trouble & paines of our nacion & of holy men.* Wher he preferred death temporal to experience of misery & chosed* rather to dye, then to sustaine the calamitie, wretchednes & shame, that they should come to, if their enemies shoulde haue the ouerhand ouer them, & yet the true fortitude & manlines in Iudas Machabeus passed the manlines of al the paignim conquerours that Aristotle could recite. Aristotle saith also: **fortis quanto est virtuosior & felicior, tanto fit in morte tristior.** [G4] A manly man the more that he hath of that vertue, & the more felicitie that he hathe, the more heuy & sorowful he is at his death,* because that by deathe he is depriued & disapointed of ye greatest felicitie, benefit, & goodnes that may com to man, which felicitie (after him) maye be gotten in this world. For though they put an immortalitie of the soule, yet of the state of soules after this present life, they litle determine, but leaue it so ragged, that a man can not tell what to make of it.* But where the Philosopher saith for a conclusion **fortis quanto est. &c.** his faithe was no better, but we by our faith know that the life to come, is much more excellent then this present life, full of misery and wretchednes, euer mutable and vnconstant. Notwythstandyng for the naturall amitie betwixt the soule and the body, they be ful lothe to departe asundre, & naturally feareth such departure, therefore in the ouercomming of this feare, & in the contempt of this life & in ieopardinge on great perils for equitie and iustice sake, & for the faith of Christ, and for the life to come: standeth principally our fortitude, this gift of the holy gost, by which the holy goste moueth our soules, & setteth vs furth to obtain & come to the end of euery good worke that we begin, and maketh vs to escape & passe al perils that maye let our good purpose. And where the paines of death, or the fear of death many times ouerthroweth & turneth the fraile minde of man that man of him selfe can not ouercome the perils of this world, & come to ye reward of his labors, [G4^v] but gyueth ouer hys good purpose, afore it be parfite and perfourmed. Here the holie goste helpeth mans minde, giuyng a certain boldnes and trust to come to rewarde euerlasting in heauen as to the most parfite ende of all good woorkes, and the very escape of all perils. To this end the true fortitude this gift of the holy gost, hath hys principall eye and respect. This excellent gifte of fortitude or manlynesse rested in our Sauiour Christ (as Esay speaketh)* and made him to put away and shake of the passions of our fraile mortalitie, which made him to feare death, and to be pensyfull and heauye, when he sweat water and blood in his agonie,* remembring the death that he should to. But anone he considered hys fathers pleasure, & by fortitude went fourth to mete them that were sent to take hym, and consequentlye suffred his painfull passion on the crosse, as he was determined for to doe. Wherefore God the father exalted him, and gaue him a name aboue all names, and that is had in reuerence of al creatures.* Many we rede of in the olde testament and in the new, that boldlye contempned deathe for iustice sake, whyche had euer their principall respect and eye to reward euerlasting: As Esaye which wyth a sawe was deuided in two partes:* Ieremye the Prophet was stoned to deathe for preaching to the people the word of God.* And **.ii. Mach vii.*** is written a marueilous story of a mother & her .vii. sonnes, in which this gift of the holy gost the gift of fortitude or manlines appereth excellently. When she with her .vii. sonnes were [H1] conuented afore the kinge and the iudges, they were required to eate certaine meates that were prohibited and forbidden by the lawe, and to fal to the rites of gentilitie, which they refused constantlye, and therfore were condemned to dye, & were brought to execution: the eldeste sonne had first his tonge cut out of his heade, then the heere and skinne of his head striped of together, his fingers and toes cutte of, and when he was almost spent, yet he was cast into a great vessell like a friynge panne, and fire put vnder, & there he was broyled and fryed vntill he was deade. His mother & his brothers lokynge on him, and one comfortynge another manfullye to dye in Gods quarell, and for the kepynge of his lawes saiynge: **Deus aspiciet veritatem & consolabitur in nobis.** God will loke vppon the truthe, and will haue comforte among vs.* The second was likewise serued, sauinge that his tonge was not cut out, and at his laste ende saide to the kynge. **Tu quidem scelestissime. &c.** O thou moste mischeuous manne,* thou destroyest vs in this presente life, but the king of all the worlde will raise vs vp againe in the resurrection of life euerlastyng, that dyeth for his lawes. The thirde shewed furth his handes and his tonge, and said I haue the possession and vse of these thinges from heauen aboue, but now I despise them for the lawe of God, because I hope and trust to receiue them of him againe. And euen so all the brothers were arayed, vntil they came to the seuenth. And that marueilous mother comforted them euerye one, [H1ᵛ] saiynge: I can not tell howe you did appeare within my bodye, for I gaue you not spirite and lyfe, and I did not ioyne together the limmes of euerye one of you, but the creatoure and maker of the worlde, that fourmed and fashioned mannes natiuitie, and that founde the originall beginnynge of all thinges, wyll restore vnto you agayne with hys mercy both spirite & lyfe, euen as you now despyse your selues for hys lawes sake. Antiochus the kinge thinkinge him selfe to be dispised and set at nought, counsayled the mother that she shold entreate & geue good counsail to the youngest sonne, and to saue his life if it might be. And she stowped downe to him mockynge Anthiochus the Kinge, and saide: My sonne, haue mercie on me that bare thee nyne monethes within my bodie, and gaue thee milke of my brestes three yeres space, and nurced thee, and brought thee vnto the age that thou arte of, I desire of thee (my sonne) that thou do loke on heauen and earthe, and all thinges that be in them, and do vnderstande that God made them all of nought, and so it maye come to passe that thou shalt not fear this butcherly hangman, but shalte be made worthy to haue such brothers as be gone afore thee. Take thi death and such part as they haue done, that in the time of gods mercy I may receiue thee againe with thy brothers. While she was thus saiyng, the yong man boldly cald vpon the tormentors, saiyng, that he wold not obey the commaundement of the kinge, but he wold obey the commaundement of gods law geuen [H2] them by Moyses. And after a sharpe lesson & commination geuen to the king, the king was inflamed with anger, & was woode against him more then against al the other brothers, & so the good yong man departed, trusting on god in all points, and at the last, the mother after her sons was spent & put to death. Of like fortitude, manlines & boldnes we read in the new testament of .s. Steuen, & saint Iames, & other in the actes of the apostles we read also of saint Peter, s. Andrew, Bartholomew, Laurence, Vincent, & many other whose passions be red in Christes church,* of which al & of others like thapostle, **Heb. xi.** saith. **Alii distenti sunt non suscipientes redemptionem vt meliorem inuenirent resurrectionem, alii ludibria & verbera experti. &c.** Some were racked & drawen in pieces, not loking for any raunsome, that so they might find a better resurrection, some suffred mocks & stripes, & more ouer fetters & prisones, & were stoned to death, some were cutte in pieces.* In al these and such other **timiditie** & cowardnes was far away & this gift of the holye gost, fortitude, manlines & strong hert lacked not, by which thei were so constant in suffryng aduersitie for Christes sake, in hope of reward euerlastyng. Amen.

¶The fourth sermon, treatyng of the fift
gift of the holy gost, called the
spirite of Science.*

THe fifte of these giftes of the holy gost, is the spirite of science, or the gifte of science or cunninge, for whiche you shall vnderstand the science is not so precisely taken here as y^e [H2^v] logitions speaking of science callyng it the knowledge of a co[n]clusion proued by demonstration,* but science as we nowe speake of it, descendeth and commeth alowe, and is properlye the iudgement in the articles of our faythe,* and in such other Godly verities as extendeth them selues to creatures and to mannes actes and doinges accordynge to saint Paules saiyng: **Faith worketh by loue,*** And so doth all the whole holy scripture more consistyng in practise and exercise then in speculation. This gift of science or cunnyng as we nowe speake of it, extendeth also to hande craftes, and occupations* as I shall declare hereafter. And it presupposeth the gift of counsaile (that I spoke of lately) by whiche we may with studie, deliberacion, and aduisement, attayne to the knowledge of mans actes, and to the knowledge of creatures.* But because that many times mennes wittes in their study and in their singuler or priuate counsailes, be ready to inuent or imagine of mennes actes, and of other creatures laiynge a parte the gifte of counsaile and good iudgement, so commeth many times to mannes minde, deception, errour, lolardye, & heresie, contrary to true science and cunnyng, gelosie, suspicion, sclaunder, and infamye, contrarye to quietnesse of liuinge. Example we haue of the people of Israell, whiche hadde inbibed so muche of Moyses lawe, and wedded their wittes so obstinately to that learnyng, and leaned so carnally to the same, that notwithstandyng all Christes doctrine, and all the preachinge of the Apostles, they [H3] thought no way to saluation, but by obseruynge and fulfillyng the workes of the lawe of Moyses, as except men were circumcised, they thought menne coulde not be saued.* And after a manne had touched anye deade thinge or anye vncleane thinge, excepte he should sequester him selfe .vii. dayes from the company of cleane people, and except he were washed the thirde daye and the .vii. daye with a certayne water made for the same purpose, he should dye,* with many such ceremonies and vsages which were then commaunded to be vsed, and were no more but shadowes and figures of our sauioure Christe, and of the time of grace that nowe is, and they shoulde nowe cease when the veritye signifyed by theim is exhibited and perfourmed,* like as nighte ceaseth when the day commeth, and darkenesse vanisheth awaye by the presence of lighte. Thys they woulde not vnderstande nor learne for any mannes exhortacion, but rather persecuted to death all them that instructed them in this veritie. In this case was sainte Paule, firste before his conuersion, and many of his contrey menne and kinsfolkes the Iewes, of whiche he saith. **Testimonium perhibeo illis quod emulationem dei habent sed non secundum scientiam. Roma. x.** I beare them witnes that they haue a zeale and loue to folowe the learnyng that God hath geuen them by Moyses, but they lacke science a[n]d cunnyng, they folow not good vnderstandynge,* in that in whiche they thinke them selues cunnyng, for the saide ceremonies were no more but **Iustitiae car[H3^v]nis vsque ad tempus correctionis imposite.** Certaine obseruances laide on their neckes, carnallye to be obserued and kept, to occupy them and holde them vnder obedience, and to keepe theim from the rites and vsages that the gentyles vsed in theyr ydolatrye, tyll the tyme of correction, the tyme of reformacion* (whiche is the tyme of Christes commyng) at whiche time they should surceasse and be vsed no more. Such a zeale and loue to learnynge hathe manye nowe adayes: And of their learnynge and knoweledge (whiche they thinke they haue) they wyll make as great glory and boast as did the Iewes of their learning. And yet their zeale and learnynge shall be without that science that is this gift of the holy gost.* In this case be they that so arrogantly glorieth in their learnyng had by study in the englysh bible,* and in these sedicious Englisshe bokes that haue bene sent ouer from our englyssh runagates nowe abidynge wyth Luther in Saxonie.* Of their studie you maie iudge by the effect. When menne and women haue all studied, and counte them selues best learned,* of their learnyng men perceiue litle els but enuie, & disdainyng at others, mockynge and despisynge all goodnes, raylynge at fastynge and at abstinence from certaine meats one daie afore an other, by custome or commaundemente of the churche, at Masse and mattens,* and at all blessed ceremonies of Christes church ordeyned and vsed for the auancemente and set[H4]tinge forthe of Goddes glorye not without profounde and great misteries and causes reasonable.* By this effecte you maye iudge of the cause, the effecte is nought, therfore there must neades be some faulte in the cause. But what saiest thou? Is not the studye of Scripture good? Is not the knowledge of the Gospels and of the newe Testamente, godlye, good, and profitable for a christian manne or woman? I shall tell you what I thinke in this matter, I haue euer bene of this minde, that I haue thought it no harme, but rather good and profitable that holie Scripture shoulde be hadde in the mother tong, and with holden from no manne that were apte and mete to take it in hande, specially if we coulde get it well and truely translated, whyche wyll be verye harde to be hadde.* But who be meete and able to take it in hande, there is the doubte.* I shall declare this doubte by an other like. The Philosopher .i. Ethi. Declareth who be mete and conuenient hearers of the science of morall philosophie. And there he excludeth from the studie of that learnyng all yonge menne and women, whether they be yonge in age, or yonge in maners and condicions, they that be yonge in yeares, be no conueniente hearers of Morall philosophye, because they lacke experience of thinges that be taughte in that facultye, which be Actes of vertue, and vertuousse lyuynge, principallye intended in Morall Philosophye,* [H4ᵛ] of such maner of liuynge, youth hath no experience, or very little, and therfore they can not discerne theim from their contraries when they heare them spoken of, neither discerne the meanes whiche be vertues from the extremities that be vyces,* no more then a blinde man can iudge colours from their contraries, or can perceiue yᵗ how muche the nigher that any meane colour draweth to white, so muche the more it scattereth and disperseth the sight, and hurteth it, or on the contrarie parte, howe muche the nyer in degrees it approcheth to the blacke coloure, so muche the more it gathereth the syghte closse together and helpeth the sight, and comforteth it. To tel thys tale to a blinde manne is all laboure loste, for he can not tell what you meane (after Aristotle) because a childe knoweth not the actes of vertue, of whiche Morall philosophye treateth (for the ende of that philosophye is well doynge, and good liuynge.[)]* Therfore to teache a childe the rules of that facultie, is a vaine laboure. And also beca[u]se youth is much geuen to folowe their affections and their lustes, they be no kindly scholers of morall philosophye, for the vehement inclinations that they haue to do their luste, maketh them that morall lessons, teachynge the exercise of vertue canne not printe in them.* And for the same cause they that be yong in maners though they be olde in yeres (as the counsaylers of Roboam Salomons sonne were)* And such as be a great meyny of our lustye yonkers now adayes olde inoughe to be wise, and yet as lewde they [I1] be as they were at twelue yeare olde, and muche worse. They be so headstrong, and so obstinately set to satisfie their concupiscence, and to take their pleasure, that they will not learne any lessons for the contrarye. And so they can not attaine to the ende of morall philosophie which is vertuous workes. Women also a frayle kinde, verye obedient to their fansies, and to earnestly and eagerly folowynge their lustes, be verye vnmete scholers of morall philosophye. Nowe to my purpose, the ende of Diuinitie is good doinge as appeareth plainelye by Moyses and the Prophetes in the olde Testament, by our sauiour Christe in the Gospels, and by the Apostles in their Epistles in manye places. And therfore diuinitie is not called a speculatiue science, but a science of practise or doinge.* Then as the Philosopher reasoneth of the hearers of philosophye I maie saie likewise, that children whether they be children in yeres, or children in condicions & vicious maners for their wilful pronitie & headines to satisfie their lustes & pleasures, whether they be menne or women, can not perceiue the differences, and diuersitie of such good works as be taught in diuinitye nother ye things that be spoken of in diuinitie, their passions doth so sequester and alienate their wittes from consideracion of them, that they shall be little or nothing the better for hearing of theim, if they come where they maye heare of them, as at sermons, lessons, and exhortacions, to which they come verie seldome, they loue nothinge worse, and thinke no tyme [I1^v] worse spent then ye time while thei be hearing the word of god, ful like them that our sauiour Christ speaketh of **Mat. xiii.** reciting ye propheci of Esai: **Auribus grauiter audierunt,** It greued them to heare the woorde of God, **et oculos suos clauserunt,** they shut fast their eyes. **Nequando oculis videant.** Lest they might se with their eyes ye works of Christ, & the right way to heauen. And least they should heare with their eares, & with good will vnderstand the liueli word of god that might saue their soules, & might be conuerted from their misliuing that so I might heale them* (saith Christe) from the sores of their soules that be their synnes. For in al such maner of sayinges you muste vnderstand y^t the impossibilitie, yea rather the difficulty to do wel, is of our self onely, & not of god. Therfore s. Austine saith they could not beleue, by which it is to be vnderstand that they wolde not beleue:* they wold not molifie their hartes to receiue holy instruction. How maye a man teache them whether charitie or loue be ye vertue or work of the body or the soule, or of both, or whether it be the worke of reason or of the wil. Likewise of fruition in whiche shall stand our beatitude & glory in heauen, whether it be the operation of the wit, or of the wil or of both. And also of Angels what maner thinges they be, & howe God speaketh to them, & one of them to another, thoughe thei haue no tonges. And how thei mai moue from place to place, considering that they fill no place, for thei be no bodies.* A hundred such things must be considered in the scriptures, whiche it is but [I2] vain labour to teach children, neither to them that be childish, & leud in condicions. I meane them that of election & of very purpose doth nought, & hath a pleasure in noughtye liuyng, in which neyther such high consideracions as I now touched, neither any moral rules or lessons of good liuing can print, or haue place, they be so blinded by yll custome, & roted in the contrarie vices, & in vicious liuing. Neither to the most part of women being very sensual parsons and much addict & giuen to folow their lusts & affections which here among you in this town not onely studieth ye scriptures but also teacheth it, and disputeth it.* S. Paule **i. Corinth. xiiii.** woulde that a woman if she wold learne anye thing for her soule health, she should aske of her husbande at home,* that he may teach her if he be so well learned, or that he maye aske of them that be learned, and so teache his

wyfe, least peraduenture if women shoulde haue resorte vnto learned men, to
reason matters, or to aske questions for their learnynge, by ouermuche familyarity
some further inconuenience might mischaunce to bothe parties. She muste not
playe the reader, she must not kepe the scooles, but rather **Mulier in silencio
discat cum omni subiectione: docere autem mulieri non permitto i. Tim. ii.** Let a
woman learne in silence without many words, & without clattering, with al
obedience & subiection. For I will not suffer a woman to be a teacher,* least
peraduenture taking vpon her to be a maistres she may wexe proude and malaperte. She must consider her creation, that a woman [I2ᵛ] was last made, and first
in faulte and in sinne. Wherfore it besemeth women to knowe their condicion &
to be subiect, and not to refourme and teache menne. Once she taught and marred
all, therfore Paule woulde haue her teache no more. But here you must vnderstand
as wel for the philosophers minde of the hearers of moral philosophy, as for .s.
Pauls minde of the students in holy scriptures, that although nether children in
age, neither in condicions, all geuen to take their pleasures, and to folowe their
lustes, be appropriate and most conuenient hearers of philosophye, because they
lacke experience of vertuous workes and by childishe plaiyng the boyes, and
plaiynge the wantons be customed in lewdenes, yet thys notwithstandyng if they
be vnder awe and feare of their parentes or of maisters, or of officers, they maye
take profite by hearynge Philosophy, in as much as if they be straightly holde to
such learning, they may be disposed to vertue and restraint from vice by the
same.* And muche like it is of the studie of scriptures, if such voluptuous persons
be compelled to haunt sermons, lessons, and exhortations, by suche meanes the
folishnes and ignorance that is knitte in the hearte of the wanton and childishe
persone maye be driuen away by the rodde of discipline. And I reade of many
blessed women that haue bene vertuously brought vp in youth, and well exercised
in holye scriptures, as they that saint Hierome wrote to,* and many others whiche
we worshyp for blessed saintes in heauen, to whiche God gaue grace to [I3] subdue
their affections and lustes, and by that they were the more mete to receiue the gifte
of science and cunnyng by the scriptures. But I rede not that they were readers,
preachers, or disputers of scriptures. Manye wise questions they vsed to aske and
were without countresaiyng satisfied with such answers as were giuen them by
them that were learned. I doubt not but they vsed to teache their maydes at home
such lessons as might make them chaste and deuout. For women may be exercised
in teaching after that maner, as appeareth by Saint Paul **Tit. ii.** saying that aged
women among other vertues, must be, **bene docentes, vt ad castitatem erudiant
adolescentulas,** well teaching, that they may enforme their yonge women to
chastitie, and to loue their husbands, and to loue their children, to be cleane in
countenaunce, in woordes, and in bodie, to be good huswiues **benignas et subditas
viris suis,** boner & boughsome* to their husbands.* So farre blessed Saint Paule
giueth women libertie to teache, but not to teache men. All beit saint Ierome in
the preamble of his exposition of the psalme: **Eructauit cor meum verbum bonum**
noteth that **Ruth, Iudith,** and **Hester** haue bookes intyteled to their names, and
that they taught men wit,* and so did the wyse woman of **Techua** conclude king
Dauid with her wyse questions that she asked hym, and taughte him by the subtyle
riddles that she proposed to hym, and mitigate hys anger wyth the pretye example
that shee brought in .ii. **Reg. xiiii.*** but in dede muche of her [I3ᵛ] wysedome in
her so doing, came of the wytte of Ioab that sent her to the kynge to intreate for
Absalon that he myghte be restored agayne into hys countrey. The blessed manne
Aquila and hys wyfe **Pryscilla** when they hadde hearde Apollo preache Christe,

they called him asyde and better taughte hym in the faythe of Christe in some
pointes then he was taught afore **Act. xviii*** But here the scripture expresseth not
whether the man Aquila, or the wyfe Priscilla taughte Apollo. And it maye well be
that they bothe instructed hym. For the holye spirite of God breatheth and
inspireth his giftes where it pleaseth hym, and by theym that it pleaseth hym,
whether it be men or women. Therefore it maye so be that it pleased GOD to
illuminate the soules of women, and by theym for the tyme to teache menne.
Sometyme for the reproch and confusion of menne to make theym ashamed of
their dulnesse and sleweth. As it is wrytten **Iudicum .iiii.** that Delbora the Prophe-
tesse iudged the people of Israell, and aduaunced theym to warre agaynst Sisara
captayne of the warres of Iabin kyng of Canaan, in so muche that Barach a noble
manne amonge the people durst not go to the battayle agaynste Sisara except thys
good woman Delbora woulde go wyth hym.* And sometyme women haue
i[n]structed men for other secrete causes, such as GOD onelye knoweth.

But thys is not to be taken for an argu[I4]ment because it is rare and syldome,
but of a common course it becommeth women to be subiecte and to learne in
sylence, and if they will teache, then to doe it wyth modestye and secretlye, and
not openlye to dyspute and teache men, and that is Saynte Paules mynde as I sayde
afore. Scripture is in worsse case then anye other facultye, for where other faculties
take vppon theym no more then pertayneth to theyr owne science, as the Phisicion treateth of thynges partaynynge to the healthe of mans bodye, and the
Carpenter or the Smith medleth with theyr owne tooles and woorkemanshyppe.
**Sola scripturarum ars est quam sibi omnes passim vendicant, hanc garrula anus,
hanc delirus senex, hanc sophista verbosus, hanc vniuersi presumunt lacerant
docent antequam discant,** as Saynte Hierome saythe in hys epistle **ad Paulinum.**

The facultie of Scripture onely, is the knowledge that all menne and women
chalengeth and claymeth to them selfe and for theyr owne, here and there, the
chatterynge olde wyfe, the dotynge olde manne, the bablynge Sophister, and all
other presumeth vppon thys facultye, and teareth it, and teacheth it afore they
learn it.* Of all suche greene Diuines as I haue spoken of it appeareth full wel what
learnynge they haue, by thys, that when they teache anye of their Disciples, and
when they gyue anye of theyr bookes to other menne to reade the fyrste suggestion
why he shoulde laboure suche bookes, is [I4ᵛ] because by this (say they) thou shalt
be able to oppose the best priest in the parish, and to tel him he lieth.* Lo the
charitie. Suppose thou haue science or cunnyng by thy studie in scriptures, yet
thou hast not this gift of the holy gost, of whych we nowe speake, for it is not
without charitie: **Scientia inflat, charitas edificat,** Such science maketh a man
proude, but charitie edifieth & dothe good. If a man thinke he knoweth any thing
by suche science wythout charitie, he knoweth not yet how he ought to know it **.i.
Corin. viii.*** he considereth not that he oughte to vse hys scyence with humilitie,
and wyth charitie towarde hys neyghboure, and that is the science that God
aloweth. For lacke of this charitie, vayne is thy studie, thy science vanisheth away
to vainglory, which agreeth not with the holy gost. And when the holy gost is
absent, then beware of studye in scripture specially aboue all faculties, for without
his special assistence, thou shalt not scape heresie, rather defoulinge the scriptures
with thy expositions and yl applicacion like Swine treading pearels vnder their
feete,* and readye to inuade, and all to teare them that haue the true knowledge
and vnderstanding of scriptures. Of such speaketh the prophet. **Psa. liiii. Con-
taminauerunt testamentum eius.*** Where he speaketh of them that without
charitie treateth the scriptures, & haue defouled them, leauing the vnitie of

charitie, and taking euery one away by them selfe in their owne confederacie, refusing the vnitie and concord of good and faithfull people. But what [K1] hath come of them? It foloweth diuisi sunt ab ira vultus eius: They haue been deuided by the anger of Gods face.* What better marke can wee haue to marke heretikes? Arrius was deuided with his confederacie, Pelagius with his faction, Nouatus, Manicheus, wycliffe* & such other which haue been deuided from the congrega- cion of good and faithfull people by excommunication here in this world, and it is to be feared least they be excommunicate from the celestiall congregacion, & be perished* for euermore, excepte peraduenture some of them did penaunce at the last caste, but whether ouer late penaunce be sufficiente, it is doubt. What profit came by the diuision and seperacion of such heretikes? It foloweth there appropin- quauit cor illius, the harte and mynde of him that deuided them by his anger, came nigher to mens knowledge by the scriptures.* For many thinges were hid and vnknowen in the scriptures, but when heretikes that vexed the church and troubled it with their questions, were prescised and cut awaye, then the harte and will of God in the scriptures, was vnderstand & knowen. For there was nothing so parfitely knowen nor so commonly knowen of the blessed trinitie and of the diuine productions, afore that Arrius* barked and rayled againste it, as was knowen afterwarde. The sacrament of penaunce had neuer be so well knowen as it is, if Nouatus* that heretike had not taughte his faction to despise the seconde table or raffe* after shypwracke, that is penaunce, the seconde helpe and remedye to [K1ᵛ] saue men soules. Baptisme is the first that riddeth a ma[n] from originall synne and from actuall synne if any be afore committed: After which baptisme if a man fall to synne agayne, penance is the second remedy. Nouatus would none therof, but that if a man synned after he was baptised, he was remediles and could not be saued.* He gloried to much in his owne sinceritie and clerenes of his lyuing. And so of the syngle lyuyng of priestes, of the inuocation of Saintes, & of theyr prayers for vs, of purgatorie, of ceremonies of the church, of images, which you without science call idols.* In all Christendome were scarce so many that could exactly & profoundly and so redely declare and reason the truthe of these matters and defend theym from barkers and from gnawers & raylers afore this wicked new learning rysse in Saxony, and came ouer into England among vs, as you shall finde now in one vniuersitie, or in one or two good towns:* So that generally by the excluding and putting awaye of errours & heresies the will of God commeth nigher and is better knowen, declared vnto vs by the scriptures wel labored and truly vnderstanded.* It foloweth in the psalme Molliti sunt sermones eius super oleum, et ipsi sunt iacula. The wordes of God in scripture which afore were hard, by the exercise and labour of catholike clerkes be made very soft, yea more softe, easye, and soople then oile, and be made harnes and dartes, or weapons for the preachers.* Of the hardnes of scriptures (in which our new diuines finde no hardnesse) [K2] riseth al heresies.* And so they did euen at the beginning in Christes time. When Christ said Io. vi Nisi manducaueritis carnem filij hominis et biberitis eius sanguinem, non habebitis vitam in vobis: Except you eate the fleshe of the sonne of man, and drink his bloud, ye shal haue no life in you.* Many of his disciples hearing these woordes sayde: This is a hard saying, & who can abide to heare him say thus?* And after that time many of his disciples gaue backe, and walked not with him, they kept him no company: then said our sauiour Christ vnto the .xii. yᵗ he had chosen apostles: wil you begone also? Peter aunswered: good mayster to whom shall we go? Thou hast the wordes of euerlasting life.* I pray you take hede, and learne here of S. Peter meekely to rede and take the woordes of GOD in his scriptures. Dyd Peter vnderstande Christes woordes, for whyche a greate manye of hys scholers gaue backe, and companyed not wyth Christ? Naye verelye, no more then other dyd.* But yet he woulde not shake of hys mayster for the obscurenesse of hys woordes, neyther despysed hys woorde thoughe it were obscure and darke, neyther tooke vppon hym arrogantlye to deuine and arede what was hys maysters mynde and meanynge by his woorde that was so darke, as manye of our yonge diuines nowe adayes wyll not stycke to doe, and rather to saye boldlye, and to confirme it wyth an horrible othe, I am sure thys is hys meanynge, and thus it muste be vnderstanded, when they be farre wyde.

[K2ᵛ] So did not Peter but taried his time, and so by sufferance and good abiding at the maundye afore the passion, when Christ by consecracion conuerted bread and wine into his precious body & bloud, then he perceiued what Christ meaned by his saying afore rehersed: **Nisi manducaueritis.** &c except you eate the flesh of a man, and drink his bloud, you shall haue no life in you. &c.* and so did other of the apostles there present then first vnderstand the word. And euen then Christe spoke certayne woordes that might haue giuen them light to vnderstand him, saying: **Si ergo videritis filium hominis ascendentem vbi erat prius**: If you shall se the sonne of man ascend to heauen wher he was afore,* as who should say, when you shall see him ascend with a whole body, then you shal perceiue that this carnall and grosse vnderstandinge that maketh you nowe to murmure and grudge, profiteth nothing at all. At that blessed supper the apostles knew that Christ should ascend whole, and that they shoulde not teare the body as they there saw it with their kniues, nor gnaw it with their teethe, that the bloud should run about their teethe, neither eate it rosted nor sod, as men eate the meate that they bye in the shambles, but that they should eat it in an other facion then they saw it then, that they should eate his body and drinke his bloude in a maner that shoulde not lothe nor abhorre theyr stomakes, vnder the fourme and facion of bread and wyne that they were daylye vsed to.* This S. Peter knewe not at the first, and yet he spoke to Christ [K3] full reuerentlye and louingly, as it were, saying: aske not whether wee will be gone and forsake you, though your wordes be so obscure that wee can not perceiue them. For this we knowe that **verba vitae eterne habes,** thou hast the woordes of life euerlasting.* As yet he dyd not vnderstande Christes woordes, but full louinglye he beleued that the wordes that he vnderstoode not, were verye good. Woulde GOD you woulde when you rede yᵉ scriptures, vse such a modesty & suche charity, that if the sentence be hard and strange, then not to determine your self to an vnderstanding after your owne fancie, but abyde a tyme with longanimitie and easy sufferaunce. **Et iacta super dominum curam tuam, & ipse te enutriet.** Referre thy mynde to Gods pleasure, caste thy care vpon GOD, and he will nourishe thee,* he will send thee light, prouiding for the some man that is wel learned & substancially exercitate in the scriptures to teache thee, specially if it be necessarye for thy soule health to knowe it. If it be not necessarye for thy soule healthe, but such as thou mayest be safe inough whether thou know it or not, and mayest come to heauen wythoute the knowledge thereof (as a thousande places in scripture be suche) then lette it passe, and say with Saynte Peter: **Domine verba vitae eterne habes.** 0 Lorde GOD thou hast the wordes of euerlasting life.* The woordes be good, because they be the woordes of GOD, although I doe not vnderstande them. Thus orderynge your selues in the studye of holye scriptu[r]e, you do like [K3ᵛ] good men, and lyke gods seruauntes, and God wyll be good Lorde vnto you. **Et non dabit in[ ]eternum fluctuationem iusto.** And wyll not suffer you finallye for euer to fleete and wauer inconstantlye,* runnyng from

one opinion to an other, from one illusion to an other, thou shalt stay thy selfe by
the ancour of faythe, and that shall keepe thee from the rocks, that be perelous
heretikes. For if thou fleete and wauer tyll thou fal on one of them, thou shalt haue
suche a crash of false doctrine and leude vnderstandyng that thou shalt not auoyde
shypwracke, thou shalte not come to the porte of safe knowledge, ne to the port of
ease, quietnes, and caulmenes euerlasting in heauen, if thou be made by suche false
doctrine to erre in the essentiall and necessarye pointes of thy belefe.

Therefore in your learnynge see that you vse charitie with humilitie and lowly-
nesse of hart, and then you shall shewe your selfe that your learnynge is the true
science gyuen of the holye goste, of whyche we now entreate. And by the same gift
you shall as well know what you shal beleue, as to iudge and dyscerne the thynges
that you shall beleue, from the thinges that you shall not beleue. And also you may
ascende to so hyghe knowledge, that you shall be able to declare the articles of
your faythe, and to induce and perswade other men to beleue, and also to conuince and ouercome countersayers, and such as woulde impugne the faith. Althoughe it be not gyuen to all menne to ascende vnto so hyghe [K4] a degree<e>
of science. And because I spoke euen nowe of Images and Idolles, I woulde you
shoulde not ignorauntlye confounde and abuse those termes, takynge an Image for
an Idolle, and an Idolle for an Image, as I haue hearde manye doe in thys citye, as
well of the fathers and mothers (that shoulde be wyse) as of theyr babies and
chyldren that haue learned foolyshnesse of theyr parentes.* Nowe at the dissolucion of Monasteries and of Freers houses many Images haue bene caryed abrod,
and gyuen to children to playe wyth all.* And when the chyldren haue theym in
theyr handes, dauncynge theim after their childyshe maner, commeth the father or
the mother and saythe: What nasse,* what haste thou there? the childe aun-
sweareth (as she is taught) I haue here myne ydoll,* the father laugheth and
maketh a gaye game at it. So saithe the mother to an other, Iugge, or Thommye,
where haddest thou that pretye Idoll? Iohn our parishe clarke gaue it me, saythe
the childe, and for that the clarke muste haue thankes, and shall lacke no good
chere. But if thys follye were onelye in the insolent youthe, and in the fonde
vnlearned fathers and mothers, it myght soone be redressed. But youre preachers
that you so obstinatelye folow, more leaninge to the vulgar noyse and common
erroure of the people, then to profounde learnyng they bable in the pulpittes that
they heare the people reioyce in.

[K4v] And so of the people they learne their sermons, and by their sermons they
indurate their audyence and make the people stubbourne and harde to be perswaded to science, contrarye to theyr blinde ignoraunce, as well in this point of
Images and Idolles, as in manye other like. They would haue that this latine worde
Imago signifieth an Idole, and so these new translations of the english bibles hath
it in all places, where the translatours would bring men to beleue that to set vp
Images, or to haue Images is idolatrye. And therefore where the scriptures abhorreth idols, they make it Images, as though to haue imagerie, were idolatrie, that
God so greatly abhorreth.* But you must vnderstande and knowe that an Image is
a thinge kerued, or painted, or cast in a moulde, that representeth and signyfyeth a
thing that is in dede, or that hath be or shal be in dede. And so speaketh our
Sauiour Christ of an Image, when the Pharisies send their disciples wyth Herodes
seruauntes, to aske hym thys question: whether it were lawfull for the Iewes to
paye tribute to the Emperour or not? He called them Hipocrites, and bad them
shewe him the coyne or money that was vsually payde for the tribute. They
brought him a denere, wee call it a peny. He asked them: **Cuius est Imago hec, et**

superscriptio Mat. xxii. Whose is this Image & the scripture about? They answered: the emporours.* Note here (good frendes) that Christ asked not **cuius est idolum hoc**? Whose is this idole? for he knewe it was none, but that it was an [L1] image, as is the Image of our soueraigne Lord the king vpon his money coyned in London, in Bristow, or in other places, whiche no man that hath witte woulde call an Idole. For Saynte Paule sayth **.i. Cor. viii. Scimus quia nihil est Idolum in mundo, & quod nullus est deus nisi vnus.** We knowe that an ydole is nothinge in the worlde, and that there is no God but one.* Where the blessed Apostle referreth muche vnto science in this matter of ydoles, and of meat offered vnto them, and spoke to them that were learned, and shoulde haue conning to discerne in this mater: sayinge in the beginninge of that .viii. Chapiter. **Scimus quoniam omnes scientiam habemus.** We knowe, for all we haue science and conninge to iudge of these meates that be offered to Idoles, what know we? **Scimus quia nihil est Idolum in mundo & quod nullus est deus nisi vnus.*** We haue this science, and this we know, that an Idole is nothinge in the worlde, and that there is no God but one. An ymage is a similitude of a naturall thinge, that hath be, is, or may be.* An ydole is a similitude representing a thing that neuer was nor maye be.* Therefore the ymage of the crucifixe is no ydole, for it representeth and signifieth Christ crucified, as he was in dede.* And the Image of Saint Paule with the sworde in his hande, as the signe of his martirdome is no Idole, for the thinge signified by it, was a thinge in dede, for he was beheaded with a sworde in dede:* but an Idole is an ymage that signifieth a monster that is not possible to be, as to sig[L1ᵛ]nifie a false God whiche is no God in dede. For as S. Paule sayde, **There is no God but one:*** As the Image of Iupiter set vp to signifie the god Iupiter, is a false signifier, & signifieth a thinge of nothinge, for there is no God Iupiter. And the Image of **Venus** to signifye the goddes **Venus** is nothinge, for that is signified by it, is nothynge, for there is no she goddes **Venus:*** As in a lyke speakynge we say **Chimera** is nothing, because the voyce is sometyme putte to signifie a monster, hauinge a head lyke a Lion, with fyre flamynge out of his mouth, and the bodye of a goate, and the hynder parte lyke a serpente or a dragon,* there is no suche thynge, althoughe the poetes faine suche a monster, therefore the voice **Chimera** is a false signifier, and that is false is nothinge, therefore we say **Chimera** is nothinge, but **Chimera** signifiynge a certayne mountayne in the countrey of **Licia**, flaminge fyre out of the toppe of it, bredynge and hauyng Lions nyghe about the hier part or toppe of the same hyl, and downewarde aboute the mydle parte, hauynge pastures where breadeth goates or suche other beastes, and at the fote of it marshes or moyste grounde breadyng serpentes:* such an hyl there is in the sayde countrey, and of the diuers disposition of the partes of the sayd hyll, the fiction of the forsayd monster is ymagened, whiche is nothynge, and therefore so we say that **Chimera** is nothing; but the same vocable put to signify the hyl in **Licia** aforesayd is somwhat, and a true signifier, for it signifieth a thinge that is in dede, [L2] as appeareth by **Pomponius Mela. lib. i.** and **Soline Cap. lii.** with their expositours,* and euen so it is true that Paule sayth that an Idole is nothing,* for there is none suche thinge as is signified by it, there is no God **Saturne,** there is no God **Iupiter,** there is no Goddes **Venus,** but I saye more, that yf a man coulde carue or paynte an Image of **Iupiters** soule burnynge in the fyre of hell, or lykewise an Image of **Venus** soule there burnynge. If Saynte Paule had sene suche a pycture or ymage, he woulde neuer haue called it an ydole, or a thynge of nothinge, for it shoulde signifie a thing that is in dede, for **Iupiters** soule is in hel in dede, and so is **Venus** soule, and other lyke taken for Goddes made of mortall men. After this maner good frendes, you must by science and connyng, learnedly speake of Images and Idoles, and not to counfounde the wordes, or the thinges signified by them, takyng one for an other. And by this you maye perceaue, that when you wyll arrogantly of a proude hearte medle of maters aboue your capacitie, the holy goste withdraweth his gyfte of science frome you, and that maketh you to speake you can not tell what, for the holy goste will not inspyre his gyftes but vpon them that be humble and lowlye in hearte. And because I sayde heretofore, that this gyfte of science as it is here taken, extendeth to mecanical science, and handy craftes. This appeareth by the text. **Exo. xxxi.** when the holy tabernacle shoulde be made in deserte, almyghty God prouided an artificer and worke[L2ᵛ]man for the same nonce called **Beseleel** sonne of **Huri,** sonne of **Hur,** of the tribe of Iuda.* I haue filled him (sayth God) with the spirite of God. **Sapientia, intelligentia, & scientia in omni opere.** I haue geuen him sapience, by whiche he might wel discerne and iudge of the thinges that god woulde haue made, in so much that he was able to teach others the thinges that he knewe by goddes reuelation and instruction. And this properly perteyneth to the gyfte of **Sapience,** as I haue sayd afore. I haue fylled hym with the spyryt of **intelligence** or wyttines, and fine and cleare perceyuinge and vnderstanding, by which he may more perfitly pearce and enter with his wit into the thinges that be taught him, then he should haue done if he had lacked the sayd gyft of **intelligence.** I haue also (sayth God) fulfilled **Beseleel** with the gifte of science.* Of whiche speaketh **Chrisost.** in a sermon of the holy goste after this maner.* When **Moyses** made the tabernacle in wyldernes, he had nede then not onelye of doctryne and learnynge, but also of the gifte of a mayster craftes man, to knowe howe he should sew togither fyne clothes and sylkes of precious colours, and howe to weaue them, plat them, and shape them together. And howe he shoulde cast golde and other metalles necessary for the ceremonies there to be vsed, and howe to polyshe precious stones, and also to frame the timber for the same tabernacle. For these and such other purposes almighty God gaue him and to his workeman **Beseleel,** the spirite of science, that they mighte frame all [L3] suche thinges accordingely. And euen so in your occupations and handy craftes, when you exercise your selues diligentlye and trulye withoute slouth, withoute disceate, gile, or sutteltie in all your exercise, ordering your selues to your neighbour, as you would be ordered your self, so longe youre occupation, exercise, and laboure is adnexed and ioyned with charitie, and semeth plainely to come of the holy gooste: for without charitie this gifte of science comminge of the holy gooste will not be, no more then other vertues infused. And contrarye, lyke as euerye good thinge hath an enemie, or at the leaste wise an ape or a counterfeiter, as fortitude or manlines hath folyshe hardines or rashe boldenes, which semeth manlines and is not so, so hath science or conninge, gile or sutteltie, whiche counterfeiteth conning, and is no true conninge, in as muche as it is withoute Charitie, and also withoute iustice. **Cicero ex platone .i. offic. Sapientia† que est remota a[b] iusticia calliditas potius quam scientia est appellanda.** Science remoued from iustice is rather to be called wylynes then science.* And to this purpose, it is necessarye that you seruauntes do youre dutye to youre maysters obedientlye with feare and quakynge, in simplicitie and playnes of hearte, as vnto Christe, not seruinge to the eye,* as to please man, but like the seruauntes of Christ, doinge the will of God with hearte and all. **Ephe. vi.*** not deceauing your maisters by your idlenes, or els beinge occupied about your owne [L3ᵛ] busines,

† Sapientia] Sciencia

when your master thinketh that you be in his labours. And lykewyse you maysters do you to youre seruauntes,* instructynge them in theyr occupations, for whiche they came to your seruyce, accordyng to the trust that theyr parentes and frendes hath put you in, that they maye get theyr lyuynge and yours with truth & iuste dealynge and honestye, and medle not to muche with other mens occupations that you cannot skyll on, leaste whyle ye be so curious in other mens matters not perteininge to your lerning, you decaye as well in your owne occupation, as in the other, so fallynge to penurye, extreme pouertye, and very beggery. For when a tayler forsakynge his owne occupation wyll be a marchaunt venterer,* or a sho-maker to become a groser, God sende him well to proue. I haue knowen manye in this towne, that studienge diuinitie, hath kylled a marchaunt, and some of other occupations by theyr busy labours in the scriptures, hath shut vp the shoppe windowes, faine to take Sainctuary, or els for mercerye and groserye, hath be fayne to sell godderds, steanes, and pitchers, and suche other trumpery. For this I shal assure you, that althoughe diuinitie be a science verye profitable for the soule health, yet small gaynes to the purse, or to the worlde aryse by it. Not that I intende to reproue the studye of scriptures, for I extoll it and prayse it aboue all other studye, so that it be vsed as I haue sayde afore, with modestye and charitie, with longanimitie and easye sufferaunce, tyll God sende the [L4] a true instructour, not infected with wylful and newfangled heresyes: From whiche I pray god to defende you all, and sende you teachers indued with such science as may instructe you in the truth, by whiche you may attayne to ioyes euerlastynge. Amen.

The fyfte sermon, intreatynge of
the spirite of Pietie.

NOwe right worshipful audience I must aunswer to your expectation, not doubt-inge but that ye loke I shoulde perfourme the promise that I haue made you in tymes paste, when I toke vpon me to declare vnto you the vii. giftes of the holye goste, whiche as the prophet **Esay .xi.*** sayth, rested on our sauiour Christ, and by hym be deriued to his faythfull people, to euery one as it doth please his goodnes to distribute them, to some more of them, to some fewer, and not so many.* And to them that receiue the giftes of one kynde and maner, yet some persones hath them more intensly, more fullye, and more perfitly, & some more remysly, more faintlye, and not after so perfit facion or maner, as I haue heretofore declared at large, which I trust in God is not all forgotten. Fyue of the sayde giftes I haue stripped and passed ouer after the capacitie of my poore witte, nowe consequentlye suc-cedeth the .vi. of the saide giftes, called **Spiritus pietatis,** or **donum pietatis,** the gift of Pietie. This word **pietas** or **pietie,** the latin terme is so ambi[L4ᵛ]guouse, & so diuersly vsed, both in the scriptures and also of the doctours, that me thinketh it very hard to make it plaine in the english tonge for your capacitie.* The transla-tours of the Bible in to englishe, calleth **pietas** godlines, and his contrary **impietas** vngodlines.* But thus speaking of **Pietie,** it semeth to comon and large to be one of these .vii. giftes distincte from the other, because that thus speakinge of it, it agreith to the other vi. giftes that I haue spoken of. For the gyft of godly counsell is a certayne godlines: the gift of Fortitude also is a certayne godlines: The gyfte also of the dreade of God is a godly gifte, and a certayne godlines, as hereafter shall appeare.* And if I should english it & call it pitie, yet there I should fall into an other equiuocation: for this word pitie is not euer taken after one maner in the englishe tonge: sometime it is taken for mercy or compassion that we haue on the miserye of our neighbour that is in paine or trouble,* & thus is **pietas** somtime taken as I shal shew hereafter & sometime otherwise, as when we say to an vnthrift or a common malefactour, it is pitie to do the good. Here it signifieth rather an offence, a fault or an il thing,* & so speking, I thinke this english may come of **pio,** a verbe, or **piaculum** taken in **malam partem,** for a crime or a sinne, as we take **sacer,** or such other, sometyme to signifie that is holye & good, and sometime that is cursed & noughte.* But we haue not yet the principal signification of **pietas** that we now speke of. Therfore more specially to speake of **pietie,** ye shall vnderstand yᵗ the paygnims in theyr writinges vsed yᵉ same terme [M1] and (as they thought) in the same signification as we vse it. **Cicero .ii. officiorum. Deos placatos pietas efficiet & sanctitas.** They were deceiued by errour and worshipped many Gods, yet this they thought good to pacifie, content, and please their gods by pietie & holines.* Albeit their pietie, holynes and integritie or clearenesse of liuyng in them, were but counterfait and vnprofitable for their soule healthe, and for salua-tion of their soules, in as muche as it lacked the foundacion of faith whiche as I saide in the firste Sermon that I made here of these seuen giftes, is presupposed necessarilye to all these seuen gyftes of<.> the holye Goost. **Lactancius firmianus diuinarum institutionum, Li. iii, ca ix.** inueighing against the erroure of the olde Philosophers, whiche sayde that mans felicitie stoode in the knowledge of cor-porall thinges as **Anaxagoras*** did, whiche when he was asked wherfore, or for what cause he was borne? answered **Solis ac celi videndi causa.** I was borne and brought into this worlde (sayth he) for to see the sunne,* and the heauen or the

bodies aboue, as meanynge that in the beholding of them with our bodelye eyes
hadde stande all our perfection, where he ought rather to haue confessed and
magnified the power of him that made the Heauen, and in contemplation of his
maiestye, that is to saie, in the interiour sight of our mindes, occupied about his
highnes, and in loue corespondente, to haue constitute our felicitie stedfastlye,
continuynge in the same, while wee be here in this corruptible bodie, till at the
last wee [M1ᵛ] maye attayne and come to the cleare fruition of the same in heauen
without any impedimente or let. Therfore if a man were asked now wherefore he
was made, he should not answere to stare vpon the skye (as Anaxagoras saide)
nother to folowe the carnall lust of this fleshe, as Aristippus* sayde, nother to be
without payne, and to take thy ease or thy pleasure generallye, as Epicure* sayde.
But rather to saye and answere that we were made and brought forth into this
world for to worshippe God, whiche begote vs to doe hym seruice. And this after
Lactancius. is called **Pietas. Dei parentis agnitio.** The knowlege of God our father
and maker* not speaking of bare and naked knowledge of GOD† as they hadde.
Quicum cognouissent deum, non sicut deum glorificauerunt. Roma. i. Whiche
when they knewe GOD did not honour him as GOD,* nother thanked hym for
his gyftes, but played the fooles, fallynge to Idolatrye, makynge Goddes of menne,
birdes, and beastes. Therfore sayth .s. Augustine .iiii ciui. ca. xxiii. **Pietas vera est**
verax veri dei cultus. And as he saythe .x. ci. ca. i it is called by the Greke word
Latria, which is properly that seruice that perteineth to the worshippyng of God,*
& may be called also by an other latine word, **Religio,** Religion which properly
signifieth the worshippyng of God, and taketh his name **(secundum Lactancium**
li. iiii ca. xxviii.[)] A **religando,** because that by the bonde of the seruyce and
worshippe that wee owe to God, GOD hathe bounde manne to hym to do hym
seruice, as to [M2] our Lord and master, and to do him worshyppe, honour and
reuerence as to our father.* Thus he hath bounde vs to hym by the faythe that he
infused and poured into vs at oure christenynge and wee haue bounde our selfe to
hym by our promysse that wee there professed, for hys sake to renounce, refuse,
and forsake the deuyll, and all hys pompe, and proude workes, and so all wee were
there made religious persones, applied and appoynted chiefelye to thys seruyce
that I nowe speake of, **pietas,** that is to saie: the true worshippynge of GOD, or the
inwarde habite, qualitie or gifte of the soule, by the holye Goste geuen to man or
woman, by whiche a manne or a woman hauing it, is inclined to goodnesse, and
made well disposed, well minded, prompte and ready to serue GOD† and to do
hym worshippe.* But because it is playne by the Prophet Esay, (where my matter is
grounded) that all these gyftes rested in the manhode of our Sauioure Christe,
whom he called the flower that shoulde rise vp out of the rodde, springynge forthe
from the roote of Iesse.* Let vs searche the scriptures whether it do appere by his
actes that he hadde this gift. **Luke ii.*** when he was twelue yere olde and able to
take some labours, he wente wyth his mother and wyth his foster father to Hierusalem. They casting no perylles,* wente homewarde after the solemnitie of the
feast, thinking that Christe hadde been in the companye of the neighbours that
then went together homwarde from Hierusalem after the maner as Pylgrymes,
[M2ᵛ] vsed to go in flockes togither.* Thus they passed the way a whole daies
iourney afore thei missed him, when thei missed him it was no nede to bid them
seke, they had lost their greatest iewel. They sought him among their frends &
acquaintance and coulde not finde him, the nexte daye they returned backe to

† GOD] GGD; GOD] GGD

Hierusalem, the thirde day they sought all aboute in the Citye, the fourth daye,
that is **post tridium,** after thre dayes they found him in the temple sittynge among
the doctours, hearynge them, and askynge questions of them. He first hearde them
reade and teache, and then asked questions, and opposed theim. Woulde GOD our
Bible clerkes woulde so do now adaies, that they woulde firste heare and learne,
and afterward to oppose, for so they should profite them selues, and theim that
they do oppose. Where nowe when they do oppose, it is wythout anye learned
maner, and more for a vayne glorie, or for to publishe and open mennes igno-
raunces, rather then to instruct them, and that appeareth, for commonlye they be
doinge & most busie with theim that be vnlearned, rather then with them that be
learned.* Our sauiour Christe occupied not him selfe soe, but gate him selfe
amonge the verye beste of the doctours that were in the Temple, firste geuinge
good aduertens and audience to their saiynges, and then opposynge them for their
learnynge. And after thys maner his Parentes founde him occupied, hys mother
saide vnto hym: Sonne, why haue you serued vs so? your father and I with sorowe
[M3] and care haue sought you. And Christe said vnto them, why sought you me?
Know ye not that I muste nedes be in those thinges that be my fathers? Or aboute
my fathers busines? Where he called the resorting and commyng to the temple,
and there to be occupied in contemplation, in preachinge, readynge, teachinge,
disputynge, or reasonyng, his fathers matters, his fathers businesse. And in this he
declared this gift of **pietie,** (that I nowe speake of) to be in him, and that by this
gifte, he was inclined so to do, and so to occupy him selfe in the seruice of his
father, and in the worshippyng of almighty God. And after when .s. Iohn Baptiste
was cast in prison, then came our sauiour Christe abroade, and preached his holye
doctrine in Galilee and other places **.Luke .iiii.*** and in his progresse he came to
Nazareth where he was nourced and brought vp in his childhode. And there came
into the churche on the Sabboth daie as he was wont to do, and stode vp and
redde a porcion of the scripture as the maner was. The scripture was of the
prophecye of Esay. **ca. lxi. Spiritus domini super me propter quod vnxit . . . me,**
euangelizare pauperibus misit me. &c.* After he had redde it, he clasped vp the
booke, & deliuered it to the clerke or minister that hadde the kepyng of it, and
sate downe like a doctour or a reader in his chaire, or on his stole and expounded
and declared the same scripture, appliyng it to himselfe as the true litterall sence of
that scripture did pretende, saiynge: **Hodie impleta est hec scriptura in oculis**
vestris. Now this [M3ᵛ] scripture is fulfilled afore your eyes.* The holye spirite of
God was on him, and did annointe him and sende him to preach to the poore
people, that be poore in spirite, and lowlye in herte. All this was the seruice of his
father, redoundyng to his worshippe, and to his fathers honour he applied all his
preachinge. **Ioh. xiiii.** The sermon that you haue hearde, is not mine, but it is my
fathers that sende me.* Also, **Ioh. xv.** In this my father is glorified, that you maye
bring furthe muche fruite, and may be made my scholers.* He did not attribute or
geue it to his own glorye or prayse that his disciples increased in knowledge, and in
the fruite of good works comming of the same, but to the glorye and prayse of his
father. Likewise that his disciples and we by them be Christes disciples, he willeth
vs to geue laudes and glorie therfore to the father, although yᵉ fathers glorie and
his by reason of his Godheade, were & is all one. Thus ye may well perceiue
through the Gospels, howe vehemently and earnestly he was geuen to the true
seruice and honour of god seking the glory of God, and not his owne glory or the
glory of his manhode. **Ego non quero gloriam meam est qui querat & iudicet.**
Ioh. viii.* which is the verye exercise and practise of this sixt gift of the holy gost

called in latine **pietas** in englyshe the **worshipping of God, or the gifte of grace by whiche we be prompte and ready, and glad to worshippe God.*** And when we be so disposed, taking example at our Sauiour Christe, commynge to his holye Temple or churche dedicate to Gods [M4] honour, where his holy word is redde and song, expounded, preached, and declared, and there occupie our selfes in contemplation and prayer like good christian people, it is a great signe that we be partakers of his plenty, hauynge this gifte of the holy goost deriued vnto vs by our Sauioure Christe. And this (I thinke) is one proper signification of **pietas,** and is as saint Ambrose **.i offi. xxvii.** sayth, the firste and principall parte of our iustice, and the beginnynge of wisdome, to know of whom we haue our wit and al other goodnes and to do him seruice accordynge to his benefite.* Albeit if we should extend and enlarge the name of **pietas,** of reuerende worshippe, we shall finde that wee owe seruice or reuerende worshippe to our countrey, & also to our parents that brought vs into this world, and nursed vs, cherished vs, and helped vs when we could not helpe our self, and also to them that be nye of kinred to vs.* So that this vocable **pietas,** semeth now to haue iii. significations, to whiche he agreeth, **secundum analogiam quandam,** as the Logition speaketh.* After a certaine order likewise, as there is an order betwixt the thynges signified, we owe a reuerende seruyce and worshippe to almyghty GOD, as to our maker, mainteyner, and redemer, as I haue sayde. Wee owe also a reuerende seruice and worshippe to our countrey. Wee also owe a reuerende honoure and worship to oure fathers and mothers, & to them that be to vs nexte of kinred. But we be not so bounde to serue our countrey as wee be to serue God, nor [M4ᵛ] so straightly bound to our parentes & kinred as to our countrey.* If the whole countrey or the whole realme in whiche thou were borne, would moue thee to do that facte, or that thinge that shuld be contrarye to Gods pleasure, and contrary to his holy scriptures, forsake thy countrey, esteme it not, take no parte with them, but cleaue faste to Gods holye worde, and resiste euen to death, the malice and frowardenesse of suche miscreantes as would moue thee to the contrarie. Did not the Apostles so? Were they not al Iewes borne? was not all the whole countrey bended to extinct the remembraunce of Christe? Howe oft were they commaunded they shoulde not once Preache or speake of his name vnder paine of stripes? yea, vnder paine of deathe? But all this would not serue, all this could not disseuer them from Christ, nor from publishyng of his fayth, and of his holy name, nother trouble, nor perplexitie, or distres, nor honger, nor nakednesse, nor peryll, nor persecution, nor sworde, axe, or anye weapon. **Ro. viii.*** Seconde, we be more bounde to our countrey then to our parentes or kynred, in so muche that if there woulde anye foreine Potentate, or alien power, attempte to inuade the Realme where thou art inhabitant, & of the nacion, yea: though thine owne father, vncle, brother, & all thy kinred that thou hast were on that partye, so irrupting into thy country, thou oughtest to forsake them al, & to fight against them al for the defence & sauegard of thi countrey, yea: & (that goeth nere to the then so) to forsake thy selfe and thine owne lyfe [N1] and healthe, and to put thy selfe in ieopardy for thy countrey sake. The paynim capitayns did so, the holy men that scriptures doth commende and repute theim **in Catalago sanctorum,** in the rolle and number of saintes did so likewise. **Codrus** king of Athens in a battaile against the Peloponensis, perceiued by an aunswere that the deuill had made speakinge in an ydole to the said Peloponensis, that they shoulde haue the victorye, if thei killed not the capitaine of the contrary parte: Wherfore the whole hoste was commaunded to saue **Codrus** the kinge of the Athenensis in anye case. This was not so secretelye done, but it came to **Codrus**

eare, which for the pietie and loue that he hadde to his countrey, disgised him self
like a poore labourer with his sith on his backe, and so came amonge the host of
his enemies, and what with shrowde wordes and misbehauiour, and with his sithe
he displeased the souldiours, and hurte one of them with hys sithe, whiche turned
to him, and with his speare staffe killed him. When this was knowen, the Peloponensis fled, and so the Athenensis had the victorie, without anye more bloudsheading.* In a certain controuersie betwixt the Carthaginensis, & the people of
Cyrene, a certayne citie in Libia, (of which it is touched. **Act. ii.** Et partes Libie
que est circa Cyrenem,)* it lieth eastward from Carthage, now I trow called
Tuneis toward Eygpt, bothe in Affricke. In a contrauersie (I saye) betwixte those
two parties for the meyres or boundes of their territoryes and dominions, [N1ᵛ]
which continued long to the great murther & destruction of the people of both
parties. At the last it was agreed betwixt bothe, that at a certaine time appointed
betwixt both yᵉ cities there shold certayne curriers be send furth, & where so euer
they met, there to be meyre stones pitched, & such markes made whereby it myght
be knowen for euer howe farre bothe lordshippes dyd extende, they that were
sente out of Carthage were twoo brothers **Phileni** called, but so it was that these
brothers were come a great waye further then the other partye thought they
should. And so the Cyrenensis pretended some fraude to be in the setting forth of
these men. But they for theyr countreys sake, and for the auoydaunce of further
trouble of the same, for to assure the contrarye partie that the thing was done
without collusion offred them selfe there to be buryed quick, that theyr tombes or
graues might be the verye meires in this purpose, with whyche the other partie
thinking no man woulde make suche an offer for the defence of a false matter was
content, and so ceased that controuersie.* In holye scriptures we haue examples
abundaunt, how that neither father nor mother, wyues neyther mens own naturall
children coulde withdrawe men from the loue of their countreys, in so much that
when some of theim were banisshed and driuen out of theyr countrey, yet when
thei herd that theyr countrey was in daunger & distresse, they sticked not to forget
al displeasures and vnkindnes, & to do the best they could to saue their countreys.
It is writ .**Gen. xiiii.*** That yᵉ holy patriarch [N2] Abraham, being but a straunger
in the land of Canaan, now called the holy lande, had such reuerend loue to the
countrey wher he was inhabitant, hearing that .iiii. kings with their hostes had
inuaded the countrey about Sodom & Gomor, & had spoyled the countrey, &
taken away many prisoners, among which thei had taken **Loth** his brothers sonne,
he assembled together all his retinue, **Expeditos vernaculos trecentos decem &
octo,*** & folowed the chase, & ouertoke these kings, & beset them about in the
night season, & slew them, & recouered all their pray, & brought home againe
Loth with all his substance, He might haue sit still at home, if the loue that he had
to his countrey in which he was then sustained for the time, as Denison, had not
pricked him forward, **Iud. xi,*** It is red of Iepthe which in dede his brothers had
banished out of his countrey, yet afterward it chanced that the Ammonites inuaded the people of Israell, and wasted & destroyed them right sore, & specially
that part beyond the riuer of Iordane called **Galaad.*** wher this Iepthe was born.
The people of Israel were sore discoraged & their enmies so enhaunced yᵗ the land
was almost destroied, then came messagers to this Iepthe wher he was in his exile,
desiring his aide & succour. He vmbraided them of their vnkindnes, saiyng: Be not
you thei that hate me & driued me out of my fathers family? & now ye be
compelled by very nede to come to me for helpe. Notwᵗstanding he was moued wᵗ
that natural & louing reuerence yᵗ he had to his country, & said to yᵉ messagers yᵗ

if thei wold make him their captain he [N2ᵛ] woulde put him selfe in ieopardie for them, and to do the best he coulde, And so he did, and destroyed their enemies, and set the lande at rest. In like maner did Dauid. **i. Reg. xxiii.*** When he was driuen out of his countrey by the furye and madnes of king Saule, he hearde that the Philisties inuaded and destroyed **Ceila,*** a certayne towne in the dominion of Saule, and prepared him self to battaile against them, all his frendes and kinsfolke that were then wyth hym entreatynge him to the contrarie. Where **Pietas erga patriam,** the loue that he hadde to his countrey wrought more in him then all the carnal loue to his frends and kinsfolkes, and also then the vnkindenes of Saule that hadde driuen him out of his countrey, where he for yll repaid good again, he fought with the Philisties, he toke all their cattell and prouision for vittailes. **Percussit eos plaga magna, & saluauit habitatores Ceile.** He made a great murther amonge them, and saued the inhabitauntes and people of the towne Ceila.* In like maner be all nacions bounde by the lawe of Nature, and by Gods lawe, to defende their countrey. And wee for our realme, In so much that if there woulde any foraine potentate (as I saide) or any other sedicious persons attempte to infringe or breake the lawes Godlye made for the conseruation and quietnes of thys realme, we be bounde to do the vttermost of our power for the suppression, and extinction of them, yea, though they were our naturall parentes or next of kinred that woulde so offende. Likewise [N3] if any malefactours, sedicious, and rebellious persons woulde raise anie vnlawefull assembly, commocion, or insurrection againste the peace, and tranquilitie, and quiet cohabitation of the people in the countrey or realme where thou art inhabitaunt: Yea, though thine owne parentes and nexte of kinred were on that partye amonge such rebellions, the pietie, and reuerende honour and loue that thou owest to thy countrey, should make thee to do the vttermoste of thy power to resist them, and suppresse their malice.* In so much that if there be any of our Englishe men in exyle or banished out of their countrey, or such as for their offences dare not come into their countrey, yet if they might perceiue in the countreys where they walke any murmuring or repliyng against the Godlie and lawdable lawes of this Realme, or if they might perceiue anye perill or perturbation, trouble, or warre, to be moued against vs: the lawe of Nature shoulde moue them to staye all suche daungers, and to the vttermost of their powers to resist them, Yea, thoughe they should put their liues in ieopardye for the sauegarde of their countrey. Example ye haue now heard of the Ethnichs,* and also of the holy Patriarches, Abraham, Iepthe, and Dauid. And holy Moyses after the offence of his people in Idolatrye, makinge the calfe **tanquam Apin Egiptiorum deum,*** praied to almighty God for mercy and pardon for their offence, saiynge: **Aut dimitte eis hanc noxam, aut si non facis dele me de libro tuo quem scripsisti. Exo. xxxij.** A vehement pietie and loue [N3ᵛ] that he had to his countrey men, that he prayed, saiynge: Either forgeue them (good Lorde) or if thou wilte not, then strike me out of that boke of lyfe that thou hast written in thy eternall predestination,* he was sure that GOD would not so do. Therfore he was the bolder so to praye, as who shoulde saye, if you wyll nedes destroy them (good Lorde) why then dampne and destroy me wyth them. He was bolde that God would not so doe, therefore he thought in maner to inforce GOD to forgeue them for his sake, and to saue them with him. Such an ardent and burnynge loue to his countrey men had saint Paule, as he testifieth of him selfe. **Roma. ix. Optabam ego anathema esse a christo pro fratribus meis qui sunt cognati mei secundum carnem qui sunt Israelite.** I haue desired and wished to be seperate & deuided from Christe for the loue that I haue to my brethren, that be

my carnall kinsmen the Israelites.* How deuided from Christ? **Origene.** Not by
preuarication or transgressynge of Christes lawes or commaundementes.* He
woulde do no synne for their sakes. For that coulde not healpe them, that coulde
do them no good. Also there was no vyolence or force that could pull him from
Christ, as he sayth hym selfe. But like as Christe being by reason of his Godheade,
in the fourme and nature of GOD, yet he did so humiliate hym selfe, hidynge hys
Godlye power, that he become manne, and suffered death for our redemption,*
and so semed for the tyme to forsake the father, and was made as a thynge
accursed, to [N4] take awaye our malediction. **Gala. iii. Christus nos redemit de
maledictione legis factus pro nobis maledictum, quia scriptum est, maledictus
omnis qui pendet in ligno. Deute. xxi.*** And so saynte Paule by example of oure
maister Christe wished to haue done that thinge in which he might seeme to be
seperate from Christe by deuotion, and not by preuarication or synne, so that he
myght saue his countrey menne, and so he dyd, when he was of all sortes to all
menne, that he myght wynne all maner of menne to Christe. Sometymes vsynge
the Ceremonyes of the Iewes to allure them, in whiche the Gentyles thought he
did nought, and so to be deuided from Christe.* And amonge the Gentylles he
vsed suche meate as they did, and kepte companye wyth theim to wynne theim to
Christe, where the Iewes that were conuerted to Christ, thought he did nought,
and so they toke him as deuided from Christe, by occasions geuen of theim, wyth
whiche he was conuersaunt, thoughe he did all for Christes sake and to wynne al
maner of menne to Christe. Nowe as for **pietas in parentes,** the worshipfull loue
and honour that we owe to our fathers and mothers,* nature teacheth vs & the
commaundementes of God, as an exposition or declaration of the law of nature
teacheth vs the same. This honour consisteth not only in cap & knee, for thi
parents might sterue for defaut, for al thy curtesy: but it standeth in ministration of
necessary helpe & comfort in their nede. But this kind of pietie or loue due to our
parents doth [N4^v] not so sore binde vs, but that we maie diminishe of it, for to do
seruice vnto God. **Etiam in operibus supererogationis,** in thinges y^t we be not
bound to do, but take them of deuotion, whiche be now called will workes,* As
saint Hierome declareth in diuerse places, and speciallie in his firste pistle **Ad
heliodorum,** exhortinge him to solitarye lyfe, and religion, to leaue the yonge
babies his nephewes, collinge him and hanginge on his necke, to leaue his mother,
though she would with wepynge eyes shewe him the brestes that gaue him sucke in
his childehode, though his father would lye prostrate ouerthwart the dore to
stoppe him the waye, he shoulde not sticke for all suche, for **Solum pietatis genus
est in hac re esse crudelem.** It is a kind of reuerend honor of God by it self in this
thing to be cruell.* He saieth likewise, **ad rusticum Monachum,** in like case.
Crudelitas ista pietas est. This crueltie is reuerende honour to God.* And in a
pistle **ad Marcellam, de egrotatione blesille,*** He bringeth in examples of the
gospel. Iohn & Iames left their father Zebede in the boate patchyng his nettes &
folowed Christ. Mathewe ye customer left his countynge borde whereby he was
wont to gette his liuynge, and his wiues liuynge, and his childrens, and folowed
Christe.* An other, **Luke .ix.** was bid folowe Christe, Christe so bade him, he
answered, Sir I praye you let me firste go home and burye my father. Christ bade
him, let other menne alone with buriynge the deade. Come thou with me, &
learne to preach the word of GOD. **Tu autem vade, & annuncia regnum dei.** [O1]
Another said he wold folow Christ, but he wold fyrst bestow his riches that he had
at home vpon his parentes or kinsfolkes, or such other. Christ bad him come on
forward, & loke not backwarde like a noughty plowman, for such shall not come

to heauen.* Of these sayth S. Hierome there. **Pietatis genus est impium esse pro domino.** It is a kinde or one maner of Goddes worship, **impium esse,** to be cruell, sore or vnlouinge for Christes sake, as he meaned, perswadinge to religion or solitarye life.* Of the same in an epistle **Ad fabiolam de vestitu sacerdotum,** vpon these wordes, **Super patre suo, et matre sua non inquinabitur,** S. Hierome saith. **Multa nos facere cogit affectus, & dum propinquitatem, respicimus corporum, & corporis, & anime offendimus creatorem.** Qui amat patrem aut matrem super Christum non est Christo dignus, discipulus ad sepulturam patris ire desiderans saluatoris prohibetur imperio. Quanti monachorum dum patris matrisque miserentur suas animas perdiderunt?* But maysters, yf in Saynte Hieroms time religion had ben lyke to religions as they be nowe a dayes, trowe ye that Saynte Hierome woulde so earnestly haue exhorted men to them, no, no, oure religiouse men they be but **parietes dealbati,** very counterfect appearing,* and not beynge religious, no more lyke the religion in Saynt Hieromes time then an apple lyke an oyster,* as is playne by his writinges, and by the Ecclesiasticall stories of Eusebius, and the Tripartite story,* and suche other. Yet one word more **de pietate.** Another way it is taken for benignitie mercy & pitie or compassion on our indigent poore, [O1ᵛ] and nedy neighbours, and thus takinge it, we vse to call the workes of mercy, workes of pitie that we do on our poore neighbours. And thus Paule **.i. Tim. ii.** taketh it, when he teacheth good and honeste wemen how they shoulde araye and trimme them selfe without golden riche and costly abilimentes, fruntlets or bracelettes, without pearles or precious stones, not platting or settyng abrode theyr lockes, like stales or baites to take the deuyll withall, but rather in theyr apparell to vse a certayne bashfulness and sobernes, not like commen wemen that studieth how gloriously and disgysedly they maye make a shewe, and set forth theyr fleshe to sale and to be vttered, but rather as good wemen shuld aray them selfe, **vt decet mulieres promittentes pietatem per opera bona,** as besemeth wemen promising or shewinge pitie by good workes.* Therefore in the same epistle he exhorteth Timothe to the same, sayinge. **Exerce te[ ]ipsum ad pietatem.** Exercise thy self to pitie, to do men good. For that is profitable for all thinges, and hath promyse of the lyfe that is now present, and of the life to come.* That mercy and pitie is rewarded in this worlde, it is sayd. **Prouerb. iii. Da pauperibus & implebuntur horrea tua saturitate & vino torcularia redundabunt.** Geue vnto the pore people, and thy barnes and store houses, or ware houses shalbe made full, and thy wyne presses shall ouerflowe with wine.* And **.ii. Corin. ix.** it is sayde, **Qui administrat semen seminanti, et pa[n]em et manducandum prestabit & multiplicabit semen vestrum, & a[u]gebit incrementa [O2] frugum iustitie vestre, vt in omnibus locupletati habundetis in omnem simplicitatem.** He that sendeth sede to the sower, wyll also geue breade to eate, and wyll multyplye your sede, and wyll encrease the gaynes of the grayne of your iustice, that you maye be made riche in all thinges, and maye habounde into all simplicitie and playnes of lyuinge.* And that the workes of pitie or mercye hath promise of the lyfe to come, it is playne in the Gospell **.Math. xxv.** when the sonne of man shal come in his maiestie and all his aungels with him, then he shall sitte on the seate of his maiestie, and all nations shall be gathered afore him, and he shall deuide them aparte, euen as the shephearde parteth the shepe from the goates, and he shall set the shepe on his righte hande, and the rancke and stinckinge goates on the lift hande. And then that kinge wyll saye to theim that be vpon his righte hande, O ye children of my father, come take possession of the kyngedome that is prepared for you: for I was an hungred and you gaue me meate, I was a thirste and you gaue me drinke, I was harbourlesse and you harboured me,* and so forth of other workes of mercye, for whiche he wyll geue to the mercyfull man or woman lyfe euerlastynge.

And here (because we speake of the workes of **pietie,** or pitie) verye pitie moueth me to exhorte you to mercye and pitie on the poore studentes in the vniuersities Oxforde & Cambridge, whiche were neuer fewer in number, & yet they that be lefte, be ready to runne abrode into the world [O2ᵛ] and to leaue their study for very nede.* Iniquitie is so aboundaunt that charitie is all colde.* A man would haue pitie to heare the lamentable complaintes that I heard lately, being among them whiche wold god I were able to releue. This I shal assure you, that (in my opinion) ye can not better bestow your charitie. Our sauiour Christ sayth. **Mat. x. Qui recipit prophetam in nomine prophetae† mercedem prophete accipiet.** He yᵗ receueth, cherisheth, or maintaineth a prophet in yᵉ name of a prophet, or as a prophet, he shal receyue the rewarde of a prophete.* All true preachers be prophetes, therfore he that cherisheth and maynteyneth a preacher, because he is a preacher, more then for anye other carnal occasion, shal haue the rewarde of preacher, which is a wonderous reward. **Dan. xij. Qui ad iustitiam erudiunt multos fulgebunt quasi stelle in perpetuas eternitates.** They that instructeth and teacheth many to iustice & vertue, shall shine like sterres into euerlasting eternitie.* As in example, yf this exhortation and sermon whiche I nowe most vnworthy make vnto you, do anye good to the soules of this audience, I doubt not but my reward shall not be forgotten, yf there be none other stoppe or impediment on my behalfe, and my parentes that set me to schole in youth, and my good Lorde Wylliam Smyth, sometyme Byshop of Lincolne, my bringer vp & exhibitoure firste in Banbury to gramer scole, with mayster Iohn Stanbrige, and then in Oxforde tyl I was maister of Arte,* and able to helpe my selfe, shall haue reward in heauen, for the gostlye [O3] comfort that you receiue by this my labour. S[o] he or she that bringeth vp any studentes to anye good learninge, by whiche they maye do good to Christes flocke, whether the facultie be diuinite, lawe phisicke, rethorike or such other, there is no doubt but they which found them & mainteyned them to such learning, shal haue reward of God for the good that cometh of theyr lerning. Wherfore in contemplation of this good consideration, and also for because that who so euer geueth so muche as a cuppe of cold water to any poore body of Christes seruauntes, shall not lose his rewarde and wages, I shal hartely pray you to extend your charitie toward the sayde scholers and studentes, and by that ye shall shew your selues to be merciful, and to haue this gifte of the holye goost, the gifte of **Pietie,** whiche after the mynde of the doctours is all one with mercy. And that the holye gooste by this his gyfte rested vpon our Sauiour Christe, it is playne by the cures that he did on them that were sicke of diseases vncurable, and also by feeding the hungry somtimes fiue thousand at once.* And also it appeareth that he vsed to giue almes to the poore, and had purses for the same intent, whiche Iudas had the keeping of, in somuch that when Christ said vnto him: **Quod facis, fac citius.** That thou dost do it spedely: some of the Apostles thought that Christ had bid him prepare for the feast commyng, or els **egenis vt aliquid daret. Iohn .xii[i].** that he shoulde giue some thyng to the poore people,* on which Christ was wont to haue mercy & pitie [O3ᵛ] and to bestow somewhat vpon them. And thus much of this sixt gift of the holy gost shalbe now sufficient. I pray God we may alwayes vse it to Gods pleasure, to whome be al honour and glorye. Amen.

† prophetae] prophetem

THe seuenth gift of the holy gost is yᵉ gift of the **feare of God,*** whiche rested in
our Sauiour Christ, as well as the other .vi. that I haue spoken of. There be in the
appetite or wyll of man .iiii. affections, or perturbations, or passions that moueth
and draweth the wyll of man hither and thither, and rather to yll then to good
cupidite or desire to haue, and **ioye** or **gladnes** for the hauinge of the thinge that
thou hast desired. The other .ii. be **feare** of hurte or displeasure, and **sorowe** for
the thinge that thou were afrayd of when it is chaunced or happened* There was a
sect of Philosophers called **Stoici,*** whose auctors were **Zeno, Chrisippus, Epictetus,*** and certayne other, and they put the hieste felicite, perfection, and
goodnes of man to be, **to liue according to vertue** and to natural reason. So that
they put nothinge good in man but **vertue,** whiche they call the very craft and way
to liue well,* other thinges (they sayd) were **commoda,** profitable for man as lyfe,
helth, and strength, but none clerely good saue onely **Iustice** or **vertue.*** And
because they saw these .iiii. affections or passions sore trouble mans reason, &
bring a man to many enormities, they said that they came of the corruption of the
body [O4] & were very nought, and shuld be cleane reiecte and cast away, & neuer
perceiued or sene in anye good man, but that in all cases and chaunces of welth &
woo, a man shuld kepe him self vpright, & take al thinges after one maner.* **Nam
perfectus Stoicus nihil mali patitur.** A perfit Stoike suffreth no il or harme, how
so euer the world go, therefore they were called **stupidi Stoici,** styffe or stubborne
Stoikes.* **Platonici** and also **Peripathetici** of **Aristotles** scole, for Aristotle was
scoler to **Plato** they were al of one opinion, & thought likewyse that al these .iiii.
affections were very nought, but yet they would not haue them cleane extinct and
destroyed, because they be naturall to man:* as it is natural for a heart to be fearful,
& to an addre to be venemous, to a spaniel to be gentle & familiar, so it is natural
for man to desire, & to be glad to be afeard & to be sory or heuy. They be **vbertas
quedam animorum,** a certaine batilnes or frutfulnes of yᵉ soul* which shuld not be
destroyed, but rather wel husbanded & bated, as if a ground or a garden be to
ranke, it is not best clene to destroy yᵗ ranknes, but rather to bate it with sand or
grauel, or such like, or els the herbes, the grasses & trees that be there set, wil
canker & be nought. So it is of these iiii. affections after these Philosophers that
they must not be cleane destroyed, but moderate and kept subiect to reason, &
measured yᵗ they runne not to fast at large, nor passe their bondes, & that they
peruert not the iugement of reason, but be ruled by reason. But surely here is not al,
for they be not vtterly vituperable & vicious: for if they were very nought, then no
measuring could make them good. [O4ᵛ] Pryde can not be good, thoughe ye kepe
him as short as ye can: Enuye can not be good for anye restrainte or measuringe,
therefore yf they be nought of them self, as these Philosophers supposed, we can
not make them good which is not so. **S. Augustine, ix. de ciui. dei. Cap. iiii.*** as
to combind and agre these two opinions, declareth that they agre in substaunce,
and varieth but onely in wordes. For declaration of which he rehearseth a propre
story of **Aulus Gellius. li. xix. noctium atticarum.*** It chaunced this **Aulus
Gellius** to be on the sea in a perilouse storme, and very rough seas, so that theyr
shyppe semed to be in extreme perill of drowninge. In the same shyppe there was a
fatherly auncient Philosopher, and of the secte of the Stoikes, which seinge the
rage of the storme and how the sees were euer stil ready to swalow them vp, begon

156

to waxe pale as ashes for feare.* There was also in company among many mo in the same shyppe, a ryche voluptuous gorbelye* of the countrey of Asia the lesse,* whiche Asia in very dede by reason of the fertilitie of the countrey, and the commodities of the same is meruelously geuen to pleasures, and out of those parties all wantonnes, insolency & pleasures crept into the citie of Rome, so that after y^t the Romaines had subdued that country, & **Galaciam** otherwise called **Gallogrecia,*** which now we call Galathians, & other countreis adioyning, Rome was neuer good, but gaue them selues* to ease & plesure, by which theyr manlines & hardnes in warre decayd gretlye, & was turned into childishnes & wenchlines.* [P1] This I tell you because of **Aulus Gellius** worde **luxuriosus asiaticus.*** To my purpose, many of them that were in the foresayde shyp (althoughe they were then at deathes doore)* tooke heede and watched verye curiouselye, whether the sayde philosopher were any thing troubled in mynde or no, then at the laste when the storme was past and when they were safe and had leasure to talk and giest, the voluptuous man of Asia aforesaide spoke to the saide Philosopher mocking him because he was afrayde and pale as death,* seynge that he himself (sayd he) was without feare, nothing regarding that peril. The philosopher answered as one Aristippus answerd to a like question dema[u]nded of him by a like person saying, that he did well inoughe, nothing to care nor to be afraid for the life of such a veri noughty knaue as he was, but that he him self ought to be afrayd for the life of Aristippus the philosopher,* a learned man, which was a more precious iewell, then twenty such ribaldes. This riche fellow of Asia was blancke and put to silence with thys aunswer. **Aulus Gellius** then asked of this Philosopher, not entendynge to anger hym or displease him, but for his learning, what was the reason of his feare? The Philosopher because he wolde teache hym, that was so earnestlye and wiselye minded to learne, drue forth out of his fardell a booke of **Epictetus** a Philosopher of the secte of the sayd Stoikes.* In the same boke **Aulus Gellius** saith, he red that the sayde Stoikes minde was that the thinges that mannes minde seeth, [P1^v] which they cal fantasies that be not in mans power whither they come to mans minde or not, and when or what time they fall into mans minde in as muche as they come of terrible and fraylefull thynges, that it can not be chosen but they wyll moue the minde, yea of a very wise man, so that he shall for a while be afrayde or shrinke for sorow or feare as though these passions did preuent the office of the mynde and of reason. And for all that, the minde to haue no opinion of hurt or yll, nor to approue or to consent to these passions or troubles of the mynde. And the saide Philosophers saithe* that this is the difference betwixt the minde of a wise man, and the minde of a foole, that the minde of a foole shrinketh and gyueth place to suche passions and applieth the assent of his minde to the same. But the minde of a wyse man although he can not chuse but must needes suffer suche sodayne passions, yet he dothe kepe a true and stedfast iudgement of suche thinges as he ought reasonablye to desyre or to exchue and auoyde without anye shakyng or wauering in hys minde. Whyche thinges if they be thus as that Philosopher **Epictetus** writeth, there is eyther no dyfference, or almoste no dyfference betwixt the opinion of the said Stoikes, and of other Philosophers about these passions, or perturbations of mens minde, for both sectes defendeth the mynde and reason of a wise man from the dominion and rule of them, & therfor paraduenture they saye that they fall not into the minde of a wise Stoike philosopher because thei [P2] do not cloude and darken the wisedome of hym, neither marre it with any spot of inconuenience but they chaunce to the minde of a wyse man the clerenes of his wysedome remaining safe. And the Philosopher

that was in the ship (whiche I nowe spoke of) myghte suffer the sayde trouble of
his phantasie and yet kepe thys fast sentence in hys mynde, that the lyfe and the
healthe of his bodye, which he was like to loose by the rage of the tempest were
not suche goodes or good thinges as maketh the hauers good men, as iustice and
vertues dothe. Bothe opinions saythe, that they had leuer loose those things, by
which the body is kepte safe and sound: then to offende and do those thinges by
which iustice is violate and defowled. Therefore the mynde of man, in which this
said sentence is fast printed, doth not suffer any perturbations or passions to
preuaile agaynste reason, althoughe they chaunce to the lower parties of the soule
of man, but rather ruleth them and maystreth them, not consenting to them, but
rather resisting them, exercising the empery, kingdome & rule of vertue. Then thus
must we do with them, we must take hede wher about they be occupied, & if the
obiect or matter that they be exercised on be good & godly, the affection is
commendable: if it be contrarye to Gods pleasure, & contrary to his lawes, the
affection about the same is very vicious & nought. When Dauid coueted & desired
to haue Vries wife in aduoutri this was a noughty apetite, a noughty desire, because
the thing that he desired was against Gods lawes.* [P2ᵛ] But when he said **Concupiuit anima mea desiderare iustificationes tuas**: My soule hath coueted & desired
vehemently to desire to know thy lawes,* this is a good affection, a good mocion of
yᵉ minde. And likewise of mirth or gladnes when men be glad in our Lorde, and
reioyseth in the thinges that pleaseth him, this gladnes is good & gratious, where
as if one be merye and glad when he hath done nought, and reioyce in thinges that
be very yll, this gladnes is damnable. And euen lyke it is of the thirde affection or
passion whyche is feare, of which my principall purpose is nowe to speake. Bestowe
him well, and he shal be good and laudable, where as if it be otherwise bestowed,
nought he wyll be as other affections be. How necessary and good feare is, the
wyseman **Prouer. xxviii.** sheweth **Beatus homo qui semper est pauidus, qui vero
mentis est durae corruet in malum.** Blessed is the man that is euer afrayde,
specially of Gods displeasure, and consequentlye of all other offences and excesses.
For he that is so hard and stiffe harted, that he nothing feareth, shal be sure to fall
to mischiefe of synnes and of paines for the same.* And **Ecclesiasticus cap. i.
Timor domini expellit peccatum, & qui sine timore est non poterit iustificari.**
Feare of God moueth a man to penaunce, and so putteth awaye sinnes past and
already committed, and it stoppeth a man from doing a mysse. **Et qui sine timore
est, non poterit iustificari:** He that lacketh feare can not be iustified, can not be
made a good manne acceptable to God, for he that will be iustified muste be
sub[P3]iect to God that shall iustifie hym as to his superiour and better. Which
subiection commeth by feare, by which a man taketh hymselfe as in the daunger of
God, where contrarye **Iracundia animositatis subuersio illius est.** The anger of
pride & presumption is a mans owne destruction.* Cain had great knowledge of
God, & by that he knew his dutie was to honour God with the increase of the
frutes that God had sent him, & had sometime familiar communicacion with God.
As when God bad him beware of the rage and passion that he was in agaynste his
brother Abell, seyng hys brothers oblacions accepted, and his own reiected, but
iracundia animositatis illius the passion and rage of his boldnes contrary to feare,
made him to kill his brother Abell to his own subuersion and destruction, he gote
Gods curse for hys labour. **Gene. iiii.*** God sayd to him: thou shalte be accursed on
earth: when thou hast laboured the ground, it shal giue thee no frutes, thou shalt
be wauering and running about from place to place vpon earth. God put suche a
marke in his face, a nodding in his heade, and trembling of his eyes that all men

abhorred him and hated him. And where he for lack of feare of God wrought mischief and murther, he was punished for the same with feare, fearing that euery man that saw him woulde kill him. But it was no godly feare, but rather a frensye feare that he had in his braine. The greatest cause of Noes floode was lacke of feare, for whyche lacke the chyldren of Sethe, whiche afore were relygious and vertuous per[P3ᵛ]sones according to the doctrine of their fathers at the last leauing their deuotion and religion to God or feare of God, and seyng that the doughters of Cain were fayre wemen burned in concupiscence of them, and maryed with them contrarie to Adams doctrine,* for he by his life time had seperate Cains broode farre of into far countries, from the issue of Sethe, for the horrour of the homicide that Cain had committed, slayinge his owne brother.* Notwithstanding in processe of time they drewe homeward toward the countrey that they came fro, & so the children of Sethe companying with them, gendred betwixt theym giantes of an vnmeasurable stature,* and as vnmeasurable in mischiefe and yll conditions, and so all the worlde which came of Cain and Sethe leauyng the feare of GOD, proued mischeuous and very nought in all carnall lust, yea agaynste nature, and in all malice and mischiefe one agaynst another. In so muche that God sayde, he repented that euer he had made man.* Not for anye perturbation of minde in God, but it is the maner of scripture to speake after the comon maner of speche of men. Nowe we see that when a manne marreth that he hathe made, it is a signe that he repenteth that euer he made it. Such maner of speaking vseth almighty God, intendyng to destroy man that he had made. Yet because **aut non continebit in ira sua misericordias suas,** in his punyshing he wyll vse mercy with correction.* He sayd **Non permanebit spiritus meus in homine in eternum, quia caro est. Genesis .vi.** My indignation [P4] and displeasure shal not abide for euer in manne kynde, I wyll not putte hym to perpetuall paynes, as the deuyll is put to, **quia caro est,** because he is fleshe, that is to say frayle and weake by the infirmitie of the fleshe, which was not in the diuell, he had none suche nourishynge of sinne as is in our fleshe, he synned by hys own wylfulnes onely, without any intisement or temptacion, and therefore hys synne is irremissyble, hys paynes shall be perpetuall, they shall neuer haue ende. But because man was tempted by the concupiscence of the eye and of the fleshe, whych wil not be ouercome wythout great conflict and battell, therefore GOD gaue vnto man a hundred and twentye yeares of repentaunce, from the first warning gyuen to Noe to make hys shyppe vnto the time that the water came in deede.* In the whyche tyme manye a one mended theyr lyues, yea and peraduenture some of them that were obstinate in yll afore amended, euen when they sawe the water come, and whyle they suffered in the water and were a drownyng. Nemrothe Cham his neuewe, whych begonne to be a myghtye manne on earthe, and a stubburn and boystuous hunter afore God.* **Genesis .xi.** reiected the feare of GOD, and contemptuousely buylded a Citye and a towre of bricke, for the stones, and suche pytche for the morter that woulde abyde all weathers, they purposed to make theyr Towre so hie that it shoulde reache vppe to the skye, because they woulde gette theym a gaye name, and a parpetuall memorye.

[P4ᵛ] And also because they woulde be sure no more to be drowned with suche a raging floode as was in the time of Noe, which was fresh in mens remembraunce, and in euery mans mouth, til that time and long after. Because he semed to contend with God, and to make himself and his subiects safe and sure whether God would or no, thys is a manifest signe that he had forgoten Gods power, and that he lacked feare of God. And hys enterprise proued thereafter, for almighty

God diuided their tounges and languages that one man vnderstoode not an other, so that when a worke man would call for his axe or hys hamer, his seruer woulde bring him morter, or els wold stand muet & bryng nothing at al, because he knew not what was asked. One neyghbour coulde not talk to an other, for one could not vnderstand an other. And so they ceased to buylde their citie, and that famous towre, and wer dispersed abrode into sondrie countries of ye world.* And where all the worlde was of one language afore, nowe euerye realme and region is of dyuers tonges and diuers languages. And this diuersitie of tonges that mankynd was then fyrst strycken wyth al, I take for one of the greatest strokes that God euer stroke mankinde with al, after the losse of the originall iustice by the synne of Adam.* For where brute beastes among themselues one perceiueth the voyce of an other, and by suche voyces as they haue, they come together or runne a sonder. Rauens and other fowles knowing theyr owne voyces flyeth to theyr feedynge [Q1] together, and change their places together. But man a reasonable creature, little vnder the angelles in the excellencie of his nature, yet perceyueth not what another reasonable creature saith except he be of his owne countrey. An Englyshe dogge perceyueth a walshe dogge, and yet the Englishe man vnderstandeth not a walshe man.* The lacke of the feare of GOD in this vsurper and verye tyraunte and extorcioner **Nemroth** brought vs to this calamitie & wretchednes. If I woulde runne throughe the holye scriptures, declaryng what mischiefe hath fallen to men, for lacke of the feare of GOD, I should soner lacke time than matter. And yet (good and worshipfull audience) let vs consider the maner of oure neighbours here in this citye. And I fear me we shall finde this gyfte of the holye Gooste, that is to saye: the feare of GOD farre awaye from a great meynye of vs. Wee haue knowen some Marchauntes and other occupiers that in their prentishippe, and while they were iourneymen or seruauntes haue serued God deuoutlye, and the worlde bus-ilye. And when they haue set vp and occupied for theim selues, haue growen to muche riches in a little space. In so muche that within seuen or eight yeres they haue bene able to be shyriffes of the Citye, but when they were fatte, that their prouender pricked theim,* they haue begon to kycke agaynste GOD, and to do noughtelye, nother doynge their dutye in their tythes and offerynges to GOD of whom they had their thrift, nother to their owne soules, kepyng [Q1^v] them selues in the feare and awe of God, nother towarde their neighbours liuynge charit-ablye.* They haue take their pleasures moste voluptuouslie, and haue contemned all others dispitefullye whiche is a signe that the feare of GOD was cleane gone, for as the wise manne sayth. **Qui timet deum faciet bona.** He that feareth God will do good dedes,* and will eschue the contraries, and his thrifte shall come according-lye, for example hereof, I reade a narration of two crafts menne. But yet because (I heare) that some yonge menne be daungerous and will peraduenture contemne or dispise such narrations as wel as some other thinges whiche they canne not <a-> amende, somewhat to comforte theim that woulde heare examples for theyr lear-nynge, you shall note what the Apostle saith. **Ephe. iiii. Omnis sermo malus ex ore vestro non procedat sed si quis bonus ad edificationem fidei vt det gratiam audientibus.** Let no yll speache or talkinge passe out of your mouthe, but if you haue anye good talkynge to edifie and healpe our fayeth that it maye geue a grace to the audience.* Sainte Ambrose expoundinge the same wordes saieth. **Bonae enim & sobrie fabulae dant gratum exemplum audientibus.** Good & sober tales geueth pleasant examples to the hearers. Sober tales (he saith) suche as be neither wilde nother wanton.* But such as a manne maye take good and pleasant examples of, as Esopes fables and suche other.* **Quid est enim aliud scita fabula**

quam amena veritatis inuolucio ad hominum vsum, atque oblectationem [Q2] **comparata?** A feete or proper tale is no more but a mery wrappyng in or coueryng of some truth inuented and sette foorthe for mennes profite, and for their plesure to allure them better to remember the matter that is spoken of.* And for this purpose harken you vnto my narration. These .ii. craftes men that I speake of came to the towne to be prentises about one season, they came forth to libertie together, and set vp their occupations aboute one time, the one was more experte in his occupation then the other, more quycke more liuelye, and more pregnant of witte, and he laboured as soore bothe earlye and late, as the other did, and yet he coulde not come forwarde, but euer almoste in beggers estate.* The other, althoughe he were not so lyuelye nor quicke of naturall wytte, and in practise of the worlde as the other hys frende was, yet he prospered and grewe to greate richesse, and to good estimation amonge hys neyghbours. I woulde euerye manne shoulde imagyn thee two men to be of their owne occupacion:* if thou be a marchaunte, thinke they were two marchaunt menne, if thou be a Grocer, or a Draper, Tayler, or Shomaker, thinke they were of thy occupation. In processe of tyme, this manne that was so farre behinde, fell in familiar communication with his olde acquaintaunce, and made hys complaynte vnto hym marueylynge of the chaunce of theim boothe, considerynge (sayth he) that when we were yong I was more likely to come forwarde then thou. [Q2ᵛ] And that I labour and studie (saith he) as many waies to haue the world, and to come to welthines, and more then euer diddest thou, & yet it wil not be, the more I laboure yet neuer the nere, I trowe thou haste founde some bagges or treasure trouy, some hid riches that bringeth thee alofte. Well saith the other man I do remember our bringyng vp very well. I know thy witte I <I> knowe thy cunnynge & thy feete in thy facultie and occupation, and I do lament thy penury and that thou commest no better forwarde. And where thou imputest to me & layest to my charge that I haue founde some hydde ryches. It is verye true. And for our olde frendshippe, I am contente to brynge thee there as thou mayeste finde like riches. And appointed to mete together on the morowe at a certayne houre to go to seke the sayde treasure. When they mette at the time appointed, this riche manne brought his frende to the churche, and there he fell on hys knees and saide his prayers deuoutly as he was wonte to do. The other man called busilye on him to shewe him this treasure. Tarye a while (sayde he) we shall anone haue a Masse or some diuine seruyce compiled or gathered of the word of God, or some sermon or exhortation that may do vs good. Anone a prieste was readye & wente to masse: After masse this poore mannes minde was on the money, and called vppon his frende whiche at the laste aunswered after this maner. Frende, thou haste hearde and sene parte of the treasure that I haue founde. Here in this place I [Q3] haue learned to loue GOD, heare I haue learned to feare God. Heare I haue learned to serue GOD. And when I haue done my duetye to God, home I go to my woorke about suche businesse as I haue, and all thinge goeth forward and so I am come to this honeste Almes that GOD hathe lende me, wyth whiche I am well contented, and do thanke God for it, it commeth of God, and not of my deseruynge. I see thy fashion, thou little regardest God or his seruice, and lesse regardest his ministers. Thou haddest leuer goe to the market then to Masse. And on the holye daye, to idle pastimes, then to heare a Sermon, if euer thou thriue it is meruayle. And surely if thou prospere and go forwarde for a season, thou shalte haue one mischaunce or another that shall set thee further backewarde in a daye, then two or three good yeares hath sette thee forwarde. Nowe let vs see whether this good mannes saiyng be not consonant and agreynge

to the scriptures. He imputeth much of his thrift to the feare of God, & to the
seruice of god, & accordyng to this sayth the prophet. **Psal. xxxiii. Non est inopia
timentibus eum.** They that feare God have no pouertie,* for eyther they be ryche,
or at the leaste wyse be verye well pleased wyth that little that they haue, which
passeth all gold, and precious stoones, **Est autem questus magnus pietas cum
sufficientia i Timo. [v]i. est Animo sua sorte contento.** Pietie or mercie with a
hart content wyth that a manne hathe, is a greate gaynes and winnynge.* **Et psal.
Beatus vir qui ti[Q3ᵛ]met dominum in mandatis eius volet nimis. Gloria &
diuitie in domo eius.** Blessed is the manne that feareth God, his will shall be verye
muche in his commaundmentes. Royaltie, wealthe, and riches shall be in his
house.* **Dispersit dedit pauperibus.** He shall be able to distribute and geue to the
poore people,* where he that lacketh such fear of GOD† shall be ready to begge
and borowe of his neighbours. Sainte Ambrose. **Li. ii. de vocatione gentium ca.
ix.** sheweth that the grace of God by the meanes of feare prepareth and maketh
readye the will of man to receiue the giftes of God, makinge our willes to consente
to the inclinacion of grace, mouinge vs to goodnesse, for there is no vertue in him
that wyll not consente to take vertue.* There muste be a consente of the will, or
els vertue wil not bee there, no more then thou canste make a horse to drinke of
the water if his appetite be not to drinke.* This consente of the wyll, is caused
diuers wayes, sometime by the exhortation of the Preacher, sometyme by lectures,
lessons, or instruction, and sometyme by feare, and yet amonge al these feare is
most of efficacitie, to make the wil of man to enclyne or consente to Goddes
pleasure, and to receyue hys Grace. Did not feare make Pharao Kinge of Egypte,
after seuen terrible plages, that he and all hys Lande (excepte the countrey where
the people of Israell dwelled) were punished wyth all, to say: **Peccaui etiam nunc
Dominus iustus est, ego & populus meus impij. Exod. ix.** I haue offended and
[Q4] done noughte nowe againe, Oure LORDE is righteous, I and my people be
wycked.* Feare made him somewhat to relent, bende and stope if he had so
continued it hadde be better for hym, he moughte peraduenture a receyued grace
at lengthe. And all sainte Stephans longe Sermon whiche sainte Paule hearde
afore the Iewes stoned sainte Stephan to deathe, at which tyme sainte Paule was
presente, and kepte the tormentours clothes.* All the preachinge of the Apostles,
and all the good examples of the good people newly conuerted to Christes fayth
wrought not so muche in hym to make hym leaue his obstinacie and malyce
agaynste christian people, as did the feare that he tooke in that terrible strooke
that he hadde commynge towarde the citie of Damascus, where he woulde haue
take vp all the christian menne and women that he could there haue founde, &
would haue brought them to Hierusalem to be put to martirdome, accordynge to
the commission that he had for that purpose.* And I doubt not but one shipwracke or peril on the sea, or to haue a shippe taken with the Frenchmen now in
this tyme of warre shuld make a marchauntmanne to remember GOD and to feare
GOD,* and to mollifye his hart, to consente and to receyue suche gyftes of grace as
God woulde inspire into hys hearte, and to serue GOD and to drawe to Godly
wisdome more then all the Sermones that hathe bene made here all thys Wytsontyde,* [Q4ᵛ] where† as for lacke of feare of GOD they little regarde God or his
giftes, but take all thinges as thoughe they came of them selues, and not of GOD,
for the more they haue, the lesse Godlye they bee. And for these considerations
saithe the Prophete, and also Salomon. **Inicium sapientiae timor domini.** The

† GOD] GGD ; where] whers

feare of God is the beginnyng of wisdome,* what vertue can make a man so blessed as this feare, for it is the begynner and getter of Godlye wisdome, and also the maister or teacher of Godlie wisedome. And euen lyke as by suche feare, the soule of man obteyneth wisedome so by the same it proceadeth and profiteth more and more in wisdome, so that it dothe conserue and kepe wisedome, and concurreth wyth wisedome so necessarily, that if feare of GOD once go awaye Godly wisedome will not tarye, but thy wisdome will vanishe away to very folly, to sinne, mischiefe, and all vnhappines. **Damascen. orthodoxe fidei. Libro. ii ca. xv.** deuideth feare into sixe members. **In cunctationem, verecundiam, erubescentiam, stuporem, terrorem, & agoniam.*** whyche shoulde be to longe particularlye to declare, but thys I shall aduertise you that euerye one of them maye be mundane, seruyle, or filiall.* Mundane or worldelye feare, which is called humane feare, or mannes feare, that commonlye troubleth the minde of worldly men, commeth of worldelye loue, and of carnall loue.* For all feare presupposeth a loue to the thing that he feareth to lacke or to lose, if a man loued it not, he would not feare to lacke it, or loose it. [R1] **August. lxxxiii. questi.*** Nowe because that worldly loue leaneth and cleaueth faste to the worlde, to worldly welth, and to carnall ease, and to carnal lust, as to the ende in whiche he putteth his felicitie, it can not be good, but must nedes be verye nought. Therfore when a man feareth to lose his temporall riches, honour, aucthoritie, office or pleasure, familiarite, mastership, or frendshyppe, delicate fare or swete morsels, in so much y^t rather than he would lose them, he woulde be redy to swarue from the rectitude and stregthnes of iustice, and to be a flatterer, and to encorage his mayster in his iniquitie, rather then to lose his maysters fauour telling truth. This is a worldly and carnall feare, and very nought and damnable, and suche was the feare that the Scribes and Phariseis had, sayinge. **Si dimittimus eum sic. &c.** If we let him scape thus, then all the people wyll beleue vpon him, and then the Romains wyll come and take our place, and our people into captiuitie.* And Adam oure fyrste father, for ouer muche loue that he had to his newe wyfe, and for feare of discomfortynge her if he shoulde not haue eaten with her of the sayde forbydden frute, broughte vs all to the calamitie, miserye, and wretchednes that we be in. And how many haue we hearde of, that for feare least they shuld lose promotion, fauour, or frendshippe that they haue loked for, hath fallen to preache and teache pernitious heresies, and many others to speake agaynste reason, and to talke that with their mouth that they haue not thoughte with theyr [R1^v] heartes. This carnall and worldly feare, yf it be with deliberation & aduisement, is very nought and dampnable, where as yf it come of the infirmitie and weakenes of the fleshe whiche naturallye abhorreth death, and abhorreth tortures, imprisonmentes, seruitude, bondage, and lacke of libertie and of accustomed pleasures, then yf this feare be but sodayne, though it trouble thy affection, wyll or appetite verye sore, there is no peryll in it, it is natural, it can not be well auoyded, specially the fyrst motions of this feare. And for the comfort of infirme and weake persones, least any man or woman susteyninge suche feare shoulde dispayre of saluation, oure Sauioure Christ to declare that he was a very<.> man, & that this carnall feare of the flesh is not euer dampnable, but naturally ensuing and folowinge the infirmitie of the fleshe, did vouchesafe to susteine suche feare in his owne affection or wyll, when afore his passion he begonne to be afrayde, and to be wery, **Marc. xiiii** he begonne to be afrayd of the death that he should to, and to be wery of the trouble that the Iewes put him to, and that he knewe they woulde put him to more greuouslye afterward, and this feare vexed him so sore, that for very agony and payne, his swete of his body was

like bloude trikeling downe to the ground. A merueilous parturbation of minde
that he was in for that space, but it dyd not longe continue. And therefore the
Euangelist Marke sayd: **Cepit pauere & tedere.** He begonne to be afrayde and to
be werye.* It begon with hym, but it dyd [R2] not continue, for anone reason
checked this sensualitie, and ruled it, directing all his wyll to the pleasure of his
father, and so he proceded forth to his paynefull passion with a verye good wyll
ruled by reason, to consummate, perfourme, and ende the thinge for whiche he
came into oure nature by his blessed incarnation.* In like maner there is no
mundane, carnall, or naturall feare comminge sodenly vpon a man, that can
dampne a man, if it continue not to longe, and if it do not ouercome reason. But if
it so ouercharge the mynde, that for any suche feare a man do forsake iustice, or do
the thinge that shalbe contrarye to Goddes pleasure, then such worldly and carnall
feare is vituperable and dampnable.* Seruyle feare hath the next place, whiche
some wryters both vtterly dampne and say it is very noughte, but it can not be so:*
for ye knowe by experience that a mayster hadde leuer haue a prentyce or a
seruaunte that woulde do his worke for feare of strokes, or for feare of beatynge,
then to haue such a prentyce that wyll nother do his worke for beatynge, nor for
feare of displeasinge of his mayster, nether yet for loue. Of the fyrste maye come
some good at length, but the other is desperate, and of him commeth noughte but
angre and vexation of minde to his maister, he must be put oute of seruyce and
caste of. Seruyle feare hath his name of a seruaunte, a slaue, or bondeman: it is
suche feare as is in the seruaunte, prentyce, or bondeman, or in a shrewde scholer
whiche wyll do no good but onelye for feare of [R2ᵛ] betynge.* So (sayth S.
Augustine) seruyle feare of God is when a man withdraweth and kepeth him selfe
frome sinne for feare of the paines of hel, and for feare least he shalbe damned with
the deuyls in hell for euermore.* Although this feare be insufficient for mans
saluation, yet it is verye good and profitable, for by this groweth a vse and a
custome of iustice, or of well doynge:* for he that oft tymes doth wel although it be
for feare, shall fynde ease thereby, and at length shal haue a pleasure in well
doynge, and a loue to iustice or well doynge, thoughe it were hard and paynfull for
hym at the beginninge, and so the seruilitie, the bondage of the feare beginneth a
litell and a litell to swage, and to be excluded, and it waxeth and beginneth to be
amicable & louing feare, by whiche a man doth well partlye for loue, and partely
for feare. And this the doctours call **timor initialis,*** and it is the meane and next
way to the filial feare, the chast and holye feare that beginneth here, and shall
remayne and continue in heauen for euermore, as the prophete sayth. **Timor
domini sanctus permanet in seculum seculi. Psalm. xviii.** The holy feare of God
abydeth for euermore, it commeth of charitie whiche neuer fayleth.* The foresayde seruyle feare of Goddes iustice and of his punyshment of synners, prepareth a
waye to the filial and charitable feare, but when charitie and louinge feare is once
gotten, the former feare of punyshment vanysheth and goeth awaye, for the more
that the loue is, the lesse is the feare of punyshment. The good that a [R3] man
doth for loue, hath no spyce of the bondage or of seruyle feare: therefore sayth
Saint Iohn **.i Ioh. iiii. Timor non est in charitate sed perfecta charitas foras
mittit timorem, quoniam timor penam habet, qui autem timet non est perfectus
in charitate.** In charitie there is no feare, but perfyt charitie dryueth out feare, for
feare hath payne annexte, and he that feareth is not perfyt in charitie.* Nowe
these wordes of S. Iohn semeth contrary to the wordes of the Prophete, **Timor
domini sanctus. &c.** The holye feare of God abydeth for euer.* To this I aunswere
fyrst bringing in this example, that lyke as one blaste of winde of the belowes

bloweth and fylleth two organ pipes or moo, so may one breath or inspiration of
the holy spyryte fyl two heartes, and styrre two tongues, the two organ pipes so
blowen by one breath, concordeth and agreeth full well, so maye two heartes
inspired with one holye spirite concorde and agre,* as ye shall perceaue so that ye
wil geue diligent audience. The Prophete in his sayinge addeth this worde **Sanctus**
or **castus**, he calleth it holye feare or chast feare, the Euangelist Saynt Iohn doth
not adde these wordes, therefore let vs put difference betwixt two feares, and so
shal we vnderstand the consonaunce and concorde of these two organ pipes, the
holye Prophete, and the blessed Euangeliste. There be men that feareth hell
paynes, least they burne there with the deuils, this feare bringeth in charitie, but
when he hath broughte in charitie, this feare auoydeth and charitie remaineth. If a
man feare onely for [R3ᵛ] punyshment, then a man loueth not him that he so
feareth, he desireth not that is good, but exchueth that that is yll. Notwithstandinge, in as muche as a man is ware and feareth that that is yll, he correcteth and
amendeth him self, and beginneth to desire that is good, and so there may be in
him holy loue and chast loue, holy feare and chast feare.* A man can not better
declare & make playne these two feares, then if a man put example of two wiues,
one aduoutresse, and disposed to take others beside her husbande, but she is
afrayde of her husbande least he punyshe her and cast her of. The feare that she
hath of her husband is onely because she loueth her wicked purpose, and feareth
leaste her husbande spye her with a faute, more then for any loue she hath vnto
hym. The other wife (in my case) is a chast wife, intendinge no nother but to liue
in coniugall chastite, accordinge to the lawe of matrimonye with her owne husbande, and to refuse all other for his sake, and for the loue of him. Both of these
wyues feare theyr husbandes, but not after one maner: the fyrst feareth leaste her
husband come and take her with the faute, the other feareth leaste her husband
wilbe gone, or will be longe awaye from her, and absent him self from her sight,
and out of her company.* The feare that the first wife hath of her husband, is like
the bondmans feare, or the lewde seruauntes feare, & this hath muche perturbation & trouble of minde, and payne annexed, whiche standeth not with charitie,
as S. Iohn sayth in his epistle, for charitie expelleth [R4] suche feare of payne &
punishment.* But because my sermon is not onely to maried men, & to maried
women, ye shal vnderstand that almyghtye God hath maried vs all to his onleye
begotten sonne our sauiour Iesus Christ, by fayth. Saint Paule, the Euangelistes
and preachers solemnised this mariage, as S. Paule saith for his part .**desponsaui
vos vni viro virginem castam exhibere Christo.** I haue maried you to one man,
that ye kepe your selfe as a chast virgin vnto Christ,* the beutifullest spouse that
euer was. **Speciosus forma pre filijs hominum.*** The great loue and charitie that
he had to vs, dyenge for vs beynge his enemies, is a very greate cause why we
shoulde loue him agayne. Then let all vs, and euerye one of vs as his spouse and
wife, examine oure selfe and our consciences, whether we be chast wiues or
aduouterers. Let euerye man aske his own conscience this question, **wilte thou
haue thy husband to come to the as yet or no, but that he shall yet longer tary?**
Now I haue knocked at the dores of your heartes, but what the conscience of
euerye one of you saith inwardly to your self I can not heare, it cometh not to mine
eares, I am a mortal man & know not the secrets of your hert, but he yᵗ is absent
bodely, & present by the strength of his maiestie, hath heard you what you think.
If a man wold say vnto you, lo Christ is here now, to morow shalbe the day of
iugement: you wuld not say (I feare me) wuld god Christ were come, would God to
morowe were the daye of dome. For they that so would say loueth God

vehemently, & if it were said vnto them, he wil yet tary lenger, [R4ᵛ] they would be afrayd least he would tary away any longer, and yf he came, they woulde be afrayde least he would go from them agayne, and would saye with S. Paule. **Cupio dissolui & esse cum Christo.** I woulde faine haue my soule losed from my body and to be with Christ.* Yet againe I aske you another question. If God him selfe woulde come and speake vnto you in his owne voice (although he ceaseth not to speake vnto vs by his holye scripture) and woulde saye vnto a man, wylte thou sinne? then sinne. Do what soeuer thinge deliteth the or please the: what soeuer thinge thou louest on earth let it be thine owne: whosoeuer thou arte angry with all let him die: whosoeuer thou wylt beate, let him be beaten: whosoeuer thou wylte iudge let him be iudged, whosoeuer thou wylt condemne, let him be condemned, no man shall resist the, no man shall say to the why doest thou so? no man shall say whye hast thou done so? no man shall say do no more as thy lyst, thou shalt haue haboundaunce of all thinges that thou desyrest, and thou shalte lyue in them and continue with them, not for a season or for a litle space, but for euermore, onelye one thinge I warne the that my face thou shalt neuer se. If you mourne for this sayinge, if youre heartes be sory to heare this, it is a signe that the chast feare remaininge for euer is spronge vp in you. But I saye to you, ye shall neuer leaue these pleasures that I haue rehearsed, ye shall euer continue with them, and they with you, what wyl you haue more? Surely the chast fear wolde [S1] wepe and wayle, and woulde saye, I hadde leuer thou wouldest take awaye all these pleasures rehearsed, and let me see thy face. The chaste feare woulde crye out aloude with the prophete in the Psalme. **O lorde God of powers, conuert vs and shewe thy face, and wee shall be safe. One thinge I haue asked of our Lorde, and that I shall require: that I maye dwell in the house of our Lorde, that I maye see the will of our God, and visite his holy temple.*** Nowe good frendes, if euerye one of vs will examine our owne Consciences after this maner as I haue nowe spoken, how many of vs shall we finde that hathe this chaste feare, this louing feare of the chaste wife, the holy feare that continueth for euermore? I pray God there be many suche amonge vs. They that haue not such feare, let theim begin at the leastwise, wyth seruile feare that I spoke of, let them liue well for feare of the paynes of Hell, that so with continuaunce they maye haue a swetenesse in well doinge, and at the laste do well for loue. For the sayde seruile feare is not vtterlye to be condempned, for it is a good gift of GOD as faith vnsourmed, or without fashion, hope vnsourmed Sapience and science vnsourmed, the giftes of tonges, the grace to do cures, and suche other as the Apostle speaketh of **.i. Corin. xii.*** Not decked nor garnished with charitie, whiche is the fashion and beautye of all other gyftes of grace.* And the sayde seruyle feare is the very waye to bring in charitie, lyke as when a manne soweth in cloothe the nedle goeth afore and maketh the [S1ᵛ] waye for the threde to come after, not because the nedle shall sticke there still in the clothe, but shall passe and go throughe, that the threde may come after and bide still there. And when a man soweth in leather, the threde hathe a bristle, or a harde heere, craftelye set and ioyned to the former ende of the threede. After the Nall hathe made the waye then afore the threde the sayde heere goeth, not because it shall there abide still, in the hoole, but because it shall leade and gyde the threade that commeth after, and muste there remaine styll.* So dothe the feare of paynes of Hell prepareth a waye to loue, in asmuch as by ofte doinge well for feare a manne shall fynde some ease in well doinge, and at lengthe shall do well for verye loue, and therefore the Prophete saide. **Initium sapienciae timor domini.** The feare of GOD is the beginnynge of wisedome, whiche is true of

the seruile feare that serueth or dothe well onelye for feare of payne, and it is true
also of the feare that groweth in processe, which is partlye for feare, & partly for
loue that is called **Timor inicialis,** & this is the next meane to the chaste feare or
holye feare that remaineth for euermore.* But nowe finallye to speake of the
seuenth gift of the holie Gost, whiche as the Prophete **Esay** sayeth, rested on our
sauiour Christ.* It is not mundane, humane, nor carnal feare, nother the seruile
feare, or the bondmannes feare. His good and gracious workes that he did on
earthe, he did not for feare of the paynes of Hell, or for feare of anye other
punish[S2]mentes. It was the holye feare that remayneth for euer. It was louynge
and reuerende feare of God, suche as all the angels in heauen haue nowe.* And
that maye begin in vs & grow vp with charitie here on earth, and shal shote vp
and growe vp with euerlastinge charitie or loue that shall neuer fall awaye or fayle,
but shall euer abide more and more in euerlastynge glory. This feare dothe not
importe anye perturbation or trouble of minde, but rather a certayne reuerence
towarde almightye God. Suche is the feare that the angels haue in heauen, where
is no trouble of minde, or vnquietnesse, but readye and ioyful obedience to
almighty God.* And such reuerende feare of the father hadde our sauiour Christe,
as appeareth in manye places of the gospell, where hee protesteth hym to dooe the
commaundementes of his father, and to fulfyll his pleasure with manye suche like.
Honorifico patrem. &c. Thus he did lowlye and reuerently magnifie his father,*
by reason of his manhode by whiche he was inferiour and lower, and subiect to his
father. And in his manhode he hadde these seuen giftes of the holye Gooste,
restynge on hym as **Esai** saide, and as I haue declared in times paste. And this gifte
of dreade or feare of GOD after scolasticall doctours, is **Humilitie,*** which was
most excellently in our sauiour Christ **Phili. ii. Humiliauit semet[ ]ipsum . . .
dominus noster Iesus Christus. &c.** Our Lorde Iesus Christe did humiliate himselfe, kepynge obedience euen to hys death on the crosse, for whiche God the
father [S2ᵛ] exalted him, & gaue him a name aboue al names, that all creatures in
heauen, earthe, or hell, shall bowe the knee to this blessed name of Iesus, and all
tonges shall confesse that oure Lorde Iesus is in the glory of god his father,* there
to be mediatour, a meane, and intreater for vs, to bringe vs as his coparteners and
coenheritours wyth him to his inestimable glory in heauen, and that we maye all
come to that enheritaunce, he graunt vs for his infinite mercy that for vs dyed.
Amen.

An homilie or sermon
of the articles of our
christian faythe.*

FAyth (as saynt Paule sayth to the Hebrewes) is ye beginnynge of heuenly ioyes
that we hope to come vnto, makinge our wits surely to assente & agree to thinges
that wee do not yet see, nor knowe by experience.* Euerlastyng lyfe shall stande in
the clere knowledge of the Godhead, and of the glorified manhode of our sauiour
Christ knitte in one persone, to the seconde persone in Trinitie, one God with the
father, and with the holye Gost. This knowledge and sighte wee shall haue in
heauen clearelye and perfitelye, whiche wee haue here but darkelye by heresaye.*
But let vs leane fast by our fayth to this that we hearesaye by Gods scriptures and
liue accordinglye, and wee shall not faile to come to the cleare knowledge in
heauen, where we shall knowe God, as he knoweth vs without corporall similitudes to conduct vs to that knoweledge, and without anye impedi[S3^v]mente.
Without faieth it is impossible to please GOD. For he that wyll come to God
muste neades beleue as the Apostle saythe. **Hebre. xi.*** Wee muste not differre†
nor refuse to beleue so longe, tyll wee can declare or proue by reason the articles or
poyntes that wee be bounde to beleue, for if wee woulde be so daungerous it myght
chaunce that by the difficultye† of the scriptures, & of the things that we shuld
beleue we myght be withdrawen and kept backe from the merite and rewarde of
our faythe for euer. He that woulde so differ to beleue, shoulde be like a manne
almoste deade for honger, whyche hauynge breade and meate offered hym, woulde
not open hys mouthe to eate thereof, tyll hee knewe who made the breade, and
dressed the meate, and howe and wyth what instrumentes or tooles it was made
and dressed. He were like to be deade for honger afore he came to that knoweledge. Better it were for him firste to take hys meate and saue his lyfe, and
afterward if nede were, at leasure to laboure for such knoweledge if he myght
obtayne it. So best it is for vs with an open harte, to beleue as wee be taughte by
Christes churche, and to feede oure soules with suche Godly foode, and to saue our
liues by fayth, & afterward by exercise to attaine to more distincte and playne
vnderstandynge of that wee do beleue accordynge to suche measure of fayth as
shall please God to distribute to euerye one of vs. There was neuer manne saued
from the beginnynge of the worlde, neither shall [S4] be to the ende of the same
but by his beliefe on Goddes rewarde, prouided for his faithfull people, by the
merite of our sauiour Christe, as by the mediatoure and meane to come thereto.
The holye menne and women that were afore Christes incarnation by the space of
fiue thousande yeres and more, were saued by their fayth of saluation by the
mediatour that was to come, and in signe thereof, they vsed their sacrifices afore
the lawe written, and also in the tyme of the lawe writte by Moyses, as figures to
proteste and signifie the misterie of the mediatour which the auncientes, and they
that hadde higher reuelation, and that were best learned among them, beleued
more distinctlye and plainelye then the younger and simpler sorte did or were
bounde to beleue.* And nowe in the plentuous tyme of grace, bothe yonge and
olde be bounde to haue expresse faythe of Christes incarnacion alreadye exhibited
and perfourmed, and of suche articles and pointes as be commonlye declared, and

† differre] diffarre; difficulty] difficilitye

168

openlye set furthe in the churche concernynge our saluation by our sauioure Christe, as the onelye meane to obtayne the same. Al be it, they that haue clearer wyttes, and they that be sette in aucthoritye and offyce, speciallye to haue the rule and cure of Christes flocke, be bound more expreslye, dystynctlye, and playnelye to haue the knoweledge of subtyller and hygher consyderations, consernynge the Articles of oure faythe, then the rude and vnlearned folcke, [S4ᵛ] so that they maye by their knoweledge and learnyng declare the truthes and the possibilitie of the same, to them that be ignorant and would learne. **i. pet. iii.** * To declare I saye but not to proue by reason the veritie of them. They muste also bee able to replye and conuince theim that frowardely woulde repugne, and countersaye anye article of our faithe. They haue euer bene impugned and persecuted by heritykes, wilfully and grosselye, leanynge to their carnall imaginations. And yet God of his goodnesse turneth all to the best agaynste their expectation. It is verye profitable and necessarye that oure faythe shoulde be set to woorke, for as sainte Ambrose saythe. **Fides inex<c>ercitata cito languescit, & crebris ociosa tentatur incommodis. super. illud. psal. cxviii. Iniqui, persecuti sunt me adiuua me.** Our fayth when it is vnexercised, anone waxeth sicke and faint. And when it is idle, it is tempted and tried with many discommodities. **Remissas excubias callidus insidiator irrumpit.** As we see that he that wililye and craftelye lieth in wayte will sone breke in to an Holde or Fortresse, where the watches bee slacke and sleapye,* euen so when our faythe the watche of oure Soule, laye idle and was not exercised and tempted by contrary heresies, spying howe to breake into the fortresse of our soules, it was easye to sowe the sedes of errours in our soules, to destroy our faith and our soules. Fortye or fifty yeares afore this present yeare of Christ .M.D. xlvi.* the com[T1]mon faithe of the churche was at rest and in maner idle without trouble. And by that, when the Germaynes suscitated and raysed vp all maner of heresies by Luther and that rable,* anone they were receiued in all countreys, for **pax fidei corruptele materia est. Ambrosius.** The peace and rest of faith is the matter and cause of corruption of faith.* Mens wits wer vnexercised & not cumbred with suche newes, and coulde not forthwith by learning spye the falsitie of them, therefore they were taken for truthes of all carnall and wilfull people, and so beleued to the vtter confusion of manye a one. The true rule of our beliefe is the whole booke of holye scripture,* but because it is to muche for euery parson to learne all that, and to beare it way, therefore the holye goste hath otherwise instruct his holye churche to gather the most necessary thinges for Christen people to beleue into .xii. articles, according to the nomber of the .xii. Apostles, which as the holy fathers wryteth, & as it is credibly thought after thei had receiued yᵉ holy gost & the gift of tonges by which they coulde speake all maner of languages, and muste departe a sondre into dyuers countries to preache the faith of Christ.* They thought it necessarye to make a gatheryng of the sayd articles and laye them together to be taught to all people, that so they might by the same shotte or gatherynge* knowe that as well they among them selues as all people of their teaching varied not but agreed in one faithe, euen like as souldiours vnder one Capitaine vseth one badge, and one [T1ᵛ] watche word.* And according to the nombre and names of the sayde Apostles I shall in my processe diuide the said articles.* They be called articles, that is to saye, truthes of God and of hys gracious effects, compact and knit into short sentences, binding vs without ambiguitie or wauering to beleue them.

THe first article saint Peter* layde to thys collation* and shotte or gatheringe, and it is this: **I beleue in God the father almightie, maker of heauen and earth.** In whiche article ye must note the order of the words. Fyrst it is said **I beleue** to declare that it is no point of our charge to discusse and reason the highe iudgement and secrets of God, nor to require and aske these busye questions, when, how, or why, but plainelye and stedfastly to leane to our fayth, beleuyng on one God. It is not sufficient to beleue that there is one God, for the deuils in hell beleue that, and so did the Paynym Philosophers, but they dyd not glorifie hym as God, but played the fooles in theyr fansies, as other idolatours did. It is not sufficient to beleue GOD as thou beleuest thy [n]eighbour or thy brother, when thou thinkest that hys saying is true, for so doth manye a synnefull person, and yet noughte wyll doe accordyng to Gods wordes, which he beleueth to be true. But we must beleue on God, or in God, that is to say, with our beliefe we must extende and set fourth our selues with loue to God so to be incorporate to him, and made one spirite with him, and thys [T2] is the good and parfit faith, adorned and decked with charitie, which onely shall saue vs. And in case thou be in deadly synne & out of charitye, yet ceasse not to say this thy belefe in this gathering or shotte of the Apostles, called the Crede, for it is the belefe of the vniuersal church, which doubtles is not without charitie, and so by the merite of the whole congregation of Christen people,* thou as the vnfrutefull membre mayst labour to come to the beliefe of the whole, & then trulye to say, that thou for thine own part beleuest in god, which afore was not true, but in the voyce of the whole church. If thou beleue on God, thou must beleue he is of infinite power, but one & no more, for it is not possible twoo powers infinite to be. Then the superstitious erroures of Paygnyms worshipping creatures as theyr gods, as **Iupiter, Mars, Venus,** Sunne, Moone, or anye element, must nedes be false.* And the heresie of **Maniche*** making twoo first causes, or twoo Gods, one of good thinges which after him were onely things inuisible, and the other he put the causer and maker of all yll thinges. He called all visible creatures yll and nought, moued by a rude imagination, because they may hurt or do yll, as the fyre burneth him that commeth to nigh vnto it, and is yll to hym, therefore he sayde it was yll by kinde, and made by the deuyll. And water because it choketh hym that is drowned in it, and so is yll to hym, therefore he sayd it was nought, by nature, and the effecte of the naughtye God. And all they that vse sorcery, charmes, wytche[T2ᵛ]craftes by inuocation and callynge on dampned spirites, that first taught men and women to vse such folishnes and to giue faith to them, loking for reuelation of secrets or for knowledge of thinges to come, or for healpe of the deuils, whych they ought to looke for onely of God. And generallye who soeuer obeyeth man more then God, doing that for the pleasure of hys Lorde or mayster, or for affection or carnall fauoure to hys worldlye frende or louer, which he would not do to please God, or doing for his louers sake that is contrary to Gods pleasure: Al such maketh their frendes theyr God, & so do all they that labour to satisfie theyr carnall lust, or theyr bellies, more then to subdue them to Gods pleasure. All suche make theyr flesh or bellies theyr Gods, and do not beleue on one God, as is afore declared. It foloweth in this first article, **The father almightye,** in which is expressed the first parson in trinitie, the original fountain of the whole trinitie, by whose frutefull memorye the second parson in Godhed the sonne of God is gotten, aske not the maner how, for the angels cannot tel. The Prophetes were ignorant thereof: Esay saith: **his generation who can declare?*** as who should say no creature. We muste beleue it, and reason no farther in it. Not that the father is elder then the sonne, neyther of greater power, but that like as the fyre is not without heate, neither the sunne in the fyrmament without brightnes: so was the father neuer without the sonne, neither had any power to do any thing but y^t the sonne had ye same power [T3] to do the same like him, and so hath the holy gost the third person in trinitie, product and brought forth by the will of the father, and of the sonne, coeternally with the father & with the sonne. Almightynes of power is here applyed to the person of the father by appropriation, although it agre to the almighty sonne, & to the almighty holy gost, not three almighties, but one God almyghtie. And by this that we beleue him to be almightie, we haue a great comfort and lighte to beleue all the articles that folowe in our creede, for if he be almighty, he may make heauen and earthe of nought, he may make a man to be borne of a virgin, he may forgiue synnes, and giue life euerlasting. **Maker of heauen and earth,** maker by creation, that is to say, without any matter or stuffe to make it of. That a man maketh, he maketh of somewhat, or of some stuffe, therefore he can be no creatour: but almighty god made heauen and earth of nothing, therefore he is iustly called the creator of heauen and earth. What is here to be vnderstande by thys woorde **Heauen,** there be two opinions, for which ye shall first vnderstand that heauen is called one maner of wise: the empiriall heauen aboue the starrye skye, and aboue all the orbes that moueth there, in which is neyther place nor vacuitie, neyther time, but onelye thinges leading a most blessed life.* Thys farre Aristotle dreamed and discussed **primo de celo & mundo,*** and it agreeth with holy scriptures, and with holy doctours, there putting the felicitye of Aungels and men that shallbe saued in the fru[T3^v]ition, that is to say in the clere sighte and loue of God, ther most aboundantly shewing his glory. This the prophet in the psalme calleth the kyngdome of GOD,† saying to God of the same. **Thy kingdome is the kingdome of all worldes,*** as who should say, whatsoeuer nomber of yeares can be thoughte or spoken of, thys kingdome passeth it, for this king almighty God was neuer wythout a kingdome, by which it semeth to be eternal and euerlasting, for it is the very clerenes of God, coeternal with him, and not created with other visible creatures, and to thys were admitted and receiued the holy angels after their creation, for so long space and such durance as God knoweth best, afore that he made heauen and earthe that Moyses spoke of. And of this minde is Saynte Basile as appeareth in the first homilye of hys exameron.* Heauen is taken an other waye, for the bodies aboue, as Sunne, Moone, Sterres, with the orbes and circles there.* Heauen is called also the thirde maner, all that is aboue the earth and so the sayde bodies aboue, with the speires of the fyre and of the ayre be comprised vnder one name of heauen, & so it is taken in the psalme when we say, the birdes of the heauen, for the birdes of the ayre.* And (after this opinion) so taketh Moyses this word **Heauen** when he saythe that in the begynning God made heauen & earth. And by the **Earth** there is to be vnderstande the water and earth together, whiche as then were not dysseuered and diuided tyll the thirde daye when the earth first appeared drye.* The seconde [T4] opinion which is more comon taketh this worde **Heauen** for the empiriall heauen replenished and ful-filled with the glorious companye of Angels, whiche was made together with the earthe, vnderstandynge by the **Earthe** the firste vnfacioned matter or stuffe, of which almighty God made, disposed, and garnyshed al other kindes of creatures that may be sene, or feled as wel in the firmament aboue, as vnder it, to his owne glorye & to do seruice vnto man.* Therfore we haue great nede to take hede that

† GOD] GGD

vsing Gods creatures for our profite or pleasure, we in no case dyshonoure God, vsing them contrary to his honour, & contrary to his pleasure & intent that he made them for

THe seconde article saynte Iohn Euangelist* layd to this shotte or gathering, which is this: **And in Iesu Christe his onelye sonne our Lorde,** euer repeting this word, **And I beleue,** so that this is the sentence: And I beleue on Iesus Christ his onely sonne our Lord. The second persone in trinitie the coeternall sonne of the father, knowing afore the worlde beganne, the syn of Adam, & of the miserable case that man shuld com to, was determined to saue mankinde from the danger of the same & therfore he was euer worthi to be called a sauiour. **Iesus** is as much to sai as a sauior, then this name was his for euer, it is ye name that ye father gaue him by production in his godhed & was newly diuulged & published bi the angell to our blessed Lady his mother, & afterward to his foster father Ioseph with ye interpretacion of y^t name saying: **Ipse enim saluum faciet populum suum a peccatis eorum.** [T4^v] For he shall saue the people from their synnes,* which onely God can do, and none other. Gods pleasure was that the same name that he had in his Godhed should also be his name in his humanite, for his humanitie was the instrument and mean by which he wrought and perfourmed our saluation and redemption **Iesus** and **Christ** signifieth one person that was borne of the virgine Mary, yet there is some difference betwixte the names. **Iesus** is his proper name, as we say Henry, Thomas, Roger, or suche like. **Christ** is the name of a sacrament as sainte Austine speaketh, or of an office **super epist. Io. tract. iii.** as we say a king, a prophet, a priest.* Christ is as much to say as anoynted, and he was anoynted before all other men, by the chiefest oyntment which is the holye gost, one God with him and with his father, of which oyntment the anointyng with oyle is the sacrament and signe.* It foloweth, **his onely sonne** which (as saint Peter writeth) was not declared by any fables. But by that that he with Iohn & Iames sawe and hearde on the holye hill where Christ shewed them the maiestie of his glorious body as it shuld be after hys resurrection: because they shuld not fear nor wauer when they saw the miserable processe of his painful passion.* Therfore (sayth he) **ii. Pet. i. Christ toke of God the father honour and glory by a voyce comming downe to him from the great doynge glorye after thys maner: this is my welbeloued sonne in whom I haue pleasure, gyue eare vnto hym.*** And Christ in manye places of the gospels calleth God hys father, and [V1] him selfe the sonne of God, he is true and verye truthe, and cannot lye, he is the onelye begotten sonne in the fathers bosome, euerlasting as the father is. He was afore Abraham was made, & afore all other creatures, not made but begotten of the substaunce of the father, very God of God the father. **Not two Gods*** but one God, and one light, and of one substaunce with the father. By whom as by his wysedome and craft the father made all creatures, as saint Iohn saith: **al things were made by him, he is our Lorde,*** which ye must here vnderstand bi his humanitie & manhod, for by reason of the Godhed we may sai so of the father and of the holy gost, although it be not so expressed in the Apostles Creede. For God is **oure Lord,** & so we should cal him by reason of his vniuersal dominion ouer al mankind, & ouer al other creatures. **The Lorde** importeth a vage dominion and vncertain power, but there is no power, dominion or authoritie so certain as the power that God hath ouer vs, wherefore it semeth we may not conueniently call him, **the Lorde.** And moreouer we vse to saye **the Lorde,** speaking of suche Lordes as haue nothing to doe with vs, as the lorde of Dale, the lord of Kilmayn and such like, whereas if we were theyr tenauntes, or otherwise held of them we woulde say my lord of Dale, or our Lord of

Dale, and so of others. Wherfore professing our due subiection to almightye God, we shoulde in common speeche cal him our Lord, not dimissing our selues from our allegeaunce to his highnes.* And I haue knowen verye honest [V1ᵛ] men that in communication long afore the new translations of the bible came abrode, vsed sometimes to sweare by **the Lord,** no more intending or meaning to sweare by God, then by any Lorde in the isles of Orchadie,* so thynking to sweare by, they could not tell what, or by nothing, albeit lest thei should offend them that be addict to the new gise: I have aduertised them to leaue suche sayinges, tyll men may be better informed. But to my purpose now, because all power in heauen and earth was giuen to Christ, and all thyng was subiecte vnder his fete, and he in his manhood taught his Apostles and all vs by them, and in his manhode redemed vs, and in the same shall iudge vs, thefore we maye iustlye by that reason call hym our lord and maister, as it is expressed in this article.

THe third article was added by S. Iames brother to saint Iohn the Euangelist, son of zebedi called Iames the more:* **That was conceiued by the holy gost, and borne of the virgine Marie,** the authoure and doer of this conception was the whole trinitie, the father, & the sonne, & the holy gost, for the workes of the trinitie outwarde amonge creatures be vndyuided, so that what so euer one person doth, the same thing doth all three persons. But in asmuch as thys blessed incarnation of Christ came of the mere goodnes, grace, mercy, and loue of God, whiche is appropriate to the holy gost, as power to the father, & wisedome to the sonne. Though all these agreeth to all three persons, therefore the scripture sayth [V2] (as very true it is) that the holy gost was the doer† thereof,* but how it was performed & done, we can better beleue then declare it: faith may do very muche in this article, and in all other articles of our faith, speche can do very litle. Saint Austine saith, that lyke as by the heate and i[n]fluence of the sunne, a worme is gendred of the moyst earth, so by the inspiration of the holy goste, santifyinge the hart of the virgin, the flesh of Christ was conceiued, formed & facioned of the flesh of ye virgin without the worke of any sede of man, workyng to the same,* and therefore Christ sayd of himself by the mouth of his prophet that **he was a worme a[n]d not a man,** because he was not conceyued as other men be. In this marueilous conception the profite and whole nature of man, soule and bodi together, was vnite and ioyned in one person vnto the sonne of God, and neither to the father nor to the holy gost because there should be no confusion, but that he that was the sonne of god shuld also be the sonne of man. **Borne of Mary the virgin** he that came to renew the nature of man cankered with sinne, chose a new maner to be borne of a mayde, and not of a corrupt woman. And when the God of maiestie tooke hys bodye, and was borne of a vyrgine, hee was no more polluted, nor defowled then when he made manne of the earthe, as when the Sunne or fyre woorketh on the claye, he amendeth and hardeneth that he toucheth and feleth† not it selfe. And it is as possyble, credyble, and lykelye, that hee [V2ᵛ] was borne of a virgine, as that he made Adam of earth, and Eue the first woman of the rybbe of Adams side, all is the woorke of God, to whom nothing is impossible. Great was the prerogatiue of that virgine Mary, and the loue that god had to her, in that that his onely begotten son, by whom he made all the worlde, he gaue vnto her to be the fruite of her wombe and her naturall sonne. God that made all thyng was made man of her purest bloud, to renewe mankinde, that by synne was brought to

† doer] dcer; feleth] fyleth

nought. While the sonne of God was in his fathers glory, not descending to our infirmitie, he was vnknowen, but when that worde of God was made man, and dwelled amongest vs: he was seene and knowen on earthe, and was conuersaunt with menne, for whose sakes he that is Lorde of all the world is made our brother, comming forth & being borne of the blessed virgine, euer close and cleane with out any aperture or diuision of her blessed body, euen like as after his resurrection he came into the chambre among the disciples, the doores beyng shut,* and like as the sunne beames commeth through the glasse and breaketh it not.

SAint Andrewe* layde his portion to thys shotte or gathering by these woordes of the fourthe article: **That suffered vnder Ponce Pilate, was crucified, dead, and buried** Thys **Ponce Pilate** was president and ruler of the countrey, and highest iudge there, set in his authority by Tiberius the Emperoure of Rome, to whom [V3] the most part of the world was then subiecte, he is here named not for any honestie to his parson but for to declare the time when Christ suffred.* The death on the crosse he chose, and neyther to haue his necke broken, nor his bones burst, as being cast downe from a hyll, as his neighbours were aboute to serue him in Nazereth **Luke .iiii.*** where he was brought vp in youthe, neyther to be stoned to death, as the Iewes would haue killed him, when he hid him self and went out of the temple. **Iohn .viii.*** And al was for our health, and for to saue vs, for (as saint Austine saith) we can not euer beare with vs rocks, stones, or swerds to defend vs from the diuell, but the sig[n]e of the crosse is soone made with a little mouing of our hand to saue vs from his falsehed. This is the signe by which with his mighty woorde is consecrate the bodye of Christ, the Fount is halowed, priestes and other degrees of the churche take their orders, and all thinges that be halowed by this signe of Christes crosse, with inuocation of hys name, be sanctified.* The crosse layd down on the grounde extendeth his partes towarde the foure partes of the worlde, East, West, Northe, and Southe* and so did the body of Christ when he was nayled on the crosse, lying on the grounde in signe and token that hys loue extended to all partes of the worlde, and that for theyr sakes he suffered so great paines as he did, whych doubtlesse very farre passed the paynes that any other man myght suffer, by reason of the complexion of his body, whych was excellently pure & quick. [V3ᵛ] for it was made of the purest substance of a cleane mayde vnde-fowled, & not mixt of such vile matter as our bodies be, and it was neuer mystem-pered by ingurgitacion or vncleane diet. Therefore it must nedes be very pure and cleane. And according to the proportion, rate, or maner of the disposition of the bodye, is the dysposition of the sences of the body, and specially of the touchyng or feling, then it must nedes folow that hys touching or feling was ex<er>ceding pure, quicke, and liuely, by which ye may be sure that the stroke or wounde that would litle agreued another man, was great griefe to him. Then consider howe his head was bobbed and beaten and pricked wyth sharpe thornes, his handes & feete bored through and torne with great nayles. And after that, the crosse & he hanging on it, hoysed vp, & let downe into the mortesse made for it, and to be shogged and shaken, hauyng no stay but his own sinowes fleshe, and skynne rent and torne in his handes and feete. Thys was a payne of all paines, specially in that pure complexioned and tender body. After this he suffered his soule to departe out of his body, and so dyed bodely, that he might delyuer vs from the death of the soule, which commeth by synne, for like as the soule giueth life vnto the bodye, so God giueth life vnto the soule, therfore like as when the soule is gone from the body, the body is dead, so when God is gone from the soule the soule is dead, and that is euer when we synne, for God and synne dwell not together, no more the[n] light and darkenesse. **Roma. v.** From thys [V4] danger we were reconsiled to God by the bloude of his sonne, for he washed vs from our sinnes in his owne blo[u]de, and so deliuered vs oute of the diuels danger which had none other holde vpon vs, but by the ropes and bondes of synne.* **He was buried** that so he might blesse the buriall and graues of al good men, for the consolacion of al them that shall be buried in the earth. Of his graue **Esay** prophecied longe afore, saying: that **hys graue shall be glorious. Esay .xi.*** as in dede it was, hewed out of a new stone intended for a worshipfull man that prouided it for hymselfe, but he was verye glad to bestow it on a better man. He was wrapt in fyne clothes and powdred with costlye spyces.* The graue was honoured wyth the presence of Angels, visited of holye women and of the disciples, and afterward deuoutely soughte of noble Emperours, and of other great men, & we Christen people in the remembraunce of the same vse a laudable ceremonie, garnishynge after the best maner that we can in our churches euerye good fryday a goodly sepulture, in whyche we repose the blessed body of Christ.*

COnsequentlye foloweth the fifth article added by saynt Phillip,* **He descended into hell,*** not hys bodye, for it remayned in the sepulchre tyll hys resurrection, but in hys soule wyth the Godhead, for the pryncipall partes of Christes manne-hoode whyche the Godheade once tooke to hym, hee neuer lefte.

[V4ᵛ] His Godhead was with the bodye in the graue, & with the soule in hell for the consolation of our first parentes, and of all Patriarchs and Prophetes, and of all good men and women, that afore his comming remayned there without anye sensible paine, but onely in the greuous payne of lacke of glory, from which they were stopped as by a payne for originall synne, because the raunsome was no rather payed. Thyther it pleased him of his goodnes to descende, for to confounde his enemies the diuels, that lyke as he had ouercome them on earth by hys blood, so he might at home among them selfes in hel triumphe ouer them taking theyr prayes and prisoners out of theyr holdes agaynst theyr wylles. The Prophet zachary sayd that Christ woulde thus doe by these wordes. **zacha. ix. Thou in the bloud of thy testament, hast let fourth out of the lake or dongeon, in which ther was no water or refreshing, theym that were bounde there*** And the blessed Apostle saynt Peter confirmeth the same in hys first epistle & thirde chapter, saying that **Christ came in spirite and preached to them that were in prison, whiche some time were hard of beliefe when they loked for Gods patience in the daies of Noe, while the shippe was a making, in which a fewe, that is to saye eighte lyues were saued by the water.*** He came in spirite in his soule, for his body remayned in the graue (as I sayd) and preached, declaryng that the misterie of his incarnation and passion was performed, by whyche hell shoulde be spoyled, and the way to heauen should be opened to all good men [X1] and women, whose soules were in captiuitie,* amonge whiche were manye of them that were alyue in that space of .C.xx. yeares that God gaue to the people to amende theyr lyues, and to Noe for a warninge to prepare and make his shyppe readye,* of whiche some would not beleue, Noe manye times and busely exhortynge them to amende theyr lyues, yet at the last when they saw the waters ryse styll, and encrease withoute any ebbyng, they repented and were sorye for theyr synnes, and so died penitente, and descended to the skyrte of hell, where were the soules of many Patriarches and Prophetes, and of other holy men and women, whiche by Christes presence had consolation inestimable, as well as they that S. Peter speaketh of in this place,* for if they of whiche it semeth lesse, had comforte by Christes descendinge to them, then muche more they that were of higher perfection, had such consolation & comfort by his presence, and by their delyueraunce out of that pryson. S. Basyl sayth on these wordes of the Psalme, **Dirupisti vincula mea,** Thou hast broken my bondes,* because thou hast set vs at libertie from the bondage of sinne, and descendinge into hell, hast losed from death mankinde, there beinge captiue, and holden in the vneuitable custodye of hel. So it was verified that was sayd in his name to synne and to hell. **Osee. xiii. O death I will be thy death, O hell I wyll bite the.** He that eateth, occupieth all that he eateth, he that byteth, taketh part and leaueth part: so dyd the soule of Christ take that part of the prisoners [X1ᵛ] in hell whiche dyed in charitie, & lefte behind him in tormentes and paynes with the deuylles, all them that besyde oryginall synne, hadde committed mortall synne, and dyed without satisfaction for the same.*

SAynt Thomas* put the syxt article of our fayth, sayinge: **The thyrde daye he rose agayne from death.** For on Sondaye earlye in the breakynge of the daye, while it was somewhat darke, he ioyned his soule vnto hys body, and rose from death to lyfe, and came forth of his chest or graue, and oute of the monument or caue in the whiche the graue was, beynge fast shutte, with a greate stone rouled to it for a dore, and surelye sealed.* And forthwith came the Aungell from heauen, and remoued the stone that was rouled to the doore of the sayde caue, and satte vpon it,* to declare that Chryste was rysen and gonne: and anone came the thre Maries,* and they sawe and hearde the Aungels, appearynge to theim lyke men, whiche told theim that Chryste was rysen,* but they scarselye beleued the Aungelles, rather thinkynge that his precyouse bodye was stolen and caryed awaye oute of the graue. Notwithstandynge (as they were bydde) they wente to geue knoweledge to the Disciples,* whiche then kepte them selues together in greate pensifenes for the losse of theyr mayster, and as close as they coulde for feare of shrewes.* Marye Magdalene made beste spede, [X2] and tolde Peter and Iohn what she hadde sene and hearde,* and consequentlye the same day, and other dayes folowinge, as well the sayde holye women as the Apostles and other Disciples, were by euidente and sensible signes, well assured that he was bodelye rysen in dede, and not fantasticallye nor faynedlye. He was the fyrste that euer ryse to lyfe immortall, neuer to die againe. Other there were that were reised frome death to lyfe by the power of God, but after certaine yeares they died againe. Christe rose by his owne power, and neuer died againe, therefore the Apostles called him **the beginninge and fyrste begotten amonge dead men. Col. i.** The beginner and cause of his owne resurrection, whiche was by his owne power, and also of oure resurrection, that lyke as he died for oure sinnes, and rose againe to iustifie vs: so we shoulde mortifie oure selfe to sinne, that we may rise againe with him, and liue to God, walkinge in a newe life whyle we be here, that finallye we maye rise with oure bodies and soules glorified to immortall lyfe. Oure olde manne was crucyfied with Christe, that the bodye of synne myghte be destroyed, that we shoulde no more doe seruice to sinne.* Oure olde man signifieth oure olde lyuinge in synne, lyke Adam the fyrste manne that synned, of whose offence descended to all his posteritie the nourisshinge and feadinge of sinne, the darte and pricke of death, whiche the Apostle manye times calleth by the name of sinne.* [X2ᵛ] this we must mortifie and kyll, that so the bodye of synne maye be destroyed. We lyue to synne when we lyue after the inclination of the sayd nurse and breder of synne, so that synne reigne in our mortall bodies to obeye the desires of sinne.* And contrary we die to sinne, when we do not the desires of sinne, neither folowe the inclinations of sinne, that so the body of sinne may be destroyed in vs: the bodye of sinne, is the whole rable and multitude of sinnes together, like limmes of one body, as fornication, vncleanes, auarice, contention, wrath, gyle, brauling, dissension, heresies, enuye, ryot or surfet, and suche other, when these be mortified in vs, then we dye with Christ. And this mortification we must buselye and continually beare vpon vs, and then we shal be sure to liue with him, by renewinge of our liuinge contrarie to vice, vsing iustice and vertue, that so we may giue light of good example to all others, that they may glorifie and laude God in vs, that finally we, and they with vs, may ryse to immortall glorye.

THen foloweth the seuenth article, whiche S. Bartholomew*† put to this gathering, and it is this. **He ascended into heauen, and sitteth on the righte hande of GOD the father almightie.** That is to saye, the condition of our nature whiche he toke of the virgin his mother, he toke vp with him, and set it on the ryght hand of his father, aboue the skye, and aboue all the orders of aungels, and aboue al thinge that is na[X3]med not only in this world, but also in the world to come.* Therefore let vs ascende vp in deuoute heart with Christ, while we be in this presente lyfe, that when the daye of the generall resurrection shall come, we may folowe him, ascendyng in body thither, as he is gone afore vs bodelye, **openinge the waye for vs. Mich. ii.*** For lyke as he rose from death to life to make vs lykewise to ryse, so he ascended to make vs to ascende. For whiche purpose we must well knowe and remember, that with Christ ascendeth not pryde, nether couetousenes, lechery, or any other synne, he was our phisition, he cured vs and made vs once hole, but he toke with him none of our malanders, therfore yf we come after him, we must leaue all these and cast them of, least they presse vs downe, that we may not ascend to that glorious place, wher Christ sitteth on the ryght hande of his father, that is to saye, equal with the father by his godhead, and in the inheritaunce and highest wealth and glory of God by his humanitie, to entreate for vs as our attourney towarde the father. To sitte, belongeth to a iudge, because oure sauioure nowe beinge in heauen, considereth and iudgeth all mens actes, and at the laste shall manifestlye and openly come to iudge them, and to geue sentence, therefore it is sayd that he sytteth.* Saynt Steuen sawe him standing on the fathers right hande, as one redy to fyght for hym, and to helpe him constantlye to suffer the persecution of the Iewes,* where ye must not ymagine any materiall body, or ryght hand or lyfte hande in the god[X3ᵛ]head, or any material stoles to sit on in heauen, it is a maner of speakinge of the scripture by a similitude, rather then that there be any such partes there in dede. And likewise to sitte or stande in heauen, signifieth no more, but there to be at his pleasure, and to shewe hym selfe as it please his maiestie.

THe eyght article saint Mathew the Apostle and Euangelist* sayd: **From thence he shall come to iudge the quicke and the deade.** In the same body he wyl come to the iudgement, in whiche he ascended into heauen, to iudge all christen and hethen,* for all we that be, hath be, & shall be, shall stande afore Christes seat of iudgement, that euery man maye receaue the duetie of his bodye as he hath done, whether it be good or yll. **ii. Cor. v.*** And so Christ sayde, that when he shoulde come in his glory with his aungels, then he shall pay euery one accordinge to his

---

† Bartholomew] Barthelomew

dedes.* These wordes are greatlye to be feared: for he sayth not, that then he wyll geue after his mercy to euery one, but after theyr owne dedes, here he is mercifull, there he wyll be all rightuous: therfore the longer that he loketh for oure amendemente here, so muche more greuouselye he wyll do vengeaunce yf we wyll not amende. This iudgemente is greatelye to be feared, for the hyghe wysedome of the iudge, and for the cleare knowledge that he hath, for al thinges be naked, bare and opened to his eyes, as well the secrete thoughtes of mynde, as open deedes, there shall [X4] nede no wytnes to accuse the synners, for theyr owne consciences and theyr thoughtes shall be the accusers, and wytnesses of theyr owne iniquitie, accusinge, or excusynge in that terrible daye. **Roma. ii.*** His fyrste comminge to take oure nature vpon him, was in infyrmitie, weakenes, and pouertie, but his seconde commynge, that shall be to this merueilous iudgemente, shall be in myghtye power and maiestie. His power is almightye in it selfe, and besyde that, all the worlde wyll take his parte, and fyghte wyth hym agaynste lewde synners, there shall be no man to speake or to entreate for them, and then he wyll be verye terrible and angrye to reproued synners, in so muche that they shall wysshe the mountaynes and hylles to fall vpon them, and to hyde them from the angre of the Lambe.* Oh merueylous agonye and furye of mynde that they shall be cumbred wyth, to be so afrayde of a Lambe. He wyll shewe him selfe very amiable, pleasaunte, and comfortable to his electe people, and therefore to theym he wyll be as a Lambe, and to the others, wonderous sore and greuous.

THe nynth article of our fayth, is of the thyrde personne in Trinitie, the holye Gooste, expressed by Saynte Iames the sonne of Alphey, called Iames the lesse, because he came later to be C H R I S T E S scholer,* then the other Iames, the Sonne of **Zebede,** of whome I spoke in the thyrde Article.*

[X4ᵛ] This is the article, **I beleue in the holy Gost.** Like as we must beleue on the father & on the sonne, so must we beleue on the holy Goost: for he that beleueth not on all three persons, taketh no profite beleuinge on one or twayne of them, for this is the catholike and common fayth, to beleue one God in Trinitie, and a Trinitie of persons, that is to saye: thre persons in one Godhead. The holy Goost the thyrde person, is brought forth by the fruitefull will of the father, and of the sonne, as the equall wyll and loue of them both, of equall mighte and power and maiestie with the father and with the sonne, on whome we must beleue. After the article of beleuinge on the holy Goost, conuenientlye foloweth two other articles concerninge the workes of grace of the holy Goost. One is of the worke of grace, in gettinge that thinge that is good, the other in amouing and auoydinge that is yll.

OF the fyrst grace Symon the Apostle, called **Chananeus** and **Zelotes,*** putteth the tenth article of oure crede saying. **The holy catholike Churche, the communion of sainctes.*** After the myndes of some holy doctors, we may not saye properlye that we beleue in the holye Churche, or on the holy Churche, for the Church is not God on whom we beleue, as is aforesayd, it is the house of God.* Albeit if we say so, it may be allowed: as S. Paule praysed the **Collossen. i.** for the fayth and charitie that they had **in Deo, & in omnes sanctos,** on God and on all holy persons,* [Y1] because that by theyr fayth and charitie, they extended theim selues to God and all good men. So in as much as we extende and set forth oure selues to conforme our selues to the vnitie of all holy churche, and to the communion and company of all holy folkes, by our fayth adourned with charitie, mouinge our selues to suche conformitie in perfection of life, we may by that reason saye that we beleue on the holye Churche, and on the communion of sainctes. This Churche is called holy, as for a distinction and difference from the Churche that the prophete speaketh of, saying: **I hate the churche of imaginers of mischiefe, dissention, and debate.*** For suche Churches be not holy, but rather yll and very noughte. It is also called holy, because the people and company of the same be washed from the vncleanes of sinne by the holy Sacramentes of the church, takinge their efficacitie and strength at the bloude of our Sauiour Christ.* It is called catholike, that is to say: vniuersall or whole ouer all the world, not mutter-inge in sundry corners or countreys, as heretikes haue imagined theyr Churches.* There can be no greater treasure, no greater honour gotten, then to haue the grace of the lyuely fayth of this vniuersall churche. This fayth saueth sinners, worketh miracles, ministreth Sacramentes: who so euer he be, or in what state or condition so euer he be, yf he be not in this fayth of the catholyke churche, he is no true christen man, neyther can be saued, lyke as there was no man nor woman saued aliue in the great floude that was [Y1ᵛ] in the tyme of Noe, but onelye they that were within his great shippe,* **The communion of sainctes,** or of holy persons,* that is to saye, like as I beleue the holy churche to be one and holye, and that yf I will be saued I muste conforme my selfe to that vnitie, not swaruinge from it by heresies or dissention, so I muste in perfection of lyfe conforme my selfe to the felowship and companye of holy persons, as well of them that be now aliue, as of them that be departed to God afore vs. For if we wyll haue communion or felowship with the sainctes or holye men in euerlastinge life, we muste studye to folowe them in liuinge, for they muste perceaue in vs somwhat of theyr vertues, that so they may vouchesafe to pray for vs to almightie God. And although we can not suffre martirdome as some of them did, yet at the lest wise we must by example of them repugne and resist yll, and vnlawfull concupiscence (and the rather by their prayers) that so we may obteyne forgeuenes of oure sinnes, hauinge a meruey-lous good helpe thereto by the holy Sacramentes of this catholike churche, whiche sacramentes all holye men and women commoneth and vseth felowlike, pore and riche all together. And by the vnitie and communion in the fayth and Sa-cramentes of this holye churche we receaue as well the merite of Christes passion and of his holy lyfe, as of the good liuinge, and good dedes of all holye people, beynge all one, knitte together by the liuelye fayth of the sayde catholike Chur-che, according to the pro[Y2]phetes: sayinge. **I am partaker of al them that feare the, O Lorde.*** And therefore euerye true lymme of the sayde Churche is partaker of all the good that is done thoroughe all the worlde, and he that is excommuni-cate and caste oute of this vnitie, looseth his parte of all the sayde good workes.

THen foloweth the eleuenth article, expressed by Iude, otherwise called Thadeus, the brother of Iames the lesse aforesaid.* **The forgiuenes of synnes.** It concerneth the amotion and puttinge awaye the thinge that is yll and moost noysome to man, that is synne, whiche by the auctoritie that Christe gaue to the Apostles, and by them to theyr successours ministers of the Churche, and by the vertue of the Sacramentes is losed and taken awaye. For while we be in this worlde, howe greate so euer oure sinnes shall chaunce to be, they may be all wasshed awaye by the strength that Christ left in his Sacramentes.

THen foloweth the twelfth and laste article of the Crede, layde to this shot or gatheringe by S. Mathy, that was chosen to make vp the perfite number of the .xii.

Apostles, after that Iudas the traiter was gone from them, & had hanged him selfe,* it is this. **The resurrection of the bodye, and life euerlastinge,** * that is to saye, glorye, rialtie,' and ioye euerlastinge of bodye and soule. It is verye necessarye for vs [Y2ᵛ] stedfastly to beleue this article, to take from vs the feare of death: for if we thoughte there were no lyfe hereafter, we might well feare death as a thinge most horrible, whiche nowe we take as a necessary meane and highe waye to eternitie, and life euerlastinge. Therefore we shoulde not vndiscretely mourne or cry for feare of our owne death, neither for the death of our frende, consyderinge that it maketh for the profyt of oure bodies and of our soules: for euer stil from the time of mannes conception in his mothers body, tyll he be buried, he maye take hurt, and may be corrupt, but he shall rise agayne vncorruptible, by the dowrye or gyfte of **impassibilitie,** * neither fyre, weapon, syckenes, neyther anye other thinge can hurte him. Lykewise in this life mannes body is dymme and darke, and geueth no lyghte, but it shall rise in glorye, clearenes, and brightnes, by the gyft of **clearnes**. Mannes body is nowe dull and heauy, and longe a mouinge, and not able to styrre it selfe withoute laboure, but it shall ryse nymble and quicke, able to moue from place to place (how farre distant soeuer they be) in a twinkelinge of an eye,* by the will and commaundement of the soule, and this shall be by the dowry or gifte of **Agilitie**: Our body is now grosse, and no more able to be present with an other bodye, then the body of a brute beaste, but it shall rise so spirituall, fine and pearsing, that it may goo thorough an other body, and be present in one place with an another body, by the gifte of **Subtilitie**: euen like as I said afore, that the body of oure Saui[Y3]our Christ came from the wombe of the vyrgyn Marye, and as he came amonge his disciples when the doores were shutte, so that his fleshe, bones, and blo[u]de were present with the ooken boordes, and yren twistes of the doore, or with the walles, withoute any diuision of his body, or of the dore, or of the yren workes, or of the walles. These wonderous indumentes, dowries, and gyftes of a body glorified, were shewed in oure Sauiour Christes body at his transfiguration, for our comforte, declaringe that like as he shewed them in him selfe then, so we shoulde assure our selfe to haue them in vs, when we shall rise to life euerlastinge. Where contrary they that shall be dampned, shall haue theyr bodies vncorruptible, for they shall euer endure passible, and subiecte to all paynes of extreme heate, extreme colde without any meane, besyde the worme and grudge of minde, frettinge and gnawinge theyr owne consciences, whiche shal neuer cease. Their bodies shall be dimme, darke, heuy, and shal supplye the rowmes of cheynes, fetters and stockes, to kepe them downe in that detestable pryson of hell. Then fynally to speake of **life euerlastinge** of body and soule in heauen, what tonge is able to tell, or what wytte can compasse how greate the ioyes of that high citie be?* to be amonge the companies of blessed spirites and holy aungels, and to beholde the countenaunce of the Godheade, euer presente with them, and not to be dismayde with feare of death, and to reioyce of the gyfte of euerlastinge incorruption,* withoute disease or [Y3ᵛ] sickenes, for there shall be no paine, sorowe, nor mourninge. There shalbe no feare of pouertie, no feablenes of sickenes, there no man shall be hurte, no man shall be angry, no man shall enuy or disdaine an other, there shall be no couetousnes, no hunger, no gaping for promotion or honoure, no feare of the deuill, there shal no diuels lie in waite for to tempt vs, no feare of hel, there shalbe no death of body or soule, but a life full of pleasure indued with immortalitie, there the blessed folke shal shine like sterres, and they that teacheth other to liue wel, shalbe like the brightnes of the firmament. Wherfore there shalbe no night, no darkenes, no cloudes, no sharpenes of colde or

heate, but there shalbe such temperature and measure of all thinges, as no eye hath
sene, no eare hath hearde, neither any mans hert hath comprehended or attained
to, but onely of them as haue be worthie, or shalbe founde worthy to haue the
same pleasures, whose names be written in the boke of life euerlastinge. In whiche
boke, that we maye be registred, he graunte vs for his infinite mercy that for vs
died. Amen.

An homilie or sermon, intreatinge
of Ceremonies and
mannes lawes.

GOod Christen people, forasmuch as now of late manye men hath so litle fauored the Ceremonyes of Christes churche, & also mannes traditions, or lawes made by man, reputing them inualide and of no strength to bynde Christen people to obserue and kepe them, that they haue runne into so great peruersitie, as to despise as wel such laudable vsages as hath ben vsed among christen people continually, sith the time of the Apostles vnto our dayes, as also to reiecte the very Sacramentes of God, the principal Ceremonies of oure faith, to the extreme daunger of their owne damnation, and of all them that haue geuen faith to theyr doctrine, because you shal not erre in like opinions, but rather shal know how necessary Ceremonies be, that so you may haue a loue to them, ye shal first hear the auncientie of Ceremonies, & then the necessitie of Cere[Y4ᵛ]monies,* And consequentlye somewhat I shall speake of **mannes traditions and lawes,** and of the strength that they haue to bind men that be subiect to the same lawes, to kepe them. For the first ye shall vnderstande, that this vocable or latyn worde **Cere-monie** (as **Valerius Maximus*** wryteth in the fyrst booke of his stories) hath his name of a towne in Italy called **Cerete,*** into which towne (when the citie of Rome was taken by the frenchmen) the preist of **Quirinus,** and the professed maidens called **Vestales virgines** with theyr Idolles, and other sacred thinges (after their maner) that they could conuey out of the citie, were caried in a wayne and there receiued, & had in very great veneration.* And thereof it was ordeyned, that thinges perteyninge to the seruyce of their Goddes, shoulde be called **Cere-monies,** because the **Ceretanes** worshipped them in that decaye, and destruction of the citie of Rome, as wel as when it floryshed in prosperitie. And the transla-tours of holy scripture vseth the same latin worde, to signifie the rites, maners, and vsages accustomed in the seruice of the true and onelye lyuinge God almighty, maker of all creatures, and about thinges dedicate, applyed, and belonginge to the same seruice, callinge them **Ceremonies**. They be externall or outwarde protesta-tions, and declarations of the inwarde worshippinge of GOD, whiche is by fayth, hope, and charitie,* and hath ben vsed in the time when the law of nature had his course, and afterwarde in the time of the law written, vnto Christes time, and finallye in the [Z1] time of grace from the firste publique and open preachinge of Christes Gospell, and so shal continue vnto the worldes ende. Almightye God alowed and commended the holy patriarch Abraham vnto Isaac, saiyng: I will geue to thee and to thy posteritie all these countreys hereabo[u]te, and all nacions of the worlde shall be blessed in thy seede for Abrahams sake, because he obeyed my voice, and kepte my commaundementes, my **ceremonies,** and my lawes. **Gene. xxvi.*** What ceremonies kept Abraham for which he was worthy thus to be commended? Verely some speciall deuout fashions or behauiour that he vsed about the sacrifices or seruices of God as he had learned of his anceters, which I thinke verely were even the same, or muche like to them that afterwarde were expresly commaunded by God, and written by Moyses. Abel Adams sonne learned of his father to honoure God wyth the fruites that God sende him, and to make obla-tions to him of the same. Enos that was sonne vnto Seth, begonne to call vpon the name of God, inuentinge deuout wordes by the waye of prayer to honour him.* Enoch the fourth generation after him, of whose goodnesse scripture speaketh,

saiynge: that he walked with God, and appeared no more amonge the sinnefull
people, for God toke him away,* doubtlesse he was no lesse ceremonious in
sacrifices, oblations, and prayers, then his progenitours were. And of Noe the
holye Patriarch it is expressely written, y^t when he came out of his ship after y^e
great flode with his [Z1^v] sonnes, his wife, and his sonnes wiues, and all the beasts
that were saued bi that shippe. Forthwith he erected and made vp an aultare for
almighty god, and offered sacrifices of part of the beastes and birdes that were
clene, burnyng them vpon the same aultare, and our Lord God smelled the
swetenesse of his oblation, acceptynge it graciously for the faith and deuocion of
the offerer, and not for the things self that were offred.* Here you haue manifest
ceremonies, the aultare was Ceremoniall, so was the distinction of the clene
beastes from the vnclene. And of the cleane fowles from the vnclene the burnynge
vp of the whole carkasses, head, fete, bowels, and al except the skinne was
ceremoniall. But afore that wee entreate of these ceremoniall lawes, I thinke it
necessary somewhat to speake of morall lawes, and also of Iudiciall lawes, which
knowen, the ceremonies may be more euident. The morall lawes commaunded by
God be they that be of the iudgement of right reason or much consonant &
agreing to the same, & that shal moue a man to fulfil & do them, although there
were no law written to compell a man to fulfil them, as this.* Thou shalt honor thy
father & mother, for reason wil that thou shalt do the best thou canst for them,
that brought thee into this worlde, and nourished thee, and cherished thee, when
thou were not able to helpe thy self. Of this kinde be the .x. commaundements of
God sonderly expressed to his elect people of Israel,* and bi them to vs, to reduce
them and vs to the lyght of naturall reason, whiche by euyll exercyse was blinded
in them, as it was through[Z2]out all the worlde in that tyme, and as I feare me, it
is in manye of vs nowe, for malyce was neuer so abundaunte.* For this purpose it is
verye necessarye that they shoulde be declared in the churches on sondayes and
holy dayes to put men in remembraunce of their duetie to GOD, and to their
neighbors other morall rules there be, whyche bynde as monicions by the waye of
honestie, as this. **Afore a white heade thou shalte rise vp and do thy dutye.** And
this, **Honour**† **the person of an olde man***, with manye others like. And of the
saide morall commaundementes dependeth bothe the Iudiciall preceptes, and the
ceremoniall.* The **Iudiciall lawes** be as it were yokes or bondes to binde the
people, to kepe and do that reason woulde to be done in an order to God and to
their neighboure, determinynge the paynes and punyshemente for transgressours,
quietynge and endynge strife, plees, and controuersies, hauynge their strengthe to
binde, not of the necessary iudgement of right reason, but only by institution, or of
that that they be made by theim that haue auctoritie to make lawes,* example of
thys. A morall lawe this is. **Thou shalt not kyll a[n]ye man, woman, or childe.**
Then if a man breake this lawe by prepensed malyce, killynge a manne, the
Iudiciall lawe sayeth that he shall dye for it, where as if he did it by chaunce
medley, wythout anye suche intended mischiefe, he myghte saue hym selfe by
some sanctuarye. **Thou shalte ho[n]our thy father and mother,** is a morall commaundemente. [Z2^v] To punishe them that do contrarye the iudiciall lawe saith:
whosoeuer hurteth father or mother shal die for it. And whosoeuer rayleth vpon
them geuing them opprobrious words shal also dye for it.
  ¶Ceremonies vsed afore Christes tyme were of foure diuers maners. Some

† Honour] Honodr

consisted in sacrifices. Some in sacraments. Some in halowed thinges, or thinges
dedicate or applied to Gods seruice. Some in obseruaunces.* Sacrifices they hadde,
of whiche some were offered for the sinnes of the people, or of particuler persons
Some of deuotion to pacify Gods displeasure, and to obtein his grace and fauour, or
for to obteine some speciall benefite of almighty GOD. Some were all burned,
some were part burned, part rosted or sodde, and parte appointed for the priestes
part, part for the owner that offred it to make merye with all. And they were
commonly of rudder beastes, of sheepe, or goates.* And amonge birdes, of doues or
turtles, and seldome of sparrowes, as in the purgation of Lepris,* which (as S. Paule
saith) can not purge the conscience of them that serueth in them, for it is not
possible sinne to be taken away by the bloude of bullockes or goates. **Hebr. x.***

¶Sacramentes they had among them as circumcision, and the paschal lambe,*
and order of the priestes ministring in the tabernacle or temple, and the water of
expiation made of the asshen of the redde Hefer & running water, to clense folke
from their irregularitie bi touching of a dead corps or of any other vncleane
thinge.* Saint Paule [Z3] calleth them neady and pore principles, for they nother
geue grace to the vsers, nother geueth to the ministers any spiritual power to remit
sinne.* The priest bi his order had power to kil the cow and to burne her, and to
mingle the asshen with running water, & to sprinkle it vpon the vnclene and so to
purge him from an externall irregularitie of his flesh, that so he might lawfully
come into the courts of the tabernacle, & stand amongst honest men, where as
afore he ought not so to do.* And for this thapostle saith, they sanctify folkes for
the clensyng of the flesh. **Heb. ix.*** Euen like as when a prelate dispenseth with a
bastard or with a man that hath but one eye, that he may be made priest, bi this
dispensation, he geueth him not any grace, but only taketh away the irregularitie
& maketh hym able to be ordered, where afore he was not so.

¶Of the thirde maner of ceremonies were sacred or halowed things to gods
seruice. As ye tabernacle & temple, ye parts of them, the courts about them, the
implementes and vtensils, as cruets, cuppes, morters, caudrons, and kettles.* And
so were certayne dayes and solemne feastes as the vii. day of the weke, the seuenth
yere, the Iubily yere,* with a great multitude more, which should be to long here
to be rehearsed.

¶The obseruances were certain religious maners of liuinges that the people of
Israell, and the holy fathers their progenitours as the electe and chosen people of
GOD vsed, to shewe them selues distincte and differente from all Idola[Z3^v]ters, of
which the world was then full. In Moses time almighty God expressely commaunded them by Moyses and Aaron to obserue & keepe a prescise maner in their
diet. They should eat no fleshe of any four foted beastes, but onely of such as were
both clouen foted, and did also ruminat his meate, or chew quyd. All other they
should repute vnclene and not eat of them.* They should nother eat porke, pigge,
hare, nor conyes, with many others. They were forbidden all fish that had not both
finnes and skales, tench, eles, congres, loches, & culles with manye others were
not for <for> them, of birdes, all raueners liuynge by prey, as haukes, gripes,*†
kites, and all kinde of rauens, or crowes, and such like, and swanne flesh, with
many others they were forbidden as things vnclene to be eaten & to be touched.*
And they sholde not drinke nor occupie the water or other liquor that any such or
any part of them had fallen into, the vessell conteynynge such liquor, should be

---

† gripes] grises

counted vnclene, and if it were an earthen vessell, it should be broken and cast away. Albeit, brokes, welles, mayrs, pondes, and cesternes made to gather water, and to kepe them, mighte be occupied for drinke, and to dresse meat, although such filthy forbidden thinges had fallen into them.* How they shold punysh them selues with fastyng.* In the feast of expiation or clensynge,* & many other seasons, and how the wiues vowe to offer, or to fast, or to do any such like thing of deuotion should be approued by her husbande as sone as he knew of it, or els not to binde her. And in case he wold say contrary on the first day that he knew [Z4] of his wiues vow, she was discharged, & he without fault, but if he deferred it til the morow then next folowing, she was bound to perfourme her vow. And if then he wold compel her to do contrary, he should beare the perill of her iniquitie, transgressing & breaking her vow. The vowes & promises of ye maids dwelling within their fathers houses, did likewise binde, if the father saide not contrary on the first day that he knew therof, if afterward he wold say nay, on his perill, the synne was his.* As concerning their raiment, thei should wear no cloth wouen of wollen & linnen threde together as be our carpets & tapstry works.* They shold also haue in the skirts of their gownes certain ribands in color resembling the skie on a clere day.* No man shold wear a womans garment, nother any woman a mans garment, for that was abhominable afore god.* Of yokinge their cattell in their plowes, of sowyng their vyneyards & their feldes, And of the very birdes neasts thei had ceremonial obseruances appointed them.* In al these this is to be taken for a generall rule that suche ceremonies as semeth to be without ani sad reason, & without any necessitie or profite in kepyng of them, or eschuyng them. Almighty God intended to remoue his people farre of from the rites of Idolatry, in which such thinges as be here forbidden were vsed.* The payn for not obseruing these ceremonies in manye cases was death, whereby thei were very dangerous painful & vntollerable as **.s. Pet.** saith, thei wer so heuy yt nother Iewes in his tyme beynge, nother their forefathers coulde bear them. **Act. xv.*** They were very many to [Z4ᵛ] the number of .vi. hundred, or aboue,*of whiche some were verye chargeable, what payne and charge was it for euerye manne to appeare in Ierusalem, three times in the yere, how farre of so euer he dwelled.* Likewise to kepe holy day all the .vii.ᵗʰ yere in deuotion, & nother to plow nor to sow, nor to gather corne,* & so in the space of two yeres together, they had but small sustenaunce.

¶Nowe wee haue hearde howe these Lawes bounde the Iewes to obserue and keepe theim vnder the paynes expressed for transgressours of the same, it is necessarye to knowe howe they binde vs christen people in the tyme of grace exhibited and geuen vs by oure Sauioure Iesus Christe. For this you shall vnderstande that the morall preceptes, because they be consonant and agreing to the light and iudgement of right reason, whiche is one in all men naturally printed in their Soules at their creation, they must nedes binde vs christian people as well as they bounde the Iewes.* Al be it the Iewes as verye ignare & rude vnperfitly and grosely vnderstode the saide morall commaundements as thinking it sufficient to kepe this commaundement. **Thou shalt not kill,** if they held their handes they thought it none offence to be angry wt their neighbour. To imagine mischefe against him. This imperfection of their grosse vnderstanding our sauiour Christ clerely taketh away, forbiddyng vs to be angry with our neighbour inwardly in our harte or by exteriour signes in word, hand, or in countenaunce **.Mat. v.** takynge away the very rote of homicide.* [2A1] The iudicialles of Moises law as giuen by him, hath this imperfection annexed, that they make a man to doe well for feare of punyshment more then for loue. And feare hath euer payn annexed, and therfore

Moyses law was called the law of feare, and by that is a painefull law.* It woulde
abhorre a mans hart to heare how many tymes the payne of deathe is inculcated
and repeted among the sayd iudiciall lawes specially, but they as giuen by Moyses
bindeth not vs Christen people, notwithstandinge because in manye pointes they
be very ciuill and holsome rules to direct comonalties, or particuler persons, wher
Christen princes and noble counsailes thynketh it good to take any of the saide
iudiciall lawes of Moyses, and to stablishe theym, to order theyr subiectes, then the
sayd subiectes be bounde to obserue and kepe them, not as giuen of Moyses, but as
newlye made by their owne superiours and rulers. But as for the Iewes ceremonies,
because they were the very figures and onelye significations of Christ to come, and
of some sacraments & ceremonies to be vsed in Christes church in the tyme of
grace now alredy exhibited and performed, giuen vs by our sauiour Christ. They
must needes surceasse, for when the veritie of the sygnes and fygures be put in
execution, the shadowes be of no efficacitie.* It is mortal sinne now to vse them
putting any trust of saluation in them, for in so doing we shoulde shewe oure selues
to be of the Iewes faith, thinkinge that our redemption by Christ is not yet
sufficiently performed, whych is [2A1ᵛ] plaine false and dampnable to be beleued.
Notwithstanding Christes churche is not clearelye without ceremonies, some ordeined by Christ, & by his Apostles, and holy fathers, by the comon consent of
noble princes and commonalties, for the adorning, aduauncing and settyng furthe
of Christes religion.* For we haue sacrifices, sacramentes, sacred or halowed
thinges and obseruances, proporcionably to the foure that (as I tolde you) were
vsed in Moyses law, one most excellent sacrifice is the busy and dayly sacrifice and
offering in the masse of the blessed bodye and bloude of our sauiour Christ, in the
forme of breade and wine. This sacrifice we be taught and commaunded to vse by
the eternall priest, after the order of Melchisedech,* our sauiour Iesus Christ at hys
last supper sacrificing vnto his father bread and wyne, turned by the vertue of his
holy and mighty worde into hys owne bodye and bloude. And in this doyng most
deuoutly is called to mans remembrance his blessed immolation on the crosse, and
is presented vnto hys father for health and grace to theym that be a lyue, and for
reast and quyetnes for all them that be departed in fayth.* A contrite and a
troubled hart for a mannes sinnes the Prophet in the psalme calleth a sacrifice
which almighty God will not despise.* And in an other psalme God sayth by the
same prophet, the sacrifice of laude & praysing shal do me honor; kyll the wanton-
esse of thy wyll, and the ranknes of thy fleshe in the loue of him,* and so thou
shalt set vpon Gods aulter, that is to say, on Christes [2A2] crosse the most
acceptable sacrifice vnto him, and who so euer voweth and payeth to God all that
he hath, all that he lyueth, all that he vnderstandeth, (as the Apostles did) he
offereth to God an holocaust, that is to saye an alburned sacrifice.* For generally
euery dede that we do, by whych we shewe our selues to cleaue and stickefast vnto
God, referred to an heauenlye ende, maye be called a sacrifice.

¶Sacramentes we haue also seuen in nomber, taking their efficacitie and
strengthe at oure sauiour Christ, and left in the church as holesom medicines
against the manyfold infirmities and diseases of our soules. These be the very few
and manifest sacraments, in which the mercy of god woulde haue his churche free
and at lybertie as saynt Austine writeth in his boke of the customs of the churche
to Ianuarye.* And yet all these be not necessary for euerye man that shall be
saued. For euery man taketh not holye orders, neyther euery man contracteth
matrimony, many a man is saued without confirmation, and also wythout the
blessed sacrament of the aulter, and without extreme vnction that we cal

Enoyling.† Baptisme is necessary, and to theym that after baptisme haue fallen to mortall sinne, penance must nedes be had.* And this seemeth to be the hardest Sacrament or ceremonie that Christe lefte in hys Churche, specially for that part of it, that is confession, in whyche we reueale and vtter to a mortall manne the synnes that afore were priuye and secrete betwyxte GOD and vs. [2A2ᵛ] But to mitigate thys confusion or shame, wee must inwardly consider the losing of our synfull bondes, and by that to be set at libertie, oute of the deuils danger, & this shall make vs not to be ashamed to tell the truth for our soules sake. Let vs with all consider that he to whom we be confessed, is most straitly bound to keepe our counsayl vnder a more priuie seale, then we be our self bounde, and so we shall not neede to stycke nor shrinke to make a plaine confession. Sacred or halowed thinges we haue very manye,* as churches and Churchyardes, Chalice, Corporas, Cruets, Vestimentes, and other ornamentes of the ministers, doynge seruice in Christes churche, besyde their daily rayment, shewing distinction of them from the laife which is a veri honest ceremony & necessary to be vsed, albeit a great many of vs priestes litle regard it, going in our apparell lyke the lay men, by that declaring that we be ashamed of our order, and woulde be glad to pull our heade out of that yoke if we might.* We haue also **obseruances** of holye dayes, as sondayes and other solempne feastes by course succedynge after the reuolucion of the yere. We obserue also certayn solempne times of fastinge, as the faste of Lent,* & the Embre daies,* and in the remembrance of Christes passion we punish our bodies with abstinence and fasting euery fridai.* The deuout ceremonies on Palme sondayes in processions* and on good fridaies about the laying of the crosse and sacrament into the sepulchre,* glorouslye arayed, be so necessary to succour the labilitie of mans remem[2A3]brance, that if they wer not vsed once euery yere, it is to be feared that Christes passion wold sone be forgotten, the crucifixes erected in churches, & crosses by the highe wayes were intended for the same purpose, although some pestiferous persons haue ouerthrowne them and destroyed them, for the very contempt of Christes passion, more then to finde money vnder them, as they haue pretended.* We obserue as a necessary ceremoni likewise a sober silence in the church in time of preachyng the worde of God, and also while di[u]ine seruice is a doying with manye suche other ceremonyes which were to long here to be rehersed.

And finally to speake of the iudiciall lawes the Iewes were neuer yoked nor troubled wyth halfe so manye gyuen to them, as we be pressed withal, what with ecclesiastical lawes and other statutes and actes aboue nomber. So that (as Sainte Austine in the booke of the customes of the church saith) the condicion of the Iewes seemeth more tollerable and easye to be borne, then the case that Christen people be in.* For the Iewes neuer knewe the tyme of lybertie, and yet they were not bound but only to the burdens expressed in Gods lawes, and not to mens presumptions as we be, in somuche that if a Iewe well learned in Moyses law, and conuerted to Christes faith, woulde consider hys former bondage whyle he was of the Iewes secte, and woulde conferre it to this bondage that he must lyue in wyth Christen people, he would thincke Christes law much more vntollerable, then Moyses law was to him. [2A3ᵛ] For what with our iudiciall lawes and our ceremon-ials, we haue more layd vpon our backs, then we can well awaye withall, and but verye fewe daies passeth ouer vs, but we breake a great many of them, and not without peryl to our soules. Then where is the swete promise of o[u]r sauiour

† Enoyling] Inoyling

Christ: Come vnto me all ye that labour and be ouerburdened and I shall refreshe you, and make you beare lighter, for my yoke is sweete, and my burden but light.* For this ye shall vnderstand, that comparing the old law vnto the new law of Christe, we may consider Christes lawe one way, as giuen of Christ, and so very true it is that Christes law is much more easye then Moyses lawe. For the iudiciall lawes be none left vs by Christe, but he biddeth vs to leaue all plees and actions, in somuche that he wylleth vs not to requyre eye for eye nor toothe for toothe as Moyses law wold, but rather if a man would afore a Iudge claime thy coate, thou shalt not sticke with him, but rather giue him thy coate and thy cloke withal.* On a time there came one to Christ that had a matter in variance betwixte him and his brother, about the diuision of theyr enheritance or londes, and would haue had Christ to take the matter in hand and to call his brother, & to bid him deuide their possessions, that either of them might know his own: But Christ would none therof, and refused to be their Iudge in that behalfe, sayinge: O man, who made me your Iudge or the deuyder betwixt you?* I came not for that entent, I wil not medle in such matters nowe, & therefore his good scholer S. Paule writeth to the Corin[2A4]thians: that it was a great fault among them that they had such iudiciall causes among them: why do not ye rather (sayth he) take wrong? why doe ye not rather suffer to be begiled?* And this we be bound to do, in case that by our extreme and gredie asking of our own, there may be like to aryse some greater inconuenience, or yl example to our neighbour, but in case by our sufferance, malicious or couetous persons may take a courage or boldnes to persist in theyr yll doing. We be not bound so to refraine to aske our own, but rather with modestie and sober behauiour we mai afore a competent Iudge redresse the iniury done vnto vs, & to require our right by iudiciall lawes, as well ecclesiastical as temporal, to which they that be subiect to the same lawes, be bound to obey, in asmuche as they be made by men, whom God hath constitute & set in power and authoriti or by his secret counsail permitted & suffered to beare rule & authoritie, & to haue the ministration & execution of the lawes.* Of the authority of prelates, successours to the Apostles saith Christe yᵗ whosoeuer heareth them hereth him, & whosoeuer despiseth them, despiseth him.* And generally of all rulers saith the Apostle, commaunding euery man to be subiect to higher powers. For ther is no power but of god, & the things that commeth of God be resonably disposed & ordred, & therfore he that withstandeth superior powre, withstandeth Gods ordinance, & they that so do, procureth their own dampnation.* And therfore of very necessitye they shoulde be subiecte to theyr heades, not onelye for feare of theyr anger and punyshemente, [2A4ᵛ] but also for discharge of mens consciences, so that they shoulde do nothing contrarie to the princes and rulers of the people, but that they should exercise the workes of Iustice and goodnes, wyth tranquillitie and quietnes wythout tortures or compulsion.* Then consideringe that for our conscience sake we must obey the iust ordinaunces of our rulers, it is plaine that if we do contrary, we hurt our consciences with inobedience, negligence and contempt, and so we sinne and deserue pain, whereof it foloweth that to obserue & kepe mans traditions, constitutions, and lawes, made by our superiours, hauinge authoritie ouer vs, as well for obseruing and keping of the ceremonies & other bound duties of the churche, as for other lawes temporall, godly deuised for the quietnes of the kinges subiectes spirituall and temporall, is necessarie for our soule health.* And that to disobey and contempne them, is pernitious and perelous, as Samuel said: Obedience is better then sacrifice, for disobedience, repugnaunce, and resistance, is like the most detestable vice of sorcerye and idolatry.* But whether we be

bound vnder payne of deadly synne to kepe all the reasonable lawes and traditions
made by men or not, it is doubtfull. For this ye shal vnderstand that some lawes
bindeth men to do suche thinges as be necessarye to obtayne the loue of GOD and
of thy neighbour, as this: thou shalt worshyp one God: thou shalt do none adultery. And these also which be necessary because God hath commaunded them:
Thou shalt be baptised, thou shalt keepe holylye [2B1] Gods holy day,* thou shalt
be confessed to a priest with all such as be necessarily deriued of them, & agreing
to them, whether they be gyuen by God or by man, edifying charitie, and com-
maundinge to exchewe, and not to do the thing that is contrarie to charitie. Nowe
because charitie is the life of the soule, without which the soule is dead, whosoeuer
transgresseth and breaketh any suche lawes, whether they be made by God or man,
killeth his owne soule, and sinneth deadly.* So that charitye is the verye true
myrrour or glasse,* by which thou maist trie and discusse & haue a great euidence,
as well of thine owne dedes as of other mens dedes, whither they be godlye or
diuelyshe, holy or sinnefull. Some positiue lawes* there be that binde not so sore
as these do, because the violation and breaking of them, maketh not directly
against the loue of God and of thy neyghbour. As the positiue lawes of fasting, the
prescise obseruing of the ordinal in saying diuine seruice, the lawes of humanitie or
curtesie. And thys: Thou shalt make no lesynges,* with a great nomber of temporal lawes, which a man transgressing, doth not euer synne deadly, except there be
concurrent a contempt or dyspisinge of the authoritie of the law, which maye
make the offence that els was but veniall to be mortall. As in theym that wee haue
heard of, that for very frowardnes and despite of superiour authoritie haue eaten
fleshe in Lent, which after Easter woulde haue ben glad to haue eaten fishe, if they
coulde haue gotten it.* Penall lawes* bindeth two maner of wayes, one [2B1ᵛ] way
because the maker of the lawes wold haue them kept, and we be bounde to obey
theym, not onelye for feare of payne, but also for our conscience sakes. But they
binde no way vnder payne of deadly sinne, in asmuch as it appeareth by the
mindes of the makers of the law, that they wold not so sore charge the consciences
of theyr subiectes, but that when they breake the said lawes, whether it be with
contempt or withoute, they shoulde suffer the temporall paines, determined &
ordained for them that offende the said lawes. And so they binde the seconde way
by the payne to be inflicte on the breakers of the same. Thys due obedience of the
subiectes to theyr heades & rulers, and other premisses considered, al noble
Princes and Prelates, and all others that commonly be called to high counsels to
make lawes, had nede maturely to consider, that in their offices they be Gods
helpers, and the mean betwixt God and hys people, and to be well ware that they
make none such humane traditions, as mai barre or deface the law of God as they
dydde, to whom Christ vmbraideth that they for their own lucratiue traditions,
disswaded from the law of the honour of theyr parentes. **Math. xv.*** And that they
doe not binde suche heauye and vnportable burdens vpon their subiects backes, as
they wil not set one finger to, to helpe men to beare **Math. xxiii.*** as the Scribes
and Pharisies did, whych then had the aucthoritie both temporall and spiritual
vnder the Romaines. And that they haue no malicious eye towarde anye partie
diuisyng [2B2] lawes for theyr neyghbours destruction, or excogitating lawes for
the impouerishynge of other men, alleuiatyng theyr owne charges, and making
others fal down vnder their burdens: The Prophet sayth to them that be constitute
and set in suche authoritie. **Psa. lvii. O ye children of men, if ye speake truelye
of iustice and ryghteousnesse, then se that ye iudge streightly,*** neither declin-
ing on the right hand by affection to your selfe, or to your friende, neither on the

leaft hand by malice or displeasure to your foes, or to them that you fauour not. Considering that the iust iudgement of God shall be against them that measureth the power that they haue receiued of God after their owne wickednes, & not according to Gods lawes. Wher they that iustly and charitably haue vsed their authority, shall haue suche reward prepared for them in heauen as no tong can tel, nor hart can think Of whiche that we may be partakers, he graunt vs, that for vs dyed. Amen.

An exposition of the first epistle of Saynt Peter
the Apostle, set fourth in traictises or
Sermons, preached in the Cathedral
Churche of Bristow, by maister
Roger Edgeworth, Doctour
of diuinitie, one of the
canons of the same
Cathedrall church.*

THe gret wise man king Salomon, yᵗ by his wit searched out the natures & kinds of all creatures on erth as far as any man might, and dysputed & reasoned of all the trees in the wood, from the highe Ceder tre growing in Libanus (where such trees be abundant) vnto the poore and lowe Isope, that groweth out of the walles, and that write and reasoned of beastes and birdes, wormes and fishes, and to whom resorted people of all nations, and from all kinges of the world to heare hys wysedome,* yet he confesseth **Ecclesiastes .i. Cunctae res difficiles et non potest ea[s] homo explicare sermone** All thinges be hard to be knowen, & no man can [2B3] perfitely expresse them by mouth.* For (as the Logition speaketh) we knowe not the substantiall and perfite dyfference and distinction betwyxte creatures of the world, that we se afore our faces euery day.* Therfore it is no merueil though our wits be very thin, feable and weake to vnderstand the holy scriptures. For the faire beuty of godlye truth comprised and contained in the scriptures, lyeth so priuely hid like a heauenly treasure, layd vp in them, that it wyll not appeare but onely to them that seeke and searche for it, wyth a whole minde, and with a clere hart.* And in asmuche as mans reason is grosse, and combred wyth many ydle thoughtes, and with muche busynes of the worlde running in mans minde, this maketh vs the more blinde & vnmete to finde the sayd treasure, specially because that in spirituall and heauenly matters (as Saint Paule saith) we se but as it were in a glasse obscurelye, and as a thyng farre of vnperfitelye.* And beside this I knowe that the thinges that be spoken of in Gods holye and liuely worde be endited by the holy spirite of God. Wherefore it is not for euery man to examine them and discusse them, after his own iudgement, for no man may worthely medle wyth hys doynge, but he that hath the holy spirite, and specially that gift of the holy spirite that S. Paule speaketh of .i. **Corin. xii. Discretio spirituum**, where he sayth, that to some man is giuen the spirit of sapience, to iudge and reason of celestial matters, to other the gift of science in lower exercise: to som is giuen faith by the same spirite. To som power [2B3ᵛ] to discerne spirites,* to know when the good spirite speaketh, and when the bad and noughtye spirite speaketh. In catholike and true expounders of scriptures, speaketh the good spirite, in heretikes speaketh the bad and noughty spirite. And in the holy scripture which is the worke of the holy spirite, of the holy gost, for he inspireth all the writers of the holye scriptures, he is the chiefe author of holy scripture,* and they that be named the doers thereof as Mathewe, Marke, Luke, Iohn, and S. Peter, whom we haue now in hand, be but as the Scribes, Notaries, Scriueners, and as it were the very quils or pennes of the holy goste. **Lingua mea calamus scribe** (saith the Prophet.)* In the holye scrip-tures (I saye) when a texte maye haue diuers expositions, and may be diversly taken, and every way good and catholike, yet to attaine to the verye prescise and true meaning of the holy gost, is no small grace, this is the grace of **Discretion, of**

191

spirites, or of putting difference betwixte spirites.* And withoute this gift no man shal be able to pas safely through the scriptures without a foyle. Nowe who shall haue this gift, and who shall lacke it, it standeth chiefely in Gods handes, and not in our merites and deseruing. For these considerations it is no merueil that it be perilous to speake of almighty God, & of heauenly or godly causes, far aboue our reache. In somuch that many wise and wel learned men haue rather chosen silence, & to hold their tonges then to take labours in expoundinge or preching ye scriptures. But this is not inough for them to whom the office of teaching is commyt[2B4]ted. As to bishops to whom is committed the whole cure of their dioceses. To Archdeacons, persons, vicars & al other hauing cure of soules, to al such it is very hurtfull & noysome to kepe silence as s. Paule full well considered saying .i. Corin. ix. **Ve mihi est si non euangelizauero** I am sure of wo euerlasting if I do not preach.* Christ biddeth **scrutamini scripturas:** search & labour in ye scriptures: he biddeth vs also, **seke and we shall finde.*** Therefore we must search & seke least we heare the reproche that Christe gaue the malicious Iewes. **Erratis nescientes scripturas neque virtutem dei:** You er, you go out of the way, for ignorance of the scriptures, & because you know not the vertue & power of god.* S. Paule calleth our sauiour Christ the vertue and power, and the wisdome of God. **Christum dei virtutem et dei sapientiam i. Cor. i.** Then considering that Christ is the vertue & power of god, who so euer knoweth not the scriptures, knoweth not ye power & vertue of God,* it foloweth that he that knoweth not ye scriptures knoweth not Christ, & the more knowledge that you haue of the scriptures, the better you know Christe, & the lesse knowledge that you haue of the Scriptures, the lesse you know Christ, & to be ignorant or not to know the scriptures, is to be ignorant & not to know Christ. An other occasion I haue to labour in the scriptures, & to expound them to you which is commen to me with master Deane of this churche, and to all my brothers Canons here (Not speakynge of my Lorde oure byshoppe,* whyche I doubte not but he full well consydereth hys dutye to GOD and to hys flocke.[)] [2B4^v] The occasion is this: although I be neither parson nor vicare nor curate of this good and worshipfull flocke, yet there is an other yoke layd as well vpon my necke, as vpon other of my brothers here, by which I feare lest there wyll come wo to vs afore God, except we preach the scriptures vnto you, performing the thing that we haue taken vpon vs, byndyng our selues to the statutes that the Kynges moste gratious Maiestye hath deuised for the ordering of all vs the ministers of this his church, in which it is prouided that maister Deane and euerye Canon, shall preache or cause to be preached certayne Sermons yearely at this church.* Therefore I wyl forget my owne imbecilitie, weakenes, and vnhablenes, and according to the porcion and measure of that talent and litle knowledge that God hath giuen me, I wyll auenture vpon the exposition and declaration of this first epistle of the blessed Apostle S. Peter, after my best power, helping and settynge fourth the veritie, repelling and reprouing falsity Trusting to Gods helpe which neuer fayleth them that trust vpon him, that my sayd labour shall be as wel profetable to me, as fruteful to them that shall heare me. The matter is harde (as all scripture is) but it is full of good learning, and of fatherly counsell, very mete for a Christen soule to learne and to folowe, therefore my labour shall not lacke, hoping and trustyng in Christes helpe, and in hys holye spirite, whych I shall muche the rather obtayne, if you wil vouchsafe to buttresse me, helpe me, and comfort me with your praiers. [2C1] **Petrus Apostolus Iesu Christi electis aduenis dispersionis Ponti Galatiae, Cappadociae, Asiae, & Bithiniae, secundum prescientiam Dei patris. etc.**

Petre Apostle of Iesu Christe, vnto the straungers dispersed in Pontus, Galatia, Cappadocia, Asia, and Bithinia, electe accordinge to the foresyghte of God the father, to haue your spirit sanctified, to haue obedience, and to haue the bloude of Christe sprinkeled vpon you: Grace and peace to you be multiplied.*

This is the salutation that this blessed Apostle Saynt Peter begynneth his letter with all. As the maner is when one frende wryteth to an other, fyrst he beginneth with recommendations (that be salutations) & consequentlye procedeth to his purpose. Accordinge to the same maner, I wyll fyrste declare these recommendations vnto you, whiche done, when I shall come to his processe, I shall tell you his principal purpose in his epistle, and prosecute the same perticulerlye and in percels as it lyeth in the letter. Fyrst we must considre who wrote this letter: Seconde, to whome he wrote it: Thyrde, frome whence he wrote it: Fourth, for what purpose and intente he wrote it.* For the fyrst it appereth, that Saint Peter Christes Apostle writte it, whiche was fyrst called Simon, Christ turned his name, and where afore he was called Simon, Christ called him Peter. **Ioh. i.*** Blessed S. Andrew, one of S. Iohn Baptists disciples, after he had diuers times heard his maister geue excellent testimonye and commendations of Christ, and on a time S. Iohn and two of his disciples, of which S. An[2C1ᵛ]drew was one, stode together and sawe Christe go by, and then sayd S. Iohn, **Lo the lambe of God,*** the sayd disciples made no more tarienge, but lefte theyr olde maister (supposinge he was content they should do so) and folowed Christe, and taried with him, where he abode al that day vndoubted with most heauenly lessons, and godly learning, although the scriptures expresse not what they were. In this appeareth the excellent prerogatiue of this blessed Apostle S. Andrew, in as much as he was the fyrst taken to acquaintaunce with Christe of all the disciples, and also his aboundaunt charitie, in as muche as he dyd not kepe to him selfe the treasure that he hadde founde, but would not rest tyll he had made his brother Peter partaker of the same. As sone as he found his brother then called Simon, he said to him, we haue found **Messias,** whiche is as much to say in English as anointed. We cal him Christ after the greke word, for **Messias** in the Hebrew, **Christus** in the greke, **vnctus** in the latin, **anointed** in the englysh, is all one.* Saynt Andrewe as I sayde broughte him to Christe, whiche looked vpon hym and sayde. **Tu es Simon filius Iona, tu vocaberis Cephas:** Thou arte Symon the sonne of Iona, thou shalte be called **Cephas** in the Hebrewe, whiche is as muche to saye in the Greke and in the latyn as **Petra.*** **Hieronimus super epistolam ad Galath, capit. ii. Non quo aliud significet Petrus, aliud Cephas, sed quod quam nos Latine & Grece Petram nominemus, hanc Hebraei & syri propter lingue inter se viciniam Cepham nuncupent.*** [2C2] And by this (nowe by the waye) is confounded the ignoraunce and erroure of certayne summalistes,* takynge for one of theyr strongest reasons for the supremitie of the pope of Rome, this text spoken to Peter, **Tu es Simon, tu vocaberis Cephas,** whiche they interpretate **caput,** a heade, as thoughe Christe sayde, thou shalte be called the head, concludynge of that, hym to be the heade of the Apostles, and consequently his successors the popes of Rome to be heade of all the churche of all countreys,* whiche thoughe it be very true, yet this texte proueth not so muche: for in the texte it is sayde expresselye, **Cephas quod interpretatur Petrus: Cephas** by interpretation is as muche to saye as a **stone,** or **of stone** (yf it be an adiectiue.)* Here such summalistes would plainlye destroye the texte of S. Iohns Gospell, to make for theyr purpose, which nede not, for ther be as well holye Scriptures as aunciente wryters, whiche proueth abundauntly the sayd primacye of the pope.* Therefore lette vs take the texte as it is meaned, for the chaungynge of Simons name into Peter, whiche soundeth in the Englyshe (as I sayde) a **stone,** or **of stone.** Christe that is the true and sure stone vpon whyche the Churche is buylded, gaue him a name deriued from him selfe, that lyke as he is the fyrme and faste stone, so shoulde Symon be all one with hym, and **of stone** with hym, as all we of the name of Christe be called Christians, and should be all one with hym. And morallye Simon the [2C2ᵛ] sonne of Ionas was called Peter.* Symon by interpretation is as muche to saye as obedient: Ionas a doue, moste gentle, hansome, and tame byrde: Obedience is the chylde of the doue,* of gentlenes and curtesye, and that we be obedient to good counsel, to godly exhortations, or to our maysters, it commeth of a gentyll and curtyse hearte, for gentlenes gendreth obedience, & they that be proude, stubborne and sturdy, wyll neuer be obedient: they that be obedient shal chaunge theyr name into the better, they shall be Peter, fyrme and faste in goodnes, by that they shall be incorporate to Christ, the fyrme and fast rocke & foundation of all our goodnes, we shalbe called Christians or Christen men and women, and by that we shalbe the children of God, the frendes of God, and the body of God with Christe, and coperteiners of his enheritaunce, and kingdome with hym. And in this that Christ chaunged the name of Symon into Peter, he declared that it was he that by his godheade had aucthoritie so to do,* and that it was he that in the olde testamente chaunged the name of Abram into Abraham, of Sarai into Sara, of Iacob into Israel, as now he called Symon, Peter, and Iohn and Iames the sonnes of Zebede he called Boanerges, **quod est filii tonitrui. Marc. iii.** the children of thondre.* It foloweth in the texte. **Apostle of Iesus Christe.** * **Apostolos** in the Greke is as muche to saye as **one that is sende:** it is the name of an office, accordynge to them that Christe chose to be sende forth thorough all the worlde, to preach [2C3] the good tydinges of remission of synnes by Christe, and of lyfe euerlastinge. But this name is not appropriate to them onely, but it agreeth also to manye other, as well in the olde testamente as in the newe.* Moyses was a blessed prophete, and he myghte also be called Apostle, because God sente him to do his message to Pharao kynge of Eygpt. **Exo. iii.** where he excused his vnhablenes desyrynge God to prouide an other to be sente thether.* And it is wrytten. **Esai. vi, Quem mittam & quis ibit nobis?** Whome shall I sende (sayde the voice of almyghte GOD) and who shall goe for vs to this people. Esaye aunswered. **Ecco ego, mitte me,** Lo, here I am, sende me.* Saynt Iohn Baptist **fuit homo missus a deo,** was sente from God, and by that he was Apostle, he was also a prophete, and more then a prophete.* And Saynt Paule calleth Christe Apostle. **Heb. iii. Considerate Apostolum et pontificem confessionis nostre Iesum.** In as muche as God the father sente hym to be incarnate for oure redemption.* Saynt Hierome on the begynninge of the Epistle to the Galathians, putteth a distinction of .iiii. manners of Apostles.* One kinde of Apostles be they that be sente, not from man, or by man, but by Iesu Christe, and GOD the father, as Moyses, Esaye, Iohn Baptiste, Peter, Paule, with theyr company. Of the seconde manner be they that be sente of GOD by man, as by a meane betwyxte GOD and them, as Iosue was made the guyde and instructoure of the people of Israell by Goddes wyll, declared [2C3ᵛ] by Moyses, whiche in Goddes behalfe put hym in aucthoritie. **Nu, xxvii.** * And so I doubt not but S. Augustine **Anglorum Apostolus,** * was sent of God by the ministerye and settinge furth of S. Gregory, [(]one of the best bishoppes of Rome that euer was after S. Peter) into this realme, to conuerte the people to Christes fayth, and so he dyd spedely, God assisting and helping forth his godly purpose. And lykewyse when the kynges maiestie, or the prelates vnder him, sende furth catholike preachers amonge the people, sincerelye to instructe them to vertue, it is to be supposed that they be Apostles sende of God by man. The thyrde maner is of them that by mans fauoure & affection, more then for learninge or any good condition in them, be sent or set furth to take vpon them the office of preachinge. And yet they lowly consideringe theyr infyrmitie and inhabilitie, and the highnes of the office, that they be put in, by prayer, and exercise of study may come to suche grace, that they maye worthely execute the Apostles office, that they toke vpon them. The fourth maner of Apostles, be neither sent by God nor good man, as pseudapostles, false preachers of heresies, scismes, discention, and diuision, of whiche speaketh Paule. **ii. Cor. xi. Such pseude Apostles or false Apostles, be subtill and disceitfull workemen, disguisynge them selues into the Apostles of Christ, and no marueil, for Sathanas self disgiseth him selfe into an Aungel of light,** therefore it is no meruayle thoughe his ministers and seruauntes do so lykewise:* They speake in Goddes [2C4] name as though God sent them, & yet God sayth not as they saye, neither sent them to do his errande. Suche was not blessed S. Peter, but he was sent by almighty God our Sauiour Iesus Christ, as he sayth here in this salutation or gretynge. **Iesus,** is as much to say as a sauiour,* and therefore in as muche as Christe by reason of his godhead, was euer a Sauiour of the worlde, he had that name from the beginning of the world, and also afore the world was made, because that he euer intended to saue the worlde, after that it shoulde perisshe. And for this cause the Aungell Gabriell, when he bad Ioseph that he shoulde not put away Mary his wife, but cherysshe her, declaringe that the chylde that she went with al was begotten, not by anye misorderinge of her virginall bodye, but by the operation of the holy goost, and that he shoulde call the chylde Iesus, because he should saue the people from their synnes. The Aungell bad him not geue him that name, but bad him that he shoulde call him so, by the name that he had euer, for he was euer a Sauiour.* Manye we reade of in the olde testamente that were called Iesus, as Iesus Naue, otherwise called Iosue, and Iesus **filius Iosedech Eccl. xlix.** and Iesus **filius Syrach. Eccl. l.*** but none of them could saue the people from theyr sinnes, but only our Iesus the sonne of Mary ye virgin. **Christ** is as much to say as anoynted, & so was oure sauiour Christe with the oyle of gladnes, that is to say: with the grace of the holye gooste, signified by the gentyll supplenes of oyle, **pre con[2C4ᵛ]sortibus tuis,** better, and aboue his felowes.* By that the Prophet compareth him to his felowes ye may playnely vnderstande, that he meaneth of the manheade of Christ, by whiche he become oure felowe, for the godheade is but one, & hath no felowe in substaunce. Kinges were annoynted, and so were priestes, and also prophetes, euery one of them for diuers offices, and with materiall oyle:* but Christ was oynted with spirituall oyntment of the holy gooste, and also not onely for anye one of those three offices, but for them all thre, for he was and is kinge and preist, and a prophete.* Therefore the prophet sayde full well **pre consortibus tuis,** aboue al other men, whiche was perfitly declared, perfourmed, and fulfylled, when he was baptised in Iordan water, & the holy gost descended lyke a doue, and lyght vpon him, and abode in him. **Ioh. i.*** Now I must (according to my promise) declare, vnto whome S. Peter wrote his letter or epistle. He wrote it to the strau*n*gers dispersed in **Pontus, Galatia, Cappadotia, Asia, and Bithinia,** chosen by the prescience and foreknowledge of God the father* **Aduenae** straungers were called among the Iewes suche as were gentils or paignims borne, & for deuotion to one God, were conuerted to the rites and lawes of the Iewes, & were circumcised, and kept their ceremonies as the Iewes did, and these

by the Greke worde were called **proseliti**.* Manye suche there were in olde time,
& euen in Christes tyme, of whiche verye many were conuerted to Christes faith
by the preaching of the Apostles, [2D1] and by the wonderous miracles that they
sawe wrought euerye daye by the power of Christes name, like as an infinite
number of the Iewes were conuerted to Christes fayth, anone after the commyng
of the holy Gost vpon the apostles by whose grace and comfort they preached
boldly, and Christe euer wrought with them, confirmynge their preachynge with
signes and miracles, aboue mannes power to do.* Notwithstanding as sone as .s.
Stephan was slain for Christes faythes sake, there rose such a persecution among
these newe christen people that they fled, & were scattered & dispersed abrode
into diuers countries all, except the apostles,* And the same apostles after thei had
made .s. Iames the lesse, the sonne of **Alphei**, bishop of Ierusalem,* they thought it
necessary to go abrode among other nacions to publish the faith of christ, at which
time there is no dout but .s. Peter went abrode among the gentils as wel as other,
for it was he that had first reuelation so to do by the vision that appered to hym in
Ioppe, vpon which he went to Cornelius captain in **Cesaria**, & to him and to his
family & company preached Christ as it is plaine. **Act. x.*** And many sure &
auncient auctours write that after thordination of .s. Iames bishop of Hierusalem,
S. Peter came to **Antioche** one of the chefe cities of Syria,* and there taried a
while preachynge Christ and proceaded further into the countreys that be here
spoken of, in the Salutation at the begynnge of thys Epistle .**pontus, Galatiae,
Capadotia**. and other, and occupied the [2D1ᵛ] tyme amonge them by the space of
fyue yeares after some, & bi the space of .vii, yeres after other and then came backe
to Antioche & there continued bishoppe and chefe instructour of Christes flock,
for the space of seuen yeres more,* and from thence chased awaye **Simon Magus**,*
and detected his errours. And afterwarde hearde that the sayde **Simon magus** was
come to Rome, and had there diuine honours done to hym as to a GOD, and had
Images erected in his honour, and that he made all the Citye to dote vpon hym
like madde men, for this occasion he came to Rome as **Eusebius** saieth. **Li. ii.
ecclesiastice historie ca. xiiii**. and there within a while quenched the blindnes of
Simon Magus, and of that deuillysh womanne that he had in his companye, by
whose disceitfull sorcerye he allured manye to geue credence to hym.* And that
Saint Peter beinge at Rome, wrote this Epistle, and sent it from Rome,* as well to
such straungers as were dispersed and scattered abroade in the countreys of
Pontus, Galatia, capadotia, &c. by occasion of persecution, as to all others in-
habitantes of the same countreys among whiche he had preached in his longe and
paynefull progresse, and had conuerted them to Christes fayeth, whiche all he
counted as straungers to the worlde.* And so in the seconde chapter of this epistle,
he prayeth them to take them selues, sayinge: **Obsecro vos tanquam aduenas &
peregrinos**. Euen like as we haue in the actes of the apostles xv.* That saint Paul
after he had planted Christes Gospel in the countreys where he hadde
la[2D2]boured preachynge, he vsed to take an oportunitie and conuenient tyme to
go throughe agayne from place to place to visite them, and to se whether they
persisted and stode as firme and fast in fayeth as he had left them. In like case
Saynte Peter hauynge so busie a piece of worke and so great a charge on his hande,
as to teache al that huge and great citie of Rome, then being lordes and rulers of
the worlde, in whiche then was in maner a confusion of all vices and synnes, of all
opinions, of all supersticions and errours by concourse of all nacions resortynge
thither, for decisions of causes which doubtles brought wyth them the supersticions, and the vices, and noughty liuynges of their countreys, as wee se by experi-

ence, where little concourse of straungers is, there is playne maner of liuyng, and
after one maner, but in port townes they be of an other sort. The Germayns and
Saxons brynge in their opinions. The Frenchmen their new fashions. Other countreis geuen to lechery, runne to the open bars or stues.* And for such confusion of
the inhabitantes<.> Saint Peter in the ende of this his first epistle calleth Rome by
the name of Babilon,* as you shal heare (by Goddes helpe) when wee shall come
to that place. For this exceadyng charge that ,s. **Peter** had take vpon him, he
might not intende to go amonge them agayne, to confirme theim, and to make
them more stedfaste in fayeth, but sent to them this excellent and noble epistle,
ful of fatherly counsayle, whiche they myght euery day read, to make them remember their maister, [2D2ᵛ] and to liue accordynge to hys doctryne that he hadde
geuen theim. But nowe riseth a doubt of no smal importaunce. Saint Paule in his
epistle to the Galatheis in the firste Chapiter, saythe that after his conuersion he
toke his iourney into Arabye, and after he had laboured a season in that countrey,
he retourned agayne and came to **Damascus*** (the chiefe citye of Siria. **Esay. vii.**
Caput Syrie Damascus.)* And then after three yeres of his conuersion, he came
to Hierusalem to see Peter, & taryed there with him .xv. dayes, & there he sawe
none other of the apostles at that tyme but onely saynt Peter and Iames the lesse
called Christes brother, whiche then was made bishop and ouerseer of Christes
churche in Hierusalem:* For all the residue of the apostles were then dispersed
abrode to preache the worde of GOD. After this Saynt Paule (as he sayeth) went
abrode into the coastes of **Siria** and **Celicia,*** where he was brought vp in youth.
For he saieth of him self. **Act. xxii. Ego sum vir Iudeus, natus in Tharso Cilicie.**
I am a Iew by kinred born in **Tharsus,** a city in **Cilicia,** which is a countrey in
mayne Asia.* For yᵉ Iewes wer not al born in Iury, but as their parents wer
dispersed into al countries, so thei had their children in diuers countreys. And then
after .xiiii. yeres, s. Pa[u]l came againe to Ierusalem to confer the gospel that he
preached, with the apostles yᵗ were the pillers of the Church, Peter, Iames, and
Iohn, whiche he founde then at Hierusalem.* Nowe good frendes take hede.
Heare we haue of saynt Paule whiche in the place alledged [2D3] swore, & toke
god to witnes, that he lyed not,* we may wel beleue hym, & must nedes so do, the
holy gost spoke in him. Here (I saie) we haue firste iii. yeres next after Paules
conuersion afore his commynge to Hierusalem, when he taryed there wyth Peter
fiftene dayes. And then we haue fouretene yeares more afore he came to Hierusalem to conferre hys preachynge wyth the other Apostles, and at bothe tymes he
founde Sayncte Peter at Hierusalem. So that by this wee haue, that Saynte PETER
was at Hierusalem, seuentene yeares and more after Christes ascention,* for .s.
Paul was conuerted in the first yere after Christes ascention in February next after
as the church representeth, at that tyme, kepyng the feast of the conuersion of S.
Paule.* Nowe (I praye you) when went sainte Peter abroade amonge them that
were dispersed in **Pontus, Galatia, Capadocia, &c?** And when was he bishoppe of
Anthiochia?* To this I saye that as for the three firste yeares that Saynte Paule
spoke of, Saynte Peter taried verye much at Ierusalem wyth Iames, there to order
the Primatyue & first churche of Christe in all the worlde. Their presence because
they were of hyghe reputation, was verye necessarye for that purpose, so that in all
that tyme I thynke he went verye little amonge the Gentyles, excepte it were by
some chaunce, or by reuelation, as he came to **Cornelius** at **Cesarea.*** His most
laboure was aboute the conuersion of Iewes, to conuerte them to Christe.

[2D3ᵛ] Then afterwarde in the .xiiii. yere that .s. Paule speaketh of (the churche
of Hierusalem beynge resonablye well stablished) there is no doubte but saint

Peter went abrode into all countreys preachynge Christe chieflye to the Iewes that were dispersed into many countreys, ther liuyinge likc straungers,* after the persecution that roose after the martirdome of saint Stephan,* and for many such troubles as fel vpon them, exhorting them to pacience, and declarynge that throughe many troubles wee muste come into the kyngedome of God. And in this time he sticked for no labours, but came to the countreys of **Pontus Galatiae**. &c. Countreys of mayne **Asia,** of which some of them be almost as farre north east from Hierusalem, as we be northwest, and to them preached Christes fayth, and returnyng backe, came againe to **Antiochia,** where he taried and ruled Christes flocke as bishoppe there by the space of seuen yeres or more. Saint Hierome sayth. **Super Gal. ii. Primum episcopum Antiochene ecclesiae Petrum fuisse accepimus, & Romam exinde translatum.*** From **Antiochia** he wente to Rome to conuince **Simon Magus** (as I saide afore.) And from Rome came backe agayne vnto Hierusalem to a counsail in the eyghtenth yere after Christes ascention, at which time .s. Paule was warned by reuelation to ascende also to Hierusalem to conferre his Gospell wyth the other Apostles, and there met with Peter, Iames, and Iohn, as he sayth in the seconde chapiter to the Galathia[n]s.* And then saynt Peter toke his leaue and retur[2D4]ned to Rome againe, where he continued, and in the countreys thereabout to his liues ende. And from thence he wrote this Epistle as I sayde.* Now if I shall perfourme the exposition of this epistle, as I haue taken vpon me, I must somewhat speake of these countreys that saint Peter rehearseth here in the salutation of his letter, for here they be written as you haue heard. **Pontus, Galatia, Capadocia,** and so furth. Therfore if they shall not be somewhat set furthe and declared, whereto be they written here? If they shall not be described vnto theim that heare or reade this epistle, let them be striken out of the boke, whye should thei cumber any more paper? To heare of them shall be pleasant to al men that deliteth in naturall histories of Geography, or Cosmographye, and to all mariners and marchauntes that haue trauersed the seas. And to them that wold haue their soules edified in vertue, it shall not be vnprofitable, by reason of some morall learnyng that may concurre amonge. For this you muste first vnderstande that **Mare mediterraneum,** the middel<y> earth sea, whiche our marchauntes calleth the **Leuant*** commeth out of the maine occean sea, runnyng into the lande at a verye narrowe entrye, called the straightes, betwixt two mountaines or rocks, one called **Calpe*** in Granado, on the south parte of Spaine, and the other called **Abila,*** in Mauritania, where yᵉ Mores inhabite. And the saide mountayne called **Calpe,** our marc[h]auntes calleth **Calis,** addynge to it for the euyll and daungerous passage by the same **Malis yll,** [2D4ᵛ] after the language of the countrey, there **Calys Malys.*** Ill Calys, because of a great multitude of ragged rockes liynge in the tresholde or bottom of the saide gate, so that when any ship shall passe in or out at the saide streicte, the mariners must be sure of an high water, and a measurable winde, els they shall finde it an yll passage and perilous. The said two rockes, cleues, or promontories, bee called **Gades** and **Columne Hercules.*** Hercules postes, and standeth one on the one side of the sayde entre, and the other on the other side and maketh lyke a gate into the Leuaunt. And as Pliny writeth, **In prohemio tercii naturalis historiae.** It is but fyue myles broade, where it is strayghtest, and passeth not tenne myles ouer where it is broadest.* **pomponius Mela** agreeth saiynge: **Libro primo. Non amplius decem milibus passimum patens.*** A wonderous worke of GOD, by so narrowe a passage to brynge into the mayne Lande so great a Sea as it maketh, runnynge furthe Eastwarde, and leauing Affrique on the ryght hande, and Europe on the lifte hand, tyll it come as farre as **Celiciae,** in maygne Asya, and there stayeth in a certayn bay called **Sinus issicus,** * the baye where the riuer of **Issus** openeth into the same sea, and it goeth no further Eastward: enuironnyng and conteinyng within it self a great multitude of the most ferti[le] ysles that we ca[n] read of, and specially the excellent Isle of **Cyprus,** * Notwythstandynge afore the said Leuaunt become so farre Eastwarde, it turneth Northwarde, longe and many a myle. [2E1] Fyrst it runneth together and entreth into a narow streict called **Hellespontus*,** muche narower then the said yate out of the **Oceane** into the **Leuaunt** that I nowe spake of, this streicte passeth not much thre quarters of a myle ouer, and whan it is past that streicte, it spreadeth abrode agayne like a sea, and is called **Propontis.** * Then yet more Northwarde it runneth togither into a narower streict then any of the two that I haue spoken of, this streict is called **Thratius bosphorus.** * The coun-trey of **Thracia,** where **Bizantium,** nowe called **Constantinople,** is cheife citie, is on the West parte of it, and the sayde **Constantinople** lieth nigh to the same streict.* This streicte is so narowe, that in caulme wether men maye heare byrdes singe frome the one point to the other, and mennes voyces also from **Europe** into **Asia,** and contrarywyse, out of **Asia** into **Europe.** * When the sea passeth that streict, then it spreadeth abroade into a marueilous great sea called **Pontus Eu-xinus,** * And yet agayne gathereth it self together into as narow a streicte as this that I spake of last, and it is called **Cymmerius bosphorus,** * and beyond him it spreadeth abroad againe into a huge meare or standing water called **Meotis,** * into whiche runneth the fierce and swifte riuer of **Tanais** * comminge oute of the mountaines of the North, and is drowned in the sayd **Meotis.** Here haue you hearde (more shortely then the matter requireth) the course and wayes of the middle earth, sea, or leuaunt, whiche you maye more sensiblye perceiue, yf you wyll conferre my [2E1ᵛ] sayinges to a table or mappe of the worlde. In the sayd Leuaunt be Ilandes, as **Pomp. Mela** reconeth about .C.xl. of whiche some be the moost excellente of the worlde, speciallye in the forthright course betwixt **Calis Malis, & Cilicia,** there is **Corsica,** where the Romaines haue their vyne cors. There is **Sardinia, sicilia,** and **Creta,** whiche we call **Candy,** there is the most fertyle and fruitfull Ilande of **Cyprus.** * And towarde the mouth of the North-warde, called **Hellespontus** (that I spoke of) is the well knowen Ile of the Rhodes, latelye inhabited with Chrysten men, nowe by the rage of the Turke, peruerted to myserable subiection and bondage.*

Nowe for the texte you shall vnderstande, that these countreys that Saynt Peter speaketh of lieth in greate **Asia,** whiche is the thyrde parte of the worlde, deuyded frome **Affrike** by the ryuer of **Nylus,** that runneth thoroughe Egipte, downe vnto the sayde myddle earth Sea, or leuaunt, & deuyded from **Europe,** by the seas runnynge Northwarde into the standynge water called **Meotis,** and by the swyfte ryuer of **Tanais,** runnynge oute of the mountaynes, in the North parte of the worlde, and descendinge into the sayde **Meotis.** * And the sayde Asia conteyneth in quantitie more grounde, then both **Affricke** and **Europe** doeth. And the sayde countreys that Sainte Peter preached in, and to whiche he wrote his lettre or Epistle, lyeth not so in ordre as Saynte Peter, rehearseth [2E2] them, but Saynte Peter rehearseth them out of theyre ordre of purpose* (I thinke) meanynge that vicinitie to Ierusalem, or prioritie in receauinge the fayth, doeth not derogate or hindre the other that wer later conuerted, but that fyrste and laste, all is one in Christe: As Sainte Paule in a lyke speaketh. **Galath. iii. Non est Iudeus, neque Grecus, non est seruus, neque liber, non est masculus, neque femina, omnes enim vos vnum estis in CHRISTO IESV.** * Furtheste of frome Ierusalem, and mooste Northwarde lyeth **Pontus,*** on the Easte side of that broade sea called **Pontus Euxinus,** that I spoke of eue[n] nowe. **Pomponius Mela, capite de summa Asiae descriptione. Circa pontum aliquot populi alio alioque sine omnes vno nomine pontici dicuntur. Hieronimus de nominibus Hebraicis. Pontus regio multarum gentium, iuxta mare ponticum, quod Asiam Europamque disterminat.*** It conteyneth dyuers countreys, and of diuers languages. There is **Colchis,** where **Iason** hadde the Golden fleice, as Poetes faine.* **Mithridates** that noble kinge, that kepte open warre with the Romaynes by the space of sixe and fortye yeares, was kinge there in **Ponto** fyrste, and afterwarde of **Armenia, Capadotia,** and of the mooste parte of all maygne, and greate **Asia:*** And I thincke verelye it is twoo thousande myle aboute by lande frome Ierusalem, where Sayncte Peter begonne to preache. In whiche all Bysshoppes, and all they that haue taken vppon [2E2ᵛ] them cure of soules, or the office of preachinge, haue example to take paines and labours in ministringe the worde of God to theyr people, and not to lie at reste & pleasures in a corner at their manours. Next to this is **Capadocia,*** where S. George the martyr was borne, as appeareth by his legend,* & this **Capadocia** hath on his North coaste the sayde sea **Pontus Euxinus,** and it runneth a long on the same sea, and hath on his east side bothe **Armenyes** the lesse and the more,* and is deuided from the greater **Armenye,** by the ryuer of **Euphrates,*** and extendeth southwarde as farre as **Cilicia** that I spoke of, and hath on the Weste side **Bithinia, Galacia, Paphlagonia.** Then by the sea coaste **Bithinia** lyeth next, and it lyeth against Constantinoble, sometyme called **Bizancium,** in so muche that the East point of the lande, making the streict called **Thracius Bosphorus,** is in **Bithinia,** and parte of **Bithinia** lyeth on the sea that is on the South part of that streat called **Propontis,** & parte of it on the North parte of that streict on **pontus Euxinus.*** And in the sayd **Bithinia** is the citie called **Nicea,** where the gratious Emperor **Constantine,** with .CCC. and .xviii. bishops, kept the moost autenticall and blessed counsell, called **concilium Nicenum,** in whiche **Arrius** heresies were condempned, and manye blessed statutes made.* Then commeth **Galacia,** sometime called **Gallogrecia,*** it lieth withoute the streicte called **Hellespontus,** southward, **super mare Egeum,*** and in this countrey S. Paule had laboured as wel as S, Peter, and had instruct them very perfit[2E3]lye in Christes fayth. Notwithstandinge by pseudapostles, and false preachers, they were broughte into the Iewes ceremonies, whiche when S. Paule knewe, he writte to them a very earnest epistle to call them home agayne, you haue it amongest his other epistles, called the Epistle to the **Galathies,** or **Galathians.*** Then commeth **Asia** the lesse, which is but a part of maigne **Asia,** that (as I tolde you) is the thyrd part, and greatest parte of the worlde, and in this countrey standeth the noble citie of **Ephesus,** in which sometyme was the famous temple of **Diana,** that is spoken of. **Act. xix.*** And to the people of this citie .S. Paule wrote his epistle, intitled, the epistle to the **Ephesies,** or **Ephesians,** The country is exceadinge welthy and fruiteful, and the people excedingely geuen to carnall pleasures, therfore S. Paule called them beastes. **i. Cor. xv. Si . . . ad bestias pugnaui Ephesi quid mihi prodest. &c.*** Here I haue breifely declared the site and standing of these countreys that .S. Peter speaketh of in his salutation and beginning of his epistle, you must not thinke that all these countreys be immediat and next to gether one to another, but there be some greate countreys betwixte them, whiche is not to my purpose nowe to speake of, but conferringe one of these to another of them, they lye by the Geographye, in that order as I haue tolde you. To all faythfull people, as well Iewes as Gentyles, dispersed as straungers here and there in the saide countreis .S. Peter wrytte his epistle, and he calleth them **electe** and [2E3ᵛ] chosen by the knowledge of God the father,* not excludynge the sonne, or the holye Gooste, for the prescience, foreknowledge, and knowledge, is all one in all three personnes in trinitie. Whom the father doth predestinate or choose to grace or to saluation, the same doth the sonne, and also the holye Gooste, predestinate and chuse to be saued.* Theyr workes amonge creatures be all one, but in as muche as Saynte Peter calleth theym that he writeth vnto, **electe and chosen by the knoweledge of GOD the father,** We muste not thynke that all they that were conuerted to **CHRISTES** fayth, in the sayde countreis to whiche Sainte Peter wrote, were electe by suche election as Christe speaketh of in the parable. **Math. xxii. Multi sunt vocati, pauci vero electi.** Manye be called, and but fewe chosen,* for here it is meaned, that fewe be chosen fynallye to be saued, and to be sure of lyfe euerlastynge. It is not to be thoughte that Saynte Peter would make to all them that he wrote vnto, anye suche assuraunce, but he taketh election more largelye, as Christe speaketh of it, **Nonne ego vos duodecim elegi, & vnus ex vobis Diabolus est? Ioh. vi.** Dydde not I chose you twelue, and one of you is the Deuylles birde.* And also, **Ioh. xv. Non vos me elegistis, sed ego elegi vos.** You haue not chosen me, but I haue chosen you:* Where we muste vnderstande by this election, the vocation and callinge to the faith, and to beleue on **Christe**: for neyther they that this [2E4] was spoken to, nor any other were chosen, because they beleued on **CHRISTE**, but because **CHRISTE** chose theym, therefore they beleued on hym, so that **GODDES** eternall election was the cause of oure vocation to fayth. And therefore Sainte Paule sayth, **Ephes. i. Elegit nos in ipso ante mundi constitu-tionem.** GOD the father chose vs in **CHRISTE**, afore the worlde was made,* he chose vs to be saued by the fayth of **CHRISTE**, whiche is the onelye and verye necessarye waye to saluation. Nowe to my purpose, all these people of these countreis to whiche Saynt Peter wrytte, were electe and chosen by the prescience and foreknowledge of GOD, to be called, and to come to Christes fayth, and to continue in the same as **GOD** knew. **GOD knewe who were his,*** that woulde finallye continue in **CHRISTES** fayth, and be saued, and who woulde fall frome the same to infidelitie agayne, or by sinne and misliuinge deface and defoule theyr fayth, and be dampned.

But here yet riseth a doubte, for Saynte Paule sayth. **Roman. vii[i], Quos presciuit & predestinauit hos & vocauit. &c.** Theim that he afore knewe and dydde predestinate, he called:* and them that he called, he iustified: and them that he iustified, he magnified, and glorified, and appointed finallye to glorie euerlasting. Therefore it shuld seme, that if they were called, they were iustified, and if they were iustified, then muste it nedes folowe that they were gloryfyed.

[2E4ᵛ] Here you must vnderstand that there is two manners of calling or chos-inge, one is, **secundum presentem iustitiam,** accordinge to a certayne iust maner of liuinge that men be of for the tyme of theyr callinge,* and as they appeare in the face of the worlde, as the scripture speaketh of Saule .i. **Reg. ix. Erat . . . Saul electus & bonus, & non erat vir de filiis Israel melior illo.** Saul was chosen, and good, and of all the issue of Israell there was not one better then he.* Then he was good, after he was noughte. So Iudas when he was chosen was good ynough, although he afterwarde betrayed his mayster and ours. For this kinde of callinge doth not so confirme men in goodnes, but that they may fall and be noughte, & so was Saul, and so was Iudas, and so were manye of them that S. Peter writte vnto, although thei were called and chosen to Christes faithe by the ministery and labour of S. Peter, S. Paule, or of others of the Apostles. There is another election, chosinge, or callinge, whiche is **secundum dei propositum,** accordinge to Goddes determinate purpose. Of this S. Paule speaketh. **Rom. viii. Scimus autem quoniam diligentibus deum omnia cooperantur in bonum his qui secundum propositum vocati sunt sancti.** To them that by Goddes determinate purpose be called, all thinges worketh for the best,* yea, sinnes that they do maketh them to repent theyr doyng, and to arise by penaunce, and to be better ware of suche sinnes thereafter, and to do no more so. Therefore I say (to the letter of S, Peters epistle) they were elect and cho[2F1]sen, as God knewe that all shoulde come to the faith of Christe, **In sanctificationem spiritus** to be sanctified in spirite by baptisme, and to haue their soules in the way of saluation **In sanctificationem spiritus** saith the vulgate and comon text, **per sanctificationem spiritus in obedientiam. &c.** saythe the newe translation and they come all to one purpose.* For by that, that we haue our spirit sanctified and made holy by Gods holy spirite the holy gost, we come to obedience and be made obedient to the faith of Christe, and be redy to fulfyll, perfourme, and do the workes of the spirite, and to bring furth the fruites of the spirite, which be **charitas, gaudium, pax, patientia. &c. Gala. v.*** And S. Paule prayed almighty GOD for his disciples, and by them for vs all **.i. Thessa. v. Ipse autem deus pacis sanctificet vos per omnia vt integer spiritus vester, et anima, & corpus, sine querela in aduentu domini nostri Iesu Christi conseruetur.** The God of peace make you all holy in euery point that your spirite, your soule, and your bodye may be kepte without complaint in the comming of our Lord Iesu Christ.* In which wordes he diuideth man into three partes, the spirite, the soule and the body where you shall note that the **spirite** sometyme signifieth the whole soule of man, and so it is taken in the prophetes words in the psalme, **In manus tuas commendo spiritum meum,*** which Christ spoke vpon the crosse. And it foloweth there: **Inclinato capite tradidit spiritum,** he bowed his head and yelded vp his spirite, that is hys soule.* But when we finde in the scriptures such a distinction [2F1ᵛ] of the partes of man, as the Apostle putteth in the place aboue rehersed, then we muste take the spirite more precisely for that parte of the soule by whiche we vnderstande and reason a matter. And that same parte Saynte Paule calleth in another place, the minde. **Mente seruio legi dei carne, autem legi peccati. Roman. vii.** Wyth my mynde I serue the lawe of GOD, but by my fleshe I serue and incline to sinne.* And lykewyse **Galathians .v. Caro concupiscit aduersus spiritum, spiritus autem aduersus carnem,*** so that he called afore the **mynde,** here he calleth it the **spirite.** Wee vse not to call the minde anye thinge els, but the reasonable porcion and parte of the soule. And sometime the Apostle ioyneth them bothe together. **Ephesians iiii. Renouamini spiritu mentis vestre,** be you renewed **in the spirite of your mynde,*** whiche is noughte els but your minde, as in an other place hee vseth lyke manner of speakinge, **Collossians .ii. In expoliatione corporis carnis.** The bodye of oure fleshe,* that is to say, the fleshe, and suche maner of speakinge we vse in the Englysh tounge, **the citye of Brystowe,** whiche is no more to saye but Bristowe. The Citye of London, is but London. The towne of Wells, is no more but Wells. And nowe to my purpose I thinke that Sainte Peter in this present salutacion taketh the spirite for the whole soule of man, comprisynge reason and the sensible powers, wyll, and sensualitie, whiche all together is **sanctified** by the holye Goste, infusinge and powring faith [2F2] and charitie into our soules, when we came to the grace of Christendome, and by thys as I sayde, wee be made obedient to Christes faythe, and readye to fulfill his commaundementes. **Et aspersionem sanguinis Iesu Christi.** And you be electe accordinge to Goddes knowledge, to haue the bloode of Iesu Christe sprinckeled and cast vppon you.* The bloode of Abell the fyrst Martyr, was shedde and sprinckeled on the grounde, when Cain his brother kylled him, but this blood sprinckelinge cried for vengeaunce. **Genesis .iiii. Vox sanguinis fratris tui clamat ad me de terra,** saieth almighty GOD, the voyce of thy brothers bloude cryeth vnto me from the grounde, as thoughe GOD sayde: Thy deede is so manyfest, that it neede none accuser, the verye bloude shedde on the grounde declareth thy manslaughter & cryeth for vengeance. **Nunc igitur maledictus eris super terram que aperuit os suum, & suscepit sanguinem fratris tui de manu tua.** Therefore (saythe almyghtye GOD) thou shalte be cursed vpon the grounde, whyche hath opened her mouthe, and hathe receyued the bloode of thy Brother from thy hande.* The bloude of Christ cryed for mercie and forgyuenes, yea for theym that crucified hym. **Pater ignosce illis quia nesciunt quid faciunt.** Father forgyue theym (saythe Christe) for they knowe not what they do.* Therfore Saynte Paule comparynge these twoo aspersions together, saythe: **Accessistis ad sanguinis aspersionem melius loquentem quam Abel. Heb. xii** [2F2ᵛ] yᵉ be come to the sprinckling of blood, that speaketh better then Abels bloud spake.* To this aspersion we come by baptisme, in which the efficacitie and strengthe of Christes passion commeth vpon vs, & putteth away synne & blame, takinge his strength so to do at the bloode of Christ shed for our redemption, that they that be sprynckled with the bloode of Christ, might auoyde and escape from the power of the diuel, as the people of Israel by the bloude of the Lambe escaped and went out of the bondage of Egipt.* We see also in Moyses lawe, that euery thing that should be sanctified, were wont to be sprinckeled wyth the bloud of the sacrifices killed for that purpose, signifying the clensing and halowing of our soules by the bloude of Christ.* **Gratia vobis & pax multiplicetur.*** This is the conclusion of Saint Peters salutacion or recommendacion, in whiche he gyueth them his blessing of grace & peace. Origene vpon a like blessing saith, I think that this blessing of peace & grace which is giuen to Gods welbeloued seruants, to whom the Apostels writeth, is no less of strength then the blessyng that the holy Patriarch Noe gaue vnto his sonnes, Sem and Iaphet, which was fulfylled by the holye Goste vpon them that were so blessed.* And lykewyse no lesse strength then the blessing that Abraham had of Melchisedeche, or then the blessynge that Iacob had of his father Isaac, or then the blessing that the twelue Patriarches hadde of theyr father Israell.* Then I saye that thys blessynge that Saynt Peter gaue theym that he wrytte [2F3] vnto, was no lesse then the sayde blessinges, for he had in hym selfe the holye spirite, and in the holye spirite he wryt hys letter, and in the same spirite he gaue his blessing. Then by the same holye spirite they shall take theyr blessynges that be blessed of the Apostles or of theym that haue the holye spirite wythin them, speciallye if they be founde worthye, and in whom the blessynge maye fall, or els the sayinge of Christe shall bee brought to passe that he saythe in the Gospell: **Si fuerit ibi filius pacis pax vestram veniet super eum, si<n> autem . . . pax vestra ad vos reuertetur:** If there be the chylde of peace, your peace shall fall vpon hym, and if no, your peace shall retourne to you agayne.* And that is wrytte of peace, is lykewyse to be vnderstande of grace, for Saynte Peter ioyneth together grace and peace, for peace is neuer withoute a speciall grace of GOD, nor grace without peace. Therefore where is lacke of grace, there canne be no peace, and where wee haue no peace, wee maye be sorye that wee lacke grace. This grace and peace the Apostle prayeth that it maye be multiplyed vppon them that he wrytte vnto, that is to saye, that it maye growe and encrease euer more and more from daye to daye. And because hys meanynge was not onelye by theym that he had seen wyth hys

bodelye eyes in the countries where he hadde laboured, but also to all other
nations that shoulde heare or see thys hys blessed Epistle. It is not to be doubted
but thys blessyng of grace and peace he wysheth also to vs, speciallye if we may
saye [2F3ᵛ] wyth the Prophet: **Aduena ego sum apud te & peregrinus sicut
omnes patres mei. Psalm, xxxviii.** I am as a straunger with thee good Lorde, and a
Pilgrame or wayfaring man as all my forefathers haue beene,* he wrytte his letter
to suche straungers, therefore if we counte oure selfe as such straungers,* not
setlyng our mindes to much in the worlde, but countynge oure selues not to haue
anye citie or stedfast abiding here but stretching and settinge fourthe our selues to
the euerlastinge citye of heauen, and to the glory to come. Then let vs take heede
to his blessed doctrine in this Epistle, & take it said vnto vs, aswell as vnto them,
that al we may by his instruction come to such grace as may bring vs to glory
euerlasting, through the help of Iesus Christ our Lord. Amen.

BEnedictus deus et pater domini nostri Iesu Christi. &c.* After his salutacion
here the apostle proceedeth to hys matter and processe in this Epistle or letter,
remembring hys pastorall [2F4] office and dutie, aswell to them that he writ vnto,
as to vs and all Christen people that shall come after vs, specially if we take our
selues as straungers and wayfaring people in this world.* He entended by his
writing to confirme theym and vs by theym in the faithe that they and wee haue
receiued by the preaching of the woorde of God, & in vertuous liuing, agreinge to
the same: He beginneth his processe with laudes and thankes to God the father of
heauen, for his aboundant and great mercy, in this that he hath regenerate and
begotten vs againe to lyfe by our sauiour Christ. Where we afore by our carnall
parentes were generate and gotten to dye. Therefore he saythe, blessed be God and
father of oure Lorde Iesu Christ (that is to saye) God that is the father of our Lorde
Iesu Christ the first person in trinitie, fountain, wel, and original beginning of the
whole trinitie, to which saynt Peter geueth his laudes and thankes, not excluding
any person in trinitie, for the father and the sonne, and the holy Gost haue all one
Godhead, equall glory and coeternall maiestie. For this you must vnderstande that
thys word **blessed** hath diuers significations according to the thinge that it is
ioyned withall. When we say blesse God, or saye blessed be GOD, it is a woorde of
thankes, and is as muche to saye as laude, prayse, and thankes be to GOD.* For by
oure blessynge GOD wee cannot increase hys glorye, neyther make hym anye
thinge the better by oure thankes although so doyng we accomplish & do our
bounden [2F4ᵛ] dutie to him, but when God blesseth vs, hys willing well to vs, or
saying wel by vs is his dede. Therefore when hee blesseth vs, he gyueth vs some
gyfte of grace or temporall subsidye and healpe by his mere liberalitye and gentle-
nesse, and not of dutie nor of our deseruinge. Thyrde when the father or a frende
blesseth the chyld, he giueth him temporall goodes, or wysheth hym well, and
prayeth for him well to doe, as Isaac blessed hys sonnes, Iacob and Esau, and
lykewyse Iacob and other holye Fathers blessed theyr children, as I sayde of Sainte
Peters blessynge in the later ende of the salutacion of this Epistle.* Saynte Peter
(as I sayde) begynneth wyth thankes, offeringe to GOD at the beginninge a
sacrifice of laude, remembryng the sayinge of the Prophet: **Sacrificium laudis
honorificabit me:** The sacrifice of laude and praysinge, shall doe me honour saithe
almighty God.* And like as hee that will doe bodely sacrifice to God, muste doe it
by the handes of a Priest, or of a Byshoppe. So this sacrifice of laude Saint Peter
offereth to GOD the father by the handes of the great Priest and Byshoppe oure
Sauiour Iesus Christe, makynge mention of hym sayinge: **pater domini nostri Iesu
Christi,** The Father of oure Lorde Iesus Christe.* And by thys Sainte Peter gyueth
vs good example to begynne all our woorkes wyth thankes and praise to hym for
hys owne glorye, and with desyringe and praying for his grace to preuent vs & to
set vs forwarde at the beginning of our workes, [2G1] and to be concurrent and
workynge wyth vs in all our affayres and proceadynges in oure businesse. **Qui
secundum misericordiam suam magnam regenerauit nos in spem viuam per
resurrectionem Iesu christi ex mortuis.** Whiche accordynge to hys great mercye
by the resurrection of Iesu Christ from amonge the deade, hathe begotten vs
againe into a liuelye hope.* Accordynge to the rate of mannes offence almighty
GOD multiplieth his mercye. And thoughe all synnes compared to almightye God
againste whom they be committed be infinite, yet consideɾynge the frowardenes of

the hart, and wyll of the sinner, some sinnes be more greuous then other be, and require proporcionablye greater abundance of mercy in the forgeuynge of them then other dothe. Therefore saynt Paule thoughe he were a blasphemer and a persecutour of christen people, yet because he did it ignorantlye for lacke of fayth, he found mercye, and was forgeuen his sinnes. i. Timo. i.* But kinge Dauid coulde not pretend ignorance in his takynge of an other mannes wife, neither in causyng Vrye the same wommannes husbande (that neuer offended hym) to be slayne vniustly.* These synnes were greate and horrible, & therefore he cryed and called for great mercye. **Miserere mei deus secundum magnam mi**sericordiam tuam. And for manifolde mercye accordynge to his manifolde sinnes.* Then let vs accordyng to this consider the miserable case that mankinde was in afore we were regenerate by Christe, and we shal perceyue that our regeneration by baptisme takyng [2G1ᵛ] his strength* at Christes passion came of mercy, yea of great mercy, and of manifold mercy. Our firste father Adam at his firste creation had the supernatural gifte of originall iustice,* geuen him for him selfe, and for all his posteritie and issue. This gift of originall iustice in him made a perfect tranquillitie and quietnes in al the powers of his soule, so that his will by this originall iustice shuld obediently do after the pleasure of god, and all the inferiour sensible powers, should likewise obeye the wyll so directed and ruled by originall iustice, the will should haue preuented the sensible powers, so that vnlawefull appetites should neuer haue bene in them. As, for to synne in adulterye with an other mans wyfe, or for to steale or take away an other mans goodes, Men shoulde haue hadde none such vnlawfull lustes. And by the same gyft the wyll should haue commaunded the sensible powers at tyme and place conuenient, to exercise their appetites accordyng to iustice. As to vse naturall generation at tymes conuenient with a mans owne wife, to eate and drinke as reason and iustice would. There shuld haue bene no discention, stryfe, or debate, betwixte man and man, but continual rest & peace. And in thys case, all mankinde should haue bene if Adam hadde kepte his obedience to almighty GOD, but as a punishemente for his disobedience to God, all hys inferiour powers disobeyed their superiours. And this gyfte of originall Iustyce was geuen hym for hym selfe, and for [2G2] all hys posteritie. And therefore lyke as God woulde hym to haue kepte it, so he woulde all hys posteritye to haue dooen, and requireth it of all menne and women that euer came of Adam by carnall propagacion, for wee all ought to haue it. And therefore almightye GOD iustelye requireth of euerye persone hauynge in hym the nature of manne, that gyfte of originall Iustyce whyche hee gaue to the whole nature of manne. And nowe the lacke of that originall Iustyce wyth the debte or duetye to haue it, is called **originall synne,*** whyche maketh all the Issue and children of Adam, the chyldrene of Goddes indignation and anger. And so wee by that bee lefte free from Iustice and bonde to synne and to dampnation. A myserable case that wee be in synne, and be made the chyldrene of anger and of dampnation afore wee haue the vse of Reason, and afore wee can dooe anye synne. And beside that wee be made subiecte to all miserie, vexation, syckenesse, and trouble whyle wee be here. For if Adam hadde kepte hys obedience to GOD, there shoulde nothynge haue disobeyed vs, nother wynde, nor rayne, heate, nor colde to distemper vs. And then to consider howe for thee lacke of the sayde gyfte of originall Iustyce, wee be so prone and headstronge to all actuall Synnes, as to pride, couetuousnesse, anger, enuye, and such other, whyche all make agaynste saluation, and worketh to dampnation euerlastynge.

[2G2ᵛ] All these miseries and wretchednes considered, it is playne that mankynde hath nede of greate mercy and manifolde and abundant mercy to releue hym. And therfore Saynt Peter sayde that **almightye God by his greate mercye regenerate vs, and gote vs again to life,*** agaynst all these mortal & deadly miseries. The regeneration & new begettyng, is by the water of baptisme, wyth ye words & the cooperation and working of the holy spirit without whiche, no man maye see the kyngdome and glorye of God. By this the dutye or debt of originall iustice is washed away, so that GOD will require it no more of vs, but he geueth vs in the stede of the sayde originall Iustice, an other gyfte equiualent, and as good to helpe vs to heauen as it was, whiche is the grace that maketh vs in the fauoure of God againe, and acceptable to hym. This gifte God sendeth into our soules, with fayth at our Baptisme, and will still at all tymes require it of vs lyke as afore he required the saide originall iustice, so that the former debt and dutye of originall Iustice, is chaunged into this latter debte and dutie, to conserue and kepe the grace geuen vs at our baptisme.* And yet the mercy of God is so great toward miserable man, that if it mischaunce vs to lose the same baptismall grace by sinne, he hath prouided vs an other helpe, the seconde table, a seconde remedy, by penaunce to washe awaye our sinnes, and to make vs cleane againe, that we may recouer his grace and fauour. So that like as originall iustice (after it was lost) was recompensed by the grace of [2G3] baptisme, so the grace of baptisme after it is lost by actuall sinne, is recompensed by grace geuen vs with remission of our sinne bi penaunce.* And so loke how necessary baptisme is to wash vs from the deformitie of orignall sinne, and to restore vs to grace, so necessary is penance to clense vs from the deformitie of actual sinne committed after baptisme & to restore vs to grace & fauour of god. And euen like as God requireth originall iustice of al men that be not baptised, as of Turkes, Saracens, Paignims, and Infidels, which all receiued it in Adam, and as for lacke of it, they remayne the children of anger & of damnation, so of al that be christened he requireth the said grace geuen with baptisme, & they that haue lost it by deadly sinne remaine the children of damnation, except thei be healed by penaunce, whiche shal geue them grace equiualent to the baptismal grace, like as I said that baptisme geueth grace equiualent to originall iustice. Al be it the disobedience and rebellion of the powers of our soules, for lacke of the foresayde originall iustice dothe remayne in vs as a payne for Adams synne, and as a nourse and a breader of actuall synne, and because almightye GOD while he dothe scourge vs, doth not forgette to be mercifull, he leaueth the sayde disobedience and rebellion of the powers of our soules, as a matter of vertue, if we will labour, and striue against it to ouercome all vices, that it woulde incline vs to. By this regeneration also all actuall synnes, mortall and veniall be cleane forge[u]en, when anye manne or woman dothe [2G3^v] worthelye receiue it. **He hathe begotten vs againe (sayeth saynt Peter) into a liuelye hope, by the resurrection of Iesus Christe.*** By whiche the Apostle meaneth, that lyke as there be two maner of fayethes, a deade fayth, and a liuelye fayeth, so there be two maners of hope, a deade hope, and a lyuelye hope: Hope is the expectation and lokynge for euerlastyng beatitude and ioye, throughe grace and our merites. Then the hope of hym that will hope and loke to come to heauen, and wyll doe no good thynge to bringe him thither, is a deade hope, and a presumption rather then hope. Thys considered the blessed manne Iob, whose hope on God was so firme and sure that he sayde. **Etiam si occiderit me, in ipso sperabo. Iob .xiii.** Althoughe he wyll kyll mee, yet I wyll hope and truste vppon hym. Yet he sayeth there, **Veruntamen vias meas in conspectu eius arguam & ipse erit saluator meus. Non enim veniet in conspectu eius omnis ypocrita.** I wyll discusse my lyfe

& accuse myne offences afore hys face. And then he wyll be my Sauioure. For there is no Hypocrite, none that wyll shewe oute warde more hope, deuotion, or holinesse, then they haue in deede, that shall come in hys sight.* Therfore lyke as wee haue powred into vs at our regeneration or Baptisme a liuelye fayeth, so wee haue a liuynge or liuelye Hoope, that lyke as Christe rysse from deathe to a lyfe immortall, so shall wee dooe, for the father of heauen so disposed and ordeyned for vs that hys sonne [2G4] shoulde dye for vs, that when hee hadde destroyed deathe, by hys resurrection he myghte geue vs good example and lyuelye Hope, that wee shoulde lykewyse ryse agayne from death to lyfe. For lyke as he dyed for to shewe and geue vs Example not to feare Deathe, so he roose agayne, because wee shoulde surelye hope lykewyse to ryse agayne **Into an inheritance that is vncorruptible, vndefowled, and neuer fadynge, conserued and kepte in store in heauen.** * The inheritaunce of Heauen (as the Apostle saythe here) hathe three excellente properties, whyche wee maye ymagine by three contrarye properties, whiche no purchaser wyll haue in anye Patrimonie, manour, or Lordshippe that he shoulde bye or purchase for him selfe to inhabite or dwell in. Firste if it bee a rotten grounde where all thynge anone moulleth, the tenauntes, and mortises of tymber buyldynge rotteth oute and loseth their pynnes. The walles or rouffes gathereth a mosse or a wylde Fearne, that rotteth out the Lyme and Morter from the stones. And where the Sea or freshe water weareth out the ground: so that all thinges that there is, in shorte space commeth to nought. Hee is not wyse that wyll bestowe hym selfe or hys money on suche a grounde. Second if there bee in the Lande or House any infectyue or pestylente Ayre, disposynge menne to manye infirmityes, and genderynge adders, snakes, or todes, or these stingyng scowts* or gnats, [2G4v] that will not suffre men to slepe, a man shoulde haue litle ioye to dwel in such a manour. Third, if it be suche a grounde where all thinge withereth, and dryeth awaye for lacke of moysture, where hearbes proueth not, and trees groweth not to theyr naturall quantitie, where the leues waxeth yelowe and falleth at Lammas tyde,* where men soweth a busshel and reapeth a peck, and for redde wheate reapeth like rye or otes, that is bestowed on suche a purchase, is but cast awaye. The inheritaunce of this transitorye worlde hath all these noughty properties rehersed, and manye worse, townes and towres, castels and manours decayeth continuallye, and where noble men haue dwelled, nowe dwelleth dawes and crowes, the vawtes and rouffes be so ruinous, that no man dare well come vnder them: Where is Troye? where be the olde Emperies and monarchies of the Assirians, of the Caldeis, Medes, Persies, and of Rome, whose Emperours had vnder them in maner all the worlde, for theyr tyme? Where is the deuotion that noble men and ryche marchauntes hath had to magnifie and encrease Goddes seruice to his honoure? If God had not preserued our mooste gratious Soueraigne Kinge Henry the eyght, whiche by his princelie zele, loue, and deuotion to God, hath erecte this Cathedrall Churche of Bristowe, and manye other suche within this Realme, God knoweth what case diuine seruice should haue bene in. All thinge waxeth olde and decayeth in processe of time, so that corruption [2H1] <and decayeth in processe of time, so that corruption> and deathe is the ende.* Seconde how frequent and many infirmities raigneth: we see dayly infections of pestilence, pockes great and small, & these new burninge agues, and innumerable others, more then the Phisicions haue written of in their bookes. These contaminate and defowleth mens bodies by infections, aches and paines euen to death. And what corruption and infection of maners commeth to the soule, by euill examples, ill wordes, and suche other occasions, it were to long to be spoken of nowe. Thirde, the comon sterilitie and barennes of the grounde, the great scarsitie of all maner of vitall and of fruites of the earth, we feele it so many times to our great paine and discomfort, that it nede not to be declared. But the inheritance that (as saint Peter saith here) is kept for vs in heauen, hath thre properties contrarie to these thre rehersed, ther is no rotting, ruine, corruption or decay, but immortalitie contrarie to all feare of death. There is no feablenes of sicknes, ther is none infection of body by corrupt ayre, nor of soule by temptacion or by euill example, for into that glorious citie and dwelling place can no vncleane thynge enter or come. Thirde, there shall nothing welow or wyther away, but shall euer be kept freshe and floorishing by that well of life almighty God. Ther shall be no lothesomnes or werynes by long vse and continuaunce as there is in all worldly <plea> pleasures, there shall all good men and women shine like the sonne. **Math. xiii.*** Oh good Lorde [2H1ᵛ] what beutie and brightnes shal our soules haue when our bodies shall be as bright as the sunne? There shal be no heauines, no labour, no payne, no sorowe, no feare, no death, but euer still shall continue health of bodye and minde. There shall neuer rise discention or debate betwixt neighbour and neighbour, no miserie, no nede or necessitye, no hunger, no thurst, no cold to hurt the, ne heate to enflame thee, no faintnes for fasting, no sluggardie for much eating, no temptacion of oure gostly enemies. The fleshe shal not resist against the spirite, ther shal be no wil to sinne, nor possibilitie to offend. But our sauiour Christ wil giue vs suche pleasure with the companye and felowship of the glorious angels, as no hart can think, nor any tonge expresse. **This ioyfull inheritaunce is conserued and kept in store in heauen** (saith sainte Peter) **for you that by vertue and power of god be kept by faith vnto saluation, whiche is readye to be shewed in the last time at the generall iudgement.*** Here he saithe that this inheritaunce is kepte in store, not for all men that be regenerate by baptisme, but onely for suche as perseuer and continue in goodnes to the ende by Gods speciall preseruation.* For perseuerance commeth principallye of God, and of our selfe but secundarelye, and is necessary for all them that will be saued. **Nam in cassum bonum agitur si ante terminum vite deseratur** saith saint Gregory. Good workes be done but all in vayne, if they be left and giuen ouer afore the ende of a mans life.* For he that gyueth ouer and ceasseth to do wel afore he haue proued [2H2] the vttermost of it, or be come to the ende, is lyke an Ape, whose condition is, when he tasteth the vtter hull or huske of an nutte, and perceiueth it sowre and bitter, casteth awaye the nutte afore he hathe tasted the swetenes of the curnell.* And our Sauiour Christ saith in the parable of hym that woulde borowe breade of hys neyghbour. **Luke .xi. Si perseuerauerit pulsans &c. If he continue still knockyng, if hys frende wyll not giue it hym because he is his frende, yet for hys importunitie & continuall crauynge he wyll ryse and gyue him as manye as he hath neede of.*** And he telleth vs what is the instrument or meane by which God dothe preserue vs, and make vs to perseuer and continue in grace and good liuynge. It is faithe and suche lyke faithe as I spoke of hope euen nowe, sayinge: that **God hath regenerate vs by hys greate mercye into a lyuelye hope,*** and so the faythe by whyche GOD keepeth vs, is a lyuelye faithe adorned with Charitie and with good woorkes accordinglye. By faithe Christe abydeth in oure hartes, by whose presence wee ouercome all assaultes of oure gostlye enemyes. Fayth maketh vs to vnderstande the fylthe and vncleanenesse of synne, that so wee maye abhorre synne, and flee from it. **Hec est victoria que vincit mundum fides nostra. i. Iohn .v.** Thys is the victorye that ouercommeth the worlde, oure faythe* (saythe Saynte Iohn) it ouercommeth the pleasures of the fleshe, tellynge vs that the fleshe is lyke a fellon giltye and most worthly condempned to [2H2ᵛ] mortalitie and death, and euer still resisting and feighting against yᵉ spirite, wherfore it deserueth rather tortures, paine and punishment, then delicates or plesures. Faith also maketh vs to know that the Apostle saith, **Si secundum carnem vixeritis, moriemini,** if ye liue after the pleasures of the fleshe, ye shall die,* wherefore if ye haue folowed your carnall pleasures eating and drinking, reuealing and rioting in this holye time of Christmas lately past,* which ye should haue spent in deuotion and holynes, ye muste repent your faulte, and do penaunce therefore. Faith maketh vs to con-temne and dispise worldly wealth and riches as the dyuels mowse snatch,* and snare, that maketh a man to catche & hold other<s> mens goodes so long till the diuell hath caught them and hold them in his danger. Saint Paule saith: **i. Tim. vi. Qui volunt diuites fieri, incidunt in tentationes et in laqueum diaboli. &c.** They that wil be made riche falleth into temptacions and snare of the dyuell,* and into many desires vnprofitable and noysom which drowneth men into death and de-struction, therefore he biddeth the sayde Timothe to commaunde the riche men of the worlde not to be to highe in their own conceite, nor to trust in the vncertein-tie of their riches, but in the liuinge God, which giueth vs all thinges abundantly, aswell to bring vs to the eternall fruition of the glorious Godhed, as to liue by in this worlde.* Fayth contempneth & despiseth honours, as a fome on yᵉ running water, as smoke, or as sleepe. The sayd fome swelleth and groweth into a great quanti[2H3]tye, but yet holow it is without any stuffe in it, and for nothing good at length. So honour and riches maketh men to swell and grow vp to great estima-tion, yet comonly holowe they be, and void without vertue or good conditions or good workes. Smoke when it riseth vp out of the chimny, it shooteth vp a great higthe, and then swelleth abrode as it were into a great cloude, but anon it vanisheth away and commeth to nothing. And euen so dothe riche mens honour and goodes, as we see by dayly experience. Sleepe is myngeled with many dreames of riches, landes, possessions, and carnall pleasures, but when they haue slepte out their dreame, and when they wake it is away they fynde nothing in theyr handes, of all that they had pleasure of in their dreames. So dothe al transitorie pleasures, in them is no stedfast securitie. Therefore auertyng and turnynge our mindes from them, we must settle our harts on heauenly ioyes that will neuer faile nor fade. To which he bring vs that made vs almighty God. To whom be glorie honour and praise for euer. Amen.

¶The thirde sermon.

IN quo exultabitis modicum nunc si oportet contristari in variis tentationibus.
In whyche you shall reioyce & be mery, although now alitle you must be sory in
diuers temptacions, persecutions, and troubles.* In whiche (saith Saynt Peter)
referring to that he spoke of immediate[2H3ᵛ]lye afore in tempore nouissimo, In
the last tyme or last day, where he said that the ioyfull inherytance that shall neuer
fade nor decaye, is conserued and kepte in store in heauen, for you that by the
vertue and power of God be kepte by faythe vnto saluation, which is redy to be
shewed in the last time, that is to say, at the general iudgement,* In which you
shall reioyce and be mery (sayth S. Peter here.) And meruel not (good frendes)
and specially you that be lerned, that I made a point betwixt the antecedent and
the relatiue:* For the graue sentences of the Apostle here in this epistle be so long,
and so coherent one part to an other, and so full of good matter, that if when I
haue entred on the declaration of the one part, I shuld nedes procede and declare
the whole sentence, I should be to long in most part of my sermons, & to tedious
for the audience, whiche I woulde be loth to be. And therfore seruing the time I
make an ende of my exhortacions, where I perceyue my selfe somwhat weary, and
the audience also weary of standing, and yet (thanked be God) not very hasty to
drawe away. Therfore so that you will giue eare and applye your mindes to that I
shall say, you shall perceiue the coherence of thys processe that I shall declare vnto
you at thys time, to that I sayde afore in my former sermon vpon this Epistle of
Saint Peter. Here you shal vnderstand that the blessed Apostle S. Peter for mans
consolation & comfort, least we shoulde to sore lament & be sory for the differring
& delay of the ioyes of heauen, for which we be regenerate, [2H4] as he had said
before now, he moueth vs to ioy & gladnes, because a weake person in yᵉ faith
wold say peraduenture, in asmuch as S. Peter saith we be regenerate to be children
of God, & to be inheritours of his vncorruptible heritage:* howe is it that he
letteth vs take so much harme with vexation & trouble and persecutions, which al
faithfull people suffred in the primitiue churche, & no man liueth without such
lyke yet to this houre, nor shal do hereafter? S. Peter answereth that it is not for
any hurt to faithful people, but rather to theyr great profite, euen like as gold when
it is cast into the fire to be tried taketh no hurt by the fyre, but rather muche good,
in asmuche as it is made purer & finer by the fyre.* Eccle. xxvii. Vasa figuli
probat fornax et homines iustos tentatio tribulation[i]s The fornace proueth yᵉ
crockers pots or pitchers & so doth the tentation of trouble proue and trye the
good men or women.* For like as the pitchers that be whole & sound be made
faster, harder and stronger by the fyre, so they that be cracked or broken, flyeth in
peces: euen so good men by trouble be confirmed & made better, where naughty
and vnstedfast parsons be al to broken through impacience, & I rede that not
onely by trouble a man is proued & tried, but also by ouermuch prosperity. For he
yᵗ is in welth many times forgetteth god & him self, & by adulation & flatering, is
brought beyonde him self. Pro. xxvii. Quomodo probatur in conflatorio argen-
tum et in fornace aurum sic probatur homo ore laudantis: euen as siluer is
proued in yᵉ blowing place & gold in yᵉ fornace, so a man is proued by yᵉ mouth of
a prayser whither he be truli vertuous.* [2H4ᵛ] for if he be neuer yᵉ prouder for
mens praising, but rather the better, it appeareth that his vertue is true vertue
whyche groweth and increaseth by laude and praysing, but if a man be prouder for
laude and praysing, his vertue is vaine and counterfaited. Then to the letter of

Saynte Peter: **The triall of your faithe more precious then golde that is tried by the fyre, may be founde worthye to haue praise, laude and glorie and honour, when Iesus Christ shall shewe hymselfe.*** There is no artificer that hath so great pleasure to worke in fine gold neither any man hauing iewels of pure gold tried to the vttermost, as almightie God the highe workeman, maker and owner of all thyng [who] will reioyce to see our faith tried by temptacion and trouble and vexation, for by that proofe it shall appeare to God and man muche more firme, fast and sure, then if there had be none suche assay or experience of it. Consider the blessed Apostles of Christ and other blessed Saintes, what persecution, paines, and punishment they suffered, euen to the death in the defence of theyr faith. And in our time what triall and proofe of mens faythe hath there bene by frowarde heretickes, impugning and reasoning againste the verye essenciall & necessarie articles of our faith, making weake men and women to wauer and doubt in theym, or clearely to renounce them, putting no faith in theym, and so of the sacramentes of the churche. And I say more, that now euery day our faithe is impugned, tried and proued by all kindes and maners of temptation to sinne. If a man see an [2I1] other mans wyfe, that is delectable to the eye, to haue his concupiscence and desyre of her, or thou wyfe in like case of anye man beside thyne owne husbande. After this delectation and pleasure, crepeth into thy soule consente to offende with her, here I saye thy fayth is tempted and proued, for whiche you must remember, that as I sayde before of the wordes of Saynte Iohn: **This is the victorie that ouercommeth the worlde, oure faith,*** for our fayth on God, and on his holy worde, telleth vs that no manne shall desyre to haue an other mans wyfe, neither any woman to haue an other womans husband, nether anye man beside her own husband. Likewise if thou se another mans good lye by the negligentlye, so that thou maist conuey it awaye and no man to se the, yf thou take it awaye, or consent thereto, here thy fayth is tryed and proued noughte, for thy fayth telleth the, that thou shalt take awaye none other mans goodes. Lykewise in thy occupyinge, if for couetousnes to get the penye, thou sell false or noughty ware, or by false weightes or measures deceiue thy neighbours, so doynge, thou shewest thy self to forget thy faith to God, and to his holy worde. **Statera iusta & equa sint pondera. Leuit. xix.†** Let thy balance be iuste, and thy weightes equall.* And. **Ezech. xlv. Statera iusta & ephi iustum,*** and also byddinge the do none otherwyse to an other man, then thou wouldest an other man should do to the.* And contrary wise, when thou art tempted to suche vnlawfull Lecherye as I spoke of, or to false pyckinge, stealynge, or [2I1ᵛ] robbinge, or to deceiue any man or woman by false occupiynge, if thou sticke stedfastlye to thy fayth, doing accordinglye to Gods holye worde, then thy faith by this temptation is proued good, and muche better in the sighte of God, then if it had neuer bene so tried. And by this it is lyke to golde tryed by the fyre, and shall be founde worthy to receiue **praise, glory, and honour,*** when Christ shall shewe him selfe in his glory at the generall iudgemente, then he wil geue to the blessed children of his father, whiche then shall be set vpon his right hand, disseuered from the refuse, deputed to dampnation on the lift hande:* to all them I saye, that hath theyr fayth tried by temptation, and proued sounde and pure as golde, Christ wyll geue **laude and praise,** sayinge to you. **I was an hungred and you gaue me meate: I was a thirste and ye gaue me drinke: I lacked clothes and ye gaue me clothes,*** and so he wyl saye, I had nede of such ware as you occupied, and you serued me faythfully and trustely, and my wife was in thy sight,

† xix.] xvii.

and in thy companye, where thou mighte haue had occasion to tempte her to yll, and yet thou dyddeste not. And to the honest wyfe, wydowe, or mayde, he wyll geue like laude and praise, sayinge: that where they were sore tempted to incontinencie, yet they didde strongely and stedfastly resist and withstande for Goddes sake, and for his holye wordes sake, for suche workes of iustice and honestye the iudge wyll praise vs, as well as for the workes of mercye, whiche be namelye expressed in the Gospell, because we [2I2] shall by them thinke lykewise to be praysed for all lyke good and godlye workes. And when he or she that haue this prayse shall saye: I neuer serued the of anye ware, and I neuer sawe thy wyfe for whom thou geueste me these thankes, he wyll saye: That you didde for the least of my seruauntes, that you didde to me, occupyinge with my seruauntes iustelye withoute gyle or deceite, thou occupied iustelye with me, and abstayninge from my seruauntes wife, doughter, mayde, or seruaunte, thou didde shewe thy selfe honest towarde my wife, doughter, or seruaunt. Nowe what ioye, and pleasure, and comforte it shall be for a Christen man to haue suche laude and praise of the highe iudge at that terrible day when folke shall haue nede of comforte, iudge who can? It passeth my braine. Oure fayth so tryed by trouble or temptation, shall be founde worthye to haue **glorye,** when the iudge shall say to vs: **Venite benedicti patris mei possidete paratum vobis regnum. Math. xxv.** Come you blessed chyldren of my father, and take possession of that glorious kyngedome,* that was prepared for you frome the beginninge of the worlde, in whiche we shal be no more seruauntes, but coparteners and coinheritours with our sauiour Christe, and with all the gloryous Aungelles, and glorious companye of heauen, where we shall haue the grace that GOD gaue vs here, consummate, perfourmed, and in his hygheste perfectyon, whiche wee call glorye, whyche honoure we shall haue (as Saynte Peter sayeth) when [2I2ᵛ] we shalbe set a lofte and in highe estate, whiche shall appeare more euidentlye by the deiection and ouerthrowinge of others, of which .**Esa. xxvi.** saith. **Tollatur impius ne videat gloriam Dei.** Take awaye the wycked synner, that he se not the glorye of GOD:* And also Christ sayth. **Go frome me you wicked persons into fier euerlasting,*** when the dampned men and women, wepinge and waylinge, and cryinge oute, when they se the exaltation of good men, shall say. **Nos autem insensati. &c. Sap. v. we dastardes estemed and counted their liues but folishnes or madnes, lo nowe howe they be counted amonge the children of God.*** All this shall redounde to the honoure of them that shalbe saued. This sayde **prayse, glorie,** and **honoure,** we shall be indued wyth all by Chryste, when he shall shew hym selfe in his glory. Therfore, **though you do not nowe se him, yet ye loue him.*** For (as Saint Augustyne sayth) we maye loue thinges that wee se not, so that we haue knoweledge of them, for no man can loue that, that he hath no knowledge of.* We know Christe by heare saye, by readinge, and hearinge his holy gospelles declaringe his gratious goodnes, for whiche we muste nedes loue hym. And **although you se him not, yet you do beleue vppon him, for whiche beleife you shall be merye,** and haue suche ioye as no tounge can tell, for it shall be the ioye of the glorye of heauen, when you shall receaue for youre rewarde, the ende and perfection of youre faith, whiche is the health of your soules.* Nowe here you knowe by Saint Peters wor[2I3]des, what is the ende of youre faith, it is **the helth of youre soules,** whiche health shall exclude al sicknes, payne, and miserie, for none suche can come into that glorye of heauen, where you shall haue the sayde health and saluation, and neuer afore, for here is no ioye but it is contaminate, defouled, and interrupted, by discomforte, payne, and trouble. And here you muste vnderstand perfect faith, garnished, and adourned with

charitie and good workes accordinge, for none other wyll serue vs to come to that
glorious rewarde of health euerlastinge. **De qua salute exquisierunt atque scrutati
sunt Prophetae.*** Here Saynte Peter styrreth vp oure deuotion, and loue that we
shoulde haue to oure soule health, that we shall obteyne and gette by the triall and
profe of our fayth, as he sayde afore. He taketh an argumente of the olde fathers
holye prophetes, that in olde tyme prophecied of the grace that should fall vpon vs
by the comminge of our Sauiour Christ, which they vehemently desired to see in
their time, but they coulde not:* As Christe saith. **Math. xiii. Multi prophete et
iusti cupierunt videre quae vos videtis et non viderunt, et audire quae auditis et
non audierunt.*** Esay. lxiiii. prayed and wysshed, **Vtinam dirumperes coelos, et
descenderes.** Woulde God thou wouldest break the heauens, and wouldest come
downe to be incarnate.* And the Prophet Dauid **Psal. lxxix. Excita potentiam
tuam, et veni vt saluos facias nos.** Wake, rayse and stirre vppe thy olde power,
whiche thou were wonte to shewe by wonderous myracles shewed in olde tyme, in
[213ᵛ] Noes time, in Moyses time.* This power of thine semeth nowe a slepe, vntill
thou renewe it againe, declaringe the veritie and signification of the saide myracles, by thy blessed comminge into oure nature by thy incarnation. And he
counteth almightie God angrie with him, because he came not, **Quousque irasceris super orationem serui tui:** in whiche he declareth the vehemencye of his
earnest loue and desyre to see Chryst, and sayde: **Shewe thy face, and we shalbe
safe.*** And yet not doubting but that he would come, he sayth in an other Psalme.
Inclinauit coelos & descendit & caligo sub pedibus eius.* Where for the certen-
tie and surenes of his Prophecie, he vseth the pretertence for the future tense,
speaking of the time to come, as thoughe it were past in dede, because he was as
sure of it, as though it had be past, as we vse to saye in common speach, of one that
is past remedye, or sure to dye, he is but a deade man. **He hath inclined the
heauens, and came downe and trode darkenes, that is to say, sinne, downe
vnder his feete.*** **Damasc. li. iii. Cap. i. Hoc est inhumiliabilem eius altitudinem
in humilitate humiliauit, & descendit ad seruos suos.** The highnes of his Godhead, whiche can not be made lowe by nature, he broughte a lowe by his humilitie
and gentlenes, whiche is the newest, the straungest, and most wonderous worke
that euer was wroughte.* Of whiche sayth **Ieremie. Cap. xxxi. Creauit Dominus
nouum super terram, foemina circundabit virum.** Oure Lorde hath wrought a
newe thinge, or a straunge thinge vpon the earth, a woman shall enuyron [214] or
compasse aboute a man,* that is to saye, the blessed Vyrgyn Marye, for she
compassed about and closed within her vyrgynall bellye, oure Sauyoure Christe, a
perfecte man in connyng, knoweledge, and vertue, euen frome the fyrst instante of
his incarnation. And Daniel that holye Prophete, **Vir desideriorum,** a man ful of
desires,* because he was so desirous to knowe of the retourne of his people of
Israell, from the captiuitie of the Medes and Persies, and of the comminge of
Messias, and what shoulde betide his people, at the later ende he was asserteyned
by an aungell sent from GOD, not onelye of the retourne of the people from
captiuitie, but also of the mistery of Christes incarnation, and of his passion, and
at the last, of the final desolation and abhominable destruction of the newe citie of
Ierusalem, by the Emperours, Vespasian, and his sonne Titus, and at the last by
Elius Hadrianus, whiche of the ruynes of the olde citie, destroyed by Titus, made a
towne there, and called it **Elia,** after his owne name.* Of these blessed prophetes
that laboured and searched so diligently for to knowe of the time of grace, that the
spirite of Christe, proceeding from the sonne, and from the father (and therefore
he is called the spyryte of Chryste, as he is called the spirite of the father) that

inspyred the sayde holye Prophetes, and spoke in theym, woulde tell them when it shoulde be, within howe manye yeares after them, **& in quale tempus**, into what manner of [2I4ᵛ] time it should be differred,* as whether tyll time of peace, or of warre. Iacob the blessed patriarch said it should come, when there should be no kinges and rulers as of the linage of the Iewes,* & so it proued, for our sauiour Christ came,† when Herode an alien and straunger was made kinge, by the aucthoritie of Augustus, then Emperoure of Rome. And Esay sayde of that time. **Et conflabunt gladios suos in vomeres et lanceas suas in falces. ca. ij.** It should be in time of peace, when all the world liued in rest and peace, and had no warre, but lyued quietlye vnder the rule of the Romaines, so that all men mighte blowe their swordes into plowe yrons, and their speare heades and moris pikes, into sithes, hokes, and sickles to cut their hay or corne.* Then Christ should come (saith S. Peter) & suffer paines and passions, **prenuncians eas quae in Christo sunt passiones,*** speakinge in the plurell number, for he suffred in soule, and in his body, and also in his limmes or members, as he doth now daylie in his elect people, and true seruauntes, and should haue for the same **futuras glorias**, two speciall glories he had after his passion, that is to say, the glory of his resurrection, & the glory of his assention.* All they (sayth S. Peter) had knowledge by reuelation, that they labored not for them selfe but for vs, not to haue them perfourmed in their time, nor vpon them selues, but vpon vs, according as they be nowe taught you by the ministers of the word of God, yᵗ haue preached to you continually, sith the holy gooste was sente from heauen vpon the Apostles in sensible [2K1] signes as fierye tongues wyth diuersitie of languages geuen by the holy Goste, **On whom the blessed Angels in heauen desire to beholde and loke on:*** Not that they lacke that glorious sighte at anye tyme, but Saint Peter vseth this maner of speakynge, because the ioyfull contemplation and sight of the Godheade, euer beinge presente with them, dothe saciate them, and perfectly content them, and yet so that they be neuer wearye of it, but euer desire to continue in that contemplation. For Christe sayth. **Math. xviii. Angeli eorum in celis semper vident faciem patris mei qui in coelis est.*** The angels see, and desire to see, desiereth to see, and seeth: For lest there sho[u]lde be anye doubt in their desire, they be saciate, and content, and assured whyle they desireth. And leste there should bee anye lothinge, or fulsomenes, or wearines in their sacietie or fulnes, while they be full, yet they desire, Therefore they desireth to see, and that without laboure or payne, for contentation foloweth their desire, and they be content without lothsomenesse, for their fulnesse is inflamed by their desire. And euen so wee shal be when we shal come to that well of life, there shal be printed in vs a delectable thirste or desire, and fulnesse of contentation withall, but there shall be in the thirste no necessitie, nother in the fulnes anye lothesomenesse, for while that we be desierous to see that glory of GOD, we shall be full of that sight, and whyle we be full, yet we shall desire to se it styll, after such a maner as we can not now perfectly perceiue, tyll we come to that [2K1ᵛ] state in which we shalbe like the angels, and then wee shall knowe it by experience, as they dooe, through the helpe of our sauiour Iesus Christe, who with the father and the holy Goste, liueth and raigneth for euer. Amen.

† came] come

The fourth treatise or
Sermon.

PRopter quod succincti lumbos mentis *vestre*. &c. Wherfore tucke vp the Loynes of youre minde, and be sober, and perfect, and trust on the grace that is offered you by the reuelation of Iesu Christe, as obedient children, not made like to the former desires of your ignoraunce, but like that holye one that called you, that so you maye be holie in all conuersation, because it is written. You shall be holye, for I am holie.* Now in contemplation of† all that the Prophetes laboured and desiered to heare and to see, they were instructed by the holye Gost, that they should be perfourmed, not for their tymes, but on vs in our times, that haue hearde the preachers of the Gospell euer sith the sensible commynge of the holye Gooste in fierye tongues from heauen. Therfore the blessed apostle Saint Peter exhorteth vs so to dispose our selues, that we maye be able and apte to receiue [2K2] this grace so that by our owne faulte wee be not frustrate and disapointed of it. And to that purpose is first required cleannes of life, whiche the apostle meaneth, biddyng vs, **Tucke vp the loines of your minde, and be sober and perfect.** He vseth a maner of speakinge often vsed in the scriptures, whiche speakyng of the soule of man applieth to it bodelye membres or limmes, and the operations and workes of the bodye. As the eyes of the soule. **Ad te leuaui oculos meos.*** and **Leuaui oculos meos in montes.** I haue lifte vp mine eies to the mountaines,* not the bodely eyes which some men lacke, but the sight of the minde, whiche serueth as well by nighte as by daie. And the Apostle. **Ephe. i. Det vobis illuminatos oculos cordis vestri, vt sciatis que sit spes vocationis eius** He praieth that God woulde geue them the eyes of their harte, (that is to say, of their minde) lightened to know what they might trust for, by his callynge.* And **ii. Cor. ii.*** He calleth the preachinge of the Gospel a smell or sauoure, because that like as the thing that is not sene is perceiued by the sauour, so the inuisible GOD is smelled out and perceiued amonge the people by the preachers. And then [(]as <(>you know) they that be vsed to stinking sauours can not liue in Bucklersbury, or in the poticaries shoppe.* So to some the true preaching is a smel or sauour that infecteth and killeth theim, as to them that maligneth, grudgeth and abhorreth true doctrine, which be worse, and more sicke for the worde, where to other it is a sauour of lyfe, and bringeth them to lyfe euerlastynge. [2K2ᵛ] And the scripture speaketh as thoughe the soule hadde a mouthe, and lymmes of tastynge, it appereth by the prophet. **Gustate & videte quoniam suauis est dominus.** Taste and see that our Lorde is swete.* And Esay speaketh as though the soul hadde wombe or bealy to conceiue child. **Esa. xxvi A faciae tua domine concepimus & quasi parturiuimus & peperimus spiritum salutis.*** He speaketh to almighty God as one longing to se the glorious and moste delectable face of God, which is so delectable that the aungels of heauen desiereth to beholde it, and hathe inestimable pleasure in the contemplacion of it, as I said a little rather, and as saint Peter saieth here in this Chapter.* By the beauty of thy face (saieth the Prophete) we haue conceiued, and haue in maner traueilled, And also be deliuered, and haue brought foorthe the spirite of health, that is to saye: **Securam fiduciam,** sure truste to come to the thinge that wee desire to see.* He vseth this metaphore and

† of] that

216

similitude of conceiuinge and labouring of childe, because that like as the mother hathe paine in traueilynge, and ioye when the childe is borne, so that the former paine is anone forgotten for ioy of the childe. **Ioh. xvi.*** so the desire to see the face of God, to see the Godhead, hath now payne annexed, for the dilation & differringe of it, we can not haue it when we will, and as the wise man saieth, **pro. xiii. Spes que differtur affligit animam.** The hope that is deferred, prolonged, and put of, vexeth the minde.* But yet the sure trust to come to that glorious sight, dothe somewhat comfort [2K3] vs for the time, but when we haue perfectly obteyned and gotten it, then the paine will be clerely past, and cleane forgotten. Saint Paule vseth like maner of speakinge to the **Gala. iiii.** callinge them his little children, because they were so childishely turned by pseudapostles and false Preachers, from the sinceritie of the true doctrine of the Gospell that he had instructed theim in. My babes (saieth he) of whiche I trauaile nowe againe vntyll Christe be newe fourmed in you.* I traueled once to bringe you from Infidelitie to the true faith of Christ, as earnestly in minde as the mother dothe bodelye for her childe. And now that you be thus inuegled, I muste labour and trauaile for you againe to bringe you to the right trade againe. Euen such maner of speache vseth Sainte Peter in these wordes rehearsed, bidding vs. Tucke vp the loynes of your mindes* The bodely loines be the breaders of carnal lust, and therefore Christe biddeth: **Sint lumbi vestri precincti.** That your loynes be girde vp with the girdle of chastitie,* that they flie not abrode to vnlawfull lustes of the fleshe, and because the exteriour actes of the bodie riseth of the inward concupiscence of the minde, Sainte Peter woulde haue the loynes of our minde girde vp, that they vage not rouing abroade by the lewde thoughts and vncleane meditations. The loynes of the minde be the witte and will, when the witte is gird in and kept close, and exercised in honest studie, and the wil desiereth nothing but that is conformable to honestie, then the loins of your minde [2K3ᵛ] be tucked vp as Saint Peter would haue them and so you shall be cleane of body from vnlawfull actes of the fleshe. And this is a great parte of cleannes of life. Sobernes perteineth to cleannes of life, and is also necessarye to that we shall be able to hope and looke for that perfecte grace and glory that is offered vs against the reuelation and glorious commynge of our sauiour Iesu Christe at the generall iudgement, at which tyme hee shall appeare in his glorious maiestye to confounde theim that contemned hym in hys infirmitie. Sobernes is the vertue by whiche a manne measureth him selfe againste the intisementes and occasions of surfete, and against the floude or streames of dronkennesse. This vertue is so necessarye for man, that\<h\> without it all goeth to hauocke, for it is the defence and sauegarde of the minde, and of the limmes of the bodye. It defendeth honestye and chastitie as a stronge warde or castell, so that when sobernes is broken and gone, chastitie is sone defowled. **Loth,** when he was dronken defowled his owne daughters whiche he woulde neuer haue done, if he had kepte sobernes.* Sobernesse is conseruer of frendship & amitie & of peace, where dronkennes breaketh them. **Spes iubet esse ratas Ad prelia trudit inertem.†** **Horac.*** It maketh all thinge sure yᵗ a man wold haue. If the dronken man wold kil the deuil, surely he wil thinke he can do it while his cups be in.* He will fight though he lack both weapon and harneis, and wyll breake a loueday* [2K4] and fall to variaunce wyth his best frende, yea, thoughe it be his owne brother. Where contrary sobernes excheweth suche rashenes and auoydeth perils. Sobernes requiteth one good turne for an other,*† and abhorreth pride and arrogancy, and

† intertem] inermem; other] order

kepeth his housholde in measure with honestie, and kepeth fidelitie trustely with euery man, that putteth trust in hym. Where dronkenes by pride of harte bringeth furthe vnkindenesse, as pride dothe euer, for a proud manne thinketh all thinges done of dutye that a man doth for hym, & so neuer regardeth to do good for good againe. The sober man kepeth his housholde in measure where the dronkarde is euer in extremities. Finally, Sobernes may be called the mother of all vertues, and dronkennesse mother of all vices.* Therfore without lothsome excesse yᵉ belly wold be filled: for what profite doth it to take to much of that that thou shalt lose by and by? Nature is content with a very litt[l]e.* Therfore if thou charge it ouer much, either thou shalt by that thou hast taken haue little pleasure, or els greate hurte. Therfore Saint Peter saieth we must be sober, and generally we muste be perfect in all workes of vertue, and so shall boldely hope to see the glorye of Christe.* Where contrary he that no good doth, and liueth viciously, may be sore afrayed of that glorious commyng, lest he come to shortly, and to soone for hym. **Quasi filij obedientie non configurati prioribus ignorantiae vestre desiderijs.** As children of obedience, or obedient children vnto the [2K4ᵛ] monicion and holesome lessons of your father, not forgettynge that I haue taught you.* Shew not your selues like vnto your olde blindenes in carnall vyces, and in all other iniquitie, to which you were geuen afore you were called out of the darkenes of ignoraunce vnto the light of faythe, by your spirituall fathers the Preachers of the worde of GOD among you, but conforme your selues to that holye one that called you, whiche was chieflye our sauiour Christe, by whose word published amonge theim by the Preachers, and speciallye by Sainte Peter that hadde laboured amonge them, they were reduced and broughte to the light of knowledge, that so (sayeth Saint Peter) you may be holy, firme, and fast in goodnesse agaynst vyce, againste trouble and vexation, for that is the signification of this woorde, **Sanctus,** firme, faste, and sure in goodnes, that is holye in all your conuersation and dealyng, lyke as he that called you is holie.* To confirme that Saint Peter alledgeth the saiynge of almighty GOD in the .xix. Chapter of **Leuiticus,** commaundynge the people of Israell, and by them all vs faythfull and true Israelites christian people. **Sancti estote, quoniam ego sanctus sum dominus deus vester.** Be you holye for I your Lorde GOD am holye.* And our Sauiour Christe in the Gospell hath a like saiynge. **Mat. v. Estote & vos perfecti sicut & pater vester celestis perfectus est.** Be you perfect as your heauenly father is perfecte.* Where this worde (**sicut**) As, importeth not equalitie, but a certaine imitation or folowinge, [2L1] as Saint Paule biddeth: **Estote imitatores dei,** folowe God* as nigh as mannes fragilitie wil permitte or suffer, though no creature can attayn to be equall with God in holiness or perfection. And here good neighbours I should by these wordes of S. Peter exhorte you to be fast, sure, and stedfast in the good opinions that you haue bene reduced vnto by catholike preachers, where afore by pseudapostles and leude preachers, you were seduced and broughte into sinistre opinions, in whiche you walked darkely and blyndely, contempninge the sacramentes and ceremonies of Christes churche, and so vsinge a leude libertye, you fell to all desires of darke ignoraunce, liuing carnally, nother regardinge prayers, fasting, abstinence, nor chastitie For surely this is the effect of suche lewde libertie, as some men would vendicate and claime by the Gospell, where there is nothinge more contrary to the Gospell.* **Et si patrem inuocatis eum quae sine personarum acceptione iudicat. &c.** In these wordes the Apostle perswadeth and reasoneth, that we oughte to be of cleane lyfe, sobre and perfecte, that we maye obediently, and reuerently hope and loke for glorye at the reuelation and comminge of Christ in his glory, sayinge: **If you call him your father that iudgeth without parcialitie according to euery persons worke, see that you be conuersaunt in feare (and in your conuersation haue feare) for the time that you be here abidinge in this worlde.** * In which wordes he willeth vs to considre almightie God as oure father, and also as our iudge. In that he is oure [2L1ᵛ] iudge, we owe vnto him feare, as to oure Lorde and maister, that maye do with vs what shall please him, and in that he is our father, we owe vnto him loue, as to oure maker and regeneratour. Accordinge to the saying of **Malachi. i. Si pater ego sum vbi est honor meus, si dominus ego sum vbi est timor meus.** If I be youre father as you call me, **Pater noster qui es in coelis,** where is the honour that you owe to me? If I be youre lorde, where is the feare that you owe to me.* Saynte Peter ioyneth them both together, meaninge that we owe vnto almightie God loue, as to our father, and feare, as to our lorde and iudge, and specially because he iudgeth withoute parcialitie or affection to any partie, hauinge respecte to a mannes workes, and not to the personne.* But yet here riseth a doubte vppon Saynte Peters wordes, that God iudgeth without parcialitie, it semeth contrary, by the wordes of Malachye the Prophet aforesaid, where the worde of God sayd by that Prophet in the fyrst Chapter, **Nonne frater erat Esau Iacob, dicit dominus & dilexi Iacob, Esau autem odio habui.** They had done nother good nor yll, as S. Paule sayth **.Roman. ix.** therefore not for any thinge of their parte God sayde, **I loued Iacob, and I hated Esau,** * and then in verye dede, for that that God loued Iacob, Iacob proued a good man, and for that he hated Esau, Esau proued nought, and all his posteritie for the mooste part. And Iacob for his goodnes, and for good workes folowinge of the same was saued, where Esau, or they of hys [2L2] issue, for theyr noughtie liuinge, were reproued and dampned:* therefore, of this it semeth that God was partiall in his election, because there was no cause in the parties wherfore one shuld be electe rather then the other, and also in the sequele that came thereof, dampninge Esau or them that were noughty and yll of his issue, and sauinge Iacob for his goodnes and vertue whiche God gaue hym. Therefore (by this obiection) it semeth not true that Saint Peter sayth, that God oure father iudgeth without parcialitie, in as muche as it semeth he was partiall in these two personnes Iacob and Esau, as well in the predestination and election of them afore they were borne, as in the course of theyr lyues, and in the maners of theyr lyuinges, and fynallye, in the saluation of the one, and reprobation or dampnation of the other. For aunswere to this obiection you muste vnderstand, that when there be anye two personnes, hauinge on theyr owne parte, or in them selues equally, the reason or cause why they shoulde be wylled, loued, or accepted, then the will of him that accepteth, or loueth the one rather then the other, offendeth by acception of personnes, or by partialitie. As if we compare any two thinges to the wyll of a creature, as to my will, or to thy will, if thou loue or fauo[u]re one more then the other, there is some iust cause, or (at yᵉ lest wise) some apparaunt cause, why thou fauoreste the one more then the other, for the goodnes in the thinge that is loued [2L2ᵛ] or els the apparaunte goodnes in it, is the cause why we do loue it. But speakinge of the will of God, there is nothinge, no goodnes in the creature, that causeth or maketh the will of God to loue it. For the thinge that is temporall & transitory, causeth not the thinge that is eternall, as is the election, predestination, and fauour or loue in God: but rather contrarywise the wil of God is cause of all goodnes in man. And therefore God can not be partiall, neither accepter of persons, because in man, or any other creature, ther is no goodnes of our owne that shuld make god, or cause God to loue vs, but that he loueth vs as he loued Iacob, before he had done other

good or yll, it commeth of Goddes mere grace and liberalitie, and not of Iacobs
deseruinge nor of ours, and in this doinge, he doth no wronge to the other partie
that is reproued, as Esau was, for generallye, iniustice or wronge hath no place,
where a thinge is geuen of mere grace, if it be geuen to the one and not to the
other, for grace or fauour may be geuen to one and not to an other without any
iniustice or wronge to the other partie. As appeareth playnely .Math. xx. of them
that were hyred to worke in the vineyarde, of whiche some came to work **primo
mane,** earlye in the morning,* and some at fiue of the clocke at night, and yet they
had equall wages, they that came laste, as much as they that came fyrst. And when
some that had laboured all day grudged therat, and complayned to the maister and
owner of the vineyarde, because they had laboured all day and [2L3] borne the
burthen and the heate of the day, and had no more wages then they that had
laboured but one houre, they were aunswered one for all. **Amice non facio tibi
iniuriam, tolle quod tuum est et vade.*** He hadde no wronge, that the other that
came laste, was made as farre forth as he that came fyrste, because it stode in the
mere libertie and grace of the mayster, to bestowe his monye as it pleased him, as
he sayde: **An non licet mihi quod volo facere?** May not I do with mine owne as it
pleaseth me.* As S. Paule saith. **Rom. ix. An non habet potestatem figulus. &c.**
Hathe not the pitcher maker of cley, power to make of one peece of cley, one
vessel to do honest seruice at the boorde, and an others to do vyle offices?* so in
oure purpose, in as muche as it stode in Goddes mere libertie, to minde or wyll to
Iacob and to Esau as it pleased him, Esau had no wronge by that that Iacob was
electe, neither almightie God was partiall in sauinge the one, and not sauinge the
other, for there was no cause geuen of thone more then of thother. And euen so
sayth S. Peter, that almighty God our father iudgeth without acception of persons,
or partialitie, crowning his owne workes in vs, rewardinge vs for the workes that he
hath made vs to do indifferentlye, to poore and to riche, to Iewes and Gentils,
otherwise then the carnall father doth, whiche vseth his owne chylde more partially, and more fauourably then his bondmen or prentises. But almightie God our
father taketh to hearte, and for his children, the bondmen or drudges of this [2L3ᵛ]
worlde, yea and also them that were his enemies afore, so that they wyll yelde and
be obedient, and they that afore were his chyldren, maye for theyr misliuinge be
excluded frome their inheritaunce in heauen, for he will iudge vs according to
oure workes, as Saint Peter saith here, **secundum vniuscuiusque opus.*** And this
is playnelie against them that regarde not workes, trusting so much to theyr faith,
that lyttle they care what worke they do. Here Sainte Peter sayth that we shall be
iudged after oure workes: And Christe in the Gospell declareth the same, **Esuriui,
& dedistis mihi manducare. &c.** I was hungry and ye gaue me meate, I was
thyrstye, and ye gaue me drinke. &c.* Therefore Saynt Peter biddeth vs **vse a
certaine feare in all oure conuersation while we be here abidinge.*** And a lytle
afore Sainte Peter willed vs to be holye in all oure conuersation and dealinge,
byinge and sellinge, eatinge and drinkinge, workinge and restynge, speakinge and
talkinge,* all these be workes and dedes after whiche we shall be iudged, therefore
in them we haue nede to vse feare of God, and surely, all the sinnefull liuinge of
people cometh for lacke of feare. Why doth one neighboure deceiue an other
nowe in this fayre time, by false weightes or measures, by false lyghtes, by false
oothes? because they feare not God that hath forbid vs so to do. Likwise of adultry,
why doth a wedded man take an other mans wife, or a wife another womans
husband? It is for lack of fear of God, that forbiddeth vs to desire in minde to [2L4]
haue an other mans wife. Likewise generally to all men and women he sayeth:

Non mechaberis, Thou shalt do no lechery.* Men speake franckly and frely when they sclaunder their neighbour, as though there were no hurte in so doinge, and all for lacke of feare, men fear not God that biddeth vs by the prophete, **Refraine thy tonge from ill, and thy lippes that they speake no gile. Psal. xxxiii*** And feare is so necessary, that without feare no man can be iustified, or made good in the syghte of GOD **.Eccles. i.*** and if he can not be iustified, then he can not be saued. It foloweth in the text **Scientes quod non corruptibilibus auro vel argento redempti estis de vana vestra conuersatione paterne traditionis sed precioso sanguine quasi agni incontaminati & immaculati Christi.*** Here Saint Peter reasoneth or swadeth, that we oughte to be of cleane life, and in all oure conuersation to liue in feare, while we be dwelling as tenauntes at wil here in this worlde. This he perswadeth by consideration of the price that was paid for oure redemption or raunsom, out of the deuils daunger, & out of our former conuersation, & noughtye liuing, which price was neither gold nor siluer, nor any such corruptible substaunce as is vsed amonge men, to redeme mens offences, or to make amends for faultes or harmes done amonge men, but you were bought & deliuered from your noughty liuing & from your vaine and folish conuersation by the precious blud of Christ, offred for vs on yᵉ crosse, like a moste pure and cleane lambe, without spot or blemishe, and neither groned nor grudged,* so [2L4ᵛ] sufferinge no more then the lambe doth, when he is ledde to the slaughter house. We must no more nowe thinke oure selues vile or little worth, for once we pleased oure Lorde God so well, that he chose rather to die for vs, then he would lose vs, it can be no smal thinge of valure that God was content to pay his owne bloude for. By his precious bloud you were deliuered from your vaine and folysh conuersation, that you learned by your fathers traditions, by your fathers teachinge. They that S. Peter writte to, some were of the Iewes, and some were of the Gentiles, as I declared in the beginninge of this Epistle.* They that were of the Iewes, had learned of their fathers to leaue the true vnderstandinge of the lawes of God and to folowe certaine precepts and rules of theyr traditions and teachinge, as to let theyr owne parentes die for hunger, & to bestow theyr goodes in offeringe at the Church. **Mat. xv.*** not that Christe forbiddeth to helpe the ministers of the Churche, but that when thou mayste helpe both, thou shouldest so do, but yf thou be not able to do both, se that thou fayle not to do thy dutye to thy parentes, cherysshinge and helpinge them, for this is thy bounden duetie. And also the curious and prescise obseruaunce of the Iewes ceremonies, may be vnderstand by these fathers traditions, whiche were but vayne, and lytle good did to the soule, for they gaue no grace to the soule, but specially after the publyshing of Christes Gospell, they seassed and did no good, but muche hurte to the soule. They that were of [2M1] the Gentilles were brought vp as their fathers were in Idolatrye, and taught to worshippe Idolles, false Goddes, whiche in dede be thinges of naught, and verye nothinge, as sainte Paule saieth. **i. Cor. viij. & .x.*** Nowe to our purpose, they were taught by their fathers and bringers vp, to worshippe that for a god, and to geue it diuine honour that was no God, were brought vp in a folishe trade, and in vayne conuersation, by their fathers lore, tradicions, and teachynge: from such vayne conuersation, wee were redemed, not by money, but by the precious blud of the lambe our Sauiour Christe, most immaculate, and vndefowled from all sinne, original & actuall. **He was knowen (sayeth saint Peter) and appointed of God afore the worlde was made, that he sholde redeme vs, And he was declared and knowen plainly now in the latter dayes,** And towarde the ende of the worlde for our sakes,* and to saue vs, that by hys instruction published and spredde abrode among vs by the preachers of hys Gospell be made faithfull beleuers on almightye God, whiche raised oure saide sauiour Christe from death to life againe, and gaue him glorie at his resurrection, and also at his glorious ascention, because you shoulde truste to <to> haue like glorye by him. And al this was not for anye indigence or neade that he hadde to be so exalted, but for oure sake, that so (sayeth Sainte Peter) your fayeth myght be on God, and your whole hope and truste in GOD that you maye receiue like glorye of GOD.* Because saint Peter sayeth that the misterye of Christes [2M1ᵛ] incarnation, & of his passion, by whiche we shold be redemed was knowen afore, and appointed afore the worlde was made.* You must vnderstand that this that saint Peter saieth of the eternall predestinacion and foreknowledge of the second person in Trinitie, the sonne of God to be incarnate, was not onely for the redemption of man, from the preuarication and offence of Adam, but althoughe Adam hadde neuer offended, yet notwithstandinge the sonne of GOD woulde haue be incarnate, takynge the nature of man vppon him to beautifye in hym selfe the whole man, aswell the outwarde man, as the inwarde man, that so mankinde, Siue ingrederetur siue egrederetur pascua inueneret. Whether he should come in by his wit, or did go furth by exteriour senses he shoulde euerye waye finde pasture,* feadynge and refresshynge pasture within by knowledge and contemplation of the Godheade to the comforte of the reason, pasture outwarde, in the flesshe and bodye of our Sauioure, to the comforte of the exteriour senses. For if Adam hadde not sinned, but hadde stande stedfast in the state of innocen-cye, he shoulde at the laste haue bene translated from Paradyse into the glorye of Heauen, and so shoulde all his posteritie wythout anye deathe, by the onely wyll or desyre of mynde, where his glorye shoulde haue bene verye leane and bare, yf no exterioure sense, shoulde haue hys owne delectation in the thing that he is exercised in, as the syghte in seinge [2M2] or the touchyng in felyng, the eare is in hearing.* Therefore to satisfye bothe the reason and the sensible powers, it was necessarye that GOD shoulde haue a bodye and shoulde be made man, that he myghte be perceyued by the senses, as wel as by the wyt. And to such beatitude & ioye wee were appoynted and chosen in Christe afore the makinge of the worlde, as the Apostle sayth. Ephe. i. Benedixit nos . . . in Christo Iesu sicut elegit nos in ipso ante mundi constitutionem. God the father hath blessed vs in Christe, as his lymmes or membres, like as he hath chosen vs in him afore the makyng of the worlde,* so that the chosynge of Christe GOD and man in one persone was presupposed, and went afore the chosing of vs hys membres to be incorporate, vnite, and ioyned to him by faith & grace as one body with hym. Like as the builder first intendeth a house of thys fashion or that fashion, & then intendeth to prouide tymber, lyme, and stone, and workemenne to make his house. Therefore sayeth the Apostle that GOD chose vs in Christe.* Firste chosynge Christe to glorye inestimable, and then consequentlye and secundarily, hee chose vs in him, as hys membres to be glorified in hym, and with him, and by hym. And therfore saieth our Sauiour vnto hys Father, speakynge of his disciples. Dilexisti eos sicut & me dilexisti. Ioh. xvii. Thou haste loued them as thou haste loued me.* Aug. Because that he loued vs in hym, lyke as he chose vs in him afore the making of the world, for he yᵗ loued his onely [2M2ᵛ] begotten sonne, surelye muste neades with all loue hys membres, whiche he hathe adopte and chosen to be hys chyldren wyth him.* And thus our Gostlye enemie the Deuyll knewe full well, for afore his fall he sawe in the Godheade that mankinde shoulde be exalted so hyghe, as to be knitte in one persone to almyghtye GOD, and yᵗ all hys faithfull people should in hym & by him be exalted aboue the nature of aungels, when he sawe it, he disdayned and enuied thereat. And furthwyth at the beginnyng of mankynde pursued and tempted our firste parentes to brynge them to synne, by that trustyng to disappoint hym, and to stoppe the glorye that GOD intended toward mankynde, and to brynge mankynde so farre out of fauour wyth GOD, that it shoulde neuer be ioyned in one persone wyth God, and consequently to stoppe & let vs al from the ioyes of heauen, for whiche almightye God hadde chosen vs in Christe afore the world was made, so that our Sauiour Christe myght saye with the prophete Ionas, which by the peryll of shipwracke that he was in, signified and figured the passion of Christe, lyke as by his beynge in the whales bealy three dayes and three nightes, was figured the sepulture of Christe three daies and three nightes, in the bealye of the earth.* When the storme rysse so perillously, that the seas were euer styll readye to swallowe vp the shippe that he was in: he saide vnto the shipmenne. **Tollite me, & mittite in mare, & cessabit mare a vobis. Scio enim ego quoniam propter me tempestas hec [2M3] grandis est super vos. Ionae .i.** Take me (sayth this blessed prophet) and cast me into the sea, and the sea will ceasse his rage, for I knowe that thys great tempest and storme lieth so sore on you for my sake.* As though our sauiour Christe sayde. Take me and caste me into the stormes of temptation and trouble, and the stormes shal ceasse, & shall not so sore trouble you. **In eo enim in quo passus est ipse & tentatus, potens est & eis qui tentantur auxiliari. Heb. ii.** In that that he suffred and was tempted, he is able to helpe them that be tempted or troubled.* For he wyl not suffer vs to be tempted aboue our power, but will get vs aduauntage to resist temptation and a way to scape from it, that we shall be able to abide it, and not to be ouerthrowen by it. **i. Cor. x.*** Nowe further to the saiyng of **Ionas.** For I know that this storme is raysed for me. So might our sauiour Christ say that the storme of temptation, that the deuill by Gods permission, raysed against our first parents and ceasseth not with the same stormes to assault all his posterytie, was raysed for Christes sake, because ye deuil knew that the godhed & manhode of Christ shold be ioyned in one person, & so shold be exalted farre aboue hym, the enuy that he had at this, made him to bende his ordinance, & to set furth all his engins of temptation against mankind to stop him from that exaltation & honor. So that the deuil first saw the exaltation of mankinde in Christe to be one person with the sonne of God, & enuiyng therat, procured the impediment (asmuch as in him laie) by the sinne of Adam. And this is [2M3^v] a signe that euen so it was in Gods foreknowledge and election, that firste he determined the sonne to be incarnate, and mankinde to come to that glorye, to be one person wyth God, and secundarilye, knowyng that Adam would fall, & would bringe all hys posteritie into daunger of damnation: the high counsaile of the Godhead appoynted our saide Sauiour Christe to be the meane to saue mankinde again by his blessed passion, that he should suffer in his passible and mortall body, which he toke vppon him for that purpose. For in very dede if Adam had not offended, Christ shold not haue bene incarnate in a mortal or passible body, nor should haue come as a redemer, when there was nothing to be redemed, but he should haue come as a glorifier to make mankynde partiners & partakers of hys glory, after the highest maner that myght be, in one persone with almighty God in Christ, & we his membres of his bodie to haue our parte of the same glory with him. But in asmuch as man had by disobedience offended almightye God, & had nede of a redemer he **shewed him self for our sakes** (as .s. Peter saith here) **now at the last cast of the world,** in a mortal bodye made of a woman, made vnder the law, that he might deliuer them that were subiect to the law, **that so by Christ our faith and our hope should be in god.*** that by him we may be bolde to trust for like grace of hym, as I saied before. It foloweth in the text. **Animas vestras castificantes in obedientia charitatis in fraternitatis amore. &c.** Chastifiyng your soules in the obedience of charitie.* Pull downe your soules & kepe them under obedi[2M4]ence, yea & in charitable obedience. For obedience coact & by compulsion, as theues in the gaole obey their keper, lest he wil punish them or cast them in sorer prison, is not the thing that god wil reward, except it be charitable, that is principally for the plesure of god, that wold the inferiours shold obey their rulers or betters, & consequently for the loue to ye party that thou oughtest to be obedient vnto. And you must kepe brotherly loue louynge one an other like as brothers, so that if one at any time hurt another, yet remember that we be all brothers in Christ redemed with one bloud & by ye remembraunce we must let the displeasure passe, forgetting it, & returning to fraternal loue again And this must come of a simple and plaine harte without dissimulation, fayninge, or flatterynge, euen after that .s. Iohn in his epistle biddeth vs. i. **Io. iii. My children let vs not loue in word and tong alone, but in dede and in truth,** specially considering that as he saith afore. **whosoeuer hath the substance of this world, and seeth his brother haue nede and closeth his hart from him, how doth the loue of god abide in him?*** In asmuch as he contemneth ye infirmitie and pouertie of hys euen christene. For this is the beginnynge of fraternall charitie, to haue pitye on our neighbours infirmitye. And to dye for our brethren is the perfection of charitie, the hyghest poynte of Charitye and of fraternall loue that is there spoken of, **In that wee knowe the charitye of GOD that hee layed awaye hys lyfe for vs, and we must ley aside our soules for our brothers.*** And our sauiour Christ in the gospel sayth. [2M4^v] **Maiorem charitatem. &c.** Greater charitie no man hath then to lose his lyfe for his frendes.* And so we here the perfection of charitye, but yet let vs more inwardlye consider the begynnynge of the same Fraternall loue. If thou be not meete and readye to dye for thy brother, yet geue thou of thy goodes to healpe and to saue thy neadye brother, and do it not of pride or boastynge, but of thy mooste entier and inwarde swetenesse of mercye towarde hym. Peraduenture thou wilt saye, why shoulde I geue my money to saue him from harme? He is none of mine, let him perishe in his owne iniquitie & noughtines, I haue nothing to do with him. If thou answer or think after this maner the loue of our father of heauen abideth not in thee. And if the loue of our father abideth not in thee, thou art not borne or gotten of God, then how canst thou glorye or be gladde that thou art a christen man? Thou hast the name, but thou hast not the dede of a christian man. **Renati non ex femine corruptibili sed incorruptibili. &c** Borne again not by any corruptible sede, but by an incorruptible sede bi the word of the liuing god & that abideth for euer.* Here ye blessed apostle .s. Peter reasoneth & swadeth vs to cleannes of life & to chastice our soules in obedient charitie, & in fraternal loue, by reason of our spiritual birthe. There is no naturall gentleman of birthe but if it soo chaunce that for the tyme hee be moued to dooe a myscheuous deede, if a discrete man woulde moue hym to the contrarye, recitynge hys Progenye and Auncestoures, saiynge: [2N1] beware what ye do, remember your blood, distayn not your kinred, shewe your self a gentleman, & not as a furious beast or a bawdy villaine, or as a churle or a thefe least al your kinred and louers will be ashamed of you. If there be anye gentlenes in the person, such vmbrayding and rehersall shall make him to leaue hys naughtye purpose, and to take a good way with him, and not to defoule his kinred with any vilany. Accordynge to that saith saint Peter, much more you should dispose your selfe to goodnes, considering your regeneration and second natiuitie, which was not by corruptible seede of man and woman, but by the vncorruptible sede, that is to say, by the word of God that abideth for euer. It is but a pore glory to be proude of the filthie substaunce that man is gotten by, nor of the bodies or bloode of theyr carnal fathers and mothers, which fadeth and continually runneth to corruption. As Esay the prophet saith. **Esa. xl. Omnis caro vt fenum, & omnis gloria eius tanquam flos agri, exaruit fenum, et flos eius decidit, verbum autem domini manet in eternum** All fleshe is lyke grasse of the medowe, and hys glori (that is to sai) carnal lust or pleasure, is like the floure of the medow that maketh a pleasant shewe for the time, and so doth carnall delectacion content and please for a while, but euen as the floure within a while withereth and falleth away, so doth carnall ioye fade and fall: it abideth not, but many times turneth to repentance, but the worde of God, that is the seede by which you were gotten and made the children of God by re[2N1ᵛ]generation by your seconde getting, abideth for euer & giueth life euer-lasting to them that be gotten bi it. And this is the holi word that hath ben preached among yo[u], (saith saint Peter) by me & by other Apostles.* By this holye woorde of God you were first instruct and taughte to leaue your old vaine errours and vices, and to renounce the deuyll wyth all his pompe and all his naughtye workes. And by the word of God concurrent and ioyned with the element of water, you wer baptised & goten to Christ, & made his children, wher afore you were the children of Gods yre & of dyspleasure, as all they be that after that waye be not new borne to God by baptisme.* The former carnall generation or birthe saueth no man nor woman, the seconde doth, and therefore it is necess-arie for all them that shal be saued, what sexe, kynde or age so euer they be of, contrarye to the secte and heresy of the Anabaptists* that woulde haue no man baptised till they were of yeares of discretion, in so much that they baptise again al them that in childhoode were christened, leauing all youth in dispeyre of saluation withoute anye way or helpe to be saued, and in worse case then the infantes of the Iewes were, which by Moises law should be circumcised on the eyght daye after they were borne, and by that circumcision should not perish but be saued.* For as saint Paul saith. **Rom. v. Si vnius delicto multi mortui sunt, multo magis gratia dei & donum . . . vnius hominis Iesu Christi in plures homines abundauit.*** Wher the Apostle compareth the offence of Adam to the [2N2] grace of Christ, for the grace of Christe is muche stronger and may extende and sprede it selfe further then the offence of one pure and frayle man might do, therefore in asmuche as death crept in among men by one Adam, then muche more by our sauiour Christ one man and God in one parson, of power infinite, the gift of grace is dilated and spred vpon all men that be made apte to receiue it, which is onely by baptisme actuallye receiued, or els in vowe or purpose. And therefore in asmuche as the synne of Adam killed all infantes, it must needes be that Christes grace in the sacrament of baptisme shal quicken the same infantes, and make theym spirituallye alyue againe in Christe, or els (as I sayde) it shoulde be weaker then Adams synne, & also because Christ saith. **Iohn .iii. Nisi quis renatus fuerit ex aqua et spiritu sancto non potest introire in regnum dei.** Except a manne be borne againe by water and the holye spirite, he cannot entre into the kyngdome of heauen.* And euen lyke as they that were circumcised in theyr infansye, knewe not what it meaned that they suffered with great paine, neither perceyued anye thinge of the promysse that God made to them that suffred it. In like maner baptysme saueth oure chyldren infauntes, althoughe they perceyue nothynge what is done vnto them, neyther the reason thereof. But Christ that saide: **Sinite paruulos venire ad me. Mathewe .xix.** Let babes or children come to me,* hathe prouyded armes to beare theym to hym, [2N2ᵛ] which be the armes of our mother holy church, by whose eares also they be cathechised or instruct, and by her mouthe they confesse their faithe, and in her faith they be saued. And this is very reasonable that other mens faith may helpe in thys sacrament of soule health, as wel as other mens faith hath helped them that haue be bodely diseased in sicknes and sores of theyr bodie, speciallye because God estemeth and regardeth more the health of the soule then of the bodye. We haue in the gospell of the Canaan womans doughter, that by the importune sute and prayer of her mother she was delyuered from the dyuell that she was obsessed with all: **O mulier magna est fides tua fiat tibi sicut vis: Math. xv. fides tua (inquit) non fides filie.*** And also **Centurio** a captain in **Capharnaum** came to Christ, praying him to helpe his seruant that was yll vexed with a paulsy, Christ offered to come him selfe to the mans house, & to heale his seruaunt. No (saith he) I am not worthye to receiue you into my house, but once say the word and my seruant shall be whole, and according to his beliefe so he sped, for his seruant was whole by and by, after the maister had confessed his beliefe.* An other that was impotent by a pawlsye, and his frendes coulde finde no waye to bringe him to Christe for preasse of people that were about him in the house. At the last they were faine to vntile the house and let him in by the roofe of the house. **Quorum fidem vt vidit, dixit, homo remittuntur tibi peccata tua, et ait paralitico tibi dico, surge, tolle lectum tuum & vade in domum tuam.** [2N3] **Luke. v. & .Mark .ii.*** He saw the faith of them that so conueyed the syckeman in at the roofe of the house, and forgaue the man his sinnes, and cured him of his pawlsy, at the contemplation of theyr faith that brought him to Christe. And this texte maketh plainly for our purpose, for here it appeareth that by the faith of other men, this sickman had aswell soule health as bodely healthe, for he had his sinnes forgiuen him for his soule health, and was rid of his pawsy for his bodely healthe. And euen so it was generallye of Christes cures that he did, which were euer full and perfite, for he healed the whole man, soule and bodye: for he vsed not to heale the bodye, but he woulde fyrste heale the soule, because that the infirmities of the body commeth comonly of the sinnes and syckenes of the soule, either originall or actuall. The Gospels hath many suche examples, in whiche it is plaine that the belief and praiers of others helpeth against bodely sickenes, then muche more it helpeth against this daungerous sickenes of the soule, that is originall synne, the common malander and mischiefe of all the issue of Adam, which if it be not cured and healed wyll surely let hym that is diseased with it, from the sight of the glorie of God for euer.* For (as I saide) God regardeth more the health of the soule, then of the body. And consideringe that the infantes haue the said originall sinne by an other mans preuarication and transgression, reasonable it is that they be releued and discharged of the same, by the meane of other mens faith, as by the vniuersal [2N3ᵛ] faith of the church, and by the faith of the godfathers and godmothers and of other assistents at the christening of the childe, so that we muste not exclude or denie the mercye & grace of God from any man or woman borne into this worlde, but that after their bodelye birthe to death, they be new borne to life by Gods holye worde, and by water with the inspiration of grace of the holye spirite, the holye Gost. And by this that I haue said you maye answer to the chiefe reason of the Anabaptistes that they vse against the said veritie, alledging that Christ sayth. **Math xviii. Qui crederit & baptisatus fuerit, saluus erit.** He that beleueth and is baptised, shall be saued: and he that beleueth not shal be dampned.* Of this they take that it is necessary for him that shall be baptised, that he beleue. Now say they, infantes lackynge the vse of reason cannot beleue, therefore they be vnmete to be baptised. I tolde you that they be saued by the beliefe of the church, and beleueth in the beliefe of the church, and in the belief of theyr Godfathers and godmothers, & other assistents representing the church, as I declared by diuers examples of the gospell, as wel of soule health as of bodely health, procured of Christ by the belief of others, or els (as the scholasticall doctours sai very well) in receyuing of the sacrament of baptisme the grace of faith is infused and powred in to the soule of him or her that is baptised, and so they haue the habyte or theologicall vertue of fayth, or the thing by which afterwarde as they increase in the vse of reason, they may beleue ac[2N4]tually and in dede.* Example, a Phisicion though he be fast a sleepe, he hath the science of phisicke, but yet if you put an vrinall in his hand, he cannot iudge the disease of the sickman, as longe as he is a slepe, albeit he hath the science in his soule, by which when he waketh he can iudge according to his learning.* And I trust you haue now herd sufficiently of the new birthe that saynte Peter speaketh of, which is more to be pondred then the carnall byrth by corru[p]tible matter, for the sede & cause of this generation is vncorruptible, it is the worde of God that abideth for euer, therfore consideringe whereof we came and be gotten to life and to God, we ought to haue special cleanenes in our life, and to chastice oure soules vnder obedient charitie, and in fraternall loue **attentius** more earnestly then we haue don, and more diligently considering the nobilitie of thys our second byrthe, by the vncorruptible seede of Gods holye worde that abideth for euer, and hath bene preached among vs, as saint Peter sayth in the ende of hys first chapter.* And now you haue heard the first chapiter of this first epistle of saint Peter declared as my poore wyt and learning wold serue me. I pray God it may be to hys pleasure and to the edifying and profyte of oure soules. Amen.

The second chapiter.

DEponentes igitur omnem malitiam et omnem dolum & simulationes et inui-
dias, et omnes detractiones, sicut modo geniti infantes rationabiles sine dolo lac
concupiscite.* In the fyrst chapiter of this epistle (which I haue passed ouer and
expounded as God put into my minde) the blessed Apostle saint Peter chiefelye
magnifyeth our regeneration and seconde byrth, by which we be borne to life
euerlasting, where throughe oure carnall parentes we were borne to dye. Fyrst he
giueth thankes to God that hath done so moche for vs as so to get vs againe to the
inheritance of heauen, that wil neuer be corrupt, that neuer wil be defowled, nor
fade or wither away, and in the meane season will bring vs to the soule healthe by
Christes faith, that al the old prophets labored to see and to obteine but thei were
answered that it would not be for theyr time, but all the labours that they tooke in
prayers, contemplacion and study, should serue for them that shuld come after,
which be wee that ha[u]e sene and heard the trouthe by theym that ha[u]e
preached Christes gospel continually, sithe the holye Gost was sent from heauen
in sensible signes of fyrye tounges, sone after Christes gloryous ascention. And for
this consideration sainte Peter exhorteth vs to be cleane of lyuinge, and while we
be here to liue in feare, considering the indifferencye of our [2O1] iudge in whom
is no partialitie. And knowynge the price that was paide for vs, whyche was no
corruptible metall, as gold or siluer, but the precious bloud of a pure Lambe our
sauiour Iesus Christ, and considering that the seede by whyche we wer regenerate
is not corruptible, as the sede of our parentes is, by which men be goten to die, but
it is immortall, as he is immortall that it commeth of, almighty God. The sede is
the immutable gospell by which we come to baptisme, that washeth vs from all our
sinnes, where I shewed you howe necessary that sacrament is to all sexes and to all
ages, as wel infants as other, that lyke as they be kylled or hurte by an other mans
sinne, so they may be reuiued by other mens faith.* Now consequently in this
second chapiter the blessed Apostle sainte Peter intreateth of the nursing or
bringing vp of them that were by the saide holy sede goten and borne to Christ,
and so to life euerlasting. This is a naturall order that saint Peter kepeth here, for
naturally the byrthe goeth afore the nourishinge. And because he that hath a
shrewd stomake, filled with nociue and yll humors, must first haue his stomake
purged, afore any meate shall do him good, therefore saint Peter like a good
Phisicion for the soule, counseleth vs first to rid the stomaks of our soules, our
hartes or consciences from all malice or wyll to hurt our neighbours.* That is
malice, and he that hathe suche an appetite to hurt an other man or woman, is
called a malicious person, otherwyse willing to do to others, then he woulde an
other [2O1ᵛ] should do to him which is contrarie to the law of nature, & to the
iudgement of right reason, for the iudgement of reason giueth that we should none
otherwise wil, intend, or do to ani other then we reasonably wold they shuld wil,
intend, or do to vs. From this generalitie he descendeth to the particulers & special
vices saying: that we must also rid oure soules from all gile and imaginacion to
deceiue our neighbours vnder the pretence and colour of some honestie or
goodnes, as I rede **Gen xxxiii[i].*** When **Dina** doughter to Iacob, and sister to the
.xii. Patriarchs sonnes of Israell, would walke abrode to see the women of the
countrey, and to be sene, as the maner of maidens is, **spectatum veniunt, veniunt**

spectentur vt ipse,* she came to the towne where **Emor** was Lorde, and a great prince there, whiche had a sonne called **Sichem*** as soone as he hadde cast his eye vpon this faire damsell **Dina** he was enamored & woulde nedes haue her, and so had his pleasure of her whyther she woulde or not. And yet his loue swaged not but euer still he loued her more and more. In so muche that he prayed and required his father to be suter to Iacob, father to the damsell, and to be woer for him that he myghte haue her to wyfe & mary with her, and so did **Emor** this yong mans father, but Iacob would make no graunt til hys sons came to the communicacion. When they herd that **Dina** theyr sister was deflowred and rauished by force, they chafed and tooke the matter very angerlye. Notwithstanding after large offers and fayre promisses made to theim by thys good gentleman **Emor**, and by the younge man [2O2] **Sichem** hys sonne. **Responderunt filij Iacob, Sichem & patri eius in dolo, seuientes ob stuprum sororis.** The sonnes of Iacob made answere to **Sichem** and to his father, in gyle, for they were in a rage for the raueshing of theyr sister.* Mark their answer and theyr intent, and you shall perceyue the gile, and what gile is. This was theyr aunswer: It is vnlawfull and a great offence for vs to mary our sister to a man that is vncircumcised, but if ye will come to our religion and be circumcised as we be, then it shall be lawfull for vs to mary together, your men with our women, & our men with your women, and so we may dwel together, and liue like frendes, and if you wil not then let vs haue our sister away, and we wyll be gone. This offer pleased **Emor** and hys sonne **Sichem** verye well. **Sichem** made no tarying, but did as they desired, and forthwith was circumcised, for the feruent loue that hee had to **Dina**, and then the father and the sonne came into the towne & perswaded all the people to agre, and so thei did agre & circumcised al the men of the town, what age so euer thei were of. But then folowed the subtile & false intent of **Dinays** brothers sons of Iacob. For on y^t third day after the circumcising of the people, when their woundes wer sorest y^t thei might not wel stir: in cam to the town with their swerdes in theyr hands **Symeon & Leui**, brothers to **Dina** bi father & mother, for **Lya** was their mother. **Gen. xxx.*** & they slew all them that were circumcised and **Emor** lorde of the town and **Sichem** his sonne with al, & toke away theyr sister with them. [2O2^v] And then came in the rest of Iacobs sonnes with their bushmentes, and made hauoke of all that was lefte. Here you see that their pretence was good and godly, but theyr intent was noughte, & this is **dolus**, gile. If there haue been anye suche gyle vsed by faire promisses and large offers to traine ani man or woma[n] to be of sinister or false opinion or heresie to kill his soule, vnder the pretence or colour of euangelicall truthe or libertye, this muste be left and layde downe as saint Peter saith here: The sutteltie and gile that is vsed in vttering of your wares by suche wiles as you vse, for the colourable setting furth of them, must be left and layde downe, and no more vsed. Ther is an other gile, whiche in comparison of thys is called **bonus dolus** good gile, such as men of war feighting in a iust cause vseth to circumuent and deceiue their enemies. Such gile **Iosue .viii.*** vsed against the towne of **Hay**, where his host were afore put to rebuke, dryuen backe, and loste .xxxvi<:> men. **Iosue .vii.*** At the second saute he set a strong bende of men to the nomber of fyue thousand in a stale at the West side of the towne of **Hay**. And then the captaine with his armie shewed freshlye against the towne, as thoughe they woulde haue fought with them. The kinge there encouraged by the victorie at the former skirmige, aduanced furth boldly against Iosue the captaine. And Iosue reculed backe and ranne awaye, as the other company had done afore, and when by his reculing he had flocked the kinge of Hay a great wai out of the town, he gaue a signe to them

that lay [2O3] in the stale, which rose vp and got into the town then being
without people, for euerye manne and woman was runne oute to pursue Iosue, and
to get somewhat in the chase, and they sette it on fyre and burned it, and
furthwith came forth on the backe of the kinge of Hay and his hoste, and then
Iosue with his host returned vpon them, & so betwyxte the captaine and the stale,
they were destroyed and taken euery mothers sonne. This was **bonus dolus** a
laudable gile, to vanquish and ouercome Gods enemies, which had discomforted
them afore. You must also lay away and put from you all simulacion or faining,
shewing one thing for an other, hauing one thing in the mouth and an other thing
closed within the hart, as Ioab did to Amasa .ii. **Reg. xx.*** suspecting that Amasa
would haue put him out of fauoure with the kinge **Dauid** when he met wyth hym,
he came louingly to him and said. **Salue mi frater,** God spede you or God saue you
my brother,* and with hys right hand he toke Amasa by the chin, as though he
woulde haue kissed him, but with his left hand he drew his dagger and strake him
in the syde, so that his guts fel about his feete, & there he died. Here was sore
simulation and fayning, this was a false flattring kisse like Iudas kisse, by whych he
betrayed his maister. This must be left & layd downe and no more vsed. There is
also an other simulation which may be called good and laudable, and suche vsed
kinge Dauid as it is wrytten i. **Reg. xxi.** when he fled to Achis kynge of Geth,
when the kynges seruauntes sawe Dauid, they [2O3ᵛ] sayd among them selues: is
not this Dauid king of the land of Israell? Dauid was sore afrayde, and when he
came afore Achis the king, he changed his countenance, and fell down among
their handes, and then flapped his handes, and layde his shoulders against the
doores, & his spytle draueled downe vpon his beard. Then sayde Achis to his
seruants: why haue you brought this mad man afore me? haue we not mad men
inoughe of our owne? Why haue ye brought this felowe to play the mad man in my
presence?* And vpon thys Dauid was let go like a foole, and so escaped the danger
of them that would haue brought him againe to king Saul, which then was his
mortall enemye. And to this fact of Dauid agreeth full well thys comon prouerbe:
Stultitiam simulare loco prudentia summa est, To fayne foolishnesse in some
case, is verye highe wisedome.* Thys is not the pernicious simulation, by whiche
men wyth flyring cheare woulde crepe into a mans bosome and yet kyll hym if they
coulde. And so muste all enuye be layde awaye, that is sorowe for an others mans
wealthe or welfare, or gladnesse for hys hurte or hynderance. For here on earthe no
man enuyeth hym that hath neyther vertue morall nor intellectuall, neyther
theologicall, but rather bemoneth hym and is sorye for hym, accordyng to the old
prouerbe, I hadde leauer hee enuyed me, then bemoned me.* Thys is that dyuelish
vice, that is not so meete for anye place as for hell. In heauen it cannot be, for
there shall be the greatest ioye possible of one neyghbour in an [2O4] other euerye
man shall reioyce of an other mans glorye, as muche as of hys owne. In hell thys
vyce shall be at rest, for there he shall see nothing to disdayne at, or to enuye at,
there shall bee no wealthe, no prosperitie, no exaltacion, or promotion to be
enuyed, but all payne, sorow, and care. And of thys shall come no ioye to the
enuyous soule, but all freatyng and gnawyng in his own conscience, and euerye
one of theym that there shall be against an other. It is the sinne that is most
contrarye to charitie, and by that moste dyspleasaunt to almightye God, and most
acceptable and pleasant to the dyuell. And of thys enuy commeth and foloweth
thys other vyce that Saynte Peter here woulde haue vs purged of that so we myghte
be able to receyue the mylke that he woulde nourse vs and feede vs wyth all. That
vyce (saythe Saynte Peter) is **detraction,** or backbitynge,* by whiche secretelye

behinde a mans backe, a mans fame or good name is defaced and defowled. Suche
backbiters that depraueth and missayeth men behinde theyr backes destroying
theyr good name, Sainte Paule reherseth amonge them that God hath let runne in
reprobum sensum into such madnes as to think no thing good, but that is nought
in dede, and to do as is vnconuenient for men to doe,* **Susurrones detractores,
deo odibiles,** they be such as God hateth or as the other translation hath **dei
osores,** suche as hateth God, for they hate theyr neygbours whom God would haue
them to loue, & so thei loue neither God nor his pleasure & commandement.*
[204ᵛ] The greatest treasure that a man hathe, is hys good name and fame,
therefore **Ecclesiast. xli.** biddeth vs, **Curam habe de bono nomine, hoc enim
magis permanebit tibi quam mille thesauri preciosi et magni:** thou must care and
take hede and prouide for thy good name, for that will stick by the better then a
thousand rich and great treasures,* and Salomon saith. **Pro. xxii. Melius est
bonum nomen, quam diuitie multe.** Better is a good name then great riches.*
Therefore he that diminisheth thy good name, doth worse then if he pyked thy
purse, or stole all thy riches, and can neuer haue his offence forgiuen, till he haue
made restitucion, and then considering howe hard it is to pull out of mens heades
that opinion that thou hast once brought into their heades by thy rayling &
backbiting tong. By this you may consider the danger of that vyce, for the frowardnes of fraile man is such, that it is more easie to bring out of his head a good
opinion once conceiued by an other, then an yll. Thou shalt tell a good tale, or a
good report by one twise or thrise afore a man beleue it, but a noughty report be it
neuer so false, is soone taken, but not so soone disswaded againe. And by this also
appeareth the danger & perill of them that giueth eare to backbiters, for they be
partakers of the offence, & so be in like damnacion beside the sinister & rashe
iudgement that they haue of their neighbour by such detraction and lewd report of
yᵉ detractour or backbiter, for to misiudge thy neighbour to be a theefe, or to be a
lecher, or adulterer, to be an heretik, or such other mortal [2P1] sinner, except the
fact be euidente and plaine, or the signes so euident, that they can not be
countersaid, is deadly sinne. Therefore (as S. Hierome saith, **Epistola ad Nepocianum de vita clericorum**) we muste beware that we haue nother itchinge tonges,
nor itchinge eares: itching tonges, busy clatering and raylinge, itching eares, euer
open and glad to be clawed with newes and noughtye tales.* But fewe there be
that forsake this vice of detraction, and a man shall seldome finde one so clere and
blameles, that he will not be gladde to reproue and blame other folkes liuinge.
And men haue so great pleasure in this vice, that thei yᵗ be not poluted or spotted
with other vices, yet they fall to this vice, as into the extremeste and last snare of
the deuill, and the lightnes of the hearer geueth occasion, aucthoritie, and courage
to this detraction & backbiting, for if there were no hearers, there would be no tale
bearers, therfore we **shoulde make an hedge of thornes before oure eares, lest we
should here any wicked tongues, Eccle. xxviii.*** Let the terrible sentence of
damnation at the general iudgement pricke our eares, as it were thornes, and then
we shalbe afraid to heare shreud tales. And the prophet rehearsyng the vertues
that maketh a man mete to dwell in the tabernacle of our lord, reckneth this for
one: **opprobrium non accepit aduersus proximos,** that hath not taken or beleued
ill saying agaynst his neighbours,* such a one is mete to dwel in heauen, then he
that is of contrarie appetite, must dwell in hell. Peraduenture you wyll say, I should
do [2P1ᵛ] a man wrong if I should not herken to his tale, I may litle do and I maye
not lende him myne eares and geue him the hearing, & what wronge can I do,
when other men telleth me the tale? it is not my sayinge, it is theyrs, let them

beware that telleth the tales. Not so my frende, for thy part is therein, for if thou wouldeste not lende thine eares and geue audience with a good wyl, but were loth to heare the backbiter, he woulde be as loth to beare tales to the, they should none fasten nor printe in the, no more then an arowe when it is shotte against a stone, fasteneth in the stone, it fasteneth not in the stone, but sometime reboundeth and flyeth backe vpon him that shot it: let the detractour learne to leaue his backbitinge, by that he seeth the loth to here him, for so thou shalt dryue shame into his face. Remember the counsayle of Salomon. **Prouerb. xxiiii. Cum detractoribus non commiscearis quoniam repente consurget perditio eorum, & ruinam vtriusque quis nouit.** Medle not with backbiters, for theyr destruction shal rise sodenly, and who knoweth the ruine of them both:* of the backbiter, & of him that geueth him the hearing? as who should saye, no man but God alone. All these vices rehersed, and suche others, must be layd away & purged out of the stomackes of your soules, whiche done, you shall euen like reasonable infantes lately borne, couet & desire to be fed with that milke that is without gile or deceit, the milke of the soul, and not of the body, by which you may grow, & waxe bigge toward saluation, specially if you haue ta[2P2]sted (sayth S. Peter) that God is swete, good, & curtise.* Here be diuersities of translations, one sayth, **infantes rationabiles,** an other sayth, **rationabile & sine dolo lac,** the thyrde redeth it, **Lac illud non corporis sed animi,*** & this laste agreeth with the second, meaning that the milke that we must desire to be nursed with all, is not the milke of the body, as nether cowe milke, nor the mylke of womans brestes that fedeth the bodye, but it is the milke of reason by which the reasonable soul is noursed and fed, and that is holy doctrine, as I shall say anone. The fyrst translation sayinge **infantes rationabiles,** saith so not without a cause, for infantes and babes haue some properties not laudable, as ignoraunce, obliuion, insolencie, and wantones, which S. Paul taxeth .i. cor. xiiii **Nolite pueri effici sensibus sed malitia paruuli estote. &c.** Be you not children lacking discretion, but as a child beareth no malice, so must we beware that we bear no malice:* this is a good propertie in which we must folow the child, & withall we muste vse reason to discerne the good from the il, that no persuasion or reasoning peruerte vs from the true and holesome doctrine, to any errour or heresie, for the true milke, the true doctrine that shall make vs to grow to health and saluation, is without gile, & without deceite, it begileth no man. Blessed S. Peter calleth by the name of milke, the first principles of our faith, and necessary rules that euery man and woman must beleue, if they shal come to God & be saued, as the mistery of Christes incarnation of his passion & resurrection, and such like as be comenly preached [2P2ᵛ] and taught in the churche, these must be vttred and shewed to al men and women after a plaine maner, by such homely and familiar examples as they may sucke, take, and vnderstande. Saynte Paule .**Heb. vi.** geueth to the Hebrewes plentye of such mylke, as fyrst for them that commeth to Christ, repentaunce, abrenunciation, and forsaking the deuyll with all his pompe, and of theyr old maner of sinful liuing, either by them selues or by the churche in their names, because of infantes that I spoke of heretofore. Another is faith on God: the third is baptisme and the effecte therof, the .iiii. is Confirmation by imposition or setting the bishops handes on him or her that is confyrmed: the fyft is the resurrection of our bodies: the syxt, is the eternall iudgemente and rewarde that God shal geue vs, accordinge to our workes.* These be the beginnings of christian doctrine, with which they that newly commeth to Christ, must be fedde plainly, and without any exquisite or high pointes of diuine learninge concerninge the same, for suche high learning is it that S. Paule calleth.

Heb. v. Solidus cibus, sad meat, or faste meate,* that shall rather hurt a beginner, then fede him or do him good, it may turne his stomack, and make him to geue vp all, as thinges vnpossible for him to digest, to attayne or learne, & to exercise and to performe in dede. And this meate agreeth well with them that be perfect, **perfectorum autem est solidus cibus, eorum qui pro consuetudine exercitatos habent sensus ad discretionem boni et mali,** that by vse haue their [2P3] wittes exercised to discerne the good doctrine, from the bad and corrupt doctrine, the truth from the falseheade,* as they be not able to do that be but beginners, like children or babes: for as yonge infantes many tymes wyll sitte moyling in the axen, & put earth or coles into their mouthes, and other thinges that may do them hurt, as sone as that shall do them good, so he that hath not his wittes exercised by often hearing the scriptures taught and declared, & that can not wey and iudge the thinges that he heareth, whether they be true or erronious, he shall as sone gape and eate into the belye of his minde earth or coles, as kyndelye feadinge, as sone errours and heresies to poyson him, as true doctrine to edifie him, and to strength him. But he that remembreth what he hath heard, and when any new maner of teachinge ariseth, will conferre it to the true preaching or teaching that he hath hearde afore of catholike clerkes, and that by suche collation can spye whether this newe waye be safe & sure or no, such a one is stronge and paste chyldhode, and may be fedde with fast meate. The preacher may be bolde afore suche men to speake of hyer matters, then he maye afore chyldren that be beginners. Saynt Paule perceauinge that the Corinthians were verye carnall and worldelye, not hauinge theyr mindes eleuate to hygh learninge, fed them with milke like chyldren, as he sayth **i. Cor. iii.*** & yet afterward hearing of theyr dissentions, and debate aboute their baptistes, **Cum quis dicet ego sum Pauli, alius autem ego Apollo,** [2P3ᵛ] where as one sayd, I am Pawles Christen man, because I was christened of Paule, an other sayth, I am Apollo his Christen man, because I was christened of Apollo.* He spied that theyr carnalitie was not all gone, therfore yet he said they were not able to take sadde meate, nor to be taught as spirituall men, but as carnall folkes, callinge them **carnall folkes,** that he calleth there **animalis homo,*** whose sences and appetites be depressed and kepte downe to sensuall pleasures, not submittinge them selues to the rule of reason, directed by the holy gooste, and these be carnall, fleshely or beastly in liuinge. Carnall, fleshly or beastlye in knowledge be they, that of almighty God and heauenlye thinges, imageneth and iudgeth by corporall phantasies, as of God, that he is a fayre olde man with a white beard,* as the paynters make him, and that the ioyes of heauen stondeth in eatinge and drinkinge, pypinge and daunsinge, these be grosse imaginations of carnall wittes. And euen so they be spirituall in liuinge, that be ordered in theyr liuinge, in theyr thoughtes, wordes, and workes, by the instincte and inclination of the holy goost, ruling and guiding them to goodnes, and such persons wil be as well ware and afrayd to come in that place where they may be hurte in soule, as they wyll be ware to come where they maye be hurte in theyr bodies, and wyll be as glad to cure and heale the soule if anye thinge be amisse, as they would be to heale the bodye if it were diseased, & [2P4] in them the feruencie and heate of the spirite waxeth not faint by multiplying of iniquitie, neither by the coldnes of charitie,* and in theim the spirite is not quenched, vnderstandinge by the spirite, that spyryte whiche is conserued & kepte whole and sounde with the soule and the bodye, (as S. Paule speaketh) and not the substaunce of the holy ghoste, whiche can not perishe or be hurte.* But we vnderstande by the spirit the graces and giftes of the holy gooste, whiche by oure vertue, or by our vyce be kindeled or quenched, as S. Hierome writeth in his epistle **ad Hedibiam**.* And they be spirituall in knowledge, that considereth of almightie God aboue all thinges, that his excellencie and glory passeth all thinges that may be sene or imagined by mannes wittes, and that he is not prescribed or determined to anye place, but that he is infinite and vnmeasurable, and all one and whole in euery place, and that of the aungels and of celestial ioyes, iudgeth aboue all corporall and bodelye creatures, and that consydereth, that after the generall resurrection men and women shall nother marye nor be wedded, but shall be as Goddes Aungelles in heauen. They that by exercyse in hearynge the holye Scriptures, haue theyr wyttes eleuate aboue the commonne sorte of people be comme to yeares of dyscretion, and loke for faster feadynge, and hygher learnynge, then the younger sorte dooth, whiche muste be fedde with mylke or suppynges that wyll be easelye [2P4ᵛ] digested.* They that Saynt Peter wrytte vnto, were but newly conuerted to Christes faith, by his preachinge amonge them in his progresse in **Pontus, Galatia, Capadotia. &c.*** Therfore specially he aduertiseth them euer to desyre that mylke of playne doctrine, concerninge the fyrst principles and necessary articles of our fayth, in whiche he had instructed them. This is milke without gile or deceipt, there is no falsehead admixte or mingled with it (saith Saint Peter)* meaninge that there is an other mylke that is mixt with gile or falsehead, as the mylke that is spoken of. **Prou. i. Fili misi te lactauerint peccatores ne acquiescas eis.** My child, if synners and noughtye lyuers geue the suck of mylke, consent not to them,* as if they say, come, let vs take a standinge for a purse, we shall get good ynough to make mery withall, or els let vs be auenged on this man or that man, he is euer contrary to our workes, let vs rydde him out of the worlde, and so we shal enioye our robberies quietly, no man shall speake agaynste vs. Thus all they that intendeth mischief, wyll geue sucke of this flateringe milke, to make others as badde as they be them selues. Therefore he sayth. **Prouerb. xvi. Vir iniquus lactat amicum suum & ducit eum per viam non bonam.** A wycked man geueth milke to his companion, and bringeth him in a shreude trade, and into an yll waye:* As he that is a baudy felowe, geuen to horehuntinge, wyll make many more suche, and bringe them to yll companye, and to noughte wyth hym, so wyll dycers, so wyll carders, and [2Q1] so wyll all vnthriftes, fyrste to pleasures, and consequently afterwarde to the very botome of all yll, and finally to perdition and destruction. This milke of temptation is not withoute gile, but hath euer falseheade and gyle annexed and ioyned with it, therefore we had greate nede to beware of it. And yf wee shall set mylke of doctrine agaynste mylke of doctrine, then considre howe the flatteringe mylke of heresie, feadinge men with fayre flattering wordes, and settynge afore men a counterfeit libertie to eate & drynke withoute any delect choyse, or difference of meat, of time or place, settinge litle by diuine seruyce and prayers, and lesse by fastynge or abstinence. This mylke is crudded and sowre, and so are theyr hartes that geueth it, and theyrs that fedeth vpon it, or sucketh it: **Coagulatum est sicut lac cor eorum,** theyr hart is crudded lyke Milke.* Ambrose vpon the same. **Vt enim lac natura sua purum speciosum ac syncerum est sed corruptione coacescit sic cordis humani natura pura ac perspicua est priusquam viciorum admixtione coacescat.** Euen lyke as milke by his owne kinde is pure, fayre and cleare, but it waxeth soure by corruption, so mannes hart is pure, cleare, and indifferente to all doctryne, but whan the teacher is soure and corrupte, it is no maruayle yf he do sone corrupt his scholer, speciallye yf the scholer haue not his wytte well exercised, to put difference betwyxte good and yll.* And howe many haue we knowen so fedde with this soure crudded milke that they haue bene made stronge and sturdie felowes, [2Q1ᵛ] paste correction or reformation, growinge towarde destruction euerlasting. This is the ende of the noughty noursinge with the badde milke, where the iust and gratious mylke of true doctrine **maketh a man to growe to saluation** (as S. Peter sayth here) **specially if you haue tasted** (saith he) **that oure Lorde God is swete and good:*** As who shoulde saye, some there be that for all the teachinge and preachinge that they haue, yet they be neuer the better, neither haue any swetenes in God nor in his holye worde, and it is no maruayle if they neuer cease to defyle him, and his holy worde with earthlye desyres and pleasures. And as we see that he that hath no pleasure in his meate, but eateth it agaynste harte, and agaynst his stomacke, shall not profyt by his meate, so he that feleth no swetenes in Christe and in his holy worde, howe can he grow to saluation by it? it will not be. Then we taste that God is swete when we delite in his wordes, and comforte our selues with his holye lessons set furth in his scriptures. And when we glory and comforte our selues in Christes byrth, his passion and glorious resurrection, and when we take pleasure in readinge and hearinge his mooste gratious lyfe and conuersation, then we taste that God is swete. And by the same we growe to saluation and health (as Saynt Peter sayth here) when for the swetenes and loue of God and for consideration of his worde, we bringe furth godly fruites, as geuinge almes to them that be nedye, remittinge and forgeuinge iniu[2Q2]ries and wronges done to vs, and when we can be content for oure soule health to pray, to faste, and to watche, these be manifest sygnes that by the swete milke of Goddes doctrine, we growe to saluation and waxe stronge in God, and by that shall be the more able to perfourme oure paynefull iourney, that we muste walke here in the wyldernesse of this worlde, labouringe and goinge towardes our countrey, whiche loketh for vs, heauen aboue, to which also we al desyre to come through the helpe of our sauiour Christ. Amen.

AD quem accedentes lapidem viuum ab hominibus quidem reprobatum a deo autem electum & honorificatum. &c. To whome ye come (sayth S. Peter) as to the liuinge stone that men haue reproued and set nought by, but God hath chosen & made him to be honored, and on hym be you builded like liuing stones into spiritual houses, in sacerdotium sanctum, & to a holy preisthod, offering spiritual sacrifices acceptable to God by Iesus Christ.* Now presuposing that we haue tasted that god is swete & plesaunt to our soules, in these wordes rehersed, the blessed Apostle S. Peter beginneth to auaunce vs, & set vs forward to higher perfection, willing vs (in as much as we be come to Christe, as to the fyrme, faste, & sure stone, & foundation of the church & of al godly religion) that we should be edified & builded on him as spirituall houses buylded on the faste rocke, [2Q2ᵛ] and that we shulde be as holy preistes, offeringe spirituall sacrifices, that maye be acceptable to God, by our Sauioure Iesus Christe. In these wordes be manye thinges to be noted and to be declared: Fyrst that our comminge to Christe, as S. Peter here meaneth, is not to come to him on fote, nor on horsebacke, but we muste come to hym by faith, fourmed and adourned with charitie, and with charitable workes, by whiche they that sometime were farre of, be made nighe in the bloude of Christe. And so came Englande to Christ, not saylinge ouer the sea, nor by peregrination to the holy lande where Christe was bodely conuersaunte for the tyme, but by fyrme and faste fayth on Christe, that they conceaued by hea-rynge the preachers that GOD sente amonge them.* And so the people of **Pontus, Galatia, Capadotia. &c.** that Sainte Peter wryteth this letter vnto, by fayth and charitie came to Christes grace, by which they dwelled in Christ, and Christe in them.* Christe is here called a lyuinge stone, by whiche you maye playnelye see, that the stone here, is not the stone that we treade on, nor the stone that you see in the pyllers or walles of the churche, for they be not alyue nor lyuinge stones, but this is a maner of speaking by a met<h>aphor or a similitude, for of all partes of the earth the stone is the fastest and the sureste to buylde on: softe earth, sande, or cleye, wyll be sone wasshed awaye with floudes or stremes, and the buyldinge sone shaken with winde or stormes, but that buyldinge that is [2Q3] well set on the harde rocke, standeth faste and shrynketh not for any violence. For this propertie of the stone, our Sauiour Christe is called a stone, as well here as in manye other places of Scripture.* This stone (sayth Sainte Peter) was reproued, despysed, and noughte set by amonge men, but it was chosen of God, and set in honour, alludinge to the wordes of the Prophet Dauid. **Psal. Cxvii. Lapidem quem repro-bauerunt edificantes hic factus est in caput anguli.** And also to the sayinge of the Prophete Esaye. **Ecce ponam in Sion lapidem summum angularem probatum electum preciosum.** * And because Saint Peter toucheth and speaketh fyrste of the reproche of this stone, accordinge to the wordes of the Psalme, and afterwarde of his exaltation and honour, according to the wordes of Esay, I wil kepe the same ordre and processe in my declaration. Because that the misticall senses and vnder-standinge of the Scriptures, whether it be morall sence, allegory or anagogicall sence, presupposeth a true literall sense on whiche they be grounded.* Therefore because that the Prophets in theyr writinges, and also the Euangelistes in the Gospels, and also the Apostles Saint Peter and Saint Paule in theyr epistles, & Luke in the Actes of the Apostles, hath manye tymes in mynde this verse of the Psalme, **Lapidem quem reprobauerunt edificantes, hic factus est in caput anguli.**

236

The stone whiche the buylders reproued and cast by, it was made the heade stone in a corner of the buyldynge.* Was there anye [2Q3ᵛ] suche stone in dede so set at nought, and caste by in the buyldinge of Salamons temple, or in kinge Dauids palace in Sion, or in anye suche other notable buyldinge spoken of in the scriptures?* Surely I thinke noo, there was none suche a stone, albeit the Hebrewes hath an olde tale, that when kinge Dauid was well minded to buylde a temple for God to be honoured in, and was aunswered that he shoulde not do that dede, because he was a bloude sheder, and hadde done manye battels, but that his sonne Salamon shoulde do it, for he shoulde be a quiet man, and a man of peace, and at reste and peace with all nations.* The sayd king Dauid prepared money, stones and tymbre sufficiente for the sayde buyldynges, and squared them, and polysshed them, and trimmed them accordingely, so that his sonne shoulde lacke nothinge for that chargeable edifice and buyldinges, all this is true. Then say they moreouer, that amonge the sayde stones that kynge Dauid had prouided, he sawe by reuelation one stone that would neuer be framed, set or layd hansomly in any place, and that therfore yᵉ builders wold cast it by, & set nought by it, & yet at the last it should haue a place at one corner in the toppe and highest part of the temple, there to be the very bond and keye stone to ioyne two walles together as one wal, & so they saye, it was at the consummation & ending of the temple that Salamon builded. And of this reuelation they say, yᵉ prophet had occasion to say, **Lapidem quem reprobauerunt edificantes, hic factus est in caput an**[2Q4]**guli.*** But because this narration hath no euidence of scripture, it is not best to grounde anye scripture vpon it, and specially this scripture that is so oft in mouth with our sauiour Christ & with the euangelistes, and in the Apostolical epistles. But we must take the said wordes of the psalme **Lapidem quem repro. &c.** spoken originally, and to the lettre of our Sauiour Christ selfe, and so he alledgeth the same wordes .Mat .xxi.* as spoken by him selfe after the parable of the good man that made a vineyard, and set it to labourers to dresse it, and kepe it, and when time came to gather the fruytes, he sent his seruauntes to gather the fruites, fyrst one company, and after an other company, and these rude felowes the labourers in the vyneyarde toke some of them that were sent to them and beate them, and slewe some of them, so that at the last the good man was fayne to sende his owne sonne, thinkinge that the vnkynde churles yet woulde be afrayde to medle with him, yet notwithstandinge him they caste out of the vyneyarde or garden, and killed hym also as they had done others that were sent amonge them afore. Now sayth Christ, what wyl the sayd goodman the owner of the vyneyarde do to these fermers and labourers in the vineyarde that haue done this mischiefe? They answered: The yl and noughty wretches he muste destroy & put them to death, & must set forth his vineyarde to other tenauntes. And then because they shuld perceiue & vnderstand more by this sonne that yᵉ goodman sent among them, he allegeth this text [2Q4ᵛ] of the psalme, makinge for his purpose, sayinge: dyd you neuer reade: The stone whiche the builders reproued and caste by, was made the heade stone for the corner of the buyldinge?* meaninge that the goodmannes sonne that was caste out of the vineyarde to be slayne, and the stone that the buylders reproued and caste by for noughte, was all one. He was the onely and derest sonne of the father of heauen, whome the vnkind Iewes cast oute of the citie of Ierusalem, and led him to the mount of Caluary, the place of execution without the citie, and there killed him, and euen he was the stone that the buylders cast by, and despised for a thinge of noughte, and yet afterwarde the same stone ioyned the two walles together as one wall, the Iewes and the Gentyles, in the vnitie of one churche:* The buylders that be here spoken of, were the scribes and the phariseis, and learned men amonge the Iewes, whiche knewe by the Scriptures that they had redde, that Christ was the verye **anoynted,** that was so longe afore promised of almightie God, by the mouthes of his holy Prophetes, for they sawe all thinges that were spoken of afore, to be performed in the **anointed** that they loked for, performed in Christ in very dede.* They saw the time that Iacob in ye blessing of his sonne Iudas apointed, & also Daniel the prophet spoke of to agre, & then put in effect & come in dede, that when ye holy one of al holy ones shuld come, ther shuld be no more kinges anointed of ye linage of Iude.* For y^t time y^t christ came, Herode was their king an alien, an Idumey, descending of Esau, & not of Iacob.* [2R1] They sawe also his wonderous workes and miracles aboue the power of anye pure man to do. Their learnynge and the experience that they had of Christes Godlye power, and of hys wisedome shoulde haue moued them to edify the people in the fayth of Christe, they should haue beleued on hym them selfe, and should haue perswaded the people likewise to beleue vpon hym, and to take hym for the true Messias, but they did cleane contrarye, peruertynge and misexpoundyng the scriptures that speake of him, and swadynge the people that he was but a dissembler, and that he was a tauerne hunter, a wyne drinker, a quaffer, a companion wyth the Publicans wyth whores & naughty liuers.* Like as a builder gathereth and ioyneth together stones and other matter or stuffe to make a house, euen so shoulde they haue gathered and layed in frame together the textes of Moyses and of the Prophetes, and suche other Scriptures of the olde Testament, appliynge them to Christ, of whom and by whome they were intended and spoken, that they so doyng, myght haue buylded the people as spiritual houses on Christ, as on the firme and sure rocke or stone. Whiche they did not, but rather dissipate and scattered abroade the buildynge, deuidynge the people into scismes and diuers opinions of hym, and rather not to be stablisshed on hym, but to be cleane shaken awaye from hym. The blessed apostles, Euangelistes, and holye doctours gathered together the texts and saiynges of the holy scriptures as stones or [2R1^v] timber or stuffe to make vp their audience, and buylde theim as spirituall houses on Christe. And so dothe Sainte Peter in this his letter that we haue now in hande by the aucthoritie of Dauid and Esay, declarynge Christe to be the precious and best beloued stone that GOD had chosen, althoughe men hadde reproued him, and set little by hym whiche yet notwythstandynge he shoulde be the hedstone to ioyne together the Iewes and Gentyles in one churche.* And not onelye then he was reproued of the builders of that tyme, the Scribes and Phariseis and their audiences and Scholers the carnall Iewes, but as well nowe adayes he is reiecte and dispised of manye Buylders and Preachers, blasphemynge and missaiynge hys godlye and myghtye power in manye pointes, as farre foorthe as they dare, for feare of the Kinges lawes. And of this it commeth that so manye miscreauntes and misbeleuers so little regarde the blessed and mooste reuerende Sacramente of the Aultare, and also the Sacramentall confession of synnes vnto a Prieste,* as thoughe Christe were not able by his Godlye power to make of breade and wine, his owne fleshe and bloude, and to geue power to a priest by his wordes to dooe the same likewise, Or as thoughe GOD were not able by his officer to deliuer men from the prison and bondage of their synnes. They that by their preachynge, readinge, or teachinge, sowe suche heresies among the people, they be naughtye builders, they cast away [2R2] the bindinge stone our Sauiour Christe, that he maie not ioyne together all people in the vnitie of one faieth, they scatter the stones, the aucthorities of the scriptures by their misunderstandinge, and false interpretation, more then gathereth theim to edifie and builde their audience on the liuelye and liuynge stone oure Sauiour Christ.* To all them that beleue not well them selues on God, **In quo & positi sunt,** * in whome wee liue and moue, and be (as Sainte Paule speaketh)* God hath made vs and set vs, and ordeyened vs to beleue vpon hym. And beside that offendeth in wordes againste Christe, and againste his blessed Sacramentes after the maner aforesayde, our Sauiour Christe is **Lapis offensionis, & petra scandali.** * As sainte Peter sayeth here, he is a stumblyng Stone, such a one as men take harme of, and be agreued withall, not for occasion geuen of hym, but by the pryde of mens hartes, and sturdinesse or hardnes in not beleuynge. The Iewes were offended and thought amisse of Christe because they sawe him in the infirmitie of his flesh. They sawe him eat and drinke, slepe, and laboure as other men did. They knewe his bryngynge vp in youthe, and where he was nursed, and who was his mother & who were his kinsfolkes. This made a great meyny of them to shake him of, and in no wise to beleue vppon him, and by that this stone fell vpon them, & al to crasshed them to naught. **Quia super quem ceciderit lapis iste conteret enim. Math. xxi.** [2R2ᵛ] On whom so euer this stone falleth, it wyl braye hym and crashe hym.* And in that place Christe sayeth, that some men falleth on this stone, and breaketh or hurteth theim selues on it. And on others this Stone falleth and brayeth theim or crassheth them as corne or grayne is brayed betwixt two mill stones, or in a querne. They that (conseruynge and kepynge their fayeth) yet falleth sometymes to synne. They fall vpon the stone, and taketh harme, and be hurt by their fall As when a christen man or woman not erring in the articles of our fayth, yet by infirmitie of the flesshe, or by temptation of the deuill falleth to synne, they fall on Christe this liuynge Stone, and hurteth theim selues right sore, bringynge them selues in daunger of death and damnation euerlastyng, and makyng them selues more vnable to resist synne an other tyme, for the oftener thou sinnest, the more redy thou shalt be to sinne againe, and the more vnable to resist temptation, but when a man or woman falleth to infidelitie or to heresie, then fare well. For this stone falleth vpon them and breaketh theim to duste and to asshen euerlastynge. **Qui non credit iam iudicatus est.** He that beleueth not is iudged already.* The sentence is geuen and past in the mynde and foreknowledge of the iudge our Sauioure Christ. Because that saint Peter saith here that Christ was **Lapis offensionis & Petra scandali.** The stone that men shoulde take hurte by, and that by him men shoulde take occasion to fall euen as the prophetes hadde saide of him afore. And as [2R3] the Gospels reherseth of him likewyse. I thinke it necessarye to demore and tarye in the declaration of that maner of speakynge of the Scriptures, and what is meaned by the same. **Luke .ii.** * It is written that when Christes foster father, and Mary his mother presented him in the temple, as the lawe was. The holye and well disposed man Symeon toke hym in hys armes with great ioye, because he knew it was he that shold be the consolation and comforte of Israell. And he knewe the tyme was then come, or very neare hande, when Christe shoulde come. He knewe it also by reuelation of the holye Gooste that then moued hym to goe to the Temple, as it is there sayde. **Et venit in spiritu in templum.** * Where after great ioye of that he hadde seene, he then desiered to be let go in peace, to dye. And among other thinges, he saide this plainely to Marye the blessed Mayde and mother of Christe, as a cordiall, or rather a corosiue. **Ecce positus est hic in ruinam & in resurrectionem multorum in Israel, & in signum cui contradiceretur. Et tuam ipsius animam pertransibit gladius.** Loe (sayeth he.) Thys childe is set to make men fall, and to make many men to ryse among the people of Israel. And he is set as a signe or a mark that folke wil countersay &

speke against. And as for your part (said he<>> to Marie his mother[)], the sworde
of sorowe shall pearce your harte, which yet shall redound and turne to the
comfort of manye others.* Here you see that this blessed man sayde that Christ
shoulde be the ruyne of many a one, and suche a [2R3ᵛ] one as should be
countersaid and spoken against of manie others. And .**Mat. xi.*** When sainte Iohn
Baptist sente two of his disciples to Christe to aske him a question for their
learnynge, whether it was he that they loked for, that aboute that time they knew
shoulde come to saue mankinde, or whether they should loke for another? Because
they shoulde not saye as the Iewes were euer ready and wonte to saye. **Tu de te
ipso testimonium dicis, testimonium tuum non est verum**. Thou bearest witnesse
of thy selfe, thy witnesse is not true.* Christe referred them to his workes that by
them he might allure them to beleue vpon him, knowynge that the blinde were
made to see: The lame were made to goe: The leprouse be made cleane, the deafe
to heare. The deade were raysed to lyfe againe, and that the poore were taughte
the Gospell and good tydynges of lyfe euerlastynge. And at laste he saied vnto
theim. **Beatus est qui non fuerit scandalizatus in me**. Blessed is hee that by me
taketh none occasion to fall, or to offende.* In whiche wordes Christe touched the
messengers and manye others by them. They sawe hym a mortall man as other
were, they could scarce beleue any Godhed in him, yet seinge that Christe knewe
their wan and fainte beleue, and the secretes of their hartes, this made them to
haue more affiance & beleue vpon him, for it is aboue yᵉ knowlege of a pure man
to knowe yᵉ secretes of an other mans minde. They knewe he spoke by them, & he
knew they wer offended by yᵗ thei saw in him [2R4] And not onely these messengers of sainte Iohn, but also manie a thousand others be offended by Christe,
and by Christes woordes euerye daye. Because men see not the bloud runne about
the Priestes fingers in the masse at the fractions of the Sacrament, they be so harde
harted, and so dul in beleue, that thei wil not beleue that Christ saide<,> true
when he saide, this is my bodye, or my fleshe and bloude in the sacrament of the
aultare because thei perceiue not by it as they do bi other fleshe and bloud in the
Shambles, not beleuing that Christe by his Godlye power causeth and maketh his
owne fleshe and bloud there secretelye vnder the fourme of breade and wyne for to
augment and encreace the merite of our fayeth, which shold be smal or none, if we
saw that with our bodelye eyes that wee see by the fayethfull eyes of our christen
hartes.* They that be addict and wedded to their carnall senses, their fyue wits be
offended and agreued to here, that they muste beleue that thinge that they see not.
And euen so they iudge by sacramentall confession of sinnes,* thinkynge men no
more bounde nowe to be confessed, nother anye otherwyse then to God, because
that afore christes time when the sacrament of penaunce was not instituted nor
ordeyned, it was inough to be confessed to god. But now that Christ hath appointed an other maner, somwhat more paineful, men can skant be euen with
Christe, nor contente wyth hym. But haue recourse backewarde, reculynge to the
Iewes custome,* and forsake the way that Christe hath [2R4ᵛ] ordeyned to remitte
sinnes by penaunce, whiche is the onely and necessarye waye to be saued for them
that after the sinceritye of baptisme hathe fallen to sinne againe, if they shall haue
oportunitie to come to it. They that wyll not submit them selues to penaunce, so
ofte hearinge the efficacity of that Sacrament, shal be condemned by the wordes of
Christe, **Mat. xii. Viri Niniuite surgent in iudicio cum generatione ista &
condemnabunt eam quia penitentiam egerunt in predicatione Ione.*** The people
of the greate Citye of Niniue were greatlye geuen to carnall pleasures, and to
vicious liuynge. Wherefore they were threatened that within forty dayes their citye

shoulde bee ouerturned and destroyed, yet by the preachynge of Ionas the prophet they did penaunce in sackclothe, in clothe of heare and asshes, and fasted both man and beaste, as well the kinge and the nobilitie, as the common people. In contemplacion wherof God was mercifull, and turned hys sentence of destruction into mercye and saluation.* They did frutefull penaunce after their maner, and christen folke despise to do penaunce as is prescribed and taught them, and therfore the Niniuites shall condemne the christen folkes at the daye of iudgement, and shall appeare more iust afore God, then christen people shal that wil do no penaunce as they be taught to do. Thus Christ sayth, but very fewe attendeth to his saiynge, or beleueth it, and whye? Because they be sclaundered or offended by Christe. Men see not Christe take the noughty liuers and destroy them [2S1] by and by, nor caste them into the fire afore their faces, but differreth it tyll the sinners be deade, or till the daye of dome, of which men heare very oft, but they se it not, therfore they counte it but tales. And because Christe forbeareth them tyll then, they care for no more, they care not what they dooe. They will beleue no more then they see lyke as dull and brute beastes. And they regarde not to come vnto Sermons to heare the worde of GOD declared, whereby they might learne to beleue that they see not. And therefore the **quene of Saba** in the south parte of the world shall rise in iudgement and shall condemne you. **Math xii.** For she came euen from the fardest and best parte of luckye and frutefull Arabie, liynge on the meridionall Ocean in the vttermost part of the worlde vnto Hierusalem to heare the wisdome and wise wordes of Salomon.* And hee whose wordes you maye heare at Sermons, is muche greater, and much wyser than euer was Salomon. It is almightye God and his increate wisdome, his onely begotten sonne our Sauiour Iesus Christe, whose wordes farre passe the wisedome of Salomon. She came manye hundred miles to heare Salomon. You be so slouthfull and negligent that you be loth to come from the Bridge to the Trinityes* to heare Christes wordes. If you came from beyonde Bedminster or Stapleton* to heare Goddes worde at euerye sermon at the trinities, yet your paynes and labours should not be comparable to the paynes & labours that this noble woman toke to come to [2S1ᵛ] heare Salomon. Therfore at the terrible day of dome she shall be praised for her diligence, where christen people shall be condemned for their slouth and negligence. At Sermons (I saye) you shall be taught to beleue that you see not, as Sainte Iohns disciples (of whiche I spoke euen nowe) were taughte by the checke that Christe gaue them, saiynge: **Blessed is he that is not offended by me.*** By whiche they perceiued that Christe meaned by them that they were offended by him, not beleuyng any Godheade or Godlye power to be in hym, because they considered no more but the infirmitie of the fleshe, whiche they sawe in hym as in other menne, but then perceiuinge that he knewe their thoughts, this made them the more inwardely and earnestlye to consider the myracles and marueilous workes to whiche he referred them, and by that to take hym as one farre aboue a pure man accordyng to saint Iohn Baptistes expectation, for he sente them to Christ (as I saied afore) to aske a question for their owne learnynge, and not for his. For he doubted nothinge what Christe was, nor of his power. And men that now a dayes geueth little credence to the commination and threatenyng that GOD geueth to the synneful people by the mouthes of his preachers, beinge offended and takynge occasion of ruine, and occasion of their hardnesse of harte in not beleuynge, by Goddes longanimitie and longe sufferaunce, because they see not the stroke of God fal by and by, in that folowing the obstinacie of the olde Iewes, for euen so it was in old tyme. The Israelites beleued not the holy [2S2] prophets which were their prechers, because thei saw not the punishementes for sinne come to passe afore their faces, that ye prophetes said wold fall vpon them. Therfore thei made a mock of the prophets words, saiyng in mockage. **Manda remanda, manda remanda, expecta, reexpecta, expecta, reexpecta, modicum ibi, modicum ibi. Esa. xxviii.** * For declaration wherof you must vnderstand that when the holye Prophetes would wythdrawe the people from vyce and Synne, they vsed the worde of Commaundement (as saiyng) God sendeth you worde and commaundeth you, thus to doe, and thus to saye, and thus to lyue. And when they preached or prophecied of Gods benefites that God woulde do for the people if they liued well, and accordynge to hys pleasure, they vsed the worde of **Expectation** and lokyng for, as saiyng, if you keepe his lawes and commaundementes, you may surely loke for plentye of corne and cattell, you may loke for health of bodye, encrease of issue, and to ouercome your enmies, with such other temporal rewardes, which most allured the carnal Iewes for their tyme.* Yea, say the carnal Iewes mockyng the prophets. Commaund & commaund again, commaund & commaund again, loke for and loke for againe, loke for and loke for again. **Modicum ibi modicum ibi,** of your threatenings yt you wold haue vs to feare, & of your faire promises yt we shold loke for, we se litle here, we se litle there. Therfore because you thus order your self to the word of god & to his prechers (saieth the pro. Esai there) euen as you said in your rayling & mocking of [2S2ᵛ] Gods worde so it shall fall vppon you, you shall commaunde and crie for helpe and none shal you haue, you shall commaunde menne to praye for you, and their praiers shall not be hearde, you shall looke for mercye and looke agayne, and little or none shall you haue here, and lesse shall you haue there, none shall you haue at all. **Propter hoc audite verbum domini viri illusores.** Heare the worde of God you mockynge men* that make so light of the worde of GOD in the preachers mouthes, or in the diuine seruice of the churche, whiche is none other but the worde of God. **Dixistis nos percussimus, fedus cum morte & cum inferno fecimus pactum flagellum inundans cum transierit non veniet super nos quia posuimus mendacium, spem nostram & mendatio protecti sumus.** You haue said or you order your selues to gods word euen as though you said thus. We haue stricke handes & made a leege or agrement with death: And we haue made a couenant and a bargayne with hell, we be agreed with death that he shall not take vs, and with Hell that he shall not hurt vs, we be agreed and be frends, we be not afrayed of death nor of hell, we be safe inough. Therfore **Flagellum inundans cum transierit non veniet super nos.** When the scourge of GOD that ouer runneth all like as a flod runneth ouer a whole cuntrey (as the vengeaunce of God doth) it shall not fall on vs nor hurt vs,* all that these commune preachers saieth, threateninge vs be but lies, we trust vpon lyes, and by liers and false flatteryng preachers that geueth vs swete words, and set[2S3]teth vs at libertie to liue as we list, & promiseth faire to vs, we be defended and safe inoughe. I thinke the prophet Esay sawe our time in spirit, or els he could neuer so plainly haue set furth and described our time. For how greatly men be sclaundered, that is to saie, offended and taketh occasion to do naughtely by Gods long suffrance and differing of his stroke, thinking all but fables and trifles that is spoken of Godds vengeaunce, and how little men regarde his preachers takinge all that they saie for very trifles & mockage, it was neuer more in experience in Esays time, then it is in our time. Therfore the said prophet Esai as for a redresse of al these enormities of the old tyme sheweth vs a remedy (if it may be taken) speaking of the same stone that .s. Peter speketh of here, & reciting the same sentence that .s. Peter grounded his saiyng on in the words of his epistle which we haue now in

hand. **Ecce ego mittam in fundamentis Sion lapidem angularem, lapidem probatum preciosum in[ ]fundamento fundatum, qui crediderit non festinet.** S. Paule
.Ro. x. & .s. Peter here readeth **.non confundetur.** * I wil set in the foundation of
Sion (by whiche is vnderstande the Catholike church of Christe, which begone in
Sion, where the holy temple was founded within the citye of Ierusalem)* a corner
stone, tried, and proued, and precious, laied in the foundation. Whosoeuer beleueth on him, let him make no haste (saieth the olde text of Esay) shall not be
ashamed sayeth .s. Peter, and also .s. Paule.* And both commeth to one purpose:
He that beleueth on this stone our sa[2S3ᵛ]uior Christe which is called a stone for
his surenes and fastnes, and stedfastnes. Let him make no haste **.s. querere re-
tributionem. glo. inter.** * to haue furthwith the rewarde for his beleue. Let hym
make no haste to see by and by the threatenynges of GODS woordes spoken by
the Prophetes or Preachers, nor to obtayne and haue by and by the rewardes that
Goddes worde, promiseth vnto theim that do well and vertuouslye. It will not be
had furthwyth, as these, **viri illusores,** these mockers of Gods word,* woulde haue
it. But it is differred till the tyme when it shall do vs more good, as God knoweth
better then we do. And therfore beleue, and at length thou shalt not be confounded, ashamed, or dismayed, accordyng to the letter of saint Peter and also of
saint Paule. And accordynge to thys saith the prophete. **Expecta dominum vi-
riliter age,** & **confortetur cor tuum** & **sustine domine.** Tarye and loke for our
Lorde God, playe the man, & be not so childish as to beleue nothinge that is
promised the, except thou haue it in hand forthwith. And then thy hart shall be
comforted saieth the prophet.* Therfore sustaine & beare with our lord And
likewyse the comminations & threatninge for oppression, extorcion, & such other
misliuyng, that these mockers of Gods worde thinketh wil neuer come because
they see it not at hande, they shall then know, when they shall fele them in dede.
Sola vexatio intellectum dabit auditui. Esay. Onelye the vexation when it commeth, will make you [2S4] to vnderstande that you haue hearde by the prophetes
and preachers.* This Stone is proued and tried (saieth Esay and also Saynt Peter.)
A mason when he shall worke a stone. Firste he will proue whether it be sounde or
not, lest if it breake when he hath laboured on it, his laboure be all lost. He wil
assay the veyne or grayne with his axe, he wil knocke on it with his sledge hammer
or mallet, and if it gerre & sounde not wel, he will caste it by, and not meddle with
it. If it rynge and sounde close like a Bell, then it is for his purpose, good for his
worke. Christ was tried with knockes & manye strokes, and yet he neuer gerred,
nor spoke any worde of anger or debate to theim that stroke him, no more then
the Lambe dothe when he is ledde to the slaughter house. Precious he was, & so
precious, that with the price of his precious bloude, he redemed and bought that
thing out of yᵉ deuils handes that al the riches of the world could not bye again.
He is laied & set in the foundation of the catholike church & yet neuertheles he is
the headstone & the hyest stone of the same, for he is the beginning & also yᵉ
consummation & ending of our beatitude, of al our grace & goodnes. And on him
were leied & set the xii. apostles immediatly & equally, according to yᵉ saiyng of
the **Apo. xxi. Murus ciuitatis habet fundamenta .xii.** & **in ipsis .xij. nomina .xii.
apostolorum agni.** The wal of yᵉ heuenly citie that .s. Iohn saw in his reuelation &
vision, had xii. foundations, or foundation stones, and in them were the names of
the xii. apostles, of the lambe our sauiour Christe.* [2S4ᵛ] And on them equallye
was founded, layed, and set the whole edifice and buildynge of Christes church.
Thus saith .s. Hierome expreslye. **Primo contra Iouinianum.** * And vpon Christ as
vpon the principall foundation, and on them and their holy doctrine al Christes

church, the whole congregation of christen people, and euery man an[d] woman of the same must builde as spiritual houses apt and able for almightye God to inhabite and dwell in. Saint Augustine deuiseth this edifice of Christes church, on Christ and on his apostles nobly well, saiyng: that when the foundation is layed here on earth, the walles be builded vppon it, and the weyght of the walles presseth and weyeth downewarde, because the foundation is beneath alowe, but in asmuch as our foundation is in heauen, we muste be builded vpwarde towarde heauen, and thitherwarde we muste wey and runne, because we must folowe the foundation, and leyne on the foundation. The earthlye buildynge beginneth at the grounde, for there lieth the foundation, but the spirituall foundation is on high in heauen.* Therfore thither toward him our spirituall buildynge must ascende, that we maye be suche spiritual houses, as saint Peter exhorteth vs to be, in the wordes of his epistle which I read now vnto you. And that all may be so, he graunt vs that for vs dyed. Amen.

¶The seuenth treatise or
sermon.

THe blessed Apostle Saint Peter prosecuteth this spiritual buylding that I spoke of
in thend of my last sermon, saying that we muste be buylded on this stone our
sauiour Christ **as an holy priesthoode, offering spirituall sacrifices acceptable to
God by Iesus Christ.** * Occasion of this saying saint Peter toke of the saying of
almighty God by Moyses, to the people of Israel **Exod. xix. If you will heare my
voice, and wil kepe my commaundement, you shall be my peculier and speciall
people of all people: all the world is myne, et vos eritis mihi in regnum sacerdo-
tale et gens sanctata. And I wyll haue you a priestly kingdome and an holy
nation.** * Alluding to this Saint Peter wryteth here **Vos autem genus electum
regale sacerdocium gens sancta populus acquisitionis.** You be a chosen kinred, a
princely or a kingly priesthod, an holy nacion, a people that are wonne.* Thys text
cannot be negligentlye passed ouer, but muste be earnestly loked on, speciallye
because that at this text manye men stumble and hurt them selues, takinge
occasion of heresie. Of this saying of almighty God in Exodo, and the rehersall of
saynt Peter of the same text here in this place, thei wil proue (if they maye) that
all men and women be priestes as well as they that be ordered by a byshops hands,
because that saint Peter writ these wordes to all them that he had preached vnto,
& by them to vs and to all other that shal come after [2T1ᵛ] till the worldes ende,
as wel to women as to men of all degres, and of all ages that were baptised and had
taken vpon them Christes lyuerye.* All such saint Peter calleth **regale sacerdotium,** kings and priestes:* and to confirme theyr opinion they alledge the saying of
saint Iohn in the first chapter of the Apocalips, wher he speaketh of Christ, saying:
**Qui dilexit nos, & lauit nos a peccatis nostris in sanguine suo et fecit nos
regnum et sacerdotes deo et patri suo.** He loued vs and washed vs from our sinnes
in his bloode, and made vs a kingdome & priests to God and to his father.* Of
these authorities the Lutherians take an argument and occasion to confounde and
deface all good order of diuine and humane thinges, allowing the women to serue
the altar, and to say masse while the men tary at home, and keepe the children and
washe theyr ragges and clothes:* and aswell they might allow the women to be
captains of their warres and to leade and gide an army of men in battell, while
theyr husbandes tary at home to mylk the Cowe, and to serue the Sow, and to
spynne and carde. To exchewe suche horrible confusion and misordring of the
worlde that would offende honest eares to heare it, and to declare that if they well
vnderstoode the textes alledged, they should finde none occasion of such errour.
We must returne to the sayd texts, and waigh the sayings of almighty God by
Moyses, to the people of Israel, and the sayinges of S. Peter and saint Iohn, so that
we may conserue and keepe that ordinate Iherarchie and good order amonge
people, that [2T2] God would haue vs to kepe, and that al the gospels and the
Apostles letters be full of. Saynt Ambrose in his first booke **de vocatione gentium,
cap. iii.** * giueth vs a very notable rule to expounde scriptures, and it is the same
rule in effecte that Tichonius putteth for the thirde rule whiche he called **de specie
et genere,** as S. Austine writeth **iii. de doctrina Christiana.** * Saint Ambrose rule
is this: In scripture many times that thing is said and spoken vniuersally of the
whole, which is verified and true onely of the part. He putteth ther many
examples, of whiche some I will reherse, leauing the other for to auoyde prolixitie
and tediousnes. The prophet saith in the psalme: **Alleuat dominus omnes qui**

corruunt et erigit omnes elisos, Our Lord God taketh vp all them that fall, and
setteth vp al them that be broken or brused.* By this texte it seemeth that who
soeuer falleth to sinne, God setteth him vp agayne, or if he be broken against the
stone, (that I spoke of afore) by sinne God setteth hym on his feete agayne,
whiche if it myght be so vnderstande and founde true, then shoulde neuer manne
nor woman be dampned, and then it myghte seeme true that I sayde of the
mockers of Gods woorde that they hadde made a leege with death, and a coue-
naunt with hell, that neyther death nor hell should hurt theym. And oure Sauiour
saythe in the Gospell: **Si exaltatus fuero a terra omnia traham ad me ipsum.** As
thoughe he promysed that when he was crucifyed, he woulde conuert and drawe
[2T2ᵛ] to him all men and women of the world* whiche is not yet performed, but
many persist and continue in infidelitie. And likewise in the negatiues it is written
in the psalme: **Dominus de celo prospexit super filios hominum vt videat si est
intelligens aut requirens deum, omnes declinauerunt simul inutiles facti sunt
non est qui faciat bonum, non est vsque ad vnum. Psa. xiii.** Our lord loked down
from heauen vpon the children of men, to se whither ther wer euer a wyse one, or
one that sought for god, al be wried away, they be al together vnprofitable, without
fruite of good workes.* There is none that doth any good, no not so much as one.
Likewise saith the Apostle. **Phil. ii. omnes que sua sunt querunt non que Iesu
Christi.** All men seeke for theyr own profite, and not those thynges that be for
Christes pleasure.* Here be hard sayinges if they be not helped bi the rule that
saint Ambrose teacheth vs to remember when we expound scriptures. The rule is
this: The scripture speaketh manye tymes of the whole meaninge, but the part of
the same, as speaking of the whole world meaneth but parte of the same, and
speaking of al men, meaneth but part of them.* Or as the Logicion speaketh in
such sayinges of the scriptures, there maye be vnderstand **distributio pro gen-
eribus singulorum, non pro singulis generum, vel e[ ]conuerso.*** As when the
prophet sayde: **that God taketh vp to him all that fall downe.*** For of all them
that falleth, he taketh vp some, and leaueth the other in their filth & myre. And
when Christ said that when he should be exalted on the crosse, he would drawe all
the men & [2T3] women of the world vnto him,* for in deede of all partes of the
worlde some he drewe vnto hym. Likewise the prophet said: all be wryed awaye,*
because that aswel of the Iewes as of the Gentils a great meany declined to idolatry
and to other vices, so that among suche as declined and wryed away, there was
scant one founde good & profitable, that woulde conuert and turne again Where
Saint Paul saith that al seke their own profit, and no man seketh for that Christ
woulde haue theym to seke for,* surelye true it is that among all men a great
manye there be suche, and euen so (saithe sainte Ambrose)* we must vnderstande
the saying of Sainte Peter that we haue now in hande, taken of the sayinge of
almightye God by Moyses to the people of Israel, **you be a chosen kinred, kynges
and priestes,*** the whole for the part, for of the multitude of Christen people there
were and be kinges, and of that multitude should be elect and made priestes, and
not that al the multitude that saint Peter or Saynte Iohn wryt vnto men and
women were all and euerye one of them priestes, no more then they were all
kinges, and yet they be equally called aswell kinges as priestes. Were they all electe
and chosen? were they all holy? were they all wone and goten as a vauntage to
God, to preach and declare the vertue and power of God that called them from
darkenes vnto his marueilous lighte of grace & of his holy gospel? Al this Saint
Peter here reporteth of them that he called kynges and priestes, and yet a great
multitude of theym, & after [2T3ᵛ] vntill our time, and now in our time (God

knoweth) sheweth litle that thei be called to that wonderous and marueilous light, but rather choseth to lye in blinde darknes, and be gladder to heare and learne suche lewde and foolish playes & leud lessons as may kepe them still in theyr blindnes. **Qui aliquando non populus dei, nunc autem populus dei qui non consecuti misericordiam, nunc autem misericordiam consecuti.** To them saint Peter sayth here, that some time they were not Gods people, but now they be Gods people, which is to be vnderstand of part of them, & not of the whole nomber. And so is the other saying to be vnderstand that where sometime they lacked Gods mercye, now they haue gotten gods mercy, which in dede the election of† they that God knew for his owne hathe gotten, where they that be reprobate and naughty and vicious hath it not.* In like maner we say that **tribus Iuda,** was **tribus regia**. The family or house of Iuda, was the house of kynges amonge the people of Israell,* yet they of that house were not al kinges, although the kings of Ierusalem were of that house euer after Saule tyll Herode the first vsurped, comminge in by intrusion by the power of the Emperour of Rome.* We say also that **tribus Leui erat tribus sacerdotalis,** the family, house, or issue of Leui was yᵉ house of pristes, for ther shuld none be prestes by Moises law, but onely of that tribe, yet for al this saying, which is true, they were not all priestes that were of yᵗ tribe or kinred although they were al ministers in the temple in some office hygher or [2T4] lower in the same.* Euen so the Apostle calleth vs kynges and priestes,* for of Christen people there be, and hath be, and shalbe some kinges and some priests, for if a man woulde egerly and frowardly by these textes of the Apostles, proue all Christen people to be priests, he must by the same graunt that al Christen men and women be kinges, which a madman woulde not saye, and so he shoulde be worse then mad, excepte they woulde transferre the name of kinges to a spirituall vnderstanding, calling theym kinges that can rule their owne passions, affections, and sensual appetites, which to do is a princely poynt, and a part of a noble man. **Prouer. xvi. Melior est patiens viro forti & qui dominatur animo suo expugnatore vrbium** Better is the pacient man, then he that is strong of bodye: and he that ruleth his own wil, is more to be esteemed, then he that conquereth townes and countreys.* For the conquest of townes and countreys is outfurth, the other is inward, when a mannes harte ouercommeth it selfe, and subdueth hym selfe vnto hym selfe, whyche the conquerours commonlye do not, but rather be ouercome of theyr owne concupiscence, ambition and couetuousnesse. Well, if ye wyll take kynges in suche a spirituall signification, then I praye you be content to take the name of a prieste in a lyke spirituall sygnifycation, and so let vs call all theym priestes that be the spiritual members of the hyghe Priest oure Sauioure Iesus Christe by parte takynge of hys priesthoode.

[2T4ᵛ] And then like as they that be spiritually kyngs, be not kinges anoynted with materiall oyle, for the office of a king, as all kinges were by the old law, and also be now adayes in the time of grace neither hath like authoritie, might, and power ouer realmes and countries, as such kynges hath. Euen so you must vnderstand of the mistical and spiritual priestes, and theyr priesthode, that it is not of such authoritie, efficacitie and strength, as is the priesthoode of them that by materiall oyle and imposicion of the bishoppes hands be consecrate and made priestes for suche offyces as almighty God by his scriptures hathe assigned to them, of which I shall speake anon.* This spirituall priesthode is no more but our baptisme, or Christendome, in whyche we be anoynted with that oyle of gladnes

† of] or

the holye Gost, gyuen vs at our baptisme, which Christe had **pre consortibus suis** afore and aboue all vs his coparteners.* And of his plenty of that grace of the holye Goste we take our part after suche measure as it pleaseth him to distribute vnto vs.* And after this maner saynt Peter here wylleth vs to be builded on the lyuing stone **as spirituall houses, and as a holy presthoode offering spirituall sacrifices acceptable to god by Iesus Christ.** * And this priesthode is common to all men, as well lay men as priestes. And Saynt Iherome in his dialoge **contra luciferianos** calleth this **sacerdotum Laicum** the lay priesthod indifferent to all men and women that be christned, & theyr spiritual sacrifices that they offer be proporcionable to theyr presthod as the sacrifice of iustice, [2V1] the sacrifice of **laude and praise of god,** the sacrifice of prayer and such other, as be common to al maner of good men and women:* And such as saynt Paule **Rom. xii.** prayeth euery person to offer to God, saying: **obsecro vos per misericordiam dei vt exhibeatis corpora vestra hostiam sanctam viuentem deo placentem.** I pray you for the mercye of God, that you giue your bodies as an holye hoste, as a liuing sacrifice pleasant to almighty God by our sauiour Iesus Christ.* These be the spiritual hostes that saynt Peter speaketh of here, and these be euery man and womans sacrifices that wyll shewe them selues to be of Christes faith and beliefe, and these be made acceptable to God by the merites of our sauiour Iesus Christe, on whom we beleue. By this you may iudge how far wide from this generall laye presthoode, and from the sinceritie of theyr Christendome they be that wil neither sacrifice to God **iustice** or rightuous dealing, but vseth al oppression, extorcion, theft and bribery, neither will giue to God the sacrifice of **laude,** praise, and thankes,* but rather blasphemy to Gods reproche, and to his dispite, and wil not vse prayers in the church nor in other places, but rather with their babling in the church, and mocking of diuine seruice letteth and hindreth other men from theyr praiers, and from attending and hearing gods seruice. They giue not theyr bodies as a holy sacrifice to God, but rather as a stincking sacrifice to the fleshe & to the diuel, not liuely but sinfull and deadly, not pleasant, but as an instrument of mischiefe, displeasant to God and [2V1ᵛ] man. There is an other priesthode whiche is one of the seuen sacramentes, called the order of presthode, farre aboue the foresayd lay priesthoode in dignitie and in authoritie. This order and dignitie of priesthode our sauiour Christe gaue to hys disciples after his last supper when he toke breade in his handes, and conuerted it into his bodye by these words saying: **This is my body.** And taking the cuppe with wine in his handes, he sayd: **This is my blood.** * And consequently he sayd to his disciples: **Hoc facite in meam commemorationem,** do you this that I haue done, and so doing remember me:* where he gaue theim authoritie to consecrate bread and wine into his blessed bodye and bloode as he had done. And in this he gaue them power on him selfe, and on his owne verye bodye and bloode, in which consisteth the chief office of a prieste, and giuing theym power to consecrate that most reuerend sacrament of the alter, he made them priestes, and wyth all in so doinge, he instituted and ordeyned the sacrament of order. And after hys gloryous resurrection, he gaue vnto the sayde Apostles power and iurisdiction vpon hys misticall body, that is, the churche or multitude of Christen people. When he came in amonge the Apostles, the doores of the chaumber beyng fast shutte, and sayde vnto them: **Pax vobis** peace be amonge you, and then he breathed vpon them and sayde: Take you the holye Gost, whose synnes you forgiue, shall bee forgiuen, and whose synnes you retay[n]e and not forgiue, shall be retayned and not forgyuen.* And as the Apo[2V2]stles tooke theyr order of priesthoode at Christes handes, giuing them the holy gost, by which they had authoritie on his own body, and also on his misticall body which is the church and the multitude of Christen people, so the Apostles by imposicion and layinge their handes on suche as they chose for to be priestes or bishops made theym priests, geuing them authoritie to consecrate Christes bodye and bloode, and to minister the sacrament of penaunce, forgiuyng sinnes, and retayning sinnes as they see it necessary, and likewise to minister all other duties of a priest.* The holye Goste spoke to the ministers of the churche that were in Antiochia: **Segregate mihi Saulum et Barnabum in opus ad quod assumpsi eos. Act .xiii.** And it foloweth, **tunc ieiunantes & orantes imponentesque eis manus dimiserunt eos.** With fasting & praying and leyng theyr holy hands on Saule (afterward called Paule) and on Barnabas they ordred theym priestes, and sent them furthe to execute priestes offices.* Saint Paule writeth vnto his scoler Timothe: **Noli negligere gratiam que in te est, que data est tibi per propheciam cum impositione manuum presbiterij. i. Timo .iiii.** Be not neglygent in the grace that is gyuen thee by prophecye, wyth leynge the Priestes handes vpon thee.* **Prophecye** he called here (after Saynt Ambrose)* the election by whyche he was chosen as one that shoulde bee a meete Minister and teacher in Christes Churche. And suche prophecye is vsed, or shoulde bee vsed to thys daye in makynge of Pryestes, where the Byshoppe [2V2ᵛ] or his sufficient depute sitteth vpon opposicions of them that shall be made priests wher he ought to haue mature and discrete examinacion aswell of his maners and conuersation, as of his learning, **oportet autem illum testimonium habere bonum ab hijs qui foris sunt. i. Timo. iii.** He ought to haue good report of the infidels* (saythe Saynte Paule) & then much more he ought to haue good reporte of the layfe, that be neither priestes nor ministers of the church, vpon which examinacion if the bishop and his officers thinke him meete to be a priest, they set him furth to the bishops handes to take orders. This allowing of his lyuing and of his learning, with hope that he will so continue and increace in goodnes, is it that S. Paul in this place calleth **prophecie. Imposition** of the bishops handes, hath with it concurring certeine holy wordes, by which wordes he (as I sayde afore) is confirmed, made strong and able to exercise that he was chosen to, takinge authoritie by which he may be bolde to offer sacrifices to God in Christes steede. And because of the perill that is in making vnworthy priestes, S. Paule warneth Timothe **.i. Tim. v. Manus cito nemini imposueris, neque communicaueris peccatis alienis.** Wher s. Paule with a contestacion as Timothe shuld answer afore God and our sauiour Christ, and hys elect Angels of heauen commaundeth him that he be not to easy and light to set his holy handes on any man to promote him to that ecclesiastical dignitie of priesthode, because he will nothing to be done in giuing orders without a foresight and a [2V3] fore iudgement, lest peraduenture if he be found reproueable and vicious, the bishop that promoted him, may repent his dede, and also least he be contaminate & partaker of the vices of hym that he hath ordered, because he hath suffered hym so lightly to passe his handes without sufficient trial of his liuing. Manye other authorities of scripture, and specially of S. Paule I could reherse, in which it doth euidently appeare how prescise he is in the sayd order of priesthoode, and howe it doth surmount the other common anointing, by which all they be anoynted that be christened, (as I sayde) for thoughe all they that be anoynted at theyr baptisme be enbrued with the holye goste, yet by imposition of the bishops handes on hym that is ordered with the holy wordes concurrent with the same, the holy goste is giuen to a prieste for to giue him authoritie in an higher office that euery man may not attain to: As for to consecrate the body and bloud of our sauiour Christe in the most reuerend sacrament of the aulter, & to minister other sacramentes, and specially the sacrament of penance,* which in this holy time all well disposed good christen people run to, as to the necessary remedy to saue their soules. Here I shuld more largely demore and tarie on this sacrament of penance, but that I remember that here afore declaring those wordes of S. Peter in the fyrste chapter, **secundum misericordiam suam magnam regenerauit nos in spem viuam.** I touched that matter sufficiently.*

¶The .viii. treatise or
sermon.

CHarissimi obsecro vos tanquam aduenas et peregrinos abstinere vos a car-
nalibus desiderijs que militant aduersus animam. &c.* These wordes which
immediately foloweth the processe that I preached of in my last sermon on Sainte
Peters epistle, be red in the church this present Sunday for the epistle in the
Masse,* where in contemplation of that he had sayde immediately afore, that they
were sometyme not the people of God, but rather Idolaters and the people of the
dyuell, and that nowe they were the people of God, conuerted to the beliefe on
one God and on our Sauiour Christ by hearyng the preachinge of Christes gospell,
and that sometyme they were without Gods mercye, and that now they had
obtayned his mercy. By reason of this he calleth them **very welbeloued,** and as his
welbeloued children and friendes he entreateth theym to vse vertue and to giue to
all them among whom they shuld be conuersant example of holy conuersation and
liuing. And afterwarde he exhorteth them to due subiection towarde theyr heades
and rulers. I beseche you (sayth he) as Straungers and Pylgrimes to kepe your
selues from carnall desyres which fight against the soule.* This obsecration or
beseching signifyeth a certayne vehemencie in desiring as it wer for Gods sake, or
for the loue of our Lady, or of al the sayntes of heauen, or for their faithes sake, by
which thei trusted to be sa[2V4]ued, of which he had spoken much afore.* So he
praieth them, and not after the imperious commaunding of Bishops & theyr
officers, which yet haue not al layd away the lowrynge browes of the phariseis.*
Not that I deny but that bishops and theyr discrete officers may commaund them
that be of theyr iurisdiction to do the thing that is conformable to Gods commaundement, and if the contumacie & sturdines of the partie proceede so far that
they will not be reformed by reason, & by fayremeanes, then to compel them by
the sensures of the church to amend theyr liues, as saynt Paule did by the notorious adulterer that kepte his own mother in law to paramour in Corinth.* And
he bid **Titus .ii. Hec loquere & exhortare et argue cum omni imperio,** that he
shuld rebuke them that be sturdy and fauty with al authority to commaund,* albeit
when desiring or beschinge maye serue, it doth best beseme a prelate or a curate,
& therefore S. Paule writing to his scoler and louing friend **Philemon,** saith:
**Multam fiduciam habens . . . imperandi tibi, quod ad rem pertinet propter
charitatem magis obsecro.** I may be bold to commaund the to do the thing that
shalbe for the profit of thi soule, but yet for the loue that I haue to thee, I had
leauer pray thee to be good to **Onesimus** thy seruant.* And euen so S. Peter might
haue bene bold to commaund them that he wrot vnto, but he had leauer desyre
them as straungers & pylgrimes We call them straungers that dwell not in theyr
owne countrey, but in a straunge place.* So saint Peter wylleth vs to count our
selues as not at [2V4ᵛ] home in our owne countrey, because that by the faute of our
fyrst parentes we be banished from Paradise, which God gaue vs to dwel in, and be
come into this vale of misery and sorowe, not to liue delicatelye, and to take oure
pleasure, but to take paine and sorow, and to do penance, and not to settle our
selues on worldly wealth and pleasures here, but to go furth like pilgrimes or
waifaring men, considering that we haue no steddye and permanent citie here, but
that we seke for an other, the citie of heauen aboue.* Like as Saynt Paule speaketh
of Abraham, Isaac and Iacob, and others. **Heb. xi.** which abiding in the lande of
Canaan, and had not receiued the promyses made vnto them, confessinge that

they wer Pilgrimes and straungers vpon earthe, signifieth that they seke for a better habitacion and dwellinge place, that is to say, the countrey of heauen aboue.* An old vse hath peruerted the name of a Pilgryme, because folke were wont to go from place to place to honour saintes in places dedicate for theyr honour, and to kysse theyr images, and they onelye in times past were call<l>ed Pilgrimes, therefore nowe men thinke the proper signification of this worde Pilgrime to be none other but such as goeth about such deuocions,* but his significacion is more generall, it signifieth a wayfaringe man or woman that abideth not still in one place, but remoueth from place to place, tyll at the laste he may come to his iourneys ende where he woulde be,* and in suche case we be, neuer at rest, but euer laboring through the troublous stormes of thys [2X1] world, to come to our inheritance and dwelling place that God hath made for vs, and that our sauiour Christe by his blessed bloud is entred in afore vs, to make vs roume. And therfore let vs do as wise pilgrimes dooe when they intende to take a great iourney vppon theim. They dispose such goodes as they haue, and set theim in safe custodye, and prouideth for their family or housholde. We knowe not when we shal be called to take this farre iourney out of thys worlde into an other worlde, as long as we be here, wee be euer onward, and entred on this iourney. Therfore it is necessary that we bestow our goodes on charitable workes, so settyng them in safe custodye, and that we order our family, that is to say: all the powers of our bodyes and of our soules, prouidyng for them accordingly, as the man did that toke his iourney into a farre countrey. **Mat. [xx]v. He called his seruauntes and deliuered them his goods*** So muste we geue to some of our familye .v. talentes to be well occupied against our lordes returne when he shall come to the iudgemente to sitte on oure audite: our bodye muste be charged with .v. senses, which we cal our fiue bodely wits They must be well employed, well spent, & well ordered: So that we close theim vp agaynst all thinges that shall be contrary to Gods pleasure. That our eare heare no yll wordes, that our eye se no vnhonest thing, that our mouth delight not in thinges that be to swete & delicate, nor speake any filthines, neither any lyes. And that we open the same our senses to all thinges perteynynge [2X1ᵛ] to Goddes pleasure, that our eare do gladly hear the worde of God, and diuine seruice, and all communication of honestye. And that we conforme our eyes and our mouth likewise to such honesty. To the seconde Seruaunt that is Reason, wee muste geue science and knowledge, in whiche he maye exercise it selfe, and haue delection in that is good and maye detest and eschewe that is yll. To the thirde seruaunt that is our Wyll, wee must geue one talent, that is the loue of god, & we must beware, lest when we haue this talent committed vnto vs, we dygge an hole in the ground and in the same hyde the money of our Lorde in earthly and worldlye thinges, as the proud man in excellencye and auctoritie, superfluous and gaye apparell, And the couetous man in worldlye wealth and riches. And the lecherous man in delectation of the flesshe. Seconde, a Pylgryme muste take diligent hede that he kepe the waye towarde hys countrey, the waye of the commaundementes of GOD that he lose not that waye. And if peraduenture he goe oute of that waye, he hadde neade of Penaunce to reduce hym into the right waye by the direction of grace, whiche communely is conferred and geuen to all Penitentes. Thirde, a Pylgryme hadde neade to beware that he make not too longe tariynge by the waye, but daylye kepe hys dayes iourneyes, proceadynge frome vertue to vertue, lyke as a Bee tarieth not styll [2X2] on one Flower, but flyeth frome Flower to flower, to gather her Waxe and Honye.* Vertue dooeth strengthen our Soules in the exyle and banishemente of thys worlde.

Fourthe, in as muche as the whole lyfe of a good christian manne is **Desyre**, therefore althoughe a Pilgryme by reason of hys bodye be in the waye, yet by hys minde he shoulde be euer in his countrey, hauynge hys minde vpon Heauen, and euer desierynge the same. And therefore Christe teacheth vs thus to praye, **Adueniat regnum tuum,** Wee desyre that thy Kyngedome maye come.* Fyfte, a Pilgryme shoulde not ouer lode hym selfe wyth superfluities, but onelye wyth such thynges that shall be necessarye for hys waye. **i. Timo. vi. Habentes alimenta & quibus tegamur his contenti simus.** Hauynge meate, and drynke, and clothe, let vs be so content.* Syxte, a Pylgrime shoulde not stryue and varye, nor goe to lawe wyth theim that be borne in the countrey where hee traueyleth, that is to saye: with worldlye persons, as **Cicero** saieth **.i. offi. Perigrini est minime curiosum esse in re publica aliena.** The office of a Pilgrime is not to be to busye in a straunge comminaltye,* but must suffer mockes and other hurtes as thei of the countrey will dooe vnto him. Wee shall finde in oure waye manye flatterynge Hostes, and Hosteses, and diuers wanton Tapsters that wyll entyce vs by their good cheare to tarrye styll wyth theim, and so for to spende [2X2ᵛ] our selues and our goodes amonge them. Saint Peter telleth vs what they be, and biddeth vs beware of them. Carnall desires he calleth them or fleshely lustes, and biddeth vs abstayne from them, because they fight agaynst the soule.* The flesh desireth ease, the flesh desireth new knacks with chaunge of pleasures. The fleshe desireth swetenes of tastynge and of touchynge. By the fleshe I meane carnal men and women geuen to folowe the inclination of the bodye. For the first, the fleshe woulde haue rest, and abhorreth paine and labour, and had leuer rust for slouthe and idlenes, then to shyne fayre and bright wyth labour. The plowmans share or culter of his plow if it be well occupied it sheweth faire and bryght and doth much good, if it lye vnoccupied in a corner, it rusteth and cankereth to naught, and doth no manne good. So with labour a man shall be shininge and bright afore God and man, and shal do muche good where the slothfull man shall be euer vnprofitable and nothinge set by, like the weuyll in the corne, and a verye spill paine. The scripture speaketh shame of him. **Eccle. xxii. In lapide luteo lapidatus est piger & omnes loquentur super aspernationem illius.** The slouthful person is stoned with a stone of myre, and euery man shall speake of the shame that he shall be put to, where by the hardines of the stone & the filthines of the mire, is signified the harde and vyle punishment that the idle person shall susteyne.* And the same sentence is aggrauate by that commeth after in the same chapter. **De stercore boum lapidatus est pi[2X3]ger & omnis qui tetigerit eum excutiet manus.** The slouthefull shall be stoned with oxe dunge, and euerye manne that toucheth him shall shake his handes from the filthe. Euery man that is conuersant with him, and partaker of his vice, must nedes make cleane his handes, and make amendes by penance. The same text is otherwyse expounded, vnderstanding by the oxen the prechers of the worde of God,* accordynge to the saiyng of Moyses. **Non alligabis os boui trituranti in horreo.** which saynte Paule vnderstandeth of the preachers whiche ought not to haue their mouthes mouselled or so bounde vp, but that they maye take their sustenaunce and liuyng by their preachynge:* then by the dunge of these Oxen may be vnderstande the sharpe and harde reprehensions by whiche they rebuke suche dull and idle sluggardes,* wyth such oxe dunge the slouthful sluggard must be stoned and beaten as is abouesaid. And he must be serued like an yl willy bondman or seruaunt. **Seruo maliuolo tortura & compedes mitte illum in operationem ne vacet. Eccle. xxxiii.** He must haue soore punishment and prisonment by the heles, and must be set to worke lest he be idle. **Multam enim malitiam**

docuit ociositas. For ydlenes is chiefe maistres of all vyces, and of all malyce and mischiefe.* And where this vice of slouth and idlenes is greatly to be feared of all christen people, yet most of the nobilitie, which be most ydlely brought vp in youth, and therfore it wyll be harde for them to leaue it in age. Secondlye I sayde the fleshe woulde take pleasure with wan[2X3ᵛ]ton knackes, rayment of the newe tricke, with curious and costlye chaunge of the same, And with newe inuentions of learninge, neuer content with the olde, be it neuer so good, but euer vagynge and rouynge curiouslie for newe and newe. It deliteth in bawdye songes, vnhonest and filthye playes, or pageantes, enterludes of scismes, dissention, & heresies,* which carnall men & women be gladder to folow, & to pay monie to hear their own bane & very poyson to their soules then to come to hear a sermon for their soules helth whiche they maye haue here many times by the kinges prouision, and cost them nothinge. They be also curious, busie, and inquisitiue to heare newes of their neighbours liuynges, and communelie lighteth more on mennes vices (if anye be) then on their vertues, and be readye to publishe them and blast them abroade, and to make all matters worse, rather then to amende them, and make them better, vncharitablye, and verye deuillyshelye. This curious and busye roauinge of mennes fansies aboute diuersities of thinges, shall neuer saciate nor please a manne, but rather a manne by suche newe fanglenes is made more hongrie and more greadie, and neuer content. For the wise man saieth. **Non saciatur oculus visu nec auris auditu impletur. Eccle. i.** There is nothinge by seynge or hearying in this worlde, that can fullye saciate the appetite of manne. But by the sighte, and by the hearing manne is rather sturred and moued, to desire yet more and more.* Therefore **Optimum est [2X4] gratia stabilire cor. Hebre. xiii.**

Beste it is euerye manne to praye for grace, and by grace to staye his harte as a shippe is stayed by the Ancre for feare of crasshinge.* For commonlye these curious and busy medlyng wittes after they haue longe roued, they fall vppon some noyfull fantasie that pleaseth theim for the tyme, & there they settle their hartes to their owne confusion and worldely shame, with daunger of damnation euerlastynge. Thirde, the flesh that is to say, carnall people, desireth the swetenes of tastinge and touchinge. Of tastynge, as of delicate and pleasaunte meates and drinkes, and the swetenes of touchinge, as bracyng and kissynge, and consequently, of the workes of lecherye. Of all these saieth Sainte Paule. **Si secundum carnem vixeritis moriemini.** If ye lyue after these desires of the fleshe, you shall dye for euer.* For they fight like cruell Souldiours againste the saluation of our Soules. And saint Paule. **Gala. v Caro concupiscit aduersus spiritum, spiritus autem aduersus carnem. Hec enim sibi inuicem aduersantur vt non quecunque vultis illa faciatis.** The flesshe coueteth and woulde fayne haue agaynste the Spirite, and the spirite agaynst the flesshe, for these bee ennemyes one to an other, so that you maye not dooe the thinges that you woulde dooe.* As he saieth also **.Rom. vii.** The good thinge that I woulde dooe, I do not, but the ill that I hate, that I do. I delite in the law of God by my inner man, but I perceiue a law or an inclination in my limmes of my body yᵗ [2X4ᵛ] haleth me like a bond man into the law of sinne. And in the same chapiter he saieth, I my selfe by my minde serue the law of God, but by my flesh I serue the lawe of synne.* A wonderous thinge it is, that there should be suche a continuall battail and deadly conflict in man, betwixt the soule and the bodie, in which commonly the body, that is the worst part of man, hath the ouer hand and the better side. And the soule very folishly taketh pleasure in the bodye, whiche is his mortall enemye, and woulde brynge hym to naughte. Myghte not he be counted a foole that would make merye in hys mortall

Enemyes house, and woulde there spende hym selfe, his money, and his tyme as his fooe his hoste woulde haue him do? And yet it is a marueile how this maye be, that the bodye and the soule shoulde bee enemies, or that betwixt them shoulde be any conflict or strife, for as saint Ciprian saith. **In prolo. li. de operibus christi.*** The soule vseth the limmes and membres of the bodye, as a smith vseth hys hammer or anveld as his tooles to worke with, then what emnitie can be betwixte theim, more then is betwixt the workeman and his toole? And also considering that the body is as it were the shoppe in whiche the soule worketh all thing that he wil. There he formeth and fashioneth the similitudes and images of all filthines and of al malicious driftes. The bodye is not the doer or causer of the synne but the soule, for to him is geuen free libertie of will, by which he may haue delectation and consent to prosecute the synne, or [2Y1] to skippe backe from it, and to auoide it. The bodye (you knowe) when the soule is gone is wythout any sence, & is mete for no vse, but is a verye stinkynge lumpe of earth and carren. Therfore (saieth S. Cypriane) when we say that the flesh or the body fighteth against the soule & the soule agaynste the bodye, it is vnproperlye spoken. **Quia solius animelis ista est que secum rixatur & cum proprio arbitrio litigat.** This contencion is onely of the soule, which striueth with it self & with his own libertye wythin it selfe. The maner foloweth there. **Desiderii sui veneno mens ebria corpus contumeliis applicat, & iunctis complexibus ambo in mortiferas suauitates elapsi obdormiunt.** The mind as it were beinge dronke with the poyson of his owne desire, applieth and setteth the body to dispiteful and noughtye workes, and so the bodye and the soule embracyng them selfes, slippeth into mortall pleasures both together, and slepeth in them. But when they awake, and the dede is past, & they remembreth them selues, most commonly ye horror of their sinne maketh them confused & ashamed. And euer such a vengeance or correction foloweth the sinner, that when he hath taken to much and surfeted in his owne lustes, he vometeth and braketh it out vpon him self, as it were one angry and wery of him self, and of his naughty doyng: God hath so prouided for the sinner, that he shall be his owne scourge. And thys is commen in all synnes, excepte Auaryce (sayeth Saynte Cypriane) in whyche it dothe not so well appeare, for the couetous persone is neuer wea[2Y1^v]rye of gatherynge and heapynge goodes together, that he maye sacrifice to his Idole mammon the God of Auarice and ambicion, he is neuer ashamed whether it bee hys owne, or other mennes, so that he maye by catchinge and scrapinge gette it to hym. And therefore it is a very true saiynge: **Omnibus viciis senescentibus sola auaritia inuenescit.** When all vices waxe olde, couetise onely waxeth yonge againe.* **Conuersationem vestram inter gentes habentes bonam. &c.*** Where Sainte Peter exhorteth them that he writte to, and vs by them, that they should be of good conuersation among them that thei dwelled among, <that> where they rayle and backebite you, saiyng euill of you, callynge you foles, because you leaue their superstitions and Idolatrye, callinge you malefactours, and naughtye liuers, reputynge the sorowe and paynes that you suffer, to be inflicte and layed vppon you for your sinnes and ill liuing. Yet when thei do consider you and wey your condicions by the good woorkes that they see you vse, they maye glorifye and laude God at the daye of their visitation, when God shall visite their Soules by his grace to take example of your good liuynge, and to followe the same, and by example of you to conuerte theim selues to the faieth that you be of. Here you may note howe the blessed Apostle estemeth good example geuynge, it is the thinge that is necessarye for all menne that wil be saued for their owne part. [2Y2] And it is the occasion and cause of the saluation of all others with whom they be conuersaunte. And the glorye in heauen shall be exceadyngly encreased by the confluence and comminge thither of them that haue bene conuerted to vertue by occasion of thy good example: where contrarye, euill example geuinge shall damne him that geueth it. **Ve homini per quem scandalum venit.** Woe, that is, dampnation euerlasting shal come to him that geueth occasion of ruyne or of sinne,* and shall damne all them that by this euil example take occasion of sinne, and by their dampnation the paines of the euyll example geuer, shall be greuouslye encreased, when he shall mete with theim in Hell, that shall come thither by his example geuinge. This knewe full well the riche glotton that was buried and laied in Hell, when he desiered Abraham to sende one home to hys brethren and their familyes, to bidde theim amende their lyues that they come not here.* This desire came of no charitie, for in Hell is no charitie, but it was onelye for the cause aforesaide. He knewe well that the euill example that hee hadde geuen theim by his lyfe tyme to eate and drinke, to reuell and riote, to go gorgeouslie and in fine, softe, and riche apparaile, to followe the lustes of the fleshe, to vse crueltie, oppression, and extorcion in the countrey to gather riches as he hadde done, shoulde brynge theim thither to him, to the great cumulation & encrease of his [2Y2ᵛ] sorowe, and so for his owne ease he willed theim well, for feare lest by their damnation, he should haue more sorowe and paine in hell. Saint Peter likewise in these wordes sheweth vs that although commonly, **Cum sancto sanctus eris, . . . & cum peruerso peruerteris.** With the holy, a man shalbe holy, and wyth a frowarde synner, a man shall be naughtye and synnefull, for lyke maketh like.* Yet the other is not impossible that the naughty maye lyue amonge the good, and the good maie lyue amonge the euill. For Iudas was naught with Christe, and with the other of the Apostles that were good. And Abraham, Isaac, Iacob, Ioseph, Iob, Thoby, and suche others, were verye good amonge theim that were naught. Euen as you see in natural example. A goodlie Rose springeth vp amonge the thornes, and a goodlye Oke amonge the rughe bryer bushes. A candle geueth best lyghte in the darke, and the Starres sheweth fayrest in the night. If your conuersation shall be seene good to theim that you shall dwell amonge, you muste beware of the .vii. faultes that be spoken of. **Prouer. vi. Sex sunt que odit Dominus, & septimum detestatur anima eius.** There be syxe thynges that oure Lorde hateth, and the seuenth his minde abhorreth.* You muste beware you haue not **Oculos sublimes,** hye lokes, by manifest signes settynge furthe your pryde, it wyll be longe afore anye such allure menne to goodnesse by their example, but rather menne shall hate theim, and also their condicions, fewe men can well agree wyth [2Y3] them, **Linguam mendacem,** You muste be no lyers, but to haue a true tongue in your head, and not accustomed to pernicious and perillous lyes who wyll set by suche a lyer, or learne anie good by his euyll example. **Manus effundentes sanguinem innoxium.** An homicide or murtherer, that will kyll or procure the deathe of theim that be innocente and haue not offended. **Cor machinans cogitationes pessimas.** He that hath a venemous harte, euer studiynge to hurte hys neighboure. Suche an harte muste neades nowe and then burste out and shewe it selfe, it will no more be kept in, then fyre couered vnder strawe, whiche muste neades burst out in one place or an other. **Pedes veloces ad currendum in malum,** Euer readye to do harme and to hurte their neighbours, as when they perceiue a man prone and ready to anger, with him thei wil be doing, as thinking it is a good sport to kindle him & make hym angry & to make him fight & brawle, or to blaspheme god, nother regardynge the deathe of their brother, nor the despite of God.* He that hath burned a pore mannes house thatched wyth strawe, might thynke he hadde greuouslye offended, then you may be sure that he hath not a litle offended that hath burned Gods house, hys euen christen. And euen suche they bee that prouoketh others to dronkennesse, or to anye other vyce, euer runnynge and readye to do shrewde turnes. And as **Titus** the noble Emperoure **Vespasians** sonne was wont to saie, that he had lost the daye, when peraduenture in the daye he had not done some [2Y3ᵛ] man good. **Amici, hodie diem perdidi, quia nemini benefeci.*** So, contrary they thinke the daye lost in whiche they haue not done some man hurte, either by backebityng men or sclaundering them raylinge or mockinge them, or picking and stealinge from them, or otherwise. **Proferentem mendacia testem fallacem.** Where afore the wiseman hadde reproued generallie a liynge tongue, Here he reproueth speciallye the lier, that will in open iudgemente geue false testimonie and witnesse, bothe to hurte his neighbour, and also to peruert iustice, whiche is hurt to the common wealthe. The seuenth and worste of all whiche God abhorreth, is **Qui seminat inter fratres discordiam.** He that soweth discorde and debate among brethren.* Wee be all brethren in God, and GOD woulde haue vs to loue like brethren, to agree in one minde and one wyll in God like brothers, to agree in opinions, **Vt idipsum dicatis omnes & non sint in vobis scismata.** That one faith, an other should saie, without scismes, diuersities of minds in thinges concerninge our fayeth, ceremonies, and vsages of Christes churche,* of such diuersity of opinions commonlye foloweth dissention and debate betwixt neighbour & neighbour, by which the vnitie of the church, the vnitie of the congregation of Christes people is dissolued and cast asunder, whiche GOD mooste desiereth to haue kept and knitte together by the bonde and knot of charitie, and abhorreth the contrarye. If we eschewe and auoyde all these seuen, our conuersation shall seme good to them that wee occupye [2Y4] wythall, and dwell amonge, so that when they consider our good workes, they may take example of the same, and haue a cause to saye well by vs, and to glorifye God by vs, whiche shall (through Christes helpe) returne to the common comfort of vs all in heauen. Amen.

The ninth treatice or
Sermon.

SVbiecti igitur estote omni humane creature propter deum.* In these wordes which I haue taken to declare vnto you, Saynte Peter willeth vs to geue example of due subiection and humilitie, whiche is the mother and keper of vertues. Be you subiect (saith he) and lowly to al maner of men constitute and set in auctoritie ouer you, whether they be faiethfull or infidels, as moost parte of them were at that time, vnder whom they liued that .s. Peter wrote his epistle vnto, in the countreys rehearsed. **Pontus, Galatia, Capadotia. &c.*** This we must do, not only for fear of punishment, but rather for discharge of conscience,* because it is gods will we shold so do. Witnesseth .s. Paule: **Ro. xiii. Non est potestas nisi a deo, . . . & qui potestati resistit dei ordinationi resistit.** There is no power but it commeth of god, & therefore he y^t resisteth power & auctoritie of office resisteth gods ordinaunce & so worketh toward his owne damnation.* **Siue regi quasi presellenti.** As well [2Y4^v] to the Kynge as chiefe ruler in his realme, in all temporall auctoritie, as to dukes and other captayns or officers sent from him to do vengeance, punish-emente, and correction, on malefactours and euyll doers, and to the laude and prayse of theim that be good.* Sainte Peter knewe no precellencye or excellencye ouer a whole realme, bearinge the sworde of Iustice, and hauynge the execution of Iustice ouer all his subiectes, but in the kynge whom he calleth Precellent, which I take for a more magnificente and noble terme then Excellent. Example. In an vniuersitie many be excellent clerkes, as it were out of the common sort, & passyng a great meyny of them that be learned, but none may well be called precellent but he that passeth them all in learnyng. So in auctoritie he is Precellent that passeth all other power and aucthoritye, whiche in his owne realme, and in the adminis-tration of Iustice ouer his owne subiectes, is onely the king, & therfore from him is deriued the ministration of iustice to all inferiour Iusticiers, iudges, & iustices. The auctoritie of a king ouer his subiects† is wel set furth .iii. Esd. iiii.* **O viri num precellunt homines qui terram & mare obtinent.** O sirs be not those men Precel-lente & highest of all in might & power, that kepeth both the land & sea, and all that is in them. **Rex autem super omnia precellit.** Such is the Kynge, for he is hyghest, & ouer al, and is lord of them. Here he vseth the word Precellent, which .s. Peter vseth. **Et omnia quecunque dixerit illis faciunt.** Al y^t the king biddeth them do thei do* And if he send them to his army in his wars, thei [2Z1] go, and there they pull downe hylles and make playne grounde, castelles and towres, they slaye and be slaine, and passeth not the kinges commaundement: when they haue ouercome theyr enemies, they bring to the king al theyr prayes, and they that goo not to warre but ploweth the ground, when they haue reaped, bringe the king his parte: And if he alone bydde them kill, they kyll: yf he bidde them forgeue, they forgeue: yf he bidde them strike, they strike: yf he bydde banishe, they banyshe: if he bidde men builde, they buylde: if he bid cutte downe, they hew downe: if he bidde them set, they sette: and all the people what power soeuer they be of, obeyeth him. And for all this he taketh his ease, his meat & drinke, and his slepe, and others watcheth and kepeth his body from harme, and they may not go euerye man his waye to do what he wyll, but at a worde they obey him. Nowe syrs howe say you, is not the kinge worthie to be called **precellent,** whose fame and royall name is set furth after this maner? Of the duety of dukes, Captaines, or great

† subiects] subieccs

officers vnder kinges, you heare: They haue aucthoritie to edifie, not to destroye, to do good, and not to do ill: to punishe vice, and to auaunce and set forth vertue: to correct them that be badde, and to laude, praise, and cherishe them that be good, yf they do otherwise, their dampnation is iuste, they well deserue it. And for them and vs, **this is goddes will and pleasure, that with well doinge we shoulde stoppe mennes mouthes,*** that folyshly will raile, and ignorantly, knowing [2Z1ᵛ] nothinge of the matter that they rayle against, with our well doinge we shoulde make theim holde theyr peace, or to say the best, and not with scolding, brawl-inge, or chidinge agayne, nor by actions on the case, nor by citations, or by suche litigious processe. If thou be sclaundered, a purgation is not the thinge that S. Peter biddeth the runne to, but he biddeth the do well, and so thou shalt stoppe mennes mouthes. Auoyde the occasion on whiche the rumoure and sclaunder rose, and the rumoure wyll sone cease, where as by contentious and litigious processe, manye men wyll speake of the matter that neuer heard of it afore, and wyl be more ready to speake the worst then the best. **Quasi liberi & non quasi velamen habentes malicie libertatem sed sicut serui Dei,*** You must geue good example and occasion to men to say well, and to leaue theyr rayling or missaying against you, not for anye bondage, or for seruyle feare, but like fre men set at the libertie, at whiche Christ hath set vs, doinge it with heart and all. And we must beware that we **vse not our libertie as a cloke or coueringe of malice and** of mischeife. Remembre what Iudas of Galiley did, that is spoken of. **Actu. v. and Iosephus antiquitatum, li. xviii Cap. i.** he calleth him **Iudas Gaulonites, homo ex ciuitate cui nomen erat Gamala,*** He seduced a great multitude, and made them to rebell, vnder the pretence of a Godly libertie, in as much as they were the elect people of God, & paid to him fyrst fruites, tithes, and other dueties. Wher-fore (he sayd) they ought not to pay tribute to any man, [2Z2] nor to recognize any other lord but onelye God. This heresie grew so sore yᵗ it peruerted a great multitude of the people to consente vnto it, but anone the auctor of it, & as many of his secte as could be found, were slaine with him, albeit the smoke of this heresy smelled longe after, for this Iudas the heresiarch set forth this heresie **tempore professionis** when by the commaundement of the emperour **Octauianus Augustus, ibant singuli vt profiterentur in ciuitates suas,** euery man went to the place where he was borne, there to haue his name taken, & to pay his head peny or tribute,* professinge their subiection to the Romaines, at which time Ioseph & Mary went to Bethle[h]em where they were borne, & they being there, came the time that Mary shuld be deliuered of child, & there Christe was borne.* And afterwarde more then .xxx. yeres, they moued a question to Christe touching this heresie. **An licet censum dare Caesari an non, Mat. xxii.** Whether it were lawful to pay tribute to the emperor or not? Christ sayd ye: declaring the same by the coine of yᵉ mony, which was the emperors image. It is but temporall, & why shuld not a temporal lord haue temporal subsedy & aide? it is his duetye so to haue, therefore pay it (saith christ) you must nedes do so.* The said Iudas pretended a liberty, by yᵗ they were of the holy line of Abraham, Isaac, Iacob & Gods electe people, but this libertie he shoulde haue vnderstand goostly and not carnally, but he turned it to carnalitie, as Iosephus expresselye sayth. **Obtentur quidem vtili-tatis defensionis communis, reuera autem proprium lucrorum gratia tota seditio gerebatur.** [2Z2ᵛ] All the commotion and fraye was made vnder the pretence and coloure of a common profytte, and common defence, but in very dede it was for theyr owne priuate and proper lucre.* What mischeif hath come in Saxony by a pretensed libertie, is not vnknowen: Euangelicall libertie setteth no man at large to liue as he list, but this it setteth vs at libertie from the bondage of sinne, and also makinge vs subiecte to god and to our kinge, and to all our rulers, constitute and set in office ouer vs, and to do vnto them oure due seruice and bounden duety frely,* **Non solum propter iram, sed propter conscientiam. Rom. xiii.** That is to saye: not for feare of strokes, not for feare of prisonment, nor for feare of death, but freelye, franckely with hearte and all, and with a good wyll, as fre men and not as bondemen, but for discharge of your owne conscience* **as Goddes seruauntes,*** consideringe it is Goddes pleasure you shoulde do so, and not as the seruauntes of the fleshe or the worlde, coueringe vices vnder the cloke of libertie.* It foloweth, **Omnes honorate,** As the Apostle. **Rom. xii.** sayth. **Honore inuicem preuenientes,** Euery man thinking another better then him selfe, for that vertue or good qualitie may be in an other that is not in the, and by that thou maye take him for thy better, and honoure him. All this S. Peter speaketh to auaunce humilitie, and to put it in euery mannes bosome as farre forth as he maye. **Fraternitatem diligite.** S. Paul sayth of the same. **Ro. xii. Charitatem fraternitatis inuicem diligentes.** Thoughe charitie exten[2Z3]deth to all men, yet principally to christen people whiche be all our brothers in Christ regenerate and gotten agayne to Christ by the Sacrament of Baptisme, as we be, **Deum timete, scilicet, Timore filiali,** as the chylde should feare his father: and next after him, **Regem honorificate,*** whiche is highest to be honoured of all powers temporall, for euer the feare of God muste go afore, so that doynge our duetie to oure kinge, or to anye other potentate or aucthoritie, we forget not the feare of God, neither do any thinge contrarye to Goddes pleasure. And then we must not onelye honour, but honorifie him, that is, we muste do the best we can to make others to do him honor, and theyr duetie to him. And it is highlye to be noted, howe intyerly to mennes hartes almighty God striketh the honour of a kynge, and the reputation that he should be had in of al his subiectes, sayinge by the mouth of the wyse man. **Eccles, x. In cogitatione tua regi ne detrahas, & in secreto cubiculi tui ne maledixeris diuiti quia & aues celi portabunt vocem tuam, & qui habet pennas annunciabit sententiam.** Where we be playnely monished and warned, that nother in angre nor in sporte or lightnes, we thinke any yl agaynst our kinge, or against a great man for that a man rolleth in his minde, it wyll burst forth one waye or another, and many times when we thinke leaste vpon it, and feare least, it wyll come forth, yea, though we speake agaynst them in our bedde, or in oure bedde chaumber, the byrdes of the ayre, the vtterers of counsell, whether they be good [2Z3ᵛ] aungels or bad, wil vtter thy counsel to thy condemnation, no man can tell howe, but euen as thoughe the birdes of the ayre, or the mouse pepinge in the hole in the walles of thy chambre, vttered the, and they that haue wynges wyll vtter the sentence: a swyft iudge wyll sone geue sentence of thy condemnation. Here the wyse man playnely biddeth men beware that **they dishonor not their kinge** neither in dede, in worde, nor in thoughte.* **Serui subditi estote in omni timore dominis, non tantum bonis & modestis sed etiam discholis.*** After that the blessed Apostle heretofore hath instruct and taught generally and comonly al them that he wrote to, and al others by them: nowe he descendeth to the specialties, geuinge certaine speciall lessons to speciall estates of men and women, fyrst beginninge with them that be in seruile state, as bondmen, prentises, and all other seruauntes men and women. All suche S. Peter exhorteth to be obediente, and subiecte to theyr lordes and maisters, aswel to theyr lordes and maisters that be good, vertuous and honest, and measurable in all theyr doinges, keping the meane in their actes and in correction, according to the iudgement of right reason (this is called modestie) as to them that be **discholi** (saith oure texte) truandes, michers that will not kepe the schole of Christes fayth and of his doctrine, to them that were infideles, and generally swaruing and going out of the schole and right learnynge of honesty, and of measure in their liuinge and in theyr punishinge Some readeth it **prauis,** [2Z4] crabbed, croked, and cumberous. Some readeth it **difficilioribus,** to hard, sore and cruell.* So that this is the Apostles minde, that what condition so euer your maisters be of, you muste do youre duety and true seruice vnto them. Seruitude commeth either of iniquitie or of aduersitie: Of iniquitie came the bondage that Cham was cursed withal, because he mocked his father lying bare, he had his fathers curse. **Maledictus Chanaan puer seruus seruorum erit fratribus suis.*** He cursed Cham in his chylde and issue, with perpetuall bondage. And after this maner, that is, by iniquitie, hath manye men geuen them selfe to perpetual bondage, to saue theyr neckes. Aduersitie made the people of Israell bonde vnto the Egiptians, and after this maner they that be taken prisoners in battel, be sometimes deputed to perpetual seruitude.* This is spoken of bondage or villanage, in which state who so euer be set, must be subiect & obedient to his lorde. And not onlye they, but also al others, as well prentises as couenant seruauntes, what state soeuer their maisters be of, & that **with al feare,*** S. Paule sayth, **Eph. vi. Cum timore et tremore,** with feare of mind,* lyke as you were your masters child, reuerently fearing to offend or displease their father, so must you haue a louinge feare, least you do the thynge that shoulde displease your maister. Such feare had good Ioseph when his maistres tempted him to be naught with her, he alledged his maysters goodnes toward him, & the benefits that he had done vnto hym, beyng but his seruaunt and very bondeman, sayinge, **Genes. xxxix.*** my mayster [2Z4ᵛ] hath committed and deliuered to me all that he hath in his house, so that he knoweth not what he hath in his house, no more but the meat that he eateth and the drinke that he drinketh when it is set afore him, there is nothing but it is vnder my hande and at my pleasure, except onelye you that are his wyfe. Then how may I do this faulte and synne agaynst my lord? Fye for shame hold me excused, I will not do it. If his maister had ben his father he coulde not haue expressed more louinge feare toward him, by this geuing example to al seruauntes to loue theyr maisters, and to feare them, and not onelye with feare of mynde, but also that the feare that is in theyr hearte shulde extende into the body, whiche S. Paule calleth **tremor,** to make the seruauntes to quake for feare. Albeit this quaking feare accordeth properly to the bondman that doth al thing for feare of strokes. And S. Peter speaketh generally of al maner of fear, saying: **in omni timore,*** so that the seruaunt should cheifely feare his maister louinglye, as the chylde the father, and if at the fyrst he haue not suche louinge feare of his mayster, yet beware of his angre, feare correction as the bondman or prentise doth, & by vsing thy self to do wel for suche seruile feare, thou shalte find ease in wel doing, & shal begin to do well for loue, & so of a good seruaunt thou shalt be made a good sonne, faithfull and louing to thy maister, and by that thy maister shall loue the better then any child he hath. **Prou. Si sit tibi seruus fidelis sit tibi tanquam anima tua,*** Euen as him self you must [3A1] do your seruice with simplicitie of hearte (sayth S. Paule) withoute doublenes, so that as you shew your self outward to be diligent and true, so you must be in hearte inwardlye, euen as you should serue Christ that bought vs, with whom it boteth no man to dissemble, you muste not serue to the eye while your maister loketh vpon you, as it were to please men, but as the seruauntes of Christ, doing the wil of God with good mind and with a good will, as seruing our Lord God that hath geuen your maisters power ouer you, and hath made you subiecte to them, not as doinge seruice vnto men, for the power that they haue ouer you, cometh of God, therefore if ye be false to theim, you be false to God that wylleth you to be true to your maisters.* And S. Paule wylleth Titus his disciple byshop of Candy, to commaund al seruantes to please their maisters in al thinges that is not contrary to Gods pleasure, **non contra-dicentes, non fraudantes (alia littera) non responsatores, non suffurantes,** no choplogikes that wil countersay their maisters, geuing them thre wordes for one, be it well be it yll, be it true be it false that your maisters sayth, you should be content & geue them no answer, but let them say what it please them: you muste be no lurchers or priuey pykers or stealers, but in al thing shewing good fidelitie, that so you may adourne & do worshyp to the doctrine of Christ in al thinges,* for ye good liuing of the scholer, is the ornament & worshyp of the maister. But now I pray you, yf the maister bidde his seruaunt to entre into religion, is the [3A1^v] seruaunt bounde to obey his maister in that? If his master bidde him take ordres and be a preist, is the seruaunt bound to obey his mayster? if his maister bidde him take a wife and be maried, is the seruaunt bound to obey him in these cases, or in suche other? No verelye: for where S. Paule or S. Peter biddeth the seruauntes obey theyr maisters in all thinges, you muste vnderstande this in all thinges parteininge to bodelye workes, and not spiritual workes, in workes parteining to the administration, guiding, and orderinge of theyr maisters housholde, and of his temporall busines, and not parteining to such a perpetuall yoke as is matrimonye. **Haec est enim gratia și propter Dei conscientiam sustinet quis tristitias patiens iniuste.** Because he had bydde seruauntes obey their maisters, althoughe they were crabbed and out of the schole of Christes doctrine, yf they were infideles, or oute of the schole of discrete iudgement in correction. In these wordes he geueth them spirituall and goostly counsayle, and comforte saying: This is a speciall gyfte of grace of the holy gooste, if anye of you suffer sorowe and payne wrongfully, **propter conscientiam Dei,** hauing in his conscience a respect to the pleasure of God,* which would not the seruaunt to grudge against his maister, and also remembring the reward that God will geue to al them that for his sake suffreth more than els thei were bound to suffre. S. Paule sayth. **Phil. i. Vobis donatum est pro Christo non solum vt in eum credatis sed ut etiam pro illo paciamini.** It is geuen you for [3A2] a speciall gifte of grace, not onely to beleue vpon him, (**i. Cor. xii. Alij datur fides in eodem spiritu,** by the holy spirite of God the holy gooste, to one is geuen faith by whiche we beleue on Christ & on his holy worde) but also for Christ it is geuen you (sayth Paule) as a speciall grace to suffre for Christes sake,* as many holy Apostles and martyrs did, for when the heat of the loue of God is inspired into the soule of man by the spirite of God the holy goost, it geueth a certaine gladnes and a certain swetenes to a man which suffreth him not to be deiecte with anye aduersitie, but maketh him bold and constant against all vexa-tion. Example we haue of the Apostles, whiche after they had receiued the holy goost at this holy time of Whitsontide,* **Ibant gaudentes a conspectu consilii quoniam digni habiti sunt pro nomine Iesu contumeliam pati. Actu. v.*** when they were reuiled, threatned, and well beaten, for their settinge forth and pre-achinge Christes faith, and were commaunded they shoulde do so no more, they went with mery hartes from the counsayle of the Scribes and Phariseis, that they were conuented and called afore, because it had pleased God to thinke them worthye to suffre suche despites for Christes sake. We se also by experience, that heate causeth and maketh boldnes in man and beaste, therefore the beastes that haue hootest hartes be moost bold, and for this cause the lion is bolder then is the horse or an oxe, because his harte hath in it a more feruente heate then the other haue in theyr hartes. So when [3A2ᵛ] the holy goost inspireth the feruencie and heate of his loue into the hart of any man or woman, it maketh that person wonderous bolde to suffer persecution and all maner of payne, yea martyrdome **propter conscientiam dei*** (as S. Peter speaketh) knowinge in his conscience that it is Gods pleasure he shoulde not reneige God, but rather constantly suffre all aduersitie for Gods sake. This feruent heate made S. Paule to say **Rom. viii. Certus sum quia neque mors: neque vita.** &c I am sure that nether death nor life, nor the aungels, nother thinges present nor thinges to come, nether any other creature, maye disseuer or put vs a parte frome the charitie and loue of God, whiche is in Christ Iesu our Lorde.* So the seruauntes that be tormented and beaten, and vexed with bitter and feruent wordes, must take it as a kynde of martirdome, this they must suffre euer, hauinge a timerouse conscience towardes God, and surely theyr rewarde shall not be forgotten at length, though they suffer for a tyme. **Quae est enim gratia si peccantes & collaphisati suffertis?** What thanke shall you haue, yf you do noughtelye and play the sluggardes, or the false bribers in youre maisters busynes, and then for your noughtye doynge be well boxed, beaten, and canueste, and so suffer as you deserue? What thanke shal you haue for your suffering? none at all. **Sed si benefacientes patienter sustinetis haec est gratia,** but if you do well and then suffer vniuste vexation and strokes, this is a matter of thankes, worthye to be rewarded.* Take ex[3A3]ample of Ioseph that I spoke of afore, he was true to his maister, he runne away and fled fornication: he was falselye accused and vniustlye condempned and cast in pryson, and layde faste in yrons, all this he toke pacientlye, and suffered very soberly and humblye, and therefore his rewarde was very greate and notable. Fyrst God sente him a grace in his fashion and behauioure by whiche he pleased the iayler and keper of the pryson, in so muche that he stroke of his yrons, and made him ouersear and ruler ouer all the prysoners there, and to geue them theyr meate that they were allowed at tymes conueniente. Then almighty god superadded an other grace, illuminatinge Iosephs wytte, with vnderstandynge of secretes that shoulde come after, signifyed to him by dreames, by which gyft he redde and expounded the dreames of the sergeaunt of the seller, and of the sergeaunt of the bakehouse that were in the iayle with hym, and by that occasion two yeares after he was called oute of pryson to interpretate the kinges dreame, and so he did, for whiche he was exalted and made ruler of all the realme of Egypte.* By this blessed patriarch Ioseph, almyghtye God geueth to all them that be in bondage, or in any paynefull seruyce, a greate solace and comforte, that they maye learne by him, that in the lowest state of men, whiche is the state of seruauntes, yet men may be highest in maners, & in good conditions. Ioseph was in bondage & in miserable seruice, [3A3ᵛ] and Pharao the kinge reigned ouer all his subiectes, but the seruice of Ioseph was more blessed and more protitable to the realme of Egipt, then the raygne of Pharao. For all Egipte had be vndone and lost for hungre, yf Pharao hadde not set al his realme vnder Ioseph, and subdued it to his rule.* You may also learne by him (as S. Ambrose noteth[)], that althoughe youre bodies be subiecte to bondage and seruice, yet youre mindes be at libertie, your maisters be maisters of your bodies, but not of your soules.* Therfore what paine soeuer your bodies suffer, your wittes may be at liberty, and may ascende towarde God, hauynge a conscience and respecte to his pleasure, and for his sake do your seruice faithfullye, and what so euer paynes you suffer wrongfullye, yet take them paciently, and you shall not lose youre rewarde of almighty God. To whom be all honour and glory for euer. Amen.

THe blessed Apostle Saynt Peter in this matter that I haue to be declared vnto you, prosecuteth further the thinge that I partelye touched in my laste sermon, whiche is of the pacient sufferaunce that the seruaunte or subiecte ought to vse towarde his maister or superiour, sayinge: **In hoc enim vocati estis**. Considre your callinge: GOD hath called you to serue (sayth S. Peter) and not to controll, to suffer, and not to remurmer, brable, or chyde agaynste your maisters, and in youre well doynge and patient sufferinge of vexation and vniuste punishment, you be the true folowers of Christes passion,* as S. Peter sayth here, in whiche he glorifieth much the state of bondemen or seruauntes, comparinge theyr pacience to Christes pacience in his passion. That man that wyl not learne pacience of Christ, can neuer be saued by Christ: Remembre the highnes of his estate, by whiche he was equal with his father of heauen, and then the abiection and vylenes of his passion and his paynes that he suffered without any cause geuen thereto on his behalfe, and this remembraunce wyll make a stony hearte to mollifye and waxe tendre. And nowe my matter of Saynt Peters epistle leadeth me somewhat to speake of Christes paynfull passion, whiche is most necessary for all christen folkes to heare of, not onely in the passion weke in time of lent,* but aswell in all times of the yeare it shoulde be euer [3A4v] in minde and in remembraunce to make vs to considre the benefit of our redemption & the punishment of the contemners of the same, and specially now in the hote time of the yeare, when all sinnes most feruently doth assault vs and tempt vs, we had most nede of shadow to saue vs from the heat of temptation: now folke be most prone to the fylthines of the fleshe, now men be prone to angre, to warre and discention, the heate of the time disposeth men therto, now men be ready to proule and go about by auarice to encreace theyr ryches, by deceiuinge or supplanting theyr neighbours, the tyme is fayre to laboure in. All these worketh towarde destruction of mannes soule, by a deuelysh heate of worldlynes, contrary to the heat of godly loue inspyred by the holye goost (that I spoke of euen nowe.) Therefore against this heat, we must take a tre to shadowe vs, & to kepe our beautie, that the deuelish heate of temptation do not marre our colour. **Prou. iii. Lignum vite est omnibus qui apprehendunt eam,*** sayeth the wyse man, speaking of the increat wisedome of the second person in trinitie, our sauiour Christe in whom the manhed is ioyned to the same wisedome in one person, he is the tre of life to al men & women that can take him. And ye spouse sayth. **Can. ii. Sub vmbra illius quem desiderabam sedi.** I reposed my self and sate downe in the shadow of him that I desired & loued.* We muste repose our selfe, and louinglye reste in the shadowe of Christes passion, that we may saue our self from synne, and gather our strength agayne, by whiche we maye be able to ouercome the deuyll, [3B1] and to resist all his assaultes. **Christus passus est pro nobis,** Christ suffered for vs,* generally for vs all, what state or degree so euer we be of, for vs (he saythe) to moue vs to compassion, and in our minde to suffer with him, in asmuche as he suffered not for his owne faulte, nor for any aduauntage for him self, but for to redeme vs & to make amendes for oure faultes, and for to auaunce vs into the fauour of God againe. Therfore he that hathe a noble and a gentle harte wyll count the paine that Christ suffered to be his own paynes, because they were taken for his sake. So dydde king Dauid .ii. **Reg. vltimo,** when he saw the angell of God striking the people, and kill them, because he had proudly caused the people to be numbred. He cryed to God & sayd: I am he that hath synned and done amisse, these be poore lambes or shepe, what hurt haue they done in this matter? as who should saye none. I besech the turn thine anger against me, and spare them.* **Esay. liii. Vulneratus est propter iniquitates nostras attritus est propter scellera nostra.** He was wounded for our iniquities, and al to torne for our yll deedes.* Therefore Christes passion is or shoulde be our passion as well because of the occasion of hys passyon, which was our sinnes, as by the vtilitie and profite that commeth of the same, not to him but to vs. **Vobis relinquens exemplum,*** to you seruantes specialli. Now to my purpose, giuing example of the despites that wer done to him, of the trouble and vexation that he suffered, of the whips and scourges that he was beaten with. And if you be [3B1ᵛ] ouercharged with heauy burdens, remembre the heauy burden of the crosse that was layd on hys shoulders when he was not able to beare it, but fell downe vnder it, he was so faint and wearye with long abstinence & with watching al the night afore, and with much rude handling by them that came wyth Iudas for to take him, & with much haling & pullinge of him from one iudge to an other, and then with the ache & smarting of mani sore stripes that he suffered, & wyth shedyng of his blood at his scourging when he was whypped. And then remember what villanie they intended against him, putting him to that deathe that they thought most dispiteful, hanging him on the crosse that he was nayled on, as we now a daies esteme hanging on the galowes, & that in yᵉ common place of execution for felons and malefactours, as we say here at Mighel hyll,* or in London, at Tiburne* or such others. And finally then consider the death that he suffered for our sakes, you must take him for your myrrour or glasse to loke in, & for your example, **that you mai folow his steps.*** He was vngiltie to dye, for he neuer did ani faut in dede, neither any gile or false word yᵗ cam out of his mouth, by which any man might be deceiued. Al this & that foloweth S. Peter taketh of the .liii. chapter of Esay, where yᵉ prophet hath the same sentence.* It is a great discomfort for him yᵗ hath a great iourney vpon him to do, to go out of his way, therfore he had nede to beware at the beginning, for a litle errour at the beginning wil be a great errour at the end. As when ther be .ii. [3B2] wayes meting together if the Pilgreme take the wrong way & go on a quarter of a mile, that mai be sone amended, he may with a litle labour com into his way againe, but if he go on stil til he be a dosen mile or .xx. mile out of his way, it wyll be a shrewd paine to coste ouer the countrey to get into the way again. The surest thing to kepe a man from masking and straying out of the way, & also to bring a man into the way if he be out of the wai, is a wise gide to go afore a man to leade him the way. Blessed S. Peter like a good shepherd fearing least his Lambes bondmen, prentises, & seruantes (to which speacially he speaketh now)* should by the rygour & roughnes of correxion be driuen out of the right waye to heauen by murmuring, grudging, chidynge and checki[n]g theyr maisters, or brawling and fighting with theym, (this is the streight way to hell) biddeth them folow the steps of theyr gyde our sauioure Christ, which suffered much more paine then they could haue layd vpon them, neuer offending nor geuynge cause to the same. And our mother holye churche in the Epistle of the seconde Sunnedaye after Easter, readeth the same woordes of Saynte Peters Epistle,* exhortynge all her chyldren, all Christen people to folowe the steppes of oure gide our sauiour Christe that we swarue not out of the way to heauen, in which [we] were sette a lyttle afore in the holye tyme of Lent by the Sacrament of penaunce, and at Easter by the moste reuerende sacrament of the aulter, the true **Viaticum** meate to strengthe vs in oure iourney. [3B2ᵛ] We must folow him, thinking that if God the father spared not his

onely begotten natural sonne, but put him into sinfull mens handes, & let him be
beaten for our sakes, then he wyll not spare hys handy workes, and his children by
adoption. If he scourged his sonne that was without syn, will he suffer them to be
vnscourged that be full of syn? It wil not be. God scourgeth euery child that he
taketh for his, therfore if you be excepted from the scourge, you be excepted from
his chyldren. For he that is a sure stedfast christen man must not onely do well, but
must also be content to suffer yll, remembring that Christ neuer sayd yl by any
man, yet he was missaied, & very il spoken to. **Cum male diceretur non maledice-
bat,** When he was missayed he missayd no man again, nor said any yl.* He was
called a Samaritane,* which was as dispiteful among them, as is now to be called
an heretik with vs. For the Samaritanes wer but as it were halfe Iewes, they came
of the Assirians and vsed the superstitions of the Gentiles, & yet mengled muche
of Moyses lawe wyth theyr errours, therefore the Iewes loued theym not, nor
companyed with them.* He was also called traytour agaynst the Emperour, tauerne
hunter. &c.* And where he knewe muche worse by theim, yet he geue them neuer
an yll worde agayne. **Cum pateretur non comminabatur**. When they layde on him
with roddes and scourges: he threatned not that he woulde be reuenged, or that he
woulde be euen with them.* **Ecclesiasticus** saythe **.xxii. That lyke as a fore the
fyre burneth the vapour and the** [3B3] **smoke riseth on high, sic et ante sanguinem maledicta† & contumelie et mine**. So afore bloode shedding yll railing
wordes, dispites, and manishyng or threatning goeth afore.* Where Christ had
vengeaunce in his hand, and might haue cast it vpon them by and by, he would
not so doe, but **tradidit vindictam ei qui iudicat iuste** (as sayth the new translation) he committed the vengeaunce to God the father that iudgeth iustli, letting
him alone with the vengeaunce, as in deede God biddeth vs doe.* **Mihi vindictam
& ego retribuam, mea est vltio & ego retribuam Deu. xxxii. Ro. xii.** Let me
alone with the vengeance, and I wil requite them.* And so he did in dede by the
Iewes, he payde theym home eueri halfpeny **vt in prouerbio**. The blod of Christ
fell vpon them and vppon theyr issue .xlii. yeares after, when the noble Emperour
Vespasian & hys sonne **Titus** destroyed the citye of Ierusalem, wyth suche an
horrible strage and murder, as woulde abhorre any yron hart to consider, as **Iosephus** in the last booke **de bello Iudaico*** expresseth it. Our translation saith:
tradebat autem iudicanti se iniuste He committed him selfe, or deliuered him
selfe to him that iudged vniustly,* to Pilate, which partly to please the Iewes that
pursued Christ, partly for feare, least he shoulde be accused of treason to the
Emperour for letting a traytour scape, as they said Christ was, because he would be
a king (they said) and that was treason against the Emperour.* But there is neyther
fauour nor feare mede nor dreade that shoulde haue made him to condempne an
innocent that neuer offended the [3B3ᵛ] lawes. Now how Christ committed him
selfe to Pilate, you must consider that fyrst he deliuered him selfe to Iudas comming to mete him, when he came with his companie to take Christe, Iudas
delyuered hym to the ministers that came with Iudas to take Christe, and they
delyuered him to the princes of priestes, scribes and Phariseys that hadde payde
money to Iudas for him: They deliuered him to Pilate which wrongfullye condempned him. This deliuerie of Christes part proceded and came of obedience to
his father and of most abundant charitie and loue towarde mankinde. Of Iudas
part it came of couetuousnes to recouer the losse of the oyntment that Mary
Magdalen bestowed vpon his fete anoynting them.* And on the Scribes and

† maledicta] maledictio

Phariseis part it came of rancke malice and enuie against Christ. I take not **prodere** and **tradere** for one. **Prodere** is to woorke the treason, and that was done when Iudas consulted with the princes of the prestes, and agreed with theim on a price, then the treason was wrought, when Christ was bought and sold. Deliueraunce was made afterwarde when Iudas mette him in the gardeine and kissed him and they sette handes on hym. Iudas was **proditor** and **traditor,** he wroughte the treason, and also made delyueraunce.* **Qui peccata nostra ipse pertulit in corpore suo super lignum.** Euen he delyuered hym selfe to the vniuste iudge whyche bore oure synnes vppon hys bodye, nayled faste vppon the tree of the crosse.* He bore our synnes vpon hys bodye (saythe Saynte Peter) not as [3B4] my surpeles beareth hys whitenesse, nor as thy gowne beareth his blackenesse, for my surpelesse beareth hys wytenesse, so that I maye saye my surpeles is whyte, and thy gowne beareth hys blackenesse, so that I maye saye thy gowne is blacke. But thoughe Christe bore oure synnes, I may not saye that Christ was a synner, for he neuer sinned in worde nor dede, as Saynt Peter sayde afore.* When we bare our iniquitie we be wicked, when we bear our sinnes we be sinners, it is not so of Christe, therefore when we saye that Christe bore oure synnes, you muste vnderstande that hee bore the payne and punyshement that we were worthye to beare for oure synnes, as the Prophet Esaye sayde of hym longe afore. **Esa. liii. Ipse autem vulneratus est propter iniquitates nostras, attritus est propter scelera nostra.** Hee was wounded for oure iniquities, and al to torn with whyppes, scourges<.> and roddes, wyth manye blowes and bobbes, and with the nailes and with the speare, and al for our greuous offences, that lyke as hee dyed bodelye, so wee maye dye to synne, so that sinne dye in vs, and haue no lyfe nor strengthe in vs, and maye liue to Iustice, so that vertue and good maner of liuyng be quick, liuelye and freshe in vs. **Cuius liuore sanati sumus,** the woordes of Esaye. With hys blewe wales and scarres in hys fleshe after the scourges, stripes and strokes that made his skinne to ryse, and to bee blacke and blewe, wee were healed from the syckenes of our soules, that that made his body sycke and sore, made vs whole & sound.* [3B4ᵛ] **Et dominus in eo posuit iniquitatem omnium nostrum.** Euen the same sentence that Saint Peter saith: **peccata nostra ipse pertulit in corpore suo.** Our Lord God the father put vpon him all our iniquities.* And still the blessed Apostle S. Peter alludeth to the same chapiter of Esay, where the prophet sayth: **Omnes nos quasi oues errauimus.** Al we went a straying lyke shepe out of the flocke, and out of the keping of our shepherd, and so saithe S. Peter: You were once like shepe strayed oute of Gods flocke, but nowe you be conuerted and turned againe to the pastor and feder, bishop and ouerseer of your soules.* And in this processe saint Peter also semeth to teach vs the parable of the gospell of the man that had a C. sheepe, of whych one was straied away, and he left foure score and nintene in deserte, and went to seeke that sheepe that was strayed awaye, and when hee hadde founde her, he cast her on his shoulders, and was glad, and when he came home with her, he called his friendes and his neighbours about him, praiyng them to be mery with him, because he hadde founde the shepe that was lost, and so they made more chere and myrth for that one shepe, then for all the rest that still kept the flocke.* Thys odde shepe that strayed out of the flocke, signifieth the tenthe kynde of reasonable creatures that God made to honour and laude hym. God made the ix. orders of Angels, al reasonable creatures, and the tenth is mankinde, which was by sinne gone at large out of the folde of Paradise, and oute of the compasse of Gods fauour. The second person [3C1] in trinitie owner of this sheepe, left all the rest of his resonable creatures and shepe or flocke the .ix orders of Angels in deserte in heauen, which the innumerable multitude of dampned angels had forsaken and left, and so to thcm it was a wildernesse, as a thinge forsaken.* And so it was to man that was made finally to inherite heauen, yet his pleasure regarded it not, but had lost it, and yet to this daye it is reputed as a wyldernes, or as a thing forsaken of the most part of people that will not walke in the streyght way that bringeth a man to heauen, but had leauer keepe the brode waye of pleasure, easelye hopping and dauncing to hell, and therefore to them heauen is a wildernes, and also in the wooddes of the wyldernes there be many birdes that singeth swetely, with many and diuers swete tunes: so in heauen where the **inhabitauntes shall prayse our Lorde God worlde without ende.*** There be also in wyldernes many swete and pleasant floures, and so there be in heauen the red roses of Martyrs, the violets of Confessours, the lilies of Virgines:* For such considerations heauen may be called a wyldernes, as Christ calleth it in thys parable. Ther he semed to leaue them when he came alowe, and was by our mortall and passible nature **minished and made somwhat lower then the Angels,*** though by his Godhead he were farre aboue them. Here in earth he found the shepe that was lost, and neither beat it nor stroke it, nor brawled with it, nor rayled nor chidde, but louingly gotte it vpon hys shoulders, when his shoulders and armes were [3C1ᵛ] racked and strained to set the holes that wer bored for the nailes in the side armes of the crosse, for then (as Esay saith, and saint Peter reherseth the same here)* he bare our sinnes vpon his tender bodie on the crosse, he suffered vpon the crosse the paines that we should haue suffered for our sins. Saint Ambrose vpon the same saithe: **Humeri Christi brachia crucis sunt, illic peccata mea deposui, in illa patibuli nobilis ceruice requieui.** The shoulders of Christ be they that be extended vpon the braunches of the crosse, there vpon them (said S. Ambrose) I laide downe my sinnes on the necke and shoulders of that noble galowes, I rest my selfe.* But because Christ in his parable saith that the shepherd cast the sheepe vpon hys shoulders **gaudens** being glad and mery,* but seyng all this concerneth his painefull passion on the crosse in which he suffred paines vntollerable: how can it be that he with ioye and gladnes cast his straied shepe vpon his shoulders? it was to his payne and not to his pleasure, as it semeth. In verye dede although he bore our sinnes (that is to say, the paines for our sinnes) to his paines, ache and smarting: yet knowing what shoulde come of it, he was gladde to take the paine and to saue hys shepe. For in this you must vnderstande that the reasonable soule of Christe (comprehending both wytte and wyll) eleuate to the contemplation and fruition of almighty God, is called the superioure & hyghest parte of the soule. The same soule applyed to inferiour and lower thinges, is called the lower porcion or lower part of the soul [3C2] As when the witte or will is applyed or inclined to the fiue wittes, or to theyr sensuall appetites or to other lower worldly busines, paines or pleasures, all beit when the witte or will is exercysed aboute anye suche lower matters in an order to Gods pleasure, they belong to the higher porcion and may be called the higher porcion of the soule largely or comonly speaking of the higher porcion. To our purpose, although the lower part of yᵉ soule of Christ had sorowe & paine wyth the sensible powers of the bodye that smarted and aked right sore with the flesh, which was most tender in Christ, because he was of most pure & tender complexion. In the higher part of his soule, both wayes had euer ioy and gladnes. As for the first way in the contemplacion and fruition of the godhead, there is no doubt, for it gaue Christes soule beatitude, euen such ioy and gladnes as he hathe in heauen now. After the second maner also, when Christ consydered hys paynefull passion as the meane appointed by the father to redeme mans soule, &

to bring home the sheepe that was lost & strayed away by sinne, he toke the paines with a good will and very gladly. We haue a like example of Saint Paule, which by the higher part of his soule, and by his deliberate and well aduised will, desired to be dissolued and to be with Christ* all beit the wyll vnite in amitie and loue to the sensuall appetite desyred to abyde styll in the fleshe and to lyue. In lyke maner were the blessed Martyrs whyche in theyr bodyes suffered vnmeasurable tormentes and greuous paynes, [3C2ᵛ] yet remembring Gods pleasure & the rewardes that they should haue for the same, they toke them gladly & with good chere. And so it standeth together that Christ bearing yᵉ paine for our sins vpon his backe on the crosse, yet bore them **gaudens** with ioy and gladnes in the higher porcion of his soul, knowing that by his paines and bi his death man shoulde be restored to fauoure agayne, that afore was attainted & out of Gods fauour. And that where we were afore like straied shepe out of the blessed flocke of Gods faithfull people, nowe we be conuerted and turned agayn to the pastor and bishop of our soules, as S. Peter said to them that he wrote vnto. **To the pastor, the shepherde, the feder of our soules our sauiour Christ,** whom afterward in his epistle .v. chap. He calleth the prynce of pastors, maister of the craft, the chief shepherd of the shepherds, the chiefe feeder of the feeders, the chiefe bishop of the bishops, the chiefe curate of all curates, and not onely of the flocke.* Him al pastors and curates aswel spiritual as temporal must folow. Here I should speake more largelye of pastors and bishops, but I shall deferre it vnto the .v. chapter of this epistle, where (God helping) that matter shalbe more largely entreated.* Now I shal exhort you as well maisters as seruantes, men and women to consider that we haue a shepherd and an ouerseer in heauen our sauiour Christ, therfore you maisters order your seruants as you would Christ should order you with mercy and fauour. And you seruantes so order your selfe to youre maysters, as thoughe you serued [3C3] Christ with simplicitie of harte without doublenes,* Serue not onely to the eye whyle your maysters loketh vpon you, playing the wantons while they be absent, for if you doe so, you are double harted, which is contrary to simplicitie and plainnes, serue as though you serued God and not man and so being in bonde seruice, you shal make your hartes free and at libertie, and shall tourne bondage into libertie of hart, and shal serue god, and seruinge hym you raygne, you bee lyke kynges ruling and commaunding and kepinge vnder your affections and wayward appetites of the body, and so you maye come to suche fortune, that you may be maisters ouer them that be free men, yea and maye peraduenture be maisters ouer your maisters children. **Seruo sensato liberi seruient Eccle. x.*** And we haue hearde sometimes of seruauntes which in processe of time haue bought theyr maisters childrens inheritaunce, or theyr goodes, but these be no dastardes but wytty seruantes, that come to such exaltacion. And so you see that God euer requiteth & rewardeth the true seruant, eyther bodely and temporally, as in this example rehersed, or gostlye giuing him quietnes of minde, by which he shall serue his maister truely, and so doing he serueth Christe, and shall come to hym, for so is hys wyll, that who soeuer serueth hym should finally be there as he is. And that we all may so serue him in our calling in the seruice that god hath appointed vs to, that we mai at the last com to him he graunt vs for his infinite mercye that for vs died. Amen.

¶The .xi. treatise or
sermon.

The third chapter.

SImiliter et mulieres subdite sint viris suis, vt & si qui non credunt verbo, per mulierum conuersationem sine verbo lucrifiant. &c.* Here in the fyrste parte of this thirde chapiter the blessed Apostle ascendeth from the informacion that he gaue to them that be in seruile state (of whiche I entreated in my laste sermon)* vnto them that be ioyned together in the yoke of marriage. First speaking to the wiues, and ordering them toward theyr husbandes, & also in theyr exteriour behauiour. And consequently he teacheth the husbands theyr duties toward theyr wiues. S. Peter saith: **Similiter et mulieres. &c.** likewise women must be subiect to theyr owne husbandes. **Likewise** (saith s. Peter) as I haue spoken of the subiection of the seruantes to their maisters, so I must aduertise & counsel the wiues to obedience & subiection according to their calling, that thei do reuerence vnto theyr husbandes wyth feare, as Saint Paule saith. **Ephe. v. Vxor autem timet virum suum.** Let the wife feare her husbande wyth such louing fear as I haue spoken of afore, more for loue, fearing to displease him, then for strokes or punishment.* And in the same chapter s. Paule biddeth wiues be subiecte to theyr husbandes as vnto our Lord & master Christ, for it is our lorde [3C4] Gods ordinance that the man should be the head of the woman, as Christ is the head of his spouse and wife the church or multitude of Christen people, therefore like as the churche is subiect, obedient, and doth reuerence to Christ, as the body to her head, so ought the wyues to theyr husbands as to theyr head in all thinges that be good and according to Gods pleasure.* Of the contempt of due subiection and obedience of the wyfe to the husband, I rede a notable story. **Hester .i.*** wher it is written that the great kynge and conquerour **Assuerus** king of the Medes and Persies, & ouer cxxvii. prouinces and realmes, made an exceding sumptuous feast to all the nobilitie and head officers of his Empery and dominions, the preparation and prouision for the same, with the inuitacion and accesse of his gests, continued .ix. score daies, the solempnitie of the feast continued .vii. daies. There was such prouision, such seruice of al officers, and such delicates of meates & drinks that wonder it is to heare of it. And like as that king kept his feast in the solemne place prouided for the same: so dyd **Vasthi** his Quene keepe her feast, to all the quenes Ladies and noble women of the Emperye, and that in the palace where **Assuerus** was wont to dwell, for the kynges feaste was kept in Haalys or tentes wonderouslye wroughte with costlye stuffe, and stronglye staied by pyllers of fyne Marble after a gorgeous fashyon all of pleasure, there the kynge kepte hys solempne banckettes, and lefte hys palace for the Quene **Vasthi** wyth the other Ladyes. [3C4ᵛ] On the .vii. daye of this feast when **Assuerus** the king had well dronke, & was well warmed with wyne, he sent his Chamberlaynes to call **Vasthi** the quene to him, willing her to put on her head her diademe or crowne and to come forthe after her goodliest maner, because he would shewe to his kynges and lordes the beautie of his quene, for she was very fayre and beautyfull, but she refused to come at him, and contempned the kinges commaundement, sent to her by his chamberleins, for this cause the king was sore dismaid, & waxed wondrous angrye,* and in a rage called all the great wisemen of his priuye counsayle that were euer at hande (as the maner of kinges is to haue such counsayle euer redy) and by theyr counsayl he did al weighty matters, because they knew the lawes of God and man: he asked theyr counsayle what sentence shoulde be gyuen againste **Vasthi** the quene for her pride and obstinacie. They aunswered all by the mouthe of **Manucha** one of the chiefe of the counsayle, whiche after thys maner spoke to the king afore the princes of the counsail. **Non solum regem lesit regina Vasthi. &c.** The quene hath hurt not onely the kinges highnes, but also all the people and princes and noble men that be wythin the dominion of kynge **Assuerus**, for the woordes of the quene will go abrode amonge all women, and make them to contempne theyr husbandes saying: **The noble and mighty king Assuerus bade Vasthi his quene come into his presence and she would not, and no more will I but when me list*** And by this example gyuen of her, all the wyues [3D1] of the Princes of the Persies and of the Medes will sette little by the commaundement of their husbandes. Wherefore the indignation and displeasure that your highnesse hathe conceiued againste her is iuste and not without a cause. And therefore (if it be your pleasure) let a proclamation be sende frome your persone, that quene **Vasthi** shall neuer more come in your presence, but that an other better then she shall take her raigne, that she hathe as one with you. And let the same commaundemente be diuulged† and proclaymed in all Prouinces and Realmes of your Emperie, euen to the furthest parte therof, that so all wiues, as well of the great men, as of the common and lower people maye geue honor and obedience to their husbandes. This counsell pleased the Kinge and the princes that were present with him, and the kinge according to the same, sent furth his letters into all countreys of his emperye, written in diuers languages, and diuers letters, that euerye man might reade and vnderstande them, conteininge this argumente, that **the men be princes and greatest in their owne houses,*** wherfore it foloweth that the wyues be subiecte and vnder obedience to them. By this storie all good wiues may note and marke what commeth of contempte and disobedience of the wyues to their Husbandes. She was deposed from her high estate and put away from her husbande, because she list not to obey nor to be subiect to his commaundement.* Almighty GOD made the first woman for two vses or purposes, [3D1ᵛ] one for to multiplye mankinde by generation, an other cause, for domesticall cohabitation, and to dwell wyth the manne for his comforte. And in bothe these two, the woman was soore punished because shee tempted her husbande to eate of the forbidden fruite. Firste where she shoulde haue borne chylde wythout payne, she was deputed to exceadynge payne wyth manye throwes and panges while shee is wyth chylde, and wyth muche more payne when shee is traueylynge to be deliuered. Seconde, to our purpose nowe, where there shoulde haue bene none inequalitie betwixte the manne and the wyfe, nowe for a punishement for her faulte shee muste be content to heare, **Sub viri potestate eris, & ipse dominabitur tui.** Thou shalte be vnder the power of thy husband, and he shall be thy ruler.* And yet let vs consider the goodnes of god, how he vseth mercy with the rod of correction, in this soore beatyng of woman kinde, with these two strokes of pain with childe, and of subiection to the husband, God hath prouided that the first is eased by the byrth of the childe into the world, which so comforteth the mother, that anone she hath forgotten all the former paine that she toke with her childe. And the second is notably releued, by this that by the dominion and rule of the husbande, the wyfe is much eased of solicitude & thought for outward prouision of necessaries, & for defence of her right, and for aunswerynge to vniuste vexation, and suche others.

† diuulged] diuulled

And also specially by this, that by the goodnesse and gentle behauiour of the wyfe, the [3D2] husbande is manye tymes made much better then he woulde els be. And this saint Peter teacheth in this place, saiynge: **Vt si qui non credunt verbo, per mulierum conuersationem sine verbo lucrifiant**. He woulde specially that they should remember their subiection and gentlenes toward their husbandes, that if there be anye of their husbandes that peraduenture beleueth not the woorde of God preached amonge theim, whiche the wyues dothe beleue, they maye be wonne and conuerted to Christes faithe, by the holye conuersation of the women without preachinge. When they consider your holye conuersation (sayth saint Peter) with louing feare of God and of your husbands.* And here is to be noted that sainte Peter wrote this epistle or letter to the countreis where some were conuerted to Christes fayth, and some were not. And as the women commonly be more tender harted then the menne, so manye tymes they were soner conuerted to Christes religion, then the men were. And in this case he exhorteth the women to shew their faithful maner of liuyng by louing obedience & subiection, that so bi their good & godly conuersation, thei might allure their husbands to yᵉ same faith yᵗ they were of, & to beleue as thei did.* And here you se now again how highly the blessed apostle estemeth honest conuersation as a meane of as great efficacitie to allure men to goodnes, as is yᵉ word of exhortation or preachyng, as he had said afore in the second chapter. **Conuersationem vestram inter gentes habentes bonam, &c.** Biddynge them be of good conuersati[3D2ᵛ]on that where men backebite you and saie euill by you, as of malefactours, when they consider your good workes, they maye glorifie God, and be conuerted to God by your good example.* And I doubt not but that in this troublelous time of new opinions and errours that hath now many a daye persecuted the mindes of good fayethfull people, the stedfast and faythfull conuersation of the honest wiues hath staied their husbandes in the right trade, and made them good men, where els they would haue erred as others haue done, as well in this citie as in other places. **Quarum non sit extrinsecus capillatura, aut circumdatio auri, aut indumenti vestimentorum cultus*** Because Saint Peter hadde bidde al wiues please their husbandes with obedience and due subiection, lest they shoulde thinke thys subiection and pleasynge of their husbandes to stand in trimmyng and dressynge their bodies curiously and wantonlye for their husbandes pleasures, he declareth that he meaneth nothing lesse, & biddeth theim that they vse not to make their heere for the nonce, settyng it abrode smothly slickt, to make it shine in mens eyes, or curiously platted in traces, or as gentle women vse now adaies, purposly neglected hanging about their eies, as it were saiyng: I care not how my heere lye, and yet while they do so, they most care howe to pull abroade their lockes to be sene. And so when they take vppon them to care least then they care most for their heere. Some there be that can not be contente with their heere as God made it, but dothe painte it and set it in an[3D3]other hue, as when it was white hoore, they dye it fayre and yelowe, or if it be blacke as a crowe, it must be set in some lighter colour, as browne, or aburne, or redde: And so muste their browes and the bryes of their eye lyddes be painted proporcionably. All this disgisyng of womens heere saint Peter calleth by one name, **Capillatura,** makynge their heere, or curiouslye dressynge their heere, which he disswadeth and counsaileth to the contrary.* And .s. Paule **.i. Timo. ii.** biddeth all women apparell and raye theim selues in comelye rayment with bashfulnesse or shamefastnes, and with sobrietie. **Non in tortis crinibus,** not wyth their heere platted or sliked abroade. And bothe the blessed Apostles biddeth women not to vse superfluitie, of these golden abilimentes (as they be nowe called) nor of ouer costlye rayment dasshed wyth Pearles or precious stones.* Sainte Peter calleth suche precious and costlye garnishinge of rayment, **Cultus indumenti vestimentorum,** as who should saye, **Indumenti indumentorum,** or **Vestimenti vestimentorum.** The dressing of the raymente of all raymentes,* to signifie the preciousnes or riches of the rayment, as we vse to saye, the flower of all flowers. A felowe of all felowes, to signifie the excellencye of the thinge. Sainte Peter and saint Paule which were sure that they hadde the spirite of God, and spoke by the spirite of God, in Goddes name, disswadeth such costlines, and biddeth women not to set their mindes theron. For as saint Cypriane saieth. **Li. de habitu virginum.*** Chastitie in virgin, wife, and [3D3ᵛ] wydowe consisteth and standeth not onely in the sounde integritie, and wholenes of their flesshe, but also in a certayne shamefastnes and honesty of their apparell, for lightly there is no more precious and costlye dressynge then is amonge them whose honestye is lyght cheape. Therfore in no case let your raymente deface and sclaunder the sinceritie and integritie of your bodies, but that like as you kepe your bodyes chaste and cleane after your callynge, whether it be virginitye, mariage, or wydowehode. So let the dressynge of your heades, and the apparelynge of your bodyes be chaste, cleane, and after a sober fashion, not lyke players disgysed after any wanton maner, least the lightnesse of your dressynge shewe the lightnes of your condicions. Almightye God by the mouth of the blessed prophet **Esai. iii.** reproueth very earnestly and greuously this costlye & gorgious dressyng & wanton behauour of women which was then vsed in Ierusalem, as it is now in our time in England, **Pro eo quod eleuate sunt filie Sion, & ambulauerunt collo extento & nutibus oculorum ibant. &c.** He punisheth them with shame contrary to their pride and iolitie, saiynge: **Decaluauit dominus verticem filiarum Syon, & dominus crinem earum nudabit.*** He bryngeth theim to shame from toppe to toe, beginnyng at the head of whiche they were so proude, and so vnto the shooes of their fete. God wyll plucke the heeres from their heade, that they toke so muche thought to set forthe and to painte it, and will make it bare, and shewe it as it is. That euerye man [3D4] maye see it was not their owne, but perwyked† or paynted, eyther here by temporall miserye & sorow & sicknes, or in hell when al the world shal wonder at their pryde. Their trimmed shoes, their nouches, brooches, and Rynges, their chaynes, dimisentes, and pendentes, their costlye edges, and precious abilimentes shall come to naught.* And then their pleasaunt odours of muske, ciuet, and of all perfumes, shall be turned into stenche. **Erit pro suaui odore fetor.*** And for ioye and myrth, shal come sorowe and mournynge, for their pryde and exaltation, shal come vylenesse and deiection. What manne or woman wyll be so madde as wittynglye to vse that hath bene the destruction of other women? If a man or a woman dye vpon the meate and drinke that he hath taken, it maye well be thought poyson that he hath taken, and a man woulde bee well ware that he eate not of the same. You heare howe for suche curious and wanton behauiour, folowed a greuous stroke of correction: therfore beware you be not poysoned with yᵉ same drinke, lest you come to a like ende. This adulteration & chaunging of gods handyworke by painting womans heere to make it seme faire and yelow, or of their leers of their chekes to make them loke ruddy or of their forehed to hide yᵉ wrinkles & to make them loke smoth, is of the deuils inuention & neuer of gods teaching.* Therfore I must exhort al women to beware of counterfeting, adulterating, or chaunginge the fashion and fourme of Goddes worke, ether by yelow

† perwyked] perwynes

colour, blacke or redde pouder, or by any other medson corrupt or chaung[e] ye natural [3D4^v] lineamentes or fauour of man or woman, because they that vse that maner of doinge semeth to go about to correcte or amende the thinge that god hath made, and striueth against God, violentlye settynge hande vppon his worke. If there were an excellent Painter or a keruer that had made a goodly image of the best fashion that he could, if a busye bodye woulde take a tole, and take vppon him to amende the ymage so made, shoulde he not do iniurye to the sayde gaye workeman, and also dispite vnto hym? Yes surelye, For he shoulde seme to count the workeman but a fole, & nothing cunnyng. Then consider almighty God the workeman of all workemen, he made the face and body of man and woman as he thought best, then I praye you what arrogancy and presumption is it for man or woman to set to the pensile or tole to make it better? Thinkest thou that God will not take vengeaunce on thee for thy striuinge wyth him to amend: yea, rather to mar that he hath made. Therfore in that y^t thou thinkest thy selfe that thou arte made fayrer<.> thou art made fowler in dede, beggynge of colours made with pouder of stones, with rindes of trees or wyth ioyce of herbes, the thing that thou hast not of thy selfe. More ouer Christe sayth. **Mat. v. Non potes vnum capillum album facere aut nigrum.** Thou canst not make one heer of thy head white or blacke.* And yet thou by thy pride wylte proue him a lyer, and make thy selfe a better workman then he, paintynge thy heere or thy face not onelye blacke or white (for women set little by such [3E1] colours[)], but also yelowe or redde (**malo praesagio futurorum,** sayth S. Cipriane) with a shreude ossinge or prophecying of the colour that thy head shalbe of in the redde fyre of hel, when thou shalt come thither. Nowe I praye the that so paintest thy selfe, arte thou not afrayde, when thou shalte appeare afore the iudge at the generall iudgemente, he wyll not knowe the, but wil put the away from the rewarde that is prouided for all good people in heauen, sayinge: what haue we here? The figure of her face is steyned or polluted into a straunge countenaunce. Howe canst thou see God with suche eyes as he made not, but as the deuyls crafte hath died and steyned lyke the fyrye glistering eyes of the serpent, with whome thou shalt burne for euermore? The fyrst that I reade of that thus painted her phisnomy was the noughtye quene Iesabell, the common butcher and murderer of all the preachers and prophetes of almightye God. She was wyfe to Achab kinge of Israell, that destroied Naboth for his vineyard* when Hieu sometime seruaunt to Achab and to his sonne Ioram, was anoynted kinge, and had slayne his Lorde and maister Ioram by Goddes commaundemente,* he came into Iezraell, where the kinges manoure was, there to do vengeaunce on Iezabell that noughty quene: she trustinge to haue grace and fauoure at his handes yf she might moue him to concupiscence, paynted her eyes and her heare and her face after the best fashion. But this woulde not helpe, they that were aboue in the chambre with [3E1^v] her, were commaunded to pitche her downe at the wyndowe, and so they did, and there she was all to troden vnder the horse feete, so that there was no more lefte but the scull of her head, and her fete, and the knockels of her handes, whiche serued for the dogges, according to the prophecie of the blessed prophete Helye. **In agro Iezraell commedent canes carnes Iezabel. iiii. Reg. ix.*** You see what payntinge serued for. But nowe maried women wyll pretende and make an excuse by theyr husbandes, sayinge: that they take all the labours in payntinge and trimming them selues to please theyr husbandes, and so doynge, they make theyr husbandes partetakers of theyr offence, and consequently of theyr dampnation for company sake. And I shall aduertise all maried men, and all them that haue doughters to kepe, that whether the tyrynge or trimminge of your wyues and doughters be for to please you as they say, or to please them selues as you say, that you suffer not theym to vse it, because it is not godlye (as I haue tolde you) and also because of the peryll that may come of it. For when they set them selues forth so curyouselye, and goeth abroade in the streates, or sytteth in theyr shoppe windows, or elles peraduenture at feastes and bankettes with vicious companye, it is not you alone that they woulde haue to loke vpon them, it is not you alone that is pleased with the sight of theim, it is not you alone that casteth theyr eyes after theim, or that draweth longe sighes [3E2] of carnall loue after them, this is not the waye to kepe theim for youre selues.* Beware therefore good husbandes that you set not youre wyues or doughters so to sale, for feare least harme come of it. And you good wiues beware of the daunger and peryll of youre honestye, and specially beware of the peryll of your soules. If yo[u] nouryshe the luste of concupiscence, and sette on fyre the breadynge of sinne so beynge as a sword or dagger to stryke an other man to the hearte, and as a verye poysonne to destroy others, you knowe the perill of it. Wo be to him or her (sayth Chryste) that geueth occasion of ruyne, woo and sorowe euerlastinge in hell.* Beare not your selues proude of youre husbandes riches, sayinge: my husbande hath landes and rentes to mainetayne all the costes that I do vpon me, my husbande hath golde inoughe in his coffers, his riches commeth in and encreaseth dayelye: The time shall comme that you shall saye wringinge youre handes, and gnasshinge youre teeth in Hell. **Sapient, v. Quid nobis profuit superbia? aut diuitiarum iactantia quid contulit nobis? Talia dixerunt in inferno qui peccaue-runt. &c.**

They that haue synned, shall saye after this manner in Hell. What dydde oure pryde auayle vs? Or what profitte hadde we by boastynge of oure ryches?* As whoo shoulde saye, none at all, but rather aggrauatethe oure dampnation. If thou be riche, lette the pouertie feele thy ryches, helpe theim wyth [3E2ᵛ] thy riches, and bestowe it not in superfluous ornamentes. Study to dresse youre soules (sayth S. Peter here) and trymme the inwarde man, **qui absconditus est cordis homo,** that is hyd within you, your soules whiche God seeth very well,* and do it so that your spirite be not corrupte or defouled with sinne, but be quiete, not troubled with inordinate concupiscence or desyre of the fleshe, nor of the minde, studyinge for to do displeasures or to do hurte. And also that your spirite be modest, kepinge a meane and measure in all your sayinges and doinges, such a soule (saith S. Peter) **est in conspectu dei locuples,** is ryche in the sight of God,* for the true riches is the riches of vertues, they wyll stycke by vs, where other be fluxe and fadinge, and wyll awaye. Suche is the riches that we ought to be glad of, for these we ought to laboure: and with suche riches S. Peter biddeth all wyues to adorne them selues, to be cleane in soule: and as for outwarde dressynge, to kepe an honeste measure as besemeth women, shewinge sadnes and honestie, in huswyfery and in good dedes. **Sic enim aliquando et sanctae mulieres sperantes in deo ornabant se subiecte propriis viris.** For so (sayth he) holye women that hoped and trusted in God, arayed theym selues here afore in olde time, whiche were subiect and obedient to theyr owne husbandes. Example he taketh of Sara, that was wyfe to the blessed Patriarch Abraham.* I thinke that yf we sawe nowe in oure time the tiringe of her, the dressing of her head, and the whomelines of her raiment, [3E3] it woulde make vs laughe, and yet it was good and huswyfely for that time I doubte not. But the rayment that S. Peter commendeth in her, was the raymente of her soule, her prompte and ready subiection and obedience to her husbande, she forsoke her countrey, and her kinred and acquaintaunce, to accompanye him, and do as he woulde haue her to do.* And in processe, when the thre aungels appeared like men to Abraham sitting at his dore, and he inuited them to his house, he badde Sara his wyfe make spede, to take floure and knede it, to make them a cake baken vnder a panne for theyr dinner, she ful obediently did as she was bid, while he runne to his herde of catell, and toke a fat yonge calfe and gaue it to his seruaunte to dresse it and to seeth it, and so with mylke and butter, and that sodde veale, he made them good chere,* I trowe theyr drynke was water, for it was in the feruent heat of the daye, and in a hote countreye,* woulde God men coulde be content with suche hospitalitie now a dayes, there should many more be fedde then be, and the hospitalitie should be more acceptable to God then it is nowe, with diuersitie of exquisite disshes, dasshed with spices and delicate wynes, and vsed for kynredde and freindes, and suche as can requyte lyke agayne: If poore people haue anye thinge, it is those scrappes that be nexte the dogges meate.* And yet more, when Abraham her husband badde her that she should not saye that she was his wyfe, but that she was [3E3ᵛ] his sister, and he her brother, she dydde so as the time serued.* And more ouer Sainte Peter noteth her obedience and subiection to her husbande, by that she called him her Lorde, and that was whan the Aungell told Abraham that Sara his wife shoulde beare him a chylde, she stode behynde the bowre doore and smiled, sayinge: What, shall I playe the wanton nowe in mine olde age, & Dominus meus vetulus est? and my Lorde is an olde man?* It was her husband that she called Lorde, in that gyuinge to all wiues example of subiection and obedience to their husbandes: And Saynte Peter sayeth to all wyues, you be all her doughters as longe as you doo well, and lyke sobre matrones as shee dydde, and so doynge, you shall not nede to feare any trouble or displeasure of youre husbandes, but shall liue quietelye and louingely together.

Viri similiter cohabitantes secundum scientiam, quasi infirmiori vasculo mu-liebri impartientes honorem.*

Nowe you haue hearde the fatherlye and holsome counsaile that Sainte Peter hath geuen to all wiues, teachynge theim howe they shoulde order theim selues to their husbandes, and to the worlde, because the husbandes shall not be to sore nor cruell to theyr wiues, nor to hie and lordelye ouer theim, he geueth also to the husbandes a holesome lesson as it were, sayinge: Similiter. Euen like as I haue exhorted the wyues to do their dueties to their husbandes, so I [3E4] muste exhorte and counsayle you to do your duties to theim, althoughe I haue tolde you that Sara called Abraham her Lorde, by her humble and lowlye hearte, yet you muste not so take youre selues as lordes ouer your wyues, nor vse theim as your seruauntes, nor as your drudges, but as your makes, and as youre felowes, specially in domesticall cohabitation, and dwelling in one house with theim, and in youre coniugall acte to gether, accordynge to science, and to the iudgemente of ryghte reason, and by wysedome.*

Saynt Ambrose. Epist. lxxxii. sayth, the wyfe muste do reuerence to the hus-bande, as to her heade and ruler, but no seruice, as his seruaunt, drudge, or bondwoman. She muste be contente to be ruled by her husbande, but not to be compelled by correction, no, not so muche as by chydynge. For indigna est coniugio quae digna est iurgio, she is not worthye to be a wyfe, that is worthye to be chydde.* Then you maye be sure she is muche moore vnworthye to be a wyfe that wyll not doo her owne woorke withoute strokes: her husbandes woorke is her owne woorke. Strokes be mete for youre leude seruauntes and bondewomen, and not for youre makes. Therefore all wyues when they wyll deserue beatinge, they reneige and refuse the honestie of a wyfe, retourning to seruantes state agayne.

They shoulde not be taken furth with the graue and sadde matrones, and with honest [3E4ᵛ] wyues, but let them come behynde with the seruauntes, because they haue not lefte theyr seruyle conditions. And then (good men) as you woulde your wyues should honoure you, so must you parte honoure with theym, honourynge the woman as the weaker vessell (sayth S. Peter.)* And yf she be crabbed and shrewshaken, yet you must beare with her as ye woulde she should forbeare you when you be oute of the waye, in your fume or in your rage. Socrates that noble Philosopher had two wyues (as S. Hierome wryteth. **primo contra Iouinianum**) with whiche he hadde muche sorowe, and specially with Xantippe, as **Aulus Gelius** wryteth, and also Saint Hierome there.* On a tyme after she had bytterly scolled and rayled at hym, he went from her, and let her alone, and as he wente forth of the dore, she bestowed the purtinence of a chaumber vessell vpon his head for his fare well, he dyd no more but with his handekercheife wiped his heade, and sayde: I knewe it woulde be thus, that after thunder clappes woulde come a showre.* And when hys scholers and freendes woulde aske hym howe he coulde forbeare her, and why he dryue her not oute of his doores? No (sayeth he) not so, I haue a iewell of her,* for she doeth so exercyse my patience, that when I come abroade, I care not what anye man sayeth or doeth to me, it greueth me not, I am so vsed to suffer her, that none other can greue me: For true it is that **trouble worketh patience.*** Manye [3F1] suche examples of Gentyles hystoryes I coulde rehearse, in whiche appeareth howe manye noble men haue borne with theyr wyues, and forborne them, though theyr conditions were leude and noughtye, ledde thereto by the verye lyghte and iudgemente of reason, withoute preachinge of the holye worde of GOD. Christen men be taughte by oure Sauioure Chryste, that howe soeuer the conditions of the man or the woman be, they must euerye one suffer the other, for better for worse, tyll death theym departe. Adultery maye departe bedde and boorde,* but the indiuisible knotte of wedlocke can not be dissolued. Saynt Hierome reciteth the sayinge of Theophrastus that noble morall philosopher, sayinge: **Vxoris nulla est electio sed qualiscunque obuenerit habenda est**. He thinketh there is no choyse of a wyfe, but what maner so euer she be of, men muste take her: men shall neuer learne her conditions (sayth he) till after they be marryed.*

A horse, an oxe, a cowe, fyrste be proued afore they be boughte, and so is cloth wollen and lynnen, so is the potte, the panne, cheyres, stooles, cuppes, and suche other ornamentes and implementes, onelye a wyfe (sayth he) is not shewed what she is, leaste peraduenture she shoulde displease and be reiecte and refused, afore she be taken or maryed. He sayeth this onelye of the women, but we haue knowen as muche vncertayntye when women haue chosen theyr husbandes, and as muche yll proofe of theim. But howe so [3F1ᵛ] euer that be, mutuall loue, and mutuall sufferaunce shall ease muche of this ambiguitie, by turninge necessitie into vertue,* and speciallye the man whiche is naturallye more stronge, and shoulde be more wyse and discrete, muste remember the infyrmitie of the woman, and muste beare with her, and muste studye for the quietnes of his house. Saynt Ambrose **Exameron. libro. v. cap. vii.** reciteth a notable example to moue all maried folkes as well men as women, to concorde and to agree together. The example is of the lamprey, and a serpente called **Vipera nequissimum genus bestie,** a serpent mooste mischeuous and venemous. If there be anye of theim with vs, it is the adder. The propertie of this serpent is this, when he lyste to gendre, specially where he breadeth nighe the Sea coaste, he commeth to the water syde and there hisseth after his maner, callynge to him his make the Lampreye, with his continuall hyssynge. The Lampreye, as soone as she perceaueth hym there, draweth to the shoore, and shalowe water, and when the adder spyeth her commynge, he vommiteth and braketh awaye out of him selfe all hys poysonne and venome, and so commeth to her cleane and holesome, and then companieth with her and then they gendre together.*

Here maye the manne and the womanne learne to beare and suffer euerye one the manners of the other. Here maye the manne learne to ordre his wife with sobrenes, and the wyfe [3F2] to be gentle and obediente. What thynge is worse then venomme of a Serpente? And yet the Lampreye feareth not that, in her make the adder, she commeth gentillye at his callinge, and louingelye embraseth hym.

Therefore good wyues, yf youre husbandes be venemous, crabbed, and cumbe-rous, or (as you call it) shrewe shaken, you muste come at his callynge, doo as he byddeth you, be gentle vnto him, and so thoughe his venome hurte others, it shall not hurte you. And you marryed men, be you prudente as the Serpente, worke wyselye, and laye awaye youre venomme, when you shall companye with youre makes, that is alwaye and euer, for you muste euer dwell with her (as Saynte Peter sayeth here), therefore you muste alwaye laye awaye youre poysonne, so that you vse none towarde her. You muste alwaye laye downe as well all your churlysshe swellynge, as all youre Lordelye and proude fasshion, lette her perceaue none suche in you, remember you be not her Lorde (as I sayde) ye be but her husbande, and her make. The Adder layeth awaye his poysonne for his make the Lampreyes sake, and so must you do away all pryde, malice and crabbednes for your wiues sake, and so doinge you shall dwell with your wyfe, **secundum scientiam**, accord-inge to science and wisedome* (as Saynt Peter sayth here) considerynge that she is the weaker vessell, the weaker creature, for all we be Goddes vesselles, [3F2ᵛ] eyther the vessels of Goddes yre, or the vesselles of his mercye. The woman for the mooste parte is weaker then the man, in mynde and also in bodye, and dysposed to more infyrmities, therefore you muste do her honoure accordyngelye. This worde **honoure** in Scripture hath a large signification: sometyme it signifieth reuerence and obedience, and so it is not taken here, for the man oweth none suche to the wyfe: Sometime it signifieth prouision of necessaryes, and so is it taken in the commaundemente of GOD, of the honoure that euerye man oweth to his parentes, for whome he muste not onelye bowe with cappe and knee, but also is bounde to prouyde for theim necessaryes if they nede. Thyrde, in this place of Saynte Peter, it maye signifie honeste intreatynge of her in youre coniugall acte, in whiche you muste vse science and wysedome, knowinge that the sayde acte, for the entent to gette chyldren to be broughte vppe in Chrystes fayth and in vertue, is good and commendable: if it be to releiue the infyrmitie of the fleshe, and to kepe you from others, it is tollerable, otherwyse to do lyke brute beastes for prolongynge of thy luste, is vycious and sinnefull, you muste geue honoure and spare her, and not mysvse her in this manner. And when you perceiue that she hath conceyued, you must abstayne, for feare leaste you destroye that GOD hath made: you muste consydre also that she is disposed to dyuers infyrmities, and when you perceaue her [3F3] in suche case, you muste geue honoure and spare her, cherysshe and comforte her: you must also honoure her with solicitude and proui-sion, that she lacke nothinge necessarye. Remember that she is coinheritoure, and copartener of the gracious gyfte of lyfe euerlastynge in heauen, as well as you, therefore vse her thereafter, not as a fylthie wretche woulde vse a calotte or a strumpette, the vesselles of Goddes indignation and wrath, apte for destruction and dampnation. The wyfe is the vessell of grace, and apte to come to the glorye in heauen as well as the man, for in Christe there is noo dyfference betwyxte man and woman. **Galath. iii. Non est seruus neque liber, non est masculus, neque femina, omnes enim vos vnum estis in Christo Iesu.** There is no difference betwixte the bondeman and the freeman, betwixte the man and the woman, all is one in the grace of fayth on Christe, and in glory to be obteined and gotten by Christe.*

Then to conclude with Sainte Peter, you must vse youre selues towarde youre wyues, dwellinge and kepinge house with them, after science and wisedome, withoute crokednes, rygoure, and malyce, honouringe them, bearinge with theim, and forbearinge them, as the weaker vessell, and disposed to manye infyrmities, and therefore vsinge them honestly, prouidinge for theim after youre habilitie and power, that they lacke not that is necessarye for theim, because they be partakers of lyke glorye as you be. And all this [3F3ᵛ] muste you do (sayth Saint Peter) **Vt non impediantur orationes vestrae,** that youre prayers be not lette and hindered frome their effecte by the contrarie,* for if there be rancoure, malice, and stryfe betwixte you, GOD will not heare your prayers, for he is the GOD of peace, and not of discention and debate. Therefore he that wyl be hearde, muste be peaceable, and no brawler. If you be not cleane of conuersation, absteininge for causes aboue mencioned, but folowe youre luste lyke beastes, you shall hindre youre prayers that they shall not be hearde. There be dayes appointed for fastinge, and holye dayes appointed for prayer and holines, if you will not at such times abstaine, but please the flesshe, your prayers will be let and hindred by fleshlye luste, that God will not heare them. And therefore S. Paul **i. Corin. vii.** biddeth the man and the wife by one assent to abstaine, that they may attende to their prayers.* You maye see howe both the Apostles, Saint Peter and Saint Paule agreith in this, hauinge good occasion by the aucthoritie of the olde testamente, for there was commaundement geuen to the people of Israell two daies before they shoulde haue the lawe geuen theim in the mount of Sinai, amonge other pointes of cleanes. **Et ne appropinquetis vxoribus vestris. Exo. xix.** that they should not come nigh their wiues.* For though the acte of matrimonie be lawfull, yet it hath some vncleannes annexed and concurrente with it, and speciallie it depresseth and pulleth [3F4] downe the witte frome contemplation of heauenly thinges, because of the vehement carnall pleasure in the acte. Nowe both these muste be remoued, when you shall geue your selues to god in fastinge, keping holy daies, and suche holines, and likewise receauinge the Sacramente of the aulter, and that was signi-fied **.i. Reg. xxi. Si mundi sunt pueri maxime a mulieribus manducent,** where kinge Dauid and his companie were sore a hungred, they came to Achimelech the highe preiste, then dwellinge in Nobe, where the tabernacle and the Arche of GOD was, he desired meate, this preiste Achimelech had none but the twelue holy loues of breade that stode afore the Arche, by a certaine ceremonie of their lawe, whiche Achimelech was content to geue them, so that they were cleane from women.* And then you may be sure that suche cleanes and muche more, is required to them that shall worthelye receiue that holy and gratious breade that came downe from heauen, oure Sauioure Christ vnder the fourme of breade, and his precious bloude vnder the fourme of wine. To whiche moste reuerende body and bloude be all honour and worshippe for euer. Amen.

IN fide autem omnes vnanimes, compatientes fraternitatis amatores.* These
wordes be redde in Christes churche for the epistle in the masse, the fifte Sonday
after Trinitie Sondaye,* and be wrytten in this thyrd Chapiter of Saint Peters
fyrste Epistle, where after he had afore geuen fruitefull and holesome exhortations
and lessons, to speciall estates of men and women, as to them that be in bondage,
and to all prentises and seruauntes, and to all seruinge men and women, and
afterwarde to wyues and to maryed men, of whiche I entreated in my laste sermon.* Nowe the blessed Apostle retourneth to generall lessons to all men and
women, vsing vs as good scholemasters and gouernours of noble mens children
ordreth them that be vnder theyr gouernaunce, fyrst exercisinge them in the
thinges that shal beseme their byrth, and consequently howe they shall exchewe
and auoyde the contraries, and such thinges as do not beseme a gentilman, so doth
S. Peter, first exercise vs in wel doynge, and seconde, in auoidinge ill doing, that so
we may be conformable to oure byrth of God by baptisme, and maye vse oure
selues according to that gentle, noble, and gratious new natiuitie and byrth. **In
fide autem omnes vnanimes.** He byddeth vs **be all of one mynde in oure fayth,**
and in all matters concernynge our fayth. The new translation hath. **In summa
omnes vnanimes.*** [3G1] In conclusion to be short, be al of one minde, and in the
epistle of the said fift sundaye after the trinitie, it is read: **Omnes vnanimes in
oratione estote.** Be you all of one minde in your praiers, whyche might seme to
haue some coherence to that went immediatlye afore, where he bade the man and
wife to agree, lest by the contrary by theyr dissension and variaunce theyr prayers
mighte be lette and hindred.* And then accordinge to the same he willeth all men
and women to be of one minde in theyr praiers, for if there be discord among
them, theyr prayers wil not be heard. But let vs take this text of Saint Peters epistle
as it is writ in the common translation. **In fide omnes vnanimes,** Be all of one
minde in your faithe, as they were that be spoken of. **Act. iiii. Multitudinis
credentium erat cor vnum et anima vna.** The multitude of them that beleued in
the primitiue churche, hadde one hart and one soule, one will and one minde.
And therfore it followeth: **Et gratia magna erat in omnibus illis,** there was greate
grace in them all.* For where is concord and vnitie, there the holye gost spreadeth
his grace aboundantly, and contrarye where be scismes and diuersitie of errours and
opinions, God withdraweth grace, and then men runne without brydell from one
opinion to another, from one heresie to an other, tyll men be set all on a rore and
out of quietnes, as it appeareth euidently in Germany, wher be almost as manie
heresies and diuers waies in theyr faith, as be cities or townes, euery citie taking his
own wai & his own fashion in their sacraments & ceremonies.* [3G1ᵛ] This
confusion S. Paule greatly feared to com among his disciples the Corinthers when
he praied them for gods sake, & for the name of our lord Iesu Christ **vt idipsum
dicatis omnes, et non sint in vobis scismata .i. Cor. i.** That they should say al one
way, so that there should be no scisme or diuision among them, but that thei shuld
be parfite in one minde, as wel in theyr doinges as in theyr knowledge or learning.* He would not they shuld varye so much as in thought or minde. Here among
you in this citie som wil heare masse, some will heare none by theyr good wils, som
wil be shriuen, som wil not, but for feare, or els for shame,* some wyll pay tithes &
offeringes, som wil not, in that wors then the Iewes which paid them truly, and

fyrst frutes & many other duties beside.* Som wil prai for the dead, som wil not, I heare of muche suche discension among you, I will not descende to the specialties, but with s. Paule & with s. Peter I pray you accord you (good maisters & frends) for feare least the anger of God fall vpon this citye, which God forbidde it should. **Compatientes**, we must one suffer with another, & beare one with another,* like the louing members or lims of one mistical body of Christ. Let vs take example of our own lims in our own bodies, if one hande be not able to do thy busines, anon commeth the other hand to worke, and if thy handes wyl not serue, thou settest to thy foote, yea, & if nede be thy teth and al. If any part of our bodie be hurt, the eyes seketh for a plaister, the fete laboreth to seke a surgion, the tonge laboreth declaring the griefe and [3G2] praying for help, & so euery part of our bodies taketh paine & laboreth one for another, and with an other, so considering that we be the lymmes of Christes body, we should louingly one bear with an other to releue the paine and laboure that we see our neighbour susteine. If there be iii. or .iiii. bearing a great burden, if ther be a good felow or two that wil com & set to theyr shulders to bear with them, this wil greatly lighten theyr burthen ease them & comfort theym, so when he that is in paine seeth other men sory & ready to set to their handes to releue him, ease him, and comfort him, this mitigateth his paine wonder<s>ly, and this is true aswel in spiritual infirmities of the soule, as in bodely paynes and infirmities. After this maner saynt Paule toke the diseases of other men. **ii. Cor. xi. Quis infirmatur et ego non infirmor?** Who is sicke or weake in his faith or in vertue or anye point of vertuous liuing, but that I am sick with him, being as sory for him as I should be for my selfe if I were so diseased. **Quis scandalizatur et ego non vror?** Who is offended, as who should say there is no man offended takinge occasion of desperacion or of any sin, by the painefulnes of trouble, or by il example of others, but that I am burned for his sake with the flames of charitie, taking compassion for him & with him?* And euen so we al shuld euery one beare an others burden, thinking an other mans misfortune as his own. Charitie requireth y^t we should after this maner take our neighbours hurt or displesure, & then you maye perceiue of this how far they be from charity [3G2^v] that reioyce of other mens harme or displeasure, and will insult and vmbraid them of it, and make it worse rather then better. **Fraternitatis amatores,** you must loue the fraternitie, the brotherheade,* not onely your brothers (as we be al brothers in God our father, and in Christ our regeneratour, that hathe gotte vs againe by baptisme) but we must also loue the brotherhead, that is to say, the company, vnitie, and knotte of the brothers all together, for although e[u]erye man and woman by him selfe muste be loued, yet we muste more loue the comontie or comon concord of them all together, then the perticular persons of the same, or then any particular companye amonge the same whole multitude. Heretikes haue gathered to them special companies which they haue called a brotherhed, as now in our time mani callith their confederacie the brotherhead, but they be but patched peces and cantels of the brotherhead.* They diuideth, disperseth, & scattereth that vniuersal and comon brotherhead that Saynt Peter here speaketh of, rather then aduanceth it or dothe it any good.* They be cantels broken of from the catholike & vniuersal brotherhed of faithful christen people, they semed somtime to be of the brotherhed, but they wer not trueli & stedfastly of them, for as s, Iohn saith .i. Ioh. ii. **If they had bene of them they wold haue taried with them,** but by theyr swaruing away, they manifestly shew them selues that they wer no true members of Christes misticall body the catholik churche,* but rather like superfluous & corrupt humors euomited & cast out to [3G3] releue & ease the

bodie that was infected by them. If men had not better loued theyr priuate &
singuler opinions, then the comon fraternitie, there should neuer so many heresies
haue sprong vp among Christen people.† When the comon knot of fraternitie is
once broken, then men take theyr libertie and run at large, euery man as his
opinion will draw him, till at the last they marre all. And euyn so it is in cities and
townes and great cominalties, except men loue better the comontie and the
comon wealth, then theyr singuler profit and auantage, the state of the towne or
citie decayeth and all goeth to ruine. Examples we rede of the Romanes, which
while they magnified the comon wealth, prospered wonderouslye, but after they
had broughte the rule and authoritie of the citie into the power of a few persons, so
that none should rule but they. And afterwarde when they were striken with
ambition and desyre of honor that euery man would be a lorde and a ruler, anon by
intestine battels, seditions, and parts taking, al cam to nought, they lost all theyr
royaltie and dominions, a great deale faster then they had got them afore. You
haue in this citie erect a certaine confederacie, which you call the companye, I
pray God it may do well, but I perceiue a certaine mundanitie in it, a worldlye
couetous caste to bring the gaines that was indifferent & comon to al the mar-
chants of this citie into the handes of a fewe persones.* Therefore good neyghbours loue the whole brotherhed & vniuersal companie of Christes faithful people,
diuide it not, & if ther [3G3ᵛ] be any cantel broken out, pray for them that thei
may returne and come home againe to the great flocke and congregation of
Christen people, and that they may hereafter loue the whole fraternitie. **Misericordes,** you must be merciful.* Our sauiour Christ in the gospell, exhorting vs to
mercye, like as our father in heauen is mercifull, putteth thre kindes of mercie.
Luc. vi. One consisteth in not iudging nor condempning our neighbour of ani
mortal crime without euident signes. For he that withoute euidence of a manyfest
facte, or of such signes as can not be countersayd & excused by any tergiuersacion
will iudge hys neighbour and inwardly condempne him as a malefactour, hath a
cruel hart and is not merciful. The second kinde of mercy that our sauiour
speaketh of ther, standeth in forgiuing offences done to vs, like as we wolde be
forgiuen, **Dimittite et dimittetur vobis,** forgiue, and you shall be forgiuen.* But
because that in the naughty world that now runneth by ouermuch suffering, ill
persons may take occasions of boldnes to do yll. It is not at al times necessary to
forgiue both the offence and the iniury. The offence and displeasure of minde, and
the yll wil to the person that hathe offended thee, muste nedes be forgiuen and
layd away, but the wrong done vnto thee, thou mayst redresse by the order of the
lawes, euer without any sinister desyre or purpose to vndo or notabli to hurt him
that thou suest at the lawes. Notwithstanding if thou forgiue the iniuri aswel as the
offence, it is a dede of super[er]ogacion* & wel done, & shal not be vnre-
war[3G4]ded at the day of iudgement, as Christ said, **quod cumque superero-
gaueris cum rediero, ego reddam tibi<=>** Luc. x. What so euer thou bestowest
ouer head aboue thy dutie when I come I shall paye it thee.* The thyrd kinde of
mercy consisteth in releuinge yᵉ nede of thy poore neighbour with thy almes of
such things as thou perceiuest him to haue nede of, whether they be bodely or
gostly. **Dare et dabitur vobis,** giue charitably and there shal be gyuen you grace in
this world, and hereafter life euerlasting,* specially if you giue as S. Paule speaketh
ii. Cor. ix. sic quasi benedictionem, et non quasi auaritiam, as a blessinge, and
not as auarice,* that is to say, abundantly and not nigardly or against your wil.

† people] poople

Chrisost. Qui elimosinam dat inuitus auare dat. He that giueth his almes againste his will, giueth it nigardly, more couetinge to saue it for him selfe, then to
releue the poore folkes by it.* We must be liberal according to our power, considering that **qui parce seminat parce et metet,** he that soweth spareli and thin, shal
reape thin, & he that soweth in blessinges with a good wil and plentifully (as
blessinges be giuen) shal reape & gather in plenty at the time of reward euerlasting,* not vnderstanding by him y^t sparely soweth him that litle hath & litle
giueth, for if his minde be prompt & redi to giue more if he had more & mighte
more spare, god wil accept him among the large giuers, and his good wil shalbe
accepte according to that he hath, and not after that he hath not .ii. Cor. viii.* as
the poore widdowes offering of .ii. half farthings was better accept, then the riche
gifts of ye ryche men that offred to the church stock in Ierusalem.* [3G4^v] And
amonge other poore and needye persons I praye you extende your mercie and
charitable almes on the poore studentes of the vniuersityes of this realm, which
like as they were neuer fewer in nombre, so they were neuer poorer of exhibicion
to finde them necessaries,* by your abioundance and plentie of that goodes that
God hath sent you, mercifullye bestowe vpon theym that you may be parte takers
of the graces that God hath giuen them, and so betwixte you and theym there may
be some equalitie (as S. Paul speaketh, exhorting ye Corinthers to do theyr almes
on the poore Christen people at Ierusalem, then lately conuerted to Christes
faith)* so that wyth distributing part of your temporall substaunce among them,
you may receiue part of the learning and other graces that God hath giuen theym,
by which they may supply & make vp that you lacke in spirituall giftes, like as you
supplye that they lack in temporal goodes. Euen like as it is written in the story of
Exo. xvi. when the people of Israel should gather Manna that they were fedde w^t
in deserte, he that gathered most had no more then he that gathered lesse, they
had but the measure called **Gomor,** for euerye person, and so God disposed that
meate that they were equallye serued & euery man had inough,* so according to S.
Paules minde, God will doe with your charitable almes bestowed on them, & with
theyr giftes of grace, that you shal haue inough, and they shall haue inough, you
shal be neuer the poorer at the yeres end, but the richer, & beside that you shal be
[3H1] encreased in grace & goodnes by them, by whiche al thinges shal go the
better forwarde wyth you and they shal haue by you more temporal help for to
sustaine them to theyr study, & theyr giftes of grace shal be neuer the lesse.* And
moreouer that is most to be embraced and regarded, **Augebit incrementa frugum
iustitie vestre,** God wil augment the encrease of the corn of your iustice.* Iustice
is holynes & good liuing, the corne & frut that cometh of iustice, is reward
euerlasting, which shalbe encreased & enlarged bi your almes so y^t you may now
gather what is ye reward of merci, pity & almes dedes, you shalbe rewarded here
temporallye w^t encrease of your riches, & gostly with encrease of grace, & finally
with abundance of glorye and ioyes euerlasting in heauen. And al this our sauiour
Christ compriseth in fewe words, **date†** et dabitur vobis giue, and all these afore
said shalbe giue$n$ you.* And I feare me that because men be so hard and streight
laced, that they wil not depart with theyr transitorie & worldly substance to them
that might redub spirituall solace to them by theyr praiers, God withdraweth grace,
& also suffreth you to decay & not to come forward in temporal substance. It
foloweth in the text of s. Peters epistle, **Modesti.*** Tully **primo officiorum**

† date] data

diffineth **Modestia** after the minde of the Stoikes: **Modestia sit† scientia earum rerum que agentur aut dicentur loco suo collocandarum,** it is a knowledge to set in theyr owne place al things that shalbe done or saide, to place al our doings & sayings according to the oportunitie of the time as occasion shal serue.* It is a foul thing & a great faut to bring in light language, & [3H1ᵛ] to speake gestingly as it wer in an alehouse when men be in communication of an earnest & sad matter. **Tulli** bringeth example of **Pericles** & **Sophocles** which wer felowes or brothers together in yᵉ office of **Pretura.*** Thei wer **Pretors** together, highest officers in the city of Rome next to the Consuls, in so much yᵗ in the absence of the Consuls they bear yᵉ consuls authoritie: They wer a mean betwixt the Consuls & the comon people, so that they shuld refer vnto the comons such thinges as were decreed bi the Consuls, & the Counsel of the senate concerning the people, & of such things as the people had to do withal, & thei had the hearing of the causes of the people & authoritie to giue sentences and make lawes & ordinances, for the ordering & quietnes of them, & to auance and to set them forth to warre as nede required. And as **Marcus Varro primo de lingua latina,** saith of that the office had his name **pretor dictus que periret exercitui:** because he should go afore the hoste & guide them. They should also speake for the people vnto the senate, & shuld defend them from wrong.* The said ii. **pretors** were on a time in counsel together about a cause concerninge theyr office, & by chaunce there came by them a welfauored & faire childe, then **Sophocles** in the midle of theyr matter said: **O puerum pulchrum Pericle,** O brother **Pericles,** lo yonder is a fair child: the other answerd him: **pretorem Sophocle decet non solum manus, sed etiam oculos abstinentes habere,** It besemeth a Pretor not onelye to haue his handes abstaining from bribery, but also hys eyes from wanton concupiscence. If **Sophocles** had said those wordes in a time when men wer about [3H2] to chuse men to do a feate, as is vsed with vs to play in an interlude, to playe a virgins part or a woers part, or suche like, when men vse to chuse fayr and welfauored yong men for their purpose, the said **Sophocles** shoulde a deserued none suche checke, but then in the middle of an earnest matter to speake of such light facions or fansies, because his sayinge was not well placed, he lacked **Modestia** that we speake of nowe, and was to be blamed.* Likewise if a man in his studie, or riding in his iourney, would muse in makinge verses, or how he should tell his tale afore a Iudge, or if a diuine woulde muse or recorde his sermon by the way riding, al this were good and laudable, but if he would so do, or would be in his dumps* when he were among his louing friendes and good felowes at a feast, or at a banket: he should seeme to be a churle and to lacke good maners, because he knewe not his time. Or if man woulde syng in the myddle of the market, or in a court at the barre afore the iudge when ther be weighty matters in hand, he should offend against modestie, & against al good humanitie, so that he maye be called modest or manerly that in al his behauiour vseth good maner and measure, and a meane. **Modestia** cometh of **modus** a measure, which is a vertue. **Nimietas** (as S. Iherome saith) is his contrarye vice,* whiche is forbid by the comon prouerbe, **Ne quid nimis** do in nothing to muche.* To muche passeth measure and passeth good maners, suche as in theyr fare at theyr borde or in their apparel and rayment excedeth theyr substaunce spending and wasting more then theyr lands or occupying [3H2ᵛ] wil extend to, or maintain, they kepe no modesty, no measure, nor good maner, they offend in **Nimietie,** they come vnto to much. How many (thinke you) of our neighbours now at the holye

† sit] est

time of Christmas comming,* wil excede modesty and good measure in theyr fare, spending so much now for ostentacion & pride, that they shall fare the worse in theyr dishe til Easter. It wer best to kepe such a measure now, that you may haue somwhat left to helpe your selfe an other time. As for modestie and measure in apparel, [it] was neuer lesse vsed, veluet & other silkes be as comonly on the pore mens backe, that liueth from hand to mouth,* as on the gentleman, or as on the alderman of this citye. The pride of the worlde is suche, that it bringeth al men almost to the extremitie of nimietie & vnto to muche. Therfore S. Peter knowyng that pride is an aduersarie to modesti, to manerlynes, and to the meane, he exhorteth vs as for to conserue and kepe modestie to vse humilitie. **Humiles** (saith he) lowly of hart,* so that when god geueth you any of these giftes of goodnes aforesaid, you be not proude of them, but thank God for theim, attributing al to God that gaue them to vs, and may take them away when he list. It is but a very folishnes for a man to be proud of that he hath not of him self, but that may be taken from him at euery twinckling of an eye, if it please the gyuer. **Humilitas dicitur ab humo,** it hath his name of the earth of the ground, which is lowest & most grosse element. We must know our state, our condicion, whereof we come & whereto we shal, which if men wold inwardly consider, they shuld neuer be proud [3H3] of any gift that god hath giuen them, whether it be kinred, landes, possessions, office, authority, acquaintance with great men, and to be in fauour with them. If men would consider howe hardlye such giftes be obtained, & how sone God can whip them awaye when it shall so please him, as dayly experience teacheth, men wold fal to the ground, thei wold be humble, lowly, & nothing proud, but attribute al to God, and take nothing as theyr own. And so doing they should deserue more benefites of him hereafter. Amen.

¶The .xiii. treatise or
sermon.

NOn reddentes malum pro malo, nec maledictum pro maledicto.* Nowe after
this godlye instruction howe we shall order our selfe in wel doing,* beseming our
byrth in Christ by baptisme. Here consequently he willeth vs to leaue & exchew
such vices as shal not beseme a good christen man, bidding vs that we shall not
redub yll for il, nor requite a shreud turn for a shreud turn, neither an ill word for
an il worde, nor checke for check, nor sclaunder for sclaunder, although after the
iudgement of the world it may peraduenture seme lawful **par pari referre,** to
requite taunt for taunt, or like for like,* but god wil none such retalliation in word
nor dede, but contrari that we shuld do good for il, & should blesse & say wel for yl
saying, as s. Peter saith here and our sauiour Christ saith. **Mat. v. Diligite inimicos
vestros benefacite hijs** [3H3v] **qui oderunt vos et orate pro persequentibus et
calumniantibus vos vt sitis filij patris vestri.** A marueilous sanctimonie that
Christ requireth of vs<.> Christen folk. He biddeth vs loue our enemies, & to do
wel to them that hateth vs & to pray for theym that pursue vs, and for them that
vniustly vexe vs at the law, that so we may be the children of our father in
heauen.* We must loue our enemies, not theyr enmitie or theyr vices & sinnes, for
them wee must hate, but the nature, the mankinde, the person must be loued, for
euery man & woman, in asmuch as they be made after the ymage of God, & may
receiue almightye God into theyr soules by knowledge and loue, muste be loued
charitablye, for the loue of charity is founded vpon the communion and indifferent
receiuing of perpetual beatitude, that is to say all creatures that nowe haue euerlasting ioyes in heauen, or that may hereafter come to that ioye, & receiue that
glory, be to be[ ]loued* by the loue of charitie. Now there is no man nor woman so
bad while they be in this world liuing, but they may be saued & may come to glory.
Therefore our charitie & loue shoulde extende to al men & women, & to our
enemies, in asmuch as they may amend theyr maners, & may do away theyr
malice, & may come to heauen, by the same reason must be loued, & we be bound
to extend our charitie vpon them. And when Christe byddeth vs praye for them
that dothe vs hurt, or woulde trouble or vexe vs, we be bound to prai for them to
God, to send them grace in this world & glory in heauen at theyr end. If we pray to
god to encrese theyr substance, or to send them healthe, or to sende them honoure
or worship, thys is more then we be [3H4] bound to do, although if we pray so for
them, we do wel, and we shal not loose our reward for our good wil, & for our
praier. It was the time of persecution, when s. Peter wrote this epistle when
christen people had much trouble & vexation, & many il words.* And because y^t
men be more redye to requite il words then il dedes, for men dare not at al times
strike when they be striken, nor rob when thei be robbed, yet words be sone paied
home & many times worse then they be giuen, of which commeth much dissention, anger, & breach of charity. Therfore the apostle specially biddeth them that
he wrot to, & vs by them, beware of that faut, & endeuour our selues to say wel
when we be ill said by, & for cursings to pai hom blessings again for which he
bringeth a vehement perswasion by that that we be called to Christes faith to haue
Gods blessing by enheritaunce whiche shall be giuen vs at oure iudgment.* Therfore s. Peter meaneth that what soeuer we desire to haue in the world to com, in y^e
same thing we should exercise our selues in thys world, blessing our Lord & maker
by laud & praising him & blessing our brothers & sisters our euen christen, saying

286

wel by them & wishing & praying them good in this world so preparing our selfes for the heauenly blessing that shal neuer fail vs. S. Peter alledged the prophet Dauid in the psal. xxxiii. **whosoeuer wil loue life euerlasting in heauen, in whiche no man dieth, and will loue to se good daies that shal neuer be darkened nor discontinued by ani night, let him refraine his tong from il saiynges,** not blaspheming yᵉ name of god, nor murmuring against him. And let him refrain his lips that they speake no [3H4ᵛ] gile nor deceit against his neighbour, but be true in thy words, & in keping thi honest promises, for vnlawful & vnhonest promises thou shuldest make none, but if thou haue made any such, thou shouldest repent thy foly & breake thy promis.* Christ saith. **Mat. xii. Ex verbis tuis iustificaberis, et ex verbis tuis condemnaberis,** by thy woordes thou shalt be iustified & ap-proued as a good man afore god, and by thy words thou shalt be dampned,* the children of Adders being noughtye them selfe can not say wel, **ex abundantia enim cordis loquitur os,** for yᵉ mouth speaketh of the stuffe of the hart.* Il wordes declareth an ill hart, & good words declareth a good hart. And therfore when the prophet & also s. Peter forbiddeth the tong from il, he forbiddeth the hart from il thoughts, as wel as yᵉ tonge from il wordes.* S. Iames saith **Iac. iii.** Be a horse neuer so strong & feirce, yet with a good bit in his mouth & with the bridle a man may turne him & winde him as he list, and likewise a ship, though it be very great and vnweldi, & be set furth in his way with a right boistous & strong forwinde, yet with a litle sterne it may be turned & wynded as the maister yᵗ holdeth the helme list. So the tonge is but a litle lim of a mans body, **et magna exaltat,** & it setteth forth many great matters,* **mors et vitam manibus lingue,** it bringeth life tempo-ral and much quietnes, if it be well bestowed and causeth life euerlasting to him that well vseth hys tonge in godlye doctrine and gostlye exhortation vttered in season, wher contrary a wicked tonge maketh muche trouble in thys worlde, and manye times death temporal and eternal foloweth of it.* [3I1] A little fire burneth a whole groue, or a greate wodde.* An yll tongue is a fire that marreth all and burneth vp, consumeth, and wasteth al goodnes, specially when the fire of hell hath set it on a flame, when the deuyll hath blowen the coale. It is an vnquiet mischiefe full of deadly poyson.* **Prohibe linguam tuam a malo.** When the Deuyll moueth thee to saye yll, then play the controller, playe the commaunder, bidde thy tongue kepe it selfe wythin hys bondes, and saye none euyll, thoughe thy courage woulde contrarye. And then **Declinet a malo, & faciat bonum.** Where the blessed apostle Saint Peter by the words of the Prophet biddeth vs vse Iustice in our woorkes and dedes, as he hath willed vs to vse iustice in our thoughtes and in our wordes.* And because there be two principall partes of Iustice, one to decline from euill, and the other to do good, hee that will see good dayes, must decline from euil, so perfourmynge the preceptes negatiue. Thou shalt not take the name of God in vayne. Thou shalt not kyll any man, woman, or childe. Thou shalt not steale nor robbe. Thou shalt do no lechery, nor such other. The seconde precept concerninge the other parte of Iustice, is to dooe good, fulfillyng the precepts affirmatiue, Beleuyng on one God, louyng him, and fearyng him: Kepyng thy holy daye holilye, worshippynge thy father and mother, and generallye so doynge to an other, as thou wouldest an other should do to thee.* **Inquirat pacem & prosequa-tur eam.** Let him seke peace with God and man, and earnestly fo[3I1ᵛ]lowe it.* The worlde can geue no peace, but will rather driue away peace, and make dissension and debate betwixt god and man, and betwixt man and man. Therfore the Prophete saith not onelye thou must seke for peace, but also thou muste pursue it, runne after it, laboure and finde all meanes possible to catche it, and to hold it,

els it will be gone, the worlde and carnalitie wil haue it awaye from thee.* And
because he that declineth and auoydeth from euill, and doth well, and also
laboureth and taketh paine to obtaine Iustice, taketh great labour and pains in so
doing. The blessed apostle sainte Peter forthwith comforteth vs, telling what is the
reward of iustice, and of good men that kepe iustice. **Oculi domini super iustos.**
This shall be their rewarde. Firste our Lorde Gods eyes wyll fauourablie beholde
them, and louinglye loke vppon theim as on his frendes, as a mans eyes runneth
muche on the thinge that a man loueth. Seconde, his eares will be open, &
mercifully inclined to heare their prayers, where contrary he will make a face and
loke with a terrible countenance vpon them that do yll, and kepe not these partes
of Iustice afore rehersed, nor careth for peace, nor will not labour for to obtaine
it.* Where the prophet applieth corporal limmes or membres to almighty god,
condescending to our infirmitie of our wittes, whiche must be led vp bi corporal
similitudes to the consideration of heuenly thinges of the maner vsed among men,
by his amiable casting his eyes vpon vs, his louing fauour, and by his frowning &
terrible countenance his anger and displeasure. Et [312] **quis est qui vobis noceat
si boni emulatores fueritis?** Here the apostle excludeth a certaine doubt that
might moue mens mindes saiyng, that if we shal thus do as you saye, not requite
euil for euil, nor checke for checke, but contrarywaies do good for yll, & blesse or
saye well for yll wordes, and euer to labour for peace and quietnes, then euery man
would treade vs vnder fote, and would hurt vs and rob vs, and do vs displeasures
one after another, & so we shold be in worse case then all other men be. To this .s.
Peter answereth, comfortyng vs as it were, marueilynge whye wee shoulde thinke
so, saiynge: who is he that will hurte you, if you be the folowers of good dedes, as
Saynte Paule speaketh. **Tit. ii. Sectatores bonorum operum.** Ensuers and folowers
of good workes, but rather wil fauour you, & cherish you?* And so wil all good
men do. Yea, good .s. Peter why askest thou that question? Doest thou maruel of
this? I praye the why was Ieremye the Prophete stoned to death? Why was Esay
sawed to deathe. Was it not for their good liuinge, and for their Preaching?* And
why wer thou thi self & thy felowes ye apostles so bitterly thretened & commaunded y^t you shold no more preach in christes name: Was it not because you
folowed the thing y^t was good? Why wer you cast into the common geyle at ye time
when ye angel of god in the night time opened the pryson dore & bade you **go and
stand in the temple and speak al the words of this christen life, Act. v.** And
afterward when **Gamaliel** had by his counsel somwhat staied the malice of y^e
officers, yet you were wel beaten & commaunded to speake no more in Christes
name.*† [312^v] And also when **Herode agrippa** would haue slain thee as he hadde
done Iames brother to saynte Iohn to gratifie the Iewes.* And finallye, when **Nero**
caused thee to be killed in dede, was not all this because thou were **Emulator boni:
et sectator bonorum operum.** A good doer?* Why was saynte Stephan martyred?*
and likewise a great multitude in the Primitiue churche, was it not for well doinge?
And in the Gospell of this present third sonday of Lent,* when Christ had cast out
a deuil out of a man that was both dombe, deafe, & blinde. The people marueiled
& praised the miracle, where others as the Scribes and Phariseis said he wrought
that myracle by the power of Belzebub chiefe of the deuils. So that where they
durste not hurte hym wyth their handes, they did the worst they coulde to hurt
him wyth their malicious tongues. And you good neighbours here in Bristowe, I
trowe you learned of them that I haue spoke of. If a man abstaine from whitemeate

† name] mane

this holye time of Lente, you will call him hypocrite, and dawe fole, and so rap at him, and strike him with youre venemous tongues, and vse him as an abiecte, excludynge him out of your companie, where he ought rather to be afrayed of your company, & to abhorre it because of your carnal lust to please the mouth and the bealy,* and for your euill example geuing to others, you be such as Iude speaketh of in his epistle. **In epulis suis macule conuiuantes.*** When you be on your Ale benche or in your bankets at the whot and strong wine, you spot your own soules [313] and spotteth others by your euill tonges and yll examples, teachinge youthe to be as euill as you bee. Then [they] haue at the preachers, then they hurte men with their rayling tongues, and more hurt they woulde do with their handes if it were not for feare of the kinges lawes. You hadde nede to amend this maner, you must be content to heare your fauts tolde you, that you maie so amend them, for feare lest the deuill leade you still in your affectate and blinde ignoraunce, till he haue brought you to the blinde exteriour darkenes in hell, where he woulde haue you. Cherishe your Preachers as besemeth good men to do, or at the lestwise if you will do them no good, do them no hurt, lest God take their parte, and execute his vengeance against you. And then to the preachers and to al good liuers I saie, that if the worst fal that you be troubled with euill persons that haue no respect to your good liuing, but that will rather inuent matters againste you, and pike quarels, by whiche they maye vnquiete you, and trouble you, let your trouble gender patience, and so you shall conuert necessitie vnto vertue, makinge a matter of vertue of it.* Count your selues blessed in that you suffer for Iustice sake. This lesson Sainte Peter learned of our maister Christe. **Math. v. Beati qui persecutionem patiuntur propter iusticiam, quoniam ipsorum est regnum celorum.** Blessed be they (saith Christe) that suffer persecution for Iustice and good liuynges sake, for their paine and sorow shall be recompenced with ioyes euerlastinge in Heauen, the paine shall be [313v] but shorte, but the pleasure shall neuer haue end.* Therefore feare you not any thing that semeth to them terrible and fearefull, that woulde peruert and ouerthrowe a carnall worldly person, and that you be not turned from your vertue, nor from any good purpose by their thunder boltes, comminations, threatenynges, prisonmente, or other punishement, let none such trouble you. **Dominum autem Christum sanctificate in cordibus vestris.** But that you sanctifie our Lord and master Christes in your heartes. **Sanctus significat firmum, sanctificare firmare.*** Make Christe sure in your heartes, so that he go not from your remembraunce, nother out of your loue, for fear of any trouble or payne. **Parati semper ad satisfactionem omni poscenti vos rationem de ea que in vobis est spe & fide.** Euer being ready to satisfie euerye man that asketh you the reason of the hope & faith that is in you.* For they that be better learned & more exercised in christen religion, muste instruct them that be ignare & not learned, as charitably and soberly teaching them by sensible & plaine examples & perswasions as they can. And if they yt wold inquire of our faith be infidels, or els peraduenture heretikes that haue swarued from the common receiued faith of Christes churche. If such wold be inquisiti[u]e & busy, questioning rather to take vs in faut by our answers, & to put vs to rebuke, then for zeale or loue to learning, as though our hope wer of things neuer like to be obteined or gotten, & our faith wer wtout reason, or of things vnpossible or vnlikely, & not worthy to be accept or receued of any wise man, yet thei may be answe[314]red reasonably. That if the thinges yt we hope & beleue wer not so obscure & remoued from our carnal senses as thei be, our merit shold be but smal: therfore because god wold reward vs abundantly for our faith, & for our hope, he wold vs to take more pain then for to adheir & stick to such things

only as we se afore our face, Many there be that be so addict & wedded to their
bodely senses that they will not beleue muche more then experience sheweth
them, or then that they may attaine to by their owne grosse reasons, by that
shewing them selues not much better then brute beastes. And of such sturdy
hardnes of hert commeth this diffidence & wauering about the veritie of Christes
body & bloud in the most reuerend sacrament of the altar. And about the state of
souls after this present life w^t many such other matters of our faith, whiche be now
adayes without brydle or staye brought into question.* But he y^t beleueth there is a
heuen & doth hope to come to heuen, must ascend while he is here, & must
beleue y^t of heuenly secretes, that he heareth by the true preachers of Christes
worde. And take this for a principal reason why thou sholdest beleue & hope as
christen people be taught, y^t when Christes fayth was first published & declared
abrode in al the world, it was first set furth bi pore men, homely & rude fishers, of
the most abiect sort of the people, for such Christ chose for his apostles. And their
doctrine was reproued & pursued of ye most mighty sort of ye world.* Great
emperours haue despised it, & haue many tymes by expresse lawes labored to
extinguish the name of Christ, & haue beaten & slaine them that beleued on
[3I4^v] Christe, or haue preached or spoken in Christes name, whiche yet notwithstandynge the more trouble that tyrantes hath stirred against Christ and his
doctrine, and against his preachers, and against his faithfull people, the more
excellently the faith of Christ hath florished, aduaunced, and gone forwarde: so
that the laboure of the pore fishers with Goddes assistence vainquished and
ouercame the auctoritie of all the potentates of the worlde, maligning against our
faythe, and against our hope. So that I count this one of the greatest myracles that
euer GOD wrought for the proufe and confirmacion of Christes faythe: And nowe
(good neighbours) if there be anye amonge you, that in time paste haue maligned
against your preachers, or against the common receiued faith of Christes church,
amend your faith assuring your selues that Christes true doctrine will haue his
waie, and will preuaile at lengthe, be your malice neuer so greatlie set againste it.
Moreouer, thus we maye saie to Infideles that woulde examine vs of our fayth, that
our faithe hath be so confirmed by such myracles as coulde not be done, but onely
by the power of GOD, therfore if we be deceiued in our beleue, god hath begiled
vs, whiche can not bee, for God is true, & very truth it selfe, and can not be witnes
of any falsitie. And for the maner how to satisfie euery person particularlie in
seuerall doubts, and how we shoulde vse our selues, the apostle S. Paule aduertiseth vs, saiyng. **Col. iiii. Sermo vester semper in gratia sale sit conditus, vt sciatis
quomodo o[3K1]porteat vos vnicuique respondere.** Let your communication be
such, that it maye be acceptable and pleasaunt to them that would learne of you,
and let it be poudred with salt, that is to saye, with sauory wisedome, that you may
knowe howe to aunswere euery person accordinge to such measure of grace, as
shall please God to geue euerye one of you, as he wyll not faile to do, for Christe
hath so promised.* **Lu. xxi. I will geue you a mouth and such wisedome as all
your aduersaries shall not haue power to resist.** * But this must be done with
modestye and with feare, without presumption, pride, or arrogancie, with modesty and good maner outwarde, and with feare inwardlie in your heartes, so that
you wade not to farre, least in your declaration you bring in more depe and obscure
matters then were asked of you, and least you trust to much to naturall reasons,
and familier examples, intendinge to proue that can not be proued by naturall
reasons, nor by examples. Although naturall reasons and familier examples may do
much to declare and to set furth the thinges that we beleue, and to declare the

possibilitie of theim that such thinges maye bee, and then ioyne ye veritie of the scripture to this possibilitie, and this shall make a man more swetelye and louingly to beleue the thing that he beleued afore.* Take example in the Article of the incarnation of the sonne of God. We stedfastly beleue that the holy Gost fourmed and fashioned in the virgins bodie of her moste pure bloude, without anye mixture or healpe of mannes sede, a perfite [3K1^v] mans bodie, parfitely distinct in all liniamentes and proporcions belonging to a mans bodye, althoughe it were of small quantitie at the beginning, yet in processe it was nourished and encreased, & growed to a greater quantity as other children dothe in their mothers bodye. This we beleue, as we beleue other articles of our faythe, and we take it for an vnfallible truth.* And the[n] if we will muse or studie howe this may be, let vs take a naturall example to helpe our beleue. We perceiue that of the moyst grounde the sunne by his heate and influence naturally gendreth firste a little worme, which in time groweth to a greater quantitie, then we may be bold to beleue that the infinite power of god may do lyke, and much more in Christes Incarnation.* Such naturall reasons and examples myght be geuen to declare other articles of our fayth, whych muste be done manerlye: that is, wyth **Modestye,** (as S. Peter speaketh) & also with fear,* lest we passe our bondes. And speciallye we must haue an eye to our owne conscience **Conscientiam habentes bonam,** hauing a good conscience, so y^t in the matters that we declare to others, we wauer not w^tin our selues, but that wee do inwardlye beleue the thinges to be true, that we say we beleue: & that in our out ward behauour & liuing, we shew it in our workes. And so whosoeuer would backebite you, or raile at you (saith .s Peter) or would vniustly accuse you afore any iudge, as though your fayeth were naught, nor worthy to be receiued of anye wiseman, thei considering your stedfastnes in Chri[3K2]stes faith, & your good conuersation and liuing in Christ, may be ashamed of them selues, and may leaue their accusementes & their rayling, & may amend their liues, and come to grace.* They that ignorantly will teach and declare the thing that is false, & that they know not, they haue no good conscience, their conscience is not sufficiently instructed, thei know not what they say, thei be no good readers, no good schole-maisters, nor good preachers. They also that for to please the world or for promo-cion, profite, or aduauntage, will be of one opinion now, & sone after of another minde, & at one time doth teach one thing, & at another time doth teach the contrary as the wind bloweth & as the world chaungeth, thei at the first had no good conscience. The science or knowlege of their hartes or minds was not good but erronious or els vafre, wilye, & suttle, which .s. Peter woulde not haue in any christen man or woman. **Melius est enim vt bene facientes (si voluntas dei velit) pati quam male facientes.** For if it be gods will that you suffer persecution, tentation, or trouble for the exercise of your faith, & for the increase of your reward, better it is that you suffer for well doyng then for euyll doinge.* For you shall haue reward of GOD for your paciente sufferynge of vexation that you haue not deserued. Where as if you were malefactours, and yll doers, you shold haue no thanke of god, for you haue euen as you haue deserued. Take example of our master Christ **which once died for our sins, the iust for the vniust,** a [3K2^v] good man for shrewes and noughty liuers, **That so he might offer vs vp to god the father,** not being noughty as we were before, for so we shoulde be no pleasaunt offerynge to almighty God: but we must be by example of him, **Mortified in flesh, and quickened in spirit:*** Like as he died for our sinnes and roose againe for oure iustification, so muste we be mortified, and muste dye to all carnalitie and sinne, so that there be none left aliue in vs. And we must be viuificate and made aliue in spirite, so that our liuyng be all spirituall, good, and godly, pliant to the inclination of the holy spirit. This example of our maister Christ saint Peter brought in to teach vs that thei that being good and vertuous, yet suffreth vexation and trouble, they folow Christ, whiche in like maner suffered iniuries, paines, and passion that he neuer deserued. Some there be that by their vexation and trouble that they suffre, amendeth their liues, leaueth their vices, knoweth<,> god & commeth to goodnes. And they maie be compared to ye blessed theife that was condemned to death for his former giltes & faults yet in his paines hangyng on the crosse, he came to the knowledge of Christe, & called for mercy & had mercye, & came to paradice, & to saluation.* Others there be that for all the paynes and punish-ementes, vexation and trouble that they suffer be neuer the better, but bee rather worsse and worsse, fretynge, chafynge, cursynge, and blaspheming against God, These be like the thiefe on the left hand, which for his faults was hanged on the crosse, and there hanginge, rayled [3K3] against Christe as others did and descend-ed into hell, to paynes euerlastynge.* The newe translation readeth this place. **Mortificatus quidem carne viuificatus autem spiritu**. speaking of Christ which was mortified in the fleshe, bodely diyng for vs, and was viuificate and euer aliue in the spirite,* for his soule neuer dyed, in signe and token that by his example we shoulde likewise do: gostly diynge to all carnalitie, and euer liuinge spiritually as I saide afore. **In quo & his qui in carcere erant spiritibus veniens predicauit**. This text is diuerslye expounded, one way thus. In which spirite, bi which he was euer aliue, Christ came and preached to the spirites that were in prison, whiche once were harde of beleue, when they loked for Goddes pacience and longe sufferance in the dayes of Noe, while the Arche or greate shippe was a makinge, in whiche shippe a fewe, that is to saie .viii. liues were saued bi the water, lifting vp the shippe a flote from the daunger of drowning. Christ came in spirite, and preached to the spirites that were in pryson.* The workes of the whole Trinitie be al one outwarde amonge the creatures (as I haue manye times tolde you) therfore in that that almighty God inspired the blessed patriarch Noe to preach vnto the people of his time, penaunce and amendement of lyfe, it maye be saide that the father in spirite preached to the people then beinge in pryson, and that the sonne in spirite preached to the same prysoners, and that the holy goste in spirite preached to the same people.* For the whole trinitie inspired Noe [3K3ᵛ] to preache, therfore it is true that euery persone in trinitie did it. And so it mai be said that Christ preached to theim, for that is true of the seconde person in trinitie is true of Christe. **Per communicationem idiomatum**.* As we say, the sonne of god is a man, and a man is the sonne of God. And so we say that the sonne of God suffred death on the crosse, & that a man made the starres in the skye, Because of the perfit vnion and k[n]ot of the godhead to the manhode in one person, and the same person that now is incarnate and made man did it. And he preached to the Prysoners that were dull in beleuyng, Noe tellyng theim Gods commination and threatenyng, to destroy the world wyth water except they would amende. And yet they were hard of beleue, and loked for more fauour at Gods hand, and for longer pacience, and forbearynge theim, and so trifled tyll the floude came vpon them and drowned them.* They were in pryson (sayth .s. Peter) whiche after this exposition must be vnderstande morally, in as much as they were bounde as prysoners by the bondes of sinne, as the prophet speaketh. **Funes peccatorum circumplexi sunt me**. The ropes of sins haue wrapt me in rounde aboute,* and likewise speaketh the wise-man. **Pro. v. Iniquitates sue capiunt impium & funibus peccatorum suorum constringetur**. His owne iniquities taketh the wicked persone, and wyth the ropes

of his owne sinnes he shalbe strayned & knit.* And in that case were the people of
Noes tyme, for all mankinde had corrupt his way, and [3K4] the maner of his
liuing. **Omnis caro corruperat viam suam. Gen. vi.** All flesh, all men left vertue
and liued insolently, & viciously.* This is one exposition of this texte of .s. Peter.
But this exposition though it be good & catholike, yet it semeth more moral then
litteral, because it taketh the name of the prison, & of them that were in pryson
morally for the custome & vse of sinne, & not for a place where a prisoner is kept
in paine & sorow to his displesure: & it taketh the prisoner for him that is
intangled, poluted, & defaced with the deformity of customable sinne. This
prisoner though he be in extreme peril & daunger of soule, yet not knowyng the
case that he standeth in, maketh merye, & fealeth no harme, nor paine, but
counteth hym self most at liberty, & at hartes ease. Therfore I thinke .s. Peter
speaketh of the spirits or soules of them that woulde not regard the exhortation of
Noe made vnto them for amendment of their liues, tyll the very floude came vpon
them. And then seing the water rise higher & higher, & men and women, and
other liuynge creatures perishe in the same floude, and that there was no place
able to saue them from drownynge, they toke remorse of conscience, and repentaunce, as well for their hardness of harte contemnynge Noes exhortion, as for
their owne naughty liuynge, & so callyng for mercy, were receyued to mercy, &
saued their soules.* Yet in asmuch as the gate to heauen was not opened bi Christ,
thei were staied in the skirt of hel,* a place prouided by GOD to receiue [3K4ᵛ]
their soules that died in the state of grace, and in Gods fauour, in whiche if they
hadde any thinge to be purged, as for venial sinnes, or for lacke of sufficient
satisfaction for mortall offences done by their life tyme, hadde first greuous paines
for their purgation, and then consequently were receiued into Abrahams bosome,
a place of tranquilitie, rest, and quietnes, where they had no sensible payne.* They
hadde none other paine, but onlye the paine of lacke of glorye, which do[u]btlesse
was a greuous payne for theim that daylie and hourely loked for it, as the wise-
manne saithe. **Pro. xiii. Spes que differtur affligit animam.** The hoope that is
prolonged and put of, vexeth and punisheth the minde.* Amonge these were
manye of them that were swalowed vp in the water at Noes floude, Yet diynge
penitent (as I sayd) of which saint Peter here maketh special mencion, vnderstandynge by them all the rest of the holye fathers that were in the same pryson, and in
the paine of lacke of glory. To these spirites or souls of theim thus beinge in that
painefull Prison, where they were payned with the honger & thirst of eiger and
gredy desire to see the glorie of God. Christe came in spirite in his soule (while his
bodye laye stil in the sepulchre) and preached, declared, and reueiled vnto them
that the high misterie of his painful passion was exhibited and perfourmed, and
mans raunsome payed by the price of his precious bloude, and there he was
conuersaunt with them to their greate consolation and comfort, and to the confusion of all the deuyls in [3L1] hell, tyll the time when it pleased him to vnite and
ioyne his soule to his body againe, agaynst the time of his glorious resurrection,*
and then toke away with him suche as were to his pleasure, as he sayde afore that
he woulde do. **Ego si exaltatus fuero a terra omnia traham ad meipsum.** If I be
lyft vp from the grounde, I shall drawe all thinges to me,* as well in hell as in
earth: for of both he drewe a great part to him. According to this speaketh the
increate wysedome of God, the seconde person in Trinite. **Eccle. xxiiii. Penetrabo
omnes inferiores partes terre, & inspiciam omnes dormientes, & illuminabo
omnes sperantes in domino.** I shall pearce and entre into all the lower partes of
the earth, and I wyll loke on all theim that be a slepe, whose bodies rest in their

graues in the slepe of peace, and I wyll geue light to all them that hope in theyr
Lord God.* And Saint Augustine in the .cxxvii. sermon, sayth. **Omnia abstulit
vtique electa, electi quamuis in tranquillitatis sinu tamen apud inferni claustra
tenebantur.** Non enim infideles quos**que** & pro suis criminibus aeternis suppli-
ciis dedicos ad veniam dominus resurgendo reparauit, sed illos ex inferni claus-
tris rapuit quos suos fide & actibus recognouit. Christ toke awaye with him all
that were electe and chosen: for suche althoughe they were in the bay or bosome
of tranquillitie, ease, and reste, yet they were kepte and holden within the clausures of hell.* For our lord Christ when he rose, did not repaire or restore to
pardon and forgiuenes all infideles, and such as for theyr crimes or mortall sinnes
were deputed [3L1ᵛ] to euerlastinge paynes and punishmentes, but them he
plucked out of the cloysters and clausures of hell, whiche he knew for his owne by
their fayth and by their dedes. For the soule of Christe ioyned to the Godhead,
from whiche it was neuer separate, descended into the said darke place, & gaue
light to them that were ther kept in prison. By occasion of that he spoke of Noes
shyppe, in whiche a fewe lyues were saued by the water, that is to saye, the liues of
Noe and of his wife, and the liues of theyr three sonnes, and of theyr thre wiues
.viii. personnes in all: the blessed apostle Sainte Peter declareth the allegorye of
the same fygure, sayinge: that like as the sayde .viii. personnes or liues were saued
from drowninge, beynge lifte vppe in the shippe a flote aboue the grounde, euen so
(sayth he) **In like fourme and maner you be saued by baptisme from dampnation
euerlastinge. Non carnis depositio sordium sed conscientiae bone interrogatio
in Deum.** The water alone is not the thinge that doth it, althoughe his propertie
be to washe away the filth and vncleanes of the body, but it is the examination and
discussion of a good conscience toward God* (saith S. Peter) because that in the
water, the worde doth make cleane the soule, as S. Augustin speaketh **tract. lxxx.
in euangel. Iohan.** Vppon these wordes, **Iam vos mundi estis propter verbum
quod locutus sum vobis. Ioh. xv.** Take away the holy sacramentall wordes from
the water, and what is the water but bare water? **Accedit verbum ad elementum &
fit sacramentum.** The worde ioyned to the ele[3L2]ment of water, maketh the
sacramente. For the water can not of it selfe haue suche strengthe as to touche the
body, and withall to clense the soule, but onely by the worde. And by the worde,
not because it is sounded or said by him or her that doth christen, but because it is
beleued.* According to that S. Peter had said. **Act. xv. Fide purificans corda
eorum.** God clensith theyr hartes by fayth,* the water and the worde concurringe
with the same fayth. Then this clensing of the soule must not be attribute to the
water, excepte we put to the worde, and then ioyne theim both together, and they
shall be of suche strength, that they may purge and make cleane the least chylde
that euer was borne, whiche (as I haue sayde in tymes past) beleueth in the fayth
of the churche, lyke as he or she that is of discretion beleueth by his own faith.* Al
these circumstances S. Peter speaketh in few wordes. **Conscientie bone interrogatio in deum,** the examination or discussion of a good & welbeleuing conscience
toward God,* comprehending as wel the cathechisation or instruction going afore
the baptisme (where yᵉ party may haue such oportunitie) as the Sacramentall
wordes with the water, & with faith and all together. According to this saith S.
Paul. **Eph. v. Christus dilexit ecclesiam et seipsum tradidit pro ea vt illam
sanctificaret mundans eam lauachro aque in verbo vite.** Christ loued his churche, & deliuered him self to sinfull mennes handes, that he mighte make her
holye, clensynge her with the lauer of water in the worde of lyfe.* This blessed
Sacramente of [3L2ᵛ] baptisme, by whiche we be regenerate and gotten agayne to

God, was signified by the water that drowned the earth, and earthly carnall people, and saued the eyght liues that then were saued. And that the water of the sayde flud saued none that were out of the shippe, signifieth that all heretikes that be out of the common receaued fayth of the churche, althoughe they were in the water, although they be christened, and glorieth to be called christen men, yet by the same water they shall be drouned into hell, by which the ship, the catholike churche was lifte and borne vp into heauen and saued, as the materiall shippe of Noe was lifte vp into the ayre aboue grounde, and saued by water.* And lyke as they that were drowned in Noes floude had theyr corpsis wasshed from exterior fylth of theyr bodies, whiche preuayled them not against drowninge: so there was in the noughty sorte of christen people **depositio sordium carnis,** a clensinge and wasshinge away of the filth of the flesh by the water of baptisme when they were christened, but it preuayled not to eternall saluation, because they lacked a faythfull conscience, well instructed, examined, and tried towarde GOD **by the resurrection of Christ from the dead,** that like as he rose from the dead, so our consciences should ryse frome deade workes of synne, to liuelye workes of grace and vertue, no more to dye or synne agayne, **which is in the right hande of God,* swalowynge vp,** consuminge, and destroyinge **death, that so we might be made inheritours of euerlastinge life.***

[3L3] That a man swaloweth he consumeth, so that it shall no more appeare in the fourme and fashion that it was of afore, so Christe made by his death, that death shuld be consumed, in as much as by his death, the deuyl that is the auctor & causer of death was ouercome, his heart was burst.* He begilinge and deceiuyng oure fyrste parentes kylled them, and made them and all theyr posteritie subiect to death, but kylling the latter man, the latter Adam our Sauioure Christe, he loste the fyrste man oute of his snares, whiche kylled his hearte and was verye death to him.* He had power to bringe all them to death that descended of Adam (whome he hadde kylled) yf they came of hym by carnall propagation, takinge of him the spotte of sinne: but abusinge his libertie, and procuringe the death of our moost innocent Sauioure Christe, that came not of the sede of Adam, by generation betwixt two parentes, nor had any spotte of sinne by Adam, he was worthy to lose his libertie, and so he loste an infinite numbre of them that he thought him self sure of, and dayly loseth his expectation, and none can gette but suche as wylfully wyll runne into his daunger. After this victorye ouer the deuyll, Christ went vp into heauen (as S. Peter sayth here) **and had subiect vnto him Aungels, potestates, and vertues,*** where S. Peter expresseth three orders of Aungels of heauen to be subdued and subiecte vnto Christ, by them vnderstandinge al the residue of the Aungels, which as S. Dionise in his boke **de celesti Hierarchia,** writeth according [3L3ᵛ] to that he had learned of his maister S. Paule, [(]by whome he was baptised and also taughte in the catholyke fayth) be diuided into .iii. Hierarchies. Euery Hierarchie conteyninge .iii. orders of Aungels, and so they make nine ordres in the whole. Saint Dionise that wrytte his booke of these heauenly creatures, was S. Paules disciple and scoler, and learned of him that could best declare the truthes of theim, in as muche as he was rapte into heauen, and there sawe suche secretes as a man might not speake:* Notwithstandinge, as muche as semed to agree to mortall mans capacitie for to knowe, & as was mete and profitable for men to lear[n]e, he declared to this blessed S. Dionise, and to others of his disciples that had theyr wittes illuminate aboue others, whiche the sayde S. Dionise committed to writing in his boke rehearsed, that the posteritie that shoulde come after him in Christes churche mighte be instructe by the same. In the sayde book he rehearsed the names of euerye order of aungels in euery one of the saide Hierarchies. The fyrste and highest Hierarchie conteyninge the .iii, orders, **Seraphin, Cherubin, and Thronos**. The seconde conteyneth, **Dominationes virtutes, & potestates**. The thirde Hierarchie and lowest, hath in it these thre orders, **Principatus, Archangelos, et Angelos**. As appereth by s. Dionise in the sayde boke. **Cap, vi. vii. viii. & .ix.*** And by S. Gregory. **Homil. xxxiiii. super Euangelia.*** All these were subiecte and subdued to Christes manhod, when he came to heauen by his marueilous as[3L4]cension. Of all these orders Saint Peter in this place rehearseth thre orders, one of the loweste Hierarchie **Angelis**, and two of the middle Hierarchie, **potestates, et virtutes,*** by them vnderstandinge all the other Aungels, which though they were euer sith theyr fyrst creation, subiecte, and subdued to Christes Godheade, yet here in this place he maketh speciall mention of theyr subiection to Christ, that he might shewe that the humanitie of Christ was so exalted and set alofte by his ascension (whiche Saint Peter here speaketh of) that it was preferred and set aboue the excellencie of all the Aungels of heauen: Accordinge to the sayinge of the Prophet, **Omnia subiecisti sub pedibus eius.*** And Saint Paul. **phil. Dedit illi nomen quod est super omne nomen vt in nomine Iesu omne genuflectatur, celestium, terrestrium, & infernorum.*** GOD the father hath geuen hym a name aboue all names, that to his name all creatures in heauen, in earth, and of hel, shall bowe the knee, and be subdued and obediente vnto him. To whome be all honour and glorye for euer. Amen.

The fourth Chapiter.

**CHristo igitur passo in carne & vos eadem cogitatione armamini, quia qui
passus est in carne desiit a peccatis. &c.*** The blessed Apostle Saynt Peter, in
diuers places of this epistle that we haue in hande, vehemently extolleth and
commendeth the most aboundant mercy of God, by whiche he hath regenerate
and gotten vs agayne to lyfe, where we were afore by oure carnall parentes gotten
to death.* And we see by experience, that one that hath a greate affection or
vehement loue to any thinge, wyll be euer busie, as it were one that coulde neuer
haue done, or that woulde be euer gladde to speake of it. So Saint Peter coulde
neuer geue thankes ynoughe, he euer inculcateth & bringeth in the remembraunce
of the benefyt of oure redemption, because we shoulde euer haue it in minde. And
because it is not ynough to remember it, but we must also in our liuinge conforme
oure selues to the same holynes, he geueth vs manye holesome morall lessons, and
fatherly exhortations, teachinge vs to lyue vertuousely and holyly, contrarye to
vices and vicious liuinge. And because our regeneration and sanctification commeth by baptisme, whiche taketh his efficacitie and strength of Christes bloude,
shedde in his payneful passion, therfore euer amonge he speaketh of the excellente
[3M1] mysterye of the sayde passion of Christe, and of his gloryous resurrection, by
whiche as he sayd in the ende of the thyrde Chapiter, whiche I declared in my
laste sermon vpon the same, he swalowed vp, drowned, and consumed death of the
soule, to make vs heyres of lyfe euerlastynge.* And in as muche as the worlde and
the spyryte be aduersaries, and euer at variaunce, euen so be worldlye and carnall
personnes, enemyes to spirituall personnes. Spirituall I call good lyuers, that worketh accordynge to the inclination and styrringe of the holye spyryte, the holye
gooste. Then considerynge that the carnall people be the more sorte, and the
greater number, and the good lyuers be fewer in number, it is no marueyle that
good people suffereth muche wo, vexation, and trouble in this worlde, that were
able to ouerthrowe a good man or woman, and to make them to leaue theyr
vertue, and to faule to angre, braulynge, or suche other inconuenience: A remedye
and a succoure agaynste this peryll Saynte Peter geueth vs in these wordes.
CHRISTO passo in carne & vos eadem cogitatione armamini. In as muche as
Chryste hath suffered in his flesshe, be you armed in the same remembraunce.*
They that were newelye conuerted to CHRISTE in the prymityue Churche hadde
muche vexation by infydeles, and also by some false Chrysten men, and euen so be
we manye tymes vexte, and euer shall be vnto the worldes ende, wyth shrewes and
noughtye lyuers, that euer goethe aboute to [3M1ᵛ] disturbe and trouble good
men, and to woorke displeasures to them that woulde serue GOD and the worlde,
in vertue and with quietnes. Saynt Peter gaue to them that he wrytte vnto, the
same defence that he woulde all vs to vse agaynste all persecution, trouble, and
vniuste vexation, that is, the remembraunce of Christes passion, the thinkinge on
CHRISTES passion.* Remembraunce of **CHRISTES** passyon, muste be oure
harnes and oure weaponne to putte awaye all extreme trouble and vexation, and
by the same we shall lykewyse auoyde and putte of all insultes and assaultes of
temptation to synne: for suche remembraunce of **CHRISTES** passion whiche he
toke for oure sake, moueth a manne to macerate and punysshe his flesshe, to

conforme hym selfe to **CHRISTES** paynes, beynge contente to take payne in oure bodyes, as Christe dydde in his, and not makynge oure selues moore precyous and delycate, then Chryste made hym selfe, for the loue that he hadde to vs.

CHRISTE fasted fortye dayes, and nother eate nor dronke,* I say not that we muste faste lykewyse withoute meate and drynke, it passeth oure power: but yet as the wyse Poete **Horace** sayth. **Est quadam† prodire tenus si non datur vltra.** We muste goo somewhat onwarde, thoughe we canne not come to the vttermooste:* we muste do the beste we canne to come toward his faste, takinge suche meate, and at such times [3M2] as by the vniuersall counsell of Christes churche be alowed to be eaten in the fortye dayes of Lente: then howe farre wyde from hys fast they be that contemptuousely taketh flesshe, or other dyattes prohibited, iudge you.* After he hadde eaten of the paschall lambe at his last supper, on the thursdaye in the eueninge with his disciples, he wente forth with theim into the place called Gethsemani, where he toke him selfe to prayer, and was in a marueylous agonye for consideration of the paynes that he shoulde to, and anone came Iudas with his companye to take hym, and then they haled him foorth frome Iudge to Iudge, from poste to pyller,* **vt dicitur,** so that he neuer eate nor dronke after, saue that in the extreme fayntnes afore hys death, when he would haue dronke, they gaue hym suche drynke as he woulde not drynke of, after he hadde a lytell tasted it,* so that from the thursdaye in the euenynge, vntyll the frydaye at three a clocke at afternone, when he expyred and dyed, he neuer eate nor dronke, notwithstanding the great laboure and vntollerable paynes that he suffred in that meane tyme.

Nowe good louinge freindes, howe we that wyll not take paynes to faste nor abstayne at tymes appoynted, but onelye whan it please vs, (that is as muche to saye, as neuer at all, as it prouith in effecte) do conforme oure selues to Chrystes paynes that he tooke, iudge you: [3M2ᵛ] eyther we muste denye Chryst, or els count hym a foole, whiche is a verye denyall of hym, or els sette lyttle by his example, to whiche Saynte Peter in his wordes rehearsed referreth vs, wyllynge vs to arme oure selues by remembraunce of the vntollerable paynes that he suffred in his mooste tendre bodye. When he was rayled agaynste, and called heretike, and traytoure, a benchewhystler, a blowboll, a felowe with ribaldes, knaues, whores, and drabbes, all this wynde shoke no corne,* all this moued hym not, but euer styll he proceded in his godlye purpose, and for yl wordes gaue to them agayn blessed wordes of godlye exhortation, and good counsayle.* If we woulde take to hearte this good example of his wondrous patience and sufferaunce, there shoulde neuer anye backebitinge or sclaunderinge, any rayling or missaying once moue vs to angre or impatience. This remembraunce of Christes passion was signified by the shield that Iosue lyft vp agaynst the kinge of Haye, of whiche it is wrytten. **Iosu. viii.** Hai by interpretation is as much to say as confusion. The king of Hai is our aduersarye the deuyll,* and he hath a capitaine of his warres called **fomes peccati,** yᵉ nurse or the breader of synne,* because manye doeth obey him, and he is the captayne of confusion, because he inclineth his subiectes to woorke agaynste the iudgemente and sentence of ryghte reasonne, and there as reason ruleth not, is nothynge but confusion, and all oute of course and [3M3] good order. GOD badde him **Pone insideas vrbi post eam,** lay a stale behynde the citie,* on the backeside because we must euer watche and laboure agaynste the armye of confusion, the multitude of mortall sinnes, as well in age as in youth, because that he ouercame

---

† quadam] quodam

the greate wyse man Salomon when he was an olde man,* notwithstandinge all his wysedome, as he hathe done manye a one moore, as well in age as in youth. When Iosue lyfte vppe his shylde on hie on a speare, that it myghte be sene a farre of, that parte of Iosue his host that laye in the stale, and also the companye that were with the capitayne ioyned together, and enuironed and closed in the whole multytude of the towne of Haye, and kylled them euery mothers sonne, manne, womanne and chylde, sauynge the kinge aliue, whom they broughte to Iosue the captayne.* Iosue by interpretation signifieth health or saluation, and signifieth in manye of his actes oure Sauyoure Christe.* Iosue his sheilde thus lyfte vppe in the syghte of all Iosue his companye, whiche gaue them courage to fyghte manfullye, sygnyfyeth the armes of Chrystes passion,* whiche lykewise lyfte vppe in the remembraunce of good Chrysten people, shall make theim to fyghte agaynste all the synnes that maye aryse or come of the temptation of the Deuyll, or of his cheyfe captayne the breader of synne, whiche by the offence of Adam remayneth in oure flesshe. We muste spare none of Goddes enemyes, mortall sinnes, [3M3ᵛ] for yf we do, it wyll be layed to oure charge, and to oure condempnation: Example we haue of Saule, whiche when he shoulde fyght agaynste the Amalachites, was commaunded to kyll all that he toke, man and beaste: contrarye to the commaundemente he saued Agag the kynge of the countrey, **i. reg. xv.** for the whiche he was reproued and caste oute of Goddes fauoure, and sone after depryued of his kyngedome, and all his issue after hym, and the kyngedome transferred to the trybe of Iuda by kynge Dauid,* whiche was of that tribe or familye, in sign and token, that when we shall fyghte agaynste vyces, we muste not leaue anye litell sinne alyue, but kyll theim all, for els as longe as one remaineth in vs, we can not be counted iuste and good men afore God.* **Sanctificate bellum et pugnate pugnam domini. Ioel .iii.*** Then we sanctifie a batayle, and make an holye batayle, when we kyll all the enemies of the soule, that is to saye, all sinnes, and when we mortifie oure fleshe, and cutte away al ill concupiscence of the same, that we may be holye in bodye and spyrite: and thus playinge the victours and conquerours, we maye saye wyth the Apostle. **Gala. vi. Mihi absit gloriari nisi in cruce Domini nostri Iesu Christi, per quem mihi mundus crucifixus est & ego mundo.*** Where the pseudapostles, agaynste whiche Saynt Paule speaketh there, reputed trouble and payne, suffred for Christes sake, to be nothinge profytable,* as many pseudapostles and false gospellars sayeth [3M4] nowe a dayes, or yf they saye it not with theyr tounges, yet they shewe it in theyr workes. Saynte Paule contrary, gloryed in nothyng so muche, knowynge the greate rewarde that he shoulde obteyne for the same: euen lyke as other of the apostles, when they were conuented afore the counsell of the Iewes, and there rebuked and sore beaten for speakynge in Christes name, **Ibant Apostoli gaudentes a conspectu consilii quoniam digni habiti sunt pro nomine Iesu contumeliam pati. Actu. v.** they wente awaye with myrthe and gladnes, that God hadde estemed them, and taken them as worthye to suffer for Christes sake paynes and despytes.* So dydde Saynt Paule glorye, communicatynge, and takinge parte of Chrystes paynes on the Crosse, knowynge (as Saynte Ambrose sayeth) that the loue of the Crosse causeth lyfe, and the loue of the worlde, bryngeth death and destruction.

Inuicem sibi mortui sunt dum nihil concupiscit Apostolus mundi, & dum nihil habet mundus suum quod agnoscat in Apostolo, sicut & Dominus ait ecce venit princeps mundi huius & in me inuenit nihil. Ioh. xiiii. The Apostle and the worlde were one crucified to another (sayeth Saynte Ambrose) whyle the Apostle hadde no concupiscence or desyre of worldelye pleasures, and whyle the worlde hadde nothynge that he coulde knowe for his owne, in that blessed Apostle. Euen as oure Sauioure Christe speaketh: loo, the Prynce of the worlde commeth, [3M4ᵛ] and findeth nothinge in me that he maye claime for his owne.* And who so euer hathe soo doone by remembraunce of Christes paines and passion, so maceratinge his fleshe, so punysshing, subduyng, & quenchinge his carnall concupiscence, he shall so doynge, conforme him selfe to Christes paynes, and shall be mortified and made deade to synne, and shall lyue to Chryste.* **Nam qui passus est in carne desiit a peccatis.** In whyche wordes Saynte Peter geueth vs an excellente lesson, and a general rule, that **he that suffreth and taketh paynes in the fleshe, ceaseth from synne, and leaueth synne,*** as it maye be declared, discurrynge generally thoroughe all synnes. When a manne or woman is tempted to lechery, by ouermuche farcinge or fyllinge the bellye with meates, and whote wines, lette him take paine to punysshe the bellye with abstinence, and anone the panges will swage: And if it be by wantonne company, or communication, then sequestre thy selfe from that occasion, thoughe it be paynefull to the soo to do, and with all occupie thy minde aboute thy occupation, or in some honest and vertuous meditation, and soo thou shalte not be ouercome with temptation, but shall scape it, and leaue it, and conuerte thy self to vertue.

Likewise in anger, whiche is a certaine kindelinge or inflamynge of the bloude aboute thy harte, suffer in thy bodye, take paine in thy bodie, lette not the occasion of that heate comme to thy harte, stoppe thy mouth, geue faire words [3N1] thoughe it greue thee, and anone thy anger wyll swage, and so thou shalt make a frende of hym that thou were moued agaynste afore, and shalt make a matter of vertue of that whyche if thou had folowed, woulde haue turned to murther or mischiefe, and to thy dampnation. Likewyse of enuy of which it least semeth, when thou seest an other man prospere and go forwarde in honestie, in substaunce, in reputation and estimation amonge the people. If peraduenture thy carnall mynde woulde thinke thy sayde neighbours preferment and thrift to be derogation and hinderaunce to thy state, and to thy estimation, and woldest be sorye to se hym so to prospere, but wouldest rather be glad to saye or do that might pull hym backe. This is playne enuy, cleane contrary to charitie, and most odious to God. What remedye. **Patiaris in carne, & desines etiam ab hoc peccato.** Suffer in thy fleshe, and in thy carnall fancye: striue with thy passion be not so folishe as to thinke that his thrifte hyndereth thee, but rather take thou payne in thy body to thriue, and to go forwarde in honestye and in riches as well as he, & compell thy minde to consider that thou shouldest loue thy neighbour, and consequentlye that thou shouldest be glad of hys auancemente and reioyce in it, as one louer should do in an other. And so thou shalte cease from that synne of enuye. And euen so you shal leaue all other vyces, if you wyll by imitation and example of Christe take payne in your bodyes, punysshe your bodyes, and stryue wyth your carnall af[3N1ᵛ]fection, accordynge to Sainte Peters saiynge. **Qui passus est in carne, desiit a peccatis.** He that hath suffered in hys bodye, hath done wyth carnall vyces and synnes, that so for the reste of hys life tyme while he shall lyue, in the flesshe in his bodye, here in this worlde hee maye liue not after the flesshe of carnall manne, whyche hathe pleasure communely in voluptuous pleasures of the flesh, but accordynge to the wyll of GOD, in sinceritie and cleannesse of lyfe. **Sufficit enim preteritum tempus ad voluntatem† gentium consummandam his qui ambulauerunt in luxuriis.** For the tyme paste is inoughe for to fulfill the wyll of

---

† voluntatem] voluptatem

Paynyms and Gentyles that haue walked, that is to say, haue ledde their liues in all maner of Lecherye and pleasures of the fleshe.* You knowe that as I haue ofte saide Saint Peter writte to the newe christened people newely conuerted, some from the Gentility, and some frome the Iewes ceremonyes also, nowe he speaketh speciallye to theim that afore were Gentyles, whiche were moste blinde, and lest knewe GOD.* To theim he sayeth be you contente, nowe no more, you haue inoughe and to muche of that voluptuousnesse that you haue vsed like Paynyms that knewe not God. And liued in all kynde of Lecherye outwarde by exteriour filthye exercise of your bodyes, **Desideriis*** and in vncleanly and wanton appetites in minde inward-lye, and as it were runnynge in **Reprobum sensum**, as Sainte Paule speaketh. **Rom. i.*** [3N2] desierynge nothyng that is good for their soules in dede, but rather contrarye, desierynge that thinge for good whiche is naught in dede. Euen as it were one that in a feruente Feauer hadde his mouthe infecte wyth nocyue hu-mours, which iudgeth that thinge to bee bitter that is swete or pleasaunte in taiste in dede. So euyll and vycious exercyse corrupteth the appetyte that it shall run on the thing that is nought, rather then to desire the thinge that is good. And these desiers that Sainte Peter speaketh of here, extendeth not onelye to the vnlawfull lustes of the flesshe, but also to vnnaturall desires and lustes, whiche Saynte Paule greuouslye taxeth. **Rom. i. Vinolentiis commessationibus.*** And because it is necessarye to amoue the cause, if the effecte shall be amoued, therefore the blessed Apostle reproueth Glotonye, of whiche commonlye ensueth lecherye, And speciallye of ouermuche drinkynge of wine, as sainte Paule saieth: **Nolite inebriari vino, in quo est luxuria.** Be not dronke with Wyne, for in wine is lecherye,* as the effecte in the cause. And therefore as **Valerius Maximus** writeth. **Lib. ii. Vini vsus Romanis foeminis ignotus fuit ne scilicet in aliquod dedecus pro laberentur quia proxim[u]s a libero patre intemperantie gradus ad inconcessam venerem esse consueuit.** The women of Rome in the olde tyme when Rome florished in highest auctoritie & dominion, knew not the vse of wyne for feare lest they should fall to anye shame or villany for [3N2ᵛ] the next step<t> of intemperancye from the God of wyne, was wont to be to vnlawful lechery.* And Terence, saieth. **Sine cerere & baccho friget venus.** Without meate and drinke Venus is colde,* the fleshely luste shall not trouble thee. In signe and token that one of them foloweth of the other, the bealy is next aboue the priuitie, to geue vs to vnderstande that if we restrayne the bealy from superfluitie of meate and drynke, the incontinency of lecherye shall be colde, and little shall trouble vs. Where contrary, he that is geuen to the pleasure of the bealy, shall not auoyd the fylthines of lecherye, **Commess-ationibus,** in extraordinary refections, banketynges, breakefastes, after non-emeates, reresuppers, and such other lewde and vnseasonable wanton bealyglee. All these feadeth lechery, and so dothe all other potations, and bibbinge, and bollynge, and reuellinge, and so doth dronkennes folowynge of the same. And in the olde tyme afore the fayth of Christe was recei[u]ed of these folkes that Saynt Peter writ to, of such excesse in meates and drinkes, folowed not onelye the vncleannes of the fleshe in lecherye, but also the vnlawefull and detestable Synnes of Idolatrye, and worshyppe of false Goddes, worshippyng that for a God that was no God, as sometyme the Sunne and Mone, and suche other creatures, and manye tymes dead men and women whose bodyes wer rotten in the grounde, or in the Sea, and their souls dampned in hell, as Iupiter, Mars, Venus, or [3N3] suche other as had exceaded in one notable work or other, whyle they were alyue. And that thys cryme moste odious to GOD, and mooste derogatynge hys honoure and glorye foloweth of reuelynge and ryatyng appeareth by the people of Israell, whiche whyle

Moyses was in the mounte wyth almyghty GOD, receiuyng the lawes, they sate
downe to eate and drynke, **Sedit populus comedere & bibere, & surrexerunt
ludere. Exod. xxii[i]**. And then they rose vp to daunce and synge, and playe on
such instrumentes as they hadde in worshyppe and honoure of their Calfe that was
newe made, whiche was plaine Idolatrye.* And **Lactancius firmianus diuinarum
institutionum. Lib. primo cap. xxi.** sayeth of suche sacrifices of the Gentilitie.
Epulisque saciati noctem lusibus ducerent.* And so you shall reade of moste
parte of their solemne feastes. I haue declared to you here afore what is an idole,
and what is Idolatrye. An Idole and an Image is not all one. Euerye Idole is an
Image, but not contrarywyse. For when Christe asked them for the coyne of their
money, and they brought hym a Denere, he asked not whose is thys idol? but
whose is thys ymage?* An Image properly representeth a naturall thinge: or a
thinge that is or hathe bene, or maye bee, as the Image of the Crucifixe. An Idole
representeth and signifieth that y^t neuer was nor can be, as when a man maketh a
picture to represent the God Iupiter, or the Goddesse Venus, whiche nother be nor
can be, for there is no god Iupiter, nor god[3N3^v]desse Venus, neither can be anye
suche. Therfore what soeuer representeth them for Goddes muste neades be an
Idole. You make an Image an Idole, geuynge diuine honoure vnto it, or lokynge for
helpe of it, or thinkynge that one Image of our Ladie can helpe thee better then an
other, for there is in the Image no suche diuine power.* The wyse Poet sayeth
verye fetelye. **Qui fingit sacros auro† vel marmore vultus, non facit ille deos: qui
rogat† ille facit.** He that maketh holye faces in Timber or in stone, maketh not
Gods, he that worshippeth them he maketh them gods.* And so thou makest an
Idole of thy wife, or of thy childe by ouermuche louynge theim or cherishynge
theim, and doinge more for theim then thou wouldest do for GOD. And slackynge
or leauinge thy duetye to God to please theim, after the maner of Saynte Paules
speakynge, when he calleth Auarice **Idolorum seruitus,** Couetousnesse is Idolatry,* because the couetous man maketh his money his Idole and his GOD,
doinge more for to gette richesse, then he woulde do to get God. And takinge
more minde on riches then on God. And doing that for his goods sake, that he
woulde not do for Gods sake. And after this manner you maie make an Idole of the
newest Image that is, if you wyll geue it suche honoure as is not kindelye for it.
Make no more of an Image, but onelye take it as a representer to signifye, and to
put you in remembraunce of the thinge that it is made after, and passe no more
vppon it. **In quo admirantur non [3N4] concurrentibus vobis in eandem luxurie
confusionem.*** Here .s. Peter toucheth a common experience which chaunceth to
them y^t from vyce be conuerted to vertue, or from a commen maner of liuyng to
more worship or to more honestie, or from pouertie to greate riches: Suche as were
their equals afore, suche as were their companions, or as leude as they were afore,
wyll mocke theim, gest at them, yea and some will bitterlye rayle, and dispitefullye
backebite theim. Example we haue **.i. Reg. x.** of Saule whiche was but a rude
persone, and sekynge hys fathers Asses that were strayed awaye, he met with
Samuell the Prophet, who by Goddes commaundement anointed him king of the
realme, and told hym afore hande certain thinges that shoulde befortune hym,
that when he sawe them come to passe, and come to effecte as they were told hym,
he myght by them assure hym selfe that Samuell was a true Prophete, and that he
declared to hym Goddes minde sincerelye and truelye. Amonge other, this was one
signe, when thou shalt come to a certayne town in thy waye (saide Samuell vnto

† auro] signo; rogat] colit

Saule) there thou shalt mete a company of Prophets. **Et insiliet in te spiritus domini & prophetabis cum eis & mutaberis in virum alium.** The spirit of our lord shall fall vpon thee sodainly, & thou shalt prophecy as thei do, and thou shalt be chaunged into another maner of man.* And as Samuel ye prophet saied, so it chaunced in dede. And Saul prophecied with them, singing & lauding god, & also speking by ye way of prophecy of things to come.* Of this came [3N4^v] the murmure and admiration, and wonder of theim that knewe hym, and were acquaynted with hym afore, euen as Saynte Peter speaketh here, they saide. **Quenam res accidit filio Cis? Num & Saul inter Prophetas? Cis** was father vnto Saule, what is become vnto the sonne of Cis? What is Saule amonge the Prophetes, or one of the Prophetes?* These menne did not thanke GOD for the gifte that God hadde geuen to Saule, but rather disdayned, and fell to mockynge of hym. Other there were that manifestlye despised hym. **Filii autem Belial dixerunt Num saluare nos poterit iste? & despexerunt eum.** The Deuylles chyldren, malicious persones sayde. Can this man saue vs from our enemies? They dispised hym and set hym at naught, and woulde not take hym as their Kynge, nor brought anye presente vnto hym as others did.* Euen accordynge to suche common practice of the worlde speaketh Saynte Peter here. They that yet styll persisteth and continueth in their old accustomed vyce and misliuynge **filii Beliall,** the deuylles birdes marueyleth at you. That you forsake theim, and that you fall not to suche confusion of all Lecherye and voluptuous liuynge as they dooe, and as you were wonte to dooe, blaspheminge and missaiynge you, because you abstaine from their noughtie conuersation, they despise you, and sette not a strawe by you,* but sayeth: Wyll you see thys Pope holye horeson?* **Num Saull inter Prophetas.** Wee shall haue a Prophete or a Preacher of hym, with suche [3O1] other blasphemynge and raylynge woordes. **Qui reddent rationem ei qui paratus est iudicare viuos & mortuos.** Whiche shall make a reakening and accompte for their raylinge, vnto hym that is readye to Iudge the quicke and the deade,* our Sauiour Iesus Christe, vnto whome the father hath geuen auctoritie to Iudge all them that shall be iudged, for if you holde your tonge and speake nothinge, that iuste Iudge will not kepe silence, nor holde his tongue, but will paye theim home for their blasphemye and raylynge, and shall geue you large rewarde for your Pacience, accordynge to that Sainte Paule sayeth that pacience tryeth a manne, a tryall worketh hoope of saluation.* And that hope shall not bee confounded, but shall be saciate with ioyes euerlastinge in heauen, accordinge to our expectation. Amen.

The fiftenth trcatice or
                                  Sermon.

VIuant autem secundum Deum in spiritu.* In these wordes that I haue nowe
reade vnto you the blessed Apostle Sainte Peter sheweth vs the commoditie that
came to them that beyng infidels hadde the Gospell and good tidings of Christes
doctrine preached vnto them And the same commoditie commeth also to all them
that beinge in deadly sinne, and so dead spiritually heareth the Gospell and the
worde of God preached vnto them, which is amendment of life. Thus he sayeth.
Propter hoc. &c. For this cause the Gospell and holye doctryne of Christes faith
was preached to you, and to them while they were afore dead by infidelitie, and for
lacke of the lyfe of grace, that they might be likewise iudged, or condemned by
carnal vicious persons as you be, and might be likewise hadde in dispite as you be
for Christes sake, and for your good vertuous liuing. And notwithstanding sinister
iudgemente of naughty men, yet they should liue Godly, and according to Goddes
pleasure, in spirite,* for commonly those two thinges foloweth of the receyuynge
of Christes fayth, and for liuynge accordinge to the same, firste that accidentallie
and by occasion of good and christian liuynge, menne suffereth muche woe and
vexation, and many dispitefull wordes. Second euen of purpose of them that
preacheth or conuerteth men to good, they [3O2] that be so conuerted maye liue
vertuouslye accordynge to Goddes pleasure. **Omnium autem finis appropinquabit.**
Because he sayd euen now that Christe is readye to come to iudge the quick and
the deade, as though he woulde not be long nor tarie. Nowe he saieth accordyng
to the same that the ende of all menne is at hande,* for as Christe saieth in the
Gospell, of that daye of iudgement no man knoweth howe nighe it is, or howe
farre of it is.* And therefore we muste euer thinke vppon it, as thinkinge euerye
mornynge it woulde be come afore night. And euen so we muste thinke of our
owne particuler iudgement at our departinge, euerie man and woman for oure
owne parte, as well for the aucthoritye of Goddes woorde, that in manye places
geueth vs warnynge to bee euer readye, as for the manifolde Pronostications and
messagers of death that wee haue euerye daye. Of whiche one is Age, whiche
daielye creapeth vppon vs, aduertisynge vs of oure ende to whiche he daielye
driueth vs, as by lacke of naturall heate, and by colde folowynge of the same. And
this commeth to manye menne by longe continuynge in thys lyfe, and by
multitude of yeres. To others it commeth afore their tyme accedentallye, and in a
manner vyolentelye, as by syckenesse, paynes, and aches, and to others by vnmeasurable solicitude and care of minde. **Eccle. xxx. Cogitatus ante tempus senectam
adducit.*** And to others by ouermuche Studye and watchynge for to get learnyng
and knowledge. [3O2ᵛ] **Vigilia honestatis tabefaciet carnes, & cogitatus illius
auferet somnum. Eccle. xxxi.** Watchyng about matters of honestye and goodnes
shall consume the fleshe, and the thinkyng on such thinges will take awaye a mans
slepe,* for of muche thought and of profounde study about weighty matters, and
likewise of musinge on terrible and troublous causes there commeth into the
sensuall appetite of manne manye passions and troubles to vexe him, and vnquiet
hym, as feare and sorow and heauinesse, or suche other, whiche manye tymes
altereth the bodye soore and vnmeasurablye, so that a mannes naturall complexion is distempered by the same, and a mannes naturall moysture is consumed, and
natural strength weakened and decayed, and so the fleshe widdereth and dryeth,
the skyne wrinkeleth and quaketh. And therefore saide the wiseman. **Pro. xxv.**

Sicut tinea vestimento & vermis ligno, ita tristicia viri nocet cordi. As a moght hurteth a garment and a worme consumeth a Tree: so dothe sorowe and heauinesse hurte a mannes harte, and consequentlye all the bodye after.* And therfore holye Iob in his greate calamitie and vexacion sayde. **Cutis mea aruit & contracta est. Iob. vii.** My skinne is withered and shronke together.* This saide holye Iob, considerynge that hys naturall moysture was consumed by age & for his manifold diseases and sores. An other pronostication & messager of our end is sickenes, soores & malenders, as weaknes of complexion, dispos[it]ion to many feuers & to be now & then vexed wᵗ one fe[3O3]uer or an other, hed ache, colick, yᵉ stone, gowts, & runninge legges,* dropsye, and palsye All these biddeth vs beware, and geueth vs warninge afore. But manye there bee that wyll take no warninge by these infirmities, but be as maliciouselye disposed in blasphemy, & couetousnesse, euen whyle they be subiecte to such diseases, as thei were in healthe. They neuer remembreth death, till they be so taken that they can nother stirre hande nor foote, and can scarsely speake or heare. As we haue knowen of these hel houndes ruffians and riatours that by there life time had neuer deuotion toward god, nether regarding masse nor other diuine seruice, nother the sacrament of Christes chur-che, which when they haue bene taken wᵗ feruent sicknes yᵗ they could not by the helpe of phisitions recouer, haue fallen to raginge, blasphemyng, & swearying, and so died desperatly. After whych soden death foloweth and preuenteth the dispo-synge of a mannes Soule to GOD, or of hys goodes to the worlde, all the sayde messagers, infirmities, and diseases, they bringe shrewde tidinges to the bodye, and bee nothinge pleasaunte for the sensuall appetite: in as muche as they putte menne to paine. And healpe to drawe menne to the graue, but to the reason they shoulde bee welcome, for they be medicynable and holesome for the soul, in as muche as they letteth menne and kepeth menne from synne, and maketh theim more feruent to please GOD, and to liue vertuouslye. When mens infirmities be multi-plyed and com[3O3ᵛ]meth one vpon another, men will make haste to know God and to come to God, amending their lyues. And .s. Paule consideringe that (**virtus in infirmitate perficitur .ii. Cori. xii.**) vertue is made parfite in infirmitie, in as much as sickenes and weakenes of body is the matter and occasion to exercise Pacience, to exercise Temperaunce and Chastitye, and also by sycken[e]sse knowynge a mannes owne infyrmitie, he shall be made more lowlye and meeke and so stronge to exercise him selfe in vertue. And also because that vertue is neuer so parfite, as when it hath some infirmitie contrarye that it maye striue agaynste, as Chastitie when it is not tempted by carnal concupiscence, is not so parfite as when it is tempted, and so pacience is moste excellent that is proued and tempted by vexacion of Shrowes, and by displeasures, and therefore Saynte Paule saith **Libenter gloriabor in infirmitatibus meis vt inhabitet in me virtus Christi.** I shall gladlye and wyth a good wyll reioyce and be proude in myne infyrmities, that so I may be conformable to Christ, hauing vertues in me more eminent and more excellent then els they woulde haue bene. **Propter quod placeo mihi in infirmitatibus meis, in contumelijs, in necessitatibus, in persecutionibus, in angustijs pro Christo.** I please my selfe (as a proud manne dothe) when I am weake and sicke, or diseased in bodye, and when I am dispitefullye vexed, and when I am in greate and extreame neade, in persecution, in distresse, or in streictes. **Cum enim infirmor tunc potens sum.** [3O4] When I am sicke and weake, then I am strong and mightye.* **Ambrosius. Verum est quia tunc vincit christianus cum perdere putatur, & tunc perdit perfidia cum se vicisse gratula-tur plaudit igitur cum illi insultatur & surgit cum premitur.** It is true that the apostle saith, for then a christen man ouercommeth and hath the ouerhande when he is thought to lose, and to haue the worse. And then falshode loseth when he is glad of his winnyng, or that he hathe ouercome and gotten the vpper hand.* And therfore saint Paule was most glad and proude in God, when men kicked and wrought displesures against him, and he rose vpward when men thought they pressed hym downe. An other common messager of deathe, is example of others that we see plucked away from vs euery daye, of all ages, of all states and degrees, As well vnthrifts and noughty liuers, as blessed men of the best sort. There is no daie, but we heare of the death of one or other, bi which we may assure our selues that we shall go after. And almightie God many times suffreth blessed men and good liuers to dye sodainely, and sometimes more miserably in the reputation of the worlde, then tyrantes, extorcioners, and bribers, and such other of the worst sort. Temporall wealth, and temporall penurye and pouertye, is common, as well to good folke, as to the bad folke, and so is that we call miserable death, & a faire deathe. For the first. **S. Aug. i. ci. dei ca. viii. Temporalia bona & mala vtrisque voluit esse communia, vt nec bona cupidius ap[3O4^v]petantur que mali quoque habere cernuntur, nec mala turpiter euitentur quibus & boni plerumque afficiuntur.** God woulde that good thinges and ill chaunces should be commen to good men and to bad, because good things shold not be to gredely desired whiche we se noughty persons to haue and enioy, nor yll things should not be shamefully eschued and abhorred, whiche moste commonlye good people hath and be combred with all.* The most diuersity is in the vse and occupiynge of prosperitie and of aduersitie. For a good man is neuer the prouder for prosperitie, nother ouercast, broken, or marde by aduersitie, where contrary, a noughty person in felicitie is corrupt by pride and arrogancy and with infelicitie, with yll chaunces & aduersite is sore vexed and punished, & many tymes brought to desperacion, yet besyde thys almyghty God showeth his meruelous worke in the distribucion or deuidinge of prosperite and aduersite, as well as of a good death and a foule death, in that that if GOD shoulde by and by correcte euerye synne wyth some manifest paine, he should leaue nothinge to bee punished at the generall iudgement, and agayne if GOD did punyshe no <no> faulte nor synne nowe in this presente life, menne woulde thynke there were no Godlye prouidence at all, or that GOD cared not for the worlde, or what that menne did in the worlde. And lykewyse, when menne praye for prosperitye, or for sufficiencye here in thys world if God would not of his liberall goodnes [3P1] graunt men somwhat of their peticions somtimes among, men wold think that he had nothing to do with them, or that worldly wealth pertained not to him, and were none of his to bestow when he wolde, and again if he should graunt them to eueri man that wold aske for them, men wold serue god for none other thing but for them, and the seruice of God should not make vs godly and deuout toward him, but rather gredy and couetouse to the world. Therefore although there be no dissimilitude betwixt the thinges that good men & naughtye men in differently suffereth, yet there is great diuersitie and difference betwixt the sufferers. As if a man chafe in his hand, or els against the fyre talow or greace, it giueth an horrible stinckynge smell, where as if you likewise chafe by the same fyre a pleasant oyntment, it giueth a fragraunt and swete sauour. And like as God sendeth welth and wo indifferently to good men and to yl men, for causes best knowen vnto his wisedome, euen so he sendeth our end and death sometime to euil men easy and worshipful in the sight of the world, and to good men shameful and vilenous as men taketh it. Many men desireth a good death, and a fayre death, and feareth and abhorreth a fowle deathe. And yet (to saye the truthe) all maner

of death is a good death to them that be good, and to sinneful persons al maner of
deathe is a fowle death, as Saint Austine declareth in his booke **de disciplina
Christiana**. Therfore if thou be afraid of a fowle death, thou muste feare a fowle
and a sinneful life, for if thou loue a fowle and a sinne[3P1ᵛ]full life, and wouldest
haue a fair end, thou louest better thy death then thy life, which I declare after this
maner. All things that a man loueth he would fayne haue them fayre and good, as
in example: If thou loue thy coate or thy gown, thou wouldest fayne haue it fayre
and good. Thou louest thy friende, thou wouldest fayne haue hym good. Thou
louest thy sonne or thy childe, thou wouldest be glad he were good. Thou louest
thy house or thy chamber, thou wouldest fayne haue it fayre and good. Then how
is it that thou woldest fayn haue a fayre and a good death at thine ending? Is it not
for like causes, that thou hast a speciall loue to it And therfore thou praiest God
(consideringe that thou must once dye) that God woulde sende thee a fayre
deathe, and that God would saue thee from a fowle deathe. Thou art afrayd to dye
yll, but thou art not afrayde to liue yl, & therfore thou louest thy death better then
thy life. Amende thy yll lyfe, and neuer feare an yll death. For **non potest male
mori qui bene vixerit,** he can not die ill that hath liued well.* But agaynste this
you will peraduenture obiect thus: hath not mani good men ben drowned by
tempest or by ship wrack in yᵉ seas & lost theyr liues wᵗ their goodes & al? Hath
not many good men ben slain amongest theyr enemies in battell? Hath not theues
kylled mani good men in theyr own houses, or els bi the hie way side? Hath not
some good men bene killed with wilde beastes, yea & mani al to torne in peces
with such wild beasts? and haue you not herd of som innocents yᵗ haue ben hanged
on yᵉ galowes [3P2] as felons, murderers, or like malefactours? Be not al these yl
deathes? be thei not fowl deathes? Aske the eyes of the carnal and fleshly man, &
they will say they be fowle deathes, & ill deathes. But examine & aske the eyes of
our faithe & they wyll iudge them and cal them fayre deathes, because that God
saith by the prophet, **preciosa est in conspectu domini mors sanctorum eius**. The
death of the holye & good men is precious & of great price & estimacion in the
sight of our lord.* Be not such deathes as I haue spoken of, the veri deathes that
blessed Martyrs (whose martirdomes we kepe highe & holy in Christes churche)
haue suffered for Christes sake? Therfore let vs endeuour our selues to haue a good
life while we be here, & then whatso euer occasion we haue to die, we shal go out
of this world to rest & quietnes that shall be without al feare of trouble, & shal
neuer haue end. The riche gloton yᵗ is spoke of in the gospel yᵗ we[n]t eueri day in
purple & soft silkes, & fared euery dai delicately, it is to be thought that he died in
a soft bed, in fine shetes & costly counterpoints or couerlets, but streight out of
them he was cast into hell, where he begged one drop of water to cole his tong, &
to refresh him & could not get it. Pore Lazar the begger died in his mangie cloutes
ful of matter of his sores, among the dogs that licked his scabs wᵗout meate or
drink, in hunger & thurst, he could not get the crummes & scraps that fel from yᵉ
rich mans bord, yet out of al this miseri he went streight into Abrahams bosom, a
place of rest & quietnes without any distemperance to trouble him or to disease
hym:* [3P2ᵛ] Take hede of theyr ende, and by that consideracion iudge whiche
was the better death, eyther the ryche gloton, which died into hel, or the deathe of
poore Lazar which dyed into health, rest, & quietnes. I dout not but your minde
giueth you that poore Lazar dyed the better deathe, excepte you would wyshe to
dye in riche clothes, & to be powdred with costly spices, and your soules to stynke
in hell, and to begge water, and none to haue gyuen you. What profeit got the
riche gloton by his gaye tumbe of fyne marble or of touche stone or els of some

costly mettal, more then the pore man by his homely buryal? litle or none. Therefore to conclude, thou shalt learne to dye well, and to dye a fayre death: if thou wilt learne to liue wel. Our Saviour Christ led the most blessed and vertuous life that any man lived, and therfore though his deth semed to his enemies the cruell Iewes most vile and vilanous, yet it was the marveylous deathe that killed deathe, and killed also the auctour and causer of all death.* Therefore finallye consideringe that the ende of us all is come at hande* (as saint Peter saithe here) let vs take example of Christ and of his holy word, and also of holy men and women that hath taken paynes to folow his steps, and let vs conforme our lyuinge vnto their liues, and let vs arme our selues with the consideracion and busie remembrance of Christes life, and of his passion & his death, as I sayd at the beginning of this exhortacion, & then there is no doubte but whether we dye by lande or by water, we shall dye a precious and a good death, [3P3] that shalbe the meane and high way to quietnes, rest, and ioyes in euerlastinge life with Christe. **Estote itaque prudentes et vigilate in orationibus,** therfore be you prudent and watch in praiers.* These wordes of sainte Peter with certaine that foloweth be red in Christes churche for the epistle of the day, on the sunday within the octaues of the ascension: which is the sunday next afore Whitsunday.* Saint Peter considering the manifold troubles of this world that vertuous faithful people be euer cumbred with al, and also considering the shortnes of our abode here, that it wil away, and is come to an ende, therefore he saithe: **be you prudent and watch in praiers.** Be you prudent (he saith), there be diuers maners of prudence. The philosopher saithe that **omnia naturaliter bonum appetunt:** Al things naturally desyreth the thing that is good for theym,* and so doth the thinges that lacketh theyr senses after theyr maner, for they naturally desireth to come to theyr natural quantitie and strength, and to furnysh and to set forth the beutie of the whole worlde, and to saue them selues by a certayne met<h>aphoricall prudence or a similitude of prudence or prouision, as you see that when a yong tree groweth nigh vnto a great tre ye yong tree wyl grow outward from the greater tree, as it were to saue it selfe from the shadow or dropping of the greater tree, naturally prouiding for his owne safegarde, by suche a naturall prudence or prouision. The brute beastes also desyreth that is good for them by a certaine comon prudence, which is and may be called **A prouision** [3P3^v] **for thinges to come bi remembrance of thyngs past.** As a Horse or a Cowe that hath be fed in a good pasture, or wintred in a warme stable, wyll draw to the same againe when thei haue nede. But man which is a reasonable creature, prouideth for the thing that is good for him self or for them that long to him bi prudence more properly taken, which is **recta ratio agibilium circa hominis bona et mala. vi. Ethi. id est ratio rectificatiua agibilium.** The reason or a qualitie or a vertue in the reason that maketh streight & setteth in order al things that man doth to obtaine that is good, & to exchew that is bad.* It is also the vertue by which a manne can gyue good counsail & make wise prouision for al thinges that longeth to a mans life. But then in as much as the wiseman saith: **Contra bonum malum est, et contra malum bonum.** Euery good thing hath an enemie, and so hath eueri vertue,* or at the lest wise an Ape or a counterfeter that semeth a vertue & is none but rather a vice: So there is a certaine prudence of hipocrites that pretendeth a grauitie and a politique cast in all theyr affaires and doinges, & yet they loke more for vayne prayse of the people, and that they may be seene to be wise and politique, then for anye right or streight intencion to do anye good by theyr policie to Gods pleasure, or to do any man good by the same. Because that Prudence and sapience be sometyme taken for one, as appeareth where the Apostle sayth. **Ro. viij. Prudentia carnis mors est**. The prudence of the fleshe is deathe. And there ryght he saythe, **Sapientia carnis inimica est deo,** The Sapi[3P4]ence or wisedome of the fleshe is enemye to God.* Therefore as Saynte Iames maketh a distinction of three maner of wysedomes, **Iacob .iij.** So we maye diuide prudence or prouidence, callynge some earthly prudence or wisedome, some beastlye wysedome, and some dyuelishe wisedome or prouision.* **Earthly prudence** or wisedome, is the wisedome of them that studyeth vehemently and farre casteth to gette the wealthe and ryches of the world, and drowneth them selues in the same euen as it were Moles or Wants that be neuer well but when they be toylynge or moylynge in the earth, and there they be wyser and can better skil then any other beast. Euen so be these worldly wise men whiche be neuer well but when they be gathering riches & mucke of the worlde, more seruing theyr riches then seruing God.* Agaynste which speaketh our sauiour Christ, **Nemo potest duobus dominis seruire . . . deo . . . et mammone**. No man can serue two maysters, God and his goodes or ryches.* The Phariseis that were couetous men, hearde thys and laughed hym to scorne, therfore they heard **ve vobis diuitibus,** you suche rych persons shall haue wo euerlastinge, for the ioye that you nowe take in your riches.* **Beastlye wisedome** they haue that obey the pleasure of the bealy, and applyeth theyr wyttes chiefelye to content the same,* in that folowing the propertye of very beastes, to which Christ sayd: **Ve vobis qui saturati estis quia esurietis**. Wo be to you that be farced and stuffed full of meates, for you shall be a hungerd, bothe here, and in the worlde to come.*

[3P4ᵛ] Esau for greedynes of a messe of potage lost hys fyrst frutes, yea & made but a trifle of it, he toke no thought for his losse, worsse then the prodigall and wastefull sonne that is spoken of in the gospel, for when he had spent al, he toke repentance, returned to his father agayne, asked mercye, and had it.* But our spill paynes that drinketh & wasteth all that theyr fathers or frendes hathe lefte them, loueth nothing wors then to heare of their ryote and waste, and wyl be readye to fighte if a man speake to them of it, and wyl sweare woundes and nayles, that if they had twise as muche more, it should go the same way, they would sell euery ynche of it. Suche men be wearye of theyr wealthe, they can not beare wealth and plentye, they can not beare so heauye a burden, therefore they must learne to beare light, to beare pouerty and beggery, and for landes, rents, and worshipfull estate must hop in a cutted cote,* **proficientes in peius** proceding and going furth euery daye into worsse and worsse.* **Diuelishe** wisedome or prudence they haue that by example of the deuyl exalt them selues to the vttermost of theyr power.* He would haue exalted him selfe aboue the sters of heauen aboue the estate of all angels, and said he would be like the highest, equall and as good as God. **Esay. xiiii** Mark the sequel that folowed of his pride, and beware of it. **Veruntamen in infernum deijcieris in profundum laci,** but thou shalt be cast into hell into the depest of the lake,* and so he was ouerturned from the gloriousest angell in heauen, and made the fowlest dyuell in hell, and [3Q1] yet proud men semeth worsse then he was, for he desired no more but to be like GOD, and equall with God, but the proude man woulde be better then God. For where God woulde haue his will fulfilled and done when it is iuste and good: the proude man would haue his will done and fulfilled, whither it be right or wrong. Against al these worldly prudences and wisedomes saith almighty God, as it is rehersed. **i. Cor. i. I shall destroy the wisedome of worldlye wise men and shall reproue the prudence and prouidence of suche prudent persons:** Hath not God (saith the Apostle) made the wisedome of the world very foolishnes? It hath pleased almightye God to saue faithfull people by the preaching of the gospell, whiche worldlye wisemen repute and take as very foolishnes, and as a foolishe thinge.* They take theyr policie and worldly prouidence as thoughe it came of theym selues and not of God, and therefore they thanke not God for it, neither honour him, but rather labour and studie to destroy his honour & to quench it, and therefore God of his iust iudgement many times taketh that awaye from theym that he gaue them so that while they thincke them selues wise, they proue verye fooles, and God turneth theyr cast and theyr drift to a frustratorie, vayne and foolishe end contrarye to theyr expectacion. The prudence and wisedome that Sainte Peter in this place of his epistle that wee haue in hande woulde haue vs to vse, is spirituall prudence, the wisedome of the spirite, of the whiche S. Paule speaketh. **Ro. viij. Prudentia autem spiritus vita et pax.** [3Q1ᵛ] The wisedome of the spirite by which man worketh according to the inclination of the holi spirit is life and peace,* that is to saye, it is the cause of life euerlasting, and of peace and quietnes here, & to ioyn them together, it is the cause of life with peace and quietnes euerlasting in heauen. Thys wysedome no sinner hathe, as appeareth manye wayes. **Fyrst,** because a sinner loseth a great inheritaunce for a little trifle of pleasure, as Esau did for a messe of potage, as I sayd afore. And it is writte. **Iob .xxviij. Sapientia non inuenitur in terra suauiter [u]iuentium,** Wysedome is not founde in the londe or countrey of them that liueth delicatelye all at pleasure.* **Seconde,** sinners lacketh prudence, for they little regarde to recouer theyr inheritance againe, where they might so doe with a little labour and payne like them that be spoken of in the psalme, **pro nihilo habuerunt terram desiderbilem,** The Israelites estemed not the delectable lande that was promised them,* but would rather haue turned backe agayne into Egipt, euen so do synners desperately litle regarde the land of life euerlasting in heauen. **Thirde,** a synner lacketh prudence, because he doth wilfully cast him selfe into the snares of him that will not fayle to draw him and strangle him to death euerlastynge. Byrdes that bee meshede in a nette, canne not gette out when they woulde wythout helpe, but the more they stryue, the sorer they be holden in the nette, Euen so saythe the wyseman. **Prouer. v. Funibus peccatorum suorum vnusquisque constringitur.** Euerye synner is wrapt and streyned wyth the ropes [3Q2] of hys owne synnes* and the more hee laboreth, striueth, and strugleth to saciate and content hys vicious appetite the harder he is holden and meshed in delectation, and in custome of hys synne, and so he prepareth and dresseth his owne death **Sapi. i. Deus mortem non fecit: impij manibus ac pedibus accersierunt eam.** God made not the death of sinne, but wicked men with hand and foote haue called it in and pulled it to theym.* **Fourth,** it is plaine that synners lacketh prudence and wysedome, by that they be not afrayde of the iustice of God knowyng that he hath iustlye condempned so manye Angels for synne, and that the Angels were made diuels for breakinge theyr obedience to God. And that so manye men and women be dampned for transgressynge and breakynge hys commaundementes, and that our fyrst parentes and all theyr posteritie were strycken wyth mortalitie and necessitye to dye, for disobedience and for synne, and that for synne all the worlde was destroyed with water, and that for synne the fiue cityes Sodome, Gomor, and theyr neyghbours were destroyed wyth fyre, brymstone, and suche horryble stynckynge tempest.* And thus it is euident euerye waye that a synner lacketh the spirituall prudence and wysedome that we speake of. Thys godlye prudence that we speake of, hathe three operacions and woorkes, of whyche commeth theyr effectes proporcionablye, one is **prouision,** the seconde is **Circumspection,** the thyrd maye be called **Caution or warynesse.***

[3Q2ᵛ] To prouision wee be moued by example of foure poore litle beastes that be spoken of. **Prouer. xxx. Quatuor sunt minima terre & ipsa sunt sapientiora sapientibus.** There be .iiii. of the least thinges breding on earth, and they be wiser after theyr maner then some wise men be.* And here we must take our examples of vnsensible thinges and of brute beasts and dumme creatures, according to the counsayl of holy Iob .xii. **Interroga† iumenta & docebunt te: & volatilia celi et indicabunt tibi: loquere terre & respondebit tibi, et narrabunt pisces maris.** Aske the beasts and they will teache thee, and so of others.* Then it may be sayde that we aske these dumme creatures questions to learne witte by them, when we consider theyr naturall disposicions, examinyng and discussing and searching out theyr naturall operacions and vertues. And then they answer vs and teache vs, when by consideracion of them we ascende and rise vp to the knowledge of god, or to som learning, to which we come by consideration of their properties. As here in our purpose we be answered by the worke of the Emyt, and taught to exchewe slouthe, and to prouide for the time to come, he is one of the foure that the wise man referreth vs to, saying: **formice populus infirmus qui preparat in messe cibum sibi.** One is the poore Emytte or Pismyre, which in haruest and in time of fayr weather prouideth meate to lyue by in winter,* of whose diligence and prouision he spoke afore. **Prou. vi. Vade ad formicam o piger, & considera vias eius, & disce sapientiam.** O thou idle man or woman, go to the Emytte, and consider [3Q3] hys labours and payne that he taketh, and learn witte.* He hath no ruler, captayne or scolemayster but onely his owne naturall inclinacion and dysposicion, where we be many waies taught to prouide, as well by almighty God in his scriptures, and by the preachers, as by our maisters and by good example giuers, and yet the said poore beast hath a cast of prouision that many of vs lacketh, for he prouideth aforehand in fair weather meate to lyue by in winter, and in fowle weather when he may not labour, and so the slouthful man may learne by him. In so muche as so little a worme, lacking a captaine, gide, or scoolemaister, taught onely by nature, prouideth so handsomely for her selfe, while she maye styrre about and laboure against the time to come. Muche more we that be reasonable creatures made after the ymage of God, and called to the sight of his glory, and that be helped with so many maisters and teachers, hauing him that made vs for our gyde and captayne, ought and must nedes for shame gather together the graynes and frutes of good woorkes, by which we may liue the euerlasting life in time to come. Thys present life is like the sommer or the haruest time: for nowe in the heate of temptacion and trouble is the tyme to gather yᵉ merites of rewardes euerlastinge, the good woorkes for which we shall be rewarded in heauen. The daye of dome, and the time after this life maye be called winter, for then will be no time to labour for a mans liuing, but euery man and woman shall be compelled to shewe furth that he hath layd vp [3Q3ᵛ] in the barne or garnard of his former workes by his life tyme, and vpon them he shall lyue, or perishe for hunger, for accordinge to theym he shall haue his rewarde. **Lepusculus plebs inualida qui collocat in petra cubile suum.** Here is som diuersitie of translations, for that in our text is called **lepusculus,** in other is called **herinacius,** and **hericius & Mus.** * And in the psalm **.Ciii.** it is sayd, **petra refugium herinacijs,** the rocke is a refuge, a place of safe garde and defence, for that beast.* It is a little rough beast, and buildeth in the rockes in Palestine, in the holy lande. I thinke we haue none of them here with vs. For the same our translation in the prouerbs of Salomo[n]

† Interroga] Ieterroga

putteth **Lepusculus** an Hare or a Leueret. This worde **Saphan** in the Hebrewe hath dyuers significations, of whyche one is a Hare, and so it is put in our comon translacion.* A Hare is a weake beast a[n]d a fraiful, euer running away, more trusting to her feete and to her form or resting place, then to her own strength. Sometime she maketh her forme in old groses, rockes, or quarryes, spent, lefte, or forsaken, and signifieth the weake good Christen people that seke not to reuenge the wrongs done vnto them, and hath this pointe of prudence and wisedome, not to trust in theyr owne strength, but to putte theyr trust principally in our redemer & sauioure Iesus Christe, sygnified by the stone or rocke in whiche (as it is sayde here) the Hare maketh hys bed or forme.* And so we all shoulde be timorous and frayfull of oure owne selues, or of our owne [m]erites, and muste commytte oure selues to the [3Q4] protection and defence of God as in a towre of strengthe to saue vs from oure ennemyes that woulde destroye vs. **Regem Locusta non habet & egreditur v[n]iuersa per† turmas suas.*** Locusta is a certayne longe Flye, bygger then the Cricket, or then the Grassehopper, they be verye many in Affrike, and in southe parte of Asia. Theyr propertie is to flye flocking together, as it wer al with one accorde, hauyng no kyng nor captayne to set theym forwarde. The Bees haue a captayne or mayster Bee whom they folowe when they wyll swarme, and so hath not these Locustes, bi which is commended vnto vs the prudence and wysedome in concorde and vnitie, felow like wythout coertion or compulsion.* For thoughe concorde and vnitie wyth obedience vnder one heade and ruler be very good and necessary, and accordinge to Gods lawes† and to hys pleasure, yet thys brotherlye loue and concorde without coertion, pleaseth him much more, & maketh the diuels of hell afrayde to set vpon vs. And therefore the spouse our sauiour Christ calleth his best beloued the holy church, the congregacion of faithful people **Terribilis vt cast[r]orum acies† ordinata, Canti. vi.** Terrible like the forwarde or the onsette of a battel wel set in order and in araye.* They that haue experience knoweth† this right well, that when two armies or hostes shall meete together in battayle, that hoste that auaunceth forward in a ray very close ioined together, shalbe terrible to the contrari part and shal make them soone afrayde, because they [3Q4ᵛ] can not spye any place where to breake the raye, but they must needes come vpon the pikes, vpon the artilery, vpon the whole ordinance and peryll of the battel, wher contrary if they be disseuered, diuided and parted abrode, then the contrary multitude runneth in among them, and scatereth them as dogges doth in a flocke of sheepe, and destroyeth and killeth where they list. Euen so when our gostli enemies seeth vs close knit together by the linkes of charitie and of concord in goodnes, thei be afrayd of vs, for they loue nothing wors then loue and vnitie in goodnes: they be in dispayre to do vs any hurt, and flye away from vs. We be euer in warre and battell agaynste the diuels our gostly enemies, and thei be euer ramping and roring and laboring to ouercome vs, and to brynge vs to dampnacion euerlasting, therfore we must needes make a close bulwerke of our selues by a frame of charitie, agreyng fast and sure amonge our selues by concord and vnitie, and so saue our selues, as the wise man exhorteth vs to doe by example of the sayde Locustes that so ordinatelye keepeth theyr aray when they flye abrode. **Stellio manibus nititur & moratur in edibus regis.** A Stote a Veyry, or a Wesyll clyngeth and cleaueth fast with his fete, which standeth him in stede of handes, and by them he scratcheth and climeth verye nimlye on the walles, on the roofes, and on all other places of great mens houses, yea and byldeth and breedeth in the kynges

† per] pro; lawes] lawee; vt castrorum acies] ut castorum acres; knoweth] knoweeh

palace:* and where he hath no winges to flie vp, he getteth vp with his handes or
feete as hie as he list to do: by this tea[3R1]ching vs this point of prudence and of
prouision, that where we may not obteyne our intente one waye, we must assaye
another way. As if a man be not of such naturall pregnancy, and quicknes of witte
as others be, yet by his diligence and busye exercise in study and contemplation,
and in prayers, he commeth sometyme to the knowlege of holy scripture, and to
such graces of vertues, by whiche he may builde his dwellinge place, in the kinges
house of heauen aboue. And you see many times, that in the trade of marchaundise, and in handy craftes, men that be not most clere of wytte, yet by their
continuall paines takinge, and by diligent appliynge their wittes that they haue
vnto their worke, they come to more conninge and knowledge in their faculties,
and to more aboundaunce of riches by their exercise, then they that ha[u]e farre
better wittes. And as we se that manye birdes that haue fethers and winges to flie
and mounte vp on hie, yet they abide and builde alowe amonge the briers, frisses,
and bushes, and sometimes vpon the grounde, while this **stellio**, this stoote or
wesel that hathe no winges, trustinge to her nayles, climeth vp to the top of the
towre: so they that be well witted, and might mount hie by their wittes, manye
times geueth them selues to slouth and idlenes, kepinge them selues alowe in
shreude vnthriftie and noughtie workes, while good simple persons, that lacketh
the winges of subtill wittes, trusting to theyr nailes, to their busie labours, commeth to greate knoweledge, and to grace and [3R1ᵛ] goodnes and finally to the
kinges house and towers in heauen aboue, as I sayde. And this for this fyrste kinde
of prudence or wysedome, whiche I called prouision. The seconde kynde of
prudence may be called **Circumspection,** by which we loke well about, and take
good hede that we do truely kepe the meane of vertue, so that while we exchew
and auoyde one vice, we fall not into the other extremitie and contrarye vice, as
that while we auoide auarice and couetousenes, we fall not into prodigalitie and
wastfulnes: and that whyle we auoyde cowardnes, we fall not into folishe hardines,
or to rasshe brainesicknes. They be not circumspecte inough, that so exchueth,
and auoideth from temporall trouble and payne, that they runne into euerlastinge
payne, or that so flieth from worldly pouertie, that they fall into euerlastinge nede
and scarcitie, when they shall begge and nothinge shall be geuen them. All such
be like a skittish starting horse, whiche coming ouer a bridge, wil start for a
shadowe, or for a stone lying by him, and leapeth ouer on the other side into the
water, & drowneth both horse and man.* Another kind of prudence is **Cautio,**
warines, lest we be begiled with vices cloked vnder the colour of vertues, as Amasa
was begiled of Ioab **.ii. Reg. xx.** This Ioab fearing least Amasa shoulde haue ben
made cheife captayne of the warres of kinge Dauid, enuied him, and dissembled
with him, and as thei were setting forward to a certaine batail, met with him, &
louingly saluted him, and toke him by yᵉ chin, as though he [3R2] would haue
kissed him, and said to him, **salue mi frater,** God spede my cosin (for in dede they
were sisters children) he had a weapon by his side, with whiche he stroke him in
the side that his guttes fell out, and so he died.* There is none so perilous gyle, as
that is hidde vnder the similitude and colour of frendship. By this kinde of
prudence we shal spie when pride disgiseth him self vnder the similitude & name
of clenlines, and when lechery is cloked & taken for loue: and we shall perceaue
that in great aboundaunce, & in worldly welth, is hid much indigence, nede, &
lacke of vertue and grace, and also that vnder the ignominie, shame, and sclaundre
of Christes crosse, is most excellent pulchritude and beautie, & that vnder the
folishnes of preaching of Christ (as many hath taken it) is couered most godlye

vertue and wysedome. Our sauiour exhorteth vs to prudence & wisdome by example of a serpent, **Estote prudentes sicut serpentes, Mat. x.** Be you wise like serpentes.* The serpent to saue her heade, wyll laye forth all the whole body in daunger and perill, and so should we do to conserue and saue Christe in vs, and to kepe his fayth and his graces in vs, we shoulde lay al our bodies in daunger, rather losing body, goodes and all, then him. And therefore s. Paule saith. **Rom. viii. who can separate or diuide vs from the charitie and loue of Christ? I am sure that nother death nor life, neither any other creature can parte vs from the loue of god that we haue in christ Iesu:*** thus sayth† s. Paule in the name of euery good christen man & woman. Second, we may learne prudence [3R2ᵛ] by the serpent, whiche when he casteth his olde slowe or skin, he crepeth into some straite place, as betwixt stones or blockes, or rockes, & there stripeth him selfe cleane out of his olde scurfe into a new skinne. And so must we do, we must get vs into the strait waye of penaunce,* and by that stripe cleane away from vs our olde faultes and sinnes. **Eph. iiii. Deponite vos secundum pristinam conuersationem veterem hominem qui corrumpitur secundum desideria erroris.** Put downe awaye from you your olde man, your olde maner of liuinge, in lustes of errours, all oute of the righte way of iustice and of good liuinge.* Thirde, the serpent when he perceiueth a charmer aboute to charme him oute of his hole or denne, he laieth one of his eares faste to the grounde, and stoppeth the other eare with his taile. By whiche propertie we be taught against the suggestions of oure goostly enemies, to stoppe one eare with the earth, that is, the remembraunce of our own vilenes and infirmitie, and the other eare with oure taile, that is to saye, with the remembraunce of our death and ende, to whiche we drawe dayly.* **Eccle. vii. In omnibus operibus tuis memorare nouissima & in[ ]eternum non peccabis.** In all thy workes remember thy last ende, and thou shalte neuer sinne, but shall euer haue a good and ready soule to god.* And that we all may so haue, he graunt vs, that by his painful passion redemed vs. Amen.

† sayth] soyth

The ,xvi. treatise or
sermon.

ET vigilate in orationibus. I haue sufficiently (as I trust) exhorted you in my
former sermon, to vse prudence and circumspection in all your affaires and
doinges,* now I must aduertise you to beware of such thinges as may be im-
pedimentes to hinder you, and lette you from well doinge. The Apostle S. Peter
wylleth you to take good hede where aboute we go, sayinge: **Et vigilate in orationibus,** And watche in prayers. Slepe not in youre prayers, for the deuill slepeth
not, but watcheth craftely to pull awaye your hearte from you, and from the thinge
that you intende to praye for. Watche and take hede that your minde thinke on
nothing els but vpon that you desire in your praier, awaye with all carnall
thoughtes out of your mindes, lette the intente of youre minde be sincere and
cleare towarde God, and praye vnto him, not so muche with the sound of your
mouth, as with the swetenes of youre minde, and so both youre prayer of mouth
and of hearte together, shal be mooste acceptable to him. And thoughe praier be
necessary at all times and in all places, yet at this time, when holye Churche
readeth this processe that we haue nowe in hande for the Epistle of the Masse,* we
shoulde be moost vigilaunte and diligent in prayer, that we mighte be the more
apte and mete to receiue into the hostrie of our soules the holie Goostes graces, at
this holye time of [3R3ᵛ] Whitsontide now comming.* And so did the blessed
virgin Marye mother of Christe, with other holy women, and the Apostles, after
that they had sene Christes ascention, they retourned to Ierusalem, and got them
into an hie halle, or a lofte, where they were **perseuerantes vnanimiter in oratione,** continuinge in prayer, withoute anye notable interruption.* **Vnanimiter,** al
of one mind, knitte together all by the bondes of Charitie, for so must they be that
do wait and loke for the holy Gost. For **Spiritus . . . discipline effugiet fictum.
Sap. i.** The holy spirite that geueth learninge, wyll flye from one that is fayned,
that fayneth him self, or is a dissembler.* Therfore he that will haue that holy
spirit, let him continue in praier, & in vnitie, concorde, and charitie in hearte and
minde. And euen so S. Peter exhorteth vs here, saying: **Ante omnia autem
mutuam in vobismetipsis charitatem continuam habentes.** Afore all thinge yo[u]
muste haue within your selues continual charitie, euery one to another, **Quia
charitas operit multitudinem peccatorum,** for Charitie couereth the multitude of
synnes.* That you may obtaine and gette of almyghtye God, that you praye for,
aboue all thynges be sure of Charitie, by whiche you may do good to others as well
as to youre selues. Accordinge to this Saynt Iames sayth. **Iaco. v. He that causeth
a synner to retourne from his errour, shall saue his soule from death, and shall
couer the multitude of his synnes.*** And the prophete sayeth, **Psalm. xxxi. Beati
quorum remisse sunt iniquitates, & quorum tecta sunt peccata.** Blessed be they
whose [3R4] iniquities be forgiuen, and whose sinnes be couered.* But for this you
must vnderstande, that oure sinnes may be couered two maner of wayes: one waye
is by the sinners owne dissimulation, hydynge, and clokinge. But after this maner
to hyde oure sinnes maketh vs not blessed, but rather accursed, in as muche as they
styll remayne, and liueth in the sinne, or to the increase of his damnation.
Another maner of couerynge oure synnes, is when they be so couered, that God
seeth them not, and that is to saye: that he imputeth them not to vs, nor leyeth
them to our charge, for after the maner of speakinge of scripture, then he seith
sinnes and loketh vpon them, when he punisheth them, and then he seith them

not when he doth not punisshe them. And therefore the prophet sayde in another placce: **Auerte faciem tuam a peccatis meis:** Tourne awaye thy face from my sinnes.* As who shoulde saye, with the eyes of thy mercy loke vppon me, and se me, but see not my synnes, but as it were one that had forgotte theim, punysshe theim not, knowe theim not, but forgeue them, and impute theim not to me, nor laye them to my charge. And in this case be they, that wythoute gyle or dissimulation vttereth theyr synnes: Of suche it is sayde. **Nec est in spiritu eius dolus:** In suche a mans spyryte there is no gyle,* where contrarywyse, they that vseth gyle and clookynge theyr faultes, howe muche the moore they laboure in defence of theyr synnes, boastynge [3R4ᵛ] their owne merites, and their owne well doinges, and seith not their owne iniquities, nother speaketh of theim, so muche their goostlie fortitude and might decaieth, and waxeth weaker. And therefore againste proude men that trusted muche in their owne good dedes, and would not be a knowen of their faultes, Christe putteth a parable of the proude Pharisei and the humble publicane: The Pharisei praised him selfe of his vertues, but he spoke nothinge of his faultes: The publicane cloked not, dissembled not, vsed no gyle, but toke vpon him as he was, and therefore the one was iustified and iudged for a good man, where the other was condempned.* Christe defended the Publicane and gaue sentence, acquitinge him as not giltie, and couered his sinnes, not any more to impute them to him, or to laye them to his charge, where the proud Pharisei euen in the temple, in the Surgions shoppe, and vnder the Surgions hande, shewed forth his whole limmes, where he was not sicke nor soore, declaringe his vertues, but his sinnes he couered and hidde from the Surgion, and therfore he was not cured, he might haue sayd, **Quoniam tacui inueterauerunt ossa mea dum clamarem tota die.** Because I helde me styll my bones wexed olde and decayde to noughte, while I cryed al day longe.* The bones of the soule be vertues, for as the bones of the bodye maketh the bodye stronge, so doth vertues make the soule stronge. These bones, these vertues decayeth and draweth to nought, whyle we be styl and cry al day [3S1] longe. A straunge maner of speakinge of the scripture. It is euen of the same maner that I spake of nowe: The Pharisei was styll and helde his tounge, and yet cried to loude: he was styll, clokinge and hidinge his faultes with scilence, and yet he was loude ynough, bosting and praysing him selfe of his vertues and of his well doinges, of whiche he shoulde haue spoken not a worde, and therfore his vertues auailed him not to saluation of his soule, but decaied to nought as his soule did. So (good neighbours) there be inough and to many of vs, that crye loude inough, boastynge and praysinge our well doinges, yf anye be, but to speake and confesse our faultes we be styll ynough, and holde our tonges. As manye men of their glottenye, of drinkinge men vnder the borde,* of ryottinge and surfettinge, and of wastfull bankettinge, and of theyr pryde & malicious taunting of pore men, & of sclaunderinge and backebiting, they take no remorse or grudge of conscience, but rather reioyce in mind, & make much boasting outwarde of the same. They vse not to reuele & vtter such faultes to theyr goostly father, and to almighty God, with contrition and sorow for them, but rather glorieth in their ill doinges, to the increase of theyr owne dampnation: If they woulde with a lowly heart vncouer them to the surgion, he woulde make them whole, where as if they be hidde, they wil rankel and fester to euerlastinge corruption. Pryde maketh a man to hide his faultes to his dampnation: Charitie putteth awaye Pryde. **Charitas [3S1ᵛ] enim non inflatur,** Charitie is not proude,* and therfore it disposeth a man to humilitie, making him contente to shewe him selfe as he is, to the surgion, and so he shall be cured and well at ease before God. **Beatus enim cui non imputauit dominus peccatum.** He is blessed to whose charge oure lorde God hath not layde any sinnes, but geuing him charitie, couereth his synnes.* S. Peter consideringe this, exhorteth vs aboue all thinges to haue charitie, for it couereth the multitude of sinnes. And therfore it may be called a holesome and healthfull garment for the soule, for diuers necessarye properties of a garment.* Fyrste like as a garment conserueth and kepeth a mannes lyuelye and naturall heate within him, so doeth charitie conserue the lyfe of the soule, so that he that lacketh it, lacketh lyfe and is dead. **i. Ioh. iii. Qui non diligit manet in morte,** He that hath not loue or charitie, abideth in death, he is all colde and stiffed.* This liuely heate of the soule is conserued and saued by kepinge the commaundementes of god, which be al comprehended in loue or charitie, according to Christes aunswer to a certayne learned man that apposed him, saying: **maister, what shall I do to haue euerlastinge life?** Christ apposed him again in his owne learning. **what is written in the lawe? howe reade you? He aunswered: Thou shalte loue God aboue all thinges, with thy whole hearte, with thy whole soule, with all thy strength, and with all thy mynde: And thy neighbour as thy selfe. Thou sayest wel** (sayeth Christ) *Hoc facet & uiues,* do that and thou shalt liue.* And all this is done by kepinge the ten commaunde[3S2]mentes of God. In the thre fyrste commaundementes we be taught howe to order our loue towarde God, and in the seuen last, howe we shall extende our loue to our neyghbours. And yf we perfourme and fulfyll these for loue, we shall please God, and deserue heauen by them, where as yf we kepe them onely for feare, we would do the contrary if we might, and be no thanke worthye. Albeit better it is to fulfyll the commaundementes for feare, then not to fulfyll theim at al: for by oft doyng wel for feare, we may gendre a loue to wel doing, & so at last we shal do wel for loue, and shall haue a swetenes in wel doinge. Second, charitie is compared to a garment, for like as a garment defendeth a man in external heat & in colde, in wet & drie wether, so doeth charitie award & defend the soule in prosperitie, & in aduersitie.* For as s. Paule saith, **Diligentibus deum omnia cooperantur in bonum.** To them that loueth God, al thinges worketh to good,* & for both prosperitie & aduersitie God is to be lauded & thanked, when al thinges that man liueth by commeth plentifully, when the fruites of ye earth proueth largely, when God maketh the sonne to shine vpon good & bad men indifferently, and sendeth rayne to the iust men as to the vniust, these and such other pertaine to temporal lyfe & prosperitie, & he that wil not loue god & laud him for them is very vnkind, By this almighty god sheweth what he reserueth and kepeth in stoore for them that be good, whyle he geuethe all suche pleasures to theym that be noughte. Then yf thou haue plentye, thanke GOD that gaue it thee, or yf [3S2^v] thou lacke, yet thanke God, for he is not taken from the, that geueth all thinges, thoughe his gyftes be withdrawen for a time. Remember what holy Iob sayde, when he was spoyled of al that he had. **Dominus dedit, dominus abstulit, sicut domino placuit ita factum est sit nomen domini benedictum.*** This is verye true charitie towarde God, that so laudeth God in prosperitie, that yet it kepeth a man vp, that he be not broken nor ouerthrowen in aduersitie. And here is hyghlye to be considered the true sentence and mynde of holy Iob, concerninge prouidence, cure, or prouision about thinges longinge to man, whiche many of the paignim philosophers imputed to desteny, or to fortune, or to influence of the sterres, or suche other causes. For Iob sayth: **Dominus dedit,** GOD hath geuen it to me. Where he confesseth that worldly prosperitie commeth to man, not by chaunce nor by desteny, nor by influence of the sterres, nor onely by mans studye and laboure, but of Gods dispensation

& disposinge. And in that he sayth, **Dominus abstulit,** God hath taken it away, he confesseth that aduersitie commeth to man also by Goddes prouidence: meaninge by this, that man hath no iust cause to complaine or grudge against God, if he be spoyled of al temporal goodes & gifts. For the things that God geueth, **gratis,** without any deseruing of vs, he may geue them for a time, or els to a mans last ende, as it pleaseth him. Therefore when he taketh them away afore our end, or when we haue most nede of them, there is no cause why we shuld [3S3] complaine. And when holy Iob sayth: **Sicut domino placuit, ita factum est, sit nomen domini benedictum,** He declareth, that considering that if a man be spoyled of all that euer he hath, yet if he loue God, he shuld conforme his wil to Gods wyll, & so not to be supped vp or ouercome with sorow, but rather to be glad, & to geue thankes to God y^t it hath pleased him to fulfil his will vpon hym, as the apostles did, **Ibant gaudentes a conspectu consilii quoniam digni habiti sunt pro nomine Iesu contumeliam pati,** they went from afore the counsell, nother wepynge nor grudginge, but with a mery heart, that it had pleased GOD to repute them worthy to suffre despites for Christes name, and for his sake.* As if a sicke man take a bytter potion, he should be glad so to do, in hope of helth that he trusteth to receiue by the medicine. And so, if God visit his louer with aduersitie, doubtles it is for some better purpose, that he knoweth better than we. Therfore, although the flesh woulde grudge, yet reason shoulde be contente & glad of it. Thyrd, like as a garment couereth a mans secretes and vncleanly partes that a man would not haue sene, so doth charitie couer the vnclenlines of the soule, so that withoute it the soule goeth naked, Therfore it is sayd. **Apo. xvi. Beatus qui vigilat & custodit vestimenta sua ne nudus ambulet, & videant turpitudinem eius.** Blessed is he that walketh as one regarding & caring for his owne saluation & sauegard, and that kepeth his raiment of vertues, lest he walke naked at ye day of the generall iudgement, that all the aungelles [3S3^v] & holy company comming w^t Christ may se his filthines.* Fourth, Charitie is the wedding liuery or garment, without which no man can be alowed to sit at Christes feast, but if he presume to come without it, he shall be taken vp, and bound hand and fote, and cast into the darke dongeon of hel. It is written. **Hester .iiii.** that it was not lawfull for any man to entre into the court of kinge Assuerus, beynge clothed in sackclothe, or such vile rayment.* **Assuerus** by interpretation is as muche to say as **beatitude,*** so it maye not be, that anye man withoute charitie, beynge as one wrapt in a sacke, or vyle ragges of vices, to come into the courte of euerlasting beatitude in heauen. This is the heauenlye vertue, by whiche mortall men yet here liuinge, be made lyke the inhabitauntes of heauen. Of this vertue it is written. **Can, viii. Valida sicut mors dilectio,** Loue or Charitie, is mightie and stronge as death.* The strength of Charitie coulde not haue ben more nobly expressed. For who can resist or withstande death? Fyre may be withstanden, weapons may be withstanden, kynges and men of greate power may be withstanden: but when death commeth it selfe alone, who resisteth or withstandeth it? There is nothing stronger then it, and therefore charitie is compared vnto the strength of it. And because that Charitie kylleth in vs that we were afore, kylleth synne, with whiche we were infect afore, and maketh vs as we were not afore, therfore it causeth in vs a certayne death, suche as he was deade with that sayde, **Mihi mundus cruci[3S4]fixus est & ego mundo.** The worlde is crucified, kylled, and deade to me, and I to the worlde.* This is the vertue that neuer falleth nor faileth, but in the highe and heauenly citie aboue, is consummate and made parfit, and set in highest perfection, that here is feable and weake, and abideth much trouble, and hath many interruptions.

It foloweth in the text of this epistle. **Hospitales inuicem sine murmuratione,** You shall kepe hospitalitie, and open householdes, or your houses open one to another without yl wil or grudginge.* Saynt Paule commendinge the constancie and stedfast fayth of the holye patriarchs, Abraham, Isaac, and Iacob, and others, amonge other vertues, specially commendeth them, **Quod confessi sunt se hospites & aduenas super terram, declarantes se patriam inquirere. Heb. xi.** because they confessed and toke them selues as gestes & straungers, or waifaring men, in ye land whiche was promised them as a peculier inheritaunce, yet they setled not theyr mindes on it, but euer had an eye to thinheritaunce that should neuer fayle, which is heauen aboue, signified by the sayd lande that they were in then:* by this geuing vs example, that while we be here, how greate so euer welth and ryches, patrimonie, landes, or reuenues God geueth vs, yet we shoulde not setle our mindes to fast on them, as in them to prefixe our ende & our felicitie, as men thinking none other heauen, but that we should euer by example of such holy fathers, set forwarde our selues to wyn the sure habitation of heauen y^t neuer decaieth nor faileth, taking our selues while we be here as straungers, [3S4^v] pilgremes, and wayfaringe men in a straunge countrey. For in verye dede, we were caste into this payneful and troubelous worlde, by occasion of the sinne of our old Adam, out of the quiet and pleasaunt seat of paradise, and sent away into exile & banishment. And so here we haue not oure owne countrey, **Dum enim domi sumus in corpore peregrinamur a domino. ii. Cor. v.** Whyle we be at home in our mortall bodies, we be pilgremes and straungers from our Lord God.* Therfore let vs not loke for that thinge in the way in our banishment, that is kepte for vs at home in our countrey. For rest and ease of oure soules, in grace and vertue, we should trauaile and labour lyke straungers and wayfaringe men,* euery one doing good one to another while we haue tyme here, and specially by liberall comonication and distribution of that we haue, one to another, for of suche helpe and releife pylgrems haue mooste nede. And though among moral vertues Iustice is moste excellent: yet as the Philosopher sayth, **liberales maxime amantur,** they that be liberall be moste beloued,* because they helpe many others, & many others fareth the better for them. One kinde of liberalitie is hospitalitie, that S. Peter speaketh of here. It is the bounteousnes & largenes in geuing meat & drinke & lodginge one to another, euery one releuing an others nede, accordinge to the power that God hath lent them, & this shall releue the nede of pore wayfaring men very greatly. There be .ii. maners of hospitalitie, one is bodely hospitalitie, ye other is spiritual hospitalitie, [3T1] the first is lauded in the Gospel, by the wordes y^t Christ shall say to them y^t shall be set on the right hand of the Iudge at ye daie of iudgement. **Venite benedicti patris mei. &c.** Come to me you the blessed of my father, & take the kyngdome that is prepared for you from the beginning of the world. For I was an hongred, and you gaue me meate, I was a thriste, and you gaue me drinke, I was a straunger, and lacked harborow or lodgyng, and you toke me in and gaue me lodgynge.* And saint Paule counseleth the Hebrewes that he wrot to among other thinges, saiyng. **Hospitalitatem nolite obliuisci, per hanc enim placueru[n]t quidam angelis hospicio receptis. Heb. xiii.** Forget not hospitalitie, for by hospitalitie some men haue pleased angels that they receiued into their houses, whiche they thought first to haue bene men, but afterwarde they perceiued that they were angels appearyng to theim in the likenes of men.* Such were they that appered to Abraham in Mambre when they tolde him that Sara his wife shoulde beare him a childe to be his heyre.* And such were they that appered to Loth in Sodom, and bade him auoide out of that towne, for it should forthwith be destroyed. Vppon

which saith **Origene** Loth dwelled in Sodome,* we reade not manye good dedes of
his, hospitalitie onely is praysed in him, he scapeth the flames, he scapeth the fires
for that onely that he opened his house to gestes and straungers. The angels entred
the house where hospitalitie was kept. The fire entred into the houses that were
shut vp againste gestes. [3T1ᵛ] But all men be not like disposed to hospitalitie, for
some men **Hospitem velut hostem vitant & excludunt.** They shun & shut out a
gest as thei wold an enemy.* Let them beware of the fire with the Sodomites.
Some other be liberall and kepeth good houses, but it is for some corrupt intente,
either because thei can not be mery without companions and good companye, and
so they do it to please them selues, which commeth of carnalitie. Some other doth
it of pride and vaine glorye, or for some temporall profite or aduauntage. As **Tully**
the noble oratour commendeth hospitality, but his motiue and consideration is
nought, it is to worldly. He saith. **ii. offi. Est enim valde decorum patere domos
hominum illustrium, illustribus hospitibus.** It is verye semely for noble mens
houses to be open for noble gestes, but his cause why he saith so, is carnal. For it
foloweth there **Reipublice est ornamento homines externos hoc liberalitatis
genere in vrbe nostra non egere. &c.** It adourneth and doth honour to our
common wealthe, that menne of straunge countreys lack not thys kinde of libertye
in oure Citye (speakynge of Rome where he dwelled.) **Est etiam vehementer vtile.
&c.** It is also wonderous profitable for them that woulde be able to do muche or
manye great thinges amonge straungers, to be in good credence of riches, of loue,
and fauoure amonge people of straunge countreys, by the meanes of their geastes,
whiche they haue receyued in hospitalitie.* So that **Tullies** minde was to get
commoditie by his hospitalite, either to him self, or to his [3T2] citie and countrey
men. This is a worldly policy comming of the worldly prudence that I spoke of
afore. And as S. Ambrose saith. **super Luk. xiiii. Hospitalem remuneraturis esse,
est affectus auaricie.** To be a great housholder or viander lokinge for acquitall, or
for to be recompenced with as good or better againe, is the affect or desire of
auarice, rather then of liberalitie.* And therfore our Sauiour Christe declaryng to
vs the verye true liberall hospitalitie of the Gospel, in the said .xiiii. chapter of
Luke. **Cum facis prandium aut coenam, noli vocare amicos tuos, neque fratres,
neque cognatos, neque vicinos diuites, nequando & ipsi te vicissim inuitent ac.
&c.** When thou makest a dyner or a supper, do not call thy frendes, nor thy
brethren, nor thy kinsfolkes, nor thy riche neighbours, lest an other tyme they
bidde thee againe, as thou hast done them, and so thy benefite be redobbed or quit
thee home. But rather when thou makest a feast, call pore people, weake folkes,
halte, and lame, and blinde, and thou shalbe blessed, because they can not quitte
thee with as good agayne. For thou shalt be quit at the resurrection of good men.*
Marke that he saieth. **Lest they bidde thee againe, and so thy benefite be
redobbed or quitte.** As who shoulde saye: if thou wylte doe this meritoriouslye to
be rewarded of GOD therfore, thou muste be well ware that thou doe it, so that
thou looke for no temporall rewarde to come thereof, but as willynge fullye to
eschue & auoyde all expectation of rewarde, or recompen[3T2ᵛ]sation in this
world, that thou maiest be rewarded in the resurrection of the iuste. For though of
hospitalitie come great rewarde temporall, and increase, yet that is not the thing
that we muste loke for, nor intende to haue, least when we haue that we lose all
the other. Of the reward for hospitalitie, there be in scriptures many gaye examples
whiche seming temporall, yet signifieth the spirituall impinguation and feading,
and profite of the soule. I read .iii. **Reg. xvii** of the blessed prophet **Helye,** that on
a time as he came towarde a towne called **Sarepta sidoniorum,** within the territory

of **Sidon,** he found a woman gatheringe a few stickes to make her a fire, he desiered her to geue him a little water to drinke, and a morsel of bread. She answered and said she had no bread. I haue no more (said she) but a handfull of meale in a steen, and a little oyle in a gearre, & I gather nowe (said she) **duo ligna,** two stickes, as a man woulde saie, a fewe stickes to bake it, and make breade for my sonne and me, and when we haue eaten that, we haue no more, we will dye. No (saide **Helye**) be not afraied. Thus saith the God of Israel. Thy steen of meal shal not faile or lack nor thy gearre of oyle shall be any thing lesse, tyll the time when GOD† shall sende rayne vpon the earth.* For in dede this fortuned in the time of the long famine that was in yᵗ countrey for lack of rayne, by the space of three yeres & an halfe (accordynge to the prayer and peticion of the same Prophete **Helye**[)], for the correction and punishement of Achab the kyng, and Iesabel his quene, [3T3] and of their false prophetes, and of their people.* And as the Prophete promised, so it proued in dede. By this example, you se howe the pore hospitalitie of the saide good woman exhibited and bestowed on Helye, was recompensed with plentie sufficiente, where all the countrey els was in greate penurye and neade. And here you shall note that this meale in the Steen that was so longe reserued and continued by the word of the Lorde God of Israell, was a figure, and signified the most reuerende and blessed Sacrament of the Aultare. The wydowe that was so longe susteined with this meal, signified Christes holy church,* the whole congregation of faythful men and womenne, whiche [signified] by that that Christe her spouse and husband was slayne and buried, and then rose again, and departed from her into heauen, and hath left her viduate and without hys visible presence, althoughe he hath left her hys blessed bodye and bloude in this blessed Sacrament, whiche this wydowe all faiethfull folkes muste bake and digest with the sayde two trees, signifiynge the remembraunce of his paynefull passion that he suffered on the crosse* (for a crosse is made commonlye of two trees,) accordynge to Sainte Paules saiynge. As oft as you shall eate this breade, or drinke of this cuppe, you shal shewe the death of our Lorde vntill he come,* and shall shewe him selfe in his glorious maiestie at the generall iudgemente, which tyme thoughe it shall be a terible and an horrible time to sinners, and to all damnable persons, yet it shal be a time [3T3ᵛ] of grace, of solace, and comfort to al his true & louyng seruauntes. This was signified by yᵗ raine that came from Heauen vppon the earth, when Helye sayde that the Steen of meale should not fayle, nor the gearre of oyle shoulde not be diminished, tyll GOD sende rayne from heauen for the comforte of the countrey, as his grace shall come for the comfort of vs all, at that daye.* This meale and Oyle were continued so longe to sustaine .iii. persons, not by any natural power, but by the supernatural power of God. And so is his bodye made of breade and wine by the worde of Christe, and by his Godlye and infinite power, aboue nature. Therefore let not naturall reason cumber it selfe in the examination or triyng how it maye be, but stedfastlye beleue that thus it is, for so God saith. And although it be called bread and the cuppe of wine, as well in the Gospell, as of S. Paule, yet there is nother bread nor wine after the consecration, but very fleshe and bloud.* Tell me how a handful of meale and a little oyle coulde continue so longe, and to feade so manye persons, and I shall tell thee, howe of a little breade and wyne shall be made a perfect body of a manne and hys bloude. Thou canst saye no more to the firste question but **Hec dicit dominus Deus Israell.** As Helye sayde. **Thus sayth the GOD of Israell.*** and thus it was in dede.

† GOD] GGD

And euen so I saye vnto thee. Thus sayeth the God of Israell our Sauiour Christe. Thys is my bodye, This is my bloude, And therefore [3T4] so it is, and muste neades be so in dede. And so shall continue **Donec veniat,** vntyll he come to the generall Iudgemente in his visible maiesty, amonge vs.* And then shall cease this blessed Sacramente, in whyche for the tyme wee see Christes body enigmatically, and in a straunge similitude by our fayeth, whiche maner of seinge hym shall then cease, when we shall see him face to face in hys owne likenesse,* when he shall cast downe and treade vnder his feete all theim that nowe so despitefullye rayle, and geste, and mock his blessed bodye that he hath left vs in this blessed Sa-cramente, for our comfort. And nowe to returne to the storie. In processe of tyme, it chaunced that the sayde good wydowes childe dyed, to her great discomforte. And she desired the Prophete Helye to praye for hym, that he mighte reuyue and lyue agayne. And so the Prophete did, the chylde reuiued, & the Prophete gaue him to his mother aliue agayne.* Loe, here was another notable recompence for hospitalitie exhibited to this good man. Firste the sauegarde of all their liues: seconde the raysynge of the chylde from death to life agayne. Likewise it is writ **iiii. Reg. iiii.*** of the blessed Prophete Helise, that he vsed to resorte to an honest house in the towne of **Suna,** where a worshipfull woman maistresse of the house perceyuynge hym to be a holy man exhorted her husbande to make for the sayde Helise a Parloure wyth a bedde in it, and a table, and a cheare, and a place to set hys candle on. And so thei did. The said prophet resorted [3T4ᵛ] thither diuers tymes and lodged in the same parlour, and hadde good cheare on a time when he was minded to pay for his cheare. he bade **Giezi** his seruaunt to aske of her whether she had anye matters to do with the kinge, or with any of the counsaile, or with anye great man in the courte, or with the Capitayne in the Warres, that hee might be suter for her, and speake for her. She aunswered, that shee dwelled amonge her owne frendes and kinred: and neaded none of his helpe in any such matters. Then saide **Giezi** to his master, you must vnderstande that she hath neuer a childe, and her husbande is an aged man, as who should saie, it shuld be most comfort for them both if they might haue issue by your praier, wherupon the Prophete promised her that she shoulde conceiue a sonne by a certayne daie that he appoynted, and so she did to the great comfort of the husbande and of the wife. This was a notable reward for their hospitalitie bestowed vpon their gest that holye Prophet. In processe of tyme the same childe fell sicke on a certayne disease that begonne with a feruent ache in his heade, and died vpon the same. Then this deuout mother layed the corps of her dead childe vpon the bed where Helye the Prophete was wonte to lye in the parlour whiche (I tolde you) was made and ordeined for the Prophete: and she shut vp the parlour dore vppon him, and gote an asse sadled, and toke a seruant with hir, and ridde with all spede to seke Helye. She found him in his house, in the hyll called **Carmelus,** and declared to him the [3V1] chaunce of the deathe of her chylde, and prayed for healpe. He bade hys seruaunte **Giezi** take his staffe and runne a pace, and to laye the staffe vppon the chyldes face: and so he did, but **Non erat vox neque sensus,** He nother spoke nor feled, it woulde not healpe.* The good woman feared so muche and woulde not depart from the Prophete, but she would haue hym to come him self. He was contente so to do. And when he came to the Corps, he layde him selfe vpon the corpes, his mouthe vppon the childes mouthe, his eyes vppon the childes eyes, his handes vppon the childes handes, and so the chyldes flesshe began to waxe warme, and he yaned seuen tymes, and opened his eyes, reuiued, and liued. And Helye gaue hym to his mother agayne alyue, and so departed. Here these honest Vianders had double acquitall for their good cheare and hospitalitie that they bestowed vppon this good man. It is also writ. **Ioh. xi.** that where Martha and Marye her sister hadde greate disconfort by the death of Lazarus their brother, their good geste our Sauiour Christe, whiche had manye times gentle interteinment with them, and wyth their brother Lazar then late departed, recompensed them with the marueilous raysynge the said Lazarus to life againe after he had bene .iiii. dayes deade and buried.* This myracle was to their great consolation and no small admiration to all the countrey. And it is writte in the Storye of my blessed patrone sainte Cu<r>thberte, in whose honoure my paryshe churche of Welles is dedi[3V1ᵛ]cate where I am vicare, that when he was cosoner or officer in the monastery (where he was) to whom it belonged to receiue & entertayne straungers, he thinkynge that he hadde receiued to the Hostrye a poore wayfarynge man, and goynge about to prouide meate for him, perceiued afterwarde that he hadde receiued into his offyce an aungell, in the likenes of a man.* And so I doubt not but many good christen menne haue bene rewarded for their hospitalitie: for Goddes power is not coarted, neither his gratitude any thinge lesse towarde manne nowe in the time of grace, then it was afore Christes incarnacion. Manye such example[s] we haue, declaryng to vs the excellencye of hospitalitie, and that true it is that the wiseman saith. **Pro. xi. Alii diuidunt propria & ditiores fiunt, alii rapiunt non sua & semper in egestate sunt.** Some men distributeth and geueth abrode their owne goods, and be richer & richer. Others scratcheth and taketh by violence other mennes goods, and be euer in nede and at beggers estate* And saint Paul saith. **ii. Co. ix.**† **Qui seminat in benedictionibus, in benedictionibus & metet.** He that soweth and distributeth abrode liberally, & with a gentle hart, shal be rewarded in blessings largely.* For it can not be false yᵗ truth saith. **Date & dabitur vobis.** Geue, & you shal haue geuen you.* But peraduenture a man wold saie. I haue nothing to kepe hospitalite withal. I am but a pore man. I haue nothing to spare. I haue nothing to geue. How shall I exercise this vertue of hospitalitie? Howe should I be a good Viander, or an hous[3V2]holder? To this I saye, that euangelicall hospitalitie, the hospitalitie of the gospel that is praised and commaunded by Christe, requireth not multitude of dishes, nor delicat chaunge of meats nor diuersitie of exquisite wynes or other drinkes. We reade of no such feasts that Christ came to. And the blessed Patriarche Abraham (whose hospitalitie is so greatly praysed) when he receiued the aungels into his house, he bade his wife Sara make haste to bake some breade vnder the asshen, or vnder a pan while he went to the hurde, and fet a yong calfe, and he sod them some veale, and serued them with sod veale, butter & milke. Here was their dinner. **Gen. xviii.*** And Christes feastes that he was bid to, were but **Manducare panem,** but to eate some meate sufficiently to susteine nature and no more.* And **Chrisostome** answereth to the saide scruple & doubt in a certaine Homelie that he made in the laude and prayse of **Priscilla** and **Aquila** for their gentle enterteining of S. Paule, of whiche it is writ. **Act, xviii.** and **Rom. xvi.*** Thei were but pore, but their hart was good & liberall. They were bold in Gods quarel, they feared no peryll, & they had greate thought and studye to do good to others. And of that it came that they saued manye a one, and deserued well of manye. For the pompose riche men can not profite the churche and congregation of Christes seruauntes, as the poore men may, that haue a good harte and a good wyll. The ryche man hath many things that greueth him, & much busines in his minde yᵗ letteth him to do ani good [3V2ᵛ] He is afrayed of

† ix] xi

his house, for his seruaunts, for his Landes, for hys riches, lest anye man hurte them or take anye thinge awaye from him. **Et qui multorum est dominus, idem multorum seruus esse cogitur.** He that is maister of much, is compelled to be seruaunt to many.* But the pore man that lacketh all these things, is lyke a Lyon, fire commeth from him, he riseth and auaunceth him selfe wyth a gentle and bolde courage againste all men that be nought. He dothe all thynges wyth facilitye and easelye that maye do good to the churche, whether neade be that men shoulde be rebuked, reproued, or blamed for euill doynge or saiynge, or whether peryls, hatred, or emnity should be susteyned and borne for Christes sake. For he that once hath dispised this present lyfe, dothe easelye ouercome all other thinges that might put him to feare. But we (God healpe vs) for the loue that we haue to this transitory life, and ease, and for feare of losynge that little that we haue, be afrayed of our shadowe, and dare not speake nor loke in Gods cause, or in a cause of Iustice, but will be more readye to speake agaynste hym that we knowe to be in the ryght, if we maye knowe that we shall please the great manne, or to haue our pleasure vppon hym, or to haue anye aduauntage by our doynge. The second maner of hospitalite may be called spiritual hospitalitie, which like as there be two maner of gestes, so proporcionably there be two maner of hospitalitie. The deuil & deadly sinne be shrewde gests for the soule of man. Almighty god and his [3V3] grace be good gestes and profitable for the soul. The deuil when he entreth into the soule of man by suggestion and temptation on the deuils behalfe, and by consent of the will of man, taketh awaye all goodnesse, spoyleth the Soule from all vertues, burneth vp all that he findeth wyth the fire of luste, and of vnlawfull concupiscence, and ouerturneth all the walles and defences of discipline, and of good instruction, that was wonte to awarde and defende the Soule frome his enemyes. Like as in example and figure it is written. **i. Macha. i.** That **Antiochus illustris** kynge of Syria sende into Hierusalem the captayne of his Tributes wyth a greate Armye of fightynge men, whiche firste spoke faire to them intreatyng of peace **In dolo,** al in gile. As to make them thinke he came for their commoditie, & to do theim good, but as sone as he was receiued, he robbed and spoyled the citye, he set it on fire, destroyed the walles, and brought all to nought.* Euen so dothe the deuill by the soule of manne, when he is once entred and harboured there. **Factum hoc ad insidias sanctificationi, & in diabolum malum in Israell.** All that turneth to the harme & hurt of al the temple of God, of all holines of the soule of man, & is a great deuil in Israel, an horrible rauener, & enemy to godly contemplation, & to al deuotion.* And you must vnderstand that in some men sin is a gest or a straunger, & in some other he is one of housholde, yea rather a king or a ruler, as in example. Incontinency or lechery was in king Dauid but as a straunger, as apereth by the [3V3ᵛ] parable or riddles that Nathan the prophet proposed to king Dauid, of a rich man that had many shepe of his owne, and yet he stole from a pore man one pore shepe that he had and no more, for meat to fede his gest or straunger that came vpon him. **Parcens ille sumere de ouibus & bubus suis, vt exhiberet conuiuium illi perigrino qui venerat ad se, tulit ouem viri pauperis & parauit cibum illi qui venerat ad se. ii. re. xii.*** All this was said for yᵉ reproch of king Dauid which hauing many wiues of his owne, yet to satisfy and feade his lecherous lust, [(]which is here called his gest or straunger) he toke the shepe of his pore neighbour, the wife of **Vry,** & abused her to satisfie his vnlawfull lust.* This adulterie and vnlawefull luste in hym was not domesticall or of housholde, but came sodainelye vpon him as a straunger, and sone after went away, as appeareth by his penaunce that he toke by and by, saiyng: **peccaui domino,** I haue sinned against god. He spared not to confesse his fault, wherupon god was mercifull to him, as the prophet then told him saiyng. **Dominus transtulit peccatum.** God hath taken away thi sinne, thou shalt not dye for it.* So blessed is he which after his offence whether it be by the flesh, or by the worlde hath grace to take repentance, and to do penance.* For in such a person sinne is not of houshold, but only as a gest or a strau[n]ger. Example we haue how sin is somtime of houshold, continuing & as a lorde or king, by Salomon of whom it is written **.iii. reg. xi. when he was an old man, his hart was made croked and naughtye by women, so that he worshipt false [3V4] Gods, and his hart was not straight and perfit wyth our Lord God, as the harte of his father Dauid was.*** His vnlawefull luste maistred hym and kepte him vnder euen to hys ende, and as it is to bee feared, to the extreame peryll of hys soule. And so in others, when their customable synne continueth† to the ende, it is a shrewde signe that it raygneth, and is a Lorde or a kynge in them. All such commers and goers, whether they be as gests or as of housholde, muste be put out of the dores or els they wyll destroye their hoste that harboreth them. Almighty God when he is harbored and lodged by his grace in your soules, is a profitable gest that all the house shall fare the better for, all shall prospere in Godlinesse and goodnes where he inhabiteth. One way to winne him and to brynge him to our house is by the liberall receiuynge of hys pore seruauntes to some sustenaunce, whiche I called euangelicall hospitalitie or viandry, for whiche he that vseth it, shall be inuited to the euerlastyng refreshyng in heauen. **Hospes eram, & collegistis me,** sayeth Christe: I was a geste or a straunger, and you called me in,* and brought about me al things necessary, which Christe reputeth as done to him self, when it is bestowed vpon his pore and neady creatures. And this must be done **sine murmuratione,** without murmure or grud-gynge. For he that is liberal or free and large of giftes with murmuryng & grud-gyng,* hath not fre liberalitie, but lasheth out as for a cloke to couer & hide his nigardnesse<.> and not without some priuy grefe in his hart for [3V4ᵛ] wasting of his substance. The murmurer & grudger wᵗ his well doing hath the property of a hog, which slepyng in his stye, & waking and going abrode to his fedyng vseth to grunt and grone as it were one neuer pleased, but thinkynge all to muche that he dothe be it neuer so little.* As it is writ of the vnkind people of Israel. **N[u]m. xi. Ortum est murmur populi quasi dolentium pro† labore.** There rose a grudge among them as they hadde bene folkes being sory for their labours.* Euen so they that geueth and yet groneth withal, semeth to be sorie for their goods, as lest they shold haue nothing lefte, or that their goodes should fayle, and be wasted and decay, if they should helpe the neady. Your hospitalitie or viandre muste also be without grudging, not disdaining yᵗ an other man is more commended then you, ether for interteining & feding more then you do, or els for making them better chere then you do, for such grudgyng groweth & commeth of enuy. And enuy commeth of vayne glory: for no man enuieth another as better estemed & taken then he, but because he would be best estemed & taken him self, which is plaine vanitie, pride, & vain glory. To auoid this euery man shold helpe an other accord-ing to his talent & abilitie. And he shal be rewarded accordynge to his good wil in yᵗ he hath, & not in yᵗ he hath not, as .s. Paule saith. **ii Co. viii.† Si enim voluntas prompta est secundum id quod habet accepta est, non secundum id quod non habet.** If the wyll be prompte and readye, GOD is pleased wyth it, if it woorke accordynge to hys substaunce, for it is not required nother [3X1] loked for,

† continueth] comtinueth; pro] pre; viii] ix

that a man shuld do more then he may, or then his goodes wyll extend to, or beare.* And contrary to all suche grudging as Saint Peter reproucth here, the Apostle Saint Paule exhorteth vs. **Rom. xii.**† **Qui prebet in hillaritate.** He that giueth, should giue with a good chere, and wyth a mery hart.* And **.ij. Corin. ix. Hillarem datorem, diligit deus.** He saythe God loueth a cherable gyuer,* and to suche he wyll requite moste comfortable thankes when he shal recken to you your good and charitable dedes, and for them shall byd you **venite benedicti patris mei,** Come you blessed children and receiue the kyngdome that is prepared for you in the glory of heauen.* Amen.

† xii] viij

COnsequently foloweth in the text of Saynt Peters epistle, **Vnusquisque sicut
accepit gratiam a domino in alterutrum illam administrantes sicut boni dispen-
satores multiformis gratie dei.*** Experience teacheth that a great housholde
wythout good officers, is a troublous and an vnruly busines. For where is no quiet
order of the subiectes among them selues, and of theym all in theyr degree toward
theyr great mayster, soueraygne or ruler, euery man taketh his owne way, and so
foloweth strife, brawling, and variaunce, and at [3X1ᵛ] the last destruction. The
housholder must be fain to breake vp houshold if his folkes amende not. The great
housholder almighti god hath a great & a chargeable familie, that is, the vniuersal
multitude & company of al mankinde, which thoughe he could rule at his plesure
according to his own wil, yet it hath pleased him to put an order in this houshold,
som head officers, som mean, some lower in auctoritie, som subiectes & seruantes,
diuisiones ministrationem sunt, idem autem dominus. i. Cor xij. There be diuers
offices & but one Lorde, whiche would euery man to do his office in his degre that
he is called to, & euery one to helpe other like members or lyms of one body,
which be euer redy one to help & cherish an other, for the safegard of the whole
bodie. **i. Cor. xij:*** But in this there is a difference betwixt yᵉ great housholde of
God, & mans houshold, that in mans houshold som ther be onelye ministers,
hauing charge ouer no more but of them selfe in that houshold, but as in yᵉ great
houshold eueri man & woman hath charge & cure ouer another, though som
more, & som lesse cure, therfore saith **Ecclesiasticus .xvij. Mandauit illis vnicuique de<o> proximo suo.** Almightie God hath giuen such a commaundement
in his houshould that euerye one shoulde care for his neighbour, one for an other.*
And for thys cause Sainte Peter in these wordes of hys epistle rehearsed, exhorteth
vs to bestowe suche giftes as God hath giuen vs, not euery man vpon him selfe, or
for him selfe, but euery one for an others profite, like good stuards in a housholde.*
He wylleth vs to be as good stu[3X2]ardes in gods house. A stuard receiueth
treasure or money of his lordes cofers, and therewith byeth all necessaries for the
houshold & distributeth or bestoweth it to euery one of his lords seruantes as they
haue nede. And so we all receiue the treasure of our great maister almightye God,
he openeth his store house of grace and wealth, and replenisheth vs all with the
blessinges of his gracious gyftes more precious then golde or siluer. To som he
giueth knowledge and cunning in spirituall causes, to some in temporall matters,
to some learning in phisicke, to some in surgerye, to som in handy craftes, to some
in marchandise or in such other occupiyng.* To some he sendeth landes by
enheritaunce, to som by purchase, and generally looke how many waies God
giueth a man to liue by, with so muche of his treasure he chargeth him withal, and
wilbe sure for a compt therof. Ther is not the poorest begger that goeth from doore
to doore, but he hath part of this treasure, and is countable for it to almightye
God, and therefore saint Peter ful wel calleth vs al Gods stuardes, willing **all men
like as he hath taken grace of our Lord God, so to bestowe the same one vpon
an other like good dispensatours or stuardes of the manyform graces of God.***
Wher s. Peter speaketh of such graces as be frely giuen as well to good men as to
the bad indifferently, whych be called **Gratia gratis data,**† keepynge the general

---

† Gratia gratis data] Gratie gratis date

name of graces gyuen to the common vtilitye and profette of the Churche, of the whole Congregacion of GODS folkes and Christen people.* [3X2ᵛ] The other grace is specially called **gratia gratum faciens,** that grace that maketh the hauer acceptable to God, and in his fauour, whiche is by an other name called **charitie.*** Of the former graces the Apostle Saint Paule speaketh. **i. Cor. xii. Alij quidem per spiritum datur sermo sapientie, alij sermo scientiae, . . . alteri fides in eodem spiritu, alij gratia sanitatum. &c.** To one is giuen by the holy spirit of God, the grace of sapience to speake in heauenly matters. To an other science to discerne & iudge in lower causes, and so of others.* Nowe because that in the vsing and bestowing of al such gyftes receiued of Gods treasure, the hauer oughte to haue a streight and a right intent. Saynt Peter saith here that if any man speake the wordes of exhortacion, according to any of the sayd giftes, he should speake them as the words of God, and not as his owne woordes, counting himselfe but onelye as the minister or stuarde, and not as the owner of the worde. And likewise he that bestoweth any corporall subsidie or helpe vpon his nedye neighbour, let him so do it as though it came of Gods sendyng, to the reliefe of the poore, and not of his owne strength or vertue. **Tanquam ex virtute quam administrat deus,** attribu- tynge it to God that gaue him the wyll and the power so to do, so that in all thinges God may be honoured, through our Lorde Iesu Christ the mediatour betwyxt God and man.* And they that so vseth them selues among theyr neygh- bours, maye be called good stewardes, where some others euer receyueth of theyr maisters treasure and neuer [3X3] paieth nor bestoweth it. An other sort of stuards payeth and dealeth, but they pay shreud payment. Of the stuarde that receiueth and neuer paieth, and of the good and iust stuarde it is wryt in the psalme .xxxvi. **Mutuabitur peccator & non soluet, iustus autem miseretur & tribuet.** A synfull stuarde, a fautie stuarde boroweth and neuer payeth, euer receiueth of his maysters treasure, & neuer thanketh GOD for it, nor bestoweth it on Gods seruantes and houshold mayny.* What treasure receiueth suche a synner of almightye God? **Aug. Accepit vt sit, vt sit homo & non pecus. &c.** Hath receiued of god his being, that he is somwhat, and that he is a man and not a beast.* He hathe taken the shape of a mans bodye, and the distinction of his fiue wits or senses, eyes to se, eares to heare, nosethrils to smell, the roofe of the mouth wyth the tonge to taste, handes to handle, and feete to go and walke, and health of body with all. But all these be comon to man and beast, yet man hath receyued more then all these, the Minde that can vnderstand and may perceiue the truth, and dyscerne the right from wrong, and may search out secretes, and may by the same prayse and laude God, and loue God. But when he that hathe receiued all suche benefites at Gods hande, lyueth not well but viciouslye, hee payeth not that hee ought, he giueth no thanke to the gyuer, nor bestoweth these giftes to Gods honour, nor to the profite of Gods poore people, nor to the wealthe of hys owne poore neyghbours, no more then other gyftes of grace that God hath gyuen hym. [3X3ᵛ] The giftes of nature, as bodelye strengthe, must be bestowed not as an instrument of mischief to fighting, quareling, brawling, or to theft or murder, or such like, but must be bestowed in good exercise, auoyding of idlenes. As the wiseman saith: **Quicquid potest manus tua instanter operare, . . . nihil est enim apud inferos quo tu properas,** What- soeuer thy hand can worke, do it buselye, for there is no worke to do in hel, whither thou makest haste by thy idlenes.* Likewise beutie of face, in whyche most part of women excedingly glorieth, shoulde not be vsed as an instrument of mischiefe to allure any person to concupiscence, by curious and wanton trimming thy self like a staale to take yᵉ diuell. And so the gifts of grace, as cunning, learning, perspicuitie & clerenes of wyt shoulde euer do good to thy neighbour, and not onely to please thy selfe. And riches that God sendeth muste be so bestowed, that in any wise we beware of couetousnes, and of nigardnes, as Christ biddeth vs. **Luke .xij. Videte & cauete ab omni auaritia, quia non in abundantia cuiusquam vita eius est.** Take heede & beware of all couetousnes, for a mans life standeth not in the aboundaunce of hys possession.* Where our Sauiour Christe forbiddeth not onely desyre to haue, but also desyre to saue. Desyre to haue dampneth many a one, as it is playne of robbers, theues and brybers, and of suche as deceyue men in byinge and sellynge, and they that gyueth false euidence, or beareth false witnes to wynne and gette a lyuing, or to gette the greate mans fauour, or els peraduenture to saue theyr [3X4] owne liues. For (after Saint Austine) this auarice and couetousnes to saue a mans owne life is an horrible auarice, & greatly to be feared, that a man for hys mortall lifes sake wyll loose him, which where he was immortal, was made mortal to make the immortal, and to giue the life euerlasting.* It were better to dye for truth, and to saue the life of the soule, by which thou mayst come to euerlastinge life, then to loose that life and to be brought to death euerlasting, we shoulde be content rather to contempne thys wretched lyfe, then to commit any sinne, & we should be content to say with him, **Nudus egressus sum de vtero matris mee, & nudus reuertar illuc.** Iob grudged not in al hys calamitie, but tooke it thankfullye, and said: I came out of my mothers belye al naked & bare, and so I wil returne thither agayne.* Naked he was without bodely aparel, but he hadde plenty of rayment that would neuer rotte. So better it were for vs to be brought to such myserye as Iob was, yea and that oure enemye or a tormentour that thursteth mannes blood should slaye vs oute of hande, then that wee shoulde by our own tounge for anye desyre of lyfe or of lucre or aduauntage slaye oure owne soules. And where Christe sayde: **Cauete ab omni auaritia. &c.** he speaketh specially agaynst thys couetuousnesse and desyre to saue, as appeareth by the parable there of a ryche manne, whose landes hadde broughte fourthe a ryche croppe of grayne: In so muche that he studyed by hym selfe and sayde, what shall I dooe nowe?† [3X4ᵛ] This will I doe, I will take downe and breake mine old barnes, and I will make them larger, and there I wyll bestowe and laye vp myne encrease and all my goodes: and then I wyl say to my self: O my soul, thou hast goodes inough laid vp for mani yeres, now take thy rest, eate & drink make feastes and bankets at thy pleasure. But God sayd to hym: Oh thou foole, this night thei wyll take thy soule from thy body, and then the goods that thou hast gotten, who shal haue them? And **euen so and in like case is he** (saith Christ) **that hourdeth and storeth for himselfe, and is not riche to godwarde.*** Generally all suche as doe not vse the giftes that God hath giuen them, but drowne them and hide them, all to theym selues, and nothing to the wealthe of theyr neighbours, theyr houshold felowes, Gods folkes, all such be slothfull stuardes, and be like him that Christe spoke of **Math. xxv.*** in the parable of a greate man that went from home into a straunge countrey, and left his goodes among his seruauntes to be employed and occupied for his profit in his absence. To one he gaue fiue talentes, to an other two, to the third he gaue one talent, and this man that had but one talent in stocke, knitte hys maisters money in a cloute and hyd it in the earth, and did no good vpon it. When the mayster came home, and shoulde syt in hys audite, where euerye man had labored vpon theyr maysters stock, and had gotten good encrease, thys last man brought the mony whole again,

† nowe] nowo

& excused hym self, laying the fault on hys maister saying: I know that you be [3Y1] a rough man, a sore cruell man, a hard man, you wil loke to gather wher you nothing cast abrod, and you wil reape wher you nothing sowed, therfore I thought good to be sure without any los, thus I haue hid it, & lo here it is, you haue your owne good againe. But for his slothe his talent was taken from him, and he was cast into exteriour darkenes, where shalbe weping & gnashinge of teeth. This was for his slothe and negligence in which he offended, fearing vndiscretly his maisters sharpenes. But other stuardes ther be (that I spoke of afore) that without feare of God payeth shrewd paymente, abusyng Goddes gyftes to theyr owne lust and likinge, and to hurt theyr felowes Gods seruantes. Of such stuardes take example. **Math. xxiiij. Si autem dixerit malus seruus in corde suo, moram facit dominus meus venire: & ceperit percutere conseruos suos, manducet autem et bibat cum ebriosis, veniet dominus serui illius in die qua non sperat & hora qua ignorat, et diuidet eum partemque eius ponet cum hipochritis: illic erit fletus & stridor dentium.** If the shrewd seruaunt say in his minde: my mayster is long a comming, & vpon that beginneth to strike and hurt his felowes, & to eate and drinke with drunkerdes, his Lorde and mayster will come when he thincketh not: & will diuide his soule from his bodie, and wil laye his part with hipocrites, his soule with false christen people, with such as beginneth well and end noughtely, that semed good Christen men, & yet dissemblers they were, and inwardly noughty liuers and dampnable into hell.* Luc, xij. readeth it. [3Y1ᵛ] **Et cepit percutere pueros et ancillas,** and beginneth to strike the children & the maides.* By the youth of the children & by the womankinde vnderstanding them that be fraile, & that easely and sone taketh occasion to do nought. In the saide exterior darknes shalbe **weping** for smoke & heate, & **gnashing of teethe** for cold.* It is said in the verse of the psalme aboue rehersed, **Iustus autem miseretur & tribuet.** The iust man, the true seruant and stuard to God is merciful & lendeth:* al the gifts of nature and of grace that God hath giuen him, he applieth to Gods honour, and to do good to hys neighbour, and such welth & riches as god hath lent him, he parteth with his needie neyghbour, and bestoweth on workes of mercye & pitie. And if he be trueli a iust man, although he be but pore in worldly riches, yet he is riche in soule. Loke in his cofer, thou shalt finde it voyd and empty, but loke & consider his soule, and thou shalt fynde it full of charitie. He hathe no stuffe nor substaunce outward, but inwardly he hath charitie, passinge all worldlye treasure. And if he finde nothing to giue outward, yet he giueth and lendeth beneuolence & good wyll, he gyueth counsell, yea and he helpeth by prayer and is soner heard of God, and doth more good then he that giueth breade and meate. He hath euer somwhat to giue that hathe his brest ful of charity. The very poore people lendeth & gyueth among them selues one to an other of the treasure of theyr good wylles, they be not al baren and vnfruteful. The blinde man is led by him that seeth, whych lendeth his eyes be[3Y2]cause he lacketh mony to lend, because yᵗ with in him he had a good wil which is the treasure of yᵉ poore. Holye Iob saithe .**xxix. Oculus fui ceco, & pes claudo,** I was an eye to the blinde, & the foote to yᵉ lame, helping them not onely with my goodes but also if nede required settinge to my helpynge handes without any attourney or proctour. Of the bestowing of the goodes of fortune he sayth: **Pater eram pauperum.*** In which woordes for the vehemencie of his mercy and pitie, he leaueth the name of a dispensatour or stuarde, and vseth the name of a father, conuerting the office of charity into the affection and feruent loue natural, vsing them on whom he bestowed his charitie, pitye, & almes, as intierly and louingly as a father vseth the childe, as though he did his charitie, not only for dread of God, but also for fatherly loue vnto his neighbours. Would God al we Christen people, in which there should abound more plenty of grace then was in men of the old time, would bestow & vse our lords tresure, the gifts of nature, of grace, & of fortune, after the example of thys blessed father: that so we might be counted good dispensatours & stuards of the maniform graces of god, as blessed S. Peter willeth vs for to be. **Charissimi nolite peregrinari in feruore qui ad temptationem vobis sit, quasi noui aliquid vobis contingat** My very welbeloued frends be not dismayde or troubled in your mindes, in the feruencie & heate of persecution & vexation y^t now is so hot agaynst you, which heate almighty God suffreth to com vpon you for your trial, to trie you & proue you. [3Y2^v] Meruel not, & be not troubled (I sai) as though any newes or straunge thing betide you or chaunced vnto you,* for it is the old maner that good men susteine harme and displeasure by shrewes, wher afore in the processe that I declared in my laste sermon, the Apostle Saint Peter had exhorted them that he wryt to, to communicate, & louingly to bestowe vpon theyr neighbours such giftes as God had giuen them.* Now consequentlye he teacheth them to take payne and to abide sorow and affliction, yea euen to death & martirdome, if ye case requyre, saying: **Nolite peregrinari,** (as our text hath it) maruel not, saith the other text.* But in asmuch as when a man is sore dismaid & troubled, his wits seme to be fro home, straying and not close together, therefore it is sayd here **nolite peregrinari,** be not you in that case as men out of them selues, in such hot and perilous times: but consider that such perturbacion and trouble commeth vnto you to tempt you, not by temptacion, that shall condempne you (for God so tempteth no man) but to trye you and proue you whether you be stedfast or wauering in your faith, and in all other goodnes as he sayde afore in the fyrste chapiter: Now you must be sory in diuers temptacions, that the triall and proofe of your faythe much more precious then golde that is tryed by the fyre, may be found worthy to haue laud, glorye, and honour at the reuelation and shewynge of Iesus Christ, at the day of iudgement.* Thys is no newes, for so suffered Christ for vs all, and so must they suffer that wyll liue a true Christen [3Y3] life, and so in the primitiue church suffred many a one martirdom for Christes sake: of which thing they that Saint Peter wryt to had good knowledge and experience. In a feruent and a cruell battel, the souldiers perceiueth and taketh an excellent comfort by the manlynes of theyr captain and by examples of mightye men that haue bene praysed for theyr noble actes. It is verye vnfytting & vnmete for a souldier to sit at ease in hys hale or tent, or in his lodgynge at hys pleasure, while his captayne laboreth sore, and is in peryll in the battell among his enemies, and it is as vnseming, that where the captaine is sore hurt and wounded, the souldier studieth to slepe in a whole skin, and beareth neuer a skar in his bodye. Our sauiour Christ is our chiefe captayne in our dayly battel against our gostly enemyes, let vs take example of him, and folow his steppes, after the counsell of saynt Peter in the beginning of thys chapiter where he wylleth vs to be armed with the remembraunce of Christes passion that he suffred in his fleshe.* And Sainte Paule biddeth vs lay away al the burden of sinne that is about vs and with pacience run to the battel that is sette furth agaynst vs,* like as the Apostles and Martirs & other blessed saintes suffred theyr bodyes to be torn, rent, and mangled, loking vpon Christ the authour of our faith, and perfourmer & maker perfite the same, and inwardly considerynge his paynes that he suffered for vs all, whyle hee might haue had ioy and pleasure, yet he suffered death on the crosse and dispised shame, he regar[3Y3^v]ded not the shame that his enemies thought thei put him to. Let vs remember him that suffered such contradiction and countersayinges against him, and let vs not be weary nor shrinke in oure mindes, considering that **if we be felowes and partakers of his paines, we shalbe likewise partakers of comfort with him. ij. Cor. i.*** And therfore if it be comfort for vs to hear of the abundant reward that we shal receiue for our paines taking, let not the pain of labours make vs afrayd, For this is sure that no man shalbe crowned as a victour, but he that wil take paine lawfully to fight, and therefore he that now refuseth to fight in this present life against our gostlye ennemyes, shall haue no crowne or garland of victorie in the life to come. And what soeuer pain we suffer for our captains sake, for Christes sake, we oughte to be gladde of them, not onely because we folowe his steps, according to our duties, but also because we be as his felowes and partakers of his passions and paines that he suffred, as s. Peter saith here **Sicut communicantes Christi passionibus gaudete,** Be you glad as men taking part of Christes passions, & made hys felowes and like vnto him, sufferynge payne and trouble as he dyd, that so at the tyme when he shall shewe him selfe in hys glorye, you maye be merye and gladde, and maye be felowes with hym, and partakers of hys ioye and glory.* Saynte Paule sayde: **Collossi. i. Gaudeo in passionibus . . . & adimpleo ea que desunt passionum Christi in carne mea pro corpore eius quod est Ecclesia.** [3Y4] Saynte Paule was in prison in Ephesus when he wrotte hys Epistle to the Collossenses, wher hee saythe the woordes rehearsed: I am gladde in my passyons and paynes that I suffer, and I fulfyll and make vppe those thynges that lacketh of Christes passyons in my fleshe.* Christes passions that he suffered in hys owne persone, were full and perfytte and nothynge lackynge, as hunger thyrste, strokes and deathe, but because he dothe esteme and repute hys Catholycke Churche as hys bodye, and taketh euerye good Christian manne as hys lymmes and members of that hys bodye, he† counteth all the hurte and harme that is done to theym, as done to hym selfe:* As hee sayde to Saynte Paule at the tyme when he went to pursue the Christen people that were in Damasco, **Saule, Saule quid me persequeris? Actuum, ix.** Saule (for so he was fyrst called) why pursuest thou mee?* Yet he was then in heauen, where no persecution coulde approche to hurte hym, but because they were hys lymmes faste ioyned to hym by faythe adorned with charitye, he tooke and regarded theyr paynes, as thoughe hee hadde suffered theym hym selfe. In lyke manner Saynte Peter in thys place of his Epistle wylleth all theym that suffereth payne for Iustice sake to reioyce and be glad, as takyng parte of Christes passions, that they may lykewyse reioyce to take parte of hys euerlastynge glorye. **Si exprobramini in nomine Christi beati eritis.** [3Y4ᵛ] You must not onely paciently & gladlye sustayne bodely paine for Christe, but also contumelious & despitefull wordes must be gladly suffered.* Elipham one of Iobs frendes that came to vysete him in his calamiti, reputed it a great benefit of God to be hid from the scourge of an yll tounge. **A flagello lingue absconderis. Iob. v.*** but he had no respecte to the life to come<.> but onelye pondred & weyed the benefites that God giueth to men in this world, which worldlye people moste regardeth and most earnestly desireth to haue, for they would haue no yll spoken to them, nor of theym. And yet they that be very good men, woulde be lothe to be yll sayd by, they woulde be lothe to be distayned, blotted, or spotted in theyr name and fame, because it is theyr highest riches and treasure, and therefore the prophet prayed: **Domine libera animam meam a labijs iniquis & a lingua dolosa.** O Lord deliuer my soule, deliuer me from vniust lippes and from a tounge that is deceyteful, from all yll speaking.* And well

† he] and

is he that can escape them, as few or none doth now adayes, such is the iniquitie of the worlde that folke thinke it no fault but a merye gest to rayle and sclaunder their neighbour, and to bring a man into an infamye, which many times turneth to his destruction and vndoyng. God amend them, they thynck to displease theyr poore neyghbour and to hurte hym, but yet many times they fayle, God preseruing his seruant, but they be sure that thei haue hurt theyr owne soules, and procured their own dampnacion, but if theyr raylynge and gestynge vpon [3Z1] vs be for iustice, for well doinge or sayinge, for Christes cause, or in Christes cause, and thou canste haue no remedye but men wyll rayle, then remember blessed S. Peters comforte, **Si exprobramini. &c.** If you be vmbraided, & called fooles for takinge that waye that you do, and for refusinge your olde trade and maner of liuinge, you be blessed here in hope, and after this presente life shal be blessed in heauen in dede, whiche (to the letter) was spoken for the comforte of them that were newelye conuerted to Christes fayth, and called Christen men and women, whiche the infideles toke for a name of despite, and they vsed other names of reproche agaynste them, as callinge them **Galileans:*** and Christ was called **Galileus**, be-cause he was broughte vp in Galile, but they that woulde not beleue on him, called hym by that name in despite, because they would not confesse hym **Christ**, nor call him **Iesus:*** As **Iulianus Apostata** vsed to call him, tyll at the laste he cryed **Galilee vicisti** to his payne.* And if they feared not to missay and rayle against the maister, lette not the disciples and seruauntes loke to scape without despite. Therfore when you vse any such deuout christian maner of abstinence as hath be vsed in olde time among christen people. As if you absteyne from fleshe, and from whitmeate in the holy time of Lent: or yf you faste Fridayes and Wednes-daies, or more dayes in the weke in that holy time,* or in this holy weke nowe present called the Rogation weke, the procession weke, yf men not willinge to runne afore a lawe, newe [3Z1ᵛ] made by them that haue aucthoritie, woulde obserue the accustomed fast, absteining from fleshe euery day in this weke, except the thursday that is dedicate in the honour of Christes glorious ascension, and taking but one meale on the Mundaye, and on the Wednisdaye, as the olde maner was, you shalbe called hipocrites, and folish phariseis, wᵗ suche other odious names:* or if a preist saye his mattens and euensonge, with other diuine seruice dayly, according to his bounden dutye, he shall be mocked and iested at, yea and not onelye of lighte braynes of the layfe, but also of men of oure owne cote and profession, leude and folyshe preistes, that nother serue God deuoutly, nor the world iustely nor diligently, but geue them selues to walkinge the stretes, and beatinge the bulkes with theyr heeles,* clatteringe lighte and leude matters, full vnseminge for theyr profession, and some of them more geuen to reading these folishe englishe bokes full of heresies, then anye true expositours of holy scriptures. Suche men be they that desteyneth the aunciente grauitie of the Churche, and suche be moste prone and ready to mocke all theim that intendeth well. To all them that be deluded or mocked, and molested with suche raylers, S. Peter geueth good comforte, sayinge: if you be vmbrayded and missaied for vsynge vertue and iustice (that is for Christes sake) you be blessed for euerlastinge blessing is promised you: And **that perteineth to honoure, to glorye, and to the vertue of GOD, and also his holye spirite resteth vpon you.** In this present lyfe [3Z2] you shall be worthye to haue honoure in youre good workes, and for well doynge and vertuous lyuinge. **Nam honor est praemium virtutis.** Honor is the rewarde for vertue,* and in time to come you shall be partakers of Christes honour. And nowe you shall haue the glorye of a pure & cleare conscience, whiche is the glory of a

Christen man and the very waye to come to glorye of body and soule. **Gloria nostra haec est testimonium conscientie nostre. ii. Cor. i.** This is my glory (saith S. Paul) the witnes of mine owne conscience, without remorse or grudge, for my conuersation hath be in simplicitie amonge you without carnall or crafty subteltie or deceipt, saith S. Paule.* Euen like glorye of your owne consciences shall reste vpon you, whiche shall comfort you agaynst the insulties and sclau[n]derous raylinge of all your aduersaries. Let them say what they wyll, you can not let them, you know your selues cleare and fautles, and the vertue and strength of God ouer the deuyll and all his membres shall also reste vpon you, and no marueyle, for his holy spirite, the holy goost, the causer of these benefites, and of all other goodnes resteth vpon you, and therefore as muche as in them is, almightie God that resteth in you, is missaid and rayled at in you, but as in you, and for your part, and as you muste take it, he is glorified, and that is said redoundeth to his glorye by you. **Nemo autem vestrum patiatur vt homicida, aut fur, aut maledicus aut alienorum appetitor.** When you take paine and be rayled on for iustices sake, you maye be gladde.

[3Z2ᵛ] But I woulde not (sayth S. Peter here) that any of you shoulde suffer for manslaughter, as a murtherer, or as a thefe, or as a sclaunderer or backbiter, or blasphemer, or as one that goeth about to take awaye other mens goodes, to spoile and robbe them.* The theues suffer imprisonment and death for theyr offences, this paine they suffer for theyr iniquitie. Heretikes be likewise put to shame, and many times to death for theyr misbeleife and heresies, and for blaspheminge and missayinge Gods holy scriptures, to the yl example and peruerting of many a christen soule, bringing them also to like damnation. There be none such to be reputed blessed for theyr paines sufferyng, because it is not for Christe, nor for iustice sake, but for theyr owne faultes, yll doinges, and ill sayinges: but yet some suche men and women that haue so suffred for theyr faultes, be so obstinate in theyr malice, and so glory in theyr errors and iniquitie, that they be not ashamed to saye they beare theyr crosse with Christe, when they beare theyr fagottes in open penaunce to escape theyr burninge. They beare theyr crosse in dede, as the thefe dydde that was hanged on Christes lefte syde, not to theyr saluation, but to theyr condempnation, which they here beginne, and in hell shall consummate, perfourme, and continue the same for euer. **Si autem vt Christianus non erubescat** (sayth S. Peter.) If you suffer as a Christen man or woman, eyther displeasures in body and goodes, or by wordes, for that thou arte a good Christen man, or liueste like a good christen man [3Z3] or woman, be not ashamed what so euer be sayd or done against the, but rather glorify God, giue laude and prayse, and thankes to God that hath geuen the grace to be thought worthye to suffer contumely or despites for Christes name, **Glorificet autem deum in isto nomine, quoniam tempus est vt incipiat iudicium a domo dei.** For nowe is the time for the iudgement of God, to beginne at the house of God.* The iudgement beginneth in our lyfe time: for whiche you muste note, that the iudgement of God is of two maners: one is priuie and secrete, the other shall be manifest and openly knowen to all men and women. The fyrste is in this life, the other shalbe at the day of dome, and the generall iudgement. For almighty God will leaue no ill vnpunished, therfore in as much as he sharpely wyll punishe sinfull persons with the intollerable paynes of hell, with the deuylles after this lyfe, he suffreth them to take their pleasure while they be here a while, and to leade a mery life in welth & in prosperitie, but at a trise sodenly they be plucked awaye, and descendeth downe into hell to that vntollerable and eternall iudgement. And when God sendeth to such malefactours any paynes or trouble, they fret and chafe, rayle and grudge agaynste GOD, and in theyr rage dyeth, and beginneth theyr hell with paynes and sorowe here, that hereafter in hell shall continue for euermore, no tounge can expresse the sorowe and paynes that there shall be. But others that by suche strokes and correction as God sendeth them, be exercised for theyr pur[3Z3ᵛ]gation, and be made better and better, & taketh them for a warning to conuert and amend their liues, such correction doth them much good. Therfore it is written, **Iob .v. Beatus homo qui corripitur a domino**, Blessed is the man or woman that is correct and punished of our lord God.* And the reason is this, for if mannes correction maye be good and holesome, then Gods correction muste nedes be much more holesome: for man knoweth not parfitly the maner and measure of holsome correction, neither is omnipotent to take awaye the punishment when it is ynoughe, or when he lyste, nor to do good and to ease a man in tyme conueni-ent: but God by his omnipotency, by that he is almightie, and knoweth all thinges, he knoweth how much or how litle he maye punishe his childe and seruaunt, and he euer punisheth hym to do him good, either to trie him, and to proue his constauncy, or to make him amende his lyfe. For there is no man liuinge that can say he is all cleare, but that he hath sinned or done amisse: and many things that in our iudgement semeth to be iust and well done, yet in the iudgemente of God they may be nought. For man seith and iudgeth after the exterior apparaunce, but God seith the secretes of the heart, and al other circumstaunces. And in as much as all mankinde was at the beginning iustly condempned for the offences of Adam, God will not easely deliuer vs from that malandre, neither from so greate a disease, which also maketh that sinnes be euer ready, we euer running headlong to them, but iustice & good [3Z4] liuing is full of labour and payne, and is hard to come to, but that loue and charitie maketh that easy to them that loueth God, whiche to other is very painefull. And this is the occasion of this priuie iudgement of God, by which he sendeth trouble and paine to good men with the bad indifferently, for all haue sinned, and haue nede of gods glorious helpe. Some by the sayde payne & trouble that God sendeth, be exercised for their purgation, a[n]d to be made better by the same, suche as be good, as Iob, Tobie, and such lyke, others be warned for their conuersion and amendment of their liues, and other that contemneth the callinge, it blyndeth toward their condempnation, as I sayd Now is the time that Goddes iudgement should begin at Gods house, the Church of Christ, the congre-gation of good faithfull people, whiche must be exercised with paine and trouble to learne the way to glory and ioy euerlastinge, where reproued & damnable persons, lead a mery life in welth and prosperitie, & feleth no paine nor displeasure, but laugheth at other mens harmes and glorieth in nothinge more, then to make them selues riche of other mennes goodes, landes and possessions, to their euerlasting impouerishing.* And if we shal yet more specially speak of the house of God, it is to be feared, lest euen like as Ezechiell the prophet saw in his vision, vi. aungels like men, with weapons in their handes to execute Gods vengeaunce on the reuersion & leauinges of Ierusalem, & they had going afore them one clothed in linnen, hauing a penner & inckhorne hanging at his back, which was com-maunded to make yᵉ sign of [3Z4ᵛ] **Tau**, vppon all them that lamented and wayled for their owne sinnes, and for the sinnes of the people: the other .vi. men were commaunded to go forth & kyl al them that had not the said signe of **Tau** marked in theyr foreheades, and to spare neither olde nor younge, man, woman, nor child. **Et a sanctuario meo incipite. Ezech. ix.** And beginne at my holye church,* sayth almighty God, because that the iniquitie of the people, rose that tyme by some

occasion of them of the churche, eyther because of ill example geuing vnto the
people, or els because they would not by holesome lessons instructe them to liue
vertuouselye, or els for feare of displeasure of great men, woulde not sharpely
reproue theyr vices, and noughtie liuinge. The day of iudgemente is at hande, as
appeareth by manye signes, continuall warre or suspition of battayle, countreys
against countreys, realmes agaynst realmes, princes agaynst princes, continuall
plague of moreine and pestilence, trouble & vexation continuallye, and feare lest
GOD hath byd the ministers, the executours of his iustice & vengeaunce, to
beginne at his churche, for wel is he that can do any hurt or displeasure to a preist,
to take their landes & liuinges, is thoughte gotten good, & no good so easely
gotten, to ieste, raile and mocke at them, and to do them despites, is thought best
pastime,* not regarding the prohibition of God, **Nolite tangere Christos meos: et
in prophetis meis nolite malignari.** Touche not mine anointed (saith God) and
maligne not, ymagin no mischeif, nor do any such harme to my prophetes, [4A1]
such as preach & teache, and tel you of the wyl of God.* So euery way Gods stroke
& iudgement beginneth at yᵉ church, albeit s. Peter in this place taketh not the
church so precisely, for yᵉ ministers of the church, but more generally for the
congregation of good faithful people, which almightye God permitteth and suffreth to be flagelled and scourged here, because he wyll not dampne them eter-
nally, but wyl shortly set them at rest in heauen aboue, where they shall be no
more scourged nor vexed, pilled nor polled. **Si autem primum a nobis, quis finis
eorum qui non credunt euangelio dei?*** If Gods iudgement beginne, and be so
sore vpon vs that beleue vpon him, what shal be their ende that beleue not
Goddes gospel, or that haue beleued it in times past, and now beleueth it neuer a
deale? If he punishe them that he loueth, howe shall they spede that he loueth
not? And if he whip & beat his children, what shal the wicked & noughty
seruauntes loke for? but to be bound hand and fote and cast into exterior darkenes,
to dampnation euerlasting. **Et si iustus vix saluabitur, impius et peccator vbi
parebunt?** And if a good man shal scarsely and with much a do be saued, where
shal the wicked & common sinner appeare?* Aristotle saith. **Quod fere fit non fit,
sed quod vix fit, fit.** That is almost done or wel nere done, is not done: but that is
scarsely done, yet it is done thoughe it be wᵗ much a do.* So if a man do manye
times well, and liue wel longe and many a day, yet at the last falleth to sinne and
liueth nought, and so dyeth, this man was almost saued, but yet he was not saued
all oute in dede, because he died in deadlye [4A1ᵛ] sinne, and out of the state of
grace, as offendinge and breaking one commaundemente or another, and he that
breaketh one commaundement, **Factus est omnium reus,** is made giltie in them
al,* as muche as concerneth euerlastinge saluation: for if a man breake one, then
the obseruinge and kepyng of al the rest shal not saue his soul from damnation. But
the iust man, the good liuer, taketh payne and labours to auoyde from sinne, and
to please God by vertuouse liuinge, and by doynge good workes, and it is not one
days worke onely, but he muste continue in well doynge, and in continuall battayle agaynst the deuil, the world and the fleshe. It is no smale busines, but
continuall payne and sorowe, as S. Paule said, **Actu. xiiii. Per multas tribula-
tiones oportet nos intrare in regnum Dei.** Through many troubles and much
busines (which can not be auoyded, ouercome, or passed through, withoute a
speciall assistence of almighty God) we must come to heauen.* And that is it that
S. Peter sayth here, **vix saluabitur iustus,** the good man, the good liuer shalbe
saued scarcelye, or with much a do.* I heard one preache in an excellent and
learned audience, whiche expounding this text of S. Peter, **Iustus vix saluabitur.**

resolued this word **vix** folishly into yᵉ .iii. letters, **v.i.x.** vnderstandinge by **v.** **virtute.** by **i. Iesu.** by **x. Christi.** as though S. Peter had meaned yᵗ a iuste man, or a good liuer shalbe saued bi the vertue or power of Iesus Christ. And this is true, for without his power no man shalbe saued: but this is not taken of the said word **vix**, so resolued by an **Ethimologie**, for it is a folish **Ethimologie** in eue[4A2]ry point, and specially because that why this letter **.x.** should signifie **Christi**, there is no reason, although the grekes **ch**, which is the fyrst letter of **Christus** in yᵉ greke, be made like our latin **x**. But this common text of Peter (which is almost in euery mans mouth) is taken of the **Prou. xi. Si iustus in terra recipit, quanto magis impius et peccator.** If a good liuer receiueth paine & punishment here on erth, how much more may the noughty liuers loke to receiue & take?* If yᵉ martirs haue suffred innumerable displeasures, & vntollerable paines for Christes sake here in this world: how muche more sorow & paines groneth & loketh for their tormen-tors that put them to those paines? And if holy Iob & the old patriarchs & prophetes, & in Christes time, the apostles, martirs, & such other receiued much pain, & suffred sorow & displesurs to please almightie God, how much more sorow may they loke for in another world, yᵗ here liueth at pleasure, & be mery & laugheth at other mens harmes, & taketh more paines to hurt them, then to do them good? The good liuers taketh paines on earth, here in this world, the sinners, malicious persons, bribers, oppressioners, & extorcioners shal suffer their paines wᵗout end, in the horrible paines of hell. And this is it yᵗ s. Peter meaned by the sayd text, yᵗ if the good man shal with much a do be saued, that is **vix**, scarsely, where shal the vicious wicked sinner apeare? he can not so come to saluation, then no remedy but he must come to dampnation, with the deuyll and all his dampned companye in hel. Then for the finall conclusion of this matter of sufferynge aduersitie, [4A2ᵛ] paynes and trouble for Christe, and for iustice sake, S. Peter concludeth saying: **Itaque & hi qui paciuntur secundum voluntatem dei. &c.** Therfore they that suffereth of ill folkes by the wil & permission of God,* this is called **Voluntas signi,** it is a signe that he is content it should so be, because he suffreth it for the time, and it semeth that he wyl so, because he suffreth it. Thei that so suffreth, let them commit their liues, their soules to almighty God their faithful maker, in good workes, let them liue well and do well, nothinge presuming on theyr owne power, & then let him alone withal, when you do the best, and you can do no more, let him alone with yᵉ rest, for he is faithfull (saith S. Peter) he is trustie and faythful, and wyl not fayle to acquite aboundauntlye the paines that you take, yea and much aboue anye mans deseruing.* And here you must not forget how S. Peter biddeth vs commende o[u]re selues to God in good dedes, then onely fayth is not ynough, you must worke charitably withall, to declare youre selues to haue a liuely fayth, viuificate, made alyue, and adourned with charitie and good workes,* whiche shalbe acquited surelye and faythfully with glory in heauen euerlastingly, whiche he graunt vs. &c.

The fyfte Chapiter.

GOod and worshipfull audience, considerynge my bounden duetie and due obedience that I owe to the s[u]periour powers, I haue absteined now from preachinge
these .v. or .vi. yeares, but nowe that it hath pleased them more fauourably to loke
vpon me, and to lycence me,* I shalbe glad to retourne to that my old exercise,
and to come among you to do my duety in that behalfe, at such times as I may
conuenientlye. Furthermore I trust you remember, and I doubt not but many here
present doth remember that about .viii. or .ix. yeares agone, I toke vpon me to
preache vnto you, here in this citie, the first epistle of S. Peter, in whiche in manye
sermons I came ouer foure chapters of the same epistle, afore I was prohibited for
to preache.* And now beginning where I lefte, I purpose (GOD helpinge) to
prosecute the residue of the said epistle. The .v. chapter beginneth thus.

**Seniores ergo qui in vobis sunt obsecro, consenior & testis Christi passio-
num, qui & eius quae in futuro reuelanda est glorie communicator, pascite. &c.
i. Pet. v.*** Because the blessed Apostle Saynt Peter woulde leaue none estate of
people destitute of learninge, and withoute gostlye exhortation, therefore after his
holesome lessons geuen afore, [4A3ᵛ] generally to all maner of people, as well riche
as poore, as to bondmen and seruauntes, & then to wiues and maried men, & then
retourning to general lessons indifferent for al men.* Nowe consequently in these
wordes rehearsed he infourmeth preistes, which God hath apointed to be among
the people, as launterns of lyghte,* to leade and guyde his people towarde the
saluation of theyr soules, whiche is the ende and perfection of our fayth, as he
sayde afore. **Capi. i.*** In all maner of doctrine the auctoritie of the mayster hath
great efficacitie, and doth verye muche in makinge the scholer to applie his mind
to that is taught him, to learne it, and beare it away. Therefore Saint Peter,
because he would here teache preistes, he professeth him selfe to be a preist as they
be, and therefore they shoulde be gladder to heare hym, and to folowe his doctrine. As yf there should be a matter of the trade of marchaundise to be intreated
of among the marchauntes of this citie, if there came in a marchaunt of graue and
longe experience, all the others woulde geue eare and lysten to his talke, and
woulde be gladde to folowe his counsell. Lykewise amonge carpenters or masons, if
the kinges cheife carpenter or maister mason of his graces workes came in place,
beynge knowen for most excellent of the realme in theyr faculties, all the carpenters, all the masons in the citie would anone resorte vnto them, to heare some
learninge of them. Euen so it is in matters of hygher learnynge pertaininge to our
soule health. And for suche considerations S. [4A4] Peter here professeth him selfe
to be a preiste, and a preiste not made at all aduentures, as these leude ministers be
made nowe a dayes of shoemakers, smithes, coblers, and clouters, as well maryed as
single, but one taught & brought vp vnder the prynce of preistes oure Sauyoure
Christe, therefore they shoulde assure theim selues that he woulde teache them
nothinge but that shoulde beseme a preiste. And yet furthermore to amplifie his
auctoritie, he calleth hym selfe a wytnes of Christes passions and paynes that he
suffred for vs. **Testis Christi passionum,*** Thoughe all Christes lyfe were a verye
passyon, and a time full of trouble, paine, and persecution, yet chiefly his passion
begonne when he prayed on the banke besyde **Gethsemani,** in the mounte

Oliuete, when he was in a marueilous agony, that made him swete so sore, that the droppes fel from him like water mixt with bloude.* Then came Iudas, and a traine with him of the presidents souldiers, & also of of the bishops men, & set hand vpon him, & led him ful boistuously, first to Annas, then to Caiphas, that was **pontifex anni illius,*** then to Pilate, then to Herode, because al the world should wonder on him, as condemned by so many iudges, and none of them all speaking one word for his dispatching or acquiting. Then they brought him backe againe to Pilate which condemned him to death,* partlye to stoppe the Iewes mouthes and their clamoure, partlye for fear lest he should haue bene accused to the emperoure for lettinge one scape that toke vpon him to be a kinge, as the Iewes bore him on hande [4A4ᵛ] that Christ did, as preparing or intending a commotion or rebellion agaynst the emperoure.* Of all this processe Peter was **oculatus testis,** a wytnesse that sawe it with his eye, to his greate discomforte, payne and heauines, and specially after that the cocke had crowen thrise, when Christ loked backe vpon him, and so pearced his hearte with his looke, that he remembred what he had done deniynge his maister, that then furth he went and wept bytterly, and afterwarde by his preaching and teaching he testified the same processe of his passion, and of his glorious resurrection and ascention, and stickt neither for threateninge, beating, nor imprisonment.* This should make all them that woulde beleue on Christe to credite him, and to do as he bad them. Another perswasion he expresseth, **Qui et eius quae in futuro reuelanda est gloriae communicator.** I am a Preist as you be, I am a witnes of Christes paines and passion which I saw with mine eyes, and thirde, I was partaker of his glory, which shalbe reueled and openly shewed in time to come,* meaninge the marueilous and glorious sight that he sawe at Christes transfiguration, of whiche S. Mathewe writeth in the .xvii. cha.* At which time he saw the glory of Christes glorified bodye for the tyme: for the which it is to be vnderstanded that there be .iiii. dowres (as they be called **dotes corporis gloriosi**) of a glorious bodye, for whiche you must consider that the soule of our sauiour Christ from the fyrst moment of his conception was glorious, & had the giftes of glory by reason of yᵉ per[4B1]fit vnion of it to his Godhed, albeit by Gods pleasure & ordinaunce it was, yᵗ the glorye of Christes Soule did not redounde and shew it selfe in his bodye, that so hys bodie might be mortal and passible to performe the pryce of oure redemption. And by like prouision of God it was, that for the tyme of his transfiguration, the like glorye shoulde redounde and shewe it selfe in his bodye, althoughe it were not permanent and continuynge, as it is nowe in hys blessed bodye, and shall be in our bodyes when we shall ryse to saluation and lyfe euerlastyng at the general iudgmente. It was for the tyme in hym, as **Passio transiens,** a qualitie passynge, and therefore for that tyme not properlye the dowrye of a glorified bodye. **Quia dos de sua ratione importat qualitatem permanentem.*** And this that I saye of these giftes or dowryes of a glorious body, is not onlye a fraske or a knack of the scolastical lernyng, but it is the true doctrine of saint Paule **.i. Co. xv.*** where he declareth the maner howe deade mens bodyes shall rise at the generall iudgement, sayinge: **Seminatur in corruptione, surget in incorruptione.** Where he expresseth the gift or dowrye of **Impassibilitie.** Nowe our bodyes be subiect to all paynes of sickenesse, strokes, and lyke harmes, then we shall ryse impassible, so that neither fire nor water, sworde, nor anye other weapon shall hurt vs, by the dowry or gyfte of impassibilitie. **Seminatur† in ignobilitate, surget in gloria.** Our bodies shall be buried in ignobilitie, that is to saye, dymme,

† Seminatur] Seminarur

darke, colourlesse, but it shal ryse in glo[4B1ᵛ]rye by the gyfte of clearenesse and brightnesse, that is to say, in suche clearenes and bryghtnes that no mortall eye shall be able to beholde it. **Seminatur in infirmitate, surget in virtute**. Our bodyes shall be sowed or buried in Infirmitie, that is to saie, dull, weake, & not able to stirre hither or thither, but they shall arise in might, strength, and subtiltie, so penetratiue & percynge, so subtill and fine, that it shal be able to pearce through the stone wals without any diuision or breaking either of oure bodyes or of the wall, euen lyke as Christ came among his disciples wᵗout breaking of yᵉ dores or wals, or any diuision of his own body **Seminatur corpus animale resurget corpus spirituale**. Our bodies be buried as of the kinde of the flesh suche as beastes haue, but it shall ryse a spirituall bodye, by the gyfte or indument of **Agilitye**, so quycke, so nymble, so quyuer, that a man shall be where he lyste in a moment or tyme vnperceptible. And so we haue of saynte Paule these foure giftes that I spake of, and of which saint Peter meaned when he said that was communicator or partaker of Christes glory, which though it wer marueilous at that time of his transfiguration, yet it shal be reueled & shewed much more manifestly, & more gloriously when he shal come in glory to iudge the quick & the dead. Part of this glory .s. Peter saw at the time of Christes tran[s]figuration, as I said, when he could not wel tel what he said or did. But he was so well pleased wyth the sight that he saw, yᵗ he wold haue ben glad to haue taried there stil, & al his company with him [4B2] as wel Moses & Helias, as Iohn & Iames. **Bonum est nos hic esse**. Here is good abiding for vs, & he wished lodgynges to be made for Christe, & also for Moses & Hely, and wold haue placed him selfe (I thinke) with Christ and his two companions with Moyses & Hely. But anone his corage was delayed when he saw a bright shining cloud couering them, by the which was signified the presence of the holy gost. And out of the said cloude came the voice of the father, saiynge: **Hic est filius meus dilectus in quo mihi bene complacitum est ipsum audite**. This is my welbeloued son in whom I delite heare him. When Peter, Iohn, & Iames hearde this voice, they fell flat on their faces, and were sore afraied. Christ came to them and touched them, bad them arise & fear not, & when they loked vp, thei saw no man but Christ their master alone.* These iii. allectiues which .s. Peter toucheth to alure them to geue credit to his writing, and to his doctrine thus declared, let vs further procede to the letter S. Peter calleth such priests, **seigniours or elders,** & ancients, specially for their ancientnes, grauitie & sadnes, in maners & conditions. In very dede **presbiter** in the greke is by interpretation **senior** in the latin, in Englishe an auncient, or an elderman.* Albeit euery olde man, or auncient man is not a Prieste, but onely suche as by prophecye, or election and imposition of a prelates hande is piked out & chosen among the moe to be addict and appoynted to God, and to be a minister of God in the Churche or congregation in thynges be[4B2ᵛ]longynge to God and to his seruice, somewhat like as in this example. In cities and townes we call theim Aldermen not euer that be the eldest men within their warde, but such as partely for their substaunce, and more for their honestye and sadnesse and wisdome be thought worthy to rule the stretes, and the people within their wardes, and so they be called eldermen or aldermen by election, although they be yonge men by yeares. But these seigniours or elders that we call priestes* be made, and euer haue ben made continually as well in the lawe of Moyses, as in the tyme of grace and the lawe of the Gospell, by the imposition and laiyng on of the prelates handes, and other ceremonies longyng to the same, by which they that be so ordered receiueth a special gift of grace, that maketh their ministerie & seruice approued & alowed of God, and acceptable to hym, and

maketh the administration of the Sacramentes effectuous and able to performe
that they signifie, that is to conferre and geue grace as they were ordeined for to
do.* And this blessed ceremonie was not done without great and Godly solicitude,
premeditation, and preparation afore by deuout prayers and fastynge, afore the
promocion of men, vnto the holye ministery and appoynted seruice of God,
accordyng to the example taken as well of our Sauiour Christe, as of his
apostles<,>. Saint Luke writeth. **Luke .vi. Factum est autem in diebus illis. Exiit
Iesus in montem orare, & erat pernoctans in oratione dei: & cum dies factus
esset vocauit discipulos suos & elegit duodecem ex [4B3] ipsis quos & apostolos
nominauit Simonem, quem cognominauit Petrum & Andream fratrem eius. &c**
Christ went vp vnto an hyl to pray, and he taried all night in his prayers to God.
And when daye came, he called to hym his scolers or disciples, and of them he
chose twelue, whiche also he named apostles. **Simon** to whom he gaue surname
Peter, and **Andrewe** hys brother, and so foorthe of others tyll he came to **Iudas**
that was the traytoure,* whom (as Sainte Ambrose noteth) Christe chose not
vnwares or ignoraunte what he would be, & how he would proue, but by especiall
prouidence, foresight, & of purpose.* For our sauiour Christ toke vpon him mans
infirmitie & frailnes, & therfor he refused not such pains of our infirmitie, as men
commonly do sustayne. He was content to be lefte and forsaken, as manye men be
of their frends sometyme that thei loued best. He was content to be vttered when
he might haue bene secrete and quiet. He was content to be betrayed of hys owne
scholer, & seruant & to be committed by him into his enmies hands. And all this
he suffered for vs, and for this purpose, To geue vs example that if thou or I be
forsaken of our owne felowe or frende, or if wee be vttered, and our secretes
reueyled and opened, or if we be betraied and put into the daunger of our aduersaries by our owne felowe, or one that we haue done for, we should moderately
take it, and well a worthe that our iudgemente hathe erred and gone amysse, that
we haue taken him of greater honestye then he is, and that we haue taken him for
one of better fidelitie and credence, then hee [4B3ᵛ] sheweth him self to be. We
must be content yᵗ our benefite that we haue done for him hath perished & is
clearly lost, we ought to be contente as well as Christ was wyth Iudas, and with all
the displeasures, dispites, and paynes that he suffered by occasion of his falsshode.
And here also .s. Ambrose noteth, that in this praier & watch of Christ all night
longe afore he chose his .xii. Apostles to be his ministers in his Churche, we maye
learne what we ought to do for our owne soule health, seing that Christ toke so
much paine, not for hym self, but for our wealth only, to watch and praye that we
might haue such ministers chosen by him that myght faythfully instruct vs for the
saluation of our soules. We may also by thys example of Christe consider what wee
ought to do, when we wyll enterpryse or set vpon any good or godly work or
busines, consideryng that Christ when he should cho[o]se his apostles to accompany him & to learn of him, and then to be sent forth to preach his doctrine,
praied, & praied alone, & praied all night long without slepe, and without meate
or drinke. Thapostles according to the example of their maister Christ vsed like
maner. As we haue **Act. xiii.** where it is written that the holye Goste spoke vnto
them that wer in **Antiochia,** prophets and doctours with other company there
seruing God & fastyng. **Segregate mihi Saulum & Barnabam in opus in quod
assumpsi eos.** Seperate & set out for me Saul (which was afterward called Paule)
& Barnabas into the work for which I haue taken them. And it foloweth, **Tunc
ieiunantes & orantes im[4B4]ponentesque eis manus dimiserunt illos.** They
altogether fasted & prayed & put on them their holy hands & sent them forth

likewise.* **Act. xiiii.** I read y^t Paul & Barnabas returning backe by the cities of **Listra, Iconium,** and **Antiochia,** confirming and staiynge the minds of their disciples, & exhorting them that they should perseuer & stedfastlye continue in their faith which thei had receued. And declaryng and persuading them that bi many tribulations & much trouble we must enter into the kingdom of god. And when they had made for them priestes in euery church, & praied deuoutly for them with fastyng thei committed & betoke them to our Lorde God, on whom they beleued.* And here (good & worshipfull audience) it is to be noted that in the Primitiue church euen in thapostles time, whensoeuer there were priestes ordered to be Gods ministers, the people vsed fasting & praiyng, fasting y^t their wits & mindes might be more clere and eleuate, & apt to pray.* And praiyng to almighty God for grace y^t thei which wer chosen & admitted to so excellent a function, ministery & seruice, might be worthy to do their duty in their seruice & calling. And euen according to the apostles examples, such fastyng & praiyng hath ben vsed hereafore euen to our time: For at such times as holi orders be geuen, we haue certein daies .iiii. times in the yere called **imbring daies,*** in whiche all christen people vsed fastinge & praiyng to god, that it may please him to inspire such grace into the harts of the pre[l]ats & pastors y^t they may circumspectly loke vpon the qualities, condicions, & learning of them that shalbe ordred, so y^t they be not accused hereafter for putting on [4B4^v] their hands to sone or vnaduisedly, or to rashly on them that taketh orders, so communicating or taking part of other mens fautes, as .s. Paul speaketh. **i. Timo. v. Manus cito nemini imposueris neque communicaueris peccatis alienis.** Put not thy handes to sone vppon no man, neither take thou part of other mennes sinnes,* for the Prelate or Bishop that geueth orders to one that is vnworthye because of hys vice or ignoraunce, & lacke of learnyng, and by that occasion liueth not like a priest or can not do his seruice and duetye like a priest, then he that gaue hym orders is partaker of his faulte, and shall beare hys parte of the iudgement, condemnation, and punyshemente for the same. This is no small perill for Prelates that geue orders, therfore verie christian charitie moued christen men and women to praye to GOD, specially at such tymes, to inspire them with the abundaunce of hys grace to take hede what they doe in this behalfe. And as well for theim that shall take Orders, and shall be deputed to that moste holye and excellente ministerye. Howe highlye the Apostle sainte Paule Goddes electe and chosen vessell estemeth and regardeth thys puttynge on of handes vppon them that shall be ordered and promoted to holye orders, appereth by his letters written to hys disciples **Tymothe** and **Titus.** He biddeth **Tymothe i. Ti. iiii. Noli negligere gratiam quae in te est, quae data est tibi per prophetiam cum impositione manuum presbiterii.** Se that thou dooe not neglecte or make light of the grace that is in thee, whiche was geuen the by [4C1] prophecy or election with imposition or puttyng on thee, the handes of the priesthode or prelates.* By this that he calleth prophecy, he meaneth election or chosynge, in as much as when men make election of any person to an office, or to performe or do any b[u]sines, they haue a certayne expectation or hope that the person so elected is able to do the thinge that he is chosen for, and wyll performe it in dede that belongeth to hys callynge. And, **ii. Tim. i. Admoneo te vt resuscites gratiam dei que est in te per impositionem man[u]um mearum.** I warne thee that thou stirre vp and exercise the grace that is in thee, the whiche was geuen thee by puttyng on thee my hands.* After that Paule being at Ephesus, met wyth certaine newe conuerted christen men, and asked them, whether they had receiued ye holy gost. No (said they) we haue not heard of him whether there be any such thing or no. Then after they were baptised in the name of Iesus (for afore thei had ben baptised only in ye baptisme of Iohn in ye name of him y^t shold come after[)].* **Et cum imposuisset illis manus Paulus venit spiritus sanctus super eos & loquebantur linguis & prophetabant.** When Paul had set his hands vpon them the holy gost came vpon them, & they spoke with tonges of diuers languages, & prophecied.* And he willed his disciple and scoler **Titus,** whome he hadde made Bishoppe of Creta (whiche nowe we call the Ile of Candye,) to constitute and make priestes in euerye Citye. **Sicut & ego dis[p]osui tibi.** As I haue prescribed and geuen thee a rule,* and taught thee (saieth he) euen as he had [4C1ᵛ] ordered Timothe & him, euen so he taught them to promote and to geue orders to others. And as he expresseth there **Oportet Episcopum sine crimine esse.*** I wyll prosecute some pointes of Sainte Paules writinge to Titus in this matter, for it agreeth muche w^t his like sayinge to Timothe.* Fyrste he requireth that a preiste be **sine crimine,** without crime. A crime is more then a sinne, or a faulte, for it is a notable or a greate faulte, worthie to be accused and to be condempned. Some sinnes be lighter, and not dampnable, suche as is† very harde for any man to escape. And therefore saied s. Iohn in his epistle. **i. Io. i. Si dixerimus quoniam peccatum.** If we saie that wee have no sinne, or no fault, we deceiue & begile our selues, & there is no truth in vs,* specially of suche sinnes as the frailtie of man customablie falleth vnto, and can not well eschue them, whiche we call veniall sinnes. The wiseman speketh. **Pro. xxiiii. Septies in die cadit iustus, & resurget.** A iust man, a good man falleth .vii. times in a daie,* the determinate nomber is put for the vncertaine number. It is as much to saie, As a good man falleth ofte, and riseth againe. The scripture calleth him a iust man, and yet saith that he falleth, by which it is plain that such fallinge destroyeth not his iustice, Therfore it must nedes be taken of such fallynge or fautes without which man doth not leade his life in this wretched world. By ignorance, by obliuion, omission, or forgetting of duties vndone, bi surreption or priuy crepinge of matters into mens mindes, [4C2] by necessitie, by fragilitie of the flesh euery daye, either willingly, or against our wills we offend, & yet rise againe, so that such frailnes of the flesh of man hurteth not, nor destroieth a mans iustice or righteousnes, if he be a iust man or a good man where contrary the wiseman saith there. **Impij autem corruent in malum.** Because that wicked persons neither good to God, nor good to man doth runne downe headlonge to yll, to sinne, and to damnation.* So that when thei haue fallen by consent to sinne, penance, and repentance is laid aside and despised. And then must neades folowe eternall dampnation. Then to Saynte Iohns saiynge. **Si dixerimus. &c.** Of ve[n]iall sinnes it is plaine, for without suche we can not leade thys fraile life. And of deadlye sinne there is no man that can certainely and surely knowe what case he standeth in afore god, and whether he be worthye hatred, or the loue of GOD, except it be by special reuelation, then a manne affirminge him selfe to be cleare and without sinne, shoulde presume to farre proudlye boasting him selfe of such sinceritie, purenesse, and holinesse, as he was not sure of, and by that in dede should be in the sinne of pride and presumption, and not cleare. Then when Saint Paule saieth that **Titus** should promote to be a Prieste, such as be without crime, that is to saye: suche as be without any enorme detestable, and notorious faulte or vice, or sinne. **Oportet enim Episcopum sine crimine esse.** For a bishop must be without blot or blemish of crime [4C2ᵛ] And that is it y^t he saith to Timothe **.i. Ti. iii. Oportet episcopum irreprehensibilem esse.** without any

† is] it

matter by whych he maye be reproued as criminall.* And here is to be noted that euen now S. Paule spoke of the orderyng of priestes, and now by and by he telleth the same tale of bishops, saiyng: A bishoppe must neades be without crime, wherfore you must note that in the apostles time a priest and a bishop were all one, euerye Bishop was a priest, and so he is yet in oure tyme, and euery priest was a bishoppe, as it is taken plainly, and proued by these words of saint Paul here.* And this S. Ierome noteth in an epistle that he writeth ad euagrium, where he saith also that afterwarde in processe of tyme, they vsed to chose one to be preferred and made ouerseer and ruler ouer other, to auoyde scismes and diuisions in the churche, for feare lest euerye one inuentynge newe wayes and makyng partes, and drawyng a congregation after him, should breake the vnitie of the church.* And such a one so elect and chosen, & set in higher roume and state then the rest, they called **Episcopum a superintendent,** that is, a bishoppe, to take hede and ouersee the others.* Euen like as if in the tyme of warre, the hooste beynge destitute, or wythout a capitayne, should chose a capitayne amonge theim sel[u]es, and call hym their Emperoure, or as if the Deacones shoulde chose one amonge theim selues, whome they knew to be circumspect, wise, and diligente, and woulde call hym an Archedeacon, or chiefe-deacon, for what thinge is it that the Bishoppe doth [4C3] but a prieste dothe the same, excepte it be geuyng of orders, confirming of children, and some other consecrations and blessinges, which by common consent of the churche were geuen to the bishops office.* Saint Augustine in an epistle that he writeth to saint Ierom agreeth to the same, saiyng: **Quanquam secundum honorum vocabula, qui iam ecclesie vsus obtinuit Episcopatus presbiterio maior sit, tamen in multis rebus Augustinus Iheronimo minor est.** Although bi the termes of honour (which now the vse of the church hath goten) a bishop is greater then a priest, yet notwithstandyng in many thinges Augustine is lesse of reputation then Ierome, albeit Augustine were a bishop, and Ierome but a priest.* Wel then we must take it indifferently as well of a bishop as of a priest, yea and also of a deacon .i. Ti. iii. y^t they must be w^{t}out crime,* euen as it besemeth gods stuard of his spirituall treasure, which requireth a more truly minister then any worldly treasure doth. A priest also must not be proud, for a proud man thinking that his preferment to ye dignite of a priest, is more because of his excellencye and deseruynge, and because he thynketh hym selfe so necessary for the churche, that the congregation hathe neade of hym, and can not be wythout hym, and so falleth to contempne and despyse others that be as good and better then hee, and that falleth into the snares of the Deuyll. As Saynte Paule sayeth, **De neophitis. i. Timo. iii.** Where he woulde not haue hym promoted to be a Bishoppe or a Prieste that is a newe conuerse.* As who should [4C3^v] saye, yesterdaye at the Carte, or in the barne among his corne and his threshers, or in the common market, and to daye at the altare to entrete the sacrament, yesterday at the open sises, sessions lawe dayes, or the courtes, & to day to minister in the church, yesterdaye at dice and cardes, and all vnthriftye games, and to daye to turne and reade the holy bokes of the scriptures, or the holy masse boke, yesterdaye to dauncyng and daliing, and to daie to consecrate priestes, wydowes or virgyns. Such sodayn chaunges s. Paul liketh not, for fear lest they that be so newly promoted, wold sone forget them selues & their callinge, **Non Iracundum,** a prieste muste not be a fl[u]mishe or passionate man,* anone in a rage for euery turning of a straw, or for a triful, for he that is as a iudge amonge the people (as priestes be) muste weighe all matters afore they take theim to harte, leste in their anger they shal not see the ryght, but rather saye or do otherwise then reason woulde. **Iratus** is he that for some cause is kindled or moued, and prouoked to anger. **Iracundus** is hee that for lyghte occasion or small cause is moued to a[n]ger, Saincte Paule woulde not haue a Prieste to be sone on fire or angrye, but rather wyth Patience, longanimitye, and longe sufferaunce to beare with his neighboure, **Non vinolentum,** no greate drinkers of wyne,* they must bee, that be promoted to holye orders, speciallye aboue all menne, because that wee be sette [4C4] in the steade and place of the Apostles, therefore wee muste obserue not onely their wordes, & preachyng, but also there abstinence. **Nolite inebriari vino, in quo est luxuria,*** sayeth Sainte Paule. The filthinesse of Lecherye and carnall luste, commeth principallye of takynge to much wyne, and hoate or stronge drinkes, and with ouermuch feadynge, for it is true that Terence sayde. **Sine Cerere**† **& Baccho friget Venus.*** Esay sayeth. **Capi. v. Ve qui potentes estis ad bibendum vinum & fortes ad miscendam ebrietatem.** Woe be vnto you, eternall payne shall come to you that bee stronge to drinke Wine, and to mengle dronkennesse, not onelye to be dronke youre selues, but also to make others dronken.* Lette vs therefore aboue all other menne, remember the wyse mannes decree and sentence. **Cogitaui . . . a vino carnem meam abstinere, vt animam meam transferam ad Sapientiam. Ecclesiastes .ii.** I haue thoughte, decreed, and determyned my selfe too abstayne my Bodye frome Wyne, that soo I myghte tourne my Soule and wytte to Wisedome.* And wee reade of Da[n]yell and his fellowes. **Dany. ii.** That they refused the meates of the Kynges reward and from hys boarde, and toke pulse and hearbes of the Gardeyn to eate, and water to drynke, and so they became wyser then all their companions, & excellently learned in all bokes, & in all sciences.* For in very dede abstine*n*ce [4C4ᵛ] wyth study breadeth science and learning, which is most besemyng and necessarye for all prelates and priestes. **Non percussorem,** they muste not be lyght fingered, or readye to stryke, or to hurte anie manne.* As they be commonly that wyll not refrayn their passion or anger, and also they that be dronken wyth wyne, whiche the Apostle excludeth here immediately afore. And some men deuoutlye vnderstande, that **Non percussorem,** that he muste not by wordes in preachyng rappe at anye man, strikynge his conscience wyth peruerse and false doctrine, and with sedicious opinions. And Sainte Peter sayeth here. **Pascite qui in vobis est gregem dei, prouidentes non coacte, sed spontanee secundum deum neque turpis lucri gratia sed voluntarie.** Prelates and Priestes muste not be to desierous or gredye of vnhonest lucre, gaynes, or wynnynge.* You muste vnderstande that the occupiyng that well besemeth som man, is vnfitting and euil besemyng some other man. And that is honeste to one man, is filthye, vnhonest, and euyll besemynge to an other manne. A Draper, a Mercer, a Shomaker, and a hardwareman maye stande in the open Market and sel hys ware to the most aduauntage and gaine, thereby sufficientlye to sustayne hym selfe, and hys familye or housholde. A Knyght, a squyre, or a well landed manne maye not so do wyth hys honestye. It were filthye, shame, and dishonestye for hym so to dooe, and hys winnyng shoulde not bee but fylthye wynnynge, horrye shyfte, and shamefull gaynes.

[4D1] So a priest that hath refused worldly trouble & toyling, and giuen him selfe onelye to the seruice of God, may not with his honesty (yea but with his shame) giue him selfe to worldly cheuesance, marchandise, chopping and changing, byeng good chepe, selling deare. That occupying or gaynes that is tollerable and somwhat honest in other, is **turpe lucrum,** shameful gaines in him. But yet

† Cerere] Cero

there is a more filthy gaines that some prelates and priestes laboreth for, to the
great infamie of the churche, and that is the gredie appetite that they haue to get
winning at dise and cardes and suche vnlawfull games, and myspendinge theyr
good houres at the same. This is **vere turpe lucrum** filthy or vnhonest gaines. The
Philosopher **.iiij. Ethi.** saithe, that **turpe lucrum est quum aliquis parui lucri
gratia o[p]probrium sustinet,** filthye and vnhonest gaines or winning, is when a
man for small aduauntage susteineth shame or an ill name, and he putteth
example of disers, and gameners, and robbers of dead mens graues:* As we had
amongest vs these that steale plates of brasse with Epitaphies from mens graues or
tombes, or yron fram the grates or par<t>closes and al such priuy pikers, and also
hoores and horehunters.* Al such saith the Philosopher, **lucri gratia negotiantur
& opprobria sustinent,** they laye forth theyr ware for aduauntage, and getteth
dispite and shame therby,* and they be all **illiberales,** churles without liberalitie or
bountuousnes, or gentle harte, as it is plaine of these gameners which studieth to
get & win of theyr own friendes and lo[u]ers, to which [4D1ᵛ] they should rather
do good then harme. For amite and freendeshyp woulde that one freende should
help an other, rather then take from hym that he had, or apayre his liuinge. And
these fylthy commen strumpets, after they haue receyued theyr promise that they
looked for, careth not† thoughe his head were of, that euen now she occupied with
all. Saynt Peters mynde is and also Saynt Paules, that we shuld not apply our
mindes nor our labours to worldly lucre, by any kinde of marchandise or chafering,
and that we should not looke for gaynes, by anye kinde of gamning or vnhonest
exercise of our bodyes. As it were sayinge to e[u]ery one of vs, as well to priests as
to religious men or women, where any be. **Labora sicut bonus miles Christi Iesu.
Nemo militans deo implicat se negotijs secularibus vt ei placeat cui se probauit.
ii. Timo. ii.** Labour & take paynes as a good Sauiour† of Christ Iesu, of Goddes
retinue, no man nor woman, beinge a Souldier to God or of Gods retinue, wrap-
peth or intangleth him selfe in seculare or worldly busynes, or occupation,* we
must not turne our spirituall profession that we haue taken vpon vs, into worldly
exercise for lucre, that by Godlye exercise we may like good warriers please him, to
whome we haue geuen and promised our selues, and for whome we haue tried and
proued our selues, as euery man must do, that wyll take suche charge vpon him.
And some there be that maketh a marchaundise of the worde of God, vsinge their
preaching & teaching all for lucre & aduauntage, **turpiter affectantes lucrum,**
vnhonestly, gredy & hon[4D2]grie for money & lucre,* thinking all that lost that
goeth beside their berdes,* or that they cannot get, it greeueth them that any men
should open theyr mouthes in a pulpet but them selues, that so they might gather
in, their sermon nobles. If a good man or woman, by testament or other wayes, wil
or geue any money, for to haue certayne sermons preached, then they make shifte,
then they make freendes, that they may be the doers of it, more for the lucers sake,
then for zele to the soule health of their audience. S. Paule ouer & aboue yᵉ
properties afore rehersed, reciteth many other necessary for a priest, whiche were to
longe to be declared euery one,* which doubtles declareth a maruaylous sinceritie,
purenes & honesty, required a prelate or a priest, & in all them that haue gyuen
them selues to be Gods souldiers & ministers, of which conditions & qualities S.
Iherom saith **contra pelagi. Li. i. Nullus aut rarus est qui omnia habet que habere
debet episcopus,** either none ther be or very few or seldom seen, that haue al the
qualyties that a bishop ought to haue.* Then it is our parte, eueri one of vs to

labour to be one of those few, that so we may not only take honour & worship by
our orders, but also may do worship to yᵉ order. **S. Iohn Chrisost. de sacerdotio. Li.
vi.** saieth. **Functio sacerdotalis angelicam virtutem requirit etenim sacerdotis
animum solaribus radijs puriorem esse oportet ne quando spiritus sanctus deso-
latum illum reliquat vt dicere illi liceat viuo ego non amplius ego, viuit autem in
me Christus.** The office of a priest requireth the vertue of an Angell, for the
priestes soule and minde must be more pure & cleare [4D2ᵛ] then the sunne beames
for fear least the holi gost leaue him desolate and without his help and assistence, so
that the priest may say with Saynte Paul, I liue now no more I, not as I was and not
as I liued afore, for Christ liueth in me.* And in the thirde booke he saithe:
**Sacerdotium in terra[m] quidem per agitur ceterum in rerum celestium classem
ordinemque referendum est.** Priesthoode is occupied and vsed on earth, but it
must be referred & taken as into the order of heauen and of heauenly thinges. And
wel worthy (saith he) for no mortal man, no angel, nor archangell, neither anye
other creature, but the very holy gost himself hath disposed this order, for he was
the auctour and causer that mortal men yet abiding in the fleshe, shoulde conceiue
in their myndes this ministery, seruice and office of the angels.* Therfore a priest
must nedes be of such pure sanctimony and holynes, as thoughe he were set euen in
the heauen & stoode euen in the middle amonge the angels of heauen. This
Chrisostome declareth by a comparison of the misteries of the old law vnto our
misteries and secretes of the time of grace, saying: **terribilia namque atque horri-
fica fuisse feruntur. &c.** Men say that the thinges that went afore the tyme of
grace, were terrible and honorable* (as no doubt they were in theyr time) such
were the smal belles and pomegranates about the skirttes of the priestes vestiments.
The .xii. rich precious stones curiously set in yᵉ golden plate on the prestes brest.
And other precious stones set vpon his shoulders, his miter vpon his head, and his
riche and large [4D3] gyrdle about his middle, and his garment preciouslye brodred
and wroughte downe side to hys feete.* Then to consider the honour of the tabernacle, and afterwarde of the temple, and speciallye of that moste and reuerend part
thereof called **sanctum sanctorum,** the holyest part or place of al holy places, and
was diuided from the larger part called **sanctum,** by a riche veyle or curtain, which
at the time of Christes death was rent and torn down from the toppe to the neither
part, as it is playn in the gospel.* Then to consider the great & wonderous quietnes
and silence in the same temple vsed, with other circumstances about the same
ceremonies, surelye it is a wonderous thinge to muse vpon and to be remembred.
But yet (sayth Chrisostome) if we conuert oure contemplacion to consider what
thinges the time of grace hathe brought to vs, and woulde discusse and examyne
them, we should iudge all the sayd nobilitie and excellencie of the old testament to
be light and smal matters, and might saye wyth Saynte Paule **ij. Cor. iij. Nec
glorificatum est quod claruit in hac parte propter excellentem gloriam.** Where S.
Paule of purpose compareth the glory and the excellencie of the ministers of the
newe testament to the glory and ryaltie of the ministers of the old testament. That
thing that floorished and was had in glorye and riallie esteemed, was not glorified in
this behalfe, in respecte of the excellent glorye of the thinges of the new testament
of Christe.* As the Apostle sayth a litle before. **Si ministratio mortis litteris
deformata in lapidibus fuit in gloria, ita vt** [4D3ᵛ] **non possent intendere filij
Israell in faciem Moisi propter gloriam vultus eius que euacuatur quo modo non
magis ministratio spiritus erit in gloria? ii. Cor. iii.** If the seruice of death, described and written with letters in the stones of the two tabels, was had in glory and
reuerence so that the people of Israell coulde not looke vpon the face of Moyses,

which was the minister of that lawe for the glorie and shyning bryghtnes of his face, which is sone taken away, for it taried not.* How then can it be that the seruice of the spirite, by the grace of the new Testament should not be in glorie muche more? He calleth the ministration and service of the olde leuits & priests of Moyses law, the ministration and seruice of death,* bycause that Moyses lawe was the occasion of death of the soule, not of it self, but by the malice and yll will of man, whiche commonly laboreth and inclineth to the thing whiche is forbidden, & so runneth headlonge to breake the commaundementes of God, whiche be set forthe by Moyses law, and consequently to run headlong to death euerlasting. And also Moyses law is full of the comminations and threateninges of the death of the body, for the breakinge of it. He that gathered stickes on the holy daye was put to deth: he that missayde his father or mother, should die for it and such other.* Yet the ministers of the same were had in glorie & great reuerence, whiche the Apostle declareth by the glory & shyninge brightnes of the face of Moyses when he came [4D4] downe from the mount from GOD, bringinge downe with him the lawes, then his face had certayne bright & shining beames comming from it which appered to the people like hornes, ascending vpward from his face, so that the peoples eyes could not abyde the sight to loke vpon him, but runne backe awaye from him, in so muche that he was fayne to put a veyle, or a couerynge ouer his face when he spoke to them, and when he went vp to talke with God, he vncouered his face, and when he should declare Goddes pleasure to the people, he couered his face agayne that they myght more easly aproche and looke vpon him and heare him, as it is playne in the story. **Exo. xx[x]iiii.*** Of this the Apostle Saynte Paule argueth. If the ministration and seruice of death, whiche also is euacuate, abolished and gon, were had in glory and reuerence as it was in deede, as appereth by the storie now rehersed, then muche more the ministration and seruice of the spyrite of the new law and Testa[m]ent, in whiche the holye spiryte of GOD is gyuen to faythfull people, whyche is also the seruice of loue, and of libertie of the soule, must needes be had in glory and in reuerence.* For in comparyson of the glory of the lawe of the Gospel and of the law gyuen by Chryst, the former<,> glory , and clearenes of Moyses law, is not seen but vanysheth awaye, euen like as the light of the Moone or of the sterres, is hyd and sheweth not by the light of the son in a clere day. [4D4ᵛ] Then saith Chrisostome conuerting his contemplacion to our misteries of the new testament of Christ, and to the ministers of the same.* Let vs consider (among other thinges) how it is committed to them here dwelling on earth in thys mortall bodye, to dispence and bestowe the treasure and riches of heauen, for it is giuen to priestes to haue suche power as almighty God would neyther giue to the angels, not to any of the archangels, or to any other angels of heauen. For it was neuer sayd to any of them, whatsoeuer thou loosest on earth, shal be losed in heauen, whatsoeuer thou bindest on earth, shall be bounde in heauen.* This bonde toucheth the very soule of men, and reacheth vp euen to heauen aboue, so that what[e]uer the priest doth in this behalfe here beneth on earth, almighty God doth ratifie and alowe the same aboue in heauen, and he beyng the lord and mayster, doth aproue the sentence of his seruant. Now what maye a man call this els but that in maner al the power in heauen is committed and graunted to the priest, for Christ sayth, whosoeuer sinnes you forgiue, thei be forgiuen, and whosoeuer sinnes you restrayne or bynde, they be restraint & bound.* Tel me (saith Chrisostom) what power can be giuen greater then this one? The father hath giuen to the sonne all power in heauen and earth. But now I see (saythe Christostome) the same power the sonne hath giuen to the prest which the father hath giuen to him.* Imagyn that if a noble king had gyuen to one of hys faythfull and true seruauntes or subiectes power to caste [4E1] into prison whom it pleased him, and to take him out of prison againe or ani other prisoner that he thought wel to do, such a man should be counted a marueilous man, and in great fauour with his souerayne and worthy to be highly estemed of all the realme. And it were a plaine madnes for anye man to despise such an auctoritye, euen so it were a manifest madnes to despise or litle regard that authoriti, without which we can not obtain our soule helth here in this world (saith Chrisostom) nor can obtaine the good promisses of the ioyes of heauen. Here you must vnderstand Christostom that he speaketh of them that be of age and dyscretion, and hath time and oportunitie to vse the sacramentes which the priest ministreth. For no man can come to heauen, except he be regenerate by water and by the holy gost, and he that eateth not the fleshe of Christ, & drinketh not his blood, can not haue life euerlasting.* Al these thynges be performed and brought to passe by the priest, then how can it well be that without theyr helpe wee may escape the euerlasting fyre of hell, or obtaine or wyn the reward of the eternall garlande and crowne of glorye? These bee they, these be they (I say) to whom the spiritual trauelyng and the byrthes or deliueraunce of soules to God be put to, and they be put in credite and trust with them. By them we put on vs Christe for our garment, when we be made Cristen men, by theym we be buried with Christe by baptisme, as Saint Paul speaketh, and be made the limmes and the members of hys blessed body.* For these considerations [4E1ᵛ] we ought to feare them, & to do them more honour, then to our carnall father, for by our carnall parentes, we be borne, **ex sanguinibus & voluntate carnis,** of bloud, & the p[l]easure of the flesh,* but these men, these priests, be the aucthors and doers of that byrth, which we haue of God, and of that blessed regeneration and trew liberty, by which we be made the children of God, by adoption and speciall grace. The Iewes priestes of Moyses law had power, not to pourge & clense the bodie from leprie of them that were infecte with the same disease,* but rather to discerne & judge, whether men were purged or not purged from that disease, and yet was their priesthod, in hie estimacion and ambitiously desired, as appered bi **Chore, Dathan and Abyron,** * which for their obstinate and greedie desyre sanke into Hell, the earth opened and swalowed them vp, with all theyr confederacie. Then consider how the priesthod of the new Testament, is amplified & made of more sanctimonie, by reason of the most holie misteries and sacramentes with whiche it is exercised, then euer was the priesthod of Moyses law. For Christes priestes doth not only declare and iudge whether men be purged fro[m] the lepres of the soule or not, but rather doeth purge them in deede, by the power that Christ hath geuen to them. Therfore (after Chrisostom) looke howe great difference there is betwixt vehement loue and desire of a thing, and the contempt or despising of a thing, so greatly thei that despiseth the holy priesthod of Christes ministers be more de[4E2]testable & to be reproued, then euer were **Chore and Dathan,** and their confederacy, which with so ardent and feruente desyre aspired to the priesthod of Moyses time. The one sanke downe into the gapinge earth, which swalowed them downe into Hell, then let not the other thinke to escape, without more shame and vengeaunce. Moreouer yet further to compare the priestes to our naturall parentes. Almighty God hath geuen to priestes more power vpon vs, then to our naturall parentes. For our parentes begetteth vs into this present temporall lyfe, but the priestes getteth vs into euerlasting life. Our carnall parentes, can nother saue vs from temporall sickenes nor from temporal death, but the priestes not only when they regenerate vs by water and with the holy spirite, or when by their holy doctrine, they recouer vs from vice to vertu, but also when we be bodyly sicke, & also sicke in our soule, they cure and heale vs, obtayning by the succour and help of their prayers, bothe health of body and soule, witnesseth S. Iames, Iaco. vlt. Infirmatur inter vos aliquis, accersat presbiteros ecclesie & orent super eum vngentes eum oleo in nomine domini & oratio fidei saluabit infirmum et alleuiabit eum dominus et si in peccatis sic remittentur ei. When any man amonge you is sicke, let him sende for the priests of the church & let them pray ouer him, & anoynt him with oyle in yᵉ name of our Lord & the praiers of faythfull persons shal saue yᵉ sick, & our lord shal set him vp agayn. And if he be in sinnes, they shalbe forgiuen him.* Natural parents cannot help theyr children, [4E2ᵛ] if they offende against princes or kinges in anye poynt of treason or greuous offence, where priestes many times obteineth grace, mercy, and fauour for theyr spirituall children, not of mortall princes, but of almighty God, when he is offended with them. Well thys excellencie of priesthod considered, which I haue now at large declared euer presupposing their excellency, power and auctority to be principallye vpon the soule of man, in such things and doinges as be toward God, to whom be all honour & glory for euer. Amen.

¶The .xix. treatise or
sermon.

WOrshipful frendes, I truste you remember that in my laste sermon that I made in
this place, I entred on the fift chapter of Saynt Peters first epistle, In which I
declared vnto you, how Saynte Peter like as he had giuen good and godly lessons
to all kynde & maners of men and women, maryed and single, masters and
seruauntes, bondmen and freemen, so because the ministers of the church shuld
not lak learning, he instructeth prelates and priests, and informeth them of theyr
d[u]tie, alluring al priestes to giue credence to his doctrine, by that he pro[4E3]fes-
seth him selfe to be a priest, and one of such experience of the affayres of our
Sauiour Christe that had sene, as well the glory of Christes glorified body at his
transfiguration, as also the vexacion that he suffred in the whole processe of his
painful passion, and that he was partaker of the same.* And then consequentlye I
descended to speake of the order of priesthode, and of the dignity of the same
which I declared at large bi the scriptures and by the auncient writers holye
fathers. And I had litle thanks for my labour, specially of them that beinge priestes
be ashamed of that name, and of likelyhood would faine be discharged of theyr
order, if they could tell howe, & most agreued they were with me, because I said
nothing in the defence of theyr shameful and incestious bawdry, which they would
couer wyth the name of matrimony, so by them sclaundring that holy sacrament.*
Then I declared many properties of a good priest, which (to exchew prolixitie) I
will now not rehearse againe, for I trust you haue not al forgotten them. These
properties of a good priest or prelate thus declared, let vs see what Saint Peter now
here in the letter willeth them to do: **Pascite qui in vobis est gregem dei,** Feede
the flocke of God that is vnder your hand.* Because that now lateli this matter of
the diuersitie of shepeheards and pastours was very well and aboundantly handled
and declared, I wil passe ouer it, presupposing these good properties afore rehersed
of him that shal be a good shepheard or pastour. We must take heede to our [4E3ᵛ]
charge **Act. xx. Attendite vobis & vniuerso gregi in quo vos spiritus sanctus
posuit episcopos, regere ecclesiam dei quam acquisiuit sanguine suo.** Take hede
to your selfe (sayth S. Paule to the priestes & prelates of Ephesus) and to all the
whole flocke, in whiche the holy goost hath set you bysshops.* Lo, here he calleth
them byshops, they were not then all in such preminence or so set in aucthoritie
or superioritie aboue others, as bishops were then sone after: and be now, but he
meaneth priestes, afore he called them **maiores natu ecclesie,** the elders of the
church or congregation.* Now he calleth the same byshops, these S. Paule biddeth
take hede to their flocke. Saynt Peter byddeth them feede their flocke, as Christe
had commaunded Peter to feede his lammes and to feede his sheepe,* his people
whiche should be lyke lammes, full of simplicitie, tractablenes and gentlenes<.>
which Christ willeth all them that wilbe saued by him to vse. So Saynt Peter
descendeth as by an ordinate Iherarchie, and giueth like charge to such as he had
constitute and ordeyned to be curates after him, willing them to feede the flocke,
prouidentes non coacte prouiding for them without **coaction*** They must wyth
discrete solicitude and studie prouide such pasture and feedinge for them, as shall
be good and holsome, & not driuing them to ranke feeding that wil bane them: to
corrupte ground, as to a certayne spire white grasse,* that growith in some
grounde, or to groundes that be morish, maresh or otherwise vnholsome, & like to
coothe the flocke, for suche the flocke moste [4E4] desyreth. And yf they be let

runne at their owne libertie, to suche feeding they wyll draw, rather then to holsome pasture. Beware that you pasture not, nor feede the people with sedicious lernynge or opynions of Heresy, for suche semyth at the fyrste shew white, fayre and† plesaunte, yet baninge it is, and shall vtterly destroye the flocke. You must not also let them runne to muche to the ranke feedinge of carnall lyberty, for that shall puffe them vp, and make them swell vp, to Pride and disobedience, and consequently to take their pleasure by all carnall lustes, and so shall rotte them and destroy them for euer. Feede Christes flocke with holie doctrine of Gods word, making them to obey their rulers, that be set in aucthorite ouer them. And here in this realme, to haue in greate reuerence the kinges Maiestie, and in all our doynges to be obedient vnto his lawes:* As well the Prelates and preachers in their sermons and exhortations, as the subiectes in performinge and doinge the same. For it is our parte to captiuate our wittes, and to credite our superiors, not thinking our selues better learned then any others be, but rather thinking yᵗ thing that is set forthe by his grace with the assent of his clergy & of his honorable counsell, to procede of higher knowledge then our wits can attain to, **Non coacte,** their feeding & prouision for gods folcke, must be frank and free without **coaction.** For al the workes of our religion must come of a good wyl, folowing the example that we haue of the old Testament. [4E4ᵛ] In the makinge of the tabernacle and the ornamentes to the same belonginge, all the people of Israel with deuout minde and with a free harte and wil, offred theyr fyrst frutes and such iewels as they had, to the furniture of the same, and the workemen also offered them selues freely to doe theyr woorkes,* as a figure and signe and token that in the spiritual edifying of the spiritual temple of God, which we be: the doers and builders priestes and curates, preachers & teachers shuld do theyr labours of theyr owne accord, withoute any gredy eye to gather riches by the same, or to despise any others by theyr doings. And yet thei shall not dye for defaut, but according to Saynt Paules doctrine, theyr audience that hath spiritual foode of them, must be diligent and liberall† to helpe them in al necessarie temporalites, and to see that they lacke not, **Neque vt dominantes in cleris.** Beware of the lowring browes and proud lookes and hartes of the old Pharisies, thei loke for dominion, they wil be like lordes & maisters, they wil be had in reuerence, they wil haue cappe and knee, and not onely that, but also wyll looke for presentes, giftes, and bribes, and doe litle or nothing therefore: Saint Peter would not that anye priestes shoulde so vse theym selues but rather to be in manner felowlyke, humblye and lowelye behauynge theym selues amonge theyr brothers, so giuyng to them as wel as to the lay fee example of humilitie, and lowlynes, affabiliti and gentlenes.* Remember our sauiour Christes saying in the parable of the yl seruant. **Mat. xxiiij** [4F1] If the yll seruaunt saye or thinke in his hart, my master tarieth very longe, he commeth not home now all is in my hande, all is in my gouernance, then he beginneth to play the lorde, & then he beginneth to strike & vex his felows, & as one that had forgotten him selfe, & also his lord or master, geueth him self to eatyng & drinking with dronkerds & riatours: then wil come home his master at the time when he was not loked for. And shal deuide him the soule from the bodie, & shall caste parte of him his soule firste, and after the whole bodie and soule together with hypocrites, that is to saie, with false christen people, reprobate, & damned, there as shall be weping and gnashinge of teeth.* By this seruaunt spoken of in this parable, be all euyll rulers vnderstanded, which as thei folow the Lordly maners of this cruell seruaunt here mencioned, so they shall

† and] ond; liberall] leberall

haue like punishement, and shal be likewise tormented in hell for euermore. Beware therefore of plaiynge the Lordes amonge your brethren, but be as one of them Ex[ ]animo,† with hart and all,* that they may likewise shewe them selues to the people that they muste teach. And thus doinge (saieth saint Peter) when the prince of pastors our sauiour Christ shall come in his glory at the generall iudgment, you shall receiue the crowne or garlande of euerlastyng glory and ioyes of heauen that shall neuer fade, welowe, or widder awaye, but shall be euer fresshe and pleasaunte, aboue that anye minde of mortall man can apprehende, perceiue, or vnderstand to our endlesse solace and comfort [4F1ᵛ] whiche. &c. It foloweth in the texte. **Similiter adolescentes subditi estote senioribus.*** When he hathe fatherlye instruct and taughte the Presidentes, the Prelates and Priestes, that they should take paine and solicitude or care to feade their flockes, and to prouide suche pastures for theim as shoulde bee most holesome, and not infectuous, coothinge or rottynge groundes too feade vppon for to bane theim. And that thys they shoulde dooe with a good will, and not by coaction or compulsion against their willes. And that they shoulde not playe the Lordes and tyrantes among their cleargie, but that they shold shewe theim selues as the fourme, the patrone, or fashion of their flocke, and to be familiar with theim as one of theim, that by their behauioure their neighbours maye learne to conforme and fashion theim selues to the maner that they see them vse, promisinge theim that for their so doinge they shall receiue a rewarde inestimable, that is to saye: the freshe and vnfadinge crowne and garlande of eternall and euerlasting glorye, when the prince of pastours our sauiour Christe shall appeare in his maiestie at the general iudgment, to reward euery man after his deseruings. Nowe consequently, the blessed apostle teacheth yongelynges, yongemen and women, howe they shoulde behaue theim selues towarde their elders as to their betters, and that they shoulde be subiecte, and submit theim selues vnto theim and to obey theim, **similiter.*** Likewise as youre Elders muste care and prouide for your Soule [4F2] health without coaction, euen from the bottome of their hartes, so muste you euen from the hart with a good will without coaccion obeye them, that so youre rulers maie doe their duties gladlye and comfortablie, and not with sorowe, or to their paine, for that shall not profite you, as Sainte Paule saieth. **Hebr. xiii. Obedite prepositis vestris & subiacete eis ipsi enim peruigilant quasi rationem pro animabus vestris reddituri, vt cum gaudio hoc faciant & non gementes hoc enim non expedit vobis.** Obey theim that be set in auctoritye ouer you, and submit and lowelye subdue your selues vnto theim, for they watche and take paine to ouersee you, as menne that should yelde and make accompte for your Soules, them you muste obey so gentlye that they maye haue ioye and be gladde to take paynes for you, and not to grone or mourne in their solicitude and pains takynge, for that is not profitable for you.* Obey theim that Preache and teache you the worde of GOD, speciallye takinge hede to their doctrine howsoeuer their liuynge be. If their condicions be noughtie, then as Christe teacheth vs. **Que dicunt seruate & facite, secundum opera eorum nolite facere. Math. xxiii.** What they saie take hede and do it, but after their doynge dooe not you, When they saye, and liue not or do not accordynge to their saiynge.* **Vt cum gaudio hoc faciant.** That they maie be glad of their labours taking among you,* like as an husbandman which is glad to do his work, when he seeth the trees of his setting & graffing proue well, & bear fruites, [4F2ᵛ] When he seeth the fieldes of his tillynge beare plentifullye suche Corne or grayne as hee

† Ex animo] Examino

hathe sene, then he perceiueth that he hath not laboured in vayne, bende his backe, and galled hys handes in vayne, and that he hath not without some cause suffered and borne the heat of Somer, and the colde of Winter: he is gladde of his paines taking, this shal make him glad and merie so to do an other time. And euen so shall the elders be glad, when they see their yonge men or subiectes, whether it be in thynges perteining to God, or els to the worlde profite, and go forwarde by their informations and labours taken amonge them, and will be sorie and soore agreued of the contrarie. And this will do you no profite, but rather hurte. It shall do theim good to be sorye for your euill doinge, or for your not profitinge, but it shall dooe you no good but rather hurte, in as muche as beside youre euill doinge, you vexe your Heades, Ouerseers, and rulers, and so aggrauate your owne vyces and leudenesse. Therfore saieth saint Peter. **Adolescentes subditi estote senioribus,** * Where you shall vnderstand that there be two maners of yongelinges. Some be yonge for lacke of many yeres, as the worde is commonly taken, others be worthy to be counted yongelinges because they haue younge, lyghte, leude, and childishe condicions, more like children, then like sadde menne or women of naturall and rype grauitye and discretion. Such a distinction of younge persones, vseth the Philosopher in the beginninge of hys [4F3] firste booke of the Ethikes,* declarynge who and what maner of menne be meete and profitable hearers of Morall philosophy, or of matters of Policye, where he hathe this conclusion. That younglinges be not moste meete hearers or scholers of Morall philosophye, whiche he proueth thus. The proper and conueniente Hearer or learner of anye science or facultye, must be suche as can surelye and euidentlye, or plainely knowe the principles and conclusions of that Science when they hear them, and that can of them geue right iudgement, whether they be wel to be done or contrarye. But younglynges can not so doe, therfore they be not meete hearers of that facultie. That they can not so do, he proueth: for the principles and conclusions of all Moral philosophye, and of all worldlye policye, be of mannes actes and doinges, whiche be not well knowen, but onelye by experience, and of them the yongmen haue none experience, and therfore of them they haue no perfite iudgemente, no more then a Prentice newe bounde to the Drapers crafte can by his hande or by his eye geue true iudgement whether the clothes in his masters shoppe be truelye and surelye wrought and coloured or not: or the Grocers prentice whether the spices and other wares in his masters shoppe be quicke or tainted or whether they maie be solde to losse or to gaynes. They muste haue longe experience afore they can come to suche knoweledge. Euen so muste they haue experience of mens doinges that shall be good morall Philosophers, or poli[4F3ᵛ]tyke persons, and suche be not these yongelings that take noo heede to grauitie and sadnesse. And thys is true (sayeth the Philosopher) whether they be younge in yeares or younge, **secundum morem,** in maners and conditions,* as be these younge ruffians and lustye bloudes. They be to obstinately and stifelye bended, and set to folow their owne passions and appetites, thinkynge the waye that they bee noseiled in, brought vp, and vsed to, to be best. They wyll not bee persuaded nor counsailed, but euen as they haue bene vsed and brought vp, that wyll they vse, and so will they continue by their good will who so euer saie naye. Teache them how to vse theim selues temperatelye in their dietes, in eatinge and drinkinge to auoide ingurgitations and riotynge by nighte and by daye, it helpeth not, how to vse theim selues chastelie according to <to> the Lawes of righte reason, or patientlie agaynste fumes or passions and anger, moderate liberalitie, against prodigalitye and waiste, they bee so wilfull, they be so wanton, they bee wedded to folowe their owne passions to folowe their

olde trade as they were wonte to dooe, more lyke childrene then like menne, that
it boteth not to exhorte theim to the contrarye. The holye Scripture speaketh of
suche youngelynges **.iii. Regum .xii.** where it is writte that after the deathe of
Salomon the kynge, succeaded hym Roboam his sonne. And when the power of
the whole Realme came [4F4] to crowne him and make him kynge, and to professe
their obedience to him, first they desiered one peticion of him, saiynge: after this
maner our father laied on vs a verye harde, and heauie burthen, therefore our
desire is, that nowe you shall diminishe and bate a little of youre fathers harde and
soore commaundemente, and of that verye heauye yoke that he layde vppon vs,
and we shall dooe you seruyce.*

This heauye yooke and burden was no vyle seruyce that Salomon putte theim
to, for it is written. **Capite .ix.** that Salomon sette or put none of the people of
Israell to anye Seruile woorke or drudgerie,* but these soore coactions were certayne money, graine, and vitailes, whiche they payed euerye moneth towarde the
furniture of the charges of Salomons house and familye, whiche were verie greate
in dede, as appeareth **.iii. Regum .iiii.*** And for thys purpose there were twelue
rulers, or maister purueyours assigned by the Kinge, ouer e[u]erye trybe one, beside
their vndertakers and gatherers, and some purloyners, by suche the people were
greuouslye oppressed, as appeareth by their humble Supplication here made. Well
the younge kinge somewhat amased at their request, badde the people departe till
the thirde Daye after, and then they shoulde haue an aunswere what hee wolde
doe.* In that tyme hee consulted, firste wyth the aunciente Fathers and graue
Counseylours that were of [4F4ᵛ] counsaile with Salomon the Kinge his father,
whiche gaue hym this counsayle. **Si hodie obedieris populo huic & seruieris &
peticioni eorum censeris locutusque fueris ad eos verba le[n]ia erant tibi serui
cunctis diebus.** If you do after the pleasures of these people this daye, and do geue
place to their peticion, and if you will speake to them soft and gentle words, they
will be your louing seruants at all times.* But he reiected this sage and wise
counsaile that these graue menne gaue him, and called to him the lustye bloudes
and yonge ruffians that were noursed from youth, and brought vp with him, and
were at hande euery daye with him for his solace and pastime, and saide vnto
them: what counsaile will you geue to aunswere this people that haue sayde to me,
make lyghte this yoke and ease vs of it that your father hath laied vppon vs? Then
they saide accordynge to their wilfull wittes lackynge experience. Thus shall you
saie vnto theim. **Minimus digitus meus grossior est derso patris mei.** My least
finger is greater and stronger then my fathers backe, or then his whole bodye. My
father layed on you a heauie yoke, and I will laye on more peyse vppon your yooke:
My father did beate you wyth scourges, but I will beate you with scorpions.* These
scorpions be scourges hauyng knottes of wire or leadde on the coardes, and
speciallye on the endes, And they be so called after a certayne venemous Worme,
whiche when he stingeth, turneth vp his tayle ouer his heade, and so styngeth, and
so perelouslye, that withoute there bee [4G1] hadde by and by a certaine Oyle of
scorpions [(]in whiche Oyle suche scorpions haue beaten theim selues to death)
there is no healpe nor remedye, but present death.* Of this compasse stroke that
the Scorpion maketh when he stingeth, the said scourges haue their name, because they winde about the bodye, and breake or teare sorest at the endes of the
coardes with the saide knottes of wires or leadde. His aunswere was as he should
saie, loke what payne of oppression or exactions, or other griefes my father did put
you to, and I will put you to more, and sorer handle you then euer did he. Here was
an aunswere euen like the wittes of his cocbrained counseilours. A folishe rashe,

and noughty aunswere, and so came of it. The people were so galled, exasperate and greued with this answer, that of y^c .xii. tribes of Israell .x. tribes shronke from him, and refused hym, and were neuer after subiect to him, nor to any of his issue. So that of the .xii. parts of hys realme he lost .x. & onely .ii. tribes Iuda and Beniamin sticked to him, and folowed him.* And all thys came so to passe, because he folowed yonge counsaile. And you muste not thinke that these counseilours were children, or younge in age, for as the Scripture saieth, they were noursed and brought vppe wyth the younge kynge Roboam.* And when he begonne hys raigne he was one and fortye yeares of age, and then of lyke age muste hys mates bee. And that is the tyme when menne shoulde haue mooste preignaunt wittes to geue good counsayle. And he [4G1^v] that hath not learned some experience or practice and trade of the world by that age will neuer be wise.* Yet it were good they had a creanser somewhat to stay them, that they runne not to eternall damnation. And though it will be hard to make an olde dog to stoupe, yet stoupe he must y^t wil be saued.* And therfore .s. Peter saieth here. **Omnes inuicem humilitatem insinuate**. All men stop & shew humilitie one to another,* euery man be lowly one to another, euen as that you wolde one crepe into an others bosome by lowlinesse, **Insinuate**, by which he meaneth an inward & harty lowlinesse that we must vse amonge vs. If thou wilt not, god will make thee to come alow, for god loueth no pride, but euer resisteth them y^t be proude. And sheweth grace to them that be lowly in hart, saith s. Peter, Iames **.Iac. iiii.** saith the same, how God hath euer resisted the proud,* you maie know how Lucifer the most excellent aungell for his pride was pulled downe and made the fowlest deuill in hell, he said he would ascende and get vp to be equal and like the highest. Nay not so (saith god) but thou shalt be cast downe to the bottom of the lake, or dungeon of hell.* Eue our first mother she wold haue ben a Goddesse, & like to god in knowlege, but God stopped her of her enterprise, & cast her into such blinde darknes & ignorance as we al be in, by occasion geuen by her.* And then what humilitie and lowlines hath done, yea, and in them which at other times were very proude & out of Gods fauour, appereth by Pharao the kinge of Egipt, which after the great stroke of vengeance [4G2] & horrible plage of hail stones, with whirle windes, thunder, and lightenynge, suche as was neuer sene sithe Egipte was firste made.* The said kinge begonne to take remorse for his obstinacye and begonne to relente, and saide vnto Moyses and Aaron. **Peccaui etiam nunc, dominus iustus est: & ego & populus meus impii, orate Dominum. &c.** I haue offended nowe agayne, oure Lorde is iuste and righteous, I and my people be nought and wycked, praye you to your lorde that these Thunders and Haylestormes maye cease, that I maye dimisse you, and let you go, so that you tarye not here anye lenger. **Exo. ix.*** Like wise when that wicked kyng Achab hearde the terrible comminations of God for the deathe of Naboth, & for other his and his wiues noughty liuinge.* **Scidit vestimenta sua, & operuit silicio carnem suam ieiunauit***que*** & dormiuit in sacco, & ambulauit demisso capite factus est autem sermo domini ad Heliam Thesbitem, dicens: Nonne vidisti humiliatum Achab coram me? quia igitur humiliatus est mei causa non inducam malum in diebus eius.** He toore hys cloothes and couered his bodye wyth clothe of Heere. And he fasted, and laye and slepte in sackeclothe, and wente loutynge and holdynge downe the heade. And then the worde of our Lorde God came to Helie, saiynge: Doest thou not see howe Achab the kinge is become lowlye afore me? Therefore because he is humiliate for because of mee, I wyll not brynge in thys mischiefe of punishemente in his tyme.*

[4G2ᵛ] And Nabuchodonosor king of the Caldeis* after his great pride that he had conceiued by his great and prosperous successe and spede that he had in his great conquestes and in his great glorye and pride that he had of his noble & large citie which he had amplified exceadingly four square, so that euery side of the square (as it is written of it[)], was xvi. mile long when he said: **Nonne hec est Babilon ciuitas magna quam edificaui in domum regni, in robore fortitudinis mee, & in gloria decoris mei? cumque sermo adhuc esset in ore regis, vox de celo ruit. Tibi dicitur Nabuchodonosor rex, Regnum tuum transibit a te & ab hominibus eiicient te & cum bestiis atque feris erit habitatio tua fenum quasi bos comedes, & septem tempora mutabuntur super te donec scias quod dominetur excelsus in regno hominum, & cuicumque voluerit det illud. Eadem hora.** Is not this Babilon the great city that I haue builded for a palaice of mi kingdom in the might of my manlines, and in the glory of my beauty. And euen while this saiynge was in the kings mouth, a voice came al in hast from heuen. This is said to thee Nabuchodonosor king. Thi kingdome shal go from thee, and thei shal cast thee out from mans company, and thy abiding shall be with wilde beastes. Thou shalt eate hey like an oxe. And seuen yeares shall chaunge and will go ouer thee, vntill thou knowe that there is a highe one yᵗ is lord in the kingedome of men, & that he may geue it to whom soeuer he wil **Eadem hora.** The same time this worde and saiynge was performed, he was striken with such amencye and madnes that he ranne abrode out of mens companye, he eat hay [4G3] & grasse like a best, he lay forth out of any house. The dewe, raine, haile, and snow fel on his body, his nails growed out like an eagle or a kites cleis & the heere of his head clotted together as longe as an eagles winges. Then after that seuen yeres were spent vpon him after this maner, almighty god that toke away the vse of his wit, restored it vnto him again, then he lift vp the eyes of his body & of his soule vnto almighty god, he lauded & praised god whose power is euerlasting, & al that it p[l]easeth him he doth as well in heuen aboue, as among them that dwelleth on erth, & there is none that can resist his hand & power, or that can saye to him, why hast thou done so?* Therfore nowe (saith he) I Nabuchodonosor laude and magnify and glorify the king of heuen, for all his workes are true, & al his waies be iudgemente. **Et gradientes in superbia potest humiliare. Dan. iiii.** And them that goeth in pride, he can humiliate & pul down, as it proued in effect by him self in dede.* When he exceaded in pride, God resisted him & pulled him downe. And when he knew him selfe and became lowly, god sent him grace euen as .s. Peter sayth here. In the new testament we haue examples of the proude Pharisey and the lowlye Publicane, one was repelled for his pryde, the other was Iustified and alowed for hys lowlinesse.*

And generallye, all the Scribes and Phariseis whyche did all their workes that they dyd, that they might be sene and praysed for their doyngs whiche euer proued nought at lengthe, and preuayled not, where contrarywise the humilitye [4G3ᵛ] of the blessed virgin Marye mother of Christe, & the meke lowlines of al Christes disciples which they learned of him obteined grace here, and glory euerlasting at their end. **Humiliamini igitur sub potenti manu dei vt vos exaltet in tempore visitationis** Considering therfore these examples how pride hath a fal, & preuaileth not wher humilite & lowlines is exalted & set aloft. Therfore concludeth s. Peter that you and all we must be made lowe in our harts vnder the mighty hand of god, that it may please him to exalt vs at the time of hys visitation,* as well euery man for him self, when euery man shall depart out of this worlde, as at his great and general visitation, at the generall iudgement, when he shal call to accompt all

that euer died sithe the beginning of the world till that time. And then according
to the philosophers rule. **Sicut simpliciter ad simpliciter, sic magis ad magis &
maxime ad maxime.*** As they that be humiliat and made lowly in hart now in this
time of battel against our gostly enemies, shalbe exalted and set aloft in glorye, so
he that is more lowlye, shall be more exalted in glorye, and he that is moste lowly
shalbe most exalted among them that for their humilitie shalbe exalted, & contrary he that here is exalted by pride, shall be made mooste lowe, in paines
euerlastinge. Yet furthermore to declare the nature of this vertue of Humilitie, you
shall vnderstande that Humilitye in vs and in Christe, of whome, and by whom
wee muste learne to be lowelye, is not in all poyntes after one maner in hym and in
vs. For in vs humi[4G4]litye is a vertue that by hys offyce restrayneth and kepeth
downe the appetite of manne frome inordinate desire of excellencye that a man
hath not yet obteined, but as it were beynge content with the state that a man
hath alreadye. An other office is to incline a mans wil or appetite not to vse or
shew to ye vttermost such power, might, honour, or auctorite as a man hath. Now
because there could be in Christ no such inordinate desire neither any excellency
able to be desired aboue y^t which he had continually from the moment of his
conception, yea, and by his Godhead euer afore ye worlde was made, therfore
humilitie in Christe was not after the first maner, but was in hym onelye after the
other office of humilitie, by whiche he kept close his mighty power, & euer shewed
him selfe curteous, gentle, patient, and as an vnderlinge to euery man. And all for
to geue vs example to kepe a low saile,* & not to haue any hy opinion of our
selues, thinkynge our feete there, as our head wil neuer come.* As they haue,
which when they can read the english Bible, thinke thei haue as perfite vnderstandyng of the Scripture as though they hadde studied in it forty yeares.* Wee muste
vse lowlinesse bothe wayes, that is to saie: by Humilitye to keepe downe our hartes
from desire of exaltation aboue our callyng. And also not to bragge or boaste of
that little that wee haue, thynkynge our selues a great deale better then other bee,
but rather thinking euerie man better than we be, as hauinge some gift of God,
that we haue not. In humilitie. **Su[4G4^v]periores sibi inuicem arbitrantes.** Sayth
S. Paule. **Phil. ii.** By humilitie you euery one must thinke an other† better then
you.* Therfore it is not without cause, that the apostle s. Peter so ernestly,
exhorteth vs to humilitie, as to the vertu contrary to pride, which the world doth
hoyst vs vp vnto, & not for any profite vnto vs but rather contrary for our
ouerthrowe and downe fall, euen as the menne of Nazareth ledde Christe to the
toppe of the hill on whiche their Citie was builded, onlie bycause they would haue
pitched him downe & haue broke his necke, but he so inuisiblie conueyd him self
away amonge them, that they had not theyr purpose. And the deuill caried our
sauiour Christ & set him on a galerie of the temple, bycause he would haue had
him pitch him self downe to the grounde,* & therfore humiliation is necessarie for
him that wilbe saued. And al thinges considered, we haue no cause to be proude at
al, but we haue manie causes to be lowlie consideringe our owne miserie, first how
miserably & how vnclenly we were gotten, & as vnclenly borne, & then how
wretched we be in our education, nursing & bringing vp, where euery beast by and
by, as sone as he commeth into the worlde can make some shyfte for him selfe to
finde the teete or other kinde of feedynge, man canne make none suche shyfte but
rather yf helpe were not, should forthwith perysh. Then in processe of our life,
how many infirmities we bee subiecte vnto, Pockes, Meesils, Axes, and Agues,

† other] order

sweatinge Pestylence, besyde troubles and vnquietnes of the mynde, [4H1] and how miserably we lyue in soule dayly offendinge him that made vs, almightie God by this vnthrifty and naughty breder of sinne, the nurse of sinne, which the Apostle calleth sinne, remayning in our flesh as the dragges of our fyrst infection and corruption, taken of Adam,* by whiche commeth gloteny, lechery, pride, malice, murder, robbery, and all other iniquitie, whiche all peyseth and presseth vs downe to dampnation euerlasting. Then what cause I pray you, haue we to be proude, none (god knoweth) but contrari great cause to come alow and study to vse humility, & by frequentinge the same to gender in vs, the habite or vertu of humilitie. And by that vertu we shalbe inclined to the contempt of the glory of thys world, and to despise the exaltation, the honour, the worshyps, welth & pleasures of this presente life, as thinges flux and fadinge, inconstant and of no valu<r>e. Christ teacheth vs the same, speaking of him self. **Io. viii. Si ego glorifico me ipsum gloria mea nihil est.** If I glorifie my self beside or contrary to the rule of goddes truth, my glory is nothing.* Then much lesse worth is our glory whiche commonly is vayne, and in thinges contrary to his pleasure. This considered s. Paule. **i. Timo. vi. Diuitibus huius seculi p[r]ecipe non sublime sapere Neque sperare in incerto diuitiarum.** Willinge Timothe to speake to the riche men, & bid them not to be proud nor to trust in the vncertenty of their riches, but to put their trust in the liuing god.* **Aug. Non expauit diuitias apostolus sed superbiam que est vermis diuitum.** The apostle was not afrayd of riches, but [4H1ᵛ] rather of pride, which is the moght, the worme that eateth vp the riche men.* And he is worthy to be called a great man, a riche man and a good man, that hauing muche riches is not ouercome with that vice of pride. And he that thinketh him self a great man because he is riche, he is a proud man, he swelleth in the flesh & is not ful, but as a thing blowen vp & redie to burst, and yet is there no sure and permanent stuffe within him. We must also come alow submittinge our selues to superiour powers, lowlie obeinge them that be set in aucthoritie ouer vs, considering that theyr aucthoritie commeth of God, & is giuen them of almightie God, eyther by his wel pleased will or at the least wyse by his sufferaunce. **Non enim est potestas nisi a deo: . . . Itaque qui resistit potestati ordinationi dei resistit. Qui autem resistunt ipsi sibi damnationem acquirunt. Ro. xiii.*** Ye may obiecte, yea, syr? I put the case that they woulde persue me for my fayth, or woulde compel me to reneyg anie article of my fayth, must I obey them vnder payne of dampnation? No syr. We must not vnderstande S. Paule yᵗ he speaketh of tirrannes, or persecutours of the faythe, but of suche rulers or men of aucthoritie, as he speaketh of there. **Principes non sunt timori, boni operis sed mali.** Of such princes, rulers yᵗ make not men afrayed for well doinge, but rather that lawde and prayse men for well doynge, and of such as be terrible to malefactours and to ill doers, them we must obey vnder payne of dampnation, in all their iust commaundementes and requestes, not onlie for feare of punishment, but also for conscience sake.* The [4H2] other we may not obey in no cause, but rather make some shift remouinge to some other place out of their daunger, if it may be, or by some other way to stay them selues for the time, but yf there be no other remedie, but yᵘ shalt be vrged or constrayned to denie, thou must rather offer thy self to die then to refuse god or his fayth. S. Peter in the seconde chapter of this epistle biddeth vs, **Subiecti estote omni humane creature propter deum siue regi quasi precellenti, siue ducibus tamquam ab eo missis ad vindictam malefactorum laudem vero bonorum** And it followith **deum timete, regem honorificate.*** On a time, when there was a contentyon amonge his disciples, & not without some cause as it seemed, because they perceiued by diuerse sayinges of our maister Christe, that he woulde be gonne from them, and that he should be betraied of one of them there present at supper with them, and that he should be ill handled of the Prelates and hie priestes, and of the Scribes, Pharisies & such other, they thought it meete to haue a president, a hed & a ruler amonge them to order them & to prouide necessaries for them. Christ hard their talke, and first extolled the aucthoriti of princes saying, **Reges gentium dominantur eorum: et qui potestatem habent super eos benefici vocantur. Luk. xxii.** Kinges of people be lordes ouer them, and they that haue power ouer them, be called souerayne lordes or gracious lordes. But you must not do so, I will haue no such lording or maistership among you, but he y^t is hiest or thinketh him self best of you, let him be as the yongest or as the least of you al. [4H2^v] And he y^t will go formest, let hym be a seruitour, take example of me. Whether is he greater that sitteth at the borde at meate, or he y^t wayteth & serueth at the table? I am amonge you as a seruaunt at the borde, & euen so must you be & you wyl be hie.* Then considering y^t, that christ would so haue it amonge his disciples that prelacie amonge them which were equalles, should come by humiliation then much more his pleasure is, that we should humiliate our selues to them, that by Gods will be set in soueraygntie, superioritie, rule or aucthoritie ouer vs. And that is it that S. Peter sayth. **Humiliamini sub potenti manu dei vt vos exaltet in tempore visitationis.** Make your selues humble and lowlye, vnder the mightye hande of God, that he may exalte you, & set you vp in honour, at the time of his visitacion,* at the generall iudgement, when he shall for youre low-lynes here in earthe, sorte you amonge the Angels in heauen, wyth euery order of Angelles, some men and women, accordinge to their good liuing here, & as it shalbe seen good, to his godly wysdom. To whome be all glorie & honour, for euer, Amen.

The twenty treatice or
                Sermon.

OMnem solicitudinem vestram proiicientes in Deum.* Where Saint Peter considerynge that the worlde dothe vnquiete manye a man, and dothe alienate his
mynde from the exercise of humilitie towarde GOD, and of other Godlie vertues
by ouermuche cumberaunce of minde, with solicitude, carke, and care of the
worlde, exhorteth vs to caste all our solicitude, thought, and care vppon almightye
God, for he hath cure ouer vs, and careth for vs. The world doth euen as Christe
speaketh of the sede sowen amonge the bushes, thornes, or briars, it can not proue,
for ye thornes suffocate it, stiful it, hinder it, and marreth it.* Solicitude and care
of the worlde is the thinge that the worlde combreth vs with. To exclude this, saint
Peter here counseileth vs to cast vppon God all our care, all our solicitude and
cumberaunce of minde, let him alone with it. Yea, sir shall I do so? This is a good
easie waie if it woulde serue I haue father and mother, a great charge of housholde
to care for, shall I let God alone with theim, & go play and make merie? Shall I
loke whether he will send them meate by the birdes, as he did to Helie by the
crowes and rauens,* or to bake a cake vnder a panne. &c. No, that were to tempt
God. &c. But I muste do that partaineth to mannes industrye and to mans laboure
and diligence, and then no further to cumber my minde, or to weare [4H3^v] away
my self with carke, but then to cast all the rest of my care vpon him, euen as the
mariners cast theyr anker vnto the lande, to more & set fast their shyp & to stay it
fast, for there is sure holde. When we haue done our diligence, let vs laye all the
rest in his lap, for he careth for vs as a mercyfull father for his children. So that
moderate sollicitude is not reproued, but **solicitudo obruens & confundens intellectum**, suche solicitude as doeth ouer whel[n]e and confounde a mans witte. And
because that **Mundus per†** **immoderantiam sauciat.** The worlde woundeth man
by excesse and superfluite,* therfore Saynt Peter byddeth vs be sobre,* contrarie to
glotenie, whiche killeth more then doth the sweard. And this sobriete is ye same
vertue that we call temperaunce, whiche is one of the .iiii. cardinall vertues, of
whiche the wise man **Sapi. viii.** speaketh, amonge the praises of sapience, sayinge:
that the godly sapience. **Sapientia increata.** The wysdome of the father, the
seconde parson in Trinitie, of whose wysedome euerie man and woman hath a
sparke, that lighteneth, and inclineth him to goodnes and to eschew yl. This
heauenly Sapience and wisdome (sayth the wyse man.) **Sobrietatem et prudentiam docet et iustitiam & virtutem quibus vtilius nihil est in vita hominibus,**
heauenly wisdom, the increate wisdome of the father of heauen, teacheth a man
sobrenes, that is temperaunce, and **prudence, & iustice,** and **vertue** or power, that
is fortitude.* And these be the .iiii. cardinall vertues, vnto which all mortall
vertues be reduced, **et vigilate,** watche, take [4H4] hede that you fall not to sinne,
beware, for you haue a shrewde whelp to bite you, to bringe you to sinne yf he may.
**Aduersarius vester diabolus tanquam leo rugiens circuit queren$s$ quem deu-
oret.*** Where s. Peter vseth the diuels owne terme, a worde of his owne confession.
**Cum venissent filij dei vt assisterent coram deo affuit inter eos etiam sathan,
cui dixit dominus vnde venis? Qui respondens ait, circuiui terram et perambulaui eam. Iob. i.** When the children of god the good angels came to stande afore

† per] par

god our lord the aduersarie the dyuel was also among them.* The good Angels be called here the children of God, in as muche as they be made like vnto him by participation of his glorie, & for the gracious fauour and loue that he had toward them, and they towarde him. The yll Angels were not yll by creation or by name, but of theyr owne frowarde wyll, declyninge and goynge away from the fauour of god. To shew that as wel all good thinges that men do, inclined by the good Angelles, as also all yll, vnto whiche they be moued by the yll spirites be openlie knowen to almightye GOD, as also the spirites good and bad, the ministers of the same workes, for it is said, **Cum assisterent coram deo filij dei, affuit inter eos etiam Sathan.** Sathan the Diuel was amonge them,* not so takinge that sayinge of holie Iob, as that Sathan was one of the good Angelles that contynuallie and styll behelde the glorye of GOD. For so onlye the good Angelles and blessed spyrytes, that be associate wyth [4H4ᵛ] them, hath that ioyful and glorious sight, but it is so sayd of Sathan, in as much as his actes and deedes be seen and knowen to almightye God. And because the good Angels do nothing but according to Gods pleasure, and to his commaundementes, therfore the Scripture taketh theyr actes, as wel knowen, and therfore it is not said that God asked of them any questions, but of the Deuyll, because his actes agre not to gods pleasure, but be in maner straunge to him, for he doth not aproue them nor alow them, but asketh of hys doinge as of a straunge thinge, like as he asked of **Cayn,** where is thy brother Abel? and, **quid fecisti?** What hast thou done?* Euen so in our purpose, Our lorde God spoke to Sathan, that is to saie, made him to vnderstande that he knoweth all thinges. And euen so you muste vnderstande the other saiynge: that Sathan answered God againe, not that he gaue anye knowledge to almighty God that he had not afore. But it is as much to saie, as that Sathan considered and vnderstode that all his doinges were plaine and open to the sight of God. Let vs consider his answere. **Circuiui terram & perambulaui eam.** I haue compassed or gone aboute the earth: and haue walked through it.* By thys circuite or goynge aboute the worlde of Sathan is vnderstand hys callidyte, wylines, and sutteltie to serche, whome he may disceyue and brynge into his snares. And this is it that saynt Peter meaneth, **Aduersarius vester diabolus tanque, leo rugiens circuit querens quem deuoret.*** Wily persons goeth compasse aboute the [4I1] bushe. **Psal. in circuitu impij ambulant,*** in a compas like as in all croked thinges, **Medium exit ab extremis.** The middel or meane goeth out from the extremities,* like as in thinges that be streyght the middel wrieth not, nother goeth oute from the extremities, as appereth playnlye in a streyght line, in whiche euery part lieth streight, and none swarueth aside out of course, so they that be iust and streight, when they entende a thing or say it, in their doinges, & setting forward toward that ende or purpose, they swarue not by wrenches and wyles, & bypathes, but goeth as streyght as they maye, to the thinge that they intende or promise, and to bringe their purpose to passe, and to good effecte. But the wylie Pie, the false shrew, in his beginninge will pretende a goodlie and Godlie matter, as for the glorie of God, for a common welth, or for some worke of merci or some other. Albeit in his processe he will exorbitate, he wyll go awry, he will compas the matter so, that it shall finallie ende in a money matter. For to get landes or possessions, or for to rob men of their liuinges, or some suche deuylishe purpose. The deuil (sayth s. Peter) goeth aboute lyke a rorynge Lyon, sekynge for his praye whome he may deuoure and incorporate to him selfe, makinge him one bodie with him selfe, for the Dyuell hath hys misticall bodie, compacte and made of suche as he hath rauende and swalowed vp by theyr sinnes, they be counted and taken as his lymmes and membres. And for to gette suche he goeth aboute by compasses, [411ᵛ] wrenches and wiles as his propertie is, not to go streyght or after a plaine fashion, but aboute the bushe by compasses, in which **medium exit ab extremis**. The midell exhorbitateth from the streightnes of trueth, as pretending some common profect, or some honesty or common wealth or some particuler pleasure or honest gaynes or suche like, but in prosecuting of hys purpose, he wyll cleane go compas and awrie from iustice & from charitie, and wyll ende finally vpon some money mater for a priuate luker to him selfe, wyth the spoylinge, robbing, or vndoing of their poore neyghbour. Examples of this we haue sene in our time more then I can haue leasure to expresse or to reherse at this time. In the actes of parliamentes that we haue had, made in our dayes, what goodly preambles hath gone afore in the same? euen **quasi oraculum apollinis**.* As though yᵉ thinges that folow, had come from the counsel hiest in heauen, and yet the ende hath ben either to destroy Abbeyes or Chauntreys, or Colleges, or suche like, by whiche some haue gotten muche landes, & haue be made men of great possessions whiche (by Gods iust iudgement) they haue but a short while enioyed, but many an honest poore man hath ben vndone by it, and an innumerable multitude hath peryshed for defaute and lacke of sustinaunce, & this miserie hath longe continued, and yet hath not an ende.* Thus the diuell goeth aboute, as he sayd by him self. **Iob. i.** When God asked of him where he had been, he sayd he had compassed aboute the earth & walked throw [412] it.* Where ye shall vnderstande, there be thre sortes of resonable liuinge creatures, of which one is in heauen as Angels and saued soules, which the diuell neyther goeth aboute by temptation to bring them to sinne, neither walketh throw them to performe his malice, actually bringing them to sin. Another kinde of reasonable creatures is in hel which the Diuel walketh through, in the middel amonge them, which he seaseth not to tormente and punishe aboue measure, he doth not compas aboute to tempte theim, for he hath brought them to his purpose alredie. The thirde kinde is here on earth, as we mortall men and women whom our goostlie aduersarie the Dyuell compasseth and goeth aboute by diuerse kindes of temptacion, to ouerthrow and bringe to sinne, and ouer some of them he doeth preuayle, peruertinge them and bringing them to sinne, which holy Iob calleth parambulacion or walkinge through them, and they may be vnderstande by the sayd earth, which the diuel said that he compassed aboute and walked through.* And that he doth like a roryng Lion, bicause that when he can not by his priuy lurking & temptations ouer come them, he goeth to worke wyth manyfest and open terrours, bearinge menne in hande that they rebell agaynst the Kynge, and a gaynste the Kinges procedinges, whiche was wonte to be their sute ancor, when they had none other argumente,* when, they shake oute the Kinge or my Lordes grace, or such other potentate to fortifie theyr waye and exorbytateth from the trew trade [412ᵛ] of true doctrine, then they rore like the Dyuell, & as the dyuels ministers, to deuoure men vp to falshed and Heresie, they know that as Salomon sayth **.Pro. xx. Lyke as the roringe of a Lyon, euen so is the feare of a Kynge, who so doeth prouoke him, synneth agaynst his owne soule.***And thus they haue shaken poore menne, and made them eyther to saye as they say, or els to holde theyr peace and say nothynge. The Deuil the aucthor of these troubles, Saynt Peter byddeth vs resist by fayth, in whiche in verye deede as Saynt Paule sayeth in the last Chapter to the Ephesians. In all thinges takynge the shielde or buckeler of faythe, wyth whiche ye maye quenche all the firie Dartes or weapons of the moste wicked Deuyll.* But Saynt Peter addeth and putteth to more then Saynt Paule doeth, exhortinge vs to be stronge in faythe, and by that to resist the fyrie Dartes of temptacion, meanynge that many haue faythe, and yet they resiste not the Deuylles rorynge and fearce temptation, and because they be not **fortes in fide,** stronge in faythe,* but verie weake in fayth, therefore they be sone ouerthrowne & ouercome. And that is the cause that Heresies so muche preuayle amonge vs, and peruerteth and turneth the most parte of people, As sayth that greate auncient Father **Tertullian libro de prescriptionibus contra hereticos. Hereses apud eos multum valent qui in fide non valent.** Where he imputeth (as he well maye) all the strength of Heresyes to the weakenes of the people, say[413]inge: Heresies be of greate strengthe amonge them that be of no strengthe in fayth, or that haue no stronge faythe. He putteth an example of these tourneamentes, as fightyng wyth Battell Axes, or Iustinge at the Tylte, or at prouinge of mastries, as Wrestlynge or suche other. Not he that is mooste stronge, hath euer the best game, or hath the victorie, but is manie tymes ouercome of a verie wretche and of a weake man, and he that doeth ouercome, doeth not alwayes ouercome, because of hys owne strengthe, but because he mette wyth a wretche or with a weake manne, that had no strength. And therfore it proueth manie times, that he that nowe ouercame, when he shalbe afterward matched with a man of good strength shall haue a foyle and be ouercome. So saieth **Tertullian. Non aliter Heresis de quorundam infirmitatibus habent quod valent. Nihil valentes si in bene valentem fidem incurrant.** Euen so Heresies getteth and hath of the weakenes of some persons that they be so stronge as they be. And should be of no strength, if they should matche or chaunce vpon a fayth that is myghtie & stronge.* Therfore yf you will resist the roring of the Deuill, and quenche the fyrie Dartes of the mooste wicked, you must doo it by faythe, and that by stronge faythe, for a faynte and a weake fayth will not be able so to doo. Howe many thynke you of this audience here present be there? A greate manie I am sure, that woulde haue sayd once within this twentie yeares, that no man li[413ᵛ]uing no nor an angell of heauen or all the diuels in Hell, should neuer haue peruerted you from the sure affiaunce and fast faith that you had towarde the blessed Sacramentes of the churche. But after that there came amonge you a great multitude of pleasaunt preachers, preaching libertie, and so pleasures folowing of such lewde libertie, how soone you haue ben ouerthrowne & turned another way, iudge you, and all for lacke of strength in faythe. Therfore I shal most hartlie pray you that wilbe saued by your faith, adorned and decked with charitie,* that you wyll be stronge in fayth, and not to folowe euerie puffe or blaste of new doctrine, that so you maye receyue **finem fidei vestrae salutem animarum vestrarum. Cap. i.** The ende and rewarde of your fayth, that is the health of your soules, that shal neuer fade nor fayle, as he sayde afore in the fyrst chapter of this epistle.* And like as in the beginninge of this present chapter, he parswaded by example of him self, the pastors, prelates & priestes: euen so now he exhorteth them that he write to, by example of the brotherhed or other faithful people to the sufferance & perseueraunce in persecution, saying: **Scientes eandem passionem ei que in mundo est vestre fraternitati fieri.** Knowing that you haue the same passion and suffering in you, that hath be layde on your brotherhed.* Here S. Peter induceth a stronge parswasion to this purpose, that we should stronglie resist all temptacion, knowinge that the same payne and passion that you haue, also haue your brotherhead that is abrode [414] in the worlde, your brothers in Christ, faythful people men and women suffer like temp[t]ation by the Diuell our goostly enemie as you doo, they suffer like persecution of infidelles and Heretikes as you do, yet they persist and stande stronglie in the fast fayth, in which they haue been instructe by true faythful people, and by trew preachers. Therfore consideringe that they stande stedfastly, it were shame for you that you should lyghtlie be ouerthrowen. And because that euen from the beginninge of the worlde, good men haue ben fauted, persecuted and tempted, and yet haue not ben ouerthrowen. Therefore you should be ashamed, yf you onely should be worse then al men, and the very refuse and dogboltes of all your brothers, not able to suffer anie thinge. And because such sufferaunce with perseueraunce in the same, hath neede of helpe to succor mans weakenes. Therefore the blessed Apostle Saynt Peter hath recurse and runneth to Goddes helpe and assistaunce, sayinge: **Deus autem omnis gratie qui vocauit nos in eternam gloriam suam in Christo Iesu modicum passos ipse perficiet, confirmabit solidabitque.** Almyghtie GOD the gyuer of all grace which hath called vs by our Sauiour CHRIST into hys eternall glorie, whiche he would vs to receyue finally after thys present lyfe. **Modicum passos,** althoughe we haue suffred but litle, for all that we canne suffer is verye lytell and almost nothing in comparison of the euerlasting [4I4ᵛ] glorie that is prepared for vs. He shall make you perfecte in that you be vnhable of your selfe addinge and puttinge to more vertues to them that ye haue alredy, he shall confirme and make sure your weaknes, for of our selues we be but weake and redy to be ouerthrowen by euery suggestion or temptacion.* Of him and by him we be stronge and able to suffre tribulacion and trouble. **Solidabit,*** And where we haue now but as loose limmes or members shaken with feare and with errours, and scarce agreinge euery man within our selues in our opinions and in matters of our fayth, but as it were one while of one mynde and a none of another mynde, and verie waueringe and vnsure. And this is the verie property of Heresies, thei be euer vnstedfast and not agreinge amonge theim selues, but some take one waie and some an other, and that pleaseth at one time, displeaseth at an other tyme: for example, how manie manners and dyuerse wayes of ministringe the Communion haue we had amonge vs? I haue knowen one whyle the Priest to take the breade vpon the patten of the Chales, and turned his backe to the Aulter, and his face downe to the people, and sayd the wordes of consecration ouer the breade, & then layde it vpon the Aulter and afterwarde donne lykewise with the Chales & the wine.* Then because there seemed to muche reuerence, to be giuen to the Sacrament by this waie, the people were al driuen out of the chauncell except the ministers, that the Communion should not be commonlye [4K1] sene nor worshipped.* And anone that way semed not best, and therfore there was veils or curtens drawen, yea and in some churches the very Lent cloth or veile hanged vp though it were with Alleluya in the Easter time to hide it, that no man should see what the prieste did, nor heare what he saide.* Then this waye pleased not and the aulters were pulled downe and the tables set vp, & all the obseruaunce saide in Englyshe, and that openlye that all men might heare and see what was done, and the breade commaunded to bee common vsed breade leuende with salte, barme, and such other.* And then sone after were all corporaces taken awaye to extenuate the honoure of the sacrament, & it laied down on yᵉ prophane borde clothe.* And at the saide tables the Prieste one while turned his face Eastwarde, an other while turned his backe eastwarde, and his face towarde the West, as the Iewes vseth to worshippe.* And anone by commaundement tourned his back Southward, and his face to the north, and finally, after the last boke that was set forth he turned his face to the South.* And this boke made swepestake of the blessed sacrament, declaring there to be nothing els but bare bread and wine.* This pulling downe of aulters & settynge vp of bords was vsed by the heritikes that were of **Arrius** sect, as saint Basil rehearseth in diuers places, & speciallye **Epistola .lxxii.** speaking of one Eustathius a disciple of **Arrius,** which

was made Bishoppe in **minor Armenia**,* As he came through Paphlagonia a
countrey in maigne Asia.* [4K1ᵛ] **Basilidis Paphlagonici altaria cum Paphlago-
niam transiret subuertit Eustathius & propriis mensis liturgiam obiuit.*** This
Basilides not yᵉ heritike, but Basilides yᵉ better, bishop of **Paphlagonia*** a familier
acquaintance of **Basilius** vsed aulters as they had bene vsed euer stil sith yᵉ
beginnyng of Christes church. The said Eustathius comming through his countrey
or dioces, pulled downe the alters, & said his masses after his fashion vpon bordes
or tables, as we did lately. And after in yᵉ next epistle he saieth. **Quam obrem cum
Dardania redirent heretici, altaria Basilidis in agro Gangrenorum subuerterunt
mensasque suas substituerunt.** When certain heritiks came back again from the
countrey called Dardania,* they ouerthrew the aulters of Basilides the bishop in yᵉ
countrey of the Gangrens,* and set vp in steede of them their owne bordes or
tables.* All such wauerynge and inconstancy in opinions, if we conuert our selues
to the god of al grace, that of his great mercy hath called vs by our sauiour Iesus
Christ, he wil solidate, stay it, & settle vs sure, contrary to al such inconstancy, to
him be glory & imperie world with out ende. Amen. Then foloweth the conclusion of this very frutefull epistle, in which first he declareth the messager by whom
he wrote this letter, because they knew the man verie well, and knew him for a
true disciple, & a true brother of theirs as he toke hym. **Per Siluanum fidelem
fratrem vobis vt arbitror, breuiter scripsi.** I haue written a short epistle to you bi
Siluanus whom you know,* you nede not to suspect him, for you knowe he is [4K2]
faithfull, and no false apostle (of which thei were then greatly afrayed) & for their
false messagers of which the world was full then. A short epistle it is in quantitie,
but very long, & abundant and plentifull in vertue & strength, and in sentence, &
good matter, as it appeared by such matter as I haue brought forth from time to
time, in exposition, & declaration of this epistle. **Obsecrans & contestans hanc
esse veram gratiam dei in qua statis.** Praiyng & beseching you for Gods sake to
conforme your selues vnto yᵗ I haue written (saieth .s. Peter.) And protesting here
& afore God that this is the true grace of the Gospell in which you stand.*
Therefore be stedfast & continue in the faith of the same, according to .s. Peter
writing in this epistle yᵗ hys holy doctrine mai take rote in you & bear fruit of good
workes. **Salutat vos ecclesia que est in Babilone collecta & Marcus filius meus.**
Here he sendeth recommendations vnto them from his companye, saiynge: that
the Churche or congregation of Christian fayethfull people gathered and assembled together in Rome, recommendeth theim to you, and wissheth you well to
doe.* And here he nameth Rome by a straunge name, callynge it Babilon,* and
comparyng it to Babilon the great Citye, in the Realme of Caldey, firste founded
by Nembroth, a hundred .xxxi. yere after the great flud.* And greatly amplified by
Semiramis the quene, wife to Ninus sometyme kyng there, **Berosus. Ipsa hanc
vrbem maximam ex oppido fecit vt magis dici possit illam edificasse quam
ampliasse.*** As yᵉ aun[4K2ᵛ]cient historiographer of yᵉ Caldees **Berosus*** writeth
antiquitatum libro quarto, saiyng, **Anno centesimo, trigesimo primo a salute ab
aquis, prima omnium gentium & ciuitatum fundata est a Saturno Babilonico
nostro vrbs & gens nostra Babilonica multiplicataque est nimis numero posteritatis. &c.*** Where he calleth **Nembroth** Saturne of Babilon, and **Belus** his sonne
Iupiter of the Caldeis, his son was **Ninus,** which was husband to **Semiramis** the
quene that after her husband reigned there marueilous vyctoriouslye by the space
of .xlii. yeares. Berosus saith, In the fourth place reigned at Babilon the wife of
Ninus, Semiramis, the Ascalonite .xlii. yeres.* This woman exceaded and passed
al men in chiualrie triumphes, riches, victoryes, & imperie. There is no man

comperable to this woman There be so many magnificent and noble things spoken and written of her life, both to her reproch & chiefly to her laude & praise. And afterward it was most amplified by the great conqueror Nabuchodonosor which said in his ioly royalte. **Da. <x>iiii Nonne hec est Babilon ciuitas magna quam edificaui in gloria mea?** Of whiche I spoke in my last sermon here made, declarynge howe GOD coulde pull downe theim that woulde not stoupe, by example of this proude Nabuchodonosor that had Daniell and other of the Israelites in captiuitie at the tyme when he made this proude boastyng.* By the name of this Babilon .s. Peter calleth Rome, bicause of the confusion & vncertenty of innumerable idolatries y^t ther in Rome were vsed as horribly as euer they wer in Babilon wher bi y^e [4K3] commaundement of king Ninus husband of the said **Semiramis** the quene was first erect a temple & an ymage of Belus the God his father, & then by the like commaundement of the quene was Ninus her husband deified, to which she had commaunded among her people diuine honours to be geuen.* And by example of her, many other great men caused like deuine honours to bee geuen to great mens ymages of their auncestours, and so began their first idolatrye, which afterward was spred through all the world, which by Christ and his apostles, and their holy doctrine was extinct and quenched. And euen like as the elect people of God, the people of Israel, amonge whiche were Ezechiel, Daniel, and many other holy men and women were a small number in comparison among the people of the city of Babilon, and there in much vexation, mockinge, and scoffinge, and great discomfort, lamenting the lacke of the holye citie of Hierusalem, and the destruction of the same, and the comfort of their owne countrey of the holie lande. They hanged vp their pipes & instrumentes of musike on the willowes in Babilon,* and could not singe the confortable songs vsed in the temple of Ierusalem, although thei were many times prouoked therto. Euen so was .s. Peter & a few new conuerses to Christes faith with him in Rome, not without muche trouble & discomfort. All they that were thus assembled with the blessed Apostle thus coarted & streicted, yet had great solace & comfort to heare of the constancy of christen people how they were daylye multiplied [4K3^v] and increased. All suche as there were with him hadde theim recommended to these good blessed people that sainte Peter writ this Epistle to. And so did sainte Marke his disciple by him instruct and baptised, and afterward fully instruct in Christes waye. In so muche that he writ the Gospell of Christe, whiche was alowed and approued for true by sainte Peter. This Marke saint Peter calleth his sonne, because that bi him he was christened and taught all thinges necessarye for an Euangeliste, or for one that shoulde preache the Gospell for to knowe.* **Salutate inuicem in osculo sancto.** Salute you one another by holy kissynge one another.* By holy kissynge (he saith,) meanynge that there be diuerse maners of kissynge, some holye and some not holye, for some do kisse for flatterynge and nothinge with the harte, but for a sinister or a leude purpose. As Absalon Dauids sonne kissed the people, allurynge them to magnifie hym, as when menne came to the courte to sue for their matters, he vsed to stande at the gates, and woulde come to the suters, and woulde knowe their causes, and then woulde kisse them, saiynge: It is pitye that the king loketh no better on these matters, wold God I had aucthorite to redresse these causes, as I woulde surelye doe if I myghte, or I woulde he should set some other man to do it, for hee is Olde, and wyll take no labours. All these and suche other flatterynge woordes and behauioure, he vsed amonge the people aspiryng to the crowne, whiche thyng he moost earnestly [4K4] attempted afterwarde, when he made his father to forsake the Citye, and to shyfte for hym selfe as well as he coulde.* Thys came of suche flatterynge cosses. There is a manner of kyssynge whiche is a faynynge kissynge. And soo Ioab kyssed Amasa. **ii. Regum .xx.** fearynge that he woulde aspire into the fauour of the kinge, that he shoulde be lyke to putte hym oute of fauoure, when he mette hym at an oportunitie, for hys purpose, came to hym flatterynge, and toke him by the chynne wyth the one hande, and kissynge hym, drewe out hys skeen or hanger wyth the other hande, and stroke Amasa in the syde so sore a wounde, that hys guttes fell about hys feete.* Here was a fayning cosse, fainyng loue, where was nought els but malyce and hatred. There is an other trayterous cosse, and suche kissynge vsed Iudas to our Sauioure Christe, not for anye loue whiche he ought to haue had towarde hym, but onelye to geue to the Souldiours and Seruauntes of hys companye a sygne that they might knowe Christe, and then set hande on him and craftelye to carye hym awaye, **Abducite caute,** as he hadde geuen theim instructions.* The traytour was afrayed (nowe that he hadde gon so farre) lest Christ should by his mighty power haue scaped frome theim, as hee myghte if hee wold inuisibly, as he did at Nazareth, when the malicious people for hys preachyng, & for reprouyng their vyces, rubbing them on the gall,* they woulde haue pytched hym downe the clefe or [4K4ᵛ] rocke on which their citi stode & was builded on. Then Iesus **transiens per medium illorum ibat.** Inuisibly he scaped awai that neuer a man spied him* This Iudas knew he could doe, and therfore he bade them beware, and conuey him away craftely.* There is an other baudy or lecherous cosse as the adulterous woman or the courtisan kisseth the youngman, as it is write. **Pro. vii. Apprehensum deosculatur iuuenem & procaci vultu blanditur.** She colled the yong man & kissed him, & with her fliering countenance flattered him.* All these maners or kissing must be left, and you must amonge you (saith .s. Peter to his scholers that he writ vnto) kiss like dow[u]es with peaceable cosses, chast cosses in signe of peace & loue.* And this was much vsed in the primatiue church, and afterward euen to our time in the holy church at the holy time of masse, when the priest in some places, & specially in c<h>athedral churches kisseth the deacon & then the deacon goeth downe to the step of the quere, & kisseth the rectors, & they go euery one on hys side and kisseth the seniors, and they vpward on both the sides the quere til all the quere haue geuen the cosse of peace one to another.* And this is daiely obserued in the cathedral church of wells at high masse, euen to this present time. And because yᵗ (as it is written in **Genises**) Our corrupte nature is prone to noughtines more then to goodnes,* & in asmuch as some haue more folowed carnalitie and carnall loue then chaste loue, the people haue misused the said cosse of peace, turninge it to wantannes. Therfore such kissing of peace [4K5] at the masse hath bene left, where hath bene present both men and women, & when the priest hath geuen the cosse of peace, saiynge to his minister, **Pax tibi & ecclesie dei.** He kisseth the paxe of siluer or other mettall,* or other honest stuffe, & that is caried about through the churche, that they that wil not chastly & louingly kisse one another, may at the lest wise kisse that pax, so by imitation & folowing the vsage of the primitiue church, & the counsell of .s. Peter here willing vs one to kisse an other in a holy cosse, or euery one kissing yᵉ said pax that an other hath kissed, which is no smal signe of concorde, amitie, & frenship. Where contrary he that loueth not another, wil not with a good wil kisse nor touch that that his aduersary hath kissed or touched. **Gratia vobis omnibus qui estis in Christo Iesu. Amen.** He begonne his epistle with harty prayer, for grace to them that were dispersed as straungers in **Pontus, Galatia, &c.** . . . **Gratia vobis & pax multiplicetur.** And euen so he endeth his epistle or letter, wisshyng & praiyng for grace to al them that be constant and remaine stedfast in Christe Iesu, to whom with the father and with the holy Gost be all honour and glorye for euer. Amen.

FINIS

Imprinted at
London by Robert Calye, within
the precinct of Christes
Hospital.

Cum priuilegio ad imprimendum
solum.

COMMENTARY

In the commentary, following the practice of the Yale edition of *The Complete Works of St. Thomas More*, first references only to books and articles are given in full. For scriptural quotations which do not vary from the Vulgate, a reference to chapter and verse is provided; where variation occurs, the relevant portion of the passage is provided from the modern Vulgate edited by R. Weber. Literal errors are recorded; omissions are indicated by . . . . The numbering of the Vulgate is followed in citing Psalms and the books of Kings. References to classical authors are taken from the texts of the Loeb edition unless noted otherwise.

Esto mansuetus . . . verum Ecclus. 5:13.

The preface

It is honourable . . . Thoby Tob. 12:6.

Bene omnia fecit . . . speake Mk 7:37.

Deferar . . . odores Horace, Epist. II, i, l. 259. See *Satires, Epistles and Ars Poetica*, ed. and tr. H. R. Fairclough (London, 1926), p. 419.

hath be Reduced form of the past participle 'been'; see *Sermons*, pp. 95, 114, 118, 181 etc.; below p. 381.

where . . . scole 'In cases where the children were able to teach the parents'.

I haue be put to silence . . . parte See Introduction, p. 30; *Sermons*, p. 338.

confederacie . . . Lathamer On Latimer's followers in the Worcester diocese see Introduction, p. 24.

bishop Barlowe . . . officers Ibid. pp. 29–30 on the Protestant William Barlow's episcopacy at Wells (1548–1553). Barlow's anti-Lutheran treatise, *A dialoge . . . of these Lutheran faccions* (1531) was reissued in 1553 (STC 1461–2); in 1554 he reverted to Catholicism. Edgeworth here reminds his readers of Barlow's earlier Protestant sympathies. See J.R. Lunn, ed. *Bishop Barlowe's Dialogue on the Lutheran Factions* (London, 1897), pp. 13–15; I. Horst, *The Radical Brethren; Anabaptism and the English Reformation to 1558* (Nieuwkoop, 1972), pp. 44–49.

The first sermon . . . treatyng of the . . . spirite of sapience, and the spirite of intelligence

The first sermon This group of six sermons on

the seven gifts of the Holy Ghost was preached at Redcliffe Cross in Bristol between c.1535 and c.1544. The first and last were preached on Whitsunday; the others may also have been Pentecostal sermons. Sermons two and four, preached in c.1537 and 1539, criticise the religious changes but sermons five and six, probably preached in the early 1540s, make little reference to them.

the vii. giftes . . . goste Several vernacular expositions of the seven gifts existed in the sixteenth century. The 'Mirror of St Edmund', the translation of St Edmund of Abingdon's thirteenth century treatise *Speculum Ecclesie*, was reprinted three times after 1521 (STC 965–7). Following Hugh of St Victor's 'De Septem Donis Spiritus Sancti' (PL 75, 410–1) and St Gregory's *Moralia* II (PL 35, 1325), the seven gifts accompany the seven virtues which heal man of sin; see *Yorkshire Writers*, ed. C. Horstman, 2 vols (London, 1895–6), I, 125, 247. *Piers Plowman* was printed three times by A. Crowley in 1550 (STC 19906–7a). In the allegory of Passus XIX (B-Text, ll.194–256) Piers, assisted by Grace, identified as the Holy Spirit, bestows the gifts which cover the professions and trades of the Christian community. The gifts are also listed in Richard Rolle's 'The Form of Perfect Living'; in two allegorical works on the religious life, *The Abbey of the Holy Ghost*, printed in 1496 and 1500 (STC 13608.7–13610), and *The Charter of the Abbey of the Holy Ghost* where they guard the Abbey ruled by the Holy Ghost (Horstman, *Yorkshire Writers* I, 45–6, 321–62); and in *Stimulus Amoris*, the fourteenth century translation of a Latin treatise partly by James of Milan now attributed to Walter Hilton, where they guide a sevenfold rising into contemplation with Christ's passion; see *The Goad of Love*, ed. and tr. C. Kirchberger (London, 1952). They receive systematic treatment in several penitential manuals translated from Lorens d'Orleans' *Somme le Roi*: in *The Book of Vices and Virtues* (ed. W.N. Francis, EETS, ES 217 (London, 1942)); in Caxton's *Royal Book*, printed in 1488 and twice in 1507 (STC 21429–30a), where they are linked to the seven petitions of the *pater noster*; and in *Jacob's Well* (ed. A. Brandeis, EETS, OS, 115 (London, 1900)), where they are linked to the corresponding virtues and vices. Edgeworth probably knew *The Pilgrymage of perfeccyon* by William Bonde (1526, 1531; STC 3277–8), in which the gifts are assigned to each day of the pilgrimage as the fruits of the pilgrim's endeavour; on Bonde's treatise see M. Aston, *England's Iconoclasts: Laws against Images*, 2 vols (Oxford, 1988), I, pp. 188–90. The gifts are also outlined in the exposition of the creed in the *Bishops' Book* of 1537; see *Formularies*, p. 49.

And treatyng . . . intelligence Following Is. 11:2 wisdom and understanding traditionally have priority. See Aquinas, *ST* 1a2ae. 68, 2, 7 (*ed. cit.* XXIV, 32–7); and the commentary on *ST* by John of St Thomas, *The Gifts of the Holy Ghost*, tr. D. Hughes (London, 1950), pp. 76–86, 123–34 (cited hereafter as John of St Thomas, *Gifts*); *DTC* IV, s.v. 'Dons du Saint-Esprit'.

The blessed . . . father John 1:1–5, 9–10. The Fourth Gospel is the principal scriptural authority for the mission of the Holy Ghost after the resurrection. See G. Johnston, *The Spirit Paraclete in the Gospel of St John* (Cambridge, 1970); *DB* II; *ODCC* s.v. 'Holy Spirit'.

verbum caro . . . vs John 1:14; cf. Col. 1:19.

semetipsum exinaniuit . . . passion Phil. 2:7–8.

whytsontide This pentecostal sermon was preached on Whitsunday, the feast held on the fiftieth day after Easter which celebrates the descent of the Holy Ghost upon the apostles; see *ODCC* s.v. 'Whitsunday'; *Sermons*, p. 162.

Expedit vobis . . . you John 16:7. For a recent interpretation of John 16:1–15 see C.K. Barrett, *The Gospel according to St. John* (London, 1955), pp. 403–9.

I haue yet many . . . knowe John 16:12–13 is here expounded conventionally as Christ's

promise of further revelation to the church. On George Joye's attack on More for his use of this text in *The subversion of Moris false foundacion* (Emdon, 1534) see Introduction, p. 61. On the reformers' interpretation of it as a reference to the content of Christ's words see J. Pelikan, *The Christian Tradition: A History of the Development of Doctrine*, 5 vols (London, 1971–), IV. *Reformation of Church and Dogma, 1300–1700* (London, 1984), pp. 211, 265 (cited hereafter as Pelikan, *Church and Dogma*). For More's views on revelation, see B. Gogan, *The Common Corps of Christendom: Ecclesiological Themes in the Writings of Sir Thomas More* (Leiden, 1982).

as we be to be taught The use of the subjunctive form 'be' followed by the infinitive seems to be characteristic of Edgeworth's speech; see *Sermons*, p. 286; below p. 430.

Christ to auoyde . . . me An exposition of John 16:13–14.

Omnia . . . you John 16:15. Vg. 'Omnia quaecumque dixi quia de meo'. On Trinitarian worship, i.e. worshipping God through Jesus Christ in the Holy Spirit, see F.S. Hendry, *The Holy Spirit in Christian Theology* (London, 1965) pp. 30–2; on the Trinity in the fourth Gospel see Barrett, *Gospel*, pp. 74–8.

All . . . me An exposition based on Augustine's *De Trinitate* VI, 5, 7 and XV, 17–19 (*PL* 42, 928, 1079–1087) and Aquinas, *ST* 1a. 37, 1–2 (*ed. cit.* VII, 79–89; see Appendix 2, pp. 252–8 on his Trinitarian theology of the Holy Spirit); see *DTC* XV, s.v. 'Trinitie'.

as Arrius . . . father Arius (250–c.356) the arch-heretic who denied the true divinity of Christ. At the First Council of Nicaea in 325, at which their doctrines were condemned, the Arians used scripture to prove that Christ neither existed from eternity nor claimed equality with God the Father. For their main propositions see J.N.D. Kelly, *Early Christian Doctrines*, 4th ed. (London, 1968), pp. 227–31; *ODCC* s.v. 'Arius' and 'Arianism'; *Sermons*, pp. 120, 127, 128, 141.

And that . . . both Arius regarded the essence of the Holy Spirit as unlike that of the Son; but the consubstantiality of the Holy Spirit was not affirmed until the Council of Constantinople in 381. Augustine elaborated the full doctrine of the Spirit in *De Trinitate* (319–419); see *ODCC* s.v. 'Holy Spirit'; Kelly, *Doctrines*, ch. 10.

the holye ghost . . . tongues A reference to the descent of the Holy Spirit at Pentecost (Acts 2:3).

Quecunque audiet . . . vobis An exposition of John 16:13.

Esaie sayth .xli . . . goddes Is. 41:23.

And the Apostles . . . have A reference to John 13:36; 14:5; 16:16–17; Mk 14:58; John 2:19; 18:36.

Of this thought . . . knowe A reference to John 14:26, with the additional implication that divine truths should not be made available to everyone.

aboundance . . . grace The reference here is to natural grace, not the sacramental grace to which this terminology usually refers; i.e. the supernatural 'plenitude of grace' which Christ as redeemer dispensed to mankind.

Psalmo .xliiii . . . tuis Ps. 44:8

Kynges . . . oyle Under the Hebrews anointing with oil, the sacrament of accession to the kingship, was held to impart a special endowment of the spirit; hence the sacrosanct character of the king as 'the Lord's anointed' (Heb. *meschiach,* Gk. *messias,* Lat. *christos,* both 'Messiah' and 'Christ' signify 'Anointed One'). The similar consecration of the priesthood descended from Aaron by sprinkling different parts of the body with oil and blood (Ex. 29:21; 40:13–15; Lev. 8:12 and 30) was probably a later extension of this rite. Anointing was always used in consecration of the high priest who was called by contrast 'the anointed priest'. See *DB* I, s.v. 'Anointing'; III, s.v. 'Priests and Levites'; *Sermons,* pp. 172, 193, 195, 238, 247.

but Christ . . . felowes A reference to Heb. 1:9 and to the Melchizedek tradition. In Ps. 109:4 is promised the Messiah and an endless priesthood after the order of Melchizedek (the King of Salem and priest of God most high over Abraham of Gen. 14:18–20); in the Epistle to the Hebrews both passages are used to prove the superiority of Christ's priesthood, prefigured by Melchizedek, over that of the Levitical priests, the descendants of Aaron. See *ODCC* s.v. 'Messiah' and 'Melchizedek'; *Sermons,* pp. 172, 186, 195, 203, 238.

They haue graces . . . hath A reference to I Cor. 12:11; cf. Eph. 4:7.

He was full . . . measure The following exposition is drawn from Aquinas, *ST* 3a. 7, 9–10 (*ed. cit.* XLIX, 30–39).

Stephanus . . . Act. vi Acts 6:8; cf. Aquinas, *ST, loc. cit.*

The blessed virgin . . . grace Luke 1:28; cf. Aquinas, *ST* 3a. 7, 10 (*ed. cit.* XLIX, 36–7).

like as the head . . . them See Rom. 12:4–5; I Cor. 12:12–23. The metaphor of the human head was traditionally used to describe the relationship of Christ's grace to all other graces; Aquinas in *ST* 3a. 8, 1 (*ed. cit.* XLIX, 52–59) extends the metaphor into a comprehensive ecclesiology in which Christ is defined as the head of the church. Christ's natural graces which he distributes to people according to their capacities are here treated as interchangeable with the seven gifts; see *Sermons,* p. 124.

capi. xi . . . him Is. 11:1–2. The messianic prophecy became the primary scriptural authority for identifying the seven gifts.

By this slyppe . . . patriarkes Cf. Luke 1:35; Matt. 1:18–20. The familiar explanation that the Blessed Virgin conceived the Saviour through the overshadowing of the Holy Spirit derives from the tradition established by Tertullian and the Church Fathers. See Ambrose, *De Spiritu Sancto* II, 38 (*PL* 16, 751); *The Royal Book,* tr. Caxton (W. de Worde, 1507), sigs O4ᵛ–P1 (*STC* 21430); *Book of Vices and Virtues,* p. 117.

by appropriation In Trinitarian theology the doctrine of appropriation is the ascription of common names and essential attributes (here the gifts) to all three members of the Trinity, even when spoken of as belonging only to one. See Aquinas, *ST* 1a. 39, 6–7 (*ed. cit.* VII, 124–9); *NCE* I, s.v. 'Appropriation'.

And on this floure . . . sayd See Aquinas, *ST* 1a2ae, 68, 1 (*ed cit.* XXIV, 6–11); John of St Thomas, *Gifts,* pp. 30–38 on the naming of the gifts as spirits with reference to Is. 11:2. From an early date in the iconographical development of the Tree of Jesse the gifts were portrayed as flowers to which are linked the beatitudes. In Bonde's *Pilgrymage of perfeccyon* (Wynkyn de Worde, 1531), they are the seven beams of the 'spiritual sterre of grace' which 'descendeth euer from the Trinite' and 'euer where these .vii. [giftes] be, there is always yᵉ holy loue of god/ and the presence of the holy goost' (fo. 31). See A. Watson, *The Early*

Iconography of the Tree of Jesse (London, 1934), Plates 1–3, pp. 128–35; E. Hodnett, *English Woodcuts, 1480–1535*, 2nd ed. (Oxford, 1973), nos 870–1.

the scholasticall doctours . . . Temperaunce The question of how the gifts are related to the virtues was debated in the early twelfth century. For a survey of scholastic thought before Aquinas see Appendix 3 of Aquinas, *ST* 1a2ae. 68–70 (*ed. cit.* XXIV, 89–111).

viii. beatitudes . . . Matth. v Matt. 5:2–11; Augustine in 'De Sermone Domini' (*PL* 34, 1234–5) first correlated the seven gifts with the beatitudes by treating the eighth beatitude as a confirmation of the others; see Aquinas' criticism of the Augustinian correlations in *ST* 1a2ae. 69, 1 and 3 (*ed. cit.* XXIV, 42–5, 50–9; Appendix 2, pp. 90–2) and *ST* 2a2ae. 121, 2 and 139, 2 (*ed. cit.* XLI, 287–9; XLII, 231–2). The beatitudes, the actions flowing from the gifts and virtues working together, are the highest action of the soul on earth.

And to the fruites . . . Gala. v Gal. 5:22–23; the nine fruits of the Holy Spirit (twelve in *ST*) are the actions of the infused virtues when they have been perfected by the gifts; on the relationship between the fruits and the beatitudes see Aquinas, *ST* 1a2ae, 70, 2 (*ed. cit.* XXIV, 68–71).

by many diuisions . . . fruites The view that the gifts precede the virtues came from the systematisation of Augustine's thought by Anselm of Laon in *Summa Sententiarum* (1138): it was questioned by Peter Lombard who classified the gifts as virtues in the *Sentences* (1148–50); see Appendix 3 to *ST* 1a2ae, 68–70 (*ed. cit.* XXIV, 100–2).

And contrarywise . . . wordes The predominant view by 1234, that the virtues precede the gifts, was developed in the 1220s in Paris principally by Bonaventura, William of Auvergne and William of Auxerre; see *ibid.* 104–7; *NCE* VII, s.v. 'Holy Spirit, Gifts of'.

Other sayth . . . giftes A reference to Aquinas' contribution to the doctrine of the seven gifts, that they precede the intellectual and moral virtues, but are posterior to the theological virtues. Drawing on Gregory's *Moralia* II, 36 (*PL* 75, 573) he distinguishes the theological virtues and the gifts from the moral virtues in his commentary (c.1152–57) on III *Sententiarum*, di. 34, 1, 1 (*Scriptum in Libros Sententiarum Magistri Petri Lombardi*, ed. P. Mandonnet,

4 vols (Paris, 1929–33), III, 1105–15). The purpose of the gifts (which constitute a supernatural flow of energy) is to perfect the infused virtues. His definitions of the theological virtues (whose object is the supernatural end itself) as prior to the gifts and a standard in relation to them, and of the intellectual and moral virtues as posterior to the gifts, became standard. See *ST* 1a2ae. 68, 8, 2 (*ed. cit.* XXIV, 36–41; Appendix 4; pp. 110–30); *Royal Book*, ed. cit. sig. P4ᵛ; *Book of Vices and Virtues*, pp. 121–2; *Sermons*, p. 227.

Marginal note *Sco. iii . . . xxxv* I.e. Duns Scotus who opposed the view of Aquinas (which Edgeworth upholds) in his commentary on the *Sentences* III, Dist. 34–5 (see *Ioannis Duns Scoti . . . Perutiles Quaestiones in IIII Libros Sententiarum, et Quodlibetales*, a. R.P.F. Paulino Berti, 5 vols (Venice, 1617), III, fos 510–30). Scotus adapted the views of Peter Lombard (*PL* 192, 823–8) and his followers and denied any distinction between the gifts and the infused theological virtues. See John of St Thomas, *Gifts*, pp. 50–72, 208 ff.

as the rote . . . fruites The representation of the tree of Jesse is stylistically related in art to the tree of virtues and vices; the imagery associated with the tree of life, of which charity is the root, stems from treatises such as Bonaventura's *Ligneum Vitae*. In Bonde's *Pilgrymage* (*ed. cit.* fos 43–44, 50–55; 67ᵛ–68) the three theological virtues, faith, hope and charity, springing from the root of grace, are compared to the trunk, branch and sap of the tree of grace; the seven gifts are branches on which flourish the flowers, the beatitudes.

the Carpenters axe . . . gifts See Aquinas, *ST* 1a2ae. 68, 3 (*ed. cit.* XXIV, 22–3); John of St Thomas, *Gifts*, p. 248.

Example . . . charitye St Paul's conversion (Acts 9:1–16), the central act of his life, became the root of his doctrine; see I Cor. 15: 5–11 and Eph. 4:7 on his receiving of grace; *Sermons*, pp. 162, 206.

quemadmodum . . . works I Cor. 3:10. Vg. 'Ut sapiens'.

I will descend . . . goste The introduction to the six sermons on the seven gifts concludes here and a discussion of the first two gifts follows.

spirite of . . . sapience Wisdom is traditionally dealt with first as in *The Abbey of the Holy*

Ghost (Horstman, *Yorkshire Writers* I, 326): 'Nam prior omnium creat[ur]ar[um] est sapiencia'. But some treatises reverse the order of Is. 11:2 and commence with fear. Sapience introduces the contemplative life and the contemplation of Christ's passion in *The Goad of Love*; in Edmund of Abingdon's *Mirror of St Edmund* it is the third and highest degree of contemplation (*ibid.* 225, 247). In Bonde's *Pilgrymage* (*ed. cit.* fos. 279 ff.) heavenly wisdom, the gift of the seventh and last day, is compared to the creation of the world, the completion of God's work; see *Royal Book, ed. cit.* sig. 2F3ᵛ; *Book of Vices and Virtues*, pp. 220–3.

a distinction A term from scholastic philosophy signifying a plurality of terms; it may be objective (the non-identity discovered between distinct things or complete substances) or subjective (the non-identity read by the mind into things).

Iacob .iii. The following comes from Jas. 3:13–15; cf. Aquinas, *ST* 2a2ae, 45, 1, 1 (*ed. cit.* XXXV, 160–1); see *Sermons*, p. 309.

you thincke your selfe . . . fellowes The singular reflexive pronoun was used in the plural sense for 'yourselves' in the sixteenth century. See B. Strang, *A History of English* (London, 1970), p. 141; *OED* s.v. 'Yourself', *pron.* I.2.; *Sermons*, pp. 122, 124, 138, 140, 141, 204 etc.

wisedome . . . heauen A reference to Jas. 3:17.

as blinde as the Molle See Erasmus, *Adagiorum Opus* (Lyons, 1541), I, iii, 55, fo. 152 (cited hereafter as Erasmus, *Adagia*). For an as yet incomplete edition and translation see *Adages Ivil to Ix100*, tr. M.M. Phillips, *CWE* 31 (Toronto, 1982); *Adages Ivil to Ix100*, ed. and tr. R.A.B. Mynors, *CWE* 32 (Toronto, 1989).

like wantes . . . beast Developed from the proverb 'as blind as the mole', the distinctive properties of the mole (a traditional symbol of avarice) here represent the spiritual blindness of the worldly man eager for material gain; 'wine and wastel', traditional symbols of earthly pursuits, symbolise the 'godly meditacions' which he ignores. See M.W. Bloomfield, *The Seven Deadly Sins* (Michigan, 1952), p. 247.

Luc. xvi . . . scorne Luke 16:13–14.

Luk. vi . . . world Luke 6:24; see *Sermons*, p. 309.

.i. Timo . . . frowardnes. &c 1 Tim. 6:17–18.

beastly wisedome . . . chere The personification of sin as the glutton who makes his belly his God is a medieval homiletic commonplace. See Owst, *LPME*, pp. 441–9; Bloomfield, *Seven Deadly Sins*, pp. 181–9.

Hi sunt . . . pascentes Jude 1:12. Vg. 'in epulis suis'.

Luc. vi . . . you Luke 6:25. Vg. 'Vae vobis'.

a messe of potage 'Dish of pulpy food or soup'. Semi-proverbial in this context; see *OED* s.v. 'Mess' sb. 2; *Sermons*, p. 309.

Gene. xxv . . . them Gen. 25:34. Vg. 'quod primogenita vendidisset'.

worse then the prodigall . . . againe A reference to Luke 15:11–32.

by oppression . . . Apes Here the ape is figured as an emblem of oppression signifying devilish wisdom. See Owst, *LPME*, pp. 169–70; H.W. Janson, *Apes and Ape Lore in the Middle Ages and the Renaissance* (London, 1952), pp. 15–22 on the Christian view of the ape as *figura diaboli*.

to wayte men a shreud turne 'To lie in wait or be on watch to inflict injury upon men'.

Rom viii . . . est Rom. 8:6; see *Sermons*, p. 309.

Luc. xvi . . . light Luke 16:8.

Saynte Iames capit. iii The following is an exposition of Jas. 3:17.

.iii. Regum .iii An exposition of III Kings 3:7–12.

Dedi tibi cor . . . thee III Kings 3:12; Vg. ' . . . post te surrecturus sit'.

Sapience . . . truth Aquinas, *ST* 2a2ae. 45, 2, 3 (*ed. cit.* XXXV, 164–7); on Aquinas' thought in 2a2ae see Appendix 4, III, *ed. cit.* XXIV, 124–30.

For Sapience . . . it This exposition of the interrelatedness of the seven gifts comes from Aquinas, *ST* 1a2ae. 68, 5 (*ed. cit.* XXIV, 24–9); Gregory, *Moralia* I, 32 (*PL* 75, 547).

Because that . . . to See Aquinas, *ST* 2a2ae. 8, 1 (*ed. cit.* XXXII, 2–7) on the empirical basis of knowledge. According to Thomistic theology the gifts are infused supernatural dispositions which make a person readily susceptible to special inspiration of the Holy Spirit towards actions that surpass the ordinary virtuous capacities of the recipient (*ST* 2a2ae 19, 9 (*ed. cit.* XXXIII, 70–1).

And that all . . . doth Hebr. 1:6.

As that . . . Hebr. i Heb. 1:1–14 with particular reference to Heb. 1:14; on this exposition of the Trinity from the proof of the coexistence of understanding with faith see Aquinas, *ST* 2a2ae. 8, 2 (*ed. cit.* XXXII, 6–9).

And by mature . . . sapientie Aquinas, *ST* 2a2ae. 45, 2–3 (*ed. cit.* XXXV, 164–9); cf. the distinctions between the gifts as they are enumerated in *ST* 1a2ae. 68, 4 (*ed. cit.* XXIV,19–25; see Appendix 4, III).

To know . . . Arrius saide On the arch-heretic Arius see *Sermons*, pp. 114, 127, 128, 141.

as Manicheus said Mani or Manichaeus (c.216–277) founded the dualist doctrine of Manichaeism which taught that there were two absolute principles: Good (i.e. God, Truth, Light) and original Evil, the author of all matter. Man is formed from matter so that, although the soul is an emanation of the good God, the body, in which the soul is imprisoned, is framed of material elements and subject to evil. See F.C. Burkitt, *The Religion of the Manichees* (Cambridge, 1925), pp. 17 ff; Kelly, *Doctrines*, pp. 8–9; G. Widengren, *Mani and Manichaeism* (London, 1965); ODCC s.v. 'Manes and Manichaeism'; *Sermons*, pp. 127, 141, 170, 171.

Sapi. ix . . . fole Sap. 9:4 and 6. Vg. 'si afuerit ab illo sapientia'.

worldly wisdome . . . i. Corin. iii I Cor. 3:19.

Psal. cxviii . . . commaundementes Ps. 118:73.

Esay .vii . . . vnderstande Is. 7:9. Vg. 'Si non credideritis, non permanebitis'; i.e. 'Unless you believe you shall not be established'. Like More, Edgeworth preferred the Septuagint and the so-called 'Old Latin' versions of this text. See Augustine, *De Trinitate* XV, 26 (PL 42, 1096); *De Doctrina Christiana* II, 12 (PL 34, 43); Epist. 120 (PL 35, 453); Hom. 43 (PL 38, 254–8); R.C. Marius's introduction to More's *Confutation*, CW 8, 1354–5; G. Marc'hadour, *The Bible in the Works of Thomas More: A Repertory*, 5 vols (Nieuwkoop, 1969–72), I, 201–2 (cited hereafter as Marc'hadour, *Bible*).

Ro. x . . . Christi Rom. 10:17; see Aquinas, *ST* 2a2ae. 8, 6 (*ed. cit.* XXXII, 16–21).

acquisite faith . . . gost See Aquinas, *ST* 2a2ae. 8, 2 & 8 (*ed. cit.* XXXII, 6–9, 22–5) on the supernatural gift of understanding based in faith (which functions to ensure that the

speculative and practical truths of the faith are taken in their right sense).

And this gift . . . gifts See Aquinas, *ST* 2a2ae. 8, 4 (*ed. cit.* XXXII, 10–13) on the importance of understanding for matters essential to salvation.

.i. Ioh .ii . . . learned I John 2:27. Vg. 'docet'

Chrisostome . . . matters A reference to 'De Spiritu Sancto', a treatise spuriously ascribed to St Chrysostom (PG 52, 817). Edgeworth used a recognised Latin translation of Chrysostom's writings such as the 1547, 5 vol, Basle edition of S. Gelenius, not the 1558 edition which he bequeathed to Oriel College (Appendix, p. 448).

Reuela . . . law Ps. 118:18.

The spirite . . . hert Chrysostom, 'De Spiritu Sancto' (PG 52, 817).

Os meum . . . vnderstandyng Ps. 48:4

that perfite Sapience . . . learned See Aquinas, *ST* 2a2ae. 45, 5 on the practical aspects of the gift of wisdom in directing human affairs according to a divine standard; *ST* 2a2ae. 8, 4 on the relation of good deeds to the gift of understanding as practical understanding (*ed. cit.* XXXV, 172–5; XXXII, 8–11).

But what . . . permit The preacher's complaint about his disregarding audience is familiar in the medieval pulpit, as is his threat of terror and reproof. See *Jacob's Well*, p. 107; Blench, pp. 237–8; G.R. Owst, *Preaching in Medieval England, an Introduction to the Sermon manuscripts of the Period, 1350–1450* (Cambridge, 1926), pp. 333–345.

Ezech. iii . . . him Ezech. 3:17–18.

Naturall examples . . . it The following passage is drawn largely from the pseudo-Chrysostom homily 'Concio Primo de Lazaro' (PG 48, 963).

sermo domini . . . name Jer. 20:8–9.

Many profites riches See Chrysostom, 'Primo Concio de Lazaro' (PG 48, 965–6).

we haue layde . . . do A reference to Matt. 25:27.

One of you . . . dyuell Matt. 26:21.

ii. Tim. ii . . . truthe II Tim. 2:24–25.

The seconde sermon of the gift of Counsail

The seconde . . . Counsail The admonitions

against insurrections in this sermon may have been inspired by the Pilgrimage of Grace (1536-7) which brought fears of popular sedition to the surface. References to the execution of Anne Boleyn in May 1536, to a famous Protestant preacher (possibly Latimer) who denied Purgatory and the dependence on the Ten Articles of July 1536 in defending the doctrine, suggest a date of preaching between October 1536 and Whitsunday 1537.

Worshipfull . . . theym A resumé of the first sermon; see *Sermons*, pp. 113-20.

the third . . . counsaile Traditionally the third gift, counsel in *The Royal Book* (*ed. cit.* sig. N6ᵛ) is linked to the third petition of the paternoster; in *The Book of Vices and Virtues*, pp. 188-190, it is the fifth gift. Edgeworth distinguishes the spiritual gift of godly counsel from worldly counsel which he illustrates with examples of unsuccessful biblical traitors, early Christian heretics and English rebels (*Sermons*, pp. 124-7).

as from the head . . . said See the exposition, *Sermons*, p. 115.

Quicumque . . . Rom. viii Rom. 8:14.

hauing al . . . Gene. vi Gen. 6:5.

the gyfte . . . reason Aquinas, ST 2a2ae. 52, 2 (*ed. cit.* XXXVI, 112-13).

.vi. Eth . . . counseller Aristotle, *The Nichomachean Ethics* VI, 5 and 10; this was the primary source of Aquinas' treatise on prudence. See *Nichomachean Ethics*, ed. and tr. H. Rackham (London, 1926), pp. 337, 357-9 (cited hereafter as *Nich. Eth.*); Aquinas, ST 2a2ae. 47, 1 (*ed. cit.* XXXVI, xiv-xvi, 4-7).

But this property . . . of Aquinas, ST 2a2ae. 52, 1, 1 (*ed. cit.* XXXVI, III).

Psal. ii . . . Christe Ps. 2:1-2; cf. Acts 4:25-6. The prophecy is Nathan's oracle in II Kings 7:8-16 in which David was promised an everlasting dynasty. In the NT the psalm was held to speak of the coming Davidic king, the Messiah; the kings of the earth (v. 2) were regarded as leaders of God's enemies personified by Herod and Pilate. See J.W. Rogerson and J.W. McKay, *Psalms 1-50*, Cambridge Bible Commentary (Cambridge, 1977), pp. 19-21; ODCC s.v. 'Messiah'.

that they should . . . Ioh. xi John 11:48.

a far cast counseil 'A shrewd trick and a cunning strategem'.

For Herode . . . ca xiiii Josephus, *Antiquitatum Iudaicarum* XVIII, 7, 2; see *Jewish Antiquities* in *Josephus*, ed. and tr. H. St. J. Thackeray *et al*, 10 vols (London, 1954-65), IX, 150-1 (cited hereafter as Josephus, *Jew. Ant.*); cf. Eusebius, *Historica Ecclesiastica* I, 11 (PG 20, 114-18) (cited hereafter as Eusebius, *Hist. Ecc.*). The attribution of John the Baptist's death to Herodias originates from the view (Mk 6:17-21; Matt. 14:1-12) that he was imprisoned because he questioned Herod's right to marry his sister-in-law. According to Josephus in *Jew. Ant.* XVIII, 5, 2 (*ed. cit.* IX, 81-5) he was murdered because of Herod's political fears.

And Pilate . . . cap. vii Josephus, *Jew. Ant.* XVIII, 4, 2 (*ed. cit.* IX, 63-5).

And at Rome . . . chapter Eusebius, *Hist. Ecc.* II, 7 (PG 7, 155); cf. the version in Matt. 27:3-10 in which Pilate hangs himself.

Vespasian and Titus Vespasian, one of the most renowned Roman generals, with the assistance of his son, Titus, restored Roman authority over Palestine in 67 AD. Josephus, a Jewish soldier, won their favour after the fall of Jotopata and celebrated their deeds in *De Bello Judaico* and the *Vita*; see *Sermons*, p. 266.

euen in the time . . . same A reference to a Christian interpolation among the Slavonic additions to *De Bello Judaico* which outlines the belief (from Matt. 27:51 and Mk 15:38) that the veil of the Temple of Jerusalem was rent at the moment of Christ's death. See Josephus, *Jewish War* V, 4 (*Josephus, ed. cit.* III, 265 ff; Appendix 27, pp. 657-8); H.W. Montefiore, *Josephus and the New Testament* (Leiden, 1962), pp. 16-22.

Sanguis . . . children Matt. 27:25.

the chiefe Townes . . . Realme The districts throughout Galilee inhabited by the Jewish people in revolt from Rome; Josephus describes their conquest by Vespasian and Titus in 67-8 AD in *The Jewish War* III and IV. See G.A. Williamson, *The World of Josephus* (London, 1964), pp. 180-216.

toke prisoners . . . xvii Chapter A reference to Josephus, *Jewish War* VI, 9, 3 (*ed. cit.* III, 497).

Qui habitat . . . scorne Ps. 2:4. A familiar translation; see Marc'hadour, *Bible* I, 106; Latimer, *Works* I, 371; J. Palsgrave, tr. *The Comedy of Acolastus*, ed. P.L. Carver, EETS, OS, 202 (London, 1937), pp. 14, 48, 69 (cited hereafter as Palsgrave, *Acolastus*).

when he rose . . . stealyng A reference to Matt. 27:64; see Josephus, *Jewish War*, ed. cit. III, Appendix 27, p. 658. The present participle 'stealyng' is here used as a passive form; a suggested reading is: 'to prevent his body from being stolen'; see *OED* s.v. 'steal'. *v.*[1].

Et dominus . . . them Ps. 2:4.

the Romayns . . . people A reference to John 11:48.

Pro. xxi . . . God Prov. 21:30.

amarum zelum . . . affection Jas. 3:14.

reasoning . . . praiers An echo of Latimer's comment of 1536: 'The founding of monasteries argued purgatory to be, so the putting down of them argueth it not to be' (*Works* II, 249); see *LP* XII, i, 1312; Kreider, *English Chantries*, p. 127.

contra dominum . . . God Prov. 21:30.

Gamaliell . . . Iewes 'The great Jewish rabbi . . . who advised the Israelites (Acts 5: 34–5) and taught St. Paul prior to his conversion' (*ODCC* s.v. 'Gamaliel'). In the *Legenda Aurea* he was recognised as a saint in the belief that he had been converted to Christianity; see J. de Voragine, *The Golden Legend*, tr. Caxton (Wynkyn de Worde, 1527), fo. 188ᵛ. STC 24880. Cited hereafter as Caxton, *Golden Legend*; on Gamaliel see *Sermons*, p. 288.

Theudas The following conflates the references in Acts 5:37 to Theudas, the leader of an unsuccessful insurrection, and in *Jew. Ant.* II, 5, 1 (*ed. cit.* IX, 441–3), to a Theudas mentioned in connection with a Jewish rebellion in 45 or 46 AD. The number of four hundred disciples is given only in Acts 5:36.

Iudas Galileus Another unsuccessful rebel mentioned in Acts 5:37; in *Jew. Ant.* XVIII, 1, 1 and in *Jewish War* II, 8 (*ed. cit.* IX, 5–7; II, 367–9) he persuaded the people to revolt while Quirinus was taking the census in Judaea. The reference to Judas' death comes from Acts 5; in *Jew Ant.* XX, 5, 3 (*ed. cit.* IX, 332–5) it is Judas' sons who are crucified; see *Sermons*, p. 259.

To my purpose . . . not An exposition of Acts 5:38–9.

Of these thre stories . . . forward W. Barlow in his treatise of 1531, *A dialoge . . . of these Lutheran faccions*, 2nd ed. (Cawood, 1553), sigs C1–2, compares the rebels of Acts 5 to Luther and the 'Euangelyke brotherne of Ger-

many' (cited hereafter as Barlow, *A dialoge*). Cf. T. Becon's Protestant treatise, written after the insurrection of 1549, 'The fortress of the faythfull' in *The Catechism of Thomas Becon*, ed. J. Ayre, PS (Cambridge, 1844), p. 595 (cited hereafter as Becon, 'Fortress'), in which they exemplify the fates of traitors.

And contrary . . . tyme Possibly a reference to the Pilgrimage of Grace, the Lincolnshire and Northern uprisings of 1536–7 against the Henrician religious changes. Edgeworth may have known rebel leaders (largely friars and local clergy) at Beverly in Holderness, near his living at Brandesburton in Yorkshire. Their leader, Sir Francis Bigod, was executed in the second Yorkshire rising, after the seige of Bigod Castle was raised on 16 January 1537. See M.H. and R. Dodds, *The Pilgrimage of Grace, 1536–7, and the Exeter Conspiracy, 1538*, 2 vols (Cambridge, 1915), I, ch. 7; II, ch 17: A Fletcher, *Tudor Rebellions*, 3rd ed. (London, 1983), pp. 17–36.

Arrius . . . Sabellius On Arius, see *Sermons*, pp. 114, 120, 128, 141.

Pelagius (c. 350–418), a British heretic who denied the existence of divine grace and original sin and attributed the attainment of salvation to man's efforts alone. He was excommunicated by Pope Innocent I; see Kelly, *Doctrines*, pp. 357–61; *ODCC* s.v. 'Pelagianism'; B.R. Rees, *Pelagius: a reluctant heretic* (Woodbridge, 1988); *Sermons*, p. 141.

Manes The heretic from Persia (c.215–275), known as Mani among Oriental writers and Manichaeus by classical writers. The name 'Cubricus' or 'Corbicus' derives from a story of the Greeks in *Acta Archelai* (c.330–340) that a slave by that name assumed the mission of a deceased heretic, Terebinthus, and renamed himself Manes the eloquent. According to Augustine, Manes later changed his name to Manichaeus to avoid his opponents' censure; see *DCB* III, s.v. 'Manes'; *Sermons*, pp. 120, 141, 170.

Sabellius (Fl. c.217), a theologian of Roman origin. 'Sabellianism' is a more sophisticated form of 'Modalist' Monarchianism, a movement which regarded the Godhead as a monad which expressed itself in three operations. This teaching was condemned at Rome in 257 and by the Council of Nicaea in 325; see *ODCC* s.v. 'Sabellianism' and 'Monarchianism'; Kelly, *Doctrines*, pp. 119–23.

Wicliffe John Wycliffe (c.1330–1384), the Oxford scholar and reformer who attacked the ecclesiastical hierarchy and the Pope's authority. His anticlericalism was endorsed by the Lollards and in 1381 his name was associated with the Peasant's Revolt. On the influence of Lollard works on the reformers, see A. Hudson, ' "No Newe Thyng": The Printing of Medieval Texts in the Early Reformation Period' in *Middle English Studies presented to N. Davis in Honour of his Seventieth Birthday*, ed. D. Gray and E.G. Stanley (Oxford, 1983), pp. 153–74; repr. in *Lollards and their Books* (London, 1985), pp. 227–48; *Sermons*, p. 141.

Kinge Edwarde the thirde Two unsuccessful attempts were made to convict Wycliffe of heresy at the end of Edward III's reign. In February 1377 he was arraigned for controversial views in his treatises on civil and divine dominion and on 22 May 1377 Pope Gregory XI issued five Bulls accusing him of eighteen erronious conclusions. Proceedings to bring him to trial in Rome were halted by the pope's death, and the trials at Lambeth in London were dissolved because of popular support for Wycliffe from the crown and citizens of London. See J.H. Dahmus, *The Prosecution of John Wyclyf* (New Haven, 1952), pp. 7–23, 35 ff; H.B. Workman, *The History of the Life and Sufferings of John Wycliffe*, 2 vols (Oxford, 1820), I, 1–18, 45–82; K.B. MacFarlane, *John Wycliffe and the Beginnings of English Nonconformity* (London, 1952), pp. 74–82.

king Henry . . . burned A reference to the rebellion of Sir John Oldcastle, a high-ranking partisan of Wycliffe, condemned for heresy on 23 September 1413. His attempted coup d'état with Lollard supporters after escaping from the Tower, was intercepted by the king and his counsellors. Oldcastle and the insurgents were put to death and in April 1414 the clergy and bishops were further empowered to imprison heretics. See More, *Dialogue*, CW 6, 409–10; *Apology*, CW 9, 91–2; MacFarlane, *John Wycliffe*, 160–83; Thomson, *Later Lollards*, pp. 4–19.

Luther in Saxony . . . realme The Protestants who met at the White Horse Inn, Cambridge, in the 1520s, shifted their centre from 1524–1540 to Wittenberg where Luther, Melanchthon and Bugenhagen were based. Tyndale completed his translation the NT there in 1525 with the assistance of William Roye;

Robert Barnes, arriving in 1530, published nineteen articles of belief, *Sentenciae ex doctoribus collectae*, under the name of Antonius Anglus and prepared *The Supplication unto . . . King Henry the Eighth* (Antwerp, 1531). STC 1470. William Barlow claimed that he visited Luther in Saxony in 1528 (A *dialoge*, ed. cit. sigs F1–F3ᵛ). Others who sought the reformers' company included Thomas Dusgate (alias Benet); Thomas Swinnerton; and John Rogers (alias Matthews). See W.A. Clebsch, *England's Earliest Protestants 1520–1535* (London, 1964); J.F. Mozley, *William Tyndale* (New York and London, 1937), pp. 51–3; P. Smith, 'English men at Wittenburg in the sixteenth century', *EHR* 36 (1921), 422–33; on Barnes's mission, Lusardi's introduction to More's *Confutation*, CW 8, 1387–96; G. Rupp, *Studies in the Making of the English Protestant Tradition* (Cambridge 1947), pp. 31–46; *Sermons*, pp. 137, 169, 245.

and his encouragyng . . . scriptures Answers to Luther's response to Henry VIII's *Assertio*, *Contra Henricum Regem Angliae* (1522), were based largely on patristic and scriptural sources. More's *Responsio ad Lutherum* was published twice in 1523 under the pseudonym of Guillelmus Rosseus; Dr Powell contributed *Propugnaculum summi Sacerdotii euangelici . . . aduersus M. Lutherum* (Pynson, 1523); Dr J. Eck, *De Primatu Petri adversus Lutherum Vidovaeus* (Paris, 1521); Bishop Fisher, *Assertionis Lutheranae Confutatio* (Antwerp, 1523). Fisher's other apologetic works were *Defensio Regie Assertionis contra Babylonicam Captivatatem* (Cologne, 1523); *Sacri Sacerdotii contra Lutherum* (Cologne, 1525), and two sermons against Luther preached at burnings of heretical books at Paul's Cross in 1521 and 1526 (see *The English Works of John Fisher*, Pt. 1, ed. J.E.B. Mayor, EETS, ES, 27 (London, 1876), 311–48; STC 10892–7). See Headley, *loc. cit.*; Schuster's introduction to *Confutatio*; CW 8, 1146–8; Doernberg, *Henry VIII*, pp. 27–45; Clebsch, *Protestants*, pp. 14–19, 27–32.

Marginal note: *King Henry . . . aucthority* In 1521, in response to Luther's *De Captivitate Babylonica Ecclesiae* (1520), Henry VIII published his defence of the church, *Assertio Septem Sacramentorum* (STC 13078). But More's reference to the 'makers' of the book implies a collaborative authorship possibly consisting of More, Fisher, Longland and Edward Lee. Several editions followed in 1522 and 1523 including German translations by T. Murner and J. Emser. See L. O. Donovan, *Assertio Septem Sacramentorum* (New York, 1908), pp. 53–93; J.M. Headley's introduction to More's *Responsio*, *CW* 5, 715–31; E. Doernberg, *Henry VIII and Luther* (London, 1961), pp. 3–26; Clebsch, *Protestants*, pp. 19–23. This is a Marian addition; references to the *Assertio* after c.1534 would have been embarassing to Henry.

Arius heresy . . . reader The story that Arius' disappointed ambitions to the chair of Achillas, Bishop of Alexandria, contributed to this subversive behaviour occurs in Eusebius, *Hist. Ecc.* I, 2 & 3; but it is probably apocryphal. Although Achillas ordained Arius presbyter of the church of Baucalis in Alexandria in c.313, it was St Alexander (next in rank to the bishop) who succeeded Achillas. The origins of the heresy are obscure, but Arianism dates from c.318 when the Christological question was already under dispute. See R.D. Williams, *Arius: Heresy and Tradition* (London, 1987), pp. 32, 40.

Inimicitia . . . man Gal. 5:19. Vg. 'inimicitiae'. While the meaning of *inimicitiae* did not change, the form changed from plural to singular in the middle ages.

Opera carnis . . . man Gal. 5:19.

Wicliff . . . Oxforde In 1365 Wycliffe was nominated Warden of Canterbury Hall, Oxford, by Simon Islip, Archbishop of Canterbury; but in 1366, Simon Langham, the new Archbishop, reinstated Woodhall, the previous head. Wycliffe's appeal to the papal court was dismissed by Pope Urban V in 1369. Further disappointments followed; in 1373 Wycliffe failed to receive the Lincoln prebend promised by Pope Gregory XI; and in 1374–5 the prebend of Caistor and promotion to the see of Worcester. See Dahmus, *Prosecution*, pp. 1–6; Workman, *John Wycliffe* I, 171–94; MacFarlane, *John Wycliffe*, pp. 27–30, 67–8.

And Luther . . . occasions Luther's attacks between 1517 and 1521 on the ecclesiastical authorities and his conflict with the Papacy gave rise to this view in England; see Barlow, *A dialoge, ed. cit.* sigs C3–C6ᵛ. More, *Dialogue*, *CW* 6, 361–2, 369, attributes to Luther the origins of the German Peasants' Revolt of 1525; see *Sermons*, pp. 169, 245, 280.

and for carnall . . . euangelicall libertie The term 'evangelical' originated with the Evangelical movement associated with Luther which opposed clerical celibacy and monastic institutions, but which was known primarily for its preaching of the gospel. First used pejoratively in England in the 1520s of those groups (including the Anabaptists and Sacramentarians) who believed in *scriptura sola* or justification by faith alone, it came to refer to the freedoms enjoyed due to the relaxation of many ceremonies and observances. More was hostile to 'evangelical liberty'; see *Dialogue*, *CW* 6, 368–9, 403–4; *Responsio*, *CW* 5, 274–7; A.G. Fox, *Thomas More: History and Providence* (Oxford, 1982), pp. 160–66. Barlow, *A dialoge, ed. cit.* sig. G1ᵛ, uses the term of those who condemn fasting and prayers; J. Standish, *A lytle treatyse . . . againste the protestacion of Robert barnes (ex aed. E. Pykerynge viduae R. Redmani*, 1540), sig. A5, says that 'carnal liberty' is preached with 'a damnable justyfycacyon of onely fayth to iustyfye' (*STC* 23210); cf. the Protestant preacher Thomas Lever who in 1550 identified it with unlawful gains; see *Sermons*, 1550, ed. E. Arber (London, 1870), p. 104; Becon, 'Fortress', *Catechism*, pp. 592, 601; *Sermons*, pp. 132, 218, 229, 259–60.

Gala. v . . . charitie Gal. 5:13.

i, Pet. ii . . . liuynge 1 Pet. 2:16. Vg. 'sicut servi dei'; see *Sermons*, p. 259.

euangelicall brothers Terms such as 'brethren' and 'the newe broched brotherhed' were used of Protestant reformers; but this is probably a reference to the Anabaptists who denied ceremonies and trafficked in proscribed books. See More, *Apology*, *CW* 9, 7, 9, 14 (n.); H. Glasier, *A notable . . . Sermon* (Caly 1555), sig. C6ᵛ, *STC* 11916; Barlow, *A dialoge, ed. cit.* sig. B7; Horst, *Radical Brethren*, pp. 38, 41, 49, 57, 78; Rupp, *Studies*, pp. 6–14; Anne Hudson, 'A Lollard Sect Vocabulary?' in *So meny people, longages and tonges: Philological Essays . . . , presented to Angus McIntosh*, eds. M. Benskin and M.L. Samuels (Edinburgh, 1981), p. 17 on the use of 'evangelical' with reference to Wycliffe (repr. in *Lollards and their Books*, pp. 165–80); Pelikan, *Church and Dogma*, p. 316; Susan Brigden, 'Thomas Cromwell and the "brethren"', in *Law and Government under the Tudors*, eds. Claire Cross, David Loades, J.J. Scarisbrick (Cambridge, 1988), pp. 31–50.

whiche counteth . . . tymes In 1536 eating flesh on fish days came to be considered a sign

of Protestantism. Latimer preached on March
12 at Pauls' Cross in favour of eating flesh and
white meat in Lent. Dispensation from ab-
stention from white meats (including *lacticina*) in the Lenten fast was first granted in
1538 because fish was scarce. See MacLure,
Paul's Cross Sermons, pp. 26–7, 186; L. Baldwin Smith, 'Henry VIII and the Protestant
Triumph', *American Historical Review* 71, ii
(1966), 157–64; Hughes and Larkin, I, 177.

that the pleasure . . . agreed A reference to the
execution of Anne Boleyn and her brother
Lord Rochford on 17 and 19 May 1536 on
charges of incest (Bridgett, 'Bristol Pulpit', 84);
these dates provide a *terminus a quo* for this sermon although the three month ban on preaching after the passing of the Ten Articles on 11
July suggests a date of preaching between
November 1536 and early 1537. See *LP* X, 908,
911, 1036; P. Thomson, *Sir Thomas Wyatt and
his Background* (London, 1964), pp. 33–6; E.W.
Ives, *Anne Boleyn* (Oxford, 1980), ch. 17.

ragged & iagged Colloquial; see Barlow, A *dia-
loge, ed. cit.* sig. L3ᵛ: 'al to hacked and iagged';
Skelton, 'Colyn Clout', ll. 53–4: 'For though
my ryme be ragged, /Tattered and jagged'; see
John Skelton: The Complete English Poems, ed.
J. Scattergood (London, 1983), p. 248.

But now . . . clerks In his defences against
Lutheranism in *The Supplication of Souls* and
Responsio ad Lutherum More used scripture to
prove purgatory as an unwritten verity
(Marc'hadour, *Bible* IV, 101–4). But by early
1536 such claims were unable to be substan-
tiated (Kreider, *English Chantries*, pp. 114–15).

Purgatory . . . sorte This definition was apparently current by May 1536 when Henry,
having admitted in April 'purgatory as formerly, or at least a third place, neither paradise or hell', allowed it to be preached again
(*LP* X, 752). See *LP* X, 282, 308, 528, 831,
1043; for innovative preaching on the doctrine, Kreider, *English Chantries*, p. 110 ff.

the scriptures . . . Purgatory In *Ein Widderruff
vom Fegefeuer* (Wittenberg, 1530) Luther concluded that there was no scriptural basis for
purgatory. More upheld Catholic doctrine in
Dialogue (CW6, 354, 425) arguing from Matt.
12:36 that purgatory was provable by scripture. But the prelates who met at Lambeth
Palace in March 1536 for preliminary discussions on the Ten Articles found the only
scriptural source in the extra-canonical book

II Maccabees (12:40–45) and very little agreement among the Church Fathers. See *ibid.* pp.
117–8; Marc'hadour, *Bible* II, 40–41.

wee reade not . . . Trinitas Most reformers affirmed the doctrine of the Trinity as a fundamental presupposition, and it did not
become a polemical issue in England; see Pelikan, *Church and Dogma*, pp. 257–8, 265, 323–
31. For anti-Trinitarianism among the radical
reformers see G.H. Williams, *The Radical
Reformation* (Philadelphia, 1962), pp. 319–25;
see Barlow, A *dialoge, ed. cit.* sigs E2ᵛ–E3, for
preaching against the doctrine. Edgeworth
may be thinking of Erasmus' mockery of
scholastic 'proofs' of the Trinity in *Praise of
Folly*; see the translation by B. Radice, *CWE*
27 (Toronto, 1986), 133.

homousion . . . thinge The celebrated Greek
term *homoousion*, of one substance (referring
to the eternal relationship which exists
between the three Persons of the Holy
Trinity), to which the Latin *consubstantialis* or
unius substantiae corresponds, was used as a
test word of theological orthodoxy at the
Nicaean Council in 325. On the grounds that
this was a non-scriptural formulation the
Arians rejected the decision of the Council;
but the doctrine of consubstantiation was subsequently adapted into the Nicaean Creed.
See ODCC s.v. 'Homoousion' and 'Consub-
stantial'; R.P.C. Hanson, *The Search for the
Christian Doctrine of God* (Edinburgh, 1988),
pp. 190–202; Williams, *Arius*, pp. 68–70;
Kelly, *Doctrines*, pp. 231–7; Pelikan, *Church
and Dogma*, pp. 322–3, 326 on the reformers'
antipathy to the non-biblical terminology *ho-
moousios*.

that I might agree . . . name The tenth article
defines purgatory, 'without determination of
any special place or expressed assertion of any
name, either to be called *sinus Abrahae* or
otherwise, but not minding to revive again a
Popish purgatory'. In the *King's Book* the
article is entitled 'Of prayers for the Souls
Departed'; see *LP* X, 225; *Formularies*, pp. 16–
17, 375; Kreider, *English Chantries*, pp. 151–2.

To denye the sayde A . . . liues Cf. the tenth
article which implies that good works and
penance are not essential for salvation; *Formularies*, pp. 16–17.

Consilia impiorum . . . menne Prov. 12:5.

I was once . . . memento Probably a reference
to Latimer who recanted sixteen articles of

belief including two on purgatory in 1532 (*Works* II, 218–20). He was charged in 1533 with preaching against the doctrine in Bristol (*ibid.* 236–9, 259–60) and attempted to persuade Henry to his views in 1536 (*ibid.* 245–9). His famous Convocation sermon of June 9 1536 concludes (Part 1) with prayers for 'those that being departed out of this transitory life, and now sleep in the sleep of peace (*Works* I, 40; *LP* XI, 123). Edgeworth probably attended this meeting of convocation as he was in London in April (Introduction, p. 25). See Kreider, *English Chantries*, pp. 101–3, 119–20; Chester, *Latimer*, pp. 114–16.

Qui nos . . . peace The second memento of the Mass occurs after the *anamnesis* and is the commemoration of those who died in the grace of the Lord 'et dormiunt in sompno pacis' (traditionally interpreted as the faithful souls in purgatory). See *The Booklet of the Mass by Brother Ghent van der Goude, 1507*, ed. P. Dearmer, Alcuin Club, 5 (London, 1903), p. 99; *The Sarum Missal*, ed. J. Wickham Legg (Oxford, 1916), pp. 223–4. The printed versions of Latimer's Convocation sermon are abridged and contain no allusions to the liturgy (Chester, *Latimer*, p. 114).

Ipsis domine . . . otherwise Ibid. In early 1536 it was permitted only to pray for, but not preach about, the souls in purgatory; see Kreider, *English Chantries*, p. 114.

Now if their new . . . alredy Luther came to make purgatory a place without specific definition known as 'Abraham's bosom' in which the souls rested until the day of judgement. John Frith's treatise (often attributed to Richard Tracey) *The preparacyon to the crosse and to Deathe* (Berthelet, 1540), sig. T8, states: 'Deathe . . . is a quiet rest from the afflyctions & troubles of this worlde, in the whiche they that be deade, be so refreshed and newely made, that from thense they shall ryse aboue al other most happye, . . . into an euerlastynge lyfe'. STC 11393; and in *A disputacion of purgatorye* [London? 1537?], sig. L1ᵛ: 'oure perfeyte purgacion is the pure bloude of Chryst whiche wassheth away the synne of the worlde'. STC 11387. The final draft of the tenth article compromises with 'their pains' and 'some part of their pains' of the first draft. By 1537–8 Henry admitted that we should 'neither mourn nor weep (for the souls of the righteous) for they be in peace and rest'; see

Kreider, *English Chantries*, pp. 122–4; *Formularies*, pp. 16–17; *LP* XIII, ii, 373; Pelikan, *Church and Dogma*, pp. 136–7; *Sermons*, pp. 130, 175, 293.

Ioh. xi The following is an exposition of John 11:6–12.

Dixerat . . . deade John 11:13–14. John 11:11 is the *locus classicus* for expounding the fates of the souls of the righteous. The second memento of the Mass teaches that Christ died that Lazarus might live.

Psal. xv . . . againe Ps. 15:9.

If we thinke . . . immortall Possibly a refutation of the minor Lutheran heresy of 'soul-sleep' (psychopannychism); i.e. that the soul was dead or asleep between death and the General Resurrection. This was debated by More and Tyndale; see N.T. Burns, *Christian Mortalism from Tyndale to Milton* (Camb. Mass., 1972), 90–111; Horst, *Radical Brethren*, pp. 161–2; More, *Apology*, CW9, 88, 349–50 (n.).

Deus Abraham . . . Mat, xxii Ex. 3:6; Matt. 22:32. Vg. ' non est deus'.

The soule is immortall . . . heauen The traditional fires of purgatory are omitted and the departed souls are prayed for, not to assuage their purgatorial torment, but to assure their safe passage to heaven.

Iud. xi Judg. 11:35–40. The vow of Jephthah, an Israelite leader, to offer a human sacrifice if he won a victory against the invading Ammonites was often used to illustrate rashness; see *Peake's Commentary on the Bible*, ed. M. Black and H.H. Rowley (London, 1962), pp. 309–10 (cited hereafter as *Peake's Commentary*).

Tua sint . . . had II Kings 16:4. In II Kings 9 David gave Ziba (Saul's servant) Saul's property to manage on behalf of Miphibosheth, son of Jonathon (Saul's nephew). But after Ziba treacherously stated that Miphibosheth sought to recover his grandfather's (Saul's) kingdom, David granted Ziba all his goods (II Kings 16:1–6); see *ibid.* pp. 333, 375.

a neded to haue be sory Reduced form of the perfective 'have' and the past infinitive 'have been'; see above, p. 370.

Ecclesiasticus . . . sorye Ecclus. 32:24.

Et de plenitudine . . . giftes John 1:16.

Exo. xviii The following account comes from

Ex. 18:13–24. Although the exact nature of Jethro's influence over Moses is unknown it is accepted that it was on his father-in-law's advice that Moses delegated his functions of judging and legislating. See *DB* II, s.v. 'Jethro'; *Peake's Commentary*, p. 226.

Moyses Like More, Edgeworth consistently uses 'Moyses', the spelling of the printed Vg. and later medieval manuscripts. The reformers preferred Moses which is closer to the Hebrew. During the Reformation the choice of spelling came to indicate religious allegiances. See More, *Apology*, *CW*9, 18, 316 (n.).

Stulto labore . . . laboure Ex. 18:18.

The thirde sermon, treating of the fourth gift . . . the spirite of fortitude

Good and worshipfull . . . matter A resumé of the contents of the second sermon.

Non est sapientia . . . God Prov. 21:30.

As longe as . . . him See the second sermon, *Sermons*, pp. 124–31.

they would not easely . . . head See M.P. Tilley, *A Dictionary of the Proverbs in England in the Sixteenth and Seventeenth Centuries* (1950, repr. Michigan, 1966), F562: 'Don't make the foot the head' (cited hereafter as Tilley, *Proverbs*).

Fortitude . . . goste See Aquinas *ST* 2a2ae. 123, 12, 3 (*ed. cit.* XLII, 36–9).

Fortitudo . . . auenture Aristotle, *Nich. Eth.* III, 7, 5 (*ed. cit.* p. 159).

Christian Philosophers The *philosophia Christi* was the essence of Erasmian humanism and the basis of a reforming programme in the 1520s (McConica, *English Humanists*, pp. 4, 9, 4–16, 24–8, 32–5). Erasmus urges that a Christian philsophy, stemming from a knowledge of Christ's teachings and guidance by the Holy Spirit, be made available to all men in his preface to his paraphrase on St Matthew, translated as *An exhortacyon to the study of the Gospell* (R. Wyer,) [1534?], sig. H1; and in the *Paraclesis* (Froben, 1516), the introduction to his *Novum Testamentum* translated in 1529 by William Roy as *An exhortacyon to the dylygent study of scripture*, STC 10494. These two treatises were published together twice in c.1534 (*ibid.* pp. 114–15); see E.J. Devereux, *A Checklist of English Translations of Erasmus to 1700*, Occasional Publications, 3, Oxford Bibliographical Society (Oxford, 1968), C63–65;

L.W. Spitz, *The Religious Renaissance of the German Humanists* (Camb., Mass., 1963), pp. 215–16; 221–4.

Esaye sayth .lxiiii . . . nostre Is. 64:6. Vg. 'quasi pannus menstruate universae iustitae nostrae'. A favourite image among the reformers who used it to deny the value of good deeds and to assert justification by faith alone. See Marc hadour, *Bible* I, 207; More, *Dialogue*, *CW* 6, 394–5; Latimer, *Works* II, 150.

All vertues . . . vices Cited as first occurrence in *ODEP* s.v. 'Vices'; this proverb comes from Aristotle, *Nich. Eth.* II, 6, 16 and 7, 8 (*ed. cit.* pp. 95, 107).

Certain conclusions . . . manlinesse Aristotle, *Nich. Eth.* III, 7, 5 (*ed. cit.* pp. 159–63).

Iudas Machabeus The following account comes from I Macc. 3: 32–59; cf. Ambrose, *De Officiis* I, 41 (*PL* 16, 82–3). Judas Maccabeus appears in the lists of nine worthies with Joshua and David as the three biblical heroes who exemplify courage. He was one of five sons of Matthias who raised the revolt against Antiochus and freed Judaea by capturing the Citadel, the last stronghold of Syrian resistance in Jerusalem. See *ODCC* s.v. 'Maccabees'; *Peake's Commentary*, p. 693.

Anthiocus the king Antiochus IV ('Epiphanes'), the notorious Emperor of Syria (175 BC) whose unsuccessful attempt to impose Hellenism on Jewish religion and customs, most notably upon the Temple priesthood, sparked off the Maccabean Revolt. See *ibid.*; *ODCC* s.v. 'Antiochus Epiphanes'; *Sermons*, pp. 134–5, 324.

Melius est . . . men I Macc. 3:59.

chosed The older form of the preterite 'chose' was preferred in translations of the scriptures.

fortis quanto est . . . death Aristotle, *Nich. Eth.* III, 9, 4 (*ed. cit.* p.173); cf. Aquinas, *ST* 2a2ae. 123, 8, 3 (*ed. cit.* XLII, 25–7).

an immortalitie . . . it A reference to the controversy over purgatory; see *Sermons*, pp. 128–9.

as Esay speaketh A reference to Is. 11:2.

when he sweat . . . agonie A reference to the Agony in Gethsemane (Luke 22:44). Devotions on the Passion often linked Christ's sufferings with the seven gifts: see *Goad of Love*, p. 78.

Wherefore God . . . creatures A reference to Phil. 2:9–10.

As Esaye . . . partes Isaiah prophecied from 739–701 BC. The legend that he was sawn in two (see Heb. 11:37) by the order of Manasseh, the idolatrous King of Judah, for making speeches on God and the Holy City contrary to the law comes from *Ascensio Isaie*, a Jewish book of the second century. See *Enc. Bib.* I, s.v. 'Apocalyptic Literature'; II, s.v. 'Isaiah'; *ODCC* s.v. 'Isaiah, Ascension of'.

Ieremye . . . God Jeremy prophecied from 626–586 BC. Of the many legends of his death it was the tradition (from Tertullian) that he was stoned to death by the Jews (cf. Heb. 11:37) at Daphne near Egypt that was accepted by Epiphanius and Jerome. See *Enc. Bibl.* II and *ODCC* s.v. 'Jeremiah'.

.ii. Mach. vii The story of the Mother and her seven sons comes from II Macc. 7:1–41; cf. Ambrose, *De Officiis* I, 41 (*PL* 16, 83). The martyrdoms occurred at Antioch at the hands of Antiochus IV ('Epiphanes') in c.169 BC.

Deus aspiciet . . . vs II Macc. 7:6.

Tu quidem . . . manne II Macc. 7:9.

.s. Steuen . . . church .s. Steuen St. Stephen, protomartyr and deacon of the Christian church, was accused of blasphemy in Jerusalem in c.35 AD and after a long discourse (Acts 7:2–53) was stoned to death without a trial; this event was witnessed by Paul (Acts 7:54–8). His holy day is December 26; see *Sermons*, pp. 162, 177.

saint Iames St James 'the Great', son of Zebedee and brother of St John the evangelist, was the first apostle to die for the faith; he was beheaded in Jerusalem in 44 AD by King Herod Agrippa (Acts 12:2). His holy day is July 25; see *Sermons*, pp. 173, 178, 288.

saint Peter Tradition claims that St Peter, foremost of the apostles, was crucified upside down in the circus of Nero in Rome in c. 64 AD. His holy day is June 29; see *Sermons*, pp. 170, 193–4, 196–8, 288.

s. Andrew St Andrew, brother of Simon Peter who, according to an unreliable tradition, was crucified in c.60 AD at Patras in Achaea on an X-shaped cross. His holy day is November 30; see *Sermons*, p. 174.

Bartholomew Apostle and martyr of the first century who, according to tradition, had missionary activities in India and Greater Armenia; he was flayed alive at Albanopolis

on the W. coast of the Caspian Sea. His holy day is August 24; see *Sermons*, p. 177.

Laurence Deacon of Rome who assisted Pope Sixtus II during Emperor Valerian's persecution of Christians and was martyred in 258 probably by decapitation with the sword. The story handed down by Prudentius, Ambrose and Augustine, that he was roasted on a gridiron has been rejected. His holy day is August 10.

Vincent St Vincent of Sargossa, archdeacon of Bishop Valerian, Spain's most illustrious martyr, was martyred in 304 AD at Valencia in the persecution of the clergy by Diocletian and Maximian. The manner of his death is legendary: he was racked, lacerated, roasted on the gridiron, thrown into prison and set on stocks. His holy day is 22 January. See *ODCC*; *ODS*; F.G. Holweck, *A Biographical Dictionary of the Saints* (Herder, 1924). J.J. Delaney, *Dictionary of Saints* (London, 1980) on all these saints.

Heb. xi . . . pieces Heb. 11:35–6. Vg. 'alii autem distenti . . . alii vero ludibria'. It was traditional to link the death of martyrs with the gift of fortitude; see Aquinas, *ST* 2a2ae. 124, 2 (*ed. cit.* XLII, 43–7); Ambrose, *De Officiis* I, 41 (*PL* 16, 83); Bonde, *Pilgrymage, ed. cit.* fos 135^r–v.

The fourth sermon, treatyng of the fift gift . . . the spirite of Science

The fourth . . . Science The monastic dissolutions in Bristol of 1539–40 and the proclamation of April 1539 restricting reading of the Bible suggest a date of preaching sometime in late 1539 or early 1540.

ye logitions . . . demonstration I.e. the Aristotelian theologians of scholasticism who treated science as a series of demonstrated conclusions; see Aquinas, *ST* 2a2ae. 9, 1 (*ed. cit.* XXXII, 26–9). Bonde, *Pilgrymage, ed. cit.* fo. 121^v, states: 'This is not the scyence or connynge of the philosophers . . . but it is the scyence of sayntes'. Scholasticism is dismissed by Erasmus in favour of *philosophia christi* in *An exhortacyon to the dylygent study of scripture* (R. Wyer,) [1534?], sig. B5^v: 'Yf scolemaysters wolde instructe theyr chyldren rather with this symple scyence then with the wyttye tradycyons of Aristotle and Averroys. Then shuld the Chrystente be more at quyetnes'.

but science . . . faythe Aquinas, *ST* 2a2ae. 9, 1, 2 (*ed. cit.* XXXII, 28–33); cf. Bonde, *Pilgrymage, ed. cit.* fo. 121ᵛ: 'First it (holy science) directeth man in all thynges concernynge our fayth'.

Faith worketh . . . loue Gal. 5:6; cited by Aquinas, *ST* 2a2ae. 9, 3 (*ed. cit.* XXXII, 34–5). More also translates *caritas* in this text by 'love' rather than by 'charity'. See Marc'hadour, *Bible* III, 100.

This gift . . . occupations Aquinas, *loc. cit.*

And it presupposeth . . . creatures A reference to the second sermon (pp. 124–31) preached c.1536–7.

Example . . . saued Probably a reference to the Jewish Christians whom St Paul met on his gentile mission at Antioch and who insisted on preserving the Mosaic law, especially the ritual of circumcision. This ceased to be obligatory on Gentiles at the first Council of Jerusalem in c.49 AD. See Gen. 17:10; cf. Aquinas, *ST* 1a2ae. 102, 5 (*ed. cit.* XXIX, 182–5); *ODCC* s.v. 'Paul, St'.

And after a manne . . . dye A reference to the water of expiation; see Num. 19:11–12; Aquinas, *ST* 2a2ae. 102, 5 (*ed. cit.* XXIX, 192–4). For other ceremonies see *Sermons*, pp. 182–5.

many such ceremonies . . . perfourmed A reference to Col. 2:17; cf. Aquinas, *ST* 1a2ae. 107, 2 (*ed. cit.* XXX, 28–9) on the Old Law as the shadow or figure.

Testimonium . . . vnderstandynge Rom. 10:2.

Iustitiae . . . reformacion Heb. 9:10. Vg. 'iustitiis . . . inpositis'.

Such a zeale . . . gost See More's call for the 'secret inspiracyon' of the Holy Ghost in *Dialogue, CW6,* 119, 178, 517; cf. Erasmus in *An exhortacyon to . . . scripture, ed. cit.* sig. B4; *Sermons,* pp. 141–2.

In this case . . . bible A reference to the early English Bible: either 'Coverdale's Bible' of 1535 or the revised versions known as 'Matthew's Bible' (1537; reissued in 1539 as 'Taverner's Bible') or the 'Great Bible' (April 1539; reissued in six editions by 1541). In 1536 all priests were enjoined to obtain a copy of Coverdale's Bible; the injunction of 1538 ordered that copies of the Great Bible be placed in every parish church. See Hughes and Larkin, I, 200; C.C. Butterworth, *The Literary Lineage of the King James Bible, 1340–1611*

(Philadelphia, 1941), pp. 94–148; J.F. Mozley, *Coverdale and his Bibles* (London, 1953); Guy, *Tudor England,* p. 182.

sedicious Englisshe bokes . . . Saxonie Bristol was a centre for the illegal book trade in the 1520s. In c.1532 Chancellor Thomas More, when examining for heresy a Bristol bookseller Richard Webb, commented that they were so freely available that they were 'throwen in the strete and lefte at mennys dores by nyght' (*Confutation, CW8,* 812; for other proceedings against heretics see 1155–1252; on the ecclesiastical commission, 178–9 (n.); for A. Hume's chronological bibliography of Protestant books printed abroad, see Appendix B, 1065–91). Tyndale's NT and Luther's works were burnt at Paul's Cross in 1521 and 1526 and proclamations prohibiting the possession of heretical books and translations of the scriptures were issued in 1529–30, 1538 and 1546 (Hughes and Larkin, I, 122, 129, 186, 272). See Doernberg, *Henry VIII and Luther,* pp. 10–13; *REB,* nos 15–22 for measures taken against possession of Tyndale's NT.

When menne . . . learned On social aspects of Bible reading see M. Aston, 'Lollardy and Literacy' in *Lollards and Reformers* (London, 1984), pp. 193–217.

raylynge . . . mattens For other comments on changing attitudes towards the fasting laws and ceremonies see *Sermons,* pp. 128, 133, 187, 189, 288–9, 298, 333.

blessed ceremonies . . . reasonable An echo of the proclamation of April 1539 limiting reading of the English Bible (Hughes and Larkin, I, 191). In 1543 it was made available only to upper class males and for household or 'private' reading by women of noble status (*Statutes of the Realm* II, 894–6); see More, *Dialogue, CW6,* 333, 335; Guy, *Tudor England,* p. 194. In the South-West, by contrast, lay Bible reading was rare; see R. Whiting, *The Blind Devotion of the People* (Cambridge, 1989), pp. 193–5.

I shall tell you . . . hadde A popular view among the apologists; see Barlow, *A Dialoge, ed. cit.* sig. L7ᵛ: 'our question is not whether it be lawful to let them (i.e. the laity) haue it: but whether it be vnlawfull to keep them from it'. More advocated an English translation of the Bible in *Dialogue, CW6,* 332, 334, 337–8; the bishops discussed it in 1530 and Christopher St German petitioned the king to commission one in 1534. Erasmus anticipated the demand for a vernacular translation in 1522 in *An exhortacyon to . . . the Gospel, ed. cit.* F2ᵛ–G2ᵛ. See *REB* nos. 26, 29, 37; G. Marc'hadour, *Thomas More et la Bible* (Paris, 1969), pp. 517–26; Horst, *Radical Brethren*, pp. 44–49; Guy, *Tudor England*, pp. 121, 123.

But who be meete . . . doubte On Standish's plea in *A discourse . . . that the scripture should be in English . . .* (Caly, 1554), sig. A3ʳ–ᵛ (*STC* 23208) see Introduction, p. 63 n. 19. Barlow's comment in *A dialoge (ed. cit.* sigs K8–L1ᵛ) is the earliest indication that an English translation was being thought of. But although More's programme for a Catholic translation (*Dialogue, CW6,* 341) was discussed in 1530, the attempt to translate the NT in 1534 was unsuccessful. In August 1537 Henry gave official approval to Matthew's Bible and in 1539 licensed Cromwell to approve the Great Bible. See More, *Confutation, CW8,* 179 and n.; Hughes and Larkin, I, 192; Marc'hadour, *Thomas More,* pp. 527–32; McConica, *English Humanists,* pp. 162–4.

.i. Ethi . . . Philosophye Aristotle, *Nich. Eth.* I, 3, 5–7 (*ed. cit.* p. 9).

youth . . . vyces A reference to Aristotle, *Nich. Eth.* III, 7, 5 (*ed. cit.* pp. 158–63); see *Sermons,* pp. 234, 354.

To tel thys tale . . . liuynge Aristotle, *Nich. Eth.* I, 2, 7–8 (*ed. cit.* p. 7).

to teache . . . them Cf. the encouragement towards self-instruction given by Erasmus in *An exhortacyon to . . . scripture, ed. cit.* sig. A8: 'Nether is it nedefull that thou be clogged with so many irxome and babelynge scyences (i.e. study of Aristotle). The meanes (i.e. the scriptures) to this Phylosophye are easy and at hande'. Wrenched syntax in the final two clauses is due to the use of the object pronoun 'them' with the verb 'maketh' used causatively. A suggested reading is 'makes them of such a disposition that moral lessons which teach acts of vertue can make no impression on them'.

as the counsaylers . . . were A reference to III Kings 12:6–15; II Par. 10:6–15; see *Sermons,* pp. 355–6 on Rehoboam.

the end of Diuinitie . . . doinge Aquinas *ST* 2a2ae. 9, 3 (*ed. cit.* XXXII, 33–5). The goals of studying divinity – good deeds – are here equated with those of moral philosophy.

Mat. xiii . . . them Matt. 13:15 with reference to Is. 6:10.

s. Austine . . . beleue Augustine, 'Quaestionum Septemdecim in Matthaeum', XIV, 1–4 (*PL* 35, 1372–3).

How maye a man . . . bodies These questions were discussed in the Schools and teaching on them was contained in the manuals of theology such as Albertus Magnus' *Compendium Theologica Veritatis.* On the properties of angels see Aquinas, *ST* 1a. 50–64 (*ed. cit.* IX); Bartholomaeus Anglicus, *De Proprietatibus Rerum* II, 2–5; see the translation of c.1398–9, *On the Properties of things: John Trevisa's translation of Bartholomaeus Anglicus 'De Proprietatibus rerum': a critical text,* 3 vols, ed. M.C. Seymour *et al.* (Oxford, 1975–88), I, 59–67 (cited hereafter as Trevisa, *Properties of things*).

Women . . . disputeth it This disapproval of women publically preaching and teaching (*Sermons,* pp. 138–40) suggests that women preachers were not a recent phenomenon in Bristol; see M. Aston, 'Lollard Women Priests?' in *Lollards and Reformers,* pp. 49–70.

.i. Corinth. xiiii . . . home I Cor. 14:35.

Mulier in silencio . . . teacher I Tim. 2:11–12.

you must vnderstand . . . same Cf. Erasmus' view in *Exhortacyon to . . . the Gospell, ed. cit.* sigs D3ᵛ–D4:
they thynke none shuld be admytted: (i.e. to reading the scriptures) . . . but a fewe suche which haue ben many yeres exercysed and beaten in the phylosophy of Arystotle / and in the dyuynyte scolastycall, vsed with in the scoles of the vnyuersytes.
Tyndale denounced the apologists' use of philosophy in reading the scriptures which he called *philautia* or 'self love'; see the preface to *Obedience of a Christian Man* in *Doctrinal Treatises,* ed. H. Walter, PS (Cambridge, 1848), p. 154 (cited hereafter as Tyndale, *Obedience*).

And I read . . . to See Erasmus, *An exhortacyon to . . . the Gospell, ed. cit.* sigs E1ʳ–ᵛ: 'saynt Hierome in the epystle to Demetryas exorteth bothe vyrgynes and wydowes/ & wedded wyues to the redynge of holy scripture . . .'; Jerome, Epist. 130 (*PL* 22, 1107–1124).

boner & boughsome Tit. 2:5. 'Well bred and obedient'. This proverbial phrase occurs in the Sarum marriage service. See 'De Sponsalibus' in *Manuale ad Usum per celebris Ecclesie Saris-*

buriensis (Rouen, 1543), ed. G. Collins, Henry Bradshaw Society, 91 (London, 1966), p. 48.

Tit. ii . . . husbands Tit. 2:3–5. Vg. 'ut prudentiam doceant adulescentulas'.

Eructauit . . . wit Ps. 44:2. Possibly a reference to Jerome's introduction to the psalms.

the wyse woman . . . ii. Reg. xiiii II Kings 14:4–20; the wise woman of Tekoa, sent by Joab to David, persuaded him by means of a parable to recall his son Absalom; see *DB* IV, s.v. 'Tekoa'.

Aquila . . . Act. xviii Acts 18: 24–6. Aquila and Priscilla were Christians who met Paul on his Corinthian mission. They instructed in 'the way of God' Apollo, an Alexandrian Jew, who interpreted the OT, preached Christianity, and conducted a mission among the Ephesians. See *Peake's Commentary*, pp. 914–15; *Sermons*, p. 323.

Iudicum .iiii . . . hym Judg. 4:4–9. Debora was an Israelite heroine who freed the tribes from Canaanite oppression by defeating Sisera and his allies near Kishon in c.1125 BC. The title of prophetess in Judg. 4:1–24 is legendary. See *NCE* IV, s.v. 'Debora'; *DB* I, s.v. 'Debora'.

Sola scripturarum . . . it Jerome, Epist. 53, *PL* 22, 544. Cited by Erasmus, *An exhortacyon to the Gospell*, ed. cit. sig. E1ᵛ; see *Sermons*, p. 139.

Of all suche greene . . . lieth A reference to 'green learning' is made in a complaint at objections to unrest by John Hamon, parish priest of Enfield in 1539 (*LP* XIV, ii, 796). For similar defamation of a preacher in a case brought before Thomas More by John Goodale against William Kygan, priest, see S. House, 'Sir Thomas More and Holy Orders: More's Views of the English Clergy, both Secular and Regular' (unpublished PhD thesis, University of St Andrews, 1987), pp. 186–70. (I am indebted to Dr. House for these references). Barlow, *A dialoge*, ed. cit. sig. L4ᵛ: 'And if the priest be ignoraunt for lacke of lernynge, or maketh not an answere satysfyeng his mynde; he is mocked and iested upon with scornefull derysyon'; cf. Erasmus, *An exhortacyon to scripture*, ed. cit. sig. B4: 'Yf any man . . . do preche and teache these thinges . . . he is a very and true deuyne/ . . . thoughe he be a weuer/ yea thoughe he dygge & delue'. On clerical disapproval of lay bible-reading in the South-West see Whiting, *Blind Devotion*, pp.

195–6; for complaints at 'heretics and newfangled fellows' in Bristol by John Kene, curate of Christchurch, see *LP* XII, 1147, iii; for other complaints *Sermons*, pp. 137, 141, 143, 146, 149, 218, 333, 358; More, *Dialogue*, CW 6, 124–6.

scientia inflat . . . i. Corin. viii I Cor. 8:1–2; cited by Polydore Vergil in *P.V . . . Adagiorum aeque humanorum vt sacrorum opus* (Basle, 1550), 144, 451, fos 217, 363 (cited hereafter as Vergil, *Adagia*).

defoulinge . . . feete An allusion to Matt. 7:6; Barlow, *A dialoge*, ed. cit. sig. L1ᵛ argues against the vernacular scriptures: 'Because of theyr abuse & makyng of theyr owne gloses & many also for theyr vnworthyness, accordynge to Christes commaundement forbiddynge to cast perles before swyne . . .'. More uses the image in a similar context in *Dialogue*, CW 6, 144 (see 122–4 on the laity's misinterpretation of the scriptures).

Psa. liiii . . . eius Ps. 54:21.

diuisi sunt . . . face Ps. 54:22.

Arrius . . . wycliffe The Nicene Council excommunicated and exiled Arius and his Libyan supporters in 325. He was recalled by Constantine from Alexandria in c. 334 and given a chance to clear himself, but died suddenly in 336 on the day before his intended restoration to the church. This story, probably apocryphal, was used by his opponents to discredit his doctrine; see Williams, *Arius*, pp. 70–81; Hanson, *Christian Doctrine*, pp. 264–5; *Sermons*, pp. 114, 120, 127, 128.

Pelagius Pelagius was excommunicated in 417 by Pope Innocent I after his teachings were condemned by two African councils in 416. Innocent's successor, Zosimus, retracted his decision that Pelagius was innocent after the Council of Carthage in 418. The Pelagians were banished in 430, and the heresy was condemned again in 529; see *Sermons*, p. 127.

Nouatus Novatian's severe views regarding the restoration of those who had renounced the church and suffered excommunication during the Decian persecution were considered heretical and he was excommunicated by St Cyprian in 251; see below p. 387.

Manicheus Manes was forced by the Zoroastrians into exile in India in 240; he returned to the capital of the Persian Empire with the protection of Sapur II, but under Bahram I he was arraigned and imprisoned; he was apparently flayed to death in 276–7. Manichaeism spread throughout the world and was outlawed by a series of imperial edicts until c.600. Persecution of the sect continued up to the fourteenth century; see *A Dictionary of Sects, Heresies, Ecclesiastical Parties and Schools of Thought*, ed. J.H. Blount (London, 1874), s.v. 'Manichaeus'; *Sermons*, pp. 120, 127, 170.

wycliffe Wycliffe declared his orthodoxy to Pope Gregory in 1384 and died in the faith. His teaching was condemned by the Blackfriars Council of 1382; but the Council of Constantine in 1415 condemned 267 errors from his works, ordered them to be burnt and his bones to be exhumed. This last injunction was not fulfilled until 1548. See Dahmus, *Prosecution*, pp. 148–53; ODCC s.v. 'Wycliffe'.

be perished 'Will have perished', i.e. spiritually destroyed; an erroneous passive form (from the p.ppl. and aux. 'be') probably formed by analogy with the subjunctive 'be excommunicate'; see *OED* s.v. 'Perish' *v*.

appropinquauit . . . scriptures Ps. 54:22.

Arrius On Arius' Trinitarian heresy see *Sermons*, pp. 114, 120, 127, 128, 141.

Nouatus Novatian, a Roman presbyter, joined the party which, after the Decian persecution (249–50), deprecated concessions with those who had compromised with paganism. He was consecrated rival Bishop of Rome to Pope Cornelius in 251 AD and suffered martyrdom under Valerian in 257–8. His successors at Rome refused absolution to idolators and extended to all 'mortal sins'. Although doctrinally orthodox (but no longer holding to the Catholic creed and baptismal interrogation) the Novatians were excommunicated; see ODCC s.v. 'Novatianism'.

the seconde table or raffe 'Raffe' is a variant form of 'raft'. The metaphor of the sacrament of penance as *secunda tabula post naufragium* was familiar in the middle ages through the writings of Tertullian, Ambrose and Jerome. But the sacrament came under attack in the Reformation; see More *Dialogue*, CW 6, 349–52; *Confutation*, CW 8, 204–5; 213–5; Pelikan, *Church and Dogma*, pp. 256, 264; *Sermons*, pp. 207, 238, 240.

Baptisme . . . saued The Novatians used Heb. 6:4–6 to prove that repentance after baptism was not possible and that evil, an act of the will, could be redeemed only by God's electing grace. In *Confutation* (CW 8, 427–8) Thomas

More accuses Tyndale of being a Novatian because of his use of this text.

the syngle . . . idols These practices which More had defended in *Dialogue* (CW 6, 51–9) were only partially endorsed in the Ten Articles and the *Bishop's Book*; but the Act of Six Articles of June 1539 reinforced clerical celibacy.

this wicked new learning . . . towns See *Sermons*, pp. 137, 140, 146, 149, 218, 333, 358.

vnderstanded The new form of the past participle of 'understand' commonly used from 1530–85; see *OED* s.v. 'Understand' *v*.; *Sermons*, pp. 339, 352 etc.

Molliti . . . preachers Ps. 54:22; cited by Vergil in *Adagia* no. 127, ed. cit. fo. 207.

Of the hardnes . . . heresies Another commonplace attitude; see Barlow, *A Dialoge*, ed. cit. sig. L4ᵛ: 'they be redy to wade forth in yᵉ depe mysteryes of scrypture, wyllynge to be teachers of thinges wherof they vnderstand not what thei speake nor what they affyrme'; More, *Confutation*, CW 8, 425–6.

Io. vi . . . you John 6:54. Vg. 'habetis'.

Many of his disciples . . . thus John 6:61.

then said . . . life John 6:67–8.

Dyd Peter . . . dyd Cf. More's attack on *scriptura sola* in *Dialogue*, CW 6, 143, 558; he alludes to 'the secret inspiration of the holy ghost' with reference to Peter's testing by Christ (Matt. 16:15–16).

Nisi manducaueritis . . . you &c. John 6:54.

Si ergo videritis . . . afore John 6:63.

At that blessed supper . . . to An exposition of the real objective presence of Christ's body and blood in the Eucharistic elements; transubstantiation was upheld in the Six Articles of June 1539; see F.J. Clark, *Eucharistic Sacrifice and the Reformation*, 2nd ed. (London, 1963), pp. 180, 536–7; *Sermons*, pp. 240, 290, 321, 365.

verba vitae . . . euerlasting John 6:69.

Et iacta . . . thee Ps. 54:23; cf. Vergil, *Adagia* no. 81, ed. cit. fo. 186.

Domine verba vitae . . . life John 6:69.

Et non dabit . . . inconstantlye Ps. 54:23.

And because I spoke . . . parentes The refusal to distinguish between an image and an idol was long considered to be a sign of heresy.

Bonde, *Pilgrymage, ed. cit.* fo. 192ᵛ, argues that Wycliffe and Luther '. . . put no difference bytwene an ydol and image'; see further Aston, *England's Iconoclasts*, pp. 188–191. The meaning 'a false God' may have been used of figures of saints as early as 1536 when the First Royal Injunctions launched the official assault on images. See R. Whiting, 'Abominable Idols: Images and Image-Breaking under Henry VIII', *JEH* 33 (1982), 39–40.

Nowe at the dissolucion . . . all The dissolutions of the Alien Houses in Bristol in 1538 and of the monasteries and friaries in 1539–40 provide a *terminus ad quem* for this sermon: St Augustine's Abbey and St Mark's Hospital were dissolved on 9 December 1539, Tewkesbury Abbey on 9 January 1540. Images were removed from parish churches in Bristol following the 1538 Royal Injunctions of 1538. See C.S. Taylor, 'The Religious Houses of Bristol and their Dissolution', *TBGAS* 29 (1907), 95; *Three Centuries of Letters in Relation to the Suppression of the Monasteries*, ed. T. Wright, CS, XXVI (London, 1843), pp. 260–1; J.H. Bettey, *Bristol Parish Churches during the Reformation, c.1530–1560*, BHA, 45 (1979), 7–9; VCH, *Gloucester* II, 60 ff; Frere and Kennedy, pp. 38–9; Aston, *England's Iconoclasts*, pp. 226–36.

nasse A West Country name, a diminutive for Agnes; see *The Oxford Dictionary of English Christian Names*, ed. E.C. Withycombe (Oxford, 1977), s.v. 'Nessie, Nest(a)'.

I haue . . . myne ydoll Aston, *England's Iconoclasts*, p. 403, cites earlier cases of images being used as if religious dolls. This extended meaning of 'ydol' as a child's plaything may shed light on the origin of the word 'doll'. *OED* s.v. 'Doll' *sb.* 1 gives a derivation from 'Dol', a pet form of the name Dorothy; cf. the derivation from 'idol' in *The Imperial Dictionary*, ed. J. Ogilvie, 2 vols (Glasgow, 1850), I, s.v. 'Doll'. See Bridget, 'Bristol Pulpit', 89 and n.

this latine worde . . . abhorreth In *Confutation* (CW 8, 173–5) More objected to Tyndale's translation of *idolum* as 'image' (I Cor. 5:10; 10:19) on the grounds that it deliberately subverted image worship. Cranmer and the reformers believed that the meanings of *idolum* and 'image' were identical in that one was derived from the Greek and the other from the Latin. The Protestant Bibles of 1535–9 are inconsist-

ent but the preference of 'image' to 'idol' suggests that the meaning of the Greek had degenerated. The apologists took issue over the reformers' translations and *idolum* and *idolatria* appear in the list of objectionable words from the NT presented by Gardiner to Convocation in 1542. Bishop Bonner renewed the attack in Mary's reign in A *profitable and necessarye doctryne* (Cawood, 1555), sig. 2H4 (*STC* 3282):

> By dyuerse false and ungodly translations this [the second] commaundement hath bene . . . alleged not only agaynst images set vp in churches . . . but also agaynste the most blessed sacrament of the Aultare callyng it an Image or Idol . . . the procedynge preachers . . . takynge . . . *Idolum* for image, and confoundynge the one with yᵉ other haue greatly abused and deceyued yᵉ people . . .

See Aston, *England's Iconoclasts*, pp. 394–6; Mozley, *Tyndale*, pp. 96–7; *Concilia* III, 861.

And so speaketh . . . emporours Matt. 22:15–21.

.i. Cor. viii . . . one I Cor. 8:4.

Scimus quoniam . . . vnus I Cor. 8:1. Vg. 'scimus quia omnes . . .'; 1 Cor. 8:4.

An ymage . . . be The church's teaching on images originated with St John of Damascus' *De Orthodoxe Fidei* IV, 15 and 16 (PG 94, 1163–75); images are treated by Aquinas in ST 3a. 25, 1, 3 and 6 (*ed. cit.* L, 192–7; 202–5). This distinction between idols and images, made despite the 1538 Injunctions against image veneration (Frere and Kennedy, pp. 38–9), was a crucial one for the apologists. See Bonner, A *profitable . . . doctryne, ed. cit.* sig. 211.

Therefore the ymage . . . dede See the articles on images in the Ten Articles and on the second commandment in the *Bishops' Book; Formularies*, pp. 13–4, 135–6; *Sermons*, pp. 301–2.

the Image . . . dede St Paul the apostle was martyred at Rome in c.67 AD during the Neronian persecution; according to Tertullian he was beheaded. Legend held that when his head bounced three times, three fountains sprang forth. In art his emblem is the sword. See Mirk's *Festial*, Pt. I. ed. T.E. Erbe, EETS, ES, 96 (London, 1905), I, 187; ODCC; ODS s.v. 'Paul, St.'

For as S. Paule . . . one I Cor. 8:4.

As the Image . . . Venus See the arguments of
Lactantius, Divinae Institutiones, I, 10–11 (PL
6, 160–84), probably Edgeworth's source here
(cited hereafter as Lactantius, Div. Inst.) and
Augustine, De Civitate Dei X, 3 (PL 41, 280–
1); Bonde's exposition in Pilgrymage, ed. cit. fo.
194ʳ⁻ᵛ.

Chimera . . . dragon OCCL s.v. 'Chimaera'
states: 'In Gk myth a fire-breathing monster
with the head of a lion, the body of a she-goat
and the tail of a snake'.

Chimera signifiynge . . . serpentes Lycia was a
district in the Southwest of Asia Minor, a
peninsula between Caria and Pamphylia, extending inland to Mt Taurus. The fiery
Chimaera was in the mountain range of
Solyma; see Enc. Brit. III, s.v. 'Lycia'.

Pomponius Mela . . . expositours I.e. C. Iulius
Solinus, Polyhistor LII; Pomponius Mela, De
Situ Orbis, libros tres I, 15 (Basle, 1543), fos
111, 168 (n. a.); the commentator is P.J. Oli-
varius Valentinus.

Paule sayth . . . nothing I Cor. 8:4.

Beseleel . . . Iuda A reference to Ex. 31:2.
Bezaleel, the son of Hur (I Chron. 2:20) and
chief architect of the tabernacle, was endowed
with special gifts for the execution of the task
among which was the gift of teaching the arts
of which he was master (Ex. 36:1); see DB I,
s.v. 'Bezaleel'.

I haue fylled hym . . . science An exposition of
Ex. 31:3.

Chrisost . . . maner Chrysostom, 'De Spiritu
Sancto' (PG 52, 818).

Cicero . . . science Cicero, De Officiis I, 19, 3,
ed. and tr. W. Miller (London, 1913), p. 64.
Edgeworth has substituted Scientia for Cicero's
term Sapientia.

not seruing to the eye 'Not merely appearing to
be serving'; a reference to Eph. 6:6 and Col.
2:23; see Sermons, pp. 261, 269.

you seruauntes . . . Ephe. vi Eph. 6:5.

you maysters . . . seruauntes Eph. 6:9. The
duties of servants and masters was a new homiletic theme introduced by the teaching on
the fifth commandment; see Formularies, pp.
155–6, 319–20; Latimer, Works II, 119, 141;
Sermons, pp. 261, 269.

marchaunt venterer 'A merchant engaged in
the organisation and despatch of trading ex-
peditions overseas and the establishment of

trading stations in foreign countries.' The
society of Merchant Venturers, incorporated
in 1552, takes its name from this Bristol term.
See P. McGrath, The Merchant Venturers of
Bristol (Bristol, 1975), pp. 7, 10–11.

The fyfte sermon, intreatynge of the spirite of Pietie

Esay .xi Is. 11:2.

and by hym . . . many I Cor. 12:11; Eph. 4:7;
see Sermons, pp. 115–16.

This word pietas . . . capacitie See Augustine,
De Trinitate XIV, 1 (PL 42, 1035–7) and De
Civitate Dei X, 1 (PL 41, 279).

The translatours . . . vngodlines The Hebrew
text of Is. 11:2 used by the reformers does not
include the word for 'piety'; this gift appears as
'the fear of God'. Pietas appears on Gardiner's
list of 1542 because of conservative objections
to its translation as 'godliness'. But 'godliness'
appears in the Douai-Rheims translation of
this text. See Concilia III, 861.

But thus speaking . . . appeare A distinction
between piety as in donum pietatis meaning
'worship, service' (from Gk. latria) and 'godliness' (applied here to all seven gifts in the NT
sense to mean the whole spiritual life of the
Christian with reference to his moral life).
OED s.v. 'Godliness' states: 'The quality of
being godly, the devout worship of the law of
God'. See Aquinas, ST 2a2ae. 101, 1 (ed. cit.
XLI, 2–3).

And if . . . trouble These various meanings of
'pity' are due to an earlier mingling of forms
and senses. Late Lat. pietas, 'dutifulness, gratitude' came to mean 'compassion, kindness'
and the ME forms 'pite' or 'piete' (from O.Fr.
pieté) meant 'pity, mercy, clemency or compassion'. The different forms and meanings
were not clear until 1600; see OED s.v. 'Pity',
sb; J.D. Burnley's discussion in Chaucer's Language and the Philosophers' Tradition (Cambridge, 1979), ch. 8.

Here it signifieth . . . thing OED s.v. 'Pity' sb. 3
states: 'A regrettable fact or circumstance, a
ground or cause for pity, a subject for regret'.

I thinke this english . . . noughte This erroneous
etymology may be inspired by the similarity of
the first element pi with 'piety' and 'pity' and
by the transferred meanings of the Latin
words. The phrase 'it is pity' is used

pejoratively as in this contrast with 'mercy' and 'compassion'. See *A Latin Dictionary*, ed. C.T. Lewis and C. Short (1879, repr. Oxford, 1969), s.v. 'Pio', D; 'Piaculum', A; 'Sacer', B (cited hereafter as Lewis and Short).

Cicero . . . holines Cicero, *De Officiis* II, 3 (*ed. cit.* p. 179).

Anaxagoras (c.500–c.428 BC) of Clazomenae in Iona, teacher of Pericles and Euripides and author of *On Nature*, whose concepts leading to an explanation of the universe strongly influenced fifth-century Greek thought.

Lactancius . . . sunne Lactantius, *Div. Inst.* III, 9 (*PL* 6, 372).

Aristippus of Cyrene, a pupil of Socrates. His grandson was probably the founder of the Cyrenaic school of philosophy which taught that knowledge is based on the evidence of the senses and that immediate pleasure is the only end of action this belief anticipated the doctrine of Epictetus. See *Sermons*, p. 157.

Epicure (371–271 BC), founder of the Epicurean school of philosophy which taught that the wise conduct of life was attainable by reliance on the evidence of the senses and which equated pleasure with the good. See *OCCL* on these philosophers.

Lactancius . . . maker Lactantius, *Div. Inst.* III, 9 (*PL* 6, 372).

Quicum cognouissent . . . GOD Rom 1:21.

.s. Augustine . . . God Augustine, *De Civitate Dei* IV, 3; X, I (*PL* 41, 130; 279).

Religio . . . father Lactantius, *Div. Inst.* IV, 28 (*PL* 6, 535). His etymology of 'religion' from *re* and *lig*, 'to tie or fasten again', is widely accepted today; cf. *OED* s.v. 'Religion', *sb.* 5: 'The recognition of man or some higher power as having control of his destiny and as being entitled to obedience, reverence and worship'. Aquinas criticised the confusion of *pietas* and *religio* in *ST* 2a2ae. 101–3 (*ed. cit.* XLI, 10–13).

pietas . . . worshippe This definition connotes the spiritual life of the Christian through the offices of the Holy Spirit; see *OED* s.v. 'Piety' sb. II. 2: 'Habitual reverence and obedience towards God godliness, devoutness, religiousness'. Bonde, *Pilgrymage*; ed. cit. fo. 104^v: 'whan so euer we behaue vs in the seruyce of God deuoutly / rendrynge to hym our duty / than know y^t it is the operacyon of this gyfte pite'.

the prophet Esay . . . Iesse Is. 11:1.

Luke ii. This account (Luke 2:42–46) is a rare application of an incident in the life of Christ. In *The Charter of the Abbey of the Holy Ghost* Christ finds in the Temple at Jerusalem, 'Riȝhtwisnesse & Wisdam'; see Horstman, *Yorkshire Writers* I, 352–3.

casting no perylles 'Anticipating no dangers'. Probably proverbial; see *ODEP* s.v. 'Youth', 'Youth never casts for peril (is reckless)'.

as Pylgrymes . . . togither As pilgrimages were denounced in the formularies as 'things indifferent to salvation', Edgeworth makes no attempt to defend them. See More, *Dialogue*, *CW* 6, 54–61; Tyndale, *An Answer unto Sir Thomas More's Dialogue called The Supper of the Lord*, ed. H. Walter, PS (Cambridge, 1850), pp. 63–4 (cited hereafter as Tyndale, *Answer*); *Formularies*, pp. 137, 301; *Sermons*, p. 252.

Woulde GOD . . . learned See *Sermons*, pp. 137, 140, 141, 143, 146, 218, 333, 358.

Luke .iiii. Luke 4:16–21.

Esay. ca. lxi . . . me. &c Is. 61:1.

Hodie impleta . . . eyes Luke 4:21. Vg. '. . . in auribus vestris'.

Ioh. xiiii . . . me John 14:10.

Ioh. xv . . . scholers John 15:8.

Ego non quero . . . Ioh. viii John 8:50. Vg. 'Ego autem non . . .'

in latine pietas . . . God On this definition see Burnley, *Chaucer's Language*, pp. 141–3; *Sermons*, pp. 147–8.

Ambrose . . . benefite Ambrose, *De Officiis Ministorum* I, 17 (*PL* 16, 42–3); cf. Aquinas, *ST* 2a2ae. 101, 3 (*ed. cit.* XLI, 8–13). The following is a treatment of piety as a virtue rather than as a gift.

Albeit . . . vs On the range of piety see Aquinas, *ST* 2a2ae. 101, 1, 3 (*ed. cit.* XLI, 4–7).

secundum analogiam . . . speaketh Probably a reference to Aristotle who uses this phrase frequently in his logical writings like the *Organon*; see *Sermons*, pp. 191, 246.

we owe . . . countrey Edgeworth follows Ambrose (*De Officiis, loc. cit.*) rather than Aquinas in placing duty towards one's country before duty towards one's parents. On the pre-eminence of duty to God see Aquinas, *ST* 2a2ae. 101, 4 (*ed. cit.* XLI, 12–19). Fidelity to filial and religious duties is the sense in which 'piety' is now most commonly used. See *OED* s.v. 'Piety' *sb.* 2, 3.

But all this . . . Ro. viii Rom. 8:35.

Codrus . . . bloudsheading The source of this story is probably Valerius Maximus, *Facta et Dicta Memorabilia* V, 7, although Edgeworth may have known the account in the *Gesta Romanorum*. See *Facta et Dicta Memorabilia Libri Novem*, ed. C. Halm (Lepizig, 1865), p. 257; *Gesta Romanorum*, ed. H. Oesterley (Berlin, 1872), no. 41, p. 340.

Act. ii . . . Cyrenem Acts 2:10. Cyrene was an ancient Gk colony in Libya founded in c. 630 BC. It was a great intellectual centre of the classical world and the birthplace of the philosopher Aristippus (founder of the Cyrenaics). It became a Roman province in 96 BC. See *Enc. Brit.* 3; *OCCL* s.v. 'Cyrene'.

In a . . . contrauersie See Valerius Maximus, *Facta et Dicta Memorabilia* V, 6, 7, 4 (*ed. cit.* pp. 258–9). Accounts are also given by Solinus, *Polyhistor* XL and Mela, *De Situ Orbis* I, 7 (*ed. cit.* fos 74, 158); G. Sallustius Crispus, *Bellum Jugurthinum* XXXIX, 4–9; see *The War with Jugurtha*, ed. and tr. J.C. Rolfe (1921, repr. London, 1980), p. 301.

Gen. xiiii The following account is taken from Gen. 14:1–16. Abraham led his forces (318 men) against the four kings from North of Canaan who had subdued the five kings of the Dead Sea cities; he recovered the spoil they had seized and rescued his nephew Lot; see *Peake's Commentary*, p. 188.

Expeditos vernaculos . . . octo Gen. 14:14. Vg. '. . . vernaculos suos'.

Iud. xi The following account of Jephthah's victory over the Ammonites comes from Judg. 11:1–9; see *Sermons*, p. 130.

Galaad Area of ancient Palestine, E. of Jordan river, corresponding to modern N.W. Jordan, bounded in the N. by the Yarmick River, and in the S.W. by the 'plains of Moab'. *Enc. Brit.* IV, s.v. 'Gilead'.

i. Reg. xxiii The following account is taken from I Kings 23:1–5.

Ceila DB II, s.v. 'Keilah' states: 'A city of Judah in the Shephelah which David delivered from the Philistines'.

Percussit eos . . . Ceila I Kings 23:5; Vg. 'salvavit David'.

if there shoulde . . . malice Probably a reference to proclamations following the Northern uprisings of 1536–7 which imposed severe penalties for unlawful assemblies and assaults of officers; see Hughes and Larkin, I, 168, 169, 179; above, p. 377.

Ethnichs 'Heathens, pagans'. A reference to *Sermons*, p. 151 and the example of Abraham's deliverance of Lot; this links him with the ethnic movements of the ancient near East; i.e. the Hurrians or Horites near Haran (Gen. 1:6); see *Peake's Commentary*, p. 188.

tanquam Apin . . . deum I.e. Apis, the ox worshipped as a God by the Egyptians; see Mela, *De Situ Orbis* I, 9 (*ed. cit.* fos 162–3) and Caius Plinius, *Naturalis Historia Libri* VIII, 184; see Pliny, *Naturalis Historia Libri* XXXVIII, eds L. Ian and C. Mayhoff, 6 vols, Bibliotheca Teubneriana (Stuttgart, 1969–70), II, 142.

Aut dimitte . . . predestination Ex. 32:31–32.

Roma. ix . . . Israelites Rom. 9:3–4. Vg. 'optabam enim ipse ego'.

Origene . . . commaundementes Origen, 'Comm. in Epist. ad Rom.', VII, 13 (PG 14, 1139).

But like as Christe . . . redemption Phil. 2:8.

Gala. iii . . . Deute. xxi Gal. 3:13; Vg. 'de maledicto'; Deut. 21:23.

And so saynte Paule . . . Christe A reference to I Cor. 9:20–22.

pietas . . . mothers See Aquinas, ST 2a2ae. 101, 2 (*ed. cit.* XLI, 6–9).

Etiam in operibus . . . workes Works of supererogation or voluntary works (*meliora opera*) such as pilgrimages and the lighting of votive candles were repudiated by the reformers. The *King's Book* defined them as 'superstitious works of men's own invention' as distinct from 'good works' or those enjoined of strict obligation. 'Will works' later became a Puritan term. See Latimer, *Works* I, 37–8; *Formularies*, p. 370; *OED* s.v. Will *sb.* V, 24c; *ODCC* s.v. 'Supererogation, Works of'; *Sermons*, p. 282.

Ad heliodorum . . . cruell Jerome, Epist. 14 (*PL* 22, 348).

ad rusticum Monachum . . . God Jerome, Epist. 125 (*PL* 22, 1076).

ad Marcellam . . . blessille Jerome, Epist. 38 (*PL* 22, 465).

Iohn & Iames . . . Christe See Matt. 5:21–22; 9:9; Mk 1:19–20; 2:14; Luke 5:10–11; 27–28.

An other, Luke .ix . . . heauen Luke 9:59–62.

S. Hierome . . . life Jerome, Epist. 38 (*PL 22*, 465).

Ad fabiolam . . . perdiderunt Jerome, Epist. 64 (*PL 22*, 610–11).

parietes dealbati . . . appearing An allusion to Matt. 23:27. See Erasmus, *Adagia* I, vii, 3 (*ed. cit.* fo. 294), '*duos parietes de eadem dealbare fidelia*' ('To whitewash two walls out of the same bucket'); *Adages*, CWE 32, 68; Vergil, *Adagia*, no. 274, *ed. cit.* fo. 121.

an apple . . . oyster Proverbial; see ODEP s.v. 'Apple'.

Ecclesiasticall . . . Tripartite story A reference to Eusebius, *Hist. Ecc.* III (*PG 20*, 211–302). Cassiodorus compiled the *Historia Tripartita*, the great medieval textbook of church history from 306 to 439 AD, from the accounts of the Greek authors, Theodoretus, Socrates and Sozomenus. See *Autores Historiae Ecclesiasticae* (Basle, 1535); OCD s.v. 'Cassiodorus'.

i. Tim. ii . . . workes An exposition of I Tim. 2:9–10; Vg. 'sed quod decet'; on these fashions in dress see J. Scattergood, 'Fashion and Morality in the Late Middle Ages', *England in the Fifteenth Century*, ed. D. Williams, (Woodbridge, 1987), pp. 255–72.

Exerce teipsum . . . come I Tim. 4:7–8.

Prouerb. iii . . . wine Prov. 3:10.

.ii. Corin. ix. . . . lyuinge II Cor. 9:10–11. Vg. 'ad manducandum'.

Math. xxv . . . me Matt. 25:31–35.

verye pitie . . . nede Concern at the decay of the universities and grammar schools is a new topic of complaint at the end of Henry's reign. A request for benefactions for scholars is included in the injunctions of 1536 and the Edwardian injunctions of 1547; see Blench, p. 245; Frere and Kennedy, pp. 10–11; Hughes and Larkin, I, 287, pp. 397–8; Latimer, *Works* I, 64–5; *Sermons*, p. 283.

Iniquitie . . . colde Based on Matt. 24:12 this proverb is a homiletic commonplace on the theme of poverty. See Vergil, *Adagia* no. 1,199, *ed. cit.* fo. 487; Latimer, *Works* I, 65; *Formularies*, p. 208; ODEP s.v. 'Charity'; *Sermons*, pp. 183, 233.

Mat. x . . . prophete Matt. 10:41.

Dan. xij . . . eternitie Dan. 12:3; Vg. '. . . multos quasi'.

and my parentes . . . Arte On Edgeworth's benefactors and his education at Banbury School and Oriel College, Oxford, see Introduction, pp. 13–15.

for because . . . seruauntes On 'for because that' ('for the reason that') see OED s.v. 'Because' A. *adv.* 1; *Sermons*, pp. 163, 236, 245 etc.

it is playne . . . once A reference to Matt. 8:1–16; Luke 6:17–19; Mk 1:31–34 and to the story of the loaves and fishes: Matt. 14:15–21; Mk 6:41–44; Luke 9:14–17.

Quod facis . . . people John 13:27 and 29.

The sixt sermon intreating of the feare of God

The seuenth gift . . . God In ME treatments this gift is known as the gift of dread since both 'dread' and 'fear' include the meaning of 'deep awe and reverence towards God'. It is called the gift of fear in treatises such as Bonde's *Pilgrymage*; and 'fear' instead of the earlier 'dread' appears in the Protestant Bibles. Edgeworth uses 'dread' only in the phrase 'dread of God' which he equates with chaste fear (*Sermons*, p. 147); see OED s.v. 'Fear' *sb.* 3d; 'Dread' *sb.* 1. The gift of fear is traditionally dealt with last. But in *Pilgrymage* (*ed. cit.* fos. 73r–v) it comes first and in *The Royal Book* the gifts rise: 'fro the spyryte and the yefte of drede vnto the gyfte of sapience. For holy drede is the begynnynge of sapyence' and 'ye gyfte of drede is the ussher at the grete masse . . . at the great menace of the sentence of God' (*ed. cit.* sigs P1v; P3); see also *Formularies*, p. 49.

There . . . happened Augustine, *De Civitate Dei* I, 4, 1 (*PL 41*, 258–9). The definition of the four passions comes from Cicero's *Tusculanae Disputationes* III, 4 and IV, 6; see *Tusculan Disputations*, ed. and tr. J.E. King (London, 1927), p. 233 (cited hereafter as *Tusc. Disp.*).

a secte . . . Stoici I.e. the Stoic school of philosophy founded by Zeno of Citium (Cyprus) at Athens in c.300 BC which taught that man should live in harmony with nature or divine reason which shows itself as fate, since this is virtue and the only good; see OCCL s.v. 'Stoics'. Edgeworth may have known Erasmus' distinction between the Stoics' and

Peripatetics' views of the passions in the *Enchiridion*; see *Enchiridion Militis Christiani* LB v. 13 E, tr. C. Fantazzi, *CWE*66 (Toronto, 1988), p. 44.

Zeno . . . Epictetus Zeno (c.333–262 BC) of Citium in Cyprus, founder of the Stoic school of philosophy; he held virtue to be the end of life; pleasure and pain of no importance; *Chrisippus* (c.280–207 BC) from Soli in Cilicia who with Cleanthes of Assos succeeded Zeno and systematised the Stoic philosophy; *Epictetus* (c.50–120 AD) of Phrygia, a Stoic philosopher whose doctrines, outlined in his lectures or *Diatribi* and in an *Encheiridion*, were made known by his pupil Arrian (b. 85–90 AD); he taught that Providence governs the universe and that all men are brothers. See *OCCL* on these philosophers.

So that they put . . . well A reference to Augustine, *De Civitate Dei* IX, 4 (*PL* 41, 259).

commoda . . . vertue Ibid. 258. The term *commoda*, 'things advantageous or beneficial', is used by Cicero in his expositions of Stoic philosophy; it refers to things like health and liberty, not good in themselves, but beneficial if they did not affect virtue; see *De Finibus Bonorum et Malorum* III, 21, ed. and tr. H. Rackham (London, 1914), p. 189.

they saw these . . . manner Cicero, *Tusc. Disp.* IV, 7 (*ed. cit.* p. 367).

Nam perfectus . . . Stoikes These quotations of commonplace sentiments are either corruptions or imperfect translations of their classical sources. *Perfectus Stoicus* could mean 'the Stoic's perfect man' (an unrealised ideal) as well as the 'perfect Stoic'; i.e. one who has acquired all the attributes of a wise man and has reached the complete stage; *stupidi* ('styffe or stubborne') could be derived from *stolidi* (which conveys the sense of intellectually sluggish and physically thick set) or from *duri* ('stern, obstinate'); see *Stoicorum Veterum Fragmenta*, ed. I. ab Arnim, 4 vols (Leipzig, 1903–4), III, 150 ff.

Platonici . . . man I.e. the Platonists, including Aristotle, who studied Platonic philosophy taught at the Academy, founded by Plato at Athens in c.385 BC; and the Peripatetics, followers of the Aristotelian school taught at the Lyceum, founded by Aristotle in c.355 BC, so named because instruction was given in the *peripatos* (covered walkway of the gymnasium). Unlike the Stoics, the Platonists be-

lieved that passion and energy should be controlled by reason. See *OCD*, s.v. 'Peripatetic'; *OCCL* s.v. 'Academy'.

vbertas . . . soul Another commonplace Stoic sentiment, although the context suggests a medieval rather than a classical source; see ab Arnim, *Stoicorum . . . Fragmenta* I, 50–52.

S. Augustine . . . Cap. iiii Augustine, *De Civitate Dei* IX, 4 (*PL* 41, 259–60).

Aulus Gellius . . . atticarum Aulus Gellius, *Noctes Atticae* XIX, 1; see *Attic Nights*, ed. and tr. R.C. Rolfe, 3 vols (London, 1948–54), III, 348–55. Other versions of the tale exist in a fifteenth century translation of the *Alphabetum Narrationum*, once attributed to Etienne de Besançon, and in Erasmus' *Apophthegmata*. See *An Alphabet of Tales*, 2 vols, ed. M.M. Banks, EETS, OS, 126, 127 (London, 1904–5), II, 505–6; Erasmus, *Apophthegmatum ex optimis vtriusque linguae scriptoribus libri octo* (Basle, 1550), III, 17, sig. n1ᵛ (cited hereafter as Erasmus, *Apophthegmata*); and the translation by N. Udall, *Apophthegmes . . . translated into Englysche*, Grafton, 1542, I, 17, fos 48–9 (cited hereafter as Udall, *Apophthegmes*). STC 10433.

pale as ashes for feare Proverbial; cited in *ODEP* s.v. 'Pale'; see Udall, *loc. cit.*

a ryche voluptuous gorbelye 'A wealthy, pot-bellied man inclined to sensuous living'.

Asia the lesse I.e. the Roman province of Asia (occupying the western third of the peninsula known as Asia Minor) ceded in 133 BC by Attalus III, bounded in the N.E. by the province of Bithynia, in the E. by Galatia and in the S. by Lycia. It was the richest, and with Africa, the most important province in the Roman Empire; see *DB* I, s.v. 'Asia'.

Galaciam . . . Gallogrecia Galatia derives from *Galatae* (i.e. the Gauls who invaded Asia Minor in 278–7 BC and settled in north-eastern Phrygia). From 64 BC a client state of Rome, it was made by Augustus in 25 BC into a province called Galatia comprising Paphlagonia, Pontus, Galaticus, Galatia (in the narrower, original sense), Phrygia, Galatica and Lycaonia Galatica. *Galatae* or Galatians, in the second sense, refers to all the inhabitants of the province of Galatia under Roman rule. See *DB* II, s.v. 'Galatia'; *Sermons*, p. 200.

Rome was . . . them selues Lack of concord due to a confusion between the referent

'Rome' in the coordinate clause and 'the Romaines', subject of the preceding subordinate
clause.

whiche Asia . . . wenchliness A reference to
the Roman Empire under Augustus, a time of
luxury and idleness for Rome but of pro-
gressive prosperity for the provinces. See
Pliny, *Naturalis Historia* XXXIII, 148 (*ed. cit.*
V, 156); *OCCL* s.v. 'Provinces, Roman'.

Aulus Gellius . . . asiaticus A coinage of Augustine's who also cites Aulus Gellius, *Noctes
Atticae*; see *De Civitate Dei* IX, 4 (*PL* 41, 259).

at deathes doore Proverbial; see *ODEP* s.v.
'Death's door'.

pale as death Proverbial; cited as first use in
ODEP s.v. 'Pale'.

Aristippus the philosopher See *Sermons*, p. 148.

a booke of Epictetus . . . Stoikes On Epictetus
see *Sermons*, p. 156.

And the . . . Philosophers saithe The following
exposition is a translation of Augustine, *De
Civitate Dei* IX, 4 (*PL* 41, 259–60).

When Dauid . . . lawes II Kings 11:2–5.

Concupiuit . . . lawes Ps. 118:20.

Prouer. xxviii . . . same Prov. 28:14.

Ecclesiasticus . . . destruction Ecclus. 1:27–28.
Vg. 'nam qui sine timore . . . enim animositatis illius subversio illius est'.

Gene. iiii The story of Cain comes from Gen.
4:3–8; 11–12 and 15.

the chyldren . . . doctrine A reference to Gen.
6:2. The descendants of Seth, the third son of
Adam, are listed in Gen. 5:6–32.

he by his life time . . . brother A reference to
Gen. 4:16–17.

gendred . . . stature A reference to Gen. 6:4.

In so muche that God . . . man Gen. 6:6.

non continebit . . . correction Ps. 76:10. By in-
terpolating 'non' into this verse Edgeworth
answers the psalmist's rhetorical question.

Non permanebit . . . deede An exposition of
Gen. 6:3.

Nemrothe Cham . . . God Gen. 10:8–9.

Genesis xi . . . world Gen. 11:3–8. The story
of Nimrod and the Tower of Babel, told by
Josephus in *Jew. Ant.* I, 4–5 (*ed. cit.* IV, 55–
57), was revived in the sixteenth century due
to the Renaissance interest in the origins of
vernacular languages. Edgeworth's source may

be P. Vergil, *De Rerum Inventoribus libri octo*
(Basle, 1532), I, 3, sig. A 7. See A. Borst, *Der
Turmbau von Babel*, 4 vols (Stuttgart, 1960),
III, i, 1094–5; D. Hay, *Polydore Vergil: Renaiss-
ance Historian and Man of Letters* (London,
1962), p. 53.

And this diuersitie . . . Adam Vergil's account
commences with Adam, the beginner of man's
posterity and lineage; see *De Rerum Inventoribus* I, 3, *ed. cit.* sigs A6ʳ⁻ᵛ.

An Englyshe dogge . . . walshe man ?Prover-
bial. This exemplum of the differences between the English and Welsh languages,
relevant to Edgeworth's West Country audience, plays on the proverbial animosity between the two races; see *ODEP* s.v. 'Heart of
an Englishman towards a Welshman'.

their prouender pricked theim Proverbial; i.e.
'abundance of food made them high spirited';
see *ODEP* s.v. 'Provender'.

Wee haue knowen . . . charitablye The association between the civic Corporation of Bristol
and the Fellowship of Merchants was traditionally close; the ordinances for merchants
made by William Cannyng in c.1466 decreed
that the master was either to be a sheriff or a
mayor. It was customary for a successful merchant to seek civic office and the sheriffs, in
whose hands the financial business of Bristol
lay, were usually elected from their fellowship.
These ties were maintained when the Society
of Merchant Venturers was incorporated in
1552. See McGrath, *Merchant Venturers*, pp.
1–8; E.M. Carus-Wilson, *The Merchant Adven-
turers of Bristol in the Fifteenth Century* BHA, 4
(1962), 9–10; *Sermons*, pp. 146, 281–2.

Qui timet deum . . . dedes Ecclus. 15:1; Vg.
'faciet illud'.

Ephe. iiii . . . audience Eph. 4:29. Vg. 'ad aedi-
ficationem oportunitas'.

Sainte Ambrose . . . . wanton Ambrose on
Eph. 4:29 in 'Comm. in Epist. ad Ephesios'
(*PL* 17, 392).

Esopes fables . . . other Although tales of the
miraculous and legends of saints lives, earlier
used for formal moralisation, were generally
condemned in the sixteenth century, fable
collections such as Aesop's were used for
elementary instruction. In 1531 Sir Thomas
Elyot recommended that children who had
mastered the rules of grammar read Aesop's
fables in Greek. See *The Boke named the Gov-*

ernour, ed. Foster Watson (London, 1907), pp. 35–36.

Quid est enim . . . of Justifications of fables were standard; this quotation probably comes from a contemporary or medieval source; cf. the defence in prefaces to sixteenth century editions of Aesop's fables such as *Aesopi Phrygis Vita et Fabule a viris doctis in Latinum linguam versae. Inter quos, L. Valla, A. Gellius, D. Erasmus* (Paris, 1534), fos 22ᵛ–23: 'Est autem fabula sermo fictus, imagine quadem representans veritatem and Fabula, est oratio ficta, verisimili dispositione, imaginem exhibens veritatis'.

but euer almost . . . estate Elision due to omission of a verb; a suggested reading is 'but lived always almost in a state of a beggary'.

I woulde euerye manne . . . occupacion 'I ask every one of you to imagine two men of your own profession'. The lack of agreement between 'euery manne', 'thee' (used as an ethic dative) and 'their' stems from the problem of address.

Psal. xxxiii . . . pouertie Ps. 33:10.

Est autem questus . . . winnynge I Tim. 6:6, probably with a reference to I Tim. 6:8.

Et psal . . . house Ps. 111:1 and 3.

Dispersit dedit . . . people Ps. 111:9.

Sainte Ambrose . . . vertue Ambrose, *De Vocatione Gentium* II, 9 (PL 17, 1124–7).

There muste be a consente . . . drinke Proverbial; see *ODEP* s.v. 'Lead'.

Peccaui etiam . . . wycked Ex. 9:27. Vg. 'Dominus iustus ego'. The seven plagues are listed in Ex. 8–10: 1–23; see *DB* III, 'Plagues of Egypt'; *Sermons*, p. 356.

sainte Stephans . . . clothes Acts 7:58; the stoning of St Stephen was the subject of a number of carols. See *The Early English Carols*, ed. R.L. Greene, 2nd ed. (Oxford, 1971), pp. 97–101 for sixteenth century versions.

All the preaching . . . purpose See Acts 9:1–9; 22:4–21; 26:10–18. St Paul, at first a persecutor of Christianity in Jerusalem, was greatly affected by the martyrdom of Stephen. His conversion occurred in 34 AD when, travelling from Jerusalem to Damascus with letters to arrest Christians, he experienced a vision of Christ in the form of a stroke which rendered him blind for three days. For the rest of his life he brought Christianity to the Gentiles. See

G. Ogg, *The Chronology of the Life of Paul* (London, 1968), pp. 1–30; *ODCC* s.v. 'Paul'; *Sermons*, pp. 116, 206.

one shipwracke . . . GOD Probably a reference to the 1543–5 war with France in which the West Country provided the backbone of the country's naval strength. Twelve ships left Bristol for Bouloigne in 1544; another eight were sent to the Isle of Wight in 1545; a total of sixty ships in the Royal Fleet at Portsmouth in August 1545 were from the West. This comment provides a *terminus a quo* for this sermon of June 1543 (when the English first engaged with the French ships) and a *terminus ad quem* of 7 June 1546 (when a treaty between England and France was signed). See Scarisbrick, *Henry VIII*, pp. 565–6, 569, 573, 587, 598; S. Seyer, *Memoirs of Bristol*, 2 vols (Bristol, 1821–3), II, 227.

Wytsontyde Like the first sermon in the series this is a Pentecostal sermon; see *Sermons*, pp. 113, 308, 315.

Inicium sapientiae . . . wisedome Ecclus. 1:16; cf. Prov. 1:7 and 9:10. More takes this maxim from Prov. 1:7 (Marc'hadour, *Bible* I, 12–13, 181).

Damascen . . . agoniam St John of Damascene, *De Fidei Orthodoxa* II, 15 (PG 94, 932); cf. Aquinas' exposition in *ST* 2a2ae. 19. 2 (*ed. cit.* XXXIII, 46–9).

Whyche shoulde be . . . filiall Aquinas, *ST* 2a2ae. 19, 8; (*ed. cit.* XXXIII, 66–9). In the scholastic tradition initial fear was considered to differ only incidentally from filial fear. Both aimed to avoid sin and alienation from God; R. Rolle in 'Contemplations of the dread and love of God' (Horstman, *Yorkshire Writers* II, 76) further identifies chaste fear with filial (or initial) fear.

Mundane or worldelye . . . loue See Aquinas, *ST* 2a2ae. 19, 3 (*ed. cit.* XXXIII, 52–3).

For all feare . . . questi Augustine, Quaest. XXXIII, *De Diversis Quaestionibus LXXXIII* (PL 40, 22); cf. Aquinas, *ST*, *loc. cit.*

Si dimittimus . . . captiuitie John 11:48.

Marc. xiiii . . . werye Mk 14:33–34.

It begon . . . incarnation Mk 14:36.

In like maner . . . dampnable Aquinas, *ST* 2a2ae. 19, 3, 3 (*ed. cit.* XXXIII, 50–3).

Seruyle feare . . . so Aquinas, *ST* 2a2ae. 19, 4, 1–2 (*ed. cit.* XXXIII, 54–5). Aquinas cites

Peter Lombard in *Glossa Lombardi* (PL 191, 1439) and St Gregory in *Moralia* IV, 27 (PL 75, 662) as denouncing servile fear. Bonde, *Pilgrymage, ed. cit.* fo. 73, states that servile fear and worldly fear 'be not the effect of grace/ & therefore they be nought . . .'.

Seruyle . . . betynge Aquinas, *ST loc. cit.*; see W. Bonde, *A deuoute Epystle . . . for them that ben tymorouse . . . in Conscience* (M. Fawkes,) [?1534], fo. 2: 'Seruile feare ys . . . comparyd to a bondman/ or a hyred saruaunte/ whiche doth feare and drede his mayster for his cruelte and lustyce . . .' (STC 3276).

S. Augustine . . . euermore Augustine, Quaest. XXXVI, 'De Diversis Quaestionibus LXXXIII' (PL 40, 26); cf. his 'In Epist. Joannis ad Parthos Tractatus Decem', IX, 4 (PL 35, 2049) upon which the following exposition draws.

Althoughe . . . doynge Aquinas, *ST* 2a2ae. 19, 6 (*ed. cit.* XXXIII, 60–3). Most ME treatments stress that servile fear does not lead to salvation; see *Jacob's Well*, p. 241: 'Þis drede allone schal neuere brynge þe to heuene'.

for he that oft . . . initialis On the distinction between servile fear (of punishment) and initial fear (of separation from God) see Aquinas, *ST* 2a2ae. 19, 8, 2–3 (*ed. cit.* XXXIII, 66–9).

Timor domini . . . fayleth Ps. 18:10; Vg. 'permanens'; cf. Augustine, 'In Epist Joannis', IX, 4 (PL 35, 2048).

.i. Ioh. iiii . . . charitie I John 4:18; cf. Aquinas, *ST* 2a2ae. 19, 9 2 (*ed. cit.* XXXIII, 68–9); Augustine, 'In Epist Joannis', IX, 4 (PL 35, 2047–8).

Timor domini . . . euer Ps. 18:10.

lyke as one blaste . . . agre Augustine, 'In Epist. Joannis', IX, 4 (PL 35, 2048–9).

There be men . . . feare On the effects of charity on servile fear and chaste or filial fear see Aquinas, *ST* 2a2ae. 19, 10 (*ed. cit.* XXXIII, 74–5).

A man . . . company Augustine, 'In Epist. Joannis', IX, 4 (PL 35, 2048–9).

as S. Iohn sayth . . . punishment A reference to I John 4:18.

desponsaui vos . . . Christ II Cor. 11:2; Vg. 'Despondi enim vos'; see Aquinas, *ST* 2a2ae. 19, 2, 3 (*ed. cit.* XXXIII, 48–9).

the beutifullest . . . hominum Ps. 44:3.

Cupio dissolui . . . Christ Phil. 1:23; Vg. 'desiderium habens dissolvi et cum Christo esse'.

O lorde God . . . temple Ps. 79:20; 26:4.

as faith . . . .i. Corin. xii. I. Cor. 12:8–10.

Not decked . . . grace A reference to I Pet. 4:8.

And the sayde . . . styll This image from Augustine's commentary on I John 4:18 in 'In Epist. Joannis' (PL 35, 2049) often appears in medieval expositions of servile fear. See *Jacob's Well*, p. 241: 'As brystell bryngeth in a threed'.

Initium sapienciae . . . euermore Ps. 110:10; a reference to Aquinas, *ST* 2a2ae. 19, 8 (*ed. cit.* XXXIII, 66–9).

Prophete Esay . . . Christ Is. 11:3.

It is not mundane . . . nowe On the identification of filial or chaste fear, the fear of God, as one of the seven gifts, see Aquinas, *ST* 2a2ae. 19, 9 (*ed. cit.* XXXIII, 72–3).

Suche is the feare . . . God On the existence of fear in heaven see Aquinas, *ST* 2a2ae. 19, 11 (*ed. cit.* XXXIII, 76–81).

Honorifico patrem . . . father John 8:49.

And this gifte . . . Humilitie Aquinas identifies filial fear as the source of the virtue of humility in *ST* 2a2ae. 19, 10, 4 (*ed. cit.* XXXIII, 72–3).

Phili. ii . . . father Phil. 2:8–11; Vg. 'Dominus Iesus Christus'.

An homily of the articles of our Christen fayth.

An homilie . . . faythe On the existence of this sermon and the following sermon on Ceremonies in Bod. MS Rawl. D. 831 see Introduction, pp. 6–7. The typographical features which distinguish them from the others in the 1557 text have been preserved: the line breaks in this sermon; the pilcrows in the sermon on ceremonies.

Fayth . . . experience Heb. 11:1; cf. Aquinas, *ST* 2a2ae. 1, 6 (*ed. cit.* XXXI, 30–1).

This knowledge . . . heresaye I Cor. 13:12; see Aquinas, *ST* 2a2ae. 1, 4 (*ed. cit.* XXXI, 20–23).

Without faieth . . . Hebre. xi Heb. 11:6.

The holye menne . . . beleue For proof that the old law made available faith in the mediator see Aquinas, *ST* 1a2ae. 98, 2 (*ed. cit.* XXIX, 8–13).

i. Pet. iii I Pet. 3:15; cf. Aquinas, *ST* 2a2ae. 2, 10 (*ed. cit.* XXXI, 102–3).

Fides inexercitata . . . sleapye Ambrose on Ps. 118:86, 'In Ps. CXVIII Expositio' (*PL* 15, 1357).

this present yeare . . . M.D. xlvi This date, the only one provided for any of the sermons, does not appear in the version of this sermon in MS Rawl. D. 831.

when the Germaynes . . . rable On Luther and his adherents see *Sermons*, pp. 127, 137, 245.

pax fidei . . . faith Ambrose, 'In Ps. CXVIII' (*PL* 15, 1357).

The true rule . . . scripture The Protestant idea of scripture as a *regula* is striking in this passage which otherwise upholds the oral traditions of the church. On John Bale's use of this terminology in *John the Baptist Preaching* (1537) see S. House, 'Cromwell's Message to the Regulars: the Biblical Trilogy of John Bale, 1537', *Renaissance and Reformation*, forthcoming.

.xii. articles . . . Christ I.e. The Western baptismal creed (known as *symbolum apostolorum*) which originates from the Roman Creed used in the fourth century. The legend (from Matt. 28:19 and John 20:19) that the twelve apostles each contributed an article before they separated at Pentecost was widely accepted until exploded by Erasmus and Valla. An important source is the preface of Tyrannius Rufinus (c.404) to his *Commentarius in Symbolum Apostolorum*. See *PL* 21, 335–86; *Rufinus. A Commentary on the Apostles' Creed*, ed. and tr. J.N.D. Kelly (London, 1955), pp. 13–14 , 29–30; Kelly, *Doctrines*, p. 44; *Early Christian Creeds* (London, 1950), pp. 101–2; A.E. Burn, *Apostles' Creed* (London, 1906), pp. 24–5; A. Harnack, *Apostles' Creed*, tr. S. Means, rev. and ed. T.B. Saunders (London, 1901), pp. 10 ff.

shotte or gatherynge Synonyms for 'collation' (from Lat. *collatio*, a meaning of *symbolum* wrongly derived by Rufinus). 'Gathering' means 'joint compilation'; 'shot' used here in the sense of 'a joint contribution made by several' (see *OED* s.v. 'Collation' *sb.* I, 1), may be associated with 'tally, reckoning, amount due' (*OED* s.v. 'Shot' *sb.* 23; cf. 'Scot-free').

as souldiours . . . word Rufinus also interpreted *symbolum* as *indicum* or *signum*, 'a token or watchword', in describing the creed as a

badge used by the true followers of Christ (*PL* 21, 337–8; Kelly, *Rufinus*, p. 30); but Tertullian, *De Poenitentia* 6, first introduced the metaphor of the soldier taking a military oath of allegiance (*sacramentum*) at the font (*PL* 1, 1238–9). Augustine links the notion of the pact with that of the password in Hom. 214 (*PL* 38, 1072). This definition appears in the Edwardian catechisms; e.g. A. Nowell, *A Catechism* (1570), tr. T. Norton, ed. G.E. Corrie, PS (Cambridge, 1853), p. 141: 'A symbol by interpretation is a badge, mark, watch word or token whereby the soldiers of one side are known from the enemies'. See Burn, *Apostles' Creed*, p. 27; Kelly, *Creeds*, pp. 52–61.

And according . . . articles Although some Reformation creeds which mention the legend of apostolic authorship distribute the articles among the twelve apostles, this form of division is unusual. But see the collection of prayers containing *The Crede by the olde lawe and by the newe* (Redman) [1535?] sigs A2–A5, STC 20200.3. The legend was rejected as an extra-scriptural tradition by the reformers who taught that the creed was only gathered from the apostles' writings. It was one of the articles recanted by Richard Smith at Paul's Cross in 1547 (Wilson, 'Catalogue', 10); Cranmer claimed it was still taught by parish priests then. (*Works*, II, 515). The Edwardian creeds resemble the version in the *King's Book* (*Formularies*, p. 226) which makes no reference to the apostles. See Swete, *Apostles' Creed*, pp. 9–11; Nowell, *Catechism*, p. 147; Strype, *Cranmer* II, 39.

saint Peter Traditionally the foremost of the apostles, St Peter was held responsible for the first article because of the tradition linking him with an apostolate which initiated the papacy. See *ODS* s.v. 'Peter'; *Sermons*, pp. 135, 193–4, 196–8.

collation Rufinus erroneously interpreted *symbolum* as 'collation' ('joint composition') rather than 'token' or 'sign' because his belief in the false tale of apostolic authorship led him to confuse Gk. συμβολη (*collatio*, also *summa*) with συμβολον (*signum* or *indicum*); see *PL* 21, 337; Kelly, *Rufinus*, pp. 30, 101–2; Harnack, *Apostles' Creed*, p. 10.

it is the belefe . . . people The new definition of the church appears in the *Bishops' Book* (*Formularies*, pp. 52–7; *Sermons*, pp. 178–9); the Protestant term 'congregation' for 'church' became standard; e.g. Nowell, *Catechism*, p. 171, states, '*Ecclesia*; . . . may fitly be called a *Congregation*'.

Then the superstitious . . . false See the arguments against idols in *Sermons*, pp. 143-4, 301-2.

And . . . Maniche On the dualism of Manichaeism – the conflict between light and darkness, whose principles were designated as two contrasting realms or states – see *Sermons*, pp. 120, 127, 141, 171.

Esay saith . . . declare Is. 53:8.

the empiriall . . . life This orthodox view of Catholic theology which identifies heaven as 'a place' and stresses the blessed life that the souls in heaven lead, but which disclaims knowledge of its spatial characteristics in relation to the physical universe, probably comes from one of the formulated descriptions of heaven found in preachers' handbooks or encyclopaedias; see *ODCC* s.v. 'Heaven'; *OED* s.v. 'Heaven' *sb.* 5.

Aristotle . . . mundo A reference to Aristotle's *De Caelo et Mundo* I, 3 on the properties of the first body. See *Aristotle on the Heavens*, tr. W.K.C. Guthrie (London, 1939), pp. 19-27.

Thy kingdome . . . worldes Ps. 144:13.

Saynte Basile . . . exameron Basil, *Hexameron* I, 5 (PG 29, 14).

Heauen . . . there OED s.v. 'Heaven' *sb.* 1 states: 'The expanse in which the sun, moon and stars are seen . . . the sky, the firmament'.

Heauen . . . ayre See Ps. 8:8; 78:2; 103:12. The visible sky and the region of space beyond. According to the Ptolomaic system this was divided into spheres which corresponded to the spaces comprised within the orbits of the seven planets including sun and moon, the fixed stars and other spheres. OED s.v. 'Heaven' *sb.* 2 and 4.

so taketh Moyses . . . drye Gen. 1:1 and 9. OED s.v. 'Heaven' *sb.* 3 states: 'The "realm" or region of space beyond the clouds or visible sky of which the latter is popularly viewed as the "floor" '. This opinion refers to the definition immediately preceding.

The seconde . . . man Apparently the second of the two opinions mentioned above and probably another reference to the OT view of heaven as the visible sky, the abode of God (conceived as in or beyond the physical

heavens) and of the angels. See *ODCC* s.v. 'Heaven'.

saynte Iohn Euangelist Author of the Fourth Gospel, the Book of Revelation and the Epistles of St John, John was one of the inner group or three disciples which included his brother, James the Great, and Peter. He probably holds second place because he promulgated the doctrine of the deity of Christ. See *ODCC* s.v. 'John, St.'

Iesus . . . synnes Matt. 1:20-21; cf. Augustine, 'In Epist. Ioannis', III, 2 (*PL* 35, 2000). 'Jesus' is the Gk form of the Heb. Joshua (lit. 'Jehova saves'); see *ODCC* s.v. 'Jesus'. This exposition follows the official teaching of the English Church. See Bonner, *A profitable doctryne*, ed. cit. sig. C4ᵛ; Nowell, *Catechism*, pp. 152-3; *Formularies*, pp. 35, 230; *Sermons*, pp. 115, 195.

Christ . . . priest Augustine, 'In Epist. Ioannis', III, 2 (*PL* 35, 2000). Like the reformers Edgeworth interprets Christ's name according to his office as saviour, see Pelikan, *Church and Dogma*, p. 56.

Christ . . . signe A reference to Heb. 1:9. 'Christ' is the translation of the Gk. χριστος meaning 'the Anointed One'; see *ODCC* s.v. 'Christ'; *Sermons*, pp. 115, 193, 195, 238.

onely sonne . . . passion II Pet. 1:16 and 18; with reference to Matt. 17:1-9.

ii. Pet. i . . . hym II Pet. 1:17.

Not two Gods A reference to the Manichaean heresy; see *Sermons*, pp. 120, 127, 141, 170.

al things . . . Lorde John 1:3.

For God . . . highnes The third article in the *King's Book* states, 'we call him *our Lord*' (*Formularies*, p. 230); worship due to God is here associated with the royal supremacy.

And I . . . Orchadie I.e. the Orkney Islands, an archipelago separated from the Caithness mainland in Scotland by the Pentland Firth strait; see Enc. Brit. VII, s.v. 'Orkney Islands'. Cf. medieval declamations of swearing; *Jacob's Well*, pp. 261, 294; *Book of Vices and Virtues*, pp. 61-2; Owst, *LPME*, pp. 414-15, 438-9 etc.; Blench, p. 244.

S. Iames . . . more St James 'the Great' a son of Zebedee; he, his brother John, and Peter were with Christ at the Transfiguration and the Agony at Gethsemane; see *Sermons*, pp. 135, 178.

the scripture . . . thereof A reference to Luke 1:35; Matt. 1:18–20.

Saint Austine . . . same Augustine, 'Sermo de Symbolo', II (*PL* 40, 1191–2); on the incarnation see *Sermons*, pp. 214, 291.

he was a worme . . . man Ps. 21:7.

after his resurrection . . . shut A reference to John 20:19.

Saint Andrewe St Andrew, brother of St Peter, is included among the first four in all gospel lists of the apostles. Ancient tradition links him with Greece; see *Sermons*, p. 135.

Thys Ponce Pilate . . . suffred Augustine, 'Sermo de Symbolo', II (*PL* 40, 1192). Pilate was the procurator of Judaea from 26–36 AD; his name is included in the creed primarily for historical reasons. See Nowell, *Catechism*, pp. 156–7; Kelly, *Creeds*, pp. 149–50.

Luke .iiii. Luke 4:29; see *Sermons*, pp. 358, 368.

Iohn .viii. John 8:59.

saint Austine . . . sanctified Augustine, *loc. cit.*; see E. Beresford-Cooke, *The Sign of the Cross in the Western Liturgies*, Alcuin Club, 7 (London, 1907), p. 5, on the uniqueness of the Roman rubric.

The crosse layd . . . Southe Augustine, 'Sermo de Symbolo', IV (*PL* 40, 1193).

Roma. v . . . synne Rom. 5:9–10.

his graue shall be . . . Esay .xi. Is. 11:10.

He was wrapt . . . spyces John 19:40.

we Christen people . . . Christ A reference to the ceremonies of the Easter Sepulchre. The Sacrament was consecrated and reserved on Maundy Thursday, placed in a pyx on Good Friday and deposited with the Cross in an Easter Sepulchre, a special place of repose on the N. side of the sanctuary (the *Depositio*). It was removed on Easter morning with an antiphon and hung in a pyx over the altar; the cross was carried to a side altar and venerated with another antiphon (the *Elevatio*). These ceremonies are described in Cranmer's 1543 treatise on ceremonies. Although they were apparently not condemned in 1548, there are few references to Easter Sepulchres after this date. But the introductory service of Easter morning was retained in the first *BCP* and is the source of our present Easter anthems. See

Cranmer, *The Rationale of Ceremonial, 1540–1543*, ed. C.S. Cobb, Alcuin Club, 18 (London, 1910), pp. 32–8 (cited hereafter as Cobb, *Rationale*); F. Procter, *A New History of the Book of Common Prayer with a Rationale of its Offices*, rev. ed. W.H. Frere (London, 1955), pp. 540–1 (cited hereafter as Procter and Frere, *BCP*); H. Thurston, *Lent and Holy Week* (London, 1904), pp. 454–72; D. Rock, *The Church of our Fathers*, ed. G.W. Hart and W.H. Frere, 4 vols (London, 1903–4), III, 77–80; K. Young, *The Drama of the Medieval Church*, 2 vols (Oxford, 1933), I, 112–48; Strype, *Ecc. Mem.* I, ii, 431; Frere and Kennedy, p. 186 n. 6; *Sermons*, p. 187.

saynt Phillip St Philip came from Bethsaida (John 1:43–51) and was probably a disciple of John the Baptist. His career after leaving Jerusalem is often confused with Philip the Evangelist. He is said to have preached in Phrygia and to have been crucified at Hierapolis where he was buried. See *ODCC* s.v. 'Philips'; *ODS* s.v. 'Philip'.

He descended . . . hell The fifth article in the *Bishops' Book*. It was included with the fourth in Henry's corrections of the formulary; this division, adopted by Cranmer in his translation of the creed of c.1538, appears in the *King's Book*. See Cranmer, *Works* II, 83, 89; *Formularies*, pp. 29, 226.

zacha. ix . . . there Zach. 9:11.

Christ came . . . water I Pet. 3:19–20; see *Sermons*, pp. 292–3.

He came . . . captiuitie On this interpretation of I Pet. 3:19 as a form of the Harrowing of Hell see below, p. 432.

amonge whiche were . . . readye A reference to Gen. 6:3 and 14–16.

they repented . . . place On this literal interpretation of I Pet. 3:19–20 and the identification of the 'skyrte of hel' see *Sermons*, pp. 129–30, 293.

S. Basyl . . . bondes Basil on Ps. 115:16 in 'Hom. in Ps. CXV' (*PG* 30, 114); Vg: 'dissolvisti'.

Osee .xiii . . . same Hosea 13:14; cited by Augustine in 'Sermo de Symbolo', VII (*PL* 40, 1194).

Saynt Thomas Called 'Didymus' in the Fourth Gospel, St Thomas offered to die with Christ on the way to Bethany. He is remembered because he refused to believe in the resurrection unless he touched the wounds of the risen Christ (John 20:25–8). His missionary work may have been in India; his body was translated to Edessa in 394. See *ODS* s.v. 'Thomas'.

and came forth . . . sealed A reference to Matt. 27:66.

and forthwith . . . it Matt. 28:2.

the thre Maries The tradition that there were three Marys at the tomb of Christ comes from John 19:25 which names (1) his mother (the Blessed Virgin); (2) Mary, the wife of Clopas, identified by some with his mother's sister (although possibly two different women are meant); (3) Mary Magdalene. Mary, mother of James and Joses, the sons of Zebedee (Matt. 28:56; Mk 15:40) who witnessed the empty tomb (Mk 16:1) may be the same as (2). Edgeworth is remembering an Easter liturgical play such as *Visitatio Sepulchri* which comprises a dialogue between the Marys and the angels and in later versions a scene containing Peter and John. It was traditionally performed after Matins on Easter Sunday as part of the Easter Sepulchre ceremonies. A Cornish passion play, *Resurrexio*, part of a trilogy, also treats the experience of the three Marys. See Young, *Drama*, I 232–3, 239 ff; O.B. Hardison, Jr. *Christian Rite and Christian Drama in the Middle Ages* (Baltimore, 1965); Whiting, *Blind Devotion*, pp. 199–202.

Angels . . . rysen Probably a reference to Luke 24:4: & 23. In John 20:11–18 the angels outside the tomb speak only to Mary Magdalene; in Matt. 28:2–7 and Mk 16:5–7 there is only one angel; see Young, *Drama* I, 217.

Notwithstandynge . . . Disciples A reference to Matt. 28:7–8.

for feare of shrewes A reference to John 19:38; 'shrewes' (which also occurs in MS Rawl. D. 831) meaning 'malignant, wicked men' or 'antireligious forces' is either a mistranslation of the Vg. 'propter motum Iudaeorum' or a deliberate substitution for 'Jews'.

Marye Magdalene . . . hearde John 20:2. See Young, *Drama* I, 306 ff. on the role of the apostles in the *Visitatio Sepulchri*.

the beginninge . . . Col. i. Col. 1:18.

Oure olde manne . . . sinne A reference to Rom. 6:6.

Oure olde man . . . sinne A reference to Rom. 5:12.

We lyue to synne . . . sinne A reference to Rom. 6:12.

S. Bartholomew The Fourth Gospel identifies Bartholomew with Nathanael. According to Eusebius he left behind in India the Gospel according to St Matthew written in Hebrew. See *ODS* s.v. 'Bartholomew'; *Sermons*, p. 135.

the condition . . . to come Augustine, 'Sermo de Symbolo', VII (*PL* 40, 1194).

openinge the waye . . . Mich. ii. Micah 2:13.

To sitte . . . sytteth Augustine, 'Sermo de Symbolo', VII, *loc. cit.*

Saynt Steuen . . . Iewes See Acts 7:55–56 on St Stephen's vision before his martyrdom; *Sermons*, p. 162.

saint Mathew . . . Euangelist St Matthew, the tax gatherer, traditionally regarded as the author of the First Gospel. According to Eusebius he preached to the Hebrews; a sixth century apocryphal work on the Lord's Infancy is falsely attributed to him. See *ODCC*; *ODS* s.v. 'Matthew'.

In the same . . . hethen Augustine, *loc. cit.*

ii. Cor. v. II Cor. 5:10; cited by Augustine, *loc. cit.*

And so Christ . . . dedes Rom 2:6.

for theyr owne . . . Roma. ii. Rom. 2:15.

they shall wysshe . . . Lambe Rev. 6:16.

Saynte Iames . . . scholer Tradition identifies 'James the Less', an apostle and son of Alphaeus, with James, 'the Lord's brother', who with St Peter was an early leader of the church at Jerusalem; but this is unlikely. The belief that he was the author of an apocryphal Infancy Gospel known as the Book of James led to his being called Christ's scholar; see *ODCC* s.v. 'James, St., "the Less" '; 'James, St., "the Lord's brother" '; see *Sermons*, pp. 196, 197.

the other Iames . . . Article A reference to James the Great sometimes confused with James the Less; see *Sermons*, pp. 135, 173, 179, 288.

Symon . . . Zelotes St Simon was called 'The Cananaean' by Matthew and Mark and 'The Zealot' by Luke; these two names represent the same word. See *ODCC* s.v. 'Simon'.

the tenth . . . sainctes On the reformers' linking of these two clauses see Swete, *Apostles' Crede*, p. 87; Nowell, *Catechism*, p. 173; *Formularies*, pp. 29, 226.

After the myndes . . . God Augustine, 'Sermo de Symbolo', VII (*PL* 40, 1196).

Collossen. i . . . persons Col. 1:4. Vg. 'in sanctos omnes'.

I hate the churche . . . debate Ps. 25:5.

It is also . . . Christ On the new treatment of the four marks of the Church – unity, holiness, catholicity and apostolicity – see Nowell, *Catechism*, pp. 172–4; P. Hughes, *The Reformation in England*, 3 vols (London, 1954), II, 31–3. The formularies omit any reference to the church as a teacher of doctrine that is holy or the church's unity being conserved by maintaining the true doctrine of the Holy Spirit. See *Formularies*, pp. 52–7, 244–8; D.H.M. Davies, *Worship and Theology in England*, 5 vols (New Jersey, 1961–75), I, *From Cranmer to Hooker, 1534–1603* (1970), pp. 26–7.

It is called . . . Churches See Nowell, *Catechism*, pp. 172–3. Cf. earlier definitions of universality 'from the beginning of the world to the end' and as applied to the Church of Rome (Pelikan, *Church and Dogma*, pp. 99–100, 106).

This fayth saueth . . . shippe An echo of the article in the *Bishop's Book*; see *Formularies*, p. 59.

The communion . . . persons The following conforms to the newly accepted definition of *sanctorum communis* (saints proper and martyrs) as a fellowship of holy persons in general (including the living as well as the departed). Saints may be intercessors, but no reference is made to worship of them, nor to the traditional third class of members of the church, the souls in purgatory; see Nowell, *Catechism*, pp. 173–4; *Formularies*, pp. 52, 57–8, 249–50; Hughes, *Reformation* II, 31.

I am partaker . . . O Lorde Ps. 118:63.

Iude . . . aforesaid Jude, one of 'the brethren of the Lord' and author of the Epistle of Jude, is usually identified with James, 'the Lord's brother', whom Edgeworth here appears to have confused with James the Less. He joined St Simon to preach in Persia where both were martyred. See *ODS* s.v. 'Jude'.

S. Mathy . . . him selfe Although it is often implied that St Matthias had been a follower of Christ during his ministry on earth, the NT (Acts 1:15–26) only refers to the apostles' election of him by lot after the Ascension to replace Judas Iscariot. He is said to have preached in Judaea and later in Cappadocia. See *ODCC* and *ODS* s.v. 'Matthias'.

The resurrection . . . euerlastinge In the *King's Book* this article is divided between the eleventh and twelfth articles (*Formularies*, p. 293).

by the dowrye . . . impassibilitie The following exposition from I Cor. 15:42–4 of the four endowments or marriage portions ('dowries') of the glorified body – *impassibilitas*, immunity from suffering or hurt; *subtiltas*, absence of density; *claritas*, a swiftness of response to the spirit; *agilitas*, movement without difficulty or labour – is standard. See Aquinas, *ST* 3a. 54, 1–3 (*ed. cit.* LV, 18–31); *NCE* 6 s.v. 'Glorified Body'; *Sermons*, pp. 339–40.

in a twinkelinge . . . eye Proverbial. See *ODEP* s.v. 'Twinkling'; *Sermons*, p. 285.

life euerlastinge . . . be This inexpressibility *topos* occurs in other treatments of the joys of heaven. See 'The Mirror of St Edmund' in Horstman, *Yorkshire Writers* I, 234; 'De Gaudiis Celi' in *Speculum Christiani*, ed. G. Holmstedt, EETS, OS, 182 (London, 1933), pp. 118–20.

the gifte . . . incorruption A reference to I Cor. 15:42.

An homily of Ceremonies and humane lawes

Good . . . Ceremonies An earlier explanation of existing ceremonies (those prescribed by the Injunctions of 1538) was Cranmer's *Rationale* or *Booke concerninge Ceremonies* drawn up between 1540–3. It was not published in Cranmer's lifetime although copies were probably circulated in manuscript. This sermon was preached just before many ceremonies were swept away by Council's Orders of Jan.–Feb. 1548 (*Documentary Annals of the Reformed Church of England, 1546–1716*, ed. E. Cardwell, 2 vols (Oxford, 1844), I, nos VII and VIII; cited hereafter as Cardwell, *Doc Ann.*). The reference to eating flesh in Lent suggests a date between the proclamation of 16 January 1548 reinforcing the Lenten fast (Hughes and Larkin I, 297), and the prohibitions on preaching of 24 April (*ibid.* 300, 303). The ceremonial is printed by Cobb, *Rationale*, pp. 3–43; and by Strype, *Ecc. Mem.* I, ii, no. CIX. See Frere and Kennedy, pp. 4, 182–7, n. 2; Procter and Frere, *BCP*, pp. 39–40.

Valerius Maximus Valerius Maximus, *Facta et Dicta Memorabilia* I, 1 and 10 (*ed. cit.* pp. 1, 6); see Aquinas, ST 1a2ae. 99, 3 (*ed. cit.* XXIX, 40–1).

a towne . . . Cerete The Etruscan town of Cære, 30 miles N. of Rome (*OCD* s.v. 'Cære'). This is a doubtful etymology; according to some authorities, *caeremonia* is linked with *Ceres*, 'the goddess of creation', stemming from the Sanskrit root *Kri*, 'to make or create', which came to mean 'to sacrifice'. *Caeremonia* was considered a 'controversial' word in 1541 (*Concilia* III, 861).

when the citie . . . veneration Livy writes of the invasion of Rome by the Gauls in c.390 BC in *The History of Rome* V, 40. The priest of Quirinus was one of the major Roman priests; the Vestal Virgins were the six priestesses charged with keeping the sacred fire of the city in the Temple of Vesta.

They . . . charitie On the relationship between divine worship and ceremonial precepts see Aquinas, ST 1a2ae. 99, 3 (*ed. cit.* XXIX, 38–41).

I will geue . . . Gene. xxvi Gen. 26:3–5.

Abel . . . him Gen. 4:4 & 26. The following promises made to Abraham and Noah are examples of the Old Covenant of which one sign was to walk justly before God; see *NCE* 4 s.v. 'Covenant in the Pentateuch'. Edgeworth may also have in mind Heb. 11:4–10.

Enoch . . . away Gen. 5:24.

Noe the holye . . . offred Gen. 8:20–21.

The morall lawes . . . this I.e. the body of requirements in conformity to which virtuous action consists (*OED* s.v. 'Moral' a.4.); cf. positive laws which are formally instituted by rightful authorities; see Aquinas, ST 1a2ae. 100, 1 (*ed. cit.* XXIX, 56–61).

Of this kinde . . . Israel A reference to Ex. 20: 1–17; on the relationship of the decalogue to the moral precepts of the Old Law see Aquinas, ST 1a2ae. 100, 3 (*ed. cit.* XXIX, 64–7).

for malyce . . . abundaunte A reference to Matt. 24:12; for the proverb based on this text see *Sermons*, pp. 155, 233; above p. 392.

Afore a white heade . . . man Levit. 19:32.

And . . . ceremoniall On the relationship between the Israelites' judicial, moral and cere-

monial precepts see Aquinas, ST 1a2ae. 99, 4 (*ed. cit.* XXIX, 42–5).

Iudiciall . . . lawes I.e. laws enforced by secular judges and tribunals (*OED* s.v. 'Judicial' *adj.* 1.b.); see Aquinas, ST 1a2ae. 104, 1 (*ed. cit.* XXIX, 252–7).

Ceremonies . . . obseruaunces On this division of the Mosaic ceremonies see Aquinas, ST 1a2ae. 101, 4 (*ed. cit.* XXIX, 124–9).

And they were . . . goates A reference to Lev. 5:6.

And . . . Lepris A reference to Lev. 1:14; 5:7; 14:22; see Aquinas, ST 1a2ae. 102, 3, 2 (*ed. cit.* XXIX, 136–7).

S. Paule saith . . . Hebr. x Heb. 10:4.

paschal lambe The passover lamb which was slain in the Temple in the afternoon of Nisan (the month of the Jewish year corresponding to April) and eaten during that night. See *ODCC* s.v. 'Paschal Lamb'.

and the water . . . thinge A reference to Num. 19:9–22; see Aquinas, ST 1a2ae. 102, 5, 1–3 & 5 (*ed. cit.* XXIX, 178–89, 192–9).

Saint Paule . . . sinne A reference to Heb. 9:9.

The priest . . . do A reference to Num. 19:3–5; 17–20; see Aquinas, ST 1a2ae. 102, 5 (*ed. cit.* XXIX, 194–7).

they sanctify . . . Heb. ix. Heb. 9:13.

As ye tabernacle . . . kettles Aquinas, ST 1a2ae. 101, 4 (*ed. cit.* XXIX, 126–7).

the Iubily yere Lev. 25:4 and 10. According to Mosaic legislation every seven years was a Sabbath year in which the land remained fallow. The Jubilee year occurred once every fifty years; slaves were to regain their freedom and land was to revert to its previous owners. See *ODCC* s.v. 'Jubilee', 'Sabbatical Year'.

They should eat . . . them Lev. 11:3–8; Deut. 14:6–8.

gripes 'Grises' has been emended to 'gripes' as the context suggests a vulture or bird of prey. See *OED* s.v. 'Gripe' *sb.* 3. *Obs.* 2. ('grier eagle').

They . . . touched Lev. 11:10; Deut. 14:10; the list of forbidden birds comes from Lev. 11:13–19; Deut. 14:12–18.

And they sholde not . . . them Lev. 11:33–6.

How . . . fastyng The line division in the 1557 text suggests that this was intended as a sentence.

In the feast . . . clensynge I.e. the annual Jewish fast day usually in October, which aimed to cleanse sin and re-establish good relations with God (Lev. 16:24; 27–32); see Aquinas, *ST* 1a2ae. 102, 5 (*ed. cit.* XXIX, 192–5); *ODCC* s.v. 'Atonement, Day of'.

and how the wiues . . . his Num. 30:3–15.

As concerning . . . works Deut. 22:11; Lev. 19:19; see Aquinas, *ST* 1a2ae. 102, 6, 6 (*ed. cit.* XXIX, 212–13; 222–3).

They shold . . . day Num. 15:38; see Aquinas, *ST* 1a2ae. 102, 6, 7 (*loc. cit.*)

No man . . . god Deut. 22:5; see Aquinas, *ST* 1a2ae. 102, 6, 6 (*loc. cit.*).

Of yokinge . . . them Deut. 22:6; 22:9–10; Lev. 19:19; see Aquinas, *ST* 1a2ae. 102, 6, 8 & 9 (*loc. cit.*)

In al these . . . vsed See Aquinas, *ST* 1a2ae. 101, 1, 4; 101, 3, 2 (*ed. cit.* XXIX, 116–17).

The payn . . . Act. xv. Acts 15:10; see Aquinas, *ST* 1a2ae. 101, 3, 2 (*ed. cit.* XXIX, 120–1).

.vi. hundred or above The total number of commandments (Heb. 'mitzot') in the Rabbinic tradition is 613 (248 are positive, 365 negative). They were codified from the Torah by Maimonides in 2 AD. The Mishneh Torah was printed in Hebrew in 1509 in Constantinople. Two Babylonian Talmuds, which included the Mishnah, were printed with Pope Leo X's approval at Venice by Daniel Bomberg in 1520–3. See *Encyclopaedia Judaica*, 16 vols (Jerusalem, 1971), 5, s.v. 'Commandments, the 613'; 12, s.v. 'Printing, Hebrew'.

what payne . . . dwelled A reference to Ex. 23:17; Deut. 16:16.

Likewise . . . corne A reference to Ex. 23:11; Lev. 25:41. On the Sabbath year see above, p. 402.

the morall preceptes . . . Iewes Aquinas, *ST* 1a2ae. 99, 2, 1 (*ed. cit.* XXIX, 34–7). Unlike the judicial and ceremonial precepts, the moral laws remained valid under the Christian dispensation.

This imperfection . . . homicide Matt. 5:22–24.

The iudicialles . . . law A reference to Aquinas, *ST* 1a2ae. 100, 7, 4 (*ed. cit.* XXIX, 86–9).

But as . . . efficacitie Aquinas, *ST* 1a2ae. 104, 3, 3 (*ed. cit.* XXIX, 258–63). This is a familiar

explanation; see the *King's Book*, *Formularies*, p. 262.

Christes . . . religion Edgeworth seems to agree here with the teaching of the *King's Book* which attributes the jurisdiction of ceremonies to kings and princes; see *Formularies*, p. 310.

after . . . Melchisedech A reference to Ps. 109:4; the name of Melchisedech, a type of Christ, is found in the Roman Canon of the Mass; see Wickham Legg, *Sarum Missal*, p. 223. See *Sermons*, pp. 114, 195; above p. 372.

And in this . . . fayth Cf. the exposition of the Mass in the *King's Book* which uses the words 'memorial' and 'remembrance' but which omits any explanation of its propitiatory character; *Formularies*, pp. 264, 268.

A contrite . . . despise Ps. 50:19.

And in an other psalme . . . him Ps. 115:17.

an holocaust . . . alburned sacrifice See Lev. 6:9–10; Aquinas, *ST* 1a2ae. 102, 3, 8–10 (*ed. cit.* XXIX, 146–51).

saynt Austine . . . Ianuarye Augustine, Epist. LV, 'Ad Inquisitiones Januarii', XIX (*PL* 33, 331). This was commonly cited to justify the abolition of ceremonies; see Tyndale, *Answer*, p. 74; Cranmer's statement on ceremonies in the 1549 BCP in Cranmer, *Works* II, 518–19.

And yet . . . had Edgeworth here follows the Ten Articles which consider only the sacraments of baptism and penance as necessary for salvation, but which retain the sacrament of the altar. The occasion of death in infancy would perhaps justify its inclusion among those considered expedient. See *Formularies*, pp. 6, 8, 11–12.

Sacred . . . manye For the following list see Strype, *Ecc. Mem.* I, ii, 413–14, 419–27; Cobb, *Rationale*, pp. 4–6, 15–28; the reduced list of church ornaments reflects the impact of the Edwardian visitations which proscribed many ornaments such as altar lights, and the ceremonies associated with them; see Procter and Frere, *BCP*, pp. 59, 366–7.

Vestiments . . . might The traditional vestments of the priest celebrating Mass: the amice, alb, girdle, stole, cope, maniple and chasuble. All except the alb and cope were abolished in the 1549 BCP (see *ODCC* s.v. 'Eucharistic Vestments'). This may be a reference to dispossessed monks and friars who became parish priests but, not being ordained, wore a habit or gown instead of eucharistic vestments. The conservatives criticised the diversity of religious habits; e.g. Barlow, A dialoge, ed. cit. sigs G3–G5ᵛ; art. 26 of Bonner's Injunctions of 1554–5 condemns the clergy who 'go in laymen's habits & apparel . . . that they cannot be discerned from laymen' (Frere and Kennedy, p. 337). But the Protestant John Hooper, nominated to the see of Gloucester in 1550, initiated a controversy by refusing at first to be consecrated on the grounds that episcopal vestments were unlawful. See Cobb, Rationale, pp. 16–18, 31; Strype, Ecc. Mem. I, ii, 419–20, 428; Cardwell, BCP, p. 267; Ridley, Ridley, pp. 222–7; The Two Books of Common Prayer . . . in the reign of King Edward the Sixth, ed. E. Cardwell, PS, 2nd ed. (Oxford, 1841), pp. 267 (cited hereafter as Cardwell, BCP).

We observe . . . Lent The Lenten fast traditionally took place forty days before Easter: one meal a day only was allowed and flesh – meat, fish, eggs and lacticina – were forbidden; but in the Middle Ages fish was allowed and abstinence from lacticina came to be dispensed in the sixteenth century. During the Reformation dispensations allowing the use of meat were sporadically granted. The observance was expressly prescribed by the BCP; see ODCC s.v. 'Lent'; above pp. 379–80.

the Embre daies Four groups each of three days observed in the church year as days of fasting and abstinence; viz. the Wednesday, Friday and Saturday after St Lucy on 13 December; Ash Wednesday, Whitsunday, and Holy Cross Day on 14 September. Possibly originating in pagan observances connected with the crops, they are now associated with ordinations; see ODCC s.v. 'Ember Days'; Sermons, p. 342.

abstinence . . . fridai The observance of Friday as a weekly commemoration of the passion and kept as a day of abstinence from meat was attacked by Latimer in 1536 (ODCC s.v. 'Friday'). The 1538 Injunctions commanded that fasting days should not be altered. See Frere and Kennedy, pp. 41–4; Hughes and Larkin, I, 188; Cobb, Rationale, p. 32; Strype, Ecc. Mem. I, ii, 428; Sermons, pp. 298, 333.

Palme sondayes . . . processions For a contemporary description of the Palm Sunday ceremonies of blessing the palms and carrying them in a procession with the Cross and the Sacrament enclosed in a pyx see Becon,

'Potation for Lent', Early Works, pp. 112–16. They were abolished by an order of Council in January 1548. See Formularies, pp. 16, 147, 310–11; LP XIV, i, 777–8, 967; Hughes and Larkin, 186, pp. 273–4; Cobb, Rationale, p. 34; Thurston, Lent, ch. 5; Rock, Church IV, 264–8; D.B. Knox, The Doctrine of the Faith in the Reign of Henry VIII (London, 1961), p. 253; Ridley, Cranmer, pp. 269, 275.

Good Fridaies . . . sepulchre I.e. the Easter Sepulchre ceremonies (Sermons, p. 175; above p. 399). The other Good Friday ceremonies of Creeping to the Cross and kissing it, which the reformers condemned, were abolished in February 1548. See Cranmer, Works II, 414–15; Aston, England's Iconoclasts, pp. 230–1; Procter and Frere, BCP, p. 40.

the crucifixes . . . pretended Cross-breaking on highways was condemned in 1529, but it continued despite a general pardon of that year which excluded these offenders; e.g. an image of the crucifix on the highway of Coggeshill in East Anglia was desecrated; the famous rood at Dovercourt, Essex was burnt in c.1532. For cases of searching for treasure see LP XIII, i, 786; K. Thomas, Religion and the Decline of Magic (London, 1971), p. 280 on 'cross digging', condemned in the statute against witchcraft of 1542. Edgeworth suggests a confusion between searching for treasure and the widespread iconoclasm which occurred after the statute's withdrawal in 1547: on 17 November the rood of Mary and John and images in St Paul's church, London were pulled down; at St Martin's, Ironmonger Lane, the churchwardens replaced the crucifix by the royal arms; at St Ewen's church in Bristol tabernacles, images and the great rood were removed. See Frere and Kennedy, pp. 116, 119–20, 126; Aston, England's Iconoclasts, pp. 212–15, 255–63; Bettey, Bristol Parish Churches, pp. 9–10; Ridley, Cranmer, pp. 261, 263–4; The Chronicle of the Grey Friars of London, ed. J.G. Nichols, CS, OS, LIII (London, 1852), p. 54 (cited hereafter as Grey Friars' Chronicle); Sermons, p. 346; below p. 441.

Sainte Austine . . . in A reference to the Mosaic law, Augustine, Epist. LV, XIX 28–30 (PL 33, 331).

Come vnto me . . . light Matt. 11:28–30.

but he biddeth . . . withal Matt. 5:38–40.

On a time . . . you Luke 12:13–14.

S. Paule . . . begiled I Cor. 6:7.

We . . . lawes On the secular jurisdiction of ecclesiastical laws see Formularies, pp. 111–13, 287–8.

Of the authority . . . him Luke 10:16.

And generally . . . dampnation Rom. 13:1–2.

of very necessitye . . . compulsion A reference to Rom. 13:5; the Bishops' Book instructs the clergy to teach that Christ forbade the apostles or their successors to assume the authority of kings; and Cranmer's questionnaire attempted to establish whether the apostles' power to create bishops came from God or from necessity (Pocock-Burnet, IV, 467–71); see Formularies, pp. 119, 121, 287 on clerical obedience due to the crown.

whereof . . . health An echo of the Bishops' Book's teaching on order; see Formularies, pp. 110–11, 114–15.

Obedience . . . idolatry I Kings 15:22–23.

thou shalt keepe . . . day On observing the sabbath see Formularies, pp. 143–6, 306–9; Cobb, Rationale, pp. 29–30.

charitie . . . deadly On the relationship of charity to the precepts of the law see Aquinas, ST 1a2ae. 100, 11 (ed. cit. XXIX, 98–103).

charitye . . . glasse An allusion to I Cor. 13:12; II Cor. 3:18.

positiue laws Positive laws, as distinct from natural laws, are those created by men; e.g. the Lenten fast was described as 'a mere positive law' as early as 1538, and in the Edwardian Royal Articles of 1547 which gave dispensations from fasting laws; the article on order in the King's Book states that the appointing of clergy and the powers of bishops come from positive laws, not scripture. See Formularies, pp. 218, 282; Frere and Kennedy, pp. 107–8; Hughes and Larkin, I, 177, 209, 214; Fox, Thomas More, pp. 161–6 on More's defence of them.

Thou shalt . . . lesynges See the articles on the ninth commandment in Formularies, pp. 165–8, 328–31.

As in theym . . . it Possibly a reference to the proclamation of 16 January 1548 which reinforced the Lenten fast in order to boost the fishing trade (Hughes and Larkin, I, 297). The fast had been attacked by Protestant preachers in March 1547 and many ate meat in Lent. See MacLure, Paul's Cross Sermons, pp. 40–1,

192; Ridley, Cranmer, pp. 263–4; Hughes, Reformation II, 85–7; this is a familiar complaint; see Sermons, pp. 128, 137, 189, 288–9, 333.

Penall lawes 'Laws which prohibit an act and which impose a penalty for the commission of it'. They are defined in the Codex Iuris Canonici and mainly concern morals, especially sexual offenses such as fornication and adultery, but also crimes such as eating flesh in Lent and non-attendance of church. On the modification of ecclesiastical laws after 1536 and the new code of 1551, Reformatio Legum Ecclesiasticarum, see R. Houlbrooke, Church Courts and the People during the English Reformation, 1520–70 (Oxford, 1979), pp. 16–19; Ridley, Cranmer, pp. 330–4; Guy, Tudor England, p. 225.

Math. xv. Matt. 15:3–6.

Math. xxiii Matt. 23:4.

Psa. lvii . . . streightly Ps. 57:1.

An exposition of the first epistle of Saynt Peter (The first sermon)

An exposition . . . church This sequence of twenty sermons was preached at Bristol Cathedral after its foundation in 1542, between c.1544 and c.1553. Edgeworth preaches secundum ordinem textus, uses the medieval biblical glosses, the Vulgate, and Erasmus' Novum Testamentum, Paraphrasis, and Annotationes.

The gret . . . wysedome III Kings 4:33–34.

Ecclesiastes . . . mouth Eccles. 1:8.

the Logition . . . day Probably a reference to Aristotle, whose writings on logic and rhetoric Edgeworth would have studied at Oxford; see Sermons, pp. 150, 246.

For the faire . . . hart An allusion either to Luke 12:31–3 or to Matt. 13:44.

Saint Paule . . . vnperfitelye I Cor. 13:12.

.i. Corin. xii . . . spirites I Cor. 12:8 &10; cf. Sermons, pp. 166, 328.

And . . . scripture On the fathers' interpretation of the divine inspiration of scripture see Kelly, Doctrines, pp. 60–4.

Lingua . . . Prophet Ps. 44:2. Vg. 'lingua mea stilus scribae'. This text, that the tongue of the human author serving as God's instrument was the pen of a ready writer, was often applied in asserting the divine inspiration of scripture; see Kelly, *Doctrines*, p. 61.

Discretion . . . spirites I Cor. 12:10.

.i. Corin. ix . . . preach I Cor. 9:16. Vg. 'vae enim mihi est . . .'.

scrutamini . . . finde John 5:39; Matt. 7:7.

Erratis . . . god Matt. 22:29.

Christum dei . . . God I Cor. 1:24.

master Deane . . . byshoppe The first bishop of Bristol Cathedral was the moderate Catholic Paul Bush. The first dean was William Snow, STP. The canons of the six stalls at the time of its foundation in 1542 were John Gough STP (1st); Roger Edgeworth STP (2nd); Henry Morgan (3rd); Roger Hughes (4th); Richard Brown (5th); George Dogeon STP (6th). See *Foedera, conventiones, literae . . .*, ed. T. Rymer, 20 vols, 3rd ed. (London, 1745), XIV, 751; J. Le Neve, *Fasti Ecclesiae Anglicanae*, corr. T. Hardy, 3 vols (Oxford, 1854), I, 213–14, 222–3; M.C. Skeeters, 'The Clergy of Bristol, c.1530–c.1570' (unpublished Ph.D thesis, University of Texas at Austin, 1984), pp. 242–7, Appendix III.

byndyng our selues . . . church The statutes of Bristol Cathedral, issued with the charter of erection on 4 June 1542, prescribe sermons to be preached in English four times a year:

And we will, that every Canon shall every year make four sermons at least to the people in the church aforesaid, in English, either by himself or by others, and that upon the Lord's Days; to wit, once between the Nativity of Christ [25 December] and the Feast of the Annunciation of the Blessed Virgin Mary; once between the Feast of the Blessed Virgin Mary [25 March] and the Nativity of John; once between the Nativity of St. John [24 June] and the Feast of Michael; and once between the Feast of Michael [29 September] and the Nativity of Christ; so that almost no one Lord's Day in the whole year shall pass without a sermon. Also, we will, that the Dean, either by himself or by his proxy, shall preach every year in our English tongue, at Easter, upon Corpus-Christi day, and at Christmas.

BRO DC/A/7/1/5: *The Statutes of Bristol Cathedral, as appointed by King Henry the Eighth*, tr. Rev. Canon Norris, 1870. The Latin reads:

Ut Singuli Canonici Singulis annis quator ad minus Sermonem ad populum in Ecclesia Praedicat Id<i>omate anglico per se vel per alios faciant idque diebus dom[o]iniis semel viz: inter Natalem Christi et Festum Annunciationis Beatae Mariae Virginis et Natalem Iohannis et semel inter Natalem Iohannis et Festum Michaelis semel inter Festum Michaelis & Natalem Christi ita ut nullus fere totius Anni Dies Dominicus abeat absque concione Decananum item Volumus ut Die paschae Corporis <Christi> et die Natalis Dominus quotannis Verbum Dei Anglico Idiomate per se vel per alius concionetur.

BRO DC/A/7/1/2

Sermons ten and fourteen were preached at Easter and sermon twelve just before Christmas as proxy for the dean; the others at the other times and between the feasts stipulated. See J.F. Nicholls and J. Taylor, *Bristol Past and Present*, 3 vols (Bristol, 1881), II, 66.

Petrus Apostolus . . . multiplied I Pet. 1:1–2.

I wyll fyrste . . . it For humanist precedents for this historico-critical method of Biblical exposition see *Ioannis Coleti Enarratio in Epistolam S. Pauli ad Romanos*, ed. and tr. J.H. Lupton (London, 1873, repr., New Jersey, 1965), pp. 124–31; *Ioannis Coleti Enarratio in Primam Epistolam S. Pauli ad Corinthios*, ed. and tr. J.H. Lupton (London, 1874, repr., New Jersey, 1965), pp. 8–10; J.W.H. Atkins, *English Literary Criticism – The Renascence* (London, 1947), pp. 58–9; Blench, p. 28.

Ioh. i. An exposition of John 1:35–41 on the first disciples.

Lo . . . God John 1:36; see also 1:29.

We cal . . . one On this interpretation see *Sermons*, pp. 115, 172, 195.

Tu es Simon . . . Petra John 1:42. Vg. 'Iohanna'.

Hieronimus . . . nuncupent Jerome on Gal. 1:14, 'Comm. in Epist. ad Galatos', I, 2 (*PL* 26, 341).

summalistes 'Beginners in philosophy'; either they or their handbooks (*summulae*) misunderstand *Cephas*. This word appears to be Edgeworth's coinage from the Latin. See C. du Fresne de Cange, *Glossarium mediae et infimae Latinitatis*, 10 vols, rev. ed. (Niort, 1882–7), VII, ii, s.v. 'Summalistae'; *Mediae Latinitatis Lexicon Minus*, ed. J.F. Niermeyer (Leiden, 1954–76), s.v. 'Summula'.

concludynge . . . countreys Edgeworth's objection to the misinterpretation of *cephas* as 'head' avoids the commonplace equation of 'apostolic' with 'papal' and cannot be considered as a defence of papal authority; see Pelikan, *Church and Dogma*, pp. 113–14.

for in the texte . . . adiectiue John 1:42. ODCC s.v. 'Peter' states: 'the name *Cephas* is probably the Aramis equivalent of the Gk "Peter" (*petra*, 'rock')'. Most English Bibles, including the AV, prefer 'stone' to 'rock' which has associations with the founding of the church at Rome.

Here such . . . pope The key text in the 1520s controversy with Luther over the papal supremacy was Matt. 16:18 in which Peter received Christ's commission. *Petra* (rock) was variously interpreted by the reformers as 'Christ the faith, God's word' (Pelikan, *Church and Dogma*, pp. 114–15). See Fisher's 1521 sermon against Luther which argues papal supremacy from John 21:15–17 (Fisher, *English Works* I, 319); E. Surtz, *The works and days of John Fisher* (Cambridge, Mass., 1967), pp. 115–17. This allusion to the dispute may be a Marian interpolation.

And morallye . . . Peter A reference to Matt. 16:17–18; Mk 3:16; the surname *Cephas* is prophetic of the moral strength that would be Peter's; see *Enc. Bib.* IV, s.v. 'Simon Peter'.

Symon . . . doue See N. de Lyra, *postilla in Textus Biblie cum glossa ordinaria*, 6 Pts (Lyons, 1520), IV, sig. 3H1ᵛ; V, sig. D8ᵛ (cited hereafter as *TB cum glo. ord.*). The full interpretation refers to Peter's name, Simon-bar-Jonah. Such moralisations of the apostles' names were common in medieval legends of them. See F.A. Lipsius, *Die Apokryphen Apostelgeschichten und Apostellegenden*, 3 vols (Braunschweig, 1883), I, 209–11.

he declared that . . . do A reference to Matt. 16:17.

and that . . . thondre A reference to Gen. 17:5 & 15; 32:28; Mk 3:16–17; Christ named John and James 'Boanerges' ('sons of Thunder'), because of their zeal. See ODCC s.v. 'John, St., Apostle'.

Apostle of Iesus Christe I Pet. 1:1.

Apostolos . . . newe 'Apostle' is a translation of the Hebrew for 'a delegate bearing a commission'; and the senses of *apostolus*, 'a messenger, one sent forth', is applied to OT prophets. The title 'Apostle' is given to the twelve disciples of Christ; in Acts and Ephesians it is also used of Paul and Barnabas. In modern usage the word often has the meaning of 'pioneer missionary', the leader of the first Christian mission to a country (e.g. St Augustine, the 'Apostle of the English'). See Colet's interpretation in 'Exposition of St. Paul's Epistle to the Romans' in *Ioannis Coleti Opuscula Quaedam Theologica*, ed. and tr. J.H. Lupton (London, 1876, repr., New Jersey, 1966), p. 56; *DB* I; ODCC s.v. 'Apostle'.

Moyses . . . thether A reference to Ex. 3:10–11; 4:13.

Esai .vi, . . . me Is. 6:8. Vg. 'ecce ego sum'.

Saynt Iohn Baptist . . . prophete John 1:6.

Heb. iii . . . redemption Heb. 3:1.

saynt Hierome . . . Apostles See Jerome on Gal. 1:1, 'Comm. in Epist. ad Galatos', I, 1 (*PL* 26, 312).

as Iosue . . . Nu, xxvii Num. 27:18–24.

Anglorum Apostolus St Augustine was missionary to Kent in 597 and first Archbishop of Canterbury. This title is given in the calendar of the Mass and in the Breviary for his feast on 26 May. See Wickham Legg, *Sarum Missal*, p. xxv; *Breviarum ad usum Sarum*, ed. F. Procter and C. Wordsworth, 3 vols (London, 1882–6), III, 303–4; *Sermons*, p. 236.

ii. Cor. xi . . . lykewise II Cor. 11:13–15.

Iesus . . . sauiour On this interpretation see *Sermons*, pp. 115, 172, 195; above p. 372.

the Aungell Gabriell . . . Sauiour A reference to Matt. 1:20–21; on the relationship of the Annunciation to the Davidic sonship which substantiates the messianic office of Jesus see F. Hahn, *Titles of Jesus in Christology*, tr. G. Ogg (London, 1969), pp. 261–4, 296–7, 304–5.

Iesus Naue . . . Eccl. l. See II Esd. 8:17 (on Joshua, son of Nun, successor of Moses); Ecclus 49:14 (on Jesus the high priest, son of Jehozadek); Ecclus. 50:29 (on Jesus, son of Sirach). 'Jesus' is the Lat. form of the Gk transcription of the Heb. 'Joshua'; and the Book of Joshua is often known as 'Iesu Nave'. This was a familiar interpretation: see *Middle English Sermons*, ed. W.O. Ross, EETS, OS, 209 (1940, repr. London, 1960), pp. 3–4; Blench, p. 11; *DB* s.v. 'Joshua' and 'Sirach'; *Enc. Bib.* I, s.v. 'Ecclesiasticus'.

Christ . . . felowes Heb. 1:9; cf. Augustine on John 1:40–42, 'In Ioannis Evang. Tractatus CXXIV', VII (*PL* 34, 1444); see *Sermons*, pp. 115, 193, 238.

Kinges . . . oyle The only OT reference to the anointing of a prophet is III Kings 19:16; on the anointing of kings and priests see *Sermons*, pp. 115, 247; *DB* s.v. 'Anointing'.

but Christ . . . prophete I.e. Christ the Messiah who according to Jewish theology was the expected, divinely appointed deliverer and ruler of Israel; he was the Davidic King prophesied in II Kings 7:12–13 and by Isaiah and Jeremiah; he combined regal offices with priestly functions, was endowed with special gifts and called by unique titles: e.g. 'a High priest after the order of Melchizedek' in Ps. 109:4; Heb. 5:10; 6:20 and 'a prophet' in Matt. 8:28 and John 4:19; see *ODCC* s.v. 'Messiah'.

Ioh. i A reference to John 1:32.

He wrote . . . father See I Pet. 1:1–2. These are the four provinces (Pontus and Bithynia are one) of the Roman Empire which in the 1st and 2nd centuries covered most of Asian Turkey. See J.N.D. Kelly, *A Commentary on the Epistles of Peter and Jude* (London, 1969), pp. 3–4 (cited hereafter as Kelly, *Commentary*); *Sermons*, pp. 157, 234, 258.

Aduenae . . . proseliti The Epistle was apparently written to Jewish Christian communities of mixed origin in Asia Minor, i.e. the Jews of the Diaspora (those living outside Israel) and proselytes or recent converts to Judaism. *Aduenae* meaning both 'foreigners and strangers' and 'Gentiles' (non-Jews) is extended here to include proselytes. Edgeworth, like Erasmus and the reformers, believes its recipients are both Jews and Gentiles (*Sermons*, pp. 200, 272, 301). See Erasmus, *Annotationes in Novum Testamentum* (Basle, 1527), fo. 672 (cited hereafter as Erasmus, *Annotationes*); cf. the likely source here, the *postilla* of N. de Lyra in *TB cum glo. ord. ed. cit.* VI, sig. 2H7. For the view that the author addresses as Jews a predominantly Gentile Christian audience see J. Ramsey Michaels, *I Peter*, Word Biblical Commentary, 49 (Texas, 1988), pp. xlv–vi. See *ODCC* s.v. 'Gentiles' and 'Proselyte'; *DB* s.v. 'Stranger' and 'Proselyte'; F.J.A. Hort, *The First Epistle of St Peter I.1–II.17* (London, 1898), App. II, on the terms for sojourner; Kelly, *Commentary*, pp. 4–5.

Manye suche . . . do A reference to Acts 2:41.

.s. Stephan . . . apostles A reference to Acts 8:1; the persecution is associated with Saul.

.s. Iames . . . Ierusalem James the Less, son of Alphaeus, traditionally identified with St James, 'the Lord's brother'. In Acts 12:17 he seems to be recognised by Peter, the original leader of the Jerusalem church, as his successor. He remained a leader until his death in 62 (Acts 15:13–22; Gal. 1:19; 2:9). See O. Cullman, *Peter*, tr. O.V. Filson, 2nd ed. (London, 1953), pp. 40–43 (cited hereafter as Cullman, *Peter*); *Sermons*, pp. 178, 197.

.s. Peter . . . Act. x. A reference to Acts 10:9–43. Peter undertook the first Jewish Christian missionary tour among the Gentiles and Jews of the villages of Samaria (Acts 8:1–25). After an intellectual conversion at Joppa he opened the church to Gentiles by admitting and baptising Cornelius, a centurion. Caesarea, a seaport like Joppa, was the seat of Roman administration in Judaea; see Cullman, *Peter*, pp. 36–7.

Antioche . . . Syria Antioch was the capital of the Roman province in Syria from 64 BC and the headquarters of St Paul in c.47–55 AD; *ODCC*; *Enc. Brit.* I, s.v. 'Antioch'.

And many . . . more The doubtful claim that Peter founded the church at Antioch appears in Origen, 'In Lucam Homilia', IV, c (*PG* 13, 1814); Eusebius, *Hist. Ecc.* III, 36 (*PG* 20, 287–9); Chrysostom, *In S. Martyrem Ignatium* (*PG* 50, 591); Jerome on Gal. 2:1, 'Comm. in Epist. ad Galatas', I, 2 (*PL* 26, 332–3); 'De Illustribus Viris' (*PL* 23, 607). Catholic exegetes arbitrarily identified Antioch (as well as Rome) with 'the other place' to which Peter went from Jerusalem (Acts 12:17). On the tradition that he was first bishop there see Cullman, *Peter*, pp. 37–9, 52–3, 226; F.T. Foakes Jackson, *Peter, Prince of Apostles* (London, 1927), p. 90 (cited hereafter as Foakes Jackson, *Peter*); *DCB* I s.v. 'Acts of the Apostles (Apocryphal)'; *ODCC* s.v. 'Antioch'; *Sermons*, p. 198.

Simon Magus A sorcerer who practised in Samaria; he was baptised a Christian but was rebuked by Peter for trying to buy spiritual powers from the Apostles. See Acts 8:9–24; Jerome, 'De Illustribus Viris', *PL*, 23, 607 (repr. in *TB cum glo. ord., ed. cit.* VI, sigs 2H6ᵛ–2H7); *ODCC* s.v. 'Simon Magus'.

Eusebius . . . hym According to Eusebius, *Hist. Ecc.* II, 13 (*PG* 20, 167–70) Simon Magus conducted secret rites with a woman called Helena.

And . . . Rome It was generally accepted that the Epistle was written from Rome; see Eusebius, *Hist. Ecc.* II, 15 (PG 20, 171–4); cf. F.W. Beare's introduction to the *The First Epistle of Peter*, 3rd ed. (Oxford, 1970), pp. 50, 209, 226–7 (cited hereafter as Beare, *First Epistle*); see *Sermons*, p. 366.

such straungers . . . worlde The *aduenae* of I Pet. 1:1 are here spoken of with the metaphorical connotation that the former Gentiles became strangers to the world on converting to Christianity; see C. Bigg, *A Critical and Exegetical Commentary on the Epistles of St Peter and St Jude*, ICC, (Edinburgh, 1901) pp. 90–91; cited hereafter as Bigg, *Epistles*.

Obsecro . . . apostles xv. I Pet. 2:11; Acts 15:36.

In like case . . . stues I Peter was apparently a diaspora letter written to encourage persecuted Gentile Christians of Asia Minor in the faith. Edgeworth, making an analogy with his own times, stresses the decadence of Rome and the provinces mentioned in I Pet. 1:1. See E.G. Selwyn, *The First Epistle of Saint Peter*, 2nd ed. (London, 1947), pp. 47–52 (cited hereafter as Selwyn, *St Peter*); Foakes Jackson, *Peter*, pp. 114–15; cf. Beare's discussion of authorship, *First Epistle*, pp. 43–50.

Saint Peter . . . Babilon Although Erasmus and Calvin argued that the Assyrian Rome was intended, the traditional view that the Babylon of I Pet. 5:13 refers to Rome is widely accepted today. Babylon was a figurative description of Rome, but the context here suggests that the corrupt, decadent Babylon, capital of the pagan world, is intended. See Foakes Jackson, *First Epistle*, pp. 117–18; Cullman, *Peter*, pp. 84–7; Bigg, *Epistles*, pp. 75–6; Beare, *First Epistle*, loc. cit.; Kelly, *Commentary*, pp. 33, 218–20; *Sermons*, p. 366.

Saint Paule . . . Damascus Gal. 1:17; cf. Acts 9:19–30. On the discrepancies between these two accounts of the three meetings between Peter and Paul see Bigg, *Epistles*, pp. 55–8; Cullman, *Peter*, pp. 37–41, 49–54.

Esay. vii . . . Damascus Is. 7:8.

after three yeres . . . Hierusalem A reference to Gal. 1:18–19; cf. Acts 9:26. St James acted as assessor to Peter when he held the leadership of the church at Jerusalem and succeeded

him after the apostles dispersed. See Eusebius, *Hist. Ecc.* II, 23 (PG 20, 195); Cullman, *Peter*, pp. 39–40, 49; Foakes Jackson, *Peter*, pp. 95–6; ODCC s.v. 'Jerusalem'. *Sermons*, pp. 178, 196 on 'James the Less'.

Saynt Paule . . . Celicia A reference to Gal. 1:21; Cilicia in the NT is the Roman province in S.E. Asia Minor situated between Pamphylia and Syria and bounded on the S. by the Mediterranean; the principality called Lesser Armenia was established there; see *DB* I, *Enc. Brit.* II s.v. 'Cilicia'.

Act. xxii . . . Asia Acts 22:3. Vg. 'natus Tarso Ciliciae'. Tarsus was made the capital of the Roman province of Cilicia in 67 BC; see ODCC and *DB* IV, s.v. 'Tarsus'.

after .xiiii yeres . . . Hierusalem The second meeting between Paul and Peter at the Council of Jerusalem in c.49 AD (Gal. 2:1–9); this visit is traditionally identified with that in Acts 15:2–4. Following their first missionary journey Paul and Barnabus were sent to Jerusalem by the Church of Antioch to settle the question of the obligation of circumcision; this historic conference concerned the terms by which Gentiles could be admitted into the church; see Foakes Jackson, *Peter*, pp. 95–6; Bigg, *Epistles*, pp. 57–62; ODCC s.v. 'Paul'; *Sermons*, p. 196.

in the place alledged . . . not A reference to Gal 1:20.

Here . . . ascension See Gal. 1:18 and 2:1. The fourteen years of Gal. 2:1 may date from the time of Paul's conversion in c.35 AD rather than from his first visit to Jerusalem. This fits with the modern dating of the Council of Jerusalem at c.49 AD; cf. Edgeworth's dating at 52 AD.

for .s. Paul . . . Paule According to Caxton, *Golden Legend*, ed. cit. fos 82^{r-v}, St Paul was converted in the year of the crucifixion on the '8 Kalendes of Feuerer'. Ogg, *Life of Paul*, p. 30, suggests 34 or 35 AD, one or two years later. The feast of the conversion of Paul is celebrated on 25 January. See Wickham Legg, *Sarum Missal*, p. xxi; L. Duchesne, *Christian Worship*, tr. M.L. McClure, 5th ed. (London, 1931), p. 218.

when went sainte . . . Anthiochia A reference to Gal. 2:11. There is no testimony as to Peter's moves after the Council of Jerusalem.

See Foakes Jackson, *Peter*, p. 117; Selwyn, *St Peter*, p. 61; Bigg, *Epistles*, p. 62.

Cornelius . . . Cesaria A reference to Gal. 1:18 and Acts 10:9–43; see *Sermons*, p. 196.

in the .xiiii yere . . . straungers A reference to Gal. 2:1. Peter's missionary and episcopal activities among the Gentile Christians in Asia Minor began in c.44 AD; he returned to attend the Council of Jerusalem in c.49 AD; see *ODCC* s.v. 'Jerusalem'; *Enc. Brit.* 14, s.v. 'Peter'.

after . . . Stephan A reference to Acts 8:1. Stephen's martyrdom occurred in c.35 in Jerusalem at the hands of the Sanhedrin, the supreme council and highest court of justice. In the reign of terror which followed many fled from the city.

Antiochia . . . translatum Jerome on Gal. 2:11, 'Comm. in Epist. ad Galatas', I, 2 (*PL* 26, 341). Peter visited Antioch briefly after the Council of Jerusalem (Gal. 2:11–21; Bigg, *Epistles*, pp. 62–3); on the tradition that he was first bishop there see *Sermons*, p. 196.

from Antiochia . . . Galathians A reference to Gal. 2:1–2 and 9. The statement that Peter preached for five years in Asia Minor and was Bishop of Antioch for seven years (after fourteen years at Jerusalem) contradicts Edgeworth's dating of the First Council of Jerusalem at eighteen years (i.e. 52 AD) after the resurrection. He recognises the problem of dating Peter's episcopacy at Antioch (*Sermons*, p. 197) but can not solve it. On the date of the First Council of Jerusalem see *loc.cit.*; on Simon Magus, p. 196.

And then . . . sayde Edgeworth appears to ignore the account (from Gal. 2:1 and 9) that at the Council of Jerusalem Peter was assigned a mission among the Jews and that he later met Paul at Antioch and possibly also at Corinth. He erroneously dates Peter's episcopacy at Antioch prior to the Council and his fourth and final visit to Rome immediately following it (Cullman, *Peter*, pp. 37–9, 54; Bigg, *Epistles*, pp. 85–7, 67). Tradition dates Peter's martyrdom in c.64 and the Epistle in c.63–64. Cf. Beare (*First Epistle*, p. 33) who suggests 111–12 AD and Michaels (*I Peter*, pp. lviii–lxvi) who suggests, p. lxiii, between 70–80 AD. See Kelly, *Epistles*, pp. 27–30; Selwyn, *St Peter*, pp. 56–62; *Sermons*, pp. 135, 170, 193–4.

Mare . . . Leuant From the late fifteenth century 'the Levant' was the name given to the Adriatic ('Cyprium Mare'), the eastern side of the Mediterranean with its adjoining countries (Greece, Turkey, Syria, Lebanon, Palestine, Egypt); it was a synonym for the Middle East. See *OED*; *Columbia Lippincott Gazetteer*, ed. L.E. Seltzer (Columbia, 1966), s.v. 'Levant'.

Calpe I.e. the rock of Gibraltar occupying the peninsula that juts S. from Cadiz province, opposite Ceuta in N. Africa: it was one of the renowned 'Pillars of Hercules' which for centuries marked the end of the classical world. The name 'Gibraltar' was not commonly used until the late sixteenth century; *ibid.* s.v. 'Gibraltar'.

Abila On the N.W. African coast in Spanish Morocco E. of Ceuta; formerly one of the Pillars of Hercules, it is now Mt (H)acho; see *ibid.* s.v. 'Ceuta'; *OL* I, s.v. 'Abila'; *Enc. Brit.* IV s.v. 'Gibraltar, Straits of'.

And . . . Malys The names *Calis, Cales* (*viz. Cades*) and *Calis Malis* used of the Bay of Cadiz or the seaport of Cadiz on the Atlantic coast of Andalusia of S.W. Spain are frequently attested in the sixteenth century; e.g. Skelton writes in 'Against Venemous Tongues' (1522): 'What shippis are sailing to Scalis Malis?' (see *The Poetical Works of John Skelton*, ed. A. Dyce, 2 vols (London, 1843), I, 195–6). *Cales Males* appears on a map by B. Boazio of 1596 (Antwerp? 1605?), (BL 157* a. 38); fo. 111; see his map in 'The Voyage to Cadiz 1596', *The Naval Miscellany*, ed. J.K. Laughton, Publications of the Navy Record Society, 20 (London, 1902), pp. 37–92. *Caliz* occurs in Abraham Ortelius' *Theatrum Orbis Terrarum* (Antwerp, 1570; facs., Netherlands, 1964), fo. 7ᵛ and on maps in *Portugaliae Monumenta Cartographica*, ed. Armando Cortesaõ, 6 vols (Lisbon, 1960), II, Plates 101, 117. In all of them Cadiz is erroneously charted as an island. Edgeworth has confused *Calpe* (the rock of Gibraltar) with *Cales* (both are often given the Roman name *Gades* on maps). Bristol sailors may have referred to the Straits of Gibraltar as *Calis Malis* as well as Cadiz. British voyages to the Levant through the hazardous Straits continued until 1552. But rocks and shallows around Cadiz are also attested. See R. Hakluyt, *The Voyages, Traffiques and Discoveries of Foreign Voyagers with other matters relating thereto contained in 'The*

Navigations' by Richard Hakluyt, 12 vols (London, 1928), IX, p. 257; Fernand Braudel, The Mediterranean and the Mediterranean World in the Age of Phillip II, tr. S. Reynolds, 4 vols (London, 1972), I, 108, 117, 613. I am indebted to Associate-Professor G.S. Parsonson, formerly of the Department of Geography at the University of Otago, for his assistance.

Gades . . . Hercules The straits of Gibraltar, indicated on many contemporary maps as Fretum Herculeum and Gaditanum et Columnarum. They connect the Mediterranean Sea and the Atlantic Ocean, their two rocks at the entrance forming the 'Pillars of Hercules'. See Enc. Brit. IV, s.v. 'Gibraltar, Straits of'.

Pliny . . . broadest Pliny, Naturalis Historia III, 1 (ed. cit. I, 231).

pomponius Mela . . . patens Mela, De Situ Orbis I, 1 (ed. cit. fo. 148).

Sinus issicus The gulf of Issus, now the Gulf of Iskenderun, on which is situated the city of Issus (where Darius was defeated by Alexander the Great in 33 BC). See Enc. Brit. V, s.v. 'Iskenderun'; OL II, s.v. 'Issicus sinus'.

Cyprus See Mela, De Situ Orbis II, 7 (ed. cit. fo. 202, n. m.).

Fyrst . . . Hellespontus I.e. the Dardanelles, a narrow strait in Turkey extending N.E. to link the Aegean Sea with the Sea of Marmara; it lies between the peninsula of Gallipoli in Europe and Asia Minor and forms the gateway to Istanbul in Turkey and the Black Sea. See Enc. Brit. III, s.v. 'Dardanelles'. The following description of the outlets of the Mediterranean follows the order given in Mela, De Situ Orbis I, 2 (ed. cit. fos. 149–50).

Propontis The ancient name for the small inland sea of Marmara (separating the Asiatic and European parts of Turkey); it is connected through the Bosphorus on the N.E. with the Black Sea and through the Dardanelles on the S.E. with the Aegean Sea. See Mela, De Situ Orbis I, 19 (ed. cit. fo. 172 n. c.); Enc. Brit. VI, s.v. 'Marmara, Sea of'.

Thratius bosphorus The strait uniting the Black Sea and the Sea of Marmara separating Asiatic Turkey from European Turkey. See Mela, De Situ Orbis I, 19 (ed. cit. fo. 173); OL I, s.v. 'Bosporus', 'Bospori Ostia'; Enc. Brit. II, s.v. 'Bosporus'.

The countrey . . . streict The land mass on the Balkans in N.E. Greece, bounded by the Black Sea and the Sea of Marmara. Byzantium, on the mouth of the Thracian Bosphorus, was chosen by Constantine the Great for his new capital in 330 AD and renamed Constantinople. See Mela, De Situ Orbis II, 2 (ed. cit. fos 181–2); Enc. Brit. IX, s.v. 'Thrace'; OCCL s.v. 'Byzantium'.

This streicte . . . Europe Pliny, Naturalis Historia VI, 1 (ed. cit. I, 428).

Pontus Euxinus I.e. the Black Sea, connected to the Mediterranean by the Bosphorus Strait, the Sea of Marmara and the Aegean Sea. See Enc. Brit. II, s.v. 'Black Sea'.

Cymmerius bosphorus The Cimmerian Bosphorus, the ancient Gk state on the Kerch Strait in present Southern Ukranian SSR, which connects the Black Sea with the Sea of Azov. It was ruled by the kings of Pontus from 110 BC to 100 AD when it came under the protection of the Roman Empire. See Enc. Brit. II, s.v. 'Bosporus, Kingdom of'.

Meotis The Sea of Azov, known to the Romans as Palus Maeotis, an inland sea of the Atlantic Basin, a large gulf of the Black Sea linked to it by the Kerch Strait. Its main effluent is the river Don. See Enc. Brit. 11th ed. (London, 1910–11), III; Chambers' World Gazetteer and Geographical Dictionary, eds. T.C. Collocott and J.O. Thorne (London, 1965), s.v. 'Azov'; OL III, s.v. 'Meotides'; the illustration in Mela, De Situ Orbis I, 21 (ed. cit. fo. 177).

Tanais The river Don which rises in the central Russian upland in Lake Ivan in Moscow and enters the head of the Tagenrog, the gulf of the Sea of Azov. See ibid. fols. 175–6; Enc. Brit. III, s.v. 'Don'.

In the sayd Leuaunt . . . Cyprus Mela, De Situ Orbis II, 7 (ed. cit. fos 204–7).

Ile of the Rhodes . . . bondage Ibid. fo. 202. Following the siege of Rhodes by Sultan Suleiman in June 1522, the Knights of the Hospital of St John of Jerusalem who for two centuries had protected the island against the Turks, were evacuated. Under the administration of the Turks Rhodes entered a state of decline. See E. King, The Knights of St John in the British Realm, rev. H. Luke (London, 1967), pp. 89–97.

greate Asia . . . Meotis Mela, De Situ Orbis I, 1 (ed. cit. fo. 149).

And . . . purpose Hort's explanation (First

Epistle, p. 16 ff.) that the provinces are named in the order in which Silvanus was to deliver the Epistle (1 Pet. 5:12), is now widely accepted; see Selwyn, *St Peter*, pp. 46–7; cf. Bigg, *Epistles*, pp. 68–70.

Galath. iii . . . IESV Gal. 3:28.

Pontus Ancient region in N.E. Anatolia adjoining the Black Sea which reached its zenith under Mithridates VI Eupator. His defeat resulted in the extinction of the Pontic Kingdom and its incorporation into the Roman Empire (63–62 BC). See *Enc. Brit.* VIII; *OCCL* s.v. 'Pontus'; above, pp. 393, 408.

Pomponius Mela . . . disterminat Mela, *De Situ Orbis* I, 2 (*ed. cit.* fo. 151). The entry s.v. 'P' in the version of Jerome's *De Nominibus Hebraicis* in Migne (PL 23, 905–975) is incomplete; see col. 962.

Colchis . . . faine A region at the eastern end of the Black Sea S. of the Caucasus in the W. part of Georgian SSR; in Gk mythology the home of Medea and the destination of the Argonauts. See *OCCL* s.v. 'Colchis'; Mela, *De Situ Orbis* I, 21 (*ed. cit.* fo. 174). The commentators in most sixteenth century editions of *De Situ Orbis* mention Jason; and *Castigationes in Pomponium Melam* (ex officina Ioannis iuntae, 1543), fos 29ʳ⁻ᵛ, cites classical sources of the legend.

Mithridates . . . Asia Mithridates VI, Eupator, 'The Great', King of Pontus from c.120 to 63 BC and Rome's greatest enemy in Asia Minor. He conquered the N. coast of the Black Sea and overran Paphlagonia, Colchis and Armenia Minor; seized Cappadocia, reoccupied it in 90 BC and nearly subdued Greece in 88–85 BC. The second Mithridatic War occurred in 83–2; he was defeated by Pompey in the Third Mithridatic War (74–63 BC). See *Enc. Brit.* VI and *OCCL* s.v. 'Mithridates VI'.

Capadocia A district in eastern central Anatolia in a plateau N. of the Taurus mountains between the mountains of Armenia and the headwaters of the Euphrates. It was a client state of Rome until 17 AD when it was annexed by Tiberius. See *Enc. Brit.* II, s.v. 'Cappadocia'; Beare, *First Epistle*, pp. 40–41.

S. George . . . legend See Caxton, *Golden Legend, ed. cit.* fo. 111. Cappadocia is mentioned in other vernacular accounts of St George and the dragon. See *The Minor Poems*

of John Lydgate, ed. H.W. MacCracken, 2 vols, EETS, ES, 107; OS, 192 (London, 1911, 1934), I, 145–54.

both Armenyes . . . more Armenia the greater, or eastern Armenia (now part of N.E. Turkey and Armenian SSR) and Armenia the less, or western Armenia (now Anatolia); see *OL* I, s.v. 'Armenia Inferior' and 'Armenia Magna'; *Enc. Brit.* I, s.v. 'Armenian SSR'.

Euphrates The largest river of W. Asia which rises in the Armenian plateau in Turkey and flows southeast towards Syria and S. towards Iraq; see *Enc. Brit.* III, s.v; Mela, *De Situ Orbis* III, 8 (*ed. cit.* fos 224–5).

Bithinia . . . Euxinus Bithinia, a region comprising part of modern Turkey adjoining the Sea of Marmara (Propontis), the Bosphorus and the Black Sea, became a Roman province in 74 BC. See Mela, *De Situ Orbis* I, 19 (*ed. cit.* fos 172–3); Beare, *First Epistle*, pp. 40–1; *OL* I, s.v. 'Bithinia'; on Constantinople see *Sermons*, p. 199.

Nicea . . . made See Mela, *loc. cit.* Another edition, *C Iulii Solini Polyhistor . . . huic Pomponii Melae de situ orbis . . . adiunximus* (Basle, 1538), fo. 176, n. h. refers to the First Council of Nicaea.

Galacia . . . Gallogrecia The Roman province (from 25 BC) in central Anatolia bordering the Taurus mountains in the S. and the Paphlagonian country in the N. See *Enc. Brit.* IV, s.v. 'Galatia'; Beare, *First Epistle*, p. 39; *Sermons*, p. 157.

super mare Egeum I.e. the Aegean Sea, the part of the Mediterranean Sea between Greece and Asia Minor. See *OCCL* s.v.

by pseudapostles . . . Galathians St Paul wrote the Epistle to the Galatian Christians to counteract the influence of a Jewish mission requiring them to keep the commandments of Jewish law. See Mela, *De Situ Orbis* I, 2 (*ed. cit.* fo. 151 and n. g); Pliny, *Naturalis Historia* V, 115 (*ed. cit.* I, 409–10); *ODCC*, s.v. 'Galatians'; *Sermons*, p. 299.

Ephesus . . . Act. xix Acts 19:24–41. Ephesus, capital of the Roman province of Asia, stood at the mouth of the river Cayster. See Mela, *De Situ Orbis* I, 17 (*ed. cit.* fo. 170). The 1538 edition (above), fo. 173, and *Pomponii Melae de orbis situ libri tres . . . cum commentariis J. Vadiani*, ed. C. Grebelius (Paris, 1540), fo. 70 n. c., refer to the Temple of Diana erected c.330 BC and regarded as one of the Seven Wonders of the World; *DB* s.v. 'Ephesus'.

i. Cor. xv . . . prodest. &c. I Cor. 15:32. Vg. 'Se secundum hominem . . .'

To all . . . father A reference to I Pet. 1:2. On the destination of the Epistle see *Sermons*, pp. 195–6. Selwyn, *St Peter*, pp. 117–18; on the exposition of divine election see Horst, *First Epistle*, pp. 14–15.

Whom . . . saued An exposition of the doctrine of election in which only the Son and Holy Spirit are predestined for salvation, as distinct from election or *calling* to the faith (in the Pauline sense of vocation); cf. the Protestant view of predestination (that the elect are assured of salvation through Christ's atonement) which could be misconstrued that all who believed are destined for eternal life; see *ODCC* s.v. 'Election', 'Predestination', 'Justification'.

Math. xxii . . . chosen Matt. 22:14.

Nonne ego vos . . . birde John 6:71.

Ioh. xv . . . you John 15:16.

Ephes. i . . . made Eph. 1:4.

GOD knewe . . . his A reference to I Pet. 1:2.

Roman. viii . . . called Rom. 8:30; Vg. 'quos autem praedestinavit hos et vocavit'. This text was the most important NT discussion of predestination after 1530; see Pelikan, *Church and Dogma*, pp. 220, 259–60.

secundum presentem . . . callinge Phil. 3:6.

i. Reg. ix . . . he I Kings 9:2. Vg. 'erat ei filius vocabulo saul . . .'.

Rom. viii . . . best Rom. 8:28.

In sanctificationem . . . purpose I Pet. 1:2. See *Novum Testamentum omne ex versione vtraque, hoc est Des. Erasmi Roterdami, & Vulgata in Biblia vtriusque Testamenti, iuxta Vulgatam translationem . . . cui in Nouo, opposuimus Des. Erasmi Rot. uersionem* (Basle, 1538), fo. 351 (cited hereafter as Erasmus, *NT*). Edgeworth would have used a parallel-text edition of the Erasmian NT and the Vulgate such as this or the one included with the 1527 edition of Erasmus' *Annotations*.

charitas . . . Gala. v. Gal. 5:22. Vg. 'pax longanimitas'.

.i. Thessa v . . . Christ I Thess. 5:23. Vg. 'servetur'.

In manus tuas . . . meum Luke 23:46.

Inclinato capite . . . soule John 19:30.

Mente seruio legi . . . sinne Rom. 7:25.

Galathians .v . . . carnem Gal. 5:17. Vg. 'caro enim . . .'.

Ephesians iiii . . . mynde Eph. 4:23. Vg. 'autem spiritu mentis vestrae'.

Collossians .ii . . . fleshe Col. 2:11.

Et aspersionem . . . you I Pet. 1:2.

Genesis .iiii . . . hande Gen. 4:10–11. Vg. 'quae aperuit'.

Pater ignosce . . . do Luke 23:34. Vg. 'dimitte illis non enim sciunt'.

Accessistis . . . spake Heb. 12:24. Vg. 'et sanguinis sparsionem . . .'.

as the people . . . Egipt A reference to Ex. 13:3–14.

We . . . Christ See *Sermons*, pp. 184, 186; in OT times blood was used in the consecration of priests (see Ex. 29:21; Lev. 8:30).

Gratia vobis . . . multiplicetur I Pet. 1:2.

Origene . . . blessed Origen on Rom. 1:7, 'In Epist. ad Romanos' (*PG* 14, 853).

the blessing . . . Israell A reference to Gen. 14:18–19; 27:6–29; 49:28; see *Sermons*, p. 238.

Si fuerit . . . agayne Matt. 10:13. Vg. 'Et siquidem fuerit domus digna veniat pax vestra super eam si autem non fuerit digna . . .'.

Aduena . . . beene Ps. 38:13. Vg. 'aduena sum apud te . . .'.

if we counte oure selfe . . . straungers A reference to I Pet. 1:1 and 2:11: on this interpretation of 'strangers' see *Sermons*, pp. 195–6.

The seconde sermon

Benedictus deus . . . Christi. &c. I Pet. 1:3.

remembring . . . world A reference to the previous sermon; see *Sermons*, pp. 195–6

thys word blessed . . . GOD This exposition suggests that the translation of *benedicere* may already have become controversial. The reformers prefered to treat it as equivalent to 'giving thanks' (as in Luke and Paul) rather than 'blessed' (as in Matthew and Mark). The words of institution in the 1549 BCP, 'blessed and given thanks', are a compromise, but the 1552 BCP omits 'blessed and'. See Gasquet and Bishop, *Ed. VI and BCP*, pp. 171–2, n.; Cardwell, *BCP* pp. 297–8; *ODCC* s.v. 'Blessing'.

as Isaac . . . Epistle A reference to I Pet. 1:3; on the blessings of Isaac and Jacob see *Sermons*, p. 203.

Sacrificium laudis . . . God Ps. 49:23.

pater domini . . . Christe I Pet. 1:3.

Qui secundum . . . hope I Pet. 1:3.

i. Timo. i. I Tim. 1:13. On St Paul see *Sermons*, pp. 116, 162.

But kinge Dauid . . . vniustly II Kings 11:2–17. David seduced Bathsheba, the wife of Uriah the Hittite, and after instructing Joab to ensure that Uriah was killed in battle, he married her. See *DB* II, s.v. 'Bathsheba'; IV, s.v. 'Uriah'.

Miserere mei deus . . . sinnes Ps. 50:3.

takyng his strength The pronoun 'his' refers to 'baptisme'.

the . . . originall iustice An exposition of the Catholic theology of Original Righteousness, defined by the *ODCC* as 'God's gratuitous impartation to man of perfect rectitude in his original condition before the Fall. The state . . . in which man was first created is held to have included freedom from concupiscence, bodily immortality, impassibility and happiness'.

originall synne The definition of original sin as lack of Original Righteousness or man's supernatural privileges derives from Aquinas; cf. the article on Justification in the *King's Book* which follows the reformers in associating original sin with concupiscence, but which asserts that baptism and penance will reconcile man to God. See *ODCC* s.v. 'Original Sin'; *Formularies*, pp. 363–4, 366–7.

almightye God . . . life I Pet. 1:3.

The regeneration . . . baptisme An exposition of the Catholic theology of Baptismal Regeneration which held that the chief effects of the sacrament after the removal of original sin were the conferring of habitual grace, the infused virtues and the gifts of the Holy Ghost, and the incorporation into the church; see the article on baptism in the *King's Book* (*Formularies*, pp. 253–5); *ODCC* s.v. 'Baptism'; Beare, *First Epistle*, pp. 56–8, on baptism and regeneration in the Epistle; *Sermons*, pp. 226–7.

the seconde table . . . penance On the reformers' denial of penance as a second plank or table after baptism see above p. 387.

He hathe begotten . . . Christe I Pet. 1:3.

Etiam si occiderit . . . sight Job 13:15–16.

Into an inheritance . . . heauen I Pet. 1:4.

scowts '?Biting insects'; possibly an application of 'scout' used to refer derisively to men and women (*OED* s.v. *sb.* 2). 'Gnat' is also used as a term of contempt (with reference to Matt. 23:24).

Lammas tyde 1 August, traditionally a harvest festival, known as 'Festum Sanctum Petri ad Vincula' in the Roman calendar; see *ODCC* s.v. 'Lammas Day'.

Where is Troye . . . ende The *ubi sunt* theme was familiar in Latin and Old English homilies and verse and survives in fifteenth and early sixteenth verse such as Lydgate's 'As a Mydsomer Rose'. Edgeworth's concluding lament on the brevity of earthly glory and power is adapted to a contemporary context with this tribute to Henry VIII. See Lydgate, *Minor Poems* II, 783; J. Longland, *A sermonde made before the kynge at grenewich, vpon good Frydaye. M.D. xxxviij.* (T. Petyt,) [1538], sig. K3. STC 16796. For other contemporary examples see Blench, pp. 228–31; on sources, J. Cross, ' "Ubi sunt" Passages in Old English: Sources and Relationships', *Vetenskap Societetus i Lund Arsbok* (1956), 25–44; E. Gilson, 'De la Bible à Francois Villon' in *Les Idées et les Lettres* (Paris, 1932), pp. 9–38.

there shall . . . Math. xiii Matt. 13:43.

This ioyfull . . . iudgement I Pet. 1:4–5.

Here . . . preseruation A reference to I Pet. 1:5; cf. *Tomus (primus) secundus paraphraseon D. Erasmus Roterdami in Nouum Testamentum etc.*, 2 vols (Basle, 1535–8); II, fo. 322: 'tamen dei presidio, qui nihil non potest, seruamini, non uestris meritis, sed fide, fiduciaque, qua non dubitatis quin deus' (cited hereafter as Erasmus, *Paraphrasis*); and the Protestant translation, *The (first) seconde tome or volume of the Paraphrase of Erasmus vpon the newe testamente* (Whitchurch, 1549), II; sig. C2ᵛ 'yet by the succour of God . . . you are preserued, not through your owne merites, but by fayth & vnfained trust' (cited hereafter as Erasmus, *Paraphrase*). Copies of this translation were enjoined to be kept in parish churches in August 1547 (Hughes and Larkin, I, 287).

Nam . . . life Gregory on Job 1:40; *Moralia* I, 37, 55 (*PL* 75, 554).

lyke an Ape . . . curnell A popular depiction in the middle ages which appears among the vernacular versions of the *Gesta Romanorum*. The common moralisation in which the rind represents the worldly tribulations of the Christian and the kernel his heavenly rewards is omitted here. See *The Early English Versions of the Gesta Romanorum*, ed. S.J.H. Herrtage, EETS, ES, 33 (London, 1879), no. LVI, p. 373; Janson, *Apes and Ape-Lore*, pp. 147–8.

Luke .xi . . . of Luke 11:8.

God . . . hope I Pet. 1:3.

Hec . . . faythe I John 5:4.

Si secundum . . . die Rom. 8:13.

this holye time . . . past This sermon was probably preached between 25 December and 25 March; see above, p. 406.

the dyuels mowse snatch 'The trap or noose laid by the devil for catching mice' (i.e. men who put their hopes for happiness in worldly wealth).

i. Tim. vi . . . dyuell I Tim. 6:9. Vg. 'in temptationem'; om. 'diaboli etc.'

therefore he biddeth . . . worlde A reference to I Tim. 6:17.

The thirde sermon.

In quo . . . troubles I Pet. 1:6. Vg. 'in quo exaltatis'.

in tempore . . . iudgement An exposition of I Pet. 1:5; on the eschatalogical phrase 'in the last time' to mean either the days of darkness before the Last Judgment or the Day of the Parousia itself see Bigg, *Epistles*, p. 102; Selwyn, *First Epistle*, p. 125.

the antecedent . . . relatiue These terms come from scholastic philosophy. The antecedent is the general initial premise of a syllogism to which the relative refers and upon which the consequence or conclusion depends. Edgeworth has discussed 'In quo exaltabitis . . . ' (I Pet. 1:6) and 'in tempore nouissimo' (I Pet. 1:5) in reverse order.

as S. Peter . . . heritage A reference to I Pet. 1:4; see *Sermons*, pp. 208–9.

like as golde . . . fyre A reference to I Pet. 1:7.

Eccle. xxvii . . . women Ecclus. 27:6.

Pro. xxvii . . . vertuous Prov. 27:21.

The triall . . . hymselfe I Pet. 1:7.

This is the victorie . . . faith I John 5:4.

Statera iusta . . . equall Levit. 19:36.

Ezech. xlv . . . iustum Ezech. 45:10.

byddinge the do . . . the A reference to Deut. 19:19.

praise, glory . . . honour I Pet. 1:7.

when Christ shall shewe . . . hande Matt. 25:31–33.

I was an hungred . . . clothes Matt. 25:35–36.

Venite benedicti . . . kyngedome Matt. 25:34. Cited by Erasmus in *Paraphrasis*, ed. cit. fo. 323; see *Paraphrase*, ed. cit. sig. C3.

Esa. xxvi . . . GOD Is. 26:10. Vg. 'videbit gloriam Domini'.

Go frome me . . . euerlasting Matt. 25:41.

Nos autem insensati . . . God. Sap. 5:4.

prayse, glorie . . . him. I Pet. 1:7–8.

Saint Augustyne . . . of This is a common sentiment in Augustine's writings; see *De Doctrina Christiana* I, 37 (PL 34, 35); 'Sermo ad Catechumenos' (PL 40, 647) on I Pet. 1:8; cited by Erasmus in *Annotationes*, ed. cit. fo. 673.

although you se him not . . . soules I Pet. 1:8–9.

De qua salute Prophetae I Pet. 1:10.

He taketh an argumente . . . not Cf. Erasmus, *Paraphrasis*, ed. cit. fo. 323: *Paraphrase*, ed. cit. sig. C3ᵛ: 'which prophecied beforehand that you should be saued through faith and the grace of the gospell without the ayde of Moses lawe'.

Math. xiii . . . audierunt Matt. 13:17.

Esay. lxiiii . . . incarnate Is. 64:1.

Psal. lxxix . . . time Ps. 79:3.

Quousque irasceris . . . safe Ps. 79:4–5.

Inclinauit coelos . . . eius Ps. 17:10.

He hath inclined . . . feete Ps. 17:10.

Damasc . . . wroughte John of Damascene, *De Fide Orthodoxa* III, 1 (PG 94, 983). See *Theologia Damascene quatuour libris explicata etc.* (Paris, 1512), sig. L2, for the translation which is closest to this version.

Ieremie . . . man Jer. 31:22; see *Sermons*, pp. 173, 291 on the Incarnation.

Vir desideriorum . . . desires The angels' appellation of Daniel in Dan. 9:23, 10:11 & 19 (translated in the AV as 'greatly beloved').

at the later ende . . . name Dan. 9:21–26. Cited by Erasmus in his annotation on 1 Pet 1:10, ed. cit. fo. 673. The prophecy of Dan.

9:24 (with reference to Jer. 85:12) of seventy weeks of years (i.e. 490 years) concerning the advent of Christ and the downfall of the Holy City, came into Christian exegesis from Josephus (*Jew. Ant.* X, 11, 7 and *Jewish War* IV, 5, 2); it found fulfillment in the destruction of Jerusalem in the wars of Vespasian and Titus (67–70 BC), and Hadrian (132–5 AD). Hadrian rebuilt Jerusalem as 'Aelia Capitolina', a pagan city which no Jew was allowed to enter. See J.A. Montgomery, *The Book of Daniel*, ICC (Edinburgh, 1927), pp. 390–401; ODCC s.v. 'Aelia Capitolina'.

Of these blessed . . . differred A paraphrase of I Pet. 1:10–11; the other 'holye Prophetes' are Jacob and Isaiah.

Iacob . . . Iewes A reference to Gen. 49:10; see *Sermons*, p. 238.

Et conflabunt . . . corne Is. 2:4; see Vergil, *Adagia* no. 337, ed. cit. fo. 308.

prenuncians eas . . . passiones I Pet. 1:11.

futuras glorias . . . assention A reference to I Pet. 1:11.

All they . . . on An exposition of I Pet. 1:12 with reference to Acts 2:4.

Math. xviii . . . est Matt. 18:10.

The fourth treatise or Sermon.

Propter quod succincti . . . holie I Pet. 1:13–16.

Ad te leuaui . . . meos Ps. 122:1.

Leuaui oculos . . . mountaines Ps. 120:1.

Ephe. i . . . callynge Eph. 1:18.

ii. Cor. ii II Cor. 2:14.

Bucklersbury . . . shoppe Proverbial; see *Proverbs, Sentences and Proverbial Phrases*, ed. B.J. Whiting (Oxford, 1968), B579: 'Bucklersbury electuary' (merchant). Bucklersbury, the centre of the London herb trade, was the area in which Sir Thomas More lived before he moved to Chelsea in 1524. The proverbial status of the name is attested by Shakespeare in *The Merry Wives of Windsor*, Act III, Sc. iii, l. 62.

Gustate . . . swete Ps. 33:9.

Esa. xxvi . . . salutis Is. 26:17–18.

He . . . Chapter A reference to I Pet. 1:12 & Matt. 18:10; see *Sermons*, p. 215.

By the beauty . . . see An interpretation of Is. 26:17–18.

Ioh. xvi John 16:21.

pro. xiii . . . minde Prov. 13:12.

My babes . . . .you Gal. 4:19.

Tucke vp . . . mindes I Pet. 1:13.

Sint lumbi . . . chastitie Luke 12:35.

Loth . . . sobernes A reference to Gen. 19:30–38. Lot's daughters made him drunk to ensure his cooperation.

Spes iubet . . . Horac Horace, Epist. I, v, l.17, ed. cit. p. 283.

while his cups be in Proverbial; 'while he is in a state of intoxication'; see ODEP s.v. 'Cups'.

wyll breake a loueday 'Will break an agreement entered into on a love day'; i.e. days appointed for the settlement of disputes without recourse to law, on which the clergy frequently acted as arbiters. Cited in John Heywood's *A Dialoge conteinyng . . . all the . . . prouerbes in the Englishe tongue* (Berthelet, 1546), sig. H2; see *John Heywood's A Dialogue of Proverbs*, ed. R.E. Habenicht (Berkeley, 1963), p. 151 (cited hereafter as Heywood, *Dialogue*).

Sobernes . . . an other Proverbial; see ODEP s.v. 'Good'.

Finally, Sobernes . . . vices This was also the verdict of the medieval pulpit; see Owst, *LPME* p. 431; *Book of Vices and Virtues*, pp. 275–9. The sentiment probably originates with Cicero.

Nature . . . litle Cited as first occurrence in ODEP s.v. 'Nature', this proverb comes from Boethius, *De Consolationae Philsophiae* II, 5; see Boethius, *Theological Tractates*, ed. and tr., H.F. Stewart and E.K. Rand (London, 1918), p. 199.

Therfore Saint Peter . . . Christe A reference to I Pet. 1:13.

Quasi filij . . . you I Pet. 1:14.

Sanctus . . . holie I Pet. 1:15.

Sancti . . . holye Lev. 19:2 with reference to I Pet. 1:16. Cited by Erasmus in *Paraphrasis*, ed. cit. fo. 324; see *Paraphrase*, ed. cit. sig. C4.

Mat. v . . . perfecte Matt. 5:48.

Estote imitatores . . . God Eph. 5:1.

contempninge . . . Gospell For similar adverse comments against the followers of 'euangelicall libertie' see *Sermons*, pp. 127–8, 229, 259–60.

Et si patrem . . . worlde I Pet. 1:17.

Malachi. i . . . me Mal. 1:6; Matt. 6:9.

and specially because . . . personne A reference to 1 Pet. 1:17. Erasmus' paraphrase of this text in *Paraphrasis, ed. cit.* fo. 324, avoids reference to *opus* (work); see *Paraphrase, ed. cit.* sig. C4: 'he estemeth no man eyther for his kynred or for his estates sake, but onely after the merites of his conuersacion.'

Nonne frater . . . Esau Mal. 1:2–3; Rom. 9:13.

And Iacob . . . dampned A reference to the account of Jacob and Esau in Gen. 25–35.

Math. xx . . . morning Matt. 20:1; the following is an account of the parable of the labourers in the vineyard.

Amice . . . vade Matt. 20:13–14.

An non licet . . . me Matt. 20:15.

Rom. ix . . . offices Rom. 9:21.

secundum vniuscuiusque opus I Pet. 1:17.

Esuriui . . . drinke. &c Matt. 23:25.

vse a certaine feare . . . abidinge I Pet. 1:17.

Sainte Peter . . . talkinge A reference to I Pet. 1:15.

Non mechaberis . . . lechery Jas. 2:11.

Refraine . . . Psal. xxxiii Ps. 33:14.

Eccles .i. Ecclus. 1:28.

Scientes quod . . . Christi I Pet. 1:18.

But you . . . grudged Erasmus, *Paraphrasis, ed. cit.* fo. 325; *Paraphrase, ed. cit.* sig. C4ᵛ enjoins turning away from ceremonies to put complete trust in God; see the following exposition of Jewish ceremonies.

They . . . Epistle A reference to the first sermon on I Peter; see *Sermons*, p. 195.

Mat. xv. Matt. 15:3–6.

i. Cor. viij. & .x. I Cor. 8:4; 10:7.

He was knowen . . . sakes I Pet. 1:20.

faithfull beleuers . . . GOD An exposition of I Pet. 1:21.

Because Saint Peter . . . made A reference to I Pet. 1:20.

Siue . . . pasture John 10:9. Vg. '. . . et ingredietur et egredietur & pascua inveniet'.

For . . . hearing A reference to the state of Original Righteousness; see *Sermons*, p. 206.

Ephe. i . . . worlde Eph. 1:3–4. Vg. '. . . in Christo sicut elegit . . .'

GOD chose . . . Christe A reference to Eph. 1:4.

Dilexisti eos . . . me John 17:23.

Aug . . . him Augustine on Eph. 1:4 in 'In Ioannis Evangelium Tractatus CX' (*PL* 35, 1923).

the prophete Ionas . . . earth Glo. Ord. in *TB cum glo. ord. ed. cit.* IV, sig. 3b2ᵛ. The 'sign of Jonah' (Matt. 12:39–40) was regarded in NT times as a prophecy of the Lord's resurrection. See ODCC s.v. 'Jonah, Book of'.

Tollite me . . . sake Jon. 1:12.

In eo enim . . . troubled Heb. 2:8.

i. Cor. x. I Cor. 10:13.

he shewed him self . . . god I Pet. 1:21.

Animas vestras . . . charitie I Pet. 1:22.

i. Io. iii . . . him I John 3:18.

In that wee knowe . . . brothers I John 1:16.

Maiorem charitatem . . . frendes John 15:13.

Renati non . . . euer I Pet. 1:23.

Esa. xl . . . Apostles An exposition of I Pet. 1:24–5 with reference to Is. 40:6–8. Vg. 'flos foeni'.

And . . . baptisme A reference to I Pet. 1:3; see *Sermons*, pp. 206–7.

contrarye to the secte . . . Anabaptists The Anabaptists believed that infant baptism, lacking scriptural authority, was merely a practical inference from the doctrine of original sin and that the infant, having no knowledge of good or evil, had no reason to be baptised; they reinstituted the baptism of all believers. The movement developed on the continent and first appeared in England as a foreign heresy associated with Sacramentarianism. A number of English-born Anabaptists were examined in 1539–40 on suspicion of denying the Real Presence; the heresy was condemned in the articles on baptism in the Henrician formularies and Anabaptist doctrines were refuted in eighteen of the Forty Two Articles of 1553. See *LP* XIX ii, 17; *Formularies*, pp. 93–4, 255–6; Horst, *Radical Brethren*, pp. 91–9, 812, 945; Williams, *Radical Reformation*, pp. 401–3. The Forty Two Articles are printed by C. Hardwick in *A History of the Articles of Religion* (Cambridge, 1859), Appendix III, pp. 277–328.

the infantes . . . saued A reference to Gen. 17:12–14.

Rom. v . . . abundauit Rom. 5:15. Vg. '. . . si enim unius . . . plures abundavit'.

Iohn .iii . . . heauen John 3:3.

Sinite paruulos . . . me Matt. 19:14.

O mulier . . . filie Matt. 15:28.

Centurio . . . beliefe Matt. 8:5–13; cf the account in Luke 7:2–10.

An other . . . Mark .ii. The story is told in Luke 5:18–26 and Mk 2:3–12. The texts are from Luke 5:20 and 24.

originall synne . . . euer See the exposition in the second sermon on I Peter, pp. 206–7.

Math. xxviii . . . dampned The text is Mk 16:16 (Vg. 'Qui crediderit . . .'), also cited in the article on baptism in the *King's Book* (*Formularies*, p. 253). Edgeworth has confused it with Matt. 15:15 or Matt. 28:19. All three texts with which the Anabaptists attacked the doctrine of infant baptism are cited in contemporary refutations of the heresy; see M. Bucer, *Handlung inn dem offentlichen gesprech zu Strassburg iungst in Synodo gehalten gegen Melchior Hoffman* (Strassburg, ex aed. C. Froschover, 1527), sig. B2ᵛ; and *A short instruction . . . agaynst the pestiferous errours of Anabaptistes* (J. Daye & W. Seres, 1549),] sig. Aᵛ (STC 4463), the translation of Calvin's reply to the 'Anabaptist Confession', *Briève instruction pour armer tous bons fidèles contre les erreurs de la secte des Anabaptistes* (Geneva, 1544). The principal beliefs of the Anabaptists are set out in the Schleitheim Articles, which are printed in *Das Separatdruck aus der Schaffhauser Beitrage zur Vaterlandischen Geschichte*, Heft, 28 (1951), ed. B. Jeny (Thayngen, 1951), pp. 11, 52. See Rupp, *Patterns of Reformation*, pp. 325–53; Horst, *Radical Brethren*, pp. 49–50, 170–2, 186–9; Williams, *Radical Reformation*, pp. 182–5; Pelikan, *Church and Dogma*, pp. 314–22.

as the scholasticall . . . dede Faith, hope and charity are the three theological or 'infused' virtues which according to Catholic doctrine, come from the free endowment of grace by God; see Aquinas, ST 1a2ae. 62, 1 and 3 (*ed. cit.* XXIII, 137–9, 145–9); on their relationship to the seven gifts of the Holy Ghost see *Sermons*, pp. 116, 120, 145, 148.

Example . . . learning This image of the physician probably derives from the use in medical examinations of the urinal, a glass vessel containing urine. Descriptions of the appearance

of urine for the purpose of prognosis and illustrations of urinals are common in fifteenth and sixteenth century medical texts. See *Liber de Diversis Medicinis*, ed. M.S. Ogden, EETS, OS, 207 (London, 1938), p. 10; and the introduction by K. Sudhoff, tr. C. Singer, to *Fasiculus Medicinae of Johannes de Ketham Alemanus*, ed. H. Sigerist, Monumenta Medicae I (Venice, 1491; facs. Milan, 1924), pp. 46–7, Plates I, II.

attentius . . . chapter I Pet. 1:22.

The fift treatise or sermon.
The second chapiter.

Deponentes . . . concupiscite I Pet. 2:1–2.

Fyrst . . . faith A reference to the treatment of I Pet. 1:3–4 and 9–23 in the three preceeding sermons; see pp. 205–8, 214–15, 216–26.

therefore saint Peter . . . neighbours A reference to I Pet. 2:1.

Gen xxxiiii The following story is taken from Gen. 34:1–29.

spectatum veniunt . . . ipse Ovid, *Ars Amatoria* I, l. 99; see *Ars amatoria Book I*, ed. A.S. Hollis (Oxford, 1977), pp. 4, 51 (n.).

Emor . . . Sichem Hamor is now believed to be not an historical individual but the eponymous ancestor of the Hamorites, and as 'father of Schechem', the founder of the place Schechem; see DB II, s.v. 'Hamor'.

Responderunt . . . sister Gen. 34:13.

Symeon . . . Gen. xxx. Gen. 30:21. Simeon was the second son and Levi the third son of Leah and Jacob; see Gen. 29:33–34.

Iosue .viii This account of the ambush by which Ai was taken comes from Josh. 8:12–22.

where . . . Iosue .vii. Josh. 7:5; Joshua's first unsuccessful attempt to take Ai is recounted in Josh. 7:2–5.

.ii. Reg. xx. II Kings 20:9–12. Amasa, commander of the army of the rebel Absalom which was routed by Joab, was pardoned by David who then gave him command of the army of Judah in place of Joab; he was slain in a treacherous manner by Joab at 'the great stone of Gibeon'; see *Sermons*, pp. 313, 368.

Salue . . . brother II Kings 20:9.

i. Reg. xxi . . . presence I Kings 21:10–15. Achish was the King of Gath to whom David fled for refuge after the massacre of the priests of Nob and before whom, fearful of the Philistines' vengeance, he feigned madness.

Stultitiam . . . wisedome Proverbial; cited in *ODEP* s.v. 'Wise man may sometimes . . . play the fool'.

I hadde . . . me Proverbial; cited in *ODEP* s.v. 'Better be envied than pitied'.

That vyce . . . backbitynge A reference to I Pet. 2:1.

in reprobum sensum . . . doe Rom. 1:28.

Susurrones . . . commandement Rom. 1:29–30. See Erasmus, *NT*, *ed. cit.* fo. 231. More translates Rom. 1:30 as 'odious to God'; the AV as 'haters of God'. See Marc'hadour, *Bible* III, 36.

Ecclesiast. xli . . . treasures Ecclus. 41:12.

Pro. xxii . . . riches Prov. 22:1.

Epistola ad Nepocianum . . . tales Jerome, Epist. 52 (*PL* 22, 538).

we shoulde make . . . Eccle. xxviii Ecclus. 28:24.

opprobrium . . . neighbours Ps. 14:3.

Prouerb. xxiiii . . . both Prov. 24:21–22.

All these vices . . . curtise An exposition of I Pet. 2:1–3.

Here . . . animi I.e. the translations of I Pet. 2:2 in the Vg.; Hugh of St Cher's gloss in *Prima (-septima) pars huius operis: continens textum Biblie cum postilla domini Hugonis Cardinalis*, 7 vols (Basle, 1498–1502), VII, sig. i1: 'rationabiles' (cited herafter as Hugh of St Cher, *TB*); and in Erasmus' *NT*, *ed. cit.* fo. 352. Edgeworth makes no attempt to choose between them. See Erasmus' discussion in *Annotationes*, *ed. cit.* fo. 675.

.i. cor. xiiii . . . malice I Cor. 14:20.

Heb. vi . . . workes Heb. 6:1–2.

Heb. v . . . meate Heb. 5:14.

perfectorum . . . falseheade Heb. 5:14.

i. Cor. iii. I Cor. 3:2.

Cum . . . Apollo I Cor. 3:4; cf. the expositions in *Sermons*, pp. 143–4, 301–2.

carnall folkes . . . homo A reference to I Cor. 3:3.

Carnall . . . beard Veneration of corporeal images of the deity is denounced in the formularies' teaching on the second commandment (*Formularies*, pp. 135, 301).

by multiplying . . . charitie A reference to Matt. 24:12; for the proverb based on this text see *Sermons*, pp. 155, 183; above p. 392.

that spyryte . . . hurte A reference to I Thess. 5:23.

S. Hierome . . . ad Hedibiam Jerome, Epist. 120 (*PL* 22, 995).

They . . . digested On the argument that the young are unfit to study divinity (or moral philosophy) see *Sermons*, pp. 137–8, 354

They . . . Capadotia. &c A reference to I Pet. 1:1; on the recipients of the Epistle see *Sermons*, p. 195.

This is milke . . . Peter A reference to I Pet. 2:2.

Prou. i . . . them Prov. 1:10.

Prouerb. xvi . . . waye Prov. 16:29.

Coagulatum est . . . Milke Ps. 118:70.

Vt . . . yll Ambrose on Ps. 118:70, 'In CXVIII Ps. Serm. IX' (*PL* 15, 1327).

maketh a man . . . good I Pet. 2:2–3.

The syxt treatise or sermon.

Ad quem . . . Christ I Pet. 2:4–5.

And . . . them A reference to St Augustine's mission which introduced Christianity into England in 597; see *Sermons*, p. 194.

And so the people . . . them See *ibid.* p. 195 on the recipients of I Peter.

For . . . Scripture See Ps. 117:22; Matt. 21:42; Luke 20:17; Acts 4:11.

This . . . preciosum I Pet. 2:4 with reference to Ps. 117:22 and Is. 28:16.

Because . . . grounded The primacy of the literal sense of scripture is recommended by Aquinas, *ST* 1a. 1, 10 (*ed. cit.* I, 36–41); see B. Smalley, *The Study of the Bible in the Middle Ages*, 3rd ed. (Oxford, 1983), pp. 300–306. Both humanists and reformers espoused the literal or philological interpretation of the scriptures. See Tyndale, *Obedience*, pp. 303–4; J.H. Bentley, *Humanists and Holy Writ: New Testament Scholarship in the Renaissance* (Princeton, 1983).

the Prophets . . . buyldynge Ps. 117:22; other references to this verse come from Job 38:6; Is. 28:16; Jer. 51:26; Hag. 2:15; Matt. 21:42; Mk 12:10; Luke 20:17; Acts 4:11; Eph. 2:1.

Was . . . scriptures A reference to III Kings

5:17 and to interpretations of Solomon's Temple as a figure of the eternal church built of living stones with Christ himself as the corner stone; see *Glo. Ord.* in *TB cum glo. ord. ed. cit.* II, sig. r8; see Blench, pp. 22–23, on Bishop Longland's sermon on this theme at Cardinal College in 1525.

albeit the Hebrewes . . . nations A reference to I Par. 22:8. The story is mentioned by Jerome in *Contra Iovinianum* I, 24 (PL 23, 243).

Lapidem . . . anguli Ps. 117:22.

But because . . . Mat. xxi. Edgeworth rejects the non-scriptural Jewish story of the stone which the builders rejected in favour of the gospel interpretation of Ps. 117:22 in Matt. 21:33–41.

he allegeth . . . buyldinge Matt. 21:42 with reference to Ps. 117:22.

He . . . churche A familiar interpretation of Matt. 21:42; see Hugh of St Cher, *TB, ed. cit.* VI, sig. I1ᵛ; *Glo. Ord.* (PL 113, 154–55).

that Christ . . . dede A reference to Ps. 109:4 and 44:8; on Christ as the Messiah see *Sermons,* pp. 115, 172, 193, 195; above p. 372.

Iacob . . . Iude A reference to Gen. 49:10 and Dan. 9:24. 'Shiloh' (Gen. 49:10) was commonly read in the sixteenth century as a title of the Messiah, with the interpretation that Judah should hold the sovereignty until the Messiah came. See J. Skinner, *Genesis,* ICC, 2nd ed. (Edinburgh, 1930), pp. 522–3; on both prophecies, *Sermons,* pp. 214–15.

Herode . . . Iacob The foundations of the Herodian house were laid by Antipater, an Idumaean, from a race that was never Jewish to the core. The Idumaeans were partly absorbed by the Bedouin tribes who claimed descent through Esau from Abraham and were acknowledged by the Israelites as brethren. Herod the Great ruled as King of the Jews from 37 to 4 BC. See *DB* II, s.v. 'Herod' and 'Idumaea'.

peruertynge . . . liuers A reference to Matt. 11:19; Luke 7:34; see *Sermons,* pp. 266, 298.

Sainte . . . churche I Pet. 2:7 with reference to Ps. 117:22 and Is. 28:16.

so manye miscreauntes . . . Prieste It is difficult to date this sermon precisely as the anti-sacramentalism of which Edgeworth complains apparently gathered momentum in Bristol from early 1547. A *terminus ad quem* is

the proclamation of 24 April 1548 granting Cranmer sole power of issuing licenses to preach (Hughes and Larkin, I, 296; below, p. 439). But it was probably preached prior to the legislation of 27 December 1547 and January 1548, passed after extensive attacks on the sacrament of altar, to enforce uniformity, before the *Order of Communion* was issued on 8 March 1548. See Cardwell, *Doc. Ann.* no. V; C.W. Dugmore, *The Mass and the English Reformers* (London, 1958), p. 116; *Sermons,* pp. 142, 240, 280, 290, 365 for similar complaints.

They . . . Christ Protestant services resumed in Lent 1547; in May 1548 services in London were held in English. This may be a reference to Latimer who preached against the Mass and the 'idol of the altar' in his famous 'Sermon of the Plougher' of January 1548, as did the Protestant preacher Thomas Hancock; see MacLure, *Paul's Cross Sermons,* pp. 192–3; Gasquet and Bishop, *Ed. VI and BCP,* pp. 104–7; Chester, *Latimer,* pp. 162–6; C. Wriothesley, *A Chronicle of England during the Reigns of the Tudors from AD 1485 to 1559,* ed. W.D. Hamilton, 2 vols, CS, NS, XI, XX (London, 1875–7), II, 2 (cited hereafter as Wriothesley, *Chronicle*).

In quo . . . sunt I Pet. 2:8.

in whom wee liue . . . speaketh Acts 17:28.

Lapis . . . scandali I Pet. 2:8. See Vergil, *Adagia,* no. 108, *ed. cit.* fo. 199.

Quia super quem . . . hym Matt. 21:44.

Qui non credit . . . already John 3:18.

Luke .ii. The following story is taken from Luke 2:25–35.

Et venit . . . templum Luke 2:27.

Ecce positus . . . others An interpretation of Luke 2:34–35.

Mat. xi. The following account comes from Matt. 11:2–6.

Tu de te ipso . . . true John 8:13.

the blinde . . . offende Matt. 11:5–6.

Because men . . . hartes An exposition of the doctrine of transubstantiation, *viz* the conversion of the bread and wine into the whole substance of the Body and Blood of Christ with only the outward appearance (i.e. the accidents) of them remaining; it was upheld in the Six Articles of 1539 although rejected by the reformers. See *ODCC* s.v. 'Transubstantiation'; *Sermons,* pp. 142, 321.

sacramentall . . . sinnes A defence of auricular confession and the sacrament of penance, which were upheld in the Six Articles and the Henrician formularies, but came under renewed attack in Edward's reign. For the Tyndale-More controversy see Tyndale, *Obedience*, pp. 260, 265; *Answer*, pp. 22–23; More, *Confutation*, CW 8, 88–92; 204–5; *Formularies*, pp. 96–100, 257–262; *Sermons*, pp. 207, 238, 280.

Mat. xii . . . Ione Matt. 12:41 with reference to Jon. 3:4 on Jonah's preaching to the Ninevites.

The people . . . saluation The story of the Ninevites comes from Jon. 3:4–10.

the quene . . . Salomon Matt. 12:42 with reference to the narrative in III Kings 10:1–10. Sheba is the OT name for the people and country of the Sabaeans in S.W. Arabia, the modern Yemen (Aden) in the southeastern part of the Arabian Peninsula. This peninsula, known to ancient cosmographers as *Arabia Felix*, extends along the Red Sea coast from El Laith in the N. to Shekh Said at the straits of Bab-el-Mandeb. The rich and fertile central highland region is the most favoured district in Asia Minor. See Pliny, *Naturalis Historia* V, 87 (*ed. cit.* I, 398); Mela, *De Situ Orbis* III (1538 ed.), fo. 185, n. b.; *DB* III, s.v. 'Sheba'; *Enc. Brit.* X, s.v. 'Yemen'.

the Bridge . . . Trinityes I.e. Bristol Bridge across the river Avon to the S. of the town and the route to the suburbs of Bedminster and Redcliffe; for a description and illustration see Seyer, *Memoir* II, 33–8, 43. The 'Trinities' is the cathedral church of Bristol on the N.W. of the town which is dedicated to the Holy Trinity and known as St Augustine alias the Trinity. Edgeworth complains that people will not cross town to attend sermons. For the first map of Bristol (1568), see G. Braun and F. Hogenberg, *Civitates orbis terrarum, 1572–1618*, 3 vols (facs. repr. Amsterdam, 1965), II, Pt. 3; see also John Speed's map of 1610 in his *Counties of Britain, 1558–1603* (1612, facs. repr., London, 1988), p. 83.

Bedminster . . . Stapleton Bedminster, one and a half miles southwest of Bristol, lying partly in the county of the city, partly in the hundred of Hartcliffe in the E. division of Somerset, is now a suburb of Bristol. Stapleton, in the union of Clifton, hundred of Barton-Regis, W. division of the county of Gloucester, is two and a half miles from Bristol and on the main road to Gloucester. See S. Lewis, *A Topographical Dictionary of England*, 4 vols (London, 1849), I, s.v. 'Bedminster'; IV, s.v. 'Stapleton'.

as Sainte . . . me Matt. 11:6 with reference to the account of Matt 11:2–6 on p. 240.

Manda remanda . . . Esa. xxviii Is. 28:10.

the worde of Expectation . . . tyme E.g. Deut. 7:12–13; 11:13–15, etc.

Propter hoc . . . men Is. 28:14.

Dixistis . . . vs An exposition of Is. 28:15; Vg. 'Dixistis enim percussimus . . .'.

Ecce . . . confundetur Is. 28:16. Vg. 'lapidem probatum, angularum, pretiosum'; cf. Rom. 9:33; 10:11; I Pet 2:6.

by whiche . . . Ierusalem See N. de Lyra, *postilla* on I Pet 2:6 in *TB cum glo. ord. ed. cit.* VI, sig. 2H8ᵛ.

Whosoeuer . . . Paule I.e. 'non festinet' (Is. 28:16); cf. 'non confundetur' (Rom. 9:33; 10:11; I Pet. 2:6).

s. querere . . . inter Glossa Interlinearis on Is. 28:16 in *TB cum glo. ord. ed. cit.* IV, sig. 2h3.

viri illusores . . . word Is. 28:14.

Expecta dominum . . . prophet Ps. 26:14.

Sola vexatio . . . preachers Is. 28:19.

Apo. xxi . . . Christe Rev. 21:14.

.s. Hierome . . . Iouinianum Jerome, *Contra Jovinianum* I (PL 23, 247).

Saint Augustine . . . heauen Augustine, 'Enarratio in Ps. CXXI' (PL 34, 1621).

The seuenth treatise or sermon.

as an holy . . . Christ I Pet. 2:5.

Exod. xix . . . nation Ex. 19: 5–6.

Vos autem genus . . . wonne I Pet. 2:9.

Of this saying . . . lyuerye An attack on the Lutheran belief in 'a priesthood of all believers'. In his 'Prologue upon the First Epistle of St. Peter' Tyndale states: 'Christ is the foundation . . . whereon all are built through faith . . . and . . . made priests'; and in *Obedience*: 'Christ is a priest for ever; and all we priests through him and need no more of any such priests on earth, to be a mean for us unto God' (*Doctrinal Treatises*, pp. 527, 255); cf. More's defence in *Confutation*, CW 8, 92, 112–13,

166; he lists this as one of Tyndale's heresies in *Dialogue*, CW 6, 353.

regale . . . priestes I Pet. 2:9.

Qui . . . father Rev. 1:5–6; Vg. 'nostrum regum'. Rev. 1:6 is cited by Foxe under Article XI of the heresies collected out of *Obedience* in 1546: i.e. 'Christ is a priest for ever and all we priests through him'; see Townsend-Foxe, V, 579.

The Lutherians . . . clothes Tyndale also claimed that every man and woman is a priest and maye consecrate the body of Christ (*Answer*, pp. 18, 176); cf. More's defence (citing I Pet. 2:9) in *Confutation*, CW 8, 190–1, 594–5.

Saynt Ambrose . . . cap. iii. Ambrose, *De Vocatione Gentium* I, 3 (*PL* 16, 1084).

Tichonius . . . Christiana I.e. Tichonius, *Liber de Septem Regulis*, Regula IV (*PL* 18, 33–34); cited by Augustine in *De Doctrina Christiana* III, 34 (*PL* 34, 83–4). 'De Specie et genere' is the fourth, not the third, rule of Tichonius.

Alleuat dominus . . . brused Ps. 144:14.

Si exaltatus . . . world John 12:32.

Dominus de celo . . . workes Ps. 13:2–3.

Phil. ii . . . pleasure Phil. 2:21. Vg. 'omnes enim'.

The rule . . . them Ambrose, *De Vocatione Gentium, loc. cit.*

Or . . . e conuerso Either a reference to one of Aristotle's logical works or to Boethius – perhaps to his commentary on Aristotle's *Posterior Analytics*; see *Posteriorum Analyticorum Aristotelis Interpretatio* II, 14 (*PL* 64, 1196–7, 756); *De Differentiis Topicis* III; *Boethius's De topicis differentiis*, ed. and tr. E. Stump (Ithaca, 1978), p. 65; see *Sermons*, pp. 150, 191.

that God taketh . . . downe Ps. 144:14.

And when Christ . . . him John 12:32.

Likewise the prophet . . . awaye Ps. 13:2–3.

Where Saint Paul . . . for Phil. 2:21.

saithe sainte Ambrose Ambrose, *De Vocatione Gentium* I, 3 (*PL* 16, 1084).

you be a chosen . . . priestes I Pet. 2:9 with reference to Ex. 19:5–6.

Qui aliquando . . . not An exposition of I Pet. 2:10. Vg. 'populus nunc'.

tribus Iuda . . . Israell The tribe of Judah, named after the fourth son of Jacob, was called 'the house of Kings' because of the descent through David, second king of Israel. After David founded the city of Jerusalem, the history of the tribe became the history of the southern kingdom of Judah. See *DB* I, s.v. 'David'; II, s.v. 'Judah'; 'Israel'.

although the kings . . . Rome Saul was the first king of Israel whose fourth son contested with David for the throne for seven years after his death. Herod the Great ruled Palestine from 37 to 4 BC with the backing of Rome. See *Sermons*, p. 238; *DB* I, s.v. 'David and Saul'.

tribus Leui . . . same A reference to Num. 18:2. All members of the tribe of Levi, descended from Levi, the son of Jacob, were ministers of the sanctuary of ancient Israel before the fall of Judah in 596 BC, the terms 'Levite' and 'priest' then being interchangeable. The title 'Levite' was later restricted to the non-Aaronic members of the tribe who were servants of the Temple; it is used in the OT with different meanings according to their changing states and functions. See *ODCC* s.v. 'Levites'; *DB* IV s.v. 'Priests and Levites'.

the Apostle calleth . . . priestes A reference to I Pet. 2:9.

Prouer. xvi . . . countreys Prov. 16:32.

materiall oyle . . . anon Tyndale denied the necessity of oiling and shaving for consecration (*Answer*, pp. 19–20). More, *Confutation* (CW8, 192–8), identifies them as ceremonies of consecration; he defines the sacrament of order as given by the imposition of the bishop's hands. This view seems to have been upheld by the conservative party in 1540 (Pocock-Burnet, IV, 478–81). The ceremonies are condemned as unscriptural in the *Bishops' Book* and ignored in the *King's Book* (*Formularies*, pp. 105, 27, 281). They were abolished in Cranmer's Ordinal of 1550. See F.J. Clark, *Eucharistic Sacrifice and the Reformation*, 2nd ed. (London, 1963), pp. 192–4; Procter and Frere, *BCP*, p. 668; *ODCC* s.v. 'Ordinal'.

This spirituall . . . coparteners Ps. 44:8. This distinction between an ordained priesthood and a spiritual or lay priesthood of all baptised Christians probably derives from Ambrose, *De Sacramentis* IV, 1 (*PL* 16, 435–7). Edgeworth challenges the reformers' view that the priesthood was only the office of a layman appointed to preach and not a sacrament; see Bonner's article on orders in *A profitable . . . doctryne*, ed. cit. sig. 2A2ᵛ; *Sermons*, pp. 115,

195 on the anointing of kings and priests; cf. p. 342.

And . . . vs A reference to I Cor. 12:11; cf. Eph. 4:7.

to be builded . . . Christ I Pet. 2:5.

Saynt Iherome . . . women Jerome, Dialogus contra Luciferianos 4 (PL 23, 158).

Rom. xii . . . Christ Rom. 12:1. Vg. 'obsecro itaque vos fratres'.

the sacrifice . . . thankes A reference to Heb. 13:15.

his last supper . . . blood See Matt. 26:26–8; Mk 14:22–4.

Hoc facite . . . me Luke 22:19.

When he came . . . forgyven John 20:19; 22–3.

And . . . priest See the conservatives' answers to question ten of Cranmer's questionnaire: 'Whether bishops or priests were first?' Archbishop Lee of York cites John 20:22; see Pocock-Burnet, IV, 472–4; Formularies, pp. 105, 277–8, 281.

Segregate . . . offices Acts 13:2–3. Vg. 'separate mihi Barnabas et Saulum in opus quod . . . dimiserunt illos'; see Sermons, p. 342.

Noli negligere . . . thee I Tim. 4:14.

Prophecye . . . Saynt Ambrose Ambrose on I Tim. 4:14, 'Comm. in Epist. ad Timotheum Primam' (PL 17, 473).

oportet autem . . . infidels I Tim. 3:7. Vg. 'et testimonium'.

.i. Tim. v . . . alienis I Tim. 5:22.

yet by imposition . . . penance Cf. the articles on orders in the formularies which rank the duties of preaching and teaching above those of consecration; Formularies, pp. 105, 277–8; Sermons, pp. 349–50.

Here . . . sufficiently I Pet. 1:3 with reference to the exposition of penance in the second sermon on I Peter; see Sermons, p. 207.

The .viii. treatise or sermon.

Charissimi . . . animam. &c I Pet. 2:11. Vg. 'obsecro tanquam'.

These wordes . . . Masse I.e. 'Dominica III post octavas pasche'. The full epistle for the Mass is I Pet. 2:11–19; see Wickham Legg, Sarum Missal, pp. 147–8. This sermon was preached between 25 March and 24 June (see above, p. 406).

that they were sometyme . . . soule An exposition of I Pet. 2:10–13.

or for their faithes . . . afore A reference to I. Pet 1:5 and 9.

So he praieth . . . phariseis A reference to I Pet. 5:3; see Sermons, p. 352.

as saynt Paule . . . Corinth A reference to I Cor. 5:1.

Titus .ii . . . commaund Tit. 2:15.

Multam fiduciam . . . seruant Philem. 1:8–10. Vg. 'habentes in Christo Iesu . . .'.

And euen so . . . place A reference to I Pet. 1:1. On this interpretation of 'straungers' see Sermons, p. 204.

we . . . aboue Proverbial. Cited in ODEP s.v. 'Life' as first use of 'Life is a pilgrimage'.

Heb. xi . . . .aboue A reference to Heb. 11:8–10.

An old vse . . . deuocions Pilgrimages were condemned in the Edwardian injunctions of 1547; see Hughes and Larkin, I, 287, p. 394; Sermons, p. 148.

it signifieth . . . be See Glo. Interlinearis on I Pet. 2:11 in TB cum glo. ord. ed. cit. VI, sig. 211; Glo. Ord. (PL 114, 683).

Mat. xxv . . . goods Matt. 25:14.

lyke as a Bee . . . Honye On this familiar image see Introduction, p. 83.

Adueniat regnum . . . come Matt. 6:10; Luke 11:2.

i. Timo. vi . . . content I Tim. 6:8.

.i. offi . . . comminaltye Cicero, De Officiis I, 34 (ed. cit. pp. 126–7); 'Peregrini . . . minimeque esse in aliena re publica curiosum'.

Carnall desires . . . soule A reference to I Pet. 2:11.

Eccle. xxii . . . susteyne Ecclus. 22:1; see Glo. Ord. in TB cum glo. ord. ed. cit. III, sig. 2n2.

De stercore boum . . . God Ecclus. 22:2 with reference to Hugh of St Cher, TB, ed. cit. III, sig. H2ᵛ.

Non alligabis . . . preachynge I Cor. 9:9 (Vg. om. 'in horreo') referring to Deut. 25:4; see also I Tim. 5:18.

then by the dunge . . . sluggardes Ecclus 22:2; the interpretation comes from Hugh of St Cher, TB, ed. cit. III, H2ᵛ–H3.

Seruo maliuolo . . . mischiefe Ecclus. 33:28–29. Proverbial; see ODEP s.v. 'Idleness'.

It deliteth . . . heresies That 'interludes of scismes . . . & heresies' count with 'filthye playes' as popular entertainments suggests that polemical Protestant plays and players were a disruptive presence in Bristol. For records of troupes of players in Bristol in the 1540s see Ian Lancashire, *Dramatic Texts and Records of Great Britain: a chronological Topography to 1558* (Toronto, 1984), App. I, pp. 326, 377, 379, 382, 386, 387, 402, 403, 407; for earlier entertainments, Owst, *LPME*, pp. 274, 362, 383, 393–4.

Non saciatur . . . more Eccles. 1:8. Vg. 'Non saturatur . . .'.

Optimum . . . crasshinge Heb. 13:9; Vg. 'enim est'; see N. de Lyra, *postilla in TB cum glo. ord. ed. cit.* VI, sig. 2Z7.

Si secundum carnem . . . euer Rom. 8:13.

Gala. v . . . dooe Gal. 5:17.

Rom. vii . . . synne Rom. 7:19; 22–23 and 25.

In prolo . . . christi The following exposition comes from the prologue to the sermons of Arnoldus Carnotensis (originally ascribed to Cyprian and Athanasius). See 'De Cardinalibus Christi Operibus Sermones' in *Athanasium et Aliorum Opuscula* (Paris, 1500), sig. G3.

Omnibus . . . againe Proverbial. Cited as first occurrence in *ODEP* s.v. 'Sins'.

Conuersationem . . . bonam. &c I Pet. 2:12.

Ve homini . . . sinne Matt. 18:7.

This knewe . . . here A reference to the parable of Dives and Lazarus; Luke 16:19–28.

Cum sancto . . . like II Kings 22:26–27; Ps. 17:26–27. Vg. 'electo electus'.

Prouer. vi . . . abhorreth Prov. 6:16.

You muste beware . . . God An exposition of Prov. 6:17.

And as Titus . . . benefeci The *celebre dictum* has a classical source in Suetonius' 'Divus Titus' in *Vitae XII Caesarum Libri VIII* VIII, 8, although Edgeworth's source may have been Erasmus' *Apophthegmata*; see *The Lives of the Caesars*, ed. and tr. R.C. Rolfe, 2 vols (London, 1914), II, 331–3; Erasmus, *Apophthegmata, ed. cit.*, fo. 485. The saying also appears in Jerome's 'Comm. in Epist. ad Galatos' (*PL* 26, 433) and in Isidore of Seville's *Chronicon* (*PL* 83, 1042) from which source it probably came into the *Anglo-Saxon Chronicle* and the Old English *Orosius*. See *The Old English*

Orosius, ed. J. Bately, EETS, SS, 6 (London, 1980), pp. xc–xci, 138–9, 325 (n.); and 'World history in *The Anglo-Saxon Chronicle*, its sources and its separateness from the Old English Orosius', *Anglo Saxon England* VIII (1980), 177–94.

Proferentem mendacia . . . brethren Prov. 6:19.

Wee be . . . churche An exposition of I Cor. 1:10.

The ninth treatice or Sermon.

Svbiecti . . . deum I Pet. 2:13.

whether . . . Capadotia. &c I Pet. 1:1; on the audience of the Epistle see *Sermons*, p. 195.

This . . . conscience A reference to Rom. 13:5.

Ro. xiii . . . damnation Rom. 13:1–2. Vg. 'enim potestas . . . itaque qui'.

Siue regi . . . good An exposition of I Pet. 2:13–14.

.iii. Esd. iiii. The following is an exposition of III Esd. 4:2–12.

O viri . . . do III Esd. 4:2–3. Vg. 'non praecellent . . . omne quodcumque'.

this is goddes . . . mouthes I Pet. 2:15.

Quasi liberi . . . Dei I Pet. 2:16.

Actu. v . . . Gamala Acts 5:37; Vg. 'in diebus professionibus'; Josephus, *Jew. Ant.* XVIII, 1, 1–6 (*ed. cit.* IX, 5–7); on the revolt of Judas of Galilee in 7 AD see *Sermons*, p. 126.

ibant singuli . . . tribute Luke 2:3; the emperor Augustus ordered a general census.

at which time Ioseph . . . borne A reference to Luke 2:4–7.

An licet . . . so Matt. 22:1 with a reference to Matt. 22:21.

Obtentur quidem . . . lucre Jospehus, *Jew. Ant.* XVIII, 1, 1, *loc. cit.*

Euangelicall libertie . . . frely Cf. *Sermons*, pp. 127–8, 229; 'euangelicall libertie', here identified with Erastian values and the Royal Supremacy, acquires a positive connotation.

Non solum . . . conscience Rom. 13:5. Cited by Robert Barnes in *A supplicacion vnto henrye the eyght* (J. Bydell, 1534), sigs B2[r–v] (STC 1471) in asserting loyalty to the king; and in the articles on order in the formularies in stating clerical obedience due to the crown (*Formularies*, pp. 121, 287).

as goddes seruauntes I Pet. 2:16.

not as the seruauntes . . . libertie Cited in ODEP s.v. 'Vice' as first use of 'Vice is often clothed in virtue's (liberty's) habit'; see *Sermons*, pp. 127–8.

Omnes honorate . . . honorificate An exposition of I Pet. 2:17 referring to Rom. 12:10; on filial (chaste) fear see *Sermons*, pp. 165–7.

Eccles, x . . . thoughte An exposition of Eccles. 10:20.

Serui subditi . . . discholis I Pet. 2:18. Vg. om. 'estote'.

Some readeth . . . cruell Both readings of I Pet. 2:18 are given by Erasmus in *Annotationes, ed. cit.* fo. 677; Hugh of St Cher, *TB ed. cit.* VII, sig. i4 mentions 'difficilioribus'; see *Glo. Ord.* (PL 114, 684).

Maledictus Chanaan . . . suis Gen. 9:25.

Aduersitie . . . seruitude A reference to Ex. 1:13–14.

with al feare I Pet. 2:18.

Eph. vi . . . mind Eph. 6:5; on the theme of servants and masters see *Sermons*, pp. 145–6, 269.

Genes. xxxix. The following is an exposition of Gen. 39:7–9.

in omni timore I Pet. 2:18.

Prou. Si sit . . . tua Ecclus. 33:31. Vg. 'Si est . . . fidelis sit . . . quasi'.

Euen as . . . maisters An exposition of Eph. 6:5–8.

non contradicentes . . . thinges An exposition of Tit. 2:9–10 citing both the Vg. and Erasmus' NT (*ed. cit.* fo. 226).

Haec est . . . God An exposition of I Pet. 2:19.

Phil. i . . . sake Phil. 1:29 with a parenthetical reference to I Cor. 12:9.

at this holy . . . Whitsontide This is a pentecostal sermon preached on the fiftieth day after Easter; i.e. between 25 March and 24 June; see above, p. 406.

Ibant gaudentes . . . Actu. v. Acts 5:41.

propter conscientiam dei I Pet. 2:19.

Rom. viii . . . Lorde Rom. 8:38–39.

Quae est . . . rewarded I Pet. 2:20; Vg. 'enim gloria est'.

Take . . . Egypte This story is taken from Gen. 39:20–41: 41; see *Sermons*, p. 261.

Ioseph . . . rule A reference to the seven years of famine described in Gen. 41:53–7.

You may also . . . soules Ambrose, Epist 37, IX–X (PL 16, 1056).

The tenth treatise or sermon.

In hoc enim vocati . . . passion I Pet. 2:20–1.

in the passion . . . lent This sermon was probably preached on Easter Sunday as decreed by the cathedral statutes; see above, p. 406.

Prou. iii . . . eam Prov. 3:18.

Can. ii . . . loued Can. 2:3.

Christus passus . . . vs I Pet. 2:21.

.ii. Reg. vltimo . . . them II Kings 24:17.

Esay. liii . . . deedes Is. 53:5.

Vobis relinquens exemplum I Pet. 2:21.

Mighel hyll St Michael's Hill on the road to Gloucester was the traditional place of twice yearly executions in Bristol and the scene of the Bristol Marian burnings for heresy. See Nicholls and Taylor, *Bristol* II, 15; K.G. Powell, *Marian Martyrs*, BHA, 31 (1972), 9–12.

Tiburne The celebrated Middlesex gallows for the execution of criminals from c.1220–1759; it was situated near what is now the corner of Edgeware and Bayswater Rd., in the NE corner of Hyde Park. Famous executions in the sixteenth century included the Holy Maid of Kent and five others in 1534; see *Enc. Brit.* X, s.v. 'Tyburn'.

that you mai folow . . . steps I Pet. 2:21.

He was vngiltie . . . sentence I Pet. 2:22 with reference to Is. 53:9.

Blessed S. Peter . . . now A reference to I Pet. 2:18.

And our mother . . . Epistle I Pet. 2:21–25 is the epistle for 'Missa per ebdomodam secunde dominice'; see Wickham Legg, *Sarum Missal*, p. 147. This sermon was preached between 25 March and 24 June (probably between 31 March and 30 April); see above, p. 406.

cum male diceretur . . . yl I Pet. 2:23.

He was . . . Samaritane A reference to John 8:48.

For . . . them I.e. the inhabitants of Samaria, capital of the kingdom of Israel (in the NT Samaria denotes the district lying between Galilee and Judaea), who were colonised by the Assyrians in 722 BC (II Kings 18:9). The Jews claimed that the Assyrians, who worshipped pagan gods (II Kings 17), were their forebears rather than the patriarchs. The Jews' hostility is proverbial, but the Samaritans were treated with respect by Christ and by the apostles after the resurrection; see ODCC. s.v. 'Samaria'; Enc. Bib. IV, s.v. 'Samaritans'; Dict. Bibl. V, s.v. 'Samaritains'.

He was also . . . hunter. &c A reference to Luke 23:2; see Sermons, pp. 238, 298.

Cum pateretur . . . them I Pet. 2:23.

Ecclesiasticus . . . afore Ecclus. 22:30; 'maledictio' suggests a confusion with Ecclus. 27:16.

tradidit vindictam . . . doe I Pet. 2:23; Erasmus, NT, ed. cit. fos 353-4.

Mihi vindictam . . . them The texts in order of citation are Rom. 12:19 (Vg. 'mihi vindicta'); Deut. 32:35.

The blod . . . Iudaico A reference to Matt. 27:25; see Josephus, Jewish War VI, 9, 3 (ed. cit. p. 497); Sermons, p. 125.

tradebat autem . . . iniustly I Pet. 2:23.

he would be a king . . . Emperour A reference to Luke 23:2.

Of Iudas . . . them A reference to John 12:3-5; this incident appears in some versions of the popular medieval legend of Judas Iscariot; see Caxton, The Golden Legend, ed. cit. fos 95ᵛ-96.

I take not . . . delyueraunce Judas is sometimes referred to as proditor. Tradere implies 'to surrender treacherously'; prodere 'to betray perfidiously' (Lewis and Short s.v.). Edgeworth may have read Chrysostom's two homilies 'In Proditionem Iudae' (PG 49, 373-392); see P.F. Baum, 'The Medieval Legend of Judas Iscariot', PMLA 31 (1916), 488-90.

Qui peccata . . . crosse I Pet. 2:23-4. The translation is ambiguous; the antecedent of the relative pronoun 'whyche' is 'he'.

for he neuer sinned . . . afore A reference to I Pet. 2:22.

Esa. liii . . . sound An exposition of Is. 53:5 (Vg. 'et livore eius') with reference to I Pet. 2:24.

Et dominus . . . iniquities Is. 53:6 (Vg. 'posuit in eo'); I Pet. 2:24.

Omnes nos . . . soules Is. 53:6; I Pet. 2:25.

the parable . . . flocke An exposition of Luke 15:3-7.

Thys . . . forsaken Hugh of St Cher on Luke 15:3 in TB, ed. cit. VI, sig. R2ᵛ.

inhabitauntes . . . ende A reference to Eph. 3:21.

There . . . Virgines For other examples of this traditional Catholic imagery in sixteenth century homilies see Blench, p. 127.

minished and made . . . Angels Heb. 2:9.

as Esay saith . . . here Is. 53:6; I Pet. 2:24.

Humeri . . . selfe Ambrose on Luke 15:4, 'Expositio Evang. Sec. Luke Libris X', VII (PL 15, 1755); cf. Hugh of St Cher, TB, ed. cit. VI, sig. R3.

But because Christ . . . mery A reference to Luke 15:5.

desired . . . Christ A reference to Phil. 1:23.

To the pastor . . . flocke I Pet. 2:25 with reference to I Pet. 5:4.

Here . . . entreated A reference to I Pet. 5:1-3; see Sermons, pp. 340-7, 351-3.

maisters . . . doublenes A reference to I Pet. 2:18 and 25.

Seruo sensato . . . Eccle. x. Ecclus. 10:28.

The .xi. treatise or sermon.
The third chapiter.

Similiter . . . lucrifiant. &c I Pet. 3:1. Vg. 'similiter mulieres subdite viris'.

Here . . . sermon A reference to I Pet. 2:18; see Sermons, p. 269.

Ephe. v . . . punishment Eph. 5:33.

s. Paule biddeth . . . pleasure Eph. 5:22-24.

Hester .i. The following story of King Ahasuerus and Queen Vashti comes from Esth. 1:1-22; cf. the version 'De Persecutione' in Gesta Romanorum, ed. Oesterley, no. 177, pp. 577-9; see Sermons, p. 318.

On the .vii. daye . . . angrye Esth. 1:10-12.

Non solum . . . list Esth. 1:16-17. Memucan's speech is taken from Esth. 1:16-20.

This counsell . . . houses Esth. 1:21-22.

By this storie . . . commaundement In the moralisation of the story in the Gesta Romanorum (ed. cit. pp. 578-9) the king is a figure of Christ, the queen a figure of the church. Edgeworth, following the literal sense, treats the story as an example of wifely disobedience justly punished.

Sub viri . . . ruler Gen. 3:16.

Vt si qui . . . husbands An exposition of I Pet. 3:1–2.

sainte Peter wrote . . . did On the household duty code or code of subordination on which the teaching of I Pet. 3:1–7 is based, see Selwyn, *St. Peter*, pp. 182–3, 434–5, 437–8; Michaels, *I Peter*, pp. 155–172. The emphasis on Christian wives of unbelieving husbands, reflecting Peter's interest in the subordinate partner, prompts the following analogy with contemporary wives who protect their husbands against heresy. Erasmus, *Paraphrasis*, ed. cit. sig. E3ᵛ; *Paraphrase*, ed. cit., sig. B2, also cites moral virtues such as obedience, but not preaching, as leading to wives' conversion of their husbands; on Edgeworth's views on women preaching see *Sermons*, pp. 139–40; on the recipients of I Peter, above, p. 406.

Conuersationem vestram . . . example I Pet. 2:12.

Quarum non sit . . . cultus I Pet. 3:3 which inspires the following complaint on extravagance and vanity in women's dress and appearance. This was a stock topic in medieval preaching; see Owst, *LPME*, pp. 390–404; Blench, pp. 241–3.

Capillatura . . . contrary A reference to I Pet. 3:3.

.i. Timo. ii . . . stones I Tim. 2:9; I Pet. 3:3.

cultus . . . raymentes I Pet. 3:3. Vg. 'indumenti vestimentorum cultus'.

Cypriane . . . virginum The following exhortation to female chastity and modesty in dress comes from Cyprian, *Liber de Habitu Virginum* V, 17 (PL 4, 444–456).

Esai. iii . . . nudabit Is. 3:16–17. The following description is adapted from Is. 3:18–23. An act of 1532–33 attempted to restrict excess and costly apparell; see *Statutes of the Realm* III, 430–32 (cited by J. Scattergood, 'Fashion and Morality', 263).

Their trimmed . . . naught Legislation restricting the wearing of ornaments was passed in 1514–15 and 1532–3; see *Statutes of the Realm* III, 179–82, 430–32.

And then their pleasaunt . . . fetor Is. 3:24.

This adulteration . . . teaching The following

exposition comes from Cyprian, *Liber de Habitu Virginum* XV–XVIII (PL 4, 454–6).

Mat. v . . . blacke Matt. 5:36.

She was wyfe . . . vineyard A reference to III Kings 21:1–16. Jezebell was known for her painted face; on her treachery and Ahab's see *Sermons*, pp. 321, 356.

when Hieu . . . commaundemente On the anointing of Jehu and the slaying of Jehoram see IV Kings 9:5–24.

he came into Iezraell . . . Reg. ix. On Jezebel's death see IV Kings 9:30–37 which cites Elijah's prophecy (III Kings 21:23); cf. *Sermons*, pp. 321, 356.

For when they . . . selues Cyprian, *Liber de Habitu Virginum* IX (PL 4, 448).

Wo be to him . . . hell A reference to Matt. 18:7; see Vergil, *Adagia* no. 111, ed. cit. fo. 200.

Sapient, v . . . ryches Sap. 5:8 and 14. Vg. 'aut divitiarum iactatio nobis'; om. 'in inferno'.

Study to dresse . . . well I Pet. 3:4.

And also that your spirite . . . God I Pet. 3:4.

Sic enim aliquando . . . Abraham I Pet. 3:5–6.

she forsoke . . . do A reference to Gen. 12:5.

when the thre aungels . . . chere A reference to Gen. 18:2–8.

I trowe . . . countreye A reference to Gen 18:1.

woulde God . . . meate The decay of hospitality and abuse of church wealth is a prominent theme of the Edwardian preachers; see Latimer, *Works* I, 64; Lever, *Sermons*, pp. 28–33, 64–5, 106; for other examples Blench, pp. 245–6.

when Abraham . . . serued A reference to Gen. 20:5.

Sainte Peter noteth . . . man I Pet. 3:6; Gen. 18:10–12.

And Saynte Peter . . . honorem I Pet. 3:6–7.

yet you muste . . . wysedome An exposition of I Pet. 3:7.

Saynt Ambrose . . . chydde Ambrose, Epist. 82 (PL 16, 273–9).

And then . . . Peter A reference to I Pet. 3:7.

Socrates . . . there The first story comes from Jerome, *Contra Jovinianum* I, 48 (PL 23, 278–9); the second comes from Aulus Gellius, *Attic Nights* I, 17 (ed. cit. I, 85). Both appear in

Erasmus, *Apophthegmata* III, 59, 64 (*ed. cit.* fos 178–9), and in Udall's translation, *Apophthegmes* I, 59, 64 (*ed. cit.* fos 23ᵛ–24; 26ᵛ).

I knewe . . . showre Proverbial; see *ODEP* s.v. 'Thunder'.

I haue a iewell of her 'She is a treasure to me'.

trouble worketh patience Proverbial; cited in *ODEP* s.v. 'Trouble'.

Adultery . . . boorde 'Adultery may bring to an end connubial relations'.

Vxoris . . . marryed Jerome, *Contra Jovinianum* I, 48 (*PL* 23, 277).

turninge necessitie . . . vertue Proverbial; see *ODEP* s.v. 'Virtue'; *Sermons*, p. 289.

Saynt Ambrose . . . together Ambrose, *Hexameron* V, 7 (*PL* 14, 213).

secundum scientiam . . . wisedome I Pet. 3:7.

Galath. iii . . . Christe Gal. 3:28.

Vt non impediantur . . . contrarie I Pet. 3:7.

i. Corin. vii . . . prayers I Cor. 7:5.

Et ne appropinquetis . . . wiues Ex. 19:5.

.i. Reg. xxi . . . women An exposition of I Kings 21:2–6. On the holy bread, or bread of the Presence see *ODCC* s.v. 'Shewbread'.

The twelfth treatise or sermon.

In fide . . . amatores I Pet 3:8. Vg. 'In fine . . .'; this was a common variant in sixteenth century editions of the Vulgate; see Marc'hadour, *Bible* II, 161.

These wordes . . . Sondaye I.e. 'Dominica .v. Post festum Sancte Trinitatis'. The full reading is I Pet. 3:8–15; see Wickham Legg, *Sarum Missal*, pp. 177–8.

he hadde afore . . . sermon A reference to I Pet. 2:18, 3:1–7 and to the two previous sermons on I Peter, pp. 269–79.

In fide . . . vnanimes I Pet. 3:8 citing Erasmus' *NT, ed. cit.* fo. 354.

where he bade . . . hindred A reference to I Pet. 3:7; see *Sermons*, pp. 276–9.

Act. iiii . . . all Acts 4:32–33.

as it appeareth . . . ceremonies Barlow claims in *A dialoge* (*ed. cit.* sigs D1ᵛ–3ᵛ), that the Anabaptists contain 'aboue xl. sectes of dyuers heresyes and sondereye opinions'; and that 'there be in Germany .iii.C. sectes aboue ye

nomber that I haue named'; More refers to this comment in *Confutation* (CW8, 662–4 and n.); see also *Sermons*, pp. 127, 169, 245.

vt idipsum dicatis . . . learning I Cor. 1:10.

Here among you . . . shame This sermon was probably preached early in Edward's reign when these practices and forms of worship were undermined: the 1547 Chantries Act denounced as superstitious the doctrines of purgatory and the Mass as a propitiatory sacrifice. *The Order of Communion*, used from Easter 1548 and incorporated into the Latin Mass in the 1549 BCP, deemed auricular confession a matter for the individual conscience; see Cardwell, *BCP*, p. 428; Dugmore, *The Mass*, pp. 116, 123–4; *Sermons*, pp. 128–9, 137, 240, 290, 333, 365.

some wyll pay tithes . . . beside The laity's impropriation of tithes and benefices was a pre-Reformation abuse; non-payment of tithes continued after the Act of First Fruits and Tenths of 1534 and became a serious problem in parishes in the 1540s (Dickens, *English Reformation*, pp. 46–7, 92, 164; C. Haigh in *Reformation Revised*, pp. 23–4, 68). This was a frequent topic of complaint among the Edwardian preachers; see Glasier, *Sermon*, sigs E2–E3ᵛ; Lever, *Sermons*, pp. 29–33, 73, 98, 124–5. The payment of tithes by the Jews is frequently attested in the OT (e.g. Deut. 14:22; 18:4; Lev. 23:30; 27:30–31); see *Encyclopaedia Judaica* 15, s.v. 'Tithes, Church'.

Compatientes . . . another I Pet. 3:8.

.ii. Cor. xi . . . him An exposition of II Cor. 11:29. Vg. 'et non infirmor'.

Fraternitatis . . . brotherheade I Pet. 3:8.

Heretikes . . . brotherhead 'Brotherhead', a synonym for 'confederacy', refers here to heretics in general, both Protestant evangelicals and Anabaptists, who called themselves 'brethren' (Horst, *Radical Brethren*, pp. 38, 40–41, 49). This is principally an attack on the Protestant dominated guilds and fraternities in Bristol (e.g. The Merchant Venturers' Association) which enjoyed increased privileges during Edward's reign; see *Sermons*, pp. 146, 160, 282, 364–5.

They diuideth . . . good A reference to I Pet. 3:8. That the church would become a remnant overtaken by heresies is a traditional complaint; see More, *Confutation* (CW8, 273, 671); *Sermons*, p. 282; cf. p. 364.

.i. Ioh. ii . . . churche An exposition of I John 2:19.

You haue . . . persones I.e. the Protestant dominated Society of Merchant Venturers, run by a Master and Wardens as a body corporate. The ordinances ensured a monolopy of overseas trade to its members. Its incorporation by Edward VI on 18 December 1552 provides a *terminus a quo* of December 1552 for this sermon. See D. Sacks, *Trade, Society and Politics in Bristol c.1500–c.1640* (Garland, 1985), II, 588–95 on the Company's composition; McGrath, *Merchant Venturers*, p. 10; above, pp. 389, 394.

Misericordes . . . merciful I Pet. 3:8.

Luc. vi. . . . forgiuen The following is an exposition of Luke 6:37.

a dede of supererogacion Cf. Article 13 of The Forty Two Articles of 1553 which states that works of supererogation 'cannot be taught without arrogancie and iniquitie'. In his Visitation of Gloucester in 1551 Bishop Hooper required the clergy to submit to the articles in draft form. But they were challenged at Worcester in 1552 in disputations held by two prebendaries, Henry Joliffe and Robert Jonson. See Hardwick, *Articles*, pp. 77–81, 101, 292–3; *Responsio . . . Henrici Ioliffi & Roberti Ionson . . . ad illos articulos Ioannis Hoperi . . . in quibus a Catholica fide dissentiebat* (Antwerp, 1564), sigs Y7ʳ⁻ᵛ; *Sermons*, p. 153.

quod cumque . . . thee Luke 10:35.

Date et dabitur . . . euerlasting Luke 6:37.

ii. Cor. ix . . . auarice II Cor. 9:5.

Chrisost . . . it Chrysostom on II Cor. 9:5, 'In Sec. ad Cor. Epist', *Comm. XIX* (*PG* 61, 532).

qui parce . . . euerlasting II Cor. 9:6.

.ii. Cor. viii. II Cor. 8:12.

as the poore . . . Ierusalem A reference to Luke 21:1–4.

And amonge . . . necessaries The Edwardian reformers also complain at the neglect of universities and ask for alms for students; see Lever, *Sermons*, pp. 31, 64–5, 81, 120–4; Latimer, *Works* I, 64–5, 178–9, 349; Blench, pp. 270–1; *Sermons*, p. 155. On the deterioration of schools and universities under Edward VI see Hughes, *Reformation* II, 153–8; on Mary I's endowment to Oxford, I.G. Philips, 'Queen Mary's Benefaction to the University', *BLR* V (1954), 26–37.

as S. Paul . . . faith A reference to II Cor. 8:14.

Exo. xvi . . . inough A reference to Ex. 16:32–36. An omer (Ex. 16:36) was a dry measure of a tenth of an ephah, or a common sized bowl; see *Encyclopaedia Judaica* 12, s.v. 'Omer'.

so according . . . lesse A reference to II Cor. 9:8.

Augebit incrementa . . . iustice II Cor. 9:10.

date & dabitur . . . you Luke 6:38.

Modesti I Pet. 3:8.

Tully . . . serue Cicero, *De Officiis* I, 40, 142 (*ed. cit.* pp. 144–5).

Tulli . . . Pretura Ibid. I, 40, 144 (*ed. cit.* pp. 146–7); cf. the version in *An Alphabet of Tales* I, 79 (*ed. cit.* p. 61).

Marcus Varro . . . wrong M. Varro, *De Lingua Latina* V, 16; see *On the Latin Language*, tr. R.C. Kent, 2 vols (London, 1938), I, 84–85.

The said ii. pretors . . . blamed Cicero, *De Officiis, loc. cit.*

be in his dumps Proverbial; cited in *ODEP* s.v. 'Dumps'.

Nimietas . . . vice See Jerome's discussion in Epist. 130 (*PL* 22, 1116–17).

Ne quid nimis . . . muche See Jerome, Epist. 108, 130 (*PL* 22, 898 and 1116); Erasmus, *Adagia* I, iv, 96 (*ed. cit.* fo. 290) and R. Taverner's translation of 1539, *Prouerbes or Adagies gathered out of the Chiliades of Erasmus* (R. Kele (1552), sigs. C4ᵛ–C5. *STC* 10440.

at the holye time . . . comming This sermon was preached between 29 September and 25 December, probably in the week before Christmas 1552; see above, p. 406.

that liueth . . . mouth Proverbial; cited in *ODEP* s.v. 'Live'.

Humiles . . . hart I Pet. 3:8.

The .xiii. treatise or sermon.

Non reddentes . . . maledicto I Pet. 3:9.

Nowe . . . doing Ellipsis due to omission of a preposition; a suggested reading is: 'Now after this excellent teaching on how to conduct ourselves through doing good deeds . . .'.

par pari . . . like Proverbial; see Jerome, *Dialogus adversus Pelagios* I (*PL* 23, 505); Erasmus, *Adagia* I, i, 35 (*ed. cit.* fo. 48); *ODEP* s.v. 'Tit for tat'.

Mat. v . . . heauen Matt. 5:44–5.

be to be loued The emendation is in line with a reading of 'be' as 'exist'; i.e. 'are to be loved'; an alternative reading is 'are beloved'; cf. *Sermons*, p. 113; above p. 371.

It was . . . words On the date of the Epistle see *Sermons*, pp. 197–8; Beare, *First Epistle*, pp. 32–3, identifies the persecution as Trajan's; Selwyn, *St Peter*, pp. 52–5, considers the persecutions were spasmodic and dates it before the Neronian persecution of 64 AD; Michaels, *I Peter*, suggests a date between 70 and 80 AD following the destruction of Jerusalem in 70 AD.

Therfore . . . iudgment A reference to I Pet. 3:9; on the Epistle's readers see *Sermons*, p. 195; above p. 408.

S. Peter . . . promis An exposition of I Pet. 3:10 with reference to Ps. 33:12–13.

Matt. xii . . . dampned Matt. 12:37.

The children . . . hart Matt. 12:34.

he forbiddeth . . . wordes A reference to I Pet. 3:10–11 and Ps. 33:14.

Iac iii . . . matters Jas. 3:3–5.

mors et vitam . . . it An exposition of Prov. 18:21.

A litle fire . . . wodde Jas. 3:5. Proverbial; cited as first use in *ODEP* s.v. 'Little'.

An yll tongue . . . poyson An exposition of Jas. 3:6 and 8.

Prohibe . . . wordes I Pet. 3:11 with reference to 1 Pet. 3:10 and Ps. 38:13–14.

Thou . . . thee The Decalogue (Ex. 20:1–17; Deut. 5:6–18), but omitting the second commandment prohibiting worship of graven images; cf. *Formularies*, pp. 137, 300.

Inquirat pacem . . . it I Pet. 3:11.

Therefore the Prophete . . . thee A reference to Ps. 33:14.

Oculi domini . . . it An exposition of I Pet. 3:12.

Et quis . . . you An exposition of I Pet. 3:13 with reference to I Pet. 3:9; Tit. 2:14.

Ieremie . . . Preaching On the deaths of Jeremy and Isaiah see *Sermons*, p. 134.

And . . . Act. v. Acts 5:18–20.

Gamaliel . . . name A reference to Acts 5:34–40; on Gamaliel see *Sermons*, p. 126.

Herode agrippa . . . Iewes A reference to

Peter's escape from imprisonment under Herod Agrippa I (Acts 12:3–11). St James the Great suffered martyrdom under Herod in 44 AD; see above, p. 383.

Nero . . . doer The tradition that St Peter was martyred in the reign of Nero in c.64 comes from Eusebius, *Hist. Ecc.* II, 25 and III, 1 (PG 20, 207, 215); see Beare, *First Epistle*, p. 31, Michaels, *I Peter*, pp. lvii–lxi; above, p. 383.

Why was . . . martyred A reference to Acts 7:57–58; see *Sermons*, pp. 162, 177.

And in the Gospell . . . Lent A reference to Luke 11:14–15. The gospel for the Mass in the third Sunday in Lent is Luke 11:14–28; see Wickham Legg, *Sarum Missal*, p. 73. This sermon was preached in March, before 25 March; see above, p. 406.

If a man . . . bealy For other references to the breaking of the Lenten fast see *Sermons*, pp. 128, 137, 189, 298, 333.

In epulis suis . . . conuiuantes Jude 1:12.

let your trouble . . . it On these two proverbs see *Sermons*, p. 177.

Math. v . . . end Matt. 5:10.

Dominum . . . firmare I Pet. 3:10 with a gloss from N. de Lyra, *postilla in TB cum glo. ord. ed. cit.* VI, sig. 212^v.

Parati semper . . . you I Pet. 3:15.

And of such . . . question For other references to the sacrament of the Mass and the doctrine of purgatory see *Sermons*, pp. 128–9, 142, 238, 240, 280, 365.

when Christes . . . world References to the Christian Church from the Ascension to the time of Paul's first visit to Rome; to the persecutions suffered by the apostles at the hands of the Sanhedrin (Acts 4:3; 5:17–40) after the stoning of Stephen (Acts 8:1), and in the reign of Herod Agrippa I.

Col. iiii . . . promised An exposition of Col. 4:6.

Lu. xxi . . . resist Luke 21:15.

Although naturall . . . afore See the defence of fables, *Sermons*, pp. 160–1.

Take example . . . truth A reference to the Anabaptist heresy concerning the Incarnation. Robert Barnes was charged with being an Anabaptist in 1540 for preaching that 'our lady (was) but a saffron bag'. The heresy was included in Henry's pardon of 1540, but resurfaced in c.1549 when it was attacked by both Catholics and Protestants. In 1550 Joan of Kent was burnt for denying that Christ partook of the real body and flesh of the Virgin because of her sinful nature. Treatises in which the heresy is denounced include Bishop Hooper's *A Lesson of the Incarnation of Christe that he toke his humanitie in and oute of the Blessed Virgine*, STC 13760–3 (printed three times in 1549); J. Standish, *A lytle treatise . . . against the protestacion of R. Barnes* (ex aed. E. Pykerynge viduae R. Redmani, 1540), sigs A3ᵛ–A6ᵛ; STC 23210; M. Coverdale, *A confutacion of that treatise, which one J. Standish made agaynst the protestacion of D. Barnes in . . . 1540* [Zurich, C. Froschauer, 1541?], sigs C5ᵛ–D1ᵛ, STC 5888; Roger Hutchinson's defence of the doctrine of the trinity in *The Image of God*, XXV of 1550 (*The Works of R. Hutchinson*, ed. J. Bruce, PS (Cambridge, 1842), pp. 145–68); J. Calvin, *A Short Instruction*, sigs F8–G7ᵛ; William Turner's *A Preseruatiue or triacle agaynst the poyson of Pelagius, lately renued . . . by the furious secte of the Annabaptistes* [S. Mierdman] (f. A. Hester, 1551), STC 24368, his reply to the Anabaptist Robert Cooche. It was disputed at Worcester in 1550 and denied there again in 1552 (*Responsio . . . Henricii Ioliffi & Roberti Ionson . . .*, sigs B5–K7). The doctrine of the Incarnation was reaffirmed in the Forty Two Articles and in Bishop Bonner's visitation articles of 1554; see Hardwick, *Articles*, pp. 90–91, 99, 278; Frere and Kennedy, pp. 338, 349; Horst, *Radical Brethren*, pp. 82, 100–111, 115–7, 138, 171–3; Williams, *Radical Reformation*, pp. 778–80.

We perceiue . . . Incarnation A reference to Augustine's 'Sermo de Symbolo', II (*PL* 40, 1191); cf. Ps. 21:7; see *Sermons*, pp. 173, 214.

wyth Modestye . . . fear I Pet. 3:15.

Conscientiam . . . grace An exposition of I Pet. 3:16.

Melius est enim . . . doinge I Pet. 3:17.

which once died . . . spirit I Pet. 3:18.

And they . . . saluation A reference to Luke 23:42–3.

These bee . . . euerlastynge A reference to Luke 23:39.

The newe . . . spirite I Pet. 3:18; Erasmus, *NT*, ed. cit. fo. 355.

In quo . . . pryson I Pet. 3:19–20 with reference to Gen. 6–8; the interpretation that

Christ preached in spirit to all souls who were disobedient in Noah's time except the eight who were saved comes from Hugh of St Cher, *TB* VII, *ed. cit.* sig. K1ᵛ. For a summary of interpretations and discussion of these texts see Selwyn, *St Peter*, pp. 316–62.

The workes . . . people See *Glo. Ord.* on I Pet. 3:19–20 in *TB cum Glo. Ord. ed. cit.* VI, sig. 213. The standard allegorical explanation from Augustine and Aquinas which has now been dismissed; *viz.* that Christ was in Noah when Noah preached repentance to the wicked generation of his time; that the spirits were then in the prison of sin, or are now in the prison of Hades, but were then alive. See Bigg, *Epistles*, p. 162; Selwyn, *St Peter*, *loc. cit.*; Michaels, *I Peter*, pp. 210–11.

Per communicationem idiomatum Lat. 'Communication of the properties'; i.e. the doctrine that the concrete properties of the human and Divine natures in Christ are mutually predicated because of their union in the person of the Saviour; see Aquinas, *ST* 3a. 16, 4 and 5 (*ed. cit.* L, 17–23); ODCC s.v. 'Communicatio Idiomatum'.

And he preached . . . them An exposition of I Pet. 3:19–20.

Funes peccatorum . . . aboute Ps. 118:61.

Pro. v . . . knit Prov. 5:23.

Omnis caro . . . viciously Gen. 6:12; Vg. 'omnis quippe caro . . .'.

But . . . soules Edgeworth rejects the previous moral or allegorical interpretation of I Pet. 3:19–20 in favour of the literal one, that the spirits are those who had disregarded Noah's exhortation but repented before their deaths and were saved. See Bigg, *Epistles*, pp. 162–3; Beare, *First Epistle*, p. 172; Selwyn, *St Peter*, p. 353; Michaels, *I Peter*, pp. 206–9; *Sermons*, p. 175.

thei were staied . . . hel Hades, Christ's place of preaching according to one traditional view, is often thought of as a temporary abode of spirits awaiting a final judgement, (Selwyn, *St. Peter*, p. 200, 319). See the discussion in *Sermons*, pp. 130, 175 on the place to which the souls in a state of grace go.

Abrahams bosome . . . payne I.e. the Limbo of the Patriarchs where they awaited the happiness of heaven; see ODCC. s.v. 'Limbo'; above, p. 381.

Pro. xiii . . . minde Prov. 13:12.

To . . . resurrection In this interpretation of I
Pet. 3:19, widely accepted today, the souls that
Christ preached to are the dead of Noah's
time; 'prison' (Purgatory or Hades) is their
temporary abode. The passage, in locating the
event after Christ's crucifixion and before his
resurrection, asserts a special form of the
Descensus ad Infernos, the Harrowing of Hell;
see Bigg, *Epistles*, pp. 162–3; Selwyn, *St Peter*,
pp. 316–17; 319–20, 327–62.

Ego si exaltatus . . . me John 12:32.

Eccle. xxiiii . . . God Ecclus. 24:45.

Saint Augustine . . . hell Edgeworth was either
using an edition which follows a different
numbering from Migne's or he refers to a
pseudo-Augustinian sermon.

In like fourme . . . God I Pet. 3:21; St Peter
interprets the Flood as a type of Christian
baptism: the water of the flood carried the ark
to safety just as the water of baptism carries
the Christian; see Selwyn, *St Peter*, pp. 202–5,
328–36; Michaels, *I Peter*, pp. 213–18.

tract. lxxx . . . beleued Augustine on John
15:3, 'Tractatus CXXIV in Ioannis Evangelium', LXXX (*PL* 35, 1840).

Act. xv . . . fayth Acts 15:9.

they may purge . . . faith See the expositions
of baptism, *Sermons*, pp. 207, 255–7.

Conscientie bone . . . God I Pet. 3:21.

Eph. v . . . lyfe Eph. 5:25–26. Vg. 'mundans
lavacro . . .'.

This . . . water Allegorical interpretations of
the water of the Flood as a type of the sacrament of baptism, and Noah's Ark and those
who were saved as a type of the Christian
church were commonplace; see Jerome (*PL*
22, 748, 1046, 1115); *Glo. Ord.* on Gen. 6:
9–12; 7:10–14 (*PL* 113, 105, 107); *Glo. Interlinearis in TB cum glo. ord. ed. cit.* I, fo. 150ᵛ;
Hugh of St Cher, *TB, ed. cit.* I, sig. c1ᵛ; More,
Confutation (*CW*8, 213). The phrase,
'catholike churche', is commonplace in the
formularies.

depositio sordium . . . God An exposition of I
Pet. 3:21–22.

swalowynge vp . . . life A reference to I Cor.
15:24.

so Christe made . . . burst A reference to Heb.
2:14.

He begilinge . . . him A reference to Rom.
5:12.

and had subiect . . . vertues I Pet. 3:22.

S. Dionise . . . speake The authenticity of the
corpus of theological writings attributed to
Dionysius the Pseudo-Areopagite (c.500) was
contested in the sixteenth century. Edge-
worth, like other Catholic scholars such as
Robert Bellarmine and C. Baronius, stresses
Dionysius's association with St Paul to empha-
sise their apostolic authority. See *ODCC* s.v.
'Dionysius' (6); J.H. Lupton's introduction to
Ioannes Coletus super Opera Dionysii (London,
1869, repr., New Jersey, 1966), pp. xxxii–xliv;
Pelikan, *Church and Dogma*, pp. 310–11.

The fyrste . . . ix. A reference to Dionysius,
De Coelestia Hierarchia VI–IX (*PG* 3, 199–
272).

S. Gregory . . . Euangelia St Gregory on Luke
15:1–10; 'Hom. in Evangelia', II (*PL* 76,
1249–55). Gregory originally established the
doctrinal authority of the Pseudo-Dionysian
writings in the West.

Saint Peter . . . virtutes A reference to I Pet.
3:22.

Omnia subiecisti . . . eius Ps. 8:8.

phil . . . infernorum Phil. 2:9–10. Vg. 'donavit
illi'.

The .xiiii. treatise or sermon.
The fourth Chapiter.

Christo igitur . . . &c I Pet. 4:1.

The blessed Apostle . . . death A reference to I
Pet. 1:3; see *Sermons*, p. 205.

our regeneration . . . euerlastynge A reference
to the exposition of I Pet. 3:18–21, *Sermons*, p.
295.

CHRISTO passo . . . remembraunce I Pet.
4:1.

Saynt Peter . . . passion On the audience of
the Epistle see above, p. 408; on the Christian
duty of *imitatio Christi* enjoined in 1 Pet. 4:1,
see Selwyn, *St. Peter*, pp. 209–10.

CHRISTE . . . dronke A reference to Matt.
4:2; Luke 4:1–2.

Horace sayth . . . vttermooste Horace, Epist. I,
i, l. 32, *ed. cit.* p. 252.

takinge suche meate . . . you The custom of
fasting a full forty days in Lent was not observed in the Latin Church until the seventh
century. By the thirteenth century it had
become customary to put vespers forward to

midday on fast days; and by the fifteenth century even the devout followed the practice of eating at noon. See *ODCC* s.v. 'Lent'; *DTC* II, s.v. 'Carême'; *Sermons*, pp. 128, 137, 189, 288–9, 333 for other criticisms of breaches in observing the fast.

from poste to pyller Proverbial; see *ODEP* s.v. 'Pillar'.

saue that . . . it A reference to Matt. 27:34; Mk 15:23.

all this wynde . . . corne Proverbial; see Tilley, *Proverbs*, W410; Whiting, *Proverbs*, W288; *OED* s.v. 'Shake', v. 14.c.

When he . . . counsayle See the gospel accounts in Matt. 26:65–8; Mk 14:63–5; Luke 22:63–5; *Sermons*, pp. 238, 266.

Iosu. viii. . . . deuyll A reference to Josh. 8:18; the moral interpretations of Josh. 8:1 come from *Glo. Ord.* and N. de Lyra, *postilla* in *TB cum glo. ord. ed. cit.* II, sigs b4ᵛ; b5ᵛ, Hugh of St Cher, *TB, ed. cit.* I, sig. D5ᵛ.

fomes peccati . . . synne 'The tinder of sin'; i.e. an inordinate quality of the body of man which rebels against the dictates of reason. This punishment, imposed by God because of original sin, can only be mitigated, but not eradicated, by grace. See H.O. Oberman, 'A Nominalist Glossary' in *The Harvest of Medieval Theology* (Camb., Mass., 1963), p. 469.

Pone insideas . . . citie Josh. 8:4.

because that . . . man A reference to the fall of Solomon (III Kings 1:4–13) due to his foreign wives who encouraged him to worship alien Gods; see *Sermons*, p. 325.

When Iosue . . . captayne Josh. 8:18–23.

Iosue . . . Christe See *Glossa Interlinearis* on Josh. 2:1 in *TB cum glo. ord. ed. cit.* II, sig. a3ᵛ; Hugh of St Cher, *TB, ed. cit.* I, sig. D1ᵛ.

Iosue . . . passion See N. de Lyra, *postilla* on Josh. 8:18 in *TB cum glo. ord. ed. cit.* II, sig. b5.

Example . . . Dauid A reference to Saul's battle against the Amalekites after which, contrary to Samuel's instructions, he spared King Agag (I Kings 15:2–10); this led to his loss of the kingdom (I Kings 15:24–28) and the anointing of David as king (I Kings 16:13); see *Peake's Commentary*, pp. 325–6.

we can not be . . . God A reference to Gen. 5:24.

Sanctificate . . . Ioel .iii. Joel 3:9. Edgeworth perhaps also has in mind II Tim. 4:7.

Gala. vi . . . mundo Gal. 6:14.

Where . . . profytable On the occasion and purpose of St Paul's Epistle to the Galatians see *Sermons*, p. 200.

Ibant Apostoli . . . despytes Acts 5:41; Vg. 'Ibant gaudentes . . .'.

Inuicem . . . .owne St Ambrose on Gal. 6:14 (citing John 14:30) in 'Comm in Epist. ad Galatas' (*PL* 17, 372); Vg. 'venit enim princeps in me non habet quicquam'.

Shall be mortified . . . Chryste A reference to I Pet. 4:1 and Rom. 6:11.

Nam qui passus . . . synne I Pet. 4:1. Vg. 'Quia qui passus est carne . . .'.

Qui passus est . . . fleshe An exposition of I Pet. 4:1–3; Vg. 'voluntatem . . . consummandam qui . . .'.

Saint Peter . . . GOD On the audience of I Pet. 1:1–2 see *Sermons*, p. 195. For the view that I Pet. 4:3 refers to Gentile Christians who were pagans before their conversion, see Selwyn, *St Peter*, p. 210; Beare, *First Epistle*, p. 180; Michaels, *I Peter*, pp. xlv–vi, 230–1; above p. 408.

To theim he sayth . . . Desideriis An exposition of I Pet. 4:3.

Reprobum sensum . . . Rom. i. A reference to Rom. 1:28.

Rom. i . . . commessationibus I Pet. 4:3 with reference to Rom. 1:29.

Nolite inebriari . . . lecherye Eph. 5:18.

Valerius . . . lechery Valerius Maximus, *Facta et Dicta Memorabilia* II, 1, 5 (*ed. cit.* pp. 59–60).

Terence . . . colde Proverbial. See Erasmus, *Adagia* II, iii, 97, *ed. cit.* fos 580–1; Vergil, *Adagia* no. 132, *ed. cit.* fo. 61; Taverner, *Prouerbes, ed. cit.* sigs E4ʳ⁻ᵛ; cf. the version in Jerome's Epist. 54: 'Sine Cerere et libero friget Venus' (*PL* 22, 554). See *Sermons*, p. 345.

Sedit populus . . . Idolatrye Ex. 32:6.

Lactancius . . . ducerent Lactantius, *Div. Inst.* I, 21 (*PL* 6, 237); see *Sermons*, p. 345.

For . . . ymage Matt. 22:19–20; cf. *Sermons*, pp. 143–4.

An Image . . . power Ibid.; also p. 170; the attack on images resumed in 1547. On 17 November 1547 Bishop Barlow of St David's exhibited an image of the Blessed Virgin Mary at Paul's Cross; and 'every precher preched in

their sermons agayne alle images' (*Grey Friars'
Chronicle*, p. 55); see Wriothesley, *Chronicle*,
II, 1; MacLure, *Paul's Cross Sermons*, pp. 40–
41.

Qui . . . gods Martial, *Epigrams* VIII, 24, ll.
5–6; see the translation by W.C.A. Ker, 2 vols
(London, 1920), II, 18–19.

Idolorum seruitus . . . Idolatry Gal. 5:20.

In quo . . . confusionem I Pet. 4:4. Vg. 'in quo
peregrinatur'.

.i. Reg. x . . . man I Kings 10:1–6.

And Saul . . . come I Kings 10:10.

Quenam res . . . Prophetes I Kings 10:11. A
predating of the first use of 'Is Saul also among
the prophets?' (1815) cited in *ODEP* s.v.
'Saul'. See Erasmus, *Adagia* II, i, 64, *ed. cit.* fo.
479; Vergil, *Adagia* no. 375, *ed. cit.* fo. 324.

Filii autem Belial . . . did I Kings 10:27. The
frenzied behaviour of Saul and the prophets
made them appear as madmen.

sette not a strawe by you Proverbial; see *ODEP*
s.v. 'Straw'.

They that yet styll . . . horeson A paraphrase of
I Pet. 4:3–4.

Qui reddent . . . deade I Pet. 4:5.

Sainte Paule . . . saluation A reference to
Rom. 5:3–4.

The fifteenth treatice or Sermon.

Viuant autem . . . in spiritu I Pet. 4:6.

Propter hoc . . . spirite An exposition of I Pet.
4:6.

Omnium autem . . . hande I Pet. 4:7; cf. I Pet.
4:5.

for as Christe . . . is A reference to Matt.
24:36.

Eccle. xxx . . . adducit Ecclus. 30:26; Vg. 'ante
tempus . . . cogitatus'.

Vigilia honestatis . . . slepe Ecclus 31:1.

Pro. xxv . . . after Prov. 25:20.

Cutis mea aruit . . . together Job 7:5.

gowts, & runninge legges 'Attacks of gout and
legs with pains spreading over them'; see *OED*
s.v. 'Running', ppl. adj. II, 6.b. For other
homiletic examples of the theme of man's infirmities see Owst, *LPME*, pp. 527–33;
Blench, pp. 231–6.

virtus in infirmitate . . . mightye An exposition
of II Cor. 12:9–10.

Ambrosius . . . hand Ambrose on II Cor.
12:10, 'Comm. in Epist. ad Corin. Sec.' (*PL*
17, 331).

S. Aug. i. ci. dei . . . all Augustine, *De Civitate Dei*, I, 8 (*PL* 41, 20–21); the following
exposition is largely a translation of this text.

de disciplina . . . well Augustine, *De Disciplina
Christiana* (*PL* 40, 676).

preciosa est . . . lord Ps. 115:15. Vg. 'pretiosa
in conspectu Domini . . .'.

The riche . . . hym The parable of Dives and
Lazarus, Luke 16:19–31.

yet it was . . . death A reference to Heb. 2:4.

consideringe that . . . hande I Pet. 4:7.

Estote itaque prudentes . . . praiers I Pet. 4:7.

These wordes . . . Whitsunday I.e. 'Dominica
infra octavas ascensionis'. The full *lectio* for
the week before Pentecost is I Pet. 4:7–11; see
Wickham Legg, *Sarum Missal*, p. 157. This sermon was preached between 25 March and 24
June; see above, p. 406.

omnia naturaliter . . . theym A common sentiment in Aristotle; see Nich. Eth. VI, 8, 4 (*ed.
cit.* p. 349).

A prouision . . . past The sentiment originates with Aristotle; see Nich. Eth. VI, 2, 6 (*ed.
cit.* p. 331); it is used by Aquinas in ST 1a2ae.
49, 1 (*ed. cit.* XXXVI, 61); and by Shakespeare in *Romeo and Juliet*, Act III, Sc. v, l. 52.
See R.W. Dent, *Shakespeare's Proverbial Language, An Index* (Los Angeles, 1981), R73.

recta ratio . . . bad Aristotle, Nich. Eth. VI, 5,
44, *ed. cit.* p. 337.

Contra bonum malum . . . vertue Ecclus.
33:15 since 'the wise man' usually refers to the
Book of Sirach; Vg. 'Contra malum bonum est
et contra mortem vita'. Cf. Is. 5:20; 'vae qui
dicitis malum bonum et bonum malum' (cited
by Vergil in *Adagia* no. 354, *ed. cit.* fo. 315).

Ro. viij . . . God Rom. 8:6–7; cf. *Sermons*,
p. 118.

Iacob .iij . . . prouision A reference to Jas.
3:15; see the exposition of earthly prudence,
Sermons, p. 117.

as it were Moles . . . God See *ibid.* for this
exemplum of the blind mole as an image of
the rich man's folly.

Nemo . . . ryches cf. Matt. 6:24 which the

text is closest to; but the context suggests Luke 16:13. Proverbial; see *ODEP* s.v. 'No man'.

ve vobis . . . riches Luke 6:24; see the exposition, *Sermons*, p. 117.

Beastlye wisedome . . . same A reference to Jas. 3:15.

Ve vobis . . . come Luke 6:25.

Esau . . . it Gen. 25:29–34; Luke 15:11–32; on 'a messe of potage' see *Sermons*, p. 118.

hop in a cutted cote 'Go about in a short coat'; possibly semi-proverbial; e.g. Udall, *Apophthegmes, ed. cit.* fo. 169ᵛ, refers to a short cape as 'this cutted facion'. Short coats, or gowns which revealed the shape of the male body, were considered a sign of affectation and were the subject of legislation which attempted to regulate apparel. But the sense here is obscure. Edgeworth often uses 'hop' pejoratively to refer to self-delusion and the phrase could mean 'feigning an appearance beyond one's means' (i.e. putting on airs and graces); but 'cutted' in this context could also be understood as 'ragged' (i.e. descending into poverty). See Scattergood, 'Fashion and Morality', pp. 255–72 and his *Politics and Poetry in the Fifteenth Century* (London, 1971), pp. 342–8, on the popular genre of poems against the 'gallants'.

proficientes . . . worsse A reference to II Tim. 3:13.

Diuelishe wisedome . . . power A reference to Jas. 3:15.

Esay. xiiii . . . lake Is. 14:15; Vg. 'ad infernum detraheris'.

.i. Cor. i . . . thinge An exposition of I Cor. 1:19–20.

Ro. viij . . . peace Rom. 8:6.

Iob .xxviij . . . pleasure Job 28:12–13.

pro nihil habuerunt . . . them Ps. 105:24.

Prouer. v . . . synnes Prov. 5:22; Vg. 'suorum constringitur'.

Sapi. i . . . theym Sap. 1:13 and 16; Vg. 'autem manibus et verbis acciesserunt.'

our fyrst parentes . . . tempest A reference to man's first disobedience (Gen. 3:19); Noah's flood (Gen. 7:10–24); and the destruction of the five cities of the plain (Gen. 19:24–25).

Thys . . . warynesse Aquinas, *ST* 2a2ae. 49, 6–8 (*ed. cit.* XXXVI, 75–81).

Prouer. xxx . . . be Prov. 30:24.

Iob .xii . . . others Job 12:7–8.

formice populus . . . winter Prov. 30:25; see Trevisa, *Properties of things*, XVIII, 53, *ed. cit.* II, 1203: 'The ampte hatte formica . . . þey maken prouysioun and gaderen stoore aʒeins tyme that comeþ'; cf. the moral interpretation of the *Gesta Romanorum* in which the ant, who harbours wealth like the rich man, is destroyed by kings and lords; see Herrtage, *English Versions of the* Gesta Romanorum, LIII, p. 372.

Prou. vi . . . witte Prov. 6:6.

Lepusculus . . . Mus Prov. 30:26; see *Glo. Ord.* in *TB cum glo. ord.* III, *ed. cit.* sig. 2c2ᵛ; *PL* 113, 1111; Hugh of St Cher, *TB, ed. cit.* III, sig. K2.

psalm .Ciii . . . beast Ps. 103:18. In the Septuagint version *eriniciis* occurs; in the Hebrew version *ericiis. Mus* occurs in Lev. 11:29; Is. 66:17.

It is . . . translacion See *Glo. Ord.*; Hugh of St Cher, *TB, loc. cit.* on the different meanings of Heb. *Saphan,* the common ancestor of the different Latin forms. By 'the common translacion' Edgeworth here refers to the Vulgate.

signifieth the weake . . . forme See *Glo. Ord.* in *TB cum glo. ord.* III and *PL, loc. cit.*

Regem Locusta . . . suas Prov. 30:27; Vg. om. 'suas'.

Locusta . . . compulsion See Trevisa, *Properties of things*, XII, 25 *ed. cit.* I, 633: 'Locusta . . . hath þat name *locusta* for he haþ longe legges . . . And þise wormes . . . haþ no kyng noþeles he passiþ forþ ordynatly in companyes'. Locusts were originally found in the grasslands throughout Africa and most of Eurasia; desert locusts inhabit grasslands from Africa to the Punjab; see *Enc. Brit.* VI, s.v. 'Locust'.

Terribilis . . . araye Can. 6:3.

Stellio manibus . . . palace An exposition of Prov. 30:28.

All such . . . man This traditional devotional image appears in *Ancrene Wisse* IV, where it illustrates the illusory nature of joys and fears; see *Ancrene Wisse*, ed. J.R.R. Tolkien, EETS, 249 (London, 1962), p. 124.

.ii. Reg. xx . . . died II Kings 20:9–10; see the exposition, *Sermons*, pp. 230, 368.

Estote . . . serpentes Matt. 10:16; Vg. 'Estote ergo'; see Vergil, *Adagia* no. 40, *ed. cit.* fo. 162.

Rom. viii . . . Iesu Rom. 8:35 and 38–9.

the strait waye . . . penaunce See Hugh of St Cher, *TB, ed. cit.* VI, sig. f8 on Matt. 10:16.

Eph. iiii . . . liuinge Eph. 4:23; Vg. 'deponere vos . . .'.

the serpent . . . dayly The snake or serpent is traditionally a figure for the sinner's refusal to listen to the preacher's exhortations; here its property of blocking its ears exemplifies ignoring temptations; see Owst, *LPME*, p. 198.

Eccle. vii . . . god Ecclus. 7:40; Vg. 'novissima tua . . .'.

The .xvi. treatise or sermon.

Et vigilate . . . doinges I Pet. 4:7; on this text see *Sermons*, p. 308 ff.

when holye Churche . . . Masse A reference to I Pet. 4:7–11; see *Sermons*, p. 308.

at this holye time . . . comming This sermon was preached between on the Sunday before Pentecost; i.e. between 25 March and 24 June; see above, p. 406.

perseuerantes . . . interruption Acts 1:14.

Spiritus discipline . . . dissembler Sap. 1:5.

Ante omnia . . . synnes I Pet. 4:8.

Iaco. v . . . synnes Jas. 5:20.

Psalm. xxxi . . . couered Ps. 31:1.

Auerte faciem . . . sinnes Ps. 50:11.

Christe putteth . . . condempned Luke 18:10–14.

Quoniam tacui . . . longe Ps. 31:3.

drinkinge men vnder the borde Proverbial; see Tilley, *Proverbs*, B487.

Charitas enim . . . proude A reference to I Cor. 13:4.

Beatus enim cui . . . synnes Ps. 31:2; Vg. 'Beatus vir cui . . .'.

charitie . . . garment A reference to I Pet. 4:8; see also Prov. 10:12.

i. Ioh. iii . . . stiffed I John 3:14.

maister . . . liue Luke 10:25–28.

Second, charitie . . . aduersitie A reference to I Pet. 4:8.

Diligentibus deum . . . good Rom. 8:28.

Dominus dedit . . . benedictum The following is an exposition of Job 1:21.

Ibant gaudentes . . . sake Acts 5:41.

Apo. xvi . . . filthines Rev. 16:15.

Hester .iiii . . . rayment Esth. 4:2.

Assuerus . . . beatitude N. de Lyra, *postilla* on Esth. 1:1 in *TB cum glo. ord. ed. cit.* II, sig. T5 and *Glo. Ord.* (*PL* 113, 740); see *Sermons*, pp. 270–1.

Can, viii . . . death Can. 8:6; Vg. 'fortis est ut mors dilectio'.

Mihi mundus . . . worlde Gal. 6:14.

Hospitales inuicem . . . grudginge I Pet. 4:9.

Quod confessi sunt . . . then An exposition of Heb. 11:13–16; Vg. '& confitentes quia peregrini & hospites sunt super terram qui enim haec dicunt significant se patriam inquirere'.

Dum enim domi . . . God II Cor. 5:6; Vg. 'dum sumus in corpore . . .'.

lyke straungers . . . men A reference to I Pet. 2:11.

liberales . . . beloued A familiar sentiment in Aristotle. See *Nich. Eth.* IV, 1, 11 (*ed. cit.* p. 191); *Rhetorica* II, 4, 8–9; see *The Art of Rhetoric*, ed. and tr. J.H. Freese (London, 1926), p. 195.

Venite benedicti . . . lodgynge Matt. 25:34–35.

Hospitalitatem . . . men Heb. 13:2; Vg. 'latuerunt quidam'.

Abraham . . . heyre A reference to Gen. 18:1–15.

Loth in . . . Sodome A reference to Gen. 19:1–15; see Origen, 'In Genesim Homiliae V' (*PG* 12, 188–9).

Hospitem velut hostem . . . enemy Proverbial; see *Thesaurus linguae latinae*, ed. *auctoritates consilio academiarum quinque germanicarum* (Teubner, Leipzig, 1900–), VI³, p. 3027, ll. 33–4.

.ii. offi . . . hospitalitie Cicero, *De Officiis* II, 18, 64, *ed. cit.* pp. 236–9.

S. Ambrose . . . liberalitie Ambrose on Luke 14:12–14. 'Expositio Evang. sec. Lucam X libris', VII (*PL* 15, 1752).

Cum facis prandium . . . men Luke 14:12–14. Vg. 'fratres tuos . . . ne forte te et ipsi reinvitent'.

.iii. Reg. xvii . . . earth III Kings 17:10–14.

For in dede this . . . people A reference to III Kings 17:1–7. Ahab, King of Israel (BC 875–c.853) married Jezabel, daughter of King

Ethbaal, previously high priest of the Tyrian Baal. She instigated a persecution of the followers of Jehovah during which Elijah emerged as champion of Jehovah. See *DB* I, s.v. 'Ahab'; II, s.v. 'Elijah'; *Sermons*, pp. 274, 356.

this meale . . . church See *Glo. Ord.* in *TB cum Glo. ord. ed. cit.* II, sig. x2ᵛ; *PL* 113, 606. The second part of this sentence, which lacks a main clause, has been emended by the addition of the finite verb 'signified'.

the sayde two trees . . . crosse See Hugh of St Cher on III Kings 17:12; TB, *ed. cit.* I, sig. S6ᵛ. This interpretation also occurs in *Ancrene Wisse*; see *ed. cit.* p. 205.

As oft as you shall eate . . . come I Cor. 11:26.

This was signified . . . daye A reference to III Kings 17:14; see Hugh of St Cher, *TB, ed. cit.* I, sig. S6ᵛ.

And although . . . bloud See I Cor. 11:26; this exposition of the Eucharist according to the doctrine of Transubstantiation denies the Lutheran doctrine of consubstantiation; i.e. that after the consecration both the bread and wine and the Body and Blood of Christ coexist. See *Sermons*, pp. 142, 240, 290, 365; *ODCC* s.v. 'Eucharist'; 'Consubstantiation'.

Hec dicit . . . Israell III Kings 17:14. Vg. 'Haec autem . . .'.

Donec veniat . . . vs I Cor. 11:26.

when we shall see . . . likenesse A reference to I Cor. 13:12.

In processe . . . agayne III Kings 17:17–22.

iiii. Reg. iiii. The following account is taken from IV Kings 4:8–37.

Non erat vox . . . healpe IV Kings 4:31.

Ioh. xi . . . buried John 11:11–14.

And it is writte . . . man See Caxton, *Golden Legend, ed. cit.* fo. 104.

Pro. xi . . . estate Prov. 11:24.

.ii. Co. ix . . . largely II Cor. 9:6. Vg. 'de benedictionibus et . . .'.

Date & dabitur . . . you Luke 6:38.

And the blessed . . . Gen. xviii. Gen. 18:2–8.

And Christes feastes . . . more Probably a reference to the Passover, the feast of unleavened bread; see Matt. 26:17; Mk 14:1; Luke 22:1.

Chrisostome . . . Rom. xvi Probably a reference to the second of Chrysostom's two

homilies 'In illud Salutate Priscillam et Aquilam' (*PG* 51, 187–208, esp. 195–6); see Acts 18:2–3; Rom. 16:3–4; *Sermons*, p. 140.

Et qui . . . many Proverbial. See Erasmus, *Adagia* II, iii, 61, *ed. cit.* fo. 565; cited as first use in *ODEP* s.v. 'Master'.

.i. Macha. i . . . nought The following account comes from I Macc. 1:30–36 (citing 1:11 & 31). On Antiochus Epiphanes ('illustrious'), king of Syria from 175 BC who attempted to destroy Judaism and attacked Jerusalem in 170 BC see *ODCC* s.v. 'Antiochus Epiphanes'; *Sermons*, pp. 133–5.

Factum hoc . . . deuotion I Macc. 1:38. Vg. 'Et factum est hoc . . .'.

Parcens ille . . . ii. re. xii. II Kings 12:1–4 citing 12:4; Vg. 'praeparavit cibos homini qui . . .'.

All this was said . . . lust A reference to II Kings 11:2–5.

peccaui domino . . . it II Kings 12:13; Vg. 'Dominus quoque transtulit . . .'.

take repentance . . . penance Tyndale's use of 'repentance' for 'penance' was another word to which More objected (*Dialogue CW* 6, 290; *Confutation, CW* 8 204–5); see *Sermons*, pp. 141, 207, 240.

.iii. reg. xi . . . was III Kings 11:4; see *Sermons*, pp. 298–9.

Hospes eram . . . in Matt. 25:35.

Sine murmuratione . . . grudgynge I Pet. 4:9.

The murmurer . . . little On the properties of the hog see Trevisa, *Properties of things*, XVIII, 87, *ed. cit.* II, 1237–9; the sow also appears as an emblem of sloth in Dunbar's 'Dance of the Sevin Deidly Synnis'; see *The Poems of William Dunbar*, ed. W. Mackay MacKenzie (Edinburgh, 1932), pp. 121–2.

Num. xi . . . labours Num. 11:1.

.ii Co. viii . . . beare II Cor. 8:12. Vg. om. 'id'.

Rom. xii . . . hart Rom. 12:8. Vg. 'Qui miseretur . . .'.

.ij. Corin. ix . . . gyuer II Cor. 9:7.

venite benedicti . . . heauen Matt. 25:34.

The .xvii. treatise or sermon.

Vnusquisque sicut . . . dei I Pet. 4:10; Vg. '. . . gratiam in alterutrum . . .'.

diuisiones . . . i. Cor. xij I Cor. 12:5 with a reference to 12:12.

Ecclesiasticus .xvij . . . other Ecclus. 17:12.

And for thys cause . . . housholde I Pet. 4:10.

To som he giueth . . . occupiyng A reference to I Cor. 12:8–10; see *Sermons*, pp. 166, 191.

all men like . . . God I Pet. 4:10.

Gratia gratis data . . . people I.e. exceptional grace or grace freely given for the benefit of others and for the church; see More's defence of the Pauline divisions in *Confutation* (CW 8, 205–6); and the exposition by Aquinas in ST 1a2ae. 111, 5 and 6 (*ed. cit.* XXX, 134–43); DTC VI, s.v. 'Grace', col. 1558.

gratia gratum faciens . . . charitie I.e. sanctifying or justifying grace given in the sacraments of baptism and penance, by which the sinner is transposed into a state of grace and inclined to good works; cf. More, *Confutation, loc. cit.*

.i. Cor. xii . . . others I Cor. 12:8.

Saynt Peter saith . . . man A paraphrase of I Pet. 4:11.

the psalme .xxxvi . . . mayny Ps. 36:21.

Aug . . . beast Augustine on Ps. 36:21; 'Comm. in Psalmos' (*PL* 36, 271) of which the following is largely a paraphrase.

Quicquid potest . . . idlenes Eccles. 9:10; Vg. 'quodcumque . . . facere instanter'. 'Nihil est enim' summarises the omitted 'nec opus, nec ratio, nec scientia, nec sapientia'.

Luke .xij . . . possession Luke 12:15.

For . . . euerlasting Perhaps a reference to Augustine, *De Doctrina Christiana* (*PL* 40, 676); see *Sermons*, p. 307.

Nudus egressus sum . . . agayne Job 1:21.

Cauete . . . godwarde The parable of the barns, Luke 12:15–21; citing Luke 12:15 and 21.

Math. xxv The parable of the talents; Matt. 25:14–30.

Math. xxiiij . . . hell Matt. 24:48–51. Vg. 'ebriis'.

Luc, xij . . . maides Luke 12:45.

In the saide . . . cold A reference to Matt. 25:30.

Iustus . . . lendeth Ps. 36:21.

Holye Iob . . . pauperum Job 29:15–16.

Charissimi nolite . . . you I Pet. 4:12.

wher afore . . . them A reference to I Pet. 4:8–10 and *Sermons*, pp. 325–6.

Nolite peregrinari . . . text I Pet. 4:12; using the Vg. and Erasmus' NT, *ed. cit.* fo. 355.

but consider . . . iudgement A reference to I Pet. 1:6–7.

Our sauiour . . . fleshe A reference to I Pet. 4:1. The depiction of Christ militant is familiar in medieval devotional writings; see 'A Treatise of Gostly Battle' in Horstman, *Yorkshire Writers* II, 421–36.

And Sainte Paule . . . vs A reference to Rom. 6:12.

if we be felowes . . . ij. Cor. i. II Cor. 1:5.

Sicut communicantes . . . glory I Pet. 4:13. Vg. 'sed communicantes . . .'.

Collossi. i . . . fleshe Col. 1:24. St Paul wrote the Epistle to the Colossians when he was in prison either in Rome or Ephesus; see ODCC s.v. 'Colossians, Epistle to the'.

Saule, Saule . . . mee Acts 9:4.

Si exprobramini . . . suffered I Pet. 4:14.

A flagello lingue . . . Iob. v. Job 5:21.

Domine libera . . . speaking Ps. 119:2.

called Christen . . . Galileans The apostles are called Galileans in Acts 2:7. The name 'Christian' is first applied to Christ's followers by outsiders in 40–44 AD (Acts 11:26) and it became the official Roman designation of members of the Church during times of persecution (see I Pet. 4:16). But it was long avoided by Christian writers because of its pagan origin. See ODCC s.v. 'Christian'; Michaels, *I Peter*, pp. lxiv–v.

Christ . . . Iesus In Matt. 26:69; Mk 14:70 and Luke 22:59 Peter is asked to acknowledge Christ as a Galilean; cf. Luke 23:6.

Iulianus Apostata . . . payne This version of the death of Julian the Apostate comes from the *Tripartita Historia* (*PL* 69, 1062–4) and was known in the middle ages through the *Legenda Aurea*; see Caxton, *Golden Legend*, *ed. cit.* fo. 86ᵛ.

As if you absteyne . . . time See *Sermons*, p. 189 on the treatment of the Lenten fast as a 'mere positive law'; on the Wednesday and Friday fasts in Lent see ODCC s.v. 'Friday' and 'Wednesday'; *Sermons*, pp. 187, 298.

in this holy weke . . . names The Rogation days were prescribed days of prayer and fasting on which intercession was made for the harvest. 'The Minor Rogations' were kept on the Monday, Tuesday and Wednesday before Ascension Day (observed on the fifth Thursday; i.e. the fortieth day after Easter). The 'Major Rogation' on 25 April took the form of a procession through the crops. The observances were abolished by a proclamation of 31 July 1547. This comment provides a *terminus a quo* of Lent 1548 for this sermon; it was probably preached between 25 March and 24 June; see Hughes and Larkin, I, 287; *LP* XXI, ii, 710; above pp. 401, 406.

beatinge the bulkes . . . heeles 'Knocking their heels against the stalls'; cited in *ODEP* s.v. 'Beat' as first use of 'To no more purpose than to beat your heels against the ground'.

if you be vmbrayded . . . you I Pet. 4:14.

Nam honor est praemium . . . vertue Proverbial; see *ODEP* s.v. 'Honour'.

Gloria nostra haec . . . Paule II Cor. 1:12.

Nemo autem vestrum . . . them I Pet. 4:15. Vg. 'autem enim . . . quasi homicidia'.

Si autem . . . God An exposition of I Pet. 4:16–17.

Iob .v . . . God Job 5:17; Vg. 'a Deo'.

Now is the time . . . impouerishing A paraphrase of I Pet. 4:17.

Ezechiell the prophet . . . church Ezech. 9:2–6 citing 9:6. The punishment was Yahweh's vengeance for the ritual sin of sun worship in Jerusalem in c.591 BC.

The day of iudgemente . . . pastime The traditional homiletic theme here becomes a complaint against contemporary conditions: the appropriation of church wealth which followed the Chantries Act of 1547; the persecution of Catholic priests and their rituals which preceded the 1549 BCP; the plague which visited London in the autumn of 1548; see *Sermons*, p. 187.

Nolite tangere . . . God Ps. 104:15; I Par. 16:22.

Si autem primum . . . dei I Pet. 4:17; Vg. 'Dei evangelio'.

Et si iustus vix . . . appeare I Pet. 4:18. Vg. 'salvatur . . . parebit'.

Quod . . . do Cited in *ODEP* s.v. 'Almost' as first use of 'Almost was never hanged'.

Factus est omnium . . . al Jas. 2:10.

Actu. xiiii . . . heauen Acts 14:21.

vix saluabitur . . . do I Pet. 4:18.

Prou. xi . . . take Prov. 11:31.

Itaque & hi . . . God I Pet. 4:19.

Thei that so . . . deseruing An exposition of I Pet. 4:19.

And here . . . workes A reference to I Pet. 4:8.

The .xviii. treatise or sermon.
The fyfte Chapiter.

I haue absteined . . . lycence me Edgeworth was not licensed to preach under the ecclesiastical seal according to the list of July 1547 (*Calendar of State Papers Domestic, 1547–80*, ed. R. Lemon (London, 1856), p. 5). Preaching without a licence under pain of imprisonment was prohibited on 24 April and 23 September 1548 (Hughes and Larkin, I, 296, 313; Cardwell, *Doc. Ann.* I, nos X, XIII). Edgeworth may have been imprisoned following the previous sermon, preached c. Lent 1548, probably without a licence. This was the fate that befell conservative preachers in the South-West. See Whiting, *Blind Devotion*, pp. 242–3; *Sermons*, p. 95.

.viii. or .ix. yeares . . . preache If this sermon was preached c.1552–3, then this comment provides a *terminus a quo* of c.1544–5 for the first sermon on *I Peter*; see above, p. 406.

Seniores . . . i. Pet. v. I Pet. 5:1–2.

Because the blessed . . . men A reference to I Pet. 2:18; 3:17; 4:7–9.

launterns of lyghte On other uses of this phrase to refer to the clergy see More, *Confutation*, *CW8*, 18; Skelton, 'Collyn Clout', *Poems, ed. cit.* p. 257.

Nowe consequently . . . Capi. i. A reference to I Pet. 1:9.

Testis Christi passionum I Pet. 5:1.

Thoughe . . . bloude A reference to Luke 22:44.

pontifax anni illius John 18:13.

then to Pilate . . . death See Luke 23:7–11.

partlye to stoppe . . . emperoure John 19:12.

Peter . . . imprisonment For Peter's denial of Christ see Matt. 26:69–75; Mk 14:67–72; Luke 22:57–62; John 18:17; 25–27; on his preaching see Acts 2:14–36; his imprisonment, Acts 4:1–12; 12:1–11.

Qui et eius quae . . . come I Pet. 5:1.

S. Mathewe . . . xvii. cha. Matt. 17:1–3.

there be .iiii. dowres . . . permanentem See Aquinas, *ST* 3a. 54, 2–3 (*ed. cit.* LV, 18–31); the Latin comes from another, unidentified source. On the four endowments (*dotes*, or marriage portions) of the glorified body (from I Cor. 15:35) see *Sermons*, p. 180; above p. 401.

.i. Co. xv. The following is an exposition of I Cor. 15:42–44. Vg. 'surget corpus spirituale'; see *Sermons*, p. 180; above p. 401.

Bonum est . . . alone The following comes from Matt. 17:4–8, citing Matt. 17:4 & 5; Vg. 'complacui'.

S. Peter . . . elderman A reference to the controversial text I Pet. 5:1. Wycliffe had rendered *seniores* as 'eldren' in Deut. 19:12; as 'eldre men' in Acts 15:16; as 'senyours' in Rev. 7:11. Tyndale translated both *seniores* and *presbyteros* as 'elders'. More distinguished between them: *seniores* signified age or seniority; *presbyteros* (of which 'this word "preste" is ye proper englesh word') signified authority. He preferred to use 'elder' for *presbyteros*, although he considered that both translations undermined the priesthood. Erasmus in *Annotationes* (*ed. cit.* fo. 683) cites Jerome's alternative to *senior* (*PL* 22, 1193); see Erasmus, *NT*, *ed. cit.* fo. 356; Tyndale, *Answer*, pp. 16–7; More, *Dialogue*, *CW* 6, 286, 289–90; *Confutation*, *CW* 8, 182–9; *Sermons*, pp. 245, 351.

euerye olde man . . . priestes An echo of More's argument in *Confutation* (*CW*8, 187) in which he uses the example of aldermen to convey one sense of *seniores*. Cf this definition of the elected priesthood which does not distinguish between *senior* and *presbyteros*. Edgeworth accepts the Protestant Bibles' translation of Vg. *seniores* as 'elders'. The conservatives had considered this an 'objectionable' word in 1541 (*Concilia*, III, 861).

by the imposition . . . . do Edgeworth upholds More's defence of the putting on of hands by which a 'special gift of grace' is conferred (*Confutation*, *CW*8, 85, 192–3) against Tyndale's assertion that this is only a custom and an 'indifferent thing' (*Obedience*, p. 275). Cf the articles on orders in the *Bishops' Book* and the *King's Book* (*Formularies*, pp. 105, 277–8, 280) and the Anglican Ordinal of 1550. See Procter and Frere, *BCP*, pp. 656–73 for a comparison.

Luke .vi . . . traytoure Luke 6:12–16.

Sainte Ambrose . . . purpose The following exposition comes from Ambrose on Luke 12:16, 'Expositio Evang. Sec. Luc.', V (*PL* 15, 1649); on 'ignoraunte' followed by a dependent clause, see *OED* s.v. 'Ignorant', *adj.* 2.c.

Act. xiii . . . likewise Acts 13:2–3.

Act. xiiii . . . beleued Acts 14:21–23.

in the Primitiue . . . pray E.g. Acts 6:6, 13:3, texts cited by Aldrich, Bishop of Carlisle, in answering question ten of Cranmer's questionnaire on whether priests or bishops were first, and if priests were, whether they made bishops; see Pocock-Burnet, IV, 472–3; *Sermons*, pp. 249, 344.

imbring daies The Ember Days became the recognised times for holding ordinations; this tradition is preserved in the Anglican Ordinal. See *DTC* XIII, ii, s.v. 'Quatre-Temps'; Procter and Frere, *BCP*, pp. 332–3, 663; *Sermons*, p. 187; above p. 404.

i. Timo. v . . . sinnes I Tim. 5:22.

i. Ti. iiii . . . prelates I Tim. 4:14.

ii. Tim. i . . . hands II Tim. 1:6.

After that Paule . . . after A paraphrase of Acts 19:1–2 & 5.

Et cum impossuit . . . prophecied Acts 19:6.

Sicut . . . rule Tit. 1:5. The Epistle to Titus was written between Paul's two Roman imprisonments when Titus was his delegate in Crete.

Oportet Episcopum . . . esse Tit. 1:7.

I will prosecute . . . Timothe The First Epistle to Timothy instructed Timothy on controlling the church at Ephesus during Paul's absence. The Pastoral Epistles are often cited in expositions of the sacraments of orders. See the *King's Book* (*Formularies*, pp. 277–81) and *The Form of Ordering Priests* (Whitchurch, 1552) printed by Cardwell, *BCP*, pp. 409–10.

i. Io. i . . . vs I John 1:8.

Pro. xxiiii . . . daie Prov. 24:16.

Impij autem . . . damnation Prov. 24:16.

Oportet enim . . . criminall I Tim. 3:2.

in the apostles time . . . here See Edgeworth's answer to question ten of Cranmer's questionnaire: that Christ 'made his apostles priests and bishops all at once'; Pocock-Burnet, IV, 474; *Sermons*, p. 249.

S. Ierome . . . church Jerome, 'Epist. ad Evangelium' (PL 22, 1193). Cited by Edgeworth in answering question ten (Pocock-Burnet, IV, 474); and by Erasmus in Annotationes, ed. cit. fo. 683.

Episcopum . . . others See Jerome, 'Epist. ad Evangelium', loc. cit. Tyndale sometimes used 'overseer' as an alternative to 'bishop' (Obedience, pp. 229, 230). Episcopus was another of Gardiner's controversial words in 1541 (Concilia III, 861). But bishops are called 'superattendants or overseers' in the Bishops' Book; 'oversee' occurs in the King's Book; and 'overseer', signifying the office of a bishop, was generally accepted by the conservative party in 1540 (Pocock-Burnet, IV, 472, 476); it was upheld at the Council of Trent. 'Superintendents' occurs in Erasmus' paraphrase of I Pet. 5:1 (Paraphrase, ed. cit. sig. C1ᵛ); episcopi (Acts 20:28) is translated as 'overseers' in the Anglican Ordinal. See More, Confutation, CW 8, 187 and n.; Formularies, pp. 109, 287; Cardwell, BCP, pp. 408–9; H. Maynard Smith, Henry VIII and the Reformation (London, 1962), p. 324; Sermons, pp. 196, 267, 344 etc.

Euen like as . . . office Edgeworth appears to treat priests and bishops as equal by virtue of their duties, without explicitly denying their distinction of rank; cf. Formularies, pp. 105, 282; Sermons, pp. 248–9.

Quanquam secundum . . . priest Augustine, Epist. XIX in Liber Epistolae beati Augustini episcopi Hipponiensis ecclesiae (J. Petit, 1515), sig. C7.

i. Ti. iii . . . crime I Tim. 3:10.

De neophitis . . . conuerse I Tim. 3:6.

Non Iracundum . . . man Tit. 1:7.

Non vinolentum . . . wyne Tit. 1:7; I Tim. 3:3.

Nolite inebriari . . . luxuria Eph. 5:18; see Sermons, p. 301.

Sine Cerere . . . Venus On this proverb see above p. 433.

Capi. v . . . dronken Is. 5:22.Vg. 'et viri fortes'.

Cogitaui a vino . . . Wisedome Eccles. 2:3; Vg. 'animum meum'.

Dany. ii . . . sciences Dan. 1:8–20.

Non percussorem . . . manne Tit. 1:7; I Tim. 3:3.

Pascite . . . wynnynge I Pet. 5:2; cf. Tit. 1:7.

.iiij. Ethi . . . graues Aristotle, Nich. Eth. IV, 1, 36–43 (ed. cit. pp. 201–3). The phrase, turpe lucrum, is commonplace; see the article on order in the King's Book; Formularies, p. 279.

these that steale . . . horehunters On the statute of 1550 (Statutes of the Realm IV, I, iii) forbidding defacing of inscriptions and images on tombs see Aston, England's Iconoclasts, pp. 267–70. On the despoiling of tombs see Nichols's introduction to Gray Friars' Chronicle, pp. xx–xxii, and p. 54 (June–July 1547): 'at this same tyme was pullyd up alle the tomes, grett stones, alle the aulteres with the stalles and walles of the qweer and auteres in the church that was some tyme the Gray freeres, and solde . . .'; p. 57 (1548): 'this yere was put downe the chappell with the charnell howse in Powlles church yerde, with the too tomes . . .'; on the removal of tombs from St Paul's in 1552 see Ridley, Ridley pp. 281–2; Sermons, p. 187; above p. 404.

lucri gratia . . . therby Aristotle, Nich. Eth. IV, loc. cit.

Labora sicut bonus . . . occupation II Tim. 2:3–4. Vg. 'deo inplicat'.

turpiter affectantes . . . lucre Aristotle, Nich. Eth. IV, loc. cit.

thinking all . . . berdes Proverbial; a predating of the first use of 1618 cited by ODEP s.v. 'All' of 'All is lost that goes beside the mouth'.

S. Paule . . . one A reference to Tit. 1:8–9; 2:1 & 7 etc; I Tim. 3:4–7.

contra pelagi . . . haue Jerome, Dialogus adversus Pelagianos I, 22 (PL 23, 517).

S. Iohn Chrisost . . . me Chrysostom, De Sacerdotio VI, 2 (PG 48, 679).

Sacerdotium . . . angels Chrysostom, De Sacerdotio III, 4 (PG 48, 642).

terribilia namque . . . honorable The following exposition is taken from Chrysostom, De Sacerdotio, loc. cit.

such were . . . feete A description of the vestments of the High Priest, head of the Levitical priesthood taken from Ex. 28; see ODCC s.v. 'High Priest'.

sanctum . . . gospel A reference to Matt. 27:51 and Mk. 15:38 on the tearing of the veil of the Temple at the moment of Christ's death; see Sermons, p. 125; above p. 376. The co-ordinating conjunction 'and' in the clause 'and . . . sanctum' either substitutes for the subordinating conjunction 'that', or the pronoun 'it' has been omitted.

ij. Cor. iij . . . Christe II Cor. 3:10; cited by Chrysostom, *De Sacerdotio, loc. cit.*

Si ministratio . . . not II Cor. 3:7.

He calleth . . . death A reference to II Cor. 3:6.

He that gathered . . . other A reference to Num. 15:32–36; Ex. 21:17.

whiche the Apostle . . . Exo. xxxiiii II Cor. 3:7–16 with reference to Ex. 34:29–35.

Of this the Apostle . . . reuerence II Cor. 3:7.

Then saith . . . same The following, including scriptural references, is a translation of Chrysostom, *De Sacerdotio* III (PG 48, 643–44).

whatsoeuer thou loosest . . . heauen Matt. 18:18.

whosoeuer sinnes . . . bound John 20:23.

the same power . . . him John 5:22.

For no man . . . euerlasting John 3:5; 6:54.

By them we put on . . . body A reference to Gal. 3:27; Rom. 6:4; I Cor. 12:27.

ex sanguinibus . . . flesh John 1:13.

The Iewes priestes . . . disease A reference to Lev. 14:2–3.

Chore . . . Abyron A reference to Num. 16:1–33. Korah, Dathan and Abiram were rebels. Dathan and Abiram disputed Moses' leadership and were swallowed up alive by the earth. Korah rebelled against Moses and Aaron demanding priestly recognition; he and his company were burnt by fire from the sacred altar; see *Peake's Commentary*, pp. 261–2.

Iaco. vlt . . . him Jas. 5:14–15. Vg. 'Infirmatur quis in vobis inducat . . . si dimittentur ei'.

The .xix. treatise or sermon.

in my laste sermon . . . same A resumé of the eighteenth sermon and a reference to I Pet. 5:1; see *Sermons*, pp. 340–50.

And I . . . sacrament This comment suggests that by 1552–3 open criticism of clerical marriage was possible; see *Sermons*, p. 338.

Pascite . . . hand I Pet. 5:2.

they were not then . . . priestes Cf. this assertion of episcopal rank with the comments in the previous sermon, pp. 342, 344.

Act. xx . . . bysshops Acts 20:28; see *Sermons*, pp. 249, 251, 344.

maiores . . . congregation A reference to Acts 20:17. Tyndale's translation of *ecclesia* as 'congregation' rather than 'church' was also contested by More; and *ecclesia* was included on the list of Gardiner's 'objectionable' words (*Concilia* III, 861). 'Congregation' appears in the Anglican Ordinal of 1552; see Cardwell, *BCP* pp. 408–9; Tyndale, *Answer*, pp. 13–16; More, *Dialogue*, CW 6, 286, 289; *Confutation*, CW 8, 164–5, 167–72, 175–8.

as Christe . . . sheepe A reference to John 21:15–16.

prouidentes non coacte . . . coaction I Pet. 5:2.

spire white grasse Possibly spearwort or banewort, a form of buttercup with long narrow leaves like spearheads which grows up to a foot high and is noxious for sheep; or a kind of spiky, sprouting, flowering plant. See *OED* s.v. 'Spearwort' *sb.* 2; 'Spiring' *ppl.a*[1].2.

And here . . . lawes This reference to the 'kinges Maiestie' suggests that sermons eighteen to twenty are Edwardian; see *Sermons*, p. 338.

In the makinge . . . woorkes A reference to Ex. 36:22–29 and 36:1.

Neque vt . . . gentlenes An exposition of I Pet. 5:3; cf. *Sermons*, p. 251.

Mat. xxiiij . . . teeth The parable of the evil servant, Matt. 24:48–51.

Ex animo . . . all I Pet. 5:3.

when the prince . . . senioribus I Pet. 5:4–5.

Nowe . . . similiter A reference to I Pet. 5:5.

Hebr. xiii . . . you Heb. 13:17.

Que dicunt . . . saiynge Matt. 23:3. Vg. 'quaecumque dixerint vobis servate . . .'.

Vt cum gaudio . . . you Heb. 13:17.

Adolescentes . . . senioribus I Pet. 5:5.

the Philosopher . . . Ethikes The following exposition comes from Aristotle, *Nich. Eth.* I, 3 (ed. cit. p. 9); see *Sermons*, p. 137.

secundum morem . . . conditions Aristotle, *Nich. Eth.* I, 3, *loc. cit.*

.iii. Regum .xii . . . seruyce III Kings 12:4; see *Sermons*, p. 137.

Capite .ix . . . drudgerie A reference to III Kings 9:22.

.iii. Regum .iiii. III Kings 4:7.

Well . . . doe The following is a translation of III Kings 12:5–11. The people's demands were presented to Rehoboam at Shechem. His seniors advised him to be conciliatory, but he followed the advice of his contemporaries to put down insubordination and so split the kingdom in two; *Peake's Commentary*, p. 343.

Si hodie obedieris . . . times III Kings 12:7.

Minimus . . . scorpions III Kings 12:10; Vg. 'dorso patris mei'.

And . . . death See the description of the scorpion in Trevisa, *Properties of things*, XVIII, 97, *ed. cit.* II, 1248–50.

The people . . . him A reference to III Kings 12:19–21.

as the Scripture . . . Roboam A reference to III Kings 12:8.

And when . . . wise A reference to III Kings 11:42; see Caxton, *Golden Legend, ed. cit.* fos 43ʳ⁻ᵛ. Proverbial; cited in *ODEP* s.v. 'Fool' as first use of 'A fool at forty is a fool indeed'.

it will be hard . . . saued Proverbial; 'it is hard to teach an old dog new tricks'; see *ODEP* s.v. 'Teach'.

Omnes inuicem . . . another I Pet. 5:5.

Iac. iiii . . . proud Jas. 4:6.

Lucifer . . . hell A reference to Is. 14:12–15.

Eue . . . her A reference to Gen. 3:5 and 16.

appereth by Pharoah . . . made On the plagues, judgements inflicted by God upon the Egyptians for their oppression of the Israelites, see *Sermons*, p. 162. The plague of hail, foretold by God to Moses, was the seventh (Ex. 9:18).

Peccaui . . . Exo. ix Ex. 9:27–28.

that wicked Kyng . . . liuinge King Ahab, prompted by Queen Jezebell, murdered Naboth for his vineyard (III Kings 21:1–16); Elijah pronounced God's denunciation of doom against him and Jezebell (III Kings 21:20–24); see *DB* I, s.v. 'Ahab'; *Sermons*, p. 321.

Scidit . . . tyme III Kings 21:27–29; Vg. 'scidit vestem sua . . . et ambulabat'.

Nabuchodonosor . . . Caldeis Nebuchadnezzar, founder and ruler of the Bablyonian empire from BC 604 to 561 was chastised by God and afflicted by a malady now thought to be 'lycanthropy'; see *Dict. Bibl.* II, s.v. 'Daniel'; cf. *Peake's Commentary*, p. 595, which states that the story is apocryphal.

Nonne hec est Babilon . . . so Dan. 4:27–30; Vg. 'transiit'.

I Nabuchodonosor . . . dede Dan. 4:34.

In the new . . . lowlinesse A reference to Luke 18:10–14.

Humiliamini igitur . . . visitation I Pet. 5:6.

Sicut simpliciter . . . maxime This is a familiar sentiment in Aristotle; see *Topica* V, 8, tr. E.S. Forster in *Organon II*, tr. and ed. H. Tredennick (London, 1966), pp. 547–8.

to kepe a low saile Proverbial; 'to live humbly'; cited as first use in *ODEP* s.v. 'Keep'.

thinkynge our feete . . . come Proverbial; cited in *ODEP* s.v. 'Thinks'.

As they haue . . . yeares For similar adverse comments see *Sermons*, pp. 137, 140, 141, 143, 146, 149, 218, 333.

Superiores sibi . . . you Phil. 2:3.

euen as the menne . . . grounde A reference to Luke 4:29–30; Matt. 4:5–6; see *Sermons*, pp. 174, 368 for similar expositions.

which the Apostle . . . Adam A reference to Rom. 5:12–14.

Io. viii . . . nothing John 8:54.

.i. Timo. vi . . . god I Tim. 6:17.

Aug . . . men This sentiment (from I Tim. 6:17) is commonly expressed by Augustine and probably comes from Hom. 177 (*PL* 38, 957).

Non enim . . . Ro. xiii Rom. 13:1–2.

Principes non sunt . . . sake Rom. 12:3 and 5.

Subiecti estote . . . honorificate I Pet. 2:13 and 17. Vg. 'propter Dominum'.

Reges gentium . . . hie Luke 22:25–27 citing Luke 22:25.

Humiliamini . . . visitacion I Pet. 5:6; Vg. 'humiliamini igitur'.

The twenty treatice or Sermon.

Omnem solicitudinem . . . Deum I Pet. 5:7; Vg. 'in eum'.

as Christe . . . it A reference to the parable of the cockles and tares, Matt. 13:38.

as he did to Helie . . . rauens A reference to III Kings 17:6.

Mundus . . . superfluite This proverb probably derives from Edgeworth's translation of a classical source.

Saynt Peter . . . sobre A reference to I Pet. 5:8.

Sapi. viii . . . fortitude Sap. 8:7; Vg. 'sapientam docet'.

et vigilitate . . . deuoret I Pet. 5:8.

Cum venissent filij . . . them Job 1:6–7.

Cum assisterent . . . them Job 1:6.

Cayn . . . done A reference to Gen. 4:9–10.

Circuiui terram . . . it Job 1:7.

Aduersarius vester . . . deuoret I Pet. 5:8.

Psal. in circuitu . . . ambulant Ps. 11:9.

Medium exit . . . extremities See Aristotle, *Nich. Eth.* II, 6, 5 & 8, 1–2 (*ed. cit.* pp. 91, 107).

Quasi oraculum apollinis A reference to the Delphic oracle at Delphi, the supreme oracle of Greece in classical times, presided over by Apollo. See *OCCL* s.v. 'Delphic Oracle'.

In the actes . . . ende I.e. the Acts of 1536 and 1538 which dissolved monasteries and friaries and transferred their lands and revenues to the Crown; the Act of 1545 which appropriated chantries, hospitals, guilds and fraternities; the 1547 Chantries Act which dissolved the lesser foundations. See H. Gee and W.J. Hardy, *Documents Illustrative of English Church History* (London, 1876), nos 61, 64, 68; for complaints at pluralities and impropriations see Lever, *Sermons*, pp. 29–32, 115–19; Glasier, *Sermon*, sigs. D4–D5ᵛ.

Iob .i . . . it Job 1:7.

as we . . . through A reference to Ps. 90:6, a text of great importance to Thomas More in *A Dialogue of Comfort*; see Marc'hadour, *Bible* I, 165. Lack of concord is due to the subsequent reference to 'we mortall men and women' as 'they'.

bearinge menne . . . argumente A reference to the troubles which followed the first BCP. In the Western risings of June 1549 the rebels demanded the restoration of old ceremonies, church lands, and the Act of Six Articles. Among the economic causes of Ket's Rebellion in Norfolk in July and August were some religious grievances. See Fletcher, *Tudor Rebellions*, pp. 40–68; Gasquet and Bishop, *Ed.VI and BCP*, pp. 217–19; Procter and Frere, *BCP*, pp. 55–57; J. Cornwall, *The Revolt of the Peasantry* (London, 1977); A.L. Rowse, *Tudor Cornwall*, 2nd ed. (London, 1969), pp. 271–3.

Pro. xx . . . soule Prov. 20:2.

as Saynt Paule . . . Deuyll A reference to Eph. 6:16.

fortes in fide . . . faythe I Pet. 5:9. Vg. 'fortes fide'.

Tertullian . . . stronge Tertullian, *Liber de Prescriptionibus* II (PL 2, 14).

adorned . . . charitie A reference to I Pet. 4:8.

finem fidei . . . epistle I Pet. 1:9. Vg. om. 'vestrarum'.

Scientes . . . brotherhed I Pet. 5:9; Vg. 'scientes eadem'.

Deus autem omnis . . . temptacion An exposition of I Pet. 5:10; Vg. 'solidabit'.

Solidabit I Pet. 5:10.

how manie manners . . . wine See *The Order of the Communion* printed by Cardwell, *BCP*, pp. 428–9. These English devotions were incorporated into the service of the 1549 BCP although there was no alteration in the Latin Mass. The sacrament was administered following the instructions on the sacrament of the altar in the *King's Book* (*Formularies*, pp. 202–9) which contains no rubrics. The prayer of consecration was to be said facing the altar, but there was no elevation of the host or showing of the sacrament to the people. Both Catholics and Protestants put different constructions upon the new rite and many parish priests incited their parishioners against it. No. 43 of Bishop Hooper's Visitation Articles of 1551 states that: 'the minister in the use of the communion and prayers thereof turn his face towards the people' (*Later Writings of Bishop Hooper*, ed. C. Nevinson, PS (Cambridge, 1852), p. 128). See Hughes and Larkin, I, 300; *Formularies*, pp. 262–9; Cardwell, *op. cit.* pp. 281, 297–8, 303; Procter and Frere, *BCP*, pp. 59–60, 66–67; Gasquet and Bishop, *Ed. VI and BCP*, pp. 233–4.

Then because . . . worshipped Following the 1549 BCP Bishop Ridley in his 1550 visitation of the diocese of London enjoined that a covered table be set up in the quire or chancel so that ministers and communicants may be separated from the rest of the people; see Cardwell, *Doc. Ann.* I, no. XXI, pp. 82–3; *BCP*, pp. 280–1; Wriothesley, *Chronicle* II, 47; Ridley, *Ridley*, pp. 214–16.

there was veils . . . saide Traditionally the Lenten cloth veiled off the sanctuary during

Lent and remained in position until the words of the passion in Holy Week. Coverings are recommended by Becon in 'Potation of Lent' 'to stir the people to remembrance' (*Early Works*, p. 111); see also Cobb, *Rationale*, pp. 33–47. In 1551–2 it appears to have been used to shroud the sacrament in some churches; e.g. Bishop Ridley at St Paul's, Holy Week 1551, 'caused the vaile to be drawen, that no person shoulde see but those that receaved . . .' (Wriothesley, *Chronicle* II, 47); *Grey Friars' Chronicle* states, p. 67: 'on sente Barnabes . . . nyght was the aulter in Powlles pullyd downe, and as that day the vayelle was hongyd [up] benethe the steppes and the tabulle sett up there and a sennet after there the comunion was mynysterd'. See Thurston, *Lent*, pp. 99–105; Hughes, *Reformation* II, 120–1; Ridley, *Ridley*, pp. 216–17, n.; 253.

aulters . . . other Destruction of altars began late in 1549. On 4 November 1550 Council ordered that all altars be replaced by wooden tables. Edgeworth refers to the 1552 BCP which permitted, without enjoining, leavened bread (the 1549 BCP had continued the custom of unleavened bread). See Cranmer, *Works* II, 524–5 on council's order to take down altars; Cardwell, *Doc. Ann.* I, no. XXIV; BCP, pp. 314, 317; Gasquet and Bishop, *Ed. VI and BCP*, pp. 230–1; ODCC s.v. 'Bread'.

all corporaces . . . clothe The rubric of the first BCP states that the bread be laid upon the corporas, or else in the paten', but there is no reference to the corporal in the 1552 BCP; see Cardwell, BCP, p. 281; *Sermons*, p. 187. The form of 'laied' is passive, but the auxiliary 'was' has been omitted.

And at the saide . . . worshippe Neither of the Edwardian liturgies contain a rubric directing the position of the priest at the consecration. The Eastward position had authority for usage according to the interpretation of three rubrics in the 1552 BCP; but the rubric authorising its use was not inserted into the BCP until 1661. The rubrical difficulties followed the replacement of altars by moveable communion tables. See Procter and Frere, BCP, pp. 69–70, 491; ODCC s.v. 'Eastward Position'.

by commaundement . . . South Upon introducing the communion table into St Paul's in 1550, Ridley 'sette the endes east and west, the priest standing in the middest at the communion on the south side of the bord' (Wrio-

thesley, *Chronicle* II, 47). The 1552 BCP directs the priest to stand at the N. side of the table. See Cardwell, BCP, p. 267; Ridley, *Ridley*, p. 253.

And this boke . . . wine A reference to the 1552 BCP's celebrated 'Black Rubric' interpolated at the end of the communion service on the eve of publication by order of the Council and without the sanction of the second Act of Uniformity. It states: 'it is not meant thereby that any adoration is done . . . either unto the sacramental bread and wine there received, or to any real and essential presence there being of Christ's natural flesh and blood'. Ridley subsequently moved the communion table into the lower quire; see Ridley, *Ridley*, pp. 281–2; see Procter and Frere, BCP, pp. 83–5; F.E. Brightman, *The English Rite*, 2 vols (London, 1915), Index s.v. 'Declaration on Kneeling'; ODCC s.v. 'Black Rubric, The'; G. Dix, *The Shape of the Liturgy*, 2nd ed. (London, 1954), pp. 670–1, on the liturgical changes incorporated into the new rite.

Eustathius . . . Armenia Eustathius, Bishop of Sebaste in Armenia (c.358–377), a pupil of Arius and a friend of St Basil the Great, Bishop of Caesarea (d. 379). He became an adherent of the views of Basil of Ancyra, and defended homoiousian doctrines at the synods of Ancyra (358) and Lampascus (365), but wavered in his attitudes to the Nicene cause. As a semi-Arian he persecuted Basilides, Bishop of Gangra, in 362 when the pure Arians were condemned; but in 374–5, rejecting St Basil's theology of the Holy Spirit, he asked to be restored to Basilides' communion; he furthered the Macedonian heresy. See Hanson, *Christian Doctrine*, 683–5; S. Le Nain de Tillemont, *The History of the Arians and of the Council of Nice*, tr. T. Deacon, 2 vols (London, 1721), II, 361, 453; DTC V, ODCC, DCB II, s.v. 'Eustathius'; DCB I, s.v. 'Basilius of Caesaria'.

Paphlagonia . . . Asia Paphlagonia was an ancient district of Anatolia adjoining the Black Sea, bounded by Bithynia in the W, Pontus in the E, and Galatia in the S. It was gradually absorbed by the Pontic kingdom; in 6 BC a postion, Inner Paphlagonia, was attached to the Roman province of Galatia; OCD; *Enc. Brit.* VII, s.v. 'Paphlagonia'.

Epistola .lxxii . . . obiuit Basil, 'Epist. 251' (written December 376), (PG 32, 935).

Basilides . . . Paphlagonia Basilides, Bishop of Gangra. Nothing further is known of him although Tillemont, *op. cit.* p. 361, implies that he was a pure Arian. See R.J. Defarrari's notes to Basil's letters, tr. by Sister A.C. Way, *Saint Basil, Letters,* Vol. II, Fathers of the Church, 28, rev. ed. (Washington, 1969), pp. 143, 207–8; Hanson, *Christian Doctrine,* pp. 60, 640.

Dardania A province of Turkey in the region of Troas. See *OL* II, s.v.

Gangrens I.e. Gangra or Cankiri, province in N. central Turkey; it was the capital of ancient Paphlagonia when it was incorporated into the province of Galatia in 6 BC; see *Enc. Brit.* II, s.v. 'Cankiri'.

Quam obrem . . . tables Basil, Epist. 226 (PG 32, 846).

Per Siluanum . . . know I Pet. 5:12.

Obsecrans . . . stand I Pet. 5:12; Vg. 'state'.

Salutat vos . . . doe I Pet. 5:13; Vg. 'vos quae est . . . cumlecta'.

he nameth Rome . . . Babilon. On the association of Rome with Babylon see *Sermons,* pp. 196–7; Bigg, *Epistles,* p. 197; Beare, *First Epistle,* pp. 209, 226–7.

Babilon . . . flud A reference to Nimrod, legendary founder (Gen. 10:8–12) of a kingdom in Mesopotamia and of four cities, two of which, Calah and Ninevah, are Assyrian. In Mk 5:6 Assyria is said to be the land of Nimrod. Edgeworth's source is Berosus, *Babylonii Antiquitates* IV; he may have used editions which include the writings of Josephus, e.g. *Hebraei Antiquitatum Iudicarum, Libri XX* (Cologne, 1534), sig. 3K4ᵛ; or the cosmographies of Mela and Solinus; e.g. *Antiquitatum Variorum Autores* (Lyons, 1552), sig. b8ᵛ.

Semiramis . . . ampliasse See Berosus, *Babylonii Antiquitates* V; see *Hebraei Antiquitatum Iudicarum,* sig. 3L1ᵛ; *Antiquitatum Variorum Autores,* sig. c5. Ninus, the son of Belus, founded the Assyrian monarchy in 2059 BC and reigned fifty-two years. Semiramis, his wife, ruled after hs death and made Babylon into the most magnificent city in the world; her exploits were denied by Berosus. See *OCD; Enc. Brit.* VII, s.v. 'Ninus'.

As . . . Berosus Berosus (fl. c.290 BC), a priest of Babylon, wrote a history of Babylon in Greek, a work which survives only in fragments. According to *The Dictionary of Greek and Roman Biography,* ed. W. Smith, 3 vols

(London, 1849), I, s.v. 'Berosus', the *Babylonii Antiquitates* with a commentary by Joannis Anni is the fabrication of the Dominican monk, Annius of Viterbo; it was printed at Rome in 1498 and often reprinted. See *OCCL* s.v. 'Berosus'.

antiquitatum . . . posteritatis. &c. Berosus, *Babylonii Antiquitates* IV; see *Hebraei Antiquitatum Iudicarum,* sig. 3K4ᵛ; *Antiquitatum Variorum Autores,* sig. b8ᵛ.

Berosus . . . xlii. yeres Berosus, *Babylonii Antiquitates* V; see *Hebraei Antiquitatum Iudicarum,* sig. 3L1ᵛ; *Antiquitatum Variorum Autores,* sig. c5.

Da. iiii . . . boastyng Dan. 4:27; Vg. 'Babylon magna quam ego in domum regni'; see *Sermons,* p. 357.

By the name . . . geuen The view that Queen Semiramis' deification of Ninus and Belus was the origin of idolatry is well attested in the Western church; see Jerome on Ezech. 23:11 ff., 'Comm. in Ezech.' (*PL* 25, 217–18); *Sermons,* p. 197; above p. 409 (on Babylon).

They hanged vp . . . Babilon A reference to Ps. 136:2.

This Marke . . . knowe A reference to I Pet. 5:13. Mark was the nephew of Barnabus (Col. 4:10) who accompanied Paul and Barnabus on their first missionary journey (Acts 12:25). According to later tradition he was interpreter for Peter, whose teaching is the basis for the Gospel of St. Mark. See *ODCC* s.v. 'Mark, Gospel of'; *ODS* s.v. 'Mark'; Bigg, *Epistles,* pp. 80–83.

Salutate inuicem . . . another I Pet. 5:1.

As Absalon . . . coulde A reference to II Kings 15:2–6. Absolom's rebellion against David began by his wooing the loyalty of the Israelites who could not get a hearing for their lawsuits; *Peake's Commentary,* p. 334.

.ii. Regum .xx . . . feete II Kings 20:9–10; see *Sermons,* pp. 230, 313 on Joab's treacherous slaying of Amasa.

and such kissynge . . . instructions A reference to Mk 14:44.

rubbing them . . . gall Proverbial. 'Touching them on a tender spot'; see Heywood's *Dialogue,* p. 153; *Proverbs in the Earlier English Drama,* ed. B.J. Whiting (Camb. Mass., 1938), p. 361; see *ODEP* s.v. 'Rub'.

as he did at Nazareth . . . him A reference to Luke 4:29–30; see *Sermons*, pp. 174, 358.

This Iudas . . . craftely Mk 14:44.

Pro. vii . . . him Prov. 7:13; Vg. 'adprehensumque'.

kiss like dowues . . . loue A reference to I Pet. 5:14.

in the primatiue . . . another The Pax or Kiss of Peace, the mutual greeting of the faithful in the Eucharistic Liturgy as a sign of their love and union. In the Roman canon it is included in the Anaphora; but it is omitted in the English canon of the 1549 BCP. This description corresponds with current practice which derives from the 1552 BCP at High Mass. See *ODCC* s.v. 'Kiss of Peace'; Procter and Frere, *BCP*, pp. 436, 460; Dix, *Liturgy*, pp. 107–110.

as it is written . . . goodnes A reference to Gen. 6:12.

Pax tibi . . . dei See the ordinary of the Mass in Wickham Legg, *Sarum Missal*, p. 226, n. 5.

He kisseth . . . mettall The pax brede, a small metal, ivory or wooden plate used to convey the Kiss of Peace at Mass; see *ODCC* s.v. 'Pax Brede'.

Gratia vobis . . . multiplicetur I Pet. 5:14; I Pet. 1:1–2.

APPENDIX

The Will of Roger Edgeworth

PRO Prob. 11/43. PCC, 34 Mellershe   [24 December 1559]
Rogeri Edgeworth

In the name of ^{god} amen The xxiiij daye of december yn the yere of ower lorde god Savior Christe 1559 I Roger Edgworth doctor of Diuinytie and Canon residensarye and Chauncelo*ur* of the Cathedrall Churche of Sainte And^{re}wes yn Well*es* in the Countie of Somerset, whole yn mynde and of good remembraunce make my Testamente continuinge therin my laste will after this manner followinge.* Firste I bequeathe my Sowle to allmightie god my maker and Redeemer, and to all the glorius company of heaven and my boddie to be buried in the boddy of the Cathedrall Churche aforesaide directly afore the Quier doore yf I dye in Well*es* and a large marble stone with an epitaf in proes to be graven yn the same stone to be layed vppon my graue.* And yf I dye oute of Well*es* then I will my boddie to be buried where hit please god to dispos. Item I bequeath to the fabricke of the Cathedrall churche of Well*es* xls. Item to the cathedrall churche of Sar*um* ^{xls} in recompens of Acomppe whiche ^{Y} say I sholde giue vnto the saide churche.* Item to my late parrishe Churche of Christchurche in wales xls. fo*ur* the necessary reperacions of the same churche.* Item I bequeath to my late seru*au*nte Phillippe Lydure all the money that he owethe me, and vis viii*d* more. Item I bequeath*e* to my late seru*au*nte powell xls in monney and stuff and allso my grey amblinge mare that I boughte in holdernes.* Item to euery one of my howsholde seru*au*nt*es* theire hole quarters wages in which quarter hit shall chaunce me to die with rewardes of nobles or crownes after the discression of my executors and no howsholde to be kepte in my howse at Well*es** paste iiij dayes next after my buriall in which tyme euery man maye bringe in and deliuer to <the company of Smith> myne Executors suche thing*es* as be vnder theire handes and keepinge. Item I bequeathe to the companye of Oriall Colledge in Oxforth where I was somtime fellowe all Chrisostomes Woorkes in five volumes to be chained in the liberary of the same Colledge with vis viii*d* for the chaininge and arminge of the same And yn case they haue the same work*es* there all reddye then I will the saide fiue volumes of Chrisostome withe Sainte Ambros work*es* in ij grat volumes to be deliuered to one master of Arte Studente in deuinytie felloe of the same Colledge borne nexte to the Castell of holte in the marches of wales beside Westechester,* And all the same vij bookes to be broughte forthe and showed before the fellowes

---

* *In the name . . . followinge* For a discussion of the will see Introduction, pp. 13, 35; on Edgeworth's livings in Wells, *ibid.* pp. 23, 27, 32. / *and my boddie . . . graue* There is no sign of this stone and its epitaph at Wells Cathedral today. / *Item . . . churche* On Edgeworth's prebend of Slape and his unsuccessful application to reside in Salisbury see Introduction, pp. 23, 28. / *Item . . . churche* On the living at Christchurch see *ibid.* pp. 21–2, 27, 35. / *Item . . . holdernes.* On the living at Brandesburton in the East Riding of York, see *ibid.* pp. 23, 27–8, 32. / *my howse at Welles* On his residence in the Chancellor's house at Wells see *ibid.* p. 34. / *Item . . . Westechester* On this bequest to Oriel College see *ibid.* p. 35.

of the same Colledge euery yere vpon the seconde daye of Nouembrer, and then to be deliuered to hym that hadd them before or to some other in like degree of Scoole borne nigher vnto the Castell of holte. Item at my burienge I will that there be present the hole quier of Welles and euery parson present to have at eveninge praier viij*d* at communyon viij*d* and to fett my corpes to the churche iiij*d** And to bringe hit to the grave iiij*d* And at my monthes mynde or lykewise to euery person at eveninge prayour vj*d* And at morninge prayer vj*d* countinge Sexton, clerkes and quiristers as they wer wonte to be taken, and at the tyme of my burienge to be giuen to two honeste prestes xvj*d* a peece, to saye the whole Salter for my negligences: Item I bequeathe vj*s* viij*d* to be giuen amonge pore folke in the parrishe of Sainte Cuthberdes in Welles. Item I bequeath to Edwarde Wawen vj*s* viij*d* in monney or stuff. Item wheras David harris of Bristowe oweth me vi*li* xiij*s* iiij*d* I will that myne executors demaunde or aske the saide Some vppon his obligacion and recouer hit if they can, And if they can recouer hit then to deliuer hit vnto ij honeste men beinge of kine to one Watkin Williams late of Aburgenye in Wales deceaced the same monne to be kepte by the same too men to the vse of the children of the saide Wattkyn Williams yf any be on liue. And if they be all ded, then to the vse of the childers children of the saide Watkin Williams, if any be on liue. And if none be on liue then the same monney to be delte in almes for the Sowle of Master Iohn Wylliams somtyme Chaplin and Crosseberer to my lorde Cardinall of Yorke, and brother to ye saide Watkin Williams of whose gooddes the monney ys.* Item I giue and bequeathe to euery one of my brother Robertes Edgeworthes* doughters towardes theire marriages a pece of my plate with the couer yf there be any to the same belonginge, and fortie shillinges a peece in monney, the same monney and plate to be deliuered vnto them at theire severall marriages yf they be marryed before the age of xx yeres. And if they be not married before then to be deliuered to them at the age of xx yeres, or else within one yere after my deceace. Any yf any of them dye before they be married, then I will that the parte and porcion of her or them so dyenge vnmarried shall remaine and goe to the Sonnes of my saide brother Robarte deceaced. Item I bequeath to euery of my godchildren xij*d* a pece yf they doe aske hitte. And of this my presente <testamente> Testamente and last will I doe ordaine and make my sister in lawe Margaret Edgworthe, the late wyfe of my brother ^Robert^ Edgeworthe deceaced, Roger Edgeworthe Sonne to my saide brother, and my cosen Richarde Stokes myne Executors, And I giue to the saide Roger Edgeworthe four his paines my siluer Alecuppe and the Couer therunto belonginge with xl*s* in monney* And to Richard Stokes xl*s* in monney or stuff. And I ordaine and make Master Iurye* my ouerseer to see this my will fully performed and fulfilled and he to haue four his paynes theryn taken xl*s* in monney. And sainte Grigores workes yn ij volumes one parte containeth the morralles an other the opuscles. The residue of all my goodes not bequeathed after my funerall charges borne and this my present Testamente

Item . . . iiijd On this form of the burial service see *ibid.* p. 35. / *And if none . . . ys* Edgeworth may have met John Williams, one of Cardinal Wolsey's chaplins and cross bearers, when attending the divorce proceedings of Henry VIII and Katherine of Aragon in 1529; see *ibid.* p. 22. / *Robertes Edgeworthes* On Robert Edgeworth see *ibid.* p. 13. / *And I giue . . . monney* This may be the same 'pott of siluer with a cover marked with I and C' which Edgeworth received as a bequest from John Clerk in 1554; see *ibid.* p. 26. / *Master Iurye* Thomas Jury was a canon residentiary at Wells Cathedral and a prebend of Milverton; in 1539 he attended convocation with Edgeworth. He was a scholar at Oriel in 1516–17, a fellow between 1523–32 and studied theology from 1530. See BRUO IV, 324; Richards and Shadwell, pp. 55–6; Le Neve, V, pp. 74, 105.

fully performed my lease of the pastures and meddowes at Mellisborowe* only excepted I will shalbe bestowed parte therof in workes of mercy and pittie for my Sowle helth and parte therof in bringinge vpp the children of my brother Robarte Edgeworthe deceaced in vertue and learninge and to other prefermentes according to the discression of myne executors in which I accompe a great parte of pittie and mercie by cause that when I am gon they be like to haue small succour. Item prouided alwayes that yf hit fortune my cosen Roger Edgeworth beinge one of myne executors to die before this my will shalbe fully performed I will that neither the wyef of the saide Roger or any of his executors shall enter medle or haue anythinge to doe with this my presente testamente and last will after the decece of the saide Roger Egeworth but that my other executors then liuinge shall have full power to performe this my will accordinge to their discressions. In witness wherof to this my presente testamente and laste will I haue subscribed my name with my owne hande and put to ^{my} Seale the daye and yere aboue written that is the xxiiij daye of december in this presente yere 1559. Item I bequeath to my Cosen Sir Richarde Edgeworthe xli in monney, & my scarlet gowne, my murre gowne and my best furred gowne.* Item to Edwarde Edgeworth xli in monney to be putt in his eldest brothers handes vntill he come to lawfull age.* By the witnes of me Thomas Iury preste by me Griffith Powell.

Probatum fuit huiusmodi Testamentum coram Magistro Waltero Haddon legem doctore Curie prerogatiue Cantuariensis Commissario apud London primo die mensis Iunij Anno Domini millesimo quingentesimo sexagesimo Iuramento Iustiniani Kidd procuratoris Rogeri Edgeworthe Executoris in huiusmodi Testamento nominati Cui commissa fuit administracio etc. de bene etc. Ac de pleno Inventario Necnon de vero et plano compoto Reddendum Ad sancta dei Evangelia Iuratus. Reseruata potestate ^{Margarite Edgwoth} et Richardo Stokes executoribus in huiusmodi Testamento nominatis / cum venerint/

[Proven 1 June 1560]

---

my lease . . . Mellisborowe The spelling suggests that this holding was situated in Melbury Abbas in Dorset (one of the four districts listed s.v. 'Melbury' in the Domesday Book); see E. Ekvall, *The Oxford Dictionary of English Place Names*, 2nd ed. (Oxford, 1974), s.v. 'Mellis'. It is two miles SE from Shaftesbury and was once in the patronage of the abbey of Shaftesbury. A manor and advowson, granted to Sir Thomas Arundell, reverted to his widow on his attainder and to her son in the first year of Mary's reign. It is likely that Edgeworth received the lands in a grant during Mary's reign. / *Item . . . gowne* On Richard Edgeworth see Introduction, p. 13. / *Item . . . age* On Edward Edgeworth see *ibid.* pp. 13, 35.

BIBLIOGRAPHY

The bibliography is selective. It does not include patristic works available in Migne's editions or classical works available in the Loeb editions. Histories of the period which contain sixteenth century documents may be listed under both primary and secondary sources.

Primary Sources: Manuscript Sources

Bodleian Library, Oxford (Bodl.)
  MS Rawl. D. 831
  MS James 29
  MS Dep. C. 136

Oxford University Archives (OU Arch.)
  Calendar of *The Chancellor's Court*
    Register 1506–1515 [Register F
    Reversed]
  Transcript of *The Register of Congrega-*
    tion and Convocation, 1505–1517
    [Register G]
  Transcript of *The Register of Congrega-*
    tion and Convocation 1518–1535 [Reg-
    ister H]

Oriel College Archives (OC Arch.)
  Transcript of *The Treasurers' Accounts*,
    Vols VII–X (1504–1525)

Public Record Office (PRO)
  Ed. VI Sc 6/740
  SP 1/54
  SP 1/125
  SP 1/142
  SP 1/242, Pt. 2
  SP 10/2/34
  SP 10/9/48
  SP 10/10/19 & 20.
  Pat. Roll 35 Henry VIII. pt. 16. m.12.
  Prob. 11/43/ PCC Mellershe.

British Library (BL)
  MS Cotton Cleop. E. V.
  MS Royal 7c. xvi.
  MS Lansdowne 11. arts. 2–5.

Lambeth Palace Library
  MS Lambeth Stillingfleet 16

Bristol Record Office (BRO)
  12966 (37)
  DC/E/1/1
  DC/A/9/1/1
  DC/A/9/1/2
  DC/A/7/1/2
  DC/A/7/1/5

Hereford and Worcester Record Office, Worcester
  Reg. Jeronimo Ghinucci, Worcester, fo.
    36.

Lincoln Archives Office
  Reg. John Longland, Lincoln, XXVII.

Salisbury Cathedral
  Chapter Act Book 14

Somerset Record Office, Taunton (SRO)
  DD/VC/66
  DD/Ca/22

Wells Cathedral Library
  Communars Rolls, 1559–1560

Primary Sources: Contemporary Printed Sources

Sermons, devotional treatises, and preachers' handbooks

An Alphabet of Tales. An English fifteenth century translation of the Alphabetum Narrationum once attributed to Etienne de Besançon. Ed. M.M. Banks. 2 vols. EETS, OS, 126–7 (London, 1904–5)

Anglicus, Bartholomaeus. *On the Properties of things: John Trevisa's translation from the Latin of Bartholomaeus Anglicus 'De Proprietatibus Rerum': a critical text*. Ed. M. Seymour *et al*. 3 vols (Oxford, 1985–8). Cited as Trevisa, *Properties of things*

Becon, T. *The Catechism*. Ed. J. Ayre, PS (Cambridge, 1844)

———. *The Early Writings*. Ed. J. Ayre, PS (Cambridge, 1843)

Bonde, William. *A devoute treatyse called the Pilgrymage of perfeccyon* (de Worde, 1531). STC 3278

Bonner, E. *A profitable and necessarye doctryne, with certayne homelies adioyned therunto* (Cawood, 1555). STC 3282

The Book of Vices and Virtues. A fourteenth century English translation of the Somme le Roi of Lorens d'Orléans. Ed. W.N. Francis. EETS, ES, 217 (London, 1942)

The Early English Versions of the Gesta Romanorum. Ed. S.J.H. Herrtage. EETS, ES, 33 (London 1879)

Erasmus, D. *Adagiorum Opus* (Lyons, 1541)

———. *Apophthegmatum ex optimis vtriusque linguae scriptoribus libri octo* (Basle, 1550)

———. *Collected Works of Erasmus* (Toronto, 1974–). Cited as CWE

———. *De Copia; De Ratione Studii*. Ed. and tr. C.R. Thompson. CWE 24. (Toronto, 1978)

———. *Dialogus Ciceronianus*. Ed. and tr. B.I. Knott. CWE 28 (Toronto, 1986)

———. *Moriae Encomium*. Ed. and tr. B. Radice. CWE 27 (Toronto, 1986)

———. *Enchiridion Militis Christiani*. Tr. C. Fantazzi. CWE 66 (Toronto, 1988)

Fisher, John. *The English Works of John Fisher*. Pt. 1. Ed. J.E.B. Mayor. EETS, ES, 27 (London, 1876)

Gesta Romanorum. Ed. H. Oesterley (Berlin, 1872)

Glasier, Hugh. *A notable and very fruictefull Sermon made at Paules Crosse . . .* (Caly, 1555). STC 11916

Heywood, John. *John Heywood's Dialogue of Proverbs*. Ed. R.E. Habenicht. University of California Publications in English Studies, 25 (Los Angeles, 1963)

Hilton, Walter. *The Goad of Love*. Ed. and tr. C. Kirchberger (London, 1952)

Jacob's well, an Englisht treatise on the cleansing of man's conscience, ed. from the MS about 1440 AD. Pt. 1. Ed. A. Brandeis. EETS, OS, 115 (London, 1900)

Latimer, Hugh. *The Works of Hugh Latimer*. Ed. G.E. Corrie. 2 vols. PS (Cambridge, 1844–5). I. *Sermons*. II. *Sermons and Remains*. Cited as Latimer, *Works* I and II

Lever, Thomas. *Sermons, 1550*. Ed. E. Arber (London, 1870)

Middle English Sermons. Ed. W.O. Ross. EETS, OS, 209 (1940, repr. London, 1960)

Mirk, John. *Mirk's Festial: a collection of homilies by Johannes Mirkus*. Pt.1. Ed. T.E. Erbe. EETS, ES, 96 (London, 1905)

The Oxford Dictionary of English Proverbs. Ed. F.P. Wilson. 3rd ed. rev. (Oxford, 1970)

Palsgrave, J. Tr. *The Comedy of Acolastus*. Ed. P.S. Carver. EETS, OS, 202 (London, 1907). Cited as Palsgrave, *Acolastus*

Proverbs in the Earlier English Drama. Ed. B.J. Whiting. Harvard Studies in Comparative Literature, XIV (London, 1938)

Proverbs, Sentences and Proverbial Phrases from English Writings mainly before 1500. Ed. B.J. Whiting (Oxford, 1968)

The Royal Book. Tr. W. Caxton (Wynkyn de Worde, 1507). STC 21430. Cited as Caxton, *Royal Book*

Taverner, Richard. *Prouerbes or Adagies gathered out of the Chiliades of Erasmus by Richard Taverner* (R. Kele, (1552)). STC 10440

Tilley, M.P. *A Dictionary of the Proverbs in England in the Sixteenth and Seventeenth Centuries* (1950, repr. Michigan, 1966). Cited as Tilley, *Proverbs*

Udall, N. *Apophthegmes, that is to saie, prompte saiynges. First gathered by Erasmus, now translated into Englyshe by N. Udall* (Grafton, 1542). STC 10443

Vergil, Polydore. *P.V. Adagiorum aeque humanorum ac sacrorum opus* (Basle, 1550)

de Voragine, Jacobus. *Legenda Aurea.* Tr. W. Caxton. *The Golden Legend* (w. de worde, 1527). STC 24880. Cited as Caxton, *Golden Legend*

Watson, Thomas. *Twoo notable Sermons . . . concernynge the reall presence* (Cawood, 1554). STC 25115

———. *Sermons on the Sacraments.* Ed. T.E. Bridgett (London, 1876)

Wilson, T. *Thomas Wilson's* Arte of Rhetorique. Ed. T.J. Derrick, The Renaissance Imagination, I. (New York, 1982)

Yorkshire Writers. Richard Rolle of Hampole: An English father of the Church and his followers. Ed. C. Horstman, 2 vols (London, 1895–6)

Works of reformation controversy

Barlow, William. *A dialoge describing the originall ground of these Lutheran faccions and many of their abuses.* 2nd ed. (Cawood, 1553). STC 1462

Barnes, R. *A Supplycacion vnto henrye the eight* (J. Byddell, 1534). STC 1471

Calvin, J. *A Short Instruction to arme . . . agaynst the pestiferous errours of the . . . Anabaptistes* (J. Daye and W. Seres, 1549). STC 4463

Cranmer, T. *The Works of Thomas Cranmer, Archbishop of Canterbury, Martyr 1556.* 2 vols. Ed. J.E. Cox. PS (Cambridge, 1844–6). I. *Writings on the Sacrament of the Lord's supper.* II. *Miscellaneous Writings and letters.* Cited as Cranmer, *Works* I and II

Frith, John. *A disputacion of purgatorye deuided into thre bokes.* [London? 1537?]. STC 11387

———. *The preparacyon to the crosse, and to Deathe,* tr. from latyn by R. Tracey in aed. T. Bertheleti, [1540]. STC 11393

Joliffe, H. and R. Jonson. *Responsio . . . Henrici Ioliffi & Robert Ionson . . . ad illos articulos Ioannis Hoperi . . . in quibus a Catholica fide dissentiebat* (Antwerp, 1564)

Joye, George. *The subuersion of Moris false foundacion: where upon he sweteth to set faste and shoue vnder his shameless shoris, to vnderproppe the popis Churche* (J. Aurik, Emdon, 1534). STC 14829

Latimer, Hugh. *The Works of Hugh Latimer.* Ed. G.E. Corrie. 2 vols. PS (Cambridge, 1844–5). I. *Sermons.* II. *Sermons and Remains.* Cited as Latimer, *Works* I and II

More, Thomas. *The Yale Edition of the Complete Works of St. Thomas More* (New Haven, 1963–). Cited as More, *CW*

Skelton, John. *The Complete English Poems.* Ed. J. Scattergood (New Haven and London, 1983)

Standish, John. *A lytle treatyse . . . againste the protestacion of R. Barnes* (ex aed. E Pykerynge viduae R. Redmani, 1540). STC 23210

Turner, W. *The huntyng of the romyshe vuolfe* [Emden, E. Van der Erve, 1555?]. STC 24356

———. *A New Book of spirituall physik for diuerse diseases of the nobilitye and gentlemen of England* (Basle, 1555). STC 24361

Tyndale, William. *Obedience of a Christian Man* in *Doctrinal Treatises*. Ed. H. Walter. PS (Cambridge, 1848). Cited as Tyndale, *Obedience*
———. *An Answer unto Sir Thomas More's Dialogue called* The Supper of the Lord. Ed. H. Walter. PS (Cambridge, 1850). Cited as Tyndale, *Answer*

Historical: chronicles and calendars

Acts of the Privy Council (1452–1628). Ed. J. Dasent *et al.* 32 vols, NS (London, 1890–1907)
Adams, W. *A Chronicle of Bristol* (London, 1910)
The Black Book of Edgeworthstown and other Edgeworth Memories, 1585–1817. Ed. H.J. and H.E. Butler (London, 1927)
Burnet, G. *The History of the Reformation in England.* Ed. N. Pocock, 7 vols (London, 1865). Cited as Pocock-Burnet
Calendar of State Papers Domestic: of the Reigns of Edward VI, Mary and Elizabeth, 1547–80. Ed. R. Lemon (London, 1856). Cited as *Cal. SP Dom.*
Calendar of the Manuscripts of the Dean and Chapter of Wells. 2 vols. Historical Manuscripts Commission (London, 1907–14). Cited as *Wells* II
Calendar of the Patent Rolls preserved in the Public Record Office: Edward VI, 1547–1553. Ed. R.H. Brodie, 5 vols (London, 1924–9); *Philip and Mary 1553–8.* Ed. M.S. Giuseppi, 4 vols (London, 1937–9); *Elizabeth I, 1558–78.* Ed. J.J. Collingridge *et al.* 7 vols (London, 1939–). Cited as *CPR*
'Chantry Certificates, Gloucestershire'. Ed. Sir John Mclean. *TBGAS* 8 (1883–4), 229–309
Chronicle of the Grey Friars of London. Ed. J.G. Nichols. CS, LIII (London, 1852). Cited as *Grey Friars' Chronicle*
Concilia, Magnae Britanniae et Hiberniae a Synodo Verolamiensi, A.D. CCCXLVI ad Londoniensem A.D. MDCCXVII. Ed. D. Wilkins. 4 vols (1737, facs. London, 1964). Cited as *Concilia*
Documentary Annals of the Reformed Church of England, 1546–1716. Ed. E. Cardwell. 2 vols (Oxford, 1844). Cited as Cardwell, *Doc. Ann.*
Duff, E.G. *Handlists of English Printers, 1501–1556.* 4 vols. Bibliographical Society (London, 1895–1913). Vol IV
Foedera conventiones, literae et cuiuscunque generis acta publica inter reges Angliae et alios imperatores . . . Ed. T. Rymer, 20 vols. 3rd ed. (London, 1745). Cited as *Foedera*
Foxe, John. *Acts and Monuments of John Foxe with a life of the martyrologist and a vindication of the work.* Ed. Rev. G. Townsend. 8 vols (London, 1841, repr. New York, 1965). Cited as Townsend-Foxe
Gardiner, S. *Letters of Stephen Gardiner.* Ed. J.A. Muller (Cambridge, 1933)
Inventories of Church Goods for the Counties of York, Durham, and Northumberland. Ed. W. Page. Surtees Society, XCVII (1897)
'Inventories of, and receipts for, Church Goods in the County of Gloucester and Cities of Gloucester and Bristol'. Ed. Sir John Maclean, *TBGAS* XII (1888), 70–113
Le Neve, J. *Fasti Ecclesiae Anglicanae.* Corrected by T. Hardy. 3 vols (Oxford, 1854). Cited as Le Neve-Hardy
———. *Fasti Ecclesiae Anglicanae: 1541–1857.* Comp. J.M. Horn. Vols 1– (London, 1969–). Vol. V. Cited as Le Neve, V

————. *Fasti Ecclesiae Anglicanae: 1300–1541*. Comp. B. Jones. 12 vols (London, 1962–7). Vols III, VIII. Cited as Le Neve, III & VIII

Letters and Papers, Foreign and Domestic, of the Reign of Henry VIII. Ed. J.S. Brewer, J. Gardner and R.H. Brodie. 21 vols (London, 1862–1932). Cited as *LP*

Machyn, H. *The Diary of Henry Machyn, Citizen and Merchant-Taylor of London, A.D. 1550 to A.D. 1563*. Ed. J.G. Nicholls. CS, XLII (London, 1848)

Records of the English Bible: documents relating to the translation and publication of the Bible in English, 1525–1611. Ed. A.W. Pollard (Oxford, 1911, repr. New Jersey, 1966). Cited as *REB*

Registers of Thomas Wolsey, Bishop of Bath and Wells, 1518–23, John Clerke, Bishop of Bath and Wells, 1523–41, William Knyght, Bishop of Bath and Wells, 1541–1547, and Gilbert Bourne, Bishop of Bath and Wells, 1554–1559. Ed. Sir H. Maxwell-Lyte. SRS, LV (1940). Cited as *Bishops' Registers*

Somerset Medieval Wills, 1531–1558. Ed. F.W. Weaver. SRS, XXI (1905)

Strype, J. *Ecclesiastical Memorials relating chiefly to religion . . . and the reformation of . . . the Church of England under King Henry VIII, King Edward VI and Queen Mary I*. 3 vols (Oxford, 1822). Cited as Strype, *Ecc. Mem.*

————. *Memorials of Cranmer*. 2 vols (Oxford, 1840)

The Survey and Rental of the Chantries, Colleges and Free Chapels, Guilds, Fraternities, Lamps and Obits in the County of Somerset (as returned in the 2nd year of King Edward VI) A.D. 1548. Ed. E. Green. SRS, II (1888). Cited as *Somerset Chantries*

Transcript of the Company of Stationers of London, 1554–1640. 5 vols (London, 1875–94). Ed. E. Arber. Cited as Arber, *Transcript*

Tudor Royal Proclamations. Ed. P.L. Hughes and J.F. Larkin. 3 vols (New Haven, 1964). Cited as Hughes and Larkin

Tytler, P.F. *England under the Reigns of Edward VI and Mary with the contemporary history of Europe, illustrated in a series of original letters*. 2 vols (London, 1839)

Valor Ecclesiasticus Temporibus Henricii VIII. Ed. J. Caley and J. Hunter. 6 vols. Record Commission Publications (London, 1810–34). Cited as *Valor*

Visitation Articles and Injunctions of the period of the Reformation. Ed. W.H. Frere and W.M. Kennedy. 3 vols. Alcuin Club, 14–16 (London, 1910). II *1536–1558*. Cited as Frere and Kennedy

Wriothesley, C. *A Chronicle of England during the reigns of the Tudors from A.D. 1485 to 1559*. Ed. W.D. Hamilton. 2 vols. CS, NS, XI, XX (London, 1875–7)

Liturgies, ceremony and worship

Cranmer, T. *The Works of Thomas Cranmer*. Ed. J.E. Cox. 2 vols. PS (Cambridge, 1846). I. *Writings . . . on the Sacrament of the Lord's Supper*. II. *Miscellaneous Writings and Letters of Thomas Cranmer*. Cited as Cranmer, *Works* I and II

The Crede by the olde lawe and by the new (Redman) [1535?]. STC 20200.3

Erasmus, D. *A playne and godly exposition or declaration of the comune Crede . . . and of the .x. commaundementes*. R. Redman, [1533]. STC 10504

Formularies of Faith put forth by authority in the reign of Henry VIII. Ed. C. Lloyd (Oxford, 1856). Cited as *Formularies*

The pater noster, ye crede and the commaundements in Englysh (J. Byddell, 1537). STC 16820

The Rationale of Ceremonial, 1540–1543. Ed. C.S. Cobb. Alcuin Club, 18 (London, 1903). Cited as Cobb, *Rationale*

Records of the English Bible: documents relating to the translation and publication of the Bible in English, 1525–1611. Ed. A.W. Pollard (Oxford, 1911, repr. New Jersey, 1966). Cited as REB

The Sarum Missal. Ed. J. Wickham Legg (Oxford, 1916)

Tudor Royal Proclamations. Ed. P.L. Hughes and J.F. Larkin. 3 vols (New Haven, 1964). I. *The Early Tudors.* II. *The Later Tudors.* Cited as Hughes and Larkin, I and II

Two Books of Common Prayer, set forth by the authority of Parliament in the reign of King Edward the Sixth. Ed. E. Cardwell. 2nd ed. (Oxford, 1841). Cited as Cardwell, BCP

Visitation Articles and Injunctions of the Period of the Reformation. Ed. W.H. Frere and W.M. Kennedy. 3 vols. Alcuin Club, 14–16 (London, 1910). Vol. II, 1536–1558. Cited as Frere and Kennedy

Classical works

Berosus, Babylonicus. *Flavii Josephi Hebraei Antiquitatum Iudaicorum libri XX . . . Accesserunt Berosi Bablyonij antiquitatum libri quinque . . .* (Cologne, 1534)

———. *Bablyonii Antiquitates in Antiquitatum Variarum Autores* (Lyons, 1552)

Mela, Pomponius. *De Situ Orbis, Libros Tres* (see s.v. 'Solinus')

Plinius, Caius Secundus. *Naturalis Historia, libri XXXVIII.* Ed. L. Ian and C. Mayhoff. 6 vols. Bibliotheca Teubneriana (Stuttgart, 1969–70)

Solinus, Julius. C. *Iulii Solini Polyhistor, rerum toto orbe memorabilium thesaurus locupletissimus. Huic . . . Pomponii Melae de situ orbis libros tres . . . adiunximus* (Basle, 1543)

Valerius Maximus. *Facta et Dicta Memorabilia.* Ed. C. Halm (Leipzig, 1865)

Bibles and scriptural interpretation
(including treatises on translating the scriptures into English)

Biblia Sacra iuxta Vulgatam Versionem. Ed. R. Weber *et al.* 2 vols. Deutsche Bibelgesellschaft. 3rd ed. (Stuttgart, 1983)

Biblia vtriusque Testamenti, iuxta uulgatam translationem . . . cui in Nouo, opposuimus Des. Erasmi Rot. uersionem (Basle, 1538)

Colet, J. *Ioannis Coleti Enarratio in Epistolam S. Pauli ad Romanos. An Exposition of St Paul's Epistle to the Romans.* Ed. and tr. J.H. Lupton (London, 1873, repr. New Jersey, 1965)

———. *Ioannis Coleti Enarratio in primam Epistolam S. Pauli ad Corinthios. An Exposition of St Paul's First Epistle to the Corinthians.* Ed. and tr. J.H. Lupton (London, 1874, repr. New Jersey, 1965)

———. *Ioannis Coletus super Opera Dionysii.* Ed. and tr. J.H. Lupton (London, 1869, repr. New Jersey, 1966)

Erasmus, D. *Paraclesis, id est, adhortatio ad Christianae philosophiae Studium* (1516). Tr. William Roye? *An exhortacyon to the dylygent study of scripture* with *An exhortacyon to the study of the Gospell* (R. Wyer) [1534?]. STC 10494

———. *Des. Erasmi Roterdami in Novum Testamentum Annotationes* (Basle, 1527)

———. *Nouum Testamentum omni ex versione vtraque, hoc est Des. Erasmi Roterdami & Vulgata in Biblia vtriusque Testamenti*

———. *Tomus primus (-secundus) paraphraseon Des. Erasmi Roterdami, . . . in Nouum Testamentum.* 2 vols (Basle, 1535–38). II. *In omneis epistolas apostolicas*

Hugh of St Cher, Cardinal. *Prima (-septima) pars huius operis: continens textum Biblie cum postilla domini Hugonis Cardinalis.* 7 vols (Basle, 1498–1502)

Patrologiae Cursus Completus: Series Graeca. Ed. J. Migne, 161 vols (Paris, 1857–66)

Patrologiae Cursus Completus: Series Latina. Ed. J. Migne, 221 vols (Paris, 1844–64)

Standish, John. *A discourse wherin is debated whether it be expedient that the scripture should be in English . . .* 2nd ed. (Caly 1555). STC 23208

Textus Biblie cum glossa ordinaria [of W. Strabo], *Nicolai de Lyra postilla, Moralitatibus eiusdem, Pauli Burgensis additionibus, Matthie Thoring replicis.* 6 pts. Ed. C. Leontorius (Lyons, 1520). Cited as *TB cum glo. ord.*

Thomas, St. Aquinas. *Summa Theologiae.* Tr. and gen. ed. T. Gilby. 61 vols (London, 1964–81). Cited as Aquinas, *ST*

Secondary sources

Educational

Annals of Eton College. Ed. W. Sterry (Eton, 1898)

Churton, R. *The Lives of William Smith, Bishop of Lincoln and Sir Richard Sutton, Knight, Founders of Brasen Nose College* (Oxford, 1800)

Clark, A. *The Colleges of Oxford: Their History and Traditions* (London, 1891)

Collectanea, I. Ed. C.R.L. Fletcher. OHS, 5 (Oxford, 1885). Pt. II. 'A Catalogue of the Library of Oriel College in the Year 1375 A.D.' Ed. C.L. Shadwell, pp. 57–70

Duhamel, P.A. 'The Oxford Lectures of John Colet'. *Journal of the History of Ideas* 14 (1953), 493–510

Emden, A.B. *Biographical Register of the University of Oxford to A.D. 1500.* 3 vols (Oxford, 1957–9). Cited as *BRUO* I–III

———. *Biographical Register of the University of Oxford from A.D. 1501–1540* (Oxford, 1974). Cited as *BRUO* IV

Lupton, J.H. *The Life of Dean Colet* (London, 1887)

Mallet, E. *A History of the University of Oxford.* 3 vols (London, 1924–7)

Nelson, W. (Ed.) *A Fifteenth Century Schoolbook* (Oxford, 1956)

Oriel College Records. Ed. C.L. Shadwell and H.E. Salter. OHS, 85 (Oxford, 1926)

Orme, N. *Education and Society in Medieval and Renaissance England* (London, 1989)

———. *Education in the West of England, 1066–1548: Cornwall, Devon, Dorset, Gloucestershire, Somerset, Wiltshire* (Exeter, 1976)

———. *English Schools in the Middle Ages* (London, 1973)

———. 'The Guild of Kalendars, Bristol'. *TBGAS* 91 (1978), 32–52

Rannie, D.W. *Oriel College, 1475–1691* (London, 1900)

Register of the University of Oxford. 5 vols (Oxford, 1885–9). I. *1449–1571.* Ed. C.W. Boase. OHS, 1 (Oxford, 1885). II. Pt. i. *1571–1622.* Ed. A. Clark. OHS, 10 (Oxford, 1887). Cited as Boase, *Register;* Clark, *Register*

Richards, G.C. and C.L. Shadwell. *The Provosts and Fellows of Oriel College* (Oxford, 1922). Cited as Richards and Shadwell

Seebohm, F. *The Oxford Reformers, John Colet, Erasmus and Thomas More.* 2nd ed. (London, 1869)

Shadwell, C.L. *Registrum Orielense, an account of the members of Oriel College.* 2 vols (Oxford, 1893, 1902)

Statuta Antiqua Vniversitatis Oxoniensis. Ed. S. Gibson (Oxford, 1931)

Sterry, W. 'Notes on the Early Eton Fellows'. *Etoniana*, 60 (1935), 158

The Dean's Register of Oriel, 1446–1661. Ed. G.C. Richards and C.L. Shadwell. OHS, 84 (Oxford, 1926)

The History of the University of Oxford. Gen. ed. T. Aston. 8 vols (Oxford, 1984–). I. *The Early Oxford Schools.* Ed. J. Catto (1984). III. *The Collegiate University.* Ed. J. McConica (1986). Cited as *EOS* and *CU*

The Vulgaria of John Stanbridge and the Vulgaria of Robert Whittinton. Ed. B. White. EETS, OS, 187 (London, 1932)

Vives: On Education. A translation of the De tradendis disciplinis. Ed. Foster Watson, (Cambridge, 1913)

Reformation history and biography

Anstruther, G. *Vaux of Harrowden: a recusant family* (Newport, Mon., 1953)

Aston, M. *England's Iconoclasts: Laws against Images.* 2 vols (Oxford, 1988–). I. *Images and Literacy in late Medieval England*

———. *Lollards and Reformers* (London, 1984)

Baumer, F. Le Van. *The Early Tudor Theory of Kingship* (1940, repr. New York, 1966)

Bettey, J.H. *Bristol Parish Churches during the Reformation c.1530–1560.* BHA, 45 (1979)

The Black Book of Edgeworthstown and other Edgeworth Memories, 1585–1817. Ed. H.J. and H.E. Butler (London, 1927)

Bowker, M. *The Henrician Reformation in the Diocese of Lincoln under John Longland 1521–1547* (Cambridge, 1981)

Bridgett, T.E. 'The Bristol Pulpit in the days of Henry VIII'. *Dublin Review.* 3rd ser., i (1879), 73–95

Burnet, G. *The History of the Reformation in England.* Ed. N. Pocock. 7 vols (London, 1865)

Butterworth, C.C. and A.G. Chester. *George Joye, 1495?–1553. A Chapter in the History of the English Bible and the English Reformation* (Philadelphia, 1962)

Chester, A. *Hugh Latimer; Apostle to the English* (Philadelphia, 1954)

Clebsch, W.A. *England's Earliest Protestants 1520–1535* (London, 1964)

Constant, G. *La Réforme en Angleterre.* 2 vols (Paris, 1930–9). Vol I. *The English Schism, Henry VIII, 1509–1547.* Tr. R.E. Scantlebury (London, 1934)

Cross, C. *Church and People, 1450–1660: The Triumph of the Laity in the English Church.* Fontana Library of English History, 2 (London, 1976)

Dahmus, J. H. *The Prosecution of John Wyclyf* (New Haven, 1952)

Dickens, A.G. *The English Reformation* (1964, repr. London, 1968)

Doernberg, E. *Henry VIII and Luther. An Account of their personal relations* (London, 1961)

Dowling, M. *Humanism in the Age of Henry VIII* (London, 1986)

Edgeworth, R.L. *Memoirs of R. L. Edgeworth . . . begun by himself, and concluded by his daughter, Maria Edgeworth.* 2 vols (London, 1820)

Eire, Carlos M.N. *War against the Idols: the Reformation of Worship from Erasmus to Calvin* (Cambridge, 1986)

Elton, G.R. *Policy and Police: the enforcement of the Reformation in the Age of Thomas Cromwell* (Cambridge, 1972)

The English Reformation Revised. Ed. C. Haigh (Cambridge, 1987)

Field, C.W. *The Province of Canterbury and the Elizabethan Settlement of Religion* (Robertsbridge, 1973)

Fletcher, A. *Tudor Rebellions.* 3rd ed. (London, 1983)

Fox, A. *Thomas More: History and Providence* (Oxford, 1982)

———— & J. Guy. *Reassessing the Henrician Age: Humanism, Politics and Reform 1500–1550* (Oxford, 1986)

Guy, J. *Tudor England* (Oxford, 1988)

Haigh, C. *Reformation and Resistance in Tudor Lancashire* (Cambridge, 1975)

Heath, P. *The English Parish Clergy on the Eve of the Reformation* (London, 1969)

Hembry, P.M. *Bishops of Bath and Wells, 1540–1640* (London, 1967)

Horst, I.B. *The Radical Brethren. Anabaptism and the English Reformation to 1558. Bibliotheca Humanistica et Reformatoria* II (Nieuwkoop, 1972)

Hudson, A. *Lollards and their Books* (London, 1985)

Hughes, P. *The Reformation in England.* 3 vols (London, 1954)

Hutchins, J. *The History and Antiquities of the County of Dorset.* 4 vols. 3rd ed. rev. W. Shipp and J.W. Hodson (London, 1973)

Ives, E.W. *Anne Boleyn* (Oxford, 1980)

Jordan, W.K. *Edward VI: the Threshold of Power* (London, 1970)

Kingsford, C.L. (Ed.) John Stow, *A Survey of London.* 2 vols (London, 1908)

Law and Government under the Tudors: Essays presented to Sir Geoffrey Elton on his retirement. Eds. Claire Cross, David Loades, J.J. Scarisbrick (Cambridge, 1988)

Lewis, S. *A Topographical Dictionary of England.* 4 vols (London, 1849)

Loach, J. *Parliament and Crown in the Reign of Mary Tudor* (Oxford, 1986)

————. 'Pamphlets and Politics 1553–8'. *Bulletin of the Institute of Historical Research* 48 (1975), 31–44

————. 'The Marian Establishment and the Printing Press'. *EHR* 101 (1986), 135–48

Loades, D. *The Reign of Mary Tudor: politics, government and religion in England, 1553–1558* (London, 1979)

————. 'The Enforcement of Reaction, 1553–1588'. *JEH* XVI (1965), 54–66

MacLure, M. *The Paul's Cross Sermons, 1534–1642* (Toronto, 1958)

Martin, J.W. *Religious Radicals in Tudor England* (London, 1989)

McConica, J. *English Humanists and Reformation Politics under Henry VIII and Edward VI* (Oxford, 1965)

McFarlane, K.B. *John Wycliffe and the Beginnings of English Nonconformity* (London, 1952)

McGrath, P. *The Merchant Venturers of Bristol* (Bristol, 1975)

Mozley, J.F. *William Tyndale* (New York, 1937)

————. *Coverdale and his Bibles* (London, 1923)

Muller, J.A. *Stephen Gardiner and the Tudor Reaction* (London, 1926)

Nicholls, J.F. and J. Taylor. *Bristol Past and Present.* 3 vols (Bristol, 1881)

Parmiter, G. de C. *The King's Great Matter: A Study in Anglo-Papal Relations, 1527–1534* (London, 1967)

Phillips, J. *The Reformation of Images: Destruction of Art in England 1535–1660* (Los Angeles, 1973)

Pineas, R. *Thomas More and Tudor Polemics* (Bloomington, 1968)

Pogson, R. 'The Legacy of the Schism' in *The Mid-Tudor Polity, c.1450–1560.* Eds. J. Loach and R. Tittler (London, 1980)

————. 'Revival and Reform in Mary Tudor's Church: a question of money' in *The English Reformation Revised*

————. 'Reginald Pole and the Priorities of Government in Mary Tudor's Church'. *Historical Journal* 18 (1975), 3–21

Powell, K.G. *Marian Martyrs*. BHA, 31 (1972)

————. 'The Beginnings of Protestantism in Gloucestershire'. *TBGAS* 90 (1971), 141–57

————. 'The Social Background to Protestantism in Gloucestershire'. *TBGAS* 92 (1973), 96–120

Redworth, G. *In Defence of the Church Catholic: the Life of Stephen Gardiner* (Oxford, 1990)

————. 'Whatever happened to the English Reformation?' *History Today* (October 1987), 29–36

Ridley, J.G. *Thomas Cranmer* (Oxford, 1962)

————. *Nicholas Ridley* (London, 1957)

Rupp, G. *Studies in the Making of the English Protestant Tradition* (Cambridge, 1947)

Scarisbrick, J.J. *Henry VIII* (London, 1968, repr. 1976)

————. *The Reformation and the English People* (Oxford, 1984)

Skeeters, M.C. 'The Clergy of Bristol, c.1530–c.1570.' (Ph.D thesis. University of Texas at Austin, 1984). Forthcoming as *Conflict and Crisis: the Clergy of Bristol c.1530–c.1570* (Oxford)

Smith Baldwin, Lacey. *Tudor Prelates and Politics, 1536–1558* (New Jersey, 1953)

Smith, H. Maynard. *Henry VIII and the Reformation* (London, 1948)

Strype, J. *Ecclesiastical Memorials relating chiefly to religion . . . and the reformation of . . . the Church of England under King Henry VIII, King Edward VI and Queen Mary I.* 3 vols (Oxford, 1822). Cited as Strype, *Ecc. Mem.*

————. *Memorials of Cranmer.* 2 vols (Oxford, 1840)

Thomson, J.A.F. *The Later Lollards 1414–1520* (Oxford, 1965)

Tjernagel, N.S. *Henry VIII and the Lutherans: A Study in Anglo-Lutheran Relations from 1521 to 1547* (St. Louis, 1965)

Victoria County History. *The History of the County of Gloucester.* 11 vols. Ed. W. Page *et al.* (London, 1907–76). Cited as VCH, *Gloucester*

————. *The History of the County of Somerset.* 5 vols. Ed. W. Page (London, 1906–85). Cited as VCH, *Somerset*

Whiting, R. *The Blind Devotion of the People* (Cambridge, 1989)

Williams, G.H. *The Radical Reformation* (Philadelphia, 1962)

Williams, Glanmor. *The Welsh Church from Conquest to Reformation.* Rev. ed. (Cardiff, 1976)

Wilson, J.M. 'The *Sermons* of Roger Edgworth: Reformation Preaching in Bristol' in *Early Tudor England.* Ed. D. Williams. Proceedings of the 1987 Harlaxton Symposium (Woodbridge, 1989)

Ecclesiastical history: doctrine and worship

Brightman, F.E. *The English Rite.* 2 vols. 2nd ed. (London, 1921)

Clark, F.J. *Eucharistic Sacrifice and the Reformation.* 2nd ed. (London, 1963)

Davies, D.H.M. *Worship and Theology in England.* 5 vols (New Jersey, 1961–75). I. *From Cranmer to Hooker, 1534–1603* (1970)

Dictionnaire de Théologie Catholique. Ed. A. Vacant *et al.* 15 vols (Paris, 1903–50). Cited as *DTC*

Dix, G. *The Shape of the Liturgy.* 2nd ed. (London, 1954)

Dugmore, C.W. *The Mass and the English Reformers* (London, 1958)

Encyclopaedia Judaica. 16 vols (Jerusalem, 1971)

Gasquet, A.C. and E. Bishop. *Edward VI and the Book of Common Prayer*. 3rd ed. (London, 1928)

Gogan, B. *The Common Corps of Christendom: Ecclesiological Themes in the Writings of Sir Thomas More*. Studies in the History of Christian Thought, 26 (Leiden, 1982)

Hanson, R.P.C. *The Search for the Christian Doctrine of God* (Edinburgh 1986)

Hardwick, C. *A History of the Articles of Religion* (London, 1859)

Leer, Flesseman-van E. 'The Controversy about Scripture and Tradition between Thomas More and William Tyndale'. *Nederlands Archief voor Kerkgeschiedenis*. NS, 43 (1959), 143–64

Messenger, E.C. *The Reformation, the Mass and the Priesthood*. 2 vols (London, 1936–7). I. *The Revolt from the Medieval Church*

The New Catholic Encyclopaedia. 10 vols (Washington, 1967). Cited as NCE

The Oxford Dictionary of the Christian Church. Ed. F.L. Cross and E.A. Livingstone. 2nd ed. (Oxford, 1974). Cited as ODCC

Pelikan, Jaroslav. *The Christian Tradition: A History of the Development of Doctrine*. 5 vols (Chicago and London, 1971–). IV. *Reformation of Church and Dogma (1300–1700)* (1984). Cited as Pelikan, *Church and Dogma*

Procter, F. *A New History of the Book of Common Prayer with a Rationale of its Offices*. Rev. ed. W.H. Frere (London, 1955). Cited as Procter and Frere, BCP

Rock, D. *The Church of Our Fathers*. Ed. G.W. Hart and W.H. Frere. 4 vols (London, 1903–4)

Stone, D. *The History of the Doctrine of the Holy Eucharist*. 2 vols (London, 1909)

Williams, R.D. *Arius: Heresy and Tradition* (London, 1987)

Young, K. *The Drama of the Medieval Church*. 2 vols (Oxford, 1933)

Textual criticism, bibliographies, dictionaries, encyclopaedias

Allison, A.F. and D.M. Rogers. *A Catalogue of Catholic books in England printed abroad or secretly in England, 1558–1640*. 2 Pts (Bognor Regis, 1956). Cited as A&R

Ames, J. and W. Herbert. *Typographical Antiquities, or The History of Printing in England, Scotland, and Ireland*. Ed. T.F. Dibdin, 4 vols. 3rd ed. (1810–19; repr. London, 1969). Cited as Ames, *Typ. Ant.*

Bennett, H.S. *English Books and Readers, 1475–1640*. 3 vols (Cambridge, 1952–70)

Columbia Lippincott Gazetteer. Ed. L.E. Seltzer (Columbia, 1966)

The New Encyclopaedia Britannica. 30 vols. 15th ed. (Chicago, 1975). Cited as *Enc. Brit.*

Gaskell, P. *A New Introduction to Bibliography* (Oxford, 1972)

Gilson, M. *Les Ideés et les Lettres* (Paris, 1932)

McKerrow, R.B. *An Introduction to Bibliography* (London, 1927)

Orbis Latinus. H. Plechl. 3 vols (Braunschweig, 1972). Cited as OL

The Oxford Classical Dictionary. Ed. N.G.L. Hammond and H.H. Scullard. 2nd ed. (Oxford, 1979). Cited as OCD

The Oxford Companion to Classical Literature. Ed. Sir P. Harvey. 2nd ed. rev. M. Howatson (Oxford, 1989). Cited as OCCL

The Oxford Dictionary of Saints. Ed. D.H. Farmer (1978, repr. Oxford, 1979). Cited as ODS

The Oxford English Dictionary. Ed. J.A.H. Murray, H. Bradley, W.A. Craigie, C.T. Onions (Oxford, 1933–). Cited as *OED*

Rostenberg, Leona. *The Minority Press and the English Crown: A Study in Repression, 1558–1625* (Nieuwkoop, 1971)

Siebert, F.S. *The Freedom of the Press in England: 1476–1776* (University of Illinois Press, 1965)

The Short–Title Catalogue of books printed in England, Scotland, and Ireland and of English Books Printed Abroad, 1475–1640. 2 vols. comp. A. Pollard and G.R. Redgrave (1926). Rev. ed. W.A. Jackson, F.S. Ferguson, K. Pantzer. Bibliographical Society (London, 1976–86). Cited as *STC*

Wilson, J.M. 'A Catalogue of the "Unlawful" Books found in John Stow's Study on 21 February 1568/9'. *RH* XX, i (1990), 1–30

Literary criticism

Blench, J.W. 'John Longland and Roger Edgeworth, two forgotten Preachers of the early sixteenth Century'. *RES* NS, v, 18 (1954), 123–43

———. *Preaching in England in the late Fifteenth and Sixteenth Centuries: A study of English Sermons 1450–c.1600* (Oxford, 1964). Cited as Blench

Burnley, J.D. *Chaucer's Language and the Philosophers' Tradition.* Chaucer Studies, ii. (Cambridge, 1979)

Cave, T. *The Cornucopian Text* (Oxford, 1979)

Chambers, E.K. *On the Continuity of English Prose from Alfred to More and his School.* EETS, OS, 192A (London, 1932)

Crane. W.G. *Wit and Rhetoric in the Renaissance: the formal basis of Elizabethan prose style* (New York, 1964)

Croll, M.W. 'The Sources of the Euphuistic Rhetoric' in *Style, Rhetoric and Rhythm.* Ed. J.M. Patrick and R.O. Evans (New Jersey, 1966)

Davis, N. 'Styles in English Prose in the Late Middle and Early Modern Period'. *Langue et Littérature: Actes du VIIIe Congres de la Fédération Internationale des Langues et Littératures Modernes.* Les Congres et Colloques de l'Université de Liège, 21 (Université de Liège, 1961), 165–84

———. *William Tyndale's English of Controversy.* The Chambers' Memorial Lecture (London, 1971)

Delcourt, J. *Essai sur la langue de Thomas More* (Paris, 1914)

———. 'Some Aspects of Sir Thomas More's English'. *Essays and Studies* 21 (1935), 21–30

Derrick, T.J. (Ed.) *Thomas Wilson's* Arte of Rhetorique. The Renaissance Imagination, I (New York, 1982)

Dibdin, T. *The Library Companion.* 2 vols (London, 1824)

Dowling, M. *Humanism in the Age of Henry VIII* (Kent, 1986)

English Humanism: Wyatt to Cowley. Ed. J. Martindale (Kent, 1985)

Evans, John, X. 'The Art of Rhetoric and the Art of Dying in Tudor Recusant Prose'. *RH* X, 5 (1970), 247–72

Gordon, I.A. *The Movement of English Prose* (London, 1966)

Gray, H.H. 'Renaissance Humanism: the Pursuit of Eloquence' in *Renaissance Essays from the Journal of the History of Ideas.* Ed. P.O. Kristeller and P.P. Wiener (New York, 1968)

Janton, P. *Eloquence et Rhétorique dans les Sermons de Hugh Latimer*. Faculté des Lettres et Sciences Humaine de l'Université de Clermont-Ferraud. 2nd ser. Facs. 27 (Paris, 1968)

Jones, R.F. *The Triumph of the English Language: a survey of opinions concerning the vernacular from the introduction of printing to the Restoration* (Oxford, 1953)

Kahn, V. *Rhetoric, Eloquence and Skepticism in the Renaissance* (Ithaca, 1985)

King, J.N. *English Reformation Literature: The Tudor Origins of the Protestant Tradition* (New Jersey, 1982)

Lewis, C.S. *English Literature in the Sixteenth Century excluding Drama* (Oxford, 1954)

Mueller, Janel M. *The Native Tongue and the Word: Developments in English Prose Style 1380–1580* (Chicago and London, 1984)

Ong, W.J. 'Oral Residue in Tudor Prose Style'. PMLA 80 (1965), 147–54

Owst, G.R. *Preaching in Medieval England, an Introduction to the Sermon Manuscripts of the Period 1350–1450* (Cambridge, 1926)

———. *Literature and Pulpit in Medieval England*. 2nd ed. (Oxford, 1961). Cited as Owst, LPME

Scattergood, J. 'Fashion and Morality in the Later Middle Ages' in *Fifteenth Century England*. Ed. D. Williams. Proceedings of the 1986 Harlaxton Symposium (London, 1987)

Seigel, Jerrold E. *Rhetoric and Philosophy in Renaissance humanism: the union of eloquence and wisdom* (New Jersey, 1968)

Southern, A.C. *English Recusant Prose, 1559–1582* (1950, repr. London, 1978)

Steuert, Dom. H. 'The English Prose Style of Thomas Watson, Bishop of Lincoln, 1557'. MLR XLI, 3 (1946), 225–36

Wenzel, Siegfried. *Preachers, Poets, and the Early English Lyric* (New Jersey, 1986)

Bibles, Bible commentaries and scriptural interpretation

Barrett, C.K. *The Gospel according to St John* (London 1955)

———. *The Holy Spirit in the Gospel Tradition* (London, 1966)

Beare, F.W. *The First Epistle of St Peter: The Greek Text with Introduction and Notes*. 3rd ed. (Oxford, 1970)

Bentley, Jerry H. *Humanists and Holy Writ: New Testament Scholarship in the Renaissance* (Princeton, 1983)

Bigg, C.W. *A Critical and Exegetical Commentary on the Epistles of St. Peter and St. Jude*. ICC. 2nd ed. (Edinburgh, 1910)

Cullman, O. *Petrus* (Zurich, 1952). Tr. O.V. Filson, *Peter*. 2nd ed. (London, 1953)

Deansley, M. *The Lollard Bible* (Cambridge, 1920)

The Dictionary of Christian Biography. Ed. W. Smith and H. Wace. 4 vols (London, 1877–87)

The Dictionary of the Bible. Ed. T. Hastings. 4 vols (Edinburgh, 1900–1904). Cited as DB

Dictionnaire de la Bible. Ed. F. Vigoroux, 5 vols (Paris, 1895–1912). Cited as Dict. Bibl.

Encyclopaedia Biblica. Ed. T.K. Cheyne and J.S. Black. 4 vols (London, 1899–1903). Cited as Enc. Bib.

Foakes, Jackson F.T. *Peter Prince of Apostles* (London, 1927)

Kelly, J.N.D. *Early Christian Doctrines*. 4th ed. (London, 1968)

———. *Early Christian Creeds* (London, 1950)

————. *A Commentary on the Epistles of Peter and Jude*. Harper's NT Commentaries (London, 1969)

Marc'hadour, G.P. *The Bible in the Works of Thomas More: A Repertory*. 5 vols (Nieuwkoop, 1969–72). Cited as Marc'hadour, *Bible*

————. *Thomas More et la Bible* (Paris, 1969)

Michaels, J. Ramsey. *I Peter*. Word Biblical Commentary, 49 (Texas, 1988)

Peake's Commentary on the Bible. Ed. Matthew Black and N.N. Rowley (London, 1962)

Selwyn, E.G. *The First Epistle of St. Peter*. 2nd ed. (London, 1947)

Smalley, B. *The Study of the Bible in the Middle Ages*. 3rd ed. (Oxford, 1983)

Thomas, St John of. *The Gifts of the Holy Ghost*. Tr. D. Hughes (London, 1950)

GLOSSARY

This selective glossary explains only words and phrases whose meanings depart from modern English or whose spellings are likely to cause problems of recognition. When a word carries more than one meaning, the meanings are listed in the order in which they occur in the text. Variant spellings of a word are given in alphabetical order. The following abbreviations are used:

adj. adjective
adv. adverb
comp. comparative
conj. conjunction
dial. dialect
intr. intransitive
n. noun
ppl. participle
p.ppl. past participle

pa.t. past tense
pl. plural
pr.ppl. present participle
refl. reflexive
trans. transitive
v. verb
var. variant
vbl n. verbal noun

ado *v.* **a doying** *ppl. adj.* continuing, in process, 187
ahungred, an hungred *ppl. adj.* oppressed with hunger, 117, 154, 212, 279
amaking, a makinge *p.ppl.* was being made, 175, 192
abiect, -e *n.* outcast, degraded person, 289; *adj.* cast down, degraded, humble in estate, 290
abiection *n.* abasement, humiliation, degradation, 264
abilimentes *n. pl.* clothing, attire, accoutrement, 154, 272, 273
abrenunciation *n.* renunciation, repudiation, 232
abroade, abrode, *adv.* **pull –, settyng –,** displaying, 154, 272; **sliked –,** displayed smoothly groomed, 272
acception *n.* favouritism due to a person's rank or influence, 219, 220
accommodate *adj.* suitable, fitting, 128
accusement *n.* accusation, accusing, charge, 291
acquisite *adj.* acquired, gained, obtained for oneself, 120
acquitall *n.* payment, repayment, requital, 320, 323
addict *p.ppl.* devoted, dedicated, 138, 173, 240, 290, 340
aduenture *n.* chance; **at all –s,** in any way by chance, 338
aduertens *n.* heed, attention, 149
aduisement *n.* counsel, advice, 119, 130; consideration, thinking, deliberation, process of considering mentally, 124, 126, 130, 132, 136, 163
adulteration *n.* debasing, corruption, making spurious, 273
adulterating *vbl n.* debasing, corrupting, 273
aduouterer *n.* adulterer, 128, 165
aduoutresse *n.* adulteress, 165
aduoutri *n.* adultery, 158
affectate *adj.* self-deceiving, 289
affiaunce *n.* confidence, trust, 117, 364
alburned, all burned *adj.* (a sacrifice) totally consumed by fire, burnt up, 118, 186
allectiue *n.* enticement, allurement, 340
amencye *n.* madness, dementia, 357
amite, amitie *n.* friendship, friendliness, 134, 217, 269, 346, 368
amonge *adv.* **euer –,** every now and then, 297; **sometimes –,** all the while, now and then, 95; occasionally, at the same time, 95; occasionally, meanwhile, 306

amotion n. removing, removal, ousting, 179

amoue v. remove, put away, 301; **amouing** pr.ppl. 178; **amoued** p.ppl. 301; **a mouinge** ppl. adj.; **long –**, slow moving, 180

apayre v. impair, damage, 346

appendeceis n. pl. additions, accessories, 95

aray, araye n. order, arrangement in line or rank, 312

araye v. attire, clothe, dress, adorn, 154, 275; p.ppl. ordered, arranged, displayed, 135, 187

Arche n. ark, 279, 292

arede v. declare by supernatural counsel, prophecy, 142

artificer n. craftsman, inventor, constructor, 145, 212

asserteyned p.ppl. informed, apprised, told, 214

assuefaction n. habituation, use by becoming accustomed, 124

auoide, auoyde v. intr. withdraw, depart, retreat, 165; **– out of**, 319, **– from**, 288, 313, 336

auoydaunce n. shunning, avoiding, hold aloof from, 151

bane n. poison, sheep rot, 254, 351, 353

baninge vbl n. poisoning, 352

barme n. yeast, leaven, 365

bashfulnes, -ness, -nesse n. modesty, shamefulness, 122, 154, 272

batilnes n. fertility, 156

bealyglee n. pleasures of the belly, 301

beggery n. beggary; indigent, mean or low circumstances; impoverishment, 146, 309

benchewhystler n. good for nothing fellow, 298

bende, n. troop, company; **a stronge –**, a well organised company of men, 229

bended p.ppl. **– to extinct,** driven to destroy, 150; **stifelye –**, stubbornly constrained, 354

beseme, -th, v. befit, become (the character of), appear well, 121, 139, 154, 280, 284, 289, 338, 344

beseming, besemyng, -e pr.ppl. befitting, becoming, 286; ppl. adj. seemly, comely; **euil –**, ill becoming, unsuitable, 345

bibbinge pr.ppl. tippling, continued drinking, 301

blowboll n. tippler, drunkard, habitual drinker, 298

boistous, boystuous adj. fierce, vigorous, full of rude strength, 159, 287

boistuously adv. roughly, violently, boisterously, 239

bollynge pr.ppl. quaffing, boozing, 301

boteth (var. of **boot**) v. avail, help, profit, 261, 354

brable v. quarrel, 264

braye v. crush into powder, 239

bringer vp n. parent, guardian, one responsible for education, 155

brye (var. of **breer**) n. eye-lash, 272

bulke n. stall, framework projecting from the front of a shop, 333

bushmentes n. pl. troops or company secretly deployed; a surprise party, 229

cabao n. ship carrying merchandise; venture in the coast carrying trade, 123

Caldees, Caldeis n. pl. Caldeans, 208, 356, 366

callidyte n. craftiness, cunning, 362

calotte n. drab, lewd woman, 278

cantel n. part, portion, 281, 282

canueste p.ppl. tossed in a canvas sheet (for punishment), 263

cap, cappe n. **– and knee,** respect, reverence, honour, courtesy, 153, 278, 352

cast, -e n. device, trick, strategem; **far –**, shrewd trick, 125, 309; purpose, design, aim, 126, 132, 282, 308; **politique –**, sagacious, prudent disposition or inclination, 308; **the last –**, near to death or ruin, at the last shift, in extremities, 141, 223; type, kind, sort, 311

cast, -e v. intr. devise, scheme, contrive, 124; **casting** pr.ppl. anticipating, 148; vbl n. planning, scheming, 132; ppl. adj. **far –**, shrewd, scheming, 118, 124

cathechisation n. catechizing, giving systematic oral instruction, 294

cathechised *p.ppl.* instructed, taught, 226

chargeable *adj.* burdensome, troublesome, 185, 327; costly, expensive, 237

chaunce medley *n.* manslaughter, misadventure (of homicide), 183

cheare, chere *n.* kindly hospitality, welcome, reception, 253, 322; **good –,**
   entertainment, 117, 143, 253, 323; **make good –,** give a welcome, receive, entertain,
   276, 325; countenance, aspect, 230; disposition, mood; **with good –,** cheerfully,
   joyfully, with good will, 143, 269, 325; fare, provisions, food, 322; **make –,** make
   merry, 267

cherable *adj.* cheerful, glad, 326

choplogik *n.* one who chops logic or uses contentious, sophistical arguments, 262

circumuent *v.* encompass with evils or malice; try to entrap in conduct or speech, 118;
   surround, encompass by hostile stratagem, 229

clatering, clattering, -e *vbl n.* chattering, 139; *pr.ppl.* babbling, chattering aimlessly,
   talking noisely, 231, 333

clausure *n.* enclosure, 294

cleue *n.* (*dial.*) cliff, steep declivity, 198

clouter *n.* patcher, cobbler, 338

coact *ppl. adj.* coerced, enforced, compelled, 225

coarted *p.ppl.* constrained, restricted 323; *ppl. adj.* repressed, 367

coaction *n.* compulsion, constraint, coercion, 351, 352, 353, 355

cocbrained *ppl. adj.* foolish, light headed, 355

coenheritour, coinheritoure *n.* joint inheritour, 167, 213, 278

coll *v.* embrace, hug, 368; **collinge** *pr.ppl.* 153

collation *n.* collection, bringing together, 170; comparison 233

colourable *adj.* hypocritical, done for appearances sake, 118, counterfeit, feigned,
   deceitful, 229

combind *v.* (form of **combine** + **bind**) combine, 156

comminacion, commination *n.* threatening of (Divine) punishment or vengeance, 117,
   122, 125, 241, 243, 289, 292, 348, 356

cominaltie, comonaltie, commonaltie, comminalitie *n.* body of common people,
   commons, 186, 253; community, 282

comontie *n.* community, 282

commoditie *n.* material benefits, wealth, 157; benefit, advantage, 304, 320, 324

commoneth *v. intr.* participate in, partake of, share in, 179

comonication *n.* (*var.*) communication, 319

company *v. intr.* keep company, associate, consort with, 141, 153, 266; cohabit, 278

compas, compasse *n.* circle, curve, 267, 362; **go –,** deviate, swerve from, circumvent,
   363; **go about by –, go – about,** take a circuitous route, make a detour, act by means of
   strategies, 362, 363

compasse *adj.* **– stroke,** circular movement, 355

compas, compasse *v.* devise, contrive, machinate, 124, 126, 362; **compasyng** *pr.ppl.* 132;
   grasp, comprehend, 180; encompass, enclose, environ, encircle, 214, 362; *intr.* **–
   about,** make a circuit, move around; hem in, beseige, 362, 363

conclude *v.* overcome in argument, convince, confute, 139

condigne *adj.* fitting, appropriate, 129

constitute *v.* set up (in an office or position of authority), 132, 343; *p.ppl.* 148, 188, 189,
   258, 259, 351

contumelious *adj.* shameful, disgraceful, reproachful, 332

contumely *n.* scornful rudeness, insolent reproach or abuse, 334

conuented *p.ppl.* assembled, gathered together, 134, 262, 299

conuenticle *n.* assembly or meeting of a clandestine or illegal character, or considered to
   have a sinister purpose, 129

conuerse *n.* convert, 344, 367

coothe *v. dial.* give rot or 'coe' to sheep, 351; **coothinge** *ppl. adj.* 353

cordiall *n.* medicine, remedy, 239

corosiue n. medicine or sharp caustic remedy, 239

corporace, corporas n. square linen piece on which the bread and wine are placed in the consecration of the Eucharist, 187, 365

cosoner n. cook, 307

coste v. intr. – **ouer** go, pass over; make a path across, 265

counterpoint n. counterpane, 307

countersayer n. gainsayer, opponent, 143

countersay, -e v. contradict, refute, 169, 240, 262; **countersayd, -said**, p.ppl. 231, 240, 282

countersaying, countresaiyng vbl n. contradiction, 139, 331

crabbed adj. ill tempered, acrimonious, irritable, churlish, 261, 262, 277, 278

crash v. break into pieces, smash, shatter, 239; **crasshinge,** pr.ppl. 254

creanser n. tutor or guardian, 356

crocker n. earthenware vessel, domestic utensil, 211

cruet n. small vessel containing wine and water for celebration of the Eucharist or holy water for other purposes, 184, 187

cull n. a fish, also known as Bull-head or Miller's Thumb, 184

cumberous adj. troublesome, burdensome, 261; harassing, causing annoyance, 278

cunning, cunnyng, -e n. knowledge, learning, erudition; practical knowledge, skill, 114, 136, 139, 140, 327, 328; ability, skill, expertness, 161

cunning, cunnyng adj. possessing knowledge, learned, clever, expert, skilled, 136, 274

currier n. messenger, 151

customable adj. customary, usual, 293, 325

customably, -ie adv. customably, habitually, usually, 343

cutted ppl. adj. cut short, 309

danger n. **in his –,** in his power or debt; under obligation to him, 210

dash v. adorn or trim; **dasshed** p.ppl. 273, 276

dastard n. dullard, someone feeble of wit, 213, 269

daungerous adj. disdainful, haughty, arrogant, 160, 168

dawe n. jackdaw, 208; fool, simpleton, dullard, 289

deale n. bit; **neuer a –,** not at all, 336

deiection n. adj. casting down, lowering of fortunes, abasement, humiliation, 213, 273

dimisent (var. of **demicient**) n. girdle (ornamented only in the front), 273

demore v. linger, delay, 239, 250

denison n. inhabitant (not native born), 151

depart, -e v. – **bedde and boorde,** bring to an end connubial relations, 277; – **with,** give away, give up, surrender, 283

deriue v. transmit, pass on, hand on, 115, 124; **deriued,** p.ppl. 115, 120, 147, 150; drawn, descended, 189, 194, 258

derogate v. lessen, disparage, depreciate, 199

derogation n. curtailment, impairment, detraction from (authority), 300

derogatynge pr.ppl. detracting from, disparaging, depreciating, 301

despite, despyte, dispite n. outrage, shameful injury, 113, 262, 265, 299, 318, 334, 336; ill will, anger, indignation, 256; contempt, disdain, scorn, 333; **have in –,** hold in scorn, contempt, 304; **do – to,** treat with injury, outrage, 336

despiteful, dispiteful adj. malignant, malicious, spiteful, 265; insulting, opprobrious, 266, 304, 332

differ, differre v. intr. differ, be at variance, disagree, hold a different opinion, 168

disciplinable adj. capable of being instructed, docile, 119

discommodity n. disadvantage, inconvenience, trouble, 169

discurrynge pr.ppl. running hither and thither, 300

dispitefullye adv. insolently, contemptuously, 160, 302, 305

distemperance, distemperaunce n. inclemency, intemperateness (of the weather), 122, 307

dogbolte n. contemptible fellow, mean wretch, 365

drabb n. harlot, prostitute, strumpet, 298

drauel v. dribble 230

disseuer, dysseuer v. separate, sever, 150, 263; separate, part (from each other), divide, 171; **disseuered** p.ppl. 171, 212, 312

drift n. design, scheme, plot, 255, 310

dycer n. one who plays or gambles with dice, 234

ebrietie n. drunkenness, the state of being intoxicated, 117

emergent adj. in the process of issuing forth, 132

empery, emperye n. absolute dominion, 131, 158, 270, 271

emyt, emytte n. ant, 311

enbrued (var. of **imbrued**) p.ppl. soaked, steeped, saturated, 115, 249

endite v. proclaim, ordain, 191

engin n. contrivance, design, 223

enigmatically adj. obscurely, ambiguously, 322

enoyling vbl n. sacrament of extreme unction, 187

enterpryse v. attempt, take upon (oneself), undertake, 341

entre n. entrance, 198

enuyron v. surround, enclose, 214; **enuironnyng**, pr.ppl. 199; **enuironed**, p.ppl. 299

Ethnich n. heathen, pagan, Gentile; neither Christian or Jew, 152

euacuate p.ppl. annulled, made void, 348

excogitating p.ppl. thinking evil, devising, contriving, 189

exercitate p.ppl. exercised (with a spiritual discipline), 142

exhibicion n. pecuniary assistance given to university students, 283

exhibitoure n. exhibitioner, educational benefactor, one who pays for an education or maintenance, 155

exorbitate v. deviate from the usual course, stray, 362

facultie n. profession, trade, 137

fancye, -ie, fansie n. delusive imagination, 138, 142, 170, 254, 284, 300

fantasie, phantasie n. spectral apparition, phantom, illusory appearance, 157, 158, 233, 254

farced p.ppl. crammed, stuffed, 117, 309; **farcinge** pr.ppl. 300

fardell n. bundle, parcel, little pack, 157

fast, faste adj. firm, settled, stable, 158, 194, 196, 218, 235; –, **meat**, solid meat, 233

fatigated p.ppl. fatigued, 131

fautie, fauty adj. guilty of wrongdoing, 251, 328

feete adj. fitting, suitable, proper, 161; n. skill, art, 161

feel v. have a physical sensation, 322; **feled**, p.ppl. perceived (through touching), 171

felowlike adv. communally, 179

felowlyke adj. equal, like a friend, 352

fet v. pa. t. fetched, 323; **far –**, cunning, devious, 125

fetelye adv. elegantly, aptly, 302

flagelled p.ppl. scourged, whipped, 127, 336

fleete v. fluctuate, waver, 142

fliering, flyring adj. obsequiously fawning, 368, 230

flocked p.ppl. driven (in the midst of), 229; **flocking** pr.ppl. **-ing together**, crowding in flocks, 312

fool n. **play the –**, act in an impious manner, 148, 170

forecasting vbl n. contriving, planning, 124

forme n. nest or lair of a hare, 311

fortalice, -ies n. small fort, 125

forwarde n. foremost part, assault, 312

foyle n. means (of setting off to advantage), 192; repulse, defeat, 364

fractions n. pl. **– of the Sacrament,** formal breaking of the bread before the *Agnus Dei*, 246

fraske *n.* trick, 339

fraye *n.* disturbance, upheaval, 259

frensye *adj.* mad, crazy, 151

frequentinge *pr.ppl.* practising, resorting habitually to, 359

frisses (*var.* of **frieze**) *n.pl.* tufts of the nap or down of plants, 313

frowardly *adv.* readily, promptly, 247

fruntlet (*var.* of **frontlet**) *n.* ornament or band worn on the forehead, 154

frustratorie *adj.* disappointing, frustrating, 310

fume *n.* fit of anger, 277, 354

fumish *adj.* irascible, hot-tempered, 344

furnysh *v.* fulfil, complete, 308

gamener *n.* gambler, gamester, player, 346

garnard *n.* store house, granary, 311

gathering, -inge, -yng, -ynge *n.* joint compilation, 169, 170, 172, 174, 177, 179

gaye *adj.* merry, light-hearted, 143; excellent, fine, 159, 274, 320; showy, brilliant, bright, 252, 307

gearre *n.* jar, 321

gerre (*var.* of **garre**) *v.* rumble, growl, chide, 243

gestingly *adv.* in jest, 284

gise *n.* fashion, style, 173

giue *v.* **gaue back**, retreated, fell back, 141; **geuing**, *pr.ppl.* **euill occasions –,** making of inducements to sin, 117

gnawer *n.* carper, captious critic, 141

godderd *n.* drinking cup, vessel for liquid, 146

gorbelye *n.* corpulent, pot-bellied man, 151

gorgeouslie *adv.* in a sumptuous fashion, 256

gospellar *n.* one who claims exclusive possession of the gospell truth, 299

gowt *n.* an attack of gout, 305

graffing *vbl n.* grafting (one tree into another), 353

gripe *n.* vulture, 184

grose (*?var.* of **grass**) *n.* grass, herbage, 312

groserye *n.* trade of a grocer, wholesale dealer in spices, 146

haal, hale *n.* pavilion, tent, 270, 331

hale *v.* drag, draw, tug, 254, 298

handfast *n.* **gyue no – to,** attach no importance to, 130

handsmothe *adv.* level or flat as if smoothed with the hand, 133

hanger *n.* kind of short sword, 368

harborow *n.* shelter, lodging, 319

harnes, harneis *n.* gear, tackle (weaponry), 141, 217, 297

haue *v. intr.* **– at,** get at, attack, 242

hauocke, hauoke *n.* **made –, of,** devastated, laid waste, 229; **goeth to –,** falls into chaos, disintegrates, 217

holocaust *n.* sacrifice completely consumed by fire, burnt offering, 186

honorifie *v.* do honour to, worship, 260

hoore *n.* hoary in appearance, 272

horeson *n.* **Pope holye –,** hypocritical, sanctimonious bastard, 303

horehunter *n.* one who chases after whores, practises fornication, 346; **horehuntinge** *vbl n.* 234

horrye (*var.* of **hory**) *adj.* **– shyfte,** fraudulent, base device(s) or trick(s), 345

hostrie, hostrye *n.* hostelry, 315, 323

hoist, hoyst *v.* raise aloft, lift up, 358

hoise, hoyse *v.* raise aloft, lift up, place on high, 174

huswyfely *adj.* fitting for a housewife, 275

huswyfery *n.* domestic duties, housekeeping, 275

ieopardinge *pr.ppl.* hazarding, risking, exposing oneself to, 134

ignare *adj.* ignorant, 185, 289

imbecilitie *n.* feebleness, impotence, 192

impassibilitie *n.* incapability of suffering an injury; incapability of feeling or emotion, 180, 339

impinguation *n.* fattening, 320

importune *adj.* persistent, pressing in solicitation, 226

incorruption *n.* freedom from physical corruption or decay, 180

increat, -e *adj.* uncreated, 241, 264, 293, 361

inculcate *v.* impress on the mind by emphatic admonition, 297; **inculcated,** *p.ppl.* 186

indifferencye *n.* impartiality, fairmindedness, 118, 228

indue (*var.* of **endue**) *p.ppl.* invested with, endowed, 113, 115; –, **with,** possessed of, 119, 146, 180, 213

indument *n.* material body or form regarded as the investiture of the soul, 180, 273

indurate *v.* render callous or unfeeling, 143

insensate *adj.* devoid of sensibility, wanting in moral feeling, 133

intangle *v.* hold fast, ensnare, 346; **intangled** *ppl. adj.* 235

intestine *adj.* domestic, civil, 282

intisement *n.* allurement, 159, 217

inuegle *v.* beguile, deceive; **inuegled;** *p.ppl.* beguiled, enticed, 127, 217

irremissyble *adj.* unforgiveable, unpardonable, 159

irrupting *pr.ppl.* bursting, breaking into, 150

Isope *n.* hyssop, 191

Iugge *n.* Joan, Joanna, 143

kindle, *v.* inflame, stir up, excite, 256; **kindled, kindeled** *p.ppl.* 345; roused, inspired, 234; **kindelinge** *vbl n.* stirring up, rousing, 300

knack, -e *n.* trinket, trifle, knick-knack, 253, 254

labilitie *n.* instability, unreliability, 96, 187

lamprey *n.* A fish like an eel in shape, lacking scales, with a mouth like a sucker, pouch-like gills, seven apertures on each side of the head and an opening on top of the head, 277, 278

lauer *n.* basin, vessell, 294

layfe, layfee *n.* laity, 249, 333, 352

leastwise, least(e) wise *adv.* **at the –,** at least, 122, 145, 162, 166

leege (*var.* of **league**) *n.* compact, covenant, alliance, 242, 246

leer *n.* complexion, hue, 273

leauer *adv.* rather, 230, 251, 268

lesyng *n.* lie, falsehood, untruth, 189

Libanus *n.* Lebanon, 191

light, lyght *n.* illumination, enlightenment, 124, 177, 183, 185, 218, 277; **false lyghtes,** false information, 220

light, -e, lyght, -e *adj.* unimportant, inconsequential, trivial, slight, 284, 333, 345; (of persons) of small account, not commanding respect, 354; – **cheape,** of small value, 273; – **fingered,** pugnacious, prompt in returning a blow, 345

lightly, lyghtlie *adv.* easily, quickly, readily, 249, 365; probably, 272

loche *n.* small European fish, 184

longanimitie, longanimitye *n.* forbearance, patience, 142, 146, 241, 345

lose *v.* **losed** (*var.* form of *p.ppl.*), lost, 118

loutynge *pr.ppl.* stooping, 356

lucre *n.* material gain or profit, 117, 118, 259, 329, 345, 346

lurcher *n.* petty thief, swindler, pilferer, 262

macerate *v.* cause the body to waste away (by fasting), 297; **maceratinge** *pr.ppl.* 300

malander, malandre, malendres *n.* sore, sickness, 177, 226, 305, 335

malaperte *adj.* presumptuous, impudent, 139

malefactour *n.* felon, criminal, evil doer, 147, 152, 255, 258, 265, 272, 282, 291, 307, 334, 359

manerlye *adv*. becomingly, properly, modestly, 284, 291

manerlynes *n*. moderation, 285

manish, monish *v*. admonish; **monished** *p.ppl*. 260; **manishyng** *pr.ppl*. 266

manyform *adj*. multiform, 327

maresh *adj*. marshy, swampy, 351

masking *pr.ppl*. becoming bewildered, losing one's way, 265

mayny, meyny, -e *n*. multitude, mass, 'crew' (often used disparagingly), 137, 160, 239, 258; attendant, servant, 328

mayr *n*. lake, pond, 185

mede *n*. reward, bribe, 266

Medes *n. pl*. Medeans, 208, 214, 270, 271

mercerye *n*. wares sold by a mercer (usually textile fabrics), 146

meshed *p.ppl*. entangled, 310

meyre *adj*. boundary, 151; **– stones,** stones set up as landmarks, 151

micher *n*. truant, 261

missay *v*. abuse, slander, revile, vilify, 266, 333, 348; **missayinge, missaiynge** *pr.ppl*. 238, 259, 298, 334; *intr*. speak abusively, slanderously, 231; **missayed, missaied, missaid** *p.ppl*. 266, 231, 259, 298, 333

mo *adv*. more, 130; **many –,** many of the same kind, 156

mock, -e *n*. taunt, act of derision or contempt, 117, 242; **–s & stripes,** taunts and lashes, 135; **make a –,** bring into contempt, 242

moe *n*. crowd, common people, 340

moiling, moyling, -ynge *pr.ppl*. burrowing, 117, 233, 309

molifie, mollifye *v*. soften, render less obdurate, 138, 162, 264

monicion *n*. instruction, direction, 183, 218

moreine, moreyne *n*. pestilence, plague, 125, 336

morish *adj*. boggy, swampy, 351

morter *n*. lime and sand mixed with water, used for plastering, 159, 160, 208; vessel for pounding with a pestle, 184

moull *v*. grow mouldy, moulder, 208

mouselled *p.ppl*. muzzled, 253

mundanitie *n*. worldliness, 282

nall (*var*. of **awl**) *n*. small tool with a slender, cylindrical, sharp pointed blade used for pricking holes in leather, 166

nashnes *n*. softness, weakness, 133

naught, nought, -e *adj*. worthless, useless, bad in condition, 156; morally bad, wicked (of actions), 158, 159, 162, 163, 164, 170, naughty, 231, 256, 261; immoral, vicious, 156, 158

nere *adv.comp*. nearer, 150, 161

newe fanglenes *n*. novelty, innovation, 254

newfangled *adj*. new-fashioned, novel, 146

nimietie *n*. excess, 284

nociue, nocyue *n*. harmful, injurious, 228, 301

nonce *n*. **for the –,** the particular purpose, on purpose, expressly, 145, 272

nonemeat *n*. food taken at nones (i.e. about 3 p.m.), 301

noseiled *p.ppl*. nurtured, sustained, 354

nouche (*var*. of **ouch**) *n*. clasped necklace, clasp, 273

noughtielye, noughtelye *adv*. wickedly, wrongly, 122, 160

noyfull *adj*. harmful, hurtful, 254

noysom, noysome *adj*. harmful, injurious, 179, 192, 210

occultation *n*. concealment, hiding, 95

occupier *n*. trader, merchant, one who deals in money, 160

occupy *v*. practice, perform, 158; *intr*. **– for oneself,** trade, do business, 160; **occupied,** *p.ppl*. use, seize, take, 184; make use of, 212, 329, 347; **occupiynge** *pr.ppl*. 306; *intr*. **– with,** dwell, reside, 213; *intr*. fornicate, 345

occupiynge, occupyinge *vbl n.; pr.ppl.* trading, dealing, 122, 212, 284, 327, 345

onsette *n.* attack, assault, 312

opprobrious *adj.* vituperative, abusive, 183

ordinance, ordinaunce *n.* established rule, body of principles, 188, 258, 270; injunction, 188, 284; contrivance, plan, 223; battle array, order, 312; decree (of God), 339

ordinal *n.* manual acquainting the priest with the Office to be recited in accordance with variations in the ecclesiastical year, 189

ordinate *adj.* ordered, regulated, 132, 245, 351

ordinatelye *adv.* in due order, according to rule, regularly, 132, 312

ossinge *pr.ppl.* presaging, betokening, 274

ouerhand, -e *n.* upper hand, mastery, victory, 134, 306

outfurth *adj.* exterior, external, 247; *adv.* externally, outwardly, 114

parclose *n.* railing enclosing a tomb, 346

parties *n.pl.* regions, districts, 131

paschal, paschall *adj.* pertaining to the Jewish Passover, 125, 184, 298

passible *adj.* capable of suffering or suffering; susceptible of sensation or emotion, 180, 223, 268, 339

patrimonie *n.* heritage, property inherited from ancestors or father, 208, 319

penetratiue *adj.* penetrating, 340

penner *n.* a case for pens (often carried with an inkhorn), 335

pensifenes *n.* heaviness of heart, melancholy, sadness, 176

pensyfull *adj.* sorrowful, anxious, 134

percel *n.* in —s, a part at a time, 193

perished *p.ppl.* spiritually destroyed, 141

Persies *n.* Persians, 208, 214, 270, 271

perwyked *p.ppl.* concealed with a periwig, 273

pestiferous *adj.* pestilential, 187

peyse *n.* weight, heaviness, 355

peyse *v.* oppress, weight down, 359

pike *n.* staff; **moris —,** staff supposedly of Moorish origin, 215

piker, pyker *n.* pilferer, robber, petty thief; **priuey —s,** stealthy thieves, 262, 346

pilled *p.ppl.* — **and polled,** plundered and pillaged, 336

pismyre *n.* ant, 311

pitcher *n.* large earthenware vessel usually with two handles, 146, 211; one who throws clay, potter, 220

pocke *n.* pustule of eruption in disease, 208, 358

politique *adj.* sagacious, prudent, 308

polled *p.ppl.* **pilled and —,** plundered and pillaged, 336

pomegranate *n.* embroidered representation of pomegranates (for decoration), 347

pope holye *adj.* hypocritically pious; sanctimonious; — **horeson,** hypocritical bastard, 303

poticary *n.* apothecary, 216

prayes *n.pl.* booty, spoil, plunder, 175, 258

prayser *n.* eulogist, worshipper, 211

precellent, -e *adj.* surpassing, preeminent, 258

precellencye *n.* pre-eminence, 258

precipitacion, precipitation *n.* sudden, hurried action, 130, 131; — **of sentence,** sudden haste in forming an opinion, 126, 132

prepensed *ppl.adj.* premeditated, 183

prescise *v.* remove, cut off; **prescised** *p.ppl.* 141

presupposed *p.ppl.* implied (as already in existence), 115, 116, 147, 222

pretertence *n.* the past tense, 214

print, -e *v.* make an impression, impress 129, 137, 138, 232; **printed,** *p.ppl.* imprinted, impressed, 158, 185, 215

priuey, priuie, priuy, -e *adj.* hidden, secret, 187, 325, 334, 335; private, 187, 270; furtive, stealthy, 262, 343, 346, 363

priuitie n. the private parts, 301

pronitie n. propensity, proneness (chiefly to evil), 138

prosecute v. investigate, go into the particulars of, treat in greater detail, 116, 193, 245, 264, 338, 343; **prosecuting,** pr.ppl. 363; persist in, pursue, 255

proue v. prosper, 208, 361; –, **well,** turn out well, 353; **prouinge,** pr.ppl. – **of mastries,** giving displays of one's power of skill, 364

prouision n. supply of necessaries, stock, store, 152, 278, 352; arrangement, decree, 254; providing (of necessaries), 270, 271; foresight, precaution, 308, 309, 310, 312, 313; **cast of –,** a type of precaution, 311; providence, divine ordination, 317, 339

pseudapostle n. false, pretended apostle, 195, 200, 217, 218, 299

purloyner n. petty thief, pilferer, 355

purtinence n. contents, 277

querne n. apparatus for grinding corn, usually consisting of two circular stones the upper of which is turned by hand, 239

quit, quitte v. make return to someone (for a benefit), repay, requite, 320; **quit, quitte** p.ppl. repaid, 320; – **thee home,** paid back to you, 320

quyd n. (dial.) cud, 184

quyuer adj. active, rapid, 340

rable n. mob, disorderly group, 118, 125

ramping pr.ppl. storming, raging in a furious or threatening manner, 312

rather adv. earlier, sooner, 175, **the –,** all the more, the more readily, 179; (all) the more quickly; (all) the sooner, 192

rauende p.ppl. devoured voraciously, 362

rauener n. ravenous, gluttonous bird, 184; ravisher, destroyer, 324

ray, -e n. rank, line, 312

recule v. intr. retreat, retire, draw back, 229; **reculing** vbl n. retreating, 229; **reculynge** pr.ppl. falling back, degenerating, 240

redound, -e v. intr. turn to, 213, 240; contribute to, 334; abound, overflow, 339; **redoundyng** pr.ppl. contributing to, 149

redub v. restore, 283; requite, repay, 286; **redobbed** p.ppl. requited, repaid, 320

refection n. taking of refreshment, 301

remediles adv. without a remedy, 141

remurmur v. resound with murmurs, 264

remysly adv. indistinctly, 147

reneige, reneyg v. renounce, deny, abandon, 263, 276, 359

reproueable adj. reprehensible, blameworthy, 249

repugne v. intr. stand, resist, 126; trans. refute, oppose, repel, reject, 169, 179

reresupper n. supper late at night, 301

ribald n. low, worthless, good-for-nothing fellow, 157, 298

rufler n. vagabond, wastrel, 118

runagate n. apostate, renegade, 137

saciate v. gratify, fill with food, 215, 254, 310; **saciate** p.ppl. 215, 303

sacietie n. full gratification, fulfilled, 215

sad, sadde adj. serious, grave, 185, 277, 284, 354; solid, dense, 233

sadnes, sadnesse n. firmness, dignity, gravity, 275, 340, 354

sanctimonie n. holiness, sanctity, 286, 349

saute n. assault, 229

scolle (var.) v. scold, 277

scurfe n. the outer layer of skin, 314

sequester, sequestre v. keep apart from society; seclude, 136, 138, 300

serued p.ppl. **as the time –,** as befitted the moment, 276; **not – to the eye,** do not appear to serve, 145, 261, 269

shambles n. meat market, table or stall for the sale of meat, 142, 240

shogged p.ppl. jolted, jerked, 174

shoofe v. shove; – **furth,** shove forward, 132; **shofyng,** pr.ppl. shoving, 130

shot, shotte n. joint contribution, 169, 170, 172, 174, 179

shrew, -e, shrowe n. malignant, wicked person; rascal, villain, 176, 291, 297, 331, 362

shreud, -e, shrewd, -e, shrowde adj.; abusive, railing, 117, 151; bad, vile, unfavourable, evil, 231, 234, 305, 313, 328, 330; unhealthy, upset, 228; cunning, artful, 274; mischevous, malignant, 286; ominous, 324; naughty, recalcitrant, 330; vicious, fierce, 361; **a – turne,** injury; mischievous, malicious act, 118, 119, 257; **– paine,** difficult, dangerous undertaking, 266

shrewshaken, shrewe shaken adj. troublesome, shrewish, 277, 278

shrinke, shrynke v. intr. refuse, hesitate, recoil, 157, 187, 331; give way, yield, 157; withdraw, retreat, 236; **shronke** pa.t. 355; p.ppl. contracted, 305

sith, -e adv. since, 132, 182, 215, 216, 228, 294, 296, 356

sith, -e n. scythe, 151, 215

skeen n. dagger or short sword (hung from the belt), 368

skil, skyll v. intr. have knowledge of or skill in, 146, 309

slackynge pr.ppl. neglecting, relaxing, 302

slickt, sliked ppl. adj. groomed sleek and glossy, 272

slowe n. skin which is cast off or periodically shed, 314

sod, sodde (pa.t. of **seethe**) v. prepare by boiling, 323; p.ppl. boiled, 142, 184; ppl.adj. 276, 323

solidate v. make firm, secure, 366

sonderly adv. singly, separately, individually, 183

sor adj. oppressive, severe; **sorer** comp. adj. 224; comp. adv. more tightly, closely, 310; more severely, grievously 355

sorte v. allot, assign, 344

spede v. meet with success, good fortune, flourish, prosper, 176, 230, 313, 336; **sped** p.ppl. dealt with, 131

spede n. prosperity, success, good luck, 356

spill paine, –, payne n. spoiler, destroyer of bread, 253, 309

spire adj. **–, white grasse,** ?spearwort or banewort; or shooting, sprouting plant, 351

staie, stay, staye v. refl. halt, stop, arrest 143, 356; trans. hold, keep, 272, 359, 361, 366; arrest, check, restrain, 153, 254, 288, 356; **staied, stayed** p.ppl. supported, held up, 270; **stayd** ppl. adj. kept, detained, 128, 293; held firm, fixed, 254; **staiynge,** pr. ppl. sustaining, supporting, 342

staie, stay, staye n. a place of sojourn, a fixed abode, 128; support, 174; control, restraint, 290

stale, staale n. lure (for entrapping people), 154, 328; ambush, 229, 298

stealyng p.ppl. **kepe from –,** prevent from being stolen, 125

steane, steen n. urn, jar, drinking cup, vessel for liquid, 146, 321

sterne n. rudder, steering, 287

stick, sticke, stycke v. intr. put in, thrust in, 128; scruple, hesitate, be reluctant; 142, 151, 153, 186, 198, 339,; persist in arguing with, 188, **– to,** remain faithful, steadfast, 187, 212, 356; **– by,** remain resolutely faithful, 231, 275

stifelye adv. **– bended,** stubbornly constrained, 354

stiffed ppl. adj. stiffened, rigid 317

stockes n. pl. fetters, 180

strait, -e adj. narrow, 314; rigorous, severe, strict, 314

straitly, adv. rigorously, severely, 187

strage n. slaughter, 125, 266

strayned p.ppl. bridled, controlled, restrained, 293

streict (var. of **strait**) n. **in -s,** in difficulties, times of hardship, 305

streicted (var. of **straited**) ppl. adj. impoverished, subject to hardship, 367

streight adj. frank, honest, 308, 328, 362

streightly adv. impartially, 189

streightnes n. honesty, 363

strike v. **stricke** p.ppl. **we haue – handes,** we have shaken hands (in confirmation of a bargain), 242

stripe n. lash, stroke with whip or scourge, 134, 135, 150, 265, 267

strip v. expose the character of, 147; refl. divest (oneself), shed 314

stubborne, stubbourne, stubburn adj. inflexible, unyielding, obstinate 143, 156, 194; fierce, implacable, ruthless, untameable, 159

stue n. stew or brothel, 97

sturdy adj. disobedient, 194, 251

sturdyness n. stubborness, disobedience, 132

styffe adj. inflexible, obstinate, 156

summalist n. beginner in philosophy, 193

supped p.ppl. consumed, swallowed up, 318

superadd v. add on besides, put on as a further addition, 263; **superadded to** p.ppl. 116, 124, 132

surcesse, surceasse v. intr. leave off, desist; stop, 122, 123, 137, 186

surfet, -e n. gluttonous indulgence in eating or drinking, 117, 177, 217

surfet v. fall ill, suffer from excessive indulgence in food, 257

surfetting vbl n. eating or drinking to excess, 316

surreption n. stealth, 343

suscitate v. raise up, stir up, call into activity, 127; **suscitated** p.ppl. 169

sute n. petition, supplication, entreaty, 226; adj. certain; **– ancor,** certain source of security, 363

suter n. petitioner, suppliant, 229, 322, 367

swepestake n. **make –,** make a clean sweep, 365

tapster n. tavern keeper, 253

tench n. thick bodied, fresh water fish, 184

tergiuersacion n. subterfuge, evasion, 282

thresholde n. entrance, 198

throwe n. violent spasm or pang; anguish, 271

timber n. timbrel, tambourine, 130

tirranne n. tyrant, 359

tocrash v. **al to crasshed . . . to naught,** broke . . . into smithereens, 239

toteare v. **all –,** tear completely to pieces, 140

touche stone n. black marble or basalt (stones similar to the variety of quartz or jasper known as touchstone), 307

tourne, turn, turne n. act of good will, 217; intent, injury; **a shrewd –,** hostile intent; malicious act, 118, 257

toward adj. impending, approaching, 121

trace n. tress, 272

truande n. vagabond, 262

truly adj. reliable, 344

tyrynge pr.ppl. attiring, 274

vacuitie n. absolute emptiness of space, complete absence of matter, 171

vafre adj. sly, cunning, crafty, 291

vage adj. imprecise, indefinite, 172

vage v. ramble, wander, 217; **vagynge** pr.ppl. 254

veyry n. stoat or weasel, 312

viander n. host, provider of hospitality for guests, 320, 322, 323

viandre, viandry n. providing of good cheer for guests, hospitality, 325, 326

vicious adj. immoral, bad, 129, 138, 158, 241, 247, 249; reprehensible, 156; profligate, wicked, 275, 304, 310, 337

viciously, -e adv. immorally, dissolutely, 218, 293, 328

vituperable adj. blameworthy, reprehensible, disgraceful, 156, 164

viuificate p.ppl. endued with life, revived, 291; ppl.adj. 294; animated, enlivened, 337

vmbraid, vmbrayde *v.* upbraid, censure, reproach, 118, 151, 189, 281; **vmbrayded, vmbraided** *pr.p.ppl.* 333; **vmbrayding** *ppl. n.* 224

vnhablenes *adj.* inability, incapacity, 192, 194

vnitely *adv.* in combination, unitedly, 119, 124

vnmete *adj.* unsuited, unfitting, unbecoming, improper, 138, 191, 226, 331

vnportable *adj.* unbearable, intolerable, 189

vnsensible *adj.* destitute of sense or intelligence, 311

vnthrift, -e *n.* spendthrift, shiftless or dissolute person, 122, 147, 234, 306

vnthriftie, vnthrifty, -e wasteful, unproductive, 313, 344; unchaste, wanton, profligate, 359

vnweldi *adj.* difficult to steer, unmanageable, 287

vocable *n.* word, term, 128, 144, 150, 182

voluptuous *adj.* addicted to sensuous pleasure, fond of sumptuous living, 118, 139, 159, 300, 303

voluptuouslie *adv.* luxuriously, sensually, 160

voluptuousnesse *n.* addiction to sensuous pleasures; indulgence in pleasure or luxury, 132, 301

vtter *adv.* outer, 209

vtter, vttre, *v.* reveal, disclose, divulge, 123, 187, 260; pronounce, speak, say, 260; speak of, report, 316; **vttred, vttered,** *p.ppl.* reported, spoken of, 118, 121, 232; sold, traded, bartered, 154; made known (of person's identity), 341; **vttering,** *pr.ppl.* selling, offering for sale, 229

wale *n.* weal, 267

want *n.* mole, 117, 309

wayne *n.* a wagon drawn by horses or oxen, 182

wayte *v.* look out for, **waytyng shrewd tournes,** lying in wait, staying on watch to inflict injury, 118

welowe (*var.* of **wallow**) *v.* waste, fade away, 353

wenchlines *n.* girlishness, 157

without *conj.* unless, 355

wittines, wittinesse *n.* intelligence, wisdom, good sense, 119, 120, 121, 125

wittynglye *adv.* knowingly, consciously, 273

wrangler *n.* quarreller, debater, 123

wrench *n.* trick, crafty action, 362

wrie *v. intr.* deflect, bend, deviate, 362; **wried away** *p.ppl.* turned aside, diverted, 246

wynded *p.ppl.* moved around in a curve, 297

yane *v.* yawn, 322

yongeling, yongelyng *n.* young person, 353, 354

yonker *n.* fashionable young man, gentleman, 137

SCRIPTURAL INDEX

The index is keyed to the Commentary. Abbreviations of names of books are given in round brackets. The order follows that of the Vulgate. Where variation occurs from the titles of the AV the latter are provided in square brackets. The numbers in brackets refer to multiple references on the same page.

OLD TESTAMENT

NEW TESTAMENT

APPENDIX